LONDON'S
LOCAL
RAILWAYS

LONDON'S LOCAL RAILWAYS

Alan A. Jackson

Capital Transport

Dedicated to the Suburban Traveller

First published 1978
Second Edition, revised and enlarged 1999

ISBN 1 85414 209 7

Published by Capital Transport Publishing,
38 Long Elmes, Harrow Weald, Middlesex

Printed by CS Graphics, Singapore

ACKNOWLEDGEMENTS

Willing and unremitting help with the original work was received from the late H. V. Borley and G. T. Moody, sadly missed, who gave freely of the fruits of their recording and observation of the London railway scene dating back to the 1910s. Others offering valuable assistance at that time included the late John Faulkner, past President and Librarian of the Railway Club, and John C. Gillham, who has a particular knowledge of west London. In connection with the extensive revision and supplementation involved in preparing this volume, help was again received from John Faulkner and also from Dr Edwin Course, past President of the Railway & Canal Historical Society, who set this student on the road to authorship at London University Extension Courses over 40 years ago. Desmond Croome, collaborator in the preparation of *Rails Through The Clay* and friend of many years, has commented helpfully on those chapters relating to the Underground system, as has another specialist in that field, Brian Hardy. The maps were drawn by Mike Harris.

When working with primary sources, old newspapers and periodicals, the task of a researcher with very limited time to spare was invariably eased and made pleasant by the patience and efficiency of the staff at the House of Lords Record Office, the Public Record Office, the Greater London and former Middlesex Record Offices, the National Newspaper Library at Colindale, the Department of the Environment Library, the Westminster City Library and the Library at the London Transport Museum. Also heavily-used and greatly valued was the access that members have to the special resources of the Railway Club Library. Mention should be made of the ingenuity and the industry of the retailers of old picture postcards and – a special word of thanks – to John L. Smith, of the famous Sutton shop, in unearthing and making available at reasonable cost many valuable images of past scenes which give rise to so much information and inspiration. Last but by no means least, it would be ungracious not to mention the encouragement, prompt decisions and excellent support given by Jim Whiting, a publisher who really cares about this sort of book.

A. A. J.

A NOTE ON SOURCES

An indication of the main sources used is incorporated in the Bibliography. Footnotes have been kept to a minimum; readers interested in sources who remain unsatisfied are invited to communicate with the author through the publisher.

Overleaf: London Chatham & Dover Railway 0-4-2T No. 99 *Mona* on a train of six 4-wheelers ready to leave Greenwich Park c.1895.

PREFACE TO THE SECOND EDITION

This book is a substantially enlarged version of one of the same title written in the 1970s, fully revised and updated. It sets out to examine the history, atmosphere and environment of those railways originating in Greater London which are or were principally used for local passenger traffic. At the publisher's suggestion, a topographical arrangement has been adopted, with a chapter devoted to each quarter, beginning in the south east and proceeding in a clockwise direction to north east London. Several lines omitted in the first edition are now included.

Since outlines of the general historical and geographical background and development of the London rail network are readily available in other books (notably that by the late Professor H. P. White), as indicated in Section 5 of the Bibliography, it has not seemed necessary to include an introductory survey.

Although all the London Underground lines are truly 'local railways', it would be impossible to give all of them adequate and comparable treatment within the bounds of a single volume; again there are suitable works readily available for those seeking information not found here and these are shown in the Bibliography. We have however included those lines which were originally owned by the old steam railway companies.

As in the first edition, the period covered is mainly that before the 1948 nationalisation, though an endeavour has been made to give details of the more important developments up to the end of the 20th century. For further information on recent and future developments on the railways covered, the reader is referred to the periodicals marked with an asterisk on page 452.

Those not well-briefed in London's geography may feel the need for assistance beyond that given by the maps of the individual lines included with the text. This is best met by obtaining a copy of one of the large-scale street atlases mentioned in Section 3 of the Bibliography; such items are not cheap, but their quality is high and their ability to stimulate interest equally so; the outlay will be well rewarded, even for the native Londoner.

The railways finding a place here were an important element in the growth and infrastructure of modern London and many of them continue to play a part in the ever-changing pattern of the capital's development. We have tried to show that even the humblest of suburban lines has a history full of interest, which once appreciated, will enrich the daily or occasional journey over it. Some readers may be surprised to find how little of the Victorian railway heritage has completely disappeared and how, even where the original lines have been closed because the purpose they served no longer exists, their formations and alignments have proved adaptable to easing the construction of new railways serving new roles, not least in improving the environment by reducing dependence on motor transport, with all its attendant noise and air pollution.

In writing this book we have had in mind not just those who enjoy learning more about railways, but all who love the infinite variety and interest of London's complicated modern history. For that reason an attempt has been made to sketch the social backcloth by showing how each line affected its catchment area and how external social factors influenced the levels and the nature of the traffic handled.

DORKING, June 1998   ALAN A JACKSON

CONTENTS

ABBREVIATIONS

BHR	Bexley Heath Railway
BR	British Railways
BTR	British Transport Records
ch	chains
CLR	Central London Railway
District	Metropolitan District Railway
DLR	Docklands Light Railway
ECR	Eastern Counties Railway
EC&TJR	Eastern Counties & Thames Junction Railway
EH&LR	Edgware, Highgate & London Railway
E&SHR	Ealing & South Harrow Railway
f	furlongs
GCR	Great Central Railway
GER	Great Eastern Railway
GLC	Greater London Council
GNCR	Great Northern & City Railway
GNR	Great Northern Railway
GWR	Great Western Railway
H&CR	Hammersmith & City Railway
H&UR	Harrow & Uxbridge Railway
K&R	Kensington & Richmond Railway
L&BR	London & Blackwall Railway
LBSCR	London, Brighton & South Coast Railway
LCC	London County Council
LCDR	London Chatham & Dover Railway
LGOC	London General Omnibus Company
LMSR	London Midland & Scottish Railway
LNER	London & North Eastern Railway
LNWR	London & North Western Railway
LPTB	London Passenger Transport Board
LSWR	London & South Western Railway
LT	London Transport
m	miles
Met	Metropolitan Railway
MDR	Metropolitan District Railway
min	minutes
M&SWJR	Midland & South Western Junction Railway
MRCE	Metropolitan Railway Country Estates Ltd
MWB	Metropolitan Water Board
N&ER	Northern & Eastern Railway
NLR	North London Railway
N&SWJR	North & South Western Junction Railway
PLA	Port of London Authority
RCLT	Royal Commission on London Traffic (1905)
SECR	South Eastern & Chatham Railway
SR	Southern Railway
T&HJR	Tottenham & Hampstead Junction Railway
UDC	urban district council
W&CR	Wimbledon & Croydon Railway

DATES AND DISTANCES

Unless otherwise stated, the closure dates given are the *last full day* of public traffic.

Distances are generally those shown in the Railway Clearing House maps and Junction Diagrams or the railway companies' official publications. With the sole exception of London Transport (and its Underground Company predecessors) who used decimals of a mile, these are always given in miles and chains and are so shown here (80 chains or 8 furlongs = 1 mile = 1.61 km).

CHAPTER ONE

SOUTH EAST LONDON

An SER train from London to Greenwich entering Greenwich station during the final years of right hand running (c.1900). Note the descending gradient from the viaduct and the central through roads. *George Potter*

Railways to Greenwich (map page 18)

Greenwich was the outer terminus of the very first public passenger railway in London, the London & Greenwich Railway, opened in 1836 and completed in 1838. Exclusively a passenger line, its early history has been well documented in other work and need not be repeated here. From 1st January 1845 the whole operation was leased by the SER, though the little company remained in existence until 3rd January 1923 to receive its rent and distribute its dividend.

Thanks to the influential opposition and obstinate prejudices of the Admiralty and the Astronomer Royal, the SER's natural desire to extend this line further east through the important town of Woolwich was continually frustrated, although the latter point had been circuitously reached via Blackheath in 1849 (the North Kent line). There was no lack of proposals for filling the gap east of Greenwich; in 1863 alone three bills were deposited for railways serving the two towns, one each sponsored by the three companies interested in this quarter of London. From the LBSCR camp came the South London, Greenwich & Woolwich Railway, a 6m 62ch branch from the Brighton's line at Peckham via New Cross, Deptford, and a covered way through Greenwich Park to terminate at the Royal Dockyard, Woolwich. The SER supported a Greenwich & Woolwich Railway which sought a 2m 61ch connection between Greenwich and the North Kent line at Charlton, crossing the Park on a viaduct. Lastly the LCDR's No. 1 bill included a 2m 18ch line from the Crystal Palace & South London Junction Railway at Nunhead to Crooms Hill,

Greenwich, the last 319 yd to be in a covered way. Beyond, the LCDR wanted a further 2m 52ch to reach the Royal Dockyard, this to cross the Park in an 843 yd covered way. There were to be connections to the SER and LBSCR where the other two companies' lines intersected. All three proposals met the predictable opposition of Observatory authorities concerned with possible wobbling of their telescopes, but by May 1863 they had conceded there might be a tunnel through the Park on a route defined by them, provided speeds did not exceed 12 mph.

Whilst the three bills were before parliament there was some horse trading between the three main line companies. The LBSCR gave up all territorial claims to Greenwich and Woolwich provided the LCDR showed no further interest in Balham and points beyond. Left with an LCDR invasion of its territory, and facing Observatory hostility to its proposed viaduct, the SER and LCDR reached an arrangement whereby the latter would have running powers over the SER into Woolwich Arsenal via Lewisham and in exchange the SER would be given less valuable running powers to Crystal Palace via new connections at Lewisham, Brockley and Nunhead. This secured the withdrawal of the LCDR Greenwich – Woolwich proposal but the 2½ mile branch from Nunhead to Greenwich, Crooms Hill was authorised to the LCDR by an act of 28th July 1863. In the following year acts of 23rd June and 14th July sanctioned the agreed running powers and connections to allow SER trains to Crystal Palace, both direct from London Bridge, from the company's new Tonbridge main line and from the Mid Kent line at Lewisham. Some work was done on making a Nunhead-Brockley curve behind St Norbert Road, but none of the necessary connections to allow SER access was completed.

In 1865 the SER finally secured an act for filling the Greenwich-Charlton gap by adopting an alignment suggested by the Astronomer Royal, who obtained power to stop the trains. But the SER was not happy with the suggested route and nothing was done until a further SER act was passed in 1872, authorising a line along the north side of London Street, Greenwich and passing along the south side of Trafalgar Road in a cut and cover subway. This removed 'all cause for alarm' at the Observatory. At Greenwich 43 arches of the original viaduct were demolished between Norman Road and the end, and an embankment made which descended to ground level opposite the original terminal. From there the line further descended to the mouth of the new tunnel. The tracks at Greenwich were on a new alignment, requiring complete rebuilding of the station.

The section between Charlton Junction and Maze Hill & Greenwich Park station was the first to open, on 1st January 1873. Temporary platforms on the new site at Greenwich were in use from 11th January 1877 for London trains but the section between Greenwich and Maze Hill was not available for public traffic until 1st February 1878 owing to delays in settling the alignment at Greenwich to the satisfaction of the Board of Trade. Even then most trains terminated at Charlton until 4th March.

The handsome new Renaissance style station house on the south side of the line at Greenwich bore some similarity with its predecessor and some of the Portland stone of the latter was reused in its construction. It was however larger and substantially a new building. Inside were four roads and a bay on the south side. Much to the frustration of the SER, the existing track layout out of London Bridge made it impossible to arrange for normal left hand running between London Bridge and Greenwich and a scissors crossing was installed at Charlton to allow reversion

Westcombe Park station, with an Up train entering, c.1905. *Commercial picture postcard*

to normal running at that point. This superseded the normal left hand running which had been in operation initially between Charlton and Maze Hill. The awkward anomaly was to last until midnight 25th/26th May 1901 when widening works on the tracks into London at last allowed normal running to be adopted through to Charlton Junction. An intermediate station between Maze Hill and Charlton, called Westcombe Park, was added on 1st May 1879 to exploit residential development on the estate of that name. With the connection to the North Kent line at Charlton Junction, the SER line in Greenwich became another alternative route into Kent, no longer just a local railway.

Westcombe Park station, 12th July 1955, looking to Charlton, showing platform extensions at London end for 10-car train scheme under construction. The telegraph poles in the previous photo are still in position. *Alan A. Jackson*

Meanwhile the LCDR was making little progress with its entry into Greenwich. Land was difficult to obtain and the construction work authorised in 1863 was overtaken by the company's great financial crisis of 1866 which landed it in Chancery for five years. An Arbitration Award of 1871 allowed the stricken company, among other things, to spend just enough to complete the branch from Nunhead as far as Blackheath Hill 'with best despatch' and this 1m 55ch length, with an intermediate station at Lewisham Road, was opened to public traffic on 18th September 1871. Finance not permitting anything more, powers for the remainder were allowed to lapse.

A second intermediate station, Brockley Lane, was added in June 1872. All the stopping places were simply and crudely built, largely in wood. Twenty six trains a day each way, about one every 45 minutes, ran on weekdays, with about one train an hour on Sundays. Some of these worked through to and from Victoria but most terminated at Nunhead, connecting into the Crystal Palace services. Things had improved very little by 1887 when there were five connections with Victoria – Crystal Palace trains on weekdays and 15 with the City – Crystal Palace services, plus two morning through workings to Victoria and one at midnight, one through to Moorgate Street, three to Holborn Viaduct, one to Ludgate Hill and seven to St Paul's (now Blackfriars). Sundays saw hourly connections at Nunhead to and from the City or Victoria.

As two of the stations were close to LBSCR and SER establishments on more direct routes to central London (Brockley and St John's), trade was hardly brisk. This no doubt exacerbated the old itch to get a foothold in Greenwich, an itch further irritated by the SER's success at building up a healthy traffic on its new line between Charlton and Greenwich which had encouraged new housing developments east of Greenwich Park. Finally, after many false rumours, a bill was deposited for the 1881 session, a move explained in almost Churchillian terms to shareholders at the half-yearly meeting by the chairman, J. S. Forbes:

> We should not have spent £450,000 to get the bottom of Blackheath Hill. The raison d'être of that expenditure was to get to the heart of Greenwich. Everybody knows what the Greenwich traffic is; it is an astounding traffic. That is a thing that the time has come for doing and we have no hesitation in recommending you to do it.

And do it they somehow did, despite the £225,000 capital required for a sinuously routed line through what was a tightly built-up area. The sanction of Parliament was obtained, extended in time by further acts of 1886 and 1888, for a new alignment, swinging north-east to a terminus at street level in Stockwell Street, Greenwich, set out to allow for a junction with the SER between the east end of that company's Greenwich station and the west entrance of the covered way through the Park. Although the LCDR's intention of making this connection was not included in the 1881 bill, it was mentioned in the Parliamentary proceedings.

The branch started at the east end of Nunhead station, opened on 1st September 1871. Here were two island platforms, the northernmost with Up and Down roads at each side, the other sharing the centre road with an additional Up road on its southern face. The centre road was used by branch trains terminating at the junction. On the Up side was a small goods yard which survived until April 1962. At the east end of the platforms the Crystal Palace lines swerved away to the south,

Greenwich Park train at Lewisham Road station c.1903. *Commercial postcard*

View from Lewisham Road Station

BR 31253 running light between the former Brockley Lane and Lewisham Road stations, 10th September 1955. *Alan A Jackson*

the Greenwich tracks proceeding almost due east over still open country in a cutting through the south side of Telegraph Hill, emerging to cross the LBSCR main line above the London end of that company's Brockley station (opened on 6th March 1871). West of this bridge, between what are now Pepys and Mantler Roads, were the branch's only freight installations, on the north side Martin's Siding, and almost opposite on the Up side, a GNR coal depot, part of that company's reward for subscribing to the LCDR Metropolitan Extension from Ludgate Hill to Farringdon Street. Martin's Siding, opened in 1885, accommodated 36 wagons and was leased to the LNWR, which sub-let to the coal merchants Charrington, Warren Ltd. The GNR depot, in service in December 1883, held some 40 wagons and was served by GNR coal trains travelling via Farringdon Street and Loughborough Junction. In later years both the yards were worked from Hither Green.

Brockley Lane station was opened in June 1872 to sneak such traffic as it could from the adjacent LBSCR establishment. Both fed on the new district of Upper Brockley, where spacious streets of substantial three- and four-decker yellow brick villas with long gardens were laid out in the late 1860s, for what Charles Booth's survey describes as the 'well-to-do middle class'. Sited on the bridge over Brockley Lane, the LCDR station had wooden platforms, with a small entrance hall at street level. Turning north-east in a deep cutting, the line traversed the southern part of Brockley, then at the edge of London. Falling at 1 in 100, it passed below Loampit Hill into Lewisham Road station, where the brick platforms were connected by a covered iron footbridge. This led to a small wooden booking office building at street level on the Up side, which was so well made that it was still in service as the 1st Lewisham Scouts' hut over a century later.

Crossing St Johns, a villa satellite of Deptford named after its church, the branch very shortly passed over the SER North Kent line near its junction with the Tonbridge main line. Now on an embankment, the branch tracks crossed the Ravensbourne River on a brick viaduct before entering a cutting. Blackheath Hill station was on the south side of that road, its brick platforms served by a booking office on the bridge that carried the street over the line.

The 46ch extension to Greenwich, opened on 1st October 1888, cleaved its way through an area packed with small houses in narrow streets and courts, obliged to twist and turn in steeply-retained cuttings and covered ways to minimise property demolition and compensation to landlords. It started in a deep cutting on the north side of Blackheath Hill and fell at 1 in 80 all the way. After some 200yd it entered a 150yd covered way under Blissetts Hill, continuing through a final section of steeply-walled cutting before reaching Greenwich station. Here the layout comprised a central locomotive run-round road between the Up and Down platforms, the former an island with an Up loop around its outer face. Both platforms and the connecting space behind the buffers were well sheltered by valanced awnings. The main buildings, of brick with round-arched windows, stood across the end of the line level with Stockwell Street, a two-storey house for the stationmaster at the south-east corner. A siding near the signal box provided space for the spare locomotive needed at busy times. The alignment allowed for a connection to the SER in an easterly direction. To avoid confusion after the working agreement between the LCDR and the SER, the station was renamed Greenwich Park from 1st July 1900.

Despite Forbes' ebullience, traffic proved to be light except on Bank Holidays and summer Sundays when the terminus was besieged by crowds seeking the exotic delights of Crystal Palace, whilst in the opposite direction the poorer people from Walworth and Southwark came to relax on the river or in Greenwich Park. But the commuting businessmen and clerks of Greenwich and Lewisham remained loyal to the more direct services of the SER which had opened a station at St John's on 1st June 1873 to compete with Lewisham Road. As for the wealthier men of Upper Brockley, their families and their servants, these found the LBSCR to London Bridge more convenient than the circuitous journey to St Paul's (Blackfriars) via Loughborough Junction.

In January 1899 the through journey from Greenwich to St Paul's or Victoria took about 30 minutes. There were then 43 Down trains between the 06.40 and 00.41 arrivals at Greenwich; in the Up direction, 54 trains left Greenwich between 05.07 and 00.10, whilst on Sundays there were 21 each way. Although some ran through to London, most workings terminated at Nunhead into connections for City stations or Victoria. In 1913 the timetable showed 55 Down and 43 Up, only 11 each way on Sundays, all stopping at each station, taking about nine minutes to traverse the branch.

Until this time the usual formation was four to six wooden 4-wheelers, probably hauled by an LCDR class D 0-4-2 well tank, but in that year a push-and-pull unit consisting of a P class 0-6-0T with a bogie coach at each end appeared on the branch. This ran until the evening of Sunday 31st December 1916 after which as part of the SECR response to a government request to provide extra capacity for war traffic, service on the branch ceased, together with the passenger services on the Crystal Palace line and Sunday trains on the Catford Loop.

Greenwich Park station c.1912 showing one of two 'Sandwich' push-pull units formed that year for working the branch, with LCDR coaches of 1897 and Wainwright P class 0-6-0.

Few were inconvenienced by the closure. LCC electric tramcars, with the multiple attraction of cheap fares, intensive service and ready accessibility, had been operating between Lewisham and Greenwich since 4th April 1908, and between Brockley and New Cross since 26th February 1910, drawing off most of the local traffic that existed. Passenger and parcels receipts at the four stations fell from £13,820 in 1905 to a mere £3,107 in 1915. It was thus no surprise that when the Crystal Palace line was re-opened after the war, the Greenwich branch was left quietly rusting, seeing no trains other than the freights into the Brockley yards and occasional forays towards Lewisham Road for carriage storage. Maintenance beyond Lewisham Road was discontinued, so that by the early 1920s platforms and rails were covered with weeds and rubbish. There was some mild agitation for re-opening, but after hearing evidence in October 1926, the London & Home Counties Traffic Advisory Committee found that the fall in receipts fully justified the SR's conclusion that the bulk of the available traffic had left the railway for good.

The closed LCDR Blackheath Hill station, looking to Greenwich Park, c.1921.
Lens of Sutton

Then someone had a bright idea. In 1926 the infant SR was making a brilliant recovery from the effect of wartime strains imposed on its constituent companies, which had borne the brunt of traffic to and from the Western Front in France. Electrification of suburban lines had been started, but in the congested and busy area around London Bridge there was a traffic problem. Whilst on much of the suburban system electric trains could run unimpeded at close intervals, unimpeded because steam-hauled freights could be accommodated in night hours, the very heavy goods traffic exchanged with the northern companies had to be run in daylight between the electric services. These trains worked to and from Hither Green yards via the City Widened Lines, Snow Hill, Blackfriars Junction, Metropolitan Junction, London Bridge station and New Cross. A particular source of congestion was the section between Metropolitan and Borough Market Junctions, west of London Bridge, where only one Up and one Down line were available to carry all the electric services in and out of Charing Cross together with the 40 or so freight movements daily.

The concept was to join up the North Kent line and the Greenwich Park branch as envisaged in 1863, making a second curve to the main line south of Lewisham, so that goods trains from the north could work from Blackfriars to Hither Green via Loughborough Junction and Nunhead, by-passing the London Bridge bottleneck. This imaginative plan also enabled Hither Green yards to receive another 20 to 30 freight trains daily from the LMSR and GWR via the West London line instead of traffic exchanges at Stewarts Lane, Battersea or Redhill yards.

The first of the two new connections carried freight from 7th July 1929 between the branch at the Greenwich end of Lewisham Road station and the North Kent line on the London side of Lewisham station, crossing the main line on a massive 240ft double span lattice-girder bridge. To reach the main line, the second link (the Courthill Loop) left the Mid Kent about 450yd from the country end of Lewisham, joining the Tonbridge line near Parks Bridge Junction. From Nunhead station (rebuilt slightly further west in red brick with a single island platform, opened in May 1925) to Lewisham Road the old branch was relaid with 45ft 95lb rail and

The bridge carrying the 1929 connection between the former LCDR Greenwich Park branch and Lewisham station over the former SER main line at St John's, looking to Lewisham, with unit 5015 on a Dartford-Cannon Street via Woolwich and Blackheath train approaching, 16th July 1955. The supporting pillar seen on the right was demolished by a collision in fog on 4th December 1957 in which 90 people were killed. *Alan A Jackson*

reballasted. The rest was abandoned by an act of 1929, and the track was taken up in that year. After unsuccessful efforts to sell the land, the cuttings between Greenwich Park and Lindsell Street, Blackheath Hill, were filled with rubble by a haulage contractor who paid the SR almost £1,500 for the privilege, completing the work by 1932. In June 1929 the Traffic Officers' Conference of the SR was recommended to abolish Brockley Lane station, the buildings reported in a bad state and 'no likelihood of a passenger service being reintroduced on the Greenwich Park branch'. At Blackheath Hill and Greenwich Park the buildings were left intact as it proved possible to let them. After the filling work was completed, the sites of the cuttings were used as yards by scrap metal dealers and transport contractors.

It was not long before the enterprising management of the SR was putting the Lewisham connections to passenger use. To allow Dartford Loop and Bromley North trains to call at Lewisham if required, the loop between Lewisham and the main line was electrified from 16th July 1933. Until that time the new route established in 1929 had only been used for passenger purposes by a few summer steam specials to the coast calling at Lewisham. Electrification of the Lewisham-Nunhead section to enable the full potential of the new works to be realised was carried out in the summer of 1935. From 30th September new rush-hour services operated between Dartford and St Paul's (Blackfriars) via Sidcup and via Bexleyheath, affording useful relief to the services into London Bridge, Cannon Street and Charing Cross struggling to cope with a huge increase in traffic from the thousands of houses built between Eltham and Dartford in the late 1920s and early 1930s. Although made more attractive by restricting stops on the inner section to Peckham Rye and Elephant & Castle, bringing Holborn Viaduct within 19 minutes of Lewisham, (just four minutes longer than Lewisham-Cannon Street), the new route was slow to attract passengers. Its popularity was not assisted by charging higher fares and the posting of travelling ticket inspectors to collect this extra revenue. A long period of suspension during the war years and immediately after (from 16th October 1939 to 12th August 1946) did nothing to help, and indeed the six or so trains in the peak periods via Bexleyheath and nine via Sidcup were never over-crowded. In the 1960s and 1970s freight workings over the Nunhead-Lewisham section were much reduced in number, the Brockley Lane yards finally closing from 4th May 1970, the signal box on 7th March 1973.

The substantial 1929 bridge over the Tonbridge line at St John's was very severely damaged by a collision in fog at about 18.20 on 4th December 1957, in which a Cannon Street – Ramsgate steam train ran at about 30mph into a stationary Charing Cross-Hayes electric train, resulting in 90 deaths. The impact toppled the front of the steam train against a steel column supporting the flyover, causing the bridge girders to collapse on to it. Above, two minutes after the collision, the 17.22 electric service from Holborn Viaduct to Dartford, very slowly approaching a red signal, was promptly stopped by its driver when he saw the bridge girders had sagged. This train was not damaged or derailed. The 'temporary' bridge installed to enable the Nunhead-Lewisham line to be reopened on 13th January 1958 is still in position at the time of writing, over 40 years later.

Further alterations to the layout at Lewisham took place from 3rd April 1976 with the opening of a new loop signalled for reversible working through St John's. This formed a flyover, allowing trains from Lewisham for Charing Cross to take the 1929 Nunhead line then descend to the Up side at St John's.

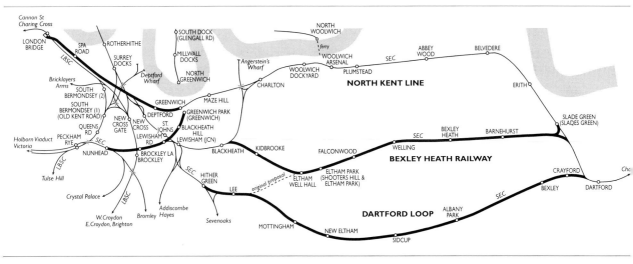

The Dartford Loop

A little to the south east of the railways just described are two others, parallel to and south of the North Kent line and providing alternative routes to Dartford and beyond: the Dartford Loop (also at first known as the North Kent Loop) and the Bexley Heath Railway. Both have long been used for traffic to and from points outside London, but what is now known as the Bexleyheath line was a truly local railway in conception and certainly merits inclusion here. Whether the Loop qualifies is perhaps more debatable but since the 1930s it has carried a great weight of London local passenger business.

In promoting a 9m 50ch railway between Lewisham and Dartford via Sidcup and Bexley in 1861–62, the SER no doubt had concerns about the vulnerability of a gap between its North Kent line and the LCDR main line east of Beckenham which its rival might be tempted to penetrate. There was also talk of providing necessary relief to the North Kent line but subsequent events showed this to be largely spurious since through traffic has never been particularly important.

Construction involved a deep cutting east of Sidcup as the line descended to near sea level when approaching Crayford and Dartford. There were no other serious engineering problems and the new railway, through open country, with intermediate stations at Lee, Eltham, Sidcup, Bexley and Crayford, came into public service on 1st September 1866. There were eleven trains each way daily, about one every two hours, plus a single fast service not calling at the Loop stations; some trains went beyond Dartford at first but after a few years the long distance trains were normally routed via the North Kent line.

All the stations were in the familiar SER rural style; weatherboarded single storey structures, with subways between the platforms rather than footbridges. Sidcup had no subway as passengers passed through the underline bridge over the road to reach the other platform. 'Eltham' was something of a misnomer, since it was actually in Mottingham, about a mile south of its namesake. This anomaly was heightened after the opening of the Bexleyheath Railway through Eltham and the suffix 'for Mottingham' later appeared, with 'for' replacing 'and' at some periods. It was not until 1st October 1927 that the Loop Line station was awarded an unequivocal 'Mottingham'. Between this station and Sidcup, a landowner gave land and money

Top: New Eltham for Pope Street station, looking to London, c.1903. Suburbanisation is already sufficiently advanced to justify a coal office behind the Up platform. *Commercial postcard*

Centre: Sidcup station approach (on the Up side) slumbers in summer haze c.1905. H Gower awaits business with his luggage and parcels van. *Commercial postcard*

Above: Sidcup interior about the same date, looking to London. *Commercial postcard*

to provide another station, duly opened on 1st April 1878. It was known first as Pope Street but this name did not please the developer and it became New Eltham & Pope Street from 1st January 1886 and simply New Eltham from 1st October 1927. This association with building development provided an early pointer to the future major business of the line.

At Sidcup the station was at Halfway Street, half a mile north of the village centre. Bexley station was conveniently near its namesake, as was Crayford, situated less than a quarter mile south of the centre of that community. For many years the Loop line appears to have had little or no effect on the development of the area it served, which remained largely rural, though the railway did attract a few middle class residents around its stations. On 1st June 1895 a new station was opened at Hither Green, where the Loop joined the Chislehurst and Tonbridge main line and this had a separate pair of platforms on the Loop line. Roads of small houses were by then appearing on the London side of the new junction station and more quickly followed.

A double line spur from west of Lee station, running east to south to join the main line was opened in 1899/1900 primarily for freight trains to and from the then new Hither Green yards; it was never regularly used for passenger traffic. At the eastern end of the Loop line, a curve south to north, allowing trains to run from Crayford round to Slade Green and on to the Bexleyheath line came into use much later, on 11th October 1942.

The years from around 1880 up to 1914 saw residential development at Lee, where new roads of houses quickly filled in the area between the original settlement and the station, whilst other residential growth spread southwards towards Grove Park. By 1914, New Eltham although small as yet, was very much a railway suburb, closely grouped around its station. At both places the houses were of medium to small size, in general for the lower middle class commuter. From around 1870 right through

Bexley, the SER main building, on the Down side, surrounded with commuters' motor cars but still gaslit and laced with telegraph poles and wires, September 1963. *BR (SR)*

to the First World War, Sidcup saw steady growth, mainly between the High Street and the line, on either side of Station Road. This was often optimistic in its projection; sales or leases were only slowly achieved, some properties remaining empty for years. At Sidcup some of the houses were larger, aimed to attract the comfortably-off, servanted middle middles who could afford the time and cost of living so far from the City. Station improvements of 1887 – a new booking office on the Up side and platform extensions – may have been a response to the building activity just mentioned. East of Sidcup, there was some new settlement in Bexley village but in general this section of the Loop saw very few commuters before the early 1930s.

Except perhaps at Lee, the arrival of electric trams and motor buses in the Loop's catchment area in the 1900s provided little effective competition then or in later years. Most rail passengers here were commuters to central London and the time factor made the cheaper road fares unattractive for the majority.

Crayford station witnessed an intensification of freight and passenger activity in World War 1. Hiram Maxim's 1888 works at Crayford had been taken over by Vickers in 1897 to become Vickers, Son and Maxim Ltd and after doing well in the Boer War, had suffered some vicissitudes, including for a time manufacture of motor cars, and then complete closure, but from 1914 the firm received huge orders for armaments, notably the Vickers machine gun. By the end of the war, Vickers' Works at Crayford and adjacent Erith (on the North Kent line) were producing 5,000 machine guns a month and aircraft were also being manufactured at Crayford. In a few short years, Crayford was transformed to an industrial town and a total of 600 cottages, including the Barnes Cray estate (1916) were constructed here in 1914–18. All this activity brought much extra freight and passenger traffic to the Loop line.

The Vickers Works, immediately east of the station (employing 15,000 by the end of the war) and two further war factories between there and the Bexley Heath Railway were served by a private siding almost a mile in length, which was opened in January 1915 worked by three small tank engines and the underframe of a LSWR coach powered by a petrol engine, all these owned by the firm.

Wartime traffic also brought about the construction of six holding sidings for Hither Green yards at the west end of what is now Mottingham station. This site became a rail-served United Dairies milk depot for some years from 1948. Another aspect of World War 1 traffic was the ambulance trains bringing wounded men to Sidcup station, whence they were moved in road ambulances to the large new Queen Alexandra Military Hospital in Frognal Avenue.

As on the Bexley Heath Railway, the SR conductor rail electrification was to usher in a new era for the Loop line. Some electric trains started during the 1926 General Strike (on 10th May) followed by a full service from 6th June. The number of trains each way daily was increased from 37 in the last steam timetable to 48, providing a basic frequency of two an hour, with extra workings in the morning and evening peaks. A few steam trains continued to run over the Loop, working fast from London Bridge to Dartford. This new service and a financial climate generally favourable both to the supply and demand caused builders and developers to transform the whole area along the railway from the beginning of the 1930s. By the summer of 1939 continuously built-up London was flowing out along both sides of the Loop line to a point over a mile beyond Sidcup station and on the north side as far as the eastern edge of Bexley village.

Between 1932 and 1938 an entirely new and extensive suburb was constructed between Sidcup and Bexley, with estates sprawling out each side of the line. Almost all these houses were erected by New Ideal Homesteads, who called their handiwork Albany Park. This firm made a £5,000 contribution to the cost of a £15,850 new station of that name to serve their development, also giving land to the SR, and the station, built on a flattened out section of the descending eastwards gradient, was opened on 7th July 1935. Platform buildings, linked by a wide, covered and glazed footbridge were wooden, but the main building, on the north side, was in the Modern style, a flat-roofed brick blockhouse with somewhat lower extensions either side. There was no goods yard. A further agreement made with the developers in 1939 provided for access and station offices, including a passimeter, on the Up side to cost £4,700 against which there would be a £300 contribution and a gift of land from the developer. This scheme was not carried through before the outbreak of war, passengers from the Royal Park Estate continuing to use the public right of way over the station footbridge to reach the Down side ticket hall.

Since a high proportion of the purchasers worked in central London all this new house construction, at an unprecedented pace and selling at very low prices, threw a huge peak hours load on the railway. By 1937 the train service outside the peak hours to and from Charing Cross/Cannon Street had been increased to four an hour and at the busiest peak hour there were a maximum of ten trains, including the service to and from Blackfriars via Nunhead started in 1933 and shared with the Bexleyheath line which has been mentioned earlier. These 'over the top' services to Blackfriars were suspended during the war but returned on 12th August 1946.

Albany Park, provided with assistance from New Ideal Homesteads Ltd and opened on 7th July 1935. Looking to Dartford, with unit 5342 on 4-car Up service, 22nd July 1975. *Alan A Jackson*

Mottingham station, looking to London, 15th August 1969. At this date, the SER buildings survived, apart from some reconstruction of canopies and substitution of SR style lighting on prefabricated concrete standards.
Alan A. Jackson

Freight traffic also benefited from the rapid residential expansion of the 1930s, both in bringing in building materials and later carrying the vastly increased demand for solid fuels to heat the many new houses. In 1933 the Loop saw three freight trains daily and there were trips from one siding to another. Sidcup goods yard was enlarged in 1933 when new housing estates were well under way along the railway at Halfway Street and east of the station. At Mottingham, where a large LCC estate was built south of the station in 1934–7, the goods yard was enlarged in 1935. A postal sorting office opened at Sidcup in 1935, bringing extra mail traffic to that station.

Developments after World War 2 included the introduction of 10-car trains from 1955 and completion of colour light signalling in 1955–70. A reversing siding was inserted at the country end of Sidcup station in 1967, allowing a few trains to terminate there. The summer timetable of that year provided the best services ever, with 13 commuter trains in the busiest peak hour at some stations, many of ten-car formation, and restoration of the four trains an hour off peak frequency. This level of service was subsequently trimmed somewhat but early 1993 saw the full introduction of the slick and smooth-running Networker sets, in a long overdue renewal of rolling stock. As elsewhere, the coal and coke traffic which was almost the only freight handled by the early 1960s, all but vanished with the spread of oil and then gas central heating into suburban homes. Bexley yard closed in May 1963, Crayford in January 1965, New Eltham in November 1965, Sidcup in August 1966 and Lee and Mottingham in October 1968.

Station rebuilding from the 1960s onwards left only Bexley in virtually unaltered SER form. Albany Park received a new ticket office, otherwise retaining much of its 1930s aura. Sidcup was substantially reconstructed in 1987–8 at a cost of around £700,000 to provide a terrazzo-tiled ticket and waiting hall and tenancy and staff accommodation on the Up side. Crayford received the ugly CLASP factory-made components treatment in 1968. Lee, Mottingham and New Eltham saw modest and sympathetic rebuilding under the Network SouthEast regime.

Although still available for services to and from Kent, the Loop is now very much a London local line, linking communities in what is very largely typical 1930s suburbia and carrying a somewhat reduced daily flow of commuters between London's south eastern outskirts and the central area. The 12-car Networker trains, each with a capacity of well over 1,000 passengers, proved more than ample to cope smoothly with peak hour loadings here and on the Bexleyheath line, still two of London's busiest local railways in the 1990s. Slack hours and weekend traffic on the Loop is now confined mainly to the leisure and shopping journeys of the car-less minority, mostly the young and the elderly, but in an attempt to promote it, the service inwards from Sidcup was increased to four trains an hour from June 1996.

The Bexley Heath Railway (map page 18)

'A long and unattractive street of small new shops and dwellings' was how Thorne saw Bexley Heath (or Bexley New Town) in the early 1870s. It then sheltered around 5,000 in houses strung along the main Dover Road amid market gardens, about 1½ miles north of Bexley on the Dartford Loop Line. To the east, at the tenth mile on the Dover Road, was Welling, and closer still to London, the 'suburban village' of Eltham, with its station on the Dartford Loop about a mile south of the High Street. Almost two miles further west, then at the very edge of south-east London, the select suburb of Blackheath offered the pattern that landowners further out wished to emulate, hoping to see the price of their acres rise from £400-£500 to the £1,000 to £2,000 which was usual at Blackheath.

This would require a railway service, but when the private interests petitioned the SER for a line into the Bexley Heath area in 1881 they received little encouragement, being advised to form their own company to minimise opposition and secure land at minimum cost. This was a tactic not unusual for main line companies to adopt in such a situation, in the hope of purchasing a ripening fruit at a discount later, when local effort was exhausted; if prospects were poor, it could be allowed to wither on the vine at no loss to them.

Dr Edwin Course has made a careful study of the genesis and early days of the Bexley Heath Railway in two papers, to which the reader is referred for greater detail than can be given here. He shows how about one-third of the capital of the independent promotion was mustered from local support, principally from active and retired professional and business men living on large and medium sized private estates scattered in the area between the Dartford Loop and the North Kent lines of the SER. Francis Brady, the SER engineer, surveyed a 7m 5f 2ch line from 5ch east of Lee station on the Dartford Loop through Eltham, Welling, and Bexley Heath to a junction with the North Kent about 1½ miles south of Erith. Although this route was sanctioned by the Bexley Heath Railway Act of 1883, the SER, after insisting that the junction be at Lee owing to alleged congestion at Blackheath, now changed its mind and desired the connection to be at Blackheath after all. Delays followed whilst the local company tried to settle terms with the SER for working its line and also sought an acceptable path through the exclusive residential district of Blackheath Park, jealously watched over by Albemarle Cator, who was finally appeased by a promise of a 140yd tunnel extension built solely to obscure the railway from the gaze of the residents.

The 1m 6f 2ch Eltham-Blackheath deviation, which was to meet the original alignment 1m 20ch from Lee, was approved by an act of 1887, but the troubles of the small company were not over. Although it had taken shares and lent money and officials, the SER was distinctly lukewarm about a line which would not only be quite expensive to make, but would abstract traffic from existing stations, whilst adding to the congestion in inner London. Difficulties were therefore made about raising the balance of the capital, involving the promoters in further legislation for extension of time. Eventually the SER was goaded into action by the deposit of two bills, one to abandon the line completely, the other seeking junctions with the SER's rival and neighbour the LCDR. With Sir Edward Watkin still occupying the SER chair, the board was incapable of resisting this sort of blackmail, so in the middle of 1890 an agreement was at last sealed under which the SER was to operate the Bexley Heath for 60 per cent of gross receipts as well as raising the remainder of the

Bexley Heath station with Up train entering, c.1903.
Commercial postcard

Welling station, Down side, in 1895 just before the opening of the line.
Bexley Libraries & Museums

Blackheath Tunnel, an unnecessary engineering work, built up above ground level to conceal the Bexley Heath Railway in its passage through the Cator Estate of Blackheath Park.
E A Course

capital. William Rigby started to make the line, but earthslips and financial troubles caused further delay, and it was not until 1st May 1895 that the service started, with oil-lit four-wheelers provided by the SER, upholstered and antimacassared in the first-class, padded in the seconds, wooden boards in the thirds. There were 14 Down trains and 12 Up, five each way on Sundays, running only between Blackheath and Erith or Dartford, calling at all stations, except in rush hours when some Blackheath–London trains were extended over the new line.

Despite its connection with the North Kent at either end, this 8¼-mile line, so long in the making, was as has been said, essentially a local railway, with a ruling gradient of 1 in 80 and severe curves. To minimise acquisition and demolition of expensive property at Blackheath, it left the North Kent 14ch east of the station on a south-east curve of only 13ch radius, tucked into a steeply-walled cutting. There followed the 437yd tunnel under the Cator Estate, its cosmetic eastern section poking its crown above the level of the surrounding land to avoid too sharp a gradient. Here the double tracks crossed the little Kid Brook, entering an area which the Earl of St Germans had been unable to develop because the Cator Estate, jealous of its privacy, had refused financial inducements to allow a road through Blackheath. St Germans accordingly petitioned against the bills for the Eltham–Blackheath deviation in order to secure a station on his land. This was granted and was connected by a new road across two farms to the Kidbrooke Park Estate, where middle-class villas were slowly grouping around the 1867 church of St James, half a mile north of the line. Kidbrooke's main building, on the Up side, was in the SER standard wooden-boarded style with rectangular sash windows, under a hipped slate roof which was extended over the platform by means of a shallow-curved canopy. On the Down side there was merely a rudimentary shelter. This general pattern was repeated at all the other Bexley Heath Railway stations. A small goods yard on the Up side at Kidbrooke saw considerable expansion and activity in World War 1 when a military depot was placed there, a development which also brought heavy peak-hour passenger traffic to what had hitherto been a very quiet station. Eventually the war depot extended both sides of Kidbrooke Park Road south of the line, served by its own narrow and standard gauge steam locomotives.

Beyond Kidbrooke, on an embankment notorious for slips, the line ran south-east towards Eltham village, swinging sharply north-east on a 12ch curve to skirt the southern boundary of the Well Hall Estate. This cruel kink, many years later the scene of a frightful derailment,* could have been avoided by a deviation to the north but for the success of Well Hall's owner (Sir Henry Page-Turner Barron) in securing a requirement in the 1887 act for a passenger and goods station exactly here, south of the estate at the junction between the original alignment from Lee and the Blackheath deviation. Called Well Hall, (Well Hall & North Eltham from 1st October 1916; Eltham Well Hall from 10th October 1927) this station's passenger platforms were sited above the Eltham-Woolwich road on the west side, just north of Eltham church and in a much more convenient location for the village than the 1866 station on the Dartford Loop about a mile to the south. Goods sidings were provided on the Up side at the London end.

East of Well Hall, the tracks ran through a cutting on the southern side of Shooter's Hill, reaching the summit south of Oxleas Wood, before crossing the Dover Road to enter Welling station. This was on an embankment at the Belle Grove or western end of the village with a small goods yard on the Down side at the country end. At Kidbrooke, builders had nothing much to offer the new line; Eltham's scattered population of 5,600 hardly justified two stations, while Welling, a thin collection of roadside cottages, was to prove no more promising in the early years.

---

* On 11th June 1972, when a railway staff excursion returning to London from Margate was driven at excessive speed through the 20mph restricted curve; four people were killed, including the driver of the diesel locomotive and two more died later.

Kidbrooke station looking towards Eltham, 30th May 1959, before replacement of the original SER buildings. Unit 4503 on Down train of mixed wooden and steel-panelled stock (8 cars).
Alan A Jackson

Eltham Well Hall, Up side entrance block, as rebuilt by the SR in 1932. The Morris Minor van waiting outside the parcels office door demonstrates that in 1968, when this photograph was taken, evening newspapers were still being delivered by rail to suburban stations.
BR (SR)

A Down train approaches the newly-opened Eltham station, provided from the roadbuilding budget as part of the cost of constructing the new Rochester Way Relief Road seen on the right; 23rd October 1985.
Alan A Jackson

Still on embankment, the tracks continued to a point at the western end of Bexley Heath* where a cutting began. The Bexley Heath goods yard was sited here on the Up side and although this transition point would have provided the cheapest site for a passenger station, the platforms were erected a quarter-mile further east in the cutting at the insistence of Robert Kersey, a BHR director and subscriber, owner of the Brampton Place Estate. Between Pickford Lane and Church Road, the station was thus a quarter-mile north of the Dover Road, a good mile from the centre of Bexley Heath at the Market Place. Most of the promoters' hopes rested on the residential development of this area with its well-drained gravel subsoil, hitherto disadvantaged by the 1½ miles distance from the Dartford Loop station at Bexley.

One further station and goods yard was opened with the line. This was about half-way between Bexley Heath and the junction with the North Kent, in open country between the Erith suburb of Northumberland Heath and Bexley Heath Market Place. It was sited in the middle of a wood on the land of Col. Frederick Barne, a BHR director, and accordingly named Barnehurst. Somewhat paradoxically, this lonely station was for many years the only one to possess a footbridge between the platforms.

Barnehurst was sited at the transition from cutting to the final embankment which carried the line down to the estuarine marshes of the Darenth and Cray, the tracks dividing at Perry Street Fork Junction to join the North Kent at Slades Green Junction (facing Erith) and Crayford Creek Junction (facing Dartford). These connections were made for operating convenience rather than through passenger working – until the 1920s, many trains turned back to London at Bexley Heath or Barnehurst.

Whilst passenger revenues in the early years were about five times those from freight, traffic was light. Despite great activity in the property market, especially at Bexleyheath,* little new housing actually appeared, and soon the SER was expressing its disappointment, all the more hurt because, in the words of the board minutes, 'the line was constructed at the insistence of the landowners'. Absolutely nothing happened at Barnehurst, (where the road to the station was still descriptively named Hills and Holes in the early 1920s), apart from the opening of a golf course on the May Place Estate, which may have produced a few passengers before the members all bought cars. Barnehurst, Bexley Heath, and Welling were all too far from London at a time when white-collar house-seekers could still find attractive and cheap property nearer in at such places as Hither Green or Ladywell. At Bexleyheath the huge Danson Park Estate of the first BHR chairman, Alfred W. Bean, remained very largely intact until it became a public open space in 1924. So miserable was business in the early years of the line that a horse-bus service between the centre of Bexleyheath and the station expired from lack of custom. Despite the anxiety to secure a station for the Kidbrooke Park estate no houses were built south of the church and it became second only to Barnehurst for quietude, at any rate until the war. Some evidence of this was noticed by a writer to *The Railway Magazine* in November 1906 who reported that no first-class ticket had been issued from it to Lewisham Junction until over six years after opening.

* The railway company used the original two-word form but in 1894 the local authority adopted the single word Bexleyheath, emulating Blackheath; railway usage did not catch up for many years.

Eltham Well Hall station looking east in 1926. Newly-laid conductor rails indicate that electric working is about to begin, or has just begun, but the station remains gas-lit and still retains its South Eastern Railway aura almost intact. *E Course*

Board of Trade Inspection of Bexley Heath Railway, 1895 at Bexley Heath station, looking east. No fewer than three Stirling 'O' class 0-6-0 locos occupy the Up line. The lack of residential and commercial development around the station at this time is very apparent. *Bexley Libraries*

Shooters Hill and Eltham Park station (later Eltham Park), erected with contributions from the estate developer, seen here around the time of its opening in July 1908. *Commercial postcard*

One major piece of suburban development did occur in the line's first two decades. In 1899 Cameron Corbett (later Lord Rowallan) purchased 334 acres of Eltham Park either side of the railway east of Well Hall station, with the intention of erecting a villa colony to repeat the success of his father's and his own efforts at Forest Gate and at Ilford. As soon as it learned of this, the SECR lost little time in seeking powers to take over the BHR. These were given in an act of 1900 and the small company was taken up at a discount from 10th July that year. Corbett was soon laying out a grid of streets with Scottish names and on 13th October 1900 he made an agreement with the SECR for 'superior passenger accommodation' for which he offered a valuable consideration. As part of the bargain, the SECR undertook to close Well Hall, which was less than half a mile west of the site of the new station in Westmount Avenue (now Road) at the centre of Corbett's estate. Subsequently the railway authorities discovered that closure contravened the BHR's agreement with Sir Henry Barron, whose heirs were not willing to modify it, obliging the SECR to try to withdraw from the arrangement with Corbett. Suing the railway for breach of contract, he was awarded damages in May 1905, but despite the proximity of the two stations, all ended well because subsequent housing development produced ample traffic for both for many years.

Substantial and capacious like Corbett's houses, Shooters Hill & Eltham Park station, designed by the railway's architect Alfred William Blomfield, was opened on 1st July 1908 (it was renamed Eltham Park on 1st October 1927). A brick booking office building on the road over-bridge was served by gently-sloping covered ways down the cutting sides to the two platforms with their brick waiting rooms, offices, and extensive canopies. In 1922 a footbridge was erected in the centre of the station, allowing the booking office to be transferred to the Up platform and the original street building to be converted to shops. Subsequently a footpath was made on the Up side, giving access from Glenesk Road. Sufficiently far to be out of sight and sound of the railway yet within comfortable walking distance, Corbett erected his most expensive houses, each with servants' annexes attached. Cheaper semis and terraces were sited nearer the line or at the outer edges of the estate. Much of the land had been covered when building ceased soon after the outbreak of World War 1. Occupants paid £26 a year rent for three bedrooms and an 80ft garden, or £38 for four bedrooms; their third-class season tickets to London cost £9 a year, but the early riser could purchase a workmen's ticket for a mere 5d return.

Partly in response to the Eltham activity, the SECR increased the service from 19 each way in 1899 to 32 in the 1900s, with about 11 each way on Sundays. But even as late as 1924 there were still only two Down through trains to the Bexleyheath line between 1700 and 1800 on weekdays, both from Cannon Street. By no means all the new residents used the railway for their journey to work; from 23rd July 1910 there were LCC electric tramcars to Woolwich, carrying many to the Royal Arsenal and other military establishments.

It was this military concentration in and around Woolwich which brought Eltham more houses and population during World War 1. With the Arsenal workforce growing from its peacetime total of 10,000 to over 70,000, the government ordered the erection of a large number of permanent and temporary dwellings around the town. Such was the activity that the three sidings at Well Hall had to be doubled in 1915, when the yard was receiving an average of 75 wagons of building materials daily. Well Hall also saw ambulance trains conveying wounded soldiers for treatment in the Royal Herbert Hospital at Shooters Hill. Although workers in the Woolwich munitions area came to live near the Bexleyheath line, most of their journeys were on a north-south axis for which they could use electric tramways, including the route between Woolwich and Bexleyheath opened on 3rd October 1903. This line offered a certain amount of competition to the railway, which it paralleled between Welling and Bexley Heath stations.

Goods traffic east of Kidbrooke remained very limited, but the passenger stations handled the produce of the many smallholdings, nurseries and market gardens until they were finally extinguished by bricks and mortar. As late as 1930 there were complaints that the waiting room at Bexley Heath station was cluttered with rose trees and crates of chickens.

Great changes were to follow the electrification of the line by the Southern Railway. In preparation for this, platforms were extended in 1924–25 to 520ft and footbridges erected at Well Hall, Welling, and Bexley Heath stations. Some electric working started on 10th May 1926 but the full timetable of three trains an hour in the peak (one Charing Cross, two Cannon Street) with two an hour at other times did not operate until 19th July. Journey time from Bexley Heath to Charing Cross, stopping at all stations, was reduced from 51 to 34 minutes.

Within a year or two the owners of the smallholdings, market gardens, orchards and nurseries were rushing to sell to builders attracted to the area not only by the vastly improved train service, but by the 9½ miles of motor roads from Kidbrooke to Eltham, Welling and Dartford, substantially completed in 1924 at taxpayers' expense, which minimised their road and drainage costs. There was much house-building activity at Bexleyheath from about 1928 but the really dramatic developments in which the firm of New Ideal Homesteads played a leading part, did not begin until the early 1930s, when economic circumstances became highly favourable to the London house building market. Within a decade the whole line from the eastern edge of Eltham to east of Barnehurst was closed in with many thousands of small semis and terraces of four or six.

Between the Edwardian fringe of Plumstead and points well south of the new Rochester Way, New Ideal, Wimpey and Wates and others laid out networks of concrete roads, lining them with little red-tiled houses offered mostly at the cheaper end of the range £425 to £750 freehold. Almost all the purchasers worked in central London and were unable to afford both the mortgage and payments on a car, so unless there were adequate bus facilities, the houses sold most readily if they were within reasonable walking distance (up to ¾ mile) from a railway station with a good service to the City and West End. Knowing the importance of this, New Ideal Homesteads offered the SR £5,000 in cash towards the £7,000 cost of a new station to serve two large estates between Welling and Eltham Park, No. 1 north of the railway, started in 1932 and No. 2 to the south, begun three years later. An agreement signed, the firm boasted in the *Evening News* of 8th January 1936:

> Where NIH build, new stations follow . . . the rapid extension of New Ideal's £1,500,000 Estate at Welling made Falconwood station a necessity.

Taking an optimistic view of the traffic potential, the SR decided to construct a rather more substantial station than at first envisaged for this site, in the cutting east of the bridge under Rochester Way. It included a flat-roofed cinema-style passimeter booking hall in red brick, facing the roadway, a covered footbridge and generous lengths of canopy on both the 540ft platforms, features which increased the cost to £12,500. Practical enough, but without the architectural elegance of contemporary London Transport stations, it came into use with its intermediate colour-light signals, on 1st January 1936.

Falconwood, another station provided with financial assistance from housing estate developers. Opened in January 1936, the Up side entrance block is seen here on 22nd December 1953 still bearing signs of its private company origins. *E A Course*

Some improvement was of course necessary to the existing wooden stations to meet the rapid growth in traffic. After an inspection by the general manager and senior officers in February 1930 the board allocated over £21,000 to reconstructing the main buildings at Eltham Well Hall, Welling, Bexley Heath, and Barnehurst. Eltham Well Hall also received a Down side entrance. Most of this work was finished by the end of 1932 but at Barnehurst, where housebuilding made a late start, reconstruction was not completed until 1935. Canopies were added on the Down side in 1937. During the rebuilding work all the stations were fitted with electric light. The new Up side buildings at Eltham Well Hall, Welling, and Bexleyheath were handsome single-storey structures in red brick under red-tiled roofs, larger than those they replaced, their style harmonising well with the new houses. The quite spacious booking halls were lined with glazed tiles. Finally, as part of a scheme to introduce 9ft wide steel-panelled rolling stock, platforms were lengthened in 1939 to a minimum of 530ft.

Housebuilding brought life to the sleepy goods yards. Materials arrived for roads; bricks, cement, tiles and window frames also came, and later solid fuels to keep the new occupants supplied with warmth and hot water. Enlargement of Welling and Barnehurst yards was sanctioned in 1932 together with an additional siding and car road at Bexleyheath. Two years later, new siding accommodation for 14 wagons was approved for Eltham Well Hall. With its usual eye for economy, the SR management moved the 5-ton crane from the closed station at Sandgate to Eltham Well Hall, and transported a redundant goods shed from Chilworth & Albury to Bexleyheath.

Traffic at Eltham Well Hall fully vindicated the SECR decision to retain it. Manual workers living on the large estates constructed nearby for the Woolwich Borough council in the 1920s went to their Thames-side workplaces by tram or bicycle, but many of their children grew up to find office or shop employment in London, joining the throngs of owner-occupier commuters and their wage-earning offspring. The area between the station and the village had been filled with private enterprise houses by about 1930, some of them dating from soon after the construction of the direct road for the electric tramway in 1910. Additional business was brought by buses which terminated in the large station forecourt, formed in 1952 into a bus terminus for six routes.

Barnehurst station, looking to Dartford, 22nd July 1975. The new brick frontage (right) provided by the SR on the Up side in 1935 has received some BR refurbishment.
Alan A Jackson

At Eltham Park, blank spaces on the Corbett estate, some of them occupied by munition workers' huts of 1915–16, were filled with houses between 1934 and 1939, whilst to the north, on the site of another wartime hut colony, Morrells' Castlewood Estate of 1935–38 offered cosy semis at £575 to £775 freehold. All this brought further business to Eltham Park, already well-established as a season-ticket station.

Welling gained from the eastern fringes of New Ideal's Falconwood and from a large council estate completed north of the line in 1920–26. From about 1928 the whole district to a depth of over a mile either side of the railway at Bexleyheath was networked with countless little streets of small houses whose owners enjoyed especially fertile gardens. By 1938 Danson Park was the only remaining major piece of open space. Typical of the somewhat down-market houses were the three-bedroomed, two reception villas five minutes from the station on the Goldsmid estate advertised in 1931 at £650 freehold. Taking its name from the station, the entirely new suburb of Barnehurst first came to life over Conduit and Three Corner Woods south of the line from 1933 onwards. 'Over 600 satisfied customers' were claimed for the £550 to £850 houses advertised on the May Place estate in April that year. Soon afterwards, New Ideal was at work on the Hill Crest estate north of the railway, while other builders were filling-in between the tracks and the golf course; within five years, Erith and Perry Street were merged with Barnehurst and Bexleyheath.

1929 had not passed before the SR was receiving complaints about over-crowding

The junction of the Bexley Heath Railway and the North Kent Line just east of Blackheath station on 9th April 1955. The substantial concrete retaining wall and sharp (13 chain) curve were required to avoid any incursion into the plot of a pre-existing house and garden (*Claverley*, Pond Road) on Cator's Blackheath Park residential development. *Alan A Jackson*

of rush-hour trains, and a year later the Bexleyheath Chamber of Commerce took up the struggle against what it called 'the continued neglect of the district by the Southern Railway Company'. Waterloo responded by offering the station rebuilding programme already mentioned, also by strengthening the train service. By the summer of 1930 off-peak frequency had been doubled to four an hour and from 30th September 1935 operation of some rush-hour trains over the Lewisham connections to City stations afforded useful relief, as we have seen earlier. Additional peak hour trains on the direct route were provided in the 1930s, so that by September 1935 the peak hour 17.00 to 18.00 saw three departures for the Bexleyheath line from Charing Cross, and two from Cannon Street in addition to the three from Blackfriars via Lewisham. This gave a total of 5,216 seats in the hour compared with 2,608 in January 1933 and 1,956 in July 1926.

During the 1950s and 1960s such limited space as was left inside the Green Belt, mainly at Bexleyheath and Barnehurst, was rapidly used up for private and local authority housing. This added further to the peak-hour congestion already experienced with the resumption of central London business activity after the war. One solution considered by the SR was the adoption of double-deck trains and the two 4-car multiple-unit prototypes, introduced in 1949, spent much of their life on the Bexleyheath line. They provided 1,104 seats (some of the tip-up type) compared with around 700 on a standard train. Often loaded, with standing passengers, to a total of over 1,500 on each journey, they proved a failure, as with one door to 22 seats (say to 30 passengers including those standing) station times were prolonged. Nor did the more sensitive souls relish the claustrophobic upper cabins with their sealed windows, which could be very unpleasant in the rush-hour scrums (though at quiet times lovers found the extra privacy pleasant). Towards the end of 1971 the trains were withdrawn from service after running some 700,000 miles. Long since BR had initiated the alternative solution of 10-car trains, each giving 958 seats. Platform lengthening for these trains started on the Bexleyheath line in 1953, the extra two cars appearing on rush-hour services from 14th June 1954, substantially alleviating overcrowding which was soon to be reduced by the effects of wider car ownership and a decline in the attraction of central London employment. It was the former, together with television's erosion of cinema and theatre patronage, that thinned out the off-peak traffic. The quarter-hour service was accordingly reduced to 20 minutes from 15th September 1958, only to be restored in what proved an over-optimistic gesture in the major timetable revisions of 10th July 1967. From that date, the Bexleyheath line had two stopping trains and two semi-fast (non-stop between Eltham Well Hall and London Bridge) in every off-peak hour. At the same time, the peak morning hour 08.00 to 09.00 was built up to eight London arrivals (two at Cannon Street, six at Charing Cross) and the Down peak (17.00 to 19.00) saw nine departures (five from Charing Cross, four from Cannon Street). On 4th May 1970, the basic service reverted to three an hour, and from 1st November that year working was much improved by the introduction of colour-light signalling controlled from a new route-setting panel at Dartford (Blackheath-Falconwood, worked temporarily from St John's box, had been in place since 15th March). Declining patronage in the evenings and on Sundays following the still increasing ownership of motor cars, saw trains at these times reduced to two an hour, in 1981 and 1983 respectively. In contrast, a welcome innovation, long suggested, was the half-hourly off peak service to and from Victoria introduced in the summer of 1994.

As elsewhere, in an age of declining domestic usage of solid fuels, the small goods yards could no longer muster enough traffic to satisfy Dr Beeching's accountants. Freight trains ceased to call at Welling from 3rd December 1962; Kidbrooke remained busy with Government traffic for some time after the war but changes of use and increased dependence on road transport caused that yard to close from 7th October 1968; and from the same day the freight yards at Eltham Well Hall, Bexleyheath and Barnehurst were also shut.

The SR had planned to rebuild Kidbrooke but other schemes took priority and its rotting timbers were passed to BR unaltered. The construction by the local authority in the early 1970s of a very large complex of tower blocks of flats, shopping precinct and a clinic, all south of the line on the site of the old military depots, promised to put extra traffic through this station and BR responded. In 1971 the SER structures were removed, to be replaced by a new ticket office, heated waiting area and lavatories, all these accommodated within the very ugly CLASP indus-trialised components. On the Down platform a new shelter was erected. As elsewhere the cheap CLASP option proved a poor investment, requiring complete reconstruction of the Up side building in brick and refurbishment of other features in 1994. At that time over 500,000 passengers a year were using this once quiet station.

Further station changes arose from the construction in the early 1980s of the Rochester Way Relief Road, which was somehow squeezed in alongside the railway between Kidbrooke and Falconwood, on the north side as far as Well Hall thence on to Falconwood on the south side, the crossing beneath the line requiring closure of Eltham Well Hall station. A new station, called simply Eltham, was erected at the cost of the road programme on the embankment at the east side of Well Hall Road, trains calling here for the first time on 17th March 1985. Heavily and crudely fashioned in red brick and concrete, with very high flat roofs above the platforms and a large car park and bus station below on the south side, the new structure seemed designed more to resist the worst assaults of vandals and hooligans than to welcome passengers. Staff accommodation and ticket offices at ground level, not completed until October 1988, were placed well away from the gaunt, intimidating platforms from which passengers could ingest the stink and roar of the new road below. As the new site was even closer to Eltham Park, that station saw its last train at 00.08 on 17th March 1985. Subsequent demolition spared the Blomfield building in Westmount Road, which is locally 'listed' and still in use as shops.

After an initial period of disappointing traffic, the BHR went on to fully justify the hopes of its promoters, and remains a very well-used railway as it enters its second century. Had it not existed, it is quite likely that around 1930 the SR would have built a similar line for electric working. At that time, the SR board was looking around for a suitable candidate for the financial aid the government was offering in its desire to relieve unemployment and here, opened up by new motor roads, the market gardens and nurseries around the old Dover Road were obvious fodder for the speculative builder. Had the BHR not been in place, there would have been an irresistible demand for a new railway from Lee or Blackheath through Eltham and Bexleyheath and it would probably have taken priority over the Wimbledon and Sutton and Chessington schemes.

The Mid Kent Railway: Beckenham & Addiscombe   (map page 41)

We now reach a railway which was to become local in character, despite the hopes of those who brought it to life; it was also one which spawned several other local lines.

'Mid Kent' seems an odd title for a railway which ran only 4¾m south from Lewisham to Beckenham, but the promoters of what had initially been named the Mid Kent & North Kent Junction had links with the SER and were aware of that company's aspirations for a cut-off line to Tonbridge, avoiding the long way round to Dover via Redhill. After discussions, the SER agreed to staff and work the proposed line, authorised in 1855, for 40 per cent of gross receipts, rising to 50 per cent after two years, when the main line company would take over maintenance costs. This arrangement lasted from the opening day, 1st January 1857, until 29th July 1864 when the SER absorbed the Mid Kent.

Closely following the River Ravensbourne and its tributary the Pool River, the Mid Kent was subject to flooding which hampered both its construction and subsequent operation but there was no major engineering involved. At Lewisham, a new station was provided to replace the old, on the country side of the new junction, with separate platforms for the North Kent and Mid Kent lines. Later the layout here was further modified by the opening of the cut off line through Sevenoaks to Tonbridge, which branched from the North Kent east of Lewisham Junction and in September 1866 was connected to the Mid Kent at Ladywell by a spur from Parks Bridge Junction which allowed Mid Kent services to by-pass Lewisham Junction station.

Decent yellow brick side-platform stations with their main buildings on the Up side were provided at Ladywell (¾m from Lewisham) and at Catford Bridge (1½m), the latter with a goods yard and a substantial two-storey Italianate station house.

Catford Bridge, looking to London c. 1870.

These two stations served and further nurtured the ribbon development that already existed along the Bromley road as far south as Rushey Green. A third station was opened for passengers and goods at Lower Sydenham (2¾m), the unfashionable east end of the plush new suburb on the eastern slopes below the Crystal Palace. The first site was close to the South side of South End Lane, but in 1906 at the behest of the Cator Estate, which contributed, the platforms were resited almost a quarter mile south, closer to the as yet undeveloped northern section of the Estate, with access to its road approaches on the Down side. Despite the Cator link, the new station had no more than the standard SER cheap and cheerful clapboard buildings. In 1854 the Crystal Palace District Gas Company established its works on the Up side just over a quarter mile north of the first Lower Sydenham station. From 1878 this was served by a siding entered from a ground frame controlled from Lower Sydenham Station Box. By 1912 what was now the South Suburban Gas Co. owned three steam locomotives, which operated over three miles of track inside the works. About three quarters of a mile south of Lower Sydenham, the Mid Kent curved sharply eastwards to terminate a quarter mile north of Beckenham village centre. This last section, passing through the Cator Estate, was subject to stringent conditions attached to the sale of the land. One of these was that no trains should stop at stations within Beckenham on Sundays, except early in the morning and late in the afternoon, a restriction not so much based on religious principle but rather to deter invasion of an area the Cator interest had in mind to develop as a respectable residential enclave by rough and noisy Cockney excursionists. This constraint was not finally removed from the railway operators until the end of the Victorian era. At Beckenham, the Cator estate subsidised the station, at first insisting there should be no goods depot but this proviso was modified after the main line was built through the area. Trees and shrubs were to be planted to screen the railway from the view of the sensitive middle class occupants of any houses the Cator Estate might build.

SER building at Lower Sydenham, Up side, c.1968. *BR (SR)*

At Beckenham, the Mid Kent was at first on its own, though soon to be joined by the West End of London & Crystal Palace Railway's eastern extension from Bromley Junction (between Crystal Palace and Norwood Junction) to New Bromley (now Shortlands). Opened on 3rd May 1858 and extended to Southborough Road (now Bickley) on the following 5th July, from the latter date until 1st September 1863 this extension carried SER trains to and from the Mid Kent. Their removal was a consequence of the conversion of the line east of Beckenham into the LCDR's Kent main line, a development which killed all hope of the SER reaching Tonbridge this way. At first SER facilities were maintained, with some difficulty; through carriages to and from the SER Mid Kent line called at stations between Beckenham and Bickley, attached to or detached from LCDR trains at Beckenham. This facility was withdrawn after 30th September 1866.

Beckenham station was jointly owned and maintained by the SER and what became the LCDR. Its main buildings, on the Up side, were in an Italianate style similar to Ladywell and Catford Bridge, the most striking feature an iron and glass train shed which covered much of the two side platforms. There was a small freight yard and a locomotive turntable. Horse bus services were soon feeding in traffic from Bromley, Hayes, Keston and even Sevenoaks, all places (except Bromley) destined to be without railway facilities for some years.

Since the SER was now blocked off east of Beckenham, other schemes emerged for using the strategic position of the Mid Kent. In 1861 the little company successfully promoted a 3¼m extension into the eastern outskirts of Croydon, with a terminus in the Addiscombe Road. And in the 1862–63 Session, in conjunction with the LCDR, the SER sought to use the Mid Kent as a jumping-off point for a 56-mile line from Beckenham to Lewes and Brighton. Both proposals were of course blatant incursions into LBSCR territory.

After two attempts, the Brighton scheme failed but the Addiscombe extension was built and was opened on 1st April 1864, worked by the SER, which secured powers to lease in its act of that year. Suburban speculators were already at work around Elmers End and at Addiscombe. W. Wilkinson, chairman of the Mid Kent, was also deputy chairman of the National Land Co., whose chairman, Charles Gilpin, was an SER director. It is therefore not surprising to find the Land Co. engaged in property transactions in the catchment area of the new railway.

In 1862 the Mid Kent also evolved a scheme for a line leaving the Addiscombe Extension to curve around the west side of Croydon before proceeding south to Caterham. This was effectively stifled by the LBSCR but that company was driven to fend off further attempts to enter Croydon by promoting its own Central Croydon branch, which we shall return to later.

At Croydon, the Mid Kent's main building was on the west side of the line, reached by a short cab approach from Addiscombe Road. The double track ended at a locomotive turntable against the north side of the main road. A four-road engine shed was built to the east of the line at the London end of the terminus.

Two intermediate stations were opened with the line. The first, immediately south of the junction with the original line to Beckenham, was named New Beckenham and had no freight yard. It had been subsidised by the Cator Estate, which intended to develop the district north of the LCDR main line by stringing villas along wide new roads. To avoid confusion, Beckenham station became Beckenham Junction. New Beckenham's original station building, on the Up side, still standing and in use

New Beckenham, looking to London, 23rd February 1963, still gaslit. *Alan A Jackson*

as a private house at the time of writing, was for the time being completely isolated in open countryside. Not surprisingly, it did virtually no business and was closed in the autumn of 1866. At that time defunct railway stations were of sufficient rarity for the Ordnance Survey to print the legend 'Station (Closed)' alongside on its maps. A certain amount of mystery attends this first New Beckenham station as the maps suggest its Up platform may have extended north of the junction, allowing trains from Beckenham to London to call, or possibly work as a shuttle between the two Beckenham stations, although, as is often the case with large scale OS maps, the extent of the platforms is not easy to determine. London to Beckenham trains on the Mid Kent, if they used the station at all, would have needed to indulge in some complex and rather futile shunting manoeuvres. Whatever, from October 1866, if not a little earlier, New Beckenham's platforms were moved north of the Junction, so that trains to and from either terminus might call without complications; there were also some shuttles working to and from Addiscombe in the early years.

The second intermediate station, 26ch south of New Beckenham, was at Elmers End, an area of scattered farm cottages and hamlets also shown on maps as Elm End, Elms End or Elm End Green. Here a freight yard was provided on the Up side and the main passenger station building was on the Down side at the end of a short approach from what is now Elmers End Road. We shall return to these two stations later to note subsequent developments.

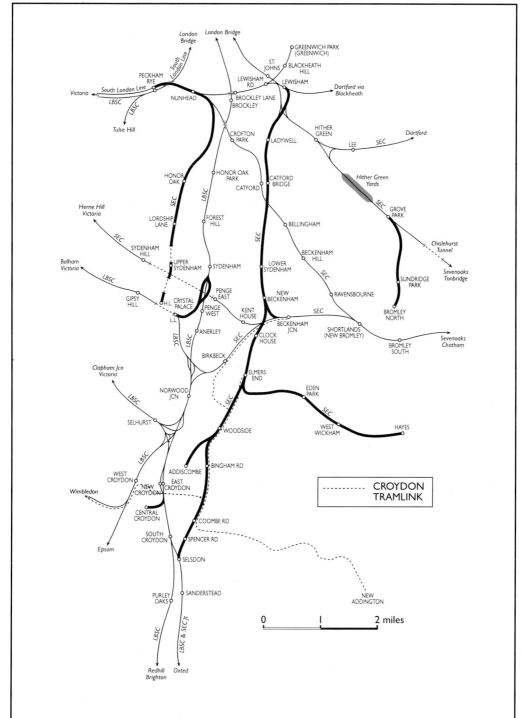

London Bridge

London Bridge

GREENWICH PARK
(GREENWICH)

ST. JOHNS

BLACKHEATH HILL

PECKHAM RYE

LEWISHAM RD

LEWISHAM

Dartford via Blackheath

Victoria South London Line

LBSC LBSC

NUNHEAD

BROCKLEY LANE

BROCKLEY

HITHER GREEN

LEE SEC *Dartford*

Tulse Hill

CROFTON PARK

LADYWELL

Hither Green Yards

HONOR OAK

HONOR OAK PARK

CATFORD BRIDGE

CATFORD

SEC

GROVE PARK

Herne Hill Victoria

LORDSHIP LANE

FOREST HILL

SEC LBSC

BELLINGHAM

Chislehurst Tunnel

SYDENHAM HILL

Balham Victoria

SEC

UPPER SYDENHAM

SYDENHAM

BECKENHAM HILL

LBSC

LOWER SYDENHAM

SEC

Sevenoaks Tonbridge

SUNDRIDGE PARK

GIPSY HILL

H.L. CRYSTAL PALACE

PENGE EAST

PENGE WEST

KENT HOUSE

NEW BECKENHAM

RAVENSBOURNE

SEC

BROMLEY NORTH

L.L.

ANERLEY

BECKENHAM JCN

SEC

LBSC LBSC

BIRKBECK

CLOCK HOUSE

SHORTLANDS (NEW BROMLEY)

BROMLEY SOUTH

Sevenoaks Chatham

Clapham Jcn Victoria

NORWOOD JCN

SEC

ELMERS END

EDEN PARK

LBSC

SELHURST

SEC

WOODSIDE

WEST WICKHAM

SEC

HAYES

LBSC

WEST CROYDON

ADDISCOMBE

BINGHAM RD

Wimbledon

NEW CROYDON

EAST CROYDON

CENTRAL CROYDON

| | CROYDON TRAMLINK |

COOMBE RD

SOUTH CROYDON

SPENCER RD

Epsom

SELSDON

PURLEY OAKS

SANDERSTEAD

NEW ADDINGTON

0   1   2 miles

LBSC

LBSC & SEC Jt

Redhill Brighton *Oxted*

Crystal Palace : Mid Kent : Addiscombe : Woodside & South Croydon
Hayes : Central Croydon : Bromley North : Croydon Tramlink

In the opening month, Bradshaw showed 11 trains each way between Addiscombe Road and London Bridge or Charing Cross, with no service on Sundays. By the following March this had been increased to 16, no doubt in response to the encouraging growth of Addiscombe. That station, less than a mile from the centre of Croydon, and only about a half-mile from the LBSCR station in George Street, was soon to secure a substantial business of its own which might otherwise have gone to the LBSCR, traffic diverted as it were through the back door of this Surrey town, which the SER had hitherto entered only on LBSCR sufferance via New Cross and the main line. The suburbanisation of this side of Croydon had been announced at the time the Addiscombe extension was promoted: on 23rd December 1861 the *Freeholders' Circular* was describing Addiscombe as 'a very eligible situation for gentlemen who wish to build or purchase a house entirely out of the smoke of London and yet within twenty minutes' ride of the City or West End.' These were of course LBSCR times, not to be bettered by the less direct SER route. A magazine called *London Society* also indicated that Croydon was already developing good quality commuter traffic, talking in 1862 of handsome villas springing up on every side 'tenanted by City men whose portly persons crowd the trains'.

Clock House, looking to London, 24th May 1975. Unit 5051 is entering with a Charing Cross–Hayes service. *Alan A Jackson*

Addiscombe Road station (later Addiscombe) exterior, c.1903. A solitary horse cab awaits hire, a canvas sheet thrown over it to keep the interior cool.

The street frontage on the overline bridge at Woodside, c.1905.

Much of the Addiscombe building was on land released by the closure and sale of the Royal Military College for the East Indian Army, whose cadets were transferred to Woolwich in 1862. Laid out by the British Land Company, the College Estate, south of the SER station, had by 1875 become a 'nest of villas' with two churches. South of this, even more spaciously planned, was the Park Hill Estate, started in 1861 by the Ecclesiastical Commissioners, although development here did not really get under way until a reliable water supply was provided in the 1870s.

From around 1870, the Mid Kent line established itself as a suburban route with a steadily growing business. At 69ch north of Addiscombe, a station called Woodside was opened in 1871 with financial assistance from local sources, to serve an extension of South Norwood which was growing down towards the Mid Kent line. Around 1885, to accommodate intensification of this growth and also the working of the extension to Selsdon Road opened in that year, Woodside was rebuilt in yellow brick with a substantial booking hall over the line, its inner wall displaying a clock to the walled, well-canopied platforms below. A bay was provided on the Down side for the shuttle service on the new line. This station secured further but sporadic business from the Croydon racecourse east of the railway, until that closed in 1890. In 1898–99 Addiscombe was rebuilt as a single storey red brick and slate-roofed block, set parallel to the main road across the end of the line. With its spacious concourse behind, serving three well-canopied platforms (two on an island), the reconstructed station made a handsome and commodious suburban terminus.

By 1914 Elmers End had almost joined up with Beckenham east of the railway but the land on the west side was occupied by the Croydon refuse destructor and sewage works, the Beckenham Council refuse destructor and electric power station, two brickworks and the Crystal Palace District Cemetery. The first of this varied group was served by a siding which left the Up side south of Elmers End station, controlled by Sykes' key and ground frame from Woodside box. North of Elmers End station on the Up side, another private siding, dating from the Edwardian years, entered the Beckenham Council site.

To the south of Beckenham Road, lower middle class housing erected in quantity from around 1885 was served by a station and goods yard named Clock House and opened on 1st May 1890. Almost an exact replica of Woodside, (even to the clock on the overbridge), it was sited on the south side of the Beckenham Road overline bridge, which carried the single storey, yellow stock brick building, from which two covered staircases led to well-canopied platforms backed by high brick walls. An opening in the wall on the Down side allowed Post Office vans to be loaded directly off the platform. At the country end of the Up platform an 18-lever signal box controlled the station, the freight siding on the Down side and, later, entry to the Beckenham Council siding mentioned above.

Immediately to the north of Clock House, the tracks passed close above the waters of the Chaffinch Brook, which regularly flooded the line to a depth of a foot or more after heavy rain. This did not cause too much of a problem for steam trains but electric trains taking power from the track were unable to proceed, even after the line had been raised somewhat in 1928, a situation requiring deployment of a standby set of loco-hauled stock shuttling to and from New Beckenham or loco haulage of dead electric trains. Much-handled and very dog-eared posters would be brought out of store to warn passengers of the delays inherent in these emergency procedures. In 1966 the local authority at long last cured the problem by culverting the stream.

Traffic at New Beckenham, much of it first and second class, blossomed under the influence of the developing residential area in the Cator Estate, where roomy villas were laid out along the wide, curving lengths of Copers Cope and adjacent roads in the late 1870s and the 1880s. The articulate residents became impatient about the lack of a footbridge and waiting rooms, the inconvenience attached to the working of the Beckenham Junction services and the increasingly dangerous nature of the Lennard Road–Park Road level crossing south of the platforms. Their complaints were taken up by the Cator Trustees and by the end of the 1890s all parties had agreed to a reconstruction of the station on the same site with a tiled foot subway under the railway in place of the level crossing, and a new road bridge across the two lines further south (Bridge Road) to connect the two sides of the Estate north of the LCDR main line. The spacious brick built station, with long, well-canopied platforms, and its main offices on the Up side, was completed in 1904. There was also a new 50-lever signal box at the country end on the Down side and a third track between the platforms to simplify the process of dividing and combining trains for the two routes to the south. Services had continued to be worked to and from Beckenham Junction over the original line, normally in the form of a portion of London-Addiscombe trains, or after the opening of the Hayes branch in 1882, between London and Hayes. Later there were also some motor train workings, shuttling between the two Beckenham stations. But the middle road at New Beckenham had a short life; the practice of working Beckenham Junction and Addiscombe portions in one train north of New Beckenham was discontinued in World War I and the track between the platform roads was removed in 1926. Sunday services on the Beckenham Junction spur ceased from 3rd April 1916 never to be restored. There were to be further changes following electrification as we shall see in a moment.

Expansion of Lower Sydenham west of the line in the 1890s mostly took the form of housing for local workers; to the east and south, open fields and woods remained either side of the railway, with sports clubs slowly taking up land. Catford Bridge station benefited from extensive villa development east of the line towards Forest Hill, some of which was contemporary with the Mid Kent. Ladywell grew up later, the land west of the line becoming covered with the small terrace homes of third class commuters in the late 1890s and early 1900s.

Addiscombe spread south and east, especially after 1902 when the opening of an electric tramway connecting it to central Croydon encouraged further residential development. In 1908 the large Ashburton Estate around Bingham Road was sold for housing but this was also served by the Woodside to Selsdon Road line which we shall look at later.

Train services were improved with traffic growth. By 1885 there were 25 journeys each way between Addiscombe Road and London, but only four each way on Sundays. In 1910, when there were 30 trains on weekdays and 14 on Sundays, Charing Cross was reached in about 50 minutes, Cannon Street in 40. From 1st April 1880 the SER worked 16 trains between Addiscombe Road and Liverpool Street, using new Up and Down spurs on and off the East London Railway at New Cross (Canal Junction). From 3rd March 1884 these trains were terminated at St Mary's (Whitechapel), using the new Whitechapel Curve, but ceased altogether after the last train on 30th September that year. The 1912 timetables illustrate the considerable variety of Mid Kent service at that time, with Down workings as far as

New Beckenham as follows:

Charing Cross/Cannon Street–Addiscombe/Beckenham Junction	10
Charing Cross/Cannon Street–Addiscombe	2
Charing Cross–Addiscombe	2
Charing Cross–Beckenham Junction	3
Charing Cross–Addiscombe/Beckenham Junction, Orpington	1
Cannon Street–Addiscombe/Beckenham Junction (1 to Orpington)	12
Cannon Street/Addiscombe	4
Cannon Street/Beckenham Junction	3
Cannon Street–Selsdon Road (1 to Edenbridge)	2
St Paul's (Blackfriars)–Beckenham Junction	1

On Sundays there were hourly trains from Charing Cross (two via Cannon Street) to Addiscombe and Beckenham Junction only.

Electrification came to the Mid Kent soon after the formation of the Southern Railway, third-rail multiple-unit trains serving Addiscombe from 28th February 1926 with full service following on 19th July. They gave a half-hourly coverage all day, seven days a week, alternately Charing Cross and Cannon Street, with four an hour at business periods, one Charing Cross, three Cannon Street. Some of the latter, missing intermediate stations, reached London Bridge in 25 minutes from Addiscombe. At the outer terminus on the east side of the line, the SR erected four-road cleaning and inspection sheds for the new trains. Operation was eased by the installation of colour-light signals between New Cross and Ladywell on 30th June 1929. Electrification plans for the Mid Kent encouraged the Metropolitan railway in 1925–26 to try to negotiate for a through electric service between Addiscombe and its system via the 1880 connections at New Cross, but this came to nothing.

Ladywell, looking south, 1890; top hatted commuters prepare to board a morning Up train composed of oil-lit four-wheel coaches.

The investigations carried out in 1925 by Metropolitan Railway officers in connection with this proposal throw some light on contemporary SR operations on the Mid Kent line to Addiscombe. The stations were described as 'old and dingy', the trains (still steam-hauled) as 'infrequent and unpunctual', the stock as 'old, dirty and in bad condition'. Trains arriving at Addiscombe were not heavily-loaded, between 50 and 90 passengers alighting from each arrival between 17.30 and 18.30. This station was said to handle about 1,000 passengers a day, of whom some 300 were taking workmen's tickets. Many residents in the eastern part of Croydon and in South Norwood were stated not to be using the line, preferring the 'faster and more comfortable' services available at East and West Croydon and Norwood Junction stations.

After the electrification of the Hayes branch in 1926 a separate half-hourly service was provided between Beckenham Junction, New Beckenham and Charing Cross/Cannon Street (alternately). But the increased number of through trains to London from Hayes and Sanderstead caused this Mid Kent service to Beckenham Junction to be severely reduced from 1935 and after traffic on 15th October 1939 it ceased altogether. No regular public workings then ran over the spur from New Beckenham to Beckenham Junction for many years but between 1965 and 1983 when the BR Southern Region South East Divisional Headquarters was located in Albemarle Road. Beckenham, some special trains were worked non-stop between Beckenham Junction and London Bridge via New Beckenham for the convenience of railway staff. The spur, which had been singled and signalled for two-way working in 1987, once again carried public trains from 29th May 1995, when an 'experimental' off-peak Mondays to Saturdays service between Cannon Street/London Bridge and Orpington via the Mid Kent line was started.

Housebuilding of any quantity in the post-electrification era was necessarily confined to the few remaining open areas around the Shirley Schools (providing more customers for Woodside); west of the line between Clock House and Elmers End stations; and a large northward expansion of Cator New Beckenham to the east of the railway between New Beckenham and Lower Sydenham. The extensive LCC estate at Bellingham, erected in two phases between 1920 and 1937 also brought a few more passengers to Lower Sydenham. Lastly there was some speculative terrace building at Perry Hill, west of the Pool River, between 1927 and 1935 which provided additional commuters at Catford Bridge. But even in total this was fairly small beans compared with the extra traffic brought to the Mid Kent after 1930 by the intensive private house-building activity along the Hayes branch, which we shall be looking at later.

The 1939 timetables showed the Mid Kent carrying half-hourly Charing Cross–Sanderstead and half-hourly Cannon Street–Addiscombe trains as well as the half-hourly Hayes service. Between 17.00 and 18.00, Hayes branch commuters were offered four trains, Addiscombe three, Beckenham Junction one and Sanderstead three, a total of 11 in an hour for stations to New Beckenham inclusive, ten as far as Elmers End. So busy were the Elmers End signalmen that in June 1939 they asked for more protection in the interest of safety; the minutes record approval of an expenditure of £2,575 on standard SR three-position closed block apparatus between New Beckenham and Addiscombe as a response. Colour light signals did not appear until 4th April 1971 on the Mid Kent, then only between Ladywell and New Beckenham. With the exception of Clock House, where three-aspect intermediate colour lights controlled from Elmers End and New Beckenham boxes had been installed in 1956, the section from Elmers End to Addiscombe retained its upper quadrant semaphores until the opening of the London Bridge Signalling Centre in 1975–76. Then, from 28th September 1975, the signalling from Catford Bridge to Woodside came under the Centre, with New Beckenham, Elmers End and Hayes boxes eliminated. Woodside remained as a fringe box, with the Addiscombe spur unchanged but closure of the line to Sanderstead made it possible to dispense with Woodside box on 24th June 1984, leaving Addiscombe as a fringe box to London Bridge. This lone outpost of low-tech remained until March 1996, when it was gutted by a fire started by vandals. After that the shuttle from Elmers End had to be worked with a pilotman and telephone.

War conditions brought train service cuts. Off peak through services between London and Addiscombe disappeared in the war emergency timetable of 1939 when the station was closed entirely during the middle of the day except on Saturdays. The Mid Kent was reduced to a half-hourly service off peak, working alternately to give Hayes and Sanderstead an hourly interval.

Freight traffic movements on the Mid Kent were dominated for many years by the appetite of the Lower Sydenham gasworks, where as late as 1958 almost 217,000 tons of coal were brought in by rail in a year. In 1951 the regular freight workings were still quite intensive. The day started with four trains between 00.20 and 02.45 carrying seaborne coal from the North End sidings at Erith to Lower Sydenham, a journey which involved reversal at Brockley Lane. Three of the trains returned to Erith. This tranche was followed by the 03.00 Bricklayers Arms–Addiscombe freight, calling at the Catford Bridge and Clock House yards, with wagons and brake for Beckenham Junction at the front. Next came the 04.07 Bricklayers Arms–Hayes, which called at the Catford Bridge and Elmers End yards as required. In the evening, the 22.55 Beckenham Junction–Catford Bridge freight was followed by a Hayes–Bricklayers Arms trip which called at West Wickham, Elmers End, Addiscombe, Woodside, Elmers End Council Siding, Clock House and Catford Bridge. The gasworks sequence then started with the 23.40 Bricklayers Arms–Catford Bridge–Lower Sydenham Gas Siding.

Declining use of domestic solid fuels, Beeching's financial appraisal and closure of town gasworks brought all this to a fairly sharp conclusion in the 1960s. Woodside yard, which had received 11,335 tons of solid fuel in 1958 was shut from 30th September 1963. Clock House and Elmers End followed from 5th October 1964. Catford Bridge and Lower Sydenham, restricted to wagonload coal only from 28th December 1964, were closed completely from 25th March 1968 and 20th June 1966 respectively. The connection to the Lower Sydenham gasworks, long disused, disappeared with the 1971 resignalling. Addiscombe yard survived until June 1968.

Some mention must be made of infrastructure changes since World War 2. Up to the 1990s many of the stations retained their Victorian buildings though canopies had often been shortened in length or removed altogether to reduce maintenance costs. Elmers End, badly damaged by bombs and missiles in the war, underwent some first aid patching-up in which the remains of the old Down side buildings were demolished; then, in 1956, here as elsewhere on the Mid Kent, platforms were extended to 675ft to accommodate ten-car trains, the extensions following the curve of the Hayes branch; new upward-sloping canopies were erected at the south end of the war-damaged Down platform as part of these works. At the same time the

Elmers End, looking to London, 28th April 1962 with a Sanderstead shuttle at the bay platform, left. At this time, the station was still gas-lit and the bomb-scarred remains of the SER Down side buildings are still in evidence. *Alan A Jackson*

tracks used by the Sanderstead and Addiscombe trains were slewed eastwards, the junction moved about 50yd south. After this operation, the signal box, which had been in the angle between the two sets of tracks, had both lines in front of it with sidings and Up bay behind. Vandals set fire to the Up side buildings in 1973 but a boldly-styled glass box entrance hall incorporating a ticket office restored some dignity when completed in 1975. In 1993 the Up bay was shortened to 63yd; the Down bay had been secured out of use in 1985.

At Addiscombe in 1956–57, in connection with the ten-car train scheme introduced on the Mid Kent from 4th March 1957, platform three was abolished, its site given over to a berthing siding; the island platform was at the same time extended up to the signal box. The carriage depot on the east side was closed in 1992 and the associated sidings in 1994.

Another probably deliberate fire severely damaged much of the lavish Edwardian Up side building at New Beckenham in the spring of 1966. A smaller structure replaced the entrance hall and ticket office. Lower Sydenham's timber inheritance from the SER was replaced in 1972 with the ugly factory-made CLASP building components, but after a fire in 1989 the station was rebuilt once more in the more pleasing neo-vernacular style adopted by BR Network SouthEast. Completed in 1991, this provided an Up side building with ticket office, waiting area and staff accommodation as well as new waiting shelters on both platforms. Yet another fire, on the Up side at Catford Bridge in May 1993, was followed by extensive renovations which resulted in the closure of the Up side ticket office in favour of a refurbished one on the Down platform.

From October 1988 staffing at stations was drastically reduced, revenue collection left to ticket machines on platforms and spot checks by inspectors on the trains. This established a pattern soon adopted on other suburban lines.

Modifications to the pre-war electric services have been considerable in recent years, reflecting significant changes in traffic flows. One important development in this area was the growth of Croydon into a major office centre in the 1960s. Another feature has been the way in which since the mid 1930s, the Hayes traffic has dominated business on the Mid Kent.

From 1945 the weekday half-hourly off-peak coverage at Addiscombe was provided by a shuttle service working in and out of the Up bay at Elmers End in connection with the Hayes service to and from Charing Cross (shuttle working on Sundays began the previous year). The summer timetable of 1948 restored a 15-minute off peak service at Elmers End, two an hour going to Hayes, one to Addiscombe, one to Selsdon/Sanderstead. But by the summer of 1950 all four were working through to Hayes, weekdays and Sundays, with Addiscombe and Sanderstead served only by half hourly shuttles on weekdays only. Off peak and commuter loadings on these two services fell off very steeply, making even two-car trains more than adequate. On a weekday evening in July 1975 only seven passengers were seen to alight from a rush hour arrival at Addiscombe. Twenty years after its first attempt had been thwarted, BR succeeded in withdrawing the little-used shuttle service between Elmers End and Sanderstead in May 1983. But not all changes have been negative; as already noted, the revival of a Mid Kent service through Beckenham Junction in 1995, brought an extra off peak facility to the inner section.

With other better-served stations readily accessible by bus or car from its catchment area, the survival of the double track line between Elmers End and Addiscombe seemed more associated with operating convenience than revenue but even this slim justification was removed by the closure of the carriage depot and sidings at Addiscombe in 1992–94. However by that time a new way of serving this district was emerging, one that also seemed likely to provide an alternative to other poorly-used local railways elsewhere in London. Croydon Tramlink was to take over the old SER alignment between Elmers End and its junction with the former Selsdon line south of Woodside station. Using this, a section of the Tramlink system was to replace the Addiscombe shuttle, providing a much more attractive service, since it offered a direct run westwards over street tracks via Addiscombe Road and past East Croydon station into the very centre of Croydon, with connections to the Mid Kent at Elmers End. Quite incidentally, it would also fulfil ambitions first expressed by the Mid Kent and SER in the middle of the nineteenth century.

Conventional rail services to Woodside and Addiscombe ceased after traffic on 31st May 1997 and changes in connection with Tramlink then saw Elmers End converted to a simple through station with the Up bay taken out of use.

The Woodside & South Croydon Line (map page 41)

This local railway was virtually a southward extension of the Mid Kent line just considered. Croydon is a town well favoured with railways, most of them very busy, but this one was a real backwater. Never properly exploited as a through route and virtually superfluous for the residential traffic for which it was used, the Woodside & South Croydon Railway had its origins in the border battles between the LBSCR and SER. In the early 1860s, the Brighton was seeking to take a share of the Tunbridge Wells traffic from the SER, whilst the latter was casting its eyes towards Eastbourne, even Brighton itself. When the SER planned a direct main line from London (St John's) to Tonbridge via Sevenoaks, avoiding the long detour through Redhill, the Brighton nurtured a Surrey & Sussex Junction scheme, a short cut from Croydon to its Uckfield–Tunbridge Wells line near Groombridge. As this proposal (which obtained an act in 1865 and was incorporated in the LBSCR four years later) was a blatant invasion of what had been settled as SER territory, the latter replied by promotion of a London–Lewes and Brighton Railway in collusion with the LCDR. From junctions with the LCDR and SER at Beckenham, this main line, sanctioned in 1866, would have run south through the very heartlands of the LBSCR. If the scheme ever were a serious one, it was lost in the financial panic of the period, in which the LCDR almost went under. That company was forced to withdraw, and turning to a more amicable attitude with the Brighton, the SER threw the plans into a dark corner.

But for its part, the LBSCR kept the Surrey & Sussex Junction powers alive, just to make sure of staking its claim, and even started to build it, a move soon to be regretted, as the enterprise was attended with many problems and much misfortune. After a number of bridges, viaducts and some tunnels had been begun, the Brighton wished a quick end, seeing no profit in it, nor any virtue, now that it had concluded pooling arrangements with the SER. Denied Parliamentary powers to abandon the line, the LBSCR eventually escaped by paying the maximum statutory penalty for not completing it in the time laid down in the act.

A Down special train just south of Coombe Lane station in 1902, hauled by SECR 2-4-0 No.61A.

The half-finished works were left to nature, but the territory crossed by the route remained the object of contentious schemes and eventually much of the Surrey & Sussex Junction was used for the Croydon, Oxted and East Grinstead Railways. These were authorised in 1878 and taken up as a joint line by the now friendly SER and LBSCR as far as the point where the line from Croydon met the SER Redhill–Tonbridge route (Crowhurst Junctions). The CO&EGR was part of a framework of railways projected at this time to strengthen the LBSCR hold, but with some judicious accommodation of the SER interest in the border territories. Other lines were to link the CO&EGR to the Tunbridge Wells–East Grinstead line at Groombridge and to extend it at either end – to Lewes, and to Woodside, on the SER Mid Kent Line. They thus realised the route of the SER/LCDR joint proposal of 1866, providing the LBSCR with an alternative route between Croydon and Brighton, with the SER allowed access only to the northern section.

The 2m 29ch link at the London end, known as the Woodside & South Croydon Railway, was authorised in 1880. It was taken-over by the LBSCR and SER for joint working from 10th August 1882 under powers given in the original act and confirmed in the SER (Various Powers) Act, 1882.

The joint line from South Croydon to Oxted opened on 10th March 1884 and the link to Woodside, which had been constructed by Joseph Firbank, followed on 10th August 1885, with its intermediate passenger station in yellow stock brick at Coombe Lane. Woodside was rebuilt in brick by the SER, with a bay platform on the Down side for the new service. SER influence predominated elsewhere. All but a few signals at Selsdon Road were of that company's pattern and the junction station at that point, with its separate sets of platforms for the Oxted and Woodside lines, was in the SER timber style. It was the SER which started to work the line, the two companies sharing the local service over alternate years from 1st July 1889.

Diverging from the Mid Kent at Woodside Junction, 12ch south of Woodside station, the new double track was on embankment to a point beyond Bingham Road. For a mile or so the line skirted the eastern edge of built-up Croydon, much of it developed by the British Land Company after 1860. The Addiscombe Park, Ashburton, and other estates east of the railway were to show the first signs of development in the 1900s, but would not be fully covered until the late 1920s. Goods stations were forbidden in this area under a section of the 1880 act which protected Lady Ashburton's estates. Beyond Upper Addiscombe Road, the W&SCR passed into a cutting, skirting the high ground south-east of Croydon known as the

Bingham Road station, Up side 24th May 1975.
Alan A Jackson

Addington Hills, then entering three contiguous tunnels, Woodside (266yd), Park Hill (122yd) and Coombe Lane (157yd). Although the first and last of these were only a very short distance apart, a change in the nature of the soil made it necessary to construct the central section of what might otherwise have been one tunnel on the cut-and-cover principle and this formed what was to become a romantic timbered dell, where the roof of the covered way supported a miniature rifle range, opened before 1914. This part of the route bordered the eastern edge of the Park Hill and Woodbury Farm estates which had already been laid out with artistically-curved roads designed to accommodate large middle-class villas, but to the east, north of Coombe Lane, there was a great deal of open parkland, much of it still uncovered today. From the tunnel the line was on an embankment through Coombe Lane station, which also bore signs of SER origins. Beyond, the line turned south-west towards the Brighton main line, at first in a cutting through the Croham Park estate where villa building started in the 1890s. Emerging at ground level, it entered Selsdon Road station, making its junction with the Croydon, Oxted & East Grinstead at the south end of the platforms.

Most trains ran only between Woodside and Selsdon Road. The 1902 timetable shows 11 each way, worked by the SECR, plus the curious oddity of a Down train which went on to terminate at Dover. Through workings, which had increased to three each way by 1914, never assumed enough importance to remove the predominantly local character of the service, which earns it a place in this book. Daily pick-up freights, two each way in 1902, worked from Bricklayers Arms to Tonbridge via the Mid Kent and Selsdon Road. In its early years the link was used by the SECR as a relief route for excursions between London and the Kent coast which returned to the main system via the Crowhurst spur. Use of this route became less frequent after the opening of the Chislehurst loops in 1902, but it continued well into the SR era.

Traffic through these still half-rural parts of east and south Croydon was very light at first, but Addiscombe gradually lapped up to the west side of the line and during the 1890s there were signs of increased building activity around Coombe Road station and between there and Selsdon Road. Either side of Croham Road, villas were erected close to the line in the 1890s and 1900s. Even so, working expenses normally exceeded revenue and in a creditable effort to exploit new suburban business at low cost, the number of journeys each way daily was increased in 1906 from about ten to 16, using the SECR Kitson steam railmotor units designed by Harry S. Wainwright. Working to and from the Down bay at Woodside, these cars, which were housed at Bricklayers Arms depot, began and ended their day on New Cross–Addiscombe trains. For this service, wooden halts with 100ft platforms were opened on 1st September 1906 at Bingham Road (between Woodside and Coombe Lane) and at Spencer Road (between Coombe Lane and Selsdon Road). Although surrounded by substantial late Victorian villas, Spencer Road Halt, reached only by footpaths, was very close to the existing stations at Selsdon Road and South Croydon. Bingham Road, adjacent to the Addiscombe terminus of the Croydon Corporation electric tramways (4th January 1902) became something of an interchange point, but general business remained very light despite the new housing. During its years of operation, the LBSCR employed pull-and-push units composed of a 'Terrier' 0–6–0T and a single coach, but in the 1910s the one-class Beyer Peacock steam railcars were transferred here from the Eastbourne–St Leonards service. Tickets for passengers boarding and leaving at the halts were issued and collected by the guard.

With its poor loadings easily diverted to alternative routes operated by the owning companies, the Woodside & South Croydon stood out as a clear victim for wartime economies. Railmotor service ceased after last journeys on 14th March 1915, when the halts were closed. Coombe Lane and Selsdon Road east platforms remained open for the few other trains until the evening of 31st December 1916, when these were also withdrawn, although Selsdon Road remained open on the Oxted line side. Empty stock, special trains, light engines and pick-up goods still worked over the line, the latter to and from the Mid Kent to call at the Selsdon Road yard, which was on the Down side of the passenger station at the London end. Local trains were not restored after the war. During 1927 the track was relaid, spawning false rumours that the line was to be re-opened for local traffic. However that summer the section was extensively used for trains from Hastings to Charing Cross/Cannon Street which worked via Tonbridge, Edenbridge and Oxted and rejoined the main line at St John's, a 70-mile journey but comparatively free of traffic. In the same year, mid week excursion trains to Canterbury West, Margate, Ramsgate, Brighton and Hastings starting from Lewisham Junction also ran via Woodside; these called at all stations to Woodside then at Selsdon Road. Similar summer workings probably continued until 1934, the year before electrification. There were also some hop-pickers' specials to and from Kent via the Crowhurst spur.

A 1925 scheme for a Southern Heights Light Railway was to have carried electric trains from Orpington to Sanderstead, connecting to SR lines. To integrate this with the rest of the system, it would have been necessary to electrify Woodside–Sanderstead, which offered a less congested route, with the possibility of convenient interchange at Elmers End with London trains and perhaps some through running via the Mid Kent. Although the Surrey Heights scheme was by then virtually dead, the SR did go ahead with the Sanderstead–Woodside electrification, the general manager cautiously telling the board in June 1934 that it was unlikely to do more than balance the books. This could not but be so, because despite a little more building development, mainly to the east of Bingham Road station, no part of the district served was very far from either Addiscombe or South Croydon stations. One cannot help wondering to what extent this decision was simply an obsession with the neatness of completing electrification of the Southern's London suburban lines.

Half-hourly electric trains, increased to three an hour in the peaks, ran between Charing Cross or Cannon Street and Sanderstead via Woodside from 30th September 1935. 'In view of the development in the area', Bingham Road Halt was replaced by a fully-equipped station at a cost of £10,000. Its brick entrances and covered staircases either side of the underline road bridge led to platforms supported on concrete piles driven into the embankment and sheltered by glazed wood and steel canopies. Spencer Road Halt, only a quarter-mile from South Croydon, was wisely discarded, but almost £7,200 was spent at Coombe Lane, reopened as Coombe Road, with extended concrete platforms and a new red brick, metal-windowed building on the Up side. Selsdon Road, renamed Selsdon (despite two uphill miles to the village) saw no changes, apart from lengthening of the Down platform and closure of the North box. The two-road goods yard here was subsequently enlarged to five roads. Sanderstead's Down platform was extended to 520ft.

Predictably, the electrification was not a success. Drastic cuts were made in World War 2 when trains ran only hourly off-peak, stopping altogether after 19.00 and after 15.00 on Saturdays, when there was no service until Monday morning. Pre-war intervals were restored in 1945 but from 26th September 1949 the through service to Cannon Street was withdrawn outside the peak hours, when two trains an hour shuttled between Elmers End and Sanderstead, connecting at the former with two of the four through trains an hour between Charing Cross and Hayes. This move further depleted the traffic, causing the complete withdrawal of service from 2nd November 1959 between 10.45 and 15.15 and after 20.45 on weekdays and 15.45 on Saturdays. A Railway Club party on Saturday morning 28th April 1962 found a 2EPB set waiting in the Up side bay at Elmers End, where some SER signs still survived. About 12 minutes were occupied in the run to Sanderstead, during which no passengers joined or alighted at the intermediate stations.

Further drastic falls in revenue led BR to propose complete closure from 4th March 1963, one of only two Southern Electric abandonments included in the Beeching Plan (the other was Horsted Keynes–Haywards Heath). After a successful protest lobby had been organised under the local MP, Transport Minister Ernest Marples announced in December 1963 a three-year reprieve followed by a review if the line was still not paying its way; it was stated that despite the existence of alternative routes, some hardship would ensue if service was withdrawn. Despite continuing unprofitability, the 1966 review led only to further pruning; from 2nd January 1967 the half-hourly Saturday peak shuttle (06.51 – 09.11; 11.51 – 14.11) was diverted to Addiscombe, and from 10th July that year, Bingham Road and Coombe Road were served only from 07.52 to 09.50 and between 16.17 and 19.10 on Mondays to Fridays, some afternoon trains reversing at Selsdon instead of Sanderstead. In April 1976 all through trains to and from London ceased, replaced by 2EPB 2-car sets shuttling between Elmers End and Selsdon or Sanderstead.

Selsdon goods yard, reduced to two roads, became a Shell oil-tanker depot in the 1960s. At the adjacent passenger station, the old SER timber buildings were demolished, leaving a station which consisted of short bits of the old canopy on each W&SCR platform and a tiny wooden booking hut on the Down side (Oxted line trains had ceased to call at their platforms in June 1959). When visited in 1975, gas lamps burned all day and the bare platforms still displayed Southern Railway signs (these also survived at Coombe Road and Bingham Road).

This quite hopeless operation, with each train carrying passenger loads which rarely if ever exceeded single figures, was kept going through the 1970s and early 1980s. Latterly there were nine morning Up trains, one starting from Selsdon, the rest from Sanderstead and seven return workings. Evening travellers had the choice of ten each way, including the 18.50 express from Sanderstead, fast from Selsdon to Elmers End. By the early 1980s fewer than 200 passengers a day were using these trains.

The inevitable end, so long postponed, came in 1983, passenger trains concluding with the 19.30 from Sanderstead on Friday 13th May, exploding detonators as it progressed and filled with people who had made little if any regular use of the line. A short length of track, between Selsdon Junction and Selsdon station was retained for working oil tank wagons into the depot on the Down side mentioned earlier. This traffic finally ceased in March 1983.

A scheme for conversion to roads was rejected, to give way to news that the Woodside and South Croydon was not to die completely. Much of the section between Woodside Junction and the site of Coombe Road station now forms part of the Croydon Tramlink light railway route mentioned earlier.

The Hayes (Kent) Branch (map page 41)

A village of some 600 inhabitants, in Thorne's words 'quiet and respectable and chiefly dependent on wealthy residents', mid-Victorian Hayes was set in one of the prettiest parts of metropolitan Kent. Although touched by several schemes, fully examined in Trevor Woodman's book, it had to wait until 1882 for its railway.

The route from Hayes to the Mid Kent line was revived in 1879 when local interests led by Col. John Farnaby Lennard of West Wickham Court (a Cator Estate trustee) in collusion with an SER anxious to filch what it could from LCDR territory promoted what is now the Hayes branch. This was to pass through a district already unsuccessfully probed by the LCDR, tapping deep into the catchment area of the LCDR's Bromley station through a district which superficially seemed ripe for high class suburban development. Authorised by the West Wickham & Hayes Railway Act of 8th July 1880, the 3m 2f 9ch branch was laid out by Francis Brady, the SER's engineer. Provision was made in the act for the line to be worked by the SER, whose director Alexander Beattie sat on the local company's board; fellow directors included Brady and A M Watkin, the son of the SER chairman. Very quickly the SER took steps to bring the small company into its grasp, securing power to purchase it for £162,000 in 1881. At this time the SER entertained ideas of extending the line to Keston and Westerham but with the realisation that costly engineering work would be involved in penetrating into and through the North Downs, this idea was quickly dropped. Indeed in view of what was to happen regarding the release of land for housebuilding, something on which the local interest amongst the promoters might be expected to have had some foreknowledge, it is remarkable that the SER proceeded with construction of any part of the line.

But proceed it did, and on Whit Monday 29th May 1882, No. 258, a Cudworth outside frame 0–4–4 back tank, worked the ceremonial opening train and the first public services. Provision soon settled down to 13 trains each way, four on Sundays, with connections to the Addiscombe–London trains at Elmers End, where the station had been rebuilt with Up and Down bays and given a new 43-lever signal box. The Up side received a single storey building fitted out with ticket hall, waiting rooms and staff accommodation. There were also new coal sidings behind the Up side bay.

West Wickham, looking to Elmers End, c.1925. *Commercial postcard*

A sleepy country branch line terminus; Hayes in the 1900s.

For some fifty years the Hayes branch was to remain a very attractive country line, climbing some 100ft in a graceful reverse curve towards the Hayes terminus as it skirted around and between the large private estates of Park Langley, Eden Park and Monk's Orchard. At Elmers End, the double track left the country end of the station on a 13ch curve which brought its direction almost due east on to an embankment, climbing at 1 in 76 and 1 in 89. Eden Park, the first station, required by the owner of that estate, William R Mace, had no freight yard. Its building was the familiar cheaply-made SER affair of wooden boards under a slate roof with platform canopies of shallow arch section supported by slim pillars at the platform edge. The Down side had but a small shelter and was connected to the main entrance by an underline subway. Outside there were few signs of human habitation. The mansion of Langley Park was a quarter mile east and the hamlet of Upper Elmers End about the same distance west. A start had been made with some villas along South Eden Park, forming a tentative southward extension of Beckenham, and the southernmost one was sufficiently close to the new station for the tenants to express concern that the signalman might be able to overlook the back of the house. Whilst the line was under construction early in 1882 they succeeded in having the station box moved to the end of the platform. For many years this station was the quietest on the branch and was missed by some trains.

Soon after leaving Eden Park, the embankment ended and the next station, West Wickham, only 67ch further on, was approached in a cutting. Similar to its neighbour, with buildings on the Up side, it was given a goods yard at the London end on the Down side and a covered footbridge connected the platforms. It was sited in the hamlet of Wickham Green and the village from which it took its name, which had 963 inhabitants within its widespread boundaries, was about a quarter mile south. Close to the station a large hostelry, *The Railway Hotel*, was erected in 1882, primarily to serve refreshments and meals to the holidaymakers who arrived by train in fine weather to enjoy the beautiful countryside.

Still on a rising gradient and now in a deep cutting, the railway then ran south east and east into the terminus, with a slight decline at the extreme end of its route. Here was a wide single platform on the south side with a wooden passenger building parallel to the line at the east end, where the track terminated at a locomotive turntable which served the run round road. The building was similar in style to those at Eden Park and West Wickham. Later the west end of the platform was given an additional face, with the bay road terminating against the west end of the station building. A goods yard was laid out on the south side. The 17-lever signal box, on the north side at the west end of the layout was moved in 1935 to the Up side and equipped with a 33-lever frame. Passengers bound for the main street of the village were obliged to climb for a quarter mile up to the Bromley Road. Scattered all round, well ensconced amid the trees of their spacious parks, were the houses of the wealthy residents mentioned by Thorne; *Hayes Place, Hayes Court, Baston Manor, Pickhurst* and *Holwood*.

Here and elsewhere along the branch nothing much changed for many years after the opening. This was no doubt a great disappointment to the promoters and the SER, but the owners of most of the large estates, who had not supported the line, kept their acres inviolate until the early 1920s, speculators not being encouraged. As already mentioned, a few costly villas in ample plots appeared along the west side of the road north from Eden Park station. There was also some building at West Wickham village, and a few more bourgeois 'seats' were cut out of the countryside around Hayes. None of this produced much traffic: indeed business was so poor at Eden Park that it was closed completely on Sundays for a time from March 1905, then reopened with a restricted service until the whole branch lost its Sunday trains as a wartime sacrifice after Sunday 31st December 1916. Although trains ran in the summer from 1920, year-round Sunday working was not restored until Easter 1923.

In such circumstances there was little improvement in the train service on weekdays, virtually unchanged at 15 journeys each way in 1900 and increased only to 18 by 1912. There were no through workings for businessmen until around the turn of the century; even as late as 1912 there were but two up in the morning and one back in the evening. One of these, the 08.37 from Hayes, offered distinguished accommodation in 1909 when it was made up with Continental Boat Train stock. Reaching Charing Cross (14½ miles) in 51 minutes after missing Elmers End, New Beckenham, Lower Sydenham, Lewisham and St Johns, it formed the 10.00 departure for Folkestone. Other oddities were recorded: in the early 1920s the branch was served by a locomotive shedded at Purley which reached its workplace via the then closed Woodside-Selsdon line, making no less than three reversals on the way. As Hayes had a turntable, tender as well as tank engines were seen in SER days. About 1906 the SECR railmotor No 4 was briefly used.

Before the two great rivals made their peace in 1898, the LCDR was offered at least one opportunity to recover such traffic as was leaking out to the SER via Hayes. A 3-mile single line was promoted in 1895 from Bromley LCDR station to a point about ¾-mile short of Farnborough. This railway, which would have given Hayes a second station on the east side of the village, received insufficient support, as did a London Southern Light Railway, which promoted three years later an electric tramway of standard gauge from Herne Hill through Bromley to Farnborough.

It was electric traction, coinciding with economic conditions highly favourable to the large-scale building of small houses for sale to the lower middle-class which was to bring about a complete and rapid transformation on the Hayes branch. The SR laid the third rail* in 1925, operating a public service with a 3-car train from 21st September. This working, for staff tuition, connected with steam trains at Elmers End, not running through to and from London until 28th February 1926. Full electric services started on 19th July, offering a 30-minute frequency seven days a week, connecting at Elmers End with half hourly workings between Addiscombe and London. A small number of through trains ran in business hours between London and Hayes. At Elmers End the train from Hayes ran into the Up bay before the Up train arrived from Addiscombe; after that had left, the branch train crossed over to the Down bay to make cross-platform connection with the next Down Addiscombe service.

The pace of building development was such that before very long it was necessary to augment the service. At last land was being released in quantity for building and the speculative builders' impact on this hitherto favoured area was severe. A Southern Railway residential guide of early 1926 found Hayes 'barely altered from what it was thirty years ago . . . perhaps a few more houses near the station on the London side' and it was necessary to go as far as Keston Park, 1½ miles south-east, a former estate of the Earl of Derby, to find new developments; here 'numerous houses of character and charm' were going up along a new road called Forest Drive, from £800 upwards. It was also noted that the northern part of Langley Park had been sold for building, but the houses were nearer to the old LCDR main line than the Hayes branch. At West Wickham the only signs of activity were a few new houses near the station (Barnfield Road), at Beckenham Road and Hawes Lane, and scattered in Monk's Orchard Park. Early in 1927 the *Sunday Express* dramatically reported the great sense of shock at West Wickham when it was discovered that the recently departed rector had sold some of the glebe land to a speculative builder, a move which made the privileged middle-class residents anxious about the future of their still delightfully rural retreat. This was indeed the year when large-scale building began to get under way, at first in the form of semis and small detached houses on both sides of the railway at the country end of West Wickham station.

Three years later the fields and copses south of the tracks between Eden Park and Elmers End were under the builder, but at Hayes itself nothing much happened until about 1931, following the sale of Hayes Place, Hayes Grove, and other private parks. Then many new streets were laid out south of the station and the large Morrell Coney Hall Estate, somewhat remote from the railway on this side, was completed between 1933 and 1935. By 1938 Beckenham had flowed over the line between

---

* On part of the branch, a *fourth* rail was laid, usually between the running rails and bonded to these, with the object of increasing their capacity to return the earth current.

Elmers End and Eden Park, while new houses, mostly the ubiquitous three-bedroom semis, now covered the area for a mile or more south of West Wickham station and almost two miles westwards towards Shirley. North of the line, long streets of red-tiled 'ideal homes' on the Langley Park estate stretched north towards Bromley whilst at Hayes, where prices tended to be a little higher, some reaching £2,500 when the average semi was between £600 and £800, the station was quite surrounded. To the south the frontier of London had been pushed well into the foothills of the North Downs, cosy suburban sitting and bedrooms looking out over seemingly limitless Kentish countryside at White Shaw Well Wood.

Copywriters for the SR guides enthused, making the best of these raw wounds on the face of what had been some of the finest countryside at the edge of London. They talked rather naughtily of:

> These beautiful estates, yielding to the pressure from the centre and what in the past has been jealously maintained for the pleasure and satisfaction of a few owners, is becoming available for homes in a beautiful country, for innumerable families . . . with a beautiful country village to work upon, and no residue of mean streets to contend with, the creators of modern West Wickham have everything in their favour, and the various estates are being planned and laid out in a tasteful manner so as to secure the best possible advantage from the natural beauties of the district.

Within nine years the railway's traffic increased almost 12-fold, reflecting the builders' bonanza:

	Passenger tickets issued		Season tickets issued	
	1925	1934	1925	1934
Eden Park	8,358	75,841	61	4,188
West Wickham	46,985	251,024	336	18,711
Hayes	21,856	177,424	159	5,831

West Wickham became the busiest commuter station on the branch, with 1,586 season ticket holders in 1935, Hayes running a poor second with 746 and Eden Park almost out of the contest with a mere 300. West Wickham had been transformed from village to small town, with a population in 1934 of 10,080 compared with the 1,301 of 1921. This huge growth produced much of the off-peak as well as commuter traffic as very few of the new home owners had cars and bus services were not well-developed or (to London) fast enough. By 1932 there were three trains an hour through to London, one to Cannon Street, two to Charing Cross, a frequency increased to four in commuter hours. Before another three years had passed, the service was built up to a 15 minute interval through the day, two an hour confined to the branch in the off-peak. The 1939 timetables provided a half hourly service between Charing Cross and Hayes, with another two trains an hour on the branch itself, weekdays and Sundays. Between 17.00 and 18.00 on weekdays there were two trains to Hayes from Charing Cross and two more from Cannon Street. Wartime conditions saw a reduction in the through trains off peak to hourly.

For a few more years people were still coming down by train to the area to enjoy the countryside, despite the relentless advance of suburbia. Whit Monday 1930 saw 21,000 passengers using Hayes station, few of whom would have been local residents, and one Lewisham firm was still bringing its staff by train to Hayes for their annual beanfeast.

To increase revenue and accommodate the swollen business, the SR decided in June 1933 to rebuild Hayes at a cost of £14,000 with shops on the street side and the ticket office and other facilities grouped around a spacious entrance hall. This work, which included a new island platform with a 200ft canopy, was completed in 1935. More coal wharves were added in the following year to feed the thousands of new tiled fireplaces and slow-combustion hot water stoves.

Not all the new building was houses and shops. In June 1928 a trailing connection was proposed from the Up line east of Eden Park for Harold Arnold & Son Ltd, contractors for the Royal Bethlem Hospital to be erected in Monk's Orchard Park. Controlled from a two-lever ground frame released from West Wickham box, this siding was built at a cost of £750, almost all met by Arnolds, whose locomotive worked the ¾-mile line south into the site. All was removed after construction was completed in 1930, this being the last of several examples of railways into large mental hospitals, some of which survived to give regular service.

Although the building boom promised well to spread further south-east into already suburbanised Keston and Farnborough, nothing more was heard of extension beyond Hayes. One reason for this was the Southern's interest in the Southern Heights Light Railway, proposed in 1925 to connect Orpington to Sanderstead via Farnborough and Biggin Hill. After the collapse of that scheme in 1932 there were suggestions that the Hayes branch be extended to Biggin Hill and Tatsfield, where, according to a correspondent to *The Railway Magazine* in February 1935, 'business men have to depend on Green Line coaches and consequently have a bad time when it is foggy'.

Standing in the path of German bombers flying towards London from French airfields, the Hayes branch did not escape damage in World War 2. Bombs fell in the area of Hayes station on the night of 15th/16th September 1940, wrecking the ticket office and the recently rebuilt frontage (Kent House station and Penge tunnel were also hit in the same attack). Then on 10th May 1941 a direct hit was registered on West Wickham station, the bomb landing between the platforms, severely mauling the SER structures. The several serious incidents at Elmers End have already been noted. In all these cases patching-up repairs and restoration of train services was quickly achieved but major reconstruction was to prove another matter.

SER rural style architecture at Eden Park, Up side, 17th September 1980. *Alan A Jackson*

Hayes (Kent) looking east to buffers c.1925 just after the SR electrification, for which the platform has been rebuilt. Otherwise the SER country branch line aura will remain a few more years.
Lens of Sutton

The war-torn building at Hayes became increasingly shabby, so annoying the Chamber of Commerce that in October 1955 volunteers were offered to repaint it, an action which appears to have shamed BR. It was neatly restored in the following year. Seventeen years after its bomb (1958) West Wickham was handsomely reconstructed in brick, with adequate canopies on the platforms. At that time this station had around 1,500 season ticket holders, much the same number as in 1935, but by then it had been overtaken by Hayes, where building in the late 1930s and the 1950s had increased the number to around 2,000.

High traffic levels were maintained throughout the war and for some years afterwards. By 1950 the branch had retrieved its pre-war basic frequency of four trains an hour, weekdays and Sundays, and around that time the Up bay connection at Elmers End was put out of use and the crossover at the start of the branch reversed to allow four-car Hayes trains to work in and out of the Down bay if required.

As almost everywhere at suburban stations, the Beeching regime saw the ending of public freight services. West Wickham yard (where over 11,000 tons of solid fuel had been brought in by rail as late as 1958) was closed from 2nd September 1963, Hayes from 19th April 1965. However the terminus continued for a little longer to handle a rather special type of traffic: greyhound dogs moving between Catford Stadium's local training kennels and Ireland.

With the spread of car ownership, loadings dwindled as many of the declining number of central London commuters drove to join the faster and superior services at Bromley South station and Beckenham Junction. Slack hour trains, which are subject to bus competition for local journeys, were trimmed to three an hour from 15th September 1958 and two from 17th June 1963, reflecting the fall in usage. Suggestions were made in the late 1970s that Hayes might become the outer terminal of a proposed new Fleet Line tube railway, running over the Mid Kent from Lewisham but, renamed the Jubilee Line, that project was in due time diverted to serve the Docklands and Stratford. The line's future as a conventional electrified passenger railway remains questionable.

Elmers End, once the junction of three rail services, is now being served only by Hayes trains and Tramlink. Should traffic levels continue to decline, it may well become a suburban terminus, with Hayes served by an extension of Tramlink over the railway alignment.

The Central Croydon Branch
(map page 41)

Another of Croydon's railway backwaters was created by the pressure of competition in the early 1860s, principally those coming from the direction of the Mid Kent and SER as just described. Between 1839 when the first station opened, and the mid-century railway boom Croydon's population had grown from about 16,000 to over 50,000. At that time it became important to stake out claims in this prosperous district on the edge of London, and SER, LCDR and other schemes for lines to or through central Croydon were on the engineers' drawing boards. As a defensive move, the LBSCR accordingly inserted into its 1864 legislation a half-mile spur pompously entitled the Croydon Central Railway. This was to start close to the intersection of the High Street and Katharine Street, where a small amount of property demolition was necessary, and ran east and north-east to a junction facing London at the south end of East Croydon station, joining the widening to South Croydon that had been authorised a year earlier.

Central Croydon was a modest terminus, its appearance of no particular merit or dignity. There were but two platforms parallel to the south side of Katharine Street, protected by sawtooth canopies, and separated by two centre roads which could be used for rolling stock storage or engine release. Under a glass canopy behind the buffers was a narrow headway connected to the main building by two short flights of steps. At right angles to Katharine Street and served by a small cab yard, this block included a two-storey stationmaster's house at the north end. Beyond the platform, the four tracks converged to two, flanked on the north side by a retaining wall below Katharine Street.

From the opening on 1st January 1868, there were 12 trains from London Bridge, mostly calling at all stations and taking 38 minutes, and 13 trains Up. Another four Down and three Up ran between Central Croydon and Kensington (Addison Road). Sundays saw only one Down and two Up between the terminus and London Bridge, plus three each way to and from Clapham Junction. A year later, this service was augmented when the LNWR Euston–Kensington (Addison Road)–New Croydon trains were reorganised as an LBSCR working between Kensington and New or Central Croydon via Clapham Junction and Crystal Palace. Two of the Kensington trains ran semi-fast, completing the run across the south-western suburbs in 31 minutes.

Central Croydon, looking to buffers, possibly just before re-opening in June 1886.

Looking south from the road bridge at East Croydon c.1890, LBSCR main line to Brighton straight ahead, Central Croydon branch and LNWR train for Willesden Junction at right.

Old habits died hard and as boarding a train at Central Croydon so often meant changing at New Croydon to increase the speed of the journey or to reach the required destination, Croydonians made little use of their new facility. In-and-out working of a much larger number of trains through triangular junctions might have done much to improve matters, but never very enthusiastic about what was to them largely a political line, the LBSCR decided to run it down, reducing the service by the beginning of November 1871 to a mere three each way on the London Bridge route and one afternoon journey from Victoria. Complete closure followed after the last train of 30th November.

Croydon's expansion continued without interruption through the 1870s and 1880s and following a request from the newly-formed corporation, the LBSCR agreed to re-open the terminus from 1st June 1886, demonstrating its lack of interest by leaving it to be served by other companies' trains. Initially there were merely five LNWR workings each way to and from Willesden Junction Low Level via Crystal Palace and Kensington, an extension of a service which had terminated at New Croydon since 1st May 1875. Calling at all stations except Wormwood Scrubs, these trains completed the cross-London run in about 55 minutes. Seven more trains each way used Central Croydon from 1st February 1887, when GER Liverpool Street-New Cross workings via the East London Railway were extended on weekdays, taking about 50 minutes.

Once again, the public made little use of a station that had proved to be less convenient for the expanding residential areas south and east of the town than the older facilities at West, East, New and South Croydon, with their vastly superior services. LNWR and GER trains were cut back to New Croydon after the weekend of 30th–31st August 1890, whereupon the site of the terminus was sold to the corporation for its new municipal buildings. This complex, which included Croydon's third town hall, a public library, and public gardens on the site of the approach tracks, was started in 1892 and completed in four years. In the course of the work a wall was erected across the truncated spur just west of the bridge under Park Lane, the rest of the line forming the nucleus of Fairfield Yard, which was used for permanent way and engineering purposes until February 1933. Soon after that the land was sold to Croydon corporation, which left it as a car park until the Fairfield Halls and other buildings were erected on it in the 1960s. The bridge under Park Lane had been filled in about 1931 and today the only relics of this curious LBSCR appendage are the retaining wall in the Town Hall Gardens and some earthworks near the site of the junction.

The Bromley North Branch (map page 41)

We have already seen something of the mutual rivalry over territory that existed between the SER and the LCDR before they finally reached agreement to work together from January 1899 as the SECR. As soon as one company served a town of any size, the other did its best to get there too. In Bromley, the story has a twist.

SER trains were in the town first, only to be ousted by the Chatham's, whereupon the South Eastern built a new line to get back. Ten miles south-east of London, Bromley, a market town with some 5,000 inhabitants, was still a quite separate place in the middle of the nineteenth century although the wooded hills around and its coach services to and from London were already securing it some popularity as a residential area for wealthy City men. Railways came first from the north-west in the form of the Mid Kent, opened from Lewisham to Beckenham on 1st January 1857. This line was worked by the SER, but the independent West End of London & Crystal Palace, an LBSCR protégé, also reached Beckenham from Norwood soon after, going on over single track to terminate at New Bromley (now Shortlands) about a half-mile west of the town centre. Over the latter, from its opening on 3rd May 1858, the WEL&CPR worked a shuttle service between New Bromley and Crystal Palace in connection with trains thence to the Pimlico (Battersea) terminus operated by the LBSCR, giving passengers from New Bromley an alternative to the London Bridge service via the Mid Kent.

The SER was interested in using the Mid Kent to get to Bromley and beyond, and a single line called the Mid Kent (Bromley to St Mary Cray) Railway, worked by the SER, was opened from New Bromley to Southborough Road (now Bickley) on 5th July 1858 through a station at Bromley on the site of the Charity Schools which was not ready until 22nd November. Now Bromley South, this was almost as far south of the town as New Bromley was to the west, but gradually the centre of Bromley grew down towards its station. The final developments of this first phase of Bromley's railway history occurred in 1860, when from 1st October it became possible to travel via the WEL&CPR (by then part of the LBSCR) to the new London terminus of Victoria, and when from 3rd December, the western extension of the LCDR reached Bickley, opening a through rail service between London (Victoria) and Canterbury, where there were road connections to Dover. The section between New Bromley (Shortlands) and Bickley, doubled in 1860, was leased to the LCDR from 1st September 1863.

For a while the SER continued to reach Bromley by means of through coaches off the Mid Kent somewhat unenthusiastically attached to LCDR trains at Beckenham, but after 30th September 1866 SER service was not available east of Beckenham.

The SER directors were reluctant to give up Bromley, their interest reviving after the completion of their cut-off main line from Lewisham (St Johns) to Tonbridge in 1868. Nor were the citizens of the town content to remain at the mercy of an LCDR monopoly. As the amenities of the area had attracted many more commuters since the opening of a station, there was much interest in improving communication with the City. An 1863 scheme for a link between the SER main line at Grove Park and the LCDR at Shortlands fizzled out, as did a more ambitious proposal of 1865 for a line from Grove Park, passing under Bromley and the LCDR in tunnel, and going on to Hayes, where it forked, one branch to the west to rejoin the SER near Elmers End, the other through the foothills of the North Downs to serve Keston and Farnborough.

By 1871, Bromley's population had doubled to over 10,000, but there were nearly 2,000 uninhabited houses. Unremitting local pressure for a direct line to the City, with the near certainty that the SER could be tempted back into Bromley produced a bill for a Bromley Direct Railway in 1873, a modest local promotion for a line of only 1m 5f 183yd southwards from Grove Park (where the SER had opened a station on 1st November 1871) to a terminus in 'New Bromley' north of the town centre, close to the main gate of Bromley Palace. The main force behind this scheme was William Dallison Starling, a prominent Bromley citizen and member of the Local Board until his resignation in 1870 over the sewerage question. Horsburgh, the local historian, describes him as 'an arrogant and pompous man', but as is often the case with such people, he got things done.

The 'Direct' in the title referred to the City, for the new line would bring Bromley within 8¾ miles of London Bridge compared with the 11¾ miles run on the LCDR to Blackfriars Bridge. To the West End, the new route gave only a quarter-mile saving to Charing Cross against the LCDR route to Victoria, any time reduction being eroded by the tedious reversals at Cannon Street.

After acquiring its act in 1874, the little company came under the wing of the SER, but although there was power to make agreements with that company for working and use, nothing was signed until 1876; a further act of 1877 extended sanction for agreements to cover maintenance, management, and the fixing, collection, and apportionment of receipts.

An SER director was in due course appointed chairman and the SER engineer acted for the small company. Lucas & Aird, the trusted SER contractors, started to build the railway in March 1877 after signing a £39,500 contract. Stations and signalling followed SER designs and practice. Eventually, under an SER Act of 1879, the Bromley Direct was transferred to that company from 21st July that year, for a consideration of £55,000 worth of SER 4½ per cent Preference Stock, that sum being the statutory capital.

Train service started without ceremony on 1st January 1878, 26 Down and 23 Up, eight Down and seven Up on Sundays, but in the following year this settled down at a slightly lower level, about 19 each way. Except during peak hours, passengers normally changed at Grove Park, where after rebuilding of the station most trains terminated in the Up side bay. Connections were not always smartly made, but the best through trains reached London Bridge in 21 minutes, Charing Cross in 30.

As constructed, the line was only 1½ miles long. At Grove Park, where there were at first only the two side platforms for the main line and branch services, the double track curved away southwards from the country end, on embankment for the first mile and climbing at 1 in 92 along the western edge of Sundridge Park estate. There followed a cutting in which a small station called Plaistow was built to appease the owner of Sundridge Park, E. H. (later Sir Edward) Scott, whose property extended from here to the main line at Elmstead Wood. West of the station, there was already some sign of residential development, small villas in three or four new roads of the 1860s forming a northern satellite of Bromley. For the remaining 35ch to the terminus the line rose at 1 in 74, crossing a busy footpath on the level just before entering the terminus (an iron footbridge was erected here about 1901).

Entirely without shame, the SER accorded Bromley one of those cheap and nasty slate-roofed clap-boarded wooden sheds that it considered adequate for both suburban and country village stations at this period. This shack, with its three brick

Sundridge Park, looking north, 2nd February 1958. At this time most SER features were intact and the only major change in 60 years or so was the SR electric lighting on the platforms.
Alan A Jackson

chimneys and valanced canopy over the alternately dusty and muddy cab approach, was sited alongside the departure platform. The other platform, also occasionally used for departures, just to confuse the customers, could only be reached by crossing the three tracks between the platforms, all of which converged at the south end on to a small engine turntable. A goods yard on the west side had a separate wooden office alongside the passenger building. To supplement the office accommodation and add insult to injury, a disused passenger carriage was later dumped on the footway of the cab road.

Citizens of a town described by Thorne as having a 'quiet air of conscious respectability' were affronted by the crudity of the station. On this there was nothing but prevarication from the SER but their other grievance about waits at Grove Park was mollified by timetable revisions of the early 1880s. Some of the more charitable souls were apt to suggest that the SER terminus at Bromley was of a temporary nature pending extension southwards into the railwayless downlands, but this was merely castles in the air.

To Plaistow's population of over 2,000 in 1871 many more houses were added in the last two decades of the century, some of them small and cheap enough to attract City clerks. By the middle 1890s the district was virtually joined to Bromley and in 1896, no doubt with every show of reluctance, the SER was persuaded to construct brick waiting rooms and lavatories on the Up side and a urinal on the other platform. A covered footbridge in the centre of the station linked the platforms to the usual SER wooden building at the top of the cutting on the Down side. A short cobbled cab road descended past this to a gate on the platform. Perhaps seeking to give the district a slightly more select status, but also to distinguish it from the LTSR station of the same name, the SER used the name Sundridge Park from 1st July 1894. Despite population growth, no changes were made at Bromley, but in the 1880s a bay for the branch was provided at the country end of the Grove Park Up platform. In 1903, with the quadrupling of the main line, Grove Park was rebuilt with three island platforms (the SR later added an Up loop platform). The westernmost faces were allocated to the branch.

From the opening until about 1903 the trains were composed of solid teak four-wheelers. That they were replaced with nothing much more modern is evident from an accident report of 1919, which reveals that the Bromley North Up train which ran into the rear of one from Dartford at Parks Bridge Junction was made up with two sets of six four-wheelers with three six-wheelers. In the early 1890s about half the trains shuttled between Grove Park and Bromley, whilst the remainder ran to and from London as the rear portions (about ten four-wheelers) of slow main line trains. Separate trains to and from London were worked in the rush hours, usually by 0–4–4T. The practice of working on and off the branch into the main line slows continued on a decreasing scale until the early 1920s.

By 1912, when Bromley's population had reached over 33,000, the service had been built up to 30 each way daily (12 on Sundays) to and from Charing Cross or Cannon Street, although the last train of the day was the 00.33 from Holborn Viaduct (the SER and LCDR were of course worked by a Joint Committee after 1st January 1899). At busy times as many as five locomotives could be seen in Bromley station and yard, the passenger locomotives usually 0–4–4T of the SER 'Q' and SECR 'H' classes.

When the SR took over the unfulfilled SER electrification scheme which had included the branch, some thought was given to the stations. It was at first suggested that it the terminus were moved a little to the north, Sundridge Park could be closed (they were so close that the headshunt of Bromley North goods yard almost reached the country end of Sundridge Park Up platform) but this plan was discarded in place of extending the existing Sundridge Park platforms to take eight-car electric trains and giving Bromley an entirely new station on the old site at cost of £32,000. As if the new SR somehow wished to make up for its predecessor's insult to Bromley's municipal dignity, when the new terminus appeared it was a surprisingly elegant and handsome structure, neo-classical in style under a pillared and coppered cupola 60ft above the street. Built in brick with stone facings under a hipped tiled roof, its two large square Georgian windows flanked a high round-arched entrance. There was a 5,000sq ft forecourt on the site of the old locomotive turntable but, as Charles Klapper once pointed out, no attempt was ever made to encourage the bus operators whose many services converged on Bromley to use the front of the station as an interchange point. This situation has been rectified in recent years – the old goods yard is now a bus station.

The 1925 Bromley North station building before and after completion.

The lofty 780sq ft booking hall with its train indicator led on to a 2,360sq ft concourse under a three-span glazed roof. Here there was an exit to Shermans Road, a bookstall and waiting rooms; iron gates guarded a 30ft wide island platform protected for most of its 520ft by a glazed umbrella awning. In the west wing of the main building was a large parcels office. Space considerations prevented construction of a balancing east wing until such time as the road layout was changed. Eleven lock-up shops contributed some revenue to offset the capital cost of this fine station, opened in partly unfinished state on 27th December 1925. During the work, which included construction of a new goods yard, Bromley Council allowed the use of its rail-served depot for public freight traffic, but this siding was taken out of use soon after the completion of the new station.

Electrification on the SR standard 660V third-rail system proceeded simultaneously, the first trial working running down the branch on 19th November 1925. Some services to and from Cannon Street were electrically worked from 28th February 1926, but the full timetable did not operate until 19th July when there were 54 Up and 52 Down trains on weekdays, 32 each way on Sundays, a basic interval of 30 minutes seven days a week with four an hour (alternately Cannon Street and Charing Cross) in the business periods. This replaced the 1925 steam service of 37 Up and 33 Down (16 each way on Sundays). With electric working Charing Cross-Bromley North timings were reduced to a minimum of 23 minutes Up and 21 minutes Down compared with 31 Up and 27 Down by steam haulage.

Bromley North had long been favoured with late night and early morning trains to and from Holborn Viaduct via London Bridge, a convenience which had encouraged newspaper, postal and market workers to live in the town. These were continued for many years after electrification, some of them still steam-worked: thus in 1933 the last electric from Charing Cross to Bromley North at 23.38 was followed down by a steam-hauled 00.40 from Holborn Viaduct, the service reopening with a 03.22 Bromley North–Charing Cross and a 04.20 Bromley North–Holborn Viaduct, both steam trains, the latter a push-and-pull set.

In the catchment area around Bromley North little space remained for new housing in the 1920s, but the excellent electric train service fostered building immediately north of Sundridge Park station. There was also some development in the late 1920s and the 1930s on the western fringes of the Sundridge Park Estate.

Wartime exigencies reduced the off-peak branch service to hourly, but the 30-minute interval was restored on 31st May 1948. The post-war pattern became half-hourly seven days a week, with alternate weekday trains terminating at Charing Cross or Cannon Street (all at Charing Cross on Sundays). Some late night working survived: the 03.30 Bromley North–Holborn Viaduct and the 01.00 down from Holborn Viaduct on Monday to Saturday nights inclusive. Normal times to Charing Cross were 25 minutes, Cannon Street 22 minutes, but some peak-hour semi-fasts reduced this by three or four minutes. Working in ten-car formation at peak periods from 4th March 1957, 4EPB and 2EPB sets had replaced the 4SUBs. The branch still required one freight working daily, usually behind a C2X 0-6-0 or N 2-6-0, to and from Hither Green Yard. There was little or no outward traffic, but domestic fuel and building materials provided inward loads. After a brief period of diesel haulage from June 1961, freight service ceased from 20th May 1968. Bromley North tracks were then reduced to the arrival and departure roads and a single berthing siding alongside the departure road on the north side, was subsequently removed.

From 4th February 1962 electro-mechanical signalling with three-aspect colour lights replaced the manually-worked semaphores but the new signal box at Bromley North became virtually redundant after the closure of the freight yard, opening only when the departure platform or the berthing siding were required for use. At all other times as soon as a train arrived at platform two, the departure route on to the Up side could be set up automatically.

Service changes after the late 1950s reflected the decline in off-peak usage. From 15th September 1958 a two-car shuttle was worked on the branch after 22.00 and all day on Sundays. This was extended to all day on Saturdays from May 1973. Sundridge Park was closed on Sundays from 16th September 1962 and all Sunday trains were withdrawn in June 1981 as well as the late evening services.

Commuter traffic was also declining. A 1977 survey showed a drop in season ticket sales from 1,708 to 768 over the previous ten years. From 14th May 1984, commuters had only one through train (to Charing Cross) with a ten-minute shuttle to connect with other services at Grove Park. All through services to London ceased from 14th May 1990. At the time of writing, the branch remains fully signalled double track, even down to the unnecessary luxury of a platform indicator at Sundridge Park for Bromley North where only one platform is normally used. This extravagance cannot last much longer; various alternative developments, such as a Docklands Light Rail service from Lewisham or an extension of Croydon Tramlink from Beckenham Junction to Grove Park via Bromley centre have already been proposed. Alignments will need to be considered in relation to schemes that commercial pressures will no doubt bring forward for alternative and more profitable uses for the railway land in the centre of Bromley, including the now listed 1925 terminal building and the goods yard site, at present still an open air bus station.

Crystal Palace Railways (map page 41)

'The most ordinary mode of transit from London to the Palace is by rail . . . special trains are despatched from the principal London stations as occasion may require.' Filled out with much detail on train services and fares, this announcement in Dickens's 1896 guidebook is a reminder that the Crystal Palace, as a permanent feature of London life for over 80 years owed its very existence and its sustenance to railways. After the Great Exhibition of 1851 was over, the board of the London Brighton & South Coast Railway were very much involved in a proposal to reproduce Joseph Paxton's Hyde Park masterpiece in even more splendid style in their part of south London. With strong backing from Paxton, and in characteristically Victorian manner, they set out with the highest motives; the benefit of the masses, who would have in the new Crystal Palace a great centre of recreation, education and culture; but at the same time they took great care that the maximum returns should come to the shareholders of the railway company. A director of the LBSCR, Leo Schuster, was persuaded without much difficulty to part with his mansion and park, Penge Place, for £86,661. Situated between Sydenham and Norwood this, together with some adjoining land, some 280 acres in all, offered a superb elevated site for the new mecca of the hoi polloi. In May 1852 a Crystal Palace Company was formed under the chairmanship of Samuel Laing MP, the LBSCR chairman, with the LBSCR a majority shareholder. The materials of the Hyde Park building were bought and in the absence of direct railway communication, had to be moved by horses over 20 miles of roads culminating in the cruel one in eight of

Crystal Palace LBSCR station; the 'East Station', looking west about 1914. This view shows the overhead wire electrification which came into use on 12th May 1911, its installation made easier by the removal of the overall roof in 1906. In the background is the 284ft South Tower of the Palace which survived the 1936 fire but was demolished in 1940.

Sydenham Hill. The project was carried out with such expedition that on 5th August 1852 Laing was ceremonially erecting the first column of the new structure. Building by Fox, Henderson & Co. then went ahead in earnest under the personal supervision of Paxton, who took up residence at Rock Hill, a large house in the northern corner of the grounds.

Although the site was close to the LBSCR's Sydenham and Penge stations on the Brighton main line from London Bridge, a new station with direct covered communication to the Palace was planned. This required new railways, the first of which was a 1m 5ch spur from south of Sydenham station to the south side of the grounds, authorised, together with an enlargement of London Bridge station, in the LBSCR Act of 1853. It opened for goods traffic on 27th March 1854 in time to carry some of the final building materials and the exhibits. To handle the heavy passenger movements expected, the LBSCR built two more platforms at London Bridge and widened its line between Bricklayers Arms and Norwood Junction to four tracks. At Sydenham, the Down line serving the new spur was carried over the main lines, an early example of a railway flyover, into a large station to be described in a moment.

Passenger service began with the first of a series of special trains from London Bridge at 10.00 on 10th June 1854, the day Queen Victoria was to declare the great enterprise open to the public. Normal service, usually of 12 four-wheel coaches, was half-hourly from London Bridge (22 trains a day each way).

At first, the Brighton directors were not denied the fruits of their efforts; daily traffic totals reached 10,000, whilst on special occasions such as the inauguration of the fountains on 18th June 1856, the demand was so great that London Bridge was choked with crowds determined to reach the delights of Sydenham Hill. On one day in 1859, 112,000 people were conveyed to the Palace by train, 70,000 via London Bridge and Sydenham.

On 4th August 1853 a second line, the West End of London & Crystal Palace, was authorised to run in continuation of the LBSCR spur via Streatham and Balham to a terminus on the south bank of the Thames opposite Pimlico. An independent promotion, set in a strategic position to attract the attention of the larger companies, it was designed to act as a main line into the West End. Relationships with the LBSCR, which agreed to work it, were cordial and a service began on 1st December 1856 to Wandsworth Common, a temporary station at the north end of the common, which closed on 31st May 1858. Pimlico (on the south bank) was reached on 29th March 1858 and Victoria on 1st October 1860. As it provided the first access to central London for the LCDR, this line is strictly outside the present terms of reference, but a full account of its history is available.*

For the two lines, the LBSCR erected a fine station at Crystal Palace with two terminal roads and two through lines serving the Sydenham spur (the 'East Station'), and two through lines and two bay roads on the West End of London & Crystal Palace (the 'West Station'). The latter line was continued southwards to Norwood Junction on 1st October 1857 and was linked to the Mid Kent (Bromley and St Mary Cray) Railway (later the LCDR) at Bromley (now Shortlands) on 3rd May 1858 to provide the main line access already mentioned. For quick loading and unloading of crowds, the through lines in the East station had platforms either side of each track. In the West Station the bays adjoined the Down through platform. At the western tip of this V-shaped complex was a large street level booking hall under a lantern roof with an elaborate five-bay iron and glass porte-cochère. Either side of this main hall, in square shaped two-storey pavilions were dining rooms, refreshment rooms, stationmaster's office and living accommodation etc., all of this sitting on a bridge over the tracks. A covered way of iron and glass led visitors to the south end of the Palace, its fairly stiff incline moderated by steps and enlivened by statues in niches which those short of breath could stop and pretend to admire. Platforms in the East Station, reached by three wide staircases with stone-capped banister rails and stone newel posts, were sheltered by a twin-span bow section all-over roof set between blind-arcaded, solidly-buttressed walls. Removed in 1906 in a fit of jitters following the 1905 Charing Cross roof collapse, the Crystal Palace roof was replaced by two ordinary centrally-supported umbrella canopies (the centre platforms had by this time been taken away to make room for two carriage sidings). *The Builder* looked at the LBSCR Crystal Palace station and found Gough's design good, although draughty and badly-lit after dark.

---

* *The Railway Magazine*, October 1956 (Charles E. Lee)

This complicated layout was controlled by three signalboxes: Tunnel, at the north end; South, on the line towards Norwood Junction (also controlling the goods yard); and East, at the Sydenham end of the East Station. Between the two stations, in the opening of the V, was a goods and coal yard supplemented by the Crystal Palace Company's own dock at the entrance to the East Station, where many strange and exotic items, including circus animals, were to be handled over the years.

From the opening, combined rail and Palace admission tickets were issued as authorised in the 1853 act. This facility, which included a substandard rail fare (at first only 5d return) lasted until Southern Railway days and made it necessary to distinguish ordinary tickets by marking them 'Crystal Palace *Station*'.* Similar inclusive tickets were later issued by most of the main line companies serving London, notably the LNWR, which enjoyed running powers to Crystal Palace West Station.

Although the LCDR was given running powers over the West End of London & Crystal Palace Railway into London, the LBSCR jealously guarded its monopoly by refusing to allow the former to share passenger business at its stations between Crystal Palace and Victoria. Nevertheless, at this period the two companies needed each other in central London and their relationship was accordingly harmonious. When the Brighton planned its South London line, linking London Bridge and Victoria stations through the new suburbs of Peckham Rye, Denmark Hill and Brixton, an LCDR protégé, the 6¼-mile Crystal Palace & South London Junction, was allowed to branch off the South London line near what was later Peckham Rye station and also to have the exclusive use of the northernmost pair of four tracks which the LBSCR would build between Cow Lane and Barrington Road Junction, Brixton. In return for these favours, the Brighton had access to LCDR tracks from Barrington Road to Wandsworth Road Junction, where it regained its own territory. All this was authorised in the Crystal Palace & South London Junction Railway and LBSCR Acts of 1862.

The Crystal Palace & South London Junction, which the LCDR agreed to work for 50 per cent of its receipts, was clearly intended to be a rather superior line. Special architectural treatment was imposed by an agreement with Alleyn's College at Dulwich and there was a firm prohibition in section 68 of the act against carriage of any 'Night Soil, Dung, Manure, Compost or other Offensive Matter'.

Seeking its own access to the City from the new branch, the LCDR obtained powers in 1863 for a cut-off between the junction with the LBSCR and their Herne Hill–City line in Walworth. This was to be used by trains to and from a Nunhead–Greenwich branch authorised in the same act, but the state of the Chatham's finances precluded its construction, although as we have seen, the Greenwich branch was painfully achieved.

Peto & Betts' work on the Crystal Palace & South London Junction was sufficiently advanced to allow trains to run through to the terminus at Crystal Palace without intermediate stops, from 1st August 1865. The service was operated to and from Victoria via the South London line between Peckham Rye and Brixton (Canterbury Road) which was opened on the same day.

---

* A similar notation occurred in north London, where tickets were marked 'Alexandra Palace *Station*', by the GNR and LNER

From Peckham Rye to Nunhead the new branch climbed steadily at 1 in 60 and 1 in 76, continuing up to the Crystal Palace at 1 in 68. Leaving the LBSCR at Cow Lane Junction, 18ch east of Peckham Rye station, the tracks ran east, south and then south west as they mounted the western flank of the Forest Hill–Norwood ridge. As mentioned earlier, at what is now St Norbert Road, an embankment was partially completed in 1865 to carry a chord authorised the previous year for direct running between Greenwich and Lewisham and Crystal Palace. Honor Oak, the first of the branch stations, was entirely timber-built. It served Camberwell cemetery and the northern end of a new villa colony on Forest Hill, sheltered from east winds and facing the setting sun. A small coal yard was placed on the Up side. The booking office was at first in a wooden shed on the Down side of the approach, reached from the west by a subway under the line where a cast-iron notice warned pedestrians of closure on Good Friday, Christmas Day 'and such other days as the Directors may from time to time determine'. In later years tickets were sold on the platform.

Beyond Honor Oak the line kept close to the west side of the ridge, invading the Dulwich College estates, and after crossing Lordship Lane, entered the station of that name. To meet conditions laid down by the College, the road over-bridge was elaborately ornamented and the station house picturesquely styled with two steeply-gabled roofs over its red brick and stone. Elsewhere cost was kept down by using timber construction. A short ¾-mile from Forest Hill station on the LBSCR main line, Lordship Lane had to share what little traffic this villa district produced.

From this point to the terminus the surroundings were romantic and well timbered, remaining so to the very end of the line's existence. Continuing south between a wood and the immense gardens of the huge houses on Sydenham Hill, the tracks passed under an elaborate timber cantilever bridge carrying a public footpath called Cox's Walk. Shortly after, the ridge was penetrated by the 400yd Crescent Wood Tunnel, from which the line emerged briefly within a curve of the ridge known as Hollow Coombe before entering the 439yd Paxton Tunnel (so called because it passed near, but not beneath, Paxton's house). A station named Upper Sydenham, almost lost in the boscage between these two tunnels, was opened on 1st August 1884. Approached by steps and path down the side of the Combe, much prone to landslips, it served an area of very large well-separated villas set in ample gardens. Traffic was always light and by 1910 it was missed by as many as 30 Up and 20 Down trains a day. Immediately south of its platforms the line crossed above the Penge Tunnel of the LCDR Penge Junction (Beckenham) to Herne Hill line of 1863.

Top Right: LBSCR E2 104 at Honor Oak Park on Crystal Palace (Low Level) service, 1926. *O.J. Morris*

Centre Right: Lordship Lane station, looking towards Nunhead, c.1930. The Southern Railway had at this date made virtually no alterations apart from 3rd rail electrification; the platforms remain gaslit. *Stations UK*

Bottom Right: BR(S) unit 4671 at Upper Sydenham on Crystal Palace (High Level) service in the 1950s. Southern Railway signs still survive. Note how the platform extensions have been constructed to a new standard higher level *R.C. Riley*

Opening out from the south entrance of Paxton Tunnel were the approaches to the terminus, built on a shelf alongside the western flanks of the Palace. More splendid in every way than Gough's LBSCR station, Edward Barry's £100,000 train shed of glass, iron and red and yellow brick could stand without shame against the huge bulk of the Paxton building. At each corner were square towers topped by four chateau-style turrets to emphasise the importance of the long carcase. Passenger accommodation, entirely under cover, was divided by a central arcade into two sections served by concourses raised above the tracks at each end of the interior, which carried the booking offices, refreshments rooms, waiting rooms and other offices. Each section had two tracks, the inner ones platformed each side for ease of loading and unloading of packed trains. The four tracks entered the building through small openings at the London end, emerging at the south on to a 44ft 10in turntable on the south side of Farquhar Road, an arrangement which helped locomotives of arriving trains to run round with the minimum of delay. Half of the station was intended for the use of first-class passengers, who were given segregated access to the first-class entrance in the centre transept of the Palace. Direct communication to the Palace, not ready until shortly after the opening of the station, was through a spacious vaulted and tiled chamber beneath Palace Parade, the roadway between the station and the Palace. This Byzantine crypt, devotedly fashioned by cathedral craftsmen especially imported from Italy, was decorated with octagonal pillars of red and cream brick interlaced with stone ribs. Steps led from it to the main floor of the Palace. It survives intact today, almost the only relic of this great structure.

The *Illustrated London News* clearly preferred the LCDR station, talking of its 'superior convenience', avoiding 'the tedious walk up half a mile of corridors and staircases imposed on those arriving by the Brighton company's line'. Nine siding roads between the station and the tunnel together with a run-round road to the turntable outside the blind-arcaded western wall of the train shed provided accommodation for goods traffic and space to store enough locomotives and carriages to move away between 7,000 and 8,000 passengers an hour. Although the names High Level and Low Level were not officially introduced to distinguish the LCDR and LBSCR stations until the formation of the Southern Railway in 1923, we shall use them here to avoid confusion.

At first there were 19 trains daily each way from Monday to Saturday running non-stop between the High Level and Victoria. Lordship Lane station was opened on 1st September 1865, and Honor Oak, Peckham Rye and Denmark Hill on 1st December. With these calls, the throughout journey of 9m 68ch to Victoria took about 40 minutes, and in 1866 there were 33 trains a day each way. A station was opened at Nunhead, 54 chains east of Cow Lane Junction, on 1st September 1871 to serve new housing development.

Large houses set amidst extensive shrubberies and lawns were built in quantity on the east side of the line between Crystal Palace and Lordship Lane in the 1870s and 1880s producing only a trickle of business for the branch, albeit of superior quality. Despite the availability of a City (Moorgate) service upon the opening of a spur from Cambria Road Junction (west of Denmark Hill) to Loughborough Junction on 1st July 1872, the High Level line did not prosper; cemeteries, very low density villa development and the extensive open areas of the jealously-guarded Dulwich College estates gave it precious little sustenance. Nor was the mid-century dream of regular mass excursions to the Crystal Palace ever fulfilled. Indeed, much of the attraction and fashion of the Palace had evaporated before the High Level branch opened; the northern transept was destroyed by fire in 1866, never to be rebuilt, while a strong and successful opposition to Sunday opening further damaged its prospects.

Such was the disappointment that the independent element in the Crystal Palace & South London Junction Co. grew somewhat restive in the mid-1870s, so much so that the LCDR was moved to action, obtaining powers in 1874 for a spur from Kent House on the Beckenham-Crystal Palace Low Level line designed to allow it a direct run from the City and Victoria to the Low Level station. An effective means of bullying the awkward elements on the CP&SLJR board, this move served its purpose and in 1875 the small company was absorbed into the LCDR, under the powers in the CP&SLJR Act of 1864.

The January 1877 timetable shows 24 trains from Victoria to Crystal Palace High Level between 06.55 and 22.52 including two fast trains which completed the journey in 25 and 27 minutes, the first one a non-stop. There were also 30 trains from Moorgate Street, Holborn Viaduct, Ludgate Hill or St Paul's between 08.12 and 12.07, usually missing Borough Road, Walworth Road and Camberwell New Road, the fastest reaching the High Level station in 26 to 28 minutes.

Although the opening of the Palace had encouraged the development of Sydenham and Upper Norwood as quality middle-class suburbs, the Palace itself was very much in decline as an attraction in the last decades of the Victorian era. The LCDR seemed to acknowledge this by renaming the terminus Crystal Palace & Upper Norwood on 1st November 1898, perhaps hoping to attract more residential traffic. A year earlier, Edward Walford had remarked 'commercially, the place has not proved so successful as was at first anticipated. The undertaking was carried out on too great a scale', and Baedeker's Guide to London noticed that '. . . the Crystal Palace no longer bulks so largely among the lions of London as it once did . . .' Indeed, paint was peeling, the roof leaked, the gardens showed signs of neglect, and the Company, feverishly selling off spare land for house building, was fast approaching bankruptcy. Neither the Saturday concerts, nor the regular firework displays by C. T. Brock & Co. did much to stimulate attendances. Only on very rare occasions, such as the Football Association Cup Final, held here from 1894 to 1914, was the ample railway accommodation put to any sort of use. On such days the two companies might share between 20,000 and 50,000 passengers a day, and the LCDR would put on its non-stop service from and to Victoria which brought first- and second-class passengers to the High Level station in a mere 20 minutes.

One of the last great occasions at the Palace was the Festival of Empire and Imperial Exhibition held between May and October 1911, after opening by King George V. This set off a railway race between the two companies. The LBSCR had inaugurated electric services from Victoria on 12th May 1911 and on a trial run had covered the 8¾ miles in 12½ minutes. This achieved, the Brighton started a 17-minute express service for the Exhibition visitors (regular electric service on the Victoria–Streatham Hill–Crystal Palace line began on 1st June 1911). Not to be outdone, the SECR promptly introduced a *15-minute* steam service between Victoria and Crystal Palace High Level, using the 0–4–4T and four-wheel coaches which comprised the normal stock on the line. These ten-coach trains, weighing 120 tons tare, carried passengers of all three classes and the schedule demanded a start-to-stop speed throughout of 39mph, a very commendable performance on a busy line of many curves and junctions, ending with a steady climb.

In the same notable year, the railways were given an opportunity of showing just how the crowd handling facilities at the Palace stations could be used. To celebrate his coronation, the King invited all London school children aged 11 and over to a 'King's Fete' on 30th June. A vast army of over 100,000 children, teachers, LCC staff, journalists and performers were brought from all parts of London in 105 special trains, 58 via the LBSCR and 47 on the SECR. Most came to the Low and High Level stations, but Sydenham Hill and Penge (LBSCR) were also used. Some of the trains bringing the north London contingents came through the City Widened Lines in charge of GNR locomotives. This movement entailed cancellation of 61 regular workings on the High Level line and substantial suspensions of other timetabled services. About 90 additional railway staff were on duty at the High Level station, in the charge of an official who directed operations from the northern concourse bridge, megaphone in hand, like the captain of a great ship controlling emergency disembarkation. All special trains ran to time, not a single child was lost or injured, and if contemporary accounts are to be believed, each trainload of 1,000 individually-labelled brats was discharged in about three minutes.

Normal service on the High Level branch at this period consisted of 21 trains daily from Victoria (usually fast to Brixton) and 28 from the City stations, with similar numbers in the opposite direction. Best times were 22 minutes Up, 25 minutes Down. Sunday service was meagre, with a train about every 80 minutes from Victoria. At the Low Level station 45 trains a day each way ran to and from Victoria via Gypsy Hill and there were also 39 Down and 36 Up London Bridge trains via Sydenham. Electric working between London Bridge and the Low Level via Tulse Hill started on 3rd March 1912, with full service on 3rd June. Like those on the Victoria services, these trains took their 6600V 25c/s traction current from overhead wires through bow collectors.

Loadings on the High Level branch continued to be poor despite the construction in the 1880s, and 1890s of smaller houses on the west side of the line between Lordship Lane and Nunhead, and around Nunhead station. There was severe competition from the LBSCR stations at Sydenham, Forest Hill, Honor Oak Park and Brockley, and also, after 19th December 1908, from LCC electric tramcars running from Forest Hill via Lordship Lane station into Camberwell Green and central London. Some traffic was also lost to LCC tramcars when from 28th November 1907, these reached Homestall Road, Peckham Rye, to tap the little streets between Honor Oak and Nunhead stations. Later, motor bus services from Dulwich Library and Honor Oak to Peckham Rye station took more business from the railway.

With its thin traffic, it is not surprising that when the manpower shortages of World War 1 began to take effect, and when the City Widened Lines were choked with wartime freight workings, the authorities considered passenger services on the High Level branch expendable. The Moorgate Street journeys, which had been severely cut in January 1915 and had ceased to run on Sundays a few years before that, were stopped altogether after traffic on Saturday 1st April 1916. With the last train on 31st December 1916 passenger working was entirely suspended. Wartime exigencies also caused the SECR to abandon after 30th November 1915 the steam railmotor service it had introduced in July 1907 between Low Level and Beckenham Junction. The LBSCR was left to cope with the useful regular traffic from the Palace's wartime role as a naval recruiting and training centre.

Although a City service to Ludgate Hill or St Paul's (now Blackfriars) was restored to the High Level station on 1st March 1919 in time to take some of the traffic generated from the demobilisation centre at the Palace, there was never again any service to Victoria, for which passengers had to change at Denmark Hill. By the beginning of the 1920s there were half-hourly trains between High Level and St Paul's with extra workings to and from Ludgate Hill in peak hours.

The High Level line was included in the SECR electrification proposals of 1920, but nothing was done until the formation of the Southern Railway. That company opened a resited Nunhead station on 3rd May 1925 and in preparation for electric working closed the supplementary signalboxes at Nunhead Bank, Lordship Lane and Upper Sydenham. This left only Crystal Palace cabin and that at Honor Oak, which was retained for working the goods yard, rearranged in 1924 with a siding to accommodate 25 wagons. Platforms at Honor Oak and Lordship Lane were lengthened for the electric trains, but at Upper Sydenham the necessary alterations cost over £1,000. A substation built there had a shaft providing power cable connections into the Penge tunnel below. Staff training runs commenced on 1st April 1925 between Nunhead and Crystal Palace High Level, but the full service of third-rail electric multiple units started on 12th July with a regular 20-minute frequency through the day (30 minutes on Sundays), to and from St Paul's. The all-stations running time was 25 minutes. As Saturday evening loads were lighter than expected, from 19th July 1926 the service after 15.00 was reduced to half-hourly. There was little scope for the capital expenditure to show any substantial returns in increased traffic; the line's catchment area remained unpromising material. A traffic census taken in February 1926 shows what poor business the electric trains were doing: from Crystal Palace High Level the 53 departures between 06.05 and 23.22 carried only 703 passengers (less than one rush hour train load for the busiest London lines), whilst only 653 arrived at the terminus from London during the traffic day. The idyllic surroundings of Upper Sydenham saw only 211 Up passengers and 216 arrivals the whole day; Lordship Lane produced 366 up and 401 down, but Honor Oak did a little better with 654 Up and 560 Down.

The decaying interior of Crystal Palace High Level station, west side, looking to London, 22nd March 1954.
Alan A Jackson

There was nevertheless some modest growth after electrification. Lordship Lane, for example, issued 30,043 ordinary and 870 season tickets in 1925, but in 1934 the totals were 57,019 and 1,742. Some minor changes were made to the stations; at Honor Oak a passimeter booth, parcel lock-up and retail kiosks were authorised in 1929. Builders did what they could, infilling where it was possible to buy the large houses and demolish them; on the Tewkesbury Lodge estate, for example, west of the tracks just north of Lordship Lane, three- to six-bedroom semi-detached houses were on offer in 1937 at £1,050 upwards.

The Southern Railway very speedily converted the LBSCR overhead wire electrics to the third-rail system; London Bridge to Crystal Palace Low Level , via Tulse Hill on 17th June and the Low Level to Victoria service on 3rd March 1929. On that day the Low Level–Beckenham Junction trains were restored, with electric traction. The London Bridge–Crystal Palace (Low Level) via Sydenham service was electrically-worked from 25th March 1928.

Saved by public subscription in 1913 after bankruptcy of the old company, the Crystal Palace received an injection of new life in 1920 when the King went down to open the Imperial War Museum and Great Victory Exhibition 'with special events culminating in the revived Handel Festival'. But the sad souvenirs of World War I were soon removed to South Kensington, leaving the Palace to subsist on a mixed diet of cat and dog shows, home exhibitions, fireworks, brass band festivals and motor cycle racing, none of which called into action any of the excess capacity at the two railway stations. Then suddenly, on the night of 30th November 1936, it all came to an end; Paxton's great glasshouse melted away in the flames of a spectacular fire, morning light revealing only the two water towers and the railway stations still standing. This occurrence attracted crowds far larger than any seen at the Palace for very many years and prompted the last special train for a Palace event – one was supplied to take home sore-eyed spectators in the small hours. Sets of LCDR 6-wheelers stored in the High Level yard for summer excursions, hop pickers' specials and national emergencies served as an excellent grandstand, withstanding in the true traditions of British workmanship of their age the pressure of the many excited spectators standing on their roofs. Saved then by the intervening roadway and the efforts of firemen through the night, the vast hulk of the High Level station also survived World War 2 with no damage other than the removal of much of its glass by the blast of neighbouring anti-aircraft guns.

After the fire, pleasure traffic to the Palace dropped almost to nothing and when as a wartime measure off-peak and Sunday trains were reduced to hourly from 1st January 1940, local passengers began to drift away to other Southern stations, trams and buses. From 6th January 1941 the branch was worked as shuttle to and from Nunhead, where connections were made into the Catford Loop service every 20 minutes at peak periods and hourly at other times. Storage capacity at High Level was used to hold passenger stock made redundant by the War, notably buffet and second-class boat train cars. A second wartime closure of the branch was predictable, and sure enough 'due to the manpower position' passenger trains were withdrawn after traffic on 21st May 1944, not to be restored until 4th March 1946 when the shuttle service was re-introduced but with some peak-hour workings to and from Blackfriars from 11th August. Finally, on 27th September 1948 all trains ran to and from Blackfriars every 30 minutes, with additional rush-hour journeys, but Sunday trains were withdrawn.

Lordship Lane on the last day of public services, 18th September 1954, Down train entering, unit 4107. The results of German bombing in World War 2 are evident. *Alan A Jackson*

Without some new source of traffic, which was not forthcoming, there could be no hope of recovery from the successive blows received, and for most of the day the trains, now only three or four cars long, ran all but empty. It was a great line for lovers. One estimate put the loading of the 88 trains into High Level daily as 400 – between four and five per train. Rain poured down through the shattered roof at High Level, encouraging a luxuriant growth of ferns and fungi on the rotting timber platforms beneath which rats, far outnumbering the passengers, scurried and scavenged unhindered. For most of the time there was only one platform in use in the huge building, where the northern stairs, concourse and rooms had long since been abandoned to rodents, birds and spiders; adding to the horror film effect, safety nets drooped from the roof to protect passengers from falling debris. At night it was one of the most eerie public places in London.

Senior officers of the Southern who had lived through the Walker electrification era must have found it distressing to recommend the first closure of a Southern Electric line, but it had to be. With all the stations and cabling in deep decay, with no hope of traffic development, and with alternative facilities readily available, the line's fate was sealed, and the local authorities were warned of the closure in January 1954. The last electric train ran on 18th September and the daily freight carrying coal and coke to the yards at Honor Oak and High Level from Herne Hill ceased about the same time. To soak up the displaced traffic, London Transport extended its 63 bus service from Honor Oak to Crystal Palace Parade via Lordship Lane and Sydenham Hill and extra trains (which lasted only a few weeks) were put on between Blackfriars and Nunhead from 20th September 1954. Coal merchants at the High Level station were moved to Gipsy Hill yard, which in turn closed to railborne traffic in January 1969.

Wooden platforms and gas lighting survive until the last day of public service at Honor Oak, 18th September 1954; 4-car unit 4639 is seen on an Up train.
Alan A Jackson

The throat of Crystal Palace High Level station (last day of public service) with an Up train about to enter the 439yd Paxton Tunnel.
Alan A Jackson

Crystal Palace Low Level station, north side, looking to Gipsy Hill, 21st March 1964.
Alan A Jackson

Dismantling the branch proved to be a slow business, occupying much of 1956 and early 1957. When it was done, the LCC bought all 48 acres of railway land from Crystal Palace to Nunhead, subsequently passing much of it to local councils for open space and housing developments. At Upper Sydenham, the sealed-off tunnel mouths became a lasting challenge to adventurous youth. In 1985 a 'Green Walk' was opened alongside and over the line of the railway, parts of which had become a nature reserve.

The High Level station itself remained intact for almost six years after the departure of the last train, patiently awaiting the imagination and finance that might convert it to some worthwhile alternative use. Since it was in London and not Paris, this did not happen and after its demolition in 1961 the vast site lay disused for a further long period whilst its future was discussed interminably. Finally, in 1986–87, the area was densely covered with housing, leaving only the main tunnel mouth and the great retaining wall below Crystal Palace Parade as reminders of what was once here.

So ends the story of a railway constructed at high initial cost in the frustrated hope of snatching some of a rival railway company's profit from the Crystal Palace traffic. As the whole route was fairly closely paralleled by an existing line, once the prospect of regular movements of very large crowds to the Palace was seen as something of an illusion, the enterprise had little else on which to build even modest prosperity. Except on rare and isolated occasions, its huge terminal station proved to be a complete white elephant, far too large for any traffic forthcoming. With the benefit of hindsight we can see that the first line to the Palace and the facilities it subsequently provided would probably have been adequate on their own to handle all the business generated, and that the decision in 1925 to electrify the High Level line was a serious misjudgement.

The Low Level station certainly proved more than capable of coping with the residual rail traffic to the Crystal Palace area after 1954, including that to the National Sports Centre opened in the park ten years later. The cavernous East station was used by the London Bridge trains, latterly running only in rush hours. During the day, the link through it was needed for the transfer of empty electric stock between Victoria and London Bridge and New Cross Sidings. It still remains open and virtually intact at rail level at the time of writing although above there have been some changes. In obeisance to the god of financial economy, BR dismantled some of the Victorian features: the glass and iron porte cochère standing over the road entrance went in the late 1960s and the north tower roof was finally cut down in 1976. The remainder was Grade II listed as of architectural and historical interest. After the collapse of some 1971 proposals carefully prepared by the Clapham Society, the Transport Trust and Sir Robert McAlpine & Sons which would have used the East Station and unwanted railway land as a National Transport Museum, apartments were eventually built in the vee between the East and the West stations in 1990–91. Before that, in 1986, with a substantial grant from the Greater London Council, a new entrance and ticket office were provided above the West station. Reflecting the style of the old Crystal Palace building, this light and pleasing structure of aluminium and glass was finished in bright blue and green.

CHAPTER TWO

SOUTH WEST LONDON

Southfields station exterior, c.1905 *Commercial postcard*

Earl's Court to Wimbledon (map page 165)

At an early stage in its history, the Metropolitan District Railway developed a policy of feeding its capital-intensive inner London section by judicious extensions into potential areas of middle class residential development. In the pursuit of this objective, attention was directed to the well-padded suburban territory occupied by the LSWR, an area which included the favoured Thames-side areas of Surrey and Middlesex.

As early as 12th April 1869 a branch had been opened from west of South Kensington station to West Brompton on the West London Extension Railway in the unfulfilled expectation of attracting LSWR and LBSCR services into South Kensington. This line carried a service to and from Gloucester Road until 1st August 1870, when the trains were extended to Blackfriars.

East Putney station street entrance and cab yard between the two diverging lines, c. 1905. *Commercial postcard*

Wimbledon Park interior, looking north, c. 1905. The four uniformed staff outnumber the passengers in view. *Commercial postcard*

For a while the District was frustrated. A proposal to tap the L&SWR at Barnes was authorised in 1872 as the Barnes & New Richmond Railway, but this was dropped when the LSWR refused a connection. Soon after this, as we shall see later, the District arrived at Hammersmith, making a junction there with the LSWR's Kensington & Richmond line in 1877, an astute move which enabled its trains to gain access to Richmond. It also reinforced the company's expansionist ambitions by enabling it to serve Ealing, the 'Queen of the Suburbs', from 1879, and very soon after that it secured access to Hounslow, both areas we shall consider later. These positions achieved, there remained only one notable gap near the inner part of the District system, the area enclosed by the meander of the Thames past Fulham, long threatened by Metropolitan Railway schemes pushing down from the H&CR Hammersmith terminus. A 1m 67ch thrust from West Brompton towards LSWR territory was authorised in 1878 as the Fulham Extension Railway, a separate undertaking with capital of £300,000.

Built by Lucas & Aird, and engineered by John Wolfe-Barry, this started at the country end of West Brompton station, proceeding in a covered way below the West London Extension and then southwestwards, first in cutting and then on a brick viaduct 'of ornamental character' to the satisfaction of the Ecclesiastical Commissioners, which terminated on the north bank of the river close to Putney Bridge and Fulham church. Putney Bridge & Fulham station (Putney Bridge & Hurlingham 1st September 1902, Putney Bridge 1932) had wooden platforms built out on steel piers and lattice girders from the sides of the viaduct, served on the west side by a large but nondescript flat-roofed entrance building at street level. Built on the eastern part of the garden of a large riverside house called *Willow Bank*, the station incorporated a footway to a new low-water pier where passengers could make connections to river pleasure steamers. Some housing demolition was necessary to make room for the two intermediate stations in the formerly separate residential villages of Walham Green and Parsons Green. Walham Green (renamed Fulham Broadway 1st March 1952), at the site of the Fulham Road tollgate, was in cutting, its platforms partially sheltered by an 'A'-shaped overall roof of glass and iron resting on blind-arched walls. With its booking hall extending out over the tracks from the road bridge, it served the Stamford Bridge grounds, leased in 1876 to the London Athletic Cricket Club & Athletic Grounds. Parsons Green had side platforms sheltered by wooden awnings, with steps down to an entrance hall in an arch of the bridge over the road. Shortly after this, near the start of the remaining 49ch to Putney Bridge, there began the long viaduct, which included a reverse curve to avoid the housing in the Kings Road and the Fulham Refuge & Female Reformatory. As far as possible the whole route was made to pass between housing through the garden land, the viaduct form minimising acquisition and demolition in an area already partially built-up.

The Fulham Extension opened on 1st March 1880 with a half-hourly service from West Brompton, increased on 1st April to quarter-hourly, alternate trains working to and from High Street Kensington. Large numbers were carried to Putney Bridge for that year's University Boat Race, thus initiating this line's strong association with sporting events. As the opening of the branch coincided with a period of rapid housing development in the catchment area, it was not long before a steady daily residential traffic had accrued. Houses 'like serried battalions of a gigantic army . . . marching and counter marching' spread out northwards from the old riverside village centre of Fulham until by 1900 they had all but filled the land between the Thames and the West London Extension and Earl's Court to Hammersmith railways. The new Fulham, which spawned its own entertainment, retail and services area around Walham Green station and a smaller shopping centre near Parsons Green station, brought the district's population from 42,895 in 1881 to 137,289 in 1901. In her *Memorials of Edward Burne-Jones* (1904) Lady Burne-Jones recalled the early 1880s: 'the District Railway had been brought near us and the speculative builder followed . . . the respectable old name of Fulham was taken from us, and West Kensington given in exchange.'

The District's receipts showed a satisfying upward curve, even if there were fewer first-class tickets than might have been wished. In his *Survey of London Life and Labour* (1899) Charles Booth found most of the new inhabitants of Fulham comfortably-off, respectable members of the lower middle class and upper working class: people in the lesser professions, minor theatricals, skilled artisans, shop-workers, clerks, foremen and transport workers, a large number of them travelling by train to work in inner London, taking good advantage of the District Railway workmen's tickets.

From its north bank bridgehead, the District was clearly poised to jump into the LSWR territory on the other side. Opportunity soon came in the form of the Kingston & London Railway, which started life as the Guildford, Kingston & London, looking for District support for its lines to Surbiton, Kingston, Guildford, Ashtead and Bookham. As authorised on 22nd August 1881 this cheeky proposal was reduced to a 7m 45.8ch line from the District at Putney Bridge across Putney Heath and Wimbledon Common to the LSWR Down side at Surbiton (the LSWR simultaneously secured powers for its own lines from Surbiton to fill the Guildford and Bookham gap). Seeing mutual advantage, a West End terminus for the LSWR, lucrative suburban trade for the District, the two companies then combined to obtain equal rights of user over the Kingston & London, the LSWR proposing in its 1882 act to make further connections at East Putney and at Norbiton to allow through running to Kingston and an 11ch branch off the District to its own West End station at Pelham Street, South Kensington. An act of 1882 jointly vested the K&LR in the two companies but it very soon became apparent that the District would be unable to raise its half share of the £650,000 capital. Wimbledon interests, feeling left out, and seeking a cheaper alternative to the West End, had put forward a Wimbledon, Merton & West Metropolitan Bill for what was in effect a branch from the K&LR at East Putney to a two-way junction with the Tooting joint line of the LSWR and LBSCR between what is now Haydons Road station and Wimbledon. Lucas & Aird, the contractors, seeing the possibilities, paid the necessary parliamentary deposit. This new link, over which the District was accorded running powers, was authorised on 18th August 1882 as the Wimbledon & West Metropolitan Railway, without the spur towards Tooting.

Unable to obtain Parliamentary approval to construct the K&LR on its own account, and unwilling to advance capital to the District, the LSWR agreed in 1885 that the K&LR should be abandoned except for the short section between Putney Bridge and East Putney, proposing instead to take over and build the Wimbledon & West Metropolitan, which it would allow the District to use to Wimbledon, where it would provide a separate station, in return for an annual rent of six per cent on cost and maintenance. The District had merely to agree to the preservation of LSWR running powers to South Kensington and High Street Kensington, with the separate terminal accommodation to be constructed at the former if required.

By its act of 25th June 1886 to which the agreement with the District covering the above was scheduled, the LSWR took over the required piece of the K&LR and most of the Wimbledon & West Metropolitan, proceeding to build a double track line together with a flying junction to the Windsor Lines at East Putney (Point Pleasant Junction) facing London, and a deviation to bring the line into the north side of Wimbledon station instead of the proposed junction west of Haydons Road.

Work started in March 1887, with Lucas & Aird getting the contract they had expected. A principal engineering feature, one of the last designs of William Jacomb, the LSWR engineer, was the eight-span wrought iron girder bridge over the Thames. Not given a name (local people dubbed it the Iron Bridge), this structure was never to carry revenue-earning LSWR trains, as that company decided not to take up the running powers and abandoned the proposed Kensington terminus in its act of 4th July 1890. A wide footway on the downstream side was opened to the public on 1st July 1889.

From the bridge, the line climbed at 1 in 70 on a brick viaduct through a partly built-up area, crossing high over the Windsor Lines before entering East Putney. Some houses were demolished. East Putney was a split station, two faces of its well-canopied platforms serving the spur to Point Pleasant Junction, which was graded 1 in 56 downhill and 1 in 60 uphill. A small entrance building in red and yellow brick snuggled in the angle of the two viaducts, fronting its cab yard on the south side of Upper Richmond Road. B. G. Wilson notes that the sharp check-railed curve bearing south-east beyond the station represents the divergence of the 'Wimbledon branch' from the planned alignment of the K&LR, which would have gone almost straight ahead into its Putney Heath tunnel. After this curve, the Wimbledon line entered a 311yd covered way beneath West Hill followed by a cutting containing Southfields station. This had an island platform with stairs at the south end leading up to a small entrance pavilion on the north side of Wimbledon Park Road, with elevations of yellow and red brick in Early English style. Platform buildings under a wide canopy from the staircase were also in red and yellow brick. At the time of opening, a spaciously laid-out estate of large villas was slowly growing on the west side and there were a few houses to the east along the Merton Road. To the south, as far as the LSWR main line there were just parklands and fields.

Now on embankment and curving east to avoid the lake and higher parts of Lord Spencer's Wimbledon Park, the tracks ran under Arthur Road into Wimbledon Park station, in every respect the twin of Southfields except that it faced the other way. Leaving this station there was a facing connection to the carriage sidings before the line curved south to run along the main lines into the 'North Station', two new platforms with a central run round and separate booking office adjacent to the LSWR's platform 1. The coal yard formerly on this site was rebuilt further east. There were signalboxes at East Putney, south of the station on the Up side, and on the platforms of the other two stations.

The District's characteristic Beyer-Peacock 4–4–0T and trains of four-wheelers began to serve Wimbledon on 3rd June 1889, providing 31 journeys a day to and from the City, 11 more than required by the 1886 agreement. A late start and finish to the traffic day (07.27 to 00.09) reflected the middle-class nature of the clientele. On Sundays trains terminated variously at New Cross LBSCR, High Street Kensington or South Kensington; most weekday trains went through to Whitechapel.

This approximately half-hourly service was shortly augmented to give a 15-minute interval at peak periods, while with the opening of the Point Pleasant Junctions on 1st July 1889 there was the additional facility of 12 LSWR trains daily each way between Wimbledon and Waterloo, using the double-track junction with the main lines at the London end of Wimbledon station. This link also had considerable value to the LSWR, both as an emergency diversion and in affording access to and from the West London Extension Railway via Ludgate Junction (north of Clapham Junction station) and Latchmere Junction. This was at its most useful in the Up direction as Down trains were faced with the steep climb from Point Pleasant and a flat crossing of main lines at Wimbledon.

At first the District's revenue was largely confined to Wimbledon and East Putney stations, though this was not to be scorned, especially that from the former with its high proportion of first-class tickets. With Wimbledon Park and Southfields as yet in abeyance, the chairman, J. S. Forbes, was able to say in 1896 that the line had increased the company's receipts by over 44 per cent in six years.

A large part of the Wimbledon Park estate was sold for building during 1898, to be covered within two or three years with a tight-packed grid of new streets east of the line between Wimbledon Park and Southfields stations, streets which were rapidly lined with 'tunnel back' housing for the lower echelons of the middle class. Briefly interrupted by World War 1, the activity here and construction of slightly more superior semi-detached houses further north either side of the railway at Southfields brought much new traffic to these two stations. In the 1910s and 1920s Wimbledon grew north-east towards the southern part of the line, leaving untouched only that part of Wimbledon Park around the lake, the All-England Tennis Courts and the Sports Club. West of the line at Southfields, building continued until 1939, much of it of higher value houses, to be followed after World War 2 by blocks of flats.

To meet the needs of this new population, services and line capacity were augmented, though not all plans were realised. By 1899 the District was working 47 trains a day each way, terminating variously at Whitechapel, Earl's Court or High Street Kensington. Always in the minority on its own line, the LSWR supplied 15 trains to and from Waterloo. District electrification at 600V dc third and fourth rail reached Putney Bridge on 23rd July 1905, trains working to and from High Street Kensington. Arrangements were made for the LSWR to electrify its tracks to Wimbledon in return for District payments of interest on the capital cost, the two companies signing an agreement on 4th December 1903. District electric working to Wimbledon started on 27th August 1905, giving a significant increase in service, most trains running through to East Ham. Current came from Lots Road, Chelsea through a substation at Wimbledon Park.

In 1904, the last full year of 100 per cent steam traction on the West Brompton–Wimbledon line, there were 103 trains a day each way on the East Putney–Wimbledon section, of which 54 were District workings. By 1911 this total had grown to 157, of which 93 were District. This began to stretch the capacity of the manually-signalled double track, but with some skill and the aid of new intermediate boxes at Cromer Road (Southfields) and Revelstoke Road (Wimbledon Park) it was just possible to cope. A further problem for the District was the landlord's propensity to delay or even stop the electric trains at times of stress, particularly on race days. In 1911, when there were 19 race days, 85 District trains had to be cancelled, and January 1912 saw 831 delays to District trains, totalling 2,415 minutes. In these difficult conditions, the District was carrying traffic which had increased by 76 per cent since 1907. The LSWR found itself under pressure to adopt a similar arrangement to that on the Kensington & Richmond; quadrupling between Wimbledon and East Putney was authorised by the MDR Act of 1912, the work to be carried out by the LSWR, which would leave the western pair of tracks for the District's exclusive use, receiving payments of interest at four per cent on capital expended. Improvements were also agreed for Wimbledon station. Although the LSWR board authorised negotiations for land purchase in April 1913, no work on the widening had been done before wartime conditions made a start impossible. With its Wimbledon & Sutton scheme very much in mind, the District obtained powers in 1913 for widening between Walham Green and Putney Bridge, with two island platforms at Parsons Green to facilitate semi-fast working. Again no start was made, although some years later the land purchased was used to make storage sidings either side of the running lines at the country end of Parsons Green station.

Some small improvements were realised. In the early summer of 1910 the District brought into use a third road on the outer (east) side of Putney Bridge station, converting the southbound platform to an island. The old through line became a reversible stub, enabling the operation of a four-minute frequency in rush hours, previously made difficult by terminal movements on the double track. At Walham Green, the single-storey street level building was replaced in 1910 by a two-storey structure in neo-classical style, the work of the District architect, H. W. Ford. This incorporated an arcade leading to a new booking hall and over-line concourse. Extra exits were provided for the Stamford Bridge sports traffic for which there were now ten booking windows, said to permit the issue of 120 tickets a minute. Football traffic had assumed importance with the arrival of the Chelsea FC at Stamford Bridge ground in 1905. Finally, at Earl's Court, from 5th January 1914, eastbound Wimbledon trains used a new flyover which brought them into the station without fouling the Ealing and Kensington (Addison Road) services. Contemporary publicity referred to this as a '£70,000 scheme for catching seconds . . . more trains and more accommodation on the Wimbledon and Putney line'. The original alignment was retained to duplicate the southbound track so that if required, two trains towards Wimbledon could be sent on to the branch, thus clearing Earl's Court station, one train being kept back as desired on the curve, or a fast train could overtake a slow one here instead of in the station. With this improvement and the contemporary addition of an extra terminal platform at the Wimbledon 'North station' by the LSWR, the District was able to start from 9th March 1914 a ten-minute all-day service to Wimbledon, increased to six minutes at rush hours.

Traffic was still growing. The small new houses at Wimbledon Park and Southfields were available for £250-£350 leasehold and typical of the bait which attracted many new District season ticket holders was an advertisement of 1914 which offered two reception rooms, three bedrooms and a bathroom in a new terrace house of 17ft 6in frontage in Wimbledon Park Road, Southfields for £285 leasehold. Here and at Wimbledon Park, the stations were rapidly becoming small suburban centres in their own right, with parades of shops to meet the needs of the new residents.

A further spurt to the popularity of this area (which was also well served by motor buses) was the decision to include the East Putney–Wimbledon line in the LSWR suburban electrification scheme. To allow the running of the third-rail trains, the District's fourth-rail system was adapted by removing the insulation of the negative return and bonding it to the running rails. A special isolating section was installed on the river crossing to prevent bridging of the section gap by the bus-lines of passing trains. This was the first part of the LSWR electrification to open, providing a 20-minute frequency on weekdays only from 25th October 1915 between Wimbledon and Waterloo via Wandsworth Town, six minutes faster than the irregular steam service it replaced. Patronage was not good, and in July 1919 when stock was required to augment busier electric services, all trains were withdrawn except for about half a dozen rush-hour trips which missed Wimbledon Park–East Putney inclusive, reaching Waterloo in 19 minutes. When regular electric working was resumed on 16th November 1919, trains ran only hourly (half-hourly at peak periods), some evening workings not going beyond Wimbledon Park. Three-car sets were sufficient for the loading. The line occupation by these and the various freight and empty stock workings caused no great distress to the District, and with the SR take-over of the Wimbledon and Sutton scheme, (to be considered later) the urgency

West Brompton, 11th May 1963. The site of the West London Extension Railway platforms is at left, with BR D6543 on a southbound empty coaching stock train; District Line station at right. *Alan A Jackson*

was removed from the quadrupling plan. The powers were allowed to lapse, but when rebuilding Wimbledon station in 1929, the SR did provide a new four-bay station for the District with its own concourse below the main booking hall.

Following the Metropolitan's reconstruction of Edgware Road station as an intermediate terminus, 7½-minute District services were started between there and Putney Bridge from 1st November 1926 (15 minutes on Sundays). Some of these trains, particularly on Sundays, went through to Wimbledon. Ten years later, Wimbledon had a four- to five-minute frequency in rush hours, seven to ten minutes at other times, whilst Putney Bridge intervals were respectively two to five and three to six minutes. Trains deceptively labelled WIMBLEDON NON STOP in fact missed only West Brompton and occasionally Parsons Green (and Walham Green in rush hours).

The onset of World War 2 saw the end of regular SR calls at Wimbledon Park, Southfields and East Putney. From 16th October 1939 the service was shaved to half-hourly at peak periods only, ceasing altogether after traffic on 4th May 1941. Through steam passenger workings had become increasingly rare in the 1930s (some LMSR trains were reported by an observer in 1938 as the first through Wimbledon Park for a considerable time). Steam-hauled freight and empty stock remained commonplace until the early 1960s, while occasional SR steam passenger trains and excursions working via the West London line were seen until the late 1950s.

With the end of regular stopping service via Point Pleasant Junction the east side platforms at East Putney remained to confuse passengers, gradually deteriorating until 1959 when the Down side buildings were demolished and the subway was closed off. Through the 1950s and early 1960s, some fast electrics came this way, usually from the Alton line, and running non-stop between Surbiton and Waterloo. Summer Channel Islands Boat Trains also worked via East Putney every year from 1953 to 1962 and it was one of these, in the latter year, which formed the last steam passenger working. Since, a few electric excursion trains have been operated to and from Clapham Junction, or Waterloo, some calling at Wimbledon Park and Southfields. Diesel-hauled excursions via the West London line to and from other BR regions are also occasionally seen. In 1963 the character of the line was further diluted by closing it at night and running milk and freight trains via Earlsfield. Today it is still used for empty stock movement between Clapham Junction or Waterloo and Wimbledon Park sidings, also of course for emergency and engineering work diversions of main line trains.

West Brompton station, London Transport, in the early 1960s with a southbound District Line train entering. The West London Extension Railway can be seen across the centre of the picture. Its West Brompton & Lillie Bridge station, which was alongside the District one, was closed after bomb damage on the night of 19/20th October 1940 and was later dismantled; some remains are visible to the right of the road bridge; a station on the same site was to be reprovided in 1999. *W.H.R. Godwin*

For many years London Transport drivers working south of West Brompton faced violent contrasts in signalling. Manual semaphores on the District's own line, converted to electro-pneumatic working with track circuits and train stops at the time of electrification, were subsequently replaced by colour-lights on the same system. Parsons Green signal frame went out of use from 9th October 1960 when all signalling here came under the control of programme machines. From 20th November that year, these machines, supervised from Earl's Court, replaced Putney Bridge box, and the Parsons Green machines also came under the Earl's Court control room from 12th December 1965. Although East Putney station had track circuits and colour-lights towards Putney Bridge from 20th November 1960 the rest of the Wimbledon line retained its Victorian manual signalling with Sykes' lock-and-block, the Underground crews enjoying in foggy weather the unusual experience of guidance from manually-placed detonators on the rails. Not until 13th September 1970 were further colour-lights installed at East Putney, three-aspect colour-lights with track circuits coming into use through to Wimbledon on the following 29th November, when the boxes at Cromer Road and Revelstoke Road were finally closed (Wimbledon Park and East Putney boxes were retained to control movements into Wimbledon sidings and to and from the Windsor Lines). At Wimbledon itself, the semaphores which remained in the station area until the early 1970s had been fully track-circuited and electro-pneumatically controlled since the opening of the new station signal box on 29th February 1948. Signalling modernisation allowed an effortless four-minute frequency to be maintained in rush hours in all weathers. Edgware Road–Putney Bridge rush-hour workings were all extended to Wimbledon in rush hours on 10th October 1960 and all Putney Bridge off-peak reversals were subsequently similarly extended.

The Up line between East Putney station and the Windsor line at Point Pleasant Junction was closed in 1990 and the retained Down connection was resignalled as a reversible line in February 1991. These changes were part of the incorporation of the Putney-Wimbledon line in BR's Waterloo Area Resignalling scheme, operated from a new control centre on the country side of Wimbledon station. Point Pleasant Junction box was closed in September 1990 and East Putney, Wimbledon Park and Wimbledon 'A' boxes were all taken out of commission on 25th February 1991.

Other than closure of West Brompton on Saturdays and Sundays after 24th/25th January 1970, there was little retrenchment on this busy line. Fulham Broadway and Putney Bridge continued to attract large and often unruly crowds in the football season for home games by the Chelsea and Fulham clubs. At the former, around 15,000 fans could be cleared in an hour by short-working extra trains into the normal service. Putney Bridge still saw an influx on University Boat Race Day, much diminished by the 1970s. Another sporting event which this line sustains is the Wimbledon Tennis Tournament, when well-behaved crowds are carried by extra trains and special bus services to and from Wimbledon and Southfields stations.

Today, with none of its stations much rebuilt, the line retains a certain period charm. The massive Thames Bridge, with its ornamental pilasters and rusticated granite and Portland stone abutments, the sinuous viaducts above the rooftops of Fulham and Putney, and the evocatively Edwardian Putney Bridge station, with its scroll-work lamps and finialled canopies, all combine to give it a special aura. Local business is supplemented by Surrey commuters moving to and from West End workplaces and on Saturdays in winter, Surrey boys give it a two-way football traffic. The line was touched with new fame in 1973 when Marlene Dietrich came this way to her performances at the Wimbledon Theatre, having discovered the journey from her West End hotel took only 30 minutes against an hour by road.

In 1994 the Wimbledon branch of the District line was served by 12 trains an hour at peak periods, four to Edgware Road, eight to Embankment and beyond. At the busiest morning peak hour approximately 2,770 passengers were entering the District station at Wimbledon, 913 at Wimbledon Park, 1,991 at Southfields, 1,854 at East Putney, 1,309 at Putney Bridge, 1,553 at Parsons Green 1,513 at Fulham Broadway and 233 at West Brompton. The journey from Wimbledon to Embankment took 28 minutes compared with 14 minutes from Wimbledon to Waterloo.

A major change occurred from 1st April 1994, when control and staffing of East Putney, Southfields and Wimbledon Park stations was handed over to London Underground. Signalling, which remained a responsibility of Wimbledon Signalling Centre, could be monitored at London Transport's Earl's Court Regulating Room. Under the new regime, the three stations were refurbished and re-signed, their ticket issue facilities modernised. The connections to the main railway system at each end and the ability to use the line for through workings over these junctions were unaffected by this development.

Tube trains may eventually be worked through these stations, operating services over a proposed new link between Wimbledon and Leytonstone via Chelsea and Hackney, whose route across London has been safeguarded.

Croydon train at Merton Park station c.1930. The Tooting platforms are on the right, with the main station building at extreme right.

Wimbledon to Croydon and the Tooting Loops (map page 109)

An important source of water power and pure water, the river Wandle attracted industry to its banks between Croydon and Wandsworth well before the railway age. It was not navigable, and but for the opposition of the mill owners alongside, it would undoubtedly have been canalised before the end of the 18th century. Instead, the district which it served was to get the first public railway to receive parliamentary sanction, the earliest railway of any sort in the London area.

Authorised in 1801, the Surrey Iron Railway, so named because its track consisted of cast-iron plates on stone blocks, ran up the valley from the east side of the river's mouth at Wandsworth through Garratt Green, Colliers Wood and Mitcham to Pitlake Meadow, Croydon, with a 1½-mile branch from Mitcham to the river bank at Hackbridge and another, owned by the Croydon Canal Company, from Pitlake to the canal basin near the present West Croydon station. Serving no less than 38 mills and factories, the line was built by the engineer William Jessop, and its double track was opened for public use on 26th July 1803. The Hackbridge branch and the Wandsworth Basin were ready on 1st June 1804 and the canal spur came into operation on 22nd October 1809.

An extension south of Croydon by the separate Croydon, Merstham & Godstone Iron Railway, authorised in 1803, was opened for public use on 24th July 1805. Although intended to run as far as Reigate, with a branch from Merstham to Godstone Green, this line never got further than the Greystone Lime Works at Merstham, via Purley and Coulsdon.

Both railways were 4ft 2in gauge between the outer faces of the rail flanges. Used only for freight, they owned no rolling stock; horses, donkeys or mules and wagons were all supplied by the users, who paid tolls on a per-ton-per-mile basis. Traffic consisted mainly of coals and manure southbound, lime, chalk and farm produce northbound. Fifty to sixty tons were pulled by one horse without difficulty on the many level stretches.

As the house on the platform demonstrates, Morden was originally a station but from November 1918, with the introduction of a push-pull service, it was reduced to halt status. About the same time, the siding (left) was taken up. This photo of about 1930 looks towards Wimbledon and shows an ex-LBSCR 0-4-2T on a 2-car push-pull unit. *Lens of Sutton*

Business done proved a great disappointment to the owners, as much of the important Croydon traffic went to the Croydon Canal. After 1825 the Surrey Iron paid no dividend, and its total profits over its 40 or so years of life amounted to no more than £10 6s 0d (£10.30) per £100 shares.

The Merstham line lay in the path of the proposed London & Brighton Railway, which obtained powers in its initial act of 1837 to purchase it. This was achieved in 1838 when the tramway was closed for public traffic, parts of it being used during the construction of the main line. The company was wound up by an act of 1839.

Early in 1844 Chaplin and Parsons, the chairmen of the LSWR and the London & Brighton Railway respectively, considered the possibility of a joint terminus near the West End; both were discontented with their respective termini at Nine Elms and London Bridge, the Brighton particularly so, since it was paying heavy tolls to the London & Greenwich and London & Croydon Railways for access. Chaplin was interested in levering away the Brighton from dependence on the London & Croydon as the latter had a scheme for a direct line to Portsmouth which would take traffic from the LSWR. A station was proposed at Waterloo Bridge which it was thought the Brighton might reach by means of a line from Purley (Foxley Hatch) to Wandsworth, LSWR, using the roadbed of the two Iron Railways. In August 1844 the LSWR secured an option to purchase the Surrey Iron Railway, but in 1845 the necessary legislation in the form of a Croydon & Wandsworth Junction Bill was sabotaged by an adverse report from the Board of Trade, while the Surrey Iron Railway Bill seeking powers to sell to the LSWR was also thrown out.

Better luck attended the Brighton in the following session when the London & Brighton Railway (Wandsworth Branch) Act was passed, but by then the steam had gone out of the issue for the Brighton, which had in July 1846 amalgamated with the London & Croydon to form the LBSCR. This abolished the toll burden and the old Croydon element encouraged a cooling of relations with the LSWR.

1846 also saw the end of the Surrey Iron, which obtained its Dissolution Act on 3rd August and then summarily closed on 31st August. The area was not to remain long without a railway. Already, in 1845, seeing the imminent death of the primitive Surrey Iron, local interests at Mitcham had sponsored a 3½-mile Mitcham & South Western Junction Railway from Mitcham Green to the LSWR near the present Earlsfield station. This met defeat from an LSWR still supporting the Wandsworth & Croydon, but was followed by another independent scheme for a Wandsworth & Croydon Railway. That had to be withdrawn when the LSWR and Brighton combined to lean on it, although all three parties did manage to agree that the promoters could build from Wimbledon to Croydon, the LSWR renting as far as Mitcham, the LBSCR leasing the remainder as far as the junction with its line at West Croydon. Subsequently the LSWR withdrew from this arrangement, but the W&CR secured its act in 1853.

As the act only contained provision for working arrangements with the LSWR, the line was built as a speculation by the contractors Peto & Betts and leased to the famous Devonian engineer G. P. Bidder, at that time a resident of Mitcham, who opened the line on 22nd October 1855. It was something of a shambles. Not only had there been two postponements whilst the requirements of the Board of Trade Inspector were satisfied, but on the very first day navvies had to rebuild the track to restore some semblance of stability to the motion of the trains. Two days later, an engine driver was killed when his train completely derailed on a loose piece of track near Mitcham. Commenting on this last incident, *Herapath's Railway & Commercial Journal* acidly observed, "We cannot help noticing that if the rails had been what is called 'fished', the accident could hardly have happened".

At Wimbledon the W&CR terminated in a single-track bay let into the Down platform of the LSWR station, then on the country side of the road bridge, with only a trailing connection to the main line. Soon after leaving this bay, the line turned south-east, taking a more-or-less direct approach to Croydon. Although in fact land was purchased throughout for double track, only a single line was laid.

Two-car push-and-pull unit 982 on a West Croydon to Wimbledon service at Mitcham Junction signalbox c.1930. The guard is surrendering the staff for the single track section south of Mitcham Junction. The Sutton line curves away to the right by the locomotive.

Mitcham, the only place of any consequence on the route, had a station at the south end of the main street where, as at Staines and Enfield, the engineers adopted the economical solution of adapting an existing house, an 18th century building, formerly the country retreat of a City merchant and now listed as of architectural and historical interest. Passengers entered through the front door, purchased their tickets in the hall, passing out through the back door to descend to a platform cut out of the side of the garden. The only other intermediate station was a single platform with low brick shelter called Beddington, but sited rather hopelessly nearly two miles north of that small village, in open country. Its remoteness from the place it was alleged to serve led to its renaming to Beddington Lane in January 1887.

From a point just west of Mitcham station to the site of the present Waddon Marsh platform, the line followed the course of the Surrey Iron Railway on land repurchased from adjacent landowners who had bought it from the old company after 1846. A junction (subsequently removed) was made with the Croydon & Epsom immediately south of the Wandle, but the W&CR single track continued for about ½-mile beside the LBSCR into West Croydon station where it was afforded a short bay let into the country end of the Up platform. Level-crossings over seven public roads are mentioned in the act, but only three survived to the 1990s. It was an easy route to build, rising only slightly at the Croydon end, requiring no substantial engineering other than short stretches of cutting at Mitcham and Waddon Marsh.

A third intermediate station called Morden (Morden Halt, 1st November 1918, Morden Road Halt, 2nd July 1951) was opened in 1857. Whilst it was the nearest station to Morden village, a 1½ mile walk faced anyone unable to secure a conveyance. Its two-storey house, with brick ticket office alongside, and bay window looking up and down the line, survived until November 1982, when both buildings were summarily demolished. The immediate surroundings remained almost entirely rural for over 70 years after its opening.

In a move which put some semblance of order into the operation of the W&CR, the LBSCR secured a 21-year lease to work, manage, and take tolls from 1st July 1856, under an act of that year which also sanctioned additional capital to double the line. Not wishing to remain impotent in an LBSCR enterprise entering its territory, the LSWR obtained parliamentary authority in 1857 for joint operation and under a territorial agreement concluded in the summer of 1859 secured the Wimbledon–Mitcham section for the remainder of the lease, with net earnings and expenses to be shared equally with the Brighton, on the understanding that the latter could continue to work into Wimbledon. By a further agreement of 1862 a joint committee was set up to manage the W&CR. After purchasing the assets of the W&CR and becoming sole owner from 1st January 1866, the LBSCR offered its neighbour a half-share, but with the emergence of a jointly-owned Tooting, Merton & Wimbledon Railway to be opened two years later, the LSWR was content to withdraw, leaving the Brighton with almost all the W&CR to itself.

Rival schemes for the borderland territory of the LSWR and LBSCR in the Wimbledon/Streatham area appeared in 1863–64, with the Tooting, Merton & Wimbledon Extension Railway securing an act on 19th July 1864. This was a nominally independent undertaking with powers to make working arrangements with the two main line companies, but the latter reached an agreement in 1864 which led to an 1865 act dissolving the independent company and vesting its line jointly in the LSWR and LBSCR.

The Tooting, Merton & Wimbledon opened on 1st October 1868 from Streatham Junction (on the LBSCR Peckham Rye to Sutton line dating from the same day). Wimbledon was approached by lines diverging at Tooting Junction, one coming into the town from the north-east, the other from the south-east after forming a junction with the W&CR at Merton. All double track, the TM&W fed the new LBSCR main line through Streatham, but as we shall see, was also to afford the LSWR its long-desired access to the City. The Tooting Junction–Merton–Wimbledon section was justified by promise of freight traffic; William Shears, a director and promoter of the 1864 scheme had copper mills at Merton Abbey (Shears & Sons), where a siding was provided from the opening of the line.

At first only LBSCR trains used the TM&W, working between London Bridge and Wimbledon by both routes to and from Tooting Junction, but the 1865 Act had given the LSWR running powers to Tulse Hill and on 1st January 1869 a Kingston to Ludgate Hill service was started. This used the new Malden–Kingston line, the TM&W and a 74ch Tulse Hill to Herne Hill spur which the LCDR opened that day. The act also allowed LSWR trains to run over the LBSCR via the TM&W to and from the Brighton's freight wharf at Deptford. Most of the twelve trains each way daily between Kingston and Ludgate Hill ran via the Merton line and there were also five trains each way on Sundays. By the 1880s the Ludgate Hill service usually terminated at Wimbledon.

South of Streatham, the LBSCR Peckham Rye–Sutton line did not take the direct route across Mitcham Common but instead swung westwards to pass close to Mitcham, the alignment then curving very sharply round into and out of the W&CR through a shared station called Mitcham Junction. This arrangement, which for many years until they were diverted via Three Bridges, slowed electric coastal expresses to 20mph, gave Mitcham a remotely-situated station which has never developed much traffic. At the country end of the Down platform was a bay used by trains which ran to and from Crystal Palace Low Level (some went through to Wimbledon) in the 1860s and 1870s. Some originating traffic was finally attracted to Mitcham Junction with the opening around the turn of the century of a golf course with a large clubhouse next to the station.

At its opening on 10th October 1868, Mitcham Junction looked very much as it does today, a simple side-platformed country station, although it has long since lost its station signalbox, which stood at the London end of the Up platform, and the bay mentioned earlier.

Returning to the Tooting, Merton & Wimbledon, we must note that there were stations and goods yards at Tooting (just west of the junction), Haydens Lane (Haydons Road 1st October 1889) on the east side of the Merton–Wandsworth road, close to the Wandle, and Merton Abbey on the southern section. A fourth station, at first without any platform on the W&CR, called Lower Merton, was sited at the junction with the W&CR a short distance on the Croydon side of its level-crossing of the Kingston Road. This anticipated the development of John Innes' Merton Park estate, where laying-out of a street grid planted with trees and hollies started in the early 1870s, but housebuilding followed only very slowly. Innes was instrumental in obtaining improvements to the station; the W&CR trains called at a new platform from 1st November 1870 and in response to his persistence, the name was changed to the more socially acceptable Merton Park from 1st September 1887, by which time it was being used by a few middle-class commuters.

As the double track of the Tooting line continued from Merton through new platforms at Wimbledon station to rejoin the northern chord, the W&CR trains began to use this 58ch of jointly-owned line, leaving the original single track to become a siding. In 1881 the LSWR reconstructed the main line station at Wimbledon on the north side of the road bridge alongside the Tooting, Merton & Wimbledon platforms.

The district served by the Tooting line saw some residential growth after 1880. Lower Tooting, which by that year had already a grid of streets either side of the line, filled out, its development eventually to be much stimulated by the arrival in May 1903 of LCC electric tramcars linking it to Westminster and Blackfriars Bridges. Tooting station was resited more conveniently on the east side of the London Road on 12th August 1894, where a more commodious red brick and tile entrance building was provided on the road bridge, with covered stairs to well-canopied platforms. Relics of the original station's Up side building, in use as a house, still survive. Wimbledon grew out towards Haydons Road station in the same period and a new residential colony, with its own church, spread around the little station between 1890 and 1914. There was contemporary development, mainly of small houses for artisans, behind the Tooting–Merton–Wimbledon road, which received an electric tramway, with a branch up Haydons Road, in 1907. Slow for long journeys and for some years requiring a change to LCC cars at the county boundary, the London United tramcars were nevertheless very cheap and frequent in contrast to the Tooting line service, which was complicated rather than lavish.

In 1893 of the 16 Down trains between London Bridge and Tooting Junction, five continued to Wimbledon via Merton Abbey, returning via Haydons Road, the remainder reversing this route. There was a late evening train from West Croydon to Wimbledon which continued via Haydons Road and Streatham South Junction to Victoria, returning to West Croydon, where it arrived about 01.00 by the same route. The contemporary LSWR Up service from Wimbledon consisted of eight trains via Haydons Road and six via Merton Abbey. For some years after the opening of Holborn Viaduct station in 1874, the LSWR trains terminated there instead of Ludgate Hill, using the easternmost platform, but when that was wanted for parcels, the LCDR offered Snow Hill (Holborn Viaduct Low Level). In January 1911 the LSWR was providing two Down trains via Haydons Road and nine via Merton Abbey, with five and six Up respectively. These were supplemented by five trains each way between Haydons Road and Wimbledon, which were mostly extensions of the Merton Abbey workings. At the same time the LBSCR was offering 17 Down to Wimbledon via Haydons Road and nine via Merton Abbey; Up trains to the same number ran in reverse order over the loop. Most of these were motor trains, with first- and third-class seats only, working between Streatham and Wimbledon. At rush hours, both companies' services were fairly well-used, but electric tramcars and motor buses (after about 1910) had secured most of the off-peak traffic by 1914. Howard Turner mentions that in 1912, as the LBSCR locos were far from home (New Cross) for almost 20 hours daily, engine pits were installed at Tooting Junction between the old and new stations to enable ash pans to be raked out.

The Croydon line saw few changes before World War I. In July 1909 Merton Park to Mitcham was being worked by train staff and ticket, Mitcham Junction–West Croydon by electric train staff, with staff stations at Mitcham Junction, Beddington Lane, Waddon Marsh box and West Croydon. There were at this time 12 trains a

West Croydon train entering Beddington Lane c.1906.

day each way and one railmotor working. The 57ch between Mitcham and Mitcham Junction had been doubled in March 1879, probably to facilitate the working of goods trains to and from the sidings and yard at Mitcham, still the only public depot on the line and situated on the south side beyond the road bridge at the Wimbledon end of the station. (Rudely severed by a landslip on the Wimbledon side of Mitcham station in 1971, the double track was cut back to beyond the Croydon end of the platforms).

Passenger business between Wimbledon and Croydon remained very light; Merton Park was the only station that saw even a small increase in residential travel. Elsewhere virtually no houses were built before 1914, apart from a few south of Beddington Lane Halt. At the turn of the century, the passenger trains usually consisted of four to six four-wheelers with open third-class, in charge of a Stroudley Terrier 0–6–0T.

Freight traffic gradually assumed more importance. Between Mitcham and Croydon were a number of sidings of which the most noteworthy was one serving Waddon Flour Mills on the north bank of the Wandle, a single line of almost ¾-mile running due south just over a mile from the Croydon end of Beddington Lane. Near this junction, sidings served gravel pits on both sides of the line, those on the south later rearranged for the British Portland Cement Works, the others for a permanent way depot. Another siding, on the north side, a little nearer Croydon entered a brewery and was followed by another into Croydon Gas, Commercial & Coke Company's works at Waddon Marsh, west of the line. After 1920, these works expanded to the east side, requiring another set of sidings. Also on that side was Croydon Power Station, rail-served from about 1925 and with its own internal system, worked by a small English Electric 500V dc locomotive taking power from an overhead trolley wire. Suffering the combined assault of noxious effusions from the gasworks and spray from the power station's cooling towers, it is not surprising that the tracks here became very corrugated. In 1948–50 a second and very large electric power station (Croydon B) was built on the west side of the W&CR north of the gasworks. This had a large complex of sidings where coal wagons were shunted by Peckett 0–4–0ST and Robert Stephenson diesels.

World War I brought changes to passenger services on both lines. Already much reduced, the LSWR and LBSCR trains between Wimbledon and Streatham via both sides of the loop were among facilities withdrawn after traffic on Sunday 31st December 1916 to make resources available for essential war transport (LSWR trains ceased on Saturday evening as there was no Sunday service). After this, the rush-hour passengers who had made up most of the traffic found their way to and from work by electric tramcar and motor bus, either all the way, or to and from the nearest station open. For Wimbledon passengers there was little hardship as the LSWR's new electric services were in any case more attractive than the 31- to 40-minute steam run to and from the City over the 10½ miles via Streatham. Economies were sought on the Wimbledon–Croydon line by the introduction of push-and-pull sets of two side-gangway coaches and Stroudley 0–4–2T. These trains, which took over the service from 1st November 1918, were manned by conductor guards who issued tickets to those boarding at what were now unstaffed halts at Merton Park, Morden and Beddington Lane. Parcels and other facilities were withdrawn from these points, but Morden, closed on Sundays for some time, was re-opened on that day.

Life on the W&CR and the Tooting loops proceeded uneventfully until the Underground proposed its Morden tube in the early 1920s. One outcome of the row that this provoked was restoration of passenger service on the Tooting loops from 27th August 1923. Seven steam trains ran each way between Wimbledon and Ludgate Hill in peak hours only (three via Haydons Road) hauled by H and M7 0–4–4T. From London Bridge there were about five each way daily in peak hours, all via Haydons Road, from Tulse Hill seven each way (three via Haydons Road)

Haydons Road station looking to Wimbledon, c.1933.

and from Streatham, ten each way (five via Haydons Road). No trains ran on Sundays. Tulse Hill trains reversed on the Herne Hill lines there, those terminating at Streatham used the old short bay on the Down side. Both services were worked by ex-LSWR push-and-pull trains (four-coach bogie sets) and the Ludgate Hill service offered ex-LCDR six-wheelers. Building development immediately before 1914 had created a demand for a station at Streatham Road, between Tooting and Streatham, but this was ignored.

When the Wimbledon–Haydons Road–Streatham line was electrified in 1929, the Merton Park–Tooting section, its traffic now completely drained off by Colliers Wood tube station, was relegated to steam freight only, the last passenger train running on 2nd March. From the following day, electric trains ran half-hourly between Wimbledon and Holborn Viaduct seven days a week (three times an hour at peak periods), 41 each way in all. Until 30th June, Sunday trains worked to and from Victoria via Brixton except for two evening trains each way, but after that, Holborn Viaduct was used all week. St Paul's (now Blackfriars) was reached in 24 minutes from Wimbledon, 19 minutes from Tooting.

Electric service for West Croydon at Waddon Marsh Halt, July 1930.
Lens of Sutton

Initially the electrics regained much traffic from road services, especially in peak hours. At Haydons Road, tickets issued and collected grew from 36,541 in 1928 to 236,845 in 1934 and seasons from 45 to 2,240. This stimulated reconstruction of the station in 1938, when the two-storey station house on the Up side was demolished and new wooden buildings were provided on each platform, that on the Up side including a passimeter booking office. The signalbox, by then open only for freight yard movements and the morning peak, was closed at the same time, and replaced by a ground frame, but it was considered necessary to enlarge the yard to accommodate another 23 wagons. Wooden stations do not of course last long without careful maintenance and further rebuilding in the Network SouthEast brick and tile neo-vernacular single-storey style took place in the 1980s. After the mid-1950s, traffic on the line fell off and today the trains are not heavily loaded even in rush hours. As we shall see when considering the Wimbledon and Sutton line, since 1995 the basic train service has formed part of the Thameslink cross-London operation, working round via Sutton to and from Luton and Bedford.

The Merton Abbey chord remained busy with freight, but the junction at the Tooting end was severed on 10th March 1934, Tooting station obstinately clinging to its 'Junction' appendage until 3rd March 1938. The Up track was removed and the section was worked as a long siding from Merton Park, with control by telephone from instruments in the Merton Abbey goods office. At Merton Park, Croydon line passengers then faced an obstacle course in the form of two closed platforms and the double right of way between their train and the street door. Occasional special passenger workings penetrated to Merton Abbey, where the two-storey station house on the Up side and the two platforms remained in good order for many years. A supplement to the working timetable issued in 1936 indicated that the Down platform could be used by excursion trains, but the line was not to be negotiated at more than 5mph, under the supervision of a pilotman.

In the late 1920s and 1930s, Merton saw industrial expansion and a siding was laid from the Merton Abbey track into the new Lines Brothers Triang toy factory in Morden Road. Other private sidings served the Eyre Smelting Works and the New Merton Board Mills at Merton Abbey. As late as 1960 there were still two return goods workings daily from Norwood to Merton Abbey and one on Saturdays to Hackbridge but, with factory closures and increased use of road transport, loadings fell and after the last revenue train ran coal down to Merton Abbey on 1st May 1975 the track was quickly taken-up.

The Morden tube extension, which passed many feet below the W&CR near Morden Road halt, contributed much clay to the filling of the Mitcham ballast pits served by the latter line. As soon as the tube opened, passenger revenue at Merton Park, Morden Road and Mitcham declined steeply, but the W&CR continued to attract a steady patronage for through journeys and at its southern stations. In 1927 there were 14 push-and-pull workings between Wimbledon and West Croydon, one extended to Crystal Palace Low Level, two from Wimbledon to Sutton via Mitcham Junction, and another from Mitcham to Crystal Palace Low Level. A similar service worked Down.

Reflecting the growth of the West Croydon industrial area, freight workings were quite complex by 1927. In that year ex-LBSCR 0–6–0T and 0–6–2T were normally employed, but the heavier coal workings required Maunsell W 2–6–4T or N 2–6–0. The first run was at 02.50 from New Cross, visiting all the sidings and yards between the two ends, finishing at Tooting Junction via Merton Abbey and returning by the same route at 08.25. This was followed Down by the 05.10 from New Cross to Waddon Marsh, carrying coal for the Croydon Gas Company and returning with empties at 11.25. Traffic for the private sidings at Waddon Marsh and Beddington Lane was carried by the 08.30 from Norwood Yard, which returned from Beddington at 15.10. The large yard at Mitcham was cleared by the 12.55 from Norwood, which returned at 18.05. Last of the booked trips was the 14.37 from Norwood to Haydons Road which left there at 17.10. There was provision for a 16.00 conditional working from Norwood if any coal was left over for the gasworks. At Haydons Road there were private sidings on the Down side opposite the Lambeth Cemetery, where traffic was exchanged with the Wandle Valley Joint Sewage Board's lines, worked by its own locomotive, and on the Down side west of the station, a siding entered the 1897 depot of the Wimbledon Council.

This varied scene was further coloured in 1930 when the LCC was building the 825-acre St Helier housing estate south of Mitcham. C. J. Wills & Sons, the

Waddon Marsh, looking to West Croydon, 13th September 1975. *Alan A Jackson*

contractors, laid an extensive temporary network of flat-bottom rails on cinder ballast to carry materials as required to the building sites. There was a connection to the W&CR through Hall & Company's siding at Mitcham goods yard. This layout, with its 30ft span bridge over the Wandle, was operated by six 0–6–0T dating from 1885 to 1926, shedded at a depot about a mile south of Mitcham. It was one of the last examples in southern England of a major public works contract relying on rail-delivered materials carried to site over specially-laid lines.

As well as the various public and private freight facilities already mentioned, the W&CR also handled the Southern's own needs for its permanent way depot on the north side of the line near Beddington Lane, and for the civil engineer's depot next to the goods yard at Mitcham, a fascinating spot where complicated new layouts were laid down on a trial basis. This depot closed in 1966.

With the sole exception of Woodside–Sanderstead, the W&CR was the only part of the Southern's suburban system not electrified by 1928. Perhaps simply to close this gap, and for no really sound reason, the general manager decided it should be converted, obtaining the board's consent on 7th July that year. With all neighbouring lines already electrified, he thought it could be cheaply done without new substations and there were of course obvious economies in eliminating an isolated steam passenger service. But the board minutes show a sad story of costs rising well above estimates as the bills came in. One reason for this situation was a decision taken following a visit Walker paid with senior officers on 2nd August.

After looking at Dundonald Road level crossing, Wimbledon, which they found 'not particularly busy' though requiring two gatemen as it was open for 18 hours daily, the party proceeded to Kingston Road, Merton Park. Here two signalmen and a porter signalman were on shifts, and a recent census had shown daily passage of 600 buses, 3,400 other vehicles and 5,000 pedestrians. Delays with the more frequent electric trains would be severe, so the chief engineer was invited to report on the possibility of eliminating both crossings by leading the W&CR into the Wimbledon & Sutton at a point south of Merton Park, an ambitious project which no doubt met a quick death once costs were assessed. But the main problem considered by the party was the handling of the important freight traffic after electrification. The existing five booked workings between West Croydon and Mitcham (two extended to Wimbledon) and one or two daily as far as Waddon Marsh would have to be moved to the night hours to make room for the proposed electric service. As such a change would incur almost £2,000 a year in extra costs, not to mention the displeasure of customers, it was proposed to construct another track between Beddington Lane and West Croydon to allow daytime freight working to continue. It was also noted that the Mitcham Ballast Sidings were not used and that much railway land here and near Morden might be made available for factories or housing. Completed in 1930 in time for the electric working, the second line was partly achieved by linking existing sidings parallel to the passenger track on the north side. Between West Croydon and Waddon Marsh the freight line was controlled by electric train staff with a separate set of electric tokens for the block sections; beyond Waddon Marsh the track was operated under permissive working.

By choosing to electrify a single line operated by conductor-guards, the SR ensured that this curious and enduring backwater would retain some character. As no corridor electric stock was available, 2-car electric sets were made up from the original side-gangway trailers of the LBSCR 1909 South London line electrification. Nine feet wide at eaves, with frosted glass vents over the quarter-lights, these vehicles had been taken off the South London line when it fairly quickly became apparent that there was a surfeit of first-class accommodation. Replaced by composite non-driving trailers in 1911, they had been given lavatories and steam heating and placed on main line duty (they were too wide to work anywhere else on the LBSCR electric system). The SR installed new electric traction equipment, forming them into motor/control trailer sets with side gangways retained but no through communication between cars. Some first-class seating was converted to third, but otherwise it was to disappear with the abolition of suburban first-class in October 1941.

Resplendent in fresh green paint, three coats of best white lead on their roofs, these sets started work on 6th July 1930, operating every 20 minutes at peak times, otherwise half-hourly, seven days a week, and sharing the reconstructed platforms 9 and 10 at Wimbledon with the Wimbledon and Sutton service. On the opening day of electric service, a new halt was added at Waddon Marsh, a 170ft island platform attached to the south end of the existing signal box, served by a passing loop which made, with sidings, a spread of four tracks at this point. Passengers approaching by footbridge were offered the bewildering choice of purchasing their tickets from the train guards or from the signalman.

Electric train staffs were used for the single-line working of the passenger trains, with exchanges at Merton Park, Mitcham, Mitcham Junction, Beddington Lane (not a passing place), Waddon Marsh, and West Croydon B box. Using the single line alongside the Croydon & Epsom, the electric trains, like their predecessors, terminated in a bay at West Croydon Up platform, an arrangement which, after the SR had rebuilt West Croydon with a main road entrance at this, the country end, led many a confused passenger to board them for what was thought to be a direct run to London. Traversing the whole length of the W&CR in just over 16 minutes, the electric trains were timed to pass each other on the double track between Mitcham and Mitcham Junction.

The market gardens and other open land in miscellaneous use which made up much of the carriage window scene between Merton Park and Beddington Lane survived electrification. Even today, there are still quasi-rural glimpses, particularly between Merton Park and Mitcham and between Mitcham Junction and Beddington Lane. As late as 1924 milk remained the principal traffic at Morden Road Halt and three years later a *Railway Magazine* writer was describing the surroundings here as 'the most rural and untouched neighbourhood of any within the same radius from Charing Cross'. Houses began to appear in the late 1920s when Merton Park was filled-up south of the W&CR, whilst to the north of the line and east of the main road were the factories already mentioned. The occupants of the houses and the factory workers, however, used the tube railway or road transport in preference to the indirect electric trains with their obligatory change at Wimbledon.

Although there were two or three patches of new housing between Morden Road and Mitcham by the end of the 1930s, the rural atmosphere was preserved when the extensive area of Morden Hall park came under the sympathetic care of the National Trust. From Mitcham to the Junction many small houses were built between 1927 and 1939 and the general residential growth of the Mitcham area required some improvement to the goods yard in 1936, but post-war maps still showed watercress beds south of the line there. Mitcham Common and Croydon Corporation's huge Beddington Sewage Farm kept the next stretch as open land. At Beddington Lane there was a small cluster of new housing close to the station. From here to Waddon Marsh the electric tramway opened in May 1906 between West Croydon, Mitcham, and Tooting with its attendant competing motor buses was probably the main influence on the plentiful new low-cost housing built between 1928 and 1935.

Purley Way, a by-pass round the west side of Croydon, was opened in 1925, crossing the railway at Waddon Marsh and helping to strengthen the growth of the industrial complex here. The 1930 halt was close to Croydon Council's housing estate which filled up land between the railway and Mitcham Road in 1928–31, but it seems doubtful if many of the tenants used the trains in preference to the cheaper and more frequent tram and bus services along the Mitcham Road.

The mixed land uses and street transport competition stunted the growth of passenger traffic that normally accompanied suburban electrification, the nature of the service also proving some deterrent to commuter settlement. Thus the two-car sets continued to provide ample accommodation for the traffic offering right through to the 1950s, when they reached the end of their useful life. In 1954 they gave way to BR 2EPB two-car sets, comfortable and smart enough, but lacking the charisma which brought railway photographers out in some numbers to record the last journeys of their predecessors. Overnight the whole line lost some colour, especially as conductor-guard operation had necessarily to be abandoned and ticket issuing arrangements provided at Morden Road. The versatile signalmen at the other two halts had more work to do.

Mitcham station with West Croydon train entering, 19th August 1957. At this time the entrance and exit of the station were through the house seen at the right hand side of the overline road bridge. *Alan A Jackson*

Goods traffic was still quite heavy in the mid-1950s, bringing on to the line LBSCR C2X, C and Q class 0–6–0, even the occasional E6 0–6–2T or W 2–6–4T. Around 1967, Type 3 (Class 33) diesel-electrics and E6000 (Class 73) electro-diesels took over, by this time on waning traffic, following transfer to road haulage and the rundown of the gasworks. Haydons Road yard closed from 5th December 1966, Mitcham from 1st May 1967, and Tooting from 5th August 1968. After the Croydon gasworks closed, there remained until 1973 two or three daily trips bringing coal from Betteshanger, Kent to Croydon B power station, but in that year a switch was made to Durham coal brought by coastal vessels to Kingsnorth (Kent). There, somewhat incredibly, it was split up into lorry loads and carried over congested urban roads to Croydon. This left gas oil for the power station's auxiliary plant as the only regular freight movement.

With its heavy staffing ratio and lightly-loaded trains, the W&CR was early on the list for closure, coming up for the first time in 1951 when it was decided that with freight still important, passenger abandonment did not make much sense, as signalling could not be much reduced. Instead there followed a series of economy cuts, starting with Sunday closure of Morden Road from 13th September 1964. From 20th June 1965 Sunday trains were withdrawn over the whole line, and from 7th November 1966 Morden Road was also closed on Saturdays. This last date also saw curtailment of evening service with last trains brought back to around 19.45 for departures each end (18.15 Saturdays) instead of 22.45. First trains now started at around 07.15, but frequency remained half-hourly through the shorter day, still with some extras at peak hours (the last of these were eventually withdrawn in May 1971). In common with others on the Southern Region, the halts lost this description in the timetables operative from 5th May 1969, although Beddington Lane's name-board still bore the forbidden word six years later.

With the drastic reduction in freight, it became possible to work the line as a siding from West Croydon, and in 1971 BR decided to test the temperature of the water. Soon after this closure notice was published, an observer found that at 16.30 on a weekday it took him nearly three times as long to travel by car as by train between Wimbledon and West Croydon stations, yet he noticed on arrival at the latter that a train from Wimbledon disembarked only 17 passengers. BR was probably surprised at the extent of the opposition. Sir Richard Thompson, MP for Croydon South, who already claimed credit for saving Woodside–Sanderstead, raised the matter in the Commons on 5th July 1972, suggesting that 1,500 commuters and 1,000 other passengers would have to meet higher fares and a longer and more tiring journey, whilst closure would add to local road congestion. A ministerial reply averred that the average use of the eight stations was about 1,700 passengers each way daily, 'very low for a suburban service of this type'. It was suggested the line was among the heaviest loss-makers in the south-east, but the minister concluded by noting that its future was not yet sealed. At the public enquiry on the same day it was stated that 80 per cent of the users would have up to 26 minutes added to daily journeys, around half having to pay higher fares. Only 11 per cent of users in the Merton area had cars, while some 250 people in Beddington Lane district would be completely isolated, their nearest bus stop 600yd across the Common, a hazard after dark. The Minister of Transport finally announced in July 1974 that the line would stay open, his department following with a statement which admitted severe environmental effects, inconvenience and extra cost to users, and added somewhat gratuitously, that buses would be an inadequate substitute. A year later, BR issued a poster encouraging people to ride the line.

The attractions of this single-track electric line, with its freight workings, manually-operated semaphore signals, varied scenery and country-style stations, were substantially eroded after the 1970s. Although the independent unelectrified freight line between West Croydon and Waddon Marsh was taken out of use from 1st February 1976, the 'as required' oil trains continued to run until some time before the closure of the Croydon Power Station in November 1981. With around a dozen railwaymen on duty at a time on a six-mile line carrying but two trains an hour, further economies were inevitable and so far as signalling was concerned these came about with the phasing of the line into the Victoria Area Resignalling Scheme. From 18th October 1981, West Croydon 'B' box was closed and the section between West Croydon and Waddon Marsh was worked under track circuit block regulations. This was followed by closure of the signal boxes at Waddon Marsh, Mitcham and Merton Park from 23rd May 1982. The level crossings at Beddington Lane, (where the box had been destroyed by fire on 26th April 1981) Merton Park and Dundonald Road, Wimbledon, converted to lifting barriers, were then supervised by closed circuit television from the new Falcon Lane signalling centre at Clapham Junction.

Further cuts were made in the train services. From October 1988 the service was reduced to one train shuttling between Wimbledon and West Croydon at approximately 45 minute intervals, Mondays to Saturdays, finishing early in the evening. By this time something rather better was under consideration: the line was to become part of the Croydon Tramlink light rail system already mentioned. With this, trams were to work into the east side of Wimbledon station, providing it with a direct link to both West and East Croydon stations.

Looking to Tooting from Christchurch Road Bridge, Colliers Wood, 21st June 1975. *Alan A Jackson*

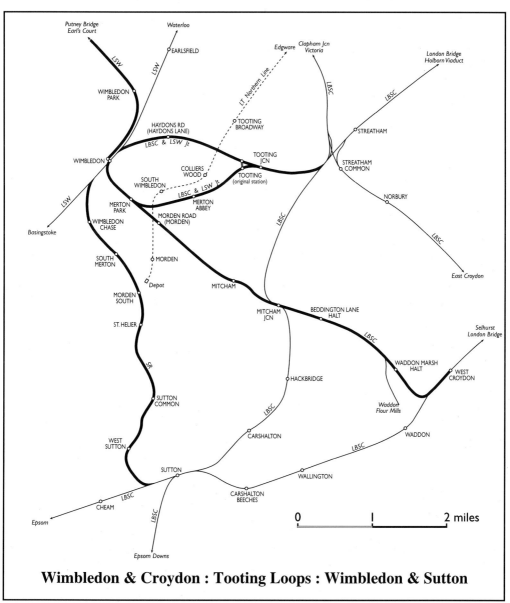

Wimbledon & Croydon : Tooting Loops : Wimbledon & Sutton

Road frontage of Wimbledon Chase station (SR 1929), with BR signage, March 1967. *BR (SR)*

The Wimbledon & Sutton Line (map page 109)

From the beginning of the 1880s, the small Surrey town of Sutton attracted schemes aimed at breaking the monopoly of the LBSCR. Sited on that company's Portsmouth main line, the town had enjoyed railway service since the opening of the Croydon and Epsom line on 10th May 1847, but its position was much improved with the availability of a direct route to London Bridge and Victoria via Mitcham from 1st October 1868. After this, the district experienced development as a residential area for middle-class commuters and by 1881 the 1851 population of just over a thousand had risen to 10,334.

Attacks on the LBSCR's hold took the form of schemes for branches from the LSWR at Worcester Park (1882) and from Wimbledon (1883, 1888, 1890 and 1891). All failed. 'Sutton', observed the parliamentary committee on the 1882 Sutton & L&SW Junction Bill, 'has to grow into greater importance before it ought to ask for amplification of its railway accommodation'. Grow it did. In 1901 the population, with that of neighbouring Cheam, had reached 20,267 and in *Black's Guide Around London* that year, A. R. Hope-Moncrieff wrote: 'its antiquity is all overlaid by the commonplace smugness of a residential suburb, the fine country round has been much cut up by schools and other institutions'. Sutton was now virtually joined to Cheam in the west, reaching out to touch Carshalton and Beddington in the east and the edge of Banstead Downs in the south. Only the railwayless north, between Sutton Common and Merton, remained neglected by the housebuilder.

Local landowners were restless, considering that if only a railway could be built across these clay pastures and through the elm copses, they stood to gain much. A meeting to consider a scheme engineered by W. Vaux Graham was convened at the Westminster Palace Hotel on 7th October 1908, presided over by landowners Sir

Henry George Smallman and H. D. Searles-Wood. Reporting on this two days later, *The Railway Gazette* considered the promoters 'peculiarly optimistic', especially as there had been no negotiations with the District or the LSWR over the proposed connections at Wimbledon. Nothing came of this initiative, but another meeting of property owners at Merton just over a year later led to a similar scheme by the same engineer being incorporated in a bill for the 1910 session. This envisaged a 5½-mile line from Wimbledon to Sutton through eight intermediate stations, and junctions with the main lines at each end. It was anticipated that the District would work the service with electric traction by extending its trains from Wimbledon. Smallman, Searles-Wood, W. E. R. Innes and other local landowners were prominent among the promoters. These gentlemen were ready to put up some but by no means all the £350,000 estimated capital cost.

From the evidence given to the parliamentary committee by Sir George Gibb, chairman of the Underground Company, and by Albert Stanley, managing director of the District, it appeared that although the District was friendly and would be quite happy to work the line, it had not committed any cash. The LSWR evinced little enthusiasm, expressing concern about further overloading of its Putney and Wimbledon line, also turning-up its nose at the proposed junction arrangements at Wimbledon.

In open opposition to a line which would filch traffic from their territory, the LBSCR, through William Forbes, the general manager, told the parliamentary committee that the railway would be 'a constant source of irritation'. As some indication of the lack of need north of Sutton he put up a Miss Mary Pochin, who solemnly declared that she had once hailed a bus which used to ply between Wimbledon and Sutton but the astonishment of the conductor was so great at being hailed that he omitted to signal to the driver to stop; the driver even turned to see what she was waving at. Forbes then outlined the Brighton's plans for improving the facilities for Sutton: electric trains would reach London Bridge in 20 minutes and Victoria in 18 minutes compared with the promoters' estimates of 32-minute run from Sutton to Waterloo. All in all, he suggested, this was a 'nice little move on the part of the District Railway, first to get to Sutton, then to Epsom, and afterwards on to Brighton'. Although he was of course laying it on rather thickly, the Brighton was without doubt genuinely rattled; in January 1910 it had steam-hauled a South London line electric train to Sutton to test clearances and was preparing plans for widening to four tracks between the western end of Sutton and Cheam (works which were completed in October 1911).

Taking note of the Brighton's attitude, Parliament passed the bill without insisting on the proposed junction at Sutton, although it was stipulated that there should be convenient access between the two stations there. The act gave the MDR powers to run over the Wimbledon & Sutton through an end-on junction with the Putney & Wimbledon line in Wimbledon station. After passing beneath Wimbledon Hill Road, the double tracks were to parallel the LSWR main line as far as the Elm Grove footbridge, just before which there was to be a junction with the LSWR Up slow line, facing London. A station at this point would serve the first site of the All-England Tennis Ground.

At Elm Grove, the line was to swerve sharply, passing beneath the LSWR, to emerge on the south side to receive a connection from the LSWR Down slow. A proposed station at Cannon Hill, closely followed by another at Green Lane, Merton

Park, would serve an area of recent residential development, the line skirting the west side of the Merton Park estate, laid out for building many years earlier. From here, the route would be south to a station serving Morden village and beyond that there was to be another station at Elm Farm on the south side of Love Lane. Sutton Common was next reached, with its station, whence there would be a wide sweep westwards to avoid the already built-up west side of Sutton as far as possible. A station at Collingwood Road (end of Sydney Road) was to be followed by another for Cheam, on the north side of Cheam Road, Sutton. Finally the line would curve eastwards to terminate alongside the LBSCR at Bridge Road, Sutton, next to the Post Office, where a footpath would link it with the LBSCR Up platform.

Despite Forbes' insinuations, the promoters at first found themselves quite isolated, receiving no encouragement from the existing railway companies and unable to raise more capital. In March 1911 they went caps in hand to Albert Stanley, who in turn approached the LSWR to see whether that company would help the District complete the line if the landowners agreed to bear part of any operating losses for a limited period. There was no response, so in October 1911 the District offered to complete the line if the promoters would guarantee about £20,000 a year. This was too much for the landowners to find, and on 8th October 1912 it was finally agreed to limit their guarantee to £6,000 a year maximum for ten years, the District to meet the balance of any deficiency below 4½ per cent return on the capital. Within a few weeks of this agreement, the local interests on the board of the Wimbledon & Sutton Railway Company were replaced by Underground Company nominees, most of the issued shares also passing to Underground representatives or share-holders. From 5th December 1912 all meetings were held at the Underground headquarters, Electric Railway House, Broadway, Westminster.

Whilst the takeover was going through, the District, by agreement with the LSWR, secured powers for a second pair of tracks for its exclusive use between East Putney and Wimbledon, partly for the Sutton traffic. A year later (1913) the District was authorised to widen its own line between Eel Brook Common, south of Fulham Broadway and Munster Road, south of Parsons Green, where there were to be two new island platforms. This work, never started, together with the third track at Putney Bridge station (completed in 1910) would have facilitated working of non-stop trains on the Sutton service.

Alterations were begun on the north side of Wimbledon station in 1913–14 in preparation for the Sutton line, and an extra bay at Wimbledon and additional signalboxes between Wimbledon Park and East Putney came into use on 9th March 1914. Negotiations with the LSWR delayed a start on the Sutton line, but much of the land was acquired and fenced. Wartime restrictions caused further delay. An act of 1913 increased the capital to £550,000 and incorporated the guarantees already mentioned, but a further act of 1915 gave the District powers to guarantee the Wimbledon & Sutton dividends and interest as a working expense.

Immediate post-war conditions were not favourable to a resumption of the scheme, but land purchases continued, including a parcel at Sutton bought in 1920. Opportunity came in the form of the Trade Facilities Act, 1921, which attempted to mitigate unemployment by offering a Treasury guarantee of capital and interest for approved public works. This brought forth a batch of proposals from the Underground Company in October 1921 which included construction of the Sutton line, now estimated to cost, with rolling stock and car depot, a total of £1.7m. The

Treasury agreed to guarantee the package which among other things included modernisation of the City & South London tube railway and its extension southwards to Morden where there would be a link to the Wimbledon & Sutton and a sharing of the car sheds. Bills for all these new works, which also provided for connection of the City & South London with the Hampstead & Highgate tube at Camden Town, were duly deposited in November 1922.

The prospect of tube and District trains busily undermining its traffic at Sutton was too much for the infant Southern Railway. At its Annual General Meeting the chairman, Sir Hugh Drummond, told shareholders it was 'a very serious matter' and in the parliamentary committee on the Underground bill, Sir Herbert Walker, general manager, talked of an 'invasion' of the Southern's territory as defined in the Railway Grouping Agreement. Sir Herbert made it clear to the committee that the SR would not object to the City & South London tube going as far as Tooting and even offered to accommodate the tube trains at Wimbledon via the Tooting & Wimbledon loop if this would secure withdrawal of the District from the Wimbledon & Sutton scheme. But the Underground representatives maintained that a combined depot for both District and tube at Morden was essential and there was no other suitable site. Taking this to mean all or none, the Lords committee rejected the whole of the City & South London extension from Clapham Common to Morden.

Incensed South London MPs, deprived of a much-needed Underground facility, sought to throw all the blame on the SR. Talks between the two parties were arranged and on 25th July a compromise was reached; the Southern agreed the tube might go as far as the north side of the London Road at Morden, with a line beyond for depot access only and no connection to the Wimbledon & Sutton, which the Southern would build and work. Running powers over the Sutton line would be available to the District, with the Southern making the necessary junctions and changes at Wimbledon and Sutton. As a further sop, the SR agreed to restore passenger service between Wimbledon and Streatham over the Tooting & Wimbledon loop, which had been a wartime casualty.

With SR opposition removed, the Morden tube extension was sanctioned and the Wimbledon & Sutton powers passed to the SR from 1st July 1924 under the SR Act of 1st August 1924. This act dissolved the Sutton company, altered the junctions at Wimbledon to the south side of the main line (the District had shown no interest in the proffered running powers) and added the necessary junction with the Epsom line at Sutton. It was altogether a remarkable concession on the part of the Southern, no doubt made under very strong political pressures and eased by an agreement with the Underground Company that there would in future be mutual consultation before competing lines were promoted.

In direct opposition to the spirit of this agreement, the Underground launched feeder bus services when the Morden tube opened in 1926, culling traffic from a wide sector of outer London suburban territory of the SR: Sutton, Cheam, Mitcham, Banstead, Wallington, Worcester Park, even Epsom. These services, combined with very low fares and through road-rail ticket facilities, drew much business from the Southern, quickly depriving it of an estimated four million passengers a year. The loss was made more serious by the rapid residential development of the district after 1928. Around the tube terminus, building of small houses spread wide and in 1929, just to the south, the LCC started to construct its new town of St Helier, over 9,000 dwellings to accommodate some 40,000.

Bridge carrying the Wimbledon & Sutton line over the London–Epsom road c.1930. Morden South station is just off the picture at the left.

In contrast to the tube extension, progress on the Wimbledon & Sutton was slow. Property had to be acquired and demolished at Merton and at Sutton, negotiations for acquisition dragging on until the summer of 1928. Approval for work to start was given by the SR board on 30th June 1927 and in October the company's engineering staff began operations on the embankment at Wimbledon. At Sutton, the main contractor, Sir Robert McAlpine & Sons, could not make a start until July 1928. Work then continued night and day until September, when a resident secured a restraint on night work from the Vacation Court.

The northern end was sufficiently advanced to allow service of the first two stations, Wimbledon Chase and South Merton, from 7th July 1929, when the Streatham-Tooting-Wimbledon trains (restored on 27th August 1923 and electrified on 3rd March 1929) were extended. Although a double track was laid, this first section was worked with train staff until about December 1929, after which trains ran empty to St Helier station to reverse. The remainder of the line opened for staff training on 1st January 1930, to the public on Sunday 5th January. Late in 1929 742 *Camelot* and other N15 and S15 4-6-0s had tested and ironed-out the track.

Construction through treacherous clay subsoil had been far from simple. Embankments at the southern end had slipped after completion and a vein of blue clay near Sutton required extensive drainage. At the extreme southern end, the engineers had to cut through much chalk and demolish Victorian villas to reach the old LBSCR line. There were no less than 20 bridges over the 5¼ miles and these, together with the drainage works, high embankments and property compensation, pushed up the capital cost to £1.042m. Although hardly justifying the railwaymen's nickname 'Wall of Death' it was a line designed for electric traction, with many sharp curves and only 35ch of level rail in its whole length; gradients were steep. From 50ft above sea level at Wimbledon the line climbed to about 200ft at Sutton.

All intermediate stations were of an economical standard pattern at rail level, a 520ft island platform for eight-car trains, partly covered with a glazed canopy carried on steel stanchions at 38ft centres. General waiting rooms, ladies' and gentlemen's lavatories and separate staff huts comprised the facilities provided. Each station had a passimeter booking office either on the platform or at road level, and at South Merton, Morden South, and Sutton Common there were no other buildings. Divided into two block sections (Wimbledon C–St Helier–Sutton), this was the first SR line to be signalled throughout with upper-quadrant semaphores. One station-master, living in an SR house at West Sutton, supervised the whole line.

In peak hours, eight-car trains ran every 20 minutes between Holborn Viaduct and West Croydon via Wimbledon and Sutton, but the basic service was half-hourly, Holborn Viaduct–Wimbledon–Sutton–West Croydon–Crystal Palace–Victoria, using three-car trains. Connections were available at Wimbledon to and from Waterloo, at Sutton and West Croydon to and from Victoria and London Bridge. The last two trains at night ran only to St Helier, returning to Wimbledon.

Traction current for the third rail came from Durnsford Road power station (Wimbledon) with conversion to 660V dc in substations at Raynes Park and Sutton; later current was taken from the National Grid via a rectifier at St Helier.

At Wimbledon a new through island platform was provided on the south side for Croydon and Sutton trains, the new line running thence for about half a mile between the main lines and the large goods yard and signal works on the south. It then turned south east on a 12ch curve traversing a 1½-mile embankment through Wimbledon Chase station to South Merton. A long siding paralleled the double track towards Wimbledon Chase, where the station served a district which had been built up between 1900 and 1914. Its well-sited frontage on the main Kingston Road was covered with white glazed blocks, but the effect of the curving street elevation was somewhat spoiled by the excrescence of a luggage lift tower which was never used. Showing some evidence of an architect's hand, the general design of this station appears to have been a prototype for new SR 'marine style' suburban stations, setting the pattern for those on the Chessington line. The name Wimbledon Chase for a site in the Merton & Morden Urban District is an interesting example of railway snobbery, matched by the Underground's adjacent 'South Wimbledon', which was in Merton High Street, also outside the Wimbledon boundary.

At South Merton, the tiny passimeter ticket office was on the platform but a concrete base was made alongside the road bridge above for a future entrance building. Although the district was fully built-up by the mid-1930s, this base has never been used. Still on embankment, the double tracks ran south to cross the main London-Epsom-Worthing road on an impressive 120ft skew span of lattice girders which took them into Morden South station, where a subway through the embankment gave access to the island platform. This station has always suffered from its proximity to the tube terminus, and its catchment area was denuded by the large acreages of the tube depot and Morden Park.

A cutting on a half-mile curve of 25ch radius led into the St Helier passenger and goods station, the most important point on the line. Twelve acres of land were conveyed free by the LCC, the SR adding just over two acres more. The freight yard had two roads and a great deal of spare space. On Green Lane, above the tracks, the station building took the form of a concrete blockhouse of quite remarkable crudity, anticipating the products of the modern brutalist school of architects by some 40

Street frontage of St Helier station (1930), still bearing Southern Railway signage 15 years after the formation of British Railways (photo 6th August 1963). *Alan A Jackson*

years. Its sole relieving feature was a narrow glass canopy which advertised the service offered. Some way from the centre of the large LCC estate, it failed to attract more than a tiny proportion of the tenants, most of whom preferred to walk or bus to the tube at Morden, or found employment locally, travelling by bus or cycle.

For almost a mile beyond St Helier, the line was on embankment until the north end of Sutton Common station was reached. Although houses were built each side of the line here in the early 1930s a very large part of the catchment area to the north-east was left as an open space. Facilities were similar to those at South Merton except that the passimeter ticket office was housed in a small hut at road level.

A short cutting and a half-mile embankment carried the line to West Sutton, the last of the stations, also below road level at the start of the deep cutting through the chalk to the junction. Its roadside building was an ugly concrete blockhouse similar to that at St Helier, but with a stubby concrete canopy. East of the station, there was a solid mass of small houses by the early 1930s and some of the streets dated back to Victorian times. On the west were open spaces and a wedge of housing towards the by-pass road, much of it completed by the early 1930s.

Sinuous and steep, the last stretch of the line featured three reverse curves of 15, 20, and 13ch radius, climbing at 1 in 90, and 1 in 49, with a final ramp of half a mile at 1 in 44 into Sutton station. As this area was fully built-up in late Victorian and Edwardian years, it was not possible without undue cost to obtain a suitable angle of slope, so the chalk cutting had in places to be lined with concrete.

Concurrently with the construction of the line, the stations at Wimbledon and Sutton were rebuilt. New road level buildings and staircases at Sutton were finished in 1928, and the enlarged Wimbledon was ready a year later.

From the time the line was opened until the autumn of 1939 builders were busy filling the area near the line with small houses, notably west of South Merton station up to the edge of Morden Park (1934–38), and west of the tracks between St Helier and West Sutton (1927–39) where, apart from some public open spaces, only the valley of the Pyl Brook was left alone. Most of the LCC estate at St Helier had been finished by 1935. Although some traffic was gained from all this activity, the success of the Morden tube with its very low fares and road-rail ticket facilities meant that the hopes of the original Wimbledon & Sutton promoters were never to be fully realised. The fact that the only peak-hour service on the line was to a City terminus, and that over a circuitous route, was a contributory cause of failure, despite the reasonably good interchange facilities at Wimbledon, Sutton and Tulse Hill (British passengers do not like changing trains, however good the connections). Towards the end of the 1950s loadings began to fall off during the day and off-peak trains, never very much used, were carrying only very light loads.

After Sunday 8th November 1959, Morden South closed on Sundays and from 17th June 1963 the line's three night trains disappeared. Originally steam-hauled, these comprised the 00.19 Holborn Viaduct–St Helier, the 01.35 Herne Hill–Sutton (connecting out of the 01.20 Holborn Viaduct–Orpington, also withdrawn) and the 03.40 Sutton–Wimbledon–Victoria (with connection at Herne Hill for Holborn Viaduct). By the late 1950s, the market, newspaper, post office and other small hours workers who had been encouraged by these services to live along the line had all taken to their cars. About 1967 the off-peak service was altered to run from West Croydon to London Bridge instead of to Victoria.

The freight yard at St Helier lost its daily train from 6th May 1963. After this, goods traffic in the form of milk tankers and coal wagons continued to be worked over the line to meet the needs of the Express Dairy's bottling plant at Morden South, where private sidings had been opened in 1954, with a junction facing Sutton at the south end of the station. The loaded milk tanker trains originated at Acton Western Region and there was also some railborne coal inwards until 1970 when the plant was converted to oil brought in by road. Internal shunting was performed by the Dairy's Ruston & Hornsby four-wheel 4B Diesel until 1972 when it was donated to Ashford Steam Centre and replaced by Hunslet Yardmaster four-wheel diesel loco *David*. The siding received its last deliveries of milk in April 1978 but continued to house empty tankers for a few months after that, seeing its final use on 30th December 1978.

Signalling economies were achieved with the line's inclusion in the Victoria Area and Waterloo Area Resignalling schemes. St Helier's signal box was closed after 22nd May 1982 and the southern section passed into the control of the Falcon Lane Signalling Centre at Clapham Junction from 4th October that year. The northern junction came under the new Wimbledon centre in February 1991.

West Sutton's road level building was completely rebuilt in 1989 at a time when all six stations received what was described as a 'facelift' but withdrawal of full time staffing soon exposed all vertical surfaces to almost 100 per cent coverage with mindless spray-painted graffiti and other vandalism. In May 1995 a railway employee described West Sutton in *Railnews* as:

> heavily vandalised and dirty. The waiting room lights still come on at night but the door is boarded up. The station is only staffed in the mornings, so the rest of the time there is no information available and no staff for security.

Left: The unassuming entrance to Sutton Common station, 6th August 1963. *Alan A Jackson*

Below: A four-car electric train climbing the 1 in 44 gradient into Sutton station from the Wimbledon–Sutton line; main line to Dorking and Horsham etc at left, 19th August 1957. *Alan A Jackson*

He added that passengers had no means of knowing what was happening when trains did not appear at the scheduled time. Such problems are not of course confined to this line; in terms of the cost of repairs and redecoration, passengers frightened off by an atmosphere of insecurity and intimidation, and of uncollected revenue from those using the trains, it seems possible that the savings from such staff 'economies' may often be quite illusory.

With bus services and private cars bringing passengers to Wimbledon, Morden Underground and Sutton stations from its catchment area, and other potential users deterred for the reasons just mentioned, off-peak loadings on this line fell away in the 1970s and 1980s. Commuting to central London has also declined, here as elsewhere. Although all Sunday trains were withdrawn after 11th May 1986, the basic two trains an hour were otherwise continued until late at night, Mondays to Saturdays inclusive. A notable improvement was introduced from 29th May 1995, when the basic provision became part of a cross-London Thameslink service to and from Luton, which split at Streatham to give two trains an hour clockwise via Mitcham Junction, Sutton, Wimbledon and Tooting, and two an hour anti-clockwise over the same circuit. Unless a change is made at Wimbledon or Sutton, this provides a painfully slow trundle to central London and traffic remains very thin.

The Epsom Downs Branch
(map page 121)

Regular horse race meetings at Epsom Downs had begun in the early part of the 18th century, patronage of the highest levels of society soon bringing the course to major importance as a centre of this sport. Thorne considered the Derby 'the prime festival of England. For it even legislation adjourned'. Nevertheless, it is somewhat surprising, given that there had been a railway service to the town below the hill since 1847, that the Epsom racecourse was deemed to justify a branch line on its own account, a line which was to serve little else but the unimportant Downs village of Banstead. That the latter community did something to tip the balance is indicated by the presence of its name in the title of the promoting company of 1861. Even more important was the implied backing of an LBSCR worried by LCDR threats for lines from Herne Hill towards Epsom and the racecourse. With a capital of £85,000, borrowing powers of £28,300 and authority to make working arrangements with the LBSCR, the 4¼-mile branch was sanctioned by the Banstead & Epsom Downs Railway Act of 1862. A jolly seal was devised for the company, comprising a locomotive, racehorse, crossed rifles and hunting symbols.

The remote situation of the terminus was well suggested by the wording of the parliamentary draftsman: 'One yard south east of the Gate opening from Epsom Downs into a Field, the property of Mr Gadsden, in the Occupation of Mr Thomas Cook, and part of Longdown Farm'. From here, racegoers were to face a good half mile uphill to the course, about half the length of the climb up from Epsom Town station.

LBSCR auto train at Belmont station (Up side), June 1906.

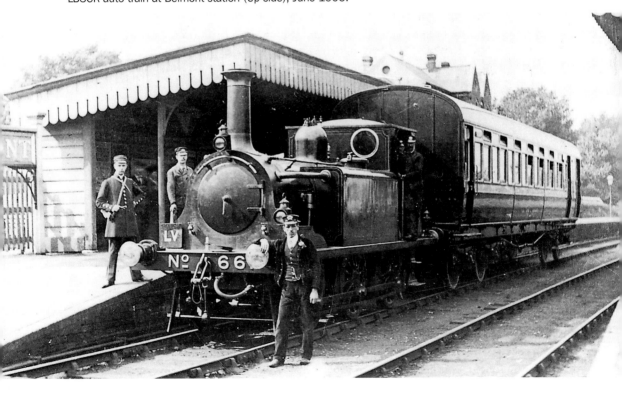

The Epsom Downs Branch
119

Sutton station, July 1882, in process of rebuilding – the Up Epsom Downs line platform (left), is still unfinished. The photographer is standing between the main lines looking towards Epsom and the top-hatted stationmaster can be seen at the end of the Down Main platform near the water column.

Leaving the LBSCR at Sutton station, the double track ran southward to the Downs, climbing quite steeply for much of the way, then, as if thinking better of it, turned west through a deep cutting and then south-west along the lower slopes, keeping mostly between the 300ft and 400ft contours. Just over a mile from Sutton, in open country, was the first intermediate station, named California because it served a public house of that name and land bought by a building speculator who had made some money in the gold rush 15 years before. Two three-storey terraces in grim urban style, one with shops on the ground floor, stood empty for many years and still survive as a memorial to his optimistic enterprise. There was in fact to be little or no business here for another 40 years or so, during which time (1st October 1875) the station was renamed Belmont, reputedly at the suggestion of the station-master's wife.

A small freight yard, dating from about 1880, occupied a cramped site between the level crossing at the south end of the station and the bridge under the Brighton Road, access requiring use of a wagon turntable. By 1910 a bridge had been built south of the station to replace the level crossing, its approach road taking up some of the goods yard site. A new yard of three roads was therefore provided to the east of the Brighton Road.

Banstead station, at the western end of the cutting, was a cheaply-made wooden affair, a tiring mile or more below the 550ft high village. A small goods yard dating from about 1880, on the south side, was approached by a steep ramp down from the road, a feature which for many years discouraged coal merchants from establishing a wharf there (in 1892 Rickett Smith was still carting his coal the whole 6½-miles from Sutton to Walton-on-the-Hill). Later two sets of private sidings were built between the yard and Epsom Downs station.

The terminus was 16¼ miles from Victoria via Mitcham Junction, 18 from London Bridge via Tulse Hill. At its maximum extent, it possessed nine platform faces, all without shelter from the elements, a total of 11 tracks including engine roads. All this to handle race traffic on six days a year, traffic which was only intense on two or three of those days. Its situation on the edge of the Downs at the 350ft contour made it a bleak spot in winter. A witness before the Commons Committee on the Epsom Downs Extension Railway Bill in 1892 thought it 'an absolute wilderness and the most god-forsaken place in the world'. Only in that year had a proper road been finished between the station and the Grandstand. Facilities for loading and unloading carriages and for horse box traffic were of course to be expected, and these could be used for handling cattle and sheep, but there was no proper goods yard, not even a crane. A large wooden building to the north served variously over the years as Royal Stables, refreshment rooms, staff canteen and railwaymen's club. The unpretentious station offices and the stationmaster's house sat across the end of the site fronting a small covered concourse.

Whilst construction was proceeding, in 1864, the LBSCR secured powers to absorb the small company, so that when the line was opened for traffic on 22nd May 1865 it was already part of the Brighton system. The initial train service consisted of eight a day each way between about 08.00 and 21.00, four each way on Sundays. Sunday trains, 'which did not literally earn enough to pay for the grease required for the wheels of the engines and coaches' were very soon withdrawn. Otherwise the provision continued without significant change for over 20 years.

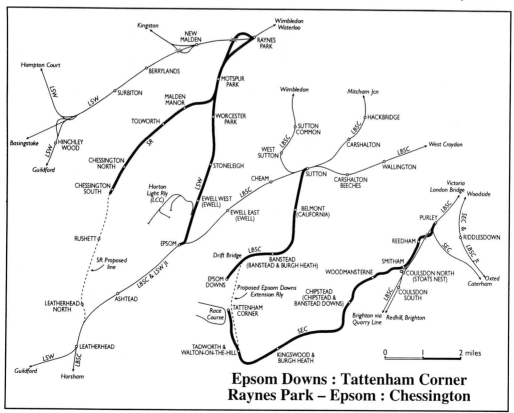

Epsom Downs : Tattenham Corner
Raynes Park – Epsom : Chessington

Even in 1890 there were but 12 trains each way daily, taking about 15 minutes, with first and last departures from Epsom Downs unambitiously placed at o8.15 and 19.50.

Almost from the start, race traffic proved something of a disappointment. Not only were the attendances at the course falling (an LBSCR report of 1869 notes a decrease in visitors to Epsom Races) but many still preferred to travel via the town, where overnight accommodation was available and licensed premises were plentiful. On Derby Day itself the deliciously prolonged pub crawl down from London by road in a vast assortment of horse-drawn vehicles remained popular right up to the motor age. Even so, because it did offer slightly more convenient access to the course for those with little time to spare, the branch did receive a sizeable share of the Derby Day crowds (variously estimated at between 100,000 and 200,000) and of the slightly smaller numbers attracted by Oaks Day. Outside the race weeks, few came on to the line except in the summer, when there was a solid trade in day and Sunday school treats. Many of the children came in special trains which ran on average about once a week at the height of the summer to bring them to the bracing air of the Downs. Near the station, swings, roundabouts, and refreshments were available to attract the children's well-warmed pennies. Acworth, writing in 1899, noted the large covered sheds at the station which offered amongst other things 'donkeys, photography and new milk'. They also served to keep the children out of the rain.

Evidence given to the parliamentary committees on the Epsom Downs Extension and Chipstead Valley Bills of 1892 and 1893 throws some light on the branch at that time. During the winter it was alleged that the terminus saw only about 20 passengers a day, a figure which increased to 30 or 40 on summer weekdays; many of them were golfers. Trains were supposed to connect at Sutton with Portsmouth expresses, which was all right going Down, but they were often late for the Up journey, when harassed schoolteachers had sometimes to endeavour to control their tired and bored charges for half an hour or more. Despite the fact that the LBSCR secretary and general manager (Allen Sarle) used Banstead station every day, the service there was not good, especially on or before race days when the number of trains calling was cut and staff were withdrawn to do duty at Epsom Downs. A Dr Edwin Freshfield related how he once took an Italian gentleman on to the branch; as they got towards the end of the journey, his guest remarked 'This is very refreshing, but it reminds me of railway travelling in my own country' (there could be no worse slur; a British railway compared with some foreign line the British never even built . . .). Sarle told the Extension Bill committee that the working expenses were 2s 7d (12 ½p) a mile and that the profit on working, including Derby Day, was only £90 in 1890 and £204 in 1892; a loss of £550 in 1891 was possibly due to relaying the track. All in all, the branch just about covered its working expenses.

Pleasure seekers and gentlemen commuters apart, there was one more aspect of regular traffic; the airy downlands attracted institutions which supplied freight business and a few passengers. The first of these colonies preceded the railway; the South Metropolitan District Schools, west of the railway alignment near what was to be California station, had opened their doors to pauper children of Camberwell, Greenwich and Woolwich in 1856, and were later to get their own siding (closed about 1889). Similar residential schools for children of the Kensington and Chelsea districts followed in 1880, sited alongside and to the south of the railway between Banstead and the terminus, and also served by a private siding (Crockett's Siding,

1880). Between 1871 and 1877 the huge and ugly bulk of the Banstead Lunatic Asylum rose up on the Downs about half a mile east of the railway, to the south-east of Belmont station. Building materials came in by daily trains from Chelsea Wharf, and were transported over the Downs via a 'tramway' which was nothing more than flat stones laid parallel in the turf to give the horse drawn carts extra purchase, and reduce bad weather difficulties. With the arrival of the motor car, this track became a temptation to drivers, and the stones were removed. Another private siding, Gadesden's, on the Up side about a quarter mile east of Epsom Downs station, was provided in 1886 to service North Looe (Lieu) Farm.

Little residential development appeared around the branch before 1914. Some workers' cottages at Belmont in the late 1880s were followed in the next decade by middle-class villas nearby, building continuing spasmodically until 1915 when a substantial Anglican church was opened at the top of Station Road, by this time lined with small shops. Banstead village attracted large houses for those just one step below the 'gentry', men of business like Allen Sarle, who could afford to run their own carriages to and from Banstead or Sutton stations for their daily trip to London. A colony of new villas began to appear along the Brighton Road, south of the station. But in 1914 there remained a great deal of fine open country, the scenery along the line beyond Belmont little changed from the time of its opening almost 50 years earlier.

We have already noted the disappointing results of race traffic. 'The Derby is not what it was' wrote Acworth in 1899, 'Year by year its importance, or at least its relative importance, diminishes'. A Lords Committee on the Chipstead Valley Bill of 1893 was told by Sarle that race traffic had fallen off in the previous decade bringing in only £2,700 on a mileage basis in 1891 despite the imposition of an 8s (40p) return fare on special trains instead of the normal 3s (15p). Yet Derby Day did remain an important occasion for the branch for over 80 years, reaching its zenith of glamour and bustle in the Edwardian era. Then, around early afternoon, Epsom Downs station presented a lively scene for a skilful photographer, whose postcard remains for us to enjoy: pride of place is taken by the royal train in its special platform on the south side, its resplendent mahogany coaches headed by a gleaming Marsh Atlantic tank engine with the royal coat of arms mounted on the buffer beam, and a gilded crown on the top lamp bracket. Nine other tracks are filled with trains turned ready to go back to London, some of them special Pullman car trains for the private parties of Lord Derby and others, the remainder ordinary suburban coaches for the *hoi polloi*. Although we cannot see them, the station buffer stops are brilliant with floral displays; behind, the station yard is filled with buskers, stalls and sideshows.

A notice of 1896 illustrates the facilities provided: special trains to be worked from both Victoria and London Bridge to Epsom Downs between 11.35 and 13.20, some of the Victoria departures calling at Clapham Junction to pick up passengers booked from Kensington (Addison Road). The company's offices at Trafalgar Square and Regent Street were to remain open until 22.00 for several days beforehand for the sale of tickets, whilst special horsebox trains were to run between Newmarket and Epsom Downs via the East London Railway.

Early in the day, to keep the crowds in some sort of order, large contingents of Metropolitan Police went to Epsom Downs by special train; extra railway staff were brought in and the rest of the branch got short shrift – many ordinary trains were stopped short at Banstead, a practice which lasted until the 1930s. Platform staff disappeared. At Banstead on Derby Day 1893, a witness described to the Lords Committee on the Chipstead Valley Bill that he had had some people down, and his man was obliged to move all their luggage himself. In 1901–02 extra signalling was installed solely for race days traffic, three intermediate block posts controlling signals with detachable arms and no spectacles or lamps. These were Sutton & Belmont Intermediate ('A', 1,408yd from Sutton Junction box), Belmont & Banstead Intermediate ('B', 1,350yd from Belmont station box) and Banstead & Epsom Downs Intermediate ('C', 812yd from Banstead station box). Even in 1923, with the old rivalries extinguished, the Epsom Downs branch carried 42 extra trains on Derby Day, including one reserved Pullman car special.

During the Edwardian years, the outposts of London were brought up to the railway between Croydon and Sutton and the many bright new houses along this frontier kept busy the electric tramway opened in 1906 between West Croydon and Sutton. Rising to this intruder, the LBSCR initiated an auto-train service which provided from 11th June 1906 seven journeys each way daily in addition to the normal service, between West Croydon and Belmont. Consisting of a Stroudley 'Terrier' 0–6–0T pulling or pushing a one-class bogie saloon coach with 50 seats (a form of steam tram in fact) these auto-trains called at all intermediate stations including new halts at Bandon and Beeches. The first of these, between Wallington and Waddon, was opened with the new service, the other, on the site of the present Carshalton Beeches station, was not ready until 1st October 1906. As elsewhere, these special units were perhaps a little faster than the street tramcar and no more expensive, but they could not compete with its frequency and convenience of access.

Belmont's prominence as the only place on the branch showing any signs of suburban growth before 1914 was reflected in the pattern of the train service: in 1910 when the auto-trains (misleadingly described in Bradshaw as 'motor cars' because it sounded trendy at the time) were providing most of the service, Belmont had 36 Down arrivals and 37 departures in the Up direction (eleven and nine on Sundays). But Epsom Downs, in the same timetable, had only 12 trains in and out daily and none on Sundays, whilst Banstead had 22 Down arrivals and the same number of departures in the Up direction (two and three on Sundays). Most of these trains connected at Sutton with services to and from London Bridge and Victoria.

Towards the close of the 19th century the high downland south of Sutton and Epsom attracted a small number of moderately wealthy and influential men who wished to possess small country estates within convenient access of London. Not exactly commuters in the modern sense, they were content to arrive in the City between 10.00 and 11.00. Among these, as we have seen, was Allen Sarle, secretary and general manager of the LBSCR, living at *Green Hayes*, Banstead, whilst another was Henry Cosmo Orme Bonsor, MP for Wimbledon and a director of the Bank of England, who purchased *Kingswood Warren* in 1885. These two travelled up together from Banstead station, and Bonsor, an energetic and dynamic personality, soon developed an interest in railway affairs. In the summer of 1891 he joined two other residents of Tadworth and Walton-on-the-Hill in forming a scheme for a railway from Epsom Downs to Walton-on-the-Hill, principally to enhance the value of the land and promote housing development. Sir John Wolfe-Barry and his nephew Arthur Barry were engaged to lay out a 2m 7f 5ch single-line extension of the Epsom Downs branch rising 240ft on a 1 in 50 gradient from Drift Bridge (between

Banstead and Epsom Downs stations) to a point on Corner Farm about 200yd south of the present Tadworth station. This 320-acre farm had been bought at the low price of £25 an acre by Bonsor's fellow-promoter James W. Benson, who had acquired *Walton Oaks*, Walton-on-the-Hill in 1889. Bonsor had taken a half-share in the land, which it was hoped to develop for building once the railway was begun. A former Tadworth baker, Walter J. Brown, also planned to build on his nearby 200-acre estate. Having ascertained that the LBSCR would be willing to work the Extension, but not to subscribe to its cost, Bonsor put up £55,000 of the required £65,000 capital, Benson the rest.

Opposition came mainly from Frederick E. Colman, owner of the 1,382-acre Nork Park Estate through which the railway was to pass for most of its length, and from the Epsom Grand Stand Association who saw the railway as a threat to their proposal to create a Straight Mile Course, and also likely to frighten horses racing and training on the Downs. Colman had been approached by Bonsor but professed no interest in land speculation, merely wishing no interference with enjoyment of his 'very beautiful and desirable residential and sporting estate' which he had bought in 1890 from the trustees of Lord Egmont. During the passage of the bill this opposition was overcome by the insertion of new clauses. A tunnel would be built for 100yd each side of the Straight Mile with no trains passing through when it was in use. Colman not only gained a private gate to the new station at Tadworth and a personal siding for 20 wagons, but was protected from further stations on his estate and from telegraph wires and poles along the tops of cuttings or over tunnels, and for his benefit all banks were to be thickly planted with trees, plantation style. Wolfe-Barry solemnly assured him that the platelayers patrolling the line (honest men, every one) would be a useful deterrent to the poachers that he feared the railway would encourage.

Once the act was passed, Bonsor and his friends argued with the LBSCR over terms for working the line, then prevaricated whilst they took up the Chipstead Valley scheme (of which more in a moment), which they used as a stick with which to beat the Brighton. This tactic moved the LBSCR to offer a rent of 50 per cent of gross receipts instead of the 55 per cent they had earlier said would barely cover working expenses. Bonsor and his friends also got the Brighton to promise to run a Sunday service despite the earlier failure on the Epsom Downs branch, and a weekday through train each way between Tadworth and Victoria as well as eight Down and nine Up between Tadworth and Sutton, all apparently to reverse in and out of Epsom Downs. Having got this far, Bonsor and Benson now had their sights set higher and refused an LBSCR demand that the Chipstead Valley scheme should be withdrawn as a condition of their working through to Tadworth. As we shall see shortly, a section of the Epsom Downs Extension Railway was to be built as part of the SER's Tattenham Corner branch, which emerged from the Chipstead Valley scheme. The Nork Park Estate siding, for the benefit of Colman's tenant-farmer (who ran a jam factory at north Tadworth as a sideline) was also provided at Tattenham Corner in 1901.

Under Southern Railway management, the Epsom Downs branch saw great changes. During January 1927, the general manager, Sir Herbert Walker, came down the line with senior officers as a prelude to electrification. They decided that the platforms at Belmont would have to be lengthened from 262ft (Up) and 257ft (Down) to at least 500ft, as would the 284ft ones at Banstead. Considering the

Epsom Downs, 18th December 1926 looking to buffers. D1 0-4-T B612 with a train of eight six-wheel coaches and two brake vans awaits departure for London. *H C Casserley*

application made for a halt at Drift Bridge, the officers saw no sign of housing development there and agreed that accommodation would only be provided if paid for by the landowners. It was noted that a full goods station could be made at Epsom Downs if required later by taking out one of the island platforms – an indication that accommodation was already excessive for the traffic offering on race days.

Soon after this, the branch was electrified as part of the Southern's third-rail suburban system. At Epsom Downs, platforms three to seven were equipped for electric working, but at normal times two roads were more than enough and the other three were used to store electric stock. As elsewhere, the train service was transformed. From 17th June 1928 when electric trains replaced steam, a regular half-hourly frequency was supplied seven days a week between London Bridge and Epsom Downs via West Croydon, calling at all stations except Brockley and Honor Oak Park. This was strengthened at peak periods on Mondays to Saturdays when there were three trains an hour. When the direct route from Sutton to Victoria via Mitcham Junction was electrified on 3rd March 1929 convenient connections were made at Sutton to give the branch a faster service to the West End. The circuitous electric service from Victoria to Sutton via West Croydon was extended to Epsom Downs on 4th May 1930, giving the branch a total of four trains an hour throughout the day, strengthened to six an hour in the morning and evening peak and at Saturday midday.

Banstead station exterior, c.1968 with the first late afternoon commuters homeward bound.

This generous and reliable facility, brought in at a time when economic conditions were strongly favouring residential construction around London, was accompanied by a vast amount of new housing in the catchment areas of Belmont and Banstead stations. Ordinary bookings at the three stations grew from 329,778 in 1927 to 927,708 seven years later, with season ticket issues moving in the same period from 2,964 to 12,937. Building on the chalk uplands south of the railway between Banstead and Epsom Downs stations had started in the middle of the 1920s, mostly fairly closely-spaced detached houses selling at around £1,000. Banstead's transformation from a small downland village to a London suburb accelerated with the completion of main drainage schemes in 1927–29. By the mid-1930s the whole area between the village street and the railway was filled with small houses, while by 1939 the mansion and untouched remnant of the Nork Park Estate was surrounded by rather more spacious development. Carshalton and Sutton's outward creep reached Belmont station, whilst Sutton and Cheam spread southwards over the 500-acre Northey Estate, where large detached houses costing between £1,700 and £3,000 were built around the Cuddington Golf Course, reaching Banstead station about 1935 and almost completely sealing off the 750-acre Banstead Downs, which had been preserved against building since the 1860s. To accommodate the traffic arising from this last development, the SR rebuilt Banstead station in brick with extended awnings of glass and steel over each platform.

At the close of the 1930s Epsom's southern outskirts were touching Epsom Downs station and the development of the Nork Estate south east of the branch had brought houses to the edge of Epsom Downs golf and race courses. Much of this housing at the extremity of the branch was in the medium and higher price ranges, but as car ownership was by no means universal even among the owners of the more expensive property, the terminal station was enjoying for the first time a regular all-the-year-round traffic at both peak and slack hours.

This was as well, because the SR had long since begun to concentrate the race traffic on the more convenient and spacious facilities at Tattenham Corner station. Nevertheless, a fair quantity of race business to Epsom Downs survived until the middle 1950s, after which the decline was rapid. The first-class specials, some with Pullman coaches, which brought businessmen down from their offices at lunchtime on Derby Day remained steam-hauled until just after World War 2, when electric locomotives took over. On Derby Day 1952 there were almost 100 ordinary and special trains each way over the branch, over half the workings concentrated between 11.00 and 19.00, all of them electric. Two years later the number of extra staff used on Derby Day was down to seven, and Derby Day 1958 saw only three extra trains compared with the 13 to Tattenham Corner. The intermediate block posts were not used after 1955. Epsom Downs station lost five of its platforms in 1972 and the 1989 changes mentioned below finally removed the branch's capacity to handle race traffic.

When considering the Derby Day service it must not be overlooked that during the 1950s the standard service to Epsom Downs was exceptionally lavish, with six trains an hour each way until early afternoon (three Victoria, three London Bridge), four an hour for the rest of the day and extras at peak periods, in all 87 each way every weekday, or nearly eleven times the number running in 1865. But in an age of increasing car ownership, with television keeping families indoors in the evenings, such generous provision became futile. From 10th September 1958 off-peak frequency came down to half-hourly to and from Victoria via West Croydon. Further changes followed in the late 1960s; the Victoria slack hour service was terminated at Sutton instead of Epsom Downs from 10th July 1967, the branch receiving instead the former London Bridge–Tulse Hill–Horsham/Effingham Junction service every half-hour. On Sundays the half-hourly service was given by trains working between Epsom Downs and London Bridge via Tulse Hill until 4th May 1969, after which day all Sunday working ceased. From May 1973 the slack-hour London Bridge service was turned at Sutton and the branch got a Victoria–Selhurst–West Croydon working every half-hour, with eight peak-period trains between Epsom Downs and London Bridge.

Other retrenchment accompanied service reductions. Banstead goods yard closed on 7th September 1964, and freight trains disappeared with the abandonment of Belmont yard on 6th January 1969. Installation of intermediate colour-lights between Sutton and Epsom Downs (both exclusive) allowed closure of Belmont and Banstead station boxes on 21st December 1969. Belmont's tatty station, showing wounds from World War 2 bombs, gave way in 1968 to one of the Southern's cheap and cheerful modular CLASP pre-fabricated boxes, looking like nothing so much as a very large packing case waiting for a crane. During 1972 the tracks at Epsom Downs were reduced to two (the former platforms 4 and 5) and after the permanent way gangs had departed only one scissors crossover remained, just outside the station. No longer was the terminus to have the artificially busy appearance imparted by the stabling of empty stock at its grass-grown platforms.

In the early hours of 16th November 1981 Epsom Downs signal box was seriously damaged by fire. At first there was hand signalling for a modified service to and from Victoria and London Bridge but after ten days the branch was operated 'one train on line', by a half-hourly shuttle to and from Sutton, using the Down platforms at Banstead and Belmont. From 4th July 1982, apart from short lengths at each end, the line was reduced to single track. This arrangement became permanent from 4th October 1982, when the branch was integrated into the Victoria Area Signalling Scheme and through working to West Croydon and London was restored.

Serious traffic decline was now evident on a line which had once had a ten minute service at peak periods and sold over 2,000 ordinary tickets daily. Thanks to the motor car and dispersal of much central London employment, irrecoverable inroads had been made since the late 1950s into the healthy peak and off peak business once generated by the between-wars suburban growth in the catchment area. By the 1980s, the shrinking army of central London commuters were increasingly using their cars to reach the superior train services at Sutton; children were being ferried to school by car instead of using the trains; cars were carrying those shopping or seeking entertainment and recreation in Sutton and Croydon; and the contra-flow movements to the hospitals and day tripper traffic to the Downs had all but disappeared. That old habits die hard was demonstrated by the trickle of punters still to be seen using the line in Derby week 1988 but these faithful were effectively banished by the 1989 development to be mentioned in a moment. One may wonder how the branch survived the 1970s. Indeed it was not until 1984 that services were given what may prove to be the penultimate cut. Off peak frequency was then reduced to hourly from 14th May, an interval that is inherently discouraging to traffic development.

At this stage in its existence the character of the outer end of the line slipped into a new guise. As a result of a property deal, the spacious site of the terminus and its immediate approaches was sold for development as a housing estate. All tracks were removed over a distance of 374yd, to a point less than a quarter mile from the long-proposed halt at Drift Bridge, where a single platform was opened on the evening of 13th February 1989. Although still called Epsom Downs, a more accurate name for the relocated station would be Drift Bridge or perhaps Nork (there was a footpath to the former). Across the end of the single track Messrs Charles Church, the developers of the housing estate, erected a two storey building which bore a family resemblance to the rather twee neo-vernacular detached houses closely packed all round. To give some indication of its purpose, the frontage was embellished by a length of canopy and supporting posts rescued from the old station.

An early evening visit here in June 1991 found the place completely deserted until the 18.25 arrival from London deposited about 25 commuters. Some seats and a 'train ready to start' button had already been vandalised, graffiti already obtruded and if the little ticket office had ever been manned, it was now firmly shuttered-up. As the tired-looking commuters quickly dispersed and the now empty train returned Londonwards, this strangely unreal railway station resumed its dreamlike air. Its relaxed, totally domesticated environment would look more comfortable with light rail. Perhaps Tramlink will find its way here one day as an alternative to the otherwise seemingly inevitable complete closure.

Tattenham Corner station in the 1930s. *Pamlin Prints*

The Tattenham Corner Branch   (map page 121)
Although the Caterham Railway for many years showed little promise, there were
signs of residential development in the Caterham valley by the early 1880s. Noting
this, and also hoping for an improvement in farm rents depressed by the difficulties
and cost of cartage over hilly roads, landowners in the adjacent Chipstead valley
projected a branch from the Brighton main line in 1884. This scheme failed to take
off, as did a later proposal for a light railway up the valley, but the success of the
Epsom Downs Extension Railway Bill revived interest in the route, so much so that
by the autumn of 1892 Bonsor and others had persuaded several landowners in the
valley to put up the promotion expenses of a bill. Arthur Barry surveyed a single line
starting from an end-on junction with the Epsom Downs Extension at Tadworth,
running down the valley to Smitham Bottom, where it was to march alongside the
main line as far as Purley station. Here there were to be junctions with both the
LBSCR and what was now the SER Caterham branch. Bonsor gave the scheme
strong support, warming the mutual jealousy of the LBSCR and the SER in the
hope of getting one or the other to work both the Chipstead Valley and the Epsom
Downs Extension as a through line from Epsom Downs to Purley on favourable
terms. He and other landowners looked to these railways to enhance the value of
their properties, eventually stimulating residential development, and were prepared
to give land in exchange for shares. But neither of the main line companies showed
any interest, the Brighton going as far as opposing the Chipstead Valley Bill, averring
that the newcomer's trains would interfere with the working of their main line traffic
at Purley. Bonsor produced an array of local landowners and residents in support,
quietly confident that the LBSCR would be obliged to pick up both schemes and
work them as one, refusing to accept a Brighton suggestion that the Chipstead Valley
station at Purley should be separate from the LBSCR establishment, the physical
link confined to a siding connection. Finally he produced his trump card; the capital
of the Epsom Downs Extension and the Chipstead Valley would be pooled, with he
and Benson (the other subscriber to the Extension) consenting to take their
proportion, almost one-third of the total needed for the two lines, as a deferred
charge. With the balance as preferred charge capital, it should not, he suggested, be
difficult to raise it from the public, and there were already some promises from
landowners. Parliament was persuaded, allowing the bill through, subject to the
insertion of a clause protecting the LBSCR against interference with its main line
traffic or the prospective widening works at Purley.

Whilst not opposing a junction with the Caterham line at Purley, the SER gave the Chipstead Valley no encouragement, partly because the company doubted its traffic prospects, but also because it feared difficulties in working the trains of both branches into the single bay platform at Purley. In the Lords Committee, the SER general manager, Sir Myles Fenton, firmly denied that the SER was spurning the Chipstead because it was constrained by some kind of territorial agreement with the Brighton – 'We have no territorial arrangement, no agreement by which we could not penetrate into any part of their district, or they into ours'. Wolfe-Barry also declared that he saw nothing to prevent the SER going up to Epsom Downs, except fear of LBSCR retaliation 'in some other way', and the fact that the SER was not contractually or even morally bound to remain east of the LBSCR main line in this district was soon to be demonstrated. Bonsor, not a man to give up easily, was determined to get a railway up to Tadworth and Kingswood. In the year following the Chipstead Valley Act he got himself on to the SER board and a year after that (1895) had reached the deputy chairman's seat. Land was acquired for both the Chipstead Valley and the Epsom Downs Extension, and in 1897 an unopposed Epsom Downs Extension Railway Bill sought powers to abandon 1m 4f 2.5ch between Drift Bridge and a point just north of Tadworth, substituting a 3f 4ch terminal spur from that point to Tattenham Corner, and giving the branch the form in which it was to be built. Any remaining problems were resolved by plans to rebuild Purley station with the widening of the Brighton main line and a bill of 1898, which went through unopposed after a petition filed by the LBSCR was withdrawn, allowed the SER to subscribe to the capital of the Chipstead Valley, which could be built as double track. The final chapters in the Parliamentary story were written in the two following years with unopposed SER bills, which respectively allowed the Extension and the Chipstead Valley to be vested in the SER from 13th July 1899, and gave the SER authority to take up the unexpended borrowing powers of the two companies.

Well before all this legislation had reached the statute book, a single line was opened between Purley East Junction and Kingswood & Burgh Heath. This was served from 2nd November 1897 by trains which called at the intermediate station of Chipstead & Banstead Downs, and during 1899 its track was doubled. A single line onwards to Tadworth & Walton-on-the-Hill, opened on 1st July 1900, was doubled by November that year. Finally, the double track Epsom Downs Extension Railway from Tadworth to Tattenham Corner was ready for Derby Day, 4th June 1901. In open and unashamed competition with the Brighton, the SECR was to have at Tattenham Corner, almost on the race-course, Britain's finest and largest station for race traffic. On that first day the company made a brave start with 13 advertised trains and 35 specials (some coming from as far away as Dover, Margate, Hastings and Reading), bringing in almost 15,000 racegoers.

'Traversing one of the loveliest districts of Surrey, where perfect quiet and beautiful pastoral scenery are to be had within half an hour's journey from London', the Chipstead Valley was certainly a romantic and interesting line. For 5½ miles the climb was steep and continuous, with a final mile of 1 in 80 to a summit ¼m south of Tadworth station. After leaving the Caterham Railway at Purley East Junction ten chains south of the station, the new branch ran for a short distance alongside the Brighton main line before crossing beneath it and continuing parallel on the west side. Just south of the underpass, on the east side was the Reedham Home for

Charing Cross–Tadworth train entering Reedham Halt, 22nd May 1926. *H C Casserley*

Fatherless Children named after its founder the Reverend Andrew Reed, and served by a private siding from the Up track. Reedham Halt, on the west side of the main line, with its 300ft platforms, was opened on 1st March 1911 to enable Chipstead Valley passengers to reach the orphanage and the new housing then sprouting up along the nearby main road; tickets were 'issued by the haltkeeper'. Close to the main line almost as far as Coulsdon North station, the branch finally turned away west through Smitham station, crossing over the Brighton Road and entering the valley. Opened on 1st January 1904, Smitham was but a stone's throw from Coulsdon North (opened in 1899 and then called Stoat's Nest). It had a goods yard but no station house, simply a single-storey wooden building on the Down side and a rudimentary shelter on the Up platform in the usual SER country style. The birth of this station was prolonged, its platforms and signal box completed almost three years before it opened to the public. From a traffic viewpoint it was rendered all but superfluous by the superior facilities of the adjacent LBSCR station, but it was obligatory under section 36 of the 1893 act, in deference to the requirements of the trustees of John Benjamin Smith. The SECR economised by closing it on Sundays from the start until about 1909.

Attacking the Chipstead Valley, the line now followed a sinuous and generally south-westerly course through pretty well-wooded country as yet almost untouched by residential development. Chipstead & Banstead Downs station was sited on the east side of the valley about 200ft below the village of Chipstead and almost a mile to the north of it. Equidistant on the other side was the small village of Woodmansterne. The station building, on the Up side, was a substantial little structure in a pleasing Domestic Revival style with three dormer windows emerging from its tiled roof on the railway side. A small goods yard was cut out of the valley slope at the London end.

Kingswood station soon after opening. The large number of wagons in the freight yard (left) may be related to railway construction work further down the branch.

After running almost due south for rather more than half a mile, the tracks turned almost west along Chipstead Bottom to climb through what is today some of the best suburban countryside on the former Southern system. At the head of the valley, Kingswood & Burgh Heath station was almost equidistant from the two small villages of its title. As Bonsor's local station, it had the most impressive building on the line, a two-storey mock-timbered station house under a pitched tile roof, sitting above a small booking office and entrance block in red brick, with an impressive arch on the road side. The wide canopy over the Up platform was later railed round with white palings to form a terrace. On the Down side there was a curious pavilion with tall arched windows and roof sloping steeply to the back wall. Also on this side, Bonsor was given a private entrance, beneath the road bridge. Situated at the London end on the Up side, the goods yard sidings extended back into the station approach.

Beyond here the tracks passed through a cutting along the northern edge of Bonsor's *Kingswood Warren* Estate, negotiating the northern tip of Banstead Heath in the 310yd Kingswood Tunnel required by the 1893 act. A second tunnel of 37yd, little more than a bridge, rejoicing in the jolly name of Hoppety, and a northward curve in deep cutting, brought the trains into Tadworth & Walton-on-the-Hill, which at 550ft above sea level, was and is the highest suburban station south of the Thames. Whilst the northern ends of its platforms were at ground level, the station building sat high above the tracks on the road bridge over the cutting. Solidly built in brick and tile, punctuated with tall sash windows, this pavilion was awarded some dignity by a central gable with an arched window which lit the booking hall below. Covered ways led down each side of the cutting to the platforms, each with its small waiting room building. Entered by a trailing connection from the Up line, the goods yard was at the north end.

On an embankment, and almost level, the branch ran to its terminus at the Tattenham Corner of the Epsom Downs racecourse, 21½ miles from London Bridge and 8m 25ch from Purley, stopping just short of the Straight Mile that had proved such an obstacle to the first alignment of the Epsom Downs Extension Railway. It will be convenient to describe this station as it was around 1920, for although by no means complete at the time of its opening, most of the features that will be mentioned were provided by the end of its first year and others were added in the first decade or so. Its passenger accommodation would have been over generous for a medium-sized industrial town; six platform faces (numbered from west to east), consisting of two platforms at the flanks and two central islands. These gravel-covered platforms, each about 20ft wide and completely unsheltered in their exposed position at the top of the downs, varied in length from about 550ft to around 700ft. Between each pair of platform tracks was an engine release road. At the west side, two long horsebox sidings stood in line with the passenger platforms, the outer one serving a brick-built horse dock and stables. On the east was a long siding equipped with a 54ft 10in locomotive turntable, and the layout was completed with the fruit farm private siding on this side and a four-road goods yard on the west at the south end of the site. This layout could accommodate about 24 normal-length trains simultaneously.

Initially the signalling arrangements were very elaborate, but from about 1922 the system was simplified, route indications being given by a main signal through sidings worked by ground levers not controlled by the signalmen. This change reduced the levers in 'A' box, which was situated on the east side at the entrance to the passenger station, from 205 to 125, and in 'B' box, which was at the extreme south end of the layout on the west side and used only on race days, from 50 to 19. The third box, 'C', was a small platform cabin at the buffer end of platforms three and four, used for train indicating purposes with indicators worked in conjunction with 'A' and 'B' boxes. A fire caused by a porter-signalman's carelessness destroyed much of 'A' box on 15th July 1924, requiring complete renewal of its equipment.

Opposite the ends of platforms three to six, behind a spacious concourse was the main booking hall and entrance building, a single-storey structure in the characteristic SER rural close-boarded style under a slate roof. Spaced around the concourse across the platform ends were other smaller buildings containing two refreshment rooms, a staff messroom and a large urinal. In the station approach and in line with the booking hall building was an extensive bungalow which incorporated a third refreshment room, luncheon room, cloak room, cycle store, telegraph office and an auxiliary ticket office. Curving to give direct access to the racecourse, the approach road skirted 'the Mound', a raised lawn which afforded the SER directors and their guests a superb view of the finishing straight of the main racecourse.

Signalling along the branch was Sykes' lock-and-block and the station boxes were supplemented on race days by temporary block posts similar to those on the Epsom Downs branch, although here their equipment was left in place all the year round. These small cabins were at Woodmansterne (1m 7yd from Smitham Station box), Chipstead Intermediate (1m 78yd from Chipstead Station box) and Tadworth Tunnel (1,441yd from Kingswood Station box).

Three distinct types of traffic were expected: racegoers and horseboxes, summer excursionists, and residential. Some effort was expended to attract the second group by providing summer refreshments at Tattenham Corner station but success was limited, hardly justifying the pious sentiments of witnesses in the 1893 bill committees that the poor of London would flock out on Sundays to enjoy the pure air of the Surrey downs, heaths and commons. After the 1902 summer there were no trains to Tattenham Corner in winter and a photograph of about 1920 shows the balcony at Kingswood, which may have been intended as a tea place, decorated with the stationmaster's family washing and bunches of pea sticks drying for his garden.

With the opening to Tadworth in 1900 the branch had about ten trains a day each way, covering the run from Purley in about 23 minutes. The first departure from Tadworth was not until 07.40, the last as early as 20.35. By 1922, with some residential development in the interim, there was a winter service of 17 Up trains and 16 Down, covering the branch in 20 to 21 minutes, while Tadworth's first and last departures had been opened out to 07.06 and 23.12. Except in rush hours, London passengers were obliged to change at Purley into and out of branch trains, worked by Cudworth 2–4–0 and various types of tank locomotive, latterly mainly Wainwright H class 0–4–4T. On race days, particularly for the Derby and Oaks, the branch was alive with trains of great variety, including fast specials from Charing Cross, Waterloo Junction, Cannon Street, St Paul's (Blackfriars), London Bridge and East Croydon, as well as excursions from main towns on the SECR system outside London. In summer, until September 1914, trains were extended 'as required' to Tattenham Corner for day trippers.

If summer pleasure traffic disappointed, estate developers did their best to make up for it. At first almost all development consisted of fairly large houses, mostly detached, in spacious gardens. Most of these Edwardian villas were to be found at Chipstead (where a new golf course proved an attraction), at Tadworth, and at Walton-on-the-Hill, where a small colony of commodious detached houses with servants' bedrooms in the roof spaces (two were designed by Lutyens) appeared around the Golf Club House between 1905 and 1914. None of this activity amounted to very much, but the proportion of first-class passengers produced was very high.

Tadworth station shortly after completion in 1900.

No race meetings were held at Epsom course from 1915 to 1918, but the railways carried military traffic to camps on the downs, where the ample accommodation at Tattenham Corner found a new use. With the cessation of hostilities, the generous siding accommodation provided a temporary resting place for scores of locomotives no longer required by the army.

Race traffic at Tattenham Corner was at its peak in the 1920s and 1930s when on Derby Day as many as 60 specials were worked by tank and tender locomotives of various types and latterly, from London stations, electric multiple-units. Other specials brought punters from such places as Reading (reversing at Purley), Chatham, Dover, Ramsgate and Hastings, whilst affluent businessmen and stockbrokers came down from Cannon Street and Charing Cross, lunching in Pullman cars. Numbers handled grew to more than twice those seen on the opening day; about 38,000, for example, arrived at Tattenham Corner on Derby Day 1923 in the ordinary trains and 54 specials, including two reserved Pullman car trains, and 40,000 returned after the races. Following some problems in handling these larger attendances in 1920 and 1921, on-the-spot improvisation was replaced by London Bridge Control, with all loco and train movements precisely scheduled beforehand.

To accommodate 50 to 60 Down specials on Derby Day it was necessary to restrict the normal branch service, especially as the Down running line between Kingswood and Tattenham Corner was used for stabling some of the trains awaiting the returning crowds. Under the new arrangements introduced in 1923, with handbills advertising 'trains running continuously' between specified times and headways in practice as close as four minutes, arrival, unloading, and clearance of platforms at Tattenham Corner was achieved in four to five minutes. After the formation of the Southern Railway, Tattenham Corner, with its more spacious layout and convenient access to the racecourse, assumed the main burden of the Derby and Oaks traffic, taking all through specials from places outside London as well as the royal trains* from Victoria. On Whit Monday and August Bank Holiday in 1927, for that year only, a number of trains were booked to run to and from Tattenham Corner, at that time normally used only on race days. On the August holiday, 12 trains arrived and ten departed from the terminus.

When it became clear in the early 1920s that the branch would become part of the Southern electric suburban system, estate developers set about their plans with confidence and increased pace, knowing that electrification would bring with it a revolutionary improvement in the train service, encouraging London white-collar workers to settle in this pleasant downland district. Not long after the end of World War 1, Richard Costain bought Bonsor's *Kingswood Warren* Estate to lay out for building. Here from 1923 onwards, in wooded parkland above the 525ft contour just south of Kingswood station, he erected houses on sites of half an acre or more for sale at £800 to £4,000. Nearby, on the Brighton Road between Kingswood and Tadworth, houses with quarter-acre gardens were advertised in 1925, and the adjacent Tadworth Court Estate was under way a year later with detached houses on quarter-acre plots selling at £1,350 upwards. For the time being, commuters buying these new homes travelled to and from London Bridge or Charing Cross in trains composed of two sets of five six-wheelers hauled by H class 0–4–4T.

* Royal trains to the Epsom course ceased after 1924 but royal use of the railway was resumed in 1946 at a time of petrol shortage and has continued ever since.

Into this already active scene came the green electrics, a provisional service from 25th March 1928, the full one from 17th June. There was some disappointment when it was learned that to avoid rush hour congestion, Tattenham Corner and Caterham trains would not be worked across the Eastern section lines to and from the Central side of London Bridge, but would terminate in the low level platforms at London Bridge instead of at Charing Cross as in steam days. (At other times the electrics ran through to Charing Cross). Apart from this blemish, the provision was as excellent as expected; three trains an hour all day long to and from Tattenham Corner, giving that station its first regular all-year-round service since 1902. Sundays saw four trains an hour, two to Victoria, two to Charing Cross, the former being the weekday Coulsdon North trains diverted, a lavish gesture which apart from the summer of 1931 continued until World War 2, when service was reduced to two an hour, one to Charing Cross, one to Victoria. London Bridge was reached in 43 minutes by the electrics, which ran non-stop inwards from Norwood Junction, and in peak hours stopped only at East Croydon between London Bridge and Purley. Tattenham Corner and Caterham trains were combined inwards from Purley, where the joining and splitting of the two branch portions was carried out with all the celerity that multiple-unit operation allows. In peak hours the trains were three three-car sets, one for Caterham, two for Tattenham Corner, the latter with an above-average proportion of first-class passengers. At Tattenham Corner most of the sidings were not electrified, but were used on race days to store electric sets shunted by a steam locomotive. Platform run-round roads were removed, together with the 'C' signal frame. Station lighting was converted to electricity, using current from the conductor rails.

Following electrification, construction of cheaper houses was begun in earnest east of the line between Tadworth and Tattenham Corner and between Chipstead and Smitham. Tattenham Corner's first houses appeared in 1928 when free yearly season tickets were on offer to all who purchased before the end of June. A 'million pound' housing scheme was started here in the early 1930s by Surrey Downs Housing Ltd offering semi-detached and detached designs at £560-£990 'amid the fairyland of Surrey 600ft above sea level on dry chalky soil swept by the sweet air from the SOUTHERN SEAS', whilst another advertisement described it as 'the estate where illness is unknown', a large claim, despite the 'medicinal pines' and the 'absence of fog'. South of the old village and close to the railway, a new Woodmansterne grew rapidly during the 1930s with many roads of small terrace and semi-detached houses and bungalows selling at between £550 and £990. To serve this development, Woodmansterne station, a simple island platform reached only by footbridge from adjacent side roads, was opened on 17th July 1932. Builders conveyed land for it free of charge, also contributing £1,500 of its £7,000 cost.

Higher up the valley, at Chipstead were more detached houses, at prices ranging from £950 to £1,500. By the middle 1930s, the areas around Chipstead, Tadworth and Tattenham Corner stations had assumed the aspect of typical London suburbs, each with its characteristic Tudor-style shopping parade, but none of these places grew large enough to justify the erection of a large cinema. Virtually all the housing, including the down-market terrace blocks, was beyond the reach of railway staff, obliging the Southern to erect a street of cottages near the line about half-way between Tattenham Corner and Tadworth stations. This had to be done in 1928 before Tadworth could be made a signing-on point for the new electric services.

Passenger accommodation was adapted to meet the suburban demand. Reedham Halt, 'inadequate for present-day traffic' was reconstructed in 1936 as a station at a cost of around £8,800. In the same year, Kingswood received a £650 concrete footbridge and a year later improvements were made to the lighting and platform canopies at Tadworth. The hitherto little-used freight yards needed no significant alteration to cope with the loads of building materials and domestic fuel.

Tattenham Corner's spare capacity again proved useful for military purposes in World War 2 when from time to time ambulance trains brought in wounded servicemen for transfer by road coaches to the large hospitals at Epsom. With the resumption of the Derby in 1946, loadings on the main race days returned almost to pre-war levels. On this occasion 34 trains arrived at Tattenham Corner from Charing Cross, Cannon Street and London Bridge between 09.00 and noon. Steam-hauled royal trains from Victoria were seen again on Derby and Oaks Days, with the full support of stand-by engines at Chipstead yard and a breakdown train in steam on the middle siding at Purley. For some years there were also steam-hauled Pullman specials from Charing Cross on Derby Day, with inclusive tickets covering lunch on the train and a seat in the grandstands. All other specials were of suburban electric stock, originating at New Cross Gate, Streatham Hill, Crystal Palace and Wallington. In 1953, when the first race on Derby Day was at 14.00 and the last at 17.20, trains arriving at the terminus between 09.00 and 13.00 totalled 31, six from Charing Cross, 17 from London Bridge, three from Streatham Hill, two from New Cross Gate, three from Crystal Palace Low Level. Returning crowds were offered 25 trains between 17.00 and 19.00, seven to Charing Cross, 16 to London Bridge and two to Cannon Street. Running non-stop, the Pullman special of twelve Pullmans hauled by an N class 2–6–0 left Charing Cross at 12.34, arriving at 13.27. Return times were 17.47 and 18.40. In the early 1950s, crowds arriving and departing on Derby Day reached almost 40,000 at Tattenham Corner station, but towards the end of the decade a combination of lower attendances and increased car ownership brought a severe decline in rail traffic. Race specials dwindled to a level where it was possible to dispense with the intermediate block posts and these were permanently closed after 1970. 1958 saw only 13 extra journeys on Derby Day and a mere two on Oaks Day. By 1976 there were only five extra workings, all on Derby Day. From 1965 the royal train was hauled by electric or diesel locomotives with much less pomp and fuss, and soon afterwards the Oaks Day working ceased. At the time of writing the Queen still goes to the Derby by train, not only because like so many other royal rail journeys in the motor and air age it is traditional, but because rail offers tangible convenience, avoiding road congestion, providing opportunity for refreshment and relaxation en route and facilitating transfer at Tattenham Corner for the ceremonial drive up the course.

Peak-hour traffic on the branch continued heavy in the post-war years, filling the ten-car trains introduced on 20th June 1955. But the general falling-off in slack-hour loadings we have noted elsewhere as occurring from the early 1960s was apparent here, bringing with it rationalisation of facilities and working economies. When on 29th November 1970 the branch was converted to colour-light signalling, a 5m 5ch section was introduced between Chipstead and Tattenham Corner, the box at the latter being the only one left open on the line. At the same time the terminal layout was drastically simplified to three platform roads and two sidings, with 22 instead of 97 levers in the box. From 15th September 1958 off-peak service, which had been

Up train approaching Woodmansterne, 28th March 1959.
Alan A Jackson

Chipstead looking to Purley, 3rd October 1964. SR electric lighting and upper quadrant semaphores are evident but otherwise there is little change since opening date.
Alan A Jackson

restored to three an hour at the end of the war was cut to half-hourly, and an hourly Sunday service was introduced on 13th September 1964, with Smitham station closed all day. As a further economy, from 6th September 1965, the ticket offices at each station were closed at 20.15 on weekdays, all Saturday afternoon and evening and all day on Sundays; at these times conductor-guards issued paper tickets on the trains from portable machines. With this change, off-peak trains reverted to the steam era practice of operating only on the branch. As some compensation, Smitham was reopened on Sundays with Coulsdon North closed instead. Use of conductor-guards was extended from 5th May 1969, when they began to man trains continuously except before 10.00 and between 15.30 and 20.15 on Mondays to

Fridays, when they opened the booking offices but still issued tickets from their portable machines. Some increase in status was granted from May 1970 when off-peak trains again ran to and from Charing Cross, in combination with the Caterham service as before. On the branch, conductor guards changed over from Up to Down trains at Reedham.

Freight traffic, never very important in this agricultural and latterly predominantly residential area, faded away in the late 1950s. After World War 2 one train had sufficed; in 1954 it left Bricklayers Arms at 03.50, returning to Norwood Yard after serving the Tattenham Corner and Caterham branches. Seven years later, when it was working to and from Norwood Yard, three journeys a week were enough and in the early part of 1962 it ceased altogether.

By the mid 1970s, off peak loads had shrunk to a level which might be comfortably handled by a small single deck bus. Pleasure traffic had dwindled almost to nothing; on a fine summer Bank Holiday in 1975, when the Downs were littered with cars, observation showed trains unloading fewer than 20 passengers each at Tattenham Corner. As elsewhere, commuters were also using their cars to reach better served stations such as Epsom and Sutton and the daily flow to and from central London was soon to thin out very considerably.

In these circumstances it was not surprising that further retrenchment and rationalisation followed in the 1980s. From 14th May 1984 the peak hour service to and from London was reduced from four to three trains an hour and the two-car half-hourly off-peak shuttle over the branch was reduced to hourly in the late evening and all day Sundays, most making connection at Purley with the semi-fast Victoria-Brighton trains. A small improvement in the slack hours service was introduced in May 1986 when one of the two trains an hour was extended to work to and from Charing Cross.

Tattenham Corner signal box was abolished on 25th September 1983, control temporarily assigned to Purley. Transfer of all signalling to the Three Bridges centre took place on 14th January 1984. With the loss of horse box traffic to road vehicles, most of the area between platform three and Epsom Lane was sold off. During 1979–80 this site was covered with small houses and garages fronting a road appropriately named Royal Drive – it was used on Derby Day by royal cars after the arrival of the royal train.

The 92-year old 'temporary' SER wooden station at Tattenham Corner was partly demolished on 1st December 1993 when the driver of the 06.16 from Victoria, who was afterwards found to be over the alcohol limit, projected his train through the buffers, over the concourse and into the booking office. Fortunately no one was hurt (the train had no passengers) but the building across the end of the line had to be completely demolished. In its place neat but much reduced facilities were completed at minimum cost in March 1994; near the head of platform three, a modest single storey pavilion in red bricks with a ridge roof of imitation slates housing a small ticket office and waiting area; a separate shelter centrally-placed across the end of the platforms; and on the east side, a small lavatory block. Viewed as a whole, this group, totally subdued by the lengthy unsheltered platforms on one side and a large open area of car parking and approach roads on the other, appeared to bear more resemblance to amenities in a municipal park than a railway station. Careful provision was made, in the form of two gated exits near the buffers of platform three, for the once-a-year passage of royal motor cars.

Motspur Park station from the level crossing, looking to London, 6th August 1960, showing the double footbridge which gives access from either side of the line. The trespass notice on the left still refers to the LSWR. *Alan A Jackson*

Raynes Park to Epsom (map page 121)

After the opening of the main London & Southampton line through Wimbledon in 1838 and the London & Croydon in the following year, Epsom, 'famed alike for purgatives and races', attracted the interest of railway promoters. An unsuccessful London & Dorking Bill of 1839, envisaging a branch south from Wimbledon, encouraged the LSWR to promote surveys by Joseph Locke in 1842–43. This was followed by a LSWR bill of 1844 for a single track branch to Epsom, which Parliament rejected in favour of an extension of the London & Croydon to Epsom because it was thought the Clegg & Samuda atmospheric traction system proposed for that line should receive a fair trial and also because there were fears that slow trains to and from Epsom might interfere with movement over the strategically important main line to Gosport (for Portsmouth).

On 10th May 1847 the LBSCR arrived in Epsom from what is now West Croydon over a 7m 74ch double track along the foot of the North Downs. As atmospheric traction between London & Croydon had proved a failure, the Epsom line was operated by conventional steam locomotives.

What happened next was closely related to the rivalry between the LBSCR and the LSWR for the Portsmouth traffic and their sensitivity about the borderlands of their respective territories. Before long moves were afoot by independent promoters to fill the gap between Epsom and Dorking, astute men who knew they could exploit this situation. An Epsom and Leatherhead Railway was authorised in 1856 over the 3m 54ch from the LBSCR station in Upper High Street Epsom and a terminus on the north side of the Kingston Road at Leatherhead. This was quickly followed by a Wimbledon & Dorking Railway scheme from the same stable, intended to absorb the Leatherhead and open up the area to the LSWR as well as the LBSCR. This new company was to have the same chairman (Thomas Grissell) as the Epsom & Leatherhead and seven of its directors. In Parliament, the proposal was reduced to a link between Wimbledon and Epsom only but the title 'Wimbledon & Dorking' remained to confuse everyone.

Leaving the LSWR at Coombe Lane Bridge west of Wimbledon, the new line was to follow the route to Epsom surveyed earlier by Locke, making a junction with the Epsom and Leatherhead just north of the High Street. *Herapath's Railway Journal* of 20th June 1857 was sniffy about the idea of a second line to Epsom, then a town with only 3,600 permanent residents, albeit swollen by many hundreds more on race days two or three times a year. It considered the LBSCR did a reasonable job with the traffic available, suggesting it was unjust to bring in a competitor 'to aid and assist horse racing, which although rational enough in the abstract has been denounced as the most swindling of all amusements'. In the same issue, a letter signed 'A Railway Manager' described the Wimbledon & Dorking promoters as 'an independent company of landowners', mocking the absurdity of their estimate that 35,000 would be carried on Derby Day over a single line in three hours. Opposition came from both the LBSCR and the LSWR though the latter finally agreed to make a double track and work it for 45 per cent of gross receipts, subscribing for 1,500 shares and nominating two directors. Legislation spanned acts of 1857, 1858, 1859 and 1860.

As for the Epsom & Leatherhead, all attempts by the local interests to secure amalgamation with the Wimbledon–Epsom scheme were frustrated by the LSWR. At the beginning of 1859 when the single line north eastwards from Leatherhead was virtually complete and agreement for the LBSCR to work it secured, shareholders voted for further negotiations with the LSWR, which would be able to provide a shorter route to London. That company, now bothered by schemes to extend the line from Leatherhead to Guildford, showed renewed interest, agreeing to better the LBSCR terms for working and taking a lease from 1st February 1859. On that day, a train service operated by the LSWR was started. Since the LBSCR was effectively blocked out, the unfortunate passengers to and from London were obliged to walk between the new line's temporary terminus at Epsom and the Upper High Street station.

Services over the line from Wimbledon began on 4th April 1859, using the aforementioned temporary station at Epsom (on the site of the present one). It was now possible for the LSWR to provide a Waterloo–Leatherhead service of seven trains Down and eight Up daily and it was also in time to secure some of the traffic for the Spring Race Meeting. Waterloo was reached in 45–50 minutes from Leatherhead, a commendable timing given the single line working south of Epsom.

It was not until 29th July 1859 that the LSWR and LBSCR finally made their peace in an agreement which admitted LBSCR trains to Leatherhead, the section beyond Epsom becoming a joint operation. This agreement established a firm boundary between the two companies' territories which made it possible at some future date for the LBSCR to go on to Dorking and Horsham, the LSWR to Shalford or Guildford. The 30 chains link between the two stations at Epsom, which had been ready early in 1859, was used from 8th August 1859 by LBSCR trains to and from Leatherhead. The company supplied that town with about six trains each way daily but these did not call at the Wimbledon & Dorking's station at Epsom. A further LBSCR/LSWR agreement of 1st January 1862 set up a joint committee to manage the Epsom–Leatherhead line, each company retaining its own receipts and sharing expenses and maintenance costs. Although the tracks from Epsom LBSCR to Leatherhead were jointly owned from 1865, the Wimbledon & Dorking station became LSWR property. This was because that company had effectively been taken over by the LSWR under an act of 1862. In 1863 the LBSCR secured powers, which it was never to use, to work the Wimbledon–Epsom line jointly with the LSWR.

So much for the somewhat tortuous origins of the line south of Wimbledon; it remains to describe it as built. At Wimbledon Junction (also called West Barnes or Epsom Junction), rather more than a mile south west of Wimbledon station, the double track opened in 1859 swerved away south across low-lying mist-haunted fields, more or less level with the land. At 2m 2ch from the junction, the first station, Old Malden, served the small village about half a mile to the west. Malden station on the main line became New Malden & Coombe in May 1859 but confusion was firmly banished when in February 1862 the station on the Epsom line was renamed Worcester Park, after an estate west of the railway. The Up platform here was furnished with a small Italianate house of stock bricks, with arched windows and a barge-boarded, wide-eaved slate roof. This contained the entrance hall, ticket and other offices, with rooms above for the stationmaster and his family. There was a small goods yard at the London end of the Up platform.

Now climbing at 1 in 180 and 1 in 100, the line reached its first summit in a deep cutting through a small wood before descending into the Hogsmill Valley. This descent brought the railway to a point west of Ewell village where, at 2m 18 ch from Worcester Park, a very similar station was provided, though here the house was on the Down side. Some years afterwards, the arrival of a stationmaster with numerous offspring caused the building to be enlarged by the addition of a second gabled two-storey block matching its predecessor in external appearance apart from some slight variations in the fenestration. No doubt anxious to recover some of the cost of this work, the LSWR gave its fecund stationmaster responsibility for Worcester Park as well, a clever strategy since it may also have sapped some of his spare energy. On the Down side, at the London end of Ewell station, a freight siding and a loading dock were provided. Around 1890 a goods shed was added at the London end of the Down platform.

Virtually unchanged after the enlargement mentioned, the passenger station (renamed Ewell West from 9th July 1923 to distinguish it from the former LBSCR establishment) remains today, now a grade 2 listed building. Here, as at Worcester Park, there was no footbridge for many years, passengers crossing the line on the level at the London end under the eyes of the signalmen. Ewell signalmen also supervised the movement of milk churns on wooden flaps erected between the platforms when the line was clear. Worcester Park did not get its footbridge until 1903, when an elegant lattice steel girder job (still in service at the time of writing) was supplied by the Wimbledon Signal Works.

Beyond Ewell, over the 1m 5ch to the junction at Epsom the line climbed at 1 in 100 and 1 in 90, turning south west to avoid the built-up area. The temporary station already mentioned was a crude wooden structure with little or no shelter from the elements but after some years a plain wooden building with gabled roof and canopy at the platform side was provided to accommodate waiting rooms and other amenities. In 1885 a facing crossover was laid between the Up and Down lines at the country end to facilitate reversal of race specials. By that time there were signal boxes at each end of the station, that at the west end controlling entry to a small goods yard on the Down side. More drastic layout changes followed in the 1890s, when two centre roads were inserted, together with a loop on the Up side. The platform on that side, shifted over to make room, was now an island. After this,

LBSCR trains to and from the Sutton line ran through the station, using the centre roads. By the early years of the 20th century, multi-gabled canopies had been added to both platforms to give shelter to the growing number of passengers.

At Worcester Park, a developer had purchased the estate of that name, laying out Great and Royal Avenues west of the railway, roads which were very slowly lined with large villas. At the station end, a small parade of shops appeared. As early as the 1860s, this suburban development was recognised by provision of a semi-fast businessmen's train from Waterloo at around 17.30, but by 1888 the gradual growth around this station and some expansion at Epsom and Ewell had justified an increase to a total of 13 trains each way daily, with Down departures from Waterloo spread between 07.25 and 23.55. Worcester Park experienced further residential expansion in the first decade and a half of the new century, mainly in the form of much smaller houses east of the line either side of the Cheam Common Road. The 1906 timetables provided 23 Down trains between 05.32 and 00.10 and by 1919 there were four trains Down between 06.45 and 08.45 followed by a departure from Waterloo at 45 minutes past each hour (all fast to Wimbledon) until 20.45 with commuter extras at 17.15, 18.15, and 19.15, all fast to Earlsfield, then hourly workings till 23.45. The existence of a considerable residential traffic is evident from the 1919 timetable, which shows five Up trains from Worcester Park between 07.13 and 08.43, all fast to Earlsfield. Sunday services were poor, only eight each way in 1909. By the 1900s, Epsom commuter business to Waterloo was justifying peak hour non-stop trains which covered the 14¼ miles in 25–26 min.

Working on and off the main line was eased by layout improvements. In 1868 the LSWR provided a dedicated pair of tracks for Epsom line trains on the south side between the London end of Wimbledon station and West Barnes Junction, where the old connection to the main lines fell out of regular use. This new double line was extended to New Malden with the opening of the Kingston Loop on 1st January 1869, when additional platforms were provided at Wimbledon on the London side of the overline bridge. After only two years the junction was again altered with the opening of Raynes Park station on 30th October 1871. Richard Garth, who had begun to develop West Barnes Park in 1868, laying out what are now Grand Drive and Blenheim Road, paid £4,000 towards the cost of building and maintaining this station but the name recognises former landowners, the Rayne family, who had long campaigned for such a station. Further changes followed in 1884 when a flyunder was constructed to bring the Up Epsom line to the Up side of the main line, where a junction was made with the Up Slow road (formerly the Up Main). A new Up platform and Up side ticket office were opened on 16th March 1884.

Freight facilities developed beyond the usual yard-to-yard pick-up goods, in a surprisingly varied fashion. In 1909 there were three daily goods trains each way on weekdays, one providing facilities to transport cattle to the Tuesday Market at Guildford. A small brickworks operated by the Worcester Park Brick Company started production on the hill above the west side of the line three quarters of a mile south of Worcester Park station in 1898. This was served by a rope-worked rail incline connected to the Up line via a short siding and trailing points. Known as 'Cunliffe's' after a signatory to the private siding agreement, access was through a ground frame released from Ewell signal box. At Ewell, a siding running out of the goods yard at the London end of the Down platform, installed around 1890 and removed in 1955, carried freight to and from corn mills on the Hogsmill stream.

From the 1920s there was another private siding on the east side of the Ewell goods yard into the Epsom Rural District Council depot. Further south on the Down side, a brickworks was opened by Messrs Stone & Co of Epsom in about 1922. This not only had its standard gauge private siding, entered through a ground frame released from Ewell box, but an internal horse-worked narrow gauge layout. Both the Ewell and Worcester Park brickworks sidings were removed in the early 1950s. Also south of Ewell station was another private siding, trailing into the Up line which gave access to the Horton Light Railway, serving the large complex of London County Council mental hospitals.*

The expected bonanza from the Epsom race traffic* proved something of a disappointment. As we have seen, the LBSCR station at Epsom Downs (1865) and the SECR station at Tattenham Corner (1901), with their extensive accommodation, provided much better access to the race course. Of the three companies in contention for this traffic, the LSWR was always at the bottom of the league, both as regards passengers carried and number of special trains worked. In 1923 only 18 specials were operated between Waterloo and Epsom, compared with 54 to Tattenham Corner and 42 to Epsom Downs and Epsom Town. Cuddington Cutting intermediate box, between Worcester Park and Ewell, specifically installed for race traffic and opened only on the busiest race days, was last used in 1924.

It was London commuters and their families, not punters, who were to provide the bread and butter for this line. By the beginning of the 20th century Raynes Park was showing clear signs of residential development, soon to be further stimulated by the arrival of the London United electric tramcars to link Wimbledon and Kingston via Raynes Park and New Malden from 2nd May 1907. It was these trams rather than the railway which sustained the emerging Edwardian community at West Barnes, later to be served by a new station. Between West Barnes and Worcester Park there was in 1914 nothing but polo and shooting grounds, fields and one or two large houses. To the south, apart from the Edwardian growth at Worcester Park already mentioned and some scattered late Victorian and Edwardian villa building along the Ewell-Kingston road, around Ewell village and on the outskirts of Epsom, the railway still passed through open countryside.

With the formation of the Southern Railway in 1923 it became possible to conceive new route developments using the lines of the absorbed companies. One example of this was the experimental operation of a number of Portsmouth trains via Worcester Park and Epsom in the summer of 1924 but a much more significant development was the inclusion of the Raynes Park–Dorking/Effingham Junction lines in the new company's suburban electrification programme for 1925. Fed through a conductor rail from substations at Raynes Park, Epsom, Dorking North and Effingham Junction, electric multiple-unit trains entered public service on Sunday 12th July 1925, providing three trains an hour seven days a week between Waterloo and Leatherhead, whence two continued to Dorking and the third to Bookham and Effingham Junction. At first both Vauxhall and Wimbledon stations were missed by the electrics but from 1st December, after public complaints, the service was rearranged to call at all stations.

---

* The history of the Horton Light Railway and the Epsom race traffic over the Waterloo-Epsom line are dealt with in the author's book *The Railway in Surrey*, Atlantic, 1999.

Before long the builders of small houses were working hard to fodder the new service. The Edwardian streets at West Barnes were extended to carry London's sprawl southwestwards towards the level crossing at Blue House Lane, where the SR had opened a station called Motspur Park on the same day as the electric working began. A simple 520ft island with a small passimeter ticket office, this was connected to an approach road on the Down side by an uncovered footbridge. Its construction cost of £7,200 was roughly equivalent to the sale price of 11 of the new houses it was designed to serve. At 20 min from Waterloo (9¾m) and with trains every 20 min. all day, sited in pastureland punctuated with hedgerows and lanes, the station formed a potent nucleus for a new residential community. And that was quickly achieved; close to it, east of the line, there appeared shopping parades and a large public house. By 1939 the BBC and London University Sports Grounds were the only reminders of a vanished countryside; the southward view from the footbridge was now dominated by two gasholders and a pumping plant supplying the fuel needs of the new district all round.

Worcester Park expanded rapidly from about 1925. To the west, within just over ten years suburban development had enveloped the village of Old Malden, its 1930s shopping parades dominating one side of the erstwhile village centre with its inn, pond and green. New housing, mostly small semis, had by 1938 flowed out either side of the railway until it coalesced into the surrounding communities of North Cheam to the east, Motspur Park to the north and Stoneleigh to the south, forming a veritable sea of red tile roofs swamping around the Victorian estate and all but obliterating the much older farming settlements.

Most dramatic of all was the appearance at the 12th mile from Waterloo of an entirely new townlet called Stoneleigh, which arose on the pastures and copses of three farms in the course of four short years. A station opened here amid empty fields on 17th July 1932 was handling well over 3,000 passengers a day by 1939. The developers, Stoneleigh Estate Company, were sufficiently convinced of its import-ance to the success of their scheme that on 17th July 1931 they had signed an agreement to contribute almost half the £7,550 cost as well as to give the land necessary to widen the railway. In its original form, with 520ft island platform and unroofed footbridge, Stoneleigh station was virtually a carbon copy of Motspur Park.

By the mid 1930s housebuilding all along the line was imposing heavy pressure on both passenger and freight facilities. Between 1927 and 1937 Worcester Park and Motspur Park stations saw a tenfold increase in season ticket issues while Stone-leigh's 103,742 passengers of 1933 grew in the next two years to an annual total of 313,647, the related gross revenue rising from £4,562 to £13,948. Some attempt was made to increase the train service to meet this growth in traffic. From 5th July 1936, following the opening of the Wimbledon flyover and the track rearrangement thence into Waterloo, the SR inserted another three trains an hour each way (increasing the frequency to a train every ten minutes) between Motspur Park and Waterloo, this in anticipation of the opening of the new line through Chessington to be mentioned later. From the same date, the 20-minute service south of Motspur Park called only at Wimbledon between Motspur Park and Waterloo, running nonstop inwards from Motspur Park in rush hours. Between 1933 and 1938 another five Up trains were somehow squeezed into the service in the morning peak, one starting from Worcester Park. These improvements gave Stoneleigh 13 Up trains from 07.19 until the basic 20-minute service started at 09.27.

Worcester Park station, Up side approach and entrance after the 1936–37 rebuilding.
Raphael Tuck & Son

Stoneleigh station looking to Epsom, 23rd January 1965, showing the 1941 footbridge and booking office and, in the foreground, the foundations of the smaller 1932 footbridge (like that at Motspur Park), which it replaced. *Alan A Jackson*

Overcrowding reached a very high level in 1934–7, with the SR seemingly taken by surprise by the full effects of the developers' activities. Passengers originating at Leatherhead and Dorking, used to corner seats in the morning but now obliged to stand as far as Stoneleigh or Ewell on the way home after a hard day at the office complained loud and long. Part of the problem was caused by over-provision of first class accommodation; less than three per cent of the new house occupiers using stations inwards from Epsom patronised the 60–78 first class seats in each peak hour train. The resentment this largely empty accommodation aroused when there were eight or more standing in the cramped third class compartments was considerable. Another irritation arose from the variable numbers of seats in each train which resulted from the assorted make-up of the electric rolling stock used at the time. But by the end of the 1930s, with the additional services just mentioned and with the new stations at Malden Manor and Tolworth siphoning off some passengers from Stoneleigh and Worcester Park, things began to improve somewhat.

The provision of more peak hour trains owed much to the lobbying of the very active local residents' associations at Stoneleigh and elsewhere. These bodies also campaigned for station improvements, another matter in which they had some success, though much was done by the SR without external prompting. By the early 1940s all the stations except Ewell West had undergone some rebuilding. At Raynes Park, noting the extensive residential development south of the station, the SR board authorised extensive new works in June 1933. These comprised: new ticket and parcels offices and a parcels and van yard on the Up side abutting the main road; a footbridge connecting the totally rebuilt staggered platforms (four faces serving from north to south, Up Epsom, Up Slow, Down Slow and Down Epsom lines); a new passimeter ticket office and entrance on the Down side; a post office; and eight lock-up retail premises to provide some revenue against the outlay. This work was completed in 1936.

Motspur Park's footbridge was enlarged in 1932 to allow access to the platform from new residential roads on the west side of the line. In 1937–38 the platform canopy here was extended at the London end and other improvements were made to a station destined to become the junction for the new line through Chessington to Leatherhead.

Worcester Park's little country station of 1859 was reported to the SR Traffic Committee in June 1935 as 'totally inadequate' for current needs. An almost total reconstruction was duly ordered. This included raised and widened platforms; slewing of the Down line; a new Up side entrance building in concrete and red brick with metal-framed windows and a flat roof to accommodate the main entrance hall and various offices; and a back-tilted steel girder canopy along much of the Down platform with a new exit from the street below. All was in place by the end of 1937 but further expenditure had to be agreed in 1939. The freight yard here was swamped by deliveries of building materials, not to mention a vast increase in solid fuels for the new houses. A very necessary enlargement was completed in 1934 and further works were undertaken in 1935/36. Even so, when the General Manager and senior officers inspected in December 1936 they found the yard filled to capacity, ordering two more sidings to be laid with a cart road and also a shunting neck to avoid delays to the passenger service.

As early as May 1935 Stoneleigh Residents' Association had started to prepare a case for reconstruction of the three year-old station. The little footbridge was already slowing down clearance of the platform in the evening peak period, making it almost impossible for incoming passengers to reach trains without unacceptable delay. In October 1937 the SR board authorised major rebuilding. This involved the erection of 12ft wide covered stairs with a railed off section for contra-flow passengers, leading to a covered bridge of the same width which was to incorporate an enlarged ticket office. Delayed by war preparation works, this project was not completed until 1941/42. Its traffic still presenting some problems, in 1946 Stoneleigh station was given intermediate colourlight signals controlled from the boxes at Worcester Park and Ewell West.

At Epsom, the pre-grouping arrangements, with two stations a mere half a mile apart, four signalboxes and two freight yards, demanded early rationalisation. The first step was the concentration of all freight traffic at the former LBSCR yard from 2nd January 1928, a year in which total reconstruction of the old wooden LSWR passenger station was begun. The sturdy and workmanlike replacement received only the most cursory architectural treatment, confined to the road frontage on the Down side. Two island platforms were provided, each 650ft long and 35ft wide, canopied with steel and glass for 300ft. The northernmost face was used by Waterloo trains and the opposite one by the Up Victoria and London Bridge services. The second island accommodated Down Waterloo line trains at its inner face and Down services from London Bridge and Victoria at its outer face. This arrangement allowed easy interchange for passengers desiring alternative routes at a station where good connections were for many years available throughout the traffic day, a facility inexcusably eroded in the early 1990s and further damaged by the fragmentation of responsibilities which followed rail privatisation. Wide covered stairways at the London end led to a subway and a spacious entrance and ticket hall cut into the south side of the embankment. One side of the underline subway was fenced off to allow unimpeded movement of parcels, luggage, mail and other passenger train traffics to and from electric lifts which gave access to the island platforms. The main frontage to the approach road was plain-faced and flat-roofed.

A new 60-lever signal box straddled the centre roads, controlling a rearranged layout which included a siding and a 200ft horse and carriage loading bay on the south side parallel with the passenger platforms. All the through lines were signalled for reversible working to allow terminating trains to return from the same platform. At the country end, each side of the running lines, two new berthing sidings were provided for electric trains, equipped with staging to allow carriage cleaners easy access. Although not yet completed this new station, which unforgivably lacked a buffet, was brought into use on 3rd March 1929, the LBSCR station (renamed Epsom Town on 9th July 1923) having closed the previous night. On the same day new electric services were begun between London Bridge and Dorking/Effingham Junction via Tulse Hill and Sutton. Main line services to and from the South Coast continued to pass through without calling, despite a 25 mph limit through the new platforms. a matter which caused considerable irritation to the late Cecil J. Allen when an Epsom resident.

After World War 2, peak hour congestion did not revert to the high levels of the 1930s. Overcrowding inwards from Epsom was ameliorated by the introduction of more spacious new rolling stock, wartime abolition of first class on local services and the new stations on the Chessington branch. As the pre-war building activity between Epsom and Raynes Park had left very little land uncovered there was

Ewell West, looking to London; Up train leaving with unit 4693, 22nd June 1963. Signal box, semaphore signals, gas lighting and freight yard are all still present at this date. *Alan A Jackson*

virtually no additional traffic to be had from this source. From the late 1950s off peak loadings were thinned out by the inexorable rise in car ownership and the use of television as a substitute for spectator sport, cinema and theatre visits. This fall was recognised from 7th January 1963 when the 20 minute frequency was reduced to half hourly in the middle of the day and evenings, all day at weekends. Even so, this line suffered less than many since the lack of parallel bus services between its stations and a wayward road layout that frustrated speedy motoring helped to sustain

The 1929 station at Epsom looking to London, 17th September 1987. *Alan A Jackson*

all day patronage, especially at Worcester Park and Stoneleigh. A notable intensification in track occupation started on 29th May 1995 when for much of the day the half hourly all-stations service was supplemented by two trains an hour working to and from Guildford/Horsham (Dorking from 30th September 1996) which did not call at intermediate stations between Epsom and Wimbledon.

Signalling modernisation began with the installation of automatic colour lights between Raynes Park and Epsom from 27th February 1966, allowing closure of the boxes at Worcester Park and Ewell West. This work included colour light starters at Epsom station Up side. Motspur Park (originally Blue House Crossing) box was retained for operating the level crossing (converted to controlled lifting barriers from 4th November 1974) and the electrically-worked points at the junction of the Chessington branch. From 30th January 1972 until 21st July 1990 when it was closed and replaced by control from the Wimbledon Signalling Centre this box assumed control of the whole of the Chessington branch. The neighbouring West Barnes Lane Crossing box was closed and the level crossing controlled by cctv from Raynes Park box from June 1978. That box was in turn closed in May 1990 when control was moved to the Wimbledon Centre. Epsom's unusual overline signal box was closed on 25th July 1990, its responsibilities assumed by the Wimbledon Signalling Centre from 29th July. Demolition did not take place until April 1992.

Colour light signalling and installation of the BR automatic warning system (January 1978) came too late to prevent the line's first serious accident, which occurred in thick fog on the evening of 6th November 1947 when the 16.45 Up from Holmwood to Waterloo ran into the crowded 17.16 from Waterloo to Chessington South whilst it was crossing from the Down side on to the Chessington branch just south of Motspur Park. Four passengers were killed and 34 injured. Some lives were probably saved by the presence of a more modern steel coach in a crucial position. The driver of the Up train, unable to see the semaphore signal, had relied on a fogman who had shown a green light, under the false impression that he had heard the signal arm move to the 'off' position.

Freight, latterly hauled by SR Moguls and Q1 0–6–0s and then diesel locos, declined rapidly after the late 1940s and was eventually almost wholly limited to domestic solid fuels. That traffic was reorganised in the 1960s. Ewell West yard was closed from 1st May 1961 and Worcester Park from 6th May 1963 though this yard had to be temporarily reopened for coal and coke traffic in the winter of 1963–4. After 1963 solid fuels for the area were handled by new depots on the Chessington branch as mentioned later. Raynes Park freight depot, in the vee between the Up and Down Epsom lines, was closed at the end of 1969 but until the end of 1983 a remnant survived in use as a civil engineer's depot, requiring occasional opening up of the ground frame housed in a small cabin on the Down side just north of Motspur Park station. This cabin had been used to control a minor level crossing, reduced to a foot crossing in December 1965. After 1983 the ground frame remained to operate an emergency crossover between Raynes Park and Motspur Park.

Peak hour overcrowding is now a thing of the past on this quintessential commuter railway, but passenger loadings have held up well in recent years despite economies that (with the exception of Epsom) have produced unwelcoming stations without staff and train running information for much of the day. Staff cuts have also engendered boarded up waiting rooms and lavatories and encouraged the mindless vandalism that breeds on lack of supervision.

The Chessington Branch

(map page 121)

As the perceptive reader will have already observed by the several references in the foregoing account, the history of the Chessington branch is closely related to some of the events just described. By the late 1920s, builders had brought the edge of London to a depth of 1–1½ miles south of the former LSWR main line between Raynes Park and Surbiton, a growth which owed much to the Edwardian electric trams of the London United Tramways and the LSWR electric services. Further south, the clay meadows and pastures in the valleys of the Hogsmill and its tributary the Rythe, and the higher woodland and commons towards Ashtead remained almost untouched by suburban building. In this extensive territory between the Raynes Park–Leatherhead and New Guildford lines there were but three villages (Hook, Chessington, Old Malden) and a sprinkling of Victorian and Edwardian villas at Motspur Park/West Barnes and Worcester Park. During 1927 the bright raw concrete strip of the Kingston By-Pass road seared the fields across the northern fringes of this district, almost at once attracting at its London end new bus services, small houses, shops and even factories.

This development was not unnoticed by the Southern Railway's passenger-conscious management. Early in October 1929 Sir Herbert Walker was reporting to his board on the desirability of a railway through the territory between the existing lines south of Surbiton. Like the Metropolitan's proposal for Stanmore, the bill prepared for the 1930 session was designed to catch government assistance under the Development (Loan Guarantees and Grants) Act of 1929. It proposed a line from a junction with the Raynes Park–Leatherhead railway 617yd south of the Blue House Lane level crossing at Motspur Park, across the Hogsmill Valley, passing north of Old Malden and west of Chessington, then running parallel to the Kingston–Leatherhead road on its east side before rejoining the existing railway 270yd north east of the Kingston Road bridge at Leatherhead, near the site of the first Leatherhead station. Seeking shareholders' consent at the February 1930 meeting, the chairman explained that 'it may be a very valuable railway to us if we get the powers to do it, because it is outside the effective bus area for people coming into London'. Certified for quick passage through Parliament in view of its expected contribution to the relief of unemployment, the bill received Royal Assent on 1st August 1930.

A long delay then ensued before any work could be done. Although the board authorised purchase of land for the first 4m 75ch of the 7m 3f 2ch route in November 1930, it was soon discovered that much of it was already being broken up into small parcels, moving through the hands of speculators who were forcing prices up in anticipation of large-scale housebuilding. As at Golders Green and many other places around London, the railway found that its own plans for extension had encouraged profiteering in land it wanted to build the line. Complicated by appeals, the process of property acquisition was to last over six years. In one case the SR was obliged to pay £7,347 after arbitration for little more than two acres, a figure seven or more times the land's value in the mid-1920s. Meanwhile, in November 1933, the board agreed that the remainder of the land should be bought as far as the junction at Leatherhead.

As we have seen when looking at other areas, the early 1930s were a propitious time for the rapid erection and sale of small suburban houses around London. By 1934 the district south of Surbiton was being well worked by builders under the additional stimuli of the Kingston By-Pass, its bus services, and the promise of the new electric railway. From 1933 Wates and others had started to fill up the land between the new railway and new motor road as far as Tolworth, leaving to nature only the immediate valley of the Hogsmill. South of the new line's route, between the Motspur Park junction and Old Malden, many small builders laboured mightily from 1932.

This activity led the general manager to suggest to the board in June 1934 that construction might start at the London end. Sir Herbert Walker estimated that with four stations and two goods yards, an electrified double track on this section to the usual SR standards of 600V dc third rail could be managed for £440,000 excluding land. Another £120,700 would be needed for five eight-car trains to work the proposed 20-minute service. This was agreed, subject to clearance with the LPTB in accordance with the understanding reached after the Battle of Morden. With land still being purchased, the first contracts were let in May 1935. Three months later the finance for the new line was included in a scheme submitted by the SR under the Railways (Agreement) Act, 1935, another unemployment relief measure, which secured the capital at a very low rate of interest guaranteed by the Treasury. The section south of Chessington was to be left until building development in that area justified its cost of construction.

Working under George Ellson, the SR chief engineer, Sir Robert McAlpine & Sons began at Motspur Park early in 1936, sharing the earthworks contract with Edmund Nuttall, Sons & Co Ltd. During April, the junction was completed with a short length of permanent track to feed the contractors' temporary way. This track also facilitated the reversal of an additional train service (three per hour) between Motspur Park and Waterloo, which started on 5th July 1936. During the following December, the general manager visited the works with other senior officers, deciding on the spot that such was the progress of the housing development they would provide 540ft side-platform stations instead of the 520ft islands of the Motspur Park and Stoneleigh type originally planned.

Construction through the very heavy and corrosive clay of the Hogsmill basin

Facing Page: Tolworth station under construction in 1938, viewed from the goods yard on the south side, looking towards Malden Manor. *F Foote*

proved both onerous and costly. Its instability required piling, dry-fill around the clay cores of the embankments, and cutting slopes as gentle as 2½ to 1, with the floors covered with ash, or even in some places concreted. Presence of sulphates in the clay caused the engineers to prescribe the use of aluminous cement wherever the work was in contact with running water. For most of the distance to Chessington the line was on embankment, but there were cuttings near the junction, between Malden Manor and Tolworth, and between Chessington South station and its goods yard. Climbing towards the country end, the line had gradients of 1 in 91 and 1 in 98 for a quarter-mile between the junction and Malden Manor and in the descent from that station on to the Hogsmill viaduct. There were seven overbridges across public roads, one underbridge at Chessington South and a three-span 140ft viaduct over the Hogsmill at the country end of Malden Manor station. All were built of steel plate girders encased in concrete (in the erroneous belief that this would save maintenance) and were supported on mass concrete piers and abutments.

Concrete was also much used in the four stations, which were an outstanding feature of this railway. All were of the same basic design, derived from Wimbledon Chase, but here for the first time SR architects attempted to integrate the street buildings of a suburban station with its platform structures. This was something that London Transport had been doing on its Underground extensions under the inspiration of Charles Holden, but the SR's success was limited, failing to emulate the calm elegance of the Holden buildings. The smooth lines and simplicity of the Chessington line station elevations, much influenced by cinema and marine architecture, certainly produced a striking effect, at its best whilst the materials remained unweathered. On the platforms, the style was set by the graceful 200ft long 'Chisarc' cantilevered concrete canopies, illuminated by porthole glasses and a mixture of blue, white, amber, and pink GEC fluorescent tubes, an early use of this type of lighting in a transport environment, and certainly revolutionary for the Southern, where electric trains often served stations lit by gas or even oil lamps.

Each street-level structure, flanked by a very small car park, included ticket office, bookstall, lavatories for each sex, parcels office and a small lock-up shop. Towers were erected for luggage lifts which were never installed. To gain the platforms, passengers traversed subways and stairs but all the Down platforms also had a separate ramp giving access from the road, intended for milk and luggage. On each side, behind the canopies, were general waiting rooms with oak furniture and an enclosed heating stove, and, on the Up platform, a porters' room. There were detail differences. At Chessington South, where the road building was above the line, the Up platform and footbridge were not completed. Both Chessington stations had less massive supports to the canopies, and street buildings with facing bricks in place of the cement-faced stock bricks used at Tolworth and Malden Manor.

The first 2½ miles to Tolworth, with the intermediate station at Malden Manor on the northern edge of the old village of Malden, was opened on Sunday 29th May 1938, served by three six-car trains an hour seven days a week, a projection of the July 1936 Motspur Park workings mentioned earlier. Tolworth station was well-sited on the west side of a 94ft span bridge over the Epsom-Kingston road close to its intersection with the By-Pass, where since 1930, builders of small semis and terraces had been busy closing the gap between the new road and the Edwardian fringes of Surbiton. At this temporary terminus all trains used the Down platform, returning to the Up line on the London side of the road bridge.

Chessington North, looking to Tolworth, May 1939.
SR Official

Malden Manor exterior, 1938; a not wholly successful attempt to create an integral design in the 'Modern' style. The entrance block shows an affinity with Wimbledon Chase, built almost ten years earlier.

From the start a buoyant commuter traffic was obtained from the new housing estates although a good deal of it was extracted from other SR stations. Useful relief was given to the Raynes Park–Epsom line which as we have seen had been somewhat overwhelmed by the rapid south-western growth of London since 1930. Many of the new house owners from the estates built from that time either side of the Kingston Road between the Hogsmill valley and Worcester Park transferred their allegiance from Stoneleigh station to Tolworth, whilst those living in the extensive accretions around Old Malden moved from Worcester Park station to Malden Manor. Tolworth also gained some passengers from Surbiton, especially those who preferred a seat to non-stop runs in crowded trains, and finally there were some new customers from buses feeding the Morden tube (belated retribution!). As noted earlier, in recognition of its new junction status and traffic growth, improvements to the 13-year-old station at Motspur Park were completed in June 1938.

Chessington South station on the first day of public service, 28th May 1939. The people are heading in the direction of the Zoo. *Lens of Sutton*

The remaining two miles to Chessington South, with an intermediate station at Chessington North, were electrified on 14th May 1939 and opened to the public on Sunday 28th May. On the preceding Friday the deputy mayor of Surbiton performed a ceremonial opening. As the official party emerged from Chessington South station, it was greeted by a baby elephant which returned with them to Chessington Zoo, where a lunch was given by the proprietor. This was a demonstration of the importance of a traffic which has ever since been encouraged by joint publicity and combined rail and admission tickets.

Some housebuilding between the line and the Leatherhead to Kingston road had started about 1934, but on the east side of the railway, with the exception of the Copt Gilders estate near the old village of Chessington, there was little building until after World War 2. Even today a very large amount of open land remains south of the line east and west of Tolworth station. Beyond Chessington South, all was still open country in 1939 but large tracts had been sold for building, notably the Chessington House Estate and 166 acres between Malden Rushett (the first station site after Chessington South), and the Leatherhead golf course. These areas were subsequently sterilised by the creation of the post-war London Green Belt.

After an inspection in May 1938 the general manager had criticised the station naming agreed with the local authority (Chessington Court and Chessington Grange), expressing the hope that the word Chessington could be omitted from one. Chessington North and Chessington South were finally adopted, but the confusion foreseen by Sir Herbert Walker persisted, as evinced by notices on the Down platform at Chessington North warning NEXT STATION FOR THE ZOO.

With the completion of the second station, the three trains an hour were extended to Chessington South, taking 31 minutes for the 14 mile all-stations run from Waterloo. Quarterly season tickets for the full distance were £4 8s od (£4.40), rather less than two weeks' pay for the average adult clerical worker.

Tolworth was given a goods yard sited at the country end on the Down side, its four roads increased in 1940 to seven, providing room for 218 wagons. The three-road yard at Chessington South, also on the Down side and a short distance south of the passenger station, opened to goods traffic on 1st July 1939.

Electrically-worked points on the Down line at the junction were controlled from Motspur Park box, but the Up track had unworked trailing points protected by a 20mph restriction. On the branch itself, upper-quadrant semaphores were worked from boxes on the Down platforms at Tolworth (20 levers) and Chessington South (18 levers) using Stevens & Sons frames recovered from LSWR boxes and instruments of standard SR three-position, 'closed-block' pattern.

At the terminus, passenger trains went in and out of the Down platform using a crossover north of the station. An Up platform had been built, complete with 'Chisarc' canopy, but no footbridge, lighting, fencing, or accommodation were provided. Electrified track continued some 20ch beyond the platforms, extended later with plain track for a further 13ch. During construction the contractors dumped spoil from the cuttings to form the embankment beyond here almost as far as Chalky Lane. In 1941–42 the embankment was carried further towards Leatherhead by Royal Engineers as a training exercise, using chalk excavated for wartime works at Andover Junction and Basingstoke, until they reached Chessington Wood, only a quarter-mile north of the next intended station. This work can still be seen today, with the remains of the railway fences.

An RAF barrage balloon station was opened near Chessington South station in 1939, followed shortly after the war by erection nearby of single-storey government office buildings on two sites and a further complex at Tolworth station. These developments helped to create a valuable contra-flow of peak-hour traffic, strengthened in 1946 by the opening of an office tower block with accommodation for some 2,500 workers close to Tolworth station.

Post-war railway planning for London, enshrined in the grandiose 1949 Report of the London Plan Working Party, included a scheme categorised as lower priority for a route 'E' tube line paralleling the Northern line between Kennington and South Wimbledon, there branching into two routes, one to go on to Chessington South via Raynes Park, using the SR tracks on the branch and taking over the service, which would be supplied from a new car depot at Chessington South. Whatever the future of the Chessington branch, it now seems unlikely that this scheme will be resurrected.

Very soon after the war, the line experienced its first serious accident as described earlier. Mishaps of this type were eliminated by the introduction of track-circuited colour-light signalling, eventually to be provided on the branch from 30th January 1972. The two manual signalboxes were then demolished and the branch was worked directly from Motspur Park box with a ground frame at Tolworth goods yard. The BR automatic warning system was installed in January 1978.

In addition to its regular-interval passenger trains, the branch has seen a fair variety of operations: steam and later diesel-hauled excursions bringing customers for Chessington leisure attractions from all over Britain, the usual SR nocturnal freights,

Chessington South station seen from the overline bridge, looking to London, 3rd March 1962. Note the uncompleted Up platform and the opening made in the brickwork at the top of the staircase for a footbridge, which was never completed. Upper quadrant semaphore signals, telegraph wires and SR electric light fittings of 1939 remained at this time but all the housing dates from after 1945. *Alan A Jackson*

parcels trains and, on at least one occasion (1954) a royal train, carrying the Queen back from the Derby via Chessington South to avoid the returning crowds at Tattenham Corner.

Freight traffic, hitherto mostly small loads of building materials, domestic coal and coke, assumed new importance in the early 1960s. The thrice-weekly working was retimed to mid-day in 1963 to allow the line to be shut at night, but this frequency was soon inadequate for in May that year a mechanised solid fuel distribution depot was opened on the site of Chessington South yard, where public traffic ceased from 18th March. Two freight trains daily were then required, usually hauled by SR Moguls, Q 0–6–0s, and even on occasion, Bulleid Pacifics. This new facility was operated by Messrs. Charringtons and together with the Tolworth depot opened later, replaced goods yards at Claygate, Surbiton, Hampton Court, Esher, Walton-on-Thames and Worcester Park. One of the more positive achievements of the Beeching era, it was served by block trains coming direct from the Notts & Derby coalfield. A similar, larger fuel depot was opened on the site of Tolworth goods yard on 4th January 1965 under the auspices of the National Coal Board. This was big enough to require internal motive power, at first a small green Barclay 0–4–0 diesel shunter, later ex BR Drewry D2310. This depot was fed by two and sometimes three trains a day in addition to the daily working to Chessington South. Motive power in the first years was usually a Class 5 4–6–0.

As domestic consumers converted in droves to oil and gas central heating in the late 1960s and the 1970s, traffic into these two depots fell away but in 1974 there were still 17 trains of 21-ton hoppers each week to Tolworth and six to Chessington South, mostly moved by SR electro-diesel locos as trip workings from Wimbledon yard. The 1980s saw further decline, with Chessington latterly served by Class 37 and even Class 58 diesels bringing in a few hoppers, sometimes just one, from Didcot. These workings ceased altogether in 1988, when the Chessington South rail-hauled coal was diverted to Purley. The depot was closed on 4th November.

Tolworth depot also began to handle aggregates traffic from about 1981, additional plant for this coming into use from March 1984 following a Government grant. Coal trains did not run after 1989, but the ex-BR diesel shunter remained in use. There were still two stone trains a week in 1992 but after July 1993 the Tolworth facilities were abandoned and freight workings over the branch ceased.

Towards the end of the 1950s the branch suffered the general decline in off-peak traffic noticed elsewhere and from 15th September 1958 frequency was reduced from three to two trains an hour. Sunday trains, for a long time sparsely used, were reduced to hourly in winter from October 1976. Further cuts were made in 1993 when evening services were also reduced to hourly intervals. The population in the catchment area has in recent years shown a slight fall and this, together with the other factors operating to reduce central London commuting, brought peak hour services down from four trains an hour to three from 1976–77, further cuts following later.

Chessington North station (1939) on 23rd April 1962, viewed from the Down side. *Alan A Jackson*

In the late 1970s about 28,000 tickets were issued on the branch each month and 1,540 season tickets, with Tolworth the busiest station at 9,800 and 460 respectively. By the early 1990s passenger numbers had fallen quite steeply, a count of passengers boarding between 06.00 and 21.00 showing not only the extent of the decline but a shift in the station league table:*

Chessington South	238
Chessington North	662
Tolworth	558
Malden Manor	836

Staffing economies had been made as early as 1971 when tickets at Chessington South were issued by the duty railman from his office on the platform and the street level booking office was closed. By the end of the 1980s the ticket offices at the other three stations were manned only in the morning peak period with no staff at all on duty at other times.

Powers for the completion of the line to Leatherhead were kept alive until 1961, after which the alignment remained zoned for railway use in the Surrey Development Plan for a further ten years. Since most of the countryside south of Chessington is part of the London Green Belt, protected from the swathes of small suburban houses that would have otherwise covered it around the proposed station sites at Rushett and Leatherhead North, the fulfilment of the SR scheme of 1929 is now very much a dead duck. Suggestions have been made for an extension to give better access to the Chessington World of Adventures, a very popular theme park establishment on the Zoo site in 1987, which even without this has boosted off-peak traffic to Chessington South especially in school holiday periods. New housing developments on the former LCC mental hospitals estate west of Epsom might also be served if a further mile or so were built, but such projects will never materialise without the (very remote) possibility of large injections of capital from interested parties.

In the sixth decade of its existence this half-finished railway continued to carry on a much reduced scale the traffic for which it was built: movement of office workers into and out of central London daily. It is interesting that this was a railway constructed when much of the new housing it was intended to serve was already in place and in use; and it is certain that without it, an intolerable strain would for many years have been thrown on road services and the existing rail facilities at Stoneleigh, Worcester Park and Surbiton. But after 60 years it had all but outlived its purpose. Passenger loadings off-peak, except at those times when the theme park is in heavy demand, had become very light; in winter trains carried much less than a busload and inter-station fare-paying traffic on the branch had all but disappeared thanks to the high tariff for local journeys. With such a scenario, the financial pressures for rationalisation and economies seemed likely to increase; proposals had already been made to demolish the Modern style SR stations (initially those at Chessington South and Malden Manor), replacing them with bus-stop style basic facilities so that land might be released for development. For the future, track singling and shuttle operation seemed possibilities for the medium term but the best solution might be integration of much of the line in a Kingston area light rail scheme, involving total abandonment of conventional electric railway operation.

* Source: Surrey County Council

Exterior of Kingston-on-Thames old station buildings, c. 1907. *Commercial postcard*

The Kingston Loop (map page 165)

Perhaps the most important of all places around London not touched by the main lines was the ancient borough and market centre of Kingston-on-Thames, strategically placed at what was for many years the last Thames bridge before London, on the main road to Portsmouth. At the end of the 1830s there were over 8,000 living in this Surrey town, served by over 60 daily road coaches to London. With the moral support of the coaching interest, the opposition of Lord Cottenham, owner of much land between the town and Wimbledon, secured the diversion of the London & Southampton Railway to the south. Francis Giles had engineered a line in 1831 which would have passed about midway between the town centre and the present Surbiton station, but the opposition caused Parliament to approve a route in 1834 which although in a sense more direct, entailed a long embankment across Norbiton Common and a deep cutting through Surbiton Hill, about a mile south of Kingston. Trains began to run between London (Nine Elms) and Woking on 21st May 1838 calling at a station named Kingston, situated just east of the present Surbiton station, where the line passed below the Kingston-Epsom road.

Within two years, speculative builders had established the beginnings of New Kingston, or Kingston-on-Railway, the middle-class villa suburb later to become known as Surbiton. There were some non-stop trains to and from London and it was not long before Kingstonians were regretting their isolation both as regards passenger and freight traffic. Grain which had formerly reached Kingston's important maltings by water was now going direct to London by rail and there was a noticeable depression in the town's retail trade. By the 1850s influential people in Kingston were ready to support almost any scheme which promised to end the indignity of a town with almost 11,000 people but no railway station nearer than one mile from its centre.

Some proposals touching the town came forward in this period, but surrounded as it was by royal parks, the Thames, and Wimbledon Common, the scope for direct links to London on useful through routes to points outside the capital was somewhat restricted. There were strong interests working to have Kingston connected by rail to the GWR and LNWR main lines, but naturally enough this met with little enthusiasm in the town. In 1857 there was a bill for a broad gauge branch from the GWR through Brentford to Richmond, offering the promise of further extension southwards to Kingston, but this was easily defeated by LSWR opposition. A bill from the same direction two years later sought powers for a Southall-Brentford-Kingston-Merton line, which would give access to Croydon via the existing Wimbledon & Croydon railway. The LSWR successfully countered by offering to construct a 3¼-mile branch from the Richmond-Windsor line at Twickenham following the Thames, to end at the west side of Kingston bridge. This was duly authorised in August 1859. After much agitation by the Kingston interests, another act in the following year sanctioned its extension for 72 chains into a terminus at Richmond Road, Kingston. Somewhat to the disgust of the LSWR, Parliament insisted that a station still be provided on the opposite bank at Hampton Wick, a mere 700yd west of the Kingston station. When the double-track branch opened on 1st July 1863 there was a second intermediate station, Teddington & Bushy Park, between the village and the north gate of the Park.

At a level just above that of the present booking hall, the three-bay, four-platform terminus under its all-over roof was at first known as Kingston New, or Kingston Town. The name Kingston soon sufficed because from the opening day of the branch, the main line station was called Surbiton & Kingston instead of Kingston Junction. A bridge of five cast-iron arches of 75ft span carried the tracks 24ft above Thames high water just north of the old road bridge. There were no other features of interest between here and the junction with the Windsor line west of Twickenham station.

It was not long before there was considerable grumbling at the roundabout approach to London, a journey of 15 miles for which some trains required as much as 57 minutes. To make matters worse, the LSWR fares were seen as expensive compared with those of the more direct horse buses (9d second-class rail to Richmond, only 6d by bus) and of the NLR, which also served the new branch. The *Surrey Comet* declared on 4th July 1863 'These fares, we feel convinced, will be as prohibitive to the development of short traffic as if a protective tariff had been framed for the very purpose'. A further irritant was a small reduction in the service required to make room for the Shepperton trains when that line opened in November 1864. Fortunately for the Kingstonians, the LSWR was not to be left in peace. From 1863 several proposals came forward for lines eastwards towards London and although all were defeated by LSWR opposition, that company was obliged to consolidate its position by obtaining powers in 1865 for a line from Kingston through New Malden to Wimbledon. This was to begin with an end-on junction with the Twickenham line, crossing the Richmond and London roads on the level, going on to the main line just west of Coombe & Malden station (now New Malden). Here the double track passed below the Southampton line, continuing alongside into Wimbledon, where end-on connection was made with the new Tooting, Merton & Wimbledon Railway described earlier. As there were misgivings about the Kingston level crossings, powers were obtained in 1866 for an alignment which brought the tracks over both roads into a high level station. This was to have two side platforms, parallel and to the north of the 1863 station and about 15ft above it. The junction was steeply made between the west end of the new platforms and the river bridge.

Built by John Aird & Sons, the Kingston & Wimbledon opened without ceremony on 1st January 1869, all trains from the high-level station running to and from Ludgate Hill, calling at the one new intermediate station of Norbiton, three quarters of a mile east of Kingston on Coombe Lane (now Road), and at new platforms at Coombe & Malden. Norbiton's large yellow brick station house on the north side of the line was similar in style to that on the west side at Teddington. In 1880 a double-line junction was made with the main lines west of Coombe & Malden station and four years later a connection was put into the new Up slow (former Up main) on the north side of the embankment so that the flyunder subsequently carried only the Down Kingston road.

Despite some continued dissatisfaction with the train service, which encouraged further railway schemes involving Kingston, the LSWR loop stimulated steady suburbanisation of the riverside area between Kingston and Twickenham in the late 1860s and 1870s, much of it taking the form of large middle-class houses. Around 1875 Teddington had many 'villas and genteel dwellings' and a new village centred on the station 'already has a church, schools, hotel and shops of a more showy description than those of the mother village'. Landowners and developers, led by Sir Thomas Freake, tried hard to persuade the LSWR to open a station to serve the new district of Strawberry Hill between Teddington and Twickenham, finally moving it into action with cash offers of one-third of its £1,500 cost, put up by those who stood to gain most. A vaguely Italianate two-platform station distinguished with some delicate-looking ironwork under its canopies was the result. This opened on 1st December 1873 and at first only Kingston and Twickenham trains called to serve 'the curious village of Strawberry Hill, made up wholly of *villas*', but by 1877 almost all the Shepperton branch trains were also stopping there. A useful aid to train working in the area was opened on 22nd October 1883 in the form of a flyover carrying the Up Kingston line over the Windsor lines into a new platform at the north side of Twickenham station, joining the Up Windsor line at the east end. In 1899, carriage sidings were constructed near the Fairfax Road level crossing at Teddington, on the Down side.

Exterior of Hampton Wick station c. 1907. *Commercial postcard*

As mentioned, the discontent in Kingston persisted after the opening of the loop in 1869. Envious eyes were cast from the town at Surbiton's excellent main line service and at favoured Richmond, with its fast trains to Waterloo and services north and north east provided by no less than five other companies. Prominent among the foreign elements anxious to penetrate the juicy LSWR territory in the Thames Valley and northern Surrey was the impecunious but ambitious Metropolitan District Railway. At one time it seemed likely that this initiative would bring Kingston its long-desired direct route to London. An independent bill deposited in 1880 proposing a Guildford, Kingston & London Railway stirred up great optimism and enthusiasm in the town, with the mayor sitting on the formation committee and the corporation offered a statutory right to appoint a director. To the consternation of Waterloo, the District was pulling many of the strings. Eventually, after much negotiation, there emerged in 1881 a Kingston & London Railway Act. In its final form, this 7½-mile line would have run from Surbiton to join the District at Putney Bridge, with connections at Norbiton to allow running from Kingston to Putney Bridge and to Surbiton. To be worked by a joint committee of the promoters, the LSWR and the MDR, this line would give LSWR trains access to High Street Kensington and South Kensington, and have intermediate stations at Coombe & Kingston (just east of the Fairfield), Roehampton (near Robin Hood Gate) and at Tibbett's Corner, Putney Heath. So interested was the LSWR that in 1882 it obtained powers to build a West End terminus at the corner of Pelham Street and the Fulham Road alongside South Kensington station. In that year the whole project was transferred to the District and the LSWR equally, but the Kingston directorship was retained. Some work was started, but with the District unable to raise its proper share of the capital and the LSWR unwilling to help it, the scheme was dropped in 1886 in favour of a shorter link between Putney Bridge and Wimbledon, for which the Kingston & London supplied the northernmost section from south of East Putney to Putney Bridge, as mentioned at the beginning of this chapter.

As something of a sop to the disappointed Kingstonians, the LSWR in the 1880s undertook substantial rebuilding of the inconvenient two-level station, making a large concourse between the buffer stops of the low-level terminal platforms and the Richmond Road with a new staircase between the two sets of platforms.

When Kingston station first opened in 1863 there were 15 Up and 13 Down trains on the Twickenham and Waterloo route and nine each way to and from Fenchurch Street, most of these involving a change at Hampstead Road (Primrose Hill). These North London Railway trains were an extension of the service started on 20th May 1858 between Hampstead Road (Primrose Hill) and Twickenham. About half of them were composed of LSWR stock, the rest of NLR; LSWR and NLR locomotives were transferred at Kew. Further variety was evident after the opening of a junction at Longhedge, Battersea, on 3rd April 1866, when trains also began to work between Kingston and Ludgate Hill.

After the opening of the link between Kingston and Malden, the NLR trains were diverted to terminate at Richmond over a new line between Richmond and South Acton opened on the same day (1st January 1869). The Kingston high level platforms saw eleven trains daily to and from Ludgate Hill, passengers from Waterloo changing at Wimbledon and those from Victoria at Herne Hill. Demand for direct service to and from Waterloo soon made itself felt; there were only two trains each way in November 1869 but the pattern gradually changed until eventually

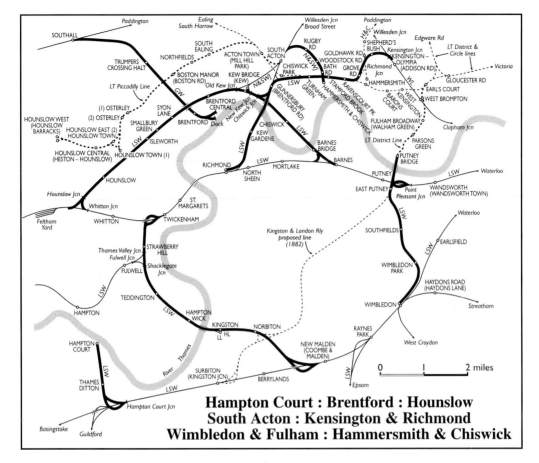

**Hampton Court : Brentford : Hounslow
South Acton : Kensington & Richmond
Wimbledon & Fulham : Hammersmith & Chiswick**

the main service was Waterloo–Wimbledon–Kingston–Twickenham–Waterloo and vice versa, referred to officially in the timetables as the *Roundabout*. By 1909 there were 39 trains from Waterloo to Kingston via Wimbledon each weekday, most of them stopping at all intermediate stations, with a running time of 37 minutes over the 12 miles. In the rush hours, when some stations were missed, the best time was 25 minutes. There were by this time only two trains (both in the evening) from Ludgate Hill. In the same year there were 35 trains from the high-level station to Waterloo, most of them coming through from Teddington. Strawberry Hill also had the Shepperton trains, which ran to and from Waterloo via Twickenham.

At this time there was a daily milk train and six freight workings between Malden and Teddington, serving the yards and sidings at Malden Crossing, Norbiton, Kingston, Hampton Wick and Teddington. Only four goods trains ran the opposite way round the loop, including two from the Midland Railway's Brent yard at Cricklewood (there was also a return working to Brent). A substantial part of the traffic was movement of coal into the Hampton Court Gas Company's works on the Up side between Hampton Wick and Teddington and those of the Kingston Gas Company in the Lower Ham Road north of Kingston station. The yard on the Down side at Malden Crossing was used by the Surrey Coal & Coke Company, which later shared it with the Twisteel Reinforcement Co. In the 1920s and 1930s the Kingston Gas Works sidings also gave access to the depot of the Anglo American Oil Co.

Hackney Carriages in attendance at Twickenham station, c.1905.

LSWR 'torpedo' front electric set on Waterloo via Wimbledon train entering Norbiton in the 1920s.

Freight traffic continued to be important until the 1950s when the Teddington, Kingston and Norbiton yards and depots were served by daily pick-up freight trains working to and from Feltham and Nine Elms yards. Through trains ran from Kingston to Feltham to convey wine traffic for other BR regions from the VP works at Villiers Road, Kingston. Facilities were curtailed in common with those of most other London lines in the 1960s: Norbiton and Teddington yards saw their last trains in May 1965, while Kingston yard closed in September 1966, apart from the siding to Fyffe's banana warehouse.

Passenger trains serving Kingston were among the very few inner suburban operations of the LSWR and as such were very vulnerable to the competition offered by the road service improvements which followed the introduction of the electric tramcar and motor bus in the first decade of the century. Clifton Robinson's London United Tramways reached the area through Twickenham, Teddington and Hampton in April 1903, crossing the bridge into Kingston and Surbiton in March 1906, finally reaching Wimbledon through Malden and Raynes Park in May 1907. Running along roads which paralleled the entire length of the railway from Twickenham to Wimbledon, the electric cars seized local traffic to an alarming extent. Another threat appeared in 1911–12, when the local authorities, banded together in the Thames Valley Councils Association, were working to get an apparently interested Central London Railway to extend its tube service over new surface lines into the area. At the beginning of 1912, under these combined pressures, the LSWR was dusting-off earlier plans for electrification. An announcement that March indicated that the Kingston Loop would be electrified 'as a dramatic answer to the appeals made from various quarters to the Central London Railway to invade the South Western preserves'. Despite this, the local authorities, Twickenham, Teddington and Hampton Wick among them, were said that month to be welcoming the prospect of competition and doing all they could to induce the CLR to alter its proposed bill for a Richmond extension to allow for working further into the Thames Valley.

An official announcement about the LSWR proposals followed in December 1912, in which it was stated that Waterloo–Wimbledon–Kingston–Richmond–Waterloo would be tackled first. For reasons of economy, the multiple-unit stock would be restricted to first- and third-class. To simplify connections with the East Putney–Wimbledon section already in use by District Railway electric trains, that company's voltage of 600dc would be used, with third-rail current collection.

Characterised by semi-streamlined 'torpedo' fronts, the electric trains of converted steam stock worked the Kingston Roundabout and Shepperton services from 30th January 1916. The three-car units (motor-trailer-motor), which ran singly in slack hours, were coupled together at peak times. They each seated about 180, some of the first-class sections including a smoking saloon formed from three old second-class compartments. Kingston Roundabout got four trains an hour each way plus two more each way between Malden and Teddington for the Shepperton branch. At peak hours there were two extra steam trains (electrics from 2nd April 1917) between Shepperton and Waterloo via Strawberry Hill. Trains ran at regular intervals past each hour, and Kingston's electric train every ten minutes compared with gaps of forty minutes to one hour in the former steam timetable. The electrics were lively both in speed and acceleration, reaching Waterloo in 28 minutes from Kingston instead of 35 (Teddington–Richmond–Waterloo, 40 to 49 minutes by steam train, now took only 32 minutes). With the new trains, all stations on the loop received electric lighting. The generous level of service introduced with the 1916 electrification remained virtually unchanged until the outbreak of World War 2, but in the 1920s Kingston–Wimbledon–Waterloo journey time was reduced to 27 minutes.

Traversing as it did an area which had seen substantial residential growth in the Victorian and Edwardian years and which possessed large acreages of royal parks, the electrification was not accompanied or followed by any large scale housebuilding although there were many small schemes to fill pockets left by the pre-1914 villa builders, much of this on the low-lying riverside land at Teddington, to the north of Kingston either side of the Richmond Road, and either side of the railway between Norbiton and Malden. Traffic on the loop grew steadily in pace with this further activity, and although the frequency remained adequate, the SR decided in 1929 that the time had come to clear away the inconvenient muddle of Kingston station. Assistance was forthcoming from the local authority, and after a delay caused by the national financial crisis, a £40,500 scheme was approved in October 1934. In the following year, all the old street-level buildings were replaced by an imposing red brick entrance and shop block prominently sited at the corner of Richmond Road and Wood Street. During the reconstruction of the high-level platforms a 520ft bay was added to replace the old low-level station, whose lines were shortened to form a loading dock, and whose site became a bus station. Some of the old cast-iron supporting pillars survived reconstruction of the high-level platforms, both of which got additional accommodation lit by steel-framed windows curving round at the ends, a buffet on the Up platform and opposite, a ladies' room with stained glass in what is now known as *art deco* style. A small passimeter booking office was added at street level for passengers proceeding from Richmond Road to the Up platform.

Teddington station also received attention in 1938, the improvements including a new building on the east side. Strawberry Hill's old wooden buildings on the Up side were replaced by a brick-built waiting room and booking office in 1935, the original booking hall becoming the Down side waiting room. Further station works have been undertaken in more recent years. Hampton Wick was completely demolished in 1968, to be reconstructed with steel and concrete platforms and the CLASP system modular buildings. A considerable amount of work was carried out at Kingston in 1988–90, providing a new ticket office and shops around a thoroughly refurbished ticket hall and entrances; rail level structures were also renovated at the same time. The elegant 1863 building at Teddington was completely restored to its original external appearance in 1991; internally the waiting rooms and ticket hall were modernised and a shop added.

Norbiton signal box, redundant after closure of the goods yard, was taken out of use from 27th July 1969. A major resignalling, in which all semaphore signals were replaced by colour lights, Kingston box was closed and Strawberry Hill and Malden Crossing boxes became gate boxes was completed on 10th November 1974. From that date, the whole of Kingston Loop came within the control of the new signalling centre at Feltham.

In an era of increasing car use, the lavish off peak service over the Loop was superfluous. From 15th September 1958 Kingston was served by four trains an hour, with a half hourly service between Teddington and Twickenham. The Sunday frequency of six trains an hour between Malden and Teddington was reduced to two an hour to Shepperton and two 'Roundabout' trains on 10th September 1962 and after September 1964 the half hourly Shepperton trains terminated at and started from Kingston. Sunday services were further modified from 5th October 1987, when Kingston via Richmond trains ceased and a Waterloo–Twickenham service ran hourly, connecting with the Shepperton shuttle.

Although for some years occasional through special excursions were still worked, the 1930–37 experiment of regular Sunday trains (also Fridays in 1930 only) between Kingston and the Kent Coast resorts was never revived.

The original Teddington Down side exterior of 1863 photographed in its centenary year with 1930s Southern Electric signs still exhibited. In recent times this building has been completely restored. *BR (SR)*

From 2nd October 1899 the Kingston Loop had had a few trains through the night except on Saturday/Sunday nights. Until World War 2, these were steam-hauled to allow traction current to be switched off for track maintenance. Calls were made at all stations Norbiton to Strawberry Hill inclusive except Hampton Wick but Norbiton and Teddington were omitted after 1st June 1981, by which time very drastic cuts had been made. With patronage fallen to very low levels, the night services were completely withdrawn from 2nd October 1989.

As an important retail centre, Kingston has in recent years become increasingly plagued by road traffic congestion and car parking problems. In an endeavour to alleviate this situation and encourage shoppers on to public transport, from 13th May 1991 the Borough Council financed a doubling of the off peak service to four trains an hour between Teddington, Kingston and Waterloo in the middle of the day from Mondays to Saturdays inclusive. The town's retail and entertainment attractions continued to provide a buoyant off peak traffic for most of the day into the 1990s, especially on Saturdays.

The entrance to Shepperton station, 31st October 1967. This building, on the Down side and now demolished, exhibits the virtually standard architectural style of all the original stations on the branch. *BR (SR)*

The Shepperton Branch (map page 171)

We now turn to a branch off the Kingston Loop that, like the Chessington branch, was really intended to go further. Chertsey's railway situation bore some similarities to that of Kingston but on a smaller scale. A small market town on the Thames, about 19 miles south-west of London, it found itself left 2¼ miles north of the London & Southampton Railway main line which here turned more sharply south-west towards a suitable gap in the Chobham Ridges. Although a branch from Weybridge was opened as early as 14th February 1848, access to London remained indirect, and the completion on 1st October 1866 of a loop through the town to the Staines & Wokingham line at Virginia Water did little to improve matters, despite the new and more convenient station that came with it. Chertsey hankered after something better for another 50 years or so.

Hope flared briefly in 1861 when a Metropolitan & Thames Valley Railway seemed about to give the town some sort of direct link to London. From a terminus on the north side of Chertsey Bridge, the M&TVR was to run through Shepperton, Sunbury, Twickenham and Isleworth and over part of the new Brentford to Southall branch to the GWR main line near Hanwell. Junctions were proposed with the LSWR Twickenham–Kingston–Malden line near the present Strawberry Hill

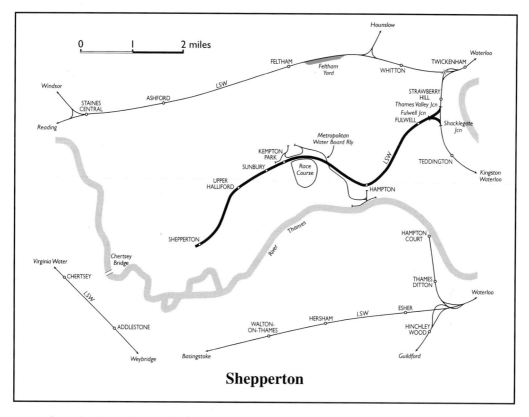

Shepperton

station. A planned spur from near the site of the present Shepperton station to the Thames (presumably to serve Walton Bridge) had been dropped by the beginning of 1862. It was hoped that the GWR would agree to build and lease the line, allowing the LSWR and the Metropolitan Railway to work over it with their own trains. The promoters were local residents and landowners, together with parties interested in increasing the prosperity of the Southall–Brentford line. As the GWR terms were not acceptable to the promoters, they turned to the LSWR. In the euphoria of deliverance from a Paddington invasion, that company conceded more favourable terms for leasing and working – retention of 50 per cent of gross receipts, guaranteeing the small company four per cent on capital up to £110,000; but the LSWR did insist that the line be restricted to 6m 52ch from the junction with its Kingston line to a point near Shepperton. An agreement with the LSWR dated 1st May 1862 scheduled to the Thames Valley Railway Act of 17th July 1862 confirmed the abandonments of the inner and outer sections of the original scheme, and required ballasting to be 'gravel at least eighteen inches deep' and the rails to be 'eighty pounds per yard and fished'. William Schaw Lindsay MP, chairman of the Metropolitan & Thames Valley Railway, lived at the Manor House, Shepperton, and the proposed terminal section to Chertsey Bridge would have crossed his land, but it seems likely that the dropping of this section was due more to LSWR opposition than to second thoughts on his part. The word *Metropolitan* was now removed from the title of a scheme successfully reduced to a 'blocking' line serving a few unimportant Thames-side villages.

John Aird & Son received the construction contract, taking £95,000 of the £110,000 issue of four per cent stock instead of cash. Airds had their eyes firmly on Chertsey; not only did they get the Shepperton terminus built as a through station, but they drummed up support from the remnants of the original promoters, and late in 1864 offered to build a connection between Shepperton and the LSWR near Addlestone at no cost to that company. But the LSWR sensed a new threat and stifled the gift horse, refusing the necessary approval for a junction.

The curious creature of all this activity was a meandering single line through small communities of which Shepperton was one of the least impressive, with a population of less than a thousand. The Reverend W. J. Scott described the branch as crossing 'a flat and somewhat dreary region of Middlesex' to terminate 'to all seeming – in a potato field, as if weary of going further in such country'. Leaving the Kingston Loop about a mile south of Twickenham, the track ran almost due west, then almost due south just beyond the western edge of Bushy Park. Before reaching the river, it turned northwest to skirt the northern boundary of *Kempton Manor*, an estate which together with that of *Sunbury Court* prevented the seemingly logical and otherwise unimpeded route along the riverside to Sunbury. For its remaining length, the direction was generally southwest to the terminus on the northern outskirts of Shepperton village. Passing loops were provided at Kingston Junction (also known as Thames Valley Junction) and at Hampton, Sunbury and Shepperton stations.

Fulwell (for Hampton Hill), the first intermediate station, stood in open country, taking its name from *Fulwell Park,* seat of the deputy chairman of the Thames Valley Railway Co, over half a mile north-west. Although the line passed close behind the large village of Hampton Hill (sometimes called New Hampton) the expense of a separate station was avoided. Hampton station was on the western edge of this riverside community, notable for its extensive waterworks. For the reason already given, Sunbury station was about a mile north of its village amid fields near the Staines to Kingston road. The terminus, about three quarters of a mile north-west of Shepperton village centre, in the aforementioned potato field, was rather nearer the smaller community of Halliford, and 18¾ miles from Waterloo via Richmond.

All stations except Fulwell received small goods yards, and all had decent yellow brick houses in a standard design that featured heavily pedimented gables and round arch windows in groups of three, quite different from anything on the LSWR. An Up platform at Shepperton soon fell into disuse, never gaining either footbridge or subway.

Passenger trains started on Tuesday 1st November 1864, worked by a single-line staff, signals being provided only at the loops. Although the Thames Valley Company, nine-tenths owned by Aird & Son, was sold to the LSWR under an act of July 1865 and wound up on 11th January 1867, the name Thames Valley line survived on OS maps and on the lips of the staff for another half century.

Under the new owners, the line (which had been built for double track) received its second road between the junction and Fulwell about 1867. Further progress had to await a stimulus, which came with the sale of the Kempton Manor Estate for conversion to a racecourse in 1869. At first unconvinced, the LSWR refused improvements, but eventually approval was given for further doubling which reached Sunbury on 17th July 1878 and the terminus on the following 9th December. The Preece single wire signal instruments then installed lasted into the British Rail era.

Sunbury, looking to London c.1921 with a Shepperton service unloading. The industrial complex (left) enjoyed a small network of private sidings and the gated siding below the signal arm serves a modest establishment at the right signed 'Fear Brothers'. There are milk churns awaiting an Up train. *Commercial postcard*

Soon after the racecourse opened on 18th July 1878 a platform was erected on the south side of the line about half a mile east of Sunbury station, near the grandstand. A second platform was added in 1879 but for the next ten years the station was available only to members. Complete rebuilding took place in 1890 and in its final form the Kempton Park racecourse station had three platforms sheltered by long canopies and connected by a covered footbridge (the third platform road, never electrified, served the outer face of the Up platform). The extra-long Down platform was able to take two LSWR first-class only Members' Special trains composed of American Line saloons. A covered way connected the station to the racecourse. Some further improvements were carried out in 1930. After 1890 the station was opened to the public on race days, when it was served by the branch trains as well as the race specials, but it could not be used other than to gain access to and from the racecourse.

To facilitate the working of race traffic, and to some extent freight movement as well, the LSWR constructed the Fulwell Curve, opened on 1st July 1894 from Fulwell Junction to Shacklegate Junction on the Kingston line about a quarter of a mile south of Strawberry Hill station. Race trains could then work over the rather longer route to Waterloo via Kingston (20m 68ch from Shepperton) but the curve was not used by ordinary passenger trains until 1st June 1901, when a single Down working (18.07 from Waterloo) was routed this way. Inside the triangle formed by the three junctions a locomotive depot known as Fulwell was built to replace the small shed at Twickenham and to service the Shepperton and Kingston lines. Opened on 1st May 1897 and enlarged in 1908 to accommodate 30 locomotives (mostly tanks), this depot eventually employed over 500 men, but it was in turn replaced by the new Feltham yard depot in 1922. From 1916 the site was partly used as an electric train depot, wholly so from 1923. Enlarged in 1936, it could accommodate up to 11 eight-car trains overnight. As an electric car depot it was known as Strawberry Hill.

Although Chertsey's population of about 3,000 hardly seemed large enough to justify the fuss, the desire for further railway accommodation persisted. There was some optimism in 1884 when the LSWR included a connection between Shepperton and the Weybridge–Virginia Water line in its bill for the next session, but once again the citizens of Chertsey were to be frustrated as the item was withdrawn from the bill soon after it appeared. In 1906–7 agitation flared up again; the Chertsey UDC petitioned the LSWR board, only to be told that the company did not see any return for the outlay. Others were persuaded to join the battle, and in 1911–12, the local authorities of Weybridge, Sunbury, Hampton Wick, Hampton, Twickenham, Molesey and Teddington tried hard to persuade the Central London Railway to bring tube services to the area (the CLR had plans to go as far as Richmond via Gunnersbury, depositing a bill in 1912 for this). The tube company did ask the LSWR whether it might run its trains over the line to Shepperton whilst assuring the local authorities 'most emphatically' that it had decided to enter the Thames Valley. By this time (November 1912) the LSWR, which already had modest plans to electrify the inner suburban services, had read the danger signals and promptly blocked such aspirations by including the Shepperton, Hampton Court and Hounslow lines in its own scheme. It also soon became apparent that the CLR's Thames Valley manoeuvre had been little more than tactics against the background of a prospective merger with the Underground Group; once the takeover terms for that had been agreed late in 1912, the Thames Valley councils were dropped like discarded toys.

Before going on to look at the LSWR electrification, a word should be said about the branch service in steam days. The first entries in Bradshaw are outside the LSWR pages under the special heading 'Thames Valley Line', not that there was much to offer – the initial service was but seven trains a day each way, all between Shepperton and Waterloo, with very long gaps. Thus anyone missing the 13.15 from Shepperton would cool his heels until 17.15 whilst the unfortunate seeing the tail of the 12.00 departure from Waterloo would have to wait until 16.10 for another. On Sundays there were four journeys each way, working only between Twickenham and Shepperton. The run from the outer terminus to Waterloo took from 50 minutes to over an hour and the luckless poor with money for no more than a third-class ticket were obliged to catch the first train of the day each way, waiting till the next day before returning. Dissatisfaction with the train service simmered for the next 40 years, partly because of the irregular sequence, but also because of the frequent need to change trains at Twickenham. In 1866 there were ten trains a day each way (five on Sundays) and 20 years later, although the number of weekday trains had increased to sixteen, ten involved a change at Twickenham or Strawberry Hill for London and the average running time for the full journey was still 50 or 55 minutes (one journey took 67 minutes). By late 1915, just before electrification, there were 23 trains each way on weekdays but even the best still required 48 minutes for the 18¾ miles to Waterloo. With the single exception mentioned earlier, all regular passenger trains ran via Twickenham and Richmond, and several combined with Kingston or Windsor services between Twickenham and Waterloo. Freight workings, which had started with one train a day, had increased to two daily by 1909.

Whether it was the poor train service, or the flat, unpromising nature of the district served, there was no really significant residential development along the line before 1914. Teddington crept westwards towards Fulwell station, mostly in the form of

Hampton Station, looking to London c.1905. The coal siding and yard by the overline bridge supplemented a freight yard at the country end of the station. *Commercial postcard*

low-cost housing for workers at the large depot of the London United Tramways, and others. There was some industrial development in the Fulwell area, accelerated in World War I, but none of this brought much traffic to the branch. At Hampton, a large estate called *Marling Park* north of the station was laid out for building in mid-Victorian times but filled only very slowly. Housing began to appear around Sunbury station at the turn of the century, some of it associated with the arrival of the Lincrusta-Walton wallpaper factory. The immediate surroundings of Shepperton station acquired a mere sprinkling of villas, a row of shops and a Railway Hotel.

This scene was enlivened on Sunday 30th January 1916 by the arrival of the 'torpedo end' electric trains bearing the easily-remembered headcode 'S'. For the first time, almost all the service was routed via Kingston, a change made to balance the Hounslow Loop service on the Richmond line and to give a combined 10-minute headway all day between Waterloo and Teddington. Altogether it was a revolutionary improvement, 35 trains a day each way, every day of the week, running at 30-minute intervals on weekdays between 05.55 and 22.55, with an extra Down train from Wimbledon at 05.09 and another at 23.53 from Waterloo. On Sundays, trains worked every half hour between Twickenham and Shepperton with headcode 'S̄'. As previously mentioned, rush-hour trains were lengthened from three to six cars, and there were steam (later electric) trains via Richmond. After 1919 all weekday trains ran via Kingston with peak-hour non-stops from Norbiton to Wimbledon covering the Shepperton–Waterloo run in 44 minutes. Rush-hour working via Richmond reappeared in 1920 and the fast trains on the other route were gradually removed. From 1916, following the electrification, Fulwell Junction signal box was open all day, (the Station Box was closed in July 1917) and the Up platform at Shepperton became a carriage siding. Stabling at Shepperton was improved in 1925 by the installation of an electrified siding and cleaning stage.

After 1926 the basic service settled down to half-hourly via Kingston calling at all stations and taking 48 minutes. Some peak-hour trains ran via Richmond, missing stops, until 1958, and some Sunday trains went that way until the same year. At various periods, as an economy, or to relieve summer congestion on the main line out of Waterloo, the branch was worked as a shuttle to and from Kingston, a practice which had been a feature of Sunday working from the early 1920s. The new timetable of 15th September 1958 gave a basic half-hourly service for seven days a week, taking 47 minutes and calling at all stations via Kingston; three peak-hour workings each way via Richmond completed the throughout journey in 40 minutes. Sunday trains reverted to the half-hourly Kingston shuttle from September 1964 and the running time of the basic weekday service was extended to a dreary 50 minutes. Improvements came with the Southern Region's radical new timetable of 10th July 1967. By missing Vauxhall, Earlsfield and Raynes Park, the basic all day half-hourly service ran from end to end in only 44 minutes, later increased to 45 with the Raynes Park stop restored. The Kingston–Shepperton half hourly Sunday service remained, as did some peak-hour runs via Richmond.

For many years after electrification steam locomotives continued to work freight and certain race specials. In LSWR days race trains were operated from various parts of the system but the post-grouping service was invariably to and from Waterloo. Until September 1939, first-class race trains made up from SECR and LBSCR compartment stock hauled by LSWR M7 0–4–4T, ran between the electric services, whilst other race trains were electrically-worked. The branch goods locomotive was employed in term time to haul a school train between Hampton and Twickenham until 1939, an unusual working which no doubt created many conversions to the railway cult. Another occasional sight was steam coming to the rescue when electric traction was in difficulty, as in the summer of 1957, when after a night of heavy rain the line was under water at Fulwell and an M7 was summoned from its empty stock chores to work a shuttle service between Teddington and Hampton for most of the next day (13th August). In more recent times, diesel locomotives have been used when this vulnerable section is flooded.

As elsewhere, the electric service stimulated housing development, but the generally flat and unattractive aspect of the district, pock-marked by gravel pits and reservoirs, its inaccessibility, and the lack of fast trains outside peak hours combined to discourage intensive development beyond Hampton. At Fulwell in the late 1920s and early 1930s large housing estates were built north-west, south and south-west of the station and there was much filling of the empty spaces left by the Victorian and Edwardian developers at Hampton and Hampton Hill. At Sunbury bungalows and low-cost houses appeared in haphazard groups between the railway and the river, and a belt of new housing linked the Staines Road north of the station with Feltham. Shepperton station became the centre of a small but fairly cohesive new suburb, and there was another much smaller group of new roads to the west at Shepperton Green. In 1931 the building activity at Shepperton was sufficient to justify the provision of a siding on the down side for materials coming in for the builder W. J. Lavender.

Freight traffic to and from the yards and private sidings at Shepperton, Sunbury and Hampton was handled by one or two trains daily, usually worked in the 1930s and 1940s by Adams '0395' and Drummond '700' 0–6–0 locomotives. In 1952 the one morning train ran from Twickenham to Shepperton and back to Feltham and a light engine worked from Twickenham to shunt Hampton yard. Although depleted traffic and rationalisation caused the closure of Shepperton and Sunbury yards on 7th October 1960, at Hampton, with its small yards on both sides of the line and where accommodation had been extended in 1930, freight working, which latterly included frozen horseflesh carried in Hungarian State Railways vans all the way from the plains of Central Europe, survived until May 1965. Another special traffic was coal and materials for the Metropolitan Water Board's pumping stations at Sunbury, Kempton Park, and Hampton. The private water companies which had established themselves at Hampton twelve years before the opening of the branch had received their coal via Thames river barges and horse carts, but the East London Water Company which had come to Sunbury in the late 1860s used the LSWR. After the Metropolitan Water Board took over the installations in June 1904 it was decided to build a 2ft gauge railway system with transhipment sidings alongside the LSWR Up line at Kempton Park and at the riverside at Hampton. The 3½-mile system opened in 1915 was worked by three very trim Kerr, Stuart 0–4–2T named *Hampton*, *Kempton* and *Sunbury*, joined by the 0–4–2T *Hurst* some years later. Eventually there were about 140 tipping, hopper and other wagons and the little trains were a pleasant surprise for the untutored traveller between Hampton and Kempton Park. With the conversion to oil-burning in the pumping stations there was no work for the railway; in 1947 the locomotives were cut-up and the line dismantled. Until 1956 the MWB also maintained a private siding on the Up side between Sunbury and Kempton Park (Hanworth Road).

Metropolitan Water Board Railway locomotive *Sunbury* in the 1920s, at Kempton Park Pumping station. *Locomotive Publishing Co.*

World War conditions produced special traffics. In 1914–18 there was a large camp at Sunbury and the racecourse was used as a motor transport store, both bringing extra work to the line. World War 2 also provided much interest for the observer, including the transport of Italian prisoners of war to and from Kempton Park camp in eight-car sets of Maunsell corridor coaches. British Thermostats built a war factory near the point where the line passed under the Feltham–Walton road, and to serve this a concrete platform with small brick buildings called Upper Halliford Halt was opened on the Down side east of the road on 1st May 1944. There was no need at this time for an Up line platform as during the war years the branch was worked as a single track, the other line serving as a parking place for crippled wagons. An Up platform and concrete footbridge followed after the war. On 29th December 1940 a bomb completely demolished the Up side at Sunbury station.

Single-line working, which lasted from 1940 to 1946 was an extension of a practice which had long applied on race days. On those occasions (and there was a meeting in eight of the twelve months during the height of the course's popularity) the Down line between Sunbury and Shepperton was worked in both directions in accordance with Electric Train Tablet Regulations, the other track being used to park race specials end-to-end, awaiting the time when they were called forward to Kempton Park station for the homegoing crowds. To facilitate this intensive working, the 1½-mile section between Hampton and Kempton Park boxes was shortened by the manning of temporary block posts at Mark Hole (on the Down side, 949yd from Hampton) and Hanworth (on the Up side 920yd from Kempton Park station). The box on the Down platform at Kempton Park was otherwise only manned when access was required to the MWB siding. There was a third temporary block post at Fulwell Cutting, between Fulwell and Hampton on the Down side, one mile from Fulwell Junction box. Using these boxes, electric race trains were operated at intervals as close as four minutes at the busiest times (Easter Mondays), working by both routes from and to Waterloo. A standby steam locomotive was stationed at Sunbury in case of emergency. Increased car ownership and television killed this business and by the later 1950s single-line working was seen only on Easter Mondays. A few special trains continued to run to Kempton Park until the early 1960s. Horsebox traffic, once a great feature on the day before the first races and the day following the last ones, with steam locomotives working through from the LNER and other lines, also dwindled to nothing in the 1950s as horse owners turned to the more convenient motor boxes.

After the mid 1960s there was a decline in commuter traffic. Season ticket issues on the whole line fell for example from 1,367 in 1967 to 1,041 in 1974. Peak hour workings were accordingly thinned out from May 1977. Further economies, this time in weekday evening and Sunday coverage, were put in place from 1st June 1981. Signalling modernisation produced more savings. From 9th March 1969 Sunbury box was closed, Fulwell Cutting box following on 1st April. In 1974 the whole branch was moved to control from the new Feltham panel box, with colour light signals replacing the old semaphores; this operation, which saw the closure of the remaining manual signal boxes (Shepperton, Shacklegate Jc and Fulwell Jc) was substantially completed on 10th November but Hampton survived as gate box until 3rd January 1975, when cctv allowed operation of the level crossing to be supervised from Feltham panel.

Station reconstruction started inauspiciously with installation of the ugly CLASP

Packing case architecture at Sunbury, Up side, 1968. The Southern Railway seat (left) has more aesthetic appeal than CLASP, but it has to be admitted that the predecessor structure here was no more elegant. *Alan A Jackson*

system building at war-damaged Sunbury in 1967. Freight yard land on the Down side here was used for an office development which formed part of the passenger station from 1989. Shepperton's semi-rural aura was disturbed in 1963 when the two-storey headquarters offices of the Ian Allan organisation were erected across the end of the tracks, their drabness subsequently given some colour when the firm purchased the first class Pullman car *Malaga* for hospitality accommodation, stabling it on the site of the old carriage dock.

Following a development deal, Shepperton station was totally rebuilt in 1988, the new structure incorporating further offices for Ian Allan Ltd. The new building's end elevation, which included a clock, was in somewhat awkward Post Modern style, intended to recall the attractive Italianate lines of its predecessor on the same site. At ground level there was a glazed waiting area and ticket hall, with a canopy on the platform side. The forecourt was attractively landscaped.

By the early 1980s the unmanned premises at Upper Halliford had inevitably succumbed to vandalism and graffiti scrawling; the adjacent concrete, noise and stink of motor road infrastructure and use added further to its repulsiveness. Somewhat surprisingly, in view of the rather thin catchment area, substantial funds were found for its total reconstruction. Completed in 1991, this featured a Neo-Vernacular ticket office and staff room on the Down platform and a large arched waiting shelter on the other side, the whole watched over by cctv cameras.

No major changes have so far been made at Hampton and Fulwell. Whilst Kempton Park no longer saw special trains, the ordinary branch services continued to set down and pick up the depleted ranks of punters at appropriate times on race days. By the mid 1990s, the branch had lost much of the character it once had; local journeys had long suffered serious depredation from a network of bus services and later from the spread of private car ownership. Outside commuter hours, passengers were very few. It seems doubtful whether this rather hopeless enterprise has ever paid its way except perhaps briefly in the 1930s and 1940s. Writing in 1918, long before anyone dreamed that it would be paralleled over part of its course by the frenzied roaring of a motorway, the Reverend W. J. Scott found the outer section as 'bearing an odd likeness to bits of the Midland & Great Northern Joint'. Well, we all know what happened to that . . .

Hampton Court station at 13.50 on a wintry day around 1908. The nature of the traffic suggests commuters returning from a Saturday morning stint at their London offices. The Tudor style goods shed is just visible at the left. *Commercial postcard*

The Hampton Court Branch (map page 165)

The magnificent State Apartments and grounds of the royal palace at Hampton Court were thrown open to the public by the young Queen Victoria in November 1838 without charge or restriction, and in the next decade visitors arrived by road and river steamer at the rate of some 178,000 a year, many of them on Sundays when there were few other comparable attractions open to them. With its main line passing only just over a mile to the south, the LSWR management thought this too good an opportunity to overlook and a bill was prepared for the 1846 session. Everyone was quite certain what it was all about: *The Illustrated London News* referred to it as 'this holiday railway' and W. J. Chaplin, the LSWR chairman, spoke of it somewhat patronisingly as affording 'a fresh means of cheap and legitimate recreation to the poorer classes'. A double line of 1m 52ch, running north from the main line near Long Ditton to the southern approach of Hampton Court road bridge was sanctioned by the LSWR (Hampton Court Branch) Act of 1846. There was some delay whilst it was considered whether the route might be used as the first part of a line to Staines and Windsor but, this proving unnecessary, work began in January 1848.

Engineering was straightforward, as the line for almost its entire length was on an embankment about 18ft high with only one major bridge (over the river Ember at the south end of Hampton Court station). Although named Hampton Court, the terminus also served the south bank riverside village of East Molesey (then spelled Moulsey) and there was a renaming to 'Hampton Court and East Moulsey' on 1st June 1869. But all the emphasis was on the Palace, even to providing the station buildings with architectural treatment in keeping, red brick and stone dressings and Jacobean curved gables (the locomotive shed was lovingly styled with steep pitched roof and prominent buttresses). The terminus was between the mouths of the rivers Mole and Ember on an artificial island created by a creek which served a watermill and connected the two rivers. A new engine shed erected about 1895 south of the Ember bridge survives today, heavily disguised as a plastics factory.

There is some evidence that for a short period after the branch opened on 1st February 1849 certain trains, if not all, were horse-drawn, with journey times far in excess of those advertised. In a letter to *The Times* of 13th February 1849, the use of a horse is described by a local doctor as 'a daily (not single) occurrence' and he relates that on 9th February the 12.45 train left Hampton Court in charge of 'an old grey horse . . . saddled and bridled' under the guidance of 'Evans, the Moulsey flyman', taking 20 minutes to reach the junction, where a main line train had been standing for 28 minutes waiting for the Hampton Court coaches to be attached. Kingston (now Surbiton) was reached in about 30 minutes from Hampton Court instead of the five shown in the time bills. In his *Short History of East Molesey*, Herbert Adams mentions that the 'flea-bitten grey' drew only one carriage, which included the guard's van. Whether this expedient arose from a shortage of locomotive power or uncertainty about the settlement of the embankment is not clear, but it does demonstrate that historians cannot always rely on published timetables as evidence of what was happening on a railway at any given time.

The first timetable, for what it is worth, gives five trains each way on weekdays, plus two more from Hampton Court with connections to Waterloo trains at Surbiton. The five through trains took about 45 minutes between Hampton Court and Waterloo – the somewhat incredible allowance of only five minutes between Hampton Court and Surbiton has already been noted (today's electric trains, with an intermediate stop at Thames Ditton, take seven). Sunday service was sparse, despite the fact that this was the only day when ordinary people could visit Hampton Court, but no doubt the three trains each way on the branch and one through working each way were duly increased in the summer months.

A little short of half-way along the branch the western fringe of the pretty riverside village of Thames Ditton was passed. This was a modest holiday resort, with some middle-class settlement, and it was not long before a demand arose for a station. Passenger facilities were provided in November 1851.

As time passed, Hampton Court gained in popularity as a pleasure resort; thus on Whit Monday 1850 some 2,000 were carried on the branch, but in the late 1860s and early 1870s the average attendance at the Palace each year was well over 200,000 and on Whit Monday 1872 there were almost 30,000 admissions, a high proportion of which would have come by train. Ordinary weekday service in 1867 was 15 trains daily each way, taking ten to eleven minutes from Surbiton to Hampton Court, calling at Thames Ditton. On Sundays about nine trains ran each way. By 1880 there were 19 trains Down on weekdays and 16 Up, taking about 42 minutes to and from Waterloo.

Houses began to appear just west of the terminus in the late 1860s and early 1870s, principally on an estate called Kent Town, which in accordance with the Victorian custom, was provided with its own church. East and West Molesey, together with neighbouring Thames Ditton were by the turn of the century firmly established as middle-class residential areas. Train service was accordingly increased, with 29 Up and 27 Down weekday trains in 1910 although the throughout timing was still between 41 and 48 minutes. A daily goods train worked the yard at Hampton Court but Thames Ditton never dealt with more than parcels traffic. A racecourse opened alongside the river at Hurst Park in 1889 brought the line more business. Horsebox traffic for this continued well into the 1930s, and punters used the branch in considerable numbers until the course closed in October 1962. Just before that, on

Whit Monday, they would give the branch its busiest day of the year, with trains running at five-minute intervals or less, a service facilitated by the opening of a special six-lever intermediate block post in the staff room on the Up platform at Thames Ditton.

The LSWR Thames Valley electrification scheme, already noticed, provided the branch with a regular service of three trains an hour for the greater part of each weekday from 18th June 1916 (service was half-hourly until 07.00 and after 21.30). Hampton Court–Waterloo time was reduced to 33 minutes despite calls at all eight intermediate stations. From 20th November 1916, for no particularly good reason, service was boosted to four trains an hour for the main part of the day. Daylight Saving, or 'summer time', introduced as a wartime measure on 21st May 1916, was used by LSWR publicity. Tired war workers and soldiers on leave from the Western Front, with girl friends, were enticed to summer riverside delights with a booklet entitled *Long Evenings on the Silver Thames* which showed them that by going to Hampton Court or other riverside stations on the new electric trains they could get in several hours on the water before darkness really set in: should the river-rocked kissing and fondling be prolonged, the electrics would still be there very late at night to take them back to town.

To facilitate the working of the intensive electric service, the LSWR built a new 1½-mile approach to the branch on the south side carrying the Down Hampton Court line on brick viaducts of 336yd and 100yd to a 160ft lattice girder span over the main lines. This was ready for traffic on 4th July 1915, in the midst of World War 1. By coincidence, the vicinity was to suffer serious damage from a German missile in World War 2, when on 2nd November 1944 the formation at Hampton Court Junction was put out of action for two days. Electrification caused the removal of the Prentice equipment for radio-controlled cab signalling, used for experiments on the branch in 1913 and 1915.

Thames Ditton Up side, showing the stationmaster's house, about 1910. *Commercial postcard*

Throughout the 1920s and 1930s Hampton Court had three trains an hour working to and from Waterloo in 32 minutes, calling at all stations. This excellent service fostered residential growth around Thames Ditton station and on the riverside land west of the terminus, a process further assisted by the opening in 1933 of a motor road from a new Hampton Court Bridge to the Kingston by-pass. Low land prices on the flat gravel plain between the branch and the reservoirs at West Molesey and the favourable economic conditions for housebuilding in the early 1930s generated the construction of low-cost houses at some distance from the station, though the developers liked to use its name. Nearer the line, in East Molesey and Thames Ditton, prices for small detached and semi-detached properties were a little higher.

All this activity led the commercially-aware SR management to look to the exploitation of its assets at Hampton Court station. Between 1935 and 1936 the platforms were shortened and the goods yard brought into a smaller area, but a proposal to use some of the land so released for the construction of an Odeon cinema which the SR was prepared to subsidise to the extent of £3,000, did not materialise. The rearrangements of this period, which also included lengthening of the platform canopies, were in part to accommodate the alignment of the approach to the new river bridge; tracks were cut back at the river end, where a handsome ornamental wall was erected across the width of the station in 1934.

Changes since World War 2 followed a pattern which has become familiar to the reader. After road competition had reduced traffic to a trickle and solid fuel distribution had been rationalised, the goods yard closed on 3rd May 1965. Wider car ownership combined with higher standards of living worked to erode the long-standing summer and bank holiday pleasure traffic. Off-peak frequency was reduced to two trains an hour on 15th September 1958, but with rush-hour loadings sustained by a post-war increase in housing density and the overbuilding of Hurst Park race-course in 1967, peak service was increased to four an hour from 10th July 1967. With an additional call (Berrylands, opened on the main line for new housing north-east of Surbiton in 1933) the Waterloo journey now took one minute longer than in 1916, but working was eased by the introduction of colour light signals on the branch from 22nd March 1970, controlled from a new power box at Surbiton. Hampton Court, reduced to a gate box, was abolished from 23rd September 1979 when cctv was installed to enable the level crossing to be operated from the Surbiton panel.

Reductions in train services followed a continuing decline in traffic: cuts in peak hour services from June 1981; Sunday trains in winter running only hourly from October 1992; and late evening frequency also widened out to hourly from October 1993. the branch still handles one special traffic, that produced by the annual Garden Festival and Flower Show at Hampton Court, an event inaugurated in 1990 and initially subsidised by Network SouthEast. An enhanced service is operated on this occasion to and from Waterloo and some special trains from elsewhere are worked through over the branch.

As the only British railway ever built expressly to serve a royal palace, the Hampton Court branch provides the fastest public transport link to this tourist attraction from central London but this fact is little known; for many years the rail service has received no properly-focussed publicity with the result that, as at Windsor, most visitors travel by motor coaches and cars, imposing extra strains on an already overloaded road system.

Ex-GWR AEC railcar at Staines West; looking to buffers, 18th July 1955. *Alan A Jackson*

West Drayton to Staines

Serving the very fringe of the Metropolitan Police District, the Staines & West Drayton Railway had much more of the country branch about it than most other London railways. Its beginnings were complex, evolving as they did from the not uncommon scenario of local interests seeking to improve railway accommodation by trading upon the rivalry between two or more main line companies. A small market town on the London to Exeter Road at an important crossing of the Thames, Staines had lost status with the arrival of the railway age, but the opening of the Windsor, Staines & South Western Railway, linking it with London on 22nd August 1848 had encouraged local industries. By the mid-1860s, these included a large brewery, mustard mills, a papier mâché factory and the world's first linoleum works, producing the floor covering invented in the town in 1860–63 by Frederick Walton. With the GWR main line only some six miles to the north across easy railway country, the business interests in the town, hoping to lower freight rates and open up new outlets, were turning their attention to a route first selected by three unsuccessful Uxbridge & Staines bills of the 1840s. After the failure of a bill deposited in 1863 for a West Drayton & Staines Railway, one of two similar schemes deposited in November 1865 became the Colnbrook Railway Act of 1866, a single standard gauge line southwards from the south side of the GWR station at West Drayton to the LSWR Windsor branch at Staines Moor, half a mile north-west of the town. The proposals included a line passing below the GWR at West Drayton to allow through running from Uxbridge to Staines. On 13th July 1866 the GWR agreed to work the line for half the gross receipts, but the powers to build it expired before the £60,000 capital could be raised.

A second act of 7th July 1873, with one of the 1866 promoters still in play, authorised a 5m 2f 9.2ch Staines & West Drayton Railway over the same route, joining the LSWR 43ch northwest of the bridge over Staines High Street, but omitting the through link to the Uxbridge branch at West Drayton. This time the LSWR reacted with some vigour to the invasion of its territory, opposing the bill by alleging that the proposed junction at Staines would be dangerous and the extra traffic impossible to accommodate at Staines station. These objections produced a clause in the act which required that the line should be built only to standard gauge, which would restrict any expansionist tendencies on the part of a still largely broad gauge GWR.

The Staines & West Drayton Railway company formed by the 1873 act suffered a long period of negotiations and frustrations before giving birth to its line. Extensions of time had to be obtained in 1878 and 1881, the last act also altering the GWR junction to one on the north side of the main line at West Drayton, a change required by the widening into Paddington. Still without much hope and forlornly casting about for sustenance, the S&WDR directors even wooed LNWR share-holders early in 1882 with a proposal that their line might form part of a *Grande Ceinture* round the west side of London which would bring LNWR trains from Watford via the proposed Uxbridge & Rickmansworth Railway, the GWR branch to Uxbridge and new lines south of Staines, on to the SER and LBSCR via Leatherhead and Dorking. This move did nothing to improve relationships with Waterloo, driving the S&WDR deeper into the embraces of the still somewhat reluctant GWR. An agreement was at last signed on 13th November 1882, which secured that the GWR would work and maintain the line after the first six months, in return for half the gross receipts. Perhaps not wishing to upset its neighbour unduly, the GWR protested that the sharing of Staines station would cause delays, insisting that there should be a 'proper and sufficient independent terminal pas-senger and goods station'. A bill deposited in the same month included provision for this separate Staines station and approach, also for a connection to the LSWR nearer to that company's Staines station coming off the West Drayton line on the south side of the Windsor branch. Also in the bill were a line into the linoleum factory and extensions to Egham and Chertsey. Predictably the LSWR opposed, but local interests were able to convince the parliamentary committees that their town required further railway accommodation after the S&WDR agreed to drop the proposed extensions. In that form the act was passed on 2nd August 1883.

Although a start was made with construction during 1882, the little company's troubles were not yet over. A squabble with the contractors drained away funds in legal action, culminating in the appointment of a receiver. When the GWR came to the rescue with more capital, all seemed well, but that was soon exhausted and no more was forthcoming.

Somehow the section between West Drayton and Colnbrook was finished in time to allow the GWR to start six passenger trains a day on weekdays from Saturday 9th August 1884. Further progress was retarded by the financial crisis, exacerbated by the withdrawal of labour when wages could not be paid. In this dark time, the engineer, A. Thuey, saved £1,150 by adapting a house owned by Charles Waring Finch (of Finch & Rickman's Mustard Mills) as the Staines terminus. Opened for public traffic on 2nd November 1885, the completed line was served by nine trains each way to and from West Drayton on weekdays. At first passenger business was distinctly thin; few wished to cross this relatively underpopulated stretch of outer London, and apart from a sprinkling of commercial and professional liaisons between Uxbridge and Staines, or those seeking destinations on the GWR west of London, the trains were all but empty. Freight traffic was also slow to develop, despite the provision of yards at Colnbrook and Staines, but things gradually improved. In May 1887 the authorised line was built across the river into the works of the now prosperous Staines Linoleum Company, yet even this had to be shared with the LSWR, which was also invited into the factory premises.

The 6½-mile single track left the GWR Uxbridge branch 21ch west of West Drayton station, falling at 1 in 104 and curving sharply to get beneath the main line. After bridging the Colne, a south-westerly course was pursued, bringing the track into Colnbrook station, which was north of the Bath Road and east of the village. Between the platforms was a passing loop and, on the Down side, dutch-gabled, the 'proper and sufficient dwelling house' required by the 1882 agreement. A signal box to the south controlled the goods yard, loop and level-crossing of the Bath Road, which was spaced wide enough for the second track that was never added.

Now going due south, the branch skirted the eastern boundary of the Poyle Explosives Works before crossing the lonely Stanwell and Staines Moors between the Wyrardisbury and Colne rivers. After climbing at 1 in 133 to bridge the Windsor line, it ran south-east, parallel to that line, before making a final curve southwards into its terminus just north of Church Street, Staines. A single long platform with a short canopy at the south end together with loading dock, run round road, goods shed and small engine shed, filled the back garden of Mr Finch's house. Behind the house another canopy sheltered passengers as they passed through the back door into the hall and out again through the front door. From the booking hall, stairs led to what remained of the domestic rooms.

With passenger business stagnant, there was a need to clutch at every straw. After closure of the ranges on Wimbledon Common, a Metropolitan Rifle Range Company was formed in 1890 to build ranges near London for those Volunteers who did not wish to go out to Bisley. That these new ranges were sited on Staines Moor, just west of the S&WDR was not unconnected with the existence of a shared director-ship. Subject to the S&WDR paying 4½ per cent interest in accordance with the 1882 agreement, the GWR agreed to construct a halt, which was opened with the ranges on 1st March 1892. A simple timber platform about 20ft long, devoid of shelter and furnished only with a seat, lamp and back fence, its only access was by field path from the range pavilion in Moor Lane. During its whole life it remained a conditional stop, where for many years trains set down and took up in daylight on weekdays only. Tempted away from geographical accuracy by the empty charm of alliteration, the Rifle Range Company preferred Runemede Range and the halt was so-called until 9th July 1934 when it became simply Runemede. Exactitude was finally established from 4th November 1935 with the renaming to Yeoveney.

By then possessing over eighty five per cent of the S&WDR issued stock of £161,640, the GWR acquired powers in its 1900 act to take over and dissolve the company, exercising them from 1st July that year. At this time there were still only about eight trains daily to and from West Drayton, where they shared the north side island platform with the Uxbridge trains. One of the Down workings ran mixed traffic, restricted to six vehicles, a feature which lasted until the 1930s. Sunday service started in 1887 with four trains each way. Once the GWR assumed full

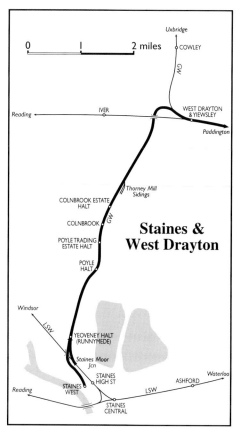

Staines & West Drayton

Colnbrook station, looking north, with loco 1436 on Staines train, 25th September 1956.
Alan A Jackson

control there were some improvements, so that by 1912 there were 14 workings each way, a few to and from Paddington and Aldgate (between 1904 and 1911 there were even through runs between Staines and Victoria). One-class steam auto-trains, introduced on Sundays from 1st October 1914, were later extended to weekdays, so that by 1st January 1916 all but one train was of this type. In October 1921 there were 16 journeys each way daily between departures from West Drayton at 07.23 and 22.28. On Sundays there were seven each way between 10.12 and 21.52.

Use of the Staines Linoleum Factory for military purposes and opening of camps around Staines provided new traffics in 1914–18, but afterwards the more relaxed tempo of what was essentially a country branch quickly returned. Freight remained more important than passengers, not that the latter were neglected. At the time when the GWR was trying to extract the last ounce of business from its investment in branch lines by opening many new halts, the Staines line was not overlooked. On 1st June 1927, Stanwell Moor & Poyle Halt (renamed Poyle for Stanwell Moor on 26th September 1927) was opened 65ch south of Colnbrook to serve the Explosives Works, Stanwell Moor village and scattered farmhouses west of the line. This had a crude wooden shelter, lacking the elegance of the more usual GWR 'pagoda'. Service on weekdays remained at about the same level through the 1920s and 1930s, but rush-hour workings of five coaches, generally hauled by 2–6–2T, ran to and from Paddington, missing the branch halts. Sunday service was built up to 14 each way between 09.02 and 21.58 from West Drayton.

A solitary passenger enjoys the spartan facilities of Yeoveney; the post for raising the signal lamp to stop a train after dark can be seen at the corner of the platform. Looking to West Drayton, 25th September 1956. *Alan A Jackson*

War again brought change. In a move which recalled the wildest dreams of the harassed S&WDR board, the authorities decided that the line had some strategic potential, seeing a role in bringing traffic from the north and midlands safely round into Feltham Yard or other points in south and south-east England should the London river crossings be severed by enemy action. To achieve this, a curve closely following the 1873 act alignment was built from a point south of Yeoveney Halt to the SR Windsor branch at Staines Moor Junction near Staines GWR station. At West Drayton double track was installed from the junction with the Uxbridge branch to the bridge under the main line, where a small signal cabin was erected. All was ready in June 1940, but no use was made of the new link until 15th September 1940 after the Metropolitan Extension at Snow Hill (Holborn Viaduct) had been blocked by bomb damage. Thereafter for a few years, surprised train crews found their freight trains routed this way to and from the GWR at Greenford, but this ceased with the end of the war and the junction at Staines Moor was taken out on 16th December 1947. Whilst saplings grew strongly between the rails there was some talk of closing the old GWR terminus (known as Staines West since 26th September 1949), diverting the West Drayton service to the SR station over the wartime link. No doubt Waterloo again showed resistance to this, pleading it could not be done until capital was available to improve the cramped Staines Central.

A traumatic change in the character of the whole area came with the establishment in 1946 of London Airport (Heathrow) when the once sequestered frontiers of Middlesex and Buckinghamshire became ever more befouled by the incessant row of low-flying aircraft with their attendant fumes. Factory estates also appeared along

GWR 0-4-2 tank loco at Staines West, 20th July 1952. The main station building here (not shown) began life as a private residence and is now in use as commercial offices. *R. C. Riley*

the branch between Colnbrook and Poyle. To serve one of these, Poyle Estate Halt, with a 50ft platform and tiny canopy supported on concrete posts was opened on 4th January 1954, just over ¼ mile south of Colnbrook. Trains stopped at rush hours, but at other times by request only. On the same day, two extra journeys were provided, making 18 each way daily, 12 on Sundays. Steam remained supreme on this untypical London line where most trains were push-pull units of two saloons (some former GWR railmotors) powered by 14xx 0-4-2T. Freight was usually handled by 57xx 0-6-0PT and 61xx 2-6-2T. South of the factory estate belt, the line retained much of its rural character through the 1950s, although its peace was increasingly threatened by aircraft noise. Yeoveney Halt, a miraculous survival from a more gentle, romantic era, was now frequented only by occasional fishermen and lovers. Stopping a train here as evening mists rose over the fields was an experience unique in the metropolitan area. Once light had faded, it was necessary to raise the lamp on the post provided; somehow the driver always *did* stop, even if occasionally he had to reverse and trundle back because the passenger was noticed only as the engine passed the platform. This choice relic of GWR country branch line practice was finally closed 'due to the cost of repair' after the last trains had called on 13th May 1962.

Other more important changes were made in these post-war years. Freight movements south of Colnbrook ceased on 30th October 1953 when all consignments were transferred to Staines SR yard. By some bureaucratic oversight, the signal box at Staines West was left open although there was never more than one train on the line at a time south of Colnbrook and the engine shed had closed in June 1952.

GWR AEC-type diesel cars appeared on some passenger workings in January 1954, taking over all weekday services outside peak hours in the following year. Steam survived otherwise until 5th October 1958, after which the whole service was operated by new BR diesel cars. Passenger traffic reached its peak; although daily journeys remained at 18 each way on weekdays, on Sundays there were now 16 trips to and from Staines West with a last departure from West Drayton at 22.43. Except for the first three weekday trains in the morning and two in the evening which called at Poyle Estate and Yeoveney halts, notice to the guard at West Drayton or Staines West was necessary if one wished to alight at these places at other times; 'passengers desiring to join should give the necessary hand signal to the driver'. Yet another halt was opened on 1st May 1961 about ½ mile north of Colnbrook. Worked on a conditional stop basis, Colnbrook Estate Halt had a short platform and shelter much as those of its immediate neighbour.

Traffic results in 1960 were such that BR could not make a convincing case for closure when this was suggested as a means of reducing the cost of the Staines By-Pass road then under construction. But as Beeching's accountants were able to show in 1962 that by their standards the branch was not 'paying its way' passenger closure was listed in the *Reshaping of British Railways* report of 1963. Extra workings at rush hours were taken off in October 1964 and the last passenger train ran on 27th March 1965 (Sunday working had ceased late in 1961). Alternative public transport was provided by buses which followed a meandering route between West Drayton and Staines.

Meanwhile freight underwent a minor revival. During 1964 the Staines West goods yard was dismantled to make room for an oil storage depot served by a siding accommodating 12 tank wagons. From October that year freight trains were again seen south of Colnbrook, bringing oil from Purfleet to the new depot. In 1975 there were 15 trains a week carrying between 1,200 and 1,500 tons of oil. Colnbrook itself was in that year receiving oil trains at an average of 75 a week (6,000 to 7,500 tons) and also about 10 tons of scrap metal a week. At the same time oil was coming into Thorney Mills, between Colnbrook and West Drayton, in an average of 24 trains a week (1,000 tons) and ten trains a week of stone (3,000 tons) were also arriving. This depot also sent out scrap metal at the rate of 360 tons a week. Traffic to and from the Cory/Shell heating oil depot at Staines continued until 16th January 1981 when the tracks south of Poyle were abandoned to the construction works of the M25 motorway. The Staines oil depot was then connected to the Staines-Windsor branch and the oil was brought in that way from 30th January 1981 until 24th June 1991, after which this rail traffic ceased.

At Colnbrook the public freight yard was closed in January 1966 and the station buildings and signal box were razed to the ground in January 1979. But the railway as far as Colnbrook and just beyond remained open for private sidings and oil trains, having its revenge on the government's roadbuilders, who were obliged to incur large sums of taxpayers' money to provide for its path under the vast concrete clover leaf junction of the M4 and M25. Oil tanker workings continued until 1982, then resumed from 1st March 1990 to 1993 when aviation fuel was delivered to a rail terminal just north of the Bath Road.

History shows the usefulness of this line for freight. Colnbrook oil terminal was again re-activated in September 1997 to receive fuel and there is also a possibility that its formation may one day be useful for rail access to the nearby Heathrow Airport.

Isleworth station, LSWR, Up side building, c.1905. *Commercial postcard*

The Hounslow Loop (map page 165)

J. N. Brewer, in his 1816 *Beauties of England & Wales* wrote of Hounslow, 'the chief dependence of the place is on the immense tide of road traffic, which rolls to and from the metropolis with surprising vehemence and bustle'. The first stage out of London, nine miles from Hyde Park Corner, and either side of the main route to Bath and the West, Hounslow was to be left stranded between the main railways to the west and south-west, and very quickly suffered a decline in business and status after these lines had opened. More self-sufficient was semi-industrial Brentford, river port and transhipment point for the Thames and Grand Junction Canal (later Grand Union Canal). Both places were obvious calling points for any railway attempting to fill the gap between the main lines; equally obvious was that the Richmond Railway (to be opened from Wandsworth to Richmond on 27th July 1846) was the most likely base for such a line, and that Staines and Windsor were the desirable objectives at the outer limits of this Thames Valley sector. There was however a slight geographical difficulty in serving all four points in a direct line from Richmond as a glance at a map of the area will show.

An 1844 proposal for a railway from Richmond to Staines received support from the Richmond Company, but this and rival schemes did not emerge from the Parliamentary session of 1846. A new enterprise, the Windsor, Staines & South Western, formed late in that year with LSWR support, was authorised in 1847 to build from Richmond to Windsor (Datchet) via Staines, together with a 7¼-mile double-track loop from the Richmond Railway at Barnes through Brentford and Hounslow, rejoining the main line at Hounslow Heath.

In a race with the GWR to reach the royal town, the main line was pressed ahead, opening to Staines and Datchet in August 1848. There was less urgency about the loop in a time of some financial difficulty, so it was not until 22nd August 1849 that the first passenger train ran between Barnes Junction and Smallbury Green, a temporary terminus a quarter-mile east of the present Isleworth station. The remaining section to Feltham Junction opened on 1st February 1850.

Joseph Locke engineered the loop line and Brassey contracted to build it. From Barnes Junction, it ran north-west, traversing the western end of the then very small village of Barnes and crossing the Thames on a cast iron bridge. Chiswick, the first station, was between the two estates of *Chiswick House* and *Grove House*, and almost a mile west of the village. Located on the Duke of Devonshire's land, its construction was enforced by the 1847 act, though for many years it was said to be of less benefit to the railway than the station that might otherwise have been built in Barnes village. After running behind Strand-on-the-Green, the line turned west to reach a station named Kew, sited on the main road from London to the west and opposite the road bridge to the village of that name on the Surrey bank. Running west and then south-west to avoid the built-up area of Brentford town, where a station was provided on the Hanwell road, the loop recrossed the main Bath road, into a station called Isleworth at the point where that parish ended and Hounslow began. Opened on 1st February 1850, it replaced Smallbury Green, closed the previous day. The station at Hounslow was 13½ miles from Waterloo, in open country to the south of the town on the road to Whitton village. Goods and coal yards were provided at Chiswick, Brentford and Hounslow.

At the opening of the line to Hounslow there were about 15 trains each way on weekdays and nine on Sundays, the Hounslow-Waterloo journey taking between 50 and 60 minutes, calling at all stations (there were a few semi-fasts taking slightly less time). For a short period (3rd April 1866 to 31st January 1867) users of the loop were able to travel between its stations and Ludgate Hill via Clapham and Longhedge Junctions, but there were only about two trains each way daily. The daily Down service over the loop in January 1867 terminated at Windsor (three) Feltham (seven) Hounslow (21, including two from Ludgate Hill) and Kew Bridge (one). There were also six North London Railway trains between Hampstead Road (Primrose Hill) and Kingston via the eastern end of the loop, a service to be mentioned in a moment.

As early as 1847 the promoters of the Richmond Railway, led by William Chadwick, had seen the importance of a connection between the loop and the northern main lines, enabling freight, particularly coal, to flow from the midlands and north on to the LSWR, and they hatched a scheme for a North & South Western Junction Railway from the loop at Brentford to join the LNWR at Harrow. Such a proposition required a great deal of careful political footwork to bring it to life, and after various adventures, alarums and excursions well described by R. A. Williams, a 3m 5f double track was opened between Kew Junction, on the loop about a quarter-mile west of Kew Bridge station, and West London Junction at Willesden, LNWR. Authorised by an act of 24th July 1851, this North & South Western Junction Railway was to be jointly worked and guaranteed by the LSWR and the LNWR. Freight began to pass over it on 15th February 1853, but passenger trains, operated by the NLR, did not appear until 1st August, working from separate platforms at Kew to Hampstead Road (Primrose Hill) or Fenchurch Street. A joint LSWR/LNWR service between Hounslow or Brentford and Euston was mooted, but it seems doubtful that it ever ran. Only slightly more substantial was the NLR service started on 1st June 1854 between Hampstead Road (connections to Fenchurch Street) and Windsor via Brentford and Staines. Infrequent, and not encouraged by the LSWR, it came to an end on 31st October that year.

To meet various threats of invasion from the north, the LSWR allowed trains of NLR stock to run from Hampstead Road to Twickenham from 20th May 1858 via Kew Junction (reverse), Chiswick, Barnes Junction (reverse) and Richmond. LSWR locomotives worked as far as Kew, the NLR taking over inwards from there. An equal number of trains worked over the same route were composed of LSWR carriages, and each company's trains called at both the Kew stations. In the summer in some years there were Sunday through workings from and to Bow.

This gesture was not enough to secure the LSWR's position and when further threatening schemes appeared in the 1859 session, the southern company pushed them away by promising (amongst other things) to build curves to eliminate the reversals at Kew and Barnes. Both curves, of 26ch double track, were opened on 1st February 1862, the first from Kew Curve East Junction on the N&SWJR to New Kew Junction on the LSWR, whilst the other joined the loop to the Windsor line just west of the Beverley Brook at Barnes (Chiswick Junction to Mortlake Junction). As already noticed, from the opening of Kingston station on 1st July 1863 the service was extended to there. The curves were not needed long for their intended purpose as they were rendered redundant by the opening of the LSWR's Kensington & Richmond Railway on 1st January 1869, a line which allowed a direct run between Willesden and Richmond via a new junction at South Acton. Although little used, the Barnes Curve was not removed until about 1881 and its site remained indicated by a row of cottage property known as 'Railway Side'. In contrast, the New Kew Curve continued busy with freight and special passenger workings and was also used by North London trains, which terminated on it at platforms opened on 1st February 1862 alongside the LSWR Kew station and connected to it by subway.

A steadily heavier freight movement passed over the original link between South Acton and Old Kew Junction, especially after connections had been made with the new Midland main line at Brent (Cricklewood) via the Midland & South Western Junction Railway, on 1st October 1868. Although a connection was opened between the N&SWJR and the GWR main line at Acton Wells on 1st January 1877 this did not prove of much use for through freight to and from the LSWR. More fruitful was a link between the M&SWJR and the new GCR main line at Neasden opened on 1st August 1899 which gave LSWR trains access to the GCR sidings at Neasden.

These links made the Hounslow loop the southern end of a strategic belt line joining the LSWR to the London docks and all the main lines north of the Thames, a circumstance which influenced the LSWR's choice of Feltham as a site for a large new marshalling yard completed in 1921–2. Before that, on 31st March 1870, the growth of freight traffic had required a third track between Kew Bridge and Windmill Road, Brentford, to accommodate trains coming off the N&SWJR. Nine years later, this track was signalled for two-way working. A second goods relief road was opened along this stretch by the Southern Railway on 7th May 1932, providing access to Brentford yard without fouling the loop tracks. Further widening between Brentford and Isleworth, authorised in the SR Act of 1930, was never completed, but in 1932 the SR extended the Up road loop at Kew from New Kew Junction to Chiswick Junction so that longer coal trains could be accommodated.

A second connection between the loop and the northern lines was made at the request of a House of Commons committee. This was the so-called Chiswick Curve opened on 1st January 1869, allowing working from the loop east of Kew Bridge (Chiswick Junction) to the Kensington & Richmond line just south of what is now Gunnersbury station (Brentford Road Junction). Passenger trains used it from 1st June 1870, running between Waterloo and Hounslow via Kensington (Addison Road), but from 1st November this circuitous service was diverted to Richmond via Kew Gardens, with a shuttle train affording connections between Gunnersbury and Hounslow.

To meet a District Railway move towards Twickenham, to be mentioned later, a line known as the Whitton Curve was opened on 1st January 1883, giving the loop its final form. This was a double track from Hounslow Junction just south of the station to Whitton Junction on the Windsor line, allowing a direct service to be worked from Hounslow to Twickenham and Richmond. From its opening day it carried trains running from Gunnersbury through Brentford, Hounslow, Twickenham, Richmond, and Kew Gardens back to Gunnersbury, replacing the Gunnersbury–Hounslow shuttle. On weekdays there were eight trains round each way increased in February 1883 to 15, with seven then added on Sundays, but from 1st November these trains ran only between Gunnersbury and Twickenham, via Hounslow.

Perhaps the most outstanding physical feature of the loop was the Thames bridge at Barnes, which the LSWR and SR put to good use during the annual Oxford and Cambridge boat race. On that day, train services over the bridge were stopped at the time of the race to allow spectators brought down from Waterloo in first-class only special trains to view the classic struggle from a comfortable grandstand. These workings continued into the 1930s; a note in *The Railway Gazette* of 29th March 1935 records that three trains were to be run that year from Waterloo, at 13.50, 13.59 and 14.06 for a return fare of half a guinea (52½p) inclusive of entertainment tax. With the increasing weight of locomotives and freight trains, it became necessary to strengthen the bridge, which was rebuilt in 1894–5 with wrought-iron bow-string girders and new brick abutments and piers. A public footpath was then added on the down train side. As on the Shepperton branch, the catchment area showed no strong residential development during the era of steam traction, when both the frequency and speed of the London service remained a constant source of dissatisfaction, especially amongst the inhabitants of Hounslow.

This town expanded only very slowly and unsuccessfully. In 1870 there were said to be 'many hundreds of empty houses in the neighbourhood' solely on account of the 'high railway fares and time wasted on the journey to London'. At this period most trains took about 55 minutes to reach Waterloo, it being a matter of complaint that the journey sometimes lasted as much as half an hour longer than that from Twickenham. Some improvements were made as the century drew to its end. By 1885 there were 29 Down and 26 Up trains on the Chiswick route to and from Waterloo, taking 35 to 45 minutes, and 21 each way on the Twickenham–Hounslow–Gunnersbury service, giving connections at Gunnersbury with the Richmond to Waterloo or Ludgate Hill service via Kensington (Addison Road). In June 1888 the Down loop service terminated variously at Staines (two), Feltham (13), and Hounslow (14) plus a half-hourly frequency between Gunnersbury and Hounslow with alternate trains going on to Twickenham.

Chiswick for Grove Park station, looking to Barnes, about 1950. *Lens of Sutton*

The latecomer: Barnes Bridge (1916) looking towards the rail bridge over the Thames, 30th March 1974. *Alan A Jackson*

Hounslow started to expand towards the railway and the Heath in the 1890s, so that by 1914 it was spilling over the line towards Whitton. A second public house, the *South Western*, had been opened south of the station to supplement the original *North Star* which dated from about the opening of the line. During the same period some of the large estates around Chiswick station were broken-up for building, houses appearing north of the station and between there and Kew Bridge. Around the bridge on the north bank, development was primarily commercial, centred on a market for local fruit, vegetables and flowers which after 1893 was housed in a building provided by the local authority. Brentford itself expanded very little but at Isleworth a new district called Spring Grove was laid out west of the line not long after it opened and there was also some villa development close to the station on the south side. The urban district of Heston-Isleworth, covering most of the line's catchment area at the outer end, experienced a 40 per cent growth between 1901 and 1911, from 30,863 to 43,313, but this owed more to the District Railway electric service and the London United tramcars than to the line we are considering.

These two powerful agents of suburban growth had both appeared in the Edwardian era. The District service will be described later, but the influence of the electric tramway was also significant. On 4th April 1901 the London United electric tramways reached Kew Bridge from Shepherds Bush and on 6th July the service was extended through Brentford and northern Isleworth to Hounslow. These tramcars, trundling along the main road every five minutes from 04.00 until 02.00, inevitably attracted much local custom away from the LSWR line which they virtually paralleled all the way from Hounslow to Gunnersbury. Almost overnight the receipts at Kew Bridge, Brentford, Isleworth and Hounslow stations dropped by a third. Nor was this the full extent of the attack, for on 13th August 1902 the LUT cars were plying along the road between Isleworth and Twickenham. It was not only the local traffic, such as that associated with the Pears Soap factory at Isleworth, the Brentford Market and shopping journeys into Hounslow and Brentford which the LSWR lost. Some London workers soon began to find it more convenient to take a tram from Brentford, Kew Bridge or Chiswick to Shepherds Bush or Hammersmith where new electric railways were available to convey them swiftly and comfortably to a large variety of destinations in the West End or the City, a route made all the more attractive by the availability of through booking facilities.

From 1st March 1910 the LSWR attempted to cut its losses by introducing steam railmotors on the long-established Twickenham/Feltham-Hounslow-Gunnersbury service. These cars had a lower carrying capacity than the LUT tramcar, having only eight first-class and 33 third-class seats, although it was possible to haul a trailer coach if business was brisk. Twickenham was reached in 20 minutes from Gunnersbury, about the same time as the more direct tramcar, and the road times to Isleworth and Hounslow were marginally bettered, but of course the trams at Hounslow were in the High Street, whilst the station was some distance to the south. In any case, as there were only 18 journeys each way (13 on Sundays) the railmotors offered no serious competition to the very frequent trams. However, the LSWR was planning something which would be more effective; by the beginning of 1912 it had decided to include the loop in its suburban electrification scheme.

In the meantime the London service, which had remained little changed since the 1880s, was slightly augmented and improved. In 1910 there were 37 Down trains terminating variously at Feltham (most often), Hounslow, Staines, Windsor, Twickenham or (one only) Ashford. In the Up direction there were 30 journeys and on Sundays 14 trains ran each way over the loop. Although a few semi-fasts reduced the through time from Hounslow to Waterloo to 37 or 39 minutes, most trains took 44 to 47 minutes. Five years later, the best time from Hounslow was 34 minutes in the Up direction and 29 back, but these were isolated examples and the average time was around 45 minutes. The 1914 Bradshaw showed only 11 railmotor runs each way between Gunnersbury and Twickenham or Feltham via Hounslow and this subsidiary service ceased altogether on 22nd February 1915. From that day, apart from Bank Holiday workings for several years, the Chiswick Curve saw only occasional excursion trains, troop trains and horsebox specials. On 29th May 1930 the SR Traffic Committee decided that these could be worked via Old Kew Junction,

LSWR steam rail motor car No. 9 at Hounslow, Down platform, c.1912 on the Gunnersbury–Hounslow–Twickenham/Feltham service, which operated from 1910 until 1915.

allowing closure of the curve together with the two controlling boxes at Chiswick Junction and Gunnersbury West. Tracks were eventually removed in July 1932 and two years later the land was sold to Chiswick Estates Ltd to be filled with blocks of flats.

Electric trains arrived on the loop on 12th March 1916, giving a substantial improvement in service. The route followed was a circular from Waterloo to Hounslow via Chiswick, returning via Richmond (headcode 'O') and also outwards to Hounslow via Twickenham, returning via Brentford (headcode 'Ō'). By the former, Hounslow was reached in 35 minutes and trains ran every half-hour from 05.22 to 00.05, every hour on Sundays. In the peak period some via Brentford ran non-stop between Barnes or Putney and Waterloo (these were steam-hauled until 31st July 1916).

With the electrification, Barnes at last received a centrally-sited station. Barnes Bridge, two 400ft platforms with timber buildings, was opened on the first day of electric working. It was situated by the riverside, at the south end of the bridge over Barnes Terrace and the river. A pleasing street level entrance pavilion in stone and red brick with an iron and glass awning blended well with the balconied Georgian and early Victorian houses of the Terrace. The booking office windows were in a tiled subway through the embankment, giving this part the appearance of an Underground station of the period. In recent years the street-level facilities have been replaced by a small ticket office on the Up platform, enabling the station to be worked by one man.

During World War 1 the loop was very busy with special traffics. Military camps were established at Chiswick and Hounslow, together with an airfield on Hounslow Heath. In the early months of the war, very heavy troop traffic passed on to the N&SWJR via Hounslow, and troop trains and military freight movements continued to keep the line busy for the next four years.

A substantial amount of residential development was fostered by the electric trains, principally between Brentford and the outer end of the loop in the late 1920s and early 1930s. Immediately south-west of Brentford, this growth was also associated with the opening in 1925 of the Great West Road and the factories which that new artery attracted. To serve this new district, a cheaply-built station with two 400ft side platforms was opened at Syon Lane on 5th July 1931. On both sides of the line between Isleworth and Feltham Junction large estates of small houses were erected for private sale by R. T. Warren, Wimpey, and others in the 1930s, so that by 1939 the whole area between the Staines Road at Hounslow and the Windsor line just west of Twickenham was a sea of new houses sold at prices between £500 and £1000. The hamlet of Whitton, transformed to a new suburb, received its own station on the Windsor line in 1930, but many of the new residents on the northern side of the district used Hounslow station.

North of Old Kew Junction a new Kew Bridge goods yard was opened in 1929 and enlarged in the following year, whilst a new goods yard opened at Hounslow in 1931 at a cost of £14,500 had to be enlarged in 1937–8. Hounslow passenger station received in 1933 a passimeter booking office for the new business on the Down side, with additional parcels accommodation, and extra sidings for electric stock stabling were completed here in 1939.

Wood Lane Crossing, Isleworth, 30th March 1974. *Alan A Jackson*

London's Local Railways

Down side buildings, Brentford, LSWR, disguised as Brentford Central, BR, 11th January 1975.
Alan A Jackson

Use of the loop by freight trains moving between the northern and southern lines continued to be brisk until well into the 1960s, making it a mecca for engine-spotters or railway observers (according to age). In the 1950s for example, as many as 30 different types of steam locomotive could be seen between Old Kew Junction and Feltham Junction, originating from all the old companies other than the GWR. The pattern of freight movement at this time varied little from that which had prevailed in earlier decades: domestic and industrial fuels southwards, cement and manufactured goods northwards. In 1953 there were some 30 trains each way between the Feltham yard and the yards at Neasden, Temple Mills, Brent, Cricklewood, Willesden and Ferme Park (Hornsey). Some journeys to and from the latter were worked via the Metropolitan Widened Lines; Chiswick and the section of the loop between Kew Bridge and Barnes was also used by 11 trains a day each way between Battersea and Hither Green and Brent yards.

Local goods traffic ebbed in the late 1950s. Chiswick yard was the first to go (14th June 1958) with Brentford Central following on 4th January 1965 and the old yard at Kew Bridge on 3rd April 1967. Hounslow New Yard closed on 6th February 1967 but the Old Yard lasted until 6th May the following year. Movements to and from Feltham Yard also declined in importance and during 1965 the connection to the third and fourth (N&SWJR) tracks east of Brentford was taken out of use. Closure of Feltham Yard followed in January 1969. Inter-regional movements by no means disappeared, and after June 1966 there were summer Saturday through passenger workings between Sheffield and Portsmouth and Bournemouth via Brent, Acton Wells, Old Kew Junction and the loop. The other arm of the Kew triangle via New Kew Junction had no advertised passenger service since the summer Saturday Nottingham–Ramsgate trains of 1965-8, but during the spring and autumn it saw twice-weekly trains of senior citizens from Newcastle and other northern towns on their way to and from cheap holidays at Eastbourne, Hastings and the Kent Coast resorts.

Off-peak passenger traffic on the electric services had been light for many years; three-car and even two-car trains have on occasions sufficed to carry it. Until the end of World War 2, the maximum train length was two three-car sets, but from 15th November 1948, eight-car trains could be accommodated at all seven stations.

'Rationalisation' and economy cuts have been very much to the fore on the Loop in recent years. From 19th August 1987 the ticket offices at all the stations except Chiswick (open in morning peak hours) and Hounslow (open most of the day) were closed and all station staff withdrawn. For a time conductor guards issued tickets on the trains but these were subsequently withdrawn after automatic ticket machines had been installed at the stations and penalty fares introduced. Alas, the prevalent late 20th century youthful vandalism which is encouraged by leaving stations and structures unsupervised soon set about persistent wreckage of the machines, causing conductor guard ticket issue on trains to be restored from mid-1994. The closure of ticket offices did however make it possible to rescind another economy measure; from 17th May 1987 Sunday trains were restored at Barnes Bridge and Syon Lane. Unstaffed stations, intimidating at night, do not encourage traffic and the management's reflex action of reducing the basic hourly service to hourly in late evening from 4th October 1993 seemed hardly likely to improve patronage at those times.

With its procession of steam-hauled freights and other special workings to and from north of the Thames now gone, with colour lights and track circuit block replacing semaphore signals in 1974 and with lifting barriers at level crossings instead of manually-worked gates, the Loop has lost much of its special atmosphere.

Further depredation of the somewhat old-fashioned aura of this line, with its many reminders of the LSWR, took place in 1989–90 when all the stations were subjected to a drastic economy treatment, euphemistically known as 'refurbishing'. At Barnes Bridge the roofing was removed from the platform approach ramps, the waiting rooms were opened out and the street level buildings were converted to offices. Surprisingly, the old platform canopies were spared. The Tite station house on the Up side at Chiswick was quite pleasingly restored and let out as offices, its platform canopy retained. A converted outbuilding housed the ticket office. At Kew Bridge the handsome Italianate street level building was sold out of railway use; the footbridge, retained without its glazing, was reached by a new entrance alongside the old station house. Brentford suffered a severe mauling. Both platforms were stripped of their canopies and small shelters with glazed arch roofs installed in their stead. The covered footbridge here was completely removed, obliging passengers to take the long way round via the road bridge and approach yard. The station house on the Down side was left in a much mutilated state. At Syon Lane all the SR structures were removed, basic shelters and a new footbridge appearing in their place. Isleworth lost its Up platform canopy and its neglected empty station house on the Up side soon became a victim of vandalism and graffiti daubing. At Hounslow the station house, also on the Up side, was let for non railway use, the ticket office moved to a converted outbuilding. Here platform canopies were retained on both sides. In 1981, further south, at the two-way junction with the Windsor and Reading line, a steeply-graded overline bridge was erected on the east side to allow development inside the railway-bound triangle.

This now rather colourless but useful line no doubt has an assured future especially as it has some value as diversionary route for through services but the decline in traffic at most of the intermediate stations is a cause for concern.

London's Local Railways

The crude corrugated iron and timber of the first District Railway provision at Northfields, just before the rebuilding of 1911. An eastbound train is leaving. *London Transport Museum*

Hounslow and Heathrow Airport

Railway promoters were much attracted to the yawning gap between the LSWR line to Staines and the GWR main line. Although it contained little population but the contiguous settlements of Hounslow, Isleworth and Brentford, served since 1850 by the LSWR loop already considered, Windsor lay temptingly to the west, while the inner end was sufficiently close to west London to make the more optimistic dream of suburban development.

Parliament had authorised a second line to Hounslow as early as 1866. This Hounslow & Metropolitan Railway formed a 3½-mile Western extension of the Acton & Brentford Railway which had been sanctioned a year earlier to run from the GWR at Acton to pass south of Ealing and join the Southall-Brentford branch just north of Brentford. Leaving the Acton & Brentford at Boston Lane, the Hounslow & Metropolitan would have passed over the Brentford branch, throwing off on the west side a four-furlong spur towards Southall. Then proceeding south-west, parallel to the LSWR Hounslow loop but about ¾-mile to the north, it kept clear of the built-up area along the Bath Road, turning west at Hounslow to terminate on the Bath Road opposite Hounslow Barracks. The act allowed for mutual facilities for passenger and goods traffic between the new line and the GWR.

In the financial panic which followed the failure of Overend, Gurney & Co it proved impossible to raise capital for this speculative venture into territory already served by the LSWR. Although extension of time was obtained in 1869, the scheme failed, but the attraction remained and similar lines were sought in unsuccessful bills deposited for the sessions of 1875 and 1876, the first with connections to the MDR and the Hammersmith & City instead of the GWR, and the second to join the H&CR only. After the Metropolitan District Railway had succeeded in obtaining powers for an Ealing extension in 1877, the landowners who were behind the Hounslow schemes sought to connect their proposed branch with that railway in unsuccessful bills in the 1878 and 1879 sessions. Commenting that the 1878 scheme was intended to go on to Windsor, *Herapath's Railway Journal* thought that the Hounslow line would not pay.

A similar bill was finally authorised by the Hounslow & Metropolitan Railway Act of 26th August 1880. In this the first directors and subscribers were named as Henry Daniel Davies (a landowner and building developer of *Spring Grove*, Isleworth), Jason Gurney (of *Percy Lodge*, Hounslow) and James Oliver Mason (of Grosvenor Road, Pimlico). Their company was to build a 5½-mile branch from the MDR Ealing Extension just south of the present Ealing Common station to the Bath Road opposite Hounslow Barracks over virtually the same route as the 1866 scheme and the western part of the unbuilt Acton & Brentford. Capital was £210,000 with borrowing powers for a further £70,000. An agreement made with the MDR on 3rd June 1880, scheduled to the act, provided for that company to work, manage and maintain the Hounslow & Metropolitan as a passenger line in return for half the gross receipts after deduction of passenger duty. The H&MR also got ten per cent of the MDR portion of fares passing from its line on to the MDR system. Both payments were limited to 4½ per cent of the H&MR's capital outlay, set at a maximum of £250,000.

At this time the MDR was flushed with enthusiasm for suburban expansion, which it saw as a means of increasing the return on its heavily capitalised inner London lines, although the company was by no means always clear how to raise money for suburban adventures. The MDR looked with particular envy at the supposedly rich residential territory of the LSWR, and with the Ealing Extension opened in 1879, and the Hounslow line secured in 1880, it spent some time in 1881 brooding on how to use the latter to reach Twickenham and Kingston. The company's intentions were clarified in a bill deposited in November which sought a 2½-mile line southwards from the H&MR at Hounslow, passing east of Kneller Hall to join the LSWR Kingston loop between Twickenham and Strawberry Hill. For good measure a spur to the LSWR 750yd east of that company's Hounslow station was included. It was apparently intended that the line should be used to work a circular service to and from Earls Court via Hounslow, Kingston, Wimbledon, and Fulham. Not surprisingly this bill met fierce opposition from the LSWR, which was able to kill it on promising to build a Hounslow–Whitton curve to provide the Hounslow–Twickenham facility. Construction was nevertheless begun in 1882 from the northern end, on land which had been bought in the name of the H&MR early that year: this may seem something of a paradox, but it was always possible to build a railway without parliamentary sanction on land obtained by voluntary agreement, provided the tracks did not cross a public highway or infringe on tidal waters. In this case the tracks were brought into a station high above Hounslow High Street's northern pavement where the rails pointed menacingly towards the first-class riverside territory of the LSWR – but although the bridge abutment was built, the lines did not cross the road. In fact parliamentary authority for this 2f 5ch spur from the H&MR was obtained in the Hounslow & Metropolitan Railway Act of 29th June 1883, by which time the work was completed and trains were running into the station at its southern end.

This first section of the H&MR, from the Hounslow High Street station to the junction with the MDR near Ealing had been given priority and its 4m 37ch of double track were in public use from 1st May 1883. At the inner end most trains terminated at Mill Hill Park (Acton Town from 1st March 1910) but until 31st December inclusive some ran through to Mansion House. Thenceforward, for most of the period of steam operation, through workings terminated at Earl's Court. Most trains on the new branch called at the intermediate stations of Boston Road (Boston Manor from 11th December 1911), Osterley (later sometimes called Osterley Park or Osterley & Spring Grove) and South Ealing, all of which opened with the line. Boston Road station was in open fields on the west side of the main road between Brentford and Hanwell; Osterley, also in open country, was near the southern gate of Osterley Park and close to the northern part of Davies' ambitious Spring Grove villa colony which had grown only very slowly since its beginnings in the early 1850s. South Ealing was on the main Ealing to Brentford road at a point already touched by the outskirts of the Queen of Suburbs.

Dull things in grey stock bricks and slate, lit by round arched windows, these stations had little architectural merit. The only other feature of note was the double span lattice girder bridge over the canalised river Brent and the GWR branch. Hounslow terminus, later to be called Hounslow Town, was reached by a brick viaduct of some 20 arches which ended abruptly at the unfinished bridge over the High Road. Two side platforms here were protected by wide wood and glass canopies; a signal box, and locomotive siding with pit, coal storage, and water tank completed the rail-level installation. Below was a substantial station house in brick, its second floor and roof reaching rail level.

Hounslow Town station, District Railway, 1905. A bus station occupies this site today.
LT Museum

Exterior of the first Osterley station (Osterley & Spring Grove) on the west side of the overline bridge in Thornbury Road, 2nd May 1959. *Alan A Jackson*

The remaining 1m 44ch from Lampton Junction with the northern end of the Hounslow spur to Hounslow Barracks (renamed Hounslow West 1st December 1925) offered little promise of traffic. It was nevertheless opened as a single line on 21st July 1884, at first covered by a shuttle service of 12 trains a day each way which worked from Osterley, where a lay-by and locomotive run-round road was provided between the running lines west of the station. Hounslow Barracks had the usual H&MR stock brick station house and booking hall, but only a single platform. There was a signal box, and another at Lampton Junction which also controlled the convergence of double and single track 200yd to the west of the junction.

Traffic results were poor in the early years, but it is amusing to reflect that many of the passengers were extracted from the LSWR stations at Hounslow, Isleworth and Brentford, only to be carried to London over that company's property between Hammersmith and Turnham Green.

No doubt the Hounslow High Street spur was completed because it was far advanced before the bill was lost, but as the awkwardness of operating this not particularly remunerative appendage soon niggled, it was closed after traffic on 31st March 1886. In its place the District opened next day a one-platform station named Heston-Hounslow on the single line at Lampton Road about half a mile to the west. This station, with its corrugated iron building, was a good deal less convenient for the centre of the town.

The District's enthusiasm for the line waned so much that until the beginning of the twentieth century it was left to languish on a diet of one train an hour (two in peak periods); in 1900 there were still only 22 trains daily each way. Building was discouraged; a District driver recalled in his old age that 'builders got it in the neck properly', so much so that some were obliged to let rent-free to keep their property from deteriorating and 'many DR men got nice little houses this way'.*

* Memories of District driver Membery, *TOT Magazine*, February 1929.

A *Railway Magazine* contributor visiting the branch in 1901 thought it must be one of the most cheaply-worked lines in the United Kingdom. Although each station was manned with ticket collector, porter, and a youth, seldom was more than one of these visible, while the stations seemed to have received no paint since their opening 18 years earlier. Only one five-coach train ran each hour for most of the day, and single line working seemed a possible further economy. He did have a good word to say about the connections at Mill Hill Park (now Acton Town): the Up branch and Down main line trains arrived here about the same time, after which the branch train went forward, the locomotive running round whilst the Down train left for Ealing; the branch train then entered the Down platform to await the arrival of the Up train from Ealing. The writer had visited the derelict Hounslow Town station, finding that the platforms outside the covered portion had disappeared, their old supporting pillars fast decaying. A short section of the spur was still connected at Lampton Junction but all other track had been removed. Beneath the roof of the station, over the remains of the platforms, the laundry of the occupants hung above their strolling rooster and his hens. In the station yard and arches of the viaduct were Urban District Council dustcarts, steam rollers and other vehicles.

This account also mentions what appears to have been an experimental installation of automatic signalling in preparation for the planned electrification of the MDR. The writer noted starting signals without arms and signals not connected to the station boxes, which remained 'off', only changing to 'on' after the passage of each train, when they were so held until the section was clear, an event announced by the ringing of an electric bell. He wrongly surmised that the numerous ramps he saw between the rails were to operate station indicators in the carriages, commenting sarcastically that none of the trains were fitted with such indicators.

It was indeed a portent, for this sleepy backwater was soon to see great changes. The opening of the London United electric tramways through the Brentford and Hounslow area which has already been noticed also caused serious depletion in MDR local traffic. The new American owners of the MDR quickly decided to buy the Hounslow & Metropolitan from Charles Morris and others, and to electrify it with the rest of the MDR. Both measures were authorised by the MDR Act of 21st July 1903. Vesting of the H&MR in the MDR took place on 1st July 1903, following acquisition for around £166,000 of a railway that had cost the original owners almost £330,000 to build.

In the face of electric tramway competition priority was now given to passenger traffic and a scheme to use the line also for freight was dropped. Preparations for this had been made in the MDR Act of 1900, which allowed the agreement of 1880 between the MDR and the H&MR to provide for the carriage of merchandise over the H&MR. The intention was to operate through goods trains between the GCR and the LSWR via a curve at Rayners Lane and a reopened Hounslow Town spur extended to join the LSWR at Hounslow. Instead, the Hounslow Town spur was reopened for passenger traffic only on 1st March 1903 with a service of two trains an hour, supplemented in the peak periods. These three-coach trains were joined at Osterley to five-coach trains which had started from Hounslow Barracks, the eight cars going through to Mill Hill Park or Mansion House. In the opposite direction, the three coaches for Hounslow Town were detached at Osterley for working to the High Street terminus by a second locomotive. These movements were facilitated by the restoration of the old loop siding between the main running lines at Osterley.

A permanent automatic signalling installation of the standard open-air Underground type was switched-in on 11th June 1905 preparatory to electric train working on the four-rail dc system from 13th June. The new services operated between Hounslow Barracks and Mill Hill Park or South Acton, trains running in and out of Hounslow Town via the original eastern curve and a new 7ch western curve (first proposed in the 1883 Bill) which rejoined the through line at Kingsley Road Junction. From this time no passenger trains ran on the through line between the two junctions.

Very soon the electric service, which was much more frequent (over 76 trains a day each way in 1907 compared with 22 in 1900) as well as faster and more reliable, was encouraging the construction of small houses at Hounslow, and between Brentford and Ealing. This growth was particularly rapid along the southern fringes of Ealing and at Little Ealing, its satellite south of the line, where a crudely-built halt with booking office hut on Northfield Lane bridge was opened on 16th April 1908. Despite the spread of little houses and the ugly bulk of the Ealing District Steam Laundry behind the eastbound platform, there were still some pleasantly shaded fields west and south-west of the new halt which attracted the patronage of Sunday School outings in high summer. But this did not last long, and in 1911 Northfield Halt was transformed to a full-scale station with concrete platforms and a spacious well-glazed entrance hall on the road bridge, named Northfields & Little Ealing on 11th December that year. Houses hereabouts, fitted with gas and venetian blinds, some of them in 'tree-lined roads', were advertised between 1904 and 1913 at £200-£300 leasehold or rents of 11s 6d (57½p) and 12s 6d (62½p) weekly.

Boston Manor for Brentford and Hanwell, looking north east, c.1912, with a two-car train at the eastbound platform.

From 1st January 1909 the basic service of two-car trains worked every ten minutes, connecting at Mill Hill Park with all Mansion House-Ealing Broadway trains. This ten-minute frequency was subsequently extended over the 1m 31ch single-line section at the western end of the branch, in and out of what was now a single platform line at Hounslow Town, where all points, sidings, the run-round road and signal box had been removed. To simplify operation it was decided finally to abandon the Hounslow Town spur, the terminus being closed after traffic on 1st May 1909. From the following morning its place was taken by a new station of the same name (renamed Hounslow East from 1st December 1925) 336yd to the north of the old, on the through line. This was less pretentious but more attractive than its predecessor, but although its garden-city style buildings by the District's architect H. W. Ford were eminently right for the surrounding suburban scene, the layout made no provision for traffic growth. The main building, of timber and brick under steeply pitched tiled roofs decorated with Tudor chimneys, snuggled tightly into the northern side of the embankment, hidden from the town centre.

A bus garage, opened by the London General Omnibus Company on 14th July 1912 on the site of the old terminus lasted until 1954 when London Transport resited it further north, adding a bus station, but missing the opportunity to provide a fully integrated road-rail interchange at this busy point despite the availability of owned land. The railway station, as we shall see, was little altered then, despite its inadequacy.

With the completion of the new Hounslow Town station, work began on extending the double track westwards from the country end of its platforms. Double-line working reached the east end of Heston-Hounslow on 24th April 1910, that station being converted to an island platform on 19th October 1912, and worked as normal double track from 1st November. This left 62ch of single line at the extremity of the branch which was soon required to carry 300 trains a day, in rush hours at intervals of six minutes but by that time train staff had been replaced by non-token working.

Another Edwardian improvement was the reconstruction of Mill Hill Park as Acton Town in 1910, providing two island platforms separated by a single track in the centre. When this was ready on 20th February, Hounslow trains shuttled in and out of the single central road, departing within three minutes of arrival. Passengers for London alighted on the left-hand platform, those for South Harrow or Ealing Broadway using the westbound platform at the right-hand side. To the north of this new station, from 10th February 1910, the Down Ealing trains used a new flyover above the two Hounslow roads.

One aspect of the road-rail co-ordination which followed the acquisition of the LGOC by the Underground Company in 1912 was the operation of a bus service between Hounslow Barracks station and Windsor via Colnbrook and Slough, realising an old District dream. This began on 14th July 1912 as an hourly Sunday service but such was the public response that it was quickly built up to a five-minute frequency for much of the day. By the autumn of 1912 it was running daily and other Sunday services to Staines, Burnham Beeches and Virginia Water had been added.

Several factors contributed to the early start of suburban development in this part of London after the end of World War 1: the opening of the Great West Road in 1925; the existence of extensive market gardens and orchards whose owners were ready to sell at low prices; and the well-established electric railway service via Acton

Town, with its frequent trains to the West End and the City. After a large housing estate had been started on the south side of the Bath Road opposite the terminus in 1926, building in this district continued until the early 1930s, by which time the formerly isolated Hounslow Barracks were completely surrounded by streets of small houses except in the south-west corner. Between the railway and the Great West Road, from Hounslow to Osterley, and either side of that road at Osterley, house building started in earnest in the early 1920s so that by 1935 the spread of development south of Osterley Park covered most of the area between the MDR and the former LSWR Hounslow Loop.

Nearer to London, the soggy valley of the Brent was left to golf courses, parks and sewage farms, but by the early 1930s there was a strip of building south-west from Hanwell past Boston Manor station into Brentford; Little Ealing had by then merged with South Ealing and the Underground's 'Northfields', whilst South Ealing had spread south of the railway for half a mile eastwards from its station.

As early as 1926 Hounslow East and Osterley stations were handling almost a million passengers a year, totals soon to grow substantially. The Underground Company's publicity of this period invited readers of the *Evening News* 'Why not live at Osterley?' quoting a house price range of £650 to £1,500, or plots at an average of £5 10s (£5.50) per foot frontage. Builders and buyers came forward after that in sufficient numbers to produce the results already sketched, so that between 1921 and 1939 the population of the larger part of the area served by the branch (Heston & Isleworth) increased from 47,500 to 102,000.

For its part, the Underground Company and its successors the LPTB, carried through a substantial amount of rebuilding and improvement between 1920 and 1939, gradually bringing the traffic capacity of the branch, with a few minor blemishes, well into line with the increased needs of the catchment area. Doubling of the remaining 62ch of single track at the outer end was completed on 28th November 1926, together with the reconstruction of the interior of Hounslow West, where from 11th December 1926 there were three tracks, one each side of an island platform and the other serving a platform capable of easy conversion to an island should traffic require. The dreary entrance building and station house of 1884 were swept away, to be replaced from 5th July 1931 by a striking Portland stone-dressed heptagonal hall with shops, in the early style of Charles Holden. Its impressive interior, decorated in gold and light scarlet, was floodlit at night. A bus lay-by and car park were provided outside.

By the late 1920s, when the Hounslow branch was carrying 170 trains each way daily, District Line capacity was severely taxed. With the availability of Government guaranteed cheap money in 1929 for projects which would relieve unemployment, the Underground Company decided to lessen the District's burden by extending Piccadilly line tube services over the branch as far as Northfields where a site was available for a much-needed rolling stock depot. To give unimpeded access to and from the depot, a second pair of tracks was to be laid between Acton Town junction and Northfields, and these were ready for use on 18th December 1932. At Acton Town the westbound Ealing & South Harrow line was carried over all the Hounslow branch tracks except the southernmost westbound road. The new depot, which could be entered from either end, was designed by Stanley Heaps, the Underground Company's staff architect, in co-ordination with Adams, Holden & Pearson. West of the overline road bridge the westbound running line was carried beneath a depot approach track. Completed early in 1932, the depot housed 304 tube and District line cars, about half this total under cover. There were 19 tracks, 450ft long, in the sheds, two allocated to car washing and two for maintenance, these equipped with lifting bays and travelling crane.

As the depot site was south of the running lines between Northfields and Boston Manor stations, the existing Northfields platforms blocked the area required for the depot approach tracks, requiring the reprovision of Northfields station on the east side of the overline road bridge. Two island platforms (District trains on the outer sides, Piccadilly on the inner) were brought into use on 19th May 1932 although the new station was not fully completed until December that year. For the street level, Adams, Holden & Pearson designed a lofty rectangular entrance hall in glass and brick, with a flat concrete lid and integral shops, all in similar style to the other new stations then being erected on the suburban extremities of the Piccadilly line. This fine structure was placed on the statutory list of buildings of special architectural interest in 1994, although its original lines had by then for some 14 years or so been cruelly marred by open steel stairways erected to meet modern 'belt and braces' safety requirements.

As the resiting of Northfields brought the London ends of its platforms a mere 265 yards or so from the country end of South Ealing, the relocation of that station further east was considered. The first proposal was to move it to the London side of the overline bridge, but by November 1930 a recommendation had been made to provide a new station about 710 yd east at the Ascott Avenue bridge. As a result it was thought necessary to make an eastern exit from Northfields into Weymouth Avenue. Accordingly a footbridge was built at the London end, together with a 6ft-wide uncovered footway along the north side of the cutting leading to a small and very basic ticket office building in Weymouth Avenue. However, as we shall shortly see, South Ealing stayed where it was, making this provision somewhat unnecessary and it was closed from 4th May 1942. The footway and little entrance building were demolished in 1959 but the associated footbridge at the eastern end of Northfields station survived until the end of 1985.

Piccadilly tube trains reached Hounslow West on 8th February 1932, but this was merely in substitution for some District workings to and from South Acton and Acton Town; the full service of Piccadilly trains running through to stations in north London did not start until 9th January 1933 to Northfields, and 13th March 1933 to Hounslow West. The basic frequency was six trains an hour, some not stopping at South Ealing and Boston Manor. District workings were confined to rush hours only, when there were eight an hour plus 15 Piccadilly trains to and from Northfields, with eight to and from Hounslow West. On 13th March some 70,000 free tickets were issued to persuade the public to sample the new service, many of the recipients using them for the 48-mile return journey between Hounslow West and Enfield West (now Oakwood) which was opened on the same day.

This was not the end of the modernisation programme. A new station was opened at Osterley on 25th March 1934, 200yd west of the original, with an entrance on the north side of the Great West Road. Although one of the least successful of the Adams, Holden & Pearson designs, marked by an ugly 70ft brick 'sign tower' carrying a concrete and glass lighting beacon, this is now a listed building. A pleasing feature was the curving of the glazed footbridge as it merged into the low booking hall. Until 1957, when some demolition took place, the old buildings in Thornbury Road remained intact, the entrance hall serving as a fruiterer's and greengrocer's shop, later as a bookshop.

Boston Manor was rebuilt with less enthusiasm. Something had to be done as the old H&MR buildings stood in the path of the proposed western approach tracks to the Northfields depot, so a new glazed hall was erected on the road bridge together with a modest brick sign tower. This opened on 25th March 1934, but the rail level saw little change and the original MDR pitched roof canopies with their period wooden valancing remained in place.

South Ealing was to suffer from the irresolution of senior management. In 1931 the old station was completely demolished, and the side platforms were converted to two island platforms to serve the new four track layout. Pending a final decision on the Ascott Avenue site mentioned earlier, a temporary wooden ticket hall and entrance was erected on the south side of the overline road bridge, which of necessity had to be rebuilt to straddle the wider alignment. Very small wooden shelters were placed on the new platforms.

Then in 1935, with traffic levels at South Ealing stabilising, perhaps even growing, the management settled on leaving it in position. Evidence of this appeared within a year: a 141ft long flat-roofed concrete canopy structure terminating in a waiting room with a glazed, semi-circular wall was added to the eastbound island platform. However total rebuilding was delayed by higher priorities and then by the outbreak of war, and the westbound island, with its small pitch-roofed waiting hut, was left quite unaltered, as were the 'temporary' footbridge and street level building of 1931. As a result of this 'as you were' decision, South Ealing attained the dubious distinction not only of having some of the longest-lived temporary buildings on the London Transport system but of being the surface station closest to its neighbour – the centre of its platforms was a mere 0.24 mile from the centre of Northfields.

After a lapse of over 50 years, a new station building was eventually erected on the site of the 1883 one, served by a new footbridge which had a diminutive canopy where it debouched on to the westbound island. This reconstruction, in use from 3rd May 1988, included a refurbishment of the 1931 platform hut on the westbound side and of the 1936 building work on the other platform. Both structures were left intact as a memorial to uncharacteristic vacillation on the part of Frank Pick and Lord Ashfield in the 1930s.

In the years immediately before World War 2 the service to Hounslow was built up to a 7½-minute frequency off peak, running through to Wood Green and stations beyond. At peak hours with the additional District workings, intervals ranged from two to five minutes. Thus at Hounslow West between 08.00 and 09.00 in 1936 there were nine Piccadilly Line departures for Wood Green or beyond and five District, terminating at East Ham, Barking or Upminster. Piccadilly Circus was reached in 32½ minutes, Mansion House in 46½ minutes. On Sundays there were Piccadilly Line trains every eight minutes. This pattern saw few significant changes until 10th October 1960 when some District trains were taken out, leaving roughly about four an hour through the peak periods. To compensate, in June 1961 some Piccadilly Line trains were altered to start from Hounslow West in the morning peak. As reasonable connections could be made by simply crossing the platforms at Hammersmith, no great hardship was caused when London Transport decided to remove the somewhat anomalous District workings in the interests of rationalisation. The last District train on the branch left Hounslow West for Acton Town at 18.00 on

9th October 1964. For many years the centre pair of tracks between Acton Town and Northfields were used during the day for testing stock from Acton Works. In rush hours all four lines returned to normal passenger service. From north to south, these tracks are designated: eastbound local (ex District line); eastbound fast; westbound fast; and westbound local (ex District line). Withdrawal of District service enabled the eastbound local to be entirely dedicated as an engineers' test track from November 1985 and although the westbound fast was normally used by Piccadilly line trains, it could also be occupied for the same purpose when required, with the public service diverted to the westbound local. In 1995 the eastbound local line was restored to use by normal passenger services. After the cessation of District trains, track and platform works at Boston Manor restricted the operation of the larger loading gauge District Line stock to the section east of Northfields depot (the airport extensions, mentioned below, were built to tube loading gauge).

The omission of Hounslow East from the pre-war rebuilding programme was to be regretted soon enough as the 1909 accommodation proved pitifully inadequate for a rush-hour traffic swollen by the build-up of feeder bus services into the bus station on the site of the old spur. Complaints led to an Adjournment Debate in the House of Commons in 1961 when the local MP, Richard Reader Harris, described how in the evening peak the congested westbound platform could not be cleared before the arrival of the following train. Fault was also found with the mean little waiting shelter on the uncanopied eastbound platform, which was compared in size to the Government Front Bench. In his reply, the Rt Hon Ernest Marples, Transport Minister, mentioned plans for rebuilding, and conceded that the platform widths were two feet less than the normal twelve. Despite this minor fuss and various announcements about rebuilding in conjunction with hotel or office projects, nothing was subsequently done apart from the construction of a new waiting room and a long canopy on the eastbound platform in 1964. Thirty one years after that some rebuilding work was undertaken on the westbound platform.

The opening of London Airport (Heathrow) in 1946 produced a new traffic magnet at the outer end of this line, which was in a position to provide the nearest rail access to central London. Connecting buses were available and passengers with only hand luggage found this a cheaper and often slightly faster way to and from central London than the alternatives of airline coach, taxi or private car. In 1973 a *Daily Telegraph* reporter established a 66 minute timing from Holborn station to an airport check-in desk, 43 min on the rail journey, 12 on the bus, which waited seven minutes before leaving. On return he managed to travel from the airport arrival gate to Holborn station in 74 minutes.

To cater for this type of lightly-loaded passenger and also 'meeters and greeters' and airport and airline staff, an extension from Hounslow West to a station under the central part of the airport was started in April 1971 after almost a quarter of a century of planning, discussion and consideration, such a delay being about par for the course for public transport expenditure of any significance in Britain in the second half of the twentieth century.

The new line branched off at the London end of Hounslow West station, where the roadside building was retained but the platforms were reprovided at subsurface level. Platform three of the terminus, on the north side, was taken out of use on 22nd October 1971 to allow work to proceed. For most of its 3½ miles, the extension was in a cut and cover trench excavated at the side of the Bath and Great South West

Roads but beyond the intermediate station at Hatton Cross there were deep level tube tunnels under the airport. The old platforms one and two at Hounslow West were closed after traffic on 11th July 1975, the new ones coming into use three days later. On 19th July 1975 trains ran as far as Hatton Cross, a spacious building close to the maintenance facilities and offices at the east end of the airport. This station was massive in appearance and costly in construction, allegedly because someone decided it must be able to withstand the impact of a jumbo jet crashing on to it. Delayed by labour problems and other difficulties, the remainder of the extension, into a terminus named Heathrow Central, was opened on 16th December 1977, 31 years after the airport, providing a destination and a traffic role far beyond the wildest imaginings of the promoters of what had now become the 'Airport & Metropolitan'.

In its first full year, traffic on the extension fell below the several estimated figures, capturing only about one fifth of the total passenger throughput of the airport in 1978, a proportion which remained little changed in the 1990s (most air passengers arrive and depart by private car, hire car or taxi). Office and other airport workers were also not to be separated from their cars in any significant numbers, a factor which led to disappointing business at Hatton Cross. Furthermore, although the service was good (up to 15 trains an hour), the journey to London, with 12 station stops before the fringes of the central area were reached, tended to be tedious even for Londoners and no doubt daunting for air travellers from other countries not accustomed to using public transport. Many, having tried it once, probably never came this way again. Nor was it possible to use the tube service for all flights, since the airport check-in and arrival times extended well beyond the Underground's traffic day. Even so, in 1979 8.8 million passengers were handled at Heathrow Central (clumsily renamed 'Heathrow Central Terminals 1,2,3' from 3rd September 1983) and 7.6 million in 1981, an economic recession accounting for the decline.

A further extension including a station serving the new Terminal 4 was opened on 12th April 1986, the trains travelling direct to it on a single line loop diverging from the 1977 line just beyond Hatton Cross and returning to the beginning of the loop via the original station, then renamed 'Heathrow Terminals 1,2,3'. The continuing growth of passenger traffic at the Airport itself produced a little more business, raising the annual total moving over the tube line to around 15 million by the mid 1990s, of which almost 2.5 million were using Heathrow Terminal 4 station.

Although the tube facility just described had the advantage of distributing airport traffic through much of central and Greater London, a fast direct service to the centre was also needed if more passengers were to be wooed away from the congested road approaches to Heathrow, where over 30 million passengers a year were requiring surface access by the early 1990s, most of them to and from London. Conventional railway services to the passenger terminals of what was to become the world's busiest international airport had been debated since the mid-1950s, initial schemes favouring a branch to join the Hounslow Loop at Whitton, using dedicated new tracks thence alongside existing lines into London (Victoria), via Putney and Clapham Junction. The opening of the tube extension in the 1970s tempered the wind behind such schemes and when the subject was taken up again in the late 1980s attention had turned towards a northern link to the old Great Western main line.

Discussions between the British Airports Authority plc and the British Railways Board produced plans for a joint venture (respectively 70 and 30 per cent later altered to 80 : 20) which received Government blessing in July 1988. This proposal was for

A Heathrow Express train at Heathrow Terminal 4 station in July 1998, a month after the full service opened.

a line into the airport from a flying junction (Airport Junction), just west of Hayes & Harlington station. It offered a seamless journey in fast electric trains to and from dedicated platforms (nos. six and seven) at London Paddington, non stop in 15 minutes, departing from each end every 15 min. At the airport, a station would be provided at the central terminal area (14.6m from Paddington) the line continuing to a station serving Terminal 4 (16.4m). The service would offer a strong contrast to the leisurely station to station trundle of the often crowded tube trains, notably in its endeavour to project the much vaunted air travel ethos beyond the airport by use of specially-designed ribbon-glazed trains, a lavish staff to passenger ratio and airline check-in facilities at Paddington. Although all four tracks out of Paddington were electrified at 25kV with overhead catenary, with the relief lines upgraded to allow speeds up to 100mph, the airport trains were normally to be confined to the 125 mph fast lines. Construction was not without its problems. The airport branch was planned to be partly in cut and cover and partly in bored tunnel but in an area not noted for its environmental attractions, the local authorities insisted on a greater length of underground line than the physiography required. Then, in October 1994 there was a disastrous subsidence during construction of the station area at Heathrow through London clay using a shotcrete lining. This not only halted airport tube services temporarily but set back the Heathrow Express construction programme by six months.

Full services on the completed line, London's newest 'local railway', started on 23rd June 1998. Should a fifth terminal be agreed for Heathrow it is intended that both Heathrow Express and the Piccadilly tube lines serve it with short underground branches from the existing lines, additions which would produce quite a complicated net of railways beneath the centre of the airport, in total estimated to bring the ground public transport share of passenger traffic to 38 per cent. Also for the future is the further complication of a rail link to the south for air passengers and others originating in Surrey, Hampshire and south west England.

GWR auto train 88 at Brentford station, c.1920, looking to Brentford Dock.

Southall to Brentford   (map page 165)

Quite soon after the opening of its main line out of Paddington in 1838–41, the Great Western Railway found its freight connections to the London port and markets far from adequate. A transfer depot had been set up at Bull's Bridge, near Hayes, where the railway and the Grand Junction Canal came together at the confluence of the canal's Thames arm. Here, in the 1850s coal was being moved from rail wagons into barges at the rate of some 50,000 tons a year, but the water transit to Brentford, involving negotiation of eleven locks in six miles, was slow enough, even when not 'enhanced in winter by frosts, and in summer by droughts'. Schemes for railways between the GWR and Brentford were deposited each year from 1845 to 1848, including elaborations in the form of extensions to Hounslow, Staines, Westminster, or to the LNWR at Pinner. None reached fruition, partly because the inhabitants of Brentford and Hounslow were loyal to the LSWR, which had arrived first, giving them reasonably direct access to central London. Attention was subsequently concentrated on a freight link to replace the canal. An 1854 proposal for a Great Western & Brentford (Thames Junction) Railway, which included the construction of a Thames-side dock on the 'Town Meadow and Ozier Bed' received parliamentary approval as the Great Western & Brentford Railway Act of 14th August 1855.

This 7ft gauge line and dock was the last railway project engineered by I. K. Brunel, now pre-occupied by his ill-starred maritime enterprises. The GWR was sufficiently sympathetic towards the scheme to suggest that there should be no difficulty about its leasing and working the branch. Some of the subscribers were GWR shareholders, but there was no finance forthcoming from the main line company despite the convenience offered, and no agreement was reached in time for the act. This lack of support was all the more difficult for the small company to bear in that they had to face fierce opposition from the canal company which added considerably to the expense of construction and secured access for the latter to the railway dock. As sitting tenants of Brentford, the LSWR also opposed, but with a good deal less effect.

Work began in the spring of 1856, but as building of the dock proved troublesome and Brunel's estimates far too conservative, further capital had to be raised after powers had been obtained in acts of 1857 and 1859. The act of 1857 mentioned the need to provide more facilities for traffic in 'Welsh Smokeless Coal' while that of 1859 also confirmed an agreement of 1st February 1859 with the GWR under which that company undertook to lease the branch for 99 years for a rent based on tonnage carried (in the case of passenger and horse and carriage traffic, a rent rising after five years to £500 a year). The main line company was to provide locomotives and stock and maintain the installations after the first year. In return for a payment by the Brentford company of £6,000, the GWR agreed to transfer the cranes and other machinery from their Bull's Bridge depot to the new Brentford dock. Except in what were described as 'urgent or extraordinary circumstances' all goods and mineral traffic arising below or at Southall or at any point on the Brentford line, which was destined for points on the branch or on the Thames, and all traffic from such points was to be routed over the Brentford Railway.

Although the narrow and twisting approach road from Brentford High Street, with its bridges over river and canal, was not ready, a formal opening ceremony took place on 15th July 1859. As the steamers *Venus* and *Jupiter* reached Brentford from London Bridge, the official party was greeted with a 19-gun salute whilst bands on each vessel played *See the Conquering Hero Comes*. Travelling to Southall and back in their special train, the guests were impressed by 'the permanence and solidity which characterises the construction'. At the banquet which concluded the proceedings, Charles Eley, secretary of the GW & Brentford, commented on the inadequacy of the canal 'for the greatly increased traffic which the opening up of the Welsh coalfields has brought upon it', adding proudly that the railway project had been completed 'despite the difficulties and obstacles greatly increased by the Russian War and the money panic which followed'.

Goods flowed along the line from the following Monday, 18th July 1859, but preparations for the passenger service were accorded low priority. A nondescript station was erected at Brentford, trains starting to work between Southall and there from 1st May 1860. To save money, the plans for a terminus at the river edge serving a ferry to Kew Gardens were abandoned.

Built for double track but at first only a single 7ft gauge track on the Down side, the 3m 77ch line fell at 1 in 102, 1 in 110, and 1 in 120 towards the river. At the east side of Southall the branch was connected indirectly to the main line through sidings, then shared the Down side island platform with the Down main line. To reach the Brent Valley without violating Osterley Park, the alignment had to go almost due east from the station until it intersected the canal and Windmill Lane at a point later known as Windmill Bridge or Three Bridges, where the roadway was carried above the canal in its 8ft deep cast iron trough and the railway passed beneath both.

South of this curious confluence of transport modes, the railway turned south-east to run between the canal and Osterley Park, closer to the former, reaching after 1½ miles the point where the Hounslow & Metropolitan would later cross it and the canal on a two-span bow girder bridge approached by brick arches. There followed after 1925 an impressive girder bridge which carried the tracks over the new Great West Road. Beyond, the line ran on an embankment to Brentford High Street, passing over the LSWR Hounslow Loop on the way; a connection between the two, authorised by the LSWR (Additional Powers) Act of 1866, was never built. Brentford's platforms were on the north side of the High Street bridge, at the western end of the town; its only building, a wooden shelter, was on the west or Up side. This platform, with signalbox at its south end, was connected to the roadway by a wooden staircase which a dissatisfied director described in 1866 as 'impracticable for ladies in rainy or windy weather'. The shocking scenes in the era of crinolines when the slightest untoward movement revealed delicate pantaloons or pantalettes are best left to reader's imagination. A separate footpath from the road to the Down platform fell into disuse after the introduction of railcars and auto-trains.

From the High Street with its box girder bridge, the line turned east on arches, twice crossing the river Brent before entering the dock area. This was at the northern tip of the Syon Park estate where the Brent joined the Thames, and eventually contained six large warehouses, a riverside wharf with a 2,270ft quay and the main dock, which had a covered basin at the west end.

Goods traffic, always the mainstay of the branch, built up rapidly from 58,000 tons in the first six months of 1860 to 66,000 in the same period following year. Whilst the importance of Brentford as a GWR London freight terminus was considerably diminished by the subsequent opening of outlets via the Metropolitan and North London Railways and the West London Extension Railway's Chelsea Dock, the Brentford installations remained sufficiently busy to justify gradual improvement.

Freight movement was facilitated by the addition of a mixed-gauge track on the Up side of the branch from 1st October 1861, this coinciding with the inauguration of mixed gauge between Paddington and Reading. Until 1875 the two tracks were worked as separate single lines, but between 4th and 7th June that year the broad gauge was removed from the Up line and the Down track was narrowed to standard. Ordinary double-line working began in March 1876. These later developments took place under GWR ownership which became effective from 1st January 1872, having been authorised by the GWR (Additional Powers) Act of 5th July 1865.

Before the independent era ended, the Brentford directors had sought to increase their empire and income by promoting or encouraging various schemes which made use of their property. The Acton & Brentford proposal of 1864 fits into the story of the Hounslow & Metropolitan, already related; the other schemes, which involved extensions towards Isleworth and Twickenham (with running over the LSWR to Richmond), and lines over the river to serve Kew Gardens, all failed.

Passenger services comprising some ten to 12 trains a day each way did not prosper, and the area served showed no tendency to develop in a way which would be helpful to a line pointing away from London. On the trains of three or four coaches, with their three-man crews, the average number of passengers 'did not exceed half a dozen' a situation that the GWR endeavoured to mitigate by including the branch in its steam railcar scheme. These cars, with seating capacity varying from 52 to 64, began to work on the line on 2nd May 1904, providing a half-hourly service weekdays and Sundays for a fare of 2d all the way. It was soon discovered that these newcomers could not haul an additional coach should this be required, so from about 1905 they were replaced with auto trains, push-pull units of 517 class 0–4–2T with one or more trailers. Apart from a brief and unsuccessful experiment with a BTH-Maudslay petrol-electric car in 1912 this was the normal mode for the rest of the period of passenger working.

GWR auto train (loco 1165) for Brentford at Trumpers Crossing Halte, c. 1906.
Locomotive Publishing Co

As part of the improved service, an intermediate stop was made from 1st July 1904 at an occupation crossing 39ch from Southall. With its pagoda-roofed huts on each of its timber platforms, this place was named 'Trumper's Crossing (for Osterley Park) Halte'. Trumper, the owner of the nearby Warren Farm, was no doubt much tickled, remembering the difficulty that the company had experienced in acquiring his land. Although in open country, the halt was reasonably close to the western edge of suburban expansion at Hanwell, and to the back entrance of the LCC mental hospital (Hanwell Asylum) but it was a good half-mile from the Wyke Green Golf Club it was alleged to serve.

The passenger potential of the branch, never very great, was neatly undermined by the opening of an electric tramway along the Boston Road between Brentford and Hanwell on 26th May 1906. As the 1904 improvements had generated little extra traffic, the line proved an easy victim for wartime economies, all passenger trains being withdrawn from 22nd March 1915. Single-line working of the freight traffic was then considered, but it is not clear whether it was in fact adopted. Under pressure from local interests, the GWR restored auto-trains on weekdays only from 12th April 1920, but with intervals extended to hourly (half-hourly at peak periods), 11 trains in all each way. In 1921 the service, which started with the 05.30 and 06.15 departures from Southall, was then half-hourly until 09.18, hourly to 17.15 and half-hourly to 20.45. At this time the intermediate stop was known as 'Trumper's Crossing for South Hanwell and Osterley Park'. A half-hourly Sunday service introduced in the summer of 1923 was withdrawn at the end of September and never again restored. From 1929 weekday trains were restricted to early morning and early evening and early morning and midday on Saturdays but the 1938 timetable showed 14 trains each way daily at these times, 11 on Saturdays. Trumper's Crossing, closed after last trains on 30th January 1926, had by then been demolished. During the empty midday hours from 1933 onwards, the branch was used by the Associated Equipment Company for testing the diesel-mechanical railcars being built at its Southall Works (between the main line and the branch). The AEC's successor, Associated Commercial Vehicles, similarly used the branch for trials of its experimental four-wheel diesel units in 1951–52.

A second wartime closure came after the last train on 2nd May 1942, but this time service was not restored with peace, although the ACV trials just mentioned excited rumours that passenger trains would run again. The ramshackle station and signal box at Brentford remained as a reminder until 1957. Other than the spread of Hanwell westwards in the 1890s and 1900s, somewhat inadequately met by the opening of Trumper's Crossing Halte, and some 1930s development west of the line near Brentford station, much better served by the new SR station at Syon Lane, no new housing appeared along the course of the branch in the whole of its 82 years of passenger working.

There was, however, a late flowering of freight business from new factories at Brentford, a development which owed more to the opening of the Great West Road on 30th May 1925 than the existence of the railway. As they were completed, from 1926 onwards, private sidings were built into the extensive premises of Macfarlane Lang (biscuits) and Firestone (motor tyres and rubber), both of them north of the new road and west of the line. Brentford Town goods yard, north of the new road where it passed under the branch, was opened on 3rd November 1930 to serve the new industrial area. During the early 1920s there were five booked freights a day with extra runs as required, but the new business caused the number of workings to more than double by the mid 1930s. Land on the Great West Road purchased for the new depot but surplus to railway requirements was subsequently developed by the GWR as an industrial estate.

More work for the Docks appeared in 1928 when the GWR assumed transport of the whole Morris Motors export output. 'Knocked down' and in packing cases, the vehicles were moved by rail from new private sidings at the Cowley, Oxford factory to Brentford, where a 150ft by 80ft shed was erected to house them whilst they awaited transfer to the Thames lighters which would carry them down-river to ships in the Port of London. During the export season from October to May, special trains were run for this traffic and the total business reached between 12,000 and 20,000 cars a year. Also at this time, the GWR augmented its accommodation at Brentford Dock by constructing a four storey warehouse fitted with overhead runways on the ground floor and electric cranes on the upper floors. This building, extended in 1938–9, enabled the company to lease accommodation to traders requiring it for bulk storage.

In 1951 there were still 25 freight trains over the branch daily, and as late as 1960 there were seven regular workings to and from Brentford Dock, some calling at Brentford Town yard. Traffic in the late 1950s was both substantial and varied: in the year ended November 1956 Kirkland records that the dock imported 52,888 tons of general merchandise and 10,960 tons of minerals, exporting respectively 127,766 tons and 9,612 tons. That year saw 20,769 tons of general merchandise and 169,077 tons of minerals (mostly coal and coke) brought into Brentford Town Yard by rail, whilst 17,586 tons of general merchandise and 24,433 tons of minerals were forwarded. Goods coming into the dock on lighters and small coasters included iron and steel, timber, wood pulp, flour, animal feeding stuffs, starch and cork; goods outwards by rail and water consisted mostly of motor vehicles and accessories (Morris cars), steel tubes, copper wire, tinplate, china clay and food products. Freight trains at this time were normally hauled by 57xx 0–6–0PT.

As an economy, single-line working using tablet apparatus was introduced in 1952, trains travelling over the former Up line between Southall and Firestone signalbox which controlled the Town yard and access to the private sidings. Traffic was transferred to the old Down road in 1956, worked under electric token regulations, and the Up line was then dismantled.

The somewhat optimistic picture painted by Kirkland in his 1960 article on this line was soon to be clouded. Drastic reductions in use of solid fuels, containerisation of shipping traffic into London, and greater use of road transport for freight movement all combined at around the same time to undermine the main livelihood of the branch. Brentford Dock, which also suffered from poor road access, was closed on 31st December 1964 after a rigorous Beeching appraisal which took into account the need to renew infrastructure and equipment. A deal was done with developers who transformed the 21 acre site into *The Dock*, an imaginative estate of high class apartments, yachting marina and riverside gardens, completed in 1978. A year after the closure of the railway dock, the tracks south of the Great West Road had gone but the Town yard remained open for public traffic until December 1970. Freight for the private sidings then continued. In 1975 Day's Roadstone terminal at Brentford was receiving an average of five trains a week (3,500 tons in total) and some ten trains of cinders, slag and coal ran weekly; in addition around 600 tons of scrap metal were taken out by rail every week.

A future for the line was firmly underwritten by the Greater London Council, which opened a solid waste transfer station on the site of the old Town freight yard early in 1977. This facility received domestic and other refuse which was compacted in the plant and loaded into box containers, each holding up to 12.5 tonnes. Fork lift trucks then placed them on Freightliner type carriers for transport by rail in up to five trains a week to a landfill site (worked-out gravel pits) at Appleford, near Didcot. Two diesel locomotives were usually required to move the 800 tonne trains up to Southall.

The LSWR bridge over Hammersmith Grove, looking north from Beadon Road, c.1905. The street level entrance to the station was on the right just before the bridge. *Commercial postcard*

The Kensington & Richmond Railway (map page 165)

Richmond, leading river resort and desirable place of residence for affluent City men, attracted numerous railway schemes in the boom years around 1860, many with the objective of undermining the LSWR's hold by providing access to west London, the West End, or the City via the North London Railway or the Metropolitan. All this activity caused the North & South Western Junction Railway to promote its own line from Kew Bridge to Richmond, with a feeding connection from its Hammersmith & Chiswick branch into the proposed Hammersmith & City Railway near Shepherds Bush. Anxious to keep the juicy Richmond fruit in its own basket, the LSWR persuaded the N&SWJR that it would fill this dangerous vacuum itself, providing connections and running powers for the N&SWJR and its users.

The result was a Kensington & Richmond Railway, a six-mile branch from the West London Railway north of Kensington (Addison Road) station, through Shepherds Bush and Hammersmith to meet the N&SWJR south of Acton and carry its trains over the Thames on a new line into a separate terminus alongside and to the north of the existing Richmond station. This separation, intended to force other companies to continue using the circuitous access to the LSWR proper via the Kew and Barnes curves, upset the LNWR, which was in a position to make difficulties about the proposed junction at Kensington. A batch of further schemes for the area drove the LNWR and LSWR into each other's arms, easing the passage of the Bill which was to receive royal assent on 14th July 1864. As authorised by the act, the Kensington & Richmond ran into the Hammersmith & City from Kensington, leaving it again just north of the Hammersmith terminus, an arrangement designed to allow GWR and Metropolitan trains to run to Richmond (the GWR was to pay for adding broad gauge to the K&R if wanted). A joint H&CR/LSWR station was to be built on the portion of the H&CR used by the LSWR trains, the H&CR to be dual-gauge at this point. At South Acton, an 'Acton Junction Line' would allow trains to work from the N&SWJR to Richmond. A second act in June 1865, extending time, rearranged the Hammersmith layout to provide a separate through line from Kensington with junctions on and off the H&CR, the intention being that some K&R trains would run over the H&CR to call at the joint station whilst others would by-pass it. This act also sanctioned a 'Chiswick Curve', to allow direct running from Hounslow LSWR onto the Kensington line just south of the present Gunnersbury station. A 'Kew Bridge Curve', for direct running between Richmond and Hounslow, authorised by the LSWR (Additional Powers) Act of 1866, was never built.

Further modifications at Hammersmith, agreed with the GWR and Metropolitan on 13th July 1867 and confirmed by the LSWR General Act of that year, provided for one junction north of the H&CR terminus, allowing trains to run from the H&C towards Richmond, and abandoned the proposed joint interchange station. In its place, the LSWR would build a station at Hammersmith Grove, south of the proposed junction, which GWR and Metropolitan trains would be able to use on payment and which would be connected by 'a convenient passageway', enclosed and covered and at least 10ft wide, passing over the H&CR into its Hammersmith terminus.

Another 18 months passed before Brassey & Ogilvy had the line ready. From 1st January 1869 LSWR trains began to run over it, working approximately hourly between Richmond and Waterloo via the Latchmere and West London Extension Junctions at Battersea (LSWR trains had been running between Kensington and Clapham Junction since 2nd March 1863, and, with the LNWR, between Kensington and Waterloo from 6th July 1865). Also from 1st January 1869, the new line carried NLR Broad Street-Richmond trains using what are now South Acton and Gunnersbury Junctions, then known as Acton and Brentford Road Junctions. A third service, operated by the LSWR from the same day, ran between Richmond and Ludgate Hill, an extension of a Kensington–Loughborough Junction–Ludgate Hill working which had started on 1st February 1868. This last very circuitous service, taking from 58 to 62 minutes, was for many years covered by about ten trains a day each way. The North London trains, which ran half-hourly as far as South Acton, splitting there, with alternate trains going to Kew Bridge, remained almost unchanged until 1909 when it was increased to half-hourly to Richmond (Sunday trains had been half-hourly since 1906).

Leaving the West London Railway 24ch north of Kensington (Addison Road) station at Richmond Junction, the K&R curved westwards in a semi-circle to pass beneath the H&CR viaduct, then going due south, following the H&CR on its west side for 700yd, its tracks rising at 1 in 108 on a low viaduct to enter the station known as Hammersmith, Grove Road. Wooden platforms here, 15ft above the H&CR, were sheltered by generous canopies supported on decorated cast-iron columns. At street level on the east side was a plain two-storey station house with round-arched windows. Complying with the act, the LSWR provided a connecting footbridge to the H&CR terminus and the eastern entrance to this can still be seen at the time of writing. The junction, which ran from 15ch north of Grove Road into the H&CR, was not used until 1st June 1870 when GWR trains started to run approximately hourly from Bishop's Road, Paddington to Richmond. From a point on the London side of Grove Road the direction changed to west, on a 1m 23ch brick viaduct, 20ft high with arches of 20ft span. At its west end was an embankment and a station at the east side of Chiswick Common named Turnham Green. This had a street building of one storey in similar style to Grove Road, situated alongside Turnham Green Terrace north of the line. For the next 75ch the tracks were mostly in cutting at 1 in 120 down, turning due south into Brentford Road station (renamed Gunnersbury 1st November 1871) where the station house, almost a replica of that at Grove Road, stood in an approach from Chiswick High Road at the west side of the line. North of the bridge under this main road was Brentford Road Junction where the important connection from the N&SWJR came in.

After passing above the Hounslow loop, the K&R was carried over the Thames on a five-span wrought-iron lattice girder bridge, which although approved by the Thames Conservators as required by the 1864 act and decorated with gothic capitals on its red brick abutments, successfully disfigured the attractive riverside hamlet of Strand-on-the-Green. On the south side, the line ran on a 22ft embankment east of the Kew Bridge-Richmond Road, entering Kew Gardens station, which was required by the 1864 act. On the Up platform was a two-storey house in the standard style, and also, to cater for the visitors to the Gardens a quarter-mile to the west, a pavilion containing a licensed refreshment bar. For another 1m 16ch the tracks ran due south to Richmond Junction, whence there was another 14ch into the separate six-track three-platform terminal on the north side of the Windsor line. The N&SWJR maintained its own booking office and clerks there until 1917.

Although completed at the same time as the rest the 30ch Chiswick Curve, from 8ch south of Brentford Road station to Chiswick Junction 23ch east of Kew Bridge station, was not regularly used until 1st June 1870. From that date the LSWR Waterloo–Kensington–Richmond trains were diverted over it to terminate at Hounslow and the Richmond connection was covered by LSWR Ludgate Hill trains and the GWR Richmond service already noticed. This arrangement was short-lived. From 1st November 1870, the GWR trains were withdrawn, the LSWR resuming a Richmond–Kensington–Waterloo working, supplying Hounslow connections by means of a shuttle service to and from Brentford Road. The subsequent history of the Chiswick Curve has already been noted in the account of the Hounslow Loop.

Housing expansion at the London end of the line by the late 1870s justified two more stations. Shaftesbury Road, opened on 1st April 1873, 64ch east of Turnham Green, served a new district called Ravenscourt Park whose name it adopted from 1st March 1888. Shepherds Bush station (1st May 1874) was 35ch west of the junction with the West London Railway, conveniently placed near the south corner of Shepherds Bush Common. Covered steps led down to each platform from the west side of the bridge carrying Shepherds Bush Road over the line. The undistinguished platforms were mostly wooden.

Further westward expansion of London either side of the line occurred in the last quarter of the nineteenth century, most notably in the form of Britain's pioneer garden suburb, Bedford Park, just north of Turnham Green station, from 1875 to 1881. Although the house building which had virtually shut in the line as far as Turnham Green by 1901 owed something to the horse tramways along the roads west of Shepherds Bush and Hammersmith to Kew Bridge after 1882–3, it was primarily succoured by the increasing variety and intensity of the train services worked over the K&R.

Ravenscourt Park station, LSWR, looking west, c.1903. *Lens of Sutton*

Turnham Green station and signalbox, LSWR, looking north along Turnham Green Terrace (Chiswick Common at left), c.1905. The entrance to the station is on the far side of the bridge, on the right. *Commercial postcard*

By its act of 11th August 1875, the Metropolitan District Railway, which had reached Hammersmith Broadway in 1874, secured passenger and coaching traffic running powers over the LSWR line to Richmond New station in return for giving up 'other routes' to Richmond, Kew, Barnes and Putney, including its Earl's Court–Barnes extension, authorised in 1872. Under the same act the District constructed a 39.5ch link from its Hammersmith station to the K&R, climbing at 1 in 46 to what was to be known as Studland Road Junction. The engineering, which included the rebuilding of Hammersmith station, was substantial. On what was to prove an enduring service, District trains reached Richmond on 1st June 1877.

Traffic was good from the start, with 54,000 carried in the first month, but some distress and a few unpleasant accidents were caused by the 2ft or more difference between the levels of the District carriage floors and the low LSWR platforms. R. A. Williams has recorded in some detail the events of this period, when ladies were sometimes obliged to sit on the floor in order to negotiate their exit to the platform; tightly sheathed in whaleboned corsets, covered in voluminous petticoats, and blushing with middle-class propriety, their dilemma must have been considerable. These difficulties were overcome, and with the opening of a further westward extension of the District from Bedford Park Junction, Turnham Green, to Ealing Broadway on 1st July 1879, the MDR became the major user of an important part of the K&R, the running powers for its 'western branches' enshrined in the MDR Act of 1877.

The District's great rival, the Metropolitan, had also been exploiting the potential of this part of suburban west London, feeding from 5th July 1875 the H&CR Shepherds Bush station with a horse-bus service to and from Turnham Green (the buses ran to Hammersmith H&CR from 12th June 1876). Further efforts were stimulated by the District's success, and using the existing running powers, the Metropolitan started an hourly service between Moorgate Street and Richmond via Hammersmith Grove Road from 1st October 1877. The eastern terminus was soon after altered to Aldgate. These trains worked in the path of one of the 10-minute Aldgate–Hammersmith trains, the diversion to Grove Road making little difference to the Hammersmith passengers who could use the interconnecting footway between the two stations.

Another company to exploit the K&R was the Midland, which gained access via the Brent Junction (Cricklewood)–Acton Wells Junction line of 1st October 1868 and the N&SWJR. Running powers were exchanged with the LSWR, which acquired the useful ability to pick up freight at Brent Sidings. From 3rd August 1875, Midland passenger trains began to work between Moorgate Street (or Kentish Town or Childs Hill & Cricklewood) and Richmond via Acton. Few passengers were attracted to this circuitous service, which ceased on the evening of 31st January 1876, but the Midland tried again on 1st May 1878, offering an even more devious route from St Pancras to Earl's Court via Cricklewood and Acton, using a new 20ch curve from the South Acton–Gunnersbury line at Bollo Lane Junction to the K&R at Acton Lane Junction, 47ch west of Turnham Green station. This curve, authorised by the LSWR General Act of 24th July 1871, was primarily intended to carry coal trains feeding the many fireplaces of west London through the Midland's own coal yards at Kensington High Street (opened 4th March 1878) and West Kensington (25th March 1878); another yard at South Kensington, for which running powers were granted from Earl's Court, was never built. Midland coal trains were the only regular freight traffic ever worked over the K&R, which had no goods yards along its route. Attended with no more success than its earlier venture, the Midland's 'Outermost Circle' passenger service between St Pancras and Earl's Court ran for the last time on the evening of 30th September 1880. Still undeterred, the Midland made a further bid for west London traffic on 1st January 1894 when it extended its Childs Hill & Cricklewood–Stonebridge Park trains to Gunnersbury, some eleven workings each way daily. Defeat was acknowledged by final withdrawal of Midland local trains on the evening of 30th September 1902, but from 1st July 1905 to October 1908 the Midland ran passenger trains from Bradford (with through coaches from other northern and midland cities) to Portsmouth via Hendon and Richmond, while in the summer of 1911 there were also LNWR Manchester–Southampton trains running via Gunnersbury.

New Year's Day 1894 saw GWR rolling stock on the K&R again, that company starting a joint service with the Metropolitan between Aldgate and Richmond via Hammersmith, Grove Road. These trains (seven Metropolitan and ten GWR each way on weekdays and 13 GWR each way on Sundays in 1903), were worked at a loss, which was increased latterly by the competition of new electric tramways parallel to much of the route. The GWR was however reluctant to give up and suggested the service might be worked more economically by railmotors connecting with the H&CR trains. The through steam workings to Aldgate were therefore withdrawn in place of a GWR steam shuttle between Richmond and Notting Hill (now Ladbroke Grove) from 1st January 1907. This ran every half hour for most of the day, hourly on Sunday mornings and half hourly on Sunday afternoons. To facilitate terminal working, a loop and crossover were provided on the Up side east of Notting Hill station. The losses continued and traffic was discouraged by the necessity of changing trains, causing the Richmond service to be withdrawn after traffic on 31st December 1910 and leaving the Metropolitan to consider whether it should run electric trains to Richmond.

Since the electrification of the H&CR in 1906, the Metropolitan had toyed with the idea of using its existing running powers to work an electric service to Richmond via Grove Road and Turnham Green. Provision was accordingly inserted in the MDR Act of 1910 (mentioned below) to allow the Metropolitan and GWR to run over and use the northern pair of tracks between Hammersmith and Turnham Green which the LSWR was to electrify if the Metropolitan or GWR wished to run an electric service to Richmond. Furthermore it was provided that the LSWR would build northern platforms at the proposed Stamford Brook station if the GWR and Metropolitan required this. Negotiations between the Metropolitan Railway and the LSWR, begun in 1911, had reached an advanced stage by the middle of 1914, but in the previous year the London Electric Railway had obtained powers for a connection between the Piccadilly tube line and the LSWR at Hammersmith with the intention of running tube trains through to Richmond. Sir Albert Stanley (later Lord Ashfield) offered the Metropolitan financial compensation in return for giving up its running powers to Richmond and this was accepted. In November 1914 the 15ch curve between the Hammersmith & City line and the LSWR at Hammersmith was severed at its north end and the rails were completely removed in May 1916.

Few changes were made in the LSWR's own services. In June 1888 the Waterloo–Richmond journey was taking about 46 minutes on trains running approximately hourly between 08.45 and 22.15. Ludgate Hill–Richmond occupied 62 to 65 minutes, again about hourly, between 08.29 and 20.55. By June 1906 this had been little altered, but there were now departures from Waterloo up to 23.40 and an additional Clapham Junction–Kensington–Richmond service taking about 50 minutes and running roughly every hour between 05.40 and 23.17. Another new facility, lasting only from 1st October 1901 to a date in 1909, was a weekday service between Clapham Junction and Twickenham via Kensington, the Chiswick Curve and Hounslow. The LSWR was now very much the minor operator on its own line; in the early 1900s it was working about 28 passenger trains each way daily, compared with 61 by the other companies between Richmond and Gunnersbury (25 District, 17 Metropolitan/ GWR and 19 NLR). In the busiest 50 minutes of the morning peak at Richmond this combination produced trains of five different companies serving six different destinations (Broad Street, Waterloo, Ludgate Hill, Whitechapel, New Cross, and Aldgate). On Sundays from 1902 some of the LSWR Clapham Junction–Kensington (Addison Road) trains were extended to Richmond and Kingston, a practice which lasted until 30th June 1912. An unusual feature of the summers of 1907 and 1908 was the operation of a daily train each way between Richmond New station and Salisbury via Hammersmith Grove Road and Clapham Junction.

As can be judged from the proliferation of services, Gunnersbury was an important station for many years. It had five tracks serving two island platforms and an extra face on the west side, all converging to double track at the south side of the bridge under Chiswick High Road. South of the station, two pairs of tracks continued for about 400yd until the westernmost pair swung away to form the Chiswick Curve.

It was in these Edwardian years that the future of the K&R was shaped. One of the sections of the MDR Act 1902 authorised the MDR and LSWR to make agreements regarding electrification, but when serious planning began it was soon realised that there would have to be separate tracks for the intensive electric service proposed by the District over the 75ch between Hammersmith (Studland Road Junction) and Turnham Green, even then carrying 148 trains each way daily. These two extra tracks were originally included in the MDR bill for the 1903 session, but in January 1903 the MDR and LSWR reached an arrangement regarding terms and conditions for working the MDR 'western branches' traffic between Studland Road Junction and Turnham Green. Sealed in an agreement dated 23rd July, these provided for the District to withdraw the quadrupling proposal in return for a certain amount of freedom in regard to the number of trains that it could run over the LSWR lines, and the fixing of fares. This agreement, designed to last to the end of 1912, could only be in the nature of a stopgap. Electrification of the Hammersmith–Richmond track by the LSWR, with the MDR paying interest on the capital, was covered by another agreement dated 4th December 1903.

After the electrification of the District's Ealing, South Harrow and Hounslow services had been completed in 1905, the 75ch of common user LSWR track was carrying some 500 steam and electric trains daily. Determined to release itself from a situation which inhibited the development of its western electric services, the MDR sought and secured a new agreement with the LSWR, dated 11th April 1910 and confirmed by the MDR act of that year. This provided that the LSWR line between Acton Lane (west of Turnham Green) and Studland Road Junction, Hammersmith, would be widened on both sides to accommodate four tracks east of Turnham Green, the two tracks on the south side to be designated for exclusive MDR and Midland use in perpetuity. The MDR was to have the use and maintenance of the southern platforms at Turnham Green and Ravenscourt Park, and the access to them; the LSWR was to control the booking offices and entrances to these stations, but both the LSWR and the MDR would appoint station staff and ticket collectors for their portions. Even such small details as the right of the MDR 'to electrically illuminate' the southern platforms and direction signs and to receive revenue from all advertisements and automatic machines were recorded. Most of the new works were to be undertaken by the LSWR, which was to receive four per cent on its outlay as well as its annual rental for running rights.

Turnham Green as rebuilt in 1911, still very much in its original condition apart from lighting and seats; looking towards Acton Town, 14th July 1994. *Alan A Jackson*

The new tracks, all LSWR property apart from two short sections, but signalled throughout by the MDR, came into use on 3rd December 1911. In the alterations, Studland Road ceased to be a physical junction and at the Turnham Green end non-conflicting junctions had been made between the LSWR and the new lines. Turnham Green had a new box with two locking frames, one a Westinghouse, pneumatically operated, under a District man, the other manual with Sykes' lock-and-block, in charge of an LSWR signalman.

Turnham Green station was rebuilt with two steel-and-concrete island platforms. The old Bedford Park Junction between the LSWR and the MDR west of the station was moved 150yd west to Fishers Lane where a bridge allowed LSWR trains to and from Richmond to pass under the Ealing line to gain access to both sides of the new northern platforms. A second island platform had also to be built at Ravenscourt Park, where the northernmost faces were now used exclusively by LSWR steam trains, and a new street-level building was provided on the south side of the viaduct. On 1st February 1912 the District opened a new island platform for its own use on the leased tracks between Ravenscourt Park and Turnham Green. Called Stamford Brook, this had a small street building south of the line at the west side of Goldhawk Road, providing convenient interchange with the London United Tramway services. This station, to be maintained and staffed by the MDR, had been included in the MDR Act of 1910.

In December 1911 and January 1912, the MDR introduced a much improved service over the new lines, 198 trains daily to Ealing instead of 119, 144 to Hounslow instead of 121 and 96 to South Harrow instead of 68. The LSWR, facing increasing competition from alternative electric rail services, electric tramcars and motor buses, now began to prune its steam services over the K&R; by 1910 the weekday Waterloo service was down to 13 each way (ten on Sundays) and Ludgate Hill to ten (one of them to and from Hounslow). There was also one train daily between Richmond, Kensington and Clapham Junction and a few between Battersea and Richmond.

Shepherds Bush, LSWR, looking east in June 1916, just after closure.

Hammersmith Grove Road, LSWR, looking north in June 1916, just after closure. Posters advertise the new LSWR electric services and exhibit names of employees killed on active service.

Stopping at all stations, Kensington was reached in 21 minutes from Waterloo, Richmond in 46 minutes. In 1912 the service to and from Richmond via the K&R ran to Clapham Junction instead of Waterloo; by July 1914 there were only two trains each way between Ludgate Hill and Richmond, a year later only one. The year 1915 saw the Richmond–Kensington–Clapham Junction service severely slashed and converted to push-pull operation (two coach bogie sets, first- and third-class only). On Saturday evening 3rd June 1916 all LSWR service over the K&R ceased, and Shepherds Bush, Hammersmith Grove Road and the northern platforms at Turnham Green and Ravenscourt Park were all closed.

Cable laying on the LSWR at Turnham Green in 1911 in connection with the provision of extra tracks for the District Railway. *Lens of Sutton*

However, 1916 was not all gloom for the K&R. From 1st October the NLR was able to introduce its electric service between Broad Street and Richmond or Kew Bridge, using the same four rail system as the MDR. Richmond–Broad Street time was cut from 56 to 44 minutes but the basic service remained half-hourly on weekdays and Sundays with some extra peak workings. There were now District trains to Richmond every 15 minutes daily including Sundays, a frequency subsequently increased to ten minutes. From 1920 the NLR electrics gave summer Sunday pleasure-seekers a fifteen-minute service, an interval extended to weekdays in 1922 and to winter Sundays in 1925.

For some years the Underground companies had planned further services to Richmond over the K&R. In 1913 the Central London Railway Act had sanctioned a 2½-mile extension under the Goldhawk, Stamford Brook and Bath roads and Chiswick High Road, to surface at Gunnersbury station, where a junction was planned, and as already mentioned, a London Electric Railway Act of the same year authorised a connection between the Piccadilly tube and the LSWR line at Hammersmith, which would enable Piccadilly Line trains to run through to Richmond. No work had been started on either scheme before World War 1, but with the return of peace, a much less costly proposal was evolved for the Central London. Sanctioned by the Central London & Metropolitan District Companies' (Works) Act, 1920, this provided for a short south-westerly extension from Shepherds Bush, the tube tracks rising either side of the K&R near Richford Street (west of the bridge under the H&CR). From there it was intended to run tube trains over electrified tracks of the K&R to Turnham Green and on to Richmond, perhaps beyond (*The Railway Magazine* talked wildly of tube race specials from Liverpool Street to Ascot). This scheme also came to nothing, which was perhaps as well because by 1927 the SR, as successor to the LSWR, had been obliged to increase its rental charges to the District and the LMSR (successor to the North London) to meet the wear and tear caused by electric trains on the Richmond–South Acton section.

In 1926, after the K&R tracks between Kensington and Turnham Green had lain disused for ten years, the SR board authorised the recovery of permanent way, telegraph and signalling equipment and told the West London Railway that it did not propose to continue the £165 annual payment still being made for maintenance of Richmond Junction (Kensington) and its signalling. Despite speculation in *The Railway Magazine* that the War Office had vetoed any obstruction of the alignment between Kensington and Studland Road Junction in view of its possible strategic value for military traffic, the course of the disused line north and east of the H&CR Hammersmith car shed, seven acres in all, was offered on a 98-year lease in a *Times* advertisement of 13th December 1929.

But if the War Office was no longer interested, the Studland Road Junction–Turnham Green section was certainly of immense strategic importance to the Underground, now its only user apart from the two or three LMSR coal trains each day. In 1925 the 1913 proposals for the Piccadilly extension over it were revived, but now the intention was to project the tube trains to South Harrow and Hounslow rather than Richmond, using the former LSWR between Hammersmith and Turnham Green as a four-track electric railway and quadrupling the Underground's own surface tracks between Turnham Green and a point beyond Acton Town. A new agreement was reached between the MDR, the SR and the London Electric Railway. Dated 10th June 1926, this was scheduled to the London Electric & Metropolitan District Railway Companies' Act of 1926 authorising the new works. It allowed the Underground companies to take over and electrify the disused pair of tracks on the north side between Turnham Green and Hammersmith, together with the stations, reserving to the SR the right to run 'occasional and special' passenger and goods trains, but not so as to 'unreasonably disturb' the Underground traffic. Just where these SR trains were going to go is not clear, but it is certain that had railway enthusiasts been as well organised in the late 1920s as they are now, there would have been SR steam trains running to their occasional delight as far as the London end of Ravenscourt Park station. The London Electric as well as the MDR were by the agreement authorised to run over the Acton Lane–Richmond line, thus opening the way for Piccadilly Line services. The SR was to continue to maintain and operate Acton Lane Junction signal box, plus the earthworks and bridges on the Hammersmith–Turnham Green line. Increased rents were payable to the SR as residual freeholders in return for what was in effect a long lease to the Underground giving it almost complete control. The Metropolitan, GWR, SR, London Electric Railway and District Railway also made a new agreement (31st July 1926) for the by now almost academic purpose of securing the Metropolitan and GWR running powers over the newly abandoned layout and to preserve the route for a Metropolitan electric service to Richmond.

Once all four tracks were electrified and the remains of the LSWR replaced by Underground equipment, the running arrangements were altered to make the centre pair of tracks fast for Piccadilly trains working non-stop between Hammersmith and Acton Town, with the outer pair slow for the District trains, which called at all stations. These alterations, which included some rearrangement of the junctions west of Turnham Green and a new eastbound platform at Stamford Brook for District trains (in use from 5th June) came into full operation on 4th July 1932. After the new junctions had been made with the Piccadilly Line, the viaduct round to Grove Road was fully restored, in a fashion which would have made it possible to re-establish a connection, presumably against the remote possibility of a Metropolitan service to Richmond. Any speculation about the future of the Kensington end of the K&R was effectively dispelled in 1937 by the erection of a large block of flats across the alignment on the east side of the LSWR's Shepherds Bush station. Around 1950 an office block was built across the old line at Grove Road and in 1954 it was blocked by a new bus garage at the country end of Shepherds Bush station. Some relics survived for a long time. At the end of the 1950s it was still possible to see the canopies, platforms and stairs of the then isolated Shepherds Bush station; the lattice girder bridge over Hammersmith Grove Road, and the LSWR station building, latterly used as a banana warehouse, were not demolished until June 1954.

Richmond station frontage shortly after completion of the Southern Railway rebuilding in the Modern style, 1938. As well as the Southern services, this station was served by the Underground (District Line) trains using the former LSWR Kensington & Richmond line as far as a point east of Ravenscourt Park and the LMSR North London electric services to Broad Street, also using that line as far as a point just north of Gunnersbury. BR(SR)

Left: Richmond train entering Kew Gardens station, 29th June 1957. The LSWR style canopies are prominent, along with SR type electric lighting and the 1911 ferro-concrete footbridge.
Alan A Jackson

Right: Exterior of Kew Gardens station (Up side) with Underground and BR symbols prominent on the canopy, 12th October 1967 *BR(SR)*

Below: Gunnersbury in the early 1960s showing the by then disused eastern island platform and the temporary roofing erected after the cyclone damage of 1954. The original LSWR station house can be seen at the right by the side of the footbridge.

Long before that, the SR had rationalised its heritage at the western end of the K&R. Gunnersbury station was reduced to two tracks in July 1932, leaving only the western or Up island platform in use. At the end of the year the refreshment room was closed. With these alterations came the closure of the Chiswick Curve and a consequential reduction to double track south of the station. Gunnersbury's appearance was sadly mauled on 8th December 1954 when its platforms formed the focal point of a small cyclone. Some of the damage was patched up in rather ugly fashion, but in 1967, BR completed a new station in combination with an 18-storey office tower at the north end of the site. At the same time the LSWR station house was demolished and double deck car parks were made on the original station area either side of the new island platform. Further rebuilding took place in 1994 in conjunction with the British Standards Institution, which was to occupy a new headquarters building next to Gunnersbury station. This work provided a new entrance and cladding of the existing ticket office, walkway and footbridge to match the adjacent offices. Today the place is virtually unrecognisable to those who knew it in the 1950s and earlier. Only Kew Gardens survives more or less intact as an example of a K&R station; although Turnham Green's street level building is the original one, its interior has been completely altered by London Transport.

Recognising the *de facto* position which had existed since 1932, the British Transport Commission formally transferred the Turnham Green–Hammersmith section to London Transport from 23rd January 1950. No longer was it necessary to show on Southern maps what W. H. Bett so neatly described as a piece of line 'petering out rather indecisively and mysteriously in the Turnham Green neighbourhood'. BR completed the severance on 28th December 1972 by closing the connections with the SR Windsor lines at Richmond.

At Richmond in 1994 the busiest peak hour saw eight District Line trains leaving, all running via Embankment, these sharing tracks as far as Gunnersbury with four North London Lines trains to Willesden Junction, Stratford and North Woolwich. The maximum number of passengers hourly entering these trains at Richmond was 1,946; the largest hourly total entering Kew Gardens station for both services 947, and Gunnersbury 618. At Richmond, the terminal platforms numbered 3 to 7 were available for use by the two services.

CHAPTER THREE

NORTH WEST LONDON

LNWR steam railcar at Woodstock Road Halt, Hammersmith & Chiswick branch, at the inauguration of the railcar service in 1909, looking to Hammersmith & Chiswick station.
Lens of Sutton

The Hammersmith & Chiswick Branch   (map page 165)

(map page 165)

At the opening of the railway era Hammersmith was little more than an overgrown village extending from the crossroads at the present Broadway to touch the outskirts of the smaller communities of Chiswick and Turnham Green. Its houses, and its inns, which provided much of its living, bordered the main road to the west country but at the riverside were the genteel villas and summer retreats of affluent Londoners who gained access by the numerous river steamers. All around were the market gardens, orchards and small dairy farms which sustained west London. Like Hounslow and Brentford, Hammersmith had been left high and dry between the two main railway arteries west of London, and it arrived at the middle of the nineteenth century with nothing better in the way of railway accommodation than the moribund freight-only West London Railway on its eastern borders.

In its opening year (1853) the North & South Western Junction Railway (N&SWJR) obtained powers to build a 1¼-mile branch from Acton Gate House Junction to a station called Hammersmith situated in a market garden on the north side of the main road, almost exactly half-way between the centres of Hammersmith and Turnham Green, but within the parish of Chiswick and nearer to that village than the Chiswick station we have already noticed on the Hounslow loop. The exact object of this initiative is somewhat obscure, but as there were only two or three houses blocking further progress to the riverbank it may have been intended to make a riverside wharf when more capital could be arranged. At all events the financing of this little branch was very soon a matter of controversy, the shareholders forming an investigatory committee when they discovered that the directors had authorised construction outside the company's guaranteed capital. Not surprisingly, the committee found that the capital had been grossly misused and could see no sound reason for building the branch.

This assertion was certainly a reasonable one as far as passenger traffic was concerned, for the line offered only the most inconvenient and indirect access to any place of importance. A traveller proceeding from the centre of Hammersmith would first have to go for one mile west along the main road to reach his train; once seated in it he would find himself moving further west then north, east, south and west again before arriving at the somewhat inconvenient City terminus of Fenchurch Street. Should he choose the alternative of Waterloo via Kew, it would still be necessary for him to navigate almost a full circle before reaching the West End. No-one in his senses would do it; the horse buses and even the river steamers were far more direct.

The south-facing junction with the N&SWJR main line reflected an expectation that the LSWR might be persuaded to work the branch but that company, together with the other main line operators, showed an understandable reluctance to provide passenger services to this 'Hammersmith'. So although there were freight movements from 1st May 1857, it was not until 8th April 1858 (after the N&SWJR had in desperation considered using horses and then managed to acquire its first and only steam locomotive especially for the purpose) that passenger trains could begin to run. This little Sharp, Stewart 0–4–0 saddle tank, which spent its nights in a tiny shed at the north end of Hammersmith station, hauled a composite coach nine times a day (five on Sundays) to and from Acton Gate House Junction, where the NLR trains stopped to pick up the coach. In the Down direction, the North London enginemen very often did little more than slow down at the Junction whilst the guard detached the Hammersmith coach by snatching the coupling, an unofficial procedure which led to frequent derailments. With the delays at the Junction, the best time from Hammersmith to Fenchurch Street was 55 minutes.

From the Junction, which was 22yd north of a level-crossing over what is now Acton Lane the single line dropped at 1 in 69, curving in a semi-circle through open country, running east and then south into the terminus. No substantial works were necessary for there were no intermediate stations and only two small bridges over a stream, whilst at the terminus an existing two-storey house on the main road served as stationmaster's residence and offices. From the road, the intending passenger saw nothing of the railway, but walking through the front door, he bought his ticket in the hall, moving through the back door into the garden, where he boarded his train from the single long platform.

The somewhat risky and illegal goings-on at the Junction came to an end on 1st November 1865 when the branch train began to run through to Acton (now Acton Central) after reversal at Gate House. In the Down direction it was propelled from Acton to the Junction. A further change took place on 1st January 1880 with the opening on that day of South Acton station and a separate 19ch line alongside the N&SWJR main line between it and the Junction. This enabled the Hammersmith trains to terminate in a bay platform at South Acton in connection with the North London service. At this time the branch trains were normally composed of three four-wheeled oil-lit coaches hauled by inside-cylinder NLR 4–4–0T of the 105 class. Two of these locomotives were housed in a two-road shed near the Junction; later on, the branch locomotives were shedded at Willesden, but the building survived to be blown down in the great 'Gunnersbury Whirlwind' of 8th December 1954.

In 1897, whilst residing at 62, Bath Road, Bedford Park, the great French impressionist artist Camille Pissarro (1830–1903) immortalised this little line, which ran alongside the house. Notable amongst several of these oil paintings is *Train at Bedford Park*, now in the Ashmolean Museum, Oxford, which depicts locomotives shunting freight wagons between Bath Road and the bridge carrying the LSWR Kensington & Richmond line. The LNWR semaphore signals then in use are faithfully reproduced.

Hammersmith's rapid growth, from 25,000 in 1861 to 72,000 in 1881 was entirely related to its transformation into a London suburb following the establishment of direct links; the Hammersmith & City Railway in 1864 and the Metropolitan District Railway in 1874. A third link, less direct, was the LSWR Kensington & Richmond line (Chapter 2) of 1869, which crossed the little Hammersmith branch immediately north of its terminus. From the many hundreds of new houses which crept out towards its tracks in the late Victorian and Edwardian years, the branch gained little or no business. Any workers using it to reach 'Soapsud Island', the laundry colony at South Acton, were hardly enough to create rush periods.

Freight movement was rather more substantial, serving the coal yards at the terminus and near the Junction. At the latter there were also private coal sidings for Eastman's Dye and Cleaning Works, and for an asphalt plant. These demanded a daily train with an additional trip for the private sidings in the evening.

Soon after taking over management and operation of the NLR on 1st January 1909, the LNWR sought economies in working the branch by replacing the trains with a one-class 48-seat steam railmotor of the type designed by its chief mechanical engineer, G. Whale. *Little Jenny*, as it was named locally, ran half-hourly on weekdays from 4th January 1909. At Hammersmith & Chiswick terminus a raised wooden platform protected by a crude canopy was erected to facilitate access to and from the car, while to encourage maximum use of the more frequent service, simple timber halts were built at all points where the line crossed roads or paths. Named Rugby Road, Woodstock Road, and Bath Road, all three were opened on 8th April 1909. On the same day, the booking office at the terminus was closed and tickets were issued on the car by a conductor-guard whose ticket stock was limited, making

Looking north from the buffer stops at the Hammersmith & Chiswick terminus of the N&SWJR on 18th June 1955. A District Line train is seen on the former L&SWR Kensington & Richmond viaduct. *Alan A Jackson*

London's Local Railways

it necessary to re-book at South Acton for all destinations off the branch other than Kew Bridge, Acton or Willesden Junction.

On 9th March 1913 the steam car was replaced by LNWR petrol-electric railmotor No. 9, operating from Willesden North Shed, but traffic, which continued to be very light, had now been further damaged by the opening in 1912 of the adjacent Stamford Brook station on the Metropolitan District Railway, so that the line was a clear candidate for a wartime closure list, its last passenger workings being made on 31st December 1916.

With the end of passenger working, the terminus became a shop and dwelling house but the platform line and run-round loop remained intact until May 1958. A daily freight ran down the branch for another 40 years, but by the late 1950s the line was worked as an unstaffed siding subject to a 10mph speed limit, train crews operating the level-crossing gates at Bath Road. Although the timetable provided for a daily train, three visits a week usually sufficed for the traffic offering. Steam power in the form of Willesden-based ex-LNWR 0–8–0s and Fowler Class 4F 0–6–0s gave way to diesels around 1962. Before then, on Saturday 10th November 1956, the branch saw its most heavily-loaded passenger train ever in the form of a special working carrying over 200 railway enthusiasts. This train of four packed BR compartment coaches, hauled by BR Class 4MT 2–6–4T 80065, was not allowed to enter the platform road at Hammersmith & Chiswick, but came to a halt on a goods road just behind the still extant N&SWJR platform.

Beeching's accountants did not take long to discover this sleepy backwater. The last freight workings were made in 1965, the yard at the Junction closing on 3rd January and that at the terminus on 2nd May. For over ten years the large area of land around the branch terminus remained uncovered but eventually houses were erected and what is now Ravensmede Way covers the site.

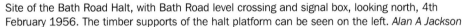

Site of the Bath Road Halt, with Bath Road level crossing and signal box, looking north, 4th February 1956. The timber supports of the halt platform can be seen on the left. *Alan A Jackson*

The Ealing Branch (District Railway) (map page 260)

We have seen in the previous chapter how a short connection at Hammersmith allowed Metropolitan District Railway trains to run over the LSWR's Kensington and Richmond Railway to Richmond from 1st June 1877. In hot pursuit of further suburban business, the District obtained an act in 1877 for its own 2m 75ch line to run north west from Turnham Green through stations at Acton Green (later Chiswick Park), Mill Hill Park (now Acton Town) and Ealing Common to a terminus adjacent to the GWR station at Ealing. Construction under the engineer J. Wolfe Barry was set back three months by severe winter weather and the line was eventually opened on 1st July 1879.

Barry's stations at the places named were all in a similar somewhat plain brick style, with two storey houses for the stationmasters and single storey entrance buildings. Entrances and ground floor windows featured protruding brick surrounds. Before long the frontages were in several cases distorted by the conversion of some of the ground floor to shops and all were heavily disfigured with advertising hoardings with a jumble of messages mostly about the railway's services and fares. At Ealing, the terminus was on the east side of Haven Green, a little to the north of the GWR station. Here the road level building consisted of a pair of the standard two-storey houses linked by an entrance frontage with two tall arch-roofed doorways. Behind, at a lower level, was a small train shed with two platforms, the southernmost with a face each side at the outer end. A major rebuilding was undertaken in 1911–13, when H. W. Ford, the District's architect, provided a two-storey classical frontage in Portland stone with a wide central entrance flanked with small shops. There was a substantial steel and glass canopy, initially adorned with a clock. A fourth platform face added at this time on the north side was later shortened to accommodate an uncoupled two-car set or locomotives. There was also a bay on the south side from about 1905.

Ford also supplied the design for the 1910 reconstruction of Mill Hill Park where the new building, placed over the line, consisted of a single storey hipped-roof stone-fronted block dominated by an arched central entrance. Extra income from retail lettings was now much to the fore and provision was made for a small shop each side of the doorway. At the same time the double line and side platforms were replaced by three tracks serving two islands. This allowed trains to be run into the centre reversible local road (with a platform face either side) to await the arrival of eastbound and westbound services on the outer faces. A new flyover bridge west of the station allowed westbound Ealing and Hounslow trains to leave at the same time. From 1st March 1910, with these new works largely completed, the station was renamed Acton Town.

Ealing's 1879 railway brought what was soon to be dubbed 'The Queen of the Western Suburbs' within 48 minutes of the City of London (Mansion House), with two trains an hour provided all day, four an hour in the peaks. This District Railway facility was very soon making a substantial impact on the area's growth and prosperity. Between 1880 and 1914 residential streets spread out south and north of the GWR main line, whilst to the east, Ealing had by the 1910s coalesced with neighbouring Acton. With a constantly growing population (over 30,000 by the early 1890s) Ealing became the first municipal borough in Middlesex in 1901.

Following the excursion into suburban areas ripe for steady development, not least Ealing, the aggregate total of ordinary and season ticket journeys on the District

increased from 30.26 million in 1877 to 34.1 million in 1882. This did not however bring any great financial rewards. Although the company was able to pay its first dividend on ordinary shares in 1878 and reach the dizzy height of 1½ per cent on ordinaries in 1880, this period of prosperity soon fizzled out.

Whilst in the full flush of its expansionist mode, the District sought powers to reach Uxbridge, depositing bills in 1879 and again in 1880, but both were thrown out after fierce GWR opposition. As a sop, the GWR conceded running powers to Windsor over the junction authorised in the MDR's Ealing extension legislation of 1877. This venture was not successful. After the junction east of Ealing station had been made in 1883 a District service of 11 trains a day each way on weekdays and nine on Sundays, using its own locomotives and rolling stock, was begun between Mansion House and Windsor on 1st March 1883. It attracted little business and from 1st October 1884 was reduced to four each way daily, ceasing altogether on 30th September 1885. The reactions of the few passengers originating in the still sparsely populated area west of Ealing to the harshness of the ride in the little four-wheeled carriages of the day no doubt contributed to this failure. Any subsequent resumption was prevented when a rebuilding of the GWR station at Ealing in 1898–99 extinguished the connecting line.

The opening of the London United electric tramway from Shepherds Bush through Ealing to Southall on 10th July 1901 and the electrification of the District Railway between Ealing and Whitechapel from 1st July 1905 further lubricated the residential growth and general prosperity of the area. Although comparisons of the census figures are misleading because of boundary changes it is clear there was a very substantial increase in population in the Ealing area between 1901 and 1911. In 1913 Ealing Broadway was offering 11–12 District trains an hour at peak periods and eight an hour (at six-ten minute intervals) for most of the remainder of the day. To attract the lucrative first class season ticket traffic, the so-called *Ealing Express* had been introduced. Leaving Ealing Broadway at 09.10 (there was a return working in the late afternoon) this passed all nine stations between Ealing Common and Sloane Square exclusive. There were other less ambitious 'non-stops' in the middle of the day. By 1921 the evening *Ealing Express* was timed to leave Mansion House at 17.07, taking 30 minutes to reach Ealing Broadway (it ran non-stop Sloane Square to Acton Town). Such was its popularity that it was then lengthened from six to eight cars.

To accommodate the Ealing & Shepherds Bush Railway, carrying Central London Railway tube trains to Ealing Broadway from 3rd August 1920, new platforms were inserted that year between the GWR and District stations. At this time a wide covered footbridge was erected to link all platforms in the three Ealing Broadway stations; the train shed of the 1879 District terminus was retained and it still survives at the time of writing, substantially unaltered. A new signalbox for the District and Central Lines was opened on the north side of the terminal tracks on 30th September 1952. In the following decade a further major reconstruction at Ealing Broadway put Ford's 1911–13 station building out of railway use. Passengers for both BR and London Transport trains were to use a single entrance and a new ticket hall with a glass-fronted ticket office situated just below street level. This was built on a concrete raft over the former GWR platforms. Above it rose a nine-storey office block with a shopping parade opening to the street. A new covered footway linked all platforms. Although the new entrance and ticket hall were opened on 5th December 1965 and the District line entrance and ticket office closed on 13th November 1966, all the new work was not completed until the end of 1968. The LT platforms were numbered in with the rest of the station from 1st July 1967, platforms 1, 2 and 3 becoming 7–9.

Ealing Common station was handsomely reconstructed in the Charles Holden 'Morden Extension' Portland stone-clad style in 1931. Its heptagonal ticket hall, under a stubby tower, opened for public use on 1st March, was decorated by the interior designer Basil Ionides in grey, green and cream, the floor inlaid with a black star motif. The rebuilt platforms included concrete canopies with clerestory illumination, the first example of this in a Holden station.

The rearrangement of tracks west of Hammersmith mentioned earlier required total reprovision of Chiswick Park station, undertaken in 1931–33. It was a difficult site and one objective was to command attention from the High Street, a short distance to the south. The new station, with four tracks but side platforms serving only the District line trains, was completed in 1933. Design here was in the hands of S. A. Heaps, the Underground's staff architect, in consultation with Charles Holden, whose 'family style' for the Underground's new 1930s stations was adopted. The street level building, on the south side of the viaduct, was dominated by a lofty and spacious semi circular ticket hall in hand-made, sand-faced, multi-red bricks. This had a flat concrete lid and very large windows, the brickwork left exposed inside. At the west side, a tower in the same bricks carried the Underground bullseye symbol and the station name. Below were three wide entrance openings and several shops set in a lengthy flat-roofed frontage. More sand-faced multi-reds backed the platforms on the viaduct and behind this, the canopies were curved and cantilevered, their concrete showing the board marks of the shuttering. As elsewhere, works in connection with the Underground Ticketing System of the late 1980s seriously eroded the careful architecture of the entrance hall.

Acton Town underwent its second rebuilding in 1932–33, with Heaps again working to Holden's new 'brick box and concrete lid' style. Here Holden's sketches had suggested a rectangular entrance hall with tall narrow windows facing the street and a long low flat-roofed entrance and shop line at road level very similar to that at Chiswick Park, extended to provide an auxiliary entrance from Bollo Lane on the east side. The entrance hall, lined with quarry tiles. led out to footbridges and gangways designed to separate inward and outward passenger flows. The platforms and tracks were also rearranged and rebuilt to accommodate the contemporary quadrupling, the new layout becoming, east to west: South Acton terminal road; District eastbound; Piccadilly line eastbound; Piccadilly westbound; District westbound (i.e. five platform faces, with two islands, and a side platform on the east).

A study of the catchment area of the Ealing extension suggests that until the 1920s and 1930s, most of its traffic originated at Ealing and to a lesser extent at Chiswick Park. The residential development around the latter was mostly in place by the time the station opened, notably the estate immediately to the north, whose name was assumed by the station from February 1887. Curiously the place is not in Chiswick at all, but the developers wanted a suitable cachet. Beyond here, the market gardens west of the line defied the builders for many years. Then in 1921 part of the site was covered by the Chiswick Works of the London General Omnibus Company and from 1922 the rest, on the north side of the N&SWJR, by its cousin, the Underground Company's Acton Works, provided to centralise the overhaul of all the undertaking's trains.

Mill Hill Park was another residential estate giving its name to a station. This was laid out north east of the railway, on the east side of Gunnersbury Lane, in 1877–80 but was not filled up until the early years of the twentieth century. West of the line here, the more compact housing of the Gunnersbury Lodge Estate and Gunnersbury Park Gardens, respectively north and south of Gunnersbury Lane, both date from 1925–27 and other housing between Gunnersbury Avenue and the railway up to Ealing Common is of similar date. What is now Acton Town station did however benefit from the start from its reasonably close proximity (just over a quarter of a mile) to the town centre of Acton, a circumstance which justified the later renaming.

The Ealing Common works and car sheds of the District Railway, on the east side of the line just south of the station, were erected in 1904–05 for the electrification. They occupied 25 acres bought from Leopold de Rothschild of Gunnersbury Park. Most of the housing east of Ealing Common station was built in the 1900s and early 1910s but that to the north west, towards Ealing itself, appeared in the 1880s and 1890s.

In the Appendices to the 1905 Report of the Royal Commission on London Traffic (vol III, p.547) we find a carefully compiled record of a typical commuter journey via Ealing Common station in 1904, just before electrification. Walking from the house to the tram stop took 7½ minutes (4mph), the electric tram to Ealing Common one mile in 7½ minutes (8 mph) at a fare of 1d, Ealing Common to Mansion House by train, (3½d workmen's fare), 9½ miles in 45minutes (12.6mph), and walking at the London end another 7½ minutes, a total of 11.5 miles in 67½ minutes (10.25 mph) at a cost of 4½ old pennies. In terms of purchasing power, the total fare may be illustrated as the cost in 1904 of five copies of *The Daily Mail*, or nine pounds of potatoes, or two small (2lb) loaves of bread. Taking into account the five minutes expended in waiting for tram and train, the average speed was 9.25 mph. A year later, after electrification, the running time on the railway would have been reduced to 35–36 minutes, even less after the subsequent introduction of the 'non-stop' working mentioned earlier. In 1996 the District Line Journey took 33 minutes, at a single fare of £1.80. Ealing's terminal platforms, still not entirely without their Victorian aura, remain well and efficiently served by the District Railway's successors.

South Acton Branch (District Railway) (map page 260)

Whilst its Turnham Green to Ealing extension was under construction in 1878, the District Railway obtained powers to build a spur from it (the Acton Loop Line) so that trains could run from the Willesden direction off the N&SWJR towards Ealing. A similar curve in the opposite direction (Bollo Lane Junction to Acton Lane Junction) was used from March 1878 by Midland Railway coal trains running to yards on the District. Although the N&SWJR had opened a station to serve the newly developing district of South Acton on 1st January 1880, the District was in no hurry to build a line whose purpose was more closely connected with the development of the western part of its system than short-distance traffic within Acton. This delay entailed a considerable amount of parliamentary cost in obtaining legislation for extension of time and revival of powers; although Ordnance Survey maps of the early 1890s reveal that some earthworks had been started near Bollo Lane, a serious beginning with the Acton Loop Line had to wait until 1898. Construction was then placed in the hands of C. J. Wills & Son, contractors for the Ealing & South Harrow Railway, the incentive for completing the link being its value in transporting construction materials to the E&SHR works. One of these trains first passed over the completed line on 15th May 1899.

It seems likely that the District saw the main use of the line as providing access to coal yards it might eventually persuade the northern companies to provide free at its western suburban stations, but this came to nothing and by 1902 it had been decided to electrify it as a projection of the E&SHR, with a station alongside the N&SWJR at South Acton for easy interchange with the NLR services to Richmond and Broad Street. This proposal was also dropped and once again the Acton Loop Line was left; although the E&SHR was opened on 23rd June 1903, no passenger trains appeared on the Loop until 13th June 1905 when a South Acton–Hounslow Barracks electric service was started, using the American-inspired 'A' stock. London passengers changed into steam trains at Mill Hill Park (now Acton Town) until the inner part of the District Railway was electrified on 1st July 1905. Connections at South Acton were indifferent; for example, in 1909, trains arrived from Hounslow at 21 and 51 minutes past each hour, and trains for Willesden and Broad Street left at 28 and 58 minutes, but passengers arriving in NLR Down trains at nine and 39 minutes past waited 13 minutes at South Acton before the District train left.

Until electric working started, the Acton Loop Line had only a single track, although the works provided for double. At the South Acton end, the junction was controlled by an N&SWJR box and working was by pilotman. When the District doubled the line early in 1905 a crossover was laid on Palmerston Road bridge and a District signalbox was opened on the new South Acton platform.

The Loop left the London end of Mill Hill Park station at South Junction, running parallel to the main line on the east side before curving round to cross Bollo Lane on a plate girder bridge and run alongside the N&SWJR on embankment into South Acton station. Here the District provided a platform of six car length and the rudimentary corrugated iron hut it considered adequate for its less important western suburban stations. This building backed on to the N&SWJR Up side at slightly higher level, steps leading the passenger to a small entrance hall which contained the District ticket office and doorways to the street and the N&SWJR platform. After a few years, ticket issue was more economically carried out from the signalbox on the platform above.

By the time the District passenger service started, the area around South Acton station was fairly well built-up, with small houses inhabited by the upper ranks of the working class, though a few larger villas and nursery gardens survived from the previous development phase. In the 1880s and 1890s, Acton had spread south towards Bollo Lane and contemporaneously the separate suburb of Acton Green had swamped the area between South Acton and Turnham Green stations. There were also some laundries and drying grounds ('Soapsud Island') serving the middle-class families of Kensington.

Both the LNWR and the Midland had obtained running powers over the Acton Loop Line, the former to Ealing Common Junction, the latter to Mill Hill Park only. Working timetables showed early-morning paths 'as required' for stores or ballast trains, but this seems to have been a survival from the construction of the E&SHR; freight traffic was virtually non-existent. All non-passenger working ceased in 1914, District Junction box closing in the following year, when the points into the N&SWJR were clipped out of use. Everything was left intact for possible use at short notice until about 1930, when the points were taken out; the box was demolished in 1934.

By 1913 the through workings between South Acton and Hounslow had been replaced by a 20-minute shuttle service working between 05.55 and 00.40. Through journeys were later restored and in 1922 there was a 15-minute service (30 minutes on Sundays), most trains running to and from South Harrow (some Uxbridge) and, on weekdays, about half a dozen over the Hounslow line. Traffic at South Acton, much of it interchanging with North London trains, reached 349,000 a year in the mid-1920s, well over twice that of some stations on the Ealing & South Harrow.

In conjunction with the projection of Piccadilly Line tube trains over the western section of the District Railway, the layout at Acton Town was considerably altered and the station completely rebuilt. A short platform (No. 5) was specially provided on the east side for the South Acton trains. The Acton Loop Line was now reduced to single track with 'one train on line' working and when this came into effect in February 1932, the District box at South Acton station was closed and demolished. For training purposes some Piccadilly Line tube trains were operated between South Harrow and Acton Town and between South Acton and the Hounslow branch, but tube car operation lasted only from 8th to 14th February 1932, when double-line working ceased. From the next day the Loop was operated by a shuttle service using either a 'B' stock motor car (No. 37, which had been specially converted to work as a double-ended unit) or a two-car unit of 'B' stock motor plus control-trailer. The latter was observed soon after the start of the new service bearing at the respective ends the absurd legends ACTON TOWN NON STOP and SOUTH ACTON ALL STATIONS.

Tunnel-type telephone wires, allowing the driver to cut off traction current without leaving his cab, were erected alongside the line on concrete posts during 1938. This paved the way for one-man operation. Two 'G' stock driving motors (4167 and 4176) were accordingly modified to operate as double-ended units; each had air doors worked from the driving cabs, two 240hp motors and 44 seats. This single-car working, known to the staff as 'the Pony', ran between 06.00 and around midnight. In the 1950s the frequency was about every ten minutes (every seven minutes in peak hours) and despite popular belief that departures from Acton Town were influenced by the staff's tea-making activities (there and back whilst the kettle boils), a timetable was observed.

District Line single car train from Acton Town arriving at South Acton station 21st February 1959.
It will take up a return load of only two adults and three children. The North London line platforms,
at a slightly lower level, appear behind the corrugated iron architecture of the District Railway.
Alan A Jackson

Those who used the interchange facility at South Acton increasingly favoured bus
or private car, and in the 1950s rarely were more than half a dozen passengers seen
on the train. Sunday working ceased after 8th June 1958 and in a search for
system-wide economies, London Transport proposed complete closure. It was
suggested that connections between the North London trains and Piccadilly/District
services might be made by taking a bus between Acton Town station and Acton,
where Acton Central station could be reached by walking 330 yards. Those unfortunates who lived near South Acton station, where some new flats had been built
and more were planned, had to walk the equivalent of the full length of the Acton
Loop Line to reach a bus road. In November 1958 the London Transport Users'
Consultative Committee opposed the closure, suggesting weighted fares as an
alternative, but were overruled by the central committee. The last car ran at
midnight on Saturday 28th February 1959.

London Transport customarily wastes little time in extinguishing rail facilities
after closure, and South Acton was no exception. The crossover connecting the
branch to the eastbound fast road south of Acton Town station was taken out of
commission from 19th March 1959 and by 13th May all track on the Loop Line had
gone. Demolition of South Acton LT station followed soon after. At the end of 1963
the embankment between Bollo Lane and South Acton was levelled preparatory to
the erection of blocks of council flats. The bridge over Bollo Lane was dismantled
in the following January, during which process it collapsed into the road, blocking
it for several days while the wreckage was cut-up where it lay. At South Acton station
about the same time a recreation ground was extended over the site of the line so
that today there is virtually no trace of it beyond Bollo Lane and very little elsewhere.
Had the North London line been incorporated into the London Transport system,
it is conceivable the Loop might have survived, as it would have offered useful
cross-town routes, including a less-congested connection between Heathrow
Central and the northern main line termini.

The Ealing & Shepherds Bush Railway

(map page 260)

Not long after its opening in 1864, the Hammersmith & City Railway, a joint enterprise of Metropolitan and Great Western, providing through trains to the heart of the City, was beginning to encourage residential spread west of Notting Hill. December 1868 saw the opening of Latimer Road station on the western edge of the smart new district of North Kensington, whilst still further west, Hammersmith was growing northwards, the pace of building hampered only by the absence of railway facilities.

To remedy this omission, a Latimer Road & Acton Railway was promoted in 1881 with a capital of £180,000. A branch from the H&CR, it was to follow a route somewhat south of the present line of the A40(M) motorway, to join the GWR near Friar's Place Green, east of that company's Acton station, 2m 15ch in all. Serving north Hammersmith and east Acton, it could hope for a steady growth in commuter traffic similar to that experienced by the H&CR; the whole area traversed lay ripe to receive the housebuilders.

Authorised in 1882 to a nominally independent company, the Latimer Road & Acton sought a working agreement with the Metropolitan and the GWR, but its potential was somewhat damaged when on grounds of alleged traffic congestion, the H&CR allowed it only an interchange platform where the two lines came together at the H&CR bridge over Wood Lane. To make matters worse, the GWR insisted on a separate station at Acton.

Enough cash was raised or promised to permit a start on construction in 1883 at the Acton end. A house standing on the site of the proposed Acton station near Friar's Place was demolished and an iron bridge erected over the N&SWJR near the present motorway bridge. This activity ceased when the money ran out; neither the GWR nor the Metropolitan were prepared to come to the rescue, and desperately seeking other suitors, the promoters were to submit bills for the 1887 session which provided for an independent terminus at Notting Hill Gate near the Metropolitan station and a link with the District between West Kensington and Earl's Court. At the Acton end, an extension towards Gunnersbury was mooted. None of this was authorised and a Notting Hill & Acton Railway Bill of 1888 for a similar route was also lost.

Much effort and money was spent on legislation after this. No less than four acts, mainly for extensions of time, were obtained between 1885 and 1893. An unsuccessful bill of 1890 sought a curve at Shepherds Bush which would have allowed direct running from Hammersmith H&CR on to the Latimer Road and Acton, though it is difficult to appreciate what the value of this might have been. Agreement was eventually reached with the GWR and Metropolitan for joint working, and this was confirmed in yet another act (1895). Despite this, capital was shy, and the veil was drawn by an abandonment act of 1900. Only the lawyers, parliamentary agents and engineers had profited.

Much the same route was revived by the Ealing & Shepherds Bush Railway, authorised to the GWR in 1905. This was primarily intended to give that company a suburban services terminus north of Shepherds Bush Common against the west side of the Central London Railway tube terminus, to which there would be subway connection. A junction with the West London Railway north of Uxbridge Road station was also proposed, mainly for freight purposes.

The Ealing & Shepherds Bush was to serve north Hammersmith and east Acton

---

in much the same way as the Latimer Road & Acton would have done, but its route passed a little further north and its access to the GWR main line was more devious because it was arranged to touch the new Wycombe main line. In 1911 the Central London Railway got powers for a half-mile connection between its Wood Lane terminus (near White City) and the Ealing & Shepherds Bush, over which its tube trains were to run to Ealing GWR. The much improved facility which this scheme offered caused the GWR to abandon its proposed suburban lines terminus at Shepherds Bush.

In a 1912 bill, the Metropolitan tried to get into the game, seeking powers to make a connection with the Ealing & Shepherds Bush between Wood Lane and Latimer Road. This failed because both the GWR and the Central London opposed through running by the Metropolitan over the Ealing & Shepherds Bush, protesting that it would obstruct the CLR service. The District added its weight, objecting to the Ealing competition. The Metropolitan finally gave up its ambitions in this area in return for a GWR agreement to a 1912 scheme for capital improvements on the Hammersmith & City Railway.

Construction of the double-track Ealing & Shepherds Bush was started by the GWR in 1912 but work was delayed by World War I and it was not possible to open it until 16th April 1917, when freight trains passed over it to and from the West London Railway at Viaduct Junction. No regular passenger working started until

North Acton, GWR, looking to London, c. 1938; the Central Line (Ealing & Shepherds Bush Railway) platforms are just off the picture on the right.

3rd August 1920 when the GWR received the boon of a through tube service between its Ealing station, the West End and the City. The tube trains called at the new station of East Acton, serving an LCC housing estate which had been started in 1912. Two other intermediate stations on the Ealing & Shepherds Bush, West Acton and North Acton, were added on 5th November 1923. All three were cheaply built and without architectural distinction; West Acton even had the standard GWR halt 'pagoda' shelters.

Motor roads called Westway and Western Avenue were carved through the area in 1922 and 1924, while during the 1920s most of the district between the GWR main line at Acton and Wood Lane was covered with LCC and Hammersmith Borough Council housing, this over 40 years after the promoters of the Latimer Road & Acton had hoped for such development. During 1937 the GWR quadrupled the section between Wood Lane and North Acton to separate tube and freight movements in anticipation of extension of Central Line tube service alongside the Wycombe line as far as Denham. GWR trains ceased to use the electric lines from 19th June 1938. Until that year they had carried one regular GWR passenger service, workmen's trains between Greenford and Kensington (Addison Road), started in 1922 and extended to Clapham Junction in 1933. These trains came very close to the site of the inner end of the Latimer Road & Acton as they passed on and off the West London line at Viaduct Junction.

The four tracks of the Ealing & Shepherds Bush Railway near Wood Lane, looking west, 6th April 1957. Wood Lane Jc signal box is beyond the concrete footbridge and the freight lines to Viaduct Jc with the West London Railway are seen between the Central Line tracks and Du Cane Road (right). An eastbound Central Line train has just passed through the flyunder which was built at this point to change the direction of running between the two tube lines. *Alan A Jackson*

The Ealing & Greenford Line   (map page 260)

When the GWR secured powers in 1897 for the section of its direct Birmingham line from Old Oak Common West (Acton) to a junction with its Maidenhead-Princes Risborough line at High Wycombe, the legislation included a two mile 24.55ch double-track line between the new main line at Greenford and Brunel's London & Bristol at West Ealing. To this the GWR Act of 1903 added an eastern curve at Greenford (26.4ch) and a western one at the southern end (36.6ch); these were something of an afterthought and parliamentary sanction followed their construction.

The initial reason for linking the two main lines at a point so close to their junction at the London end was principally to allow freight trains to run off the new High Wycombe direct line through Ealing Broadway on to the Midland, LNWR and North London lines via Acton Wells Junction and also to provide for expresses on the new line to call at Ealing Broadway. But in practice it became very much a local line, hence its inclusion here. Indeed from the start the possibility of developing suburban traffic was not overlooked; the additional curves authorised in 1903 were largely designed for this purpose.

From its junctions with the old Bristol main line the Greenford line ran in a cutting through the higher ground north of Ealing, emerging at Castle Bar Park to cross the claylands of the Brent Valley on a high embankment, passing over the Ruislip Road and the Brent on a 320ft brick arch viaduct. It continued northwards above ground level as far as South Junction, where the Greenford East and West Loops diverged. At the time of construction, most of the area traversed was open country. Only at the southern end did built-up London touch the new railway. Greenford, then a small crossroads settlement, was away to the west on the country bank of the River Brent, near the point where the river turned south, and almost a mile from the railway. Its new station, sited at the junction between the West Loop and the new main line, was about halfway between Greenford village and the then separate community of Greenford Green to the north.

By the beginning of 1903 work on the new railways was sufficiently advanced to permit operation of trains between Old Oak Common and Ealing or Hanwell via the north-south connecting line. Some urgency was evident as the Royal Agricultural Society had prepared 100 acres of show grounds at Park Royal (so named by Edward VII when he performed an opening ceremony on 25th May 1903) and to serve them the GWR had erected a substantial station with long stone platforms on the new main line about halfway between the present North Acton and Hanger Lane stations. Almost immediately after the royal visit, freight trains began moving in materials and equipment for the first Show, some coming in via the new north-south link. A service of passenger trains, 14 each way daily, weekdays, was started on 15th June 1903 between Paddington, Westbourne Park, Park Royal, the Greenford East Loop and Ealing Broadway. During the period of the Agricultural Show (23rd – 27th June) this was augmented to provide a 20-minute service. Over those five days, some passenger trains were also worked between Southall and Park Royal via the Hanwell curve and the Greenford East curve. Not surprisingly in view of the lack of development in the Brent Valley, passenger traffic fell sharply once the Show-ground closed and all these trains were withdrawn on 4th July 1903.

Indeed the Show itself was something of a flop, despite the combined efforts of the GWR, the LNWR and the District Railway to serve the new grounds with dedicated stations. Nor was the event any more of a success in 1904 and 1905, a sequence which caused the Royal Agricultural Society to give up the site in despair. Possibly the farmers and traders felt ill at ease in a place which was neither town nor country and no doubt the limited interest of Londoners in matters agricultural was not sufficient to bring them out in any quantity for what was for many a difficult journey across the city. In an attempt to rescue something from its large investment in Park Royal, the GWR made some use of the sidings as a freight depot and also enticed Queens Park Rangers FC to play in the showground from August 1904. When this move proved unpopular with the football fraternity, the GWR built QPR a new ground on railway land immediately north of the station, leasing it to the club on favourable terms. This venture proved moderately successful, producing a steady flow of winter Saturdays football traffic until 1915, when the whole area north of the station was taken over for war purposes.

The combined effects of very heavy rain and the pounding of freight trains for the 1903 Show wrought such havoc with the earthworks of the newly-built railway that it was closed between Old Oak, Park Royal and West Ealing from 10th August 1903 to allow an army of over 500 men to rebuild the works and construct new halts. After passenger trains returned on 1st May 1904 a complex pattern of workings developed, to be much varied from time to time. The intricacies so fascinated the Rev. W. J. Scott that he contributed an article on the subject to the 1908 *Great Western Railway Magazine* which ran to no less than four instalments.

The first service (1st May 1904) operated between Westbourne Park, Park Royal and Southall, calling at new halts erected at North Acton (adjacent to the present LT station), Twyford Abbey (by the Hanger Lane bridge), Perivale (on the west side of the Horsenden Lane bridge), and Castle Bar Park for Greenford (1m 1ch north of West Ealing at the point of transition from embankment to cutting). This last halt could only be reached by a fieldpath but it served the 17-acre GWR sports ground east of the railway, and on the west side, the Central London and West London Schools for Pauper Children, where Charlie Chaplin spent some time as a pupil. All four halts had short timber platforms with centrally sited corrugated-iron 'pagoda' waiting huts. With no other amenities beyond oil lamps and name boards, and without staff, they set a pattern for the many which were to follow all over the GWR system. They were expressly designed to accommodate the 52-seater steam railcars which the company had chosen to use in the as yet undeveloped districts west of London and on its rural branch lines.

The initial train service was worked by one such car ('rail motor-car' in GWR parlance), based at Southall shed and operating about 14 trips daily (about every 70 minutes) from the 07.00 ex-Southall to the 22.42 ex-Westbourne Park. Although built, the eastern curve at West Ealing was for some reason not available for use, hence the choice of Southall as the outer terminus. At the London end, Westbourne Park was the starting point because Paddington did not have the capacity to take the railcars, though they did start and finish there on Sundays, when there were nine trips each way.

In a commendable effort to stimulate traffic, leaflets about this service were distributed to London property auctioneers for onward transmission to developers and landowners. A second railcar, which arrived on 1st July 1904, was put to work to run ten times daily each way (roughly hourly) between Park Royal and Acton via Castle Bar Park. After Greenford station had opened for regular traffic on 1st

October 1904, most of the railcar trips worked in and out of there using the Greenford West Loop, and some of the Acton journeys were extended from the same date via Acton Wells Junction to Willesden Junction High Level. A further halt was opened on 1st March 1905 at Drayton Green, 57ch south of Castle Bar Park and just north of the triangular junction. Close to existing housing in north east Hanwell and the western edge of West Ealing, this attracted a trickle of residential traffic. Later the area was enlivened by the construction of an engineer's depot inside the triangle and a four-road coal yard east of the halt to serve the domestic needs of West Ealing and north Hanwell.

Changes made to the railcar services on 10th October 1905 saw the end of the lightly-patronised Southall via Castle Bar trips apart from a few Sunday workings this way between Paddington and Southall. The basic service now ran Westbourne Park–Park Royal–Greenford–Castle Bar Park–Acton–Willesden Junction. 1906 saw further alterations, set out in great detail by Scott, but which it would be tedious to relate here.

With the opening of the Uxbridge (High Street) branch on 1st May 1907 the service was changed again, eventually settling down to run between Denham (or Gerrards Cross from July 1909) and West Ealing via Uxbridge (High Street), Denham (again) and Greenford. The Westbourne Park–Park Royal–Castle Bar Park–Acton–Willesden Junction trains were cut back to Acton GWR during a coal strike in March 1912 and never again ventured beyond that point.

Twyford Abbey Halt closed completely from 1st May 1911, giving way to a new halt called Brentham & North Ealing a short distance further west, better placed to serve the 1901–14 housing estate south of the line known as Brentham or West London Garden Village. Also, immediately west of the junction between the two main lines, at Old Oak Lane, a halt of that name, with full length platforms came into use on 1st October 1906 mainly for the convenience of railway staff at the adjacent engine and carriage depots.

Loadings in these early years did not tax the limited capacity of the steam railcars. On the first day, 1st May 1904, a fine Sunday, about 400 tickets were sold on the Westbourne Park–Southall service, a figure only subsequently approached on sunny weekends and Bank Holidays when west Londoners were tempted to taste the rural delights of the Brent Valley. Such trippers were encouraged by cheap fares and, from August 1904, a Sunday and Bank Holiday railcar service by both routes between Kensington (Addison Road) (now Olympia) and Greenford. From 16th April 1905 this was extended back to Clapham Junction and later in 1905 into the GWR side of Victoria station. Brent Valley trains were not seen at Victoria after 1915 but from about 1930 the GWR worked unadvertised workmen's trains from Clapham Junction to Ealing Broadway via Greenford, services which were mostly patronised by staff employed at Messrs J. Lyons' factories at Cadby Hall (near Olympia) and Greenford.

Regular use of the route via the Hanwell and Greenford East loops ceased after 1905, this then seeing only football and other specials. The two western loops were followed in combination by occasional weekday trips until 1910 and by some summer Sunday trains until August 1914. After that, all regular passenger trains to various destinations used the Greenford West Loop and the West Ealing Loop, as is still the case at the time of writing.

It has taken some time to describe even the main pattern of the services up to 1914 but in practice they did not amount to much in terms of frequency. Thus in 1910 there were 20 railcar trips each way daily between Greenford and West Ealing or Hanwell (one), offering either connections or through working to Westbourne Park, Uxbridge (High Street), Denham, Acton, Willesden Junction and Southall (one). Sundays saw four each way between Victoria and Greenford via Castle Bar Park, five between Paddington and West Ealing via Castle Bar Park and two between Uxbridge (High Street) and Acton/Southall. The Acton–Westbourne Park service ceased in 1914, after which the stops between Greenford and Old Oak Lane were served by main line local trains and the West Ealing–Greenford section was covered by trains between Ealing Broadway/West Ealing and Greenford or stations north west of Greenford.

It did not take the GWR very long to realise that use of a small tank engine (usually a 517 class 0–4–2T) with one or two trailers fitted for push-pull working offered greater flexibility and economy than the steam railcars. Like the steam railcars, these so-called 'motor trains' or 'auto trains' could be staffed with a conductor, saving the cost of ticket offices. By the early 1920s they had taken over almost all the Brent Valley services.

With some new housing appearing between West Ealing and Greenford on both sides of the line from 1925 onwards (most of it in the 1930s) trips were increased to

Greenford auto train (BR loco 1456 and car *Thrush*) at platform 3, Ealing Broadway, 17th April 1954. *Alan A Jackson*

around 32 each way daily, taking 10–12 minutes. The Elthorne Heights Estate, west of the line between Castle Bar Park halt and the river Brent was started in 1923/4 by the Great Western Land Company (which had no direct links with the GWR). Here detached four bedroom houses were advertised at £1,000–£1,250. Immediately north of this, also bringing some business to Castle Bar Park halt from 1932, was the Cuckoo Estate, where small three-bedroom houses were sold at £750. Three years later the LCC started its Hanwell Estate, making use of the large area occupied by the Residential Schools and by 1938 some 5,300 were living here. Between the wars, Ealing advanced up to the east side of the railway and the edges of the GWR Sports Ground.

To the north, Western Avenue, one of the state-funded unemployment relief roads, was opened through the Brent Valley as far as Greenford in 1927 and on to Uxbridge in 1935–37. This main road construction soon hastened the development of estates of small houses between the old village of Greenford and its station, which had started in the 1920s. Light industries were also encouraged by it and a whole new district grew up around Greenford station, where season ticket issues rose from 469 in 1923 to 4,068 five years later. This development stimulated the GWR into providing South Greenford halt, 61ch north of Castle Park. Approached by footpaths either side of the embankment leading from Western Avenue, the new facility was opened on 20th September 1926. At first the main users were road construction workers and patrons of the Perivale Park Golf Course and the West London Shooting Grounds. The 'South' in the name was a typical piece of railway management geography, accurate only in relation to the 1904 Greenford station, as the site was three quarters of a mile *north east* of the old village centre.

House and factory building led to some improvements (from 20th June 1932) along the main line through Greenford, including the opening of another halt, at Park Royal West (just west of the District Railway bridge) on that day. Another feature of the 1932 summer timetable was a sensible extension into Ealing Broadway of all services through Greenford and Castle Bar, providing connections to main line services and the Underground. This 1932 timetable brought 27 more trains each way, most of them turning round at Northolt. At Ealing Broadway, a siding was built for the auto trains between the Up and Down Relief lines and equipped with an engine inspection pit and a water crane. A further innovation was the provision of two late night theatre trains departing Ealing Broadway at 23.02 and 23.52. From this time the auto-trains were worked by the new 48xx 0–4–2T or by 54xx 0–6–0PT. At rush hours, a second trailer was added (the halt platforms between West Ealing and Greenford had been lengthened to allow for this in 1930).

In part these improvements were designed to counter the bus competition which had started in 1930 when residential development had attracted a Royal Highlander service between Ealing Broadway and Greenford, passing close to West Ealing station and Drayton Green halt and tapping the new housing south of Ruislip Road to the west of the railway. From 1933 London Transport perpetuated this service, which has always operated much more frequently, if more slowly, than the trains. Trade at South Greenford and the halts on the main line was drawn off by a General bus service along Western Avenue which provided a connection to Park Royal Underground station from May 1932. Another bus service started at about this time served the roads on the west side of Castle Bar Park and Drayton Green halts, passing through West Ealing to Ealing Broadway.

The main line featured in the 1935–40 London Railways New Works Programme, and after the delay caused by World War 2, Central Line tube trains were projected alongside it from North Acton to Greenford from 30th June 1947. These trains were carried above the Greenford East and West Loops on single track concrete and lattice girder viaducts which left the original GWR double track junctions unaltered. A single line spur was built from the Greenford West Loop to allow the Ealing auto-trains to ascend between the east and westbound electric lines to terminate in a bay set into the eastern end of the island platform which formed the new Greenford Central Line station. This platform, 33ft above the roadway, was reached by a single escalator of 30ft rise, the first on the Underground carrying passengers up to their train. The old GWR halts on the main line were replaced by new stations at Perivale and Hanger Lane, both on new sites.

At first the 35 trains a day each way over the Greenford–Ealing Broadway line (22 on Sundays) continued to use the old GWR platforms at Greenford which were connected to the Central Line ticket hall by an underline subway but when the tube service was extended to West Ruislip on 21st November 1948, all auto-train trips west of Greenford were withdrawn and an hourly train (with additional workings at the peak periods) then ran each way in and out of the unelectrified bay road at Greenford Central Line station, using the spur mentioned earlier. Until 17th June 1963 the old GWR station at Greenford remained open for parcels trains and some main line calls.

Class 54xx 0-6-0PT No.5401 propels an afternoon Northolt to Westbourne Park train on 16th June 1947. Old Oak Lane Halt was closed two weeks later. *J.J. Smith*

Throughout the 1950s the Greenford–Ealing line retained much of the delightfully relaxed aura of a GWR country branch line. That regressive GWR attitudes remained very much alive at Paddington was demonstrated in 1951 when a new series of steam-hauled auto-trailers of saloon type with large windows and sliding ventilators were introduced. Two of them, named *Thrush* and *Wren* were allocated to the Ealing–Greenford service, which continued to be operated with a mixture of BR and GWR cars for another six years. Diesel power reared its smelly head on Monday morning 25th August 1958 in the form of four new two-car sets (double-ended power cars plus single-ended driving trailers). On the previous evening, the steam auto trains trundled off to Southall and were never seen on the line again. The new arrivals maintained the hourly frequency with peak hours extras which their predecessors had provided before the economy cuts of June 1958. Subsequently cuts were made in Saturday services and there were no Sunday trains after 6th September 1964. Before long, most trips were undertaken by single cars. The diesels completed the 3½m run in 13 min.

Until the Beeching cuts of the early 1960s, Drayton Green and Castle Bar Park were under the supervision of the West Ealing stationmaster. The former was unstaffed but at Castle Bar Park there were two women porters taking turns for two shifts. South Greenford, supervised by the Greenford stationmaster, was unstaffed. These arrangements ensured that the passenger facilities were kept tidy and free from vandalism.

After the withdrawal of staff and supervision in the 1960s, the three halts were all reconstructed with concrete platforms. The nostalgic pagodas at Drayton Green and Castle Bar Park were replaced with ugly red brick shelters and those at South Greenford with the flimsier bus stop type, very soon to lose their glass. The small wooden ticket offices erected by the GWR for commuter service at Drayton Green and Castle Bar Park gave way to brick and concrete accommodation strongly fortified with steel shutters and heavy duty padlocks against youthful vandals. The word 'Halt' did not appear on the new nameboards but the GWR heritage tenuously survived in the form of that company's seats, their wood soon heavily scored by the sharp knives of the vandals, who also quickly did their best to wreck and disfigure everything else newly-provided.

The two loops at Greenford were singled in about 1970 and the connection at Hanwell was also reduced to a single line junction. Although all four loops remained in use, the West Ealing coal yard was closed to public traffic from 4th January 1965. An interesting change to the appearance of the line occurred in 1976–77, when the cutting north of Drayton Green was converted to a covered way to allow construction by the GLC of houses (Copley Close) over the line, part of the process of infilling land between Cavendish and Browning Avenues to provide 639 new homes.

Train services have been substantially improved in recent years. From 1980 the basic frequency was increased to half-hourly off peak, 20 minutes at peak times. To achieve a reduction of two minutes in the running time, the three halts were converted to request stops. From 16th May 1988 the Greenford–Ealing Broadway shuttle was extended into Paddington. On Saturdays there were three trains an hour (20 min intervals) from Greenford, respectively fast from Ealing Broadway to Paddington; Paddington all stations; and Ealing Broadway only. October 1993 saw replacement of the odoriferous and rattly first generation diesel cars by smooth and good-looking Class 165 turbo sets.

Greenford auto train (BR loco 1474) at Drayton Green c.1955.
Lens of Sutton

BR 2-car diesel set for Greenford leaving South Greenford, 18th June 1960. At this date, apart from the train, this was in every respect a typical GWR rural halt.
Alan A Jackson

BR 2-car diesel set from Ealing Broadway entering the central bay between the two tube line platforms at Greenford, 5th September 1959. The Old Oak-High Wycombe main lines are at the left of the picture, which looks towards London.
Alan A Jackson

Train approaching Wembley Exhibition station in July 1925. Just visible on the right are cars of the 'Never Stop' railway. *H C Casserley*

The Wembley Stadium Loop   (map page 260)

In the years immediately preceding World War 1 the idea of a British Empire Exhibition came forward several times but it was not until 1920, when the government and others had agreed to contribute to a fund which would guarantee the organisers against loss that sufficient force built up to bring the concept to fruition. Its objects were then stated to be to 'take stock of the resources of the Empire' . . . to 'make the peoples of the Empire better known to one another, . . . to display scientific practice and research', and . . . to 'enable established industries to show what they have to offer'. The chosen site was Wembley Park, six miles from Marble Arch, served by three railway stations; the Metropolitan's Wembley Park, the GCR's Wembley Hill and the LNWR/Underground at Sudbury & Wembley (later Wembley Central). Electric trams and several bus services also passed close by.

The 280-acre Wembley Park estate had been purchased by the Metropolitan Railway in 1890. An attempt to open up the area as a sports and leisure centre to increase rail revenues had flopped badly; in particular its main feature, Sir Edward Watkin's English version of the Eiffel Tower, erected here in 1892 had not reached above the first platform level and was ignominiously dismantled in 1906. After that, the Metropolitan set its mind to developing the area 'as a building estate in the interests of the railway company'. By 1914 just over 100 houses had been erected in the western part of the site but activity had then ceased and was slow to resume after 1919. There was thus a large area of land still uncovered within the fork formed by the Metropolitan Railway and the former GCR Neasden–Northolt line. In January 1922, 216 acres here were sold to the company organising the Exhibition.

Sir Sam Fay for the GCR and R. H. Selbie for the Metropolitan had agreed in 1921 that the GCR might construct a 'siding' into the Exhibition Grounds following a promise by the GCR that most of the freight brought in over it would be routed via Quainton Road and the Met & GC Joint line. Later the GCR decided to build a loop about a mile long, diverging from the Down Main of the Neasden–Northolt line just east of Wembley Hill station, crossing the Up line, then running north into the Exhibition site before turning back north-east and then south east to rejoin the former GCR Up Independent line at Neasden North Junction, then the Up Main at Neasden South box. This new line was to be signalled for this clockwise direction only and both connections were to be controlled by Neasden North Junction box. When the LNER, as successors to the GCR, decided to build a passenger station on the new railway, which would give it the only station actually inside the Exhibition Grounds, the Metropolitan protested in 1923 that this action was opposed to the spirit, if not the letter of the agreement made between the two companies in 1913 that the GCR would not seek to exploit local traffic between Marylebone and Harrow. But the LNER insisted that the Wembley Loop was connected to its own Neasden–Northolt line, to which the agreement did not apply. The Metropolitan, taking legal advice, was firmly told it had no case to pursue.

Construction of the single track loop, started in December 1922, required removal of around 40,000 cu yd of clay as the station area was approached in a deep cutting. Here a single platform, as yet without any shelter or other buildings, was provided on the west side of the single line. At 600ft long and 22ft 6in wide, it was just big enough to hold a nine coach train of suburban steam stock. As a three minute service was planned between Wembley and Marylebone, the LNER installed automatic colour light signalling and ac track circuits between the London terminus and Wembley Hill station and also around the Loop, closing two manual signal boxes. This allowed very close working, including a maximum of four trains on the Loop at any time.

The first part of the Exhibition Grounds to be completed was the Empire Stadium, which still stands today, on the highest part of the estate, occupying the site of Watkin's ill-fated tower at the southern edge of the area and very close to the north side of the railway between Neasden and Northolt. The largest building of its type in the world at the time, it was selected by the Football Association as a permanent home for its Cup Finals from 1923. The Stadium, which could seat 120,000, and the new railway were ready in time for that event, Bolton Wanderers v. West Ham United, held on 28th April. The railway managers had reckoned on the Cup Finals attracting far more people on one day than the Exhibition would normally see, but even they were to be surprised: over 200,000 made their way out to Wembley and when the Stadium was filled, football-besotted men and boys continued to surge in until the pitch itself was swamped. After herculean efforts by the police, it was cleared to allow the match to start somewhat later than planned.

The LNER had timetabled 51 trains from Marylebone to the Loop station, 15 between 13.00 and 14.00 and nine between 14.00 and 14.30. Mostly of eight bogie coaches and monopolising platforms 3 and 4 at Marylebone, these were filling to capacity from around 11.00. Arrived at the new station, in trainloads of 800–1,000, the crowds very quickly exited through 16 gates on to a road leading directly to the Stadium, about five minutes walk away. All worked smoothly in the outward direction.

However, following the chaos mentioned, the thousands unable to gain access to the Stadium drifted back to the station, anxious to return home. As they pushed in, loaded trains were still arriving. These had to be promptly reloaded and despatched, but many trains had already proceeded to Neasden sidings to await the end of the match. Hurried arrangements were improvised to recall them to take the frustrated spectators back to London. Inevitably the major dislocation of the booked arrangements that ensued caused some delay to the returning trains. As the match finished late, the trains taking back the lucky spectators were also heavily delayed as the timetable fell apart. Some of the crowds were dealt with by the LNER at its Wembley Hill station and large numbers used the Metropolitan at Wembley Park station.

The British Empire Exhibition was opened on 23rd April 1924 and with it, the Loop for a second time, now with a completed station, equipped with a lengthy canopied brick and concrete shelter and other small buildings in an architectural style similar to that adopted for the Exhibition generally. Every day through the Exhibition season, eight-ten trains of five-six coaches an hour were worked to and from Marylebone, mostly with ex GCR 4–6–2T, covering the journey in 12 minutes, the loop eliminating the delays involved in reversal. When the Exhibition closed on the evening of 1st November 1924, 17.5 million people had paid to enter the grounds, providing a special traffic which the LNER had of course to share with the Metropolitan, the LMSR, the Underground and the road services. Despite a reduction in the cost of the combined rail fare and admission charge, there was a great deal less interest for the second season in 1925, with a total of only 9.7m tickets sold between 9th May and 31st October. During the 1925 season, the LNER operated a similar service to that of 1924 round the Loop mostly using its new suburban N7 0–6–2T.

On Cup Final Day in 1925, the LNER was greatly put out to find employees of the Metropolitan Railway distributing leaflets at Marylebone station suggesting the Metropolitan route from Baker Street was the best way to the Stadium. Alex Wilson, for the LNER, wrote to Selbie, the Metropolitan's general manager, protesting:

> When all is said and done, your company get the lion's share of the Wembley traffic and you must not begrudge us any few odd crumbs that may fall from the rich man's table . . .

But the LNER did have the advantage of sidings which ran right into two of the largest Exhibition buildings, the Palace of Engineering (with its railway exhibits) and the Palace of Industry, as well as another along Commonwealth Way serving the Canada and Australia buildings. These enabled it to gain much of the freight traffic involved in erecting the structures, making the roadways and other features and setting up the displays. After the final closure in October 1925, rail access gave the LNER a lever towards obtaining the dismantling business and the traffic involved in the subsequent conversion of the site into industrial units and warehouses. An Exhibition Goods Yard here survived until 3rd December 1962.

The LNER, with its Loop and Wembley Hill stations, was also best placed to serve the Stadium, which was now converted to accommodate greyhound racing as well as other sports. After 1924 (118,000), Cup Final attendances settled down to 90–95,000, almost all travelling by public transport and of which the Metropolitan carried about one third, leaving the balance to the LNER and the other alternatives.

After closure of the Exhibition in 1925, the loop and its station (renamed Wembley Stadium in 1927) were regularly reopened for passenger services to principal events at the Stadium, notably the FA and Rugby League Finals and the England v. Scotland International Matches. These occasions provided a feast for trainspotters as there were many special workings from distant places supplementing the Marylebone service. Some use was even made of the loop during the war, as for example for the FA Cup Final of 1943. On the occasion of the April 1948 FA Cup Final, 14 trains ran, carrying 9,500 on to the loop and 12,500 away after the match.

Station and Loop were renovated for the 1948 14th Olympic Games, held at the 1923 Stadium and the adjacent 1934 Empire Pool. By the 1960s, diesel multiple unit sets were able to cope with a reduced level of patronage on the special services round the loop from and to Marylebone. The 1923 line and its station were last used for the Rugby League Cup Final of 18th May 1968 but the official date given for closure of the Loop was 1st September 1969. Rails from a point just north of the platform were lifted at around that time and the connection at the Wembley Hill side was broken early in 1970.

In recent years, following use of the Empire Pool (renamed the Wembley Arena) for entertainments and other events as well as swimming, the opening of the Conference Centre in 1976 and later the Exhibition Centre, Wembley has seen traffic more evenly distributed through the year. Although some still passes via Marylebone and Wembley Stadium (formerly Wembley Hill) station, the majority is handled at Wembley Park station. The long battle to win extra revenue from Wembley has in the end gone to the Metropolitan, the originators of the whole exercise.

The LNER Wembley Stadium loop and passenger platform, looking north east in the mid-1950s. *Lens of Sutton*

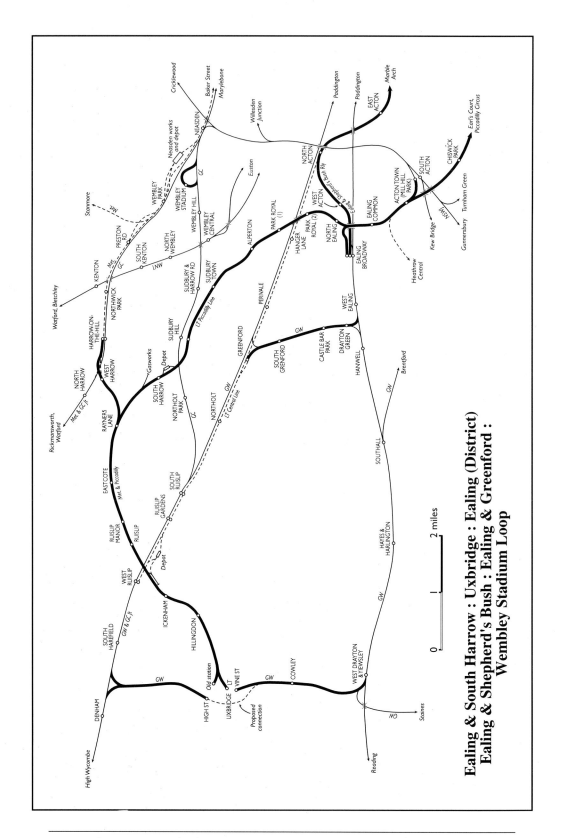

Ealing & South Harrow : Uxbridge : Ealing (District)
Ealing & Shepherd's Bush : Ealing & Greenford :
Wembley Stadium Loop

Cowley station, looking to West Drayton, almost ready for public opening, September 1904.

The Uxbridge Branches (Great Western Railway)   (map page 260)

Like its Middlesex sister Hounslow, the town of Uxbridge was a place of some importance at the beginning of the nineteenth century. A staging point on the Oxford road 15 miles from London, with breweries, corn mills and market, it was also well served after 1798 by the Grand Junction (later Grand Union) Canal, which not only moved freight to its metropolitan markets, but took passengers up, if somewhat slowly. Although a focus of many railway schemes, Uxbridge passed the Victorian era with only minimal railway accommodation, a fact which surely contributed to its contemporary decline. Then, at the turn of the century it quickly found itself with two more stations and an electric tramway link to west London. All three railway services were essentially of a local nature and did little to revive the town's prosperity; we shall examine later the facilities provided by the Metropolitan and District Railways; here we are concerned with the contribution of the Great Western, by whom the burghers always considered themselves poorly treated.

Whilst Brunel could have brought his London to Bristol line into the southern part of Uxbridge without too much difficulty, he preferred not to cut across the lower part of the Colne valley, taking instead the level route through West Drayton, some 2½ miles south. After the opening of a station there on 4th June 1838, road conveyances plied from Uxbridge High Street for those choosing the faster if less convenient alternative to the Oxford road coaches. Local interests were soon seeking a rail connection, finding it necessary to get up an independent scheme. A 2½-mile single line along the Colne from West Drayton was authorised in 1846 as the Great Western & Uxbridge Railway, but capital could not be raised and although the GWR took powers in the following year to purchase the undertaking, it had no incentive to build and allowed the scheme to lapse.

Finally goaded into action by local support of the Oxford and Brentford schemes of the early 1850s, the GWR secured a third act in 1853 authorising a 2m 51ch single line of 7ft 0in gauge over the 1846 route with a deviation at the Uxbridge end to a new terminus near the Vineyard. Leaving the main line west of West Drayton station, the branch was to climb at 1 in 116 to cross the canal and the valley road, soon afterwards passing behind the east side of Cowley village into a cutting, terminating on a short rise of 1 in 66. In a central position on the south side of Vine Street, the terminus had two tracks with four platform faces and a very narrow headway beyond the buffers. Over it all was one of the timber and glass A-shaped roofs favoured by the GWR at this period, a feature which lasted until 1932–3. The side platforms were removed when the roof was replaced with a conventional umbrella canopy protecting about two coach lengths of the widened island platform. The single-storey, hipped roof building across the headway, in local yellow brick, had a wooden canopy on the outer side until 1941 when it was demolished by a bus. West of the passenger station was the small goods yard, awkwardly situated for shunting at the top of the gradient.

Public traffic on this, the first GWR branch in the London area, began on 8th September 1856 when there were 15 arrivals at Uxbridge daily and 13 departures (ten and 11 on Sundays). All connected with Up and Down main line trains, and the balancing workings were goods trains which may have carried passengers. By 1870, with most trains into Paddington operating over standard gauge rails, re-gauging became increasingly desirable, especially for the working of freight. The job was completed on 9th October 1871. Doubling followed in 1880/1881, probably in response to the first threats of District Railway invasion of this part of the GWR monopoly.

Initially most of the trains, some of them mixed, were confined to the branch, but from an early date there were daily through workings to and from Paddington for the convenience of businessmen. Working over the Metropolitan Railway to the City via Bishop's Road, Paddington, was started in 1879 to meet the competition and threat of the District Railway, which had reached Ealing Broadway that year. Although there were rarely more than three trains Up in the morning and a similar number back in the evening, these Uxbridge (Vine Street)–City workings were continuous from 1881 to September 1939.

After the electrification of the Metropolitan in 1905, electric locomotives of that company hauled the GWR carriages between Paddington and the City, a somewhat piquant situation since the Metropolitan was by then in direct competition with the GWR for Uxbridge traffic. For a few years from July 1897 there were also through trains between Vine Street and Victoria via West London Junction and Latchmere Junction, Battersea.

As well as the 20 trains a day each way on the branch, there were around 1900, 12 Up and ten Down journeys to and from Paddington or the City and two between Uxbridge and Victoria with Paddington coaches. A 1911 timetable shows 31 trains a day each way, mostly confined to the branch, plus 14 Up and 13 Down through London workings of which two Up and one Down were Victoria trains taking one hour ten minutes, while five Up and three Down were Liverpool Street workings. The best time from Uxbridge to Paddington was 20 minutes. Apart from an early morning working which appeared in 1906, the line saw no steam railcars until these took over most of the Sunday service in October 1914.

Cowley, an agricultural community of some 500 inhabitants (1871), 1½ miles north of West Drayton, did not get its station until 2nd October 1904. With its characteristic liberality, the GWR then provided wide 400ft platforms and decent brick buildings; the main structure, single-storied, with an ample canopy, was on the Up side and a small waiting room and men's urinal in similar style on the Down. Since there was no goods yard, a block post was dispensed with and the whole line continued to be worked as one section. Another economy was the absence of a footbridge, the porter on the Down side having access to a lockable box of Uxbridge tickets. By 1913 this station was handling around 40,000 passengers a year but its best period of growth was during the 1920s and 1930s when there was some housing development, mostly west of the line. In 1937 over 65,500 passengers were handled. Even then, much of the catchment area was taken up by nurseries, cemeteries and a sewage works.

One of many proposals for cracking the GWR monopoly of Uxbridge was the long-lived scheme for a link between Uxbridge GWR and Rickmansworth LNWR, mainly to provide for freight transfers. First authorised in 1861, the Uxbridge & Rickmansworth lived in paper and talk for about 40 years, providing sustenance for lawyers and politicians through no fewer than 11 acts of parliament.*

But Uxbridge was far more interested in getting itself on to a main line, or at any rate in achieving a direct link to London, and every encouragement was given by the town to the many schemes which emerged after 1879, most of them with open or covert support from the District or the Metropolitan. When the 1891 census revealed a fall in population this was attributed to the deficiency in railway accommodation and used as evidence of the need for something better.

At the end of the 1890s the GWR found itself facing District-inspired schemes linking Uxbridge and the Chiltern towns to London, and worse, a proposal for an independent railway from London to South Wales via High Wycombe and Denham which might make use of the District as one means of gaining access to central London. GWR powers were accordingly secured in 1897 to block this by constructing a direct main line between Acton and High Wycombe, affording a shorter route to Oxford and Birmingham by using the existing line from Wycombe through Thame to Oxford. Although a connection with the unbuilt Uxbridge & Rickmansworth was included, this proposal again by-passed Uxbridge and when a protest deputation from the town waited upon the GWR board they were told that although a line nearer the town had been investigated, use of the Alderbourne valley route would affect too many interests, not least the scenic Burnham Beeches. As a sop, Uxbridge was promised a branch from the new line, which would join the existing branch to form a loop which would carry circular services to and from the City section of the Metropolitan Railway via Greenford and via Ealing Broadway, a proposition which was eventually mentioned to the parliamentary committee on the GWR Bill of 1897. Not all the Uxbridge representatives found this an acceptable substitute for the sting of competition from a second railway company in the town; one was churlish enough to cast doubts on the GWR's intentions, asserting that although it might build the promised line, it would not use it. He was not far wrong. Parliament, also apparently convinced of the merits of competition, passed the 1899

* Useful summaries of this saga will be found in *The Railway Magazine*, January-February 1945 (H Langford Lewis) and December 1959 (J Spencer Gilks).

Uxbridge High Street station, 1907, looking to buffers and the half-built underline bridge for the proposed connection to the West Drayton Line.

Harrow and Uxbridge Act, the final step for a line first proposed in 1881 and opened in 1904 and one which now provides the town's only railway connection. We shall be looking at this shortly but it should be noted here that, aided by the extension of the London United electric tramways to Uxbridge in the same year, it reduced the 162,000 tickets issued at Vine Street in 1903 to 120,100 in 1913.

In fulfilment of its promise, the GWR sought and obtained powers for the northern branch into Uxbridge in 1898, a 2m 7f 2.2ch line, which was to have junctions with the new Wycombe route facing both London and Denham. Following the Colne valley to join the existing branch in the town, it was in effect a substitute for the southern part of the long-planned Uxbridge & Rickmansworth, for which powers finally lapsed in 1901. A longer but cheaper route for this GWR branch, detouring west of the town to join the West Drayton line 34ch south of the terminus, near Walford Road, was authorised in 1899. Work started on the whole 3m 2.35ch, but when it opened on 1st May 1907, trains ran only to a second Uxbridge station (High Street) on the east side of the main road between the Grand Union Canal and Fray's River. Construction work south of this point which included a cutting, an embankment, a 1,275yd brick viaduct and an iron girder bridge over the High Street was stopped before completion. Sensibly, the GWR decided that there was not enough traffic potential to justify the proposed circular service now that both District and Metropolitan electric trains served Uxbridge. Powers for the uncompleted section were formally abandoned in 1914.

Denham West Junction with the new Birmingham line was immediately east of the Grand Union Canal Viaduct; the 2f 6.76ch spur to Denham East Junction, opened at the same time as the branch, was never used for regular passenger workings. Nine steam railcar trips worked each way daily between Denham, Uxbridge (High Street), and West Ealing, with some going on to Ealing Broadway or Willesden Junction. Sunday railcar working between Uxbridge (High Street) and Kensington (Addison Road) via Park Royal or Ealing Broadway was started in July 1907, continuing sporadically on summer Sundays until 1914. Some weekday journeys were extended to Gerrards Cross in July 1909; the cars then ran down the main line from London to Gerrards Cross, ran back to Uxbridge (High Street) and returned to Gerrards Cross before working up to London along the main line.

Freight working on the branch did not start until 11th May 1914, when a small coal yard was opened at street level to the west of the passenger station, approached by a spur from a junction about a quarter-mile north of the terminus. Tracks on the little-used east curve at Denham were removed for war purposes about 1916 and never again laid throughout. From 14th May 1942 a single track was opened over the alignment from Denham South Junction to serve an oil tank depot.

From Denham South Junction the branch ran on an embankment almost due south to cross Fray's River near Denham Lock, then following the west bank of the river, coming to an end at a bridge across the north end of the High Street. North of this bridge, at the west side of the line, there was a single timber platform with a canopied wooden building, cantilevered at the back from the embankment and containing ticket office, waiting rooms, lavatories and the stationmaster's office. Access from the street was by a covered stairway to the south end of the platform. At street level, under the bridge, the GWR erected a flat-roofed brick building most of which was leased out as a café.

Since very little business was attracted by the slow and restricted passenger service of steam railmotor cars, it was no surprise when the GWR offered suspension of passenger trains as a contribution to economies required to help the war effort at the end of 1916. Much of the line was also singled to supply rail for Army use. Passenger services were resumed, on weekdays only, from 3rd May 1920 over what was now a single track branch through an area never able to generate even the scanty settlement that might justify an intermediate halt. Apart from the demolition in 1922 of the bridge over Uxbridge High Street, there was little to disturb the sleepy between-wars life of the branch until the construction of a bridge carrying the Western Avenue arterial road over the line in 1939–40. Train services in this period, normally working between Uxbridge High Street, Denham and Gerrards Cross, a 13 min journey, continued as steam railmotors until the mid 1930s when they were replaced by typical GWR auto trains, latterly powered by 54xx 0–6–0PT. After the signalling had been removed in the early 1920s, the branch was worked by use of a small metal token, with one engine in steam at a time, or two coupled together. By 1938 there were just nine services each way daily with a surprising five extra workings at midday on Saturdays, thought to be justified by shopping traffic. At the end of the 1930s, when the station was staffed with two porters under the supervision of the stationmaster at Vine Street, about 10,000 tickets a year were issued at High Street, say around 30 a day, this figure almost certainly including season ticket journeys.

Uxbridge Vine Street station, looking to buffers, in the 1930s. *Lens of Sutton*

For the second and last time all passenger trains were withdrawn after traffic on Thursday 31st August 1939; on the following day, the GWR was heavily engaged in the evacuation of schoolchildren from London and this and the immediately following outbreak of war provided convenient justification for not resuming a little-used service. Freight trains, mainly incoming coal, continued to run daily if required, reversing in the engine run-round loop of the old passenger station by means of ground frame levers. To enable the tracks in the former passenger station area to be removed, a run-round loop was installed a short way up the branch in 1956 but in post-war conditions the depot here had become superfluous and all freight working to High Street ceased from 24th February 1964. Some trains continued to use the track between Denham West Junction and the oil depot until a final working on 30th April 1965.

In contrast to this decline, from the late 1920s the original Uxbridge branch enjoyed a modest prosperity in an area experiencing steady industrial and residential development. By 1938, when there were 46 trains daily each way and 26 on Sundays, the whole route, apart from a stretch at Cowley, was clothed with houses and factories. Seventeen trains, three on Sundays, ran through to and from London, discerning passengers finding them more comfortable and marginally faster than the London Transport services via Rayners Lane. On the branch, auto trains with one or two cars in charge of fussy little 0–4–2T or 0–6–0PT ran to and fro, taking seven minutes for the journey. On the outbreak of war in 1939 the two trains each way between Uxbridge and Liverpool Street (Metropolitan Line) were withdrawn, running for the last time on Saturday 16th September, but Paddington workings continued. Wartime demands brought additional freight traffic to the branch.

At the end of the 1950s the line was still quite busy, with 35 trains each way daily, about a dozen of them to and from Paddington at peak hours, taking about 30 min. GWR AEC railcars replaced the steam auto trains in the mid 1950s at a time when freight business still required three workings daily. The aura of the GWR was still very apparent but it was to be an Indian Summer both for the line and those at Paddington striving to maintain GWR traditions. The appearance on the line of new BR diesel railcars in 1958 raised hopes of a new era which were soon to be dashed. From 27th July 1962 passenger workings were reduced to peak hours only and after Saturday 8th September that year ceased altogether. The next month saw the line reduced to single track. Any residual London traffic via West Drayton fell away quickly; the alternative bus route (available on the parallel road since the 1930s) was not only slower but exposed passengers to the elements as they transferred between road and rail. For journeys to London, Uxbridge was soon relying entirely on the latter-day intruder.

Cowley station closed completely with the end of passenger trains but at Vine Street parcels trains continued to visit the platforms until 11th July 1964. Freight traffic into Uxbridge yard ceased on 24th February that year. One small section survived for a while; a 26ch length at the southern end was used until 1976 by trains serving a siding added about 1964 for the Middlesex Oil & Chemical Works at Yiewsley. Beyond that point, all tracks and railway structures were quickly demolished and before many years had passed, much of the alignment had been built over.

The Ealing & South Harrow Railway bridge over Twyford Abbey Road, looking north west, c. 1912. The entrances to Park Royal & Twyford Abbey station (1903–31) can be seen at the right hand side of the bridge. *Commercial postcard*

The Uxbridge and Harrow Branches (Met and MDR)   (map page 260)

A substantial wedge of Middlesex between the LNWR and GWR main lines remained without railways until the very end of the nineteenth century. As late as December 1901, the Reverend W J Scott was able to hope that 'this wooded country, so close to London' would not be covered 'with rows of the small yellow brick houses one sees at Wood Green or Leyton'. It is true that the Metropolitan reached Harrow in 1880 and was at Pinner five years later, but this merely scraped the north-western edge of the area. Several reasons may be cited for the slow exploitation of land so near the western edge of London: the GWR and LNWR, for many years content to enjoy their profitable long-distance traffic, were able to postpone the hazardous task of developing suburban business through their inconveniently-sited termini; speculative builders were deterred by the lack of railways in an area mostly covered with deep hard clays that discouraged house construction until main drainage schemes were implemented, while industry was notably absent, except on a few sites alongside the Grand Junction Canal.

During the final quarter of the nineteenth century this railway desert began to attract a variety of schemes, some supported or directly promoted by the MDR in expansionist mood, others put up independently by parties who wished to challenge the GWR monopoly at Uxbridge, with its unsatisfactory branch line access; or to develop land for housing; or even to form possible corridors for new main lines coming to London from the north and west. But it was the District that took the lead role.

On 1st July 1879 that company reached Ealing, a vantage point from which it could contemplate further objectives: Harrow to the north, Uxbridge and High Wycombe to the north-west. The boardroom mood at this time was quietly optimistic; ordinary shareholders had received their first dividend (if only ½ per cent) in 1878, receipts and traffic were climbing, and there were high hopes for the new lines to Ealing, Richmond and Fulham. A new policy was announced in the chairman's report of 30th January 1880:

> The enormous outlay of the parent line can only be fully utilised and made ultimately profitable by judicious and comparatively cheap lines constructed in direct continuation of those already existing; and into districts possessing not only a present considerable population but also affording attractive outlets for the denser population of London constantly moving westward.

These remarks introduced a proposed extension from Ealing to Uxbridge, then served only by the little GWR branch of 1856. In 1861 an extension of that branch northwards to Rickmansworth had been authorised to an independent scheme, and there had been other earlier proposals which would have given this important Middlesex town direct access to London. The District's Uxbridge Extension Bill deposited in November 1879 provided for an 8m 5f westward extension from Ealing which for its last five furlongs would run into Uxbridge alongside the GWR, a brazen assault on its territory which that company successfully opposed. Notwithstanding this defeat, the District board deemed it 'necessary and prudent' to try again the following year with a route only slightly different. Again the bill was thrown out.

Railway interest in Uxbridge remained strong, with the business community working hard to secure some competition for the GWR, which reacted by doubling its branch as a precautionary measure in 1880/1881. November 1881 saw the deposit of no less than four bills affecting the town, none directly promoted by the District. Two of the proposals followed much the same route as the earlier District bills: the Uxbridge & Rickmansworth (Ealing Extension), and the High Wycombe, Beaconsfield, Uxbridge & London, which was to be linked with the GWR at High Wycombe, with the Uxbridge & Rickmansworth near Uxbridge, and the District at Ealing. The other two bills went further north. The Harrow & Uxbridge was a straightforward branch from the Metropolitan at Harrow-on-the-Hill via Ruislip, but the Beaconsfield, Uxbridge & Harrow, the only bill of the four to succeed, was more ambitious, proposing a line westwards from junctions with the LNWR and the Metropolitan at Harrow to Beaconsfield through Ruislip. Uxbridge would be reached via the Uxbridge & Rickmansworth, which was to be joined near Denham. Although the junction with the LNWR was deleted, the rest emerged as the Beaconsfield, Uxbridge & Harrow Railway Act, 1882. No capital was raised; the powers, which lapsed in 1887, were not renewed.

Harrow, about four miles north of Ealing across Alperton Vale was an obvious target for the District. Until the arrival of the Metropolitan from Baker Street and Finchley Road on 2nd August 1880, its only railway accommodation was a poorly-served station on the LNWR at Wealdstone, over a mile north of the town. There had been some attempts to remedy this deficiency. An unsuccessful London, Harrow & Rickmansworth Railway Bill of 1864 had proposed a line from Rickmansworth through Pinner, Roxeth (now South Harrow), Greenford Green, and Alperton to join the LNWR at its crossing of the Brent, with a spur to the GWR at Old Oak. At its northern end this line would have joined the existing Watford and Rickmansworth branch and the authorised Amersham & Chesham Railway. A few years later the GNR was making unsuccessful attempts to reach Harrow from Edgware, but nothing more happened until 1876 when a Harrow & West End bill was deposited. This was a branch from the GWR at Ealing to Roxeth and Harrow, London Hill, hoping to carry District trains from that company's Ealing Extension, which was in the same session, as well as GWR workings. The bill was rejected as were no less than four similar ones promoted in 1877, 1878, 1879 and 1884. Of these, the first three were entitled Harrow & District and included junctions with the Metropolitan at Harrow, whilst the last three also provided for connection to the MDR at Ealing. The 1884 scheme went on to join the GNR, its ambitious promoters seeking running powers over the GNR into Farringdon as well as over the District, Metropolitan and GWR, arrangements postulating some interesting circular services.

The next proposal to affect the still railless claylands of West Middlesex came from a new direction. A Harrow, Ealing & Willesden bill, deposited in 1886, sought a line from junctions with the LNWR and Midland & South Western Junction at Willesden, west through Alperton and then north-west, through Sudbury to terminate at Roxeth (South Harrow), throwing off a branch from Alperton to Castle Bar Park, Ealing. It was hoped to run into London both via the Midland and the LNWR, carrying passengers from the houses whose construction the railway's promoters hoped it would stimulate. New housing at rents of £250-£300 per annum on the southern slopes of Harrow Hill was mentioned in evidence, and one promoter was an Alperton builder and contractor who told the parliamentary committee that he had houses to let at £40-£60 per annum, so that there appeared to be scope for both first- and third-class traffic. On a technical objection skilfully raised by its counsel, the LNWR rid itself of the proposed connection, bringing the whole bill to grief, but the committee recorded that it did not wish it to be thought that its opinion was that no further railway communication was required in the district.

Although now in a far less buoyant state, the MDR was still concerned about the vacuum which remained so near to its western extremity. The board authorised survey of an extension to Uxbridge in November 1892, but decided not to deposit a bill. An Ealing & South Harrow Railway bill was however deposited the following year, ostensibly by local interests anticipating District support. A 5m 2f 9.7ch line, this was to run from the MDR Ealing Extension at Hanger Hill Farm, Ealing, to Roxeth, now for the first time christened 'South Harrow'. Arthur J. Barry was the engineer, and agreements were sought with the District, whose shareholders approved the bill. It passed unopposed, obtaining royal assent on 25th August 1894. The preamble to the act explained that construction estimates were based on double track to MDR standards, but until goods traffic could be brought onto the line, it might be made cheaply as a 'single track light railway' for £75,000 instead of £160,000.

This goods traffic was expected to arrive from outside London. At the MDR half-yearly meeting of 9th August 1894, the chairman, James Staats Forbes, spoke obscurely of 'some other railway company northwards' having sufficient interest in the E&SHR 'to materially assist construction', adding that the idea seemed to be 'a connection between a great northern railway and this little railway' to enable the former to use District access to central London. In these circumstances, he slyly suggested, it would be necessary for the District to subscribe capital.

Forbes' reference was probably to the London extension of the Manchester, Sheffield & Lincolnshire Railway (later the Great Central). Work on this had begun that year with the intention of entering London over the Metropolitan Railway as far as Finchley Road, a move facilitated by the fact that both railways shared the same chairman, the famous Sir Edward Watkin. Watkin fell ill in 1894, resigning his chairmanships, and his successor on the Metropolitan made things less easy for the London extension of this 'great northern railway'. It seems likely that Forbes was hoping to profit by this, offering an alternative route into central London. But in the event the newcomer obtained powers in 1895 and 1896 for a second pair of tracks alongside the Metropolitan, thus removing a major cause of friction. Forbes had a second string to his bow. another trunk line scheme, the London & South Wales Railway, aiming to break the GWR coal monopoly, deposited its bill in autumn 1895. Engineered by J. Wolfe Barry, this was to enter the London area via High Wycombe, Denham, Ruislip and Harrow, with junctions to the Metropolitan at Great Missenden and to the Midland at Welsh Harp, Hendon. Neither of these two companies could be relied upon to afford the newcomer access to central London, so Forbes set out to attract this further prop for the E&SHR, promoting an extension from South Harrow to Uxbridge and High Wycombe, and a small terminus for it at South Kensington. These proposals were however withdrawn before the end of 1895 when the South Wales apparently showed no interest. In any event the new main line scheme collapsed a few weeks afterwards, with the GWR promising to improve its access to South Wales.

Despite this setback, the District still felt impelled to make its bid for Uxbridge and High Wycombe, promoting in 1896 through a nominally independent company an extension of the E&SHR through Ruislip, Ickenham and Uxbridge, passing south of Chalfont St Peter and north of Beaconsfield. At Uxbridge it would have junctions with the diuturnal Uxbridge & Rickmansworth. The terminus at High Wycombe, which required property demolition, was to be higher than the GWR, without physical connection. By this time it had been decided that the E&SHR should be part of the District system, built by that company, and the 1896 bill included spurs at Alperton to the M&SWJR at Neasden and also from North Ealing to a proposed GWR Acton–Wycombe line, facing towards London. An extension of time was sought for the E&SHR, also running powers over that line for the High Wycombe's trains, over the GWR into Acton, and over the Uxbridge & Rickmansworth. Business interests in Uxbridge, ever keen on breaking the GWR monopoly, subscribed towards the expenses of the High Wycombe Bill. Once again we read of the District Chairman talking about 'judicious and timely extensions', now pointing to the example of the Metropolitan Railway, enjoying 'relative prosperity' from the same policy. A new threat to the inner London lines, motor bus and electric tramway competition, added further urgency. Thus persuaded, the MDR shareholders agreed the new bill in February 1897, with working by the MDR.

Now very much alive to the dangers of competition from the Oxford–Princes Risborough–High Wycombe direction, the GWR promoted in the same session a bill for a main line from Acton to High Wycombe, and it was the powerful opposition of the GWR that secured the deletion of the Uxbridge–High Wycombe section of the District-sponsored bill. The remainder, from South Harrow to Uxbridge, was authorised as the Harrow & Uxbridge Railway Act of 6th August 1897, which included confirmation of an agreement dated 19th July in which the District undertook to manage and work the double-track line. The District's own act of that year also confirmed an agreement to work the E&SHR, so that on paper at least the District was in Uxbridge at last, although that is by no means the end of the story.

A loop between the original GWR main line and the new route from Acton to Wycombe, included in the act for the latter, was in effect a final mutilated realisation of the several Ealing–Harrow and Ealing–Uxbridge proposals already mentioned. In the following two years the GWR secured powers for the Denham–Uxbridge branch and the Great Central Railway was authorised to link Northolt on the new GWR main line with Neasden on its original Metropolitan entry into London. These lines, subsequently built, completed the final pattern of the railway network in West Middlesex, with one small exception.

Attempts to raise capital for the South Harrow to Uxbridge line met with no success. As the shaky finances of the District were over-extended on the E&SHR and the capital-intensive Whitechapel & Bow, it became all too clear in the autumn of 1898 that unless a saviour could be found, Uxbridge would not get its competitive line. After informing Forbes, who raised no objection, the Uxbridge parties began to woo the Metropolitan, receiving sufficient encouragement to promote a bill for the 1899 session which sought powers to link that railway at Harrow with the Harrow & Uxbridge at Rayners Lane, with a curve at the latter which would allow through running from South Harrow to Harrow-on-the-Hill, and a flyover for the Down line at the point of junction with the Metropolitan. At the committee stage, Forbes began to object, seeking to make the Harrow & Uxbridge a joint District and Metropolitan enterprise, but he soon had to admit that the District was quite incapable of raising half the capital and had in any case decided to concentrate its efforts on the Whitechapel & Bow. It was finally agreed that the Metropolitan would manage and work the line from the date of Board of Trade authority, taking all receipts and paying the Harrow & Uxbridge Company three per cent on the capital cost of what the H&UER were to build as a 'first class double line' for passengers and goods.

From the wreckage of its hopes the District secured running powers for up to three trains an hour each way daily and eight goods trains each way in return for a minimum annual rent of £2,000. Some anxiety was expressed that having no interest in it, the H&UR would not make the Rayners Lane to South Harrow portion of the original act, but counsel for the promoters gave an assurance that it would be built and worked, whether or not the District used its running powers. The arrangements described were incorporated in the Harrow & Uxbridge Railway Act of 9th August 1899, the 1897 agreement with the District was repealed, and the way was at last clear for some real progress to be made on what now seemed to be a reasonably viable group of railways.

That summer, C. J. Wills & Son had two steam navvies and 325 men at work on the Ealing & South Harrow, the stations were started, and most of the bridges were completed. Work then tapered off and by the end of 1899 seems almost to have stopped, probably owing to the parlous financial state of the District. In his report of 8th February 1900, Forbes cautiously told shareholders that the E&SHR and the Whitechapel & Bow would be open 'within two years', sugaring the pill with a promise of freight business for both.

Under the MDR Act of 1900 the E&SHR was transferred to the larger company from 1st July that year. This act also sanctioned further capital, which was somehow secured, enabling work to proceed until the project was brought to virtual completion in the spring of 1901. On 4th April that year the Board of Trade inspector passed the line for public traffic, but the District was in no state to open it. Its main London system, increasingly vulnerable to competition from electric tramways and tube railways, was in dire need of modernisation and electrification, yet the board could hardly muster sufficient cash for day-to-day running costs. At the time when the clouds seemed at their blackest, deliverance arrived from the west. Whilst the E&SHR was being prepared for Board of Trade inspection in March, the District had passed into the control of the dynamic American railway and tramway financier and entrepreneur, Charles Tyson Yerkes and his associates. In that summer Yerkes formed the Metropolitan District Electric Traction Company to finance the electrification of the whole system, the money coming entirely from the USA.

As the E&SHR was lying ready for use, Yerkes and his advisers decided it would form an ideal test bed for the District electrification, but there was at first some delay whilst the District and the Metropolitan, who shared operation of the Inner Circle, decided which system they would use, and who would supply the electric power. During the winter of 1902–03, electrification was completed between Mill Hill Park (now Acton Town) and South Harrow using the 550V dc system with centre positive and outside negative conductor rails which a Board of Trade arbitration tribunal had chosen, much to Yerkes' satisfaction. A generator used for the Inner Circle electrification experiments of 1899–1900 was installed on the canal bank at Alperton where coal could conveniently be brought by barge. Yet another act was required to sanction electric working of the E&SHR and this, which also included the purchase of more land to ensure the stability of cuttings through the Middlesex clay, was passed in 1903.

Two seven-car trains, built by Brush of Loughborough from drawings prepared in the USA, were straight-sided, monitor-roofed, arch-windowed and of distinctly transatlantic appearance. Each train consisted of three motor cars and four trailers, one having British Thomson-Houston Sprague multiple-unit control, the other Westinghouse pneumatic control. After the trials on the E&SHR it was the former which was eventually selected for the main District fleet. When delivered on 11th March 1903 the cars, with their gate platforms and central sliding doors, were in bright yellow picked out in maroon, with the company's name in full over the windows, USA style. During the year three were painted white above waist, red below, and six others bright red, but very soon all were in the red livery finally chosen for the District electric stock. They were kept in a shed at the London end of South Harrow station, where the electrical equipment was fitted and various experiments made, including an unsuccessful attempt to set one alight by starting fires inside and below it with electric arcs. In the shed and sidings the rails were of the American flat-bottom type, spiked to the sleepers, but elsewhere on the E&SHR the traditional British bullhead laid by the contractors was left undisturbed.

By May 1903 conductor rails had been installed on the running lines, with the negative return protected by boards. Yerkes' plans to make the District a true American 'rapid transit' operation called for a completely new approach to signalling and the system now installed on the E&SHR was later adopted with only minor modifications for the whole of the Underground company's network. Basically this consisted of electro-pneumatically operated signals (lower quadrant semaphores in the open air, colour-lights in tunnel) held in the line clear position until operated by 110V track circuits, and protected by train stops. Similar to that proved on the

Boston Elevated Railway, it was designed and manufactured by the Westinghouse Brake Company under the patents of H G Brown. On the E&SHR it replaced the conventional mechanical system with Sykes' lock-and-block and station boxes which had originally been provided, requiring only two boxes, at Hanger Lane Junction and South Harrow, to control junction, terminal and siding movements.

From Hanger Lane Junction where the authorised north to west curve towards Ealing was not built, the line turned sharply to the north-east, reaching the first station, North Ealing & Hanger Hill, which had a substantial house on the Down side and a crossover at the country end, enabling the line to be worked independently during the trial period. The site was close to Hanger Lane in a part of Ealing so far almost undeveloped, with Hanger Hill Farm close by. After skirting the eastern boundary of Hanger Hill House grounds (later a golf course) the tracks crossed above the new GWR Wycombe line before entering Park Royal & Twyford Abbey station, where there was nothing but a simple corrugated-iron shack on the Up side reached by a flight of steps from Twyford Abbey Road below. The surroundings were open, but Park Royal, the new 102-acre permanent London showground for the Royal Agricultural Society, was immediately to the east. From here the line crossed Alperton Vale, the Brent and the canal before entering Perivale–Alperton station in the centre of Alperton village. Here the corrugated-iron booking office was in the roadway below platforms partly protected by clumsy wooden canopies. The surroundings were a little more lively than at the first two stations, a few houses and some long-established factories on the canal banks, but Perivale was over a mile across fields to the west.

Park Royal and Twyford Abbey station, District Railway (Ealing & South Harrow Railway), soon after opening in 1903, looking to London. Note that the construction materials are almost entirely timber and corrugated iron, to reduce costs to the minimum.

The line now turned north-west, soon running into Sudbury Town for Horsenden, another corrugated-iron hut, this time on the Up platform, which was more or
less level with the surrounding land. Its name was rather a joke as Sudbury at this
time consisted of nothing more than a few well-dispersed houses, a farm and a
brewery set around the Priory, all a good half-mile north of the station. At the
western end of this settlement was another iron hut station, set in open country,
Sudbury Hill for Greenford Green. Later the GCR Northolt to Neasden line was
built beneath an E&SHR cutting just beyond here, a cut and cover operation not
without difficulty in the unstable heavy clay. North of the cutting, on the Up side,
were the electric car sheds and sidings at the London end of South Harrow station,
which was almost five miles from Hanger Lane Junction. The well-built station
house on the Up side was similar to that at North Ealing and there was a crossover
at each end of the platforms. At the northern end, on the London side of the bridge
over the Harrow to Northolt road, the rails met those of the Metropolitan Railway's
Uxbridge line at what was known as Northolt Road Junction. 'South Harrow' was
a railway renaming of Roxeth, the community on the southern slopes of Harrow
Hill whose inhabitants served the needs of Harrow School, the big houses higher up
the hill, and the works of the Harrow District Gas Company.

Invited with other reporters to see Mr Yerkes' American style railway, *The Times'*
man thought the cars more like trams than railway carriages, with far fewer seats
than comparable steam suburban trains. Told that they expected to carry almost as
many standing passengers as seated ones during the busy periods and that this was
the usual thing on American railways, he remarked 'whether the London traveller
will take kindly to this arrangement remains to be seen'.

Following a satisfactory Board of Trade inspection on 16th June 1903 it was
intended to open to the public on Monday 22nd June, but heavy rains shifted the
earthworks so much that it was only possible to run between Mill Hill Park and Park
Royal on 23rd June, the opening day of the Royal Agricultural Society Show. Until
the show ended on 27th June, a shuttle service of four trains an hour worked to and
from Mill Hill Park, but although the weather cleared up, the attendance at the
Show was the lowest for 28 years. Despite the electric rail service and special GWR
workings on their new line, the shows of the following two years were similar failures,
causing the Society to give up Park Royal as a bad job in 1905.

Restoration of the line north of Park Royal was speedily accomplished, enabling
the full length to be opened on Sunday 28th June 1903, but the clay continued to
give trouble for a long time, requiring speed restrictions and even on occasion,
single-line working. The 08.05 departure from South Harrow that Sunday inaugurated the District Railway's first permanent electric service on London's first surface
electric railway. At first only hourly, with some extras in the mornings and evenings,
the frequency was soon increased to half-hourly with connections into the steam
service at Ealing Common and Mill Hill Park. Few passengers were attracted, and
the lack of any service beyond South Harrow did not help matters. Sudbury Town
saw only 60,000 bookings in its first year and the stationmaster, who had a house at
Alperton and was, American-fashion, responsible for these two stations and Park
Royal, was not exactly busy.

Although the Metropolitan had reached South Harrow at the end of 1903 there
were no regular services over this section until 1910. Pending further developments,
the MDR protected itself with trap points, but when the Metropolitan's first electric

'Underground to Anywhere: Quickest Way: Cheapest Fare' is the enticing message at the door of the corrugated iron shed that was the original station at Sudbury Town, portrayed here on a commercial picture postcard published around 1908. The London platform is nearest the camera and the stationmaster's house can be seen at the right. The direction of the shadows and absence of activity suggest that the picture was taken early on a Sunday morning.

cars were delivered early in 1904 it was arranged that they should be tested on the South Harrow–Rayners Lane section, for which purpose a short section of the Down road was electrified, using power from the Alperton plant.

The contractors, Bott & Stennett, had begun to build the Harrow & Uxbridge in September 1901, but it was not until 4th July 1904 that the public were able to ride between Harrow-on-the-Hill and Uxbridge. As the Metropolitan's new power station at Neasden was not yet ready, steam trains were used, running to and from a bay platform at Harrow-on-the-Hill, some to and from London in the peak periods. At the formal opening on 30th June a decorated train of two saloons, two bogie firsts and two brake coaches hauled by 0–4–4T No. 1, its coal painted white, left Harrow, backed down the South Harrow line to show the flag, and then took the guests on to lunch in a marquee at Uxbridge station. A *Financial News* reporter remarked that 'the line passes through a charming rural district, which looked its best and suggested infinite possibilities of snug residences to spring up in due time'. And spring up they did, though not in any great numbers until the 1920s and 1930s, as we shall see.

Leaving the Metropolitan's main line west of Harrow-on-the-Hill, the branch ran south-west to Rayners Lane Junction, where the South Harrow line came in from a viaduct of 71 brick arches and three iron bridges which covered most of its 1.17m. About half-way between Rayners Lane Junction and Uxbridge was Ruislip, the only intermediate station, with a large station house on the Up side, a half a mile below the village. Its yard had facilities for coal, cattle, horse and carriage traffic and (appropriately) furniture vans. Passing east of Ickenham village, the line then ran south-west to terminate at Belmont Road, Uxbridge. Here the plan was that of a through station with two 473ft side platforms, 20ft wide, firmly placed on the alignment of the 1897 High Wycombe proposal. (With suggestive imagery, *The Railway Magazine* of September 1903 had remarked 'The Fulmer Valley lies temptingly open . . .'). To the south of the station there was a large goods yard and shed. The main passenger building, in red brick, which included a refreshment room, was also on this side of the line.

Other than the Roxeth viaduct there were few features of interest, as the line passed through fairly level open pasturelands for most of its length, with few houses to be seen until Uxbridge was reached. Signalling was the usual Metropolitan Railway Spagnoletti electric lock-and-block, controlling mechanical semaphores from boxes at Rayners Lane, Ruislip, and Uxbridge. Conductor rails had been laid in anticipation of electric working through a substation at Ickenham. Electric trains composed of end-platform stock designed for urban service on the Inner Circle worked incongruously through the fields to Uxbridge from 1st January 1905, but steam trains did not entirely disappear from the branch passenger services until the end of May.

With the completion of the District's main electrification in 1905, the E&SHR was integrated with the rest of the system, taking its power from the huge new plant at Lots Road, Chelsea, through a substation at Sudbury Town. Until the summer of 1909 there were no public workings beyond South Harrow, but then the District running powers on to the Uxbridge line were exercised in the form of pleasure party specials worked from Ravenscourt Park and West Kensington and hand-signalled between South Harrow and Rayners Lane Junction. Regular service of District trains to Uxbridge started on 1st March 1910, remaining hourly for most of the day until 1919. Sunday trains were about every 45 minutes but in summer, when cheap tickets were issued, frequency was increased to half-hourly in the afternoons for the benefit of pleasure traffic. As the District trains were short, the Metropolitan waived its statutory right to a minimum payment of one shilling (5p) a train-mile. Towards the end of 1910 the District tried out late-night theatre trains to Uxbridge on Wednesdays and Saturdays, and for a short time an Uxbridge portion was included in the 17.15 Mansion House–Hounslow Barracks. This had disappeared by 1911 when the only through District working between central London and Uxbridge was the last train Down at night.

Since its opening in 1855, the South Harrow works of the Harrow & Stanmore Gas Co. had received its coal in road carts coming up from the canal wharf at Greenford Green, then from Harrow (Met) yard, but in 1910 a siding, crossover and signalbox were provided just north of Northolt Road, South Harrow. From 4th October, Metropolitan steam locomotives propelled a coal train daily (at first averaging seven trucks) from Rayners Lane to the works, returning with gas coke. A minimum 14,000 tons of traffic annually was guaranteed by the gas company.

Varying at first at four, three or two trains an hour, the basic E&SHR service settled down to every 20 minutes in 1911. Running time between Acton Town and South Harrow, at first 24 minutes, became a mere 14 after 1906 when single-car operation was introduced in the middle of the day and all intermediate stations except Alperton were treated as conditional stops. Park Royal, the least used, closed earlier and opened later than the others. In the hope of attracting pleasure traffic, Sunday service was increased from two to six an hour in 1911, but wartime constraints brought this down to four in 1916 and three a year later. South Harrow trains usually ran to and from South Acton or Acton Town, but at peak periods some worked to and from central London. By 1913 South Harrow was generating a trickle of commuter traffic, which justified the introduction on 1st January 1915 of a morning business 'express' named *The Harrovian* in the timetable folders (the staff called it *The Pansy*). Leaving South Harrow at 08.15 and missing some intermediate stations, this covered the congested 15¼ m to Mansion House in 39

The Ealing & South Harrow Railway did have decent brick built stations at each end of its line. South Harrow's street frontage to South Hill Avenue, Roxeth is seen here on a commercial picture postcard published about 1908.

minutes, and although it survived until the introduction of tube trains on the line in 1932, it was never matched by an evening return train. Between London and Acton Town, rush-hour trains normally consisted of eight cars, five working to and from Hounslow, three to and from South Harrow.

In the early years there were about 25 trains daily each way between Harrow-on-the-Hill and Uxbridge (15 on Sundays), some running through to and from London in the rush hours. The fastest train in 1911 was the 07.22 from Uxbridge which reached Baker Street in 38 minutes, Liverpool Street in 54. By 1916, with suburban growth just evident, the service had been increased to about 48 trains a day each way, 28 on Sundays; most trains terminating at Harrow had London connections.

At the MDR meeting on 6th August 1903 the chairman had looked forward to rapid suburbanisation of what was 'almost an unknown territory to Londoners, even of the West End', but in the event house building along both routes to Uxbridge was at first very slow. A few streets of small houses appeared close to South Harrow station around 1910–14, with similar developments at Sudbury Hill and Sudbury Town, and Wembley spread towards Alperton station. Traffic between Harrow and Uxbridge was at first extremely disappointing, and despite efforts at promotion, which included a Metropolitan booklet on the residential and holiday attractions of the district, in 1908 the Metropolitan was losing £3,000 a year, not counting interest on capital. Economies made late in that year included removal of through trains to and from Baker Street, leaving the line worked by a three-car shuttle service which allowed closure of Ickenham sub-station. To build up traffic, the Metropolitan opened a series of halts which it was hoped would attract pleasure seekers until housing development got under way.

The first of these simple structures, asked for by the parish council, was at Ickenham, close to the old village. Constructed at minimum cost, its timber platforms on concrete pillars, only three-car length, opened on 25th September 1905 with nameboards reading *Ickenham Halte*. Holidaymakers formed the main traffic here for many years, the villagers serving lunches and teas in their gardens or cottage rooms, sending them home with cut flowers at 6d (2½p) a bunch. Delayed by a 1918 proposal to resite the halt near the Air Board Stores, platform lengthening, by then much needed for the quite heavy summer traffic, was finally completed for the 1922 season.

Two more halts came into use on 26th May 1906, sited in the rural seclusion between Harrow and Ruislip, both of them at first conditional stops. Eastcote, on the Northolt Road, about a mile south of the village, rapidly assumed popularity as a destination for children's treats and summer excursions, so much so that it had to be extended from three-to six-car length in 1910. In July 1913, 93 children's parties were dealt with, 16,000 in all or up to 3,000 a day, a statistic which caused the board to sanction some modest improvements to the structure. Building of estate roads started here at the end of 1912, materials subsequently coming in through a wagon siding worked by Annett's key until a signal box was opened in 1913. Another intermediate block post was established at the Ickenham Ground Frame about 1914. The second of the 1906 halts was at Rayners Lane, just west of the junction with the South Harrow line, serving nothing but two or three well-dispersed houses, a sewage farm and a rifle range. Operating convenience rather than traffic demand was the reason for extending its platforms from three to six car length in 1918.

Responding to pressures from Ruislip Manor Ltd, which gave land and started to develop a 133-acre estate between the Eastcote Road and the railway in 1911, Ruislip Manor halt, at first only accessible by fieldpath, was opened on 5th August 1912. A siding to bring in building materials was laid from Ruislip station, extended into the estate area with light railways. By 1914 roads had been laid out and some 200 houses built, many of them unsold. More successful was West Harrow halt, a delayed response to the quite considerable amount of house building west of Bessborough Road which had begun around 1905. Only a quarter mile west of the junction with the Metropolitan main line, West Harrow, perched on an embankment and entirely in timber, built at a cost of just over £1,000, a little more than that of two of the new houses served, was opened on 17th November 1913. Within three years, it was handling 40,000 passengers a month. Noting that receipts had grown from £3,770 in 1915 to £16,308 in 1927, the board agreed to a minor reconstruction in 1928 which included concrete platforms of eight-car length.

Thanks to the economy measures described, and the small additional traffic generated by the halts opened up to that year, the Metropolitan's Uxbridge branch showed a small credit balance for the first time in 1912. Further progress was checked by the outbreak of World War 1; house building then slowed down and before long stopped altogether, not to resume for some time after the return of peace.

During the war years, railwaymen quietly cultivated potatoes alongside these still very rural lines, grateful not to be in Flanders' trenches. When the railway had been built, sufficient land was taken for four tracks between Harrow and Uxbridge, and this provided six acres within the fences which in 1917 were turned over to cultivation, together with Metropolitan fields at Eastcote and Ickenham.

For some time after the war, pleasure traffic remained the major feature at Eastcote and at some of the other stations. In 1919 one train ran all the way from Surrey Docks to Eastcote with a children's outing, and between April and August 1925, 40,000 arrived at the halt in pleasure parties. Reporting in December 1926 that drawing-up at the six-car length platforms was endangering the children, the general manager persuaded the board to extend them to 420ft (eight cars); a 120ft shelter was provided on the Up side at the same time. South Harrow was another popular resort for children's excursions, special trains coming in the 1920s from Shepherds Bush, Ravenscourt Park and elsewhere to the Roxeth fields and sports paddocks, bringing up to 3,500 a day in high summer.

The Metropolitan's Harrow & Uxbridge Railway terminus at Belmont Road, Uxbridge was built as a through station aligned for further extension to High Wycombe, for reasons explained in the text. This view, apparently taken just before the opening in July 1904, also shows (right) the spacious goods shed and yard. *Commercial postcard*

The tiny pavilion of a design that served as entrance and ticket office for several Metropolitan Railway suburban stations, seen here at Eastcote in 1933 attracting some new suburban house-wives. The tobacco kiosk looks rather out of place on the bridge over the line, and not particularly waterproof. The tea shop on the right is a relic of an earlier era of pleasure trippers – at this time the countryside they sought is rapidly being covered with houses.
London Borough of Hillingdon Libraries

One of the first pointers towards the coming residential boom was the sale of the 400-acre Swakeleys Estate at Hillingdon in September 1922 and of the 200-acre Hillingdon Court Estate in the same year. By the end of that year, the Halden Estates Company, which planned to erect £750 detached houses at Hillingdon Court was negotiating with the Metropolitan for a siding and passenger halt. This was agreed subject to the donation of land for a future goods yard and a guaranteed minimum annual income representing 10 per cent of the cost of construction and staff wages. Hillingdon halt opened on 10th December 1923, its siding following soon afterwards. No longer needing the 7½-acre plot that it had bought at the Swakeleys sale for a goods yard, the Metropolitan sold this in 1927 to its subsidiary, the Metropolitan Railway Country Estates Ltd, for its Hillingdon Mount Estate.

During the 1920s residential development along the Metropolitan line was steady, if sporadic. That at West Harrow has already been mentioned, and when local authorities pressed for service enhancements there in 1925 the response was to extend trains terminating at Harrow to Rayners Lane, making minor improvements at the latter point. At Eastcote, serious building started in 1923, soon taxing the capacity of the ten-wagon siding. After it had been told of wagons held back at Harrow daily for lack of room, the board authorised improvements in September 1923. Land bought by the railway company next to the station in 1923 was sold for development three years later to Metropolitan Railway Country Estates Ltd.

Ruislip Manor was slow to start. As the Ruislip Manor Co did not prosper, much of its land was sold off in large blocks, but when nothing had happened by mid-1926, the Metropolitan threatened to close the halt. This was averted when the owner of the Windmill Hill Estate agreed to make an annual grant of £50, and he and others began to use the spur siding adjoining the halt to bring in building materials towards the end of 1926.

For reasons analysed in another book* suburban growth around London took off at the end of the 1920s. One of the most favoured sectors in the following decade, the whole catchment area from Harrow to Ruislip and from Ealing to Rayners Lane then experienced large-scale construction of small houses by private firms until most of the fields and woodlands were covered by semis and short blocks. West of the line at North Ealing the Hanger Hill estate appeared from 1928, while at Twyford and Alperton the activity was intense from the same time. Between Sudbury's two stations new streets either side of the line were largely filled up between 1930 and 1936. By 1939 there was very little open land left between South Harrow and west of Ruislip, where Nash, Crouch, Davis and other firms had carpeted the fields south of the railway with a patchwork of new streets; north of the tracks, the whole area up to the Metropolitan main line was suburbanised by about 1936. A major contributor to this last was the Metropolitan's offspring, the Metropolitan Railway Country Estates Ltd, whose 213-acre 'Harrow Garden Village' around the once-isolated Rayners Lane station, was begun in May 1929 on land acquired in 1928 with loans from the railway company. A Metropolitan Railway advertisement in the *Evening News* of 24th January 1931 invited readers to 'view the development of this delightful estate on the Metro . . . houses by well known builders available at popular prices. Free first class return tickets from Baker Street'. For those tempted by this offer there were 110 trains daily to Rayners Lane and the same number back, a

* Jackson, Alan A., *Semi-Detached London*, Wild Swan, 1991

journey of '21 minutes from town'. Other MRCE schemes along the line evolving about the same time were Hillingdon Mount, already mentioned, Eastcote Hill, Manor Farm (Eastcote Road, Ruislip) and Elm Grove (Ruislip). Among those aiding MRCE in the creation of the new suburb of Rayners Lane were T. F. Nash Ltd, who acquired the 250-acre Tithe Farm Estate. A long siding was constructed into this during 1931 to bring in building materials, the Metropolitan receiving £1,600 in six annual instalments for the cost of connection at Rayners Lane.

During the two decades after 1931 the population of Ruislip & Northwood Urban District grew by almost 326 per cent, the largest accretion in London for the period, most of it logged up by the end of 1939. London Transport estimated that the number of residents served by the Harrow to Uxbridge line rose from 48,300 in 1931 to 95,000 in 1938; at Rayners Lane alone, traffic jumped from 22,000 in 1930 to 4,000,000 in 1937, marking the transition from a tree-girt country lane to bustling suburb with large shopping centre and super cinema. At Ruislip Manor, the 17,000 passengers of 1931 grew to 1,262,500 in 1937. Nearly 1,500,000 more journeys were made from South Harrow in 1936 than two years earlier, whilst at Park Royal the 1,300,000 travellers of 1936 were three times the 1933 total.

As most of the new householders were London office workers, train services and station accommodation had to be reshaped to cope with peak movements. In 1931 the 1920 service of four trains an hour with rush-hour extras on the South Harrow line was increased to six and then in the autumn of that year to eight (six on Sundays). From 1920, two trains an hour ran through from the District line to Uxbridge, weekdays and Sundays, but this was increased to three in 1932. On the Metropolitan line in the 1920s there were some 50 to 60 trains each way daily between Harrow and Uxbridge, but as early as 1928 the general manager foresaw that the need to strengthen this substantially would require additions to substation capacity. As Ickenham and Harrow substations were 4½ miles apart, voltage was low between them and in March 1928 the board agreed to a new substation at Eastcote with two 1,200kW rotary converters. Taking advantage of a government grant of interest at five per cent on the capital, under the 1929 Development (Loan Guarantees and Grants) Act, the Metropolitan resignalled between Rayners Lane and Uxbridge in 1930, installing long-range Westinghouse automatic three-aspect colour-lights which required signalboxes only at Rayners Lane, Eastcote, Ruislip and Uxbridge, with a ground frame at Hillingdon yard. At Rayners Lane, the original 22-lever mechanical locking frame at the intersection remained until the early hours of 22nd November 1934 when it was severely damaged by a runaway ballast train. A replacement box at the country end of the Up platform controlled the whole layout including the South Harrow gasworks siding and a new reversing road between the Up and Down lines west of the station. At the gasworks, the 14-lever mechanical frame was abandoned, replaced by a plunger operated by the engineman's foot, which gave a 'train ready to start' indication in the new Rayners Lane box when the once or twice daily steam working was ready to return to Harrow-on-the-Hill. In full operation from 17th November 1935, Rayners Lane cabin had a power frame of 35 levers incorporating route lever working. Its opening allowed removal of the lock-and-block on the South Harrow–Rayners Lane section, the last example of this on lines wholly worked by London Transport.

As pressure increased, it became impossible to find more paths over the District line for the Uxbridge, South Harrow and Hounslow trains into central London, so when cheap government money was on offer to combat unemployment, it was decided to extend Piccadilly tube trains to South Harrow (and, as we have seen, Hounslow). Work on this started in 1930, in conjunction with an extension to Cockfosters at the other end of the Piccadilly Line. Tube trains reached South Harrow on 8th February 1932, shuttling to and from Acton Town. Through services began on 4th July, providing the Ealing & South Harrow line with its first all-day through workings to and from inner London; the old 7½-minute District shuttle with two through morning Up City trains and four back in the evening was replaced by tube trains at 5½-minute intervals, supplemented in rush hours, a total of 170 each way daily between South Harrow and the Piccadilly tube. Six- or seven-car trains were used at peak hours, three at other times, all composed of new rolling stock fitted with four air-operated sliding doors each side of each car. Between South Harrow and Uxbridge, a 20-minute District service replaced the half-hourly workings to and from Ealing Common, but from 23rd October 1933 Piccadilly Line tube trains ran to Uxbridge, where like their predecessors, they were relegated to the almost unsheltered platform on the north side. These trains ran every 20 minutes, soon increased to four per hour (three on Sundays), with extra workings at peak periods. Tracks were raised at stations to give a suitable compromise platform height for both types of stock. Many tube trains ran the full 31½ miles from Uxbridge to Cockfosters, at that time the longest tube train journey in London. The tube extension was fed through a distribution station, control room and substation at Alperton, and unmanned substations at Sudbury Hill and North Ealing. Car sidings were laid at South Harrow on the site of the 1903 installation.

Publicised by such naive slogans as 'Live at Ruislip where the air's like wine, it's less than half an hour on the Piccadilly Line', further house building followed these service improvements, much of it either side of Field End and Victoria Roads south of Eastcote and Ruislip Manor stations. Not three years elapsed before an MP was asking in Parliament about overcrowding on the Piccadilly Line in north-west London. New rolling stock was promised, but nothing appeared, apart from the 1936 experimental trains, which started work on the Uxbridge line on 8th April 1937.

All the District's outback stations of corrugated-iron and timber disappeared in a modernisation programme in response to the huge increase in passengers. Park Royal & Twyford Abbey was closed after traffic on 5th July 1931 to be replaced the following day by a temporary station just under a mile south on Western Avenue, better placed to serve the new housing and factories which had appeared in this area from 1929 onwards. With traffic showing a growth from an initial annual total of about 60,000 to almost 1,300,000, Sudbury Town was chosen for the prototype of a new generation of surface stations for the Underground system. Designed by Charles Holden and others working under his supervision, these were to gain recognition as some of the finest examples of British public building of the inter-war period. In restrained functional style, with meticulous attention to detail and passenger flow, graceful and appropriate, the new Sudbury Town which opened on 19th July 1931 was built around a large flat-roofed passenger hall in Buckingham brick and white reinforced concrete. Similar but less confident rebuilding of Alperton and Sudbury Hill followed in 1932. At South Harrow the new station of 5th July 1935 had an entrance on the main road, the architects solving the problem of an embankment site with a design of some elegance. Park Royal got its new

Like the District Railway, the Metropolitan was for some years reluctant to spend more than the minimum on new stations for suburbs that had yet to develop; their provision may be compared with that of the GER on the Churchbury and Fairlop loops. This is Ruislip Manor, looking north, on 26th April 1934. Timber platforms and crude wooden sheds are still thought good enough, despite the arrival of new housing on both sides of the line (which seems to form a frontier of quality here). Note too the interesting mixture of Metropolitan diamond and Underground Co bullseye symbols still awaiting standardisation by the new London Passenger Transport Board.
London Transport Museum

permanent station on the site of the temporary one on 1st March 1936. Also in the Holden style, its 40ft diameter passenger hall, marked by a rectangular sign tower, dominated this part of Western Avenue. Only North Ealing remained unaltered, retaining its original signs and early Underground ambience up to the end of the 1950s, when some minor refurbishment took place.

During 1937–38 the Metropolitan Railway's formerly rural halts at Rayners Lane, Eastcote and Ruislip Manor were transformed into modern Holden style stations. The Metropolitan had considered plans as early as 1928 for complete rebuilding of Rayners Lane with two island platforms to form an intermediate terminus providing cross-platform interchange with the District, but nothing was done apart from the provision of an additional waiting shed on the old wooden side platforms. The opening of a timber building on 14th March 1935 to replace the tiny roadside booking hut of 1906 was an expedient pending agreement of road widening plans, which finally allowed the LPTB to go ahead with a new station, opened on 8th August 1938. Designed by Holden and Uren, this had as its main feature a tall rectangular hall astride the railway, jutting 25ft from the building line, so that pedestrians could walk in and out of it from the footpath and flanking shops. Rather less impressive new buildings in Holden style at Ruislip Manor and Eastcote were completed in 1938 and 1939 but at the former, the work at rail level was left unfinished. At Hillingdon, where receipts moved from £2,025 in 1924 to over £12,000 in 1930, the board ordered some improvements in the latter year. Building pace at Ickenham did not justify reconstruction before 1939 and although platforms were lengthened, this remained very much the country halt, with its homely little booking office on the road bridge. In the mid-1960s London Transport slowly transformed it to a suburban station, opening a passenger hall built on a raft over the line on 19th September 1971.

Bold decisions had to be taken at Uxbridge where, using the entry provided by the existing large goods yard, the LPTB erected an entirely new rail and bus station fronting the High Street. Approached through a deep cutting, this had three tracks with four platform faces under an impressive overall roof of glass and concrete. At the High Street end, a spacious passenger hall with a licensed refreshment room was linked to the roadway by a shopping arcade. When this new facility was opened on 4th December 1938 the tube service to Uxbridge was increased from four to eight trains an hour.

Suburban growth also required expansion of freight installations. At Ruislip, where the 1904 passenger station remained unchanged apart from a new covered footbridge and roofing and shelter extensions in 1928, the yard was enlarged in 1928–29. After the board heard reports of an average of 17 wagons blocked daily at Harrow unable to get into Hillingdon, that yard was improved in 1930. Nash's private siding at Rayners Lane has already been noted, but this was preceded by another laid in 1929 for the builder E. S. Reid, who met its £1,000 cost. For the new suburb the Metropolitan opened a public yard west of the station in July 1929 where by the end of the year traffic had risen from 230 to 1,157 tons a month, requiring expansion in 1930.

At Uxbridge the wholesale grocers Alfred Button & Sons had leased buildings in the goods yard since 1913 on condition that the Metropolitan would get a minimum level of traffic, but when the firm wanted to expand this property in 1926 whilst sending the bulk of their traffic by road, the Metropolitan insisted that the company withdrew all but one of the road vehicles that had been used to carry goods from the London docks and markets, consigning the bulk via the railway. This was agreed, and for some years much of it passed through the Metropolitan's Farringdon goods depot, but when the LPTB took over in 1933 this movement was seen as an embarrassment to the rapidly growing passenger traffic. Reconstruction of Uxbridge station brought closure of the yard at the end of April 1939.

Freight movements over the Uxbridge line survived well into the postwar years, ex GCR class N5 0-6-2T giving way in the 1950s to BR standard class 4 2-6-0s and these in turn, in 1963 to diesel locomotives. The closure of the South Harrow gasworks on 4th April 1954 brought to an end the local trips described earlier and a Beeching rationalisation killed off the remaining public freight workings, diverting all railborne solid fuel (virtually the only residual business) to a new concentration depot at West Drayton. As a result the yards at Rayners Lane, Eastcote, Ruislip and Hillingdon were closed from 10th August 1964.

At West Harrow, where the ugly station structures of timber and old rail had become unstable on their embankment perch, a total reconstruction was completed in September 1990. Clad in white vitreous enamel metal panels, the new platform buildings included small waiting rooms. At street level, the Metropolitan Railway's garden shed-like ticket hut gave way to a ticket and entrance hall in brick and glass which bore a passing resemblance to a very large greenhouse. This new building was sited below the London platform and passengers for the Uxbridge direction, having bought their tickets, were still obliged to pass under the railway bridge and climb the separate staircase to the westbound platform.

Somewhat more splendid was the replacement of the shabby station at Hillingdon, long overdue for rebuilding. Here some forward-looking architecture from the Cassidy Taggart Partnership won a design competition. Completed in 1992–3 and

funded from the roadbuilding coffers of the Department of Transport, this transformation came about because the 1923 station most fortuitously stood in the way of a desired realignment of the A40 London-Oxford road (Western Avenue). It was a rare and precious example of public expenditure in the interests of speeding up motor traffic being obliged to benefit rail transport facilities. The new platforms, moved 71 metres nearer to Uxbridge, with ticket office above their London end, were reached by a lengthy elevated covered walkway from the former ticket office site in Long Lane. Two hydraulic lifts with a 16ft 6in rise were installed to facilitate access by those with impaired mobility. This end of the platforms, the footbridge over the line and the new ticket office area were protected by a graceful ridged overall roof and a second similar roof at a slightly lower level covered a further length of the platforms with their waiting areas enclosed in glass block walls. These stepped roofs, reminiscent of the Victorian trainsheds, created a bright and airy space beneath, luminous with direct and reflected light from their fritted glass and white metal framework. Since the pattern of the glass was varied to correspond with the changing angle of the sun's rays, it provided protection from solar heat and radiation without degrading the light. Visually, the whole structure formed a creditable adornment to the Uxbridge line, in its own generation standing comparison with the fine 1930s architecture elsewhere. Unfortunately, any contemplation of its interesting and pleasing design, from within or without, was assaulted by the persistent roar which arose from the malodorous chasm enclosing the adjacent A40 road.

The elegant 1993 station at Hillingdon, looking to Uxbridge. *Capital Transport*

Further modernisation of signalling was undertaken in the post-war period: on 17th October and 12th December 1948 the Metropolitan's 1930 installation between Harrow and Uxbridge was replaced by standard London Transport two-aspect colour-lights, increasing line capacity to 30 trains an hour. On the Ealing & South Harrow, the original semaphores were gradually replaced by standard colour-lights until the last, at Hanger Lane Junction, went out of use on 21st November 1953, a date which marked the end of semaphore signals on wholly-owned London Transport electric running lines. Some points at South Harrow remained mechanically-worked until 14th November 1957 when the signal box there was closed in favour of remote control from Rayners Lane. The South Harrow–Ealing section was controlled from the Earl's Court Regulating Room after another programme of signalling improvements, completed on 17th July 1978.

On the Metropolitan Line between Harrow and Uxbridge, a further signalling modernisation scheme was started in 1987. Uxbridge box was closed and its work transferred to an auxiliary panel at Rayners Lane from 4th May that year; under this scheme, supervision and operation of the whole line was eventually to be moved to the Signalling Control Centre at Baker Street station.

To give permanent way trains from Ruislip depot better access to the LT system and to increase operational flexibility in movement of empty stock, a single line connection, unelectrified and hand-signalled, was laid through sidings from the Uxbridge line west of Ruislip station into the Central Line Ruislip depot between Ruislip Gardens and West Ruislip stations. This came into use on 24th July 1973. From 28th September 1975, mainly to facilitate its use for reversing Piccadilly Line trains at Ruislip, it was signalled and electrified.

Train services underwent some modification from the late 1950s onwards, partly to reflect the general decline in off peak loadings and later the severe staff shortages experienced by London Transport in the mid 1970s. Frequency after 21.00 was reduced to 20 min Mondays to Fridays and before 09.00 and after 19.00 at weekends. Piccadilly Line tube trains were progressively withdrawn west of Rayners Lane: between 10.00 and 16.00 on weekdays from 2nd March 1959, on weekday evenings and Sundays from 16th/22nd October 1967, after midday on Saturdays from 5th December 1970 and all day Saturdays from 5th October 1974. By 1995 the number reaching Uxbridge had declined from 106 a day in 1958 to 30.

Things then improved. From 30th May 1995 the midday Metropolitan Line service Mondays to Saturdays was increased to six trains an hour (8/12 min. intervals); a 15 minute service was introduced on Sundays in shopping hours in response to changes in Sunday trading legislation; and from September 1996, Piccadilly tube trains once again ran through all day to Uxbridge. The important point to absorb is that even at its lowest point, the service given to Uxbridge and intermediate stations through north west London's 1930s suburbia was always better than that received by comparable areas south of the Thames, such as Waterloo–Raynes Park–Epsom. Although post 1948 traffics would never at any point have come near to justifying commercially the ambitious line capacity advancements put forward in that year, the London Transport services through South Harrow and Rayners Lane to Uxbridge continue to make a substantial contribution to the success of the popular residential and retail centres they serve and in whose development they have played such a large part. The shades of Henry Raynes, C. T. Yerkes and R. H. Selbie must view the outcome of their initiatives with continuing satisfaction.

The Stanmore Branch (LNWR) (map page 293)

Like the Chipstead Valley, the Harrow–Stanmore branch owed its existence to the drive and pertinacity of a single capitalist. With a population of only 1,400 and three stations within little over a two-mile radius, Thorne's 'neat, clean, genteel' village of Great Stanmore seemed a poor candidate for a railway of its own, but in the 1880s, this picturesque district of north Middlesex, already a favourite place of residence for the moderately wealthy, attracted the attention of the hotel and restaurant magnate Frederick Gordon (1835–1904). The particular object of Gordon's interest was Bentley Priory, a mansion set in a vast richly-timbered estate, once the home of Queen Adelaide, latterly of Sir John Kelk, the prosperous railway and building contractor. In 1882 Gordon bought the estate with the intention of converting it into a country resort for his London hotel guests, a project which could not be expected to prosper without some improvement in railway communication. Meanwhile the Priory opened as an hotel on 6th June 1885.

Edgware, Stanmore & Harrow Railway and Edgware & Harrow Junction Railway Bills deposited by other interests in November 1881 had failed, as did the Ealing, Harrow & Edgware Bill deposited in 1884. Obliged to promote his own line, Gordon engaged William Beswick Myers to survey a route from the LNWR at Harrow. Opposition from Lord Wolverton of the Glyn banking family was overcome when Gordon purchased part of his estate, land which he opened as a golf course in 1893.

The 2m 4f 7.25ch branch was authorised in 1886 as the Harrow & Stanmore Railway, to a company consisting of Frederick Gordon, Edward Hegley Byas, John Pound and Charles Edward Keyser, with a capital of £60,000 and borrowing powers of £20,000. From a junction with the LNWR Up slow line at Harrow, facing away from London, the branch was to run due north between Kenton Lane and the west side of Stanmore Park, finally passing through the southern part of the Bentley Priory estate to terminate on the west side of Green Lane, 190yd north of St John's parish church.

When Gordon failed to raise capital for this line he promoted a second bill in 1887 for a shorter route of 2m 1f 2.25ch, which left the 1886 alignment 2f 6.25ch from Harrow, passing to the east of Stanmore Park to terminate 375yd south-east of the parish church on the west side of Old Church Lane. In its new act of 1888, the Harrow & Stanmore's capital was reduced to a more manageable £36,000 with borrowing powers of £12,000. Gordon took up 3,180 of the 3,600 £10 shares and 40 more went to his relatives.

Myers settled a junction with the LNWR which agreed to work the line, leaving Gordon to find the money. By its act of 1891 the main line company was authorised to enter into agreements with the Harrow & Stanmore, and an agreement dated 29th January 1891 scheduled to the act required the H&SR to build and maintain for one year a single line with passenger and goods station at Stanmore and interchange sidings at Harrow, also an intermediate station if this were required by the LNWR. In return, the main line company would work the branch in connection with its system, provide staff and rolling stock and after the first year undertake maintenance and repairs, all this for 60 per cent of gross receipts. The LNWR (Additional Powers) Act, 1899 confirmed the purchase of the H&SR by the LNWR on 1st July 1899, and an agreement scheduled to the act revealed the price as £34,000 in cash with H&SR liabilities as £36,000 in £10 shares, £12,000 in debenture bonds, and a mortgage of £2,800.

The pretty conceit that was Stanmore LNWR station, of which only a small part survives. Since the LNWR van carries a poster advertising the new line to Watford, this photo probably dates from 1912. *Commercial postcard*

Meanwhile, at 12.17 on 18th December 1890, the first train left Harrow for Stanmore, inaugurating a timetable of ten Down and nine Up trains Mondays to Fridays with one extra each way on Saturdays. The first departure from the terminus was at the reasonably gentlemanly hour of 08.20, but the last Down run from Harrow was at 20.15. To secure his railway, Gordon was obliged to pay careful attention to local feeling; one demand was that there should be no Sunday trains, although he did manage to obtain a concession that the ban should be limited to 40 years. Stanmore's station building, as we shall see, was another costly obligation in this direction.

At Harrow station the branch platform, labelled HARROW JUNCTION CHANGE FOR LNW RAILWAY, differed in fittings and appearances from the rest of the building, an indication of the line's independent origins. For the first part of its route, the branch descended at 1 in 95 and 1 in 528, but just before half-way started to climb at 1 in 80, 1 in 85 and entered the terminus at 1 in 285. Situated about a quarter of a mile from the village centre and 94ft above the junction, Stanmore's station met the sensitivity of the privileged and affluent residents with truly delightful gothic elevations intended to blend into its surroundings of leafy parklands and expensive mansions. A low red brick and tile building with freestone embellishments, it bore a strong resemblance to a tiny country church, its principal feature a square tower decorated with spire, stone-faced clock and buttressed portico. The interior consisted of a single platform 310ft long, protected for most of its length by a cast-iron and glass awning supported by stanchions bearing the arms of the Gordon family. Facing the platform was a locomotive run-round road; behind it, on the east side, a goods shed and four sidings.

As working was on the single-staff system, the only signals were at each end, those at Stanmore two arms on a single post controlled from an open ground frame at the buffer stops (this was later replaced with a standard LNWR frame at the London end). Push-and-pull operation with Webb 2–4–2T started about 1907, after which the locomotive was invariably at the Harrow end of the train. The redundant locomotive line at Stanmore was used to stable stock. Freight trains were also propelled on the branch, latterly under a 13-wagon restriction. There was no intermediate goods yard but a siding was provided just north of Kenton Lane, where until about 1920 Marylebone's refuse was unloaded to deposit on the fields of Marsh Farm. Another change in the early years was the complete reconstruction of Harrow & Wealdstone station in connection with the LNWR widening and suburban electrification scheme. Completed in 1912, this work included a 540ft island platform (No. 7) for the Stanmore trains, with the Up slow line on the opposite face (No. 6). The position of the new suburban lines at the extreme west side of the station combined with the nature of the junction rendered it unduly costly to include Stanmore in the electrification scheme, a circumstance which to a large extent sealed the fate of the line, allowing other railway companies to exploit the district during the building boom between the wars.

As yet there was no sign of any traffic potential. Gordon's enterprises at Stanmore failed and the line's business was very light. A few houses appeared near the station, some built by Gordon but the Bentley Priory hotel flopped and Gordon moved in with his second wife and 11 children. He became a regular passenger on the 08.20 Up train, returning home from London in the evening. After his death in 1904, Bentley Priory became for 20 years a school for young ladies, before passing to the Air Ministry. Gordon laid out a road named after himself across the part of Stanmore Park that he had bought and three-bedroomed houses here were advertised in 1906 at rents of £26 a year, but there was no general development of small houses at this time in the country between Stanmore and Harrow & Wealdstone stations.

Some inroads were made into such traffic as did exist on the branch by the establishment of motor bus services in the area. In 1922 an hourly service was started between South Harrow and Golders Green via Harrow & Wealdstone station, Stanmore and Edgware, and since 1913 there had been a 20-minute bus service between Kilburn and Watford via Stanmore Hill. From 1924 the South Harrow–Edgware buses, increased to half-hourly frequency, were feeding the new Underground terminus at the latter point, with through tickets to London available which were cheaper than the Stanmore–Euston fare via Harrow & Wealdstone.

From about 1923 a number of roads were made east of the branch at Stanmore station, and in the late 1920s and early 1930s Kenton was creeping north to fill the triangle between the branch, Kenton Road and Kenton Lane. This last development, of semi-detached and terrace blocks, was soon to provide extra loads for the Stanmore branch. In response to demands from the builders, the LMSR opened a halt called Belmont on 12th September 1932, sited where the branch passed under Kenton Lane about 1¼ miles from the junction. The single platform, on the west side of the line, supported an ugly wooden waiting shelter and a wooden ticket office under a pitched roof. Branch trains called here on weekdays between 07.00 and 22.00, and soon the somewhat primitive facilities were proving inadequate. Wealdstone spread eastwards to the branch in the early 1930s, whilst Davis Estates and others built north from Belmont towards Stanmore Park, selling at prices between

£595 and £865. By this time a second competitor was in the field. The Metropolitan Railway had opened its branch to Stanmore on 10th December 1932, but although this had the advantage of through rush-hour trains to and from the West End and the City, initially the fares were at main line rates leaving the road-rail facility via Edgware Underground as the cheapest route for Stanmore residents.

With building of low-cost houses proceeding apace, Belmont became and was to remain the main traffic centre for the Stanmore branch. Bricks for house building were brought in to a temporary siding nearby. A reconstruction scheme announced in 1935 was completed on 5th July 1937, when a 300ft island platform station with centrally-heated waiting room replaced the halt. A wooden booking office, built out on stilts at the side of the road bridge was linked to the platform by an uncovered footbridge. The passing loop, with its spring-loaded points and ancillary sand drags, controlled from a signal box on the platform, made it possible to have two trains on the branch at a time, providing a ten-minute service in the peak. As a further refinement, electric token block working with long and short section tokens started in September 1938; the extraction of the long section token from the Belmont frame locked it, also securing the slip points at Harrow to prevent a second train from entering the branch. The signals were then set to give one through road on the west side of the Belmont loop. With the long section token placed in the Belmont frame to unlock it, it was possible to withdraw a blue section token to give to the driver of a Stanmore train. This done, the Harrow No. 1 box signalman was able to take out a red token which allowed a second train as far as Belmont. The two trains met there and the tokens were exchanged after being used to unlock the appropriate starter signals and crossover locks. Should any driver attempt to pass the Belmont starter signals at danger, he would find his train in the sand drag.

Before serious building began in the 1920s, 30 trains a day each way sufficed, but the service was then gradually improved so that by 1933 the morning intervals were only 15 to 20 minutes with service after that irregular, gaps varying from 15 to 65 minutes. Sunday trains were started on 6th May 1934 at approximately 20-minute intervals between 09.00 and 23.00. With the new loop in operation, the 1938 timetable showed 71 trains each way on weekdays leaving Stanmore between 06.43 and 00.25 and Harrow between 06.43 and 00.54. A ten-minute service applied in rush hours and at Saturday midday. A similar pattern was operating in 1946 but with earlier and later trains (05.45 to 01.05 from Harrow) and on Sundays there were half-hourly departures from Harrow between 07.35 and 00.05.

Webb 2–4–2T pushing or pulling one, two, or three coaches were replaced about 1934 with new 2P 0–4–4T which were also used on the daily freight run. Fowler 2–6–2T arrived in 1935, to remain the usual locomotives for most of the rest of the branch's life. The only other type of steam locomotive regularly seen were Ivatt 2–6–2T which were allocated to the line from their introduction in 1946. Webb tanks reappeared after World War 2, finding some difficulty in propelling three modern bogie coaches up the hill to Stanmore.

British Railways experimental ACV diesel railcar units took over the passenger service from 15th March 1954, and with some breaks these rattling and uncomfortable sets of three four-wheeled vehicles remained on the branch until 13th June 1955 when they were moved to the Watford–St Albans branch. Diesel car working was resumed on 6th August 1957, using both the ACV and the then new BR Standard types, steam locomotives coming to the rescue from time to time.

LMSR class 2P 0-4-4T 6409 ready to return from Stanmore, c.1938. *J G Dewing*

Sunday working was a victim of the coal shortages of winter 1946–47, but was restored the following June. Patronage was so light that Sunday trains were withdrawn permanently from 27th July 1947. In these early post-war years the LNWR rubber doormat at Stanmore station still showed little sign of wear and by 1952, with daily loadings on the branch averaging 700, it was not difficult for the BR accountants to establish an annual 'loss' of £4,000, which made it eligible for closure. Not surprisingly, the many rail user residents of Belmont rose up in anger, securing the retention of the section between there and Harrow.

After 13th September 1952 the delightful little station at Stanmore saw only the daily freight train, which brought in bananas and domestic fuels, and later, stores for the main line electrification. Holders of unexpired season tickets from Stanmore were allowed to use them on London Transport buses between Harrow & Wealdstone station and Stanmore church (route 114) or between Belmont station and Stanmore church via Wealdstone (routes 18 and 114). In 1955 the west side of the Belmont loop was taken up, working on the branch reverting to one train on line from 9th July. Freights to Stanmore continued until August 1964 when the last of the engineering stores were moved away. Track lifting began soon afterwards.

Despite the introduction of the diesel cars which brought some increase in

Experimental ACV lightweight diesel railcar set at the Belmont island platform, ready to leave for Harrow & Wealdstone, 17th April 1954. An LMSR 'Hawkseye' station name sign, a type standardised in 1938, survives at right. *Alan A Jackson*

loadings, off-peak travel became very light towards the end of the 1950s for the usual reasons. Only some 900 ordinary tickets were issued each month for journeys between Harrow and Belmont in 1957, but this figure, which related only to local issues, was about twice that of steam days. Peak-hour patronage remained fairly heavy, with some trains in 1958 loading to over 100 passengers.

Ordinary bookings to and from Belmont faded away almost completely in the early 1960s when rail fares were allowed to climb above those of competing bus services, whilst operating difficulties brought frequent cancellations. Belmont duly appeared in the sad and lengthy list of potential casualties included in Dr Beeching's *Reshaping of British Railways* of 1963. During that summer a 15-year-old schoolboy collected 1,080 signatures in favour of retention, but was obliged to admit to the enquiry that only some 450 of these were regular users of the line. The Beeching decision was duly confirmed, the last train running on 3rd October 1964, after which the remaining passengers had to seek the alternative bus services which had already drained off most of the business. This was not quite the end. BBC television films were made on the branch in 1965 and 1966 and the first few chains out of Harrow & Wealdstone were used as a siding and as a tamping machine test track until 1968.

Few clues remain for the railway archaeologist. Belmont station was demolished in July 1966. This was no loss architecturally, but it is sad to record that despite the efforts of local residents, the planning authorities allowed the pretty little building at Stanmore to be incorporated in a housing and garage development. What survives is almost unrecognisable and the delightful Victorian atmosphere has gone. Harrow Council bought most of the track bed, using it for a variety of purposes including electricity substations, housing, car parks and schools, even a cemetery extension. Solid reminders of Gordon's enterprise remain in London's Northumberland Avenue, but there is little enough to see at Stanmore.

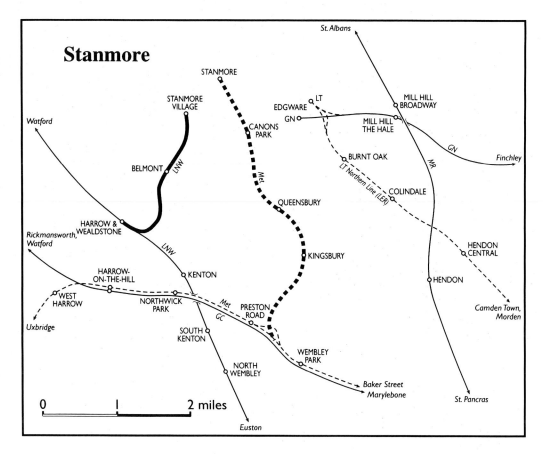

Stanmore

St. Albans

STANMORE

STANMORE
VILLAGE

LT

EDGWARE
GN

MILL HILL
BROADWAY

Watford

CANONS
PARK

MILL HILL
THE HALE

BURNT OAK

GN

BELMONT

LNW

Finchley

Met

LT Northern Line (LER)

COLINDALE

QUEENSBURY

MR

HARROW &
WEALDSTONE

Rickmansworth,
Watford

KINGSBURY

HENDON
CENTRAL

HARROW-
ON-THE-HILL

LNW

KENTON

HENDON

WEST
HARROW

NORTHWICK
PARK

Met

PRESTON
ROAD

Uxbridge

GC

SOUTH
KENTON

WEMBLEY
PARK

Camden Town,
Morden

NORTH
WEMBLEY

Baker Street
Marylebone

0   1   2 miles

St. Pancras

Euston

The Stanmore Branch (Metropolitan Railway)   (map above)

As early as 1892 a Metropolitan extension from Wembley through Stanmore to
Watford had been suggested, and it came up again in 1908 when the Watford &
Edgware interest saw it as a means of getting its line built; the idea was revived by
Bushey residents in 1911, but on each occasion the Metropolitan shunned the
advances. Although it later reached Watford by another route, it did however retain
interest in Stanmore as an objective. A second railway to that place might seem an
extravagance, even in the 1930s when the area was becoming thoroughly suburbanised, but the LNWR branch just described left untouched the western side of
Edgware which had begun to grow in the late 1920s, also missing a large district
west of Edgware Road which had seen industrial activity in World War I and which
now seemed ripe for intensive housing development. So, thinking that there might
be some pickings to be had, reinforced by the prospect of getting substantial parcels
of land free or at nominal price from All Souls' College and the promise of
government assistance with finance under schemes to relieve unemployment, the
Metropolitan began in the summer of 1929 to look at possible extension in this
direction. The aim was to draw from the Underground Company some of the
business that it was at last getting from its 1924 Edgware extension, at the same time
staking out a rival claim to the still open country north of Edgware in which the
Underground had long had an interest. London was on a northward march, nothing
seemed likely to halt it, and the Metropolitan had no wish to be left behind.

In September 1929 the Metropolitan board was told that all landowners along the route had been approached and serious opposition was unlikely. Property demolition could be confined to a few houses in Whitchurch Lane, Edgware. The picture of low land costs proved to be too rosy, as after work had started, it was necessary to compensate some developers at Canons Park and around Kingsbury for disturbance to housing estates already in the process of being laid out. Basing his assumptions on traffic growth at North Harrow and Preston Road between 1923 and 1928, the general manager forecast to the board that the new branch should produce a net profit of at least £20,000 a year within a few years. Again this was somewhat optimistic, as we shall see.

A bill for the 1930 session proposed a 4m 3.7ch branch from about half a mile north-west of Wembley Park station to a terminus on the eastern side of Stanmore, passing through potential suburban areas around Kingsbury Green and western Edgware. At the February meeting shareholders were told that the Stanmore catchment area, which was being rapidly developed for housing, was legitimately 'their territory'. An astute questioner from the floor made the awkward point about adding to the already serious congestion between Finchley Road and Baker Street, fears that the chairman tried to assuage with talk of more rolling stock and longer trains. He did not mention that the board had been concerned with this problem for over ten years, having tried earlier to secure government assistance for a 1925 scheme for a main line size tube between Willesden Green and Edgware Road. This had however come up against the difficulty that the Ministry of Transport's new 'Requirements for Tube Railways' would have prevented the operation of compartment stock on the planned line; the Metropolitan's long-distance services were entirely worked with such stock, which was preferred by the passengers. Nothing was done, although alternatives were considered and some stopgap measures taken; the misgivings of the questioner were to be justified and, as we shall discover, London Transport eventually had to undertake surgery.

Understandably, the LMSR objected to a second station in Stanmore on the grounds of wasteful competition, but were not in a very strong position as the Metropolitan could show without difficulty that it wished to serve a different district and also that its facilities would offer greater convenience to Stanmore travellers.

The Stanmore bill was one of four for new London lines in the 1930 session whose passage was facilitated because they were certified as likely to contribute substantially to the early relief of unemployment. Royal assent was given on 4th June and Treasury approval to a grant under the 1929 Development (Loan Guarantees & Grants) Act followed just over a month later. This was to amount to five per cent of the net expenditure for five years and 2½ per cent for a further five years. Petitions against the bill from the Wembley Urban District Council secured among other things that the abutment walls of the road bridges should be faced with brindle bricks up to dado height and bricks of 'varied and approved tints' above, whilst the de Havilland Aircraft Co. wanted any embankment past its Stag Lane airfield to be not more than 25ft high, with no obstructions more than 25ft above existing ground level.

In its *Metro-Land* annual for 1931, the company enthused over the new line, which the writer noted would pass through a district little known in the first part of its course except to the 'Sports Grounds players who use Preston Road station'. The central part was described as 'open pastureland crossed by a few footpaths' whilst the last section, approaching Stanmore, would pass through pleasant parkland. 'Houses there are at present practically none, but they will speedily follow the line . . . the work presents few engineering difficulties, the district for the most part being fairly level and of an altitude varying from 135 to 220 feet'. This statement about ease of construction was no doubt recalled with a bitter smile later. Substantial earthworks were required through the area's heavy clay and some short cuts were evidently taken to keep costs within estimates, since the formations subsequently required expensive maintenance and remedial treatment. In 1995 the whole length of embankment between Canons Park and Queensbury had to be stabilised.

In a 1933 advertisement the Metropolitan suggested that the district served, 'essentially pastoral in character' (they liked the word, but there was more hay than sheep) would 'provide room, under healthy, happy conditions, for a considerable population', an assertion somewhat at odds with the conclusion that 'the pleasant lanes, meadow tracts and byways that abound' would become 'deservedly popular with the pleasure-seeker'.

Hendon Rural District Council was less enthusiastic. Examining the bill in December 1929 it remarked somewhat sourly that the new railway would cut through 43 football and hockey grounds, would displace 14 houses each side of Whitchurch Lane, some of them only six months old, and would cross a fine avenue of trees, a dairy farm, the avenue to Canons Park and land scheduled as an open space.

Construction by Walter Scott & Middleton started early in 1931 under the Metropolitan Railway's chief engineer, E. A. Wilson. Temporary railways served by Manning Wardle 0–6–0T dating from 1876–1908 were laid along ground level, eventually to be linked to a siding alongside the main line at Wembley Park, and serviced by a depot west of the proposed Kingsbury station. Public roads were crossed on the level, with traffic controlled by flagmen. Delays caused by the prolonged wet weather in 1931 were recouped by 24-hour working during the following spring, summer and early autumn. On the first Sunday of December 1932 two Metropolitan Railway K Class 2–6–4T arrived to consolidate the new permanent way.

An official ceremonial opening took place on Friday 9th December when the Minister of Transport, the Minister for the Colonies (the local MP), and other notables joined the Metropolitan chairman, Lord Aberconway in a six-car train of new multiple-unit compartment stock, to which was added the company's official saloon and a Pullman car. This train ran to allow an inspection of the new stations and a formal 'switching-in' of Stanmore signals from Wembley Park signal box, returning the company to luncheon at Baker Street's new Chiltern Court restaurant. One of the speeches, by J. H. Thomas, Dominions Secretary and former GWR engine driver, was notable for the sentiment, still apparently tenable, that in the development of the nation, prosperity had run side-by-side with the prosperity and development of its railway system.

Public service started the next day, 10th December 1932, worked with multiple-unit compartment stock. Except in rush hours, when some trains ran to and from Baker Street, passengers were obliged to change trains at Wembley Park. There were 72 trains each way daily on the branch with a reduced service on Sundays, the best travelling time for the 11¼ miles from Stanmore to Baker Street being 22 minutes.

Left: The handsome station building provided for its Stanmore terminus by the Metropolitan Railway, seen here just before opening in 1932. Designed by the company's staff architect, C W Clark FRIBA, its Domestic styling was in keeping with the high quality housing of the area it served.

Right: Interior of Stanmore Metropolitan Railway terminus, with special train for Press inspection, December 1932. The unsuccessful goods yard is at the right. *C F Klapper*

From the junction, seven miles from Baker Street, the new line ran north-east on embankment, traversing its sharpest curve (15ch radius) and twice crossing the Wealdstone Brook which had been diverted into new channels. At this point, the alignment was to some extent determined by the presence of a new housing estate north of Preston Road station, the site of Uxendon Farm, Barn Hill, and the watercourse. Continuing north-east towards the Edgware Road and the still small communities of Roe Green and Kingsbury Green, the line entered a deep and wide cutting, passing below the Kingsbury-Kenton road. Here was Kingsbury station, which strictly should have been called Kingsbury *Green*, as that place was but half a mile east of the line, whereas Kingsbury itself was well over a mile away, close to Neasden station, which was called Neasden & Kingsbury until the new station opened. The entrance block, on the south side of the road bridge, was in the centre of three cottage-style red brick-and-tile two-storey blocks of shops, with flats above. There were five shops in each of the side blocks and three each side of the main entrance. From the entrance hall with its passimeter ticket office, covered stairs led down to platforms either side of the cutting, each platform with a short canopied red brick building containing a neat waiting room with tiled fireplace and wooden bench seats along the walls. Electric lamps held in pretty iron scroll work lit the platforms at night. When the station was opened there were no significant population centres nearby other than the small settlement at Kingsbury Green and, a little to the north, Roe Green, the interesting 1917 garden village for workers in the adjacent wartime aviation factories.

Crossing open land and skirting the east side of Willesden Isolation Hospital, the branch now turned north-west on embankments which continued almost to the terminus, encountering its maximum gradient of 1 in 70. Passing between the western boundary of Stag Lane airfield and the Hendon Isolation Hospital, the direction changed to almost due north. After crossing above Whitchurch Lane, where some suburban building was already in evidence, Canons Park (Edgware) station was entered.

At street level on each side of the northern abutment of the bridges was a canopied entrance to a booking hall beneath the first arch of the six-span masonry viaduct supporting the platforms. Either side of the entrances were small two-storey blocks of shops with flats over. Platform structures were similar to those at Kingsbury.

For its final section the line turned slightly north-west, entering the ancient Canons Park. Here it was closest to the LMSR branch, just over half a mile to the west. Encountering the upward slope of the Elstree Ridge, the tracks entered the terminus in a cutting. The station itself, the summit of the line, was scooped out of the side of the hill, its main building fronting on to the south side of the London Road, almost half a mile east of Stanmore village centre. Any extension towards Elstree and St Albans was going to involve expensive tunnelling through Elstree Ridge, but the terminus was planned to require very little alteration should that be required. The terminal platform was an island protected by a canopy which also covered the waiting room, staff accommodation and the lower landing of the covered staircase to the roadside building, a large three-storey block with its first floor at ground level. East of the platform was the only goods siding on the branch, together with two stabling roads. As traffic in domestic fuel and building materials was well entrenched with the LMSR, freight business at uncompetitive rates did not justify working a train up the line, and the facility was withdrawn on 31st March 1936.

The roadside buildings at Kingsbury and Stanmore were executed in a domestic style of 'pleasing and unassuming simplicity' by the company's architect, Charles W Clark, who also designed houses on Metropolitan land at Pinner and elsewhere. Stanmore, with its handsome hipped roof, four chimneys and Georgian windows would not have looked out of place on a country gentleman's estate. Both buildings were in red multi-coloured bricks set on a few courses of dark brindled bricks which formed a mock plinth. Their long red-tiled roofs were broken by dormer windows, one of which lit the entrance hall. These halls were tiled in khaki tone below plaster friezes, whilst the doors, clock and other features were elegantly framed in hardwood.

Canons Park was less impressive; here the roadside buildings were flat-roofed, the horizontal motif of bridge and roof emphasised by the pattern of the brickwork and a dark granite plinth. All three stations had platform buildings in matching red brick with workmanlike glass and steel canopies valanced in metal.

Spoil from the station area at Stanmore and the Kingsbury cutting provided much of the fill for the embankments. There were seven underbridges, the largest with a span of 89ft, and eight overbridges (four of them footbridges). All main bridges apart from one in steelcrete were of plate girder construction with concrete slab floors. Set in a 30–32ft wide formation, the double track consisted of 45ft 95lb bullhead rails and in accordance with Metropolitan practice, the 600V dc conductor was placed outside the inner running rails, current returning to a negative conductor between the running rails.

Signalling was conventional, with three-aspect colour-lights, ac track circuits, train-stops and short-range colour-lights or electric discs for shunting, but there was one novel feature. All points and signals were worked from Wembley Park box, using a Westinghouse centralised traffic control system for the first time in Great Britain (first in the world for a suburban application).

Power from Neasden at 11,000V three-phase ac was converted to traction voltage in new rotary substations at Preston Road ($3 \times 1,500$kW) and Canons Park ($2 \times 1,500$kW). Publicity for the opening made much mention of 65 new multiple-unit compartment cars which could be used to form seven complete eight-car trains or be broken up into four-car formation for slack-hour working. Five of the third-class cars were used to bring existing seven-car MW trains to eight-car length. This steel-panelled stock by Birmingham Railway Carriage & Wagon formed the ceremonial train described earlier, but the branch passengers also saw much of the older type of compartment stock. From January 1934 until November 1938 the off-peak shuttle was operated by single-unit 52-seater compartment cars converted from older stock in 1910 for the Uxbridge branch. Thereafter, until the arrival of tube stock, a two-car set was made up to accommodate traffic increases. The 1934 timetable shows three off-peak shuttle workings to and from Wembley Park each hour and three through workings composed of three- or four-car trains.

As it was constructed at just the right moment to coincide with the London suburban housing boom, building development did 'follow the line' as had been prophesied. Between 1931 and 1938 the population served between Kingsbury and Stanmore increased from 17,800 to 33,100, producing a 253 per cent increase in tickets sold (742,000 in 1933 to 2,622,000 in 1938). Train services were augmented accordingly so that by 1935 there were 98 each way on weekdays (45 of them to and from Baker Street) and 50 each way on Sundays.

Neither Stanmore nor Canons Park reaped anything like the maximum from their burgeoning catchment areas for reasons to be discussed in a moment. Kingsbury's trade became fairly brisk in 1933–38 when the whole of the surrounding area was clothed with small houses. After 1933 the station shopping parade was joined by others of varying styles and ugliness on both sides of the road, also by a cinema, the whole forming the focus of an entirely new community centred around the railway.

But perhaps the branch's greatest success in its early period was the new district built on and around the Stag Lane airfield after it closed for flying in October 1933. Plans for this 'new township of 100,000 houses and 150 shops' had been announced in local newspapers as early as April 1932 as 'awaiting the railway'. As there had been nothing there other than the flying field and hangars (they remained as factories) a name was required, and the not too imaginative choice of an estate agent was Queensbury. A station to serve it had been a condition of free conveyance of land by All Souls' College in 1929 (which wanted it to be called Kingsbury Downs) and on Sunday 16th December 1934 a wooden halt was opened. In 1936, with the growth of the surrounding area justifying something better, London Transport built a spacious new entrance hall and access passage through a large neo-Georgian block of shops and flats erected alongside the line by John Laing & Son. In the 1950s, the crude platform shelters were rebuilt in brick and concrete, leaving some evidence of the original halt in the timber platforms beyond the canopied sections until they too were rebuilt in 1978–9. With the station and the opening of other large blocks of flats and shops, followed in 1938 by a 1,500-seat cinema, this western end of the 80ft wide boulevard through the new suburb became its focal point. West of the railway, in the last three years before World War 2, Kenton grew northwards and houses and factories appeared alongside the 1935 dual carriageway motor road which replaced the tree-shaded Honeypot Lane. As there was no facility for railborne freight and as their workforce depleted the ranks of those who used the railway daily, these factories, with others (some of World War 1 origin) near the Edgware Road, much reduced the impact of Queensbury on the health of the branch.

A second influence militated against complete success for the new line. The Underground Company had encouraged its subsidiary, the LGOC, to operate feeder buses based on the Edgware extension stations. Providing a frequent service, together with road-rail bookings, these buses exploited to the full the new housing areas west of the Edgware Road, passing the entrances of the Metropolitan stations at Stanmore and Canons Park. The convenience of this road-rail facility, with its direct access by a shorter route to both West End and City via Euston, and above all its cheaper fare structure, encouraged a substantial proportion of the new home owners to use the Edgware tube in preference to the Metropolitan, some of them even coming to it from the west side of the Stanmore branch. The fare anomaly arose because the Metropolitan had in 1928 aligned its outer district fares and season ticket rates to those of the LNER; its ordinary fares were thus 1½d a mile, whilst the Underground's were closer to bus and tram fares, averaging 1d a mile with special reductions to encourage settlement at the outer ends of tube extensions. The single fare from Edgware to Charing Cross was 7d (3p) compared with 1s 2d (6p) from Canons Park, the latter route of course somewhat longer. This gave more than enough margin to cover the cost of the feeder bus ride whilst still offering the daily traveller a worthwhile saving over walking to a much nearer Metropolitan station.

After much agitation, London Transport took the opportunity of a general five per cent fare increase on 11th June 1939 to even out the rates. Fares on the former Metropolitan services came down to 1d a mile (no less than 700 fares from Stanmore branch stations were reduced) whilst the old Underground Company's substandard fares on the Edgware tube were increased to 1d a mile. But old habits die hard, and diversion of traffic to the Stanmore branch stations was not significant. Even in the 1950s many commuters were still using the very frequent (three to four minute) 18 bus across to Edgware station from places as far west as Belmont, and the former Metropolitan stations were never crowded even at the busiest times.

As expected, the imposition of Stanmore through trains inevitably worsened the existing peak-hour congestion between Finchley Road and Baker Street, where the Metropolitan's four-track main line came down to double. A variety of proposals had been considered by the Metropolitan Railway from 1915 onwards, but the solution finally adopted by London Transport used a plan formulated by the Underground Company in the early 1930s. This took the form of a 2.14-mile small-diameter tube railway from the Bakerloo Line at Baker Street which would surface for cross-platform interchange with the Metropolitan Line services at Finchley Road. By extending the Bakerloo trains over the existing Metropolitan tracks to Stanmore, capacity would be released on the old inner section. It was thought that the Bakerloo could accommodate dual termini north of the Thames because the original service to Queen's Park and beyond was not heavily loaded and could sustain a reduction in frequency if trains were lengthened from six to seven cars. Works for this scheme were duly incorporated in the 1935–40 London Railway Programme, construction starting in April 1936. A burrowing junction north of Wembley Park was included to allow Stanmore trains to reach local roads rearranged in the centre of the four tracks between Preston Road and Finchley Road, and this came into use on 6th November 1938 together with a rebuilt station at Wembley Park.

Operation with tube type rolling stock began on 27th March 1939 when three-car trains ran between Stanmore and Wembley Park for staff training. A through service over the 14.8 miles between Stanmore and Elephant & Castle started on 20th November 1939, six-car trains operating the whole route all day, reaching a maximum of seven an hour at peak periods on the Stanmore branch section. Not all went smoothly. Wartime commitments delayed the delivery of train describers and until 12th December 1939 when paper stickers showing 'M' over the background of the old Metropolitan diamond device appeared in the front windows of Stanmore trains, there was much confusion at inner London tube stations as to the destinations of trains. Drivers unfamiliar with the new route were hampered by blackout conditions, with the result that irregular running continued well into 1940. Nor were tube train drivers accustomed to such rural features as the electrocuted stag spotted after dark on the line between Canons Park and Queensbury in the autumn of 1944.

Platforms at the branch stations were altered to a compromise tube/surface stock height of 2ft 9in above rail, despite the fact that there was to be no more regular working of full-size stock over this line. Signalling was also changed to conform to LPTB practice, two-aspect signals replacing the old (some were retained with one lens covered), repeaters added and electro-pneumatic train stops installed. Centralised traffic control was discarded, a new 47-lever power frame with mechanical interlocking opening at Stanmore in 1939. Six new stabling sidings laid on the site of the old goods roads at Stanmore were used during the war years to house tube cars surplus to requirements pending completion of the 1935–40 New Works Programme. In 1949 land alongside these sidings was purchased for the construction of a new Bakerloo Line car depot in connection with the scheme authorised that year to extend the southern section from Elephant & Castle to Camberwell Green. Revised cost estimates led to the deferment of this proposal in September 1950. The 1939 resignalling of the branch proved unsatisfactory in that it restricted train intervals to a minimum of 3½ minutes, so delays building up in central London could not be rectified by retiming trains on the branch. To remedy this, complete resignalling for a minimum two-minute interval was undertaken in 1955.

Such a close frequency was not dictated by traffic levels. Patronage began to decline in the 1950s when the timetable was rearranged to provide for alternate trains to work only on the branch. The construction of a large complex of government offices close to Canons Park station in the late 1940s added a useful element of contra-peak flow until growth of car ownership removed most of it.

From 1st May 1979 Stanmore services were diverted away from the Bakerloo Line through new tunnels between Baker Street and Charing Cross via Bond Street and Green Park. Two thirds of the 2½–3min peak hour service at Charing Cross (formerly Strand/Trafalgar Square) then ran through to Stanmore, the remainder reversing at Wembley Park, Willesden Green or West Hampstead. Stanmore had a 3½–4 min frequency at rush hours and 7½ min during the middle of the day. This development, given the name Jubilee Line, was a belated recognition of the fact that although it made good sense to integrate the 1932 Stanmore branch with the central area Underground system it had been a mistake to do this by overloading and complicating the Bakerloo Line.

Although it is doubtful whether traffic on a branch line built in the very last years of competition between London railway operators has ever justified its construction and maintenance costs in the narrow financial sense, Wembley Park–Stanmore does continue to play a useful role in relieving the strain on the north London road system. For the perceptive visitor, the branch still retains some of its original atmosphere, rewarding the attentive eye with delightful reminders of Metro-land suburbia, particularly at Kingsbury station.

Edgware GNR, in August 1920 looking to buffers. The sign (left) reads 'EDGWARE FOR CANONS PARK'. The proverbial man and a boy are the only sign of life on the single lengthy platform.
H J P Rutherford

The Edgware, Finchley and Barnet Branches (map page 304)

To the north of Kings Cross and Euston, a low range of hills with a moderately steep southerly slope runs across from Willesden through Hampstead and Highgate to the western outskirts of Wood Green. Behind there is high ground northwards through Finchley towards Barnet, where the town centre is at the summit of a 430ft hill. This barrier, long known as the Northern Heights, was carefully avoided by the early main lines. The London & Birmingham of 1837 passed it on the west; the Great Northern, completed in 1850 to Maiden Lane, swung to the east, seeking a ruling gradient of 1 in 200. Barnet, a coaching town on the Great North Road with an important cattle market, had to make do with a station 1½ miles from its centre.

Other places left unserved in the Northern Heights gap included the straggling villages of Edgware and Finchley, agricultural communities whose farms provided hay for London's huge army of horses. Edgware, as the first stage out of London along Watling Street, had also been a place of some importance in coaching days, but with the eclipse of road transport, its many inns and drinking houses saw little trade except at haymaking time, and by the middle of the nineteenth century its population of around 1,500 was slowly declining.

Proposals to connect Edgware to London by rail were brought to Parliament in 1860 and 1861, but these poorly-engineered schemes failed. Coming up with something rather better, including a station in the centre of Finchley, the Edgware, Highgate & London Railway obtained an act in 1862. Intended to attract GNR interest, it succeeded in getting that company's agreement to a junction at what is now Finsbury Park, and the main line company also consented to staff and work the railway for 50 per cent of gross receipts, subscribing one-third of the £220,000 capital; in return, it was awarded three of the eight seats on the board.

Imbued with a desire to retain some measure of independence, the little company was soon in financial difficulties, its situation aggravated by the appearance of the Midland Railway, whose authorised main line of 1863 kept very close to the western edges of the Northern Heights and attacked the south Hertfordshire plateau at Elstree, cutting right through the district the EH&LR hoped to serve. This threat the Edgware company countered by sponsoring a scheme for a 6¾-mile single-line extension to Watford and a branch from Highgate to Muswell Hill. (The latter's objective was Alexandra Palace, and we shall be returning to it in chapter 4). Both lines were to be worked by the GNR, and both were authorised in 1864. In a further attempt to strengthen its prospects, the EH&LR promoted another line from Finchley to Barnet along the east side of the Dollis Brook valley, for which it gained GNR support after a brief row with 'big brother'. An act for the Barnet line was finally obtained on 16th July 1866, not before Parliament had had to consider a rival Midland branch from Cricklewood and a GNR counter-thrust in the form of a strategic loop to the main line from Potters Bar through the western edges of Barnet to a junction with the EH&LR just west of Finchley. To consolidate its position, the GNR now made a good offer for the Edgware company and its offshoot the Watford & Edgware, the takeover coming into force on 1st August 1867. Despite the fact that some land had been bought, the GNR had little desire to trespass in LNWR territory, so the Watford line was formally abandoned by an act of 1870.

After all the financial, political and engineering delays it had suffered, the 8¾ mile EH&LR was eventually opened on 22nd August 1867 from Seven Sisters Road (now Finsbury Park) to Edgware through stations named Crouch End, Highgate, East End Finchley, Finchley & Hendon,* and Mill Hill. The line began each side of the GNR main lines, the Down track climbing on arches between the two Down slow tracks to join the Up line from Edgware, which was carried over all the main lines before descending to the extreme east side of Seven Sisters Road station.

All the intermediate stations had two side platforms except Mill Hill, which had but one, on the north side. Edgware, built as a through station in anticipation of the extension to Watford, had its main platform on the west and another side platform opposite, which before long fell into grass-grown disuse. There was also a large station house on the main platform, and a sizeable goods yard on the west side, together with a small engine shed, which was to be blown down in the Great Blizzard of 1881.

Beyond the north end of Highgate tunnels the line was single, but the 13-arch brick viaduct over the Dollis Brook between Finchley and Mill Hill was built wide enough for double track, as were the other structures on this section. Starting to climb at Finsbury Park, the line's gradients steepened to 1 in 60 east of Crouch End

---

* Renamed 'Finchley' February 1872; 'Finchley, Church End' July 1896.

London's Local Railways

station, 1 in 59 east of Highgate, reaching a summit north of the Highgate tunnels. The station here, attractively sited in a fold of the hill between the two pairs of single bore tunnels, was set out as an intermediate terminus, the tracks splaying to allow a central shunting road long enough to accommodate a short train. Of the 18 trains each way daily, eight reversed at Highgate, the rest going through to Edgware. Some served Kings Cross, others ran only to and from Seven Sisters Road station.

The double line was brought to East Finchley on 1st December 1867, Highgate then ceasing to be a terminus for some trains. Doubling was extended to Finchley & Hendon on 1st November 1869 this station then becoming the intermediate terminus, rebuilt with an island platform on the Down side, the western face used by Edgware trains in both directions. Meanwhile, in February 1868, trains from the EH&LR began to run through to Farringdon Street, and from March to Ludgate Hill, using the newly-opened City Widened Lines. As operations were somewhat inhibited by the absence of a direct connection from the Down line to the single line at Finchley & Hendon, Edgware's through trains to and from London were very few.

Northwards from Finchley, the double track to Barnet was opened on 1st April 1872 through stations called Torrington Park Woodside and Totteridge. Approaching its High Barnet terminus, the line mounted the side of the Dollis Valley at 1 in 61, cutting right across the former horse race track (once a feature of Barnet Fair) and crossing the Great North Road before coming to an end on the east side of Barnet Hill. Cabs and pedestrians from the hilltop town had to negotiate a steep approach from the main road, a feature which, in icy weather, was to cause many a dignified season ticket holder to complete an unwisely hurried progress to the morning train on his backside. The terminus, 11m 17ch from Kings Cross, had two platforms, the eastern one taking the form of an island. Carriage sidings on the east side and a goods yard to the south completed the layout. From the opening day there were 24 trains each way daily, all but one terminating at High Barnet, the exception going on to the Edgware line, which was otherwise now worked entirely as a shuttle to and from Finchley.

From the late 1860s these facilities encouraged suburban growth as far out as Finchley and within the next decade or so built-up London was pushing beyond Finsbury Park, requiring station accommodation at Stroud Green, where a wooden building on the embankment was in use from 11th April 1881. Finchley's high ground and good drainage attracted the better-off middle class commuters and their families; the village of 7,416 in 1871 had by 1901 become a small town of over 22,000.

A gradual increase in the train service, with morning and evening peaks becoming a feature in the late 1870s, threw considerable strain on the congested approaches to Kings Cross, a situation somewhat relieved when North London Railway trains to and from Broad Street all day appeared on the branch on 18th January 1875.

Increasing traffic led to layout changes. About 1880 Highgate station was rearranged with a central island platform instead of side platforms, served by a new booking office on the footbridge which gave access to entrances both sides of the line. At Finchley a double-line junction was laid in June 1896, facilitating through workings between Edgware and London, but although these were then increased, they never exceeded six each way daily. A new villa colony near Torrington Park Woodside, caused this station to be renamed Woodside Park for North Finchley in the public timetable dated 1st May 1882. Seven years later, waiting rooms were

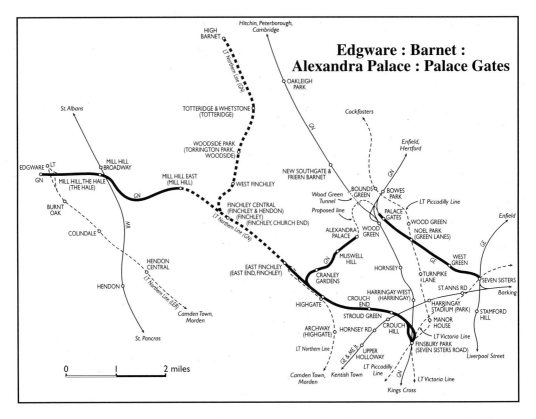

erected on the Down platforms both here and at Totteridge & Whetstone. Further south, suburban snobbery required the renaming of East End, Finchley, which became East Finchley from 1st February 1887. From 1889 onwards there were sporadic campaigns to secure a station in the 1½-mile section between this station and Finchley. Such calls were still being made in the 1940s, but as before, they fell upon deaf ears.

At High Barnet in 1896 a new entrance and ticket office (still in use over a hundred years later) were provided halfway down the pedestrian approach slope from the town, at the level of the footbridge, but the original cab entrance at platform level remained in use at peak periods.

The Edgware line remained a sleepy backwater, for some obscure reason known locally as 'the Pig'. Its relaxed atmosphere was hardly affected by the addition of a wooden halt at The Hale, a single platform on the north side just west of the Midland main line bridge, on 11th June 1906, an optimistic attempt to divert some traffic from the new suburb that was growing around the Midland Railway's Mill Hill station. A goods yard was added at The Hale in August 1910, when a booking office was placed on an extended platform and a man was posted to look after both goods and passenger business.

Goods traffic on the Edgware line received a boost in 1886 with the opening of the North Middlesex Gas Works, served by sidings at the south side of Mill Hill station. Further business came here with the construction of an infantry barracks north of the station; the sidings put in for the building work were retained for army traffic after the depot opened in 1904.

The precipitous approach to High Barnet terminus, with the original buildings at the lower level and the later ticket office in the middle foreground. This commercial postcard was published around 1905 but the buildings shown all survive in only slightly altered form almost a century later.

H. A. Ivatt's steam railmotors 1 and 2 were tried out on the Edgware–Finchley service from 19th February 1906. The diminutive 0–4–0T mounted on the same frame as a 53-seat car was fine for most of the day, but at holiday times when more capacity was required, the steam unit was not powerful enough to draw an extra coach. After just over a year, locomotive-hauled trains once more reigned supreme.

Suburban development on the Barnet–Finsbury Park line after 1870 required additional freight facilities. Loads were mostly house coals, building materials, perishables, and of course the ubiquitous milk churns (Down full, Up empty) as more and more of the local dairy farms were built over. By May 1879 additional sidings had been laid at Finchley and the accommodation there was further expanded in 1880 and 1907. More goods roads were added at East Finchley in 1898 and 1902, the business there becoming sufficient to justify a separate daily train.

Finchley's population reached 39,419 in 1911 when Church End station (now Finchley Central) had 60 trains each way daily, 14 of them to London between 06.00 and 09.30 serving Kings Cross, Farringdon Street, Moorgate, and Broad Street. After the opening of the tube railway from Charing Cross to Golders Green in 1907, some of the rush-hour traffic of the High Barnet line was extracted by electric tramcars and motorbuses which fed the tube from North Finchley, offering through bookings to tube stations from 1914. From March 1907 electric tramcars running parallel with the steam railway all the way from Highgate to High Barnet provided a more convenient, frequent and cheaper facility which drained-off most of the railway's purely local traffic. Motor-buses joined the trams in this activity from around 1914.

When the building boom of the late 1920s and 1930s filled up most of the open land remaining around the line, rush-hour services came under severe pressure and the LNER, not altogether enthusiastic about its GNR inheritance, dusted-off the latter's electrification plans only to find finance eluding its grasp. Changes were therefore few and undramatic.

From 1931 F. J. Ingram laid out the Woodside Park Garden Suburb west of the Dollis Brook and its name was added to the boards at Woodside Park station. Southwards, between the Dollis Brook and Ballards Lane, new houses appeared in large numbers between 1925 and 1936 over the fields and nursery gardens in an area known as Nether Street. Considering this description unattractive, the developers preferred West Finchley, which became the name for the new station they persuaded

Woodside Park station, GNR, looking to High Barnet about 1905. A small crowd including three nuns in full garb awaits an Up train. Apart from the fashions, the advertisements, the goods yard and the absence of conductor rail, this scene is little changed over 90 years later.
Commercial postcard

Highgate station GNR, looking to Barnet, *c.* 1903. The little hut behind the fence houses a representative of the Imperial Property Investment Company of Moorgate, no doubt anxious to interest prospective commuters in desirable residential prospects in this well-wooded middle-class area.
Commercial postcard

the LNER to open on 1st March 1933 where Nether Street crossed the line. As this was the LNER, construction was done as cheaply as possible, using second-hand materials from closed stations. A final improvement, which assisted running during the fogs to which the area was prone, was the introduction in 1932 of multiple-aspect colour-light signalling over the two miles between Finsbury Park No. 7 box and Park Junction, Highgate, allowing closure of the manual boxes at Stroud Green, Crouch End, Archway and Highgate.

During the 1930s passenger trains usually consisted of two Gresley 'quad-art' sets (two four-car articulated sets), some still gaslit. D. S. Barrie recorded that the Gresley N2 0–6–2T used to reach speeds up to 33mph with fully-loaded evening rush-hour trains on the climb to Highgate. Earlier, the GNR had deployed sets of 11 or 12 large four-wheelers with upholstered third class, hauled by Sturrock and Stirling 0–4–2 well tanks and 0–4–4 well and side tanks. The early years of the century saw the arrival of Ivatt 4–4–2T and the first of the Gresley 'quad-art' coaches appeared in 1911. By about 1914 the most usual passenger engines were H. A. Ivatt's N1 0–6–2T of 1907. Broad Street trains, confined to rush hours from the early 1920s, were for many years in the charge of the NLR 4–4–0T, but the LMSR introduced Fowler Class 3F 0–6–0T in the 1930s. Passenger accommodation on these trains was even less comfortable than the spartan 'quad-arts' as almost until the outbreak of World War 2 Broad Street commuters suffered the joys of NLR four-wheelers with half-partitioned thirds. Second-class facilities were withdrawn on the Barnet and Edgware lines at the end of 1937.

A 1938 timetable shows 57 trains a day from High Barnet, terminating variously at Kings Cross, Finsbury Park, Moorgate (13, confined to morning peak), and Broad Street (12, morning peak). Some of the Up peak-hour trains passed stations between Finchley Church End (now Finchley Central) and Finsbury Park, whilst the evening rush hours saw some non-stop working between Finsbury Park and East Finchley. Notwithstanding cheap off-peak fares, the irregular steam service proved utterly unattractive to a population still largely dependent on public transport. Compared with the adjacent Golders Green–Edgware line, which had generated 181 annual journeys per head of population served, the High Barnet/Edgware/Alexandra Palace group of lines produced a miserable 26 per head. As we shall see, London Transport hoped to change all that.

High Barnet station, LNER, looking to buffers, about 1938. Work has not yet started on the electrification for Northern Line tube services and LNER and LMSR steam trains, respectively bound for Kings Cross and Broad Street, stand peacefully at platforms 1 and 3.
Lens of Sutton

Freight traffic, almost entirely inwards, remained buoyant in the 1930s, although by the end of that decade road-making and house-building materials were becoming less important. In 1938 there were some eight goods trains daily to Barnet and Edgware behind GNR 0–6–0 and 2–6–0 tender engines. Edgware goods yard had been enlarged in 1926 to deal with building materials and domestic fuels for the suburban growth which had followed the arrival of the tube trains from Golders Green two years before. The Underground extension encouraged the LCC to site a large housing estate immediately south of Edgware. Watling was given its own station on the new Underground line, but much of the estate construction material was brought over the LNER line from Finchley into special sidings at The Hale, installed in 1926 to serve the contractor's temporary site railway system. Another aspect of the vast suburban expansion of the inter-war period was a revolutionary change in the distribution of milk. Large combines absorbed the many small dairy firms, introducing road and rail tankers and glass bottles instead of the unhygienic inefficient churns from which milk had been ladled into the housewives' jugs. In 1928 the United Dairies' milk depot at East Finchley was adapted to receive milk brought nightly from Staffordshire in trains of glass-lined tank cars, each tank carrying 3,000 gallons. This traffic, which even at the start fed some 750,000 suburbanites on the Northern Heights, continued for 20 years before giving way to road tankers.

The single-line Edgware section, its passenger business further diluted by the Underground extension, continued its relatively quiet existence. In 1938 there were 26 trains a day each way, only four more than in 1901 despite the fact that Edgware's population had grown in that period from 868 to almost 15,000. New housing had certainly brought a few extra passengers to The Hale, and rather more to Mill Hill (which had been respectively renamed Mill Hill for The Hale and Mill Hill East from 1st March 1928) but through trains to London were reduced, and in 1938 there was only one in the Up direction with no corresponding evening return. Rolling stock on the line varied from LNER vestibuled main-line stock to ancient GNR four- and six-wheelers, but in September 1929 there was some local excitement when the brand-new Sentinel steam railcar *The Rising Sun* appeared. This seated 59 passengers in some comfort, but like its GNR steam railmotor predecessors it suffered from an inability to cope with sudden surges of extra traffic, and was withdrawn during the following year. During its stay, *The Rising Sun* covered a single trip to High Barnet and back at midday, whilst a tank engine took over passenger working on the single line and placed wagons in the goods yards. At the end of the traffic day, the railcar worked in revenue service back to Finsbury Park.

Between Finchley and Edgware operation was by train staff with one engine in steam, signals being confined to an ancient fixed distant outside Edgware and a tall post on the platform there to prevent drivers from crashing through the buffers on dark nights. Unusual measures were therefore necessary when the line was required to cope with the exceptionally heavy traffic generated by the annual Royal Air Force display at Hendon aerodrome. Thus on 25th June 1932 through trains were running from Kings Cross and Moorgate to Mill Hill for The Hale every few minutes starting at 13.30 and during the afternoon normal service had to be suspended because some 1¼ miles of the single line were occupied by the trains which were to return to London from 17.24 onwards. Flagmen were present to control moving up, which was conducted at a very low speed.

In this 1937 view, Mill Hill East for Mill Hill Barracks, gaslit, sleepy and deserted, awaits the arrival of construction workers to provide double track for the proposed tube train service to Edgware and Bushey Heath. *Lens of Sutton*

Totteridge & Whetstone station, LNER, looking to London, probably in the 1930s. *Lens of Sutton*

East Finchley LNER, looking to London, probably in the early or mid 1930s. The nameboard has received a supplementary indication 'And The Hampstead Garden Suburb' but there is little else in the scene to indicate that this is already a thriving residential area with an electric tramway and Edwardian shopping parades just outside the station. All the railway infrastructure shown here was soon to be swept away and replaced with the impressive 1939 station for the Underground, designed by L H Bucknell in the Holden style. *Lens of Sutton*

The proximity of the Northern Heights lines to the Underground routes termi-nating at Edgware, Highgate (now Archway) and Finsbury Park led to their being incorporated in the major railway development plan drawn up by the London Passenger Transport Board and the main line companies north of the Thames soon after the formation of the Board in 1933. In view of its contribution to the relief of unemployment, this plan, announced in 1935 and modified two years later, received government blessing and a Treasury guarantee for the principal and interest involved. An important share of the finance was to be devoted to the Northern Heights. From the tube railway terminus at Highgate, tunnels were to be built to bring the trains to the surface alongside the LNER just south of East Finchley station, which would be rebuilt. A connection to be made between the LNER line and the Underground terminus at Edgware would allow trains to run into London via East Finchley from a new extension to Bushey Heath along the alignment of the Watford & Edgware Railway, which had been protected from house-building. At Drayton Park, the Northern City lines were to be brought up to run into the east side of Finsbury Park LNER station. The intention was to operate three new services of tube trains: between Moorgate and Alexandra Palace or East Finchley; between Bushey Heath and Kennington via East Finchley and Charing Cross; and between High Barnet and the Northern tube line via Camden Town. For the Bushey Heath service, the Edgware line was at last to be doubled and the junction station at Finchley Church End (Finchley Central) was scheduled for complete reconstruc-tion. All LNER lines involved would get power-operated signal boxes with automatic colour-light signalling to tube railway standards, and the tube stock used would be partly owned by the LNER, which was to retain the freehold of its lines. Work on all this began in November 1936, but completion of the scheme was frustrated by the outbreak of World War 2.

To allow doubling and electrification to proceed, trains between Finchley and Edgware were replaced by a 'railway bus', complete with railway ticket structure, on some Sundays from the autumn of 1938, and completely from 11th September 1939. Tube trains reached East Finchley on 3rd July 1939 but the very impressive new station, with its two island platforms and Eric Aumonier's statue of an archer firing his rapid transit arrow towards London, was not fully completed until the following year. Thanks to the slow start of active hostilities between Great Britain and Germany, it proved possible to finish the electrification to High Barnet, and on 14th April 1940 tube trains began to operate a vastly improved service to and from that terminus. In peak hours there were trains every ten minutes from High Barnet and every five minutes from Finchley Central (so renamed from Finchley Church End on 1st April 1940). On weekdays 212 tube trains served High Barnet and there were 396 at Finchley Central and stations south in comparison with the 114 each way in the LNER 1938 timetable. All the electric trains ran via Charing Cross, but a service to the City branch of the Northern Line was started on 24th January 1941 and was increased to a ten-minute interval in peak hours from 19th May 1941. As we shall see in the next chapter, steam trains continued to run up to Alexandra Palace, and they also worked temporarily between East Finchley and Finsbury Park (Kings Cross, Moorgate and Broad Street in peak hours). They ceased to soil East Finchley's bright new concrete on Sunday 2nd March 1941, after which passengers requiring stations between Highgate and London on the surface could use the newly-completed tube station (opened on 19th January 1941) beneath the surface platforms at Highgate and the steam service between Alexandra Palace and Finsbury Park. The planned reconstruction of Finchley Central with a building on the overline road bridge was not started and the old GNR station remains in use today.

With some pressure from the War Office, Mill Hill barracks were served by reopening the Edgware branch as far as Mill Hill East on 18th May 1941. Despite the fact that a second track had been laid with conductor rails as far as Mill Hill for The Hale, the tube trains used only one line and the other was removed soon afterwards. The service was to and from Morden until 19.00 on weekdays; at other times the branch was shuttle-operated. Although the railway bus was withdrawn, rail tickets were available on ordinary service buses working between Edgware Underground and Mill Hill East. Tickets for journeys via Finchley Central were also issued at Edgware Underground and Mill Hill LMSR stations, which provided the curiosity of railway tickets headed LNER issued at an LMSR booking office for travel on an LPTB bus.

About 1942, to accommodate army traffic, the goods yard on the north side of the line at Mill Hill East was extended. Since the cessation of steam passenger services parcels had been carried by road, and depots for road collection were established at all stations except West Finchley. At Edgware, however, parcels continued to be brought in and taken out by rail.

In general, passengers were well pleased with the improved service although it was much more difficult to get a seat for the first part of the journey home in the evening. They missed too the 'Minute Bell' which had stimulated generations of City men to break into a trot down the steep slope of the High Barnet approach road; more romantic travellers were saddened to see LPTB roundels replacing the old black-and-white nameboards; 'Totteridge & Whetstone' had been contracted to 'Totteridge'; 'Woodside Park and North Finchley for the Woodside Garden Suburb' was replaced by 'Woodside Park'; and the imposing 'Finchley Church End change here for Mill Hill, The Hale and Edgware' was now just 'Finchley Central'. As for the latter, 'No one could ever imagine anything but tube trains calling at such a station' a reader of *The Railway Magazine* sneered in 1940.

For a few more years, goods trains brought steam locomotives (latterly N2 0–6–2T) over all the LNER lines, and after the war, tender engines were seen on occasional seaside excursions or railway enthusiast trips. Working of freight trains amidst the busy tube service presented some difficulties and curiosities. As the signal overlaps at the two-aspect colour-light signals were arranged to fit the braking performance of the tube trains, the goods trains were restricted to a 20mph limit and 14 wagons, while disc distants were installed in the rear of the colour lights to give a minimum braking distance of 500yd. All steam locomotives were supposed to be fitted with tripcocks to allow the London Transport train stops to bring them to a halt should they pass a signal at danger, but this rule was sometimes ignored. To penetrate beyond Mill Hill East it was first necessary to procure the key of the Edgware ground frame from Finchley Central signal box (an earlier procedure had been to carry a train staff normally accommodated at the Mill Hill East ticket office). The Mill Hill East platform signal was then passed at danger and after the tripcock had operated and been re-set, the train proceeded westwards with the driver keeping a sharp outlook for children on the track. If, as sometimes happened, the train became derailed, or the locomotive failed, the guard would take the ground frame

East Finchley as rebuilt for Underground train services in 1939/40, looking to London 23rd March 1957 with a Morden train at platform 4. The centre roads provide access to and from Highgate depot. *Alan A Jackson*

key (or the train staff) back to Finchley Central by bus, returning in due course on the rescue locomotive. Tube cars moving between the Northern City Line and Acton Works were attached to goods trains made up at Highbury Vale Yard, often travelling right through to Edgware and back before returning to London Transport hands at Highgate depot. This was the former Wellington Carriage Depot, used in steam days for storage of spare main line coaches and minor repair work, and was situated just north of the Highgate tunnels on the east side of the line. With openings made at the north end, the buildings were converted in 1939–40 to serve as tube car sheds, further stabling being provided in open sidings on the east side. In exchange the LNER got a new depot sited alongside the main line at Wood Green.

With the full revival of road transport after the War, freight traffic was soon mostly solid fuels and building materials. Nevertheless in 1956 there were still nine trains each way daily to East Finchley and seven beyond there, including coal for the lineside gasworks at Mill Hill East. In 1953 the old GNR station at Edgware still employed about 20 staff on goods and parcels work; passenger enquiries and bookings were also dealt with, bringing in a revenue averaging £100-£200 a month. But all this was in the nature of a swansong; the Mill Hill gasworks was closed in 1956 and in the following year all domestic fuel traffic was transferred to a new centralised distribution depot at Enfield Chase. From 1st October 1962 the yards at High Barnet, Totteridge, Woodside Park, Finchley Central, East Finchley (West Sidings) and Mill Hill East were all closed to rail traffic. When erection of a tower office block at Edgware in 1961 required demolition of the old station buildings, parcels and passenger agency facilities there were withdrawn, although the goods yard and that at Mill Hill The Hale remained open until May and February 1964 respectively. Freight working beyond Finsbury Park ceased with the closure of the yards at East Finchley and Wellington Sidings in June 1964 and the track beyond Mill Hill East was lifted later that year.

The London Green Belt, a feature of post-war planning, enshrined in government-approved development plans, made it unlikely that the proposed tube services beyond Mill Hill East to Edgware and Bushey Heath would generate a sufficient traffic. A preliminary announcement was made in 1950, foreshadowing the death sentence proclaimed in February 1954. As the proposed Moorgate-Alexandra Palace tube service was also dropped at the same time (for a different reason), the little stub of the Edgware branch and the High Barnet line north of East Finchley now became a simple appendage of the Northern Line out of Camden Town, with the short section south of East Finchley retained for access to the car sheds at Highgate Wood.

Recent decades have seen several changes immediately south of East Finchley station. The old LNER sheds which had been converted to a Northern Line car depot were completely rebuilt in 1969–70 to provide eight covered tracks under a single ridged roof, with improved access at the north end which considerably facilitated empty train movements. Following train service cuts, Highgate Wood stabling sidings were closed from 6th December 1982; tracks at the south end of the car shed had been removed shortly before this. In declining use, this almost new depot, housing nine trains, was itself closed after 25th March 1984, together with the 1939 Park Junction signal box, the last manual box on the Northern Line. Apart from one reception road retained for engineer's trains, the whole site was mothballed. This somewhat secluded, wooded area with its abandoned buildings was soon discovered by drop outs and vagrants who, unable to believe their luck, took it over. Arsonists and vandals also enjoyed themselves. Then, after a few more years had passed, their occupation and amusement was brought to an end. In connection with an increase in train services on the Northern Line, the installation was renewed, coming back to life from 23rd January 1989. Eight covered tracks, one open track, engineer's train siding and a tamping machine siding were then controlled by electric interlocking in a new relay room, train drivers operating trackside plungers to initiate movements. Park Junction box was demolished in 1995.

There has been little significant change to the rest of the infrastructure in recent years. Closure of West Finchley station was considered and rejected in 1983 and in 1992 some rebuilding was undertaken. Platforms were reconstructed and a new brick-built entrance and ticket office were provided on the northbound platform. The secondhand footbridge and the pretty timber waiting shed on the southbound side, with its valanced canopy, imported by the LNER, were both carefully restored and retained. Further north, at Totteridge, serious ground movements occurred in the station area in the summer of 1982, entailing temporary closure of the southbound line and platform. Subsequent stabilisation work was accompanied by a certain amount of rebuilding of the station but the original Victorian scale and style were very largely retained.

This is typical: even today, the transformation into another part of the Underground system is incomplete. For the seeing eye, once the East Finchley's stunning 1930s architecture is left behind, there is still a strong flavour of the past; the Great Northern Railway country branch comes alive, not only in the stations, where, as elsewhere the steam railway heritage is commendably cared for by London Transport, but even in the survival of several Victorian manual signal boxes, well-maintained and put to other uses. Woodside Park station, in particular, is worth travelling a long way to see; it has hardly changed in appearance since the 1890s.

CHAPTER FOUR

NORTH EAST LONDON

Alexandra Palace after the fire of 9th June 1873, showing the extreme end of the branch railway, apparently unaffected by the conflagration despite its timber platforms.

Railways to the Alexandra Palace (map page 304)

The psychological impact of the Crystal Palace on its new site was such as to ensure north London interests would inevitably seek to emulate it, and an 1860 scheme, involving GNR directors was the first of several. Capital could not be raised, but the 1862 International Exhibition held in the Cromwell Road, Kensington provided a new stimulus. A group of businessmen purchased 240 acres of open country on and around the 310ft knoll that rises between Hornsey and New Southgate, their declared intention being to erect a north London Crystal Palace, using the materials from the International Exhibition, and naming it Alexandra Palace after the wife of the Prince of Wales (later Edward VII). The park was opened to the public on 23rd July 1863 and a year later work started on a building designed by John Johnson and Alfred Meeson. Financial problems and the unstable nature of the subsoil (gravel over soapy clay) caused many setbacks and the builders, Kelk & Lucas, were not finished until 1866. As the original enterprise had by then collapsed, the Palace was to remain empty and unused for over six years. Work on completing the park went forward, and the associated racecourse was opened in June 1868.

To serve the Palace, the Edgware, Highgate & London Railway had obtained powers in 1864 for a 1m 11ch branch starting near its proposed Highgate station and terminating at Muswell Hill near the boundary of the new park. Section 23 of the act, which contained sanction for the collection of one sum for railway fare and admission to Palace and park, noted that the railway was 'chiefly intended for the Conveyance of Passengers to and from the Alexandra Park at Muswell Hill belonging to the Alexandra Park Company (Limited)'. Two years later new companies had been formed, and an act of 1866 noted in its preamble that the landowners, the Muswell Hill Estate Company Ltd, had let for 999 years to the Alexandra Palace Company Ltd land which was 'being laid out in an ornamental manner and for public resort and recreation' whilst another part was 'being laid out as building ground'. This act authorised railways in the park, one extending the EH&LR branch from Muswell Hill alongside the northwest wall of the Palace, and others (which we shall come to later) linking the Palace to the Great Eastern Railway.

A third party seeking access to the supposed goldmine on the Northern Heights was the North London, Highgate & Alexandra Park Railway, whose Act of 1865 authorised a line from Caledonian Road station NLR to the EH&LR at Highgate, with running powers thence to Muswell Hill. This would have given a slightly more direct route to inner north London and the City, to which the GNR was understandably opposed, and no more was heard of this scheme once the EH&LR had been absorbed into the main line company. Yet another interested company was the Metropolitan & St Johns Wood Railway, a line authorised in 1864 from Baker Street to Finchley Road; a year later this company had promoted an extension from Swiss Cottage to Hampstead, with plans to go on to Highgate and Alexandra Palace, but the section beyond Hampstead, involving cuttings across the Heath inevitably encountered powerful opposition, and was not sanctioned.

In pace with the slow gestation of the Alexandra Palace there was no hurry to build the branch, although land was bought from 1867 onwards. Eventually, in the autumn of 1871, when there was some assurance that the Palace was at last to open, a start was made on the railway. About the same time work also began on the separately owned line from Muswell Hill to the Palace, and that was completed before the rest, in the summer of 1872.

The double track from Highgate, with its intermediate station at Muswell Hill, opened with the Palace on 24th May 1873. As the Muswell Hill Estate Company possessed no locomotives or coaches, the line was worked throughout by the GNR, the Estate company recovering what it could by imposing an exorbitant 2d single fare for the half-mile from Muswell Hill to the terminus. Issue of such tickets was however not frequent, the most popular ones being the shilling (5p) returns from Kings Cross, which included Palace admission.

By far the most convenient, if rather roundabout, access to the Palace, the branch at first enjoyed a very satisfactory traffic, indeed on the opening day there were so many passengers in the first-class compartments that they were deemed 'unfit to be entered at all by ladies or delicate persons', and on the following Whit Monday the largely rail-borne crowd of over 60,000 exceeded that at the Crystal Palace.

Alas, a few days later, on Monday 9th June 1873, North London's proud new attraction was completely destroyed by a fire which originated in a charcoal brazier used by workmen on the roof. Within 1½ hours the building was transformed to a 'melancholy and gutted ruin', despite the efforts of the GNR which, with an interest in the fate of the Palace not entirely altruistic, despatched two of its fire engines by rail from Kings Cross which reached the scene before any of the road appliances. Indeed the loss was a bitter blow to the GNR as well as to the underinsured Palace proprietors; at this period there was no suburban development to support the branch apart from a scattering of large villas whose owners could well afford to go down by carriage to the better-served stations at Wood Green or Highgate. So it was that once public interest in viewing the blackened ruins had waned, the train service, already reduced from 18 to seven each way, ceased altogether. After 31st July 1873, the only activity was a daily pick-up goods to Muswell Hill yard, if traffic required.

Although some half million pounds of assets had been lost it was decided to try again. Designed by John Johnson, a new palace, seven acres in extent, rose from the embers in only ten months. Grandiloquent in aspect, it lacked the delicate elegance of its smaller predecessor. For the opening on 1st May 1875 the full train service was restored, together with North London trains working to and from Broad Street via Canonbury. Only 21,000 attended the opening, but the following Whit Monday brought 94,000 to the Palace and Park, most of them coming by rail. *The Builder* reported journeys of over an hour from Kings Cross to the Palace on that day, and a chaotic evening with a derailment at Copenhagen Tunnel which blocked the whole line back to Alexandra Palace, causing many to walk off the railway at Holloway station, and others to spend the night on the trains.

The reopening revived interest in providing access from the Metropolitan Railway. In 1875 and again in 1876, bills were presented for a branch from Swiss Cottage to Highgate, with stations at Childs Hill, Hampstead Village and The Spaniards, but although the Metropolitan was sympathetic, that company was deterred by a lack of GNR interest and the scheme failed.

After autumn events in 1876 the Palace remained closed through the winter and with it the terminal station, but in those early years it enjoyed a modest success and the Muswell Hill Estate Company, as owners of the railway in the grounds, paid dividends of 2½ and three per cent in 1878, a year when almost 500,000 were carried on their section of the line. Like its sister south of the river, the 'Ally Pally' did not sustain public interest sufficiently to make it profitable. Despite its huge Willis organ (one of the largest concert instruments in Europe), the Japanese, Egyptian, and Moorish villages, the Italian garden, the 200-seat circus and the many other attractions and amenities inside the building or in the Park, the place gradually lost popularity and fashion, attracting large crowds only on the three Bank Holidays. Its owner, the London Financial Association, was itself inhibited by the possession of great quantities of unmarketable securities in hopeless railway enterprises. The Association went into decline in the late 1880s, its misfortunes exacerbated by lack of success in developing parts of the Park for residential purposes.

In 1877 the Association had secured parliamentary powers to sell 80 acres north of the Palace for house building (legislation was necessary as the 1866 act had authorised the railway on the understanding that the 240-acre Park was to be devoted to public recreation in perpetuity). A small amount of the 80 acres was sold-off in March 1878, but development was slow and Bacon's map of 1880 shows empty roads marked 'Alexandra Park Muswell Hill Estate'. Further sales in 1881 and 1883 found no buyers. In the 1880s and 1890s the London Financial Association wasted much money in promoting unsuccessful bills to secure powers to sell the whole of the Park for building.

Stroud Green GNR, c.1905. The station entrance and ticket office is behind the horse van on the right. Note the competition between coal merchants handling railborne fuel for suburban grates (left). The wooden station structures have long since gone but the underline bridge and railway alignment either side are still accessible for pedestrian exploration. *Commercial postcard*

The midday sun shines on an anorexic looking horse and ancient cab awaiting custom outside Muswell Hill station in the mid-1900s. Houses are offered to let or for outright sale and Gray Brothers have 11 types of railborne coal to sell householders, the most expensive (Inland Wallsend) at £1. 3s (£1.15p) a ton, a sum roughly equivalent to the weekly wage of the labourers who built the houses around here. *Commercial postcard*

During the early years, access to the terminus was restricted to those holding the combined rail and admission tickets or prepared to buy entrance tickets on arrival. With an eye to future residential development, the Muswell Hill Estate Co. obtained parliamentary powers in 1886 to incorporate the holders of stock and shares in the railway undertaking into a separate body to be known as the Muswell Hill & Palace Railway. This had the effect of enabling the terminus to be operated as a public railway station although as someone sourly remarked, there were perhaps not more than 20 souls in the vicinity to make use of it. Plots still sold only very slowly and for a few more years the station was closed when the Palace was shut to the public.

For the Palace things went from bad to worse. It was closed from late August 1882 until March 1885 and there were further periods of continuous closure between September 1885 and May 1889. During these times the racecourse remained open for a few days' racing each year and other events were organised in the racecourse area, all this bringing sporadic bouts of traffic to Muswell Hill station. When the Palace closed in August 1889 after a none too happy season, it was to remain lifeless until March 1898. Hoping to encourage some residential traffic, the GNR nevertheless opened the terminus in March 1891, but receipts were so low that it was shut again in April 1892. In 1898 the GNR, perhaps seeing that suburban development was at last a definite possibility, agreed with the owners that the station should remain open continuously. Trains ran into the terminus again from 1st April that year when the Palace reopened from its long sleep, and almost 100,000 travelled on Easter Monday to see a balloon ascent, a parachute race, fireworks and other events.

After unsuccessful attempts in 1897 to enhance the attraction of its building land by promoting costly railway connections from Alexandra Palace station to the GER and GNR stations at Wood Green, and a fairly disastrous season in 1899, the owners in desperation offered the whole property to the local authorities. By an act of 1900 under which trustees were constituted, the local authorities were allowed to borrow money to contribute towards the purchase. The transactions were completed in February 1901, when 173 acres passed to the trustees and the balance was sold off for building. Under the new regime the white elephant perked up a little, enough for a short time to keep the annual revenue account in balance. Perhaps deceived by this temporary revival, the GNR made an agreement with the Muswell Hill & Palace Railway Company on 3rd April 1911, under which the main line company was to purchase the undertaking from 14th August 1911 for £18,416, releasing the small company from its obligation to pay five per cent interest on the £1,584 which the GNR had spent on improving the Alexandra Palace station. This agreement was confirmed by the GNR Act of 1911.

After swamping Crouch End, Hornsey and Stroud Green in the last two decades of the nineteenth century, the outward tide of London moved on strongly towards the isolated villas amid the trees on Muswell Hill. By 1901 roads had been laid out towards Hornsey, either side of the road called Muswell Hill, and on the east side of Muswell Hill Road to the south of the branch. This activity led to the opening on 2nd August 1902 of a second intermediate station, named Cranley Gardens after one of the new residential avenues. Through the 1900s and 1910s, the new suburb of Muswell Hill grew rapidly north of the railway, filling up at last many acres of the old Alexandra Park north of the terminal station. For a short period all this building brightened the fortunes of the GNR branch, providing it with a regular daily traffic for the first time. There was also a useful freight movement in the form of building materials, domestic fuels, and goods for the new retail centre at Muswell Hill Broadway. So intense was the building activity around Muswell Hill station about 1900 that a network of light railways was laid down, spreading out from a junction with the branch. Over these lines, contractors' locomotives hauled main line wagons along the housing frontages, pausing at each plot whilst the requisite quantities of bricks, timber, ironwork and so forth were dumped.

But scarcely had the new passenger traffic established itself when it was seriously diminished by improvements in road transport. First came electric tramways: in December 1905 from Turnpike Lane to the bottom of Muswell Hill and through the Park to the Palace doors; and in April 1906 from Wood Green to the east entrance to the Palace. Then, with even more effect, motor buses began to penetrate the very heartland of the branch, establishing direct communication between Muswell Hill and the new tube railway stations at Highgate (now Archway) and at Finsbury Park, with their direct services to the West End and the City. In April 1914 a four-minute service of small single-deck buses was started by the London General Omnibus Company between Finsbury Park and Muswell Hill via Crouch End, and shortly afterwards, an eight-minute frequency was available between Highgate (Archway) Underground and Muswell Hill, passing Cranley Gardens station. The GNR hounded the General into court with charges that excessive loads were being imposed by the buses on its overbridges at Cranley Gardens and Crouch End stations, a move which at least kept down the size of the buses used, for even a five-tonner was alleged to be dangerous for flimsy structures built to carry farm carts. In those days of cheap labour there was little difficulty in intensifying the service to make up capacity, and as the buses offered the attraction of through bookings via the Underground the hold they established strengthened steadily through the 1920s.

Curiosities of railway working such as through trains between the Alexandra Palace branch and Woolwich via Ludgate Hill and to and from Victoria were also affected by the competition from tube railways and motor buses. Both workings had disappeared by 1910, when the branch supported 61 trains each way daily, 15 more than seven years earlier. Not all these worked through to the terminus at Alexandra Palace while 20 of them were NLR trains to and from Broad Street. The GNR workings ran either to Kings Cross or Moorgate Street via the City Widened Lines. Last arrival at Muswell Hill was 00.16 but the first departure, as late as 07.14. provided firm evidence of the middle-class nature of the area. Eight minutes were taken from Alexandra Palace to Highgate, seven more to Finsbury Park. In the Down direction an additional two minutes were allowed to give the steam locomotives time to tackle the climb up to Highgate. These timings were to remain virtually unchanged for the next 30 years.

The special passenger traffic which had long been a feature of this line, trains for Sunday school treats, boy scout rallies, and other Palace events, was given a new twist with the outbreak of war in August 1914. The Palace closed on the 8th, briefly becoming a holding centre for mobilising army reservists who arrived and departed by rail; no sooner had these left for France than their place was taken by Belgian refugees who came in their hundreds from October onwards, many in special trains which worked through to Alexandra Palace station from Tilbury, Folkestone and Dover. In May 1915 when the refugees had gone, the Palace became an internment camp for 3,000 enemy aliens, and immediately after the end of the war it housed 4,000 civil servants engaged on clearing up the administrative aftermath.

Heavy use of the City Widened Lines for wartime freight caused off-peak cancellations to and from Moorgate and Kings Cross and from 11th January 1915 most of these trains disappeared, leaving only a shuttle between Finsbury Park and Alexandra Palace in slack hours. North London Railway off-peak trains also ceased, briefly reappearing after the war before succumbing to an early LMSR economy campaign. After 1919, GNR services were fully restored, continuing with little change for the next 20 years. Thus in 1939 there were 43 Up trains on the branch between 07.10 and 23.12, including departures from Alexandra Palace for Broad Street between 07.59 and 09.45. The Down service was similar. Although Sunday trains were fully restored on 1st February 1925 after suspension from 1st October 1915, they had finally yielded to bus competition by 1930.

In the early days, the GNR used Sturrock 0–4–2 well tanks and Stirling 0–4–2 and 0–4–4 well and side tanks. These were displaced in the early 1900s by Ivatt 1500 (later C12) 4–4–2T which in turn gave way to the powerful Ivatt N1 and Gresley N2 0–6–2T in the 1910s and 1920s respectively. North London trains were normally headed by William Adams' outside cylinder 4–4–0T, but these were superseded in the 1930s by Fowler's ubiquitous Class 3F 0–6–0T. First and third class was still provided in 1939, the second having disappeared at the end of 1937. On the Broad Street services the old NLR four-wheeled coaches were made to last well into the inter-war period. The articulated bogie stock of the LNER trains, comfortable enough whilst no standing passengers intruded into the very restricted leg room, remained gas-lit to the end.

Highgate in LNER days; N2 0-6-2T 4741 bursts out of the eastern tunnel with an Alexandra Palace train in the mid-1930s. The sign hanging below the station nameboard gives no additional topographical assistance, but merely advertises 'The Daily Mirror'. *H C Casserley*

Alexandra Park reopened to the public in March 1920, the Palace in 1922. On 7th October in the latter year, a huge boy scout rally saw the arrival of 60,000 by train through the three stations serving the Palace; 12 special trains were somehow inserted into the ordinary service on the GNR branch. But the popularity of the Palace, which the trustees were unable to keep in good repair, was again in decline. A writer in the 1924 *Hornsey Journal* blamed the poor transport facilities; after remarking that trams on the hill were few and far between at night, he continued:

> There is a railway station actually inside the building it is true, but it is dirty, dark and dismal, and the trains are so infrequent that this means of access scarcely counts on the few days when crowds are expected. Everyone avoids the station who can possibly do so, for the railway service does not even offer the attraction of cheapness.

In evidence to the 1930 parliamentary committee on the Underground bill for a tube railway extension through Wood Green which would compete with the LNER, the vice-chairman of the trustees correctly averred that the LNER service to the Palace had not seen any improvement for over 20 years. On Sundays there were often as many as 6,000 visitors to the Park, but the LNER provided no trains. A recent Bank Holiday had seen 30,000 at the Palace and Park but only some 150 had arrived at the station as the service was slow and inadequate.

At this point we can turn to look at the line as it was in the 1930s. From Park Junction with the Barnet and Edgware line north of Highgate station, the double track curved east alongside Gravel Pit or Highgate Wood, soon entering Cranley Gardens station. This served the southern parts of the Muswell Hill district and its two side platforms with their small wood and brick buildings were on the west side of Muswell Hill Road. There was a wooden booking office building on the bridge with an open footbridge to both platforms immediately behind it. A second entrance, guarded by a ticket collector's box, led directly from the Down platform to the main road. Discreetly hidden by a line of trees behind the Up platforms was the goods yard, opened on 29th June 1897.

Beyond the road bridge, the tracks crossed from the west to the east side of the Highgate/Wood Green ridge, emerging on to a 17-arch brick viaduct which offered extensive views across north London. After passing under Muswell Hill itself and now heading almost due north, the train entered Muswell Hill station, only one minute's walk from the Broadway, the centre of this middle-class suburb. From the brick booking office building on the road bridge, stairs led directly to each of the side platforms. On the Down side there was a short canopy and a rush-hour entrance from Dukes Avenue; the Up side had a canopy of about four coach lengths and behind it was a small goods yard which required a back shunt by trains coming from Highgate. Like the other two stations, Muswell Hill had a small signalbox. The busiest on the line, it was given a passimeter ticket office in 1927, the first on the LNER.

The final 40 chains were mostly in a shallow cutting with the Palace coming into view on the right. After passing over a small road into the Park, the train arrived at the little terminus, heavily overshadowed by the huge bulk of the Palace's north-west face. Lacking even a hint of the grandeur and scale of the Crystal Palace stations, it had little to show other than some architectural styling on the street frontage and the signalbox. When opened, its platforms were beneath a terrace alongside the north-west front and this structure, with its blind-arcaded outer wall, survived the 1873 fire. The interior, with its wooden platforms was in such an advanced state of decay and rot by the 1900s that the GNR had to set about rebuilding it. The terrace was demolished apart from the flight of entrance steps near the station and what had been a long island platform was shortened to about two train lengths and given conventional umbrella awnings. The old Up side bay road with its side platforms became a carriage siding. At the Muswell Hill end, alongside the passenger lines on the north side, was a two-road yard reached by a facing connection placed between the platform end and the signalbox. The main traffic here was coal for the Palace heating system which consumed vast quantities of fuel – as much as five tons were required to take the chill off the Great Hall for a single concert or organ recital.

This little line, together with the longer branches to Barnet and Edgware, received the promise of a bright new electric prosperity in June 1935. It was to become part of the London Underground system under the five-year new works programme then announced, carrying tube trains projected from Drayton Park via Finsbury Park and Highgate. A rush-hour service of 28 eight-car tube trains was proposed between Moorgate (Northern City) and Finsbury Park, with 14 onward to Highgate (LNER) and thence seven to High Barnet and seven to Alexandra Palace. For the rest of the day, there would be 12 eight-car trains an hour between Moorgate and Highgate (LNER), six going on to Alexandra Palace, six to terminate at East Finchley.

London Transport's publicists carefully pointed out that the Barnet/Edgware/ Alexandra Palace group of LNER lines was attracting only 26 annual journeys per head of population served compared with 181 on the adjacent Golders Green– Edgware tube line. A substantial traffic increase was forecast once tube trains were running to the three LNER suburban termini.

This 1935 scheme was in fact largely a re-hash of old plans. A northern section of the Highgate tube as far as the surface railway station at Highgate had appeared in a bill as early as 1901 and during the 1920s, projections further north had been publicly mooted by Underground officials. The Finsbury Park and Moorgate tube line, originally the Great Northern & City Railway, had in fact been planned to carry electrified services to and from GNR suburban stations and had been built to main line loading gauge for that reason. Its 1892 act, supported by the GNR, provided for a connection climbing to the surface between Drayton Park and Finsbury Park, where the tube trains would have shared platforms with the GNR. But the two companies squabbled over terms and eventually the GNR bottled-up the GNCR in an underground terminus which it built beneath its Finsbury Park station, isolating it from the outside world except for a back shunt connection for rolling stock purposes into the Highbury Vale sidings. In 1924 the LNER revived the idea of electrified suburban trains using the Moorgate tube and obtained powers for the necessary connections south of Finsbury Park. Delayed by the difficulty of raising capital on acceptable terms, the scheme was dusted-off in 1929 when government legislation designed to relieve unemployment afforded an opportunity to finance it. The LNER, however, had to fight for this government assistance in competition with the Underground Company, whose scheme for extending the Piccadilly tube from Finsbury Park to Cockfosters eventually won the favour of government and Parliament.

Work on the 1935 Plan for the Northern Heights lines, due for completion in 1940, came to a halt at the beginning of that year having already been slowed down by wartime conditions. As described in Chapter 3, only the sections from Highgate (Archway) to High Barnet and Mill Hill East were brought into use.

With the outbreak of war the Alexandra Palace branch trains were reduced by as much as 62 per cent on Mondays to Fridays. Through working to and from Moorgate and Broad Street ceased from 10th September 1939 in the expectation that wartime commuter traffic to the City would fall heavily after firms had evacuated their staff to the countryside. Broad Street trains returned on 4th December, but ceased for good after the night of 3rd October 1940 when they were interrupted by severe bomb damage to the North London lines. In 1940 the branch once again played its wartime role of carrying refugees from the Low Countries to temporary shelter at the Palace. Troops returning from Dunkirk were also brought up the hill by train for billeting in the Palace and Park.

When tube trains reached High Barnet in April 1940, LNER steam trains ran only to East Finchley in the rush hours, the rest of the service diverted to Alexandra Palace. Trains called at the new Highgate tube station below the LNER station from September 1940 for air raid sheltering, but public traffic here did not start until 19th January 1941. Escalators were then available from tube level to a new booking hall under the LNER lines, but the escalator for the further climb to street level had to await the post-war era (25th August 1957). From 3rd March 1941 all steam trains west of Finsbury Park worked to and from Alexandra Palace, giving the branch an enhanced service for a time.

There can be little doubt that had the war been delayed for only a year the Alexandra Palace–Moorgate electrification would have been ready at the end of 1940 and the branch would be open today. The only major work unfinished was the completion of the northbound connection at Drayton Park and, at Finsbury Park, the additional platforms, with their underline bridges at each end. Conversion of the GNCR tube to give it signalling, platform height and current collection standard with the other tube lines was completed in May 1939 and at Drayton Park the civil engineering work for the southbound line from the surface was finished, including a 10ft 6in diameter covered way descending beneath the Broad Street lines at 1 in 50. Earthworks for the northbound link were well advanced, whilst at Finsbury Park the abutments for the road bridges were formed and the girders for one lay ready for rolling-in. Structural steelwork to support Finsbury Park's additional island platform had been erected over the site for the new ticket hall and was to remain in position, steadily rusting, until September 1972. Conductor rails had been placed in position for much of the distance to Alexandra Palace and East Finchley, together with lineside cabling. By 1941 substation buildings were in place at Muswell Hill station and Crouch Hill. A new signal box building (not equipped and put into use until 1953) was finished at Drayton Park and the London Transport box at Park Junction, just beyond Highgate, came into daily service from 30th July 1939. At Crouch End and Highgate, platform edges had been reconstructed in concrete with the platforms lowered to compromise tube/main line height, whilst Highgate had also received a Holden style building with flat concrete canopy on its island platform, its walls embellished with LT bullseye roundels.

'To conserve motive power and fuel', further cuts were made to the Alexandra Palace steam train service from 7th September 1942. All through trains to London were then withdrawn, leaving only three an hour shuttling to and from Finsbury Park at peak hours Monday to Saturday. On Mondays to Fridays the last train was at 19.00, on Saturdays at 17.00. With the return of peace there was some improvement, so that by 1950 the midday gap had been reduced to 11.30 – 15.30 but there were still no trains later than those in the September 1942 timetable. More damage was done to the line's image in the winter of 1951–2 when the branch was closed completely to passenger traffic after the last train on 27th October, allegedly as an economy measure in a period of manpower shortage. Local pressures secured a restoration of train services from 7th January 1952 and after a slight augmentation the following month there were 15 trains Down (one to Highgate only) and 17 Up daily (two from Highgate). After the 09.42 from Alexandra Palace there were no Up trains until 17.05 and there was a corresponding gap in the Down service from Finsbury Park. Saturdays saw 15 Down workings and 16 Up between the 07.00 from Finsbury Park and the 17.25 from the Palace. The seeds of destruction were sown.

In this last decade of operation, the usual formation was a couple of gaslit coaches and N2 or N7 0–6–2T working push-pull. From time to time trainspotters (an easily bored breed) were given variety in the form of C13 4–4–2T and ex GCR F2 2–4–2T. Punctuality was erratic, especially in winter weather and a contemporary traveller remembers explanations for delays and cancellations which varied from the mundane 'breakdown' or 'fog' to the trendy 'export freight on the line'. It was not a service to inspire traffic despite the existence of through bookings from all Underground stations, introduced in anticipation of the tube conversion. This facility was not publicised and in traffic circulars London Transport booking clerks were periodically exhorted to warn any passengers requesting such tickets about the limited nature of the train service. In the 1950s requests at Finsbury Park for stations on the Edgware or Barnet lines by changing at Highgate were still met with printed tickets, but persistence was required as the clerks often tried to sell an LT ticket via Kings Cross. Any casual travel which still survived must have been finally smothered by the introduction of mileage fares in 1952; after then, the circuitous nature of the route caused fares from Alexandra Palace from Broad Street or Kings Cross to be 50 per cent above those to nearby Wood Green & Alexandra Park station (now Alexandra Palace) on the main line.

In contrast to all this discouragement, London Transport was working single deck buses at 35 journeys and hour between Finsbury Park and Muswell Hill stations, with a further 17 an hour on the inner section from Crouch Hill. Between Muswell Hill and Highgate stations two bus routes provided no less than 40 journeys an hour.

Interior of Stroud Green station, with LNER N2 2663 on a two-coach train for Alexandra Palace, 11th August 1945. The conductor rails were laid in 1939–40. *H C Casserley*

Alas poor Highgate! Looking west from the top of the tunnel on 5th July 1981. This view shows the partial conversion to a surface station for the proposed Northern Line extension from Drayton Park to Muswell Hill and Alexandra Palace, on which work ceased in 1940, never to be resumed. Although there is little sign of it here, below this site is the present Northern Line Highgate tube station. As can be seen, the area is even more thickly wooded than it was in the 1900s. Not surprisingly the place is alleged to be haunted, perhaps by the spirits of frustrated commuters who once dwelt at Muswell Hill. *Alan A Jackson*

When there was no sign of restarting work on the 1935–40 Railway plan local interests grew restive. Parliamentary questions in 1948 received the reply that there was need to restrict capital investment. Before long a reassessment had begun. Wartime bombing had severely reduced the quantum of offices in the City, adding impetus to a drift to the West End which had started before 1940. Post-war Labour governments did not exactly encourage rebuilding of City offices and the consequent heavy fall in commuter traffic between the branch and Moorgate and Broad Street, combined with the successful diversion of most other business to road services, influenced the decision-making. Buses were doing well on roads as yet uncluttered by large-scale car ownership and a surfeit of lorries, and the pre-war philosophy that electrification would generate suburban traffic, exemplified by the Barnet line results, was conveniently forgotten at 55 Broadway.

In the autumn of 1953, for what London Transport unblushingly called 'reasons of reduced traffic', this part of the 1935–40 Railway plan was announced as cancelled. The local authorities and the Alexandra Palace Trustees, the latter protesting that the Palace had yet to be restored and reopened, were solemnly told that the average of 700 passengers Monday to Friday (45 a train), or 22 a train on Saturdays, did not justify keeping the line open, let alone electrifying it. A dubious assertion that although £300,000 had been spent on the works another £2m would be needed to complete them was not challenged.*

* Both figures are at 1939 prices.

Cranley Gardens station, 3rd July 1954, the last day of passenger service; the two-coach train with its N2 0-6-2T is bound for Alexandra Palace. *Alan A Jackson*

It was easier in 1953 than it would be nowadays for such a decision to be imposed without proper discussion and analysis and the Transport Users' Consultative Committee duly applied the rubber stamp. On 3rd July 1954, just before 17.00 eight gas-lit coaches, packed with railway enthusiasts and sentimental local residents stood at Finsbury Park under the stern eyes of police dog handlers and their charges. The N2 hauling this last train made a spirited attack on the Northern Heights, but some jerky starts from Stroud Green and Crouch End resulted in a drawbar fracture beneath the leading coach when the departure from Highgate was attempted. After some delay the train was propelled to Alexandra Palace by the N2 from a following freight. Arrival back at Finsbury Park, with the original locomotive restored for the downhill run, was a mere 35 minutes late. A punctual arrival would of course have been something of an anti-climax for the final journey on this line.

Those conductor rails still remaining had been removed by February 1955, when only the discerning eye could detect what might have been but for Hitler's strategy. With the end of the rail service, bus frequencies were heavily strengthened to eliminate all opportunity for criticism, the peak-hour frequency of the 41-seat single-deckers between Muswell Hill and Finsbury Park becoming 46 an hour, one of the most intensive in London. A so-called 'express' bus with a 6d (2½p) minimum fare and through season tickets to tube stations appeared in October 1955 on this route. In icy weather, this and the other buses left passengers to fend for themselves on the one in nine gradient of Muswell Hill.

Goods trains and the occasional enthusiasts' special kept the branch alive a little longer, but Muswell Hill yard closed from 14th June 1956 and Cranley Gardens from 18th May 1957, after which coal and coke came to the area by road from the rail-served concentration depot at Palace Gates, to be mentioned later. When the line closed, the bridge over the railway at Muswell Hill station was filled in, allowing use of 56-seat double-deck buses from 6th January 1960, running at 38 an hour in peak periods. From October 1967 the through bus-tube season tickets were limited to existing holders and on 6th September 1968 the 'express' bus disappeared. In May 1969, with the conversion of the Muswell Hill–Finsbury Park route to single-deck flat-fare buses running at 18 an hour in the peaks, the through road-rail tickets were completely withdrawn. On the Muswell Hill–Cranley Gardens–Highgate route at this time, two services provided a peak frequency of 20 buses an hour. Such was the fall in traffic.

When all freight working to Edgware and High Barnet came to an end in May 1964, the tracks between Finsbury Park and the tube car sheds at Park Junction, became semi-derelict, coming to life only occasionally to transfer tube cars between the Northern Line and the Northern City at Drayton Park. There were also some trials of tamping equipment by London Transport. The section between Finsbury Park No. 7 box and Park Junction was latterly operated as a single line and progress of the LT battery locomotives with BR pilot on board was at walking pace whilst a sharp lookout was kept for old prams, oil drums, car tyres and other detritus of inner London civilisation. Bridge maintenance on this section had been neglected for some years and this, together with plans for electrification of the suburban services through Finsbury Park, hastened the end. The final LT rolling stock transfer was on 29th September 1970, these movements being made with greater complication from 5th October via Kings Cross and the City Widened Lines until London Transport gave up working the Drayton Park–Moorgate tube in October 1975. At the end of 1971 the rails between Finsbury Park and Highgate were removed and the tunnel mouths at Highgate sealed, leaving the London Transport depot at the end of a stub from the through line south of East Finchley.

Through electric trains from the GN to Moorgate via Finsbury Park and Drayton Park began on 8th November 1976, at last fulfilling the 1892 plan for electric working between Moorgate and Great Northern suburban stations . . . except for those on the Northern Heights.

After closure, Haringey Council eventually adopted much of the railway alignment between Finsbury Park, Highgate and Alexandra Palace as a 'Parkland Walk' but by the time this was achieved, some buildings had blocked the route on the site of Cranley Gardens and Muswell Hill stations. Suggestions for using the route as a light rail scheme came forward from time to time, initially from London Transport itself and this may yet become a reality. Meanwhile, although much of the Victorian railway infrastructure and the physical preparations for electrification have disappeared or been altered beyond recognition, some relics of what was 'Almost a Tube' may still be found, though it is advisable to explore in broad daylight and preferably not alone.

We now turn to the second aspirant for the rewards of the expected bonanza in Alexandra Park. The Great Eastern Railway responded in almost reckless manner to the advances of the Muswell Hill Estate Company, which was seeking all the access it could get. That company's act of 1866 included powers for a 1m 2f 9ch line curving north west and then north through the Park to a point just south of what is now the North Circular Road, where it would make end-on junction with a 3m 1f 7ch branch authorised by GER Act of the same year from the proposed Enfield Town line at Seven Sisters (Tottenham). The loop round the back of Alexandra Palace (where the Muswell Hill Estate and Railways Act included a chord which would have allowed through running from Highgate to Seven Sisters) would have entailed some interesting engineering to bring the tracks down from the top of the hill into the Lea Valley. When a financially embarrassed GER came to parliament in 1869 with a bill to discard various schemes of dubious merit, it is not surprising to find the Alexandra Palace branch in the list of abandonments. Accepting the realities of the situation, the Muswell Hill Estates & Railway Company obtained powers in 1871 to abandon the bits of railway in its 1866 act rendered useless by the GER withdrawal.

A BR diesel car set on a special working from Hitchin via the Cuffley Loop at the still gaslit Palace Gates station, looking towards the end of the line, 13th September 1958. *Alan A. Jackson*

Although the GER was no longer interested in a mountain railway up to the Palace, it did feel the need to fill the gap between the Enfield Town branch and the GNR main line, territory in which others were beginning to show interest, especially as it was now in the path of the tide of bricks and mortar seeping northwards from London. Thus the GER Act of 1874 included a branch from Seven Sisters more-or-less on the 1866 alignment but stopping short after 2m 5f 4.5ch at a point in Bounds Green very close to the GNR Wood Green station (now Alexandra Palace) although with no provision for a connection. That there was still some intention of catering for Palace traffic was seen in the extra spaciousness of the terminal station, which was somewhat deceitfully named Palace Gates. Until the coming of electric tramcars in the early years of the twentieth century passengers arriving here for the Palace were faced with an uphill walk of all but three quarters of a mile before they were in sight of the eastern entrance doors.

The double-track branch opened as far as Green Lanes station on 1st January 1878, the first train leaving Liverpool Street at 09.10 to arrive at the temporary terminus 30 minutes later. The remainder of the branch to Palace Gates was ready for public traffic on the following 7th October.

At Seven Sisters the wooden branch platforms were on an embankment, curving away to the west at the country end. On the Down platform a small brick building housed waiting rooms etc; the Up side was linked to the Enfield Town platform by footbridge between the two embankments but it was also possible to walk round the platforms at the London end where they came together under a small canopy. A subway connected all four platforms to a footpath which led to the main booking office and entrance in West Green Road, but at the west end this subway opened into Birstall Road, where a small booking office was established in 1906. Latterly only used for workmen's traffic, this closed in 1942. Over the 53 chains to West Green station the line fell at 1 in 100, passing under West Green Road to enter platforms sited in a wide cutting. This station, which served the hamlet of that name, still separate from Tottenham when the line opened, had low buildings in yellow stock brick and timber boarding on the north side of the road bridge and a signal box and goods yard on the Down side, with sidings which came almost to the road, above and behind the platform.

Beyond here the branch continued on a north-westerly course, now climbing for the rest of its distance with gradients as steep as 1 in 51 and 1 in 66. Green Lanes station was on an embankment with wooden platforms and platform buildings served from a small brick booking office at street level close to the centre of the village of Wood Green. Its signal box was on the Up side at the country end of the bridge over Green Lanes and the goods yard was also on that side of the line, at ground level a little to the south east. Palace Gates station, 7m 66ch from Liverpool Street, had generously-proportioned yellow stock brick buildings connected by a wide covered footbridge. With its 750ft platforms (260ft under canopies) and main entrance on the west side, it was built as a through station, and was at ground level, in open fields almost exactly half-way between what is now Bounds Green Road and the GNR Wood Green (now Alexandra Palace) station. At the country end the tracks led on to a small engine shed and carriage sidings on the Up side, and to a goods yard on the west, the whole site occupying eight acres. The signal box was on the Up platform and two sets of staff cottages were built near the station entrance. Saxby & Farmer lower-quadrant signals and Tyer's block telegraph system lasted the branch the whole of its life with only minor modifications and renewals.

As we have seen, the Alexandra Palace proved a miserable failure as a popular resort, so the branch's pleasure traffic never amounted to very much except on special occasions such as Bank Holidays and exhibitions. There was however a significant flow of commuters as the fields between Seven Sisters and Green Lanes filled up with small terraced houses in the late 1870s and the 1880s. By 1914 streets of such houses clothed the line half a mile deep each side for the whole of its length except for a short stretch north of West Green. East of Green Lanes station, the extensive Noel Park Estate of the Artisans', Labourers' and General Dwellings Company was laid out under architectural supervision in 1883, though not fully completed until the 1900s. During its construction, sidings were extended from the north end of the 1883 Green Lanes freight yard into the site. This development was thought important enough to justify a change in the station's name from Green Lanes to Noel Park from 1st May 1884. Building activity along this line was not uninfluenced by GER fares policy, for although the 2d workmen's return was not available, 3d returns to the City were issued before 07.00 and 4d returns (4½d from Palace Gates) between 07.00 and 08.00.

Nor was the GER ungenerous with the train service. By 1908 a total of 41 Up and 38 Down through trains between Palace Gates and the City alternated with Enfield Town–City trains. Off-peak service was half-hourly, with strengthening in the peak periods, so that there were, for example, six trains from Liverpool Street to Palace Gates between 18.00 and 20.00. Stopping trains averaged 31 minutes for the 7¾ miles, but some rush-hour trains, missing stops, did the run in 25 minutes. In peak hours the formation at this time was all four-wheelers, eight six-a-side third-class coaches, six second-class, and three firsts, offering a total of 888 seats, but some of the early morning trains were all or nearly all third-class with a total of 972 seats. At other times 12-coach trains were worked. After 1910 through trains between the branch and Liverpool Street were gradually reduced; Sunday trains worked only on the branch from 1912.

As elsewhere, the Jazz Service of 12th July 1920 brought major alterations. The principal feature was the introduction of two two-car 'auto' or push-and-pull sets which provided the half-hourly slack period working and at peak hours connected with Enfield line trains at Seven Sisters, alternating with through trains between Palace Gates and Liverpool Street, making up a combined ten-minute frequency. Special signalling arrangements were necessary at Seven Sisters to allow the auto-trains to terminate at the Up branch platform, thus affording the maximum convenience for passenger interchange. A 'Syx' electro-mechanical train stop protected the main line, not only preventing over-running, but allowing Enfield line trains to approach the junction without a check. Access to the branch platform was controlled by a calling-on arm at the country end.

At the rear end of the second of the two compartment coaches in the auto-trains was a cab containing compressed-air equipment which enabled the driver to control the regulator, brake and whistle of the F7 2–4–2T at the other end. Through trains, hauled at first by 'Buck-Jumper' 0–6–0T, were composed of 16 four-wheelers including two firsts and two seconds, but during the 1920s Gresley 'quint-art' bogie articulated sets and N7 0–6–2T took over. After 1926 travel on the auto-trains was given added interest by the importation of clerestory-roofed GER main line bogie stock complete with lavatories (later boarded up). In the 1930s there were three auto-trains in use, one with three clerestory-roofed vestibuled bogie coaches, the others each made up with a composite bogie suburban carriage and an ex-GER main line bogie coach. School children, often the only passengers outside peak hours, enjoyed such unwonted luxury with less vandalism than it would now provoke, but the author recalls that the faded comforts of the main line cars did much to encourage teenage dalliance on long summer afternoons, when it was always better to travel to Palace Gates than to arrive.

Palace Gates push & pull auto train No.2 in the Up branch platform at Seven Sisters c.1939.

A North Woolwich–Palace Gates train under the capacious footbridge at Palace Gates, in charge of BR 67205, 24th August 1950. *E A Course*

An interesting traffic surviving until the 1930s were the trains of horse boxes carrying grooms and racehorses from Newmarket to the racecourse at Alexandra Park, which was reached by walking the horses through the streets from Palace Gates station. Latterly these trains were usually hauled by B12 4-6-0s in charge of Cambridge crews.

Through trains between the branch and Liverpool Street had ceased by 1939 but until 6th July 1942, when it was withdrawn under the exigencies of wartime, a frequent shuttle service was maintained. Restored with some brave publicity on 31st May 1948, it disappeared for ever from 15th January 1951 'owing to fuel cuts'.

The branch supported another service, not so far mentioned. With the opening of a curve from Seven Sisters to the Tottenham and Hampstead Junction Railway at South Tottenham on 1st January 1880, trains were worked over this and Tottenham West and South Junctions from Palace Gates to Stratford and Fenchurch Street. On the following 1st September the service was diverted to Blackwall, but ceased after traffic on 28th February 1881. Six years later, on 1st June 1887, a most useful cross-London facility was established by operating trains from Palace Gates to North Woolwich. This proved of great value to dock workers and railwaymen employed at the vast Stratford complex; the trains were also used by North Londoners employed at Woolwich Arsenal, especially during World War I. In the opposite direction, on Sundays and Bank Holidays, East Londoners came this way to relax at Alexandra Palace. Eleven trains each way, roughly at hourly intervals, were provided in 1910, with six each way on Sundays. Calling at all stations, they accomplished the 12½-mile run in 42 minutes. In 1938 there were 14 trains each way on weekdays, with a generous Sunday service of hourly trains from late morning to early evening.

Reductions came with wartime and from 5th July 1942 there was no service outside peak hours on Monday to Saturday apart from a few trains for Sunday workers. The latter ceased from 23rd March 1947 but about a half dozen peak hour trains ran each way daily until 7th January 1963 when the service was cut back to run between Tottenham Hale and North Woolwich.

These North Woolwich trains were similar in character to those working between Palace Gates and Liverpool Street, but after the departure of the 'Buck-Jumpers' in the 1920s they were usually hauled by F7 2–4–2T, N7 0–6–2T or G4 and G5 0–4–4T. From 1st January 1962 some of the workings were handled by Rolls-Royce three-car diesel sets, but N7s continued to appear, making this the last outpost of steam on the Great Eastern sector of BR in the London area.

Declining passenger patronage, which caused the eventual withdrawal of services from the branch stemmed from two factors: changes in employment patterns (local road journeys to new factories instead of radial rail journeys to inner London workplaces), and the vastly improved road transport provision with the arrival of the electric tramcar and the motor bus in the 1900s and 1910s. Electric trams were working between Wood Green and Finsbury Park from 22nd July 1904, and between Wood Green and Tottenham on 20th August, whilst a branch tram service from Wood Green to Alexandra Palace East, passing close to Noel Park and Palace Gates stations, started on 11th April 1906. At Finsbury Park, tramcar passengers could make an easy transfer to new electric tube railway services to the City and West End. Between 1910 and 1914, motor bus services were started along the road between Seven Sisters and Wood Green, passing West Green station, and also between Noel Park station and the West End. Further damage followed the 1932 opening of the Piccadilly tube from Finsbury Park through Turnpike Lane (less than a mile west of West Green station) and Wood Green to Bounds Green, the last two stations being very close to Noel Park and Palace Gates. This drew off any remaining passengers whose workplaces were in the West End, the Finsbury, Holborn, or Kings Cross areas.

Some rush-hour traffic remained both to the City and the Stratford, docks, and North Woolwich stations. Indeed, the LNER had sufficient confidence in the future to announce in June 1937 that Noel Park station was to be rebuilt, noting that it had been used by 250,000 passengers in 1936. Later in 1937 the underline bridge here was renewed in connection with a road-widening scheme and although a small start was made on reconstructing the station, work stopped on the outbreak of war in 1939.

Destruction of City offices and other workplaces in the inner area by the German air attacks of 1940–41, the serious damage to the Royal group of docks and the evacuation of many businesses to outer areas reduced the traffic to a trickle and led to the cuts of 1942. With road services back to peacetime standards and a very slow reconstruction in the City and East End, the restoration of the shuttle service in 1948 proved to be a short-sighted extravagance.

In these declining years of passenger traffic the completion of a link with the former GNR lines at Bounds Green brought about a substantial change in character of other train movements. Although a connection had been authorised by the LNER Act of 1924, the powers were allowed to lapse in 1929 before any work had been started, but in the following January, mainly to allow GE section suburban stock to move to and from a washing plant at the new Bounds Green carriage depot, a single-line connection was made in the sidings between the depot and the former GER terminal yard at Palace Gates. This soon proved useful for other purposes, even carrying some east coast excursion trains from former GNR suburban stations during the summer of 1939. Two years later to relieve the normal routes, the LNER started to work coal trains to Temple Mills (Stratford) through Palace Gates, usually splitting the trains in two for movement over the branch in charge of two 2–4–2T or a J39 0–6–0. At best this was awkward and time-consuming, so under the pressures of wartime demands it was decided to build a through connection between the GER branch and the Hertford loop. This was a single track signalled for two-way working, controlled from Palace Gates and Bounds Green boxes by direction levers associated with track circuits. It came into regular daily use from 9th July 1944, carrying four through freight trains each way between New England (Peterborough) and Temple Mills. Loaded southbound, empty northbound, these were limited to 50 wagons by the curvature and gradients of the branch. From the summer of 1953 the connection was again used by excursions from GNR suburban stations to Clacton and Southend, usually calling at stations on the branch, whilst in May 1959, when major engineering work blocked Broxbourne Junction, Cambridge line trains were worked to and from Liverpool Street via Palace Gates, Hertford North and Royston.

Goods traffic only briefly outlasted passenger services: West Green yard closed on 5th October 1964, Noel Park on 7th December, while through freights ceased from 28th December. Palace Gates yard and the 1944 connection survived the branch, thanks to the construction of a domestic fuels concentration depot in the old GER yard. This Charrington depot, opened in July 1958, was one of the first of its kind, handling coal and coke in full trainloads and equipped to bag the fuel ready for road distribution over a wide area. It dealt with up to 55,000 tonnes a year, replacing the coal yards at New Southgate, Oakleigh Park, Noel Park, West Green, Stoke Newington, South Tottenham, Hornsey, Cranley Gardens, Muswell Hill and Highgate.

With the declining use of solid fuels, traffic fell away causing closure and demolition of the depot in 1984. Even then the Palace Gates branch did not completely disappear hereabouts; the area from a point just north of the demolished Palace Gates station to the junction with the Hertford line was retained as part of the layout of the Bounds Green Inter City trains depot of 1976–77.

Following closure and dismantling of both the GNR and GER branches and the rebuilding of Wood Green main line station for the Kings Cross suburban electrification scheme, little survived to remind the visitor of the extensive railway accommodation which had once existed for North London's Palace of the People and its Park. Such rail traffic as remained, further diminished when the Jockey Club deprived the race course of its licence in 1970, was to pass through the main line station. In recognition of this what had been Wood Green & Alexandra Park was duly renamed Alexandra Palace from 17th May 1982. Ugly and brooding on its hill, victim of yet another disastrous fire in July 1980, the great building piled up a substantial debt liability for its initially enthusiastic new owners, Haringey Council. Under that regime, it was eventually restored to meet modern entertainment, recreational and commercial needs. If sufficient traffic can be generated by the new facilities behind the Victorian frontage, the future may yet see some restoration of more convenient rail facilities in the form of light rail, as suggested above.

Up train entering the island-platformed Bowes Park station c.1905. *Commercial postcard*

The Cuffley Loop
(map page 365)

Although intended as a by-pass for the vulnerable Great Northern London approaches and built to main line standards for much of its length, the Wood Green–Hertford–Stevenage loop has never carried regular long-distance passenger services despite the capital lavished upon its outer section. Left for 47 years as a suburban branch, it was operated as two separate passenger branches even after completion as a loop. For these reasons it earns mention in this book.

We shall see later how the Middlesex market town of Enfield was at first reached, somewhat circuitously, by the Eastern Counties Railway and subsequently more directly by its successor, the Great Eastern. In 1865, a year after the GER Act for the direct approach, the GNR sought and obtained powers to build a relief loop to its main line, which would extend from the north end of Wood Green station through Enfield to Hertford, whence trains would return to the main line via the existing Hatfield to Hertford branch and a new spur from that towards the Welwyn Viaduct. Probing into this borderland, the GER in the same year received authority to build a branch from Tottenham on the proposed direct Enfield line, to Winchmore Hill. Before any work was done on the GNR line, the board reconsidered what it could afford, obtaining a Board of Trade certificate in 1869 to abandon the section beyond Enfield.

The GNR then started construction of what was nothing more than a country branch aimed into potential middle-class suburban territory threatened by the Great Eastern. The local character of the line was well illustrated by the wicked curving ascent out of Wood Green, where Down trains had to storm a 1 in 55 grade to reach the three-span plate-girder bridge over the main lines. Up trains were brought in more gently on the opposite (eastern) side of Wood Green station. At Bounds Green the Up and Down lines came together, running northeastwards on embankment to Palmers Green station. This place was then nothing more than 'a little gathering of houses on the road to Enfield' but the station was placed on the road to Southgate, a village ¾-mile away to the northwest on the foothills of the Barnet Ridge, much favoured by wealthy businessmen, for whose benefit a privately-operated horse-bus feeder service was started. At the transition from embankment to cutting on the north side of the road, the station house was a pretty barge-boarded, twin-gabled bungalow, with covered staircases at the back leading down to the platforms. Run-round facilities were installed to allow trains to terminate here, together with a small goods yard on the Up side at the London end, all controlled from a signal cabin under the stairs to the Up platform. When the goods yard was enlarged about 1936 this cabin was replaced by a box on the Down side, where a goods shed and siding had been added. Other than extension of the Up platform canopies and the provision of a separate canopied waiting pavilion on the Down platform this station was to remain virtually unchanged for over a hundred years.

After traversing the foot of the high land along the edge of the Lea basin in a cutting, the branch reached Winchmore Hill, almost the twin of its predecessor in siting, layout and architecture except that its goods yard was north of the passenger station on the Down side. Today the street-level building is but a remnant; elegantly carved wooden finials and barge boards on the gables have long since rotted away, and in 1965 subsidence caused the whole of the Down side wing to be demolished. At the time of the opening, the country at Winchmore Hill, 'undulating, abundantly wooded and agreeable' was already a favourite place of residence for City men 'whose comfortable houses are seen on every hand'.

A final stretch, mostly on high embankment on a falling gradient, brought the line

Winchmore Hill station GNR, c.1910. A solitary cab awaits hire to a destination in this well-scattered middle-class residential district. *Commercial postcard*

to its terminus at the western edge of Enfield. This was at street level, with a two-storey twin-gabled house in the same style as the others, placed firmly across the end of the tracks, as if to emphasise that all thought of further extension had been abandoned. Inside, an island platform, sheltered by a wide canopy for much of its length, was flanked by engine run-round roads and sidings. There was a goods yard at the London end.

An evocative portrayal of the impact of this line on the quiet gentrified country at the northern edge of London is found in a book written by the observant daughter of Winchmore Hill's doctor. Miss Cresswell watched the generally well-behaved navvies building a tall embankment across the valley of the Salmons Brook, noticing how, when exposed to the air, the London clay changed from a bright cobalt blue to an orangey colour. She rode by invitation on the contractor's locomotive *The Fox*, bumping along the temporary way between Winchmore Hill and Palmers Green in the evening light through cuttings soon to be ablaze with poppies thriving on the newly-excavated clay. At last:

> It was the night of the 31st March 1871, the permanent way was completed, the station was finished and smelled strongly of fresh paint, everything was ready. It was late in the evening, all was very quiet, the familiar sound of the working engine and attendant trucks attracted no attention, but suddenly the village was startled by a loud explosion, a perfect volley of explosions!

The last work train was departing over a chain of detonators. Next morning regular passenger and freight working started. About 16 trains arrived and departed daily at Enfield on weekdays (five on Sundays), most of them after 1st May running to and from Moorgate Street, a few to Victoria via Ludgate Hill; two additional trains terminated at Palmers Green. North London Railway trains provided extra journeys from 1st February 1875 between Broad Street and Enfield or Palmers Green, while from the same day the Victoria service was worked by LCDR locomotives and coaches. Further variety was available from 1st June 1878 when some GNR trains began to work between Enfield and Woolwich via Ludgate Hill and Blackheath. SER locomotives and stock took these over from 1st August 1880, some workings then calling at Cannon Street on the way. By then the combined services at Enfield totalled over 27 each way, departures starting at 07.42 and finishing at 23.10. There was no workmen's traffic as yet, but Palmers Green had two extra early morning trains. From the early 1880s the GNR Stirling Radial 0–4–2T with their bumpy little four-wheel coaches were replaced by small Stirling 0–4–4T. The latter were in turn succeeded about 1890 by the larger Stirling tanks of the same wheel arrangement, known as 'Wolves' from their staccato bark.

Bacon's map of 1880 shows Wood Green starting to grow between Green Lanes and the railway to Enfield with some other new housing in and around Brownlow Road, Bounds Green. For the latter, the GNR opened a station called Bowes Park on 1st November 1880, with an island platform linked by footbridge to new roads either side of the line. A centre track at the country end, controlled from a small signal box, provided for rush-hour reversals. By the end of the 1890s this station was extremely busy, with new streets extending from the railway to the Enfield Road almost all the way to Palmers Green and also about a quarter-mile depth of new housing on the west side of the line. Patronage justified the extension in 1911 from Wood Green of five Up trains in the morning and nine Down in the evening.

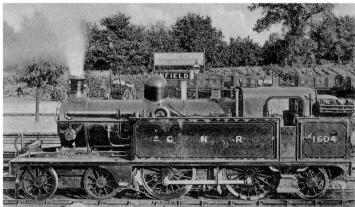

Above: North London Railway 4-4-0T No.58 on a Broad Street–Enfield train (six four-wheel coaches and two four-wheel brake vans) at Palmers Green, c.1910
H. Gordon Tidey

Left: GNR 4-4-2T 1504 at Enfield station, c.1905
Commercial postcard

The first GNR station at Enfield, looking to buffers, c.1905.
Commercial postcard

Palmers Green & Southgate station GNR, looking to London c.1905. *Lens of Sutton*

Villa development at Palmers Green was less rapid until about 1900, when side streets sprouted out each side of the Enfield Road from Wood Green to Winchmore Hill, encouraged much more by the new electric tramway than the railway. The Metropolitan Electric Tramways' 1907 opening from Wood Green to Palmers Green and on to Winchmore Hill in 1908 and Enfield a year later caused much damage to the GNR short-distance traffic whilst increasing the railway's commuter loadings. As much of the new housing was directed at the middle-class market, the new traffic was lucrative, with a high proportion of first- and second-class bookings. In 1905 the *Evening News* saw Palmers Green and Southgate, 30 minutes journey from the City, as the places where the bank clerk or the man with a responsible position in a merchant's office could find the home he desired. A typical house had five bedrooms, two reception rooms, study, kitchen and scullery, with a long garden, all for a rent of £70 a year. By 1914 the combined efforts of railway, electric tramcar and willing builders had brought the frontier of London a good half-mile north of Winchmore Hill station, touching Enfield itself. That place, however, was only very slowly losing its small country town atmosphere. At Bycullah Park, north of the terminus, where in the 1870s a special 15-minute train service had brought thousands to Easter steeplechases and fairs, a large villa estate was laid out in the following decade. There was very little else before 1900 to produce traffic for the GNR, apart from some streets of artisans' cottages on the north side of the town. Schemes in the 1870s to encourage suburban development by extending both the GNR and GER towards Forty Hill and a junction with the Lea Valley line got no support.

At the beginning of the twentieth century Enfield had 49 arrivals and a similar number of departures, including 16 NLR journeys each way to and from Broad Street and two SER trains each way on the Woolwich service. The latter were hauled by brass-domed dark green 0-4-4T but, rendered redundant by electric tube railways and motor buses, lasted only until 30th April 1907, the Enfield–Victoria trains following them into oblivion on 30th September. In late Victorian and Edwardian years the GNR locals were hauled by Ivatt's 4–4–2T running Down chimney-first and returning bunker-first. Just before 1914 these were replaced by Ivatt N1 0–6–2T then a few years later the squat-chimneyed Gresley N2 0–6–2T arrived to monopolise the service for the rest of the steam era. From 1912 the old close-coupled sets of 11 or 12 GNR four-wheelers gave way to eight-coach rakes of the first Gresley articulated coaches, known as 'Bogie Locals'. North London trains were easily distinguished by their scarlet-ended guards' brakes fitted with 'birdcage' observation glasses, one at each end of the rake. The gas-lit NLR four-wheelers were first-, second- and third-class, the last being semi-open, with wooden seats. In the 1890s there were usually three first-class coaches (96 seats), four seconds (200) and three thirds (150), an allocation which gives some indication of the type of traffic carried. These trains were hauled by black Adams/Park outside-cylinder 4–4–0T, which always found some difficulty with full trains on the Down flyover at Wood Green, so much so that their exhausts were easily heard over two miles away at Palmers Green. Not until the late 1920s were they retired in favour of Fowler's sprightly 'Jinty' 0–6–0T.

Increasingly concerned with the problem of operating a congested main line south of Hitchin, especially during emergencies and engineering work, the GNR board finally decided to make the long-considered loop, securing an act in 1898 for an Enfield–Stevenage line. Whilst this was a more costly solution than quadrupling the two double-track sections of two and 2½ miles on the Wood Green–Stevenage section of the main line, it was hoped that the loop would generate additional business, especially suburban traffic of good class between Enfield and Hertford, in an area well beyond the reach of the electric trams. Yet, as we shall see, once the line was built, this aspect was virtually ignored by the railway operators.

After much discussion and indecision, contracts were let in January 1906 to the Stockton-on-Tees firm of H. M. Nowell for the first 4¾ miles of the 20 miles north of the terminus. In undulating clay country, the engineers faced construction of cuttings up to 42ft deep and embankments of similar height, which required angles of rest as low as 1 in 3.

As extension from the original terminus would have involved a level-crossing, a junction was made about half a mile to the south, at the country end of a new station called Grange Park. Perched on a wind-swept embankment with a view east to cuckoo-haunted woods, the timber platforms of the latter were reached by gas-lit slopes connected by an underline subway to a single-storey slate and brick booking office at road level on the Down side. Suburban activity here started boldly in 1909 with the erection of three impressive shopping parades and the first villas in roads called the Chine and the Grangeway, all on the Grange Park estate east of the line.

North of the station three sidings, later to be used for storing passenger stock, ran parallel to the new double line on the Down side. A new station for Enfield was provided just east of the old, immediately south of the bridge over Windmill Hill. In red and engineering bricks, its large booking hall at street level on the Down side was connected to the well-canopied wooden platforms by ample staircases. With the opening of the extension the old terminus became the general merchandise and coal depot for the area, including the new suburb of Grange Park; its passenger platform, which remained intact for many years, returned to use briefly in October 1940 when an unexploded bomb fell on to the through line.

Curving slightly north-west from Enfield station, the new line traversed the western edge of the town on a long embankment planted with 'plane and other suitable trees' on both sides, its bridges over side roads decorated with stone copings and red facing bricks; the cosmetic treatment was required by clauses in the 1898 Act 'for the protection of Enfield Urban District Council'. At Gordon Hill, on its outermost northern edge, Enfield got its third GNR station. Very much at the brim of London, this place retained a frontier atmosphere until the end of the 1960s. In a wide cutting, spanned at the northern end by a massive five-arch road bridge, were two well-canopied island platforms, with spacious waiting rooms and other brick-built offices. A covered footbridge and walkway led to a single storey brick ticket office building at the top of the eastern cutting slope; nearby on Gordon Hill itself stood a two storey house for the stationmaster (now demolished). It was clear the GNR envisaged development into a terminus for suburban services, but only the Up island was used as such and the outer road on the Down side, connected to the through lines only at its northern end, accommodated berthed carriages and vans and was fenced off from the Down platform to avoid any misunderstandings. In 1973, when this road was connected to the Down line at the southern end, the original connection was removed. We shall return to the fate of these bay roads later. Terraced villas and cottages had reached the top of Gordon Hill by 1895–8 and in 1911, just south of the station, on the Up side, the GNR opened an 11-acre staff sports ground to which special cheap tickets were available from all its London area stations.

Beyond Gordon Hill the alignment was across undulating countryside, entering an area still remote and free from urban taint, destined to remain unspoiled for many years after the opening of the railway, its stations seeing only golfers, walkers and lovers. Before reaching Crews Hill station, the tracks were carried 70ft above a tributary of the river Lea on the 495ft Rendlesham Viaduct with its 14 graceful brick-and-concrete arches. Higher ground was now encountered, and the station, at the transition from embankment to cutting, was a simple affair with small uncanopied brick buildings on wooden platforms, covered stairs leading from the London end to a subway beneath the embankment, and a small wooden booking office on the Up side. A modest goods yard was sited on the Up side north of the station. Crews Hill served a golf course, a scattering of nurserymen's greenhouses and a stud farm which provided some horsebox traffic.

Crews Hill, looking to Hertford, 1963. The freight yard is behind the country end of the Up platform. Apart from the electric lighting, upper quadrant semaphores and the screen of poplars, this scene shows no substantial change since the station was opened 53 years earlier.
Stations UK

Entering Hertfordshire, the line emerged from deep cutting on to another embankment, crossing 30ft above a side valley of the Cuffley Brook on the 390ft 11-arch Soper's Farm Viaduct before running into its temporary terminus at Cuffley. This station, on the north side of the road between the two villages of Cuffley and Goff's Oak, was similar to Crews Hill in all respects, including the siting of its goods yard.

Passenger service to Cuffley started on 4th April 1910, calling at all the new stations, with over 50 arrivals daily at Gordon Hill, the last as late as 00.44, and a similar provision in the Up direction. Cuffley however closed early (19.30) and had only 16 trains each way including a solitary North London Railway train* to and from Broad Street. On Sundays there were but three trains in and out of Cuffley, increased to five in the summer of 1910. There was some excursionist traffic at Cuffley in the summer; the local newspaper reported 6,000 arriving over the Whitsun holiday weekend in 1911. As traffic built up, service was increased, so that by 1914 there were about 69 each way, 20 going through to Cuffley, the rest reversing at Gordon Hill. A 1913 scheme for a garden city at Cuffley, 2,750 houses on 550 acres, got little further than planning stage, but Cuffley's great moment came with the war, when it gave earthly rest to the scorched steel tracery of SL21, the first bombing airship to be shot down over England. On the following day, Sunday 3rd September 1916, the little station saw a level of traffic never repeated until the area finally became suburbanised in the 1960s.

Some difficulty was encountered in raising capital for the remainder of the loop, but construction was eventually begun in 1911 by Robert McAlpine & Sons (Cuffley to Hertford), followed a little later by H. Arnold & Sons (Hertford to Langley Junction). Work continued slowly until labour and material shortages brought it to a virtual halt late in 1916. Activity was resumed in the following year, and by December a single running line was available without stations or signals. Regular freight workings, at first of empty wagons only, started on 4th March 1918, the whole 14¾ miles from Cuffley to Langley Junction under the control of Tyer's No. 5 Absolute and Permissive single line tablet instruments. This system, used for the first time in Britain, allowed a limited number of trains to follow each other, those in the rear being duly warned as to time intervals, and of course there was no question of any working in the opposite direction until all the tablets had been returned to the instrument at the far end of the single line section. Lineside telephones were available for emergency use.

The partially completed loop, in all 23 miles, and only 1½ miles longer than the main line between the two junctions, came into its own on the morning of 6th February 1920 when passenger trains were diverted over it for the first time after two freight trains had collided, blocking the only two roads in Welwyn North tunnel. To avoid the appalling delays which use of the single line section produced on this occasion, the GNR quickly installed the second track and normal signalling, including a flyunder for the Down road at Langley Junction. This work was brought into use on 23rd December 1920 but the only regular traffic over the northern section was four or five freight trains daily, mainly coal Up and empties Down.

---

* This train was withdrawn from 1st May 1918 together with other off-peak NLR workings. An LMSR train ran in weekday rush-hours between Broad Street and Cuffley from 2nd May 1938 to 9th September 1939 inclusive.

Stations at Hertford and Bayford had been substantially completed by 1917 but the GNR was incredibly slow in making use of its new investment, not operating regular passenger trains north of Cuffley until 2nd June 1924. The London service, worked by N2 0–6–2T and Gresley 'quad-art' bogie compartment coaches, terminated at the new Hertford North station, which was also used by the Hatfield–Hertford branch service, the old terminus at Hertford (Cowbridge) closing the previous evening. North of Hertford about four trains ran each way daily, terminating at Hitchin and calling at new halts at Stapleford and Watton as well as at Stevenage. Watton (Watton-at-Stone from July 1924 to avoid confusion with Watton in Norfolk) was Sir Nigel Gresley's local station. This service did not lack interest, as for much of its pre-war existence it was worked by steam railmotors and steam railcars, but it really lies outside the scope of this book.

Between Cuffley and Hertford the line penetrated a remote part of Hertfordshire which remained thinly populated for many years after the start of the train service. Reaching the head of the valley of the Cuffley Brook, the tracks passed through the north eastern outcrop of the Barnet Ridge in the lonely 1½-mile Ponsbourne Tunnel, the longest on the GNR. Five 10ft diameter shafts (one of them 140ft deep) carried engine smoke to erupt incongruously into the quietness of Wormley Wood. Half a mile from the northern portal was Bayford station, reached only by a bridle path from the scattered village of some 400 people west of the railway. Small waiting huts on the platform and a slightly larger booking hut at road level on the Up side above the line were the only buildings. A little-used goods yard was sited on the Up side north of the station.

After Bayford, the tracks descended into the valleys of the Mimram and Lea, running over two viaducts, Horns Mill, 50ft high with seven arches above the Hatfield Road and the river Lea, and the Hertford viaduct, with 20 brick arches and a skew girder span over the Hatfield branch and the river Mimram. Coming out on the east side, the Hatfield branch kept company with the new line into the station, which was on the west side of the town. This station, only half-finished and left so for over 50 years, was intended to have four roads and two island platforms, but only the western island had tracks either side; the other, which was without buildings, had a track on its western flank. The main island which was normally the one used, had a substantial building with pleasant brickwork, terra cotta detailing and moulded corbels for its large awning. A subway to a miserable little booking office at street level completed the station, altogether a very poor thing compared with the elegant and impressive GER terminus on the other side of the town. At the south end of the platforms were connections to the Hatfield line and some sorting and carriage sidings; general merchandise and coal traffic continued to be handled at the original GNR station at Cowbridge, nearer the centre of the town.

To complete the loop, the GNR proposed to quadruple south of Gordon Hill, with improved junctions at Wood Green burrowing below the main lines. This work was authorised in 1914, but finance could not be found by the impoverished LNER which kept the powers for the Wood Green junctions alive into the 1940s. Another unfulfilled proposal was a north to east spur at Hertford for through running between Langley Junction, Cowbridge and the GER Hertford branch.

Hertford now had a route to London 1½ miles shorter than that of the GER, but neither the GNR nor the LNER ever showed any inclination to develop traffic on this costly line. The fastest time for the 19¼ miles between Kings Cross and the county town was never reduced below an unremarkable 44 to 47 minutes minimum, achieved by only two trains a day, the rest taking ten or more minutes longer. On the inner section, train services showed no significant improvement in the 1930s over those of 1914, 24 trains a day to and from Hertford North, a further 22 to and from Cuffley and another 41 at Gordon Hill; additionally two trains terminated at Grange Park and another two at Bowes Park. The only non-stop workings of any note were one daily from Finsbury Park to Enfield Chase, and another Up from Gordon Hill to Finsbury Park in 15 minutes. Other factors were of course at work, including the attitude of major landowners to selling their property north of Gordon Hill for building, but the unenterprising train service undoubtedly played its part in preserving this lovely corner of London's country from the inter-war speculative building boom. Virtually nothing happened north of Gordon Hill apart from some 1930s bungaloid accretions at Goff's Oak and Cuffley. Passenger traffic on this section consisted almost entirely of summer pleasure-seekers coming out from urban north London at weekends to enjoy the countryside, often taking advantage of ticket facilities which allowed them to travel either by the Cuffley or the Lea Valley lines and return by the other. Steadier revenue came from the greenhouse nursery-men east of the line at Crews Hill and Goff's Oak who provided business in coal and fertilisers inwards and tomatoes, flowers and other garden products outwards.

Things were a little more lively south of Gordon Hill, where building went on steadily through the 1920s and 1930s until Grange Park, Winchmore Hill and Southgate coagulated into a continuous mass of small red-roofed houses. This development was not stimulated or enjoyed by the LNER alone; in 1932 the Piccadilly tube was extended from Finsbury Park to Arnos Grove, Southgate, with a station on the main road at Bounds Green only a few hundred yards from backstreet Bowes Park. the latter, once one of the busiest on the GNR suburban system, lost almost all its traffic overnight. Nor was that the end of the pillage. A further extension of the tube to Cockfosters was completed in 1933 with stations at Southgate village centre and west of Enfield. Bus services with favourable fare facilities ensured that not only was almost all the available traffic brought into these new stations, but a goodly picking also from the steam railway's catchment area at Palmers Green, Winchmore Hill and Enfield itself. Financially weak and unable to obtain government assistance for suburban electrification in this area, the LNER did nothing; indeed the outbreak of war provided excuse for reducing services which were not to be restored to their former level for many years. Broad Street trains, which had run in rush hours only throughout the 1920s and 1930s, generally terminating at Gordon Hill, ceased altogether on 4th October 1940 after temporary suspension from 11th September to 3rd December 1939 inclusive. Some peak-hour operation between Broad Street and the Hertford loop was resumed on 30th July 1945 with stock and locomotives provided by the LNER. Moorgate services, suspended from 11th September to 31st December 1939 and again, after bomb damage, from 30th December 1940, were resumed on an attenuated basis to Aldersgate on 1st October 1945 and to Moorgate on 6th May 1946. The basic service to and from Hertford was reduced to approximately hourly throughout the war and for some time afterwards, although there were extra workings at peak periods.

War years saw the line carrying a good deal of special freight and passenger movement, some of it using the connection to the Palace Gates line at Bounds Green, mentioned earlier. Operations suffered major disruption on 26th October

1944 when a German V2 missile severed both tracks at the country end of Palmers Green station, but with some remarkable organisation and hard work, the tremendous hole was filled and traffic resumed after only 24 hours. In the meantime shuttle services with a locomotive at each end of the train had kept passengers moving.

The late 1940s and early 1950s were doldrum years for a line which smelt of decay and decline as grotty 'quad-arts' were trundled to and from Hertford North by filthy and now wheezing N2 tanks. Towards the end of the 1950s the coaches were being repainted and repanelled, while from 1954 onwards some five-car sets of new standard BR suburban stock were seen on the line. A variety of locomotives appeared on the through and local freights from ex-GNR 0–6–0 upwards, and in the 1950s L1 2–6–4T shared local passenger working with the N2 0–6–2T.

Electrification, first proposed by the GNR before 1914, was announced in the BR Modernisation Plan of 1955, but even now there was to be a long delay before anything happened. In the meantime, in 1959 the tracks on the loop were rebuilt to allow maximum speeds to be raised from 40/50mph to 70mph and on 15th June that year diesel-hauled passenger trains and railcars were introduced with a much improved timetable which provided a basic half-hourly service with extra skip-stop workings in the peak periods. Around the same time builders at last began to make some progress at Cuffley, erecting several estates of small houses for commuter families between the railway and the old village on the hill.

The Hertford–Hitchin trains, which had ceased after traffic on 9th September 1939, were restored on 5th March 1962 with about four or five journeys each way at peak hours Mondays to Fridays and approximately hourly for part of Saturdays and Bank Holiday Mondays. The two intermediate stations remained closed but their yards continued to deal with public goods traffic until 1965. After that, at Watton, a Cory oil tanker siding was active until the end of 1991.

N2 0-6-2T 69547 on an Up train at Grange Park station, looking to Enfield Chase, 24th March 1958, a scene showing little change over the previous 40 years, and virtually none to the buildings and fittings since the station was opened in 1910. *Alan A Jackson*

Under the Beeching regime freight working was rationalised, the yards at Palmers Green, Winchmore Hill, Crews Hill, Cuffley and Bayford all closing from 1st October 1962 to be replaced by a new centralised solid fuel depot in the old station yard at Enfield Chase. Here rail hopper wagons discharged about 59,000 tons of fuel annually into road trucks standing below them. These then took the fuel to the old goods yards where the local merchants retained their rented staithes. But domestic heating was at the brink of a major change and it was not long before the Enfield depot saw its traffic falling as solid fuels gave way to gas and oil. The inevitable closure took place from 1st July 1974, BR advising helpfully that the nearest public freight stations would then be St Pancras or Welwyn. The tracks at Enfield yard were taken up in 1975 and the carriage sidings on the Down side here were lifted four years later. This enabled the whole area to be sold off for residential development in 1983.

As the Hertford North–Cowbridge connection had been closed in 1963, after 1974 local freight was confined to the oil tankers mentioned above. Through freight working had also diminished perceptibly in the 1960s and early 1970s, particularly after closure of the large Ferme Park yards at Hornsey between 1968 and 1973. And the loop's role as an emergency by-pass to the main line was less in demand after the 1959 completion of quadrupling between Greenwood (New Barnet) and Potters Bar.

In preparation for electrification, the manual lock-and-block signalling on the loop was replaced by colour lights in 1971–2 (the last of the picturesque GNR somersault semaphores, at Palmers Green, had disappeared in 1955). All movements came under the Kings Cross Signalling Control Centre from 4th July 1976 and the modernisation scheme was finally completed in 1977. Most signals were three-aspect, with some four aspect ones between Wood Green and Gordon Hill and two aspect displays between Hertford and Langley Junction, where minimum headway lengthened out to five minutes.

Work on the electrification started in 1973, only 70 years after the GNR's first moves in that direction. Electric services between Moorgate and Hertford North began on 8th November 1976, using the former GNCR inwards from Drayton Park, where a change was made from 25kV overhead catenary to 750V dc conductor rail for the tube tunnel section. Initially the service provided nine trains per hour at peak periods to and from Hertford North, three per hour off peak, two per hour on Sundays, and additional workings as far as Gordon Hill. With the introduction of electric trains, the diesel car shuttle to and from Stevenage was augmented at peak hours, running hourly at other times, always with convenient connections at Hertford North. A full electric service beyond Hertford started on 14th May 1979, operating at hourly intervals (two an hour in the peaks) and calling at Watton at Stone after that station was reopened on 17th May 1982. Modifications subsequently somewhat diluted the generous initial electric services; in particular Bowes Park, still suffering from tube competition, was reduced to an hourly train off peak in 1995 and Watton at Stone, Grange Park and Bowes Park were closed on Sundays after 3rd October 1993.

Apart from its own equipment, electrification brought few visual changes but there was some modernisation of lighting and modest tidying up and replacement of neglected structures, notably at Bowes Park, where in 1975 the footbridge was replaced and a new ticket office provided on the island platform. At Gordon Hill,

Intermediate suburban terminus: Gordon Hill sleeps in the afternoon summer sun, 21st July 1973; looking towards Hertford. The closed-off Down bay is being used for storing empty stock. *Alan A Jackson*

where the Down side buildings were demolished and replaced with a wooden waiting hut, both bay roads were electrified, giving this station the appearance its GNR planners may well have envisaged. But this was to be a brief hour of glory. From May 1981 the Down bay was taken out of use; its track subsequently removed, the area quickly became totally overgrown. From 5th October 1981 the Up bay saw only emergency workings until 11th January 1987, after which it again housed a handful of peak hour departures and arrivals. Sadly in recent years this once dignified station has suffered much punishment at rail level from vandals whilst above, its spacious forecourt is untidily cluttered with parked cars and bottle banks.

Acting as an ancillary to the East Coast Main Line south of Stevenage seems now very much a secondary role for what is primarily a suburban and outer suburban electric railway with a buoyant traffic although still very much in competition with LT's Piccadilly tube line south of Enfield. Even so, electrification, along with modernisation of signalling and trackwork do render any necessary main line diversions a far less onerous proceeding than was once the case. For the railway-minded explorer, the GNR atmosphere still lingers here and there, perhaps to be tasted most strongly at Enfield Chase, where the generously-canopied timber platforms are approached through an entrance hall with beamed ceiling and leaded glass fenestration. The once peaceful remoteness of Crews Hill between trains, punctuated only by the whispering of the poplars behind the platform, is now severely degraded by the restless noise of the nearby M25 motorway. Further out still, the bare, isolated platforms of Bayford and the somewhat forbidding Pons-bourne tunnel (where during the German air assaults on London, the royal train would sometimes take shelter for the night) have since electrification lost much but not quite all of their mystery and romance.

Ex LNER N7 0-6-2T 69665 leaving Liverpool Street with a train for Enfield Town in September 1958. *R.C. Riley*

The Enfield Town Branches (map page 350)

Moving east from the GNR main line, we find a through route following the west bank of the river Lea out of London. This was opened in 1840 from a junction with the Eastern Counties Railway at Stratford by a company known as the Northern & Eastern. In its anxiety to keep to the easy flatness of the valley floor, it neglected the old market town of Enfield, which had to make do with a station at Ponders End, a good two miles east of its centre. Only a little more fortunate were the middle-class residential villages of Tottenham and Edmonton, strung along the Hertford road, an early example of ribbon development. Popular rural retreats for City merchants, professional men and artists, these places got stations on their easternmost fringes (the present Angel Road and Tottenham Hale).

Enfield and Edmonton, with populations of over 9,000, soon demanded more direct railway accommodation. Local pressures led to the deposit in 1845 of an Enfield, Edmonton & Eastern Counties Railway Bill (the N&ER had been leased to the ECR in 1844), and in 1846 of an Enfield & Edmonton Railway Bill. The latter was successful, with arrangements made for the ECR to take over the project and build the line.

Thomas Earle began work on the contract in 1848. From just north of the N&ER Edmonton station the 3m 7ch single track traversed market gardens on an almost level and direct north-westerly course to terminate east of the crossroads at the centre of Enfield, where a three-storey late seventeenth-century mansion, latterly a school attended by John Keats, was conveniently available to become the station house and offices. At Lower Edmonton, a single platform occupied a central position at the edge of the village green, with C. F. Cheffins' sober two-storey house behind it, on the west side of the line. Although the main turnpike road had been diverted to cross above the line south of the station, there was a level-crossing at the south end of the platform and a footpath was cut through the platform itself. This was at ground level and when a train was due, it was covered with an iron plate.

Without 'formal or public demonstrations', the line opened on 1st March 1849. An infrequent service, often involving a change at the junction, and the long way round through Stratford to the Bishopsgate terminus offered little competition to the horse coaches and buses which continued to ply along the direct main road from Edmonton through Tottenham to the City. But for anyone with a sense of fun and adventure there was always the possibility of a ride on the rather splendid little steam railmotor *Enfield*, which appeared on the branch soon after its opening. This was a 2–2–0 locomotive and a 36-seat, four-compartment coach on one frame, built at Fairfield Works, Bow, by W. B. Adams, and was normally attached to a nine-ton 116-seat carriage and used for the through journeys between Enfield and London. With its 5ft driving wheels, the ungainly *Enfield* could cover the 10¾ miles from Edmonton to Bishopsgate in 27 to 30 minutes, touching 50mph and using only 12lb of coke a mile compared with a normal locomotive's consumption of 30–33lb. But despite this brilliant performance *Enfield* was not a consistent success and was eventually converted to a 2–2–2T.

After the formation of the Great Eastern Railway in August 1862 there was some improvement in the London service, with 14 trains each way daily in 1864, but the long way round through Stratford tried everyone's patience and the dissatisfaction of all the communities along the high road led to schemes for improved access to the City. Several proposals for a direct line along the road route emerged in the early 1860s: from Angel Road to the NLR near the present Dalston Junction station in 1861, from Edmonton to Finsbury Circus in 1863, and a scheme for a NLR branch from Dalston to Edmonton in 1864. None was successful, but when planning new facilities in connection with its proposed City terminus, the GER took the precaution of filling this now obvious gap. This was done by projecting a line south from the Enfield branch at Edmonton, parallel to the main road, but far enough west of it to avoid major property demolitions. At Stamford Hill it crossed under the main road, running south east to Hackney along the western edge of the open land at Hackney Downs. At Hackney, a junction was made with a second new line coming

Workmen's train for Liverpool Street at Lower Edmonton Low Level in the 1880s. *Enfield Libraries*

from the N&ER at Copper Mill, the two then running together to join the ECR main line at Bethnal Green, thus forming a much more direct route from the City not only to Enfield, but to Hertford and Cambridge. A brick viaduct between Hackney Downs and Bethnal Green minimised the destruction of property in the inner area. Other features of the scheme included doubling of the original Enfield branch outwards from Lower Edmonton and links at Tottenham with the proposed Tottenham & Hampstead Junction Railway, and at Hackney with the NLR. Although the last was never built, a footway connection was established between Hackney Downs GER and Hackney NLR stations on 1st December 1885, remaining in use until the Broad Street-Poplar service ceased on the evening of 13th May 1944.

These proposals were included in the GER (Metropolitan Station & Railways) Act of 29th July 1864, but their realisation was much delayed by the GER's financial problems, work on the Hackney Downs to Lower Edmonton section not starting until early in 1870. Other associated new lines appearing in the GER (Additional Powers) Act of 19th June 1865 and never started were a branch from Tottenham to Winchmore Hill and a loop from Lower Edmonton to the N&ER at Ordnance Factory (Enfield Lock).

Although Liverpool Street was delayed by the financial situation and still unfinished, the section from Bethnal Green Junction to Stoke Newington opened on 27th May 1872. This had intermediate stations very closely spaced: at Cambridge Heath, just south of the bridge over the Regents Canal; at London Fields, serving south Hackney; Hackney Downs, immediately on the London side of the junction with the Copper Mill line; and Rectory Road, serving the southern part of Stoke Newington. At Stoke Newington the station was well-placed on the main road, at the east side, close to what was to become an important retail centre. As will be appreciated when details of the train service are studied, the section south of Hackney was soon to become very congested. Quadrupling between Hackney Downs and Bethnal Green was completed in June 1894, the new fast lines on the east side of the viaduct serving only Hackney Downs and Bethnal Green stations.

The 1872 underline bridge over West Green Road, Tottenham looking west, c.1906. The entrance to Seven Sisters station is on the far side of the bridge behind the left abutment. The message blazoned on the bridge plates reads: 'GREAT EASTERN RAILWAY/ SEVEN SISTERS STATION/ TRAINS TO THE CITY EVERY FEW MINUTES/ WEEKLY PACKETS OF TICKETS EQUAL TO 4D PER DAY.'

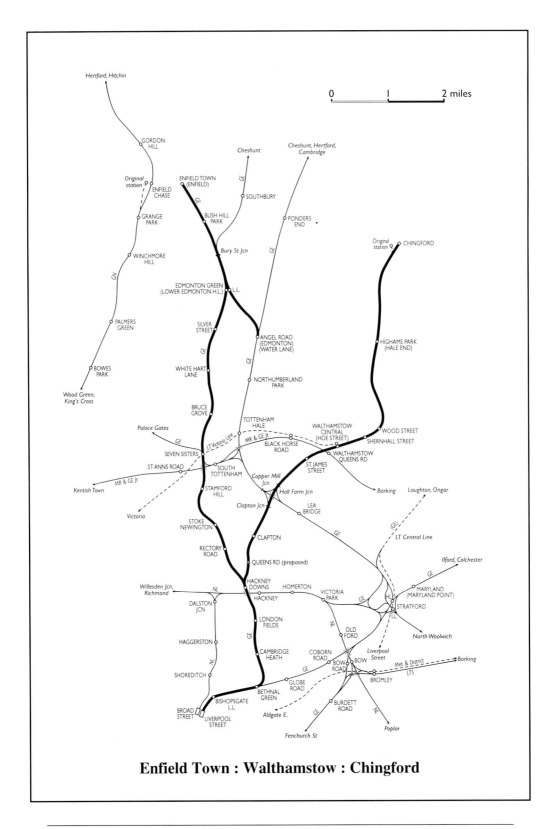

Enfield Town : Walthamstow : Chingford

The remainder of the new route to Enfield opened to Lower Edmonton on 22nd July 1872 and to Edmonton Junction on 1st August 1872, when trains ran to Enfield over a new double line. At Enfield, now only 10m 55ch from Liverpool Street, the mansion 'with its beautiful façade and tracery-work of carved brick (probably unrivalled in England)' was demolished, but the central part of the frontage went to what is now the Victoria & Albert Museum. In its place there appeared a rather dull single-storey building, two gabled sections linked by a lantern-roofed entrance hall, facing a small yard surrounded by substantial iron railings and flanked by a two-story cottage for the stationmaster. Within there was an island platform.

Intermediate stations on the northern section were: Stamford Hill, in the initially very select Amhurst Park residential district, and just west of the main road; Seven Sisters, serving south Tottenham and sited just north of the bridge over the 1868 Tottenham & Hampstead Junction Railway; Bruce Grove, almost on the main road in the centre of Tottenham; White Hart Lane, serving the still rural northern edge of Tottenham; Silver Street, in Upper Edmonton; and Lower Edmonton, west of Edmonton Green and just south of the junction with the old branch. The original Edmonton station, renamed Lower Edmonton Low Level, remained open as a terminus for a few workmen's trains to London, some of which went via Stratford, the rest via Copper Mill Junction and Hackney Downs. The single track of the original line between Lower Edmonton and Angel Road, now worked on the electric train tablet system, was also traversed by some freight trains.

GREAT EASTERN RAILWAY.

OPENING OF THE NEW LINE TO EDMONTON.

On **MONDAY, 22nd JULY, 1872**, a further portion of the New Railway extending from Stoke Newington to Edmonton will be OPENED for PASSENGER TRAFFIC, and Ordinary Trains will run between Bishopsgate, Stamford Hill, Seven Sisters, Bruce Grove, White Hart Lane, Silver Street, and Edmonton

EVERY HALF-HOUR.

DOWN.

Every Half-hour from 7.15 a.m. to 11.45 p.m. on WEEK DAYS; and on SUNDAYS from 7.45 a.m. to 10.15 a.m., and from 1.15 p.m. to 11.15 p.m., as under:—

Bishopsgate	dep. 15 & 45 min. after every Hour.	
Bethnal Green	,, 18 & 48 ,, ,, ,,	
Cambridge Heath	,, 21 & 51 ,, ,, ,,	
London Fields	,, 23 & 53 ,, ,, ,,	
Hackney Downs	,, 26 & 56 ,, ,, ,,	
Rectory Road	,, 29 & 59 ,, ,, ,,	
Stoke Newington	,, 31 & 1 ,, ,, ,,	
Stamford Hill	,, 34 & 4 ,, ,, ,,	
Seven Sisters	,, 37 & 7 ,, ,, ,,	
Bruce Grove	,, 40 & 10 ,, ,, ,,	
White Hart Lane	,, 43 & 13 ,, ,, ,,	
Silver Street	,, 46 & 16 ,, ,, ,,	
Edmonton	arr. 49 & 19 ,, ,, ,,	

UP.

Every Half-hour from 7.2 a.m. to 11.32 p.m. on WEEK DAYS; and on SUNDAYS from 7.32 a.m. to 10.32 a.m., and 12.32 p.m. to 11.2 p.m., as under:—

Edmonton	dep. 2 & 32 min. after every Hour.	
Silver Street	,, 5 & 35 ,, ,, ,,	
White Hart Lane	,, 8 & 38 ,, ,, ,,	
Bruce Grove	,, 11 & 41 ,, ,, ,,	
Seven Sisters	,, 14 & 44 ,, ,, ,,	
Stamford Hill	,, 17 & 47 ,, ,, ,,	
Stoke Newington	,, 20 & 50 ,, ,, ,,	
Rectory Road	,, 22 & 52 ,, ,, ,,	
Hackney Downs	,, 25 & 55 ,, ,, ,,	
London Fields	,, 28 & 58 ,, ,, ,,	
Cambridge Heath	,, Even Hours and Half-hours.	
Bethnal Green	,, 33 & 3 min. after every Hour.	
Bishopsgate	arr. 36 & 6 ,, ,, ,,	

TRAINS RUN BETWEEN LONDON AND STOKE NEWINGTON—
From BISHOPSGATE every Quarter of an Hour from 7.0 a.m. to 12.0 night on WEEK DAYS; and on SUNDAYS from 7.30 a.m. to 10.30 a.m., and from 1.0 p.m. to 11.30 p.m.
From STOKE NEWINGTON every Quarter of an Hour from 6.50 a.m. to 11.35 p.m. on WEEK DAYS; and on SUNDAYS from 7.35 a.m. to 10.35 a.m. and 12.50 p.m. to 11.5 p.m.

FARES:

BISHOPSGATE TO	SINGLE. 1	2	3	RETURN. 1	2	3
Bethnal Green	3d.	2d.	1d.	4d.	3d.	2d.
Cambridge Heath, London Fields	4d.	3d.	2d.	6d.	4d.	3d.
Hackney Downs, Rectory Road, Stoke Newington	6d.	4d.	3d.	8d.	6d.	4d.
Stamford Hill, Seven Sisters, Bruce Grove	7d.	5d.	4d.	10d.	7d.	5d.
	8d.	6d.	4d.	1s. 0d.	9d.	6d.
White Hart Lane	9d.	7d.	5d.	1s. 2d.	10d.	8d.
Silver Street	10d.	8d.	6d.	1s. 3d.	1s. 0d.	10d.
Edmonton	1s. 0d.	10d.	8d.	1s. 6d.	1s. 3d.	1s. 0d.

WORKMENS TRAINS leave Edmonton for Bishopsgate, on Week Days, at 5.2 and 6.2 a.m., calling at the intermediate Stations.
WORKMENS WEEKLY TICKETS AT ONE SHILLING EACH are issued by these Trains.—For particulars see Hand bills.

Bishopsgate, July, 1872. **S. SWARBRICK, General Manager.**

PRINTED AT THE COMPANY'S WORKS, STRATFORD.

Timetable and Fares poster issued for the opening of the line between Stoke Newington and Edmonton (Lower Edmonton), Monday 22nd July 1872.
Alan A Jackson

Stamford Hill station entrance building on the overline bridge in Amhurst Park, looking west, c.1904. *Commercial postcard*

Substantial and moderately spacious, but exceedingly plain, the standard pattern intermediate stations of yellow brick were enlivened only by their pretty saw-tooth platform canopies of matching length, trimmed with wooden valancing. As far out as Lower Edmonton, none was as much as a mile from its neighbour. Freight facilities were provided at Manor Road Sidings (on the Down side between Stoke Newington and Stamford Hill); at White Hart Lane (on the Up side, with a refuge siding opposite); and on the Up side at Enfield. At the turn of the century another yard was built at Lower Edmonton between the old Low Level station and Edmonton Junction.

At Seven Sisters there was no junction with the Tottenham & Hampstead Junction Railway until 1st January 1880, after which trains could run between Seven Sisters and South Tottenham stations. Although an embankment was built to form a Stamford Hill–St Ann's Road connection, this was never completed, and the Seven Sisters–St Ann's Road north western curve authorised in the GER (General Powers) Act of 1890 was not even started. A flimsy-looking bridge over the T&HJR here was an afterthought authorised in an act of 1866 in place of the level-crossing envisaged in the 1864 act, which was just as well, in view of the intensive traffic eventually generated on both lines.

In releasing the GER from any obligation to rehouse the large number of unfortunates displaced by the construction of the Liverpool Street terminus and the new lines serving it, Parliament had inserted in the 1864 act a requirement for a 2d return train to be run daily for workmen between Lower Edmonton and London. There were no great colonies of horny-handed sons of toil beyond Bethnal Green; Hackney Downs still had a rural air, breezy Stamford Hill only a few large tree-shrouded villas in huge gardens, while Tottenham and Edmonton were semi-rural and largely middle class. Writing four years after the opening of the new Enfield line, James Thorne remarked that Tottenham had 'many outlying farms and much of the land still under the plough . . . flowers are grown for the London market'. Edmonton was noted for its market gardens at this time. Not surprisingly there was some resistance in these districts to the proposed workmen's trains; in 1869 the local newspaper suggested they would only encourage a large body of people who could not fail to add to poverty and mortality and bring an increase in local rates.

But the GER did not renege. On the contrary, from the very first day of operation the statutory requirement was interpreted generously and there were two 2d return trains from the temporary terminus at Stoke Newington to Bishopsgate, leaving at 05.20 and 06.20, calling at all stations. When the remainder of the line was opened these were extended to start from Enfield, which was operationally more convenient than Lower Edmonton. Until 1920 this provided the remarkable bargain of a daily return run of 21½ miles for 2d (under 1p).

The introduction of the full train service to Enfield was delayed by the inadequacy of the London terminal arrangements. Although the opening of the new approach tracks as far as Bishopsgate Low Level station on 4th November 1872 helped a little, it was not possible to add more trains until the West Side suburban platforms of Liverpool Street were ready on 2nd February 1874. Within two years from then the Enfield line had a basic frequency of four trains an hour (two of these reversing at White Hart Lane) with strengthening in peak hours. Supplementing the statutory 2d returns were fares only slightly more costly for early morning users and the frequent cheap service from closely-spaced stations rapidly changed the whole character of the district as far north as Lower Edmonton. Whilst elevated Stamford Hill retained its middle class aspect, the market gardens and little bourgeois demesnes either side of the main road through Tottenham and Edmonton were quickly covered with thousands of low-rent houses set in serried ranks. Twelve years after the opening of the line, the GER general manager, William Birt, described what happened to the Royal Commission on the Housing of the Working Class:

> . . . speculative builders went down into the neighbourhood and, as a consequence, each good house was one after another pulled down, and the district is given up entirely, I may say, now to the working man. I lived down there myself and I waited until most of my neighbours had gone; and then, at last, I was obliged to go.

Census returns for Edmonton serve to illustrate the rate of growth. From 14,000 when the line opened, the population increased 70 per cent by 1881 to 23,463 and by 1901 had reached almost 62,000. As we have noted, the workmen's 2d trains were not the only ones offering cheap travel, but 2d trains were increased to three daily in 1883, to five in 1890 and by 1898 there were seven, all this a simple response to overcrowding rather than benevolence on the part of the GER. The 2d trains all ran before 07.00, return journeys being possible by any train after 16.00 or noon on Saturdays. In an attempt to get some more revenue, the GER had twelve 3d trains running by 1900 between 07.00 and 07.30 followed by half-fare trains arriving at Liverpool Street between 07.30 and 08.00, the latter used by 'the better class of workmen, warehousemen, shopmen, and not a few poorly-paid clerks'. After 08.00 ordinary fares applied, and as there were no third-class season tickets, the second-class accommodation was generously provided.

Rectory Road, looking to Enfield Town, Up train entering. The newspaper placards at the bookstall indicate a date of 1904. This station exhibits the almost standardised platform canopies used on the Enfield Town and Chingford branches. *Commercial postcard*

At the turn of the century these Enfield line trains were hauled by 0–6–0T of a design dating back to 1886 and nicknamed 'Jubilee Jumpers' or 'Buck Jumpers'. There were also a few Holden 0–4–4T dating from 1898–1901 to be seen on Enfield trains. All coaches were four-wheelers and the workmen's trains usually consisted of 15 compartment coaches offering a total of 852 seats. First class was upholstered in blue cloth, second in red, but third-class passengers got hard sprung seats covered with American cloth, backed by partitions open above luggage rack level. This last feature was much exploited by itinerant musicians playing mouth organs, concertinas, or merely giving voice. In an atmosphere of cheap shag and inadequately washed bodies, men of strong character also attempted to conduct hymn singing and prayers over the tops of the partitions, although these were by no means universally appreciated. A letter in the *Tottenham Herald* in June 1894 complained of 'religious fanatics' on the 06.19 from Seven Sisters to Liverpool Street.

For some years the GER alleged that the 2d trains were covering their working expenses, but this was evidently no longer the case in 1904 when the general manager, J. F. S. Gooday, gave figures to the Royal Commission on London Traffic. He also refuted the suggestion that the GER gained something from the freight traffic that the ingress of population had brought with it. As Acworth had noted some years earlier, the Enfield line was certainly not a cheap one to work with steam traction; the 45lb of coal gobbled up each mile by the engines on the 46-minute all-stations run compared with the 30lb or so per mile necessary to keep them moving at around 40mph for a similar non-stop journey.

Although he had no particular responsibility for the situation he described, having been general manager only since 1899, Gooday expressed some concern at the social effects of his company's policy, remarking at one point to the Royal Commission, apparently in all seriousness, that 'the aggregation of so vast a population of one class in one locality seems likely to be productive of social danger'. But this was England, and the red belt created by his blue engines was to prove no more of a social danger than the upper class concentration in Mayfair.

In any case, the territory served was not exclusively plebeian. Enfield had always supplied a leavening of first- and second-class traffic. In the late 1860s and early 1870s a subscription list 'for the attention of gentlemen passengers' was pinned-up in a newsagent's shop next to the station each Christmas to the benefit of drivers and firemen. Efforts were made to develop this lucrative middle-class business in the late 1870s. The 700-acre Bush Hill Park Estate west of the line just south of the terminus was sold in 1872 to the Bush Hill Park Land Company for conversion to a villa colony for which a station in the GER's best suburban style was opened on 1st November 1880. In the following decade housing of the terrace type appeared east of the new station, some 600 cottages existing by 1892, mostly of five-room design. An *Evening News* advertisement of July 1901 mentions 'cottages for working men at Bush Hill Park (2d or 3d return), 6s 9d rent.' A second booking office was opened in 1894 to serve this artisan area, Bush Hill Park becoming one of those places where the railway formed a social boundary, with both classes using the same station, but rarely meeting because they passed through it at quite different times of the day. Even in the 1950s, Bush Hill Park appeared better cared-for than most other stations on the line, with plenty of clean seats on the platforms and well-kept gardens.

Bush Hill Park, GER, Down side entrance block and stationmaster's house, c.1905.

Main entrance block and station-master's house, Enfield Town station c.1908.
Commercial postcard

On the remnant of the original Enfield branch, workmen's trains continued to be the only passenger service. Loadings were sufficient to justify an additional platform at Lower Edmonton in 1899, built alongside the original but south of the level crossing. A small booking office here issued weekly or fortnightly blocks of the special workmen's tickets, in numbers restricted to the accommodation available – rather better treatment than today's air passengers get. There were five trains each way between here and Stratford in 1908, another five to Liverpool Street, one via Stratford. Seven years later, there were two fast 2d trains and two fast 3d trains via Angel Road and Stratford or via Hackney Downs. Patronage fell sharply after 1919 as local employment opportunities increased and competition from road services consolidated; the remaining single morning train disappeared in 1931 but one train ran to the Low Level on Monday to Friday evenings until 8th September 1939. Occasional passenger diversions and freights continued to use the line until close of traffic on 5th December 1964.

Passenger traffic decline was also evident on the newer line. During 1905 electric trams replaced the former horse and steam service along the main road parallel to the railway between Stamford Hill and Edmonton and two years later the LCC's electric cars were plying from Stamford Hill to the City near Liverpool Street station. With motor buses joining in from about 1910, the road services drained away much of the railway's off-peak traffic. There was also some erosion at rush hours, especially after the introduction of through tramcar service to the West End and City via Finsbury Park in August 1912 and from Edmonton to the City via Stamford Hill in June 1920. Evidence of the effect of electric tramcar competition was the reduction in basic service to half-hourly 12-coach trains (quarter-hourly inwards from Seven Sisters) by 1907. Peak hour working remained intensive, and in that year the line was carrying ten trains (usually of 17 coaches) between 07.00 and 08.00, six from Enfield, one from Bush Hill Park, one from Cheshunt (via the Churchbury Loop and Lower Edmonton High Level) and two from Palace Gates (via Seven Sisters). Some of these ran semi-fast reducing the 40-minutes all-stations timing for the 10¾ miles Enfield run to 27 minutes. At this period, Enfield Town, with its locomotive depot and carriage sidings, had a daily provision of 56 Up trains and 63 Down, whilst Seven Sisters had 97 Up and 98 Down. The traffic day extended from 04.00 to 01.00. Seven Sisters, the busy junction with the Palace Gates branch, was given an additional entrance and ticket office in Birstall Road, for passengers from the west side in 1906, no doubt another response to tramway competition. This remained open for issue of workmen's tickets until 6th July 1942.

Stoke Newington station main entrance building in High Street, c.1908. No fewer than seven railway staff are posed by the doorway and there are two horse cabs in the yard. *Commercial postcard*

It was the existence of parallel electric tramway facilities which enabled the GER, in response to government pressure, to close the inner area stations London Fields and Cambridge Heath to effect manpower economies in World War 1. Somewhat surprisingly, and unlike similarly-placed stations in south London, both reopened in 1919 and remain in use today, though since 1992 at peak hours only.

Tramcars and motor buses, if slower, were certainly no less comfortable than the severely spartan third-class accommodation provided by the GER. Although a train of bogie carriages had been tried out in 1900, four-wheelers were the rule until after the end of World War 1. In them, the workmen's ticket-holders and third-class passengers sat five-a-side on hard seats covered with a shiny dirt-resisting cloth. Second-class buttocks enjoyed sprung cushions, whilst first-class passengers got more leg room and sat only four each side. In 1899 James Holden, the locomotive, carriage and wagon superintendent, introduced six-a-side four-wheelers and later rebuilt the older carriages to this width, thus providing a 21 per cent increase in carrying capacity at low cost. A prototype train composed of four-wheeler bogies mounted on bogie frames was produced in 1913 for suburban traffic.

These changes were in part designed to meet the problem of increasingly concentrated rush hours, which were causing severe overcrowding on some trains. Consideration was given to electrification of suburban routes to improve the service and build-up off-peak traffic, but the capital required for this frightened the GER board. Instead the company adopted a scheme put forward by its superintendent of operations, Frederick V Russell, which for one-fortieth the cost of electrification promised a 75 per cent increase in inward rush-hour trains and a 50 per cent increase in evening departures from Liverpool Street. This was to be achieved by making certain minor alterations, principally in terminal and track arrangements at Liverpool Street and Bethnal Green. At Enfield Town, where the platforms had been lengthened in 1903/05 to take more coaches, a third platform was added on the east side. Introduced on 12th July 1920 and soon known by its newspaper title, the 'Jazz Service' gave 12 trains an hour in the evening peak as far as Seven Sisters and nine thence to Enfield Town. Off-peak, weekdays and Sundays there were four-coach trains every ten minutes. Standard rush-hour trains were composed of 16 gas-lit four-wheelers offering 848 seats, still mostly hauled by the 'Buck Jumpers'. Stopping patterns, indicated by coloured headcodes, were varied.

Good as it was, the Jazz did little to revive declining patronage. Competition from road transport was only one of the factors now operating. Industry had established itself in the Lea Valley before 1914, and encouraged by the construction of new

---

The Enfield Town Branches

Bruce Grove station, looking east to High Road, Tottenham, c.1910. Note the deliberate attempt to bring the architecture of the signal box into keeping with the other station buildings.
Commercial postcard

motor roads and the post-war boom in road transport, factories proliferated in the 1920s and 1930s, creating a whole new pattern of journeys to work by bus, tram, bicycle or on foot. After the 1926 general strike, the slack-hours timetable was thinned out and loadings on the Enfield line suffered further losses after the opening of the Piccadilly Line tube from Finsbury Park to Arnos Grove on 19th September 1932. As this offered a much more attractive service to Kings Cross and the West End, its stations at Manor House, Turnpike Lane and Wood Green were soon winning many former Enfield line passengers from the district between Stamford Hill and White Hart Lane, some coming on buses and trams, others walking across.

Like its predecessor, the LNER found difficulty in obtaining capital for electrification and was disheartened when the Underground was favoured for the assistance that various governments devised to counter mass unemployment. Small improvements were made. From 1926 all trains were hauled by the more powerful N7 0–6–2T introduced by the GER in 1915, and beginning in 1925, the old GER four-wheel 'cattle trucks' gave way to Nigel Gresley's articulated bogie sets, known as 'quint-arts', two per train of ten separate bodies. Ten-minute interval departures from each terminus in the slack hours were maintained until 1939, though by then the practice of running alternate trains fast between Liverpool Street and Stoke Newington with a connection at Seven Sisters for Palace Gates had disappeared. Sunday trains were only half-hourly by 1939. During 1934–5 all manual signals except those at Seven Sisters were replaced by three- and four-aspect Westinghouse Brake & Signal Co. colour-lights controlled by track circuits. Together with the improved performance given by the N7s, this reduced the all-stations time from end to end to 34 minutes. In the early 1940s, with the war closing City offices and workshops, the frequency was widened to half-hourly (ten minutes at rush hours), whilst train lengths were reduced respectively to five and six coaches.

A visit to the line in 1955 found it little changed from the railway so familiar to the author in schooldays twenty years before. At Liverpool Street, platforms 1 and 2 were buffered with N7s, Westinghouse pumps busily panting. There too were the familiar Gresley carriages, as drably uninviting as ever, each compartment with its dusty, severely straight-backed, hard-padded benches and limited knee-room. First-class compartments were still available, though the fares had been withdrawn on 6th October 1941 (second had gone at the end of 1937). This weekday mid-morning train carried an average of half-a-dozen passengers and although its station stops of some 20 seconds were almost up to Southern Electric standard, the ambling jogtrot between stations was another matter. At White Hart Lane, the porter disobligingly refused a proffered ticket, instructing that it should be left at the street level passimeter booth which had been installed here and at some other stations on the line by the LNER in the early 1930s to economise in staff.

White Hart Lane still had the wide exit doors which the GER had installed for the crowds attracted to home matches at the nearby Tottenham Hotspur football ground. At its height, this traffic had brought as many as 10,000 to the station on trains running at intervals of rather less than five minutes, the closest possible headway whilst this line was operated with steam. A returning crowd of this size would be cleared in little over half an hour. After electrification, the football business remained at a high level for some years and in 1961, in the period just before the start of a home match, trains would be arriving every four minutes from Liverpool Street, with others coming in from Hertford East and Bishops Stortford via the Churchbury Loop. A new entrance for returning spectators was added in 1962. At this time a railway officer informed the author that to limit damage and hooliganism, it was the policy to load the new electric trains so tightly at White Hart Lane and Liverpool Street that the football supporters were unable to move their arms and legs during the brief journey to and from the match.

Bush Hill Park on 13th September 1958, looking to London, with a Liverpool Street–Enfield Town train entering, hauled by N7 0-6-2T 69667. *Alan A Jackson*

A word should be said about the decline and extinction of the freight facilities, never an important feature of this line. The private sidings on the Up side just north of Seven Sisters station, installed for a lager brewery and ice factory in 1882 and later used by the Tottenham Council, had fallen out of use by the late 1940s. Closures elsewhere began with Enfield Town yard, whose traffic was diverted to Enfield Chase and Churchbury from 14th September 1959 ahead of electrification. The site, east of the passenger platforms, was then leased for the erection of a seven-storey office block with shops at ground level, which was completed in 1964 as Bovril House. Bush Hill Park Sidings, north of the station on the Down side, were put out of use in May 1964 and the depots at Manor Road, Stoke Newington and Lower Edmonton (high and low level) were shut the following 7th December. General freight facilities were withdrawn from White Hart Lane in January 1968 but the yard remained open for solid fuel traffic to merchants' staithes until 2nd July 1977.

When it seemed almost too late (and indeed in a sense it was) the Enfield Town service was at long last electrified; resignalling in preparation for this had been completed in May 1960. Fed from a 6.25kV 50-cycle ac overhead wire system (converted to 25kV in 1980/83) the new trains appeared in public service on 14th November 1960, working to the steam timetable. The full electric service was started on the 21st of that month but such was the complexity and intensity of the technical troubles encountered with the new stock that it was not possible to achieve the planned timetable until 18th June 1962. From that date a ten-minute slack hour frequency was implemented, with all-stations trains reaching Enfield in only 29 min from Liverpool Street, semi-fasts in 25 min. Between 17.00 and 18.00 there were six trains to Enfield, three more calling only at Lower Edmonton on their way to Hertford East and Bishops Stortford over the reopened Churchbury (Southbury) line, which we shall consider later. A similarly generous frequency applied in the Up direction in the morning peak.

The ten-minute slack hour service proved incapable of generating additional traffic in what was a fully-built up area where most short journeys were easily and conveniently achieved by excellent bus services. Few people wished to travel to or towards Liverpool Street during the day. The headway was therefore widened out to 20 min from June 1965. When the Victoria line tube railway opened through south Tottenham to Walthamstow on 1st September 1968 it very quickly attracted passengers from stations to the north of Seven Sisters, where a convenient interchange was available from 1st December 1968. On that date the original West Green Road entrance of Seven Sisters station was replaced by a new combined BR and LT ticket hall in Seven Sisters Road, reached from the south ends of the Enfield line platforms by making use of part of the old Birstall Road subway. Fast trains on the Bishops Stortford and Hertford East services were then stopped at Seven Sisters and passengers quickly adopted this new and more direct route to Kings Cross and the West End. The Seven Sisters interchange was a major factor in the scaling-down of peak hours services which followed its opening.

The Enfield line's inner London stations presented a particular problem; their peak hours traffic fell away steeply in the early 1970s and the off-peak patronage was low. Sunday trains had been withdrawn from Cambridge Heath, London Fields and Rectory Road in June 1965 and the decline continued through the 1970s. Stamford Hill was closed on Sundays from October 1981. From 5th October 1981 calls at stations south of the Seven Sisters (apart from Hackney Downs) were restricted to the half hourly all-stations Southbury line services (Enfield Town Trains ran semi-fast, stopping at Hackney Downs, Seven Sisters and then all stations). A 1983 survey of Hackney residents in the line's catchment area showed that a high proportion were unaware of the destinations served or the frequency of the Enfield line services.

In an experiment funded by the GLC and marketed as the 'Jazz Service' (again) from 3rd October 1983, the frequency at all stations to Enfield was raised to four an hour between 10.00 and 16.00 (19.00 on Saturdays). With the Southbury line services, this gave a ten minute service at these times as far as Lower Edmonton. A brave try, it failed miserably, having little or no effect on the low level of off-peak traffic south of Seven Sisters. After over 2½ years, reality was recognised in the timetable applicable from 12th May 1986, which gave Enfield Town only two trains an hour off peak, four an hour to stations between Bethnal Green and Lower Edmonton; Sunday services became hourly. 1991 saw an attempt to close the Enfield line stations entirely on Sundays, a proposal quickly withdrawn in the face of strong protests. Business at the inner area stations continued to be disappointing and despite expensive rebuilding in 1985–86, Cambridge Heath and London Fields were closed except at peak hours from 11th May 1992.

It would be an exaggeration to say that electrification changed the line's image overnight; it was too ingrained into the north London urban scene for that. The change in traction brought with it only two major new structures; a quite presentable new station for Enfield Town, officially opened on 25th April 1958 and a power-operated signal box with a conspicuous sun baffle, erected at the north end of platforms 2 and 3 at Hackney Downs in 1959. For some years the electric trains ran over a line which retained much of its GER atmosphere. Between trains, the closely-spaced stations, with their soot-stained brickwork, their platforms gloomy under rotting saw-tooth canopies and their cavernous stairways and underline subways, still seemed to be haunted by the ghosts of corduroy-trousered artisans and consumptive clerks clutching their cheap tickets.

BR eventually found the money to initiate a modest programme of station modernisation in 1974–80, making a start at Stoke Newington and Stamford Hill. A second phase of rebuilding, which saw the disappearance of a great deal of the remaining GER structures, followed in 1981–86, launched with substantial assistance from central and local government funds. The two most notable rebuildings were at Seven Sisters and Rectory Road; details of these and the other works are given in the list overleaf, which also records the quite remarkable number of contemporary fires. No fewer than six of the 12 intermediate stations were seriously damaged in this way, between December 1972 and July 1984, often overnight, in suspicious circumstances. At Silver Street a fire made a second rebuilding necessary. Lack of supervision also ensured that almost as soon as new construction work was completed it was defaced by the wall-scrawling fraternity and vandalised in other ways.

A journey in the summer of 1996 found punctual four-car trains well-filled north of Seven Sisters with Edmonton Green particularly busy in early afternoon. Little activity was however evident at Silver Street, Bruce Grove, Stamford Hill, Stoke Newington, Bethnal Green and Rectory Road, where the costly GLC reconstruction of 1985 exhibited sad signs of persistent vandalism. Inwards from Edmonton Green, the railway environment was depressing, with tracks weedgrown, accumulations of uncleared litter between platforms and unwelcoming and tatty street entrances often failing to give prominence to their purpose. Station premises appeared neglected and unwelcoming, in strong contrast to those of London Transport in similar inner suburban locations. The time may be approaching when a drastic reappraisal would be appropriate for a line which has since the late 1950s absorbed such a very large amount of capital investment without much tangible return either to railway revenue or urban renewal. One possible development could be a thinning out of the stations, which are spaced far too close together for modern needs.

Enfield Town Line: Station Fires and Reconstruction
(Since c. 1960 all platforms have been extended to take 8-car electric trains).

Bethnal Green: Rebuilt 1985–86, platforms reduced to two (on north side); all GER structures at rail level removed. Crude metal covers over stairwells, simple pitch-roofed waiting pavilion on Down platform.

Cambridge Heath: Gutted by fire 27th July 1984: GER canopies destroyed, station closed until September 1984. Closed again, for rebuilding, 17th February – 16th March 1986. New street front-age and ticket hall. All platform buildings demolished and small shelters substituted.

London Fields: Gutted by fire 13th November 1981, closed and neglected. Rebuilt 1985–86, all GER structures demolished, new waiting shelters; entrance, subway and staircases refurbished. Reopened 25th September 1986.

Hackney Downs: New street entrance hall and ticket office by BR architect Sandy Boal, funded by Urban Aid Programme and GLC grant, 1981. New waiting rooms, platform awnings and train indicators funded from same sources 1982–85. GER canopies preserved on Down Enfield platform.

Rectory Road: Closed by fire early morning 9th December 1972, reopened 17th January 1973. Completely rebuilt 1984–85. Street level building (opened 1st May 1985) in brick under a tiled roof; BR double arrow logo in brickwork. New footbridge, small tiled-roof, glass and brick pavilion shelters on each platform; all GER structures demolished. Three quarters of the cost met under Urban Aid Programme.

Stoke Newington: Ticket hall and office modernised. New and much smaller canopies along walls of cutting replacing GER structures. Completed 1974–75.

Stamford Hill: New ticket office in refurbished street level building 1979. Platform improvements with new shelters 1984 with GLC funds. All GER structures demolished.

Seven Sisters: Rebuilt 1979–80. GER platform structures demolished, new heated waiting rooms with lavatories at each end of Down platform, new 300ft awning, stairs to Seven Sisters Road covered over. From May 1985 escalator connection and retiled subway from combined BR/LT ticket hall to Down platform, funded by GLC.

Bruce Grove: Rebuilt 1979. Down side canopies and structures demolished, roofing over stairs removed. GER canopies retained on Up side. Ticket hall in arch under the line rebuilt.

White Hart Lane: Gated exit/entrance on Down side for football crowds, 1962. Station gutted by fire c. 1977. Ticket hall, entrance and ticket office rebuilt on Up side. New steel staircases (unroofed) on both sides. Work completed 1978–79. GER canopies remain on both platforms but valancing cut away.

Silver Street: New ticket hall and entrance building; GER structures on Down platform demolished, work completed 1979. Gutted by fire 12th June 1984. Ticket hall and entrance again rebuilt 1985–86. GER canopies remain on Up side.

Lower Edmonton/Edmonton Green: New flat-roofed ticket hall and entrance building on Up side facing Edmonton Green shopping centre. GER buildings and entrance in Church Street (Down side) closed. GER platform canopies remain on both platforms. Work completed 1977–78. Renamed Edmonton Green 28th September 1992.

Bush Hill Park: Ticket hall and entrance on Down side gutted by fire August 1981. Rebuilt in brick with flat roof 1982. GER canopy retained on Up side.

Enfield Town: Rebuilt 1957–58 by BR architect H H Powell. Flat-roofed structure in brownish-red facing bricks across end of line with large entrance hall lit by clerestory, mechanised ticket office, parcels office, cycle store, ladies' waiting room and men's lavatories. Concourse area re-roofed with asbestos cement decking. Platforms 1 & 2 (island) given a central canopy 418ft long, glazed for 6ft back from edges each side. Side platform 3 unaltered, no shelters. All GER structures removed (except signal box).

The Churchbury or Southbury Loop (map page 365)

Well before the arrival of railways in London, the Hertford road along the Lea Valley showed signs of ribbon development, a growth nurtured by the business of the road, adjacent market gardens supplying the needs of London and the popularity of the valley for holiday trips and retirement homes. As early as 1864, the GER, considering a second line up the western side of the valley near London might bear some fruit, included in its Additional Powers Act of 1865 an 'Ordnance Factory Railway' which was to leave the Bethnal Green-Edmonton line authorised the previous year at Lower Edmonton, proceed along the west side of the Hertford road and cross it to make a junction with the 1840 Northern & Eastern line near Ordnance Factory station (now Enfield Lock). Perhaps the promoters also hoped that the 1850s enlargement of the Royal Small Arms Factory would lead to further developments, but industrial expansion in the Lea valley was thirty years away, and the powers for the loop were wisely abandoned in an act of 1869. Proposals of the 1870s to link the GNR and GER Enfield branches to the Lea Valley line also came to nothing.

Noting that its direct line from Enfield to Liverpool Street with its cheap trains and frequent service had worked wondrously to enlarge Tottenham and Edmonton, the board reconsidered the position at the beginning of the 1880s, reviving the old dream in an act of 1882, which provided for a 5m 7.5ch line from north of Lower Edmonton to Cheshunt on the Cambridge line. With stations much closer to the main Hertford road than those on the older line, this loop was expected to open up a first- and second-class ticket-holder district which seemed ready for building development. Construction was however deferred until 1889/90 and it was not until 1st October 1891 that passenger and freight operation could start. There were 17 Down passenger workings and 18 Up, with five each way on Sundays, the service running only between White Hart Lane on the Enfield line and Cheshunt, calling at all intermediate stations and taking about 23 minutes.

Construction through the comparatively level land of the valley was not costly in terms of engineering works but the GER chose to spend lavishly on stations designed for heavy suburban traffic. Substantially-built in stone, red brick and tiles, with distinctly urban elevations, their long, well-canopied platforms looked quite out of place amid the market gardens and brickfields. Each had a full set of offices, including 'Waiting Rooms, First-Class, Ladies', a facility unlikely to be much in demand in what was a distinctly artisan and working-class area, although it was perhaps indicative of the company's hopes for the district. Features displayed by these pleasing buildings were ridge tiles, ogee gables, chimney buttresses, false pediments, tile-hung gables and windows with segmented arches with glazing bars reminiscent of Bedford Park. They were clearly intended to blend in with the large middle-class villas that they were expected to serve.

From Bury Street Junction, 60ch north of Lower Edmonton, named after a hamlet west of the line, the double track veered north-east, soon reaching a station called Churchbury on the south side of the bridge carrying the Ponders End-Enfield road over the railway and about a quarter-mile west of Ponders End High Street. Its main building, sitting over the line, was the most impressive of the three intermediate stations, presumably because as the nearest to London, it was expected to reap the greatest measure of suburban business. Covered staircases led down from it to platforms at each side of the line, well-canopied for much of their length. On the Up side at the London end, the small goods yard had ample room for expansion.

There were only a few cottages between the station and the Hertford road, whilst on the west side there was nothing but two brick works, using the brick earth that lay on the gravel terrace to make yellow stock bricks for the houses at Tottenham, Edmonton and other places in north London. The southernmost of this pair was to be served by a long siding off the Down line.

Keeping fairly close to the west side of the valley road, the line entered Forty Hill station at the point of transition from a low embankment to a very shallow cutting. The platforms stood on the north side of the bridge over a narrow country road called Turkey Street which connected Enfield Wash with Forty Hill, a northern outpost of Enfield town. Covered staircases led to a tiled subway under the line and the main building, a square pavilion on the Up side in the approach road to the goods yard at the country end of the station. A small entrance on the Down side was close to the half-dozen cottages and inn that constituted the hamlet called Turkey Street. Another handful of workers' cottages built in the 1850s was all that existed between the east side of the station and the main road a quarter of a mile away.

From Forty Hill, the general direction was north-east towards Waltham Cross, but to avoid property demolition in this already large village it was necessary to go to its extreme northern end before crossing above the Hertford road to reach the Lea valley line. At this point, on the west side of the bridge over the main road, were platforms on a curve built over arches in blue engineering brick which carried the tracks to the elaborate plate girder bridge with its brick arch abutments and six supporting iron columns. Entrances were made on each side of the line, the main one on the south side with a covered staircase leading to the solid red brick main building on the Up side. As there was already a station named Waltham Cross on the old line, half a mile to the south-east, this one was called Theobalds Grove after the former royal palace and park and the eighteenth century mansion about ¾-mile west of the railway. The goods yard, at the London end of the station on ground level, was reached by a steeply-graded 15ch single track from the Up road. From the road bridge the embankment dwindled down on to the marshes bringing the tracks to Cheshunt Junction about ¾-mile south of Cheshunt station, where a bay platform was provided on the Down side, 5m 15ch from Bury Street Junction.

No improvements were made, or were necessary in the first ten years apart from

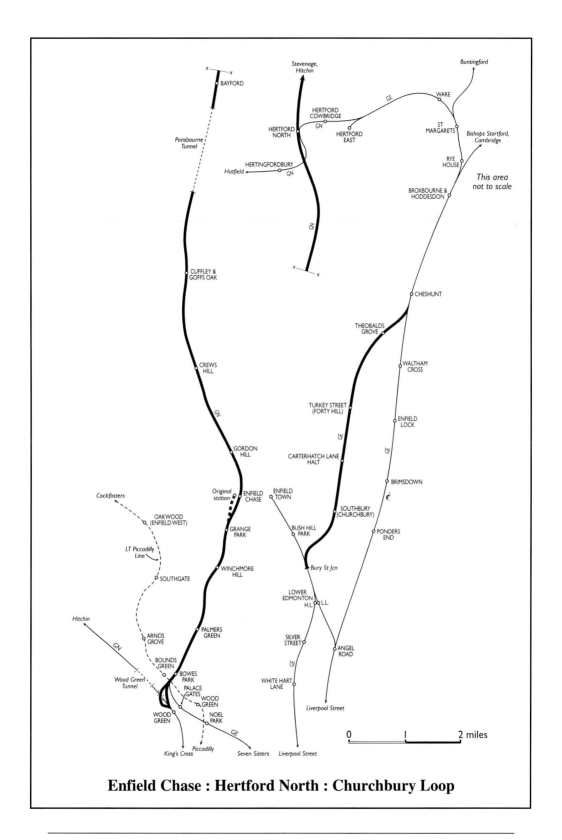

Enfield Chase : Hertford North : Churchbury Loop

the addition of one or two trains. Doubtless the unenterprising character of the service, with the requirement to change to reach London on all but a few morning trains did much to discourage such traffic potential as existed, but the fact was that at this time the district served lacked residential attractions and was too far from town to entice season-ticket holders. Builders showed no inclination to buy up the nurseries, market gardens and brickfields along the line except in penny packets along the main road.

In 1907 there were 21 Down journeys and 23 Up, all but three morning rush-hour workings running between Cheshunt and White Hart Lane. Sunday service remained at five each way between those stations. Why White Hart Lane? Brian Perren has suggested it was chosen because it was the maximum distance the single train used for the service could work up the Liverpool Street line, given the constraints of an hourly interval and adequate running-round time at termini. Freight business was possibly slightly more remunerative than passenger; the brickworks and nurseries needed coal and coke, the nurseries and market gardens took in fertilisers, and all three provided some outward traffic. Through freights were seen on the line as well as the daily pick-up working.

Low passenger revenue was seriously eroded after the opening of the Metropolitan Electric Tramways from Lower Edmonton to Enfield Lock (Freezywater) on 11th December 1907 and onwards to Waltham Cross centre on 17th April 1908. Not only did the electric cars provide a cheaper and much more frequent service for the local journeys that had made up most of the new line's business; they offered the great boon of accessibility, passing as they did through the very centre of the then thinly built-up area each side of the main road. Almost overnight the GER receipts fell to half what they had been, which in any case was not much. Forty Hill and Churchbury, within a quarter-mile of the tramway, fared the worst, with Theobalds Grove, half a mile north of the tram terminus slightly less affected. After pausing, as if they were unable to comprehend what had happened, the GER decided upon complete abandonment of the passenger service, the last trains running on 30th September 1909. Reluctance to act promptly was understandable, for this was something quite new for the GER, and was the first passenger closure in the county of Middlesex. There was something of a minor sensation over it, with Winston Churchill, then President of the Board of Trade, called upon to answer a question in the Commons. He gave the now familiar reply that this was the undertaking's business, no concern of central government, passing on to Branch, the local MP, a copy of a letter from the GER general manager. This explained that the district had not developed as expected, its principal occupations were market gardening and nurseries, with most of the population locally employed, but the electric trams were to blame, for they had abstracted such traffic as existed.

Freight working continued, no doubt just covering costs, though much of it, equally well handled by the Lea valley line yards, showed no net gain to the GER. A brighter era briefly dawned when from 1915 the Lea valley became a centre of war industries. This activity was principally sited around Angel Road, Edmonton, at the Royal Gunpowder and Royal Small Arms Factories at Waltham Abbey and Enfield Lock, and at the Ponders End Shell Works. Production requirements were such that the factories could not subsist on local 'walking' labour, and although most of the workforce came in by tram or the existing train services from the London end of the Lea valley, the GER was called upon by the government to re-open the loop for passengers. This it did on 1st March 1915, using A. J. Hill's new auto-train, the first on its system. After trials on the Southend-Shenfield line in 1913, a Y65/F7 2-4-2T had been fitted with a compressed-air control system for auto-working, with subsequent trials on the Mildenhall and Ramsey branches; the accommodation consisted of two clerestory-roofed coaches, a first- and third-class composite, and a third-class driving trailer. It was this unit, providing 76 third-class and nine first-class seats, which was moved to the Churchbury loop. The conductor issued tickets on the train, tramcar-style. A second and similar train arrived on the loop in December 1915 when the service was built up from an initial 15 journeys each way between Cheshunt and Lower Edmonton (where passengers changed for Angel Road) to 18, six of the latter going on to White Hart Lane. For this service, which operated on weekdays only, a timber halt was opened at Carterhatch Lane, 69ch north of Churchbury, on 12th June 1916. Wartime traffic was not substantial, declining rapidly with the rundown of the war factories, so the GER withdrew the service again after the last train on 30th June 1919. The halt was demolished, the auto-units sent south to work the Palace Gates shuttle. Towards the end, their place had sometimes been taken by normal trains hauled by 0-6-0T or 0-6-2T.

Its main interests concentrated on long-distance passenger and freight, the GER's successor, the LNER, unlike its southern neighbour, lacked incentive for developing London suburban business. Thus when the area served by the loop was opened-up by the completion of the Great Cambridge Arterial Road (now the A10) from Tottenham to Wormley in 1924, the board remained impervious to suggestions that because the new housing the GER had looked for seemed likely to arrive at last the railway should be re-opened. And the houses came; with their ready-made drainage, services, and all-weather access for delivery of materials, combined with considerable publicity value, the London arterial roads completed as unemployment relief in the 1920s proved a strong magnet for speculative builders, and the Great Cambridge Road was no exception. If further encouragement were needed, this was given by the extension of a 12-minute motor bus service along the new road as far as Southbury Road in April 1934, and on to Turkey Street two years later. By this time, row after row of small houses had appeared to line the new road, soon followed by estates filling in much of the area crossed by the railway between the Cambridge Road and the old Hertford road. Close behind came industrial development, attracted by easy road transport access and low land costs in an era when the economic situation favoured industrial growth in the London region. Some extra business came to the goods yards, but the LNER remained inflexible on restoration of passenger service. Its attitude was not wholly inexplicable; any addition to the 58 trains an hour passing Hackney Downs in the peak was unthinkable without electrification or other major works for which capital could not be raised without government assistance, and that assistance tended to favour the Underground until around 1935. Nor did the LNER see much popularity to be gained from decanting passengers from the loop at Lower Edmonton or White Hart Lane to join already crowded Enfield Town trains. Nevertheless one feels that had this been south of the Thames, the loop, with hundreds of new houses and many new factories closing in on it, especially at the London end, would not have been left to stagnate.

After World War 1, coal and goods yards were still served daily by freight trains working in both directions over the Down line, the other track being used for wagon storage. Most of the traffic was in solid fuels and building materials but through the

1930s and 1940s some of the factories made use of the rail service. In 1927, when there were three through Down freights in the early hours and three local workings on Tuesdays to Fridays, the signal boxes at Bury Street Junction, Churchbury and Theobalds Grove stations were open from 03.00 to 19.00, 07.00 to 15.00, and 05.00 to 13.00 respectively. Forty Hill box was switched out, to be opened only for shunting operations without use of the block instruments. Subsequently Bury Street box was closed, the points then being worked from a two-lever ground frame controlled from Edmonton Junction box. Churchbury station box also closed, as did Forty Hill, which was demolished. After these economies, the signalman for Theobalds Grove box travelled with the Down pick-up goods. Some of the GER signals were replaced by LNER upper-quadrants. but the GER track on its ash and gravel ballast was left undisturbed until 1950 apart from essential replacements.

Leased out for non-railway purposes, the three stations remained more or less intact. Forty Hill and Theobalds Grove were used as domestic accommodation, occasionally visited by press photographers in the silly season when the occupants were persuaded to take tea on the tracks or to string washing between the platforms. Churchbury was for many years a joinery works, its platform canopies boarded in. Later it acted as a store for a builders' merchant, whose stock of wc pans, piping, tiles and other goods could be seen stacked under the canopies.

When there were interruptions between Cheshunt and Clapton, the loop provided a valuable diversionary route. Examples of such use occurred in February 1919 when melting snow submerged the Lea valley line at Tottenham to a depth of 3ft; in January 1928, when a small underline bridge at Angel Road collapsed after a cloudburst; in October 1929 after a collision at Tottenham; and in 1940 and 1944 when the Lea valley route was blocked by enemy action. The 1928 diversions lasted for several days and it is recorded that on this occasion if on no other, the three stations were temporarily re-opened, (no doubt at some inconvenience to the tenants), their names chalked on blackboards, and with hurricane lamp illumination after dark. Double-line working was usually the rule during these diversions, after the empty wagons had been dragged out. In 1947 double-line running was restored permanently.

The British Transport Commission's Railway Modernisation Plan of December 1954 included a promise that train services from Liverpool Street to Hertford East and Bishops Stortford would be electrified, and it soon became clear that this was to include resumption of passenger services over the loop, now to be known as the 'Southbury Line', following consultations between the BTC and the local authorities in which it had been agreed that Churchbury and Forty Hill stations would be respectively renamed Southbury and Turkey Street after the roads they served. Whilst the decision to re-open was a recognition of further development in the area since 1945 and of the strength of local pressures for rail service, maintained for at least a decade, a major factor evident in the upgrading of track and signalling to main line status was the part the loop could play in increasing the flexibility of Eastern Region operations in the London area.

Work on rebuilding the right of way to main line standards started in the early summer of 1956 when the six-year-old track and concrete sleepers were uprooted, together with all the ballast. Bridges were rebuilt or strengthened and junctions realigned to allow 50mph running instead of the previous 20mph. When this work was finished, the overall speed limit was raised to 60mph from 40mph. At first it was thought the stations might be rebuilt, but financial pressures and the discovery

Unit 296 on Up special train at Theobald's Grove station on 20th November 1960, the day before reopening for public service. *Alan A Jackson*

that their substantial construction remained sound led to a decision simply to refurbish, bringing platforms to standard height, and fitting-out with cold cathode lighting which exhibited the station name along the platform. At Southbury the old canopies were repaired and the original buildings thoroughly cleaned up. Turkey Street lost its canopies and platform buildings, receiving instead only two small brick shelters. Theobalds Grove retained all its buildings although the canopies were reduced to less than one car's length each side. A pleasant touch was the appointment to stationmaster here of the son of the first booking clerk. Three- and four-aspect searchlight signalling with continuous track circuiting replaced the old double-line block system. Finally the line was wired for 6.25kV* overhead traction supply (25kV from a point north of Theobalds Grove). Some through diesel-hauled trains worked over the loop non-stop from 2nd November 1959.

The three stations opened for enquiries on 14th November 1960, an official ceremony followed on 16th November, and public service, using 19 four-car sets of new multiple-unit stock, started on 21st November. The eight-car trains which included composite first- and second-class trailers, operated every 30 minutes every day of the week between Liverpool Street and Broxbourne, where they divided for Hertford East and Bishops Stortford. Liverpool Street to Lower Edmonton was covered non-stop in 15 minutes, half the time taken by the all-stations steam service, with calls at every station beyond. Extra trains at peak hours provided approximately 20-minute intervals. As noted earlier, the planned level of service was not reached for some time owing to serious technical difficulties with the new rolling stock.

With the opening of the Victoria Tube line in 1968 an additional stop was made by the Southbury Loop trains to allow interchange at Seven Sisters. Electrification of the Lea Valley route between Cheshunt and Clapton on 5th May 1969 brought further change; the normal pattern of service then became Lea Valley trains via Tottenham Hale between Liverpool Street and Hertford East and Bishops Stortford–Liverpool Street electrics via the Southbury Loop with interchange connections between the two at Broxbourne.

* Uprated to 25kV in 1983–84

Freight traffic faded away during the first decade of the loop's renaissance. Theobalds Grove yard, closed to all except coal on 3rd January 1966, saw its last train at the end of the following May and was leased to a scrap metal merchant. Turkey Street depot was shut from 1st June the same year, but Southbury lasted until December 1970. As commuter traffic at the three stations was not substantial there was no immediate pressure to convert these yards to car parks. At first it seemed that the very long period of passenger closure, combined with the continuing growth in local employment opportunities in the post war years was making it very difficult to build up traffic for the electric service. Southbury and Turkey Street each saw only about 500 joining trains each day in 1974 but at Theobalds Grove the figure was around 1,500. Thanks to a considerable amount of new housing in its catchment area, this was also the busiest commuter station, with season ticket holders increasing from 456 in 1961 to 706 in 1974. At the other two stations, the number of season ticket holders, about 250 at each, showed little or no growth in the same period.

As elsewhere, vandalism and security measures were principal agents in stimulating station works. In 1978 Theobalds Grove was given a modernised ticket office and ticket hall, and new entrance doors protected by a canopy. Further work here in 1987–88 involved demolition of some GER structures and erection of new waiting shelters and awnings. In the same period Turkey Street's heavily-vandalised GER street level building was demolished and replaced with more secure accommodation built into an arch next to the subway; new waiting shelters were erected on the platforms here and at Southbury.

To one who knew this line during its long period of closure a journey over it in an electric train at first assumed an almost dreamlike quality. It was difficult to realise that the romantic sight of a deserted railway which so stirred childhood imagination had really been breathed back to life. That feeling has now gone, as has that strange half rural, half suburban, almost pioneer atmosphere that could be sensed around the stations; such open land as now remains is very largely taken up with sterile playing fields and motor roads, including, across the northern end of this railway, the ineluctable, all-enclosing, all-roaring M25.

Chingford Station, c. 1903, main entrance block and stationmaster's house Down Side, and cab yard, facing Station Road. *Chingford Historical Society Collection*

The Chingford Branch   (map page 350)

The Chingford line's history shares much with that of its Enfield sister, for it was another of the feeders for the new Liverpool Street terminus, destined to receive cheap trains which were to lead to social development of very similar pattern.

Although Chingford was to remain a very small and unimportant place for another 70 years, Walthamstow already had some 5,000 inhabitants by the middle of the nineteenth century. Like Tottenham, Edmonton and Enfield, it was a place of rural retreat for London businessmen; it too depended on the Northern & Eastern Railway for access to the City, a horse bus connecting with all trains at Lea Bridge station.

The 1860s saw the first stirrings of organised suburban development in the area. This was essentially directed at the middle-class market, so that when Parliament insisted on a workmen's train obligation for proposed GER lines through Waltham-stow, James Higham, one of the developers, rose up in anger at the threat of plebeian invasion. So anxious was he that the right sort of people came to Walthamstow that in conjunction with other developers, he promoted his own line, alongside the GER scheme of 1864. But it was the GER which got parliamentary approval in that year for lines which were part of the new suburban system associated with their City terminus at Liverpool Street. The first of these, in a separate act, was a branch from Leyton (Loughton Branch Junction) to a point three quarters of a mile south of High Beach, a holiday resort in the Epping Forest, passing through east Waltham-stow and Chingford Green. This was intended to carry good class residential traffic as well as the excursionists to and from the Forest. As mentioned earlier, the main act – the GER (Metropolitan Station and Railway) Act, 1864 – included a line from Bethnal Green to Hackney Downs, where one section continued north to Lower

Edmonton and another forked north east to join the N&ER at Copper Mill Junction. This act also contained powers to extend the latter line across the N&ER through Walthamstow to a junction with the proposed High Beach branch. It was in this main act that Parliament included the obligation to run one 2d return workmen's train daily between Walthamstow and the City as some recompense for the destruction of working-class housing in inner London. Thus the GER had two proposed lines through the area, each likely to nurture a different class of housing development.

The ambitious plans of the youthful GER were soon overshadowed by a difficult financial situation, which was to lead to the appointment of a receiver in 1867. An embankment had been built from west Walthamstow down into the Lea valley, but work ceased when the GER found itself unable to pay the contractors. In 1868 it was necessary to obtain an extension of time for the 1864 lines. Houses were now appearing in some quantity and Higham had been hammering at the GER board-room door, even offering to muster cash to secure a railway as far as Walthamstow. All this no doubt influenced Parliament, for in granting the extension of time, it insisted the GER build a branch into Walthamstow from its Lea valley line.

Money was somehow scraped together for this, a single track over the alignment used by the contractors for the embankment mentioned earlier, and trains began to run between Lea Bridge station and a temporary terminus called Shern Hall Street on 26th April 1870. Situated in the centre of the chain of small villages that formed Walthamstow, this station had an earth bank platform on the south side of the railway in the cutting between the 60yd Nag's Head tunnel and Shern Hall Street itself. Two other stations were provided in Walthamstow. The west end was served by a single wooden platform on the south side just east of the bridge over St James's Street, which gave it its name; at Hoe Street, just half-a-mile from the terminus, there were substantial buildings on a platform on the south side, facing open fields. Hoe Street station was destined to become the main traffic centre of the new suburb, and there were already some small houses under construction immediately south of it.

Trains worked the branch hourly, connecting with the Bishopsgate via Stratford service on the main line. This lasted for just over two years, during which time the GER managed to complete an important part of its 1864 proposals. From 1st August 1872 it was possible to work a half-hourly service between Shern Hall Street and Bishopsgate over the newly-completed double track between Hall Farm Junction and Hackney Downs. This had one intermediate station, opened on 1st July 1872 following the completion of the Hackney Downs–Copper Mill Junction line on 22nd June. Clapton station, on the east side of the Upper Clapton Road, served what was then the north-eastern edge of continuously built-up London. It had no goods yard until 2nd July 1900 when one was opened on the Up side, south of the bridge over the river Lea. Between Clapton and Hackney Downs stations were two short tunnels, the southerly one passing under the Downs. During the 1890s, against an intermediate signal box called Queen's Road between the tunnels, the GER erected a platform, but never completed the proposed station.

Powers to abandon the planned branch from Leyton to High Beach Green were obtained in 1869 subject to the presentation in the following session of a bill to extend from Shern Hall Street over the northern end of the High Beach Green alignment as far as Chingford Green. This was duly sanctioned in 1870, together

London's Local Railways

with the Lea Bridge–St James's Street spur, which had been built in advance of parliamentary authority. At Wood Street, Walthamstow, the extension deviated to the east of the 1864 alignment, probably for reasons connected with land purchase. Passenger trains served the Chingford terminus in Bull Lane (now Kings Road) over a single track opened on 17th November 1873. As a further attempt was to be made in the next parliamentary session to obtain an extension to High Beach, the building on the single platform was a temporary wooden structure and locomotives slaked their thirst at an old farm pond.

From the opening day, trains ran from Chingford to Bishopsgate (and from 2nd November 1874 to the new Liverpool Street station) via Hackney Downs over a newly-doubled line between Shern Hall Street and Hall Farm Junction. With the extension, Shern Hall Street platform was closed, to be replaced by a permanent station at Wood Street serving the eastern part of Walthamstow. This had substantial buildings in yellow stock brick and two platforms from which stairs led down to a street-level booking hall. Hale End (now Highams Park), a second intermediate station between here and Chingford, was a less solid structure.

On 2nd September 1878, the branch reached its final form with the opening of a permanent terminus at Chingford, some distance north of the original. At the very edge of the Forest, 10m 37ch from Liverpool Street, it possessed a large station house on the Down side, and two main platforms with bays at their outer edges; the track leading to it was the only piece of a High Beach extension sought in 1874 which parliament had allowed. As was sometimes the case with such parliamentary pruning, the original plans were followed and the centre was a through station, its two roads going on for some 75yd beyond the platforms to be used as an engine dock and watering point pending further progress northwards. An extension bill deposited in 1882 for a line via Sewardstone to a point a quarter of a mile north of High Beach was badly timed. On 6th May 1882, Queen Victoria came to Chingford in the GWR royal train (hauled by the GER's first blue locomotive, a modest 0–4–4T) to declare the Forest open to the public. In the excitement, opposition to the desecration of the Forest by a railway was easily aroused, killing the extension then and for all time.

Although the temporary station at Bull Lane, Chingford was shut, it was not demolished until the early 1950s. Its approach tracks served for many years to store wagons moving in and out of the goods yard built in 1878 between the old and new stations.

Until the turn of the century, pleasure traffic formed the main business at Chingford and a buffet, directed to its needs, survived on the Down side until 1972. Residential trade was apparent by 1910 when £375 semi-detached houses were ready on the Forest Estate, east of the station, and an entrance was opened on that side to Beresford Road.

During the last decades of the nineteenth century very strong housing growth in Walthamstow required expansion and improvement of the somewhat sparse accommodation installed in 1870 and 1873. Pressure first became apparent at St James's Street, the nearest point to London. A Down platform had been erected here with the doubling of the line in 1873, and it received a waiting room two years later. From 27th May 1890 a second ticket office and entrance were in use at the eastern end of the Up platform, a facility which survived (although latterly with very restricted opening hours) until October 1967.

Hoe Street also acquired a Down platform in the 1873 doubling but there was no booking office or entrance on that side until 1897, a belated response to the northward growth of the suburb. The original small goods yard on the Down side was virtually replaced by a larger one opened south of the line on 15th July 1880. A footpath across this linked the GER platforms with the adjacent Walthamstow station of the Midland's Tottenham & Forest Gate line after its opening from South Tottenham to Woodgrange Park on 9th July 1894. That line, with its services to Moorgate and East Ham, passed below the Chingford branch west of Hoe Street station. With the completion of the Walthamstow Council electric power station off the inappropriately-named Sylvan Road in 1901, coal was delivered to its private sidings via Hoe Street yard. Immediately north of Wood Street station, carriage sidings were laid out together with a small engine shed, facilities later expanded to meet the needs of an increased train service. From 20th April 1893 a goods and coal depot was available on the Up side south of Wood Street station, its business consisting largely of domestic fuels and building materials.

As on the Enfield line, the crowds presenting themselves for the 2d trains soon obliged the GER to provide more accommodation. The number of such trains increased from three in 1883 to six in 1890, seven in 1897, eight in 1899 and finally ten in 1904, all reaching Bishopsgate Low Level or Liverpool Street between 05.00 and 07.00. Many of their patrons, obliged to save every penny they could, preferred to use them even if they had to wait for their place of employment to open at 08.30 or even 09.00. Despite pleas about the consequent distress to young girls, especially in winter, the GER resisted all pressures to extend the 2d concession to a later hour, but it did start half-fare (4d return) trains in 1885 which arrived in London between 07.30 and 08.00. This rate was also available from midnight to 05.00 on the all-night service started between Wood Street and Liverpool Street on 21st June 1897. Unique in London, these half-hourly trains, which gave the line a continuous service from very early Monday morning until very late Saturday night, brought many printers, newspaper workers and other night toilers to live in the west Walthamstow area. Reduced to hourly as a wartime economy from 15th January 1917, the trains continued to run until 1966, when for the first time since 1897 there was a prolonged interval at night.

The half-fare trains, marginally profitable provided they were full, were especially popular in Walthamstow, patronage so increasing around the turn of the century that the GER general manager could tell the 1904 Royal Commission on London Traffic 'Walthamstow is largely the home of the half-fare traveller and at this place the half-fare forms the principal traffic'. At this time there were nine half-fare trains, offering a total of 7,400 seats, but the last two were severely overcrowded. By 1920 the loadings on these trains were more than double those of the 2d trains, with as many as 20 to 30 passengers crammed into third-class compartments meant to seat 12. In May that year the general manager admitted loadings in excess of 1,460 on evening peak trains to Chingford, over four-fifths in the third-class accommodation. Probably in an endeavour to recover its losses on some of the sub-standard fare trains, the GER set Chingford line third-class fares season ticket rates at an abnormally high level. Most rush-hour trains had at least eight of their 15 cars allocated to first- and second-class passengers; the latter cars, always subject to invasion by third-class ticket holders, were patronised by the higher-paid clerks, civil servants and junior managers who boarded at Highams Park and Wood Street.

As far as Wood Street frequency had reached half-hourly by early in 1874, but at peak periods there were trains every 15 minutes. On the country section beyond, a two-hourly off-peak and hourly peak service sufficed, strengthened at summer weekends and holiday times. By 1902 there were seven trains an hour to and from the three Walthamstow stations in the rush hours and although the basic half-hourly frequency in the off peak was unchanged, it had been extended to Chingford to meet the tentative emergence of residential traffic there and at Highams Park. Soon after this, the rush-hour service was built up to 12 an hour in the morning (07.00 to 08.00), ten from Wood Street, and between 18.00 and 20.00 there were 15 Down trains, five of them terminating at Wood Street. An all day slack-hour interval of 15 minutes applied from July 1909. Most rush-hour trains consisted of 15 gaslit four-wheelers offering a total of 768 seats, but there were also a few 16- and 17-car sets, some all thirds. Motive power was normally a 'Buck Jumper' 0–6–0T.

As at Tottenham and Edmonton, the combination of cheap and frequent trains from closely-spaced stations led speculators to erect low-rent housing in quantity, which was filled almost as soon as it was ready. East of the Lea valley, each side of the line as far as Wood Street, there was by 1901 a mass of tightly-packed streets half a mile or more deep. From just over 11,000 inhabitants when the railway first opened, Walthamstow's population grew by 95 per cent in the subsequent decade and by 113 per cent in the 1880s. The figure had reached 95,131 in 1901 with almost 50 per cent of the working adults in the UDC area travelling by train to workplaces in inner London. To an even greater degree than at Tottenham and Edmonton, the colonisers were the upper strata of the working class: junior clerks, artisans, uniformed public servants, shopworkers and warehousemen. Not until around 1910 was large-scale industry established here.

One of the most prominent developers in the 1890–1914 period was Thomas C. T. Warner, who told a parliamentary committee in 1901 that he had covered some 300 acres with houses and half-houses (maisonettes) let at rents of 6s 6d and 7s 0d (32½p and 35p) a week, his 2,184 weekly tenants mostly 'artisans and clerks working in London'. Giving evidence to another parliamentary committee two years later, Walthamstow UDC bemoaned the fact that of 18,600 houses in its area, 11,654 were let at rents up to 9s 6d (47½p) and 3,421 up to 11s 6d (57½p), none producing enough rate income to cover the cost of the local authority's services.

Not everyone worked in London. Until electric tramcars rendered it redundant there was some patronage for a Walthamstow to Stratford service. This was started on 7th June 1880 at two-hourly intervals, with some trains going through to Chingford for pleasure seekers, but with the arrival of the electric trams, midday trains were cut back to Wood Street in 1910 and the service ceased on 3rd October 1914. This was not the end of passenger working over the Lea Bridge–St James's Street spur, as from 1914 there were summer services between North Woolwich and Chingford and between Lea Bridge and Chingford.

Another cross-town facility was from Chingford or Wood Street to Highgate Road from 1st August 1885, using the curve opened in that year between Hall Farm Junction and Copper Mill Junction. At first there were some 12 trains daily each way weekdays and Sundays in summer; to encourage pleasure traffic, ordinary returns were issued at a fraction over the single fare. These trains were extended on 4th June 1888 to a single platform at Gospel Oak, from which passengers could transfer to the North London Railway or go out to Parliament Hill Fields. Patronage,

Liverpool Street train leaving Highams Park station c. 1905 watched by some young trainspotters.
Commercial postcard

never very great except at summer weekends and public holidays, fell-off badly with the intensive bus and tram competition from 1910 and there were only two trains a day each way by the end of 1918; the service ran for the last time on Sunday 5th September 1926. After that until August 1939 trains ran between Gospel Oak and Chingford only at Easter, Whitsun and August Bank Holidays, nor were they restored after World War 2.

For some years the little wooden station at Hale End was the quietest on the Chingford line, although it gained some pleasure traffic after Highams Park and its lake were added to the public area of Epping Forest in 1891. To mark this, the station, which had received a second platform in 1878, was renamed Highams Park (Hale End) on 1st October 1894. During the 1890s some terraced housing appeared south and west of the station, whilst west of the line a distinctly urban encroachment was the arrival in 1898 of the British Xylonite Company from Homerton. This had a fairly neutral effect on passenger flow, but was to provide some business for the goods yard on the Down side. With the construction of more houses, traffic at the station slowly increased and in 1900 it was rebuilt in more substantial form. Further development followed east of the line, so that by 1908 some 5,000 new residents were established around the station. In 1922 J. F. Gairns described Highams Park as 'a busy station for residential traffic of a good class'. Here again the social layering of the branch showed similarities with the Enfield line.

The overcrowding of the Liverpool Street trains which followed the increasing concentration of peak-hour traffic in the 1910s and early 1920s was no less evident on the Chingford branch, making the line a worthy candidate for the 1920 'Jazz Service' improvements. To accommodate the additional trains, Chingford's platforms were lengthened and a new signal box and four more carriage sidings were

Clapton main entrance block, on the overline bridge in Upper Clapton Road, looking north, c. 1905. *Commercial postcard*

erected there. The Wood Street carriage sidings and locomotive shed were expanded and additional signalling appeared at various points along the line. Track circuiting was installed at Chingford station, also between Wood Street and St James's Street. From 12th July 1920 the new arrangements allowed rush-hour trains to run at approximately five-minute intervals, alternate workings terminating at Wood Street where, to facilitate quick turnarounds, an Up side siding was converted into the Up running line, the original line becoming a terminal road with spurs to both Up and Down tracks. Many Wood Street trains now ran non-stop between St James's Street and Liverpool Street. To save time at the terminals, locomotives were coaled from baskets. There were 848 seats in the rush-hour trains of 16 four-wheelers, but slack-hour service was given by 318-seat trains (six four-wheelers) running every ten minutes instead of 15. Stopping at all seven stations, the Jazz reached Chingford in 33 minutes from Liverpool Street, or 29 when running semi-fast.

Whilst the Chingford branch was not exposed to the parallel electric tramcar and motorbus competition which afflicted the Enfield line, there was some decline in patronage from the early 1920s. This could be attributed to increasing employment opportunities in the Lea valley industrial zone and the growth of commercial institutions in and around Walthamstow. It was to some extent counterbalanced by steady growth in middle-class commuter traffic associated with new private enterprise housing at Chingford, South Chingford and Highams Park designed to attract the inner London white-collar worker. Population at Chingford rose from 9,482 in 1921 to 22,076 ten years later. For its new season-ticket holders, the LNER rebuilt the booking hall at Chingford and provided a Down side exit at Highams Park in 1934.

As former users of the inner stations went by bicycle, bus or tram or on foot to the new factories, industrial troubles in the 1920s forced the reduction of the slack-hour service to 20-minute intervals on several occasions, causing many casual travellers to desert the railway for bus or tram when making local journeys in Walthamstow and Chingford.

Nor was the peak-hour Jazz a popular success. It was a poor substitute for electrification; the combination of ageing, uncomfortable four-wheel coaches and the inability of the overloaded 0-6-0T and 0-4-4T to maintain time brought many complaints. Much of this dissatisfaction was dissipated by the arrival of the pugnacious N7 0-6-2T (hauling virtually all trains by 1928) and new Gresley 'quint-art' sets. The latter, marshalled into ten-car (872-seat) trains ousted the GER 'cattle trucks' between 1927 and 1931 and were to last until electrification 30 years later. Their second-class seats became thirds after the end of 1937; first-class tickets were withdrawn in October 1941. Apart from the troubles mentioned, off-peak services between the wars were at ten-minute intervals, alternate trains fast between Clapton and Liverpool Street.

Another improvement made by the LNER was the replacement of the 1891 Sykes' lock-and-block manual signalling with Westinghouse Brake & Signal Co. three-aspect colour lights and track circuits. Hackney Downs to Clapton Junction was so converted on 24th February 1935, the rest on 30th January 1938, worked from the boxes at Hackney Downs, Clapton Junction and Chingford, instead of the six formerly used. The existing mechanical frames in the retained boxes were fitted with electric locks and circuit controllers.

Wartime conditions reduced off-peak service to half-hourly but rush-hour loading still required about nine trains an hour inwards in the 1950s, by which time a 20-minute slack-hour frequency was operating. In this last decade of steam traction a semi-fast train stopping only at four stations took 26½ minutes for the 10½-mile run from Chingford to Liverpool Street; those trains calling at all nine stations required 34½ minutes. Five-car sets, half the length of rush hour trains, were the rule in the off peak. As the ageing 'quint-arts' and N7 locomotives were suffering from lower standards of maintenance, service deteriorated, sorely trying the patience of the regular passengers. A town meeting at Chingford in 1955 heard protests about dirty carriages and mechanical breakdowns, the MP for Epping suggesting that the branch had 'the most decrepit engines and the most ramshackle rolling stock imaginable'. Following this up in the House of Commons, he described how one train had been held up two hours when a door fell off at Clapton whilst another stopped in the Bishopsgate tunnel for half an hour, its passengers gradually becoming smoke-dried. He complained that despite increasing population since 1939, Chingford had only 84 trains a day compared with 125 then, and 50 on Sundays compared with 68.

Business was still quite buoyant in the mid 1950s, when Highams Park was dealing with around 1,000 tons of freight and 5,000 parcels monthly. Ticket issues each month at this station totalled some 50,000 with another 1,500 seasons. But with the return of road transport to a peacetime scale, freight traffic fell off. Most was inwards, coal, coke, timber, building materials and general merchandise, but in the early days there had been some milk taken out from the farms at Highams Park and Chingford. Yard closures started under the Beeching regime with the withdrawal of coal facilities at Hoe Street, the yard there closing finally in November 1964

One of 'the most decrepit engines', so described by the MP for Epping in 1955, N7 69604 on an Up train from Chingford entering Liverpool Street on 23rd September 1958. *R C Riley*

although coal traffic to the power station continued until December 1967. No goods facilities were available at Highams Park and Chingford from 4th October 1965. At Clapton, freight traffic ceased from 7th December 1964, while Wood Street yard closed from 6th May 1968.

Unusually for a London line, the Chingford branch saw pleasure traffic both inwards and outwards for many years; until the more prosperous 1930s, Chingford was a popular resort for north Londoners at summer weekends and Bank Holidays, demanding extra trains to carry the crowds out to the Forest. As late as 1920 up to 100,000 used the station on a Bank Holiday and 46 additional staff were on duty to handle the traffic. Summer excursion fares from the branch stations to east coast resorts were introduced by the GER in 1890, and the LNER ran special seaside trains in the summer months, a practice continued by BR. There were also special through workings, to Lea Bridge for the motorcycle speedway events, and to Northumberland Park for matches at Tottenham Hotspur football ground. These last used the Copper Mill curve, continuing until that was rather suddenly taken up in 1960.

In the BR Modernisation Plan of 1955 the branch was listed for electrification. Work began early in the following year to prepare for operation from overhead lines carrying 6.25kV ac at 50c/s (this was to be uprated to 25kV from 20th November 1983). Three-car multiple-unit sets, seating 272 made up the trains which entered service on 14th November 1960 but as on the Enfield line, these were soon in trouble from technical problems and needed to be helped out by steam traction until the end of 1961 (steam continued even longer for freight trains, not giving way entirely to diesel locos until well into 1962). After a greatly prolonged breaking-in period, the technical problems with electric traction were finally overcome, full electric service starting on 18th June 1962 with a ten minute basic frequency, supplemented at peak hours. Between 08.00 and 10.00, 18 trains from the branch arrived at Liverpool Street and there was a similar number of return workings in the evening peak. Semi-fasts from Liverpool Street reached Chingford in 22 min, all-stations trains taking two minutes longer. It soon became obvious that this provision was absurdly over generous; as on the Enfield line, traffic patterns had long since changed and inwards from Walthamstow Central much had been permanently lost to road transport. In 1965 the basic frequency was widened out to 20 min and the long-established all-night trains were withdrawn. Although the curve to Lea Bridge had been wired for electric working it was never so used, and the rails were taken up in 1967.

Some minor changes were made with electrification. At Chingford, the two main platforms were linked by a path across the outer ends, sealing off the 'extension' and allowing the subway to be closed. The eastern platform face (No. 4) was not electrified and fell out of use. Wood Street Sidings were rearranged. Hoe Street station, renamed Walthamstow Central on 6th May 1968, underwent partial re-building to accommodate the terminal traffic of the Victoria line tube which was opened to here on 1st September 1968. It had at first been intended to bring the tube to the surface at the London side of Wood Street, making that station the terminus, but this had been dropped as an economy. At Walthamstow Central, a combined LT/BR ticket hall on the Down side, with covered access to a new bus station, was soon much busier than the original Up side entrance. Reached by stairs from the platforms, the top landing of the escalators serving the tube station was beneath the BR tracks.

In 1974–75 St James's Street and Wood Street stations were rebuilt in glass reinforced plastics, brick and aluminium, the result seeming to be designed more to deter vandals than attract the eye. Waiting rooms, staff accommodation and ticket offices were all replaced; platform shelters took the form of light steel-framed canopies and the ample GER awnings were swept away. By the 1990s, the main entrance hall at St James's Street, long unstaffed, bore a wounded, sad look. Chingford received a new ticket hall and ticket office under a suspended ceiling in 1978, all within the existing building. At Highams Park a new ticket office and enlarged Up side waiting room were provided in 1979, again using the GER structure. Clapton benefited from injections of finance by the GLC and other local authority sources; in 1982–83 a modern glass-fronted ticket office, a new station bridge from the ticket hall to the Up platform and a rebuilt and enlarged waiting room were all completed without entirely destroying the GER atmosphere. Some of the latter also remained on the platforms at Walthamstow Central. The carriage sidings at Wood Street, declared redundant, were taken up and the site was sold for development in 1986.

As on the Enfield Town line, the tube service was soon diverting much traffic from stations inwards from the interchange point. This caused BR peak hour frequencies to be reduced, beginning in May 1974. Weaving through the drab workaday districts it had helped to create to reach lower middle class suburbia at Highams Park and Chingford on the edge of Epping Forest, the branch now presents difficult problems for transport planners. Its outer section remains busy, but the loadings between Liverpool Street and Walthamstow Central are light for exactly the same reasons as those on the Enfield Town line south of Seven Sisters. This decline, and schemes for a new south west/north east tube railway could eventually lead to a significant reshaping of the present infrastructure and transport mode on both routes.

The level crossing and station at Woodford, where the original building was on the Down side but a substantial ticket office and additional entrance has by this time been provided on the Up side. Looking south to London, c. 1910. *Commercial postcard*

The Loughton, Epping & Ongar Branch (map page 386)

We now enter GER suburban territory offering strong contrasts to that just considered. Except at its two innermost stations, the line to Loughton and beyond served a favoured residential area along the eastern edges of Epping Forest, ending in what was until quite recent times a country branch of the quietest kind. Writing in 1920, George Potter commented that although much of the route passed through residential districts, '. . . these are well wooded, and the traveller does not have the feeling that all the available land has been completely swallowed up by the erection of modern houses'. First- and second-class business was encouraged and more first-class seasons were sold on this than on any other GER suburban service. Often as many as one-third of the seats on the trains were first class. No workmen's tickets were ever issued by the GER beyond Leytonstone. This shaped the nature of the development just as much as the cheap fare policy on the Enfield and Chingford lines. Returning to Potter, we find him expressing the view that among London's many suburban lines, few could take 'a higher place for prettiness of scenery and outlook as seen from the carriage windows'; once Loughton was passed, he viewed only 'pastures and cornfields interspersed with woods and coppices . . . there is beauty indeed in Essex'. Some of this survives; there are not many other places where one can see sheep and pheasants scattering over fields at the approach of a tube train.

An early scheme for a line to Epping from the London & Blackwall Railway and the ECR at Ilford came to nothing. Subsequent proposals for the area were at least partly inspired by hopes of residential development. The Woodford Railway, promoted in 1852 to run from a junction with the NLR at Victoria Park to Woodford had on its board Edward Warner, a prominent landowner who had plans drawn up for building over his estates at Woodford and Hale End. Coming to Parliament alongside an ECR bill for a Woodford and Loughton branch, the independent scheme lost out, but the ECR Act of 1853 stipulated that the Loughton branch could not be opened until 'an additional line of rails' had been laid between the ECR and Woolwich Railway junction at Stratford and the junction at Bow between the ECR and the London & Blackwall Railway.

Leaving the old N&ER about half a mile north of Stratford, the ECR Loughton branch ran north-east between the small villages of Leyton and Leytonstone, reaching the Roding valley at Wanstead. Turning north and keeping to the west side of the valley, it terminated on the south side of the High Street in the centre of Loughton, then a village of 1,500 people on the eastern fringe of the Forest, 12 railway miles from Fenchurch Street. Cheaply-built, the double track followed ground contours fairly closely, rising steadily to a modest summit at Buckhurst Hill, crossing four public roads on the level in four miles south of that station. A 1 in 110 descent from the summit to Loughton was the steepest gradient on the line. Indicative of the expectations was the generous provision of stations, although when the line opened on 22nd August 1856 there was little sign of pending changes in the rural and semi-rural nature of the territory traversed. No goods facilities appear to have been available initially, nor was there a telegraph until 1858.

Low Leyton station, just north of the junction, at the southern tip of the village, was to be renamed Leyton on 27th November 1867. It was closely followed by Leytonstone, conveniently adjacent to the centre of that settlement. The new manifestation of the Devil was well kept at bay here, a section of the 1853 act stipulating that no trains were to stop at stations within the parish of St Mary Leyton between the Sunday church hours of 10.30 – 13.00.

About half a mile north of Leytonstone, the tracks passed beneath two roads in a cut-and-cover tunnel, the only one on the branch. Snaresbrook & Wanstead the next station, was about midway between those places, but Woodford, a straggling village extending for about three miles along the Stratford to Loughton road, got two stations. The first, called George Lane, Woodford served the extreme southern end, whilst Woodford station was just east of Woodford Green and Woodford Wells. Buckhurst Hill, the last of the intermediate stations, was about a mile east of the small community either side of the Loughton road. At the terminus of the 11m 39ch branch in Loughton High Road, (Lopping Hall) a goods yard had appeared by 1858 and at the extreme end of the line, fed by three tracks, was a small engine turntable. Soon after the opening, at the suggestion of Horatio Love, the ECR chairman, a field on the east side of the line here was let to an operator to provide 'a place of refreshment and amusement for the excursionists'.

Most of the level-crossings were sited at stations. The platforms at Buckhurst Hill and Leytonstone were staggered either side of the crossing gates so that trains halted with their locomotives at the roadway's edge. Woodford also had staggered platforms, the Up south of the Down, both south of the crossing.

Opposite top: Eagle Lane level crossing and signal box, between Snaresbrook and George Lane (South Woodford) stations, c. 1905. The train is on a Down service. *Commercial postcard*

Opposite centre: George Lane (now South Woodford) station and level crossing, looking south east, c. 1905. In this predominantly middle class area, a weatherproof footbridge was considered a justifiable extravagance. *Commercial postcard*

Opposite bottom: Loughton, looking north, 1911. The original approach to the 1856 terminus is seen on the left, in use as carriage sidings. The 1865 extension to Epping and Ongar diverges to the right through the re-sited Loughton station completed in that year.

Epping station and signal box, looking to Ongar, c. 1910. *Lens of Sutton*

Epping, a small agricultural and market town of just over 2,000 inhabitants, stood along the Newmarket road clear of the northern tip of the Forest, remote from metropolitan influence. About five miles to the east, on the Dunmow road was the similar but smaller town of Chipping Ongar. Both places were objectives of an independently promoted scheme of 1858 for an 11¼-mile extension beyond Loughton. The Epping Railways Bill, which contained the stern provision that signals were to be erected 'to prevent Danger at the point of Junction with the Eastern Counties Railway', received royal assent in 1859. Three years later the little company was absorbed by the ECR as had been foreseen in the act, but construction had to await the birth of the Great Eastern Railway. That company opened a single line from Loughton through Epping to Ongar on 24th April 1865.

Theydon Bois station and goods yard, looking towards Epping, 1911. *NRM*

To avoid the higher ground, the extension left the older line about a quarter-mile south of the terminus, swerving east through a new two-platform Loughton station very close to the junction. With the opening of the Ongar line the old terminus was closed and the approaches were used to extend the goods yard and carriage sidings; excursion sidings were also later erected on the site for the considerable holiday traffic to the Forest and such trains seem to have terminated here (Chingford station was not yet open). Following the west side of the Roding valley, the extension ran north east through the remotely-situated station of Chigwell Road which was a good mile north of Chigwell village. This passing place, which originally had only one platform, on the Down side, was quiet enough to justify closure in the manpower shortage of World War 1 and was still lit by oil lamps after the end of World War 2. Just beyond it, the line turned into the uplands north of the Roding valley, a long stretch of 1 in 86 bringing it to Theydon (Theydon Bois from 1st December 1865), a station serving the several communities bearing that name either side of the line. In 1885 this station was rebuilt with a passing loop and given an Up platform. After a short traverse of the valley of a stream feeding the Roding, the track started the long climb at 1 in 78 to its summit between Epping and North Weald stations, a dizzy 340ft, which until the opening of the Thaxted branch in 1913 remained the highest point on the somewhat undramatically engineered GER. At Epping, the station, which was a good quarter of a mile south of the town centre, had a passing loop, and served as an intermediate terminus. There was also a goods yard at the London end on the Down side; an engine shed was added in 1892.

Beyond here the railway entered thinly-populated countryside, served by two small stations, North Weald, close to the small village north of the line, and Blake Hall, with not so much as a hamlet within half a mile, its namesake two miles away. The terminus at Ongar, with its single long platform on the south side and goods yard behind, was at the north end of the High Street which formed the major part of the town.

Down train about to leave Ongar, c. 1903, looking to Epping. *Commercial postcard*

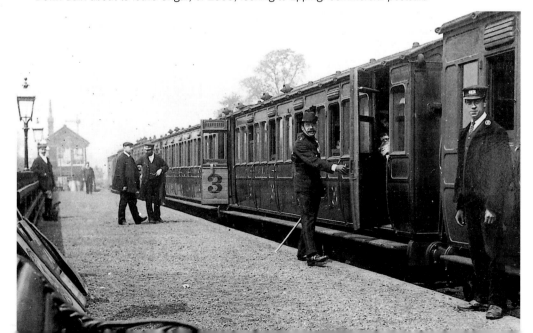

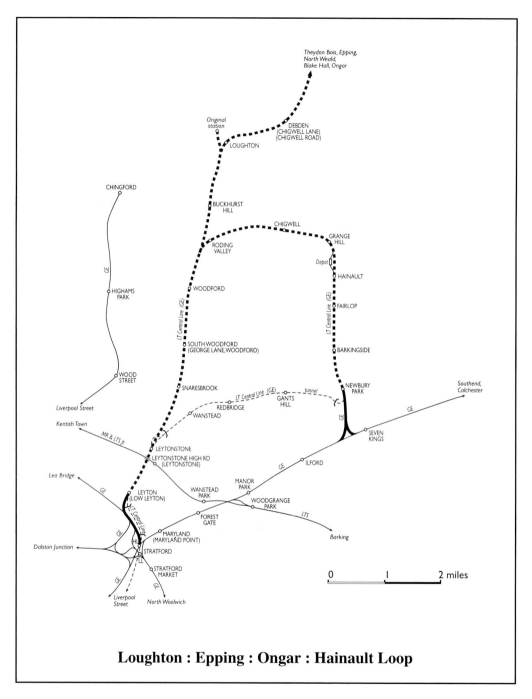

Loughton : Epping : Ongar : Hainault Loop

Extensions beyond Ongar were promoted on several occasions, and mooted more often. The Epping Railways (Dunmow Extension) Act of 1860 would have taken the line north to Great Dunmow along the upper valley of the Roding, but powers lapsed when capital could not be raised. Twenty-eight years later there was an ambitious scheme to build from Ongar through Great Dunmow to Bury St Edmunds. Subsequent proposals were made under the Light Railways Acts: the

25-mile Central Essex Light Railway (1901), with interchange stations at Ongar, Great Dunmow and Yeldham; the Ongar & Shenfield Light Railway, promoted in 1919 by the Essex Light Railways Syndicate; and the Mid-Essex Light Railway (Ongar-Dunmow) of the Essex Light Railway & Property Co. Ltd (1920). None of these was able to acquire the capital to make a start, and with the arrival of the rural motorbus in the early 1920s the need for further railway provision in remotest Essex faded fast. For its part, the GER nursed an idea for completing a link between Ongar and Chelmsford, forming a strategic loop for its main line, but this was never formalised.

At the opening of the Loughton branch, the ECR provided nine trains each way daily, all but one using Fenchurch Street (Sunday trains terminated at Bishopsgate). Even at this early date there was some recognition of residential needs in that two of the only three semi-fast workings were timed to run Up at 09.15 from Loughton and Down at 17.10 from Fenchurch Street. Most of the trains were diverted to Liverpool Street when the new terminus opened in 1874, but a rush-hour service, mostly semi-fast, continued to and from Fenchurch Street. By that year Loughton had gained some 40 trains each way daily, whilst Epping had 18 and Ongar 12. In the 1890s steady suburban growth at the inner end justified 62 Down trains daily as far as Snaresbrook (where 11 terminated). A further train finished its run at Woodford, 28 ended their journeys at Loughton, eight at Epping, the remaining 14 running through to Ongar. After the opening of the Ilford to Woodford loop, the service south of Woodford was augmented by trains which ran on and off the loop. Thus in 1907 we find that Leytonstone had 70 Down trains and 63 Up, whilst at Woodford there were 72 and 67. In that year Loughton had 50 Down and 48 Up workings, Epping had 22 each way and Ongar still had 14 arrivals and 14 departures. The best time among these trains for the nine miles from Liverpool Street to Woodford was 21 minutes, all-stations trains taking 33 minutes. Loughton, 11½ miles, was reached in 25 minutes by semi-fasts, but stopping trains took 40 minutes; 35 minutes was the best time for the 16½ miles to Epping (53 minutes for all stations), whilst Ongar, at 22½ miles, was gained in 56 minutes by the best trains, 77 by the slow ones. In the peak hour from 08.24 to 09.24 there were 14 trains off the branch to London, four of them into Fenchurch Street; two of the total originated at Ongar, one at Epping, six at Loughton, one at Buckhurst Hill, two at Snaresbrook, while the remaining two came off the loop at Woodford.

With the growth in residential traffic, the GER rebuilt stations on the inner section and made other improvements. At Leyton in 1878–9 a new main entrance on the High Road overline bridge replaced that on the Down platform which became an exit only. In 1888 the entire station was reconstructed, while another exit and entrance was added at the country end in Union (now Langthorne) Road in 1901. A very commendable rebuilding at Leytonstone in 1891–2 saw the end of the staggered platforms and included a public pedestrian subway which became a scene of carnage in a 1944 rush-hour air raid. Snaresbrook got a bay platform for Up trains in 1893, and ten years later an entrance for ticket-holders was added on the Up side in response to building development. George Lane, given a footbridge in 1881, was rebuilt two years later. Woodford was reconstructed with a bay and booking office on the Up side in 1892 as middle-class housing was spreading around the station. A new Buckhurst Hill station with parallel platforms was opened north of Queens Road in 1892. Additional carriage sidings were provided at Loughton and new sidings made at Woodford. Sykes' lock-and-block signalling was installed between Loughton and the junction at Leyton in 1901–2, and about the same time an intermediate box called Leytonstone South was added on the London side of Leytonstone station. To relieve overcrowding at South Woodford, another goods depot was established at Eagle Lane. This yard and signal box, on the Up side, just over a quarter-mile south of George Lane station, was opened on 15th May 1899.

Beyond Loughton, the main change before 1914 was the completion of a double track as far as Epping in January 1893, the work including a second platform for Chigwell Lane on the Up side together with a footbridge.

The GER worked the line with 15-car trains of four-wheelers, which normally included five first-class cars compared with three per train on the Romford line and only two in the 15-car Enfield Town and Chingford trains. Ten of the 15 coaches were usually detached at Loughton or Epping as not only was the traffic on the outer section very much lighter, but stations beyond Epping were too short to take 15 without drawing-up. From 1911 bogie carriages, some of them new, others constructed from pairs of the old four-wheelers, were brought on to the line in eight-car sets (reduced to two on the outer section). These trains were customarily hauled by S. D. Holden's class G69 2–4–2T, introduced in the same year. Other locomotives seen on passenger trains in the last years of the GER were 1100 class 0–4–4T and the ubiquitous 'Buck-Jumper' 0–6–0T. Gresley articulated sets finally saw off the four-wheelers in 1928, and although the LNER brought the more powerful N7 0–6–2T on to the Ongar line, the 2–4–2T did not entirely disappear until the completion of electrification in 1957.

As already suggested, the business traffic was probably the most remunerative of any on the GER system. Under pressure from the LCC, the Railway & Canal Commissioners allowed workmen's fares at Leyton and Leytonstone in 1911 on the grounds that the areas served were similar in character to that around Maryland Point on the main line, where workmen's rates had always been available. However, the GER sturdily and successfully resisted all other attempts to impose workmen's facilities on the branch; only at these two innermost stations did the housing and social mix show any similarity to that at Tottenham and Walthamstow, though even then the main growth between 1870 and 1900 contained a strong leavening of white-collar families – one witness to a Royal Commission in 1904 thought the area 'practically a dormitory'. Between 1882 and 1902, season ticket issues at Leyton and Leytonstone increased by 303 per cent, including a notable 171 per cent growth in first-class seasons. There was no large-scale suburban building from Snaresbrook to Loughton until the early 1900s, when new villas and shopping parades began to appear near the stations. Until the mid-1920s almost every house built in this sector was in the higher price range, for middle-class occupation; thus in 1911, rather more than 44¼ per cent of Wanstead's housing stock had seven or more rooms and almost 11 per cent of the population were in the professional classes.

Suburban expansion here continued at an accelerated pace in the late 1920s and 1930s, spreading out to Loughton, even to Theydon Bois, where there were some new streets west of the station. Much of this later growth was of cheap speculatively-built houses selling at £600 or less, situated on the low-lying land to the east of the line. One large estate off Snakes Lane Woodford was built so near the Roding that it was under water in January 1939. By the outbreak of World War 2, much of the land between the Roding and the Forest, bisected by the railway, was covered with houses as far out as Loughton. Discontent with the LNER steam service, strained by the extra traffic, began to boil up in the early 1930s. A public meeting held at Loughton in May 1935 heard a railway official confess that the facilities offered were not up to requirements. As we shall see in a moment, a promise of something better was about to appear.

On the outer section, the peace remained almost undisturbed during the LNER régime. There had been some extra activity during World War 1, mainly from the construction of army camps and at North Weald an airfield for the defence of London, but in 1921 the GER was able to introduce conductor-guard working as a Sunday economy and the two coaches used on weekdays were never overcrowded. There was some housebuilding between the wars at Epping, but in general the country beyond Theydon Bois remained untouched by suburban influences. World War 2 saw a revival of activity at North Weald, where the Royal Air Force station was expanded.

Penetrating as it did into deepest Essex, the outer end of the branch carried a lot of farm produce, particularly milk. This latter traffic grew large enough to justify daily milk trains on Mondays to Fridays to and from Ongar in 1911, with Saturday workings added in 1916. Full churns were loaded at each station as far as Theydon Bois on the Up run and empties were unloaded on the return working. Although some of the milk was put out at stations south of Loughton, most of it went through to Stratford for distribution in inner London. In 1918 some 5,000 17-gallon churns were reaching Stratford from the branch weekly, and at Ongar alone, farm carts, some travelling up to eight miles in all weathers, fed 1,300 churns a week to the railway. Inwards freight, much of it solid fuels and building materials, flowed steadily until BR diesels arrived to replace the GER and LNER 0–6–0s after World War 2. Snaresbrook Yard was closed from 1st August 1949 and Leytonstone from 2nd September 1955. The remainder went under the Beeching axe: South Woodford from 25th November 1963, North Weald from 6th January 1964, Buckhurst Hill from 10th April 1964, Eagle Lane, Woodford, Loughton, Debden, Theydon Bois, Epping, Blake Hall and Ongar all closing from 18th April 1966, and Leyton, Goodall Road, served by trains from Temple Mills, from 6th May 1968 when it was converted into an engineer's depot.

With the Forest so close to the line on the west side, summer pleasure traffic remained an important feature at stations between Buckhurst Hill and Epping until the 1950s, both the GER and the LNER encouraging it with cheap fares. Large tea rooms and pleasure gardens were placed strategically on the roads from the stations to the Forest, as at Coppice Row, near Theydon Bois station. Children came in their hundreds in special trains chartered by Sunday Schools and other organisations, including Dr Barnardo's Homes, whose trains from Stepney to Theydon Bois continued into the LNER era. In the opposite direction, excursions were worked through to east and south coast resorts, the latter via the East London line. These continued, steam-hauled, and later diesel-powered, well into the 1960s, long after tube trains had taken over the ordinary workings.

Tube train operation of the branch was first mooted in the early 1930s. A major objective of the 1935–40 London Railways New Works Programme was to bring the eastern suburbs of London into more direct communication with the West End, at the same time relieving the very heavy pressure on the LNER lines through Stratford. Much of the overloading arose from the hundreds of acres of cheap houses which by the late 1930s had filled the area bounded by the Loughton line, the Woodford-Ilford loop, and the main line. To meet the needs of this new population, it was proposed to extend the Central London tube railway below ground to Leyton via Stratford, where it would briefly surface for cross-platform interchange with the LNER main line. At Leyton, the tube trains were to surface and take over the working of the Ongar line and the Hainault loop (to be reached by a new tube railway below Eastern Avenue as far as Newbury Park). Work on this part of the Programme, financed at 2½ per cent interest, with interest and capital guaranteed by the Treasury, began in October 1936 but the exigencies of war brought it to a halt in 1940.

A new station at Loughton, slightly east of the old, was sufficiently advanced to allow it to open on 28th April 1940. Its two island platforms on the embankment served three roads, and although decorated with London Transport totems and designed for the new service, it saw nothing but the drab LNER steam trains for the first 8½ years of its life. To emphasise its continuing ownership, the LNER instructed the architects, J. Murray Easton and Robertson Fellows, deliberately to avoid undue similarity with contemporary London Transport stations. A barrel vault theme was adopted for the core block and the centrally-supported platform canopies had a bold sweep seldom before seen in concrete work, combining grace and strength in a most impressive manner.

Such was the importance attached to easing the congestion on the eastern suburban services that the post-war Labour government allowed work to resume in 1945 despite economic and supply problems. Tube trains reached Stratford on 4th December 1946 and Leytonstone on 5th May 1947. The new tracks reached the surface about a quarter-mile south of Leyton station, where a new frontage was constructed for the High Road entrance. Leytonstone received substantial rebuilding with a sub-surface booking hall, pedestrian subways beneath the platforms and an island platform on the east side to allow two Up trains to stand in the station at the same time. As elsewhere on the line, the level-crossing was abolished before the tube service started. Steam trains shuttled between Leytonstone and Ongar until 14th December 1947 when they were cut back to Woodford to make way for the

N7 0-6-2T 9630 working a Leytonstone–Epping steam shuttle service after the arrival of Central Line tube trains at Leytonstone on 5th May 1947. *Lens of Sutton*

London's Local Railways

Top: Ex GER F5 2-4-2T 67203 accelerates out of Ongar station bound for Epping on 18th May 1957. *R C Riley*

Below: Ex GER F5 2-4-2T 67202 and 67218 on Up and Down trains passing on the loop at North Weald, 16th November 1957 looking to Ongar. *R C Riley*

extension of tube working. For this, Snaresbrook, South Woodford, and Woodford received new ticket halls and restyled frontages. At Snaresbrook the site of the bay road and goods yard became a car park, opened in September 1949. Leytonstone's yard went the same way. Additional ticket halls were provided on the Up (now 'Westbound') side at Snaresbrook and South Woodford in 1948. Loughton's new station received its electric trains at last on 21st November 1948, with a service every four minutes in peak periods and every ten at other times. At Buckhurst Hill, the GER station of 1892 remained virtually unchanged.

Commuters who had been looking forward to electrification found it a not unmixed blessing. They lost the semi-fast workings and suffered a substantial reduction in seats. A tube passenger from Woodford in 1948 faced a journey to Oxford Circus taking up to 30 minutes longer, despite the elimination of the transfer at Liverpool Street, and at peak hours was much more likely to stand for part of the journey, even if the trains were cleaner. This discrepancy remained significant when more modern tube stock was introduced; before electrification there were 11 steam trains leaving Liverpool Street for Woodford and beyond between 17.00 and 18.00 on Mondays to Fridays, offering a total of 9,952 seats, but in 1961, in the same period of the peak, the 18 tube trains had only 5,904 seats.

Although there were misgivings in some quarters about extending tube operation into the London Green Belt, the electrification was carried through to Epping on 25th September 1949. A substantial business was expected at Chigwell Lane, renamed Debden on that day, after a large LCC housing and industrial estate already opened there. Two reversing and storage roads were placed between the running lines just east of the platforms to give a terminal facility, trains running to and from London every ten or twelve minutes, and every six in the peak periods. Between here and Epping there were through workings to and from London only at 40-minute intervals (12 to 15 minutes in the rush hours) but a shuttle between Loughton and Epping gave the stations on this outer section a 20-minute headway.

For another eight years, GER tank engines and drab LNER coaches shuttled between Epping and Ongar whilst the authorities weighed the difficult balance between operating convenience and the poor traffic potential. Finally it was decided to electrify the single line, operating it as economically as possible. No substation was provided, that at Epping producing just sufficient power to enable two four-car trains to run simultaneously between Epping and Ongar, passing at North Weald, this being enough to give what was considered a reasonable peak hour frequency. Tube trains made their appearance at the remote-seeming Ongar platform on 18th November 1957, looking like fish out of water. Since 14th August 1949 the Epping–North Weald section had been track-circuited and this system had replaced train staff and ticket on the remaining stretch of the single line from the following 25th September. With it, BR had provided a passing loop and second platform at North Weald. There were no changes to the typically GER rural stations for the arrival of the tube trains, apart from replacement of oil lamps by electric light and installation of standard LT signs and totems.

With electrification, the whole line south of Epping had been track-circuited and signalled to LT surface line standards, the principal indications given by two-aspect long range colour lights with repeaters. Signal cabins with power frames and miniature levers were opened for the tube service at Leytonstone, South Woodford, Woodford, Loughton, Debden and Epping, but the old GER boxes remained at North Weald and Ongar with the modifications just mentioned. Ongar box and shunting neck were eventually abandoned from 23rd March 1969.

Steam locos and later, diesels, continued to run over the line north of Leyton with freights and passenger excursions until 1966. Even then LT did not have the line entirely to itself; some passenger workings were still worked each way between Epping/Loughton and Liverpool Street/Stratford. Operated for the convenience of railway workers, these trains were available to the public, running outside tube traffic hours until finally withdrawn on 31st May 1970. The diesel car sets used on these services in their last years provided a useful fall-back when the exposed Epping–Ongar tube trains were defeated by bad weather, though this flexibility was lost when the original junction at Leyton was removed on 29th October 1972 in response to London Transport's rigid policy of isolating itself from the national rail network.

Almost the only special traffic available on the Ongar line was that generated by the Air Shows at North Weald airfield. For some years London Transport operated a special 15 min service to and from Loughton on these occasions, with alternate trains going through to Ongar. This involved the use of five four-car trains and special care and vigilance to avoid overloading Epping substation or excessive voltage drops. Latterly there was a shuttle service between Epping and North Weald.

As far as regular patronage was concerned, Epping showed some signs of residential expansion after the arrival of the tube service. Debden became very busy as we shall see shortly and from the late 1950s onwards, the planning authorities allowed Ongar a considerable measure of additional housing.

But the outermost section remained a problem. Despite the growth at Ongar, traffic never justified the electrification. North Weald and Blake Hall soon secured for themselves the unenviable position of the least-used stations on the LT system; Blake Hall, which attracted only some 260 passengers a week, lost its Sunday trains from Sunday 23rd October 1966. Facing heavy costs for track works, LT sought complete closure beyond Epping in 1970, when off peak trains were said to be carrying an average of less than ten passengers each (although some peak hour services loaded up to 200). As no alternative bus service could be arranged, the Transport Users' Consultative Committee recommended retention, a finding endorsed by the Minister, though no grant was offered. Essex County Council agreed in 1976 to meet a quarter of the annual loss if costs were cut by operating only one train at a time instead of the normal two. This was accepted and applied from 18th October 1976, producing a somewhat ludicrous 35/40 min peak hour interval for a tube railway service. With the passing place no longer required, the North Weald signal box and loop were taken out of use in 1977 (the level crossing there had been closed to vehicles in May 1962).

When the Essex Council subsidy was withdrawn, fares were boosted to a high level and in 1979–80 passengers using the Ongar trains endured five increases in eight months. This and the speed restriction of 30 mph over the whole line imposed by the poor state of track and engineering works discouraged traffic so much that by 1980 the annual loss was over £0.6m on a service carrying only 650 passengers daily each way. After a second formal application to close the line in 1980 had failed, in a search for further savings, the isolated and little-used Blake Hall station was closed completely after traffic on Saturday 31st October 1981 and from 6th December 1982 (after withdrawal of a temporary District Council subsidy) trains ran only Mondays to Fridays at morning and evening peaks (five and six services each way respectively).

From 30th October 1989 in a sudden outburst of light headedness ('to evaluate demand') an all day (including Sundays) service was restored, with an initial week of free travel and a large illuminated Underground sign at Ongar station. This did no good at all and the Monday–Friday peak hours only pattern was resumed on 8th April 1991 (just three morning trains each way plus one each way at North Weald, and four each way in the evening). But even the commuters had found other alternatives, using their cars to reach better-served LT or BR stations, and by 1993, in the evening rush hour, some departures for Ongar from Epping were loading as few as 12 passengers, with none at all on the inward return runs. Ongar was then producing only 85 passengers a day, North Weald a mere 50. A third formal application to close the line in 1993 was successful, and the end came with the last train offering the now very lively and bumpy ride from and back to Epping's platform 2 on 30th September 1994. Attempts were then to be made to operate the line privately, but with heavy engineering works overdue, a refusal by LT to have the private trains in its Epping station, frequently unreliable Central Line connections at Epping, and the line's history of low traffic, any such enterprise would seem to need a great deal of faith and good fortune.

Some changes south of Epping since the introduction of Central Line tube services remain to be mentioned. North of the line around Chigwell Lane the LCC had opened its Debden Estate in 1947, a major project which eventually included a total of almost 4,500 dwellings accommodating a population of some 16,000. Then there was development south of the line in the 1950s and later an extensive industrial estate which included the Bank of England Printing Works; offices followed in the early 1970s. All this activity brought a great increase in traffic to what had been a very quiet rural station. Direct access from the industrial estate to the westbound platform was opened in 1956, a new station footbridge in 1957. Then, in 1974–75, with half the cost met by the government, a major rebuilding scheme was undertaken, involving a larger ticket hall, new canopies on both platforms and new lighting.

In connection with the architecturally-disastrous Underground Ticketing Scheme, Snaresbrook received a new ticket office and associated buildings in the late 1980s, with sad consequences for its GER heritage. Elsewhere this pleasing aspect of most of the line's stations received more consideration, as at Buckhurst Hill, where in 1995 damaged windows were replaced and expertly etched in replica GER style; in the retention of GER seats; and in the sympathetic preservation of the GER buildings and canopies at Leyton and elsewhere. Alas, Leyton did suffer some desecration from an external predator. A start was made in 1991 with construction of the M11 Link road, which was to run alongside the railway on the west side from a point just north of Leytonstone station to the site of the former Leyton goods yard west of Leyton High Road. This was to cut a great swathe through back gardens and little side roads and at Leyton station required closure of the 1901 Langthorne Road entrance from 3rd March 1995. No compensation was offered by the government for its replacement.

After the closure of Eagle Lane goods yard in 1966 the site had been used for dumping tube tunnel segments. These were removed in 1986 preparatory to sale of the land to Wimpey for erection of small houses.

Signalling was modernised as part of a major programme covering the whole of the Central Line. Stratford–Leytonstone, including a lengthened westbound loop at Leytonstone, was completed on 1st May 1995 but the remainder of the scheme was not in use until 9th November 1997.

By the mid 1980s off peak patronage north of Loughton had fallen substantially and the service of five trains an hour in the middle of the day was accordingly reduced to three in 1986. Commuters living near stations north of Woodford were now using their cars to reach stations closer to central London, where residents were soon complaining of the street parking around the station areas. This change in travelling patterns, facilitated by wider car ownership, was in part a response to the higher fares operating in the Essex County Council area, but it also reflected an increasing lack of tolerance with the long and slow journeys to outer stations in rolling stock expressly designed for high load capacity short distance travel. This last aspect received greater emphasis when the new Central Line stock entered service in 1993–95. All-stations travel out to Buckhurst Hill and beyond in nasty little longitudinal seats with upright backs, listening to irritating repetitive automatic announcements and in summer, noisy ventilation fans, then became even more of an acquired taste. The 1930s policy mistake of extending costly all-stations urban tube service deep into outer suburbia (and beyond) is nowhere more apparent than on these eastern extremities of the Central Line, which unlike those of the tube lines in north and north west London, lack any faster and more comfortable alternative rail routes.

The Fairlop or Hainault Loop
(map page 386)

As early as 1846 the Eastern Counties Railway obtained powers for an Epping Extension which was to have left the main line at Ilford, following the Roding valley as far as Woodford where it would join the route subsequently constructed from Stratford, which has already been noticed. Nothing happened; for many years the district north of Ilford slumbered in rural peace, London influence showing only in some retirement and other middle-class development at Chigwell and Woodford from around 1865. When Ilford's rapid suburban growth began during the last quarter of the century much of it spread northwards from the main line, prompting the 1895 promotion of an independent Ilford, Barkingside & Chigwell Row Railway. Although the bill for this was deposited for the 1896 session, it was withdrawn when the GER promised to build a similar line itself, an end result which may well have been the real intention of the promoters. True to its word, the GER secured parliamentary authority in its 1897 General Powers Act for a 5m 7f 7ch loop from Ilford through Barkingside, Fairlop and Chigwell to join the Epping and Ongar line at Woodford. A 1f 8.7ch eastern curve completed the triangular junction at Ilford.

Some of the Churchbury optimism still remained. Fairlop loop stations were built to similar high standard, but unlike Churchbury, this was also an expensive line to make, its route lying across the grain of the country through gravel overlaid with clay, requiring 15 steel girder and four brick arch bridges, a short tunnel, cuttings up to 50ft deep and long stretches of embankment. Construction started in 1900 under the Manchester contractor C. J. Wills, working to the plans of the GER chief engineer, John Wilson. Much difficulty was experienced in stabilising the clay earthworks and when the line was at last ready, through freight trains were worked over it from 20th April 1903 to consolidate the formation. After the deep cuttings at Chigwell and Grange Hill had been shaped, hundreds of old sleepers were set alight, smouldering for weeks in an attempt to burn and settle the unstable clay.

Chigwell station, LNER, c. 1931, looking east. The station master's house (left) is on the Down side of the line, which passes under the Chigwell Road. Barclay's Bank appear to occupy rather vulnerable premises shared with a tobacconist and confectioner; and is that the bank manager's Baby Austin? *Commercial postcard*

Passenger and local freight operations started on 1st May 1903. At first the service worked from either Fenchurch Street or Liverpool Street and then back to London, both ways round the loop. Trains stopped a short time at Fairlop before returning to town, the complete tour taking about 1½ hours or about 30 minutes on the loop itself. Trains at Ilford to and from loop stations numbered about 20 daily each way, nine each way on Sundays. Composition was normally Holden 0–6–0T or 2–4–2T with up to 16 four-wheel coaches.

Either side of the summit at Grange Hill, the loop had long stretches of 1 in 100 and the sharpest curve was 10-chain radius. Direction was designated Down from Ilford to Chigwell, Up from Chigwell to Woodford. From Woodford Junction, which was facing for Down trains, the double track curved east on a high embankment across the Roding valley, spanning the river on a three-arch brick viaduct. On the north side, a quarter of a mile from the junction, Chigwell Bank box broke up the long stretch between two stations. On the other side of the river, the line entered a cutting in which Chigwell station was situated, its site about half a mile south of the village centre, on the east side of the main London road. Two well-canopied platforms were reached by covered staircases from a handsome brick booking office building on the road bridge and both platforms had waiting rooms and lavatories in the same red brick. There was no goods yard, but a short distance to the east, a ground frame gave access to a siding and wharf on the north side of the line, used for loading fruit grown in an adjacent orchard owned by the GER for supplying its hotels. This facility had been removed by the end of the 1920s. On the south side near Chigwell was a refuge siding, later to be buried by an earth slip.

Soon after Chigwell the line entered a 260yd tunnel followed by a cutting which led into Grange Hill station. This cutting, 50ft deep at the tunnel end, gave much trouble during construction and subsequently, until London Transport built retaining walls. Grange Hill was almost the twin of Chigwell with its booking office building on the south side of the bridge carrying the Woodford–Lambourne End road over the line, but in addition there was a goods yard here, on the west side, behind the platform, with connection at the London end.

From Grange Hill the tracks ran south for about two miles, mostly on embankment across the western fringe of Fairlop Plain. Stations here were very closely spaced in anticipation of continuing northern expansion of Ilford. Hainault, the first of the series, sat on a brick arch viaduct, its small entrance pavilion at road level on the west side. Within half a mile radius there were hardly half a dozen houses, but the passenger accommodation was no less lavish than elsewhere on the line. The small goods yard was on the west side just south of the platforms. Separated by only 30ch from its neighbour, Fairlop station was almost identical, except that the goods yard was at the north end on the east side, complemented by a cattle dock and siding on the opposite side. This was the nearest station to the huge Claybury mental hospital which the LCC had opened in 1893, but there was little else within its catchment area apart from a farmhouse and a mission room.

Barkingside station, at the end of the embankment, at least had a village and Dr Barnardo Girls' Home to serve, both a quarter-mile west of its platforms. The main building was on the level at the west side, and in front of it the goods yard extended from its connection south of the platforms almost up to the approach road. Newbury Park, the last of this trio of putative suburban stations, was in a cutting, 1m 61ch north of Ilford. At the time of its opening, new houses were being erected near here at the north-eastern edge of burgeoning Ilford, and the population had grown enough to justify the opening of an Infants' School close to the new station in 1895. In general design and appearance very similar to Chigwell and Grange Hill, Newbury Park had a booking office building on the road bridge at the southern end of the platforms. Goods facilities were provided on the west side of the line at the north end of the station. The cutting continued southwards to Newbury Park Junction, where double-track curves branched towards Ilford (Ilford Carriage Sidings Junction) and towards Seven Kings (Seven Kings West Junction) on the main London–Colchester line.

At the planning stage, the GER had envisaged the loop not only as opening up a new area for residential development, but also as a freight by-pass for the congested main line between Ilford and Stratford, but in practice very little use was made of the eastern curve, with through freight trains and passenger services over it limited to the occasional seaside excursion or special. As constructed, the loop presented difficulties to heavy goods trains and there was no attempt to make connections for direct working between trains off the Loughton line and Temple Mills yard or between that line and the strategic cross-London link at Victoria Park.

Instead, everything was done to prepare for heavy passenger traffic, misplaced optimism in this direction being most evident in the location and design of the stations, all of which had substantial buildings and 640ft platforms graded level and capable of accommodating 1,000-seater trains of 20 four-wheelers. Architect and civil engineer, briefed to allow for heavy season ticket traffic, provided adequate weather protection in the form of long canopies, covered footbridges or subways, rail-level buildings in red brick and tiles with lavish waiting and lavatory accommodation each side of the line. With the intention of creating buildings worthy of the new districts they were to serve, decoration was elaborated with curves and cupolas, gables and curly ironwork carrying the GER monogram. Barkingside was indisputably the most handsome of the six stations, its main west side structure featuring stone-arched windows, stone quoins and a deep stone plinth under hipped roofs, the central portion crowned with a dainty Baroque cupola carrying a weather vane. The reason for the extra expenditure is obscure but may have been connected with its proximity to Doctor Barnardo's Homes and VIP visits thereto. This station and Newbury Park were within the Ilford Council's electric lighting district, but the other four had to make do with gas and oil lamps.

Indicative of the undeveloped nature of the areas served were the three pairs of semi-detached garden-city style cottages for railway staff placed near each station. Set a little apart from them was a small detached villa for the stationmaster with a pillared porch and larger garden. Wooden houses, some still in use at Grange Hill, were erected for the navvies constructing the line.

Once again the GER had badly misjudged. After a frenzy of activity from about 1890, the market for London suburban houses declined, bringing a noticeable slowing down in the northward growth of Ilford. Had it not been for the Ilford Council's electric tramcars, unkindly started on 14th March 1903 just before the railway was ready, there might have been a little business at Barkingside and Newbury Park stations, but the trams, which ran parallel to the line through the centres of the existing settlements, not only stole all the local traffic between Barkingside and Ilford, but carried much of the commuter load direct to Ilford station, leaving the railway with a pitiful trickle from the still thinly-populated new roads south east of Newbury Park station. North of Barkingside, with the exception of Chigwell, the new stations stood isolated in open country, their massive urban forms looking uncomfortable and misplaced. With no housebuilders in sight, the GER board contributed in 1904 to the cost of acquiring Grange Park Forest, Hainault, as a public open space, a desperate gesture which was to do it little good. Writing at the end of 1907, Cecil J. Allen, then a GER employee, painted a truthful picture. After remarking that the growth of North Ilford was very slow, he continued,

> and now the extraordinary sight may be seen of two palatial stations – Hainault and Fairlop – within a quarter of a mile of each other and yet with scarcely a house in sight, while the daily number of passengers to and from them could often be counted on the fingers.

Soon after these words appeared in *The Railway Magazine*, the GER accepted the inevitable, closing Hainault and its goods yard to all traffic after the last train on 30th September 1908. This move failed to stem the loss on working, calculated in 1911 at £8,000 a year.

Further retrenchment occurred in World War 1, when Barkingside was selected as the most suitable candidate on this line for a list of stations to be closed to release more railwaymen for the army. Passenger and goods trains called here for the last time on 21st May 1916, the few regular patrons no doubt finding the frequent and cheap Council tramcars to Ilford station a tolerable alternative. When the station reopened (on weekdays only) on 1st July 1919 little business was done, and all year round Sunday service was not restored until August 1934.

World War 1 brought new and unusual traffics. Wounded soldiers came in long ambulance trains to Newbury Park for transfer to the 1912 Ilford Emergency Hospital at the west side of the station, whilst at Hainault Farm and Fairlop Plain men and materials arrived to form and maintain a fighter air station for the defence of London. After the war, with the departure of the Sopwith Camels, the grass airfield remained open for civil flying, becoming the focus of a 1936 City of London Corporation scheme for a 948-acre six-runway London airport to replace Croydon. But for the onset of World War 2, this would have been built and with it a planned new Fairlop station, some 500yd south of the old, linked to the terminal buildings by covered ways. And Heathrow might have been left in peace . . .

Towards the end of the GER era, train services over the loop were modified to eliminate most of the through workings to and from London apart from rush hours and on Saturday afternoons, when there was some sports ground and other pleasure traffic. At other times trains then mostly ran between Ilford and Woodford with a few London to Ilford services extended to Fairlop and some Down Woodford via Stratford workings going through to Chigwell, Grange Hill or Fairlop. Sunday trains, generally confined to the loop, were approximately hourly before World War 1, then, as a wartime economy, were reduced to two-hourly. On 1st May 1921 the hourly interval was resumed, and with the growth of the residential areas served and the popularity of country excursions, some extras were introduced in 1932. A half-hourly frequency followed a year later.

During the building boom of the late 1920s and early 1930s, Ilford's growth entered a second more powerful phase, covering over the area crossed by the Eastern Avenue motor road which had been opened in March 1924. Between that year and 1936 almost all the land between the eastern bank of the Roding and the loop was

Roding Valley halt, LNER, north side, fronting Station Way, January 1937. In the background is some of the new housing (Cherry Tree Rise) that prompted its opening.
London Transport Museum

filled with small houses up to a point well north of Barkingside. East of the railway, Fairlop Plain remained untouched and elsewhere on this side, apart from some building at Newbury Park from 1931 onwards, and some lighter activity either side of Hainault station, there was no development of any consequence before 1940. Fairlop's immediate surroundings were still free of housing estates in that year although there was some building towards Claybury along the Chigwell Road a quarter-mile west.

The activity at Hainault caused the LNER to re-open the station for passenger and parcels traffic on weekdays from 3rd March 1930, but it had been in use some time before then. A note in the working timetable for March 1927 mentions that tickets available at Hainault were issued to the employees of Messrs Hughes' works and also to the public at Hainault and from certain suburban stations 'on application'. It was also possible for holders of season or ordinary tickets available at Fairlop from the Woodford direction and at Grange Hill from the south to alight or join trains at Hainault. The freight yard there remained closed, never to be restored.

In the 1900s Woodford had started to grow northwards from the station either side of the Loughton line, expansion which was resumed with greater vigour in the early 1930s, soon reaching and passing Woodford Junction. Responding to agitation from estate owners and others, the LNER opened a halt on the loop a short distance from the junction, on 3rd February 1936. Named Roding Valley, it was equipped only with simple shelters and an open iron footbridge – the LNER lacked the enthusiastic approach to suburban business evinced by the Southern Railway, and clearly had no wish to emulate the confident optimism of its GER predecessor.

Some improvements were made to the train service for the new residents, many of whom were London season-ticket holders. From 22 trains each way round the loop (a few running through to London or other points en route) and about 15 each way on Sundays in 1927, the service was built up in ten years to 44 round the loop to Woodford and beyond and the same number to Ilford and beyond, plus three from Newbury Park to Ilford and beyond, with half-hourly service each way for most of Sunday.

The Fairlop or Hainault Loop

Much more than this was however required to improve the lot of the thousands of central London workers who had been enticed to purchase low-cost new houses either side of Eastern Avenue between Newbury Park and Wanstead and who depended on crowded buses to get to Ilford and other stations. Of those within easy access of the loop stations, something like 40 per cent wanted a direct transit to points west of St Pauls. Backed by the local MPs, a powerful pressure group arose to represent this discontented mass, whose number grew each day as more houses were built, crowding into congested trains at Ilford, and obliged to make a second transport change at Liverpool Street.

Even the long-distance oriented and impoverished LNER could not continue to ignore the highly unsatisfactory situation which had arisen by 1929. Early the following year the company commissioned a consultants' study of an Ilford–Liverpool Street tube railway, but shied away when told of the capital cost and low return this would bring. Not that the Ilford & District Railway Users' Association had much interest in the usefulness of an LNER tube; it was campaigning for an extension of the Central London Line from Liverpool Street to Romford via Eastern Avenue, with a branch to Claybury. Continued lobbying eventually brought LNER and Underground heads together, but the lack of return on capital remained a problem. After the formation of the London Passenger Transport Board there were further joint consultations under increasing pressure from central government, resulting in the inclusion of Underground extensions into North Ilford in the 1935–40 London Railway New Works Programme, which was to be financed by government-guaranteed loans in recognition of its contribution to the relief of unemployment.

Under this proposal, the Central London Line was to be projected from its terminus beneath Liverpool Street station to Stratford, where the trains were to come to the surface to afford easy interchange with LNER suburban services to Shenfield, to be electrified at the same time. Descending again to deep-level tube, the Underground trains would go on to Leyton where they were to surface to join the Loughton line and provide the service on it, as described earlier. From Leytonstone, a new tube would be made under Eastern Avenue as far as Newbury Park, where the Underground trains would take over service on the Fairlop loop (London Transport named it the Hainault loop after deciding to use the latter place as the terminal). Work on these projects, which began in October 1936, was well advanced when stopped under wartime constraints in 1940.

At that time tube tunnels had been completed beneath Eastern Avenue and following an initiative of Lord Beaverbrook, these were converted to a 2½-mile long factory for the Plessey Company, producing aircraft components. In the air-conditioned atmosphere of a brisk spring day, safe from bombing, it accommodated 2,000 workers, mostly girls, at any one time in the 24 hours. Transport within the 12ft diameter tunnel was by means of an 18in gauge tramway operated by electric battery locomotives. Another almost-finished installation found wartime use. The Underground depot on the west side of the loop between Grange Hill and Hainault stations served from June 1943 to January 1945 as an assembly point for railway rolling stock operated by the US Army Transportation Corps. Earlier some tube cars had been stored there. Fairlop Plain again provided a military airfield, completing the strange assortment of new traffics brought on to the loop in wartime conditions.

After the war, at a time when there were very severe restrictions on capital expenditure, the government gave priority to completion of the Central Line eastern extensions. Much work was needed in the tunnels after Plessey's departure, but tube trains were operated along the 4.11-mile new section between Leytonstone and Newbury Park from Sunday 14th December 1947, calling at three tunnel stations, Wanstead, Redbridge, and Gants Hill, each of them well placed to serve the inter-war housing. LNER steam trains between Ilford, Newbury Park and Woodford ran for the last time on Saturday 29th November, allowing engineering work to proceed unhindered in the interim, when passengers used a special bus service calling at all loop stations except Roding Valley. A new western spur to the main line at Ilford, opened in September 1947 to serve the loop and the new electric car sheds for the Shenfield main line electrification, was used only briefly by passenger trains. This curve was severed by an extension of the depot in 1948, but as we shall see, the eastern curve remained in use for a little longer.

At Newbury Park, the tube tracks emerged either side of the old GER line south of the station, which was not substantially altered apart from the opening of a temporary ticket office in what was to be the bus forecourt on the east side. On 6th July 1949 a permanent ticket hall, entrance, and staff canteen were opened here, passengers reaching the GER platforms by a new concrete footbridge across the centre of the station. These new buildings were flanked by a combined bus station and car park. The former, used by eastbound buses on routes 66 and 139 (now 296) had been designed by Oliver Hill in 1937 and included a coppered barrel vault roof in reinforced concrete of 60ft span, 30ft high and 150ft long, apparently inspired by airship sheds of the 1930s. This new work, on the site of the seven GER staff houses, was but a part of the complete rebuilding envisaged in 1937, and still not undertaken over 60 years on. Only one further change was made here; in 1956 the GER street building, with its covered staircases to the platforms (where the old ticket office had apparently remained open until late in 1954) was demolished to make way for the new road bridge carrying the widened Eastern Avenue. Despite the dualling of the road, no provision was included in the roadworks to allow the Oliver Hill bus station to be used by westbound buses, as had been intended before World War 2.

With the arrival of the tube trains at Newbury Park, Hainault depot, designed for 344 cars, came into partial use, with the tracks as far north as Grange Hill electrified to permit empty stock movements. Nine-car sidings also provided at Newbury Park north of the goods depot on the west side were subsequently removed.

London Transport designated Leytonstone–Newbury Park–Woodford as *Inner Rail* and the other track as *Outer Rail*, following Inner Circle practice. Trains ran to and from Newbury Park about every four minutes at peak periods, every 7½-minutes at other times. Steam passenger trains had disappeared entirely from the loop and passengers for stations beyond Newbury Park used a truncated version of the bus service already mentioned.

Despite the provision of the much requested link to the West End, the new facility proved a mixed blessing, especially in the early days. Passengers soon found that the total capacity offered in the trains was less than in steam days, especially as regards the number of seats. The addition of many who had formerly travelled by bus direct or to and from Ilford station made things worse and there was added discomfort in frequent breakdowns of the 20-year-old rolling stock, which had been stored in the open during the war years. Until the new depots at Hainault and Ruislip were fully operational, maintenance could not be organised to provide a sufficient quantity of fault-free trains.

Hainault was reached by Underground trains on 31st May 1948, Woodford on 21st November. Little alteration was made to Barkingside and Fairlop stations other than retiling of booking halls and installation of LT signs and lighting. Originally scheduled for complete rebuilding, Hainault received a new island platform on the west side, and a passimeter booking hall built into the embankment at road level blended into the old GER subway between the platforms; like Newbury Park, it was destined to exhibit two conflicting architectural styles for at least another 50 years. At Grange Hill, where the street level overline building had been demolished by a German V1 missile on 12th July 1944, there was a reconstruction in the rather arid late 1940s style, but the GER stationmaster's house survived. Chigwell saw little change apart from rebuilding of the ticket office but Roding Valley lost its halt status and underwent some rearrangement in 1949.

With the extension to Hainault, peak-hour service was increased by four trains an hour to Leytonstone, two of which continued to Hainault, giving that section 17 trains an hour at the busiest times. Otherwise Hainault had a 7½- to 10-minute frequency according to the time of day. Between Hainault and Woodford a shuttle of three-car trains worked every 7½ minutes at peak hours, 24 to 30 minutes otherwise. This replaced the original concept, found to cause operating problems, of working trains right round the loop in both directions to and from the rest of the Central Line.

Standard LT open-air signalling was installed, with train stops, two-aspect long-range colour-lights, repeaters and fog repeaters, most of it controlled by track circuits. To allow the requisite stopping distances for steam-hauled freight and excursion trains, distant signals of the externally-lit disc type, showing a swallow-tailed bar on a yellow ground, were placed along the open-air section. New signal cabins were opened at Newbury Park (59 levers), Hainault (83 levers) on 12th May 1948, and a subsidiary cabin at Grange Hill controlled from Hainault on 29th October 1948. Fairlop LNER box closed on 20th April 1948, after which all the goods yards were controlled by ground frames. At Newbury Park, the Outer Rail tunnel mouth was protected by electric train detectors in the station platform.

For the first decade or so of tube operation, the frequent electric services to both City and West End, with easy connections to the remainder of the Underground system drew out the maximum available patronage but there was very little scope for generating new traffic. Much of the uncovered land adjacent to the line to the east and north was by that time in the postwar London Green Belt, statutorily protected from housing development. It is true that the LCC had sited a large new estate just east of Grange Hill station but this was on land bought for the purpose in the 1930s and had been opened in 1947. Covering some 247 acres, it was eventually to house about 11,000 and much increase business at Grange Hill and Hainault stations. A large area of open land on the west side of the line between Hainault and Grange Hill was also later built over, some of it sold surplus to LT depot requirements in 1976. There were smaller infilling developments elsewhere.

Freight trains, hauled from the early 1960s by diesel locos, at first worked in and out via the eastern curve at Ilford but this was disconnected on 17th March 1956 to provide space for a BR new electric train depot. Thereafter the freights entered via Woodford, reversing on a short length of the original line south of Newbury Park road bridge. Although the road overbridges south of that point provided clues, the GER alignment was soon obscured, with much of the original formation filled to ground level to form allotment gardens. Freight traffic on lines such as this was now doomed; Fairlop's sidings closed on 24th March 1958 and the late evening path for the working disappeared entirely from the timetable from 4th October 1965 with the abandonment of the yards at Newbury Park, Barkingside and Grange Hill. As elsewhere, the sites of the old goods yards made useful station car parks. The stub line south of Newbury Park remained in place until 1992 when major track and signalling changes were made in the area in connection with the Central Line resignalling scheme.

Few changes have been made to the stations in recent years and significant signs of the GER origins survive to please the eye, notably at Barkingside, though in 1987 the lofty entrance hall of that station suffered considerable desecration in the name of the Underground Ticketing System. Near New Barns Farm, rather under halfway from Chigwell to Roding Valley, the M11 motorway was aligned to pass beneath the railway, which from September 1972 was carried over it by a 152ft span concrete bridge. This new road would soon be feeding car commuters from remoter Essex and East Anglia into the Central Line at stations nearer London.

By the late 1950s, television and wider car ownership were eating deeply into off-peak traffic; a little later, office dispersal was also draining off the London commuter flows. Weekend business, much of it to sports grounds, was lost to the car. Fairlop, penalised by its proximity to Hainault, and still with virtually no houses nearby, was closed on Sundays after Sunday 28th September 1958 and on Saturdays after Saturday 24th January 1970. It was considered for total closure in 1982 but was reopened again at weekends from 21st April 1990 in the hope of attracting some traffic bound for Fairlop Waters, a nearby leisure complex east of the line. In 1969 Saturday receipts at Roding Valley averaged only £24, Sundays £9, and after a short period of local authority subsidy, this station was closed at weekends from 2nd August 1970. London Transport restored weekend calls from Saturday 13th April 1991 but since this was achieved by dispensing with staff, the effects on revenue and the condition of station structures seemed likely to be counter-productive. At some of the other stations between Newbury Park and Woodford, ticket clerk attendance has been reduced to a single shift basis in recent years.

The quiet nature of the Woodford–Hainault section made it an obvious choice for testing the automatic train equipment devised for the new Victoria line tube and the shuttle service between these points was operated with this refinement for an extensive period from 5th April 1964. Poor loadings on this section caused it to be considered for complete closure in 1970 and again in 1982. From 6th December in the latter year trains ceased to run north of Hainault after about 20.00 each evening.

After a 1991 attempt to widen intervals up to 45/46 min, even at peak periods, some improvement followed local complaints: from 2nd November 1992 the whole service terminated at Woodford, running across Hainault, with intervals of 18–24 min at peak hours, 20 min at other times and mostly 30 min at weekends.

By the mid 1970s Fairlop, Roding Valley, Barkingside and Grange Hill were respectively the third, fourth, eighth and eleventh least-used stations on the whole London Underground system, none of them gathering as many as 1,000 passengers a week. Indeed north of Newbury Park, the line still forms the outer boundary of continuously-built up London, its semi-rural aspect emphasised when tube trains are occasionally delayed by horses and deer straying over the tracks.

The LTSR station building at South Street, Romford, c. 1905 (right), looking north. The GER station entrance can be seen at the left. The connecting footway between the two stations is visible above the arch of the underline bridge. *Commercial postcard*

Romford, Upminster & Grays   (map page 406)

On the north side of the Thames Estuary, nineteenth century railway objectives were three in number; Tilbury, where a ferry would carry passengers to the Londoners' favourite river resort of Gravesend and its Rosherville Gardens, destination of well over a million steamboat passengers a year in the 1830s and 1840s; the inlet at Thames Haven (which had potential for development as import docks); and Southend, which had begun to develop as a bathing resort at the end of the eighteenth century. Foreshadowing events, a scheme of 1833 had proposed a link between the planned Eastern Counties Railway at Romford and Thames Haven. This 16-mile line was authorised in July 1836 as the Thames Haven Railway & Dock Company but although the powers were renewed in 1846, construction was never started.

After the London Tilbury & Southend Railway had acquired its full independence in 1880, the Great Eastern Railway felt tempted to exploit the developing residential and pleasure resort of Southend and the deep water docks at Tilbury, whose construction had been authorised to the East & West India Dock Company by an act of 1882. Apprehension about the GER's intentions played a part in the LTSR's promotion of a cut-off line between Barking and Pitsea, which would provide a faster route to the seaside town, leaving the original LTSR line via Grays free for the Tilbury Dock traffic. This direct line through Upminster, authorised in 1882, was opened throughout on 1st June 1888. The year 1882 also saw a move to break the LTSR monopoly of the Tilbury Dock traffic in the form of an independent Romford & Tilbury Railway, supported by local landowners. This envisaged a 12-mile double track from the GER at Romford to the LTSR at Grays, with a branch into the new Tilbury Docks. An associated scheme proposed a Tilbury & Gravesend Railway, tunnelling beneath the river. This was sanctioned in August 1882 but the considerable amount of capital required was not attracted and powers were abandoned in

1885. Despite GER support, the Romford & Tilbury also sank, defeated in the Lords but the GER, determination unalloyed, launched its own Tilbury branch in its General Powers Bill of 1883. This line was to branch off from the east end of Romford station, passing west of Upminster and east of South Ockendon before running directly into the Tilbury Docks, then under construction. Failing in its attempt to negotiate with the GER over this challenge, the LTSR put in its own bill, seeking running powers into Romford station for a 2m 5f 5ch line from a junction on the west side of Upminster station on the new cut-off line. South of Upminster the LTSR proposed a line to connect with its main line at West Thurrock about a quarter mile west of Grays station. The GER scheme received support from the Romford Local Board and the Dock Company, the latter no doubt hoping that a little competition would reduce freight rates. Landowners on the other hand saw the LTSR schemes as marginally more helpful to residential development around Upminster. It was the LTSR which emerged as the victor, its two cross country lines receiving sanction on 20th August 1883. This effectively blocked any opportunity for others to grab a share of the Tilbury Dock business. But, once completed in 1886, the Tilbury Docks failed to attract traffic. By 1888 the Dock Co was bankrupt. Cautiously, the LTSR made no start on the Romford-Grays links whilst keeping the powers alive. Eventually fears of GER intentions nagging, a decision was made to build, but as cheaply as possible, laying only a single line. Despite the generally flat nature of the countryside traversed, there were some unavoidable engineering works; a heavy retaining wall to provide space for a separate station at Romford; a 105ft span brick bridge over the Ingrebourne west of Upminster; and the Stifford Viaduct over The Mar Dyke south of Ockendon. The 6¾ mile southern section opened first, on 1st July 1892. It had one intermediate station at Ockendon, 3¼ miles from Upminster, serving the only community of any size along the route. Situated at the west end of the village of South Ockendon, it had two platforms on a passing loop and a small goods yard on the east side. On that side there were substantial brick built ticket and other offices with a two storey house at the south end.

Apprehensive about LTSR trains coming on to its main line to enter Romford station the GER made difficulties, seeking to ease its frustration by offering to lease the Romford-Upminster line from the LTSR at three per cent of its capital cost in return for running powers from Upminster to Tilbury. When this dubious proposition was spurned by the LTSR, the two companies eventually agreed to a separate LTSR station at Romford east of the GER platforms, subject to the GER receiving a small rent for the site. It was also agreed the GER would provide freight facilities at Romford for three years, after which the question of independent accommodation could be raised.

This agreement necessitated a widening of the GER embankment on the south side to provide room for the LTSR's single wooden platform and a run-round loop, the infill held by a 1,260ft retaining wall parallel with Victoria Road. At the west end, the LTSR erected a three-storey building with a 40ft frontage to South Street facing the main entrance to the GER station across the road. This building accommodated the street level ticket office (later moved to platform level), waiting rooms, parcels and other offices as well as the stationmaster's residential quarters. Up above there was no weather protection on the platform apart from some canopied circulating space behind the buffer stops. At a point five chains east of the platform, a connection was laid to the GER Up line for exchange of freight traffic.

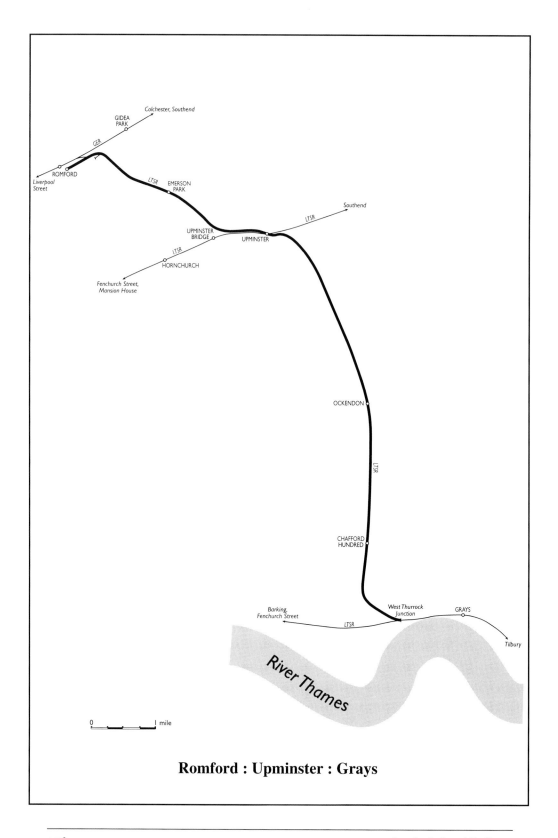

Colchester, Southend

GIDEA
PARK

GER

ROMFORD

Liverpool
Street

LTSR

EMERSON
PARK

Southend

LTSR

UPMINSTER
BRIDGE

UPMINSTER

LTSR

HORNCHURCH

Fenchurch Street,
Mansion House

OCKENDON

LTSR

CHAFFORD
HUNDRED

Barking,
Fenchurch Street

West Thurrock
Junction

GRAYS

LTSR

Tilbury

River Thames

0   1 mile

Romford : Upminster : Grays

At Upminster station, east of the platforms on the north side, a small engine shed was built for the branch locomotives. Train services between Upminster and Romford began on 7th June 1893, numbering eight each way daily between Romford and Grays plus one between Romford and Upminster. On Sundays there were five each way over the whole length and short workings on each section. From Romford to Grays, the LTSR's oil-lit four-wheelers were hauled by Sharp Stewart 4–4–2T in 32–38 minutes but it seems likely there were few through passengers. Signalling arrangements, supplied by the Railway Signal Co, allowed only one train at a time on the three sections controlled by the boxes at Romford, Upminster, Ockendon and West Thurrock Junction.

Leaving behind the eastern edges of Romford town, the line ran across open country to join the LTSR main line just west of the separate bridges over the Ingrebourne. Residential development was just starting around the old agricultural village of Upminster, where the Romford–Grays trains used the northern face of the Down island platform, which was connected to the Up side by a subway.

In July 1896 under the Romford station agreement, the LTSR opened a separate freight yard in Victoria Road, Romford near the point where the two lines diverged. After this, the connection to the GER fell into almost total disuse. From the new yard, one train daily worked through to Tilbury Docks whilst a second, on Wednesdays only, carried animals bound for Romford Market. Freight trains were hauled by LTSR 0–6–2T or the company's only two tender engines, the Sharp, Stewart 0–6–0s built in 1898 for the Ottoman Railways. Poultry and calves in sacks for the Market were also accepted as passenger train traffic, most of this business coming off main line trains at Upminster.

An ancestor of Monsieur Hulot walks along the LTSR platform to board an Upminster train in charge of a Midland Railway tank engine; looking north east, 1921. *H J Patterson Rutherford*

After the Midland Railway had taken over the LTSR in 1912, the freight side was actively developed and further business arose when Hall & Co. of Croydon opened private sidings for building materials on the west side of the line off Manor Road, Romford in 1923. Hall's enterprise was well placed for the resumption of the residential construction which had begun in the district between Romford and Upminster in the 1890s, mostly on the higher ground between the GER main line and the LTSR branch west of the Ingrebourne. An estate called Emerson Park, 220 acres in extent, situated east of Butts Green Road, was purchased for development in 1895. Four years later, the first houses were being advertised. Estates known as Heath Park (near the confluence of the LTSR and GER) and Great Nelmes (adjoining Emerson Park to the north) were advertising house plots in 1904 and 1908 respectively. At Great Nelmes, plots 60ft by 300ft were offered for detached houses with the privilege of 'exclusive use' of Great Nelmes Woods. These developments, along with the Gidea Park Garden City on the north eastern edge of Romford from about 1910 and the Upminster Garden Suburb, north of Upminster station, from about 1903, were all designed to attract the comfortably-off middle class. Though they did not settle hereabouts in any great number, those that did were very articulate and were soon badgering the rival railway managements for additional passenger facilities.

The LTSR responded by opening a single platform on the north side of the cutting just east of the Butts Green Road bridge over the Romford–Upminster line. Protected by a lengthy and prettily-valanced umbrella canopy for much of its length which seemed to anticipate a future island platform, this facility was opened on 1st October 1909. A large wooden nameboard announced it as 'Emerson Park and Great Nelmes' but tickets referred to 'Emerson Park Halt'. A fortnight after its opening, a short loop of about four car length was provided on the north side of the running line a quarter mile west to facilitate reversal of 11 additional trains to and from Upminster. Within five years, the privileged residents of the new area were enjoying another facility: a connection off the 00.10 theatre train out of Fenchurch Street, which delivered them at Emerson Park Halt at 00.54, ready for a hot cocoa and bed.

Generous provision for a Romford–Upminster service; a seven-coach train pauses at Emerson Park and Great Nelmes Halt, LTSR c. 1910. *Commercial postcard*

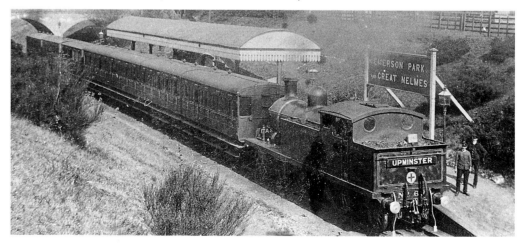

The GER reaction to all this was to start a horse-bus service between the Emerson Park Estate and Romford station, following up with what was to be its last suburban station in the London area: Squirrels Heath & Gidea Park, opened on 1st December 1910 (the two place names were reversed from 1st October 1913 and 'Squirrels Heath' was later dropped altogether). By diverting its buses to run Hornchurch–Emerson Park–Heath Park–Gidea Park station, and wording its station nameboards 'Alight Here for Great Nelmes and Emerson Park', the GER did its level best to draw off the new residential revenue, much of it first or second class.

Such was the confidence in development of traffic that the Midland Railway Bill for the 1914 parliamentary session included a loop from a widened Barking–Upminster line to connect with the Romford branch, which would be doubled. But this was not to be; as World War 1 intensified, the railways had more urgent concerns; the housebuilding around Emerson Park came to a stop; and afterwards life around Upminster would never be quite the same again.

Residential development in the area certainly resumed in the early 1920s but most of the new properties were now small and designed for those further down the social scale than the Edwardian pioneers. By the early 1930s, the triangular area formed by the two railways and the Ingrebourne was almost completely built over with small houses and bungalows and between 1928 and 1939 hundreds more in similar style were erected north of the Hornchurch and Upminster Roads, covering the land between them and the railways. All this brought many new passengers to Emerson Park Halt but their tickets were almost all third class.

Apart from a few new roads at Cranham in the fork between the two lines east of Upminster station, the flatlands around the Upminster–Grays railway remained undeveloped between the wars. Had this been the GWR, there would have been pagoda halts at Cranham and West Thurrock to develop what trade was to be had but the LMSR was little interested in promoting lightly-remunerative local passenger traffic. Although Upminster itself spread south as far as Corbets Tey, this development did not touch the Ockendon line and the new residents found their way north to Upminster station.

On the Ockendon line, most journeys were between Upminster, Grays, Tilbury and Gravesend, the latter encouraged by the availability of through tickets covering both rail and ferryboats. As for freight, the expected use of the line for dock traffic did not materialise, most of it passing to the former GER via Barking and Forest Gate Junction. The statutory requirement to run two freight trains a day via Ockendon was strictly followed but since the Dock traffic did not achieve the guaranteed tonnage prescribed in the legislation, the PLA was obliged to pay compensation to the LTSR. Occasionally the route's strategic value was demonstrated when flooding or other emergencies blocked the LTSR main lines.

The rapid suburban expansion of London between the wars provided the outdated steam railways with increasing problems in handling commuter traffic and when government financial assistance was made available for projects likely to reduce unemployment both the LMSR and the LNER seized the opportunity. The LMSR dug out the Midland's 1914 plans and widened Barking–Upminster to four tracks, electrifying two to carry District line trains as far as Upminster but the Romford branch was left untouched. This scheme involved a major rebuilding of Upminster station, including extension of the LTSR island platform; the provision of a second island to the north for the new Down Local road and the Romford–Grays trains;

improvements on the former Up platform with bay for terminating Grays trains at the eastern end; and a large new entrance and ticket office building on the overline road bridge at the London end. All this work was substantially completed in time for the extension of the District line services on 12th September 1932. Traffic was there for the taking, and on 17th December 1934, on the new local lines a little west of the point where the Romford branch diverted, Upminster acquired a second station, named Upminster Bridge, an island platform serving new housing either side of the Ingrebourne.

The LNER also quadrupled the former GER main line, first as far as Gidea Park, then on to Shenfield. When four new 650ft platforms were provided at Romford in 1931, the former LTSR arrangements were not altered, but from 2nd April 1934 the old LTSR station building was closed for public use except at rail level. This followed an agreement between the LMSR and LNER to rationalise at places where they were in competition and the former LTSR platform now came under LNER control, all passengers passing in and out of the main station via the wooden footway which ran along the south side of the underline road bridge. Although this facility had been provided with the LTSR station in 1893, until 1934 its use had been restricted – there were no through fares via Romford GER/LTSR. The LTSR street building survived until July 1986, when it was demolished following a fire.

By the end of the 1930s the Romford–Upminster line was surrounded by a fully built-up area, though trees and bushes hid much of it from the eyes of passengers, giving quite a false impression. In particular the rural atmosphere of Emerson Park, buried in its dell, was now totally deceptive. Such was the growth of traffic from the new housing north west of Upminster that even the pinch-penny LMSR was moved to introduce some improvement. This came on 1st August 1934 with the arrival of push and pull units powered by former Midland Railway Johnson 0–4–4T (affectionately known as 'One Lung Charlies') which provided some 36 trains a day each way compared with the former 29, four of the new workings shuttling between the Halt and Upminster. Sunday service on the line remained at nine each way, about half working to and from Grays. At this time there were 12 weekday departures from Upminster for Grays or Tilbury, about 14 the other way. Some of these trains ran to and from Romford. With push and pull operation now total, the loop north of Emerson Park was dismantled early in 1936 and from 1st March that year a 'key token' replaced the old train staff.

Wartime brought no major changes apart from a reduction in the number of short workings to and from Emerson Park and these disappeared altogether in 1948. To increase flexibility of working Tilbury Dock traffic should normal paths be damaged by air attack, a running connection was put in between the LNER and LMSR east of Romford station on 21st July 1940. This replaced the original junction, which, together with the LTSR signal box, had been removed in the 1930s, but it was little used until the arrival of diesel cars on the Upminster line.

After the war, the Romford–Upminster line faced a series of threats. Its vulnerability was first indicated in February 1951, when at a time of serious coal shortages, the service was reduced to 16 each way daily and from the end of the following August, when Sunday trains were withdrawn permanently. Steam traction in the form of the remaining 'One Lung Charlies' and N7 0–6–2T, last ran on Saturday, 15th September 1956. On the following Monday diesel railcars doubled the frequency to 32 each way daily, basically half hourly, from 06.05 to 21.22, reducing

BR 42504 on Upminster–Grays–Southend service at Ockendon, 8th May 1960. The signalman is waiting to hand the single line staff to the driver. *Frank Church*

the running time from Romford to Upminster to eight minutes and ending through running on to the Grays line. In connection with provision of a new Underground car depot east of the platforms, Upminster station underwent further reconstruction at this time. With platform faces 4 and 5 allocated exclusively to District Line trains, a new platform 6 was carved out of the cutting slope on the north side for the Romford trains, coming into use on 20th May 1957. Another consequence of the LT depot was the removal of the crossing west of Upminster station in 1959, which left the wartime connection at Romford the only outlet; this was regularly used by the diesel cars when proceeding from and to their depot at Stratford.

Following a census taken in the summer of 1964, the Romford–Upminster line was included in the notorious Beeching list of proposed passenger closures. Formal notice of abandonment from 4th January 1965 appeared in August 1964 along with details of proposed new and augmented bus services. Beeching's census-takers had counted 588 passengers joining Upminster trains between 06.05 and 21.10, 321 of them alighting at Emerson Park, where 139 boarded, making a total of 406 arriving at Upminster through the day. In the reverse direction, the corresponding figures for the same June Monday were 397, 121, 346 and 622. Maximum activity at Emerson Park focussed on the 08.24, which took up 101 commuters for Romford and the 08.37, which loaded 37 for Upminster. Some trains in the middle of the day were found to be carrying but three or four passengers.

Opposition to closure was well organised; hearings before the Transport Users' Consultative Committee established hardship, and in October 1965 the Minister issued a reprieve, recognising that the line's contribution to commuter travel outweighed the net gain on closure calculated by the accountants. Despite this, a second attempt at the kill was mounted in 1969, prompted by identification of an annual cash deficit of £70,000 and a net saving from abandonment of £40,000. Again the defence was successful; another reprieve was granted in 1972 after it had been noted traffic was responding to local publicity and that savings were to be had by restricting the trains to two-car sets.

Freight traffic was no exception to the general trend at London local stations. Upminster lost its yard from 7th December 1964 and freight trains disappeared from the line with the closure of Hall's Romford sidings and the former LTS yard in Victoria Road, Romford from 4th May 1970.

Diesel car working became increasingly unreliable, causing many cancellations and it was with some relief that users heard in August 1984 of the intention to electrify this 3¼ mile line as part of a programme to eliminate the anomaly of diesel car sets working out of Stratford depot to operate three lines* within what was otherwise a totally-electrified zone. The conversion was done at minimum cost: between the outer end of Romford station and the point of divergence the gantries on the main line were used to support the 25kV overhead traction supply; a cheaper method of mast erection, used on the East Coast main line was adopted; and reconstruction of two low overline bridges was avoided by inserting neutral sections. Emerson Park's platform was extended to accommodate the three-car Class 305 electric sets to be used. Resignalling eliminated the last of the semaphore signals in the area, and electric working started on 12th May 1986. Driver-only operation was introduced in the following year.

A few years before the electrification, juvenile vandalism had emerged as a serious problem. In an effort to protect drivers and passengers from injury arising from collisions with objects placed between the rails, some of the diesel units had been fitted with powerful headlights in 1980. Emerson Park became a centre for the perpetrators. Its little ticket office, burnt out in 1987, was replaced with an ugly structure at considerable cost and the automatic ticket and permit to travel machines subsequently installed were soon totally wrecked. On the trains, manned only by a driver, the interiors were defaced by paint sprays or the contents of fire extinguishers. When exhausted, the extinguishers were thrown on the track, which was also used as a dump for torn-out train seats, supermarket trolleys or anything else that might cause satisfying noise or damage. Some drivers refused to work after dark. In 1993 and again in 1994, the harassed management announced that they were considering withdrawing all but a few commuter trains and the service was sometimes stopped as a result of vandalism. Police action restored calm but a police presence could not be continuously maintained. On a service already making a cash loss, the depletion in off-peak travel and revenue arising from such events was a serious matter which, if they persisted, seemed likely to once again bring closure into focus.

On the other side of Upminster, the single line railway enjoyed something of change of fortune in the immediate post-war years. The LCC Aveley Estate, at South Ockendon, opened in 1950, was to cover 391.25 acres, accommodating a population of almost 22,000. This development clothed the railway on both sides with houses and industrial buildings for about 1½ miles south of Ockendon station. Ideally the station should have been moved to a more central position in the new community to stimulate maximum patronage of the train service but no funds for this were made available by the authorities. Whilst many of the adult residents at Aveley found employment locally, or soon enough acquired cars to reach workplaces along the Thames Estuary, there was some increase in traffic through the day, from shopping and entertainment travel and from youngsters commuting to shop and office employment further afield.

* The other two were the Southminster and North Woolwich branches.

After the introduction of diesel cars on the Romford section. Grays trains worked in and out of the Up side bay at Upminster, at first powered by a variety of steam locos: N7 0–6–2T, LTSR 4–4–2T and 0–6–2T, ex GNR C12 4–4–2T and BR 2–6–4T. Most trains were formed of three-car push-pull sets. Then from 6th January 1958, diesel cars were introduced, providing a basic half hourly service (hourly on Sundays) with a journey time of 15 min and additional workings in the peak period. Some trains ran through to Tilbury Riverside.

Sustained by the new industries of Aveley, Ockendon yard remained open until May 1968. Freight did not entirely disappear from the line even then as oil and cement trains were diverted over it as occasion required.

It was this strategic value and possibly the extra traffic brought by Aveley that caused BR to include the line in its LTS electrification scheme. The conversion was completed in time to allow the four-coach electric sets to work hourly (every 30 min between Ockendon and Upminster) from 17th June 1963. On Sundays there were hourly trains between Fenchurch Street and Tilbury Riverside via Ockendon. Between West Thurrock Junction and Grays station (where they could terminate in a Down side bay) the electric trains were able to use a new third track, worked by tokenless track circuit block. Trains continued to pass at the Ockendon loop in peak hours until the signal box there was gutted by fire on Christmas Eve 1977. After a period of working with one train on line, the new signalling was commissioned in November 1978. There were colour light signals at Ockendon, where use of the loop was restored and the whole line was worked with tokenless track circuit block under control of Upminster box. Both the Grays and the Romford lines came under the new Upminster Integrated Electronic Control Centre when this was opened on 17th April 1995, replacing all the manual boxes in the area. This change, which included a new track layout between West Thurrock Junction and Grays, was completed on 8th April 1996. Off peak traffic between Upminster and Grays has declined since the 1960s but some increase may be expected from more recent developments. First to appear was the Lakeside retail centre, with its 250 shops, opened in October 1990. Sited south of Aveley, below the level of the railway and west of it, Lakeside is close to the M25 motorway and with its huge car parks, is primarily succoured by road transport. Closely behind and still in progress at the time of writing was Chafford Hundred, a new community of 5,000 homes between the railway and Grays. Planning permission for this was granted on condition the developers provided a new station and this came into public use on 30th May 1995. Using 'traditional' design and materials in the hope of achieving what was described as 'a welcoming, comfortable feel to complement the growing new community', it had a single 12-car length platform on the Down side, a brick building featuring a gabled glass-walled atrium as its centre piece, a forecourt and a 150-space car park. Bus services provided a link to the Lakeside Shopping Centre.

In preparation for traffic growth, the peak service was doubled in September 1995, with some trains running through to and from Fenchurch Street via Ockendon and Chafford Hundred. This may be a portent. Certainly this section of the former LTSR cross-country line does seem likely to have a more assured future than the northern part and various options have been discussed, including doubling throughout and diversion of all the services between Fenchurch Street and Grays–Pitsea stations over it, perhaps leaving the stations between Barking and Grays to an extension of the Gospel Oak–Barking service.

Millwall Extension Railway Manning Wardle 2-4-0T No.6 on North Greenwich train of two ex-GER oil-lit four-wheel coaches at Millwall Junction station, c. 1905.

Railways to Blackwall & North Greenwich (map page 416)

'It will be apparent even to the most sceptical, that few undertakings embrace more important advantages than the present'. A potential investor, reading these words in the 1835 prospectus for a railway between the City of London and Blackwall learned that the 'advantages' were those to be derived from constructing a short cut to the meandering and dangerous river passage round the Isle of Dogs; it was claimed that not only would this reduce the cost of transporting goods to and from the East and West India Docks, but would cut an hour each way from the journey of those using the numerous Thames estuary steamer services, all of which called at Brunswick Wharf, Blackwall. Pickings from this river steamer traffic between London and the estuary towns and beyond were certainly worth having in the early 1830s when around 1,750,000 passengers a year were travelling this way to Gravesend, Margate and Ramsgate alone. Brunswick Wharf was also an embarkation point for the numerous emigrants to the colonies. Along the Commercial Road there were almost 100 return bus journeys daily between London and Blackwall, some of them operated by the West India Dock Company.

Proposals for improving communications between the West India Docks and the City of London dated back to 1825, when an iron flange tramway along the Commercial Road had been suggested. Although this was formulated into a parliamentary bill in 1828, it failed for lack of support. Two schemes for railways between the City and the West India Docks were evolved in 1835, one, whose prospectus is quoted above, with George Stephenson as engineer, the other, engineered by Sir John Rennie, having the title The Commercial Railway. It was the latter which succeeded in obtaining an act on 28th July 1836. Just over 3½ miles of line were proposed from the Minories at the eastern edge of the City, to Brunswick Wharf, Blackwall, running south of the Commercial Road; if the dock companies requested, there were to be branches into both the East and West India Docks. Since the inner part of the area was already built over, the width of the formation was restricted to 25 yards, except where there were railway installations, passing places or loading points. The railway company was authorised to use locomotives, stationary engines or 'other power', but any steam engines employed were to 'consume their own smoke' and their funnels were to be fitted with a 'gauze of wires' at a maximum of one eighth of an inch apart, to reduce the fire risk to the sails and timber of vessels. The West India Dock Co. was empowered to hold shares in the railway and the chairmen and deputy chairmen of both the East & West India Dock Companies were to be given seats on the railway's board.

A further act in 1837 extended time for acquisition of land and allowed the East India Dock Company to subscribe, correcting what appears to have been an error of drafting in the original statute. Both dock companies did in the event subscribe capital, but were limited by the second act to a maximum of £50,000. Another part of the 1837 bill did not succeed. All along, the promoters had wished to have a worthwhile entry into the City but were obstructed in this intent by the Corporation. A proposed terminus in Lime Street was rejected by the Corporation on the grounds that it would increase street congestion.

Realising that the success of its passenger business depended on a convenient City terminus, the company made another attempt in 1839, when a less ambitious invasion of only 415 yards across the boundary to a terminus 'at or near' Fenchurch Street was allowed. This 1839 act also changed the name of the undertaking to the London & Blackwall Railway. In return for the use of its hallowed territory, the City Corporation obtained many protections, amongst them a ban on stationary and other steam engines within its boundary, except on the east side of the Minories. Another section of this act allowed the railway company to negotiate with the newly-amalgamated East & West India Docks Company over the use of Brunswick Wharf.

This was to be the first railway to cross an area of London already fully built over with streets and houses. Not until the Isle of Dogs was approached was there any open land, so on the western section, as far as the West India Dock, the tracks were placed on a brick viaduct of 285 arches, mostly of 30ft span, to eliminate level crossings and minimise demolition. Streets and water were spanned by iron girder bridges, the Limehouse Basin and Limehouse Cut of the Regent's Canal by structures of three and one 87ft spans respectively. There was very considerable scope for compensation in the 1836 act, so much so that despite the restricted width, land owners and property owners waited upon the directors daily with demands 'compared with which the exactions of the country gentry were liberal arrangements'. After leaving this costly viaduct, the line was in cutting for most of the distance to the Blackwall terminus.

William Tite designed for Blackwall a handsome brick and Portland stone two-storey building presenting a 105ft long, 45ft high frontage of 'Roman-Doric character' to the river. Parallel to the railway on the south side, but partly extending beyond the buffers, the accommodation included ladies' and gentlemen's waiting rooms and lavatories, a booking hall, and above it, a large room borrowed by the customs men when ships serving foreign and colonial ports berthed here. Along much of the length of the platform the frontage was extended in the form of a blind arcaded brick wall supporting one side of the 'light and elegant' all-over roof which offered some protection to carriages stored in the station overnight until it fell into disrepair and was replaced around the turn of the century by the usual umbrella-type valanced awnings. At first there was but one track, with a wide platform bounded by the brick wall mentioned, but the introduction of steam traction in 1849 required alterations in the layout. Three tracks were then made, with a narrow island platform between two of them, its northern face much longer than the southern one. The third road was used as a carriage siding until eventually a platform took its place. No such extravagance was shown at Minories, a temporary terminus pending further advance into the City. A two-track, side-platform station, this had an overall roof which provided less protection than the one at Blackwall. Five small stations were erected to serve the populous district traversed: Shadwell, Stepney, Limehouse, West India Dock and Poplar (re-sited in 1845). Others were subsequently added at Cannon Street Road (21st August 1842), Leman Street (1st June 1877) and Millwall Junction (18th December 1871), but the first of these lasted only six years and the others closed from 7th July 1941 and from 4th May 1926 respectively. With stations so closely-spaced and the potential fire danger to the timber and ropeyards clustered against the viaduct and to the vast expanse of sailcloth and rigging in Limehouse Basin, it was thought wise to avoid the use of steam locomotives. This advice, given to the directors in an 1837 report by the engineer George Parker Bidder, was endorsed by both George and Robert Stephenson, the latter suggesting that rope-haulage would also be cheaper as space was restricted and land costs were very high. Robert told the parliamentary committee in 1836 that considering the 'immense value of the property on every side' he thought the railway would have to be abandoned rather than use steam engines.

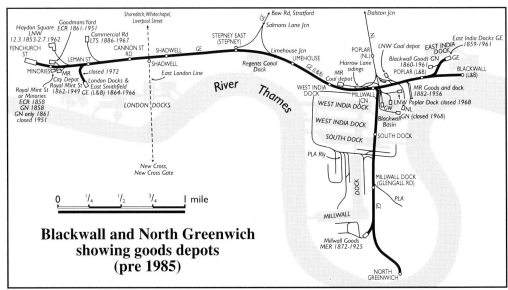

Blackwall and North Greenwich showing goods depots (pre 1985)

Bidder and George Stephenson were appointed engineers for the line in January 1838, a decision having been made for a 5ft gauge rope-hauled system. The gauge was that of the neighbouring Eastern Counties Railway which was to open about the same time, and with which future connection for traffic exchange was expected.

Public service on one track only started on 6th July 1840, the second line following on 3rd August. From the latter date, a 15-minute frequency was worked every day of the week between 08.30 and 20.45. Widened out to earlier starts and later finishes, this frequency was to remain unaltered until 1883. The intermediate stations at Limehouse, West India Dock and Poplar opened with the line on 6th July; Stepney was not ready until August and Shadwell came into use from 1st October.* Two classes of accommodation were offered in the blue-painted six-wheeled coaches but some of the inferior class had open sides and no seats under the rudimentary roof.

At each end of the line were a pair of steam winding engines. Minories had Maudsley & Field marine condensing engines developing 110–115hp, but the engines sited between Poplar and Blackwall were only 70–75hp machines as the line fell some 68ft from the viaduct to its eastern end. Two hemp ropes, each about seven miles long, wound on to one drum as they were uncoiled from the drum at the opposite end of the line, guided at about 30mph along the tracks by cast-iron sheaves of 3ft diameter spaced 33ft apart. Both the 'north line' and the 'south line' were equipped in this fashion and used alternately for traffic in each direction.

The method of working was rather curious. At the start of each day there would be one coach standing at each intermediate station. As the rope began to move, these would be attached to it, proceeding as one-car 'trains' to Blackwall without further stops. Also, as the rope moved, a complete train attached to the same rope left Minories, detaching a single coach at each station it passed. When the residue of two coaches reached Blackwall, it would be marshalled with the collection of single coaches already arrived there to form a return train. The whole operation was then carried out in reverse, using the same track; the single coaches dropped at each intermediate station on the outward journey returned one by one to Minories, followed by the train, which again discarded a single coach at each station on its way. A similar sequence was performed on the other line. By this means an end-to-end journey could be made in 10 to 15 minutes, compared with about one hour on the river when conditions were favourable. Modifications were made to the rope working from time to time but there were always some journeys that could not be completed without going to a terminus and working back along the line. All movements of the ropes were controlled by signals on Cooke & Wheatstone's single needle telegraph instruments, used here for the first time on a public railway. Blackwall station, beyond the engine house, was entered on a slight upward gradient, enabling the incoming coaches to be detached from the rope and sent in on a slowing momentum. This feature also allowed a gravity-assisted departure, with some muscular contribution by the staff. A similar arrangement existed at Fenchurch Street, in conformity with the City's ban on steam engines.

The City terminus, just south of Fenchurch Street, and named after it, was opened on 2nd August 1841. Behind an unassuming frontage by William Tite was a modest two-platform train-shed. In deference to the City's collective conscience, a provision

---

* Shadwell closed after traffic on 21st May 1916, reopened from 5th May 1919 and was permanently closed from 7th July 1941.

in the 1839 act forbade railway operations here on Sundays, Good Fridays and Christmas Days, but the Sunday trains which had always worked to and from Minories came into Fenchurch Street from Sunday 5th June 1842, the ban having been lifted by the act of that year, which noted that the extension had been totally enclosed. With the sinful railway working decently obscured behind fenestrated walls and a roof of slate and iron, the God-fearing City Corporation went to church with a clear conscience. In his evidence to the 1846 Royal Commission on Metropolitan Railway Termini, the superintendent of the London & Blackwall Railway averred that the short extension into Fenchurch Street which had cost £250,000, had increased its business by 50 per cent. It also caused the collapse of traffic at Minories, which was closed permanently after the last train on 23rd October 1853.

Although rope haulage provided speeds which were high for the period and was clean and relatively safe, it proved expensive and troublesome in operation. Manpower requirements were high, with two men on each coach to attend to the speedy conclusion of rope-gripping and slipping, and maintenance costs were also heavy. When after a very short time the original ropes wore down, they were replaced by steel wire rope which caused much distress by twisting. Travel on the Blackwall in this period was always something of an adventure, demanding patience and a well-developed sense of humour. The directors were soon regretting their decision, longing to break out of their isolation and attract the traffic of other lines to their well-situated City terminus. In 1845 they supported a London & Blackwall Railway Extension Bill seeking powers for a line from Stepney to join the Eastern Counties Railway near the River Lea at Old Ford; from here the promoters cheekily proposed running powers over the ECR as far as Stratford, whence they would build their own line northwards to Epping. These suggestions were vigorously resisted by the ECR, which was also not keen on the idea that some of its trains might be diverted from the Shoreditch terminus into Fenchurch Street. But during the passage of the bill, the ECR opposition was withdrawn on condition that the running powers were dropped and the Epping line be left to the ECR to build as the company thought fit. The London & Blackwall Railway Extension Act of 1845 gave the London & Blackwall company power to lease the Extension and to purchase it, which was done in February 1846.

To allow the expected through running, the act required the Extension to be built to standard gauge (the Eastern Counties had been converted to standard by October 1844), and in preparation, the original line was narrowed to standard gauge and worked with steam locomotives from 15th February 1849. Between 1848 and 1860 the Blackwall company acquired nine handsome passenger locomotives, all 2–2–2 well tanks by Jones, Potts & Co or George England & Co, also two England 2–4–0T for freight working. All were painted blue and shedded at Blackwall. The last one survived until 1883. The old 5ft gauge Blackwall coaches, retrucked for standard gauge working, were still in use in the mid-1860s when complaints were being made about their condition. Residual fears of fire led to the erection of a light iron roof to trap sparks and hot cinders on the section of viaduct through Limehouse Basin. Speeds were generally better than in cable days, and from 22nd June 1849 until 5th November 1854 a service was run non-stop between Fenchurch Street and Blackwall in five minutes, in connection with the Gravesend steamers, a time which could not be matched by public transport today or by car, except perhaps on a clear road at dead of night.

The Extension opened on 2nd April 1849, but was of limited use as the ECR continued to create difficulties. Although exchange platforms had been built, few ECR trains called and the ECR facility was closed from 6th January 1851. Regular traffic over a junction here between the two railways did not pass until 13th April 1854. Meanwhile, the Blackwall worked a 15-minute service between Fenchurch Street and its new station at Bow Road (known as Bow & Bromley), apparently going forward to the exchange platforms (Victoria Park & Bow) only on the rare occasions when it was possible to make a connection with the ECR trains.

The Blackwall was eventually released from its isolation by the arrival of the East & West India Docks & Birmingham Junction Railway (later more neatly renamed the North London Railway). This line, partly subsidised by the East & West India Dock Company, opened between Islington (later Highbury & Islington) and a junction with the London & Blackwall Extension at Bow near what was known later as Gas Factory Junction) on 26th September 1850. From that date, a 15-minute service was worked between Fenchurch Street and Islington, extended, with the opening of the line to Camden Town (now Camden Road) on 7th December. These trains, which brought a substantial accretion of traffic to the Blackwall, much of it of a commuter nature despite the roundabout route, were extended west to Hampstead Road (now Primrose Hill) on 9th June 1851. Until physical connection was made with the LNWR on 15th February 1851, some rolling stock and train crews were temporarily hired from the Blackwall Company. With the start of the North London service, Blackwall Railway trains between Fenchurch Street and Bow & Bromley were withdrawn and the latter station was closed.

As both parties came to realise the advantages of co-operation, relations between the Blackwall and the ECR gradually improved, so much so that the two companies sponsored a railway called the London, Tilbury & Southend, designed to secure the pleasure traffic to Gravesend and Southend and make better use of the western section of the Blackwall. The first section of the LTSR, from Forest Gate Junction on the ECR to Tilbury was opened on 13th April 1854, the trains running through to Fenchurch Street via Stratford and the 1848 link at Bow. From this time, the section of the Blackwall between Bow Junction and Fenchurch Street falls outside our terms of reference and the reader needing its later history must look to histories of the London, Tilbury & Southend.

The new friendliness between the Blackwall and its neighbour was sustained after the ECR's absorption into the GER from 1st July 1862. Negotiations followed which led to the London & Blackwall Lease Act, 1865 which authorised the L&BR to lease its undertaking to the GER, a lease which was to operate from 1st January 1866 for 999 years, with the GER guaranteeing the Blackwall dividends of 4½ per cent on its ordinary capital. The small company retained a nominally independent existence until finally absorbed into the LNER in 1923. Another part of the 1865 act opened up the Blackwall to much heavier freight use by granting running powers to the Midland, the LNWR and the GNR (the NLR was merely assured of the passenger running powers enjoyed since 1850 and the goods powers of 1853, in return for which it undertook to run into Fenchurch Street every 15 minutes, an obligation removed by the 1865 act).

Two more links were made between the eastern end of the Blackwall and other lines. In October 1851 for coal, and on 1st January 1852 for all freight, the East & West India Docks & Birmingham Junction Railway was extended from Bow to West

India Docks, with a coal depot at Poplar and a spur to the Blackwall line. Use was at first confined to freight, but after the opening of Broad Street station, a passenger service was started on 1st August 1866 between that terminus and a new NLR station at Poplar. North London trains ceased to run into Fenchurch Street after traffic on 31st December 1868, the GER substituting a passenger service between Fenchurch Street and the NLR at Bow which ran from the following day, lasting until close of traffic on 3rd April 1892. A more convenient connection for passenger trains between the Blackwall and the NLR at Poplar opened on 1st September 1870 and was used until 30th June 1890 by an extension of the Broad Street–Poplar (NLR) service to Blackwall in connection with river steamers. This Poplar connection lost much of its former value after the opening of the Limehouse Curve on 5th April 1880; seeing little use after the cessation of the NLR trains to Blackwall, it was removed in August 1890. The double-track Limehouse Curve, first authorised in 1865, completed the triangle at Stepney, enabling trains to run direct from Blackwall to the GER at Bow Junction and, via Gas Factory Junction, on to the NLR at Bow. Extending from Salmons Lane Junction on the Stepney–Bow line to Limehouse Junction, just west of Limehouse station, it was used from 1st September 1880 by a Palace Gates–Stratford–Blackwall service, but this was unsuccessful and ceased after traffic on 28th February 1881. Passenger trains were seen again on the Curve in the summers of 1890 and 1891 when a Sunday service carried dockers and their families to a few hours' cheap excitement at Southend.

Although the Blackwall Railway promoters had envisaged freight movement between the docks and the City, the reasons why this had not materialised are not difficult to find. Double transhipment over such a short distance, with mixed rope and animal haulage would be unduly costly compared with the traditional lighterage, and in any case the layout of the two-horse cartage dock complexes was not conducive to the provision of an adequate railway layout without major rearrangement.* This last factor continued to limit freight activity to and from the old docks even after the Blackwall had been linked to the main railway system and converted to steam traction. But despite this disappointment, the location of the Blackwall line assured it of a strong growth in freight traffic once it had been connected to the other railways. Using the running powers established in 1865, other companies added their own goods depots and yards to those built by the Blackwall. Between 1853 and 1866 ten installations appeared along the L&BR at the City end and between West India Dock station and Blackwall,† owned by five different companies (LNWR, GER, Midland, GNR and LTSR), all but one of which worked their own locomotives to and from their depots (Haydon Square, LNWR, was served by NLR locomotives). As early as 1862 the GNR and Midland depots at Royal Mint Street were alone handling some 310,000 tons of freight a year.

Passenger business in the early years was not unsatisfactory, although many

---

* Although the Blackwall Railway built a branch from near Leman Street to the Wool Warehouse of the London Docks in 1864 (the Dock Company guaranteed 5 per cent on the capital) it did not prove possible to lay further tracks in the dock area. A second branch from near Poplar (L&BR) station into the East India Docks served mainly a GNR goods depot, extending only for a very short distance on to the North Quay of the Export Dock.

† The locations and dates of these depots are shown on the map on page 416.

Millwall Extension Railway train for Millwall Junction at North Greenwich, with unidentified Manning Wardle 2-4-0T, c. 1905. *Lens of Sutton*

steamboat users continued to go on board in the City despite the saving in time that the train offered. Seeking to capture some of the river trade, the Blackwall Railway in 1843 bought from Thames Ironworks steam vessels *The Railway*, *The Brunswick* and *The Blackwall* to start an hourly through-fare service between Fenchurch Street, Woolwich and Gravesend. But the once-thriving regular steamer services between London and the estuary towns collapsed as soon as railways were opened along the river, and the Blackwall turned its energies, as we have seen, to attracting other railways on to its system. On the river, pleasure sailings continued to bring uncertain and seasonal grist to the Blackwall mill until 1914.

Almost from the opening, rather more than half the passengers carried between Fenchurch Street and Blackwall were local as distinct from river users, and in the early years there was a considerable amount of Sunday pleasure traffic to Blackwall, where the crowds strolled by the river, watching the shipping and refreshing themselves at the *Railway Tavern* and the *Brunswick Hotel*. Through the nineteenth century the line was used mostly by workmen moving between the intermediate stations and the docks, sailors, craftsmen and others with business at the docks, and, until the telephone came into general use in offices in the 1890s and 1900s, messengers between the City shipping offices and ships. About the time the latter traffic started to fade, the Blackwall really began to feel the tramway competition which had begun with a horse-drawn service along the Commercial and East India Dock Roads in December 1872. Reductions of the Blackwall service were initiated as early as October 1883 when Sunday intervals were extended from 15 to 30 minutes. In 1902 the weekday frequency became 20 minutes instead of 15, and the Sunday trains ceased altogether from 4th October 1908, probably a direct result of the opening of the electric tramway from Aldgate to Poplar on 15th December 1906. A further cut to half-hourly on weekdays was offered as part of the GER contribution to manpower economies at the height of World War 1. It is unlikely that these reductions caused much hardship, so it is surprising to find that quarter-hourly intervals were restored in 1919 even though the traffic day was shortened from around 07.00 to 20.00 (07.00 to 15.00 on Saturdays). For years these trains were handled by the 150 class, the smallest of the GER's 0–6–0T, with 1300 class 2–4–2T sometimes appearing.

The newly-formed LNER was not long in deciding that the Blackwall service was expendable, announcing in 1926 that the passenger service would be withdrawn after 30th June. However the issue was decided by the coal shortages caused by the miners' strike and by the General Strike that year, so that in practice no trains were run after the last working on the evening of 3rd May.

Goods traffic kept the line busy for another decade or so, but quickly diminished when both docks and railway installations suffered severe damage from German air attacks early in World War 2. From 1949, as the map on page 416 shows, all remaining depots and yards were closed. At Blackwall the scene was radically changed in 1947 by the erection of a huge electric power station on the site of the passenger terminus and the East India Export Dock. The few freight movements that remained in the early 1950s were being worked on and off the line via the Limehouse curve; the old London & Blackwall Railway viaduct across the base of the triangle between Stepney East station and Limehouse carried only the former Up line, used as a siding since 1951 from the Limehouse end for occasional transhipments of crane-lifted scrap metal between railway wagons and lighters in the Basin below. This section, together with Limehouse curve, went out of use on 5th November 1962.

Poplar Dock was silted up when visited by a party of railway students in November 1954, but a fine specimen of a Midland Railway signal box and Midland signals were discovered intact, one of the latter with no role other than that of warning drivers not to take their trains over the edge of the dock into the mist-shrouded river. Although not officially closed until 1956, all activity here had ceased long before that date. Connections into the docks at Millwall Junction remained in use until the early 1960s, as did the extensive sidings west of that station, but most of the docks traffic, including the bulk grain moving out to Welwyn Garden City to be made into the breakfast cereal called 'Shredded Wheat', was routed via the old NLR line and Bow. Tracks east of Millwall were taken up in 1967 and a direct line was built from Poplar NLR yard to the western Poplar docks across the bed of the Blackwall Railway. This link, opened in May 1968 to replace the old high-level NLR access lines, was used by trains entering via Victoria Park over the former NLR line, which was singled from 19th August 1979. Connected to it were some remnants of the Blackwall Railway tracks which extended through the site of Millwall Junction as far west as Ming Street. These lines were visited by freight trains (latterly carrying scrap metal) until 1981, the last movement into Poplar docks taking place on 30th August that year. The track between Poplar and Victoria Park was lifted in 1984.

To the west, the London & Blackwall and the Extension Railway formation between Fenchurch Street and Bow continued to be very busy with fast and frequent electric passenger trains to Barking, Tilbury and Southend.

For many years the old London & Blackwall viaduct east of Limehouse remained, neglected, weed grown and trackless, but its usefulness was far from over, for as we shall see at the end of this chapter, it was destined for a second life, carrying a new railway to Blackwall and beyond.

Poplar station, London & Blackwall Railway, looking west, 20th November 1954. The track on the right leads to the former GNR Blackwall and GER East India Dock goods depots. *Alan A Jackson*

Millwall Junction signalbox and station, looking east, 20th November 1954. The North Greenwich line diverges right, where the goods brake van is standing; the London & Blackwall Railway to Blackwall runs straight ahead, and the connection to the North London Railway is at the left. *Alan A Jackson*

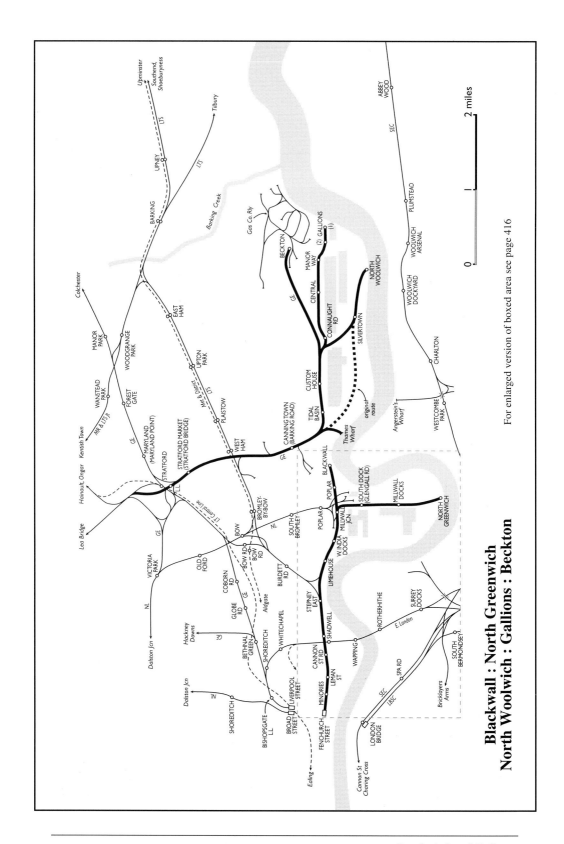

Blackwall : North Greenwich
North Woolwich : Gallions : Beckton

For enlarged version of boxed area see page 416

2 miles

A somewhat curious offshoot of the London & Blackwall was the Millwall Extension Railway, a single track authorised by the London, Blackwall & Millwall Extension Railway Act of 19th June 1865 and which, although a mere 1m 49ch in length was initially split amongst three companies and operated in four separately-owned sections. Its main task was to serve the Millwall Docks which had been opened in the southern part of the Isle of Dogs on 14th March 1868, the first docks in London to be provided with a complete internal railway system, much of it with sharp radius curves. In the hope of securing some of the traffic between central London and the town on the opposite bank, the MER was extended beyond the Docks to the southern tip of the Isle of Dogs to terminate at a station accurately, if somewhat misleadingly called North Greenwich.

The Millwall Canal Company (Millwall Dock Company from 1870) was of course the principal party in promoting the MER, but it was actively assisted by the London & Blackwall, and later, the GER. This collaboration was immeasurably eased by the fraternal relationship of the respective general managers of the dock company and the GER, a happy state of affairs only matched by the ill-feeling of the East & West India Docks Co., which saw the project as encouraging a rival by making use of its land for a railway 'prejudicial and injurious to their undertaking and calculated seriously to interfere with the Trade and Shipping Interest of the Port of London in connexion therewith'. However, agreement was eventually reached with the London & Blackwall on 21st March 1865 by which E&WID opposition was withdrawn provided the railway through its premises was built, owned and controlled by the company and not worked with locomotive power. It was stipulated that if the London & Blackwall wished to operate a locomotive-hauled passenger service on the Isle of Dogs, another line would have to be built under the Dock company's property instead of the proposed surface railway. Both dock companies eventually contributed to the construction and working of the line, controlling it through a joint committee on which the GER was also represented.

From Millwall Junction, a new station between West India Dock and Poplar (L&BR) stations, the first five chains of the North Greenwich branch were owned by the L&BR, the next 41ch were the property of the London & India Docks Co. and were followed by 52ch owned by the Millwall Dock Co. The final 31ch were again part of the L&BR. Three swing bridges of rather flimsy construction combined with light track and the vast quantity of tarred wood and sail near the line caused the dock companies to reject the use of steam locomotives within their boundaries, and when the line opened for goods traffic from Millwall Junction to Millwall Dock on 18th December 1871, horses were used. From the same day, a half-hourly service was worked, using single cars hauled by two Millwall Dock Co. horses, calling at the intermediate station and crossing place, South Dock, and a station named Millwall Dock on the south side of Glengall Road, serving the workmen's colony of Cubitt Town. The original passenger vehicles were four large Starbuck tramcars which later went to the Wisbech & Upwell Tramway. Millwall Junction had three platforms, those from the Up Fenchurch Street line and branch splaying into the fork of the junction. Brick station offices occupied the wider part of the triangle and connection with the outside world was by footbridge. The other two stations, built partly in brick, but mainly in wood, had only one platform. From June 1872 the passenger service was increased to four journeys an hour, starting at 07.30 and ending at 16.30.

With the opening of the Millwall Dock–North Greenwich section on 29th July 1872 a full passenger service was started with GER locomotives taking over the single car from the horses at the southern boundary of Millwall Docks. The locomotives had been moved on to the line with their fires out, hauled by horses. This final part of the branch was on a 682yd brick viaduct terminating at a single wooden platform at North Greenwich where there was an engine run-round road, a small engine shed and carriage sidings, but no goods facilities. The tracks finished at a substantial barrier just above the river's edge.

The first locomotive was *Ariel's Girdle*, built by Kitson's and shown at the Great Exhibition of 1851 before being purchased by the ECR. Originally a 2–2–0 well tank, it was rebuilt in 1868 as a 2–4–0T with 4ft driving wheels. Its place on the North Greenwich line was taken in 1878 by a Kitson four-wheeled tram engine with a vertical boiler.

Doing its best to secure a Greenwich traffic, the GER transferred its Blackwall–Greenwich steam ferry service to the pier at North Greenwich in 1874 after purchasing the ferry rights from the Poplar & Greenwich Ferry Co. The latter's pier, about 200yd from the railway, was replaced in 1877 by a new pier near the station. Through bookings were arranged between Fenchurch Street and what the GER was pleased to call 'South Greenwich' at an advertised journey time of 36 minutes. This gave the Millwall Dock Company the ability to draw on labour south of the river, leading in time to a substantial traffic in workmen. In accordance with the terms of the 1865 act, a penny fare workmen's train had been run since 1872. Another feature was the carriage of crowds to see Millwall Rovers Football Club after its formation in 1885. On occasion these trains loaded up to five crowded coaches, placing considerable strain on the tiny locomotives of what was virtually a light railway. This problem disappeared after 1910 when the football club moved to its present New Cross ground.

Anxious to provide an alternative to the dangerous and uncertain ferry operations in winter fogs, the LCC built a pedestrian and cyclist tunnel between Greenwich Church Street and North Greenwich. This opened on 4th August 1902, the GER agreeing to close its ferry (after 31st October) when offered £8,000 of the ratepayers' money as compensation.

Horse operation through the dock area continued for eight years after opening, when, with some strengthening of the swing bridges and a change of attitude by the dock companies' insurers, steam traction was introduced. The Millwall Dock Company purchased three small Manning Wardle 2–4–0T with 3ft 6in driving

North Greenwich train of three ex-GER coaches at Millwall Dock station, Glengall Road, Millwall Extension Railway. 'Coffee Pot' Manning Wardle 2-4-0T bears its PLA number 29 (ex MER 4), c. 1910.

wheels. Of a type used by civil engineering contractors on temporary railways, these engines imposed minimal strains on the flimsy track and were used for all passenger trains together with hired GER coaches from 23rd August 1880. Known locally as 'coffee pots' from their tall smokestacks and spark arresters, they were first painted dark yellow, later altered to brick red, lined in black. Rebuilt in 1905, they passed into Port of London Authority ownership when that body was formed in 1909, continuing to haul the branch trains of two or three oil-lit four-wheel GER coaches until November 1922.

For most of the period a 15-minute service was operated from about 07.00 until 18.00, then half-hourly until about 22.00. Sunday trains, usually half-hourly with a church interval from 10.00 to 13.00, did not call at South Dock, and ran from 29th August 1880 to 28th December 1913. Some workmen's trains and other early morning workings were started in July 1883. Operation was by train staff and ticket, with staffs exchanged at each end and at South Dock.

All the rolling stock was stored at North Greenwich, and although the GER provided guards, the drivers, firemen and cleaners were all dock employees. According to Thomas Peacock, two cleaners 'paid unremitting attention to the brasswork, washed the engines down with soft soap every fortnight and once a week scoured the couplings and buffers with emery paper'. It is not clear whether this commendable endeavour was in any way associated, financially or otherwise, with the fact that these engines carried advertisements for Pears Soap affixed to their tanks and smokeboxes.

In a rash attempt at modernisation, the PLA purchased in 1922 three redundant steam railmotors from the GWR to replace the little Manning Wardles. Two of the cars had four-coupled driving units and were Swindon products of 1904, the other had a six-coupled driving unit (later converted to 2–4–0) and was originally built for the Port Talbot Railway Co in 1906. These vehicles, specially fitted with electric light and reduced in weight, were not an unqualified success on the Millwall Extension. Some bridges had to be strengthened before their arrival and facing points had to be equipped with locking bars; they were tight on curves, and to loading gauge, rendering anything close to the track vulnerable to damage. Their introduction did little to revive the flagging fortunes of the passenger service, which had been reduced to half-hourly in 1915 and was now a victim of motor bus competition. The PLA and the LNER took a long hard look, deciding to abandon from 30th June 1926, but as on the Blackwall line, the date was fixed by the General Strike, the last trains running on 3rd May.

Between North Greenwich and Glengall Road the line was completely closed. Parts of the viaduct were demolished ten years later, but the station at North Greenwich, in use as a store, remained more or less intact until the mid-1960s. During 1929, the PLA completed a new entrance to the south West India Dock from Blackwall Reach which severed the central section of the railway, but a link to Millwall Dock was retained by constructing a diversion round the west side of the Dock, which was opened in January 1929. Although their importance decreased with the growth of road motor transport and the later decline of the inner dock system, the dock railways, connected to the Blackwall line at Millwall Junction and thence to the former North London lines, remained in use until 1970. With the subsequent removal of tracks and equipment, the death of the Millwall Extension Railway seemed complete, but as we shall see later, it was to reappear in a new guise.

An Up train leaving North Woolwich behind N7 0-6-2T 69640 on 24th June 1961. The 1847 terminal building can be seen, to the left of the goods yard, still busy at this time. *R C Riley*

The North Woolwich Branch (map page 424)

There are some similarities between the lines we have just considered and the North Woolwich line and its appendages. Both started life as alternatives to river passenger services, handling pleasure traffic before becoming servants of the dock complexes and riverside industry. Sub branches were necessary in each case to reach dock extensions and industrial installations. Both systems for some years provided service to important places on the south bank of the river in connection with ferries and river steamers.

A proposal of 1833 for a railway from Commercial Road, Limehouse to a point in East Ham opposite Woolwich came to nothing but ten years later another scheme, promoted primarily to move seaborne coal from the riverside to places on the ECR, was more successful. The Eastern Counties & Thames Junction Railway, which obtained its act on 4th July 1844, was to be about 2¾ miles long, running from Stratford, ECR (Eastern Junction) to the mouth of the river Lea (Bow Creek) opposite Blackwall. Included in the act were a junction with the Northern & Eastern Railway 'near the engine house thereof' at Stratford and a passenger and goods pier in the Thames at the southern terminus. This site, at Bugsby's Reach, became known as Thames Wharf; to the north of it, between the Lea and the new railway, was the shipbuilding and ironworks of C J Mare & Co, which opened in 1846 becoming the Thames Ironworks & Shipbuilding Co in 1857.

Construction of the single line was delayed by flooding of Plaistow Marsh and other land east of Bow Creek, but it was eventually opened for freight on 29th April 1846. Business built up quickly and the track was to be doubled in conjunction with the extension to North Woolwich, to be mentioned in a moment. Coke ovens were set up at Thames Wharf to convert sea coal into locomotive fuel for the ECR and the N&ER.

Although somewhat indirect, the new line came closer to the important military and market town of Woolwich than any other railway and a 2½-mile extension across the marshes to a point immediately opposite this desirable objective could be cheaply built. This scheme, backed by George Parker Bidder, Samuel Morton Peto and the original Eastern Counties & Thames Junction directors, received sanction in an act of 21st July 1845 after meeting no opposition in Parliament, although the Board of Trade had suggested with some lack of foresight that it was unwarranted on grounds of public need.

Whilst preparations for the North Woolwich extension were going ahead the Eastern Counties & Thames Junction obtained powers to build a branch across the river Lea to the pepper warehouses of the East India Dock Co, and also a quarter-mile curve to the main line at Stratford, pointing towards London. The preamble to this 1846 act noted that the Eastern Counties Railway had purchased the EC&TJR, using the powers given in the original act of 1844. A year later, with the North Woolwich line under construction, the ECR also bought that undertaking, paying £2.10s (£2.50) for each of its 1,200 £25 shares.

Both the double track extension to North Woolwich and the new curve at Stratford were opened on 14th June 1847, together with the second track on the original section. An hourly passenger service ran between Bishopsgate and North Woolwich, supplemented after a few years by summer extras. From the junction at Thames Wharf, the route kept close to the river as far as its terminus opposite Woolwich, where at first there was nothing but the station, a hostelry known as the *Barge House*, some empty and decaying houses and the ferry pier built by the ECR. A contemporary writer though it 'singular to hear the whistle of the locomotive and the clatter of the iron wheels where, twelve months since, the heron, the plover, and the bittern roamed in undisturbed solitude'. Intermediate stations named Stratford Bridge and Barking Road were built where the Stratford and Barking roads crossed the line. Both were subsequently resited, but the sober and dignified Italianate building across the end of the tracks at North Woolwich survived to be damaged by German bombs in World War 2.

A small housing development, harbinger of many miles of mean streets, was soon in progress between the railway and Bow Creek, north of the Barking Road. Only a year after the opening of the line to passengers, a directory records:

> A new town called CANNING TOWN, is being formed; the streets being laid out, about 200 houses already erected. The neat cottages erected here each have a garden back and front, an entrance porch, a sitting room, kitchen, and wash house, fitted up with oven, boiler &c; and three chambers fitted up with handsome painted iron bedsteads. They possess that grand desideratum for the working classes, the maximum of comfort with the minimum of expense.

One street was named after Bidder, principal promoter of the North Woolwich Railway. Barking Road station was duly renamed Canning Town, although not until 1st July 1873. Its removal to the north of Barking Road took place in 1888, by which time the densely packed workers' houses were well established east of the railway at this point.

Two steam ferries came from a Barking shipyard to transport ECR passengers to and from Woolwich town while a third vessel was added later. Those not holding railway tickets were charged one penny to cross the water. Gravesend Steam Packet

Company steamers also called at the ECR pier and much of the early traffic on the railway was to and from the river services. At Bishopsgate, Woolwich passengers were allocated a special booking office, whence they proceeded to trains with rolling stock superior to that on most other ECR lines, 8-wheel coaches 40ft long and 9ft wide. From 1st June 1854 a second ECR service was worked half-hourly between Fenchurch Street and North Woolwich via Stratford Bridge. By that time the Bishopsgate trains were also half-hourly, and both services worked on Sundays, with the usual church intervals. The 1862 timetable showed North Woolwich as having the most lavish GER suburban service, with 81 trains daily (31 to and from Bishopsgate, 50 to and from Fenchurch Street).

The half-mile freight branch to the Blackwall pepper warehouses opened in June 1848 was soon to prove a useful support to the revenues from the North Woolwich passenger service. Using powers obtained in the 1847 Act, the ECR leased the warehouses from the Dock Company to form the Blackwall goods depot. Access to the bridge over the Lea involved a climb at 1 in 30 while there were further hazards including the 180ft-radius curves which restricted the line to four-coupled locomotives for much of its life.

Before the North Woolwich line had been completed, Bidder and his associates formed a land company which secured most of the riverside marsh all the way from Bow Creek to Gallions Reach and from the Barking Road to the river. At this time it was mostly pasture with only two or three houses, and could be obtained for a few pounds an acre. This was an astute move which was to help cushion the severe loss of passenger traffic following the opening of the South Eastern Railway's line from London to Woolwich and Gravesend on the south bank in July 1849. One of the early moves – the offer of reduced-rate season tickets to anyone caring to rent a house on the lonely and malarious marshes – was a complete failure, but the opening of pleasure gardens opposite North Woolwich station in May 1851, brought some business to the line at weekends and holidays. The facilities offered included bowling greens and a dancing saloon which, it was carefully noted, was readily convertible to a locomotive shed should the need arise. With the passing of years these gardens deteriorated to a vulgar resort, with standards of behaviour which shocked Victorian busybodies. A voluntary committee 'rescued' them to be placed in the care of the LCC, which in 1890 converted them to the Royal Victoria Gardens, the public park they remain today. Although a row of cottages appeared at North Woolwich about the time the line opened, White's *Essex Gazetteer* shows that in 1848 the stationmaster still found it necessary to live at East Ham. Efforts to attract industry to sites alongside the railway were rewarded in 1851 by the establishment of a glass factory and wharf, followed a year later by the arrival from Greenwich of S W Silver & Co's waterproofing works. Expanding its activities to the manufacturing of cable, ebonite and other rubber-based products, this firm gave its name to the small new community (Silvertown) which grew up around the works, about a mile west of North Woolwich. Towards the end of the nineteenth century, Silver's works were taken over by the India Rubber, Gutta Percha & Telegraph Works Co. Similar products were manufactured by W. T. Henley, who in 1853 bought 12 acres at North Woolwich, where a submarine cable and electrical works were erected.

Perhaps the most enterprising and ambitious of all the proposals to develop the area held by the land company was the scheme to build alongside the railway a deep water dock larger than any other in London, and the first to be adequately served by rail. These plans, in which Bidder, Peto, Kennard, and David Waddington, the chairman of the ECR, were all closely involved, were announced in 1849, Bidder was appointed chief engineer of what was to be named the Victoria Dock. As the entrance to the dock was to be formed near Bow Creek, it was necessary to carry the railway over it on a swing bridge. Because traffic would be interrupted as ships moved in and out, an avoiding line was built at the dock company's expense along the northern and eastern edges of the dock, branching from the original route at Thames Wharf Junction and joining it again at Silvertown, about three quarters of a mile west of the terminus. Under its statutory title of 'The Woolwich Abandoned Line', the discarded section around the south side of the dock passed to the dock company. Eventually the swing bridge, which had become something of a nuisance, was dismantled, leaving the remainder of this section to be worked as a long siding from the Silvertown end. Known as the Silvertown Tramway, this performed a useful role for many years in serving the numerous industrial installations which appeared between the dock and the river edge.

The Victoria Dock was opened on 26th November 1855, the avoiding line with its intermediate station of Victoria Dock, Custom House, carrying its first traffic at the end of that month. Industrial and dock development eventually required the provision of further stations: Victoria Docks, Tidal Basin in 1858 at the north western corner of the dock; and Silvertown, at the junction between the old and new lines, on 19th June 1863. By 1900 the latter was an important industrial centre with some 20 large firms and many smaller ones, chemicals, creosoting, and manure manufacturing brushing shoulders with jam, soup, candle, cocoa, and sugar factories. (Tate & Co. had established itself here in 1871, Lyle & Sons ten years later.)

To service the new dock, the ECR opened on 15th August 1854 a 1½-mile link between the NLR at Victoria Park and the North Woolwich line at Stratford. At first used only for freight, this carried passengers from 16th October, when the NLR started a service between Victoria Park and Stratford Bridge.*

Interchange with ECR main line trains was achieved through a new Low Level station at Stratford on the south side of the main line, which became known to travellers as the 'North London Station'.

Another connection was established with the construction of the LTSR between Barking and Bow. This opened on 31st March 1858, crossing above the North Woolwich branch about half-way between Canning Town and Stratford Bridge, the two lines connected by a curve between Lower and Upper Abbey Mills Junctions, allowing direct running between North Woolwich and Fenchurch Street via Bromley. A service over this route was started on 1st June 1858 in part replacement of the old one via Stratford Bridge.†

By 1864 the North Woolwich branch was carrying a total of about 40 passenger trains a day each way.

* The Victoria Park–Stratford Bridge service, popularly known as 'Stratford Jack', was taken over by the GER from 1st November 1866, reverting to the NLR a year later. This working by each company in alternate years continued until 1st November 1874 from which date the GER maintained it. On 1st October 1895 it was extended over a newly-provided additional track to a new third platform at Canning Town, some trains going through to North Woolwich.

† The Fenchurch Street–Stratford Bridge–North Woolwich service had operated between 1st June and 15th October 1854 and again from 1st May 1855. From 1st June 1858 alternate trains from Fenchurch Street went via Bromley.

A second large dock, called inevitably the Royal Albert, was opened to the east of what had now become the Royal Victoria on 6th May 1880 by the London & St Katharine's Dock Company (which had absorbed the Victoria Dock Company in 1864). This new dock was entered from Gallions Reach but was connected by a cut to its predecessor, requiring a second diversion of the North Woolwich branch. Work on the new line started with the construction of the dock in 1875, a cut-and-cover operation in dry ground which presented no difficulty. Known in the acts as the 'Substituted Line' and opened for traffic in June 1876 it passed through a 1,800ft brick-lined subway, partly double and partly twin tunnels, beneath what was to be the water channel between the two docks. Built at the cost of the dock company, it was vested in the GER, the dock company taking in return the old surface route (the 'Transferred Portion'), the severed sections of which they later rejoined by making the Connaught Road rail and road swing bridge over the shipping channel. The GER retained power to use the old route free of payment, and for many years freight trains too heavy to tackle the 1 in 50 tunnel ramps came this way, their speed restricted to 15mph. The small dimensions of the tunnels later prevented the GER from using its six-a-side passenger stock on the North Woolwich services.

After some 50 years the somewhat alarming discovery was made that ships were scraping the top of the tunnels as they passed through the cut. The subway was lowered and while the work was proceeding, from 30th September 1935 to 28th March 1936, passenger trains passed over the old surface line.

The new Albert Dock was served by a passenger railway running along its north side as far as the river bank at Gallions, to which we shall return later. On the south side of the dock was a goods line, branching from the 'Transferred Portion' and turning east over the top of the subway at its southern end.

F5 2-4-2T 7095 on a Palace Gates train at North Woolwich, c. 1938, looking to buffers.
Lens of Sutton

London's Local Railways

The street frontage of Canning Town station, c. 1904. Separate booking offices are indicated for Up and Down trains, and 'Trains every half hour' with 'Through bookings to Stations on the North London Line' are advertised. *Commercial postcard*

'Stratford Jack', the GER service from Victoria Park to Canning Town (some workings went on to North Woolwich) at the GER platform, Victoria Park Station, c. 1905. *Commercial postcard*

A third dock in the group, opened on 8th July 1921 by the Port of London Authority (which had taken over the dock companies in 1909), was named after King George V. Entered from Gallions Reach, it had water connection to the Royal Albert, which was parallel to it on the north, but this time no alterations were required in the North Woolwich lines. The dockside quays and warehouses were amply served by lines connected to the Royal Albert Dock south side railway.

This substantial provision of dock facilities, with the continuing industrial development largely associated with the docks and riverside wharves, assured the North Woolwich line of a steady flow of freight. Passenger liners using the docks also brought traffic, not only for their fuelling and provisioning, but boat trains, often as many as four for each ship.

Many hundreds of workmen crossed the Thames twice daily, many of them using North Woolwich station to get to and from their workplaces. After the introduction of the LCC Free Ferry on 23rd March 1889, most used this in preference to the penny GER ferries, which somewhat surprisingly survived until 30th September 1908. Electric tramways opened by the West Ham Corporation to a terminus at the north side of the Victoria Dock in 1904 and 1912 secured some of the railway's traffic from this direction but left it still an important passenger carrier. At this time a generous and varied train service was available. Thus in 1907 there were journeys to and from Fenchurch Street at 15-minute intervals all day including Saturdays; one of the four trains each hour worked via Abbey Mills Junctions and Bromley, another ran via Stratford Market and Bow Road, calling at all stations, whilst the third and fourth ran to and from Custom House, serving the Gallions line. One of these last two worked fast between Fenchurch Street and Canning Town. There was also an hourly train each way between Liverpool Street and North Woolwich via Stratford Market, calling at all stations ; an approximately hourly service between Palace Gates and North Woolwich; seven trains each way daily between Stratford Market and Custom House on the Beckton service; and the shuttle between Victoria Park and Canning Town via Stratford Low Level about every half-hour. The latter carried bookings between GER and NLR stations.

The 1910 timetable shows no less than 96 trains each way daily at Canning Town, Mondays to Saturdays inclusive. Of these 52 ran to and from Fenchurch Street by both routes and 11 between North Woolwich and Palace Gates. On Sundays there were 46 trains each way, including six on the Palace Gates service and 24 to and from Fenchurch Street. The Canning Town–Victoria Park trains, not included in these totals, ran 35 journeys each way on weekdays and 27 on Sundays. Ten years later Canning Town had some 110 trains each way daily, 86 to and from North Woolwich (15 Palace Gates, 34 Fenchurch Street, four Victoria Park, seven Liverpool Street, 26 Stratford or Stratford Market). Stratford Market, a very busy station, was substantially rebuilt in 1894 with dormer windowed offices at street level and four platform faces including a central island.

Discouraged by the many level crossings and swing bridges, motor bus operators left the area alone, apart from a service between East Ham and Woolwich Ferry, which had little effect on the railway. Sunday trains to and from Victoria Park ceased after 30th September 1923, but the lavish provision on weekdays was maintained through the 1920s and 1930s, with Canning Town reaching a peak of activity just after World War 1, when there were over 130 trains each way including those terminating. This station, which had a bay platform on the Down side for the shuttle service to Victoria Park, was rebuilt at street level in 1932–33. The new brick building with hipped roof on the overline bridge included a spacious entrance hall with a three-windowed ticket office.

A new road through the dock area eventually brought a challenge to the railway's passenger business. Constructed under an unemployment relief programme, this Canning Town–Silvertown link included impressive concrete viaducts to span the railway and water barriers. Its eastern end was opened on 21st April 1934 and it was completed with the Silvertown viaduct and approaches in July 1935. Three years later, London Transport established a trolleybus service along this Silvertown Way, extending the existing Stratford–Canning Town route to the North Woolwich ferry terminal. Offering a decided contrast to the cramped and gas-lit GER carriages, the quiet, smooth-running electric buses made serious inroads into the railway revenue; this now entered a decline from which it never recovered, and which was to be accelerated by the effects of World War 2.

At the end of the 1930s there were still over 90 weekday trains to and from North Woolwich (15 Palace Gates, 37 Fenchurch Street via Bromley, four Victoria Park, 35 Stratford or Stratford Market) and 14 to and from Gallions (seven of them running through to and from Fenchurch Street). The Custom House–Stratford section also got four trains each way to and from Beckton. On Sundays there was an approximately hourly service between Chingford and North Woolwich (summer only) and a train about every hour between Fenchurch Street and North Woolwich. Sundays also saw 13 trains each way to and from Palace Gates.

The importance of freight has already been noticed. As dock traffic grew, the line between Stratford Bridge and Tidal Basin was quadrupled to allow the many goods trains to work alongside the intensive passenger service. A small beginning was made with this widening in 1860 and there were extensions in 1879–1883, and in 1890, the work reaching completion in 1892. By the turn of the century the branch served numerous goods depots, some operated by 'foreign' companies, as well as many riverside wharves and factory sidings. On the west side just south of Stratford Market station, the forage, fruit and vegetable market opened by the GER on 1st October 1879 was fed by an extensive layout. Traffic here reached over 52,000 tons in 1897. Immediately to the south of this was a GER coal depot. On the Down side, just south of Abbey Mills Lower Junction the West Ham and Plaistow Goods Depot was opened by the GER on 1st October 1906, extending as far east as Pretoria Road. On the opposite side, from connections with the Up and Down goods roads 270yd south of Abbey Mills Lower Junction, were reception and outward sidings linked with a branch of over half a mile which ran north and then south to serve the gas and electricity works on the east bank of the Lea. Canning Town Down side was the site of an LNWR goods yard opened in 1880. Beyond here, south of the Barking Road, was a GER depot dating from the opening of the line and rebuilt in 1904. Nearby, also on the Up side, the lines to the GER depot at East India Dock, Blackwall, branched off. To the south of this, off the old Silvertown alignment, were the GER Thames Wharf coal sidings on the site of the 1847 depot and also a Midland Railway Thames Wharf depot of 1870. In the latter year the Midland established a depot at Victoria Dock where there were also GER (c.1855), GNR (c.1885) and GWR (1902) depots. The Victoria Dock lines were reached through Port of London Authority sorting sidings south of the line between Tidal Basin and Custom House stations where movements were made by the PLA's own locomotives. There were

LNER F6 2-4-2T 7790 at Custom House, looking west, c. 1937. The indicator board on the locomotive reads 'ALBERT DOCK'; there is no station of that name, but the train is destined for the
PLA branch to Gallions, which ran along the north side of the Royal Albert Dock.

also two other GER depots, dating from the opening of the line, west of Silvertown
station, and at North Woolwich. Private sidings abounded off the Silvertown
Tramway and between Silvertown and North Woolwich. Apart from the Midland's
Victoria Dock depot which had closed on 3rd April 1939, all these freight facilities
were active at the outbreak of World War 2.

In the 1920s the weight of the goods and passenger traffic was such that the
level-crossing gates on the branch were closed against road movement for about
nine hours out of the 24 and at the busiest time of the day for 47 minutes in each
hour. Rail was supreme as long queues of road trucks formed, waiting to enter or
leave the docks area. At this time most freight was worked between Temple Mills
Yard, Stratford and the yards and sidings at Thames Wharf and Silvertown or the
PLA sidings at Victoria Dock. There were also through trains between the latter
points and the LNER main line at Clarence Yard, Finsbury Park, and between the
PLA sidings and the former LNWR yard at Canning Town and destinations on the
LMSR. Locomotives of the latter company worked trains either via South Totten-
ham or via Victoria Park, also carrying traffic to and from the GWR and SR systems.
So serious was the congestion that when the railway companies received government
encouragement to produce new works schemes for the relief of unemployment, the
LMSR presented a Bill for an independent line between Wanstead (on the Tottenham & Forest Gate line) and the PLA sidings at Custom House, alleging that this
would avoid delays in negotiating 12 junctions on the 6¾-mile LNER route between
South Tottenham and the docks. Needless to say this 1930 Bill was vigorously
opposed by the LNER, and although it passed the Commons committee in modified
form, it was thrown out by the Lords. Promising improvements, the LNER got its
way, but did little or nothing before war came.

A northbound train in charge of LNER L1 2-6-4T 67701 leaving Stratford Low Level on 16th February 1957 after passing beneath the main line platforms. The two tracks on the right are now used by the Richmond–North Woolwich electric services. *R C Riley*

Almost from the start of World War 2, freight and passenger movement fell steeply. In accordance with contingency plans, labour and plant were sent from London docks to the provincial seaports, and in the late summer of 1940 the Royal group of docks were viciously attacked by the German air force. Damage was so great that from 7th September 1940 all passenger trains were terminated at Custom House, not reaching North Woolwich again until 1st January 1941. Wartime destruction and reductions in traffic caused the abandonment of the Fenchurch Street services in October 1940. Passenger loadings at Tidal Basin, a station badly mauled by bombing, were down to four per cent of the 1939 total in 1942, when receipts were less than £1 a day, and it was closed from 15th August 1943. Another wartime casualty was the remnant of the once busy service to and from Victoria Park, latterly cut back to Stratford Low Level; the old GER platforms at Victoria Park were used for the last time on 31st October 1942.

Some life returned to the docks in 1942 when they and the railways became busy with preparations for the invasion of North Africa; this was followed by similar activity for D-Day. Once again the PLA sorting sidings were bustling; freight train movements reached 40 a day, with up to 1,500 wagons handled.

Throughout the war the passenger service consisted of a shuttle between North Woolwich and Stratford with a few peak-hour workings to and from Palace Gates. A Sunday workmen's service ran until close of traffic on 16th March 1947. LNER N7 0–6–2T or GER 2–4–2T hauling Gresley 'quint-art' sets were now the usual rule.

Traffic patterns were changing. The mean little houses which crowded up to the line at Canning Town and between Silvertown and North Woolwich were sadly reduced or smashed about by the German bombs, forcing many of the dock workers to seek accommodation further afield. After the war they did not return to the trains, most of them coming in daily by road. For another 20 years the train service remained more than sufficient for the business offering. In 1960 for example, an hourly service with 10-minute frequency in the peak periods had replaced what had been a very largely peak-hours only service of only 26 trains a day each way. In 1962 there were 37 Down trains (six starting from Palace Gates, one from Cheshunt, the rest from Stratford Low Level) and 38 Up (nine through to Palace Gates, the rest terminating at Stratford Low Level). Other through workings had been withdrawn from 21st November 1960 with the introduction of electric service to Chingford and Enfield. Steam locomotives (N7 0-6-2T and L1 2-6-4T) hauled the indestructible quint-arts on all services until Rolls-Royce 3-car diesel sets were introduced on some workings from 1st January 1962. For a few more months the N7s continued on this their last regular assignment. These trains no longer called at Stratford Market, which had finally succumbed to road competition on the night of 4th May 1957, but in the 1950s and for a time in the 1960s, the branch still saw up to five boat trains a week between Liverpool Street and the docks, with BR locomotives working to and from the quayside over the PLA system. Saturday trains on the branch ceased after traffic on 4th January 1969, but in 1974 three-car diesel sets were still working 37 journeys each way daily, one third of them to and from Tottenham Hale.

Stratford Market station on its last day, 4th May 1957, with a North Woolwich train hauled by BR N7 0-6-2T 69661. War damage to the canopies remains unrepaired. *Lens of Sutton*

Stratford Southern Junction and signal box, looking north to Stratford Low Level station, 10th August 1979. The curve to the left of the picture allowed a direct run from the North Woolwich line to Liverpool Street or Fenchurch Street (via Bow Jc). Another curve to the right, beyond a signal box already dismantled by this date, gave direct access to the Colchester and Loughton lines. *Alan A Jackson*

For some years after the war, goods traffic remained buoyant with about 60 trains a day running on and off the branch at Stratford. After Bishopsgate depot was destroyed by fire in December 1964, Stratford Market depot assumed new life, taking all perishable traffic from the Continent via Harwich, with customs clearance on the spot. Some thousand tons of fruit and vegetables were then handled every week at the 660ft platform. Thames and Blackwall Wharves were modernised in 1961, each receiving two new electrically-operated rail-mounted cranes to transfer freight to and from the 10 barge berths, rail, and road vehicles. Freight to and from the docks declined slowly until the early 1960s, then very rapidly as the containerisation revolution had its effect. Seasonal traffic included the movement of East Anglian sugar beet into Tate & Lyle's sugar refinery at Silvertown, which required as many as four trains daily at the peak. The yards and sidings at Thames Wharf, Bow Creek, Blackwall, Silvertown and Canning Town (LNWR) each still had enough traffic in the 1950s to justify allocated shunting pilot locomotives, which were sub-shedded at Bow Creek and Silvertown. Stratford Market, West Ham & Plaistow , West Ham electricity works, Berk Chemicals, and Cohen's private sidings were all worked by pick-up freight trains. All goods workings were diesel hauled by 1965.

Most of the remaining freight facilities were closed as the 1960s came to an end: Thames Wharf (Midland) on 4th October 1965, Canning Town (LNWR) and the Blackwall and East India depots on 6th March 1967, Canning Town (GER) on 1st July 1968, and North Woolwich on 7th December 1970. After a century of use the connection to the former LTSR line was taken out in 1958 and the eastern curve at Stratford Low Level went in 1973. The 'top line' between Custom House and Silvertown, last worked in October 1967, was dismantled soon afterwards. From 25th August 1969, passenger trains used only one track (the former Down line) east of Custom House; the other was allocated to the much reduced freight workings to the Silvertown factories and Ward's scrapyard. With this change, North Woolwich and Silvertown signal boxes were closed. All freight movements ceased early in 1993 and the former Up line was taken out of use on 29th March that year. At Stratford Market, full load freight facilities and coal traffic were withdrawn from 5th November 1984 but the GER fruit and vegetable market lingered on, road-served, until May 1991 when it was transferred, together with historic Spitalfields, to a purpose-built complex at the edge of Hackney Marshes on the site of the former GER wagon works at Ruckhold Road, Leyton. After some use by engineer's trains, the Stratford Market sidings were lifted in 1988 and the whole site, together with its pub, licensed to open between 07.00 and 10.00, was taken for the rolling stock depot completed in 1996 ready for the Stratford extension of the Jubilee Line tube.

BR N7 0-6-2T 69608 on North Woolwich train at Stratford Low Level station, 21st May 1955, looking north west. The bridge carrying the main lines out of Liverpool Street and the Central Line tube tracks runs across the picture above the locomotive. Note the wartime pillbox at the right. *Alan A Jackson*

Much affected by the decay of activity at the Docks, passenger traffic between Stratford and North Woolwich continued to decline in the late 1960s and early 1970s. When BR was driven to suggest further service cuts in 1976, the Greater London Council, already much involved with planning redevelopment of the rundown Docklands areas, came to the rescue with a grant which enabled a Monday to Friday half hourly frequency to be maintained between Tottenham Hale (or Stratford Low Level) and North Woolwich until early evening.

But the GLC had more ambitious plans and what followed owed much to its initiatives. From 14th May 1979 the train service was rearranged with diesel railcar sets operating Mondays to Fridays at 20 min intervals at peak hours and half-hourly off peak between North Woolwich and Camden Road, reopening to passengers the former GER line between Stratford Low Level and Victoria Park (closed 1942) and the former NLR line thence to Dalston Junction (closed 1944). These trains over what was renamed the 'Crosstown Link Line' called at a new island platform station at West Ham under the LT station and later connected to it by a covered way. With GLC funding, Silvertown, Custom House and Canning Town stations were all rebuilt during 1979. At Silvertown the former Up platform was completely demolished and the rebuilt platform and waiting room were on the north side. Canning Town's dreary war-damaged platforms were replaced by an island with a glass-walled waiting shelter. This was reached by open stairs from the road overline bridge, where a little later a flat-roofed ticket office and entrance building replaced the much more attractive LNER station of 1933. Few changes were made at Stratford Low Level apart from a new waiting room on the Up platform and a new subsidiary ticket office for passengers interchanging between the main line or the Underground and the North Woolwich line.

Entirely new stations funded by the GLC and the Docklands Partnership were opened near former NLR station sites on 12th May 1980 at Hackney Central and Hackney Wick (just east of the former Victoria Park platforms). Both were of similar design with a sloping walkway to a brick building housing ticket hall, waiting and staff room. An open footbridge provided access to the Up platforms, which had an enclosed waiting room. Local opinion formers ungratefully commented that the stations were 'open, wind swept and inhospitable places with open footbridges and minimal platform cover'. At the formal opening ceremony, Sir Peter Parker drew attention to the lack of lavatories, commenting enigmatically that to have none at all was better than offering vandalised facilities.

During the first year of operation, the quality of the new diesel car service was seriously eroded by staff shortages, the resulting cancellations doing much to discourage new traffic; as a driver explained when the line was visited in August 1979 and we watched a disappointed man tear up his free promotional ticket in disgust at the absence of an advertised train, 'we have the drivers, we have the train sets, but we can't get enough guards'. He went on to explain how hapless passengers were left stranded at the unstaffed stations east of Stratford, unaware when, if ever, their timetabled train would arrive. A half-hourly Saturday service was introduced on 16th July 1983 but did not run east of Stratford. Some notice seems to have been taken of the criticism of the low-cost new stations of 1980; Dalston Kingsland, opened on 16th May 1983 to replace the old Dalston Junction station, was a much better job, given a pleasing appearance by large areas of red brick and adequately sheltering the passenger's path from street to the canopied waiting areas. This station

North Woolwich station exterior, fronting Pier Road, 7th December 1974. This fine building, which escaped destruction in the punishing 1940 German air attacks on the docklands, is now restored as a museum of the Great Eastern Railway. The sole remaining platform, used by the electrified service to Stratford and Richmond, is reached through a replacement building to the left.
Alan A Jackson

stood exactly on the site of the original NLR Kingsland station (9th November 1850–31st October 1865) and generated a satisfying degree of traffic from its very convenient position in a busy retail centre on Kingsland High Street opposite Ridley Road Street Market.

At North Woolwich, where the layout was reduced to one track, the rebuilt platform on the south side was served by a new single-storey ticket office building with a heated waiting room which was completed on the former freight yard site early in 1980. With funding from the London Docklands Development Corporation, the heavily-vandalised and war damaged 1847 terminal building was acquired by the Passmore Edwards Museum Trust and handsomely restored to house a well-arranged museum of the Great Eastern Railway. Opened in September 1984, this was sustained by revenue funding from the London Borough of Newham.

Signalling was modernised in 1984; the remaining manual boxes, at Custom House, Abbey Mills and Stratford Southern Junction, were closed and from 18th November the whole line was controlled from the Stratford Panel, with track circuit block working to Custom House and one-train working thence over the single line to North Woolwich. Around the same time the old semaphore signalling between Stratford and Dalston was also replaced with three aspect colour lights controlled from Stratford, allowing closure of the two existing boxes.

This work prepared the way for the introduction from 13th May 1985 of 750V dc third rail two-car electric trains working weekdays and Sundays at basic 20 min intervals between North Woolwich and Richmond, taking 61/62 min. Designated 'North London Link', this amounted to an almost total diversion through north east London of the former NLR services to the City terminus at Broad Street station, leaving the Dalston Junction–City line to rush hour Watford services only. Funded by the GLC, the electrification completed the Council's bold plans of the late 1970s with one exception: a tunnel under the Thames from Silvertown to Woolwich Arsenal station. Not everyone was pleased; there was some grumbling in the Hampstead area at the loss of direct access to the City, exacerbated by the unsatisfactory interchange with Moorgate trains at Highbury but it soon became apparent that the new service was going to produce a higher level of traffic than before.

The newly-electrified section over the 8½ miles between Dalston Western Junction and North Woolwich included a station at Homerton, on the site of one which had last seen passenger trains on the same day of the month 41 years earlier. Long-planned, it was said that this station, funded by the GLC and the Department of the Environment, had to await electrification because the diesel sets could not be given an additional stop without creating pathing problems west of Dalston Junction. Sited in a densely populated and deprived area with two large hospitals, Homerton was soon generating a satisfactory traffic. Dalston Kingsland and Hackney Central also did well. Less successful was Hackney Wick, which had a very thin catchment area consisting mainly of industrial units and recreational open land. By mid 1987 it was reported that over the North London line as a whole there had been an increase of some 2,400 passenger journeys a day, a figure which exceeded that used by the GLC in making a case for electrification. In October 1989 the former Southern Region slam-door electric stock first used was replaced with sliding door Class 313 units which gave a smoother ride and an increase of 50 per cent in capacity. But there was a down side: plagued by cancellations, unpunctuality and a low standard of car cleaning, service quality remained poor well into the 1990s.

For a second time, Silvertown station was rebuilt in 1990, given a new ticket office and waiting area as 'Silvertown & London City Airport'. Immediately to its north, the two single track tunnels beneath the channel connecting the Victoria and Albert Docks had long been prone to flooding (at times up to 5ft above the rails) but with the high level lines now closed and electric working, almost any depth of water brought an interruption to rail services and this nuisance could no longer be tolerated. It was finally tackled in 1994–95 when major structural repairs and waterproofing were undertaken, backed up by a modern drainage and pumping system; the cost was funded by the owners, the London Dockland Development Corporation.

The opportunity to carry out this improvement arose when the line had to be closed for another reason. Substantial works in the Canning Town area in connection with the extension of the Jubilee tube line from Green Park to Stratford required suspension of the train service between Stratford and North Woolwich from close of traffic on 28th May 1994 until 29th October 1995. With the reopening on the latter date, Canning Town station was resited on the south side of the road bridge to provide convenient interchange facilities with the new tube, bus and DLR stations at this point. West Ham emerged from this closure with a rebuilt platform and improved interchange facilities with the LT services to the City and Barking/Upminster.

Long periods of closure, operating problems and a poor public image have combined to seriously erode the impact of the electric services on this line, discouraging maximum traffic development; at the time of writing they present a challenge to management as the second decade of electric working begins. Beyond those matters capable of internal solution, the line's future will depend very much on the successful regeneration of what is still a very run-down area for the time being somewhat overprovided with public transport, and also perhaps upon the completion of the rail crossing of the Thames at this point.

The Beckton Branch   (map page 424)

The North Woolwich line sprouted two branches of its own, the first of these serving the huge riverside works of the Gaslight & Coke Company, one of those splendid manifestations of Victorian energy hidden away in unfashionable corners of the metropolis. Sited on desolate marsh to the south-west of Barking Creek, the works were well placed to receive sea-borne coal, but poorly served by land – nothing more at first than a rough road from Barking. Construction started in November 1868, the first gas was produced on 25th November 1870, and full production began the following month. A 'village' of some 130 workmen's cottages, houses for foremen and officials, a church, chapel and recreation ground was built nearby and what Thorne called 'this busy if not altogether lovely colony', which was often cocooned in its own private fog, received the name Beckton after the first Governor of the company. By 1900, it was contributing half the rateable value of Barking.

A Gaslight & Coke Company Act of 1871 authorised the construction at the company's expense of a single line from the North Woolwich branch at Custom House Junction, about a quarter-mile east of Custom House station. Other than the level-crossings of Connaught Road and East Ham Manor Way there were no intermediate stations or special features on the 1m 56ch across the marsh. Beyond East Ham Manor Way, the track was double on the company's own land.

Freight traffic started on 14th October 1872, followed on 17th March 1873 by workmen's trains operated by the gas company, but the line was leased to and worked by the GER from 18th March 1874. A clause in the 1871 Act required the operation of a penny workmen's train each way on weekdays between Barking Road and Beckton before 06.00 (Down) and after 18.00 (Up), but in practice these and other passenger trains worked to and from Stratford Market or Stratford Low Level at times suited to the shift changes at the gas works. Throughout the line's history all passenger trains were in fact workmen's trains, tickets issued in the afternoon being available for return the following morning. It is doubtful whether the small booking office at Beckton saw much use, except perhaps in the early years. Latterly, tickets were always collected from Down trains at Custom House.

At Beckton station, 2m 1ch from Custom House, the long and (of course) gas-lit platform, with its wooden shelter and small signalbox, was on the north side of the line about a half-mile inland from the river wall. From here the tracks continued into the works, which were sited east and north of the station, and were eventually to occupy about 360 acres. They were served by about 40 miles of internal standard gauge lines, fully signalled and latterly worked by over thirty 0–4–0T steam loco-motives (replaced by Planet diesels from 1959). Most journeys were to carry coal between the two collier piers and the retort houses. A full-scale locomotive works and erecting shop was maintained by the gas company for many years.

Freight on the branch comprised gasworks supplies and materials inwards and some coke outward, but the bulk of the coke went by water. Around 1892 the GER opened a freight yard (West Ham South Depot) on the north side of the branch just east of Connaught Road level crossing.

Access to the gasworks for employees not living at Beckton was much improved by the opening of two electric tramways in the 1900s. East Ham Corporation's line from the Town Hall to New Beckton (Cyprus) via East Ham Manor Way was inaugurated on 22nd June 1901 and extended to the Royal Albert Dock on 25th March 1903. At the level-crossing with the railway both tramcars and trains were

Beckton station looking west, 1948.
Mowat Collection

controlled by semaphore signals worked from Beckton Tramway Crossing box. A second tramway, coming south from Barking to terminate close to the northern boundary of the gasworks, opened on 1st December 1903, to be extended to the centre of Barking on 15th December. Whilst these tramway facilities must have had some effect on the travel patterns of Beckton workers, some of the journeys would be entirely new as the demand for labour increased with the continuing expansion of the works. The railway remained the most convenient route for those who lived at Canning Town or Stratford.

At this time there were seven trains each way, originating at Stratford Market; by 1918 the terminus was Stratford Low Level, but the number of trains was unaltered. Weekday arrivals at Beckton were 05.37, 06.58, 13.33, 16.11 and 21.33. Departures were at 06.20, 12.28 (Saturdays), 14.31, 16.18, 17.24, and 22.15. Sundays saw arrivals at Beckton at 05.38 and 21.33, with departures at 06.27, and 21.42. It will be seen that although office workers had a convenient afternoon departure they had to rise early or make a more circuitous journey via Gallions and the East Ham tramcar. In 1939 the branch had only four trains each way and still the two on Sundays, the journey time being 20 minutes for the five miles from Stratford, calling at all stations. Both tramcar services had by then been replaced by motor buses and bus journeys from Stratford and Canning Town were possible via the Barking by-pass built in 1927. Few now used the trains, and it was no great hardship when the LNER closed the line after severe bomb damage in September 1940. Service was briefly resumed after repairs, but passenger trains ran for the last time on 28th December that year.

Freight traffic continued at much the same level as previously for another two decades, but there were a few brief hours of wartime glory. A shortage of fuel to heat huts and water at the many airfields and camps in eastern England during the winter of 1943–44 brought Beckton to the rescue with 21 trains a week carrying off its coke mountain to 113 sites via 86 wayside goods yards.

West Ham South yard was closed on 7th December 1964, leaving the branch to the much diminished freight requirements of the gasworks, by then only a dozen wagons a day, even though the working timetable included an unaltered layover of one hour, relic of busier days long before. As coal gas production was run down, rail traffic faded to nothing, bringing complete closure in February 1971.

The Gallions Branch (map page 424)

The Rudyard Kipling character who asked 'Is it Tilbury and a tender, or Gallions and the Dock?' neatly summarised one function of the second shoot from the North Woolwich branch. When the London & St Katharine Docks Company planned to build the Royal Albert Dock in the misty uninhabited marshes east of Canning Town, it was realised that the normal dock railways for freight would not be enough. Some sort of passenger facilities would be required to serve the liners expected to berth in the dock. The dock company therefore built on its land a 1m 61ch double-track line between the North Woolwich branch at Connaught Road and the river edge at Gallions, punctuating it with four closely-spaced stations. This 'Royal Albert Dock Railway', which passed close to the northern boundary of the new dock area, was not ready in time for the opening of the dock on 6th May 1880, but a limited train service worked from 3rd August. Having brought the line into the world, the dock company decided to make an honest woman of itself, belatedly turning to Parliament in 1882 for authority 'to maintain and use' the railway 'as if the same had been authorised by this act'. The act also gave powers to make working arrangements with the GER, restricted the line's traffic to passengers and parcels, and required a penny workmen's train in the Down direction before 07.00 and back again after 18.00 each day.

At Custom House station the GER built a bay on the up side for the Gallions trains, renting it out to the dock company. The new line began 34ch east of here at Royal Albert Dock Junction, whose signal box also controlled Connaught Road, the first station, another 220yd further east. Like all others on the dock railway, this was fully staffed by the dock company, which issued its own tickets, and it had all the signalling and amenities of a normal passenger station. Beyond it, the tracks swung north-east before running almost dead straight eastwards as far as Manor Way. About half-way along this straight section was the second station, simply and aptly named Central. At Manor Way, the station (which did not open until July 1881 and was called Manor Road until 1882) was at first on the west side of the road bridge over the line. Gallions station followed very quickly, sited about half-way along the north side of the dock entrance basin. Here the dock company erected a pleasant-looking hotel in the style of a large country house (described by Baedeker as 'small, but first class') for the use of liner passengers and their relatives and friends. Beyond the platforms the tracks went on to join the dock freight lines, eventually passing on to a pier which in later years was used as a coaling jetty by William Cory & Son Ltd, who had their own locomotives.

As already mentioned, the first trains ran on 3rd August 1880, probably in the first few weeks to and from Central only but Bradshaw, showing the service for the first time in November 1880, indicated an approximately half-hourly frequency between Gallions and Custom House, taking 10 minutes, with the last train of the day leaving Gallions at 19.00. The service first appeared in GER timetables in April 1881 when 33 trains a day were shown, but only to and from Central. By July that year, both Bradshaw and the GER timetables were agreed on 33 trains a day each way between Custom House and Gallions, including eight each way to and from Fenchurch Street. This service, which probably began on 1st July 1881, included 13 each way on Sundays (four running to and from Fenchurch Street). All local trains were worked by three 2–4–0T bought by the dock company from the LNWR, these continuing in use until the GER took over all workings on 1st July 1896. Fares, first,

Royal Albert Dock Co 2-4-0T
loco No.7 on Custom House
train at Gallions terminus
c. 1900. *Lens of Sutton*

second, and third class, to all stations on the dock line were the same in each case and tickets were collected at Connaught Road. During the early part of the twentieth century, the railway was at its busiest; there were in 1900 about 53 trains each way, 35 locals between Custom House and Gallions, 16 to and from Fenchurch Street (two via Stratford Market), the others to and from Stratford Market or Stratford Low Level. Two Down workings from Liverpool Street were not balanced. Sundays saw only a shuttle between Custom House and Gallions. The heavy weekday provision catered primarily for dock workers, overseers and office staff, many of whom returned to their Canning Town homes for midday dinner, thus creating four peaks daily.

Sunday trains ceased after 27th June 1915; from the end of 1917 there was no service on bank holidays. From early 1918 until the end of World War 1 a special service was worked over the branch in connection with a ferry carrying munitions workers between Gallions pier and the northern installations at Woolwich Arsenal. At this period the basic service on the line was about half-hourly, but only seven trains worked to and from Fenchurch Street.

With the change in traffic patterns created by the electric tramcar and motor bus services already mentioned, the need for a local service diminished and it was discontinued from 6th July 1932. As successor to the GER, the LNER maintained through workings to and from Stratford or London, while PLA staff and signalmen continued to work the line.

In 1938 there were 15 Down trains, eight from Fenchurch Street (two via Stratford), four from Victoria Park and three from Stratford Low Level. Eight Up trains worked to Fenchurch Street (one via Stratford), two to Victoria Park and six to Stratford Low Level. This service provided trains spread throughout the day, concentrated at rush hours, but there was nothing from Saturday lunchtime until Monday morning.

Over the years some changes were made in the stations. Gallions was replaced from 12th December 1886 by a larger station of the same name, sited 275yd east. This had an island platform, the south face for the dock company's local trains, the north for the GER workings. About a year later, Manor Way station was moved to the east side of the road bridge and underwent further rebuilding when the old wooden bridge was replaced by a more substantial structure in 1926. Around the same time the somewhat elaborate wooden building at Gallions was demolished and a smaller one put in its place. Central, the least used of the stations, was reduced to halt status form 1st November 1933.

When German aircraft swarmed over the docks on Saturday afternoon 7th September 1940, passenger service had ceased for the week. A stick of bombs put the line completely out of action, and although repaired and used for wagon and van storage, it never carried passenger trains again. Formal abandonment was authorised by the PLA Act of 1950, but Cory's used the tracks for some time after.

The DLR: or New Life for the Old

Brief reference* must now be made to London's latest local railway. Happily this provides a fitting conclusion to both chapter and book since, for all the controversy and criticism it has generated, the Docklands Light Railway, in the extent to which it has made use of the formations of the several lines just described, nicely illustrates the abiding nature of London's railnet.

Planned as a transport system expressly to further the regeneration of London's North Bank docklands, the DLR had a chequered childhood. Its initial underfunding, apparently based on an investment appraisal that totally ignored its ability to turn negative land values to extremely positive ones, produced a railway unable to cope with the crowds arriving on its opening day. Almost at once, if it were to be of any use at all, its capacity had to be upgraded at very considerable further cost and it was later considered politically expedient to back it up by the very expensive extension through its catchment area of the Jubilee Line, a conventional tube railway.

Something of a curiosity amongst railways, the DLR, despite its name, has long seemed to share more characteristics with a full-scale urban electric railway than with the modern light rail systems of the USA and Western Europe. Though enthusiasts will point to its sharp curves, steep gradients and rolling stock as evidence to the contrary, this impression has grown stronger as the system has developed. Necessarily, by the choice of a conductor rail traction supply, its right of way is rigidly segregated throughout; even when it uses a road (Royal Albert Way) its central reservation is very convincingly isolated from it. The inner portion to the Bank involved extremely costly deep level tube construction; all its stops are at high-platform stations, some of them surprisingly elaborate. Nor is there anything 'light' about its civil engineering or its sophisticated signalling and control systems.

But our main theme here is the manner in which the DLR in large part runs alongside, above, and in some cases actually on the roadbeds of the London & Blackwall, the London & Blackwall Extension, the Millwall Extension, the North London Railway through Poplar and Bow, and the North Woolwich, Gallions and Beckton branches. This feature is important in the way it influenced the pattern of the DLR layout and even the planning of the northern Docklands development as a whole, shaping these just as strongly as the topography of the principal docks. Knowledge of the DLR's relationship with its predecessors can also enrich the interest of a journey over it. A careful student will wish to unravel this topographical puzzle by comparing large scale maps of various dates but here we shall do our best with verbal description.

The first stage of the DLR, seven and a half miles of line and 15 stations, electrified at 750V dc, with bottom contact third rail, was opened to the public on 31st August 1987. Shortly after leaving the little Tower Gateway terminus, close by Fenchurch Street station, the double track occupies the southern side of the widened London & Blackwall viaduct (formerly occupied by two of the four approach tracks to Fenchurch Street), passing through the DLR Shadwell station, which is about 220yd/201 metres west of the L&BR's Shadwell. At Limehouse station, the DLR parts from the main line, taking over the original roadbed of the L&BR, using its

---

* Brief because its origins and development are fully treated in the publishers' *Docklands Light Rail Official Handbook* (Bibliography section 6).

1840 viaduct as far as a point on the east side of West India Dock Road. From here, it rises steeply but, eastwards, does not deviate much from the course of the L&BR. Beyond the DLR Poplar station, the new railway, again at ground level, turns sharply north to join the roadbed of the former NLR to Bow, passing beneath Poplar High Street. The DLR's All Saints station occupies the precise site of the NLR Poplar station but its next stop, Bow Church, is on the south side of Bow Road whilst the NLR's impressive station abutted the north side of the overline bridge. Having passed under Bow Road, the DLR now veers east to climb up alongside the northernmost part of the Blackwall Extension Railway before running along the south side of the former Eastern Counties Railway main line into Stratford station, making use of one of the two tracks formerly connecting the latter to the Fenchurch Street line.

South of its junction at Poplar, the Isle of Dogs section of the initial DLR at first follows a completely new alignment across the West India Docks before veering east to join the formation of the Millwall Extension Railway at a point just under a quarter mile north of the DLR Crossharbour station. There the platforms are more or less on the same site as the MER's Millwall Docks (Glengall Road) station of 1871, which was also above street level. Continuing south, the DLR then follows the MER roadbed through Mudchute DLR to the Island Gardens terminus. This last section is laid on the 27-brick arch 1872 viaduct of the MER but the DLR ends slightly to the north of the original North Greenwich terminus, which was very close to the water's edge, its site now occupied by a boat club.

The second above ground section of the DLR, from Poplar eastwards to Beckton, five route miles, with ten new stations, was opened on 28th March 1994. This takes up the approximate line of the London & Blackwall Railway almost as far as the site of that company's Poplar station, but is carried above it at a higher level. It then veers north east, crossing Bow Creek on a new alignment before turning south and east to accompany the North Woolwich branch to a point just beyond Custom House station. The Canning Town DLR station is slightly south of the original 1847 station site but at a higher level and the DLR's Royal Victoria is about 300yd/274 metres east of the Tidal Basin station of 1858–1943. At Custom House, the old and new station sites are alongside. Just beyond Royal Albert station, the DLR takes up the approximate line of the Gallions branch, with Beckton Park DLR virtually on the site of the latter's Central station of 1880–1940. After this the DLR diverges north away from the Gallions branch at a point near the site of the former Manor Way station, allowing the passenger a glimpse of the Gallions Hotel, which still stands, looking somewhat lonely and neglected at the time of writing. Soon turning west, as if it had lost its way, the DLR runs for a short distance parallel with Winsor Terrace, following if not precisely over the roadbed of the terminal section of the former Beckton branch. However the DLR's Beckton terminus is just under half a mile west of its namesake's former platform, Away to the east, the new DLR Beckton depot occupies part of the extensive gas works site.

So it is that some of London's oldest local railways have played an important part in the planning and realisation of one of its newest, and as we have seen earlier in this book, this process is also occurring in south London with Croydon Tramlink. In this way, even those local lines that have been abandoned live on in another guise and there will no doubt be more examples as the London rail system adapts and develops to meet twenty-first century needs.

SOURCES AND BIBLIOGRAPHY

Note: This bibliography is not comprehensive but will give an indication of the sources used and also where the reader can find further information and background. Only some of the secondary sources listed in sections 5–7 were consulted in the preparation of this book.

1: GENERAL AND PRIMARY SOURCES

Parliamentary papers, private bills and acts and evidence before parliamentary committees (House of Lords Record Office).

Railway companies' minute books, reports and other papers (Public Record Office and, for London Transport and predecessors, the Greater London Record Office).

Railway companies', BR and LT public and working timetables and appendices.

Passenger statistics and freight loadings supplied to the author by BR.

Traffic Circulars, London Transport Railways and predecessors.

2: NEWSPAPERS AND PERIODICALS

Contemporary accounts and reports in:

Branch Line News, British Railways Magazine, Daily Telegraph, Edgware Gazette, Electric Railway, Electric Railway Society Journal, Estates Gazette, Evening News (London), *Great Western Railway Magazine, Herapath's Railway & Commercial Journal, Illustrated London News, Law Reports, Railnews, Railway & Travel Monthly, Railway Gazette, Railway Magazine, Railway News, Railway Observer, Railway Times, Southern Railway Magazine, Surrey Advertiser, Times, TOT Magazine, Tottenham & Edmonton Advertiser, Transport & Travel Monthly, Underground News.*

3: MAPS AND PLANS

Ordnance Survey maps, various editions and scales, pre 1940

Edward Stanford's *New Map of Metropolitan Railways and Improvements sanctioned in 1866*, 1866.

New Large Scale Atlas of London & Suburbs . . ., George W Bacon, 1880 and 1888

Stanford's map of the County of London, 1905

Stanford's Indexed Atlas of the County of London, 1911

Bacon's Atlas of London & Suburbs 1904, 1912, 1928

Bartholomew's Reference Atlas of Greater London, Seventh Edition 1940, Ninth Edition, 1954, Eleventh Edition, 1961.

Geographia Ltd, *The Authentic Map Directory of London & Suburbs*, First Edition 1924, Third Edition 1933.

Geographia Ltd, *London Map Directory . . .*, First post war Edition, 1964

Nicholson Greater London Street Atlas, Comprehensive Edition, 1995

4: STATE PAPERS

The Royal Commission on London Traffic, Report, Evidence, Appendices (eight vols), 1905–06

Reports of the London Traffic Branch, Board of Trade, 1908–15

London & Home Counties Traffic Advisory Committee, Report upon the Public Inquiry held in October 1925 with respect to the Travelling Facilities to and from North and North East London, HMSO, 1926

London & Home Counties Traffic Advisory Committee, Public Inquiry with regard to the alleged inadequacy of travelling facilities to, from, and within, certain areas of East London, Minutes of Evidence and Report, HMSO, 1926

London & Home Counties Traffic Advisory Committee, Public Inquiry with regard to the alleged inadequacy of travelling facilities to, from, and within, certain areas South East of London, Minutes of Evidence and Report, HMSO, 1926

5: SECONDARY SOURCES: GENERAL

Acworth, W M, *The Railways of England*, various editions from 1888

Allerton, R J, *London County Council Housing Service Handbook*, 1962

Anon, *The Country at London's Door*, 1926 (Southern Rly)

Country Homes at London's Door, 1927 (Southern Rly)

Southern Homes, 1932 (Southern Railway)

Improving London's Transport, 1946 (*Railway Gazette* Supplement)
North London Railway, A Pictorial Record, 1979 (HMSO)
Barker, T C and Robbins, Michael, *A History of London Transport, Vol 1, The Nineteenth Century*, 1963, and *Vol. 2 The Twentieth Century to 1970*, 1974
Barran, Sir David, *London Rail Study*, 1974
Bayman, Bob and Connor, Piers, *Underground Official Handbook*, Third Edition, 1994
Borley, H V, *Chronology of London Railways*, 1982
Brown, David and Jackson, Alan A, *Network South East Handbook*, 1990
Clark, R H, *A Southern Region Chronology and Record 1803–1965*, 1964
Connor, Piers, *Going Green: The Story of the District Line*, Second Edition, 1994.
Course, E A, *London Railways*, 1962
  London's Railways Then & Now, 1987
Croome Desmond F, and Jackson, Alan A, *Rails Through the Clay, A History of London's Tube Railways*, Second Edition, 1993
Crump, Norman, *By Rail to Victory*, 1947
Darwin, Bernard, *War on the Line*, 1946
Dickens's Dictionary of London, 1896
Dobson, C G, *A Century and A Quarter*, 1951 (Hall & Co.)
Edmonds, Alexander, *History of the Metropolitan District Railway Company to June 1908*, 1973
Faulkner, J N and Williams, R A, *The London & South Western Railway in the Twentieth Century*, 1988
Gray, Adrian, *The London, Chatham & Dover Railway*, 1984
  South Eastern Railway, 1990
Howard Turner, J T, *The London Brighton & South Coast Railway* (three vols, 1977, 1978, 1979
Jackson, Alan A, *London's Termini*, Second Edition, 1985
  London's Metropolitan Railway, 1986
  'London Transport under the Greater London Council', in *Modern Railways*, February, 1986
  'BR in London: the GLC contribution' in *Modern Railways*, April 1986
  Semi-Detached London, Suburban Development, Life & Transport, 1900–39, Second Edition, 1991
  (ed.) *The Memories & Writings of a London Railwayman . . .*, 1993
Jeafferson, J C, *Life of Robert Stephenson*, 1864
Klapper, C F, *Sir Herbert Walker's Southern Railway*, 1973
Lawrence, David, *Underground Architecture*, 1994
Leboff, David, *London Underground Stations*, 1984
Lee, Charles E, *Workmen's Fares . . .*, 1944
  The Metropolitan District Railway, 1988
London County Council, *Housing . . .*, 1928
  Housing 1928–30, 1931
  London Housing, 1937
Moody, G T, *Southern Electric 1909–79*, Fifth Edition, 1979
Peacock, Thomas P, *Great Western London Suburban Services*, New Edition, 1978
Pratt, Edwin A, *British Railways & The Great War* (two vols), 1921
Robbins, Michael, *The North London Railway*, Seventh Edition, 1974
Surrey County Council, *Rail Line Improvements in Surrey (SWT Operating Area), Final Report*, 1995
Taylor, Derek and Bush, David, *The Golden Age of British Hotels*, 1974
Thornbury, W and Walford, Edward, *Old & New London* (six vols.), 1897
Thorne, James, *Handbook to the Environs of London* (two volumes) 1876
Waters, Lawrence, *Britain's Rail Super Centres: London – The Great Western Lines*, 1993
Welch, H D, *The London, Tilbury & Southend Railway*, 1963
White, H P, *A Regional History of the Railways of Great Britain: Vol 3 Greater London*, 1987
Williams, R A, *The London & South Western Railway*, (two vols) 1968, 1973

6: SECONDARY SOURCES: LOCAL STUDIES

Anon, *A Short History of the Plessey Tunnel Factory 1941–2*, 1942
  Return to North Woolwich: The North Woolwich Railway and Transport Around the Royal Docks, 1987
Bayliss, Derek A, *Retracing The First Public Railway*, 1981
Blake, Jim and James, Jonathan, *Northern Wastes: The Story of the Uncompleted Northern Line Extensions*, 1987

Body, Geoffrey, *The Blackwall and Millwall Extension Railways*, nd
Connor, J E, *All Stations to Poplar*, 1980
  Stepney's Own Railway: A History of The London & Blackwall System 1984
Course, Edwin, *The Bexleyheath Line*, 1980
Cresswell, Henrietta, *Winchmore Hill, Memories of a Lost Village*, 1907
Davies, Reg and Bevan, David, *Rails to the People's Palace and the Parkland Walk*, Third Edition, 1994
Elliot, Alan, *Wimbledon's Railways*, 1982
Frost, K A, *The Romford-Upminster Branch*, 1964
Frost, Ken, 'Grays-Upminster-Romford', in *Railways South East: The Album*, 1994
Goode, C T, *The Railways of Uxbridge*, 1983
  The Hertford Loop Line, 1984
  To The Crystal Palace, 1984
Goudie, F W, *Metropolitan to Jubilee: Wembley Park to Stanmore*, 1986
Hamilton, J E, *The Industries of Crayford*, 1980
Heselton, Kenneth Y, *Sunbury and the Thames Valley Railway*, 1975
Hodge, Peter, *The Hertford Loop . . .*, 1976
Horsburgh, E L S, *Bromley, Kent, From the Earliest Times to the Present Century*, 1929
Jowett, E M, *Raynes Park: A Social History*, 1987
Kidner, R W, *The Dartford Loop Line 1866–1966*, 1966
  The North Kent Line, 1977
Lake, G H, *The Railways of Tottenham*, 1946
Lee, Charles E, *Early Railways in Surrey, The Surrey Iron Railway . . .*, 1944
Peacock, Thomas B, *PLA Railways*, 1952
Pearce, Alan; Jolly, Stephen and Hardy, Brian, *Docklands Light Rail Official Handbook*, 1994
Pond, C C, *The Walthamstow and Chingford Railway*, 1982
Robbins, Michael, *Railway Development in South West London*, Transactions London & Middlesex
  Archaeological Society, vol 34 (1983), 259–269
Ruegg, R, *Summer Rambles Round Woolwich*, 1847
Scott, Peter G, *Harrow & Stanmore Railway*, Second Edition, 1981
Sherwood, Tim, *Change at Clapham Junction: The Railways of Wandsworth and South West London*, 1994
Skinner, M W G, *Croydon's Railways*, 1985
Spence, Jeoffry, *The Caterham Railway*, 1952
Thomas, R H G, *London's First Railway: The London & Greenwich*, 1972
Townsend, Charles E C, *Further Notes on Early Railways in Surrey*, Newcomen Society, 1950
Wilmot, G F A, *The Railway in Finchley: A Study in Suburban Development*, Second Edition, 1973
Woodman, Trevor, *The Railways to Hayes . . ., Kent*, 1982
Young, John N, *Great Northern Suburban*, 1977

7: MAGAZINE ARTICLES ON SPECIFIC LINES & LOCATIONS

BRJ = *British Railway Journal**, ER = *Essex Review*, GEJ = *Great Eastern Journal**,
GWRJ = *Great Western Railway Journal**, LRR = *London Railway Record**, R = *Railways*,
RM = *Railway Magazine**, RSE = *Railways South East*, RTM = *Railway & Travel Monthly*,
RW = *Railway World*, U = *Underground*, UN = *Underground News**

Anon, (Lee, Charles E?), 'The Gauge of the Surrey Iron Railway', RM August 1967
Anon, 'The Expansion of the Great Eastern Railway: The New Line from Woodford to Ilford', RM
  June 1903,
  'Milk Traffic on the Ongar Branch, Great Eastern Railway', RM November 1918
Baker, Ian, 'Railways Around Tooting', LRR January 1955
  'North of Wood Green', LRR April 1995
  'From Harrow to Uxbridge', LRR July 1995
  'Tracing the Line to Alexandra Palace', LRR April 1996
Braidley, Philip W, 'Construction of the Metropolitan Stanmore Branch', U vol 1, 12
Burnham, T G, 'Branch to Bromley North', RM February 1975
Connor, J E, 'The Railways of Beckton', LRR November 1994, January 1995
  'The Gallions Branch of the PLA', LRR April 1995
  'The Palace Gates Branch', LRR July, October 1995

'The Greenwich Park Branch', LRR April, July 1996

Croome, Desmond, 'The Strange Story of Northfields (Weymouth Avenue)', UN 406 (October 1995)

Davis, P R, 'A Long-Forgotten Airport Scheme', U vol 10, 3

Derrick, J, 'The Woodside & South Croydon Joint Line', LRR July 1995

'The Alexandra Palace Line', LRR January 1996

Edwards, W E, 'The Stanmore Railway', RM February 1922

Faulkner, J N, 'The Shepperton Branch of the Southern Region', RW February 1964

'Easter Monday at Kempton Park', RM April 1955

'To Guildford via Cobham', RM September 1959

Frost, K A, 'Railways Around Romford', RSE Winter 1988/89

Gairns, J F, 'The Ealing & Shepherds Bush Railway, RM July 1920

'The Hackney Downs Group of Lines, Great Eastern Railway', RM October 1922

Gillham, J C, 'The Railways of Kew and Gunnersbury', RM September 1956

Holmes, J G, 'The North Woolwich Branch', RM May-June 1946

Hopwood, H L, 'The Enfield-Stevenage Loop Line', RM July 1920

'The London & Blackwall Railway', RM May 1927

Jackson, Alan A, 'The South Acton Branch', RM December 1958

'North-West from Ealing', RM September 1959, October 1959

'The Wimbledon & Sutton Railway', RM December 1966

'Beyond Edgware', RM February 1967

'Almost A Tube', (Alexandra Palace Branch), RM May 1973, June 1973

'Chessington: Southern Electric Swansong', RM January 1974

'Rails to Tattenham Corner', RM June 1975

'Brent Valley Railcars', RW May 1979

'Racing to Residential: the Wimbledon & Epsom Line', RW July 1980

'Romford to Grays', RW December 1979

'The Horton Light Railway', RM October 1981

'Central Line to the West', RSE Winter 1987–88

'Northern to Morden', RSE Winter 1988–89

'Newbury Park: Not Quite What It Was Meant To Be', LRR April 1996

Jenkins Stanley C, 'Denham to Uxbridge (High Street)', GWRJ 1, 1992

Jenkins, Stanley and Turner, Chris, 'Uxbridge Vine Street', GWRJ 13, 1995

Kirkby, Dick, 'Derby Day', RSE 12, Summer 1993

Kirkland, R K, 'The Great Western and Brentford Railway', RM February 1960

'The Staines Branch Western Region', RM April 1955

Morss, Jeffrey, 'The Palace Gates to North Woolwich Line', RM September 1962

Norris, P J, 'The Bromley North Branch', RW February 1957

Paar, Harry, 'Hidden Aspects of The Fairlop Loop Line', GEJ, 81, January 1995

Potter, G W J, 'The New GER Loop Line', [Fairlop Loop] ER vol 12, 1903

'The Loughton and Ongar Branch of the Great Eastern Railway', RM September 1920

Riley, R C, 'The Steam Railmotors of the SECR', R January-February 1951

'Railmotors of the LBSCR', R August 1952

Sams, J G B, 'The West Croydon and Wimbledon Railway', RM March 1927

Sekon, G A, 'The First Railway With Non-Stop Trains: The London & Blackwall Railway', RTM April 1912

Smith, William H, 'The Crystal Palace (High Level) Branch, BRJ 28 (1989)

Treby, Edward, 'The Edmonton-Cheshunt Line', RM March 1958

'By Central line to Ongar', RM September 1968

'The Central Croydon Branch', RW March 1974

'From Custom House to Gallions', RM February 1975

Turner, Chris, 'Uxbridge High Street', GWRJ 10 (1994)

Webster, V R, 'Railway Byways in East London', BRJ 27 (1989)

Wilson, B G, 'The Railway Development of Wimbledon', RW March 1961

Wilson, P W, 'By Railway to Tattenham Corner', RM July 1901

INDEX

Note: Stations are indexed under their most recent names. For train services refer to entries for main stations; for signalling details, refer to individual lines and stations; for locomotives and rolling stock, refer to the individual lines. Page numbers in *italics* indicate illustrations. There may be more than one reference on the page indicated.

ATLAS
OF
DOG BREEDS
OF THE WORLD

Bonnie Wilcox, DVM,
and
Chris Walkowicz

H-1091

Distributed in the UNITED STATES by T.F.H. Publications, Inc., One T.F.H. Plaza, Neptune City, NJ 07753; in CANADA to the Pet Trade by H & L Pet Supplies Inc., 27 Kingston Crescent, Kitchener, Ontario N2B 2T6; Rolf C. Hagen Ltd., 3225 Sartelon Street, Montreal 382 Quebec; in CANADA to the Book Trade by Macmillan of Canada (A Division of Canada Publishing Corporation), 164 Commander Boulevard, Agincourt, Ontario M1S 3C7; in ENGLAND by T.F.H. Publications, The Spinney, Parklands, Portsmouth PO7 6AR; in AUSTRALIA AND THE SOUTH PACIFIC by T.F.H. (Australia) Pty. Ltd., Box 149, Brookvale 2100 N.S.W., Australia; in NEW ZEALAND by Ross Haines & Son, Ltd., 82 D Elizabeth Knox Place, Panmure, Auckland, New Zealand; in the PHILIPPINES by Bio-Research, 5 Lippay Street, San Lorenzo Village, Makati, Rizal; in SOUTH AFRICA by Multipet Pty. Ltd., P.O. Box 35347, Northway, 4065, South Africa. Published by T.F.H. Publications, Inc. Manufactured in the United States of America by T.F.H. Publications, Inc.

ATLAS
OF
DOG BREEDS
OF THE WORLD

Bonnie Wilcox, DVM,
and
Chris Walkowicz

Third Edition, Revised

About the Authors

Bonnie Wilcox, D.V.M., and Chris Walkowicz, each having established distinguished careers in the dog fancy, combine their talents and experience to bring forth *The Atlas of Dog Breeds of the World*. This volume, the product of four years of research and writing, is the third book co-authored by this team. *Successful Dog Breeding* (1985) and *The Complete Question and Answer Book on Dogs* (1988) have both received recognition by the Dog Writers Association of America, the former being chosen as the Best Dog Book of the Year 1985. The authors have also established themselves as monthly columnists for international dog magazines. Dr. Wilcox, a practicing veterinarian for over 20 years, pens "Tell Me Why," for *Dog Fancy*, while Ms. Walkowicz writes "Breeders Forum" for *Pure-Bred Dogs/American Kennel Gazette*. Ms. Walkowicz, a full-time freelance writer and editor, has authored over 200 published articles as well as two breed books: *The Bearded Collie* (1987) and *Your German Shepherd Dog*. Dr. Wilcox, also a breeder of German Shorthaired Pointers, received her B.S. and D.V.M. degrees from the University of Illinois School of Veterinary Medicine. Both authors, whose association with pure-bred dogs as owners and breeders extends some 20 years, live with their husbands, children and dogs in Illinois.

To Rebecca, Clayton and Amy Wilcox
Dean, Teresa, Michael and Josh Walkowicz
who understand that Moms can be more than cookie bakers.

May you, sometime in your life,
know the love of a very
special dog.

Acknowledgments

A big thank you to our correspondents, who have contributed their time, knowledge and photos of their chosen breeds. Without you, we would have had no direct source of correct information on some of these breeds, particularly in countries outside the United States.

To Isabelle Francais, who supplied many of the marvelous photos from all over the world, and added color to this kaleidoscope of dogs.

To John R. Quinn, who rendered the dog illustrations used to make this volume complete. Mr. Quinn was able to recreate, with enviable accuracy, many of the extremely rare and possibly extinct breeds for which photographs were not available. Much gratitude for his talent and dedication to this project.

To the Quad City branch of the National League of American Pen Women, especially Willetta Balla, Judie Gulley, Betty Klaas, Rhonda Krahl, Connie Heckert, Delores Kuenning, Jan Oliver and Sidney Jeanne Seward, who (thankfully) have been ruthless in their critiquing sessions.

To our translators who have come to our rescue and untwisted our English tongues. They have made it possible for us to ask our questions and to understand the answers we received.

Contents

Authors' Preface

"But the poor dog, in life the firmest friend,
The first to welcome, foremost to defend,
Whose honest heart is still his master's own,
Who labours, fights, lives, breathes for him alone."
Lord Byron

Although most dog owners already recognize—and appreciate—these attributes, it is difficult for us to truly understand our own dogs and their history without a general knowledge about evolution of the human/dog relationship, its roots and transformation.

The authors believe, as do most animal behaviorists, that if more pets were chosen through knowledge rather than seduction by a pair of deep, soulful eyes, fewer pets would end their existence at an animal shelter. . . or worse. An understanding of the individual breeds can best be attained by a study of the parent groups and their accompanying predispositions/inclinations/proclivities. Only after such research should a pet be chosen to fill and complete a family and its individual lifestyle.

Our intent is for this book to help all dog enthusiasts more fully appreciate their own breed choice. These insights will help dog owners see what causes the pleasing characteristics—as well as the ones that irritate them. Ingrained breed nature instills the sweetness, intelligence, loyalty, sturdiness, working and protective qualities that we desire in the various breeds. This very nature also motivates digging, yapping terriers; chasing, yelping herding dogs; aggressive, barking flock guards and mastiffs; straying, howling gun dogs and hounds; and independent, aloof sighthounds and pariahs.

Most people, however, have deep feelings for their pets and, according to surveys, consider them an important part of the family. For these dog lovers, it is interesting to discover and to share what makes their dogs "tick." We intend to unfold a world of dogs—and their roots—hoping to further strengthen this bond between people and their pets. The information and photographs from owners all over the world demonstrate that the love between masters and their dogs transcends the boundaries, tensions and stone walls between countries.

Frequently, people tend to focus on the world of dogs from the narrow viewpoint of their favorite breed, as if it were an isolated phenomenon. Even the professional breeder or exhibitor may attend a kennel club show and watch the Pomeranians, Schipperkes and Norwegian Elkhounds, all in different group divisions, and be unaware that these breeds share a close common background. Through this volume, dog lovers will have the opportunity to look at the great diversity of dogs through a wide-angle lens.

Many people do not realize that more than 400 breeds of dogs share our world with us. Some of them are common in their homelands; others are unknown even to the people who share their native countries. Yet all of these breeds have carved a niche and a relationship with humankind. Moreover, every one was created for a specific purpose. These are truly "Dogs For All Reasons."

—B.W./C.W.

How To Use This Book

In undertaking a volume that intends to survey the breeds of dog known to man, we, as authors, were pleased to hit upon the notion of "Dogs For All Reasons" to guide us through the immense and fascinating world of dogs. Therefore, each breed of dog in this volume is categorized according to its stem group, original purpose and geographical development. The traditional groupings employed by the major registering bodies have not been used here. Our pursuit of "Dogs For All Reasons" has produced eight categories, into which all 400 + dog breeds fall: Flock Guards, Mastiffs, Scenthounds (referred to in the text simply as Hounds), Gun Dogs, Northern Breeds, Herding Dogs, Terriers, and Southern Dogs. For instance, the Chow Chow, which the American Kennel Club groups as Non-Sporting and The Kennel Club of Great Britain groups as Utility, has here been placed among the Northern Breeds due to its place of origin and traditional purpose. This includes even the breeds which are considered "toys" in most registries.

A chapter devoted to each of the eight categories of dogs describes the group's general characteristics and gives the reader an historical perspective on the group's evolution. Complete lists of the breeds in the group are included at the end of its chapter.

The next section, "The Dogs of the World," is a collection of articles arranged alphabetically. Inasmuch as some breeds are very similar in historical origins and characteristics, we have combined some related breeds into single articles. The Breed Name Cross-Reference list will show the reader where in the alphabetical section these breeds can be found.

When the information is available, ranges for height and weight are given for each breed, from the smallest female to the largest male. Height is rounded off to the nearest half-inch, and weight is given in pounds. Registry is noted for the Federation Cynologique Internationale (FCI) world registry; the two main registering bodies of the United States: the American Kennel Club (AKC) and the United Kennel Club (UKC); The Kennel Club of Great Britain (TKC); and the Canadian Kennel Club (CKC). In addition to the notations in this volume, however, many of the breeds are registered by their own country's kennel clubs, by private registries, or by specialty clubs. The country listed is not always the country of origin, but is that which most cynologists credit with breed development and promotion.

Personal communications from correspondents are included in the body of the text without footnotes; additionally, all other references have been incorporated into the text for smooth and easy reading. Complete lists of sources, contributors, and owners of the dogs portrayed in the book are included at the back of this volume.

Throughout this work, *breed names* are capitalized; however, words referring to *types* of dogs are lowercased (e.g., the American Foxhound is one breed of foxhound).

Breed Name Cross-Reference

Since this list is designed to help the reader locate the dog breeds mentioned in the alphabetically arranged articles in "The Dogs of the World," it does not, of course, contain the titles of all the articles found there. The column on the left states the breed name; the column in the center is the title of the article in which the dog is discussed, and the column on the right indicates the page number.

Because dogs have different names in different lands, this list will aid the reader in locating the name of the article that pertains to the breed in question. To illustrate: the Pyrenean Mountain Dog, as the breed is known in Great Britain, is known more commonly in the United States as the Great Pyrenees; in France, its native land, it is called the Chien de Montagne des Pyrenees. Thus, the reader is able to look up the British or the French name to find the name employed in this atlas (in this case, Great Pyrenees).

Articles that combine two or more breeds of similar origins and characteristics are also covered in this list. For example the article entitled "Elkhounds" treats the Norwegian Elkhound and its two closest relations, the Black Norwegian Elkhound and the Jämthund. Looking up any of these three breed names will direct the reader to the article entitled "Elkhounds."

Dogs For All Reasons

Although many beasts have served humanity throughout time, only one serves by choice. Only one animal is willing to forsake its own kind and follow us. Dogs have always been and remain "man's best friend"—and mankind, occasionally, is dog's.

Cynologists and archeologists have found evidence of the canine/human relationship existing almost as early as the species of *Homo sapiens*. Dogs served the hunter, the shepherd and the warrior. They were guardians of the home, beasts of burden and companions on the journey of life. Dogs have long fed human need, their souls—even their bellies. Although few civilizations now incorporate dogs in their menus, dogs still assist their masters in all the ancient ways and in many new ones.

How did this relationship come to exist between people and dogs? What caused the development of so many diverse breeds?

The answer to this special bond can best be explained by studying the wolf. Wolves are the most social of all mammals: cooperating in the hunt, mating for life, sharing in puppy care, playing with and teaching their young. The dog has a built-in capacity to love and serve his "pack" or family. Cynologist John McLoughlin, in his history of dogs, *The Canine Clan, A New Look at Man's Best Friend*, summed up the phenomenon best when he said, "The dog can love us, not because we are so lovable, but because their wild wolf ancestors had such a mighty devotion for one another."

Each breed, each individual dog is valued by someone or by a group of people. It serves a purpose, even if its destination is "only" to stave off loneliness.

Oft-quoted legends portray this special relationship:

God summoned a beast from the field
and He said,
"Behold man, created in my image.
Therefore, adore him.

You shall protect him in the wilderness,
shepherd his flocks,
watch over his children, accompany him
wherever he may go,
even unto civilization. You shall be his
ally, his slave
and his companion.

"To do these things," God said, "I
endow you with these instincts
uncommon to other beasts: faithfulness,
devotion, and understanding surpassing
those of man himself.
Lest it impair your loyalty, you shall be
blind to the faults of man.
Lest it impair your understanding, you
are denied the power of words. Let no
fault of language cleave an accord
beyond that of man with any other beast
or even man with man. Speak to your
master only with your mind and through
honest eyes.
Walk by his side, sleep in his doorway,
forage for him, ward off his enemies,
carry his burdens, share his afflictions,
love him and comfort him.
And in return for this, man will fulfill
your needs and wants which shall be
only food, shelter and affection.
"So be silent, and be a friend to man.
Guide him through the perils along the
way to the land that I have promised
him.
This shall be your destiny and your
immortality."
So spake the Lord.
And the dog heard and was content.

★ ★ ★

At the creation of the world, an
earthquake carved a huge chasm,
leaving man on one side, and animals on
the other. Man called to the beasts for
companionship. As the dog saw man on

Like no other creature, dog serves man by choice. The Collie, which serves man as a herder, protector and companion, is one of the world's most famous canines.

the other side alone, he paced up and down the great divide, whining. When man called, "Come!", the dog leaped, narrowly missing and barely hanging onto the edge. Man leaned over and pulled him to safety, and thus began the closest relationship between man and beast.

★ ★ ★

Bible lore credits the dogs with Noah as using their noses to plug the holes which sprang in the Ark. This is why their noses are so cold!

★ ★ ★

A Spanish legend says the Three Wise Men were each accompanied by a dog to welcome the Christ Child. These dogs were Cubillon, Melampo and Lubino, and it is said that any dog that bears one of these names is blessed.

Dog & Man, by Sloan and Farquar

Although the early relatives of dogs and humans were certainly less sentimental than the foregoing legends, the human-dog relationship was the

The evolution of the dog is closely linked to the history of man—where man has gone, dog has followed, to the North Pole, into the desert, into the woods, and through the prairie. These two American Cocker Spaniels live a contented life on the farm with their owner.

first of all the beasts. When families lived in caves, it is certain canine types were utilized—as scavengers and for hunting; as playmates for the cavekids and for warming cold toes; probably even on the cave menu.

Eventually the relationship grew closer and the dog prototype was looked on as a friend, rather than just a means to a comfy life.

A parallel history exists between *Homo sapiens* and dog. When society was pastoral, flock dogs were developed. When hunters needed assistance, sporting breeds answered the call. When civilizations moved to war, mighty dogs accompanied them, and the diversification of the breeds began.

Many anthropologists believe that the "thinking human" first developed in the area somewhere between northern India and northern Iran. This is also the geographical location that is believed to be the site of the oldest domesticated canines. From this background, it is possible to imagine either a single or twofold origin for the dog and to envision how the animal changed and spread throughout the world.

Human's first success at domestication was the dog. For centuries, the pattern persisted—primitive hunters and their dogs stalked and cut animals out of wild herds, sharing the bounty.

The first domesticated dog probably performed mainly as a herder. The herding progenitor retained many characteristics of the wolf: small, upright ears; foxy (wedge-shaped) faces; a stand-off coat; and the square, athletic body, built for endurance rather than speed. The neotanous (infantile) trait of the curled tail was purposely selected, along with the infantile temperament, i.e., more trusting and companionable than the adult wolf.

Geologists have found cave drawings and other proof of close association occurring during the Stone Age—50,000 years ago. In the United States, remains of dogs (dating to 9,000 years ago) were discovered in the Jaguar Cave, situated in the Beaverhead Mountains of east-central Idaho. Bones of two classes were found: one a small Beagle size, and another closer to the size of a modern-day retriever. Other burial sites in late Mesolithic and Neolithic settlements, circa 600 BC in Denmark, and lake settlements of Switzerland and Austria have disclosed the re-

Dogs have evolved for specific functions: to hunt, to herd, to guide, to defend. Despite a breed's particular original function, it can learn to perform a variety of tasks; this English Setter, a member of the gun dog group, does a fine job of keeping an eye on the farm livestock.

mains of sheepdogs, hunting dogs and miniature dogs. Artwork that depicted dogs was used to decorate stoneware, pottery and paintings from early Egypt, Assyria and Greece, as early as 3200 BC. Canine paw prints appear in a clay brick from Ur (ca. 2100 BC).

In Neolithic times, the Finno-Ugrian peoples first migrated from Tibet westward into Europe, then north to populate the great northern plains. They became Lapps, Samoyeds and other northern tribes. Later still, these nomads crossed the land bridge to populate the North and South American continents. With them, to all points of the world, came dogs of northern type, selected and molded for a variety of tasks.

Meanwhile, civilized Tibetans were selecting dogs for other traits. Smaller and shaggier dogs were used for herding. Others—larger and, eventually, giant—were selected for guardian chores. These became the stem breeds of the eastern herding dogs, as well as the fount of

flock guards and mastiffs. As migrations moved west into Europe and east to the Orient, these varieties moved with them—still retaining the tail curled over the back.

As civilization traveled south into the warm Fertile Crescent, it became more efficient to have a smaller and smoother coated pariah type dog. Within native populations of pariahs in the Middle East, a natural variation occurred and still exists: from the large flock-guard type, to the medium husky size and the collie type, and the svelte racing variety. This pattern indicates that these tendencies traveled with them from other parts of the world.

Nature influenced the development of breed types—when the dog lived in a cold clime, he grew a thick, warm coat. When he ran the hot desert sands, tufts of hair protected his feet.

His owner, too, helped to dictate his transformation. Breeders selectively bred for larger, faster, stronger, tinier—leaner or meaner.

Taxes and other impositions dictated canine fashion. In parts of the world, long-tailed dogs were taxed, and it became more economical to own a dog with a short stump or none at all. When genes didn't cooperate by transmuting this expensive appendage into short stubs, many a dog lost his tail to the knife—or even to teeth. For a fee, the whelps were nipped by the town's tail-biting "specialist."

Dogs of the nobility were pampered pets, or favored hunting companions, that enjoyed luxuries most of the populace could not imagine. The dogs of the poor, however, endured suffering and existed mainly to help their masters put food in their mouths or to ease their workloads.

The nobility further protected their advantages with cruel laws designed to prevent a royal hare stewing in a peasant's pot. The poor paid dearly for the luxury of their poverty, and so did their dogs. To prevent poaching by the commoners, their dogs' knee tendons were cut, so they could not run down a hare or deer on royal land. Expeditation, cutting off the toes from one foot, accomplished the same purpose. The "dog gauge," a ring of 7 inches x 5 inches, through which the dog must fit to escape mutilation, separated the fortunate toed from those who would soon be de-toed.

It's a miracle dogs (or their masters) survived to modern times! Treatments for various diseases (human and canine) called for mixtures of ox dung and vinegar; quicksilver, brimstone, nettlefeed and sewet [sic]; new pressed wine or egg white in the ear; a nail or needle to pull out worms. These methods were prescribed to cure everything from infertility or rabies to acne.

To the pharaohs in Egypt, the dog was a symbol of fidelity and a guardian. Anubis, the Egyptian god of death, who enfolded the dying in his arms, had the body of a man and the head of a dog. Even the Dog Star, Sirius, heralded the overflow of the Nile, and the shepherds moved their flocks to higher levels when the guardian star appeared.

Since these times, and even earlier, a wide variety of sizes and types bred true. The definition of a breed is "a race of animals from the same stock, kind or sort." The individual breeds recognized by the various world registries have bred true for many generations. Registry organizations, such as the Federation Cynologique Internationale (FCI), American Kennel Club (AKC), Canadian Kennel Club (CKC), The Kennel Club of Great Britain (TKC), and United Kennel Club (UKC), and those of various countries throughout the world, demand that newly recognized breeds be purebred and that their owners maintain stud books which list matings prior to the time of application for recognition. Many of these dogs boast pedigrees fancier than their masters' family trees. Pedigree is derived from the French *Pied de Grue*, meaning foot of the crane.

The Shih Tzu as a breed has made quite a stir in the dog fancy today—it was indeed one of the nobility's pampered pets centuries ago.

Bred in the Middle Ages by monks, the Basset Hound comes to modern man as a keen trailer of rabbit and hare. The breed's sluggish, sad-eyed expression is no indicator of this scenthound's abilities—it has been also known to work coon, squirrel and opossum.

In Roman times, however, before pedigrees or registrations became important, the earliest listing classified dogs as House, Shepherd, Sporting, Pugnacious or War, Dogs Which Ran By Scent and Swift Dogs Which Ran On Sight. The first breed "catalog" was attributed to Juliana Barnes (Berners), the prioress of Sopwell nunnery, in the 1486 *Boke of St. Albans*: "Greyhound, Bastard, Mengrell, Mastif, Lemor, Raches, Kenettys, Terroures, Butcher's Houndes, Dunghill Dogges, Tryndeltaylles, Prycheryd Currys, [and] Small Ladyes Poppees That Bere Awaye The Flees."

These translate into our current sighthounds, mongrels, mastiffs, Bloodhounds, Beagles, Bulldogs, terriers, long-tailed shepherd dogs, pariahs and toys of today—all of which still occasionally "bere flees."

While the "Small Ladyes Poppees" and the hounds of the hunt enjoyed sumptuous quarters, foods cooked especially for them, and personal servants, the dogs of the underclass scratched for their existence. No wonder certain breeds carry themselves with regal bearing,

while others are scrappy, feisty and independent! Dog expert Edward C. Ash noted: "The dog of well-educated people somehow or other collects some of their education, habits and manners, and the dog of a man who lives by his wits appears verily to vie with his master, behaving with the greatest cunning, sometimes with more wisdom than its biped companion."

Throughout time, individuals have shown their bond to dogs even unto death. Egyptian masters mourned the loss of their pets by shaving all the hair of their heads and bodies. They erected tombs in miniature for their beloved pets, and even fitted their dogs with golden masks, similar to those placed on esteemed personages. The Toltec Indians felt the most perfect, unselfish love was that of a dog for its master. When its owner died, the pet was buried with the master. The selfless beast's devotion carried through life unto death, when the dog interceded with the god of death, relating the master's good deeds. Some cultures fitted deceased dogs with glass eyes so they could see in the afterworld.

The Shar-Pei, a breed of ancient China, has a mastiffy appearance and a respective dominant temperament, but belongs to the northern group as its genes are traced to Nordic, Chow-type dogs. Trained properly, the Shar-Pei is affectionate and personable.

The largest funeral for a dog was hosted by Emperor Norton I of the U.S., Protector of Mexico. Ten thousand people mourned the death of the Emperor's mongrel, "Lazaras."

Concern of masters for their pets in the afterlife has been chronicled by anthropologists who have found evidence of cave dwellers, and later Indians, and their dogs buried together. In the ruins of Pompeii were the remains of an elderly person. Cradled in the skeletal hand was a pet dog, comforting and being comforted to the fiery end. A dog cemetery from 700 BC has been unearthed in Israel. All the skeletons appear to be of sighthound type.

Even today, true dog lovers take it upon themselves to ensure their pet a peaceful departure from life and arrange a burial or memorial of their companions. Pet cemeteries and cremations are common, as are the accoutrements of death: caskets, stone markers and memorial donations.

In some societies, the bond was so strong that dogs were actually chosen over humans. The Fulgian Indian Dog, which guarded the camp and aided in hunting otters and birds, was crucial to the tribe's welfare. The oldest women were assigned to care for these dogs. When food was scarce, these women would be cannibalized, but never the dogs. A tribesman was quoted, "Dogs catch otters . . . old women are good for nothing."

In more modern times, however, the odds leaned to the humans. Wars were hard on dogs, as well as people. Breeds suffered decimation, some to extinction, others to minimal numbers. People were occupied with keeping themselves alive, rather than concerned with breeding pure-bred dogs or even feeding them. Later, with care and nurturing, several endangered breeds again flourished.

In our modern world, as communications expand and walls between countries come down, we learn more and more about other nations, the people and their canine companions. Currently, FCI recognizes nearly 400 dog breeds and varieties worldwide. Those that are unknown in the United States are often termed "rare breeds," which some are, indeed. Others are common-place in their homeland, but still relatively un-heard of in some areas of the world. The popularity of many lesser known breeds is increasing, however, in their native lands and the United States.

Most dogs fit neatly within one of the following genres: flock guard, mastiff, scenthound, gun dog, terrier, northern, herding or southern dog. Some of our modern breeds, however, could have their family tree traced back to two or more of these groups through various ancestral crossbreedings.

In this book we have categorized the individual breeds according to the group of their stem breeds, original purpose and/or geographical development. The toy breeds are also classified according to their stem breed.

One of the largest of the flock guards, the Great Pyrenees is surely a people-dog. The flock guardians are as courageous and industrious as they are loyal and beguiling.

The Flock Guards
Keepers of Their Kingdoms

About 8,000 years ago in what is now the Middle East, primitive people evolved into the true modern *Homo sapiens*. This new "thinking" person domesticated herbivores and swine, undertook crude agriculture, molded pottery and conceived the idea of community living. The domesticated flocks represented their wealth, a continual and reproducible food supply.

However, the domesticated plant eater was at constant risk. Carnivores—wolves, bears, and lions—found them easy prey. And, of course, shepherds fought the threat of raids from neighboring villages.

Early herdsmen noted the natural protective qualities of some dogs. Selective breeding began, the largest specimens being chosen to confront a hungry bear or a 125-pound wolf.

Mass alone was not enough, for the job demanded agility as well as power. A flock guardian (not to be confused with a herding dog) needed courage and watchfulness, as well as wholehearted loyalty to his charges. He would stay with the flock all year, facing the same climatic extremes. Food was not always plentiful, yet vigilance had to be maintained. Even facing starvation, he could never turn to the flock for food. Thus the group became "easy keepers," able to survive and keep their large bodies strong with minimal food. They had to earn their keep, or they were eliminated. Flock guarding had stringent job requirements—size, dedication and toughness.

Historians tell us that Neolithic tribes migrated from the high plateaus of Turkey and Iran about 6,000 years ago. They spread in all directions, to Africa, Europe and the East. Accompanying them were dogs of an ancient type (called *ku-assa*, or the horse dog) used to guard their vast herd/flock wealths. Soon throughout the Neolithic world, primitive villages and shepherds used large dogs to help keep their food supplies safe.

Canine protection proved most beneficial in the mountainous regions. The largest and boldest predators roamed the mountains. The forest, rocks and crevices, as well as the distances between pastures and from the village, made keeping track of the entire flock difficult work for shepherds.

Crop cultivation spread through the fertile flat ground. Domestic flocks and herds were often relegated to the poorer pastures and high mountains.

From the great high plains of Turkey and the Caucasus Mountains of southern Russia, to the rugged Carpathians of eastern Europe, through the Balkans, the high Alps, the Pyrenees range of Spain, Portugal's Estrela Mountains, even the low Atlas chain of northern Africa—all have their flock-guarding type, bred true for four or five millenia.

Despite thousands of years and miles separation, all the breeds are amazingly similar in type. They are always large (the higher the mountains, often the larger the specimen), ranging from an economical 60 pounds to a robust 140 pounds.

These flock-guarding dogs were the stem type from which all the mastiff-type dogs developed. They were valued for their ferocity and watchfulness, independent thinking, hardiness, devotion to duty and loyalty to master. Flock guards possessed courage, speed, agility, craftiness, endurance, and stamina. They were free from wanderlust and the hunt or chase urge, attacking only when their property was threatened.

The dogs belonged to the village, sleeping here and there, and feeding on scraps. They guarded their entire territory.

They were then, as well as now, great, imposing beasts—tall, muscular and large-boned. Many have rear dewclaws, which are sometimes retained. The body is balanced, with a long tail carried low. The body might be a bit longer

The Italian contribution to the flock guards, the Maremma Sheepdog, is a fine example of the group. The Maremma spends his nights with the flock, protecting and guarding it, while the shepherd goes home to sleep.

than tall, with very little tuck-up. Although large, they are not ponderous and heavy skinned like the mastiffs. The flat head, with a tendency to a deep median groove, is generous and strong, yet more refined. The stop is pronounced, accompanied by a slightly tapering muzzle. The small drop ears are in distinct opposition to dog's enemy, the wolf.

In their native lands, the ears of working dogs were often cropped short. Sometimes tails were partially docked. The dogs were left outdoors year round, and grooming was not on the shepherds' agenda. Docking and cropping eliminated matting and problems of sanitation. Cropping

increased the visibility of the dog's reactions when his ears raised at the base during an alert. This practice is dying out, however, and many exhibited dogs must remain natural.

An ample coat protects them from the elements—the closer coats of the Turkish plains and northern African hills, to the heavy-corded rugs in the high cold peaks. Coats are moderate in length, with thick underwool and, occasionally, a slight wave to the hair. Although the dun or tan/gray color has been accepted by breeders in a few lower elevations, white is the preferred color for many reasons. White distinguishes them from the wolf and allows them acceptance into the flock, as well as making them visible from distances when apart from the sheep.

They are almost indistinguishable from sheep in the middle of the flock. Studies show most guarding "sheep dogs are sheep-sized, sheep-colored, sheep-shaped."

As civilization creeps into areas where the shepherd and his flock guardian have toiled secluded for centuries, the working specimens become fewer and fewer. Fortunately, the breeds are being preserved. Many countries and breed clubs have fostered an interest in saving these magnificent dogs. Through difficult times, wars and poverty, the aristocracy of Turkey protected their purebred dogs. The Veterinary School at Brno has fostered the rebirth of the Czechoslovakian version, and several have gained recognition by the American and English Kennel Clubs.

Although the breeds have long served their native lands, they have achieved the admiration of American shepherds and cattle owners only recently. The wolf is disappearing in Europe and Asia, but it still exists in America and plagues stock, along with its cousin the coyote,

Known in its native Poland as an outstanding mountain worker, the Owczarek Podhalanski is extremely attentive and alert.

causing serious financial and breeding program deprivation. The U.S. government spends many millions a year in an attempt to control this destruction, with annual losses still totaling over a million sheep. Several of the breeds have been imported to the United States for development as flock guardians.

Biologists at Hampshire College in Amherst, Massachusetts, have a study program using these dogs. In their first year they procured ten pups of three different breeds of European and Asian working stock. They bred and raised the first generations, noting behavior, and placed them all on farms and ranches.

Ray and Lorna Coppinger of the college note they brought: "two screaming, quarreling, Russian-type Ovcharka [sic] pups from eastern Turkey to Ankara by bus, while we cut at miles of red tape with dull scissors in Budapest, trying to get four Shar Planinetz [sic] pups we'd bought in southwestern Yugoslavia onto a direct flight to Boston. In Italy, we dickered in millions of lire for the great white Maremmano-Abruzzese sheepdog."

The Livestock Dog Project at Hampshire College has monitored Great Pyrenees, Maremmas, Russian Owtcharkas, Anatolian Shepherds, Sarplaninacs, Tibetan Mastiffs, and Castro Laboreiros. The U.S. Sheep Experiment Station in Dubois, Idaho, has also researched and trained guarding dogs against predators, using Great Pyrenees, Komondors and Akbash Dogs.

The training programs begin when pups are eight weeks old. A shelter is erected near the sheep, where the pup can see its future wards, but not harm them or be harmed.

Youngsters are not left in charge of sheep until they reach about one year of age, although there are exceptions. A future flock guard must be a natural guardian and exhibit proper behavior: nonaggression and attentiveness to sheep, as well as defense of the flock. They should never use their teeth on the sheep. These dogs are protectors rather than herders. When young, the pups tend to play with the sheep. Care must be taken to stop rowdy galloping, harmful to both sheep and dogs. The pup may be injured, and the sheep may lose wool, suffer torn ears or be chased to death.

However, if it's the sheep that reacts aggres-

Spanish shepherds carrying baby lambs with Spanish Mastiff following closely behind. The Spanish Mastiff shares a similar history to other flock-guarding canines from Portugal and Spain and can still be found on hills of Spain close by its well-protected flocks.

sively, the dog shows submissive behavior as it would toward its mother: lowering haunches, turning a back knee out, and licking the sheep's face.

Escape routes of the training pen are not blocked, and pups could easily leave the area. Therefore, they are judged by their desire to stay with the sheep. Most of these dogs instinctively perform well. For instance, one male is recorded to have saved a wet, newborn lamb that was isolated from its mother, curling up with it to keep it warm.

Charles Darwin, *The Zoology of The Voyage of H.M.S. Beagle*, told about these dogs: "It has no wish to leave the flock, and just as another dog will defend its master, man, so will these the sheep. It is amusing to observe, when approaching a flock, how the dog immediately advances barking, and the sheep all close in his rear [*sic*], as if round the oldest ram."

As Darwin wrote in 1833 about the dogs' stringent training in their country of origin: "The method of education consists in separating the puppy, while very young, from the bitch, and in accustoming it to its future companions. An ewe is held three or four times a day for the little thing to suck, and a nest of wool is made for it in the sheep-pen; at no time is it allowed to associate with other dogs, or with the children of the family."

Flock-guarding dogs have been raised to think of the stock as their family. The best ones show total dedication to their charges, not to their fellow dogs, nor even to their master or master's family unless trained for that chore. Flock guards often are raised among the sheep they will grow to protect. The dogs begin to interact, even to the point of suckling on ewes and performing sexual play as they normally would with their own kind.

As a group, the dogs are difficult to breed. First heats usually occur between one and two years. The bitch is sometimes not receptive in the first heat, and if bred, pseudopregnancy is common. They rarely have a litter until their second heat. The bitch may actually be antagonistic, so that the interested male becomes submissive. Libido in males is low, complicating matters.

27

Shepherds in various European countries allow their pups to get acquainted with the flock at a very early age. Some owners relay that their flock guards think they are sheep themselves. This Sarplaninac pup seems to get on fine with his woolly pals.

The flock-guarding breeds are much more interested in the sheep or their other charges than in propagating their own species. Once in whelp, however, they become good mothers. In fact, non-breeding females sometimes allow young of other species to nurse.

It is interesting to note a case where Border Collies were raised with flock guards. Though environment was identical, the herding dogs were quicker to respond to commands and the guardians slower; the Collies "eyed" and stalked, where the guards did not. The guarding dogs were non-retrieving and not as responsive to directions. The Collies eagerly did both. As they grew older, the guardians preferred the sheep to playing with their "littermates." Each was growing up exactly as nature intended.

The guarding characteristics of various breeds and individuals range from mild resistance to hostility against intruders. The most aggressive dogs are assigned to remote pastures with flocks suffering high losses. Even then, posting signs and showing the dog its boundaries are suggested. Some dogs insist on guarding adjacent areas; however, they may guard the neighbor's sheep as well!

As guarding maturity is reached, males—even some females—raise legs to urinate rather than squat, and scent marking becomes more deliberate, placed around boundaries. Barking becomes an alarm, rather than puppy yapping. They are active for longer periods and sleep less. The dogs display more interest in the sheep than their handler. Patroling escalates and dogs stay on the job around the clock, taking advantage of any shelter when necessary.

A high-pitched, crisis bark, charging at the trespasser and tail held high in warning are indicative of typical guard behavior. While observing the dogs and collecting choice pups in Yugoslavia, the Coppingers reported that one of their group tested a guard by approaching the flock. The huge dog casually rose, approached, and gave alert signs of lowered head. He meant business, and no further challenge was given.

Records show that the dogs are achieving favor with the New World stock breeders. Most canid predators will not approach when there are multiple guards or one of a larger size. Even though confrontations were not always observed, statistics show fewer casualties to the flocks. In more than one case, the dog had to be removed from the flock for a period of time (such as for a veterinary visit), and kills occurred while it was away.

These dogs have shown amazing success in trial situations, winning the enthusiastic praise of stockmen! They are an attractive alternative to expensive, harmful and unappealing methods, such as poisons, traps, fences, chemicals or special guns.

FLOCK GUARDS

Akbash Dog	Turkey
Caucasian Owtcharka	USSR
Middle Asian Owtcharka	USSR
Kangal Dog	Turkey
Anatolian Shepherd Dog	Turkey
Greek Sheepdog	Greece
Sarplaninac	Yugoslavia
Karst Shepherd	Yugoslavia
Rumanian Sheepdog	Rumania
South Russian Owtcharka	USSR
Komondor	Hungary
Kuvasz	Hungary
Slovak Cuvac	Czechoslovakia
Owczarek Podhalanski	Poland
Maremma Sheepdog	Italy
Great Pyrenees	France
Pyrenean Mastiff	Spain
Spanish Mastiff	Spain
Perro de Pastor Mallorquin	Spain
Estrela Mountain Dog	Portugal
Cão de Castro Laboreiro	Portugal
Rafeiro do Alentejo	Portugal
Chien de l'Atlas	Morocco

Above: Flock guards must be agile and attentive. The Estrela Mountain Dog of Portugal is a cousin to the Spanish Mastiff of Spain and a lively guardian. **Below:** Maremma Sheepdog pups getting acquainted with the family lambs.

The Mastiffs

Let Slip the Dogs of War

Somewhere in Tibet or northern India, about seventy centuries ago, a giant trod the earth. This was not just another "big dog," but a true giant, the mastiff prototype. One in every 10,000 births is a giant, in humans as well as dogs.

Flock-guarding dogs in the 100-pound-plus range were already well-established in human settlements. As humans became more civilized, they began to manipulate animal and plant breeding. The rare giant pups were selected by these early breeders and the type was soon fixed.

Acromegalic traits in dogs are as distinct as those in humans and often correlate similar features. The giants are massive due to substantially increased bone growth. The growth hormone further causes an increased size in the distal extremities, resulting in huge paws and bulky skull with heavy jaw and brows. Overgrowth and thickening of the skin produces the wrinkled, scowling expression, heavy flew and dewlaps, large drop ears, and a tendency to an abundance of skin on the body. (One might imprudently assume he is slow and clumsy.) Sadly, like his human giant counterparts, the acromegalic dog also is predisposed to heart trouble, back, hip, and gastro-intestinal problems, and a generally shortened life span.

The classic mastiff has a deep, abrupt stop and a muzzle that is strong but proportionately shorter than the capacious back skull. Generally the type is smooth-coated—allowing no grasping—and carries its tail low. The mastiff has a superior power of scent and a strong sense of territory, with no tendency to chase or herd—all gifts from flock-guarding ancestors.

The colors originated as sable (red), fawn, black/tan, or brindle without white markings. The rare dilution factors that produce the chocolate, blue, or pale gray hues were present even then. Originally, these frightening behemoths were used to guard flocks—later, home and property. As selective breeding continued with

the most fierce and aggressive, they were adapted to warfare and combat. From this prototype came all of the European mastiff types of today, most of the world's fighting breeds, and other modern dog giants. But this mastiff was also the progenitor of the true hounds, and later the gun dogs. Since the scenthounds and the mastiffs are so closely related genetically, ancient references to "hounds" were often actually describing the lighter bodied mastiff.

From his start in Tibet, the warlike leviathan traveled with tribes as they migrated into other parts of the world, from the Himalayas to the Pyrenees. This mastiff migration followed two major routes, one west through the Middle East and the Mediterranean, and the other northwest via China and Russia. The progress of the northern mastiff parallels the migration of a variety of fierce, nomadic people originally from the Turkistan areas of southern Russia. During the millenia before Christ these nomads migrated east into western China, conquering as they went.

Their mastiffs were lighter in body, perhaps because the wandering lifestyle required a nomadic dog. The most distinct trait of the northern dog was the first appearance of the brachycephalic (undershot) jaw. Whether this was a spontaneous trait (a mutation) or came from crosses with Chinese dogs is unknown. There is reference to a huge, fierce, short-faced "hound," called the Shejos, in China as early as 600 BC.

As the political winds changed, the nomads migrated back to the West. A group called the Alans arrived in eastern Europe five or six centuries BC to settle what is now Albania, and others arrived in waves around 400 AD. Thus the brachycephalic eastern mastiff was possibly the first of his type to arrive in Europe, and he certainly predated the Christian era. The Germanic tribes especially welcomed this canine's toughness and incorporated it into their dog

Used to guard flocks and property, the early relatives of today's mastiff breeds were adapted for fighting and combat. Breeders focused on the traits they considered to be paramount: strength, aggressiveness, and size. This vocal, able-bodied mastiff is an American Bulldog.

populations. Romans wrote of the "broad-mouthed" fighting dogs found on the British island when the Romans arrived in the early centuries AD.

By the Middle Ages the racier, undershot "mastiffs" were known throughout Europe as Alaunts or Alains. This name may have referred to the nomadic Alans, or perhaps came from the word *Allemanni* for people of Germanic origin.

The southern branch of the mastiff family followed the spread of civilization from Tibet, south and east through the Fertile Crescent. The Sumerian, Babylonian, Assyrian and Phoenician cultures all used mammoth war dogs, the fiercest being the "molossian," supposedly from the Greek island of Molossus.

Dogs were heavily utilized—as tools—in warfare. Both Greek and Assyrian armies sent dogs ahead of their men to draw fire and disclose the whereabouts of the enemy. The dogs sometimes wore collars fitted with huge curved blades or fiery torches. Leading the charge into enemy cavalry, the war dogs slashed, burned and spooked the horses. Another ploy was to have the warrior-master go ahead into battle while his war dog, clad in full armor, was forcefully restrained by a slave. As the warrior became engaged in hand-to-hand combat with an enemy, the enraged dog was released to go to the rescue of his master.

These fearsome canines defended their masters to the death and beyond, as shown by Aelian, a Greek cynologist of the early third century AD: "When Darius, the last of the Persian kings, was killed by Bessus in his battle with Alexander, and lay dead, all the men left the

Like human giants, mastiffs have oversized heads, huge feet, and a superabundance of wrinkles (flews). The Dogue de Bordeaux epitomizes these giant features.

The dogs spread to other lands, aided by the seafaring Phoenicians, who may have also introduced this type to England centuries before Christ. After his trip to the Far East, Marco Polo told of the Kubla Khan's vast kennel of 5,000 war mastiffs.

In Rome, the molossian dog found popularity—not only in the army—but also in the pit against bears, lions, and even men in the arena as entertainment. His skill and ferocity in mortal combat were legendary. Romans so depended on these dogs as guards that when some failed to bark as Gaul soldiers scaled the capitol, they were crucified.

"Let slip the dogs of war," a Latin phrase, was an appropriate cry for the Roman tradition. As the Roman legionnaires moved north in their conquest of Europe, the molossian went with them. Through this southern route, the heavier bodied mastiff with a conventional head was introduced to Europe. Many of the modern mastiff breeds trace their ancestry to a combination of the northern Alaunt as well as southern Molossus blood wedded in Europe.

By the Middle Ages, modern warfare had made the war mastiff obsolete. But new tasks were assumed by the great dogs. The molossian was adapted as an estate guardian. The terms bandog and *acathena* refer to the fact that the mastiff was tied during the day and allowed loose at night to roust poachers or intruders. Originally, these canine terrors were believed to be bred from bears and wolves. Little wonder that Cerberus, the canine guard to the gates of Hades, is proclaimed to be a mastiff.

Johannes Caius, writing *Of Englishe Dogges* in 1576, describes the Bandogge as "vaste, stubborne, ougly,...of a burthenous body,...terrible and frightful to behold." Besides describing their use as a guard, he tells of their formal training to fight bears, apes, and other beasts or even "men with pikestaffs and clubs."

Estate-owning nobility became so paranoid about poachers, they feared even their groundskeeper's dogs might be after their game. Thus, for hundreds of years it was illegal to own a large dog unless he had three toes on the front feet chopped off. If the lucky dog fit through the gauge, he was determined too small to harm game and kept his toes. King's men performed

corpse behind but the dog alone he had bred remained faithful. The dog belonging to King Lysimachus chose to die by the same fate as his master, although he could, had he so wished, have saved himself. Again, when there was civil war in Rome, a Roman citizen called Calvus was killed. Many of his enemies strove in rivalry to accomplish the glorious deed of cutting off his head, but none could do so until they had killed the dog who stood by his side."

A parade in Alexandria staged by Pharaoh Ptolemy II displayed a regiment of 2,400 war dogs. These warring beasts, described as "large dogs, the size of asses, and fierce as lions," were led by several soldiers, holding them back with chains. The dogs were arrayed in satin cloth and silver collars, which had iron points. When ancient kings sent military aid to their allies, it often included hundreds of dogs equipped with iron collars and armor plates.

In Japan, dog fighting has been an unrelenting passion—the Tosa Inu, Japan's contribution to the mastiff group, has fulfilled its nation's passion head-on.

the inspection and carried out their grim duty with chisel and mallet. The animals did not give up their toes easily, however. Some of the larger and fiercer dogs chewed up the inspectors!

In Spain and elsewhere, dogs were employed to help control bulls when they were brought into town to market. The Alaunt was touted as well adapted to this job of butcher's dog. If a bull got out of line, the dog grabbed him by the ear and held him helpless until the men could gain control. Hence, another bloodthirsty sport was born for medieval spectators—organized bull-baiting.

By the 15th century, a distinctive bull-baiting breed had been developed. Perhaps through crosses of Alaunt, mastiff, and other unknown brachycephalic dogs, the first bulldog (often called *bullenbeisser*, German for bullbaiter) was created. The genes for white markings were probably introduced with these crosses. The bulldog was low-stationed with an undershot jaw, allowing him to grab and hang on without his upper jaw being in the way. He pinned the bull by grasping the vulnerable nose instead of the ear. If the dog let go or failed to clasp the nose, he would be gored, and if the bull raised his head, the dog would be thrown. Spectators

held blankets between them to catch the dogs on the fly. To win—in fact, to survive—the dog had to quickly gain hold, maintain the grip and lower the bull's head to pin him. The popularity of the sport in England was expressed by Queen Elizabeth I's decree that no plays or other entertainment should be offered on Thursday evenings, so that everyone, including Her Majesty, could go to the bull-baiting.

The trait of holding on to the nose and gamely never letting go was highly prized. Mutilation of a dog's feet when he had a grip on the bull's nose, to prove tenacity despite pain, was said to greatly increase the value of his pups. Ash, writing in 1939, describes a famous bulldog of his time. The dog was "descended from Bratten's 'Peter' who pinned the bull on his raw stumps after his feet had been cut off one by one by his owner for a wager." One unproven legend tells of a determined bitch, mutilated bit by

Above: An American Pit Bull Terrier demonstrating the breed's strength and coordination. **Below:** Argentina's bulldog, the Dogo Argentino, is a manmade breed which has performed a variety of tasks: guard dog, guide dog, sled dog, and hunter.

These Bulldog pups reveal a number of traits specific to the mastiff group: excessive wrinkles, large heads (relative toward bodies) and a fearless, aggressive tendency with their own kind.

bit, limb by limb, until only her jaws remained firmly clenched on the bull.

Bull-baiting proponents claimed the bloody sport made the meat more tender. Whether for juicy roasts or juicy fights, the craze continued for 700 years until the advent of British humane laws in 1835 that finally stopped it.

Unfortunately for the dogs, as bull-baiting waned, other blood sports were introduced. The "humane" laws protected the bull, but the dog who had been humanity's companion since the canine evolution stayed in the pits. Dog-fighting reached its peak in 18th-and 19th-century England, with matches advertized in the papers and huge wagers being made. Again special breeds were developed for the purpose, the mastiff and/or bulldog being crossed with smooth, game, terrier types (called Bull and Terrier) to increase quickness and agility. Since many of these terriers were all white, the blending of the breeds generated more white markings or even all-white coloring in the mastiffs.

Not every mastiff was developed for an evil purpose. Selecting for more benign personalities, many European countries developed draft dogs, rescue workers, and genial companions from these original mastiffs. During the European Renaissance, the Great Butcher Dog was common. This more placid mastiff helped drive cattle to market, guarding the livestock as well as the owners, and often carrying the sales money home around his neck! Few highwaymen challenged such a beast. Also employed as the serf's "horse" in carting and hauling, the dog with a more mellow temperament was desired. This dog had less loose skin, but the same square, bulky, muscular body, and his tail was sometimes docked.

By choosing and crossing with dwarf varieties, breeders even created "miniature" giants. The mastiff group has much greater variation than the flock guards for two reasons. The mastiff was not isolated in rural areas and was allowed opportunity to meet and mate with a variety of dogs, drawing from other gene pools. In addition, the double origin initially provided a greater variety of genes. Despite the wide variation, each individual breed goes back in whole or in part to the common gigantic ancestor from Tibet.

Above: The American Staffordshire Terrier *(left)* and the Staffordshire Bull Terrier *(right)* share similar origins. Notice that the Staffordshire Bull Terrier has uncropped ears and is somewhat smaller than its American counterpart. **Below:** The Rottweiler can be counted among the mastiff breeds which were traditionally used to work cattle; today it more commonly performs as a guard and police dog.

Above: The Entelbucher, one of Switzerland's four mountain dogs, is a territorial herder, protective but not aggressive. **Below:** The Great Dane is one of the tallest of the mastiff group, as this Harlequin attempts to display.

MASTIFF

Mastiff

Tibetan Mastiff	Tibet
Aryan Molossus	Afghanistan
Mastiff	Great Britain
Great Dane	Germany
Saint Bernard	Switzerland
Moscow Watchdog	USSR
Newfoundland	Canada
Landseer	Scandinavia
Tosa Inu	Japan
Fila Brasileiro	Brazil
Leonberger	Germany
Doberman Pinscher	Germany
Danish Broholmer	Denmark

Draft/Cattle

Rottweiler	Germany
Appenzeller	Switzerland
Greater Swiss Mountain Dog	Switzerland
Bernese Mountain Dog	Switzerland
Entelbucher	Switzerland
Belgian Mastiff	Belgium

Bulldog

Neapolitan Mastiff	Italy
Bulldog	Great Britain
Bullmastiff	Great Britain
Dogue de Bordeaux	France
Boxer	Germany
Dogo Argentino	Argentina
Staffordshire Bull Terrier	Great Britain
American Staffordshire Terrier	USA
American Pit Bull Terrier	USA
Bull Terrier	Great Britain
Miniature Bull Terrier	Great Britain
Perro de Presa Mallorquin	Spain
Perro de Presa Canario	Spain
American Bulldog	USA
French Bulldog	France
Pug	China
Boston Terrier	USA

The Scenthounds
In Full Cry

Long before the Christian era, dog breeders created, from existing mastiff stock, the first hounds to hunt by scent. They selected for the mastiff's sensitive nose and tenacity. Breeders retained the dogs' hanging ears and loose, heavy skin while exchanging some of the bulk for speed and endurance. Over the years, the ferocious temperament of the original dogs was mellowed into a sweeter, more benign attitude that allowed for control during the hunt. Unfortunately, many of the larger hounds still retain their mastiff ancestor's tendency for hip and intestinal disorders.

The scenthounds stem mainly from their European ancestors, originating from Celtic breeding. The Celts were a tribal people that lived during the centuries before the rise of Rome.

Mastiffs of the Alaunt type were owned and bred by Celtic clans and used in their warfare. Before 500 BC the Celts were principally in southern Germany, but they soon spread throughout western Europe and all the British Isles, their mastiffs and hounds by their sides. As the Romans, and later barbarian invaders, overtook Europe, the Celts were destroyed or absorbed by other cultures. Eventually only the tribes in Ireland, Britain and Brittany remained. Today, their majestic hounds and the distinctive Celtic languages of Irish, Highland Scottish, Welsh and Breton are their legacy to modern society.

It is these great huntsmen who probably first used the mastiff for hunting by scent. The old-style scenthounds, of the mastiff type, were seeded throughout the Celtic travels. Some remained in pure form while other types, especially those in areas accessible to the Phoenician hound trade, were crossed with sighthounds. Before the discovery of gunpowder, the hound searched out and chased game until the hunter could kill it with spear or arrow, or until the dogs themselves could close in for the kill.

Scenthounds themselves existed many centu-ries before the first concerted breeding programs to establish types had begun during the Middle Ages. The St. Hubert Hound was the first breed brought to prominence during the sixth century. St. Hubert, a pagan huntsman, was converted to Christianity while out on a Sunday hunt, when he saw a vision of a stag with a gleaming cross rising between its antlers. He later became the Bishop of Liege and achieved sainthood, and the monastery in the Ardennes region of Belgium was named for him. These monks developed and bred a strain of scenthound called the St. Hubert Hound, using Celtic dogs originally from Gaul (France).

Always black and tan, the monks' dogs were medium sized, heavily built with body a bit longer than high, having heavy heads with deep flews. Although slow and methodical, they were noted for their melodious "voice" and incomparable scenting ability. The breed is the direct ancestor to today's Bloodhound, which is still referred to as a St. Hubert in his native Belgium. These hounds became well known throughout Europe and were the basis of many other hound breeds.

By the eighth century, several variations of the St. Hubert had appeared. A variety that was nearly all white (tricolored with a majority of body white) became known as the Southern Hound. Although now extinct, the breed was commonplace through the 16th century and used in England for hunting hare while on foot. The Southern Hound was heavy, slow, and possessed long ears and heavy flews as did the St. Hubert progenitor. Also known for his deep bass bay and exquisite sense of smell, the Southern Hound was the basis for many of the European hound breeds as well.

Emerging in the eighth century was the Talbot Hound, a pied or liver variation of the St. Hubert. Early Dalmatians were often referred to as Talbots, so the term may be a reference to the color variety rather than type.

The 13th century marks the initial rage in Great Britain of fox hunting. Dogs smaller and faster than the St. Hubert Hound with good voice were desired to trail the cunning and elusive fox.

Because many types of hounds were developed to hunt in packs and were kenneled in large groups, they were selected for their non-quarrelsome behavior. It was necessary for the dogs to be amiable with pack members, orderly and mannerly for the hunter to manage in the fields as well as in the kennel. These dogs were, however, independent of spirit, since the pack was often sent to hunt alone for hours without direction from their master. A brand was often shaved into the side of the hound's coat, to enable the Hunt Master to make identification quickly at the end of the day.

The dog continued to be malleable according to the wishes and needs of its master. Each country has developed its own breed(s) of scenthound, usually following a general type, but in great variation, depending on the game sought and the method of following the hounds. Some have become lighter of body for faster and for

39

mounted hunting; various crosses with gaze-hounds have produced even greater speed. Yet others have maintained the heavier body for methodical tracking. Some types were bred for shorter legs to slow the dog's work. While many are smooth-coated, most countries have a few rough or wire-coated scenthounds. The scenthound family has become the most numerous in dogdom for recognized breeds; these are best discussed by country of origin.

France is *the* country of the scenthound; it spawned the genre and boasts the most breeds.

In America, dogs were needed to hunt raccoon. The coonhounds basically developed from the foxhounds in the late 18th century. The first of these coonhounds was the American Black and Tan, illustrated here treeing with a Redbone Coonhound—in full cry!

In fact, in France this family usually does not use the word "hound" in breed names—assuming that, if it's French, it's a scenthound. For many centuries after the Middle Ages, France was not a unified country but a collection of feudal estates, each run by a powerful nobleman. These aristocrats had nearly as much power as the king. Hunting was a passion with the nobility as well as royalty and many kept extensive kennels, developing their own strains of hound.

Although horseracing may be dubbed the "sport of kings," the companionship of dogs and their considered importance fell not far behind. During the reign of Charles I of Lorraine in the 15th century, 70 forests and nearly 800 royal parks were confiscated for the sole purpose of raising and training the king's dogs. Louis IX, of the 1450s, planned all of his wars for summer and fall, leaving his winter free for boar and stag hunting and the spring for hunting with falcons, accompanied, of course, by his hounds.

Originally, most of the early types of hounds were bred to hunt wolves as well as wild boar. These dogs hunted in large packs, sometimes as many as a thousand or more, and had to have great tenacity, courage, and stamina as well as the prerequisite fine nose. The quality of the voice on the trail was of prime importance as well, and strains were selected for the tonal quality and the carrying ability of their bay. While the peasants—without even two pieces of crockery that matched—often went hungry, the royal packs were not only well fed, but were selected for their matching pitch, among other abilities. These early types used on large game are often referred to collectively as the *Grand Chiens Courant*, the Great Hounds of the Chase. Other strains were used to hunt stag, roe deer and fox, for which they needed more speed. Smaller or short-legged varieties were produced to do slower work in heavy cover or for following on foot, especially for rabbit and hare.

The cost of raising and caring for the huge kennels was staggering, and they could not be maintained after the fall of the nobility. While dozens and dozens of breeds were lost after the French Revolution several remained in smaller numbers or have been brought back from the brink of extinction and still exist today.

Above: These three Black Mouth Curs pictured with their day's catch—two wild boars.

Below: Short, crooked legs allow the Basset Hound to keep his nose low to the ground. The breed is certainly of British fame but is closely related to the French bassets.

The general characteristic of all French hounds is one of great grace and beauty. Although Gaul was the source of the pure scenthounds that were the progenitor of the St. Hubert, the French coast was also one of the stops of the Phoenicians. The hounds of France have a definite hint of sighthound in their background. They have a long, lean and chiseled head, not as heavy as the St. Hubert Hound, yet not as slim and pointed as the pure sighthound. Their ears are set very low and are often unusually long and folded; yet the head and neck lack the heavy flews and wrinkles of the St. Hubert type. They are up on leg, being racier and lighter in bone. Although in no way weedy or lacking in strength, they weigh considerably less for their height than English or German hounds. Many of the French hounds have both wire-coated (called *griffon*) and/or short-legged (called *basset*) varieties. Their names are often descriptive and, hence, easily translatable, usually referring to the province where the breed originated, as well as the size, coat and color.

41

Beagles, like many of the scenthounds, are versatile and enthusiastic hunters. Although usually associated with hunting rabbit or squirrel, this Beagle has cornered this coon well.

HOUNDS

Griffon Nivernais	France
Griffon Vendeen, Grand	France
Griffon Vendeen, Briquet	France
Basset Griffon Vendeen, Grand	France
Basset Griffon Vendeen, Petit	France
Grand Bleu de Gascogne	France
Griffon Bleu de Gascogne, Petit	France
Basset Bleu de Gascogne	France
Poitevin	France
Gascon Saintongeois, Grand	France
Gascon Saintongeois, Petit	France
Griffon Fauve de Bretagne	France
Basset Fauve de Bretagne	France
Chien d'Artois	France
Basset Artésien Normand	France
Billy	France
Levesque	France
Ariégeois	France
Porcelaine	France
Beagle Harrier	France
Chien Francais Blanc et Noir	France
Chien Francais Blanc et Orange	France
Chien Francais Tricolore	France
Anglo-Francais, Grand	France
Anglo-Francais, Moyen	France
Anglo-Francais, Petit	France
Sabueso Español de Monte	Spain
Sabueso Español Lebrero	Spain
Segugio Italiano a Pelo Raso	Italy
Segugio Italiano a Pelo Forte	Italy
Istrian Hound, Wirehaired	Yugoslavia
Istrian Hound, Smoothhaired	Yugoslavia
Posavac Hound	Yugoslavia
Bosnian Roughhaired Hound	Yugoslavia
Balkan Hound	Yugoslavia
Yugoslavian Mountain Hound	Yugoslavia
Yugoslavian Tricolored Hound	Yugoslavia
Greek Harehound	Greece
Transylvanian Hound, Tall	Hungary
Transylvanian Hound, Short	Hungary
Black Forest Hound	Czechoslovakia
Polish Hound	Poland
Deutsche Bracke	Germany
Dachsbracke, Westphalian	Germany
Hanoverian Hound	Germany
Bavarian Mountain Hound	Germany
Dachshund, Standard	Germany
Dachshund, Miniature	Germany

Switzerland, where the scenthound is known as the laufhund, contributes nine individual breeds to this group. Essentially, all these hounds are similar, barring variations of size and color.

Breed	Country
Bloodhound	Belgium
Austrian Brandlebracke	Austria
Styrian Roughhaired Mountain Hound	Austria
Tyroler Bracke	Austria
Dachsbracke, Alpine	Austria
Schweizer Laufhund	Switzerland
Schweizer Niederlaufhund	Switzerland
Bruno Jura Laufhund	Switzerland
St. Hubert Jura Laufhund	Switzerland
Jura Niederlaufhund	Switzerland
Berner Laufhund	Switzerland
Berner Niederlaufhund	Switzerland
Luzerner Laufhund	Switzerland
Luzerner Niederlaufhund	Switzerland
Strellufstöver	Denmark
Finnish Hound	Finland
Drever	Sweden
Schillerstövare	Sweden
Hamiltonstövare	Sweden
Smalandsstövare	Sweden
Haldenstövare	Norway
Hygenhund	Norway
Dunker	Norway
English Foxhound	Great Britain
Beagle	Great Britain
Harrier	Great Britain
Basset Hound	Great Britain
Otter Hound	Great Britain
Kerry Beagle	Ireland
American Foxhound	USA
American Black and Tan Coonhound	USA
Redbone Coonhound	USA
English Coonhound	USA
Bluetick Coonhound	USA
Treeing Walker Coonhound	USA
American Blue Gascon Hound	USA
Majestic Tree Hound	USA
Plott Hound	USA
Leopard Cur	USA
Mountain Cur	USA
Treeing Tennessee Brindle	USA
Stephens Stock	USA
Black Mouth Cur	USA
Russian Hound	USSR
Russian Harlequin Hound	USSR
Estonian Hound	USSR
Latvian Hound	USSR
Lithuanian Hound	USSR

Gun Dogs
Ready, Willing and Able

Hunting dogs are the equivalent of the melting pot in the canine world. Grouped for their skills, they have diverse backgrounds and varied physical appearances. Even the term "gun dog" is a modern appellation. Long before the invention of firearms, these dogs accompanied hunters who used nets, falcons and bows. At that time they were exclusively "bird dogs," any larger prey being the quarry of hounds.

Many years later with the discovery of gunpowder, firearm use widened the scope of these dogs to finding or retrieving furred and hooved game. Today, they are subdivided into four broad, sometimes overlapping groups: the pointers, the land retrievers, the shaggy water dogs and the setters/spaniels.

The pointers are the most closely related to the scenthounds and are descended directly from them. They are, for the most part, smooth-coated, of basic hound body and head type, and predominantly white with spotting or ticking. They, like their ancestors, also can possess a wire coat.

Even their names become enmeshed. The German word *bracke* and the French *briquet* refer to scenthounds, while *braque* in France and *bracco* in Italian identifies their gun dogs. *Griffon* can mean either a hound or a gun dog (or even a ten-pound toy!) as long as his coat is coarse and shaggy.

While the pointers have inherited the fine nose and strong desire to hunt from the hounds, they differ in their intense desire to please, which was selected in breeding programs. Pointers instinctively look to their masters for direction. The added traits of retrieving and hesitation upon scent of game fine-tuned these breeds for gun work.

Although most Americans think of the English Pointer when this group is named, this one is perhaps the "odd man out" in the dozens of European pointing types. The English developed specialist dogs; the pointer found and

pointed the game, the retriever was brought up to retrieve the shot bird, and the water retrievers were reserved for water work.

Contrarily, the Continental ideal was a dog who could assist in all phases of the hunt. Europeans wanted their "pointers" to work the cover to find game, of course, but also relied upon them to perform well after the shot. They were expected to retrieve shot birds, trail wounded running birds, track wounded ducks on water, retrieve from the water, retrieve furred game if necessary, and even be willing to bloodtrail wounded game. Some of these all-purpose dogs started out very heavy-boned, methodical and houndlike, while the English version of the pointer was racy-bodied and fast.

The pointers in a particular geographical area tended to follow the type of the hounds, due to the available gene pool. In places where a heavier hound was favored, the resulting gun dog was heavy and slow. Where faster, lighter hounds were the root stock, the pointer was of the same type. Later in their development, some of these heavier types were refined with crosses to the elegant English prototype.

Many of the pointer and spaniel breeds have the tail docked at birth, not as short as that of the Doberman and Boxer, but about half the tail's length. The dogs wag their tails vigorously when on the scent, often incurring tail-end injuries which are notoriously hard to heal properly. Poodles, which were originally bred as water retrievers, are also docked. However, the fashion for most setters and retrievers is to leave the tail intact.

Dewclaws, even in the front, are generally clipped off. Removal was for the practical prevention of injury. When the dog hunted in heavy cover, his dewclaws snagged and ripped. These injuries developed into infections and eventual death before the days of antibiotics and veterinary surgeons. Therefore, removal was the customary "ounce of prevention."

The Gordon Setter has been known in its native Scotland since the early 17th century. Setting dogs are traced back to Celtic origin and were found wherever the Celts traveled.

A mystery concerning this group is the preponderance of the liver (brown with brown nose) color. We know this was a common gene carried by the mastiff group, and the liver gene color has been present since the eighth century in the hounds called Talbots.

Nevertheless, it was a color that never gained prominence in any of our current hound breeds, appearing in only a few. Yet the majority of the pointer types, as well as many of the spaniels and water dogs from Europe, have the brown nose and the liver color, at least in spots. If brown were a dominant gene, a "single dog origin" might be assumed, with its influence spreading throughout Europe. However, since the gene for brown is recessive to black, any cross of brown to black eliminates the brown. Thus we know that the color had to be purposely selected, with brown bred to brown by choice in diverse and remote areas. A plausible explanation might be that the gene for brown was closely associated with the genes for crack

gun dog performance, as opposed to the hound's, and early pragmatic breeders found that breeding brown dogs produced superior gun dogs. Another reason for the brown may be that the camouflage effect of that color was desirable for hunting dogs working in the autumn.

The land retrievers, most of British origin, are mastifflike in type. Well-known breeds such as the Labrador and Golden Retrievers are heavy bodied and a bit low on leg. They have the heavier, wide bracoid head (long with square muzzle and median groove), along with a higher incidence of hip dysplasia, as do their mastiff progenitors.

The water dogs' history is more clouded, but they probably are related most closely to the shaggy herding dogs that came originally from the Orient. These sheep dogs were most likely crossed with hunting dogs to create the new group. They show up very early, being commonplace by the Christian era, around the Mediterranean and into Europe. Sporting a shaggy single coat, the hair covered the body and was curly or corded.

The cutting of water dogs' curly coats in a pattern was described by the 1500s. A mass of curly dog wool is not only odorous when wet, but very heavy. Thus a large portion of the coat was sheared off, with only that over the ribs and joints left long. (The thinking of the day was that cover over those areas would prevent the pneumonia and arthritis, often suffered from working long hours in cold water.) This coat pattern gave birth to the coiffure of our modern show Poodle, as well as that of the Portuguese Water Dog.

Water retrievers/dogs were specialized for a host of chores. Used most frequently for water-fowl shooting, they were also adept at flushing and retrieving on shore. Some were used on boats as aids to the fishing communities. The water dogs, or their shaggy progenitors, may have been the source of the rough coat in the wirehaired griffon-type hounds of Europe. As early as the first century AD, efforts were made to miniaturize these water dogs. The diminutive

form yielded the charming family of shaggy bi-chons, which are popular companions today.

By medieval times in Europe, setting dogs—an old gun dog type with a fringed coat—began to appear, accompanying falconers. A tapestry made in 1400 depicts a falconer's beautifully constructed white dog with long fringed tail, feathering on legs and belly; only the small flat drop ear is free of long coat.

The Greek historian Xenophon, writing in the sixth century BC, tells of hounds that paused upon the scent of game instead of giving chase. Although this was considered an abomination in the hound, this obviates that the genes for "set-ting" have been around since early times.

The exact origin of the setting dog (also called Èpagneul or Spaniel) is a mystery, probably a great mixture that will never be sorted. The coat, fringed on the ears, legs and tail, is reminiscent of the flock guarders, rather than the shaggy sheep and water dogs. Their passion for the hunt and their superb noses speak of the hound, or the pointing dogs that came from these hounds. Perhaps they were combinations

Few dog lovers would deny that the gun dog group contains many of the world's most intelligent canines. Perched on the shore, these Nova Scotia Duck Tolling Retrievers prepare to outfox an approaching flock of ducks.

Pointers have inherited much of their fine nose and hunting desire from the hounds; they were developed to perform a specific function: to point. Demonstrating its pointing ability is Portugal's only pointer, the Perdigueiro Portugueso.

of the two types, both of which owe their genes originally to the mastiff.

Setting dogs were seeded wherever the Celts migrated: France, southern Germany, the Netherlands, as well as Ireland and Scotland. Since the history of the Celts and hounds are tied together inextricably, the setting dog may have a parallel Celtic background. The much repeated deduction that the spaniel originated in Spain because of his name is probably erroneous. They were known throughout central and northern Europe, particularly France, as well as the British Isles, and seemed to follow the general route of the Celts. Although traded between the capitals of Europe by kings and noblemen courting favors, there is no indication that Spain was the fount of this type. The French verb *espanir* means to crouch or flatten oneself, and seems a more plausible source of the name since it so accurately describes the spaniel's early hunting style.

These early dogs—called "couchers," "setters" and, later, "spaniels"—would slow, crouch and creep in upon scent of the birds. This characterization allowed the hunters with their falcons to approach closer before putting the game birds to flight. The falcons were then released to capture the birds. Another hunting ploy was to have the dogs indicate a covey by creeping in and lying motionless, as the hunters drew their nets over canine and fowl, catching many birds at a time. These setting dogs developed into all of our modern setters and spaniels. What is called a spaniel in Europe is, in reality, a setter that points its game. Later, the English created the flushing spaniels from these couching setters.

Shorter hair appears on the face, body and leg fronts, with fringing of the ears, tail, belly and back of legs. Miniature varieties of the spaniels have been around ever since their beginning as pampered pets and "sleeve" dogs.

47

Above: In both Great Britain and America, the Labrador Retriever has acquired a fine reputation as a duck dog and hunter. **Below:** The Weimaraner is an ancient gun dog of Germanic origin—in the early 17th century, the breed was used to hunt large game: boars, bears and wolves.

Above: Setters have been well known throughout Europe for many years; most of today's setter breeds have developed from similar stock. Illustrated here are the Irish Setter, Gordon Setter, and English Setter. **Below:** Since the 19th century, the English Cocker Spaniel has been popular in Great Britain. Both the English Cocker Spaniel and its cousin, the American Cocker Spaniel, are categorized as flushing spaniels because they spring or "cock" the game for the net.

The Grosser (Large) Münsterländer is a black and white setter of Germany which is popular in both its native land and Great Britain. In appearance and type, it is most similar to the German Longhaired Pointer.

GUN DOGS

Water Dogs

Barbet	France
Poodle, Standard	France
Poodle, Miniature	France
Poodle, Toy	France
Irish Water Spaniel	Ireland
Curly-Coated Retriever	Great Britain
Wetterhoun	Netherlands
American Water Spaniel	USA
Portuguese Water Dog	Portugal
Maltese	Malta
Bichon Frise	France/Belgium
Löwchen	France
Bolognese	Italy
Havanese	Cuba
Coton de Tulear	Madagascar

Pointers

Belgian Shorthaired Pointer	Belgium
Wirehaired Pointing Griffon	France
Braque d'Auvergne	France
Braque d'Ariége	France
Braque du Bourbonnais	France
Braque Dupuy	France
Braque Francais de Grande Taille	France
Braque Francais de Petite Taille	France
Braque Saint-Germain	France
Pointer	Great Britain
Old Danish Bird Dog	Denmark
Hertha Pointer	Denmark
Česky Fousek	Czechoslovakia
Dalmatian	Yugoslavia
Vizsla	Hungary
Bracco Italiano	Italy
Spinone Italiano	Italy
Perdiguero de Burgos	Spain
Perdiguero Navarro	Spain
Perdigueiro Portugueso	Portugal
German Shorthaired Pointer	Germany
German Wirehaired Pointer	Germany
Stichelhaar	Germany
Weimaraner	Germany
Pudelpointer	Germany

The Wetterhoun of the Netherlands was originally an otter dog; today it is used effectively as a gun dog in land and water.

Retrievers

Flat-Coated Retriever	Great Britain
Labrador Retriever	Great Britain
Golden Retriever	Great Britain
Nova Scotia Duck Tolling Retriever	Canada
Kooikerhondje	Netherlands
Chesapeake Bay Retriever	USA

The creation of American duck hunters and recognized by the five major registries, the Chesapeake Bay Retriever hits the water with passion.

Setters

German Longhaired Pointer	Germany
Large Münsterländer	Germany
Small Münsterländer	Germany
English Setter	Great Britain
Gordon Setter	Great Britain
Irish Setter	Ireland
Irish Red and White Setter	Ireland
Stabyhoun	Netherlands
Drentse Patrijshond	Netherlands
Brittany	France
Épagneul Francais	France
Épagneul Picard	France
Épagneul Bleu de Picardie	France
Épagneul Pont-Audemer	France
Deutscher Wachtelhund	Germany

Flushing Spaniels

Sussex Spaniel	Great Britain
Field Spaniel	Great Britain
English Cocker Spaniel	Great Britain
American Cocker Spaniel	USA
English Springer Spaniel	Great Britain
Welsh Springer Spaniel	Great Britain
Clumber Spaniel	Great Britain
Russian Spaniel	USSR
Boykin Spaniel	USA
English Toy Spaniel	Great Britain
Cavalier King Charles Spaniel	Great Britain
Continental Toy Spaniel, Papillon	France/Belgium
Continental Toy Spaniel, Phalene	France/Belgium

The Northern Breeds
The Horsepower of the North

The northern breeds' story begins with the pre-historic wolf, before the first Ice Age, when the Northern Hemisphere was an unending, cold grassland. The vegetation was so abundant and the boundaries so limitless that it supported millions of grazing animals. Vast herds of deer, goats, sheep, cattle and horses thrived on the range. The giant herbivores, the woolly mammoth, the giant sloths, llamas, bison, musk oxen, and rhinoceroses prospered. Their major enemy, the Gray Northern Wolf, grew large with the never-ending food supply.

Wolves were—and still remain—social (cooperative) hunters, working as allies to bring down prey larger than themselves. They creep toward the herd, intently and silently seeking a vulnerable animal—the sick beast, with its head held lower, or the slower aged, young or weak. After a target animal had been selected, the wolves moved in to frighten and stir the entire group. Natural herders with great stamina, they could bide their time, trotting all day if necessary, to keep up with the panicky quarry. Then they actually began to "herd," manipulating and cutting out the target animal. Once it was isolated and beyond the group's protection, they closed in for the kill. This cooperative hunt was unique to wolves.

This spirit extended to their family life. Pairs mated for life; cubs were raised, fed and protected by the entire pack and played with all members.

The cold clime produced a heavy, thick coat of straight medium-length hair that shed ice and provided warmth. The unlimited food supply enabled the wolf to grow large and heavy boned, up to 130 pounds.

Around the time of the Mesolithic era, another—albeit primitive—social hunter appeared on the scene. Early humans had also learned to cooperate in hunting the larger herbivores. While the wolves concentrated on smaller, deer-sized animals, humans pursued the huge, stupid behemoths, often chasing whole herds into pits or stampeding them over cliffs. After our primitive ancestors made use of one or two beasts, scavenger wolves relished the carnage.

Over many thousands of years, the wasteful hunting methods of humans contributed to the extinction of the large herbivores. For the first time, humans and wolves were hunting the same food source. However, since game was plentiful at that time, competition was scarce.

Hunting side by side gave each species the opportunity to observe and become accustomed to the other. *Homo sapiens* admired the canine ability to divide and efficiently cut the herd. Wolves recognized the cave dweller's ability to kill—and that waste was left for scavengers.

Soon wolves lurked nearby during the hunts, waiting for the "leftovers." Over time, these camp followers developed a shorter jaw with smaller teeth than their hunting cousins. (This has been recreated in modern wolves who are bred in captivity and raised on commercial food.) They were then forced to scavenge, since they were no longer efficient at killing their own game. Their herding skills led them to join in the stampede.

After generations of living in proximity, a mutual trust developed and true domestication occurred. Wolf pups were brought into camps and hand raised. These cubs reached maturity and aided in the hunt and in controlling domesticated flocks and herds. Although herding was the first canine skill used by early humans, many other useful qualities were utilized. These early wolf-dogs served as draft animals to pull the sledges. They searched for and located the herds as well as assisting in the kill. In addition, their presence at the campfire was a deterrent to predators. Even at the dawn of history, a furry and live presence in the tent provided companionship and helped keep toes warm.

Today, the northern dog has retained many of the characteristics of his wolf cousins. He has

The ice-ridden landscapes and the brutally harsh weather may have caused man and dog to combine forces for survival. The Greenland Dogs are close cousins of the Nordic hauling huskies and were used on the island as sleigh dogs and hunters. This pack works in "fan hitch."

their small pricked ears and wedge-shaped head framed with a ruff. The body is powerful, lean and square, with strong muscling and trim loin that allows for efficient trotting over vast distances. He is jacketed with a short, plush stand-off coat that protects him from the worst of weather, but needs no special care. Occasionally, the banded hair coloring is present.

Nordic (northern) dogs possess an independent yet social personality. Most of the draft dogs are friendly and affectionate and do not make good guard dogs. Overall, some of them are aggressive with other dogs and livestock.

The Nordic tail, which curves up over the dogs' backs, is the main feature that separates them from the wolf ancestors. Mature wolves always carry their tails low; cubs have high tails. Barking is also a puppy tendency demonstrated by many northern adults. These neotanous (in-

fantile) traits likely were selected during primitive breeding and adoption processes—since the more infantile the wolf, the more manageable he remained.

As sheep, cattle and reindeer were domesticated, the dogs originally used for herding/killing were honed into a herding-only dog. The modern Nordic dogs used for herding are probably the closest to the original domesticated dog. Although used extensively throughout the centuries, modern travel and farming methods have reduced these dogs to a few isolated types.

As the demand for herding diminished, these dogs gained ground with their skills in hunting and draft work, and their warmth as companions. Termed Nordic, Northern or spitz, the type remains distinct in many areas all over the world today.

Above: The Norwegian Buhund is an ancient Nordic herding type dog which originated in the Scandinavian countries but did not gain   much recognition until the 20th century. **Below Left:** The Swedes and the Finnish together partake in the origin of this little spitz, the Norbottenspets. **Below Right:** Lorna Demidoff and her Siberian Husky team, pictured on the grounds of the Monadnock Kennels in New Hampshire.

Above: Even in its homeland, the Greenland Dog is not populous. In addition to employment as a sled dog, the breed was used to find seals' breathing holes in the ice. **Below:** The Japanese Spitz, a miniature lap spitz, weighs in at 13 pounds. In appearance, the breed bears a striking resemblance to the Miniature American Eskimo.

Above: Perhaps the most striking characteristic of the northern breeds is the full, plush coat. The Chow Chow, a breed which traces its origin to 1000 BC, can have one of the most impressive and beautiful of coats. **Below:** A 20th-century American creation, the Chinook was developed to be a sled dog par excellence.

NORTHERN DOGS

Hunting

Finnish Spitz	Finland
Karelo-Finnish Laika	USSR
Norwegian Elkhound	Norway
Norwegian Elkhound, Black	Norway
Jamthund	Sweden
Karelian Bear Dog	Finland
Russo-European Laika	USSR
Lundehund	Norway
Norbottenspets	Sweden/Finland
West Siberian Laika	USSR
East Siberian Laika	USSR
Akita	Japan
Ainu Dog	Japan
Kishu	Japan
Kai Dog	Japan
Shikoku	Japan

Draft

Alaskan Malamute	USA
Siberian Husky	USSR
Greenland Dog	Scandinavia
Eskimo Dog	Canada
Chinook	USA
Northeasterly Hauling Laika	USSR

Herding

Samoyed	Scandinavia
Nenets Herding Laika	USSR
Norwegian Buhund	Norway
Iceland Dog	Iceland
Swedish Lapphund	Sweden
Finnish Lapphund	Finland

American Eskimos over a snowy terrain.

The Lundehund, also known as the Norwegian Puffin Dog, is perhaps one of the most fascinating of the world's canines.

Companion

German Wolfspitz	Germany
German Spitz, Giant	Germany
German Spitz, Standard	Germany
German Spitz, Small	Germany
German Spitz, Toy	Germany
Keeshond	Netherlands
Pomeranian	Great Britain
Schipperke	Belgium
Eurasian	Germany
Volpino Italiano	Italy
American Eskimo, Standard	USA
American Eskimo, Miniature	USA
American Eskimo, Toy	USA
Shiba Inu	Japan
Sanshu	Japan
Japanese Spitz	Japan
Chow Chow	China
Shar-Pei	China

HERDING D

enforcement, and personal protection dogs. They can be strong-natured and willful, but with proper training they also make fine obedience and working dogs, demonstrating their intelligence and willingness both to work and to please.

In the canine family, herding dogs remain among those with the closest affinity to humans. These breeds, unlike flock guards, work under the direction of their masters and are more dependent. This trait carries through in the personality of their modern non-working counterparts. They are biddable and obedient, today making some of the best obedience ring workers. These dogs need their people, just as the shepherds and the cattle breeders need *them*.

Bonding and socializing is important with these breeds. Work and play with them, and they will die for you. Ignore them and they will withdraw.

For many years herding dogs were the helpmates of the peasant or working classes, and no records or formal pedigrees were kept. They were in demand by all agricultural communities. Crossbreeding occurred regularly, since all "breeding programs" were based on work ability and convenience only. Because of proximity-enforced inbreeding, types were established in certain areas. Not until dog shows came on the scene was breeding true to "type" encouraged by show enthusiasts.

In addition to the above hodge-podge, translations of breed names and standards often were careless when breeds were introduced outside their native countries. Therefore, the whole area of sheep dogs and shepherds is confusing and hopelessly tangled.

The English Shepherd, once known as the farm shepherd, is a natural driver and heeler. A hard worker and versatile shepherd, this breed is used on cattle as well as sheep, hogs, and even poultry. Early British settlers to the States brought the forebears of the breed which, despite its name, is considered American in origin.

Men clad in ar
sheep from the
tory of British .
ous hindrances
perhaps no jog
men" were pe
1570s.

Most of the
duced by selec
their norther
breeds were
manifested th
retained the p

Other herd
cient sheep o
stem had the
of drop ears
coat. Brough
ous migratio
source of the

In modern
in few of the
group's bree
as a fault, t
Most carry t
ture of their
like a sheph
dock the app
tail-set ques
kept out yea

Most of t
bling them
are lithe, s
coat varies a

Although
ing with re
sheep. Son
for heeling
were the pr
Today herc
ranches. A
taught only

Two of the most popular of the herders, the Collie and the Shetland Sheepdog, are contributions of Great Britain to the dog world. The Sheltie is about half the height of the Collie but is otherwise extremely similar in appearance.

Above: The Belgian Sheepdog Laekenois, the rarest of the four varieties, has been employed as a herder as well as a guardian. Its population is most prominent in Holland. **Below:** Originally utilized in the Pyrenees mountains of France, the Berger de Pyrenees is extraordinarily adaptable to extremes in weather. Pictured here in the snow is the goathaired coat type.

HERDING DOGS

Lapinporokoira	Finland
Belgian Sheepdog, Malinois	Belgium
Belgian Sheepdog, Groenendael	Belgium
Belgian Sheepdog, Tervuren	Belgium
Belgian Sheepdog, Laekenois	Belgium
Bouvier des Flandres	Belgium
Bouvier de Ardennes	Belgium
German Shepherd Dog	Germany
Giant Schnauzer	Germany
German Sheeppoodle	Germany
Hovawart	Germany
East European Shepherd	USSR
Tibetan Terrier	China
Lhasa Apso	China
Shih Tzu	China
Tibetan Spaniel	China
Pekingese	China
Japanese Chin	Japan
Puli	Hungary
Pumi	Hungary
Mudi	Hungary
Croatian Sheepdog	Yugoslavia
Bergamasco	Italy
Cão da Serra de Aires	Portugal
Catalan Sheepdog	Spain
Polski Owczarek Nizinny	Poland
Berger de Picard	France
Briard	France
Berger de Beauce	France
Berger de Pyrenees	France
Berger de Pyrenees, Smooth Muzzled	France
Berger du Languedoc	France
Armant	Egypt
Dutch Shepherd, Longhaired	Netherlands
Dutch Shepherd, Shorthaired	Netherlands
Dutch Shepherd, Roughhaired	Netherlands
Saarlooswolfhond	Netherlands
Schapendoes	Netherlands
Bearded Collie	Great Britain
Border Collie	Great Britain
Collie, Rough	Great Britain
Collie, Smooth	Great Britain
Shetland Sheepdog	Great Britain
Old English Sheepdog	Great Britain
Lancashire Heeler	Great Britain
Welsh Corgi, Cardigan	Great Britain

Along with the Old English Sheepdog, the Bearded Collie, having evolved from the Polski Owczarek Nizinny, is fast becoming one of the most recognizable shaggy sheep dogs.

Welsh Corgi, Pembroke	Great Britain
Vasgotaspets	Sweden
Australian Kelpie	Australia
Australian Cattle Dog	Australia
Stumpy-Tail Cattle Dog	Australia
Australian Shepherd	USA
English Shepherd	USA
Catahoula Leopard Dog	USA
Blue Lacy	USA
Kyi Leo	USA

The Terriers
True Grit

Terriers are mighty dogs in small packages. Admirers call them "small warriors," "tough guys," and "swashbucklers." In their early days, their prey was savage, and the terriers had to be equally tough. Even today, they have a certain dash and pugnacity. They are described variously as hard-bitten, intrepid and audacious.

True terriers are small to medium dogs that were developed mainly for vermin hunting, often going underground after the quarry. Thus "terrier" came from the Latin *terra*, meaning earth.

These small warriors were used to catch and kill rats in the barn, stable and home. Their services rid the farmyards and pastures of pests that plagued the stock, crops and food supplies, and helped reduce vermin in the teeming cities. In the pastures, they searched out the underground lair of the badger or fox and dug in after the animal. Otters and foxes were maneuvered from their hiding places in the rocky cairns. Snakes were easy prey to these quick, agile dogs, and marmots and weasels, too, fell victim. With their tough-guy attitude, terriers also made excellent watchdogs for the home, and guardians—as well as untiring companions—for youngsters.

Unfortunately, the terrier-type dog was also a victim, as one of the combatant choices in dog-fighting. Besides the "sport" of fighting, there were other competitions that made use of this feisty dog. The "poor man's" sport of rat killing earned the fame and fortunes of many early terriers and their owners. The upper class trained them for formal fox hunts. When the fox had hidden in a hole or drain to escape the hounds, the small terriers were put to the ground (these terriers were carried on horseback, as they were too little to keep up). They darted after the fox, rooting him from his hiding place, and the chase was on once again.

They are rarely used in fox hunts in this modern age, but in some places, terriers still hunt live quarry to prove their gameness and courage. Most modern terrier owners who desire competition prefer to prove their dogs' abilities in formal terrier trials. Artificial burrows are created with "prey" placed in a cage and then in the burrow. While the dog actually cannot engage in combat with the animal, the desire, keenness and aggression toward its quarry can be seen.

Many of the dogs called terrier more correctly belong in other groups. The American Staffordshire Terrier, Boston Terrier, Bull Terrier, and Staffordshire Bull Terrier are actually of mastiff derivation. The Tibetan Terrier is a herding-type dog of Oriental spitz extraction. Yet, Dachshunds (although truly hounds) fit the terrier definition of being tough and going to ground. Many of the terrier breeds that started out as true working dogs, such as the Yorkshire Terrier and Toy Manchester Terrier, have been miniaturized and are now rightly referred to as companion dogs—although they still maintain many of their terrier mental characteristics.

Terriers were bred to stay comparatively small, so they would fit in the burrows and to lessen the expense of feeding. They often have a rough, wiry coat that not only protects them from the elements but also minimizes necessary grooming. Even the terriers that have a comparably smooth coat usually sport one that is thicker and rougher than most smoothhaired dogs (i.e., Smooth Fox Terriers, as compared to Dalmatians). A few have long hanging coats.

Terriers were not used merely to find or chase their quarry like the hounds or gun dogs, but were often required to make the actual kill. Even if they didn't join in mortal combat, facing a frightened and cornered wild animal in the dark many feet underground is not for the faint-hearted. This takes a dog with a bold, fearless, confident and pugnacious temperament. The terrier has presence; he is a dog that, even though only 15 or 20 pounds, acts like he is 120!

The traditional ritual of sparring terriers in

Originally bred to hunt fox, the Jack Russell Terrier is exceedingly successful as a raccoon and varmint hunter, with no qualms about going to ground.

the show ring (the only group where this is done) is to prove they have the true temperament. The judge asks the handlers to bring two or three of the dogs at a time on leash into the center of the ring to face one another head-to-head. Whereas the hound might lower the tail peacefully and a gun dog might sniff interestedly, terriers must show they are ready for a contest if the situation should arise. While not nasty or quarrelsome, they should be up on their toes, leaning forward, heads up, looking the opposite dog right in the eye. The ears and tails are in an erect, dominant position. Each should look and rumble a bit, as if to say, "I'm usually a perfect gentleman, but if *you* want to start something then I'm game!"

The terrier is typically lean and long-headed with a square, strong jaw to seat firmly the punishing teeth. To prevent injury, the eyes are set deep in the sockets. Ears are generally pricked or semi-pricked (button ear). Tails, usually carried straight up, are docked, leaving about half or less, depending on the breed. (This left a

good handle to extract the dog from underground!) Terriers that work above ground are built with squarer proportions, while the dogs that go to ground tend to be a bit shorter on leg.

Dogs of terrier type have been known in the British Isles since very ancient times. As early as the Middle Ages, European forms were described by writers, storytellers and painters. Like our other modern dogs, terriers are not of a pure or single origin. Whichever dogs best fit the purpose of the owner were those chosen, and looks and shape did not matter. The basic terrier stock was most likely from small spitz/Nordic dogs.

Even in modern times, these dogs share many of their northern predecessors' characteristics, both in type and temperament. They are busy, active and very vocal dogs who naturally chase and alarm.

The erect, or nearly erect, ears and the tail that almost curves over the back also indicate northern influence. There were probably crossbreedings to the smaller mastiff dogs to gain the heavier jaw and aggressive temperament apparent in some of the terriers. Some breeders now feel the wire coats were the result of crosses to water poodle dogs. This may be the case, since Poodles, with their heavy curling coats, create a double wire coat much like the terrier's when crossed with smooth-coated dogs. The Poodle, in turn, goes back to mastiff/herding dogs, so there is a double line to those two types. Other terriers, in part, owe their ancestry to small sighthounds which yielded a racier dog.

The smooth terrier needs very little coat care other than an occasional brushing. The proper wire coat also requires a minimum of fuss. Terriers with correct wire coats have a soft dense undercoat and an outer jacket of very straight, hard, wiry hair. This outer hair grows to a length of only two or three inches and then dies, when it can be pulled or "stripped" with the fingers or a stripping knife. The dead hair is easily removed once or twice a year, and a new wiry coat soon replaces the old. This process prevents matting and shedding and keeps the dog appearing neat and trim. The wire coat is water-resistant—mud simply can be shaken off when it dries—and it provides good protection in the brambles and briars. A true wire coat never grows very long as the hard hair breaks off easily; early wire terriers often were referred to as broken-coated terriers.

Many modern terrier owners prefer to have the coat trimmed with electric clippers. While an abomination to dedicated terrier breeders, the care of such a trim is easier for the pet owner. The new coat, when it grows back after cutting, is softer and silkier and not of proper texture. Nearly all wire-coated terriers exhibited on the bench are hand-stripped, and the proper technique of creating the smart appearance of modern show winners is a definite art.

England is the origin of most terriers; many that developed in other parts of the world used English breeds in their creation. Exceptions are the German pinschers and schnauzers. These dogs, by the definition of terriers as vermin catchers and watchdogs, are included in the terrier group in this book. Early pinschers and schnauzers were likely the same breed type, the former being smooth-coated and the latter having the wirehair. Miniature versions of both the pinscher and the schnauzer have become popular companion dogs.

The Yorkshire Terrier, although once a true working dog, has been miniaturized and is a quality companion.

Above: The Soft-Coated Wheaten Terrier belongs to the family of Irish terriers. History finds the Wheaten in the homes of the Irish farmers as a companion and hunter. **Below:** The American Hairless Terrier resulted from a single hairless female in a litter of Rat Terriers. These two specimens belong to the Scotts of Louisiana, the founders and promoters of this new breed.

Sharing similar histories to the other British terriers, the Cairn Terrier has been around for about 500 years. These terriers were useful in extracting foxes from their hiding places in the cairns, hence the breed name.

TERRIERS

Manchester Terrier	Great Britain
Toy Manchester Terrier	Great Britain
Fox Terrier, Smooth	Great Britain
Fox Terrier, Wire	Great Britain
Jack Russell Terrier	Great Britain
Lakeland Terrier	Great Britain
Patterdale Terrier	Great Britain
Airedale Terrier	Great Britain
Bedlington Terrier	Great Britain
Welsh Terrier	Great Britain
Border Terrier	Great Britain
Dandie Dinmont Terrier	Great Britain
Norwich Terrier	Great Britain
Norfolk Terrier	Great Britain
Sealyham Terrier	Great Britain
Yorkshire Terrier	Great Britain
Cairn Terrier	Great Britain
Skye Terrier	Great Britain
Scottish Terrier	Great Britain
West Highland White Terrier	Great Britain
Irish Terrier	Ireland
Kerry Blue Terrier	Ireland
Soft-Coated Wheaten Terrier	Ireland
Glen of Imaal Terrier	Ireland
German Pinscher	Germany
Harlequin Pinscher	Germany
Miniature Pinscher	Germany
German Hunt Terrier	Germany
Schnauzer, Standard	Germany
Schnauzer, Miniature	Germany
Affenpinscher	Germany
Kromfohrländer	Germany
Austrian Shorthaired Pinscher	Austria
Dutch Smoushond	Netherlands
Brussels Griffon	Belgium
Belgian Griffon	Belgium
Petit Brabancon	Belgium
Czesky Terrier	Czechoslovakia
Australian Terrier	Australia
Silky Terrier	Australia
Rat Terrier	USA
Toy Fox Terrier	USA
American Hairless Terrier	USA
Brazilian Terrier	Brazil
Japanese Terrier	Japan
Black Russian Terrier	USSR
Moscow Longhaired Toy Terrier	USSR

Above: Jack Russell Terriers after a hard catch! **Below:** One of the largest in the terrier group is the Airedale Terrier, pictured here as a pup.

69

Southern Dogs
Dogs of the Desert Wind

At the dawn of history, the Southern Hemisphere of the world was semi-arid and less than hospitable to herbivores. This, plus the existence of other predators, meant a more limited food supply. The southern wolves, such as the Pale-Footed Asian Wolf, were much smaller and lighter boned than their northern cousins. Forced to share the meager food supply, the southern wolf did not exhibit the strong group cooperation and family ties. Adaptations for the warmer climate such as a short, smooth coat and large, upright ears appeared. Their ears were large with the blood vessels near the surface to dissipate heat. From this early southern predator came the domesticated dog of the South.

Humankind had evolved faster in the south. Perhaps as long as 10,000 years ago, nomadic tribes in Africa and southeast Asia had tamed sheep and goats, as well as dogs to help herd these flocks. These were, by far, the earliest domesticated canines, predating those of the northern varieties by nearly several thousand years. This early southern canine was basically a herding dog with distinctive physical traits.

The southern dogs were of moderate size (around 30–40 pounds) for efficient keep and short coated to withstand the heat. The body was squarish and up on leg; the head was wedge-shaped and sharply angled with the rather large pricked ears that tilted forward, sometimes creating forehead wrinkles. They sometimes retained the wolf traits of once-a-year estrus and infrequence or absence of barking. Some possessed the low tail of the wolf, although others showed the neotanous trait of the tail curled over the back.

This creation of the southern dog is thought to have occurred in what is now northern Iran. From that starting point, early people migrated to all parts of the globe. With them went their dogs. These nomads went north and east to populate Siberia, crossing the land bridge into the Western Hemisphere. From there they spread through North and South America. Some of these migrations took the tribes south and west into Africa. Still others slowly moved east to settle what is now Malaysia, Oceania and across another land bridge into Australia.

In all of these areas, the southern dog was seeded, very often reverting to a feral state. It was in this venue that he earned his name of pariah, scavenging on the fringes of civilization. As a competitor for the limited food sources and, as an eater of garbage and carrion, he generally became detested. The Chinese, Indian, Moslem and Jewish cultures all looked upon this scavenger as unclean and to be avoided.

In more recent times, as these breeds were unearthed, many experts classified them as true wild dogs, separate species from the domesticated dog. Modern research has shown that they *are* the true feral form of the southern dogs domesticated so long ago, altered and adapted for a variety of lifestyles. Despite their "wild" state, they were—and still are—converted back to domestic living.

Although, numerically, these dogs represent the largest group of dogs in the world, they have the fewest known and established breeds, probably because they have been shunned for so long. In fact, many of these dogs, which tended to breed true in an ecological niche untouched by human intervention, are described in this book. Yet others have been tended and selected by people to fill certain needs or crossed with the better known northern dogs to create new breeds.

During the rise and fall of the pariahs, the great ancient civilizations of the Fertile Crescent had developed. These cultures rapidly learned to modify and change nature's products for their own use. They began practicing selective animal breeding.

War mastiffs were in wide use. In ancient Egyptian culture, archaeologists found records of eight specific and distinct types of dogs, in-

Bred by tribes of the southern Sahara, the Azawakh was employed as a camel and goat guardian. Truly "Dogs of the Desert Wind," the Azawakhs are built like fine Arabian horses, possessing a lightfooted, lithesome gait.

cluding mastiffs, small house dogs, pariahs in various forms, medium-sized hounds, and "new" dogs of the chase. The Egyptians and other cultures also used tamed jackals for hunting. As civilization progressed and people enjoyed more leisure, hunting became not just a necessary chore but a pastime developed to an art.

In the hot, arid and treeless areas where early civilizations settled, hunting was accomplished mainly by sighting and running down prey such as gazelle and antelope. To create a dog specialized for this task, the early racy pariahs were se-

lected. Traits that increased speed and minimized wind resistance were sought. Soon the pariah dog was longer legged with more angulation, had wider back vertebrae and more loin muscles. This dog had lighter bone and a deeper chest to allow increased lung capacity, which are all adaptations for speed and the double-suspension gallop.

The head was lengthened and narrowed to slice through the wind and to increase the cooling mechanisms of the nasal passages. But he maintained his upright ears and the wedge-shaped head with forehead wrinkles. This prototype sighthound speedster can be seen today in several breeds.

The swiftness of the sighthound brought a sport to dog lovers that has spanned the years, probably since before Ovid's written description at the time of Christ. Humans, being human, have always relished contests and, from the start, delighted in boasting, "My dog's better'n your dog." The most ancient of dog sports certainly was racing, and enthusiasm for the races have continued to this day. Initially, the dogs pursued a hare; nowadays the thrill of the chase must suffice, as the hare has been replaced by a stuffed bunny or other inanimate lure. English coursing events became organized in 1776, eventually resulting in the Waterloo Cup, the Derby of dogdom.

Races draw enthusiasts from the ranks of Irish Wolfhounds, Scottish Deerhounds, Salukis, Afghan Hounds, Whippets, Italian Greyhounds, and of course, the *creme de la creme*—the Greyhound. Racing competitors stand as far apart from their show brothers as do field trialers from bench competitors, occasionally appearing

to be different breeds altogether. Racing dogs are alert to the extreme (sometimes not making them good pets), deep-chested and powerfully built.

Sighthounds that run down prey alone in open country are distinctly different from ancestral wolf cousins which always trotted in groups after their target.

Their relative, the jackal, has a long, narrow head, is lighter built than the wolf and is adapted to withstand heat. Jackals tend to be higher strung and do more solitary hunting. The jackal is not as closely related biologically as the wolf is to the dog, but crosses can and have occurred. Many cynologists believe that some crossbreeding to the jackal occurred in the development of the sighthound. Gazehounds tend to have an aloof and reserved personality, quite different from other types of dogs. If there were crosses, they were very early with the type being set, since there is very little variation in the group as a whole. Later, the heads became even longer and narrower, the ears dropped or folded back to the neck, and the size and tuck-up be-

A strong bond between the Moslem nomads and their Sloughis exists even to this day. A registration is underway at a Moroccan dog show.

The Pharaoh Hound, like all the sighthounds, possesses great speed and agility. The Pharaoh Hound descends from the pariah-type dogs and is able to hunt by sight as well as scent.

came more exaggerated to create the classic sighthound type.

The Phoenician civilization was at its peak during the years of 800 to 2000 BC. These people were great sailors and had trade routes throughout the known world. They sailed around the entire Mediterranean from their main cities, in what is now Lebanon, to Turkey, Greece, Italy and even the Straits of Gibraltar and Spain, to the north and south, to the northern coast of Africa including Egypt, Libya and Morocco. But they also ventured into the Atlantic to Portugal, Brittany and the British Isles. They were commercial traders for nearly everything—metal products, cedar wood, glass, and their famed purple-dyed cloth—at each port of call.

The fleet sighthounds were in high demand. The Phoenician hound trade was known throughout the ancient world. Wherever Phoenicians landed, whatever strange and new society they encountered, the barter for the dogs of the chase overcame language and cultural barriers. Because of this, the sighthound was seeded over a wide area of Europe, the Middle East, and Africa. In some places, like the islands of Sicily and Ibiza, he remained to breed true for many thousands of years. In other areas the sighthound was used in crosses to native types, creating new breeds. Because of these crosses, long and wire coats also were developed.

As the centuries passed, the desert Bedouins kept and bred choice dogs of the desert type. These dogs of the chase were an exception to the "unclean" rule among the Arabs. They were prized by their owners, lived in tents with the tribal chieftains and were given as treasured gifts. The pedigrees were carried only in the memories of their owners, but passed from generation to generation by word of mouth.

The sighthound became the dog of nobility in other areas of the world as well. Several distinct types were created by the upper classes of Russia. Although fallen into disfavor since the Revolution, some of these breeds are making a comeback in the Soviet Union. The rough-coated sighthounds of Ireland and Scotland hunted with—and were loved by—kings and the

Above: Whippets—some believe a cross of English terriers to the Greyhound—are very social dogs, delighting in the company of people and dogs, such as the Basenji, a fellow southern canine. **Below:** The beloved house pet of Peruvian Indians who surrounded their dogs with orchids, the Peruvian Inca Orchid is still bred by natives today.

nobility, with oft told legends to their credit.

A strange mutation occurred at some time along the line of evolvement from pariah to sighthound. Some pups were born hairless, or nearly so, except for sparse tufts on the feet and head. Always on the lookout for the unusual or different, fanciers kept and bred these types.

The exact origin of the first hairless dogs is unknown, but the dominant hairless dogs are all of pariah/sighthound types. This suggests the North African/Middle East areas, where a hairless species called *Canis Africanis* evolved. Breeds once known included the African Sand Dog, African Elephant Dog, Small African Greyhound and the Nubian Dog. Hairless dogs also have been raised in the Middle East, India, China, Mexico and South America: the Turkish Hairless, Indian Rampur, Guatemalan Hairless and Buenos Aires Hairless, besides the more "common" rarities seen today. They were common during the height of Aztec and Incan advanced cultures. They may have emigrated from Asia with the Indians or may have mutated sepa-

Every hairless breed has a "powderpuff" (coated) variety as well. In order to cut the effect of the lethal homozygous gene, the powderpuffs are essential to the propagation of the breed. These are Chinese Cresteds.

rately, but their basic form is similar to hairless dogs elsewhere in the world. In the Aztec culture, the hairless dog was a food source. Raised in pens and grain-fed, they were an important part of the Aztec diet. It was only much later that they became pets.

Hairless dogs of pariah type share many similarities. The hereditary factor that produces the hairless condition is a dominant lethal gene. Dogs carrying the double-dominant die before birth, so there is never a homozygous hairless dog (one that always reproduces the hairless condition). Dogs born hairless are heterozygous for the trait, meaning they can produce both hairless and coated progeny. About one out of three pups born from a hairless-to-hairless mating are double-recessive for normal hair and are called "powderpuffs," with the powderpuff being the original type and the hairless the mutant. Legend has it that the coated pups are born in

every litter to keep their bald siblings warm. Hairless dogs possess a tendency to have missing teeth, with as many as all of the premolars being absent. It was once believed that these breeds also carried a warmer body temperature.

Puppies born of hairless-to-hairless matings often suffer extreme abnormalities. One in four is stillborn or reabsorbed prior to birth. The hairless variety also has the primitive mouth (teeth extending forward, missing premolars and occasionally missing eyeteeth) with less dental enamel. Hard foods can cause problems, and soft, moistened foods are recommended. Bathing to prevent blackheads and protection from the sun are also advised. Knowledgeable breeders realize the importance of utilizing the powderpuff in the breeding program to aid in correcting these problems. A few types of these ancient hairless dogs have evolved into modern breeds.

The elegant and flowing appearance of the Afghan Hound should not be misinterpreted; as a hunter in his native Afghanistan, the breed was used on swift and powerful game, including wolves, foxes, and gazelles. Of course, the breed's hunting abilities by no means detract from its overall beauty.

SOUTHERN DOGS

Pariah

Dingo	Australia
Telomian	Malaysia
New Guinea Singing Dog	New Guinea
Canaan Dog	Israel
Basenji	Zaire
Carolina Dog	USA
Tahltan Bear Dog	Canada
Hawaiian Poi Dog	USA
Pharaoh Hound	Malta
Ibizan Hound	Spain
Cirneco dell'Etna	Italy
Podengo Portugueso, Grande	Portugal
Podengo Portugueso, Medio	Portugal
Podengo Portugueso, Pequeño	Portugal
Chihuahua	Mexico

Sighthound

Sloughi	Morocco
Saluki	Iran
Azawakh	Mali
Greyhound	Great Britain
Whippet	Great Britain
Galgo Español	Spain
Magyar Agar	Hungary
Borzoi	USSR
Chortaj	USSR
Tazy	USSR
Taigan	USSR
South Russian Steppe Hound	USSR
Kangaroo Dog	Australia
Afghan Hound	Afghanistan
Scottish Deerhound	Great Britain
Irish Wolfhound	Ireland
Rhodesian Ridgeback	South Africa
Italian Greyhound	Italy

Hairless

Peruvian Inca Orchid	Peru
Inca Hairless Dog	Peru
Chinese Crested Dog	Africa/China
Xoloitzcuintli	Mexico
Xoloitzcuintli Toy	Mexico

The prototype sighthound has a long, narrowed head to assist it in slicing the desert wind with speed and grace. The Whippet is a fine example of this sleek and pointed body type.

The Dogs of the World

This chapter is divided into specific articles, arranged alphabetically and each concerned with one individual breed or group of closely related breeds. The reader is advised to consult "How to Use This Book" for a more detailed explanation of the most effective approach to this chapter.

Affenpinscher, dark gray.

AFFENPINSCHER

COUNTRY: Germany
WEIGHT: 7–8 pounds
HEIGHT: Less than 10 inches
COAT: Medium long, harsh and wiry
COLOR: Black preferred, black/tan, red or dark gray also allowed
REGISTRY: FCI, AKC, TKC, CKC
GROUP: Terrier

A true toy terrier, this breed has been in existence for more than 300 years. His origins are difficult to pinpoint, but he is seen in nearly his present form in 17th-century paintings. He may be a miniature form of the wire terrier prototype which came from Nordic dogs, such as the Schipperke. These, crossed with the little pinschers or with small brachycephalic Puglike dogs from Asia found in Europe, could have created the Affenpinscher. In fact, earlier Affens may have had a longer muzzle, because the Affenpinscher and smooth Miniature Pinscher were at one time considered two coat varieties of the same breed and even occurred in the same litter.

Whatever his ancestry, this quaint little dog has earned the description of "monkey dog." His rather flat, turned-up nose, alert cropped ears, prominent round eyes, bristling eyebrows and bushy mustache and beard all add to this description. The French often call this dog *Diabletin Moustache*, literally the mustached little devil!

Belying his very small size, he is every inch a terrier in personality. He is alert, yet quiet, game and sturdy. The FCI standard translates: " . . . a charming mixture of fearlessness, obstinancy, loyalty and affection which he will show in rapid change from amusing earnestness to raging passion."

Regular brushing and tidying up is all the Affen requires to look neat. The tail is docked short. Although not among the most numerous of dogs, he has his proponents internationally. American and Canadian recognition was granted in 1936 but, perhaps because of the wealth of terrier types already in Britain, he remains virtually unknown there.

Afghan Hound.

AFGHAN HOUND

COUNTRY: Afghanistan
WEIGHT: 50–60 pounds
HEIGHT: 25–27 inches
COAT: Long, straight, thick, silky; short on face
COLOR: Any color; white on head undesirable
OTHER NAMES: Tazi
REGISTRY: FCI, AKC, UKC, TKC, CKC
GROUP: Southern

The history of the Afghan Hound is ancient, though the legend which claims the Afghan as the dog Noah took into the Ark may be a bit exaggerated. Migration of northern African sighthounds into the mountains of Afghanistan included some hounds with longer hair. In the cold mountain air, the heaviest coats were selected and bred from necessity, eventually creating the Afghan. The breed spread into the border areas and even into India and aided both the hunter and the shepherd.

His unique, upright tail with the curled end served as a marker in the heavier underbrush, and his high-set hip bones enabled him greater flexibility in the mountain ranges. The aristocratic, elegant Afghan was no pussycat, hunting big—even tough—game: wolves, foxes and gazelles. In times past, he was a favorite of the Afghani nobility as an adjunct to the sport of falconry.

His old native name is Tazi, and his obvious resemblance to the like-named Tasy of Russia (even to the ring in the tail) indicates similar histories. The proximity of southern Russia and Afghanistan geographically increases the likelihood of close ancestry.

Originally, sale of the national dog to outsiders was prohibited, and the first specimens to arrive in the United States and England did not appear until the turn of the 20th century. An English Captain Banff imported the exciting hound, "Zardin," from Afghanistan around this time. Exhibited at the Crystal Palace Show in 1907, he won spectacularly and started a true interest in the breed. Good breeding programs existed in Britain by the 1920s. AKC and CKC recognition followed in the 30s.

The Afghan coat bears singular requirements: the topknot and the distinct shorthaired saddle on the back which forms as an adult. It is permissible for the dog to display a shorthaired cuff on the feet. Frequent, fastidious combing is a necessity. An ungroomed Afghan is not only unkempt but uncomfortable.

As well as being a highly celebrated show dog today, the Afghan participates in lure coursing. Despite their high numbers as show competitors, they have not achieved the same status as a pet, due to their size, coat care and exercise demands. Their temperament is aloof, though they can be the greatest of clowns at play time. From their origin on Mount Sinai to today's show ring, the Afghans are majesty at its peak. "At a glance, one can see the Eastern inscrutability; the conviction that they are royalty; the certainty that they are above lesser breeds."

Afghan Hound.

Afghan Hound.

AINU DOG

COUNTRY: Japan
HEIGHT: 18½–21½ inches
COAT: Moderately short, thick, stand-off, with undercoat
COLOR: Sesame, brindle, wolf gray, red, brown or white
OTHER NAMES: Hokkaido Dog, Ainu-Ken
REGISTRY: FCI
GROUP: Northern

When the Ainu tribe arrived in Japan nearly 3,000 years ago, they had dogs of Nordic type with them, and these became the Ainu Dog. The Ainus were an ancient people who migrated to and were the first settlers in Japan, ten centuries before Christ. They were a white race of unknown origin, and at one time lived on all the islands of Japan.

The Ainus were slowly pushed out over the centuries by the influx of Yamato (Japanese) people and now live only in their own settlements on the northernmost island of Hokkaido. (They live in their own groups, with their own separate and quite primitive culture.) Their dog has changed little over the centuries. The Ainu Dog is probably the oldest of the Japanese breeds and may have been altered somewhat through crosses with matagi dogs.

The breed is known for its strength and was a draft dog originally, but is used today for hunting and guarding. The Ainu is extremely courageous for his size, willingly attacking a 650-pound bear. He is generally kept in the home.

As is common with most of the Japanese breeds, this dog is clean and mannerly yet quite ready to warn of danger. As a working dog for so long, he tends to be a bit coarser and more primitive than the other Japanese breeds. His character is sharp and fearless. He also differs by having smaller ears, a broader head and a fiercer expression. Also of interest is that, although not particularly desired, these dogs occasionally have the black tongue. This may hint at ties to the Chow Chow and mainland China. If loved and cared for, he is said to be obedient to his master and an irreplaceable friend.

Facing page: Ainu Dog, red.

Airedale Terrier.

water. By the 1860s, these crosses were standardized and called Working, Waterside or Bingley Terriers. Classes were first offered at agricultural shows in 1879. In fact, the Airedale agricultural show had an extremely large entry of Waterside Terriers and was responsible for giving the breed its current name.

The patriarch of the breed is Ch. Master Briar, 1897–1906. One of his sons was exported to Philadelphia to initiate the breed in the USA. The Airedale boasts many Best In Shows in the USA and England, but loyal fanciers exist throughout the world.

According to *Hutchinson's Dog Encyclopaedia*, "the breed has long been held in high favour by the armies of European and Asiatic countries being easy to train and once trained, showing great determination of character and devotion to duty, and almost superhuman intelligence, chiefly in carrying despatches on the field of battle and finding the wounded. In fact, the dog's intelligence was so high in the latter respect that they became a source of embarrassment to the Japanese victors during the Russo-Japanese War by always finding and directing to the Russians first and the Japanese soldiers last, for the Airedale's power of scent is remarkable."

They are used on large game in Africa, India and Canada, as well as the USA. The breed was chosen as one of the first to be used for police work in Germany and England. During World War I, the breed was enlisted by the British and Russian armies. During that time it aided the Red Cross, locating wounded and carrying messages. A few also served in the Second World War. When trained for defense, these dogs are usually unbeatable for their weight. It is said the Airedale "can do anything any other dog can do—and then lick the other dog."

Their sweet disposition comes from their hound background. Mature dogs have a certain dignified aloofness, both to strangers and to their own kind. Exceptional playmates for children who are old enough for high-spirited play, their disposition can be molded by their masters.

The Airedale coat, which is not only hard and wiry, but sports a bit of a curl, requires consistent regular grooming. The ears have a half drop and the tail is docked.

AIREDALE TERRIER

COUNTRY: Great Britain
WEIGHT: 44 pounds
HEIGHT: 23 inches for males
COAT: Wiry, hard, dense with a bit of a curl; undercoat
COLOR: Black/tan, saddled
REGISTRY: FCI, AKC, UKC, TKC, CKC
GROUP: Terrier

The extinct black and tan Old English or Broken-haired Terrier is probably the progenitor of the Welsh, Irish, Wire Fox and Airedale Terriers. Sporting Yorkshiremen used Airedales and their crosses for fox, weasel, otter, badger, water rat and small game in the valleys of the rivers Colne, Calder, Warfe, and Aire. They ranged from 17–30 pounds and excelled in agility, eyesight, hearing and courage, but they lacked the nose and swimming ability of the Otterhound used in the same area. The crossing of the terrier and hound formed the stem of the Airedale, a large terrier that would also work in

Airedale Terrier.

AKBASH DOG

COUNTRY: Turkey
WEIGHT: 80–140 pounds
HEIGHT: 28–34 inches
COAT: Smooth or long, both double coat; thick, with fringing on tail and back of legs, and often a slight wave
COLOR: Solid white (a bit of light biscuit around ears is not to be penalized); complete black pigment of eye rims, nose and lips preferred, but dark brown acceptable.
GROUP: Flock Guard

As one of the oldest breeds of the flock-guarding group, the Akbash Dog still carries the same physical and mental traits that characterized these dogs thousands of years ago. They were probably brought to the *yaylas* (mountain pastures) of Turkey with migrations of peoples from the East. Since sighthounds, mastiffs and flock-guard dogs accompanied these Oriental migrations, all could have contributed to the gene pool. Turkey (Asia Minor) was on the mi-gratory routes between West and East, and stories have been told and records kept of these guardians from very early times.

Lucien G.M. Columella, a first-century AD Roman author, wrote: "Sheepherders wish to have white dogs in order to avoid confusing them with wild animals, since, when the wolf attacks in the twilight, it is important that there be a color difference between the dog and the wolf; otherwise the sheepherder might strike his dog, thinking he was killing a wolf."

A Phrygian civilization (Asia Minor, 750-300 BC) graffito shows a large guarding dog wearing a spiked iron collar. Turkish flock-guarding dogs still wear huge iron-spiked collars as added protection for the vulnerable neck area against predators.

The Akbash is a fleet-moving dog, with acute hearing and eyesight. Natural and owner culling has developed strong, sturdy animals. These dogs are bred to be animal-oriented, rather than toward people. Their independence is sometimes misunderstood by the uninformed as stubbornness or stupidity. They are bred to think, rather than obey with robot precision. A strong

Akbash Dog.

Akbash Dog.

tendency to natural suspicion fosters development of the proper guarding attitude.

Proper bonding with sheep requires calm, quiet, steady temperament. Livestock guardian candidates are never brought inside the home or made into pets. They need to be introduced to their future animal at a tender age.

If pups want to play with sheep, trainers cure this by adding an "old cantankerous ewe or feisty ram . . . to discipline the overly exuberant puppy," so they learn not to injure the young lambs in rough play.

In modern society, the Akbash usually accepts other farm animals (i.e., dogs, cats, horses and other domestics), if reared with them from puppyhood, and is sometimes protective of them. When raised with children, the dogs are good with them. Pets should be confined to an area, rather than being chained which intensifies aggression.

Matings are not readily accomplished. Dogs are so attached to the flock that they are not easily sidetracked, even for affairs of the heart. One bitch owner had to rent an entire flock and the shepherd to convince its guard dog to cooperate.

The animal refused to leave his flock!

Double rear dewclaws are often seen on Akbash Dogs and may be removed. In conformation, the smooths, without padding of coat, falsely tend to appear slighter in build than the long coats. Many Akbash Dogs have the ranginess, fleetness and arch to the loin that give just a hint of the running hound in their background. In the past, the ears were cropped like many breeds of this group to diminish the ability of a predator to grip and hold. Thus many imports have the ears lopped off. Ears on modern dogs are usually left natural.

The handsome Akbash has been successful in USA flock-guarding programs, and American breeders are determined to preserve the working qualities. Their active American-based Akbash Dog Association International promotes the breed for guard work, obedience and exhibition at rare breed shows, as well as for livestock protection on farms and ranches. In addition, the Akbash Dog is showing up in more and more activities, such as therapy dogs and independence dogs (aiding the handicapped).

Akitas.

AKITA

COUNTRY: Japan
WEIGHT: 75–110 pounds or more
HEIGHT: 24–28 inches
COAT: Stiff, moderately short; stand-off, with undercoat
COLOR: All colors allowed, including white, pied, or brindle, with or without mask
OTHER NAMES: Akita Inu
REGISTRY: FCI, AKC, TKC, CKC
GROUP: Northern

Most of the native dogs of Japan are of the classic northern type. They have square bodies, wedge-shaped heads, small upright ears, short, thick stand-off coats, and the tail is curled up over the back. The eyes tend to be triangular and recessed, "suggesting the burning spirit within." Their temperaments are always calm and considerate, with great dignity.

The breed differences lie in the sizes, colors, uses and backgrounds, and a few other minor features. In fact, they are so much alike that in Japan, these native breeds are shown in one classification, divided into sub-groups: large (Akita), medium (Kai, Kishu, Ainu, Shikoku) and small (Shiba).

Both the terms *inu* and *ken* translate into the word dog. Many of the Japanese breeds originally carried one of these terms after their names, but modern usage tends to drop the superfluous suffix.

In the late 19th century, when the National Isolation Policy was repealed, other breeds were brought into the country and, naturally, some

Akita, tan.

crossbreeding occurred. The Japanese government became concerned over the impending loss of their native breeds and formed the Society for Preservation of Japanese Dogs, declaring all native breeds as national monuments.

The largest of these breeds is the well-known Akita from the Akita prefecture in northern Japan. The breed traces back many centuries to the polar regions when the spitz group found its way to the northern mountains in Honshu. The largest and most powerful specimens were selected and bred with the type appearing about 300 years ago. Akitas were originally developed as fighting dogs, as popular in the Far East as they were in Europe. As that sport lost favor, the nobility found new uses for this brave breed in their hunts for deer, wild boar or even black bear. This dog has achieved praise as a bold hunter of large game, a guard and a loyal companion.

A huge statue of an Akita stands in the busy Shibuya Station in Tokyo, erected in the 1920s as a tribute to a dog who appeared daily to greet his master as he returned to the station from work, continuing ten years after the master died. The statue is named *Chuken Hachi-ko*, or Loyal Dog Hachi.

The Akita is a tough, robust fellow, needing firm, loving discipline. He can be obstinate and reacts against harsh methods. The breed cannot be forced but, once shown what is desired, he is quite cooperative. The Akita is aggressive with other animals and will defend its territory against all intruders, human or otherwise. Yet he is an affectionate companion to his family. The Japanese say he is "tender in heart and strong in strength."

To preclude boredom and mischief, sufficient exercise is necessary. The Japanese spitz dogs are hardy and can endure extremes of climate.

The breed's popularity continues as a companion and guardian. He is sometimes called *Shishi Inu*, meaning large dog. The breed is a favorite in Japan, and is fairly well known in the USA as well as in England and the European continent. As noted by Fujino Junko, "the characters of these dogs suggest ancient Japanese people—austere, valiant, faithful, good-natured and gentle, highly affectionate and sensitive to the kindness of their masters."

Akitas, black and white.

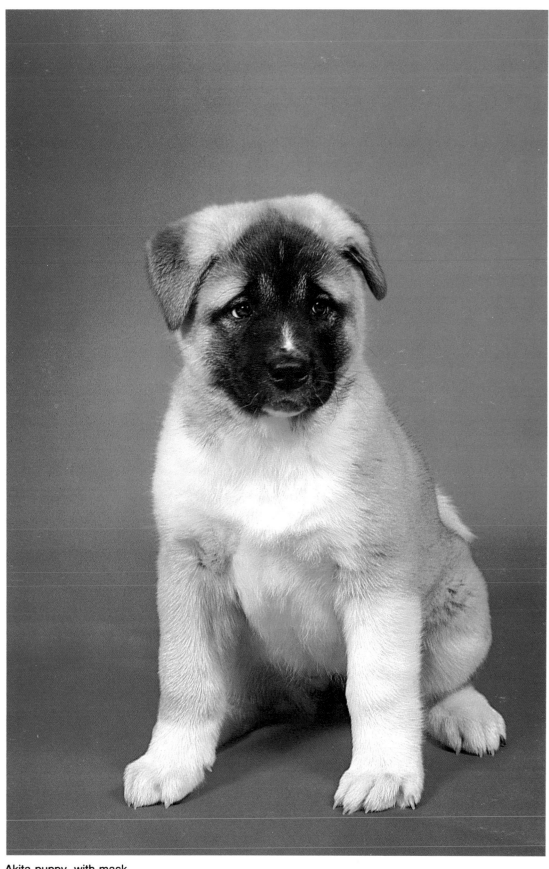

Akita puppy, with mask.

Alaskan Malamute.

ALASKAN MALAMUTE

COUNTRY: USA
WEIGHT: 75–85 pounds
HEIGHT: 23–25 inches
COAT: Short, stand-off
COLOR: Black or various shades of gray, with lighter mask and underside common
REGISTRY: FCI, AKC, UKC, TKC, CKC
GROUP: Northern

The draft or combination draft/hunting dogs of the North have been an essential part of the northern people's culture since the Stone Age. Because most northern tribes were nomadic, they could not have existed without their dogs to move their belongings from place to place. In the harsh and bitter cold, dogs were the only domestic animals that could survive.

Historians argue whether the ancestors of the northern Eskimo tribes came over a land bridge from Asia or across the North Pole from Scandinavia. But the fact that Nordic-type dogs accompanied these people is without argument. Each tribe or area developed its own type of dog, so perfected that many remain distinct today. The *Mahlemuts* (later spelled Malamute) were an industrious and skilled Inuit people of upperwestern Alaska (across from Siberia). Since they were nomadic, they moved their families to the site of each new kill, relocating when the need for another food source arose.

This lifestyle necessitated dogs strong enough to haul all of the tribe's possessions and to transport goods to and from the trading post. Speed was not vital, however, and a leisurely pace was quite acceptable. The Mahlemut tribe was never mentioned without a reference to their sledge dogs. Early European explorers and Russian whalers of the last century told that the Mahlemuts had dogs of "beauty and endurance," and that they were "fond of their . . . dogs. The dogs work hard and have great endurance."

During the settling of Alaska by white people, from 1750 to 1900, dogs were used for hauling and transportation in large numbers. These newcomers did not pay much attention to type, as long as the dogs (named after the tribe) could work. In addition the upsurge of dog-sled racing did the Malamute dog no good. In an attempt to create a faster animal, racing drivers crossed them with established speedsters, and the breed was nearly lost.

At that time, however, some Eskimos kept their dogs pure to type. Fortunately, interest in the promotion of the pure Malamute rose among American dog fanciers, and the breed has been maintained. Eva "Short" Seely became interested in sled dogs, obtaining good Malamutes (and Siberians) and breeding them, even sending her stock with Admiral Byrd to Antarctica. World War I had an effect on these northern dogs as well as on European breeds, but in a different manner. Their numbers were depleted by search-and-rescue, the Byrd expeditions and supply-packing work during the War. The stud book was reopened after the War and additional foundation stock was added to those already registered. Once again, the breed thrived.

The Malamute is as distinct from the Siberian Husky as the draft horse is from the horse of the desert. The Malamute is a dog that denotes power rather than quickness. Never so large as to appear clumsy, he must personify substance and strength. The body is slightly longer than its height, moving the center of gravity back, which allows powerful leaning into heavy loads. A clean, quiet, affectionate companion, the Mal needs firm, early handling to understand who is boss.

Raised and exhibited in much of North America and Europe, the Malamute is a popular dog for home sledding. Many owners and their Mals compete in weight-pulling contests. The dogs take to it quite naturally—in fact, enthusiastically—with many capable of shifting one-ton loads over a short distance.

They prefer outdoor living, with sufficient entertainment provided by their people, and are ready to join in almost any athletic activity. If bored, a Mal will express his displeasure by howling and digging to the South Pole!

Alaskan Malamute.

Alaskan Malamute.

Alaskan Malamute.

Alpine Dachsbracke, profile.

A short-legged hound for closer hunting and tracking was developed in Austria, as in other countries. But in the high altitude of the Alps, a larger dachsbracke was necessary, and the Austrian version is slightly bigger than his German cousin, the Westphalian. Like the other dachsbrackes and bassets, this breed has a normal hound body with short but not curved or twisted legs. He was created from the indigenous hounds of Austria.

The Alpine Dachsbracke is solid, robust, and heavily muscled, giving him an athletic and agile appearance. The coat, although not wiry, is harsh and dense. His stern, with a brush of hair, is extremely long, nearly reaching the ground. Unlike the Westphalian, this variety has no white markings. The standard lists solid black (without the tan markings), chocolate or gray-blue as disqualifications.

Mainly a coldtrailing hound on deer tracks, in full voice he is equally useful after rabbit and fox. The official standard of the breed calls him a "multiple utility dog of the Alpine hunter." A real professional at his craft, he has found little following outside of local gamekeepers and hunters.

Alpine Dachsbracke, red with black ticking.

ALPINE DACHSBRACKE

COUNTRY: Austria
WEIGHT: 33–40 pounds
HEIGHT: 13½–16½ inches, ideal 14-14½ inches
COAT: Short, coarse and hard
COLOR: Stag red, red with black ticking or black/tan, any white is undesirable
OTHER NAMES: Alpenlandischer Dachsbracke
REGISTRY: FCI
GROUP: Hound

American Black and Tan Coonhound.

AMERICAN BLACK AND TAN COONHOUND

COUNTRY: USA
HEIGHT: 23–27 inches
COAT: Short and dense
COLOR: Black with tan points
OTHER NAMES: Black and Tan Coonhound
REGISTRY: AKC, UKC, CKC
GROUP: Hound

Famed scouts and Indian fighters, Simon Kenton and the Poe brothers from the Ohio Valley, were among the first to foster the Black and Tan in the late 1700s. From Poe's stock and the later efforts of Simion Shirk and his grandson, Holmes Lingo, in the early 1800s, evolved the Old Glory strain of Black and Tans, the breed's most famous line which lasted in pure form for more than 130 years, until the mid-1940s. Other promoters of the breed, such as the Merritt Brothers of the 19th century and Don Stringer's Ten Oaks line of the 1920s–1940s, contributed to the modern development of the American Black and Tan breed.

American coonhounds were basically developed from foxhounds, with dashes of French, German and Irish dogs for specific needs. In fact, the AKC position early in this century was that these dogs were Foxhounds, and officials refused to register them as coonhounds. Therefore, breeders of these dogs turned to the United Kennel Club, which has sponsored coonhounds and their competitive events ever since.

The Black and Tan was the first "coonhound" to split off from the American Foxhound umbrella and, ironically, is the only one to be accepted by AKC. Black and Tans developed from early methodical, exquisitely cold-nosed "foxhounds." Most cynologists feel that a large percentage (at least) of the Kerry Beagle was in the stem stock.

The raccoon, an animal unknown in Europe, is a native of the Americas. "Coon" hunting became and has remained a passion with Americans, and the development of specific dogs for this sport ensued. The coon, when pursued, will finally climb a tree where the dogs hold it until the hunters arrive. This quarry is nocturnal, so hunting is done at night. A group of hounds are cast and, when one of them encounters a fresh coon trail, he "opens" or begins to bay.

Since each hound has a distinctive bawl, the handlers can identify which hound has opened on the trail. Then all the other hounds join the leader in following the scent and combine their voices. The hunters can follow the progress of the chase through the dark by the musical sounds of the hounds, heard for many miles as they pursue the quarry. When the dogs finally tree the raccoon, their voice tone changes, and the hunters then head toward the sound. Eavesdroppers on a typical hunt can hear, "There goes Babe. She's on the trail." Or, "Ol' Joker's got 'im treed."

The American Black and Tan is a big, rangy, strongly headed hound with abundant earage. He possesses a beautiful bugle voice and is a methodical hunter that leaves no stone unturned. E.S. Traverse, a knowledgeable houndsman, writes about the classic Black and Tan as "a cold-nosed hound that opened on tracks the other hounds didn't even know were there, with the determination to finish the track even if it led to Hell's backdoor." Because of these attributes, the Black and Tan has trailed boar, big cats and other similar game, as much or more than on raccoon, so that his specific talents can be fully utilized.

Today a few breeders foster the breed on the bench and occasional specimens are seen at AKC shows. The exhibition specimens have tended to become more refined and racy in type, and it would seem a shame to create a breed split in this fine old hound by forgetting its original use, purpose and proud history. Although called American Black and Tan Coonhound by the UKC, which registers 12,000 each year, the 600 registered by the AKC go by the shortened name of Black and Tan Coonhound.

The Black and Tans are calm, affectionate and good with children. They love being with people and are willing to please. Early socialization is suggested to insure confidence. Droopy ears must be kept clean to avoid odor and infections. Like most hounds, when they catch a scent, they're off and running, so owners are well advised to secure the dogs in an enclosure when not being worked.

The original coonhound, the American Black and Tan is possessed of a versatile, buglelike voice and hunts boar and big cat with the same vigor with which it hunts coon.

American Blue Gascon Hound.

AMERICAN BLUE GASCON HOUND

COUNTRY: USA
WEIGHT: 75–105 pounds
HEIGHT: 25–30 inches
COAT: Short, thick and dense
COLOR: Basically white body with tan points and heavy black ticking creating the "blue"; there are allowed natural variations in color including degree of ticking and roaning, amount of solid black spots, absence of tan marks, and sometimes a grizzled appearance
OTHER NAMES: Big 'n Blue
GROUP: Hound

Those hound aficionados favoring the big, strong-voiced, cold-nosed hound of the old "Gascon" type were forced to keep changing their allegiance. It wasn't the breed so much as the preservation of a type that these hunters wanted.

One of the most successful promoters of this type of hound was Wilson "Bluetick Bill" Harshman. For 30 years he hunted, bred, wrote about and organized events for these dogs. In the 1930s, Harshman wrote about the English Coonhound in a magazine, and later was the man most responsible for the bluetick faction breaking away. He wrote a book called *Big 'N' Blue,* a marvelous collection of stories and legends about the Old Line strain. This was how the American Blue Gascon came by its nickname.

In the 1950s, the sport of competitive night hunting was born. This called for the faster, racier, hotter nosed hound without the patience and thoroughness of the old type. Judging was based on the ability to tree the greatest number of raccoons in the shortest period of time, not the individual ability of each hound. The Redbone and Walker Hounds proved to be highly competitive in these events, and many Bluetick breeders began streamlining their hounds to cop the prizes as well. Those who loved the old Gascon type became alarmed and, in 1976, created the new American Blue Gascon Hound Association.

Ups and downs for the breed followed, but

currently there is a strong central organization to sponsor and maintain this type of hound which was never meant to compete with the speed of the streamlined hounds. The Blue Gascons were and still are prized as game-taking hounds; i.e., they are used on real animals in actual hunting situations. Capable of pursuing a wide variety of quarry including fox, badger, coyotes, wolverine and wild boar, the Big 'n Blue dogs are particularly suited to the big-game hunter going for bear, bobcat, jaguar or mountain lion. "They also make splendid coondogs for the man who hunts for the enjoyment of hearing and seeing good hounds work, or to experience that special bond between a man and his hound."

To insure the maintenance of the type, the breed organization requires all dogs to be examined for type, even those of registered parents, before permanent registration can be granted. The group has not sought UKC recognition, fearing loss of type if control escapes the breeders' hands.

This is not a hound for everyone, but he is excellent for specialized needs. His extremely large size and loud voice, which can be heard up to five miles, necessitate large spaces and remote areas. He is best suited to adverse terrain and poor hunting conditions, such as dry canyons, swamps and bayous, high altitudes or where game is quite scarce. The person who appreciates an American Blue Gascon is a sports enthusiast to whom the hunt is more important than the kill.

Stories, both modern and long past, show the heart of these hounds—tales of "Green's Scout," "Blue," and "Sport." Scout and Blue were two well-known hounds of the late 1930s and early 1940s. One day they hit a bear track in the Wasatch Mountains of Utah and were never seen or heard from again. Sport's spectacular leap of 150 feet from a bluff into water won his owner a field trial in the early 1920s. More recently, "Sugar Creek Blue Ben" kept a lion treed for three days during sub-zero weather in the Bitterroot Mountains of Montana.

It is no wonder that the Blue Gascon is admired for its stamina, perseverance, desire and hunting abilities. These are truly dogs of great heart. They are bold with people they know, aloof with strangers and sometimes protective.

AMERICAN BULLDOG

COUNTRY: USA
WEIGHT: 65–105 pounds
HEIGHT: 19–25 inches
COAT: Short, smooth
COLOR: Preferred in following order—red brindle, all other brindles; solid white, red, fawn or fallow; piebald
OTHER NAMES: Old Country Bulldog, Old English White
GROUP: Mastiff

The old-time bull-baiters did more than provide a day's entertainment. One of the excuses given for baiting was to tenderize the meat. Notices of a bull-baiting were considered advertising for a fresh meat sale, long before refrigeration made that commodity available. Dogs were expected to fight until the bull submitted—or their own

American Bulldog.

death. When tossed, the owner would attempt to catch the dog on a leather apron or, amazingly, on a bamboo pole which the dog then slid down. No matter what the injuries—cracked ribs, injured back, ripped or gored hide—if the dog could walk, it was expected to continue its bloody battle. After the bull was called on a technical KO, and before he was killed, the young canine apprentices were allowed to rush the victim for a "taste of blood."

The American Bulldog, as opposed to today's familiar English version, is very similar to the old 17th-century bull-baiter. If that's confusing, it's because the modern English Bulldog has been changed, modified, improved or exaggerated, depending on who's making the statement.

The original "bulldogge" was first brought to American shores in early colonial times. Here he did not undergo the "improvement" of his English cousins and has come down to the present day in his generally original form.

The American Bulldog remains higher on the leg, more agile and swifter than its English counterpart. This dog can leap eight feet into the air and "turn on a dime." He has tenacity, an iron jaw, small flap or rolled ears and, usually, a long, low tail.

The American version is now an all-around dog, used for protecting homes, with some owners hunting raccoons, squirrels and even wild hogs and bears with their Bulldogs. They boast longevity of up to 16 years, and these dogs are still capable of wrestling down a cantankerous bull. Farmers find all these qualities attractive for a working farm dog and companion.

Reputable breeders recount myriad tales showing the heroism of these dogs. They do not wait for a command, but assess the situation themselves and react appropriately. To protect their masters, they have fought wild dogs, bulls and even fire. It is said that "fighting off one of these dogs is like fighting an animal that possesses an alligator's head and a python's body." Yet when called off by their handler, they immediately obey. No wonder they are said to have "true grit, true devotion and true love." This breed genuinely loves children.

Other types of American or "original" Bulldogs are being bred in the USA. While some are merely dogs crossbred in an attempt to produce

American Bulldog.

something that looks like the former dog, others are truly descendants of early dogs. Some of these latter are called Old Country Bulldogs or Old English Whites and are common in the southern states where they are used as boar dogs.

A small underground faction continues to illegally fight these dogs. This activity is not encouraged or promoted by the breed organization or by reputable breeders.

American Bulldogs are registered with the Game American Bulldog Club (GABC). Some recently have been placed on military bases as Marine mascots.

American Cocker Spaniel, buff.

AMERICAN COCKER SPANIEL

COUNTRY: USA
WEIGHT: 24–28 pounds
HEIGHT: 15 inches maximum
COAT: Long and silky, very abundant, especially the feathering
COLOR: Solid black (including black/tan); any solid color other than black (called ASCOB) such as chocolate, red, buff, sable, cream; particolored; not more than a third of the ground color of any of the other allowed colors, including tri
OTHER NAMES: Cocker Spaniel
REGISTRY: FCI, AKC, UKC, TKC, CKC
GROUP: Gun Dog

The American version of the Cocker Spaniel evolved from early spaniel imports. By the 1930s, this Cocker was much smaller than his English ancestors and had other conformation differences, so the breed was given separate status. Not long after that, in the 1940s, he had changed even more dramatically so that he bore almost no resemblance to his English counterpart.

Early AKC spaniel trials included classes for Cockers, and the little spaniel was used frequently for gunning. During the middle of this century, a Cocker served as friend and playmate in many a household during the week and as a working assistant to the hunter on the weekend. For many years, no competitions were held for the Cocker's field ability, but with AKC's new hunting tests for spaniels, owners once again can try their dogs with game. His modern propensity is mainly as a pet and a show dog. In the 1940s, the Cocker rose to first in AKC registrations and remained there for some time. Displaced by the Poodle for a number of years, he has since regained the top spot in AKC registrations.

For a breed to go to the top in registrations and stay there, he must have a lot of good things going for him. The modern American Cocker is a happy, trusting, intelligent, as well as handsome, companion dog.

His head is domed, with a short, deep muzzle and abrupt stop. Short of back and up on leg, his usual dramatic angulation allows tremendous reach and drive in a small package. The luxurious coat, with thick feathering on legs and belly nearly reaching the ground, creates a picture hard to resist by dog show judge and puppy buyer alike. But prospective owners should be aware of the care necessary to keep that lovely coat "in the pink."

Buyers should also seek the merry temperament, avoiding any fear or stand-offishness exhibited by the parents. As so often happens when puppies are in high demand, the unscrupulous and unknowledgeable "backyard" breeders and disreputable puppy millers rush to fill the demand. Conscientious Cocker fanciers have some of the finest tempered animals in all of dogdom. But it is no secret that there are frightened and snappish examples of this breed produced when the sale of puppies is the only goal.

Hunting instincts are still present inside that well-coiffed body. The superabundant coat, however, does make field work difficult. The Cocker is a good obedience worker, because of his happy nature and desire to please. He fits into almost any household, adapting to a variety of age groups and lifestyles.

American Cocker Spaniel, parti-color.

American Cocker Spaniel.

American Cocker Spaniel, chocolate.

American Cocker Spaniel, parti-color.

American Cocker Spaniels.

AMERICAN ESKIMOS

American Eskimo, Standard

COUNTRY: USA
WEIGHT: 18–35 pounds
HEIGHT: 14–19 inches
COAT: Thick, straight spitz type
COLOR: Pure white preferred, white with biscuit or cream permissible
REGISTRY: UKC
GROUP: Northern

American Eskimo, Miniature

COUNTRY: USA
WEIGHT: 10–20 pounds
HEIGHT: 11–15 inches
COAT: Thick, straight spitz type
COLOR: Pure white preferred, white with biscuit or cream permissible
REGISTRY: UKC
GROUP: Northern

American Eskimo, Toy

COUNTRY: USA
WEIGHT: 6–10 pounds
HEIGHT: Males less than 12, females less than 11 inches
COAT: Thick, straight spitz type
COLOR: Pure white preferred, white with biscuit or cream permissible
GROUP: Northern

Standard American Eskimo.

The only spitz breed created and fostered in America, the American Eskimo is probably related to and descended from white German Spitz dogs. In fact, many people still refer to this breed as "spitz," a carry-over from 100 years ago. During their beginnings in America, most of these Nordic beauties were rather large. When they began to be registered by the United Kennel Club in the early part of this century, owners adopted the name "Eskimo" as a tribute to their ancient Nordic ancestry and "American" for their immediate foster home. The Standard and Miniature sizes have been bred since the start of the 20th century. A toy-sized American Eskimo has evolved, and fanciers are working toward gaining acceptance for that miniscule variety in the UKC show ring. Except for size, all three forms of the breed are judged by the identical standard of perfection.

Like all of the European spitz, the American Eskie is noted for being sturdy, hardy, and long-lived. These canines are natural watchdogs, tending to bark if there is something wrong or unusual. With their owners, they are very affectionate and willing to please, making them ideal obedience prospects. Eskies do, however, tend to be reserved with strangers at first, the watchdog instinct impelling them to be sure before allowing a breach in their protection of family and

108

home. They have a need to be near their owners and feel a part of things. Because of the northern heritage, the breed can be a bit stubborn and willful but cheerfully submits to the owner's wishes if taught from the beginning, firmly and consistently. Because of their intelligence, energy and desire to please, they also make outstanding trick dogs, performing in circuses and shows.

The coat, as is true with all of the spitz dogs, is described as self-cleaning, i.e., the harsh-textured, straight hair shakes off dirt or mud when dry. The dense underwool precludes the dog from getting wet to the skin from the environ-

ment. Thus, they have little doggy odor and, even though white, stay "spic and span" clean. But, again, like their cousins from Europe and the North, there is need for routine brushing, especially in the spring when the undercoat is being shed.

True to their species, the Eskies love to be outdoors, using their doghouses rarely, often curling up in a snow bank with their tails covering the tip of their noses. Although a perennial favorite in the United States, the Eskie is unknown elsewhere, probably due to the fact that many countries have developed their own type of white spitz.

American Eskimo puppies.

Above: Toy American Eskimo. **Below:** Standard American Eskimo.

Standard American Eskimos.

American Foxhound, tricolor.

AMERICAN FOXHOUND

COUNTRY: USA
HEIGHT: 21–25 inches
COAT: Close and hard, not too short
COLOR: Any color
REGISTRY: FCI, AKC, UKC, CKC
GROUP: Hound

Because America was a great melting pot for immigrants, it was also a large mixing cauldron for dogs as well. Immigrants from all over the world, if they could afford the passage, brought their dogs with them. Colonial America was a vast wilderness in which hunting was not only a hobby but often a necessity. Hounds from many countries proved most useful in this young land and, in the spirit of democracy, little worry was wasted about pedigree and purity as long as the dogs were good hunters. Thus, the exact development of the American hounds is only generally known with much overlap, conflict and even fabrication of history.

Since so many of the settlers on American shores were British, it is only logical that the majority of the hounds came with them. English Foxhounds formed the general basis for the American version, but there were Irish, French and other additions as well.

One of the first packs was brought to America in 1650 by Robert Brooke of Maryland. They were black and tan and did well on the slower gray fox which went to ground sooner. Often recorded as English hounds, these dogs now are felt by many to be of the Irish Kerry Beagle type because of their color, size and style of working. With the introduction of the speedy English red fox to America in the 1700s, hunters soon wanted a hotter nosed animal with more speed, so dogs with more of an English type were used. Brooke's line became the basis for the Black and Tan Coonhound, which would be developed later.

George Washington was a dedicated fox hunter and maintained a choice breeding program and good records. French hounds given to him by Lafayette were used for their abilities and their beautiful voices. Many other breeders developed their own strains and types over the years, based on how the hounds were to be used.

Pioneers often hunted the fox with one hound and a gun, requiring a methodical dog with great nose and persistence. This type of hound was more akin to the French hounds or the German schweisshunds and was often used later for bigger game such as wild cats, boar, coyote and bear. Others pursued the fox, or *renard*, in a group with a pack of hounds. For the formal style of group hunting, many clubs did (and still do) use purebred English Foxhounds. But others, especially those who liked informal group night hunts, developed their own strains of rangier, leggier foxhounds.

These pack hounds are the closest to what is

American Foxhound.

known by AKC as the American Foxhound. They are taller, a bit lighter boned, and longer eared than their English ancestors, but are close enough to often be mistaken for one another. Other hound fanciers favored competitive events with both night field trials and drag trials being developed. This necessitated the use of hounds that were not only faster and hotter nosed, but were more individualistic and competitive than those who happily cooperated in a pack.

For decades, this whole gamut of early "fox-hounds" slowly separated into a variety of breeds and types. Hounds of the slower, indi-vidually hunting type developed into the cold-nosed American breeds such as the Black and Tan, the American Blue Gascon and the Majes-tic Tree Hound, as well as the Plott Hound. From the speedier, competitive dogs came the faster, treeing breeds like the Treeing Walker and the Redbone Coonhound. And from the middle ground, there remained a wide diver-gence of true Foxhounds.

Various strains of American Foxhounds have persisted over the years. Famous lines such as the Henry Birdsong and July hounds date from the early 1800s, as do the Walker strains from which the Coonhound of that name later devel-oped. Any mixed breed hound that bears the solid tan color is often called a "July." The July-type Foxhound, often of a solid red or tan color, is still used throughout the country for hunting coyote and other game. Colonel Haiden Trigg of Kentucky developed a renowned strain of blueticked, white-collared hounds in the late 1800s based on Walker, Birdsong and July dogs. The Trigg hound is often erroneously referred to as a separate breed. Modern hunts have de-veloped their own strains, such as the currently well-known black/tan Penn Merrydales.

The AKC Foxhound is very small in actual registration numbers, even though the various strains, not registered with any formal body, represent a large population of American practi-cal hunting hounds.

American Hairless Terrier.

AMERICAN HAIRLESS TERRIER

COUNTRY: USA
WEIGHT: 7–14 pounds
HEIGHT: 9–14 inches
COAT: Hairless
COLOR: Pink skin with gray, black, golden or red spots
REGISTRY: None
GROUP: Terrier

In 1972 one entirely hairless female appeared in a litter of medium-sized Rat Terriers. She was normal in every other way and became the beloved pet of Willie and Edwin Scott of Louisiana. They and several acquaintances grew so fond of their pet "Josephine" that they wanted to produce more of the hairless pups. Jo produced one hairless female in her first litter, but through the next several litters, the little terrier failed to whelp any more exhibiting the hairless trait. Finally, at the age of nine years, she

crowned her attempts by having a litter with two hairless pups, one of each sex. These became the foundation of a breeding program to produce and stabilize the breed, which the Scotts named the American Hairless Terrier.

The Scotts, with the help and cooperation of geneticists and veterinarians, are still working toward their goal of establishing this breed. They want to keep the true type and temperament of the Rat Terrier while maintaining the hairless trait. Hairless advantages naturally include no shedding and the complete absence of fleas—both things many owners would covet! The gene responsible for this form of hairlessness has been proven, through careful breeding trials, to be an autosomal recessive. This is distinctively different from the semi-lethal dominant genetic pattern seen in the pariah-type hairless breeds. The recessive hairlessness is not associated with missing teeth and skin problems often seen in the dominant form.

Hairless-to-hairless breedings always produce 100-percent hairless puppies. Hairless-to-coated matings produce variable results, depending on chance and whether the coated dog is a carrier of the hairless trait. Hairless pups are born with a bit of sparse fuzzy hair all over their body. The pup begins to shed this fuzz, starting with the head, proceeding backwards, becoming entirely—and eternally—hairless by the age of six weeks. American Hairless Terriers do not have tufts of hair on the head, feet and end of tail, as do the Chinese Cresteds. They do, however, have normal eyebrows and whiskers.

The breed can be born with short or full-length tails, each being left in its natural state. The only special care required is preventing sunburn and keeping them warm in cold weather. The ears stand in a natural state, and are called bat, similar to the Rat Terrier's. These dogs make excellent companions for anyone, especially children or the elderly.

Right and Below: American Hairless Terrier.

American Pit Bull Terrier, brindle.

AMERICAN PIT BULL TERRIER

COUNTRY: USA
WEIGHT: 50–80 pounds
HEIGHT: 18–22 inches
COAT: Short, smooth
COLOR: All colors
OTHER NAMES: American Pit Bull, Pit Bull Terrier
REGISTRY: UKC
GROUP: Mastiff

The ancient molossus was the root of all fighting dogs, producing the bull-baiting dogs, which later were crossbred with terriers for ratting, badger hunting and dog-fighting. For many years, the term "pit bull" was given to any dog of the fighting pits. The United Kennel Club originally registered these breeds of dogs and, at one time, regulated dog-fighting.

Pit Bulls are still registered with UKC, but dog-fighting is illegal and any that still occurs takes place "underground" without the kennel club's approval. In fact, both AKC and UKC outlaw any dog and/or owner involved in dog-

Above: American Pit Bull Terriers; brindle (left), liver (right). **Below:** American Pit Bull Terrier, fawn.

American Pit Bull Terrier, parti-color.

fighting, and the old "battle scars" are no longer allowable in the show ring. Although fight advocates claim most contests are over in a couple minutes and that few dogs die, some matches continue for as long as two hours. It is a sad, but true, fact that the Commission on Animal Care and Control of Chicago estimates 1,500 dogs die annually due to organized dogfighting. The fights draw gamblers and high stakes, with one raid netting 20 people who had $500,000 along with assorted illegal weapons and drugs.

These dogs have been the victim of a witch-hunt in recent years. Because of their instinctive hostility toward other animals, it has been assumed they will attack people. This aggression has been sought, encouraged, and malevolently intensified by some disreputable owners. These people have misdirected the dog's instincts toward all animals *and* people. The breed has received bad press, and legitimate, dedicated owners of Pit Bulls have paid the price, along with their dogs, since the breed has been outlawed in several communities. Other breeds have also been placed on the "most wanted" list. Like all dogs, particularly those originally bred for aggressive purposes, the Pit Bull should be selected from temperamentally sound parents, bought from responsible breeders, socialized from puppyhood, trained and handled properly.

Not all Pit Bulls are bad, but they *are* strong and, when tested, they *do* attack with a bone-crushing, mutilating bite. They are too much dog for the average dog owner, and should only be purchased by people who are willing and strong enough to channel that power into productive areas. Nevertheless, they are loving and protective of their families, and owners report them particularly responsive to training: herding, obedience, schutzhund and weight-pulling. An incredible Pit Bull weighing less than 70 pounds set a record by pulling 2,000 pounds. A host of admirers included Helen Keller, Theodore Roosevelt, Thomas Edison (whose dog, "Nipper," was the RCA model) and Jimmy Carter, who had one as a boy. Actors Michael J. Fox and James Caan are current owners.

Since the early 1900s, the AKC has called the breed American Staffordshire Terriers; UKC registers them as Pit Bulls. Pit Bulls are robust, courageous and stoic, although they are also laid-back and calm. Ears are cropped, and grooming is almost non-existent. The "Pit Bull smile" and humorous play ingratiate them to their masters and others.

AMERICAN STAFFORDSHIRE TERRIER

COUNTRY: USA
WEIGHT: 40–50 pounds
HEIGHT: 17–19 inches
COAT: Smooth
COLOR: Any color—solid, parti or patched, but black/tan, liver or more than 80 percent white not to be encouraged
REGISTRY: FCI, AKC, UKC, CKC
GROUP: Mastiff

The American Staffordshire Terrier's ancestor, the Staffordshire Bull Terrier, was developed in England and brought to the United States in the mid-19th century to compete in the fighting pits. "Cockney" Charlie Lloyd is credited with bringing over "Pilot," "Paddy" and other dogs who figured in the formation of the American strain. Breeders increased the size and height of the British version, and ears were cropped to accentuate the more massive head and to prevent them from being ripped in a fight. Over the years, this dog has been labeled with a variety of

American Staffordshire Terriers, parti-color.

American Staffordshire Terrier, gray.

names: Bull-and-Terrier, Half-and-Half, Pit Dog, Pit Bull Terrier, American Bull Terrier and even Yankee Terrier. While some of their brethren were sentenced to life in the pits, other more fortunate American Staffordshire Terriers guarded the frontier families and homesteads.

In 1900, dog-fighting was generally outlawed in America, and a group of fanciers, who were opposed to any association with the crime, wanted to promote other characteristics of the breed. The American Staffordshire served its country during WWI, with "Stubby" becoming the most decorated war dog and earning the rank of sergeant. It was important to the new breed image to avoid breed names associated with the pits. Breeder Joe Dunn headed the movement to bring together a club, which resulted in the name (and the breed) Staffordshire Terrier being recognized by AKC in 1936. The word American was added, in 1972, to differentiate from AKC's newly recognized Staffordshire Bull Terrier. A modest demand for AmStaffs exists in America, but they are rarely seen in Canada.

During the breed's early years of AKC competition, an engaging group of kids entertained American children. These "Little Rascals," (or "Our Gang") had a constant pal in "Pete," their black-eyed Staff, also claimed as a Pit Bull.

Even at the nadir of dog-fighting, the hostility was toward other dogs, not to people. This dog was specifically chosen for his acceptance of being grasped or restrained by his handler, even during the frenzy of a fight.

The modern version of the breed is affectionate and reliable with people and, in fact, the high tolerance which served them well in the blood sport gives them unusual patience with children. They barely notice an infant chewing on their ear or a toddler playing "horsie." An occasional bump with a crutch or wheelchair is taken with good humor, making them good companions for the handicapped. Despite this amiability with humans, some Staffs retain their terrierlike pugnacity toward other animals, and owners must be capable of maintaining control.

Their coat requires only a couple swipes with the brush to stay neat. The breed has an uncanny ability to discern between friend and foe. All these qualities, plus their robust good health, make them a good choice whether on farms or in apartments.

American Staffordshire Terrier, fawn.

American Water Spaniel.

AMERICAN WATER SPANIEL

COUNTRY: USA
WEIGHT: 25–45 pounds
HEIGHT: 15–18 inches
COAT: Thick, close curls or a marcelled effect all over, except smooth on the head
COLOR: Solid liver or dark chocolate
REGISTRY: FCI, AKC, UKC, CKC
GROUP: Gun Dog

The origin of this All-American has not been recorded. Among his forebears were various forms of water dogs and spaniels which accompanied immigrants and settlers. Originally, the breed was called the Brown Water Spaniel.

Development occurred in the late 1800s, basically along the great Mississippi flyway, where the waterfowl migrated north and south each year. He was used as a jump-shooting retriever especially in northern Minnesota, which is full of small lakes and pot holes (ponds). To get close enough to shoot the ducks feeding at these waterholes, the hunter and his dog had to crawl the last 50 or so yards. The hunter then "jumped" the ducks and shot, the brown spaniel retrieved them whether they fell on land or in water. His small size also made him an easy dog to tote in a skiff for hunting in open water or from a blind. The natural camouflage of his brown jacket matches the fall flora. He hunts small game as well.

As the 20th century progressed, British retrievers became more prevalent, and the little American brown spaniel, as he was known at the time, began to disappear. Doctor F.J. Pfeifer is credited with rescuing the breed from obscurity through the creation of a written standard and promotion with a breed club. His efforts paved the way for AKC recognition; in fact, his own dog, "Curley Pfeifer," was the first AKC registered American Water Spaniel.

Although very few specimens are seen at dog shows, they still enjoy moderate but steady favor among hunters and as family pets. The brown spaniel is a dog of the common folk, and has the great charm and easy trainability of the true spaniel. The parallel waves of "marcelled" hair are the desired coat type, although a tighter curl is also allowed. The ears are covered with profuse curls, as is the tail, and only his face is smooth haired. The body is a bit longer than tall. He is essentially unknown outside of North America.

ANATOLIAN SHEPHERD DOG

COUNTRY: Turkey
WEIGHT: 80–150 pounds
HEIGHT: 27–30 inches
COAT: Short to medium
COLOR: Usually black-masked fawns, some brindles, tricolors, whites and blacks
OTHER NAMES: Anatolian Karabash Dog
REGISTRY: TKC
GROUP: Flock Guard

With a history spanning centuries of breeding and use—without benefit of any recorded pedigrees or even official names—the large Turkish guarding breeds have been named and categorized by Westerners. They are all ancient Turkish guard dogs, but there is argument over whether they should be "split" or "lumped." Some owners have selected stem stock from specific localities in Turkey, where one set of characteristics was fixed, and made individual breeds from each. Other dog buyers came into Turkey and chose representatives of Turkish guard dogs (in Turkish, the generic *çoban kopegi* or shepherd dog) from various locales. This broad approach has created the breed known as the Anatolian.

The Anatolian was once used as a combat dog and for hunting big game (i.e., lions and horses). They stem directly from ancient flock-guarding and mastiff dogs of the Middle East. The breed is now used as the front-line defense for Turkish flocks. His strength and speed are legendary in his homeland, allowing him to take on such formidable opponents as wolves.

The breed is dominant with all other dogs, males asserting influence over females. With wolves their natural enemies, Anatolian Shepherd Dogs tend to be suspicious of all dogs with upright ears.

American Robert C. Ballard remembers his adventurous search for his Anatolian pup: "Finally we were invited outside to see the stud. He was big—about 130 pounds, rather ferocious looking—overall a fine specimen. Most memorable, though, was the chain leash, heavy enough for tractor towing, and the stance of the handler who was braced as if expecting the dog to lurch or lunge at any moment." Ballard brought the

Anatolian Shepherd Dog, black masked fawn.

first examples of this breed to America toward the end of the 1960s.

Turkish lore says that the dog receives his collar after detecting, outrunning and killing his first wolf. Actually, these collars help to protect them against the wolf. While in Turkey, a tourist observed that other dogs respected and did not challenge those with collars. He bought one for his Anatolian, which was then elevated to a level of respect. Local canines and citizens alike assumed the dog had won the collar in mortal combat.

These dogs are loyal to their masters, but suspicious of strangers, and demonstrate guard instincts at an early age. Obedience training and socialization are strongly urged for acclimating the breed to life as a controllable family dog.

The Anatolian is gentle and playful with children of the family. However, it will tolerate no teasing from strangers. Owners stress that these dogs are not "gentle giants." Formal introductions should be protocol with neighbors, friends and the veterinarian. Breeders suggest leaving a note for delivery drivers not to enter an Anatolian's turf.

A fiercely loyal guard dog, the Anatolian is possessive toward family, property and livestock. It is not unusual for an Anatolian to seek a high vantage point—a hill of dirt if necessary—to survey its domain. Highly territorial, a dog with no family or stock to protect will guard even its dirt mound!

Barks or howls greet an intruder. If the challenger is wise enough to retreat, Anatolians do not attack. However, upon provocation, they have offered fair warning and don't run from a fight. In one instance, hounds made a fatal error, taking a direct route through a flock after a raccoon. The guarding dog systematically killed each hound as it came through the fence.

A blunt muzzle and low-set ears show the mastiff influence on the Anatolian. Its structure and movement give a lionlike impression. This is particularly true when the ears are cropped to erect stubs, as they sometimes are in Turkey. The tail is curled over the back when the dog is alert.

Size is impressive, with pups showing rapid growth. Typical records show pups weighing 15 pounds at seven weeks, and 42 pounds just five weeks later. They are sturdy dogs, working into their teens, at home in rugged terrains and extreme climates from 60 degrees below zero to 120 above.

This dog is hardy, an easy keeper and a free-thinker. During hot weather, it may dig an underground shelter to reach cooler ground. The breed seems to have a keen sense of smell, as one owner reported his dog pawing eagerly through a stack of papers on a chair. When the dog reached one handled by his breeders, he rested his head on it!

Enthusiasts in the United States are actively promoting the breed, and several Anatolians are participants in flock-guarding programs. Their club members hold specialty shows for the breed and admirers are working diligently toward AKC recognition. The breed is recognized in England, with numerous entries at larger shows, such as Crufts.

Anatolian Karabash Dog Club of Great Britain contends that dogs must have tan with black mask (karabash meaning black head). The Anatolian Shepherd Dog Club of Great Britain and the Anatolian Shepherd Dog Club of America maintain that color variety is normal and predictable.

Anatolian Shepherd Dog, cream.

ANGLOS-FRANCAISES

Grand Anglo-Francais

COUNTRY: France
WEIGHT: 66–71 pounds
HEIGHT: 24–27 inches
COAT: Short and smooth
COLOR: Black and white, orange and white, or tricolor
OTHER NAMES: Large French-English Hound
REGISTRY: FCI
GROUP: Hound

Anglo-Francais de Moyen Venerie

COUNTRY: France
WEIGHT: 49–55 pounds
HEIGHT: 20 inches
COAT: Short and smooth
COLOR: Black and white, orange and white, or tricolor
OTHER NAMES: Middle-sized French-English Hound
GROUP: Hound

Anglo-Francais de Petite Venerie

COUNTRY: France
WEIGHT: 34–44 pounds
HEIGHT: 16–18 inches
COAT: Short and smooth
COLOR: Black and white, orange and white, or tricolor
OTHER NAMES: Small French-English Hound
REGISTRY: FCI
GROUP: Hound

Grand Anglo-Francais.

The bulk of the working packs in France today falls under the category that the survey committee termed Anglo-Francais. Resulting from the crossing of French and English hounds, these dogs are rarely exhibited and are strictly utilitarian.

The Grand is the result of crossing the bigger French hounds with the English Foxhound. He carries more bone and less ear than his pure French cousins. FCI actually recognizes three color variations of Large: the Black/White, the Tricolor and the Orange/White.

Harriers and the medium French hounds, such as the Poitevin and Porcelaine, contributed to the Middle-sized Anglo-Francais. As a fast hound, he is useful for all types of small game over a variety of terrain. Except for size, this type is similar in appearance to the Grand. The Moyen, also, is divided into three color classifications.

The Petite was the result of blending the smaller French hounds, for instance the d'Artois, with the Beagle. Like his larger brothers, the Petite is a good tracker, and packs are useful when hunting rabbit, pheasant or quail.

These smaller dogs were not sufficiently pure to create a standard, but FCI does recognize them. They look much like the large and medium sizes, a mid-type between the hounds of France and England.

The Petite has readily adapted to indoor life, where it has proven to be tranquil and clean. This variety also separates into three color varieties. At one time, there were wire-coated (griffon) versions of all the sizes and colors of the Anglo-Francais, but interest in these variations waned and the wires seem to have disappeared.

Above: Grand Anglo-Francais. **Below:** Anglo-Francais de Petite Venerie, tricolor.

Above: Anglo-Francais de Moyen Venerie, tricolor. **Below:** Anglo-Francais de Petite Venerie, orange and white.

Appenzeller.

APPENZELLER

COUNTRY: Switzerland
WEIGHT: 49–55 pounds
HEIGHT: 19–23 inches
COAT: Short, smooth
COLOR: Black and tan, with white at toes, tail tip, chest, and blaze. The tan always lies between the black and the white.
OTHER NAMES: Appenzell Mountain Dog, Appenzeller Sennenhund
REGISTRY: FCI
GROUP: Mastiff

As Caesar's legions swept into Switzerland through the Mons Jovis (St. Bernard) pass, their dogs accompanied them to guard the stock and encampments. A descendant of these molossus breeds, the Appenzeller is one of the four Swiss sennenhunds, which offer a choice of sizes to please "big men" to "junior petites." The Appenzeller was most likely developed through crossing with the smaller herding dogs like the Puli. The Eastern influence is suspected due to its tail curled over the back, as well as the mental traits of high energy and watchfulness.

As sure-footed in the mountains as the goats they watched, these dogs were valued by farmers for sundry tasks. When market day came, Appenzellers were harnessed to carts and hauled the goat milk and cheese to town.

In modern times, the breed is dependable and alert as an alarm dog. He adapts easily to his family's needs and, in fact, is happiest when working at some chore, side-by-side with his master.

Owners stress the need for more space, and a more active lifestyle than the other three Swiss mountain dogs. When given the opportunity to expend his energy, the Appenzeller is content to stay within home boundaries. The breed's extroverted demeanor is accentuated by its vocal enthusiasm for life.

As well as farm work in his native Switzerland, the Appenzeller serves as a rescue dog in avalanches and other catastrophes. He participates in obedience and schutzhund trials as well. His prowess as a herder and companion, and the pride of his owner, is depicted on the traditional handworked collars which the dogs still wear on special occasions. Brass figures of cattle and hikers decorate the wide leather neckpieces.

All four Swiss sennenhunds have handsome, rich, glossy coats and pleasant personalities. They differ mainly in size, tail characteristics, and coat length.

Appenzeller.

Ariégeois.

ARIÉGEOIS

COUNTRY: France
WEIGHT: 66 pounds
HEIGHT: 22–24 inches
COAT: Short and smooth
COLOR: Tricolor, with the black and tan mostly on the head; a few body patches allowed, but the body is basically clear white without ticking
REGISTRY: FCI
GROUP: Hound

This comparative newcomer to the world of hounds originated in 1912. Ariége province, for which the breed is named, is in the very south of France on the Spanish border, midway between the Atlantic and the Mediterranean. Breeders used Bleu de Gascogne, Gascon Saintongeois, and Chien d'Artois in the formation of this hound. Hunting in packs, they are hare dogs par excellence, demonstrating skill over all terrain. They have gained little notice outside their own region, perhaps because the locals referred to them as half-blood or bastard hounds (*batards*) due to their recent blending of breeds.

The Gaston Phoebus Club in southwestern France has promoted the breed, since its recent birth, through pack trials at the Ceron Villa. The Ariége hound is a handsome and vigorous dog, serene and affectionate in the home. He looks very similar to the Grand Bleu de Gascogne without the ticking and in a smaller package.

Ariégeois.

Armant, black.

ARMANT

COUNTRY: Egypt
WEIGHT: 50–60 pounds
HEIGHT: 22 inches
COAT: Long, shaggy and rough
COLOR: Black, black/tan, gray and grayish yellow
OTHER NAMES: Ermenti, Egyptian Sheepdog
REGISTRY: None
GROUP: Herding

Napoleon's armies brought the Armant's ancestors to Egypt, where these Briard types bred with native dogs. Named after a village in northern Egypt, the Armant was used first as a drover and guardian of the herds. The breed excels as watchdogs, and these dogs are sometimes called *sabe*, Arabic for lion, symbolizing their ferocity and the legend of their leonine descent.

The Armant is a large, square, powerful dog with a strong muzzle. His mask is dark, and the shaggy coat forms a mustache and topknot. The topknot, muzzle and chest are white. The small ears may be drop or prick and the tail long or docked.

With battles erupting in the Middle East, the current status of the breed is unknown. Recent travelers have found examples of this dog, but type varies greatly and the purity of breeding programs is not known. Others may still exist in isolated areas. The FCI has dropped them from their list of recognized breeds.

Armant, black/tan.

ARYAN MOLOSSUS

COUNTRY: Afghanistan
WEIGHT: Up to 200 pounds
HEIGHT: 34 inches
COAT: Short, plush and dense; abundant undercoat
COLOR: Dark sables; very little white
GROUP: Mastiff

Probably closely related to both the Kangal Dog of Turkey and the Tibetan Mastiff, this ancient breed was utilized by primitive tribes to settle land and tribal disputes. When villagers argued over grazing areas, goat herd ownership or other grievances, a dog from each tribe was placed in the pit to fight out the dispute. Owners of the winning dog were declared victorious. . . with no further argument. This primitive prelude to a third-party decision of a jury or judge eliminated warring and unnecessary loss of life.

The canines were bred, raised and trained by "dog specialists" not affiliated with any tribe. When disputes were percolating, tribal leaders, who were astute experts in such matters, went to the "dog man" and dickered for the best animal. The chosen title contender stayed with his breeder until the day of the contest, when he fought in a pit at the dog compound or was delivered to neutral ground. Only the men came to watch the fight. Tails were painted or dyed so that the opponents could be easily identified during the fracas. Dogs often fought to the death; if not, the loser was necessarily destroyed.

These dogs were extremely large and fractious, with their tails held high and loosely curled over the backs. Loose skin hanging on the head and throat protected them during the vicious melee. Nobody but the owner ever handled them—or cared to, due to their fierce reputation, although they were even-tempered with their "promoter."

These dogs have been moved into the highest mountains and hidden from the Russian army recruitment. Because of expense in upkeep, their numbers were always limited, with breeders retaining just a few title contenders. Their current status is endangered by the Russian occupation of the country, which has overturned old tribal customs.

AUSTRALIAN CATTLE DOG

COUNTRY: Australia
WEIGHT: 35–45 pounds
HEIGHT: 17–20 inches
COAT: Medium-short, harsh, straight, dense
COLOR: Blue speckled, with black, blue or tan markings on head; red speckled, with darker red markings on head
OTHER NAMES: Australian Queensland Heeler, Blue Heeler
REGISTRY: FCI, AKC, UKC, TKC, CKC
GROUP: Herding

Australian Cattle Dog, blue speckled.

Derived through intensive and careful cross-breeding over a 60–year period, the Australian Cattle Dog was the result of the deliberate introduction of various breeds serving specific purposes. The AuCaDo came into being because imported herding dogs were not capable of controlling the tough cattle on long treks to market. Most existing herding dogs, i.e., the Smithfields or the Black Bobtail, drove by barking and running after the cattle. The Black Bobtail, according to Robert Kaleski, ". . . bit like an alligator and barked like a consumptive," spooking the wilder cattle native to Australia and running the meat off them. The dogs used for driving these cattle had their problems too. All the running and barking on the journeys from the outback wore them out, and they were in as poor shape as the cattle by the time they arrived at market.

A native wild dog, known as the Dingo, was a silent worker that conserved energy, driving herds by biting or nipping at strays. The Dingo performed well in high temperatures, but was naturally aggressive and too wild to train.

During the 1830s the running, biting, barking Smithfield Collie was experimentally crossed with the silent-working Dingo. The offspring were called Timmon's Biters, which eliminated the barking problem, but accentuated the biting.

Later, in 1840, Thomas Hall, a squatter with two blue-merle, smooth-coated Collies, took a daring step by breeding his purebred Scottish imports to the Dingo. The half-breeds were impressive workers, and the best were retained. The red or blue get, called Hall's Heelers, were hardy, silent drovers with prick ears. Further breeding experiments incorporating the Dingo, Timmon's Biters and Hall's Heelers were conducted by others.

Dr. Allen McNiven conducted an extensive breeding program and found that it takes 12 generations to get a good AuCaDo. He noted, "Most of the first generations run off." McNiven had men from the outback follow a Dingo slut for two weeks prior to whelping. When the pups were about two weeks old, a male would be taken from the litter while the dam was away hunting for food. They chose only the heavy-boned Red Deer Dingo because of its good head and intelligence. This male would be bred to one of McNiven's Blue Merle Collies. As Dingoes mate for life, he would breed no other females.

The next breed to be added to the melting pot was the Dalmatian, changing the merle to its current speckle, and adding loyalty to their masters and a rapport with horses. This combination, however, diluted the heeling ability. A drop of Bull Terrier blood was not enthusiastically received, infusing an excess of toughness. Cattle owners bred out the Bull Terrier influence; but a hint of this breed still is seen in the AuCaDo temperament and shape of the head. Still later, another cross brought in the black/tan Kelpie, which revived heeling capabilities. This was the final cross, and the Australian Cattle Dog has been pure since 1893.

An oddity inherited from their Dalmatian progenitor causes them to be born white. Although the pups do not show their true colors until several weeks of age, color may be ascertained by the paw pads. Reddish brown or brown pads indicate a red, and blue or black pads belong to blue speckle pups. The darker the pad, the darker the dog becomes.

The Dingo influence is shown in the breed's speed, keen hearing and sense of smell, as well

Australian Cattle Dog, blue speckled.

as the general hardiness and ability to withstand heat. AuCaDo dams display their wild heritage by attempting to burrow to whelp their litters, and by weaning pups at four weeks.

Owners say the dogs have cast-iron stomachs and will attempt to eat anything. They're described as watchful, sensible and courageous, willing to tackle hard tasks. They take firm, but not harsh discipline. "Don't beat him too hard, or you will break his heart past mending . . . though the more he is knocked about by cattle, the more eager he becomes to bite."

Their silent work enables them to sneak up on stock—in fact, one theory for development of the silent drover was to obtain help in cattle rustling! A current owner's young AuCaDo doesn't partake in such dubious activities, but has worked horses, goats and ducks. "He's so silent in his approach, he's managed to pluck all the ducks."

It was a Queensland Heeler which became the oldest dog on record: 29 years, five months. "Bluey" served his master by working the flocks nearly 20 years!

The breed was approved to compete for AKC championships in 1980. The Australian Cattle Dog Club of America encourages competition in versatility trials.

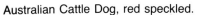
Australian Cattle Dog, red speckled.

Australian Kelpie, black with tan.

AUSTRALIAN KELPIE

COUNTRY: Australia
WEIGHT: 25–45 pounds
HEIGHT: 17–20 inches
COAT: Short, smooth
COLOR: Black, red, blue or fawn; with or without tan
OTHER NAMES: Kelpie, Barb
REGISTRY: TKC
GROUP: Herding

The harsh, unaccustomed environment of Australia forced settlers from England and Scotland to select working dogs that fit the land's conditions—much larger spaces, great numbers of fractious merino sheep, plus the intense heat. The *mob* (Aussie lingo for a flock of sheep) had to be *folded* (brought into the pens at the ranch or station) each night, in those early days, to protect them from Dingoes, aborigines and straying. This required a real workaholic "mustering" or gathering-style sheep dog, rather than the shepherding type from the old country.

Many counties and even some estates in the British Isles had established their own strain of sheep dog, most bearing the name of the locale or owner. The majority of these strains are lost today, but they were still active during the 1800s when Australian immigration was at its height. Many breeds were brought to Australia, and those that suited the new land were used and crossed with others.

One of the first types that proved ideal for the Australian conditions was the Rutherford strain of North County Collies. These dogs were smoothhaired, prick or semi-prick eared, and black or black/tan, and were described by G.S. Kempe as "stoutly built, bold tempered . . . . with very thick head and jaws."

Several members of the Rutherford family emigrated from Scotland to Australia, and they received a steady supply of these dogs from their relatives back home. Others soon recognized this type's skills and wanted pups from the strain. It is doubtful they were kept 100-percent pure, as pragmatic sheep owners bred their good working sluts (i.e., bitches) to the best working dogs they could find, no matter the background. But the Rutherford strain formed the

Australian Kelpie, red with tan.

For its size, the Australian Kelpie is a solid, capable dog with tremendous working abilities.

base for the breed we know today as the Kelpie.

In the late 1800s, a rancher named Gleason swapped a horse for a black/tan sheep dog pup bred in Victoria of imported parents from the Rutherford strain. He named her "Kelpie," Gaelic for water sprite, and found her to be a fine worker. She became known as "Gleason's Kelpie," and it was her offspring that gave the breed its name. This original Kelpie was bred twice to "Moss," a black Australian dog from the Rutherford strain, and then to "Caesar," a black/tan dog from pure Scottish parentage. From this last litter by Caesar was created the most renowned "Kelpie" of all. A black/tan female, also named "Kelpie," was given to G.T.W. King. His Kelpie (the second) later won the first sheep dog trial held in Australia. This coup created a greater interest in the strain.

The Kelpie breed evolved from this beginning, with crosses to other strains throughout the years. The breed is essentially all English without introduction of the Dingo. Many fine working black dogs resulted from the line created by back crosses to Moss, particularly one named "Barb." For many years, there was a general belief that the black ones were a separate breed called Barbs. There were other strains known by the names of the best-known dog or its owner, but soon all were combined into a single grouping under Kelpie.

Around the campfire in the outback, the story of the "immortal Coil," as related in *The Australian Kelpie Handbook*, is still spun. Coil was a famed sheep trial champion and working Kelpie who had "all the qualities necessary for such work, very keen and active, with a good eye and forceful when required."

In the 1898 trial at the Sydney showgrounds, he completed the full course in the first round and was awarded an unheard of 100 points, the maximum possible. But he had to compete again the next day to win the title, and that night was run over by a cab, which broke a front leg.

With the permission of the judges and stewards, the next day Coil completed the full course in six minutes and 12 seconds, "with the injured limb swinging to and fro," and received a second maximum 100 points (a record to this day), all before having his leg set! Although difficult for compassionate people to understand, the

Australian Kelpie, black.

story illustrates the breed's intense desire to work which blocks out everything else.

An estimated 70,000 to 80,000 Kelpies are in service on Australian ranches today, still the top herding dog in that country, and sheep workers say a good Kelpie is equivalent to two men on horseback. The labor-saving statistics are staggering, and many American ranchers are learning the worth of these dogs. Although a natural header with sheep, the Kelpie can be taught to drive in order to work cattle. Kelpies bred for cattle work are forceful, and many both head and heel. They can be most useful in gathering sheep and bringing them into the pens, forcing them through the dipping vats, loading them into trucks and railcars, and even "backing" them (leaping on their backs) if they get jammed in the loading chutes. A team of Kelpies can be sent out to round up a herd of dairy cows or cattle while the owner waits at the gate. They can assist in running them through the veterinary chutes, loading them and driving them down the road to another pasture.

Kelpies have been used effectively, also, with hogs, horses, goats, poultry and even reindeer.

Although they are friendly and trainable, their high energy and great drive to work make them unsuitable to a house-bound or apartment environment. They bond strongly to one owner and, although loyal and intelligent, they are independent thinkers, which is necessary for their work. Some dog owners may find their independence hard to deal with, although it helped one American family out of a jam. When a Simmental-cross bull got into the lot with yearling cattle, it was impossible for the family to sort out the willful cattle. Rain had turned the lot into 12 to 16 inches of mud. But their three-year-old Kelpie went right to work. He carefully worked the yearlings into the barn, isolating the bull, then drove the animal to his pen.

Workaholics they remain, and tale after tale abound of the breed's prowess despite personal discomfort. Kelpies are registered with the Working Kelpie Council in Australia and in the USA by the National Stock Dog Registry. They are rarely exhibited. They are used in areas other than herding, and are now useful in search-and-rescue, dog guide and drug detection work.

AUSTRALIAN SHEPHERD

COUNTRY: USA
WEIGHT: 35–70 pounds
HEIGHT: 18–23 inches
COAT: Moderate in length and harshness, straight to slightly wavy, with dense undercoat
COLOR: Blue merle, red (liver) merle, black, liver, red, with or without white and/or tan markings
REGISTRY: UKC
GROUP: Herding

The Australian Shepherd is a true herder, an excellent working dog, bred from old herding breeds. The nomenclature "Australian" is deceiving, since the breed is "made in America" and perfected to type in the USA. The Berger de Pyrenees, brought to America by the Basques, is one obvious ancestor. Other herding dogs, such as the Smithfield, Collie and Border Collie, also contributed to its prototype. It is believed the Aussie's immigration to America (in the late 1800s) was not by direct route, but through a detour to Australia, where Basques accumulated flocks of hardy Australian sheep. When the Americans saw dogs working these sheep, they assumed the dogs, also, were Australian. They were received enthusiastically as hard-working stock dogs and sometimes the only companion for an isolated shepherd.

The Australian Shepherd is well known and in demand on American farms and ranches. Aussies have been a fixture around stables and with horse people for many years as well. Northwest Indian tribes hand down tales of "ghost-eyed dogs," an apt description for the breed with its blue eyes. Despite the fact that they have been in America for more than a hundred years, they have not solicited recognition as a show dog and are only recently entering that arena. The Australian Shepherd Club of America is a strong parent organization and emphasizes working abilities, awarding titles to qualified animals. The breed's herding instincts remain strong.

People who wish to have a doormat dog are instructed to consider a stuffed animal or a "pet

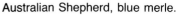

Australian Shepherd, blue merle.

Australian Shepherd, black with white and tan markings.

rock" instead of an Australian Shepherd. The breed is intelligent, active and protective, a combination of qualities which require a dominant owner who is willing to take the time to turn these tendencies into attributes. Those "hot-blooded" specimens are the choice for active work and families. More laid-back Aussies suit the family looking only for a companion.

Aussies not only have become entertainers but have attained success in tracking, narcotics detection, search-and-rescue, and as hearing dogs for the deaf. They love all physical activity and are quick to learn such sports as Frisbee™, flyball and obedience.

Eyes may be brown, amber, blue, flecked or even odd-eyed. The tail is naturally or surgically bobbed. The breed tends to be reserved with strangers. Yet its proponents feel there's no other dog like the Aussie. In fact, as noted in *Stodgehill's Animal Research Magazine*, one stockman states he only maintains his sheep as an excuse to continue raising Aussies!

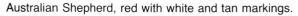

Australian Shepherd, red with white and tan markings.

AUSTRALIAN TERRIER

COUNTRY: Australia
WEIGHT: 12–14 pounds
HEIGHT: 10 inches
COAT: 2½ inches, harsh, straight, dense
COLOR: Blue/tan or clear sandy
REGISTRY: FCI, AKC, UKC, TKC, CKC
GROUP: Terrier

The histories of the two native Australian terriers are tied inextricably—one to the other. Both the Australian Terrier and the Silky Terrier were developed in the 19th century by Australians using various British terrier breeds. Records show that blue and tan broken-coated terriers of about ten pounds were renowned watchdogs around Tasmania, even in the early 1800s. Other terriers of that era in Australia were sandy colored.

The likely descent of the Australian Terrier was from terriers of Scotland and northern England brought to Australia with settlers. The Scottie (or the Cairn) created the hard coat and short leg—with the Skye strengthening the gene for shortness of leg, plus contributing coat abundance and body length. Later crossbreedings added the Dandie's topknot and the Yorkie's blue fading color and small size. Some experts believe that a bit of Irish Terrier was used to set the red color in the sandies, and Manchester crosses occurred much later to improve the depth of the tan in the blue/tans.

Dog shows in the 1800s had classes for both black/ tan and blue/tan broken-coated terriers, for under and over seven pounds. These classifications were the early Australian Terriers before they had any official name or standard. The smaller size was often referred to as the Broken-Coated Toy Terrier.

Selection from these early mixtures developed the modern Australian Terrier. He was welcomed for his skills at dispatching the hated rabbit and at killing snakes. The little dog faced his slithery opponent, then leaped high, turning around in the air. As he landed behind the snake, he grabbed it at the back of the head and killed it.

The Aussie was slow to make headway outside Australia, with British approval not coming until 1936. Although Canada recorded registrations

Australian Terrier, blue/tan.

in 1938, it was 20–some years later before the Americans embraced him. He is now recognized internationally.

He is all terrier—though tiny—with the inborn confidence and spirit of his type. Yet he tends to be quiet and affectionate, making a fine house dog. His coat requires the same care as other broken-coated terriers. The breed is eager to please and is a good choice for children, the elderly or handicapped. Although many terriers contributed to his genetic make-up, the twinkle in the Aussie's eye is all his own.

AUSTRIAN BRANDLBRACKE

COUNTRY: Austria
WEIGHT: 33–49 pounds
HEIGHT: 18–23 inches
COAT: Short, thick; hard and shining
COLOR: Black and tan, or red; may have limited white marks on neck, chest and feet
OTHER NAMES: Osterreichischer Glatthaariger Bracke, Austrian Smoothhaired Hound
REGISTRY: FCI
GROUP: Hound

The hounds of Austria are the same general type and often of similar origin as the German hounds. They have the same sturdy, unexaggerated body type including the stopless face and high-set, smooth ear. Austrians also appreciate the fine tracking qualities of scenthounds and enlist them for bloodtrailing as well as hunting live game.

The Brandlbracke has the raciest body of the Austrian hounds, being leggier and lighter of bone than the Bavarian dogs to the north. He stems directly from the Celtic brackes of old, and is closely related to both the Belgian St. Hubert and the Jura Hounds of Switzerland. He

Austrian Brandlbracke, black and tan.

Austrian Brandlbracke, black and tan.

has been recognized as a distinct type since 1884. His elegant head, carried high, is straight and wide, crowned with prominent eyebrows, and tapering to the muzzle. There should be no flew or hanging eyelids.

The Brandlbracke is usually of the black and tan pattern, with the tan actually being a rich shade of red. *Brand* is literally fire in German, and the diminutive *Brandl* indicates the little marks of fire red. The sleek, black body with the trace markings of bright red gave the breed its name. A small white ring may be around the neck, with a star on chest and white feet.

The breed dwells exclusively in the hands of hunters, who appreciate it especially for silent trailing. While work on the cold scent is his specialty, he can also be utilized for hunting hare and fox, for which he gives tongue. Prized by Austrian hunters, he is unknown outside his native land.

AUSTRIAN SHORTHAIRED PINSCHER

COUNTRY: Austria
WEIGHT: 26–40 pounds
HEIGHT: 14–20 inches
COAT: Short, smooth
COLOR: Red, brindle or black/tan often with white markings
OTHER NAMES: Osterreichischer Kurzhaariger Pinscher
REGISTRY: FCI
GROUP: Terrier

A sturdy dog with roots similar to the German Pinscher, this terrier is in the same height range, although broader and heavier. The standard demands a chest so wide that he appears wider than tall when viewed from the front.

Left: Austrian Shorthaired Pinscher, black/tan with white markings. **Below:** Austrian Shorthaired Pinscher, red with white markings.

Austrian Shorthaired Pinscher.

AZAWAKH

COUNTRY: Mali
WEIGHT: 37–55 pounds
HEIGHT: 23½–29 inches
COAT: Very short, soft
COLOR: Sable (brown, light fawn to dark red) with white markings
OTHER NAMES: Tuareg Sloughi
REGISTRY: FCI
GROUP: Southern

A true terrier who is a likeable and courageous country companion, the Austrian Pinscher does not thrive in city life, unless given plenty of exercise. An urban owner could have a problem with the dog's predisposition to overzealous barking. He is fearless against predators, enthusiastically goes to ground, and is an alert, noisy alarm dog.

The Austrian Pinscher may be tailless or have a tail rolled up on the back. Ears can be pricked, tipped or rosed. The hair, while shortish, tends to have some fringe on the belly and thighs. Despite a long history, he is quite rare today.

Bred by the nomadic Tuareg tribes of the southern Sahara as hunting and guard dogs for over a thousand years, the Azawakh was developed for the chase and will course any game. The German term "windhound" is descriptive of this breed and its close relatives. The Azawakh is described by a breeder as "fleetfooted enough to catch gazelles, hares and the European mouflon (wild sheep), courageous enough to ward off big predators, untiring like a camel and beautiful like an Arab horse."

These dogs defended goats and camels and vigorously protected the herds against jackals, hyenas and wild dogs. They still carry out these duties in their homeland. Their true value lies in the chase; however, the nomads appreciate their beauty and look upon the Azawakh as a symbol of high standing and wealth.

The dog must never kill the prey, merely curbing its flight. If the game were killed, it would spoil in the desert heat. The Tuareg hunter has no guns nor even bow and arrow—providing food for the encampment only with a knife and a sighthound.

Pups are cultivated from birth for the hunt. They are fed on milk, never on flesh, and continue this diet throughout their lives. As three-month-old babies, they are introduced to their calling by beginning with rats and progressing to hares.

Eventually, at full growth, the Azawakh is taken on horseback to course gazelle. The hound is seated in front of his master on the saddle until the game is sighted and the chase is begun. When the dog is released, he begins his "breathtaking course," which sometimes lasts five to six hours. Finally, the Azawakh hamstrings the quarry, waiting for his master to join

Azawakh, light fawn with white markings.

Prized by their nomadic owners, the Azawakh is hailed as having the stamina of a camel and the beauty and agility of an Arabian horse. As this painting illustrates, the breed is used in Mali for hunting and falconry.

him and complete the kill.

This breed has been the product of strict culling and selection, based on the nomad's stark existence. When a litter was born, only one male was kept for hunting purposes, and, occasionally, a bitch for reproduction. The others were killed. This practice made it nearly impossible for outsiders to obtain an Azawakh. Asking a nomadic huntsman to sell his sighthound was tantamount to asking him to sell his oldest son.

An ambassador to the Upper Volta and Ivory Coast, Dr. Pecar earned the title of "Great African Hunter." He much admired the exotic beauty of these hounds, and spent considerable effort and time attempting to obtain a pair to no avail. When it was necessary for him to return to his home country of Yugoslavia, he was presented with a handsome male in admiration for his prowess as a hunter. Later he attempted to arrange a trade of his services for an Azawakh female. Fortunately—for Dr. Pecar and European sighthound fanciers—a bull elephant had been terrorizing a Tuareg tribe. The doctor destroyed the animal and was awarded a half-starved bitch, otherwise destined to die. But she was to become the beginning of the European breed.

The Tuaregs required their dogs to have white markings—the ones without white were considered worthless. Black nails and black eye rim pigmentation surrounding the large dark eyes were also required by the nomads—along with five obligatory warts on the head!

Owners state that to know one is to love the breed. Nevertheless, Azawakhs are not for everyone. They are a proud, even haughty breed that does not take well to harsh discipline. They are aristocratic, "a friend, never a slave." True to their native land, they love sun and warmth and require protection in cold climes. One breeder warns that they love food and will become food thieves, eating themselves into obesity, particularly if not given the opportunity for the necessary long runs.

Their gait is typical of the sighthounds, almost balletlike in movement, lightfooted, floating. They are built similarly to a good Arabian horse, high on leg, short-coupled, with small feet. This is quite different than many other desert hounds. Their speed reaches 43½ mph.

The Azawakh has a solid foundation in Europe and is bred in several countries, including Switzerland, Germany and Yugoslavia. FCI accepted the breed in 1980. It has been considered one of the purest sighthounds, because these dogs were not crossbred by the Tuareg tribes nor were they sold outside the Azawakh Valley and territories of the Oullimiden Tuareg, in what are now the countries of Mali, Upper Volta, Nigeria and Mauritania.

Above: Head study of fawn Azawakh. **Below:** Red Azawakh running. The breed's gait is gazellelike, or more than gazellelike as it is used to course gazelles in its native land.

Barbet, fawn.

BARBET

COUNTRY: France
WEIGHT: 33–55 pounds
HEIGHT: 18–22 inches
COAT: Thick, long, and "tassled"; curly or wavy
COLOR: Black, chestnut, fawn, gray; with or without white markings; white
OTHER NAMES: Griffon d'Arret a Poil Laineux
REGISTRY: FCI
GROUP: Gun Dog

Exact roots of the Barbet are forever lost, but most likely they stem from corded sheep dogs from Asia and, possibly, early griffon hounds. Woolly water dogs were found throughout 14th-century Europe, answering to various names, i.e., the *wasserhund* meaning water dog. Although not the source of all water dogs, the Bar-bet is very likely closest to the original type. The Barbet is most generic of water dogs, with a woolly sheep-dog coat and hair all over, allowing him to withstand hours in water and chilly marshes. He resembles a pointing dog, but is slower and heavier of body, without the keen nose or sleek beauty. Sixteenth-century cynologist Fou-illoux dubbed him the Barbet, from *barbe*, a French designation for beard; his pseudonym, *laineux*, translates into woolly.

Elizabethan references to shaggy-coated water dogs in France and England describe their use for retrieving and their coat care. Dr. Johannes Caius says personalities were "efficient and playful." Perhaps it is their impishness that entices them to muddy, swampy places, giving them the nickname of "Mud Dog."

They not only retrieved ducks and other game in deep water, but recovered the arrows when huntsmen shot and missed, much like the Portuguese Water Dog. They drew favor from the French royalty. Zella Llewellyn writes that both Louis XV and Henri IV hunted with Barbets, and Henri's mistress, Corisande, was reproached by M. de Bellievre, the chancellor of Marie de Medici, for attending mass in the company of "a madman, a monkey and a Barbet." More prosaically, the breed also aided sailors in a similar manner to its look-alikes, the Porties.

Jean-Claude Hermans, president and founder of the Barbet Club in France, credits the Barbet with being the foundation (crossed with other types) that produced the Briard, the Newfoundland and the Poodle. The modern Barbet is an excellent water dog, using his webbed feet to advantage in swimming, never tiring after long

Barbet, black.

Barbets, fawn.

hours. His personality is noted as gay, obedient and intelligent. These qualities and his fidelity make him a valued companion. Although its stamp has come down through the poodles, the various water spaniels, and even the bichon dogs, the Barbet, as a distinct breed, was nearly lost. Hermans tells us, "Despite . . . good qualities, the breed was abandoned during the 19th century, replaced by its direct descendant the Poodle as a companion dog; the sailors chose the Terre-Neuve (Newfoundland), and the hunters the Korthal griffon."

The Barbet's specialization may have been his undoing. Almost unknown outside his native France, the breed is promoted by a few enthusiasts at home. Today there are only about 200 left in all of France.

Basenji, red.

BASENJI

COUNTRY: Zaire
WEIGHT: 22–24 pounds
HEIGHT: 16–16½ inches
COAT: Short, smooth
COLOR: Red, black/tan, black—all with white markings
OTHER NAMES: Congo Dog
REGISTRY: FCI, AKC, UKC, TKC, CKC
GROUP: Southern

Admired by the pharaohs, these ancient dogs stem from the earliest pariahs. They were used as hunting dogs much like their larger relatives, the Pharaoh and Ibizan. As the great Egyptian culture declined, these hunting partners were adopted by tribes throughout the Congo.

The breed's keen nose (a Basenji can scent at 80 yards) and sharp eyesight were useful to the natives, who used the dogs to drive game into nets or to track wounded prey. Because the Basenji hunted silently, he often wore a bell.

Centuries later, the Basenji was found in the bush by British explorers, nearly in its original form. The Englishmen called the breed the African Bush Dog. The breed's independence, resourcefulness and hunting ability had helped the Basenji to survive on its own.

Finally, in 1936, a pair imported from the Congo by a Mrs. Burn, Bongo of Blean and Bokoto of Blean, produced the first English litter. When these pups were exhibited at Crufts in 1937, they created so much interest that special police had to be employed to keep the crowds moving past the Basenji benches. The Basenji was obviously on its way to acceptance. It was Mrs. Burn who gave the breed its current name, *Basenji*, translating to bush thing from the African dialect. The Basenji was recognized by AKC in 1943.

A popular hunting dog for small game in his native land, he is valued for his silent approach. Today the barkless dog is valued for the same attribute in apartment complexes. Nevertheless, he is not totally silent, communicating with a growl when displeased and a singular yodel when happy. The Basenji is exceptionally clean, licking itself in the manner of a cat, adding to his appeal as a pet. Owners note the use of his feet to cling, play and communicate.

Current owners find them happy playmates and avid coursing dogs. They retain many of the characteristics of the pariahs: the aloofness, the wrinkled brow and the cycling once a year. Basenji bitches come into season between August and November (which would be late winter and early spring in Africa) allowing their young to be several months old by cold weather.

These dogs prefer being with their family and, if left to their own resources, may resort to deviltry and destruction for their amusement. Crate training is suggested by breeders.

Basenji.

Basset Artésien Normand, tricolor.

BASSET ARTÉSIEN NORMAND

COUNTRY: France
WEIGHT: 33 pounds
HEIGHT: 10½–14½ inches
COAT: Short and smooth
COLOR: Tricolor or orange/white
OTHER NAMES: Artesian Norman Basset
REGISTRY: FCI
GROUP: Hound

Short-legged dogs were present in northern France for many years where they were generally known as Norman Bassets, although many also came from Artois (Artésien). Frenchman Fauilloux's memoirs from the 17th century mention his use of short-legged dogs from Artois for hunting badger.

By the end of the 19th century, when identification of individual breeds was begun throughout the world, two types of "Norman" bassets existed that were unrelated to one another. The Count Le Coulteux de Canteleu was breeding strong-bodied, straight-legged bassets with particular emphasis on hunting qualities rather than on "classic" appearance. In head type, they were similar to the Chien d'Artois, with the small flat ear. Near Rouen another breeder, Louis Lane, was emphasizing aesthetic characteristics, and his hounds had noble heads with large drooping ears. But they also had less energy, due to the extremely dwarfed front legs, so curved that the dogs were half disabled. Many other breeders of the area, wanting the best of the extremes, crossbred the two types.

By 1898, when the first written standard was adopted, most of these bassets carried characteristics from both types. The man who spearheaded the modern blend was Leon Verrier. In the early years of this century, his hounds dominated the exhibitions, and were the type most sought by the newly formed association for the breed. During the 1920s, his dogs were often referred to as Artois Bassets (Basset d'Artois), despite their double origin. WWI wiped out Verrier's kennels, but he continued his influence as a judge and leader. Under his presidency, the name of Basset Artésien Normand was chosen, which accurately pinpoints their historical origin. After WWII, the breed was reduced to very few pure specimens, but several dedicated breeders, especially Leparoux de Combree des Maine et Loire, saved the Artésian Norman Basset from extinction.

The desired type is an athletic dog, with an elegant head and long, smooth muscles. The muzzle is long, refined and arched. Ears are low-set, thin and curved. Most modern specimens approach the top of the standard or even larger. While not carrying over-abundant skin, some wrinkles appear on the cheeks, and this hound does have a bit of dewlap.

The Artésien Normand is a happy, good-natured dog who is courageous and headstrong in the hunt. He, like so many of his basset cousins, was designed to go into heavy cover. Originally bred for rabbit shooting, he is now adapted to hunt a variety of prey. His additional qualities of kindness, obedience and patience with children have found him a place as a house dog.

Basset Artésien Normand.

Basset Hound.

BASSET HOUND

Country: Great Britain
Weight: 40–60 pounds
Height: 14 inches or less, 15 inches disqualifies
Coat: Short and smooth
Color: Any hound color
Registry: FCI, AKC, UKC, TKC, CKC
Group: Hound

Alix M. Freedman asserts that French noblemen were so "out-of-shape they could only follow a slow hound with short legs and crooked knees."

The Basset was bred by monks in the Middle Ages to hunt in heavy cover, whether for the heavy-bellied nobility or not is conjecture. His short, crooked legs allowed him to hold his nose close to the ground. Like a Dr. Seuss creation, the Basset has the head and bone of a Bloodhound, the coloring of a Foxhound and the legs of a Dachshund.

Basset Hound.

Developed to individual perfection in England, the breed we know simply as the Basset Hound is closely related to the whole family of French Bassets discussed earlier. Bassets of the Normand and d'Artois type have been noted in England at least since Shakespearean times. In *A Midsummer Night's Dream*, the bard has Theseus, the Duke of Athens, saying:

> My hounds are bred out of the Spartan kind;
> So flew'd, so sanded; and their heads are hung
> With ears that sweep away the morning dew;
> Crook-knee'd and dew-lapp'd like Thessalian bulls;
> Slow in pursuit, but match'd in mouth like bells. . . ."
>
> (IV, 1, 118)

Who could doubt the type of dog being described!

But the fostering of a separate, individual breed came several centuries later. In 1866 the Comte de Tournow sent a pair of Basset Normands, "Basset" and "Belle," to Lord Galway of England. A litter bred from this pair went to Lord Onslow, who proceeded to develop an exceptional pack by crossing with further imports from the Coultreux pack of Normandy.

Soon importation ceased, and the English version of the Basset developed on its own. Except for the legs, this hound closely resembles the St. Hubert Hound, with the same superb nose (considered to be the best, next to the bloodhound's) and coldtrailing ability. From England, he was brought to America, where he has been enthusiastically accepted.

A fine trailer of rabbit, hare and even wounded pheasant, his short-statured bulk proves especially useful in heavy, impenetrable cover. He can be taught to tree coon, squirrels and opossum. AKC sponsors field trials (rabbit trailing) throughout the USA for Basset Hounds, and the breed is also well represented in the North American show ring. The Basset, like the Dachshund or Beagle, is one of the few

Basset Hound.

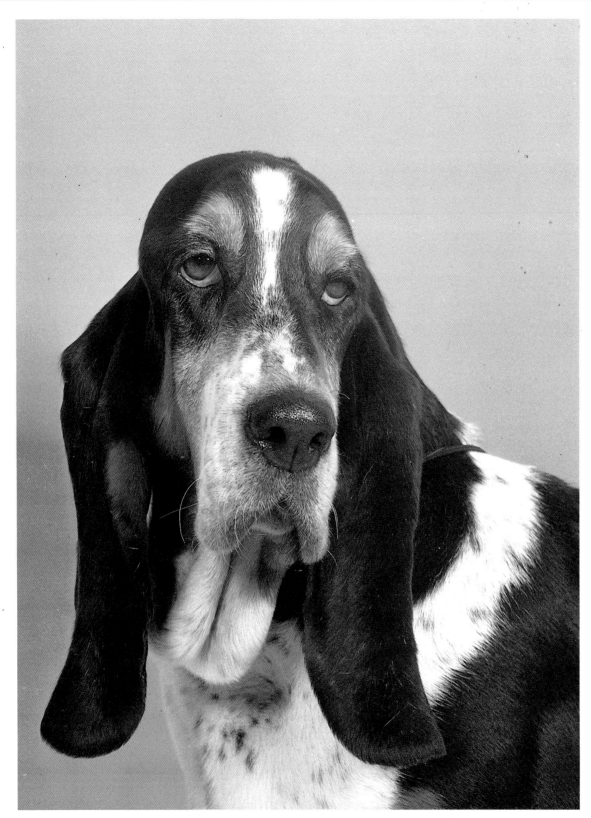

Basset Hound.

hounds that has achieved a fair degree of popularity as a companion dog. This may be due in part to his frequent use in various advertising campaigns. The Hush Puppy™ spokesdog is a Basset, and his soft, sad, appealing face seems to sell a lot of shoes!

In hunting situations, Bassets can be a bit lazy or stubborn, according to some hunt masters, and may get "hung up" on scents—or "go riot" after the scent of a deer. These hounds so love the deer that they cross highways or lose their masters in the woods during a chase. Trailing deer, therefore, is discouraged. But despite the idiosyncracies, true basseters are sold on their breed. As these dogs fill their noses with a bouquet of scents and take off on the trail, their melodious voices blend to create the music of the gods to the basseters. Their slower approach is actually an advantage, as they are less likely to frighten and bolt the game.

Type, in both England and America, is divergent. Like his cousins in Artois and Normandy, there is a variance between hunting type and those bred strictly for appearance. Bassets in formal hunt packs in England and those used for field trialing, or as pets in America, resemble the Coultreux strain with the lighter bone, higher, straighter leg and minimum of hanging skin. Dogs for exhibition, like those originally bred by Louis Lane for their "aesthetics," are massive and extremely low-stationed, with more crooked legs and a super-abundance of wrinkles, flew and dewlap.

Like all hounds, the Basset can be independent in nature, and his baritone musical voice, so loved by connoisseurs of hunting, may be an irritant to neighbors. And, again, in tune with his hound heritage, discipline is a must! Despite these hindrances, the Basset still makes a fine pet. A few in America have proven the critics wrong by winning at the highest level of obedience competition. Many continue to give double service, with the family pet used as a rabbit dog on an occasional weekend hunt.

Pack existence called for a good-humored, sociable dog, and this transfers well to life as a companion. Grooming is minimal. He loves dinner time, but takes the Garfield™ attitude toward exercise, so routine walks must be scheduled to avoid obesity.

Basset Hounds.

155

Bavarian Mountain Hound.

BAVARIAN MOUNTAIN HOUND

COUNTRY: Germany
WEIGHT: 55–77 pounds
HEIGHT: 20 inches or less
COAT: Short, thick and shiny
COLOR: All shades of black-masked fawn or brindle
OTHER NAMES: Bayrischer Gebirgsschweisshund
REGISTRY: FCI
GROUP: Hound

Schweisshund literally means bloodhound, which is a generic term for a dog, such as the Hanoverian or Bavarian, that follows a bloodtrail. When large game is wounded during a hunt, it may travel many miles in heavy cover only to hide and die a long, slow death. The development of dogs for trailing the wounded animal are common on the Continent. The honor code of the German hunter demands an obligation to find all shot game—dead or wounded. A deer injured with an arrow or bullet may leave only occasional drops of blood many yards apart. The dogs, although brought in even hours later, can follow the cold trail for many miles and lead the hunter to the wounded animal. Sometimes the search goes on for days, but it is never abandoned until the wounded animal is found, dead or alive. This sort of hunting, actually trailing, is not often employed in the USA. It requires a dog with an excellent cold nose and great coldtrailing ability.

Bavaria is a mountainous state in southern Germany near the Austrian and Swiss borders and includes the Bavarian Alps. The hound from this region is a shorter and finer version of the Hanover, probably obtained from crossing the latter with Tyrolean Hounds. The Bavarian is smaller, even shorter on leg, smoother of skin and sharper of temperament, but otherwise very similar to the Hanoverian. He is a tracker par excellence and a fine hunter of the chamois deer, but because he has less size and substance, he can move with more agility in the altitudes of the Bavarian Mountains.

These dogs are calm, quiet, poised and very attached to their master and family. But when hunting, they are "hard, single-minded and persistent." They are highly specialized and must be worked steadily to bring out the best of their talents. Thus, they are not dogs for the casual hunter. Most are owned and utilized by foresters and game wardens.

Bavarian Mountain Hound, black-masked fawn.

Beagle.

BEAGLE

COUNTRY: Great Britain
WEIGHT: 18–30 pounds
HEIGHT: 2 varieties: under 13 inches and 13–15 inches; over 15 inches disqualifies
COAT: Short, smooth and dense
COLOR: Any hound color allowed
REGISTRY: FCI, AKC, TKC, CKC
GROUP: Hound

The history of the Beagle is clouded. Since very early times, small hounds similar to the Beagle have existed for the hunting of hare in the British Isles, particularly in Wales. The original form probably came with the Celts, although certainly crossing with types such as the hounds of Artois or others created this modern breed. Throughout the world, dogs are requisitioned by sporting enthusiasts to be hunted individually or in small packs for squirrel, rabbit and hare, and Beagles are particularly suited for this task. They are determined, keen hunters, and their "music" during a hunt brings goosebumps to neophytes and the oldest pro alike.

During the days of King Henry VIII and his daughter, Elizabeth I, Beagles were sometimes wire-haired. They were also very small, often diminutive enough to be carried to the field in the pocket of a hunt coat. It has even been reported that 10 or 12 couples of Beagles could be carried in saddle baskets! Over the years the size has somewhat increased, but the little "pocket" Beagles still occasionally crop up in a litter. American top size is 15 inches, although in England they allow them up to 16 inches.

Hounds of the Beagle sort were brought into the States throughout the Colonial period, but type varied until further imports from England arrived in the 1880s and 1890s. The Beagle's ability to drill a trail and work the rabbit back around to the waiting hunter have contributed to his demand as a hunting companion. But his small size and happy personality have also been a factor. Needing little grooming, they are easy to maintain and are wonderful playmates for children.

Laboratories traditionally use Beagles in research of diseases, medicines and other medical matters. Large colonies are bred for this pur-

Facing page: Beagle. **Above:** Beagle puppy.

pose, often with certain specific characteristics or proclivities, such as to cancers. This breed is chosen for this heart-rending but medically pertinent task due to its easygoing personality and its adaptability to kennel or pack life, as well as its overall sturdiness.

These same qualities, plus longevity, secure it a permanent place in the heart of dog lovers. In the USA, the Beagle has remained in the top ten registrations for many years, boasting a brief stay in the number one spot during the 1950s. His cocky show strut and merry performances in obedience make him a joy to watch. He is a much-loved pet and companion, although one may have to deal with his hound's voice and a bit of a stubborn streak. This hound's inquisitive, happy-go-lucky nature and voracious appetite can take him out of his master's good graces, however. To avoid this, training and crating in the owner's absence are advised by breeders.

Beagles are so popular that a verb has been coined, and fanciers are said to be "beagling." The breed is seen frequently in the winner's circle at dog shows, and nearly 3,000 sanctioned Beagle Field Trials are offered each year. Even with all these dogs involved in competitions, the great majority of Beagles enjoy a hunt individually or in pairs with their masters.

BEAGLE HARRIER

COUNTRY: France
WEIGHT: 44 pounds
HEIGHT: 17–19 inches
COAT: Short and smooth
COLOR: Mostly tricolors with a lot of tan; but color is of no importance
REGISTRY: FCI
GROUP: Hound

Baron Gerard of France created this breed by crossing two English hounds, the Beagle and the Harrier. A pack hound used on hare or deer, it looks like the English-type hound from which he came. This dog has the higher set, flat, smaller ears of British dogs. He is stockier and more compact of body than the French hounds and is heavily boned for his size. Small packs of Beagle Harriers are still seen in France with hunters who prize him for his abilities. He is rarely exhibited.

Beagle Harrier.

Beagle Harrier.

Bearded Collie, blue with white markings.

BEARDED COLLIE

COUNTRY: Great Britain
WEIGHT: 40–60 pounds
HEIGHT: 20–22 inches
COAT: Long, harsh, dense
COLOR: Black, brown, fawn, blue, with or without white markings in the Irish pattern. Tan points may occur on all colors.
REGISTRY: FCI, AKC, TKC, CKC
GROUP: Herding

The Bearded Collie evolved from Polski Owczarek Nizinnys, which were left on the shores of Scotland in the 1500s and bred to native herding dogs. One of the earliest notes on the breed described them as: "A big rough tousy-looking tyke with a coat not unlike a doormat, the texture of the hair hard and fibry and the ears hanging close to the head."

In 1898, Alfred Ollivant's book *Owd Bob* carried a description that closely suits the modern Beardie. "Should you, while wandering in the wild sheep land, happen on a moor or in market upon a very perfect gentle knight, clothed in dark grey habit, splashed here and there with rays of moon; free by right divine of the guild of gentlemen, strenuous as a prince, lithe as a rowan, graceful as a girl, with high king carriage, motions and manners of a fairy queen,

Basket of Bearded Collie pups.

should he have a noble breadth of brow, an air of still strength born of right confidence, all unassuming; last and most unfailing test of all, should you look into two snow-clad eyes, calm, wistful, inscrutable, their soft depths clothed on with eternal sadness—yearning, as is said, for the soul that is not theirs—know then, that you look upon one of the line of the most illustrious sheep dogs of the North."

The modern breed as we know it today was introduced to the public sector in the 1940s by its British devotee, G. Olive Willison. An accidental acquisition of a Bearded Collie pup, "Jeannie," so entranced her, she was determined to continue the breed and, after diligent searching, she finally obtained "Bailey" as a mate for Jeannie. Willison's Bothkennar Beardies set the modern lines. Most, if not all, pedigrees lead back to Jeannie and Bailey of Bothkennar.

Beardies met with amazing success in Canada and the USA and were accepted under the ranks of CKC and AKC dogs in nearly record time. They have a steady following, keeping them near the middle of all registrations.

The Bearded Collie breed is one of the few that carries a dominant fading gene. Pups that are born black can begin graying by eight weeks. Blues turn silver, browns lighten to a cinnamon or milky chocolate and fawns become a champagne color. They continue fading until about the age of one year, when the process reverses and they darken again, although they rarely become as dark as they were at birth. The exceptions, of course, are the dogs that do not carry the fading gene. These are called "stay-blacks" (or browns, and so on). Any white markings on these dogs should appear only in the Irish pattern.

Grooming is necessary on a weekly basis, brushing to the skin to remove tangles and prevent mats. Many, seeing the breed for the first time, ask if they are miniature undocked Old English Sheepdogs.

They are becoming one of the most recognizable shaggy sheep dogs, along with their cousin, the OES. The breed's winsome appearance causes them to be in frequent demand for commercials. Beardies are handsome show dogs and loving family pets. Some are therapy dogs and are greeted enthusiastically by residents of nursing homes and hospitals. The breed's parent club is active in encouraging natural instincts and has instituted herding trials.

Beardies are bouncy, bubbly and sometimes boisterous. They are also strong-willed, sturdy and sensitive. Many owners find them both a challenge and a pleasure to train in obedience.

Bearded Collie, fawn, working dog.

Bedlington Terrier.

BEDLINGTON TERRIER

COUNTRY: Great Britain
WEIGHT: 17–23 pounds
HEIGHT: 15–17½ inches
COAT: Mixture of hard and soft hair that has a tendency to curl, crisp but not wiry
COLOR: Blue, blue/tan, sandy, sandy/tan, liver, liver/tan
REGISTRY: FCI, AKC, TKC, CKC
GROUP: Terrier

Boasting a longer traceable pedigree than any other terrier, the curly-coated Bedlington gives a lamblike illusion. The breed hails from the mining area in the north of England and was first called the Rothbury Terrier in the 1830s. He was originally bred from the wire-coated terriers used locally, probably crossed with hound (i.e., Otterhound) and perhaps Whippet as well. One of the breed's forefathers, "Peachem," is mentioned as both a Bedlington and a Dandie Dinmont. The Bedlington carries a long drop ear and an arch over the loin, both hinting of sighthound. He is also unusual in that he carries the blue or liver colors, probably an inheritance from his sighthound ancestors as well.

He was a favorite with miners and nailmakers for ratting and badgering. In the hunt, he swam after otters and ran down rabbits. A game fellow, he slowly drew a following outside Northumberland, with an English national association for him starting in 1877. At that time, the breed was known to be a tough game dog who would fight to the death if necessary. Gypsies and tinkers kept them as pit fighters, as well as poaching assistants. His skills in poaching caused him still to be known in some remote parts of England as the Gypsy Dog. One of the breed, Ainsley's Young Piper, saved his mistress's toddler from an angry sow. At the age of 14, toothless and almost blind, the same dog drew a badger when other terriers had failed.

Although type has vastly improved over the years, his popularity as a lady's companion tempered his tough working qualities. It was his great heart and lovable nature that endeared him as a pet, and he was no longer selected for his hunting attributes. The American Kennel Club's *The Complete Dog Book* even admits that "when his jealous nature is aroused, he will fight for his place in one's affection"—hardly the same thing as a cornered fox or badger!!

The coat requires periodic trimming to maintain the Bedlington guise. For the show ring, he is hand-scissored to his modern shape, not stripped like other terriers. His terrier heart still makes him a fine alarm dog.

Bedlington Terriers.

Bedlington Terrier.

BELGIAN GRIFFONS

Belgian Griffon

COUNTRY: Belgium
WEIGHT: 2 varieties—up to 6½ pounds and up to 11 pounds
HEIGHT: 7–8 inches
COAT: Hard, long and disheveled
COLOR: Black, black/tan or red/black grizzle
OTHER NAMES: Griffon Belge
REGISTRY: FCI
GROUP: Terrier

Brussels Griffon

COUNTRY: Belgium
WEIGHT: 6–12 pounds
HEIGHT: 7–8 inches
COAT: Long, hard and disheveled
COLOR: Clear red
OTHER NAMES: Griffon Bruxellois
REGISTRY: FCI, AKC, TKC, CKC
GROUP: Terrier

Petit Brabancon

COUNTRY: Belgium
WEIGHT: 6–12 pounds
HEIGHT: 7–8 inches
COAT: Short and dense
COLOR: Red, red/black, red/black grizzle, black or black/tan
OTHER NAMES: Piccolo Brabantino
REGISTRY: FCI
GROUP: Terrier

The descriptions of these little terriers from Belgium are analogous. In fact, AKC recognizes only the breed known as the Brussels Griffon. Its American standard allows all of the color varieties, black through red, as well as the smooth variety (Brabancon). FCI, conversely, divided them into three breeds: smooths (Petit Brabancon), rough reds (Brussels Griffon) and roughs of other colors (Belgian Griffon). Therefore, in Europe they are shown separately, with no interbreeding between the varieties. In America, al-

Petit Brabancon, red.

Belgian Griffon, black.

though the same parameters exist, they are combined into one breed with different color and coat varieties. The history of all three is indistinguishable.

The Affenpinscher was probably the main ingredient in the creation of this "Belgian street urchin." Jan Van Eyck depicted the little Belgian dog in a painting in 1434. A peasant's dog, he was fairly standard in type by the 1600s. Later the breed drew the affection and patronage of French King Henry III, Belgian Queen Henrietta Maria and Queen Astrid. At that time, he was universally rough-coated and longer muzzled, and quite a bit larger than modern specimens, more the size of a Fox Terrier. The Belgian terrier is stouter of build than the Affenpinscher.

In early times, he was called *Griffon D'Ecurie* (Stable Griffon), for he earned his keep by killing the rats and mice in the stable, particularly in those for urban hansom cabs. Their engaging personalities soon created the fashion of riding about town on the driver's seat, next to the cabbie. This gained him wider exposure and, as his popularity as a companion dog increased, he was reduced in size. Many breed historians feel that

crosses to English Toy Spaniels shortened the face and decreased size, as well as removing many of the Griffon's working abilities. Pug blood was also used in the breed's modernization, with the smooth coat and sturdy build coming from that source. Barbets, Smoushond, Yorkshire Terriers and Pekingese are also mentioned as possible members of the family tree. These happy mix-ups that created so many breeds before formal pedigrees were kept may be conjecture or fact.

Their affectionate temperament makes them welcome throughout the world. They reached England in the late 1800s and the United States around the turn of the 20th century.

The Belgian terriers are likeable fellows, intelligent, sensitive, alert with a jaunty good nature, making them precise obedience workers. Their gamin faces invite attention, and they need and enjoy association with people. The breed is not aggressive or quarrelsome. The coat on the wire varieties requires periodic stripping. In America, all three varieties customarily have tails docked short and ears cropped to a very short point, in the fashion of many European terriers.

Brussels Griffon, red.

Above: Body study of the Brussels Griffon. **Below Left:** Body study of the Belgian Griffon. **Below Right:** Head study of the Petit Brabancon.

Belgian Mastiff, fawn with white markings.

BELGIAN MASTIFF

COUNTRY: Belgium
WEIGHT: 99–110 pounds
HEIGHT: 26½–31½ inches
COAT: Short, smooth
COLOR: Fawn, brindle; may have dark mask and occasional white markings
OTHER NAMES: Mâtin Belge, Chien de Trait
REGISTRY: FCI
GROUP: Mastiff

The Belgian contribution to draft dogs was a bobtail mastiff of the butcher's dog type. The breed was used for carting in Belgium and was a calm and obedient dog. The FCI lists this breed in suspension, and the Belgian Kennel Club states that it may be extinct.

169

BELGIAN SHEEPDOGS

Belgian Sheepdog, Groenendael

COUNTRY: Belgium
WEIGHT: 62 pounds
HEIGHT: 22–26 inches (ideal)
COAT: Medium-long
COLOR: Black
OTHER NAMES: Belgian Sheepdog
REGISTRY: FCI, AKC, UKC, TKC, CKC
GROUP: Herding

Belgian Sheepdog, Laekenois

COUNTRY: Belgium
WEIGHT: 62 pounds
HEIGHT: 22–26 inches (ideal)
COAT: Rough, harsh, shaggy, 2¼ inches long, shorter on muzzle and around eyes
COLOR: Fawn to mahogany, with black overlay
OTHER NAMES: Laekense, Laeken
REGISTRY: FCI, TKC, CKC
GROUP: Herding

Belgian Sheepdog, Malinois

COUNTRY: Belgium
WEIGHT: 62 pounds
HEIGHT: 22–26 inches (ideal)
COAT: Moderately short, dense
COLOR: Fawn to mahogany, with black overlay
OTHER NAMES: Belgian Malinois
REGISTRY: FCI, AKC, UKC, TKC, CKC
GROUP: Herding

Belgian Sheepdog, Tervuren

COUNTRY: Belgium
WEIGHT: 62 pounds
HEIGHT: 22–26 inches (ideal)
COAT: Medium-long
COLOR: Fawn to mahogany, with black overlay
OTHER NAMES: Belgian Tervuren
REGISTRY: FCI, AKC, UKC, TKC, CKC
GROUP: Herding

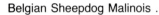
Belgian Sheepdog Malinois .

Above Left: Belgian Sheepdog Tervuren. **Above Right:** Belgian Sheepdog Groenendael. **Below:** Belgian Sheepdog Laekenois.

The hard-working shepherds' dogs from Belgium have rated raves since the Middle Ages. In those days type varied widely and breeding was based on herding ability. An owner who desired a litter from his good working bitch simply sought out another superb sheep dog, preferably that of a close neighbor. It made little difference if the bitch was fawn and medium-coated, with a refined muzzle and prick ears, and the male was black and shaggy-haired, with a heavy muzzle and half-drop ears. The pups, no matter who they resembled physically, would inherit the working abilities and be in demand. Because of the localized matings, inbreeding was common and dogs began to take on certain standard characteristics. Similar varieties of herding dogs evolved during the same period in Holland, France and Germany.

In 1891, Professor Adolphe Reul of the Belgian School of Veterinary Science cataloged and established standards for the various types of

Belgian Sheepdog Malinois.

Belgian Sheepdog Groenendael.

Belgian Sheepdogs. He found them remarkably similar in type with the main differences being color, length and texture of the haircoat. The professor divided them into varieties and advised breeding them as separate breeds. At one time as many as eight were documented. Today, however, only four remain: the Malinois (shorthaired fawn), the Groenendael (longhaired black, known in the USA simply as the Belgian Sheepdog), the Tervuren (longhaired fawn) and the Laekenois (wirehaired fawn), all named after the regions in which they were most populous. The standards are identical except for the haircoat.

According to Pagel, the Malinois were the first to establish type, and became so well known that other varieties at one time were called "other-than-Malinois."

The shorthaired *Chien de Berger Belge Malinoix a poil court fauve charbonne* has been given a shorter handle: Belgian Malinois (pronounced *mal-i-nwa*). The Malinois, with its "charcoaled" fawn coat, is a sheepherder par excellence from the area of Malines, giving the variety its tongue-twisting official name. Although still rare in the USA, Malinois are gaining some prominence in police work. Only recognized by AKC in 1965, the breed is slowly gaining a following.

A restaurant owner, Nicholas Rose, is credited with fostering the Groenendael. Rose bred his black bitch, "Petite," to another black herding dog, Piccard D'Uccle, and produced Duc de Groenendael, the keystone sire of the modern Belgian Sheepdog. Wartime was detrimental to breeding programs, but the Groenendael continued to serve its country in finding wounded soldiers and carrying messages on the front. Tales related by American soldiers of these dog heroes paved the way for their introduction to the North American continent. In fact, it was their prowess in war and police work that caused people to confuse them with the German Shepherd Dog. To this day, the term "Belgian Shepherd" is often a misnomer given to black German Shepherds. Today in America, the Groenendael is seen frequently in dog shows, obedience and schutzhund work. The breed also makes a fine family dog.

Brewer M. Corbeel, located near Tervuren, bred his two longhaired, black-tipped fawns, "Tom" and "Poes," producing "Miss," who was purchased by M. Danhieux, developer of the Tervuren variety. Danhieux bred Miss to Piccard D'Uccle, the black foundation of the Groenendaels, and who carried the fawn factor. During the War years, the Terv came close to being only a fond memory, until a lovely specimen, Willy de la Garde Noir, revived interest in the breed. The Terv has made rapid progress since the 1950s in both show and obedience in the USA.

The Laekenois is the rarest of the varieties. This type hails from the area of Boom near Antwerp, which is noted for its lovely and costly linens. The breed's name came from the Chateau de Laeken, one of Queen Marie Henriette's royal residences. The Laekenois was her favorite breed, which she could see helping the shepherds who grazed their flocks on the castle

Belgian Sheepdog Tervuren.

grounds. This contributed to his popularity at that time. The Laeken was used not only for herding but for guarding the fields of Boom where the valuable linens were put out to bleach. The breed still demonstrates its guard instincts and assists both the Belgian army and police. Today the variety is quite rare, and most of its population is in Holland. In 1987, there were 20 specimens in Switzerland, six in Germany and one in Italy as well as a handful of breeders in France and its native Belgium. Although recognized by the Canadian KC, the breed is still scarce in that country as well.

The Laeken likes to be "top dog." To be the dominant partner in the relationship, a Laeken owner should begin training early.

The different varieties—except the Laekenois—have been recognized for many years outside their native Belgium, with the Groenendael being the most numerous. In Canada and in Eu-

173

rope, the Belgian herding dogs are still considered varieties of the same breed, thus allowing interbreeding. In the USA, however, they have been defined as separate breeds since 1959 and crossbred litters are not registerable. This has created a pickle for breeders because Groenendaels imported from Europe can and do carry the recessive for fawn. It proves to be an unpleasant surprise to Americans to find a "Tervuren" in a litter of purebred Belgians. On the Continent, this "odd man out" could be registered, shown and bred as Terv variety. In the USA the pup would have to be listed as a fawn Belgian Sheepdog, a disqualifying color, and thus be barred from exhibition.

The Belgian dogs are agile and versatile, demonstrating their abilities today in fields other than herding: police and military work, search-and-rescue, dog guides, schutzhund and obedience. They are sturdy and thrive on outdoor excursions, no matter what the weather.

Above: Head study of the Belgian Sheepdog Laekenois.
Below: Body study of the Belgian Sheepdog Groenendael.

Belgian Shorthaired Pointer.

BELGIAN SHORTHAIRED POINTER

COUNTRY: Belgium
WEIGHT: 55 pounds
HEIGHT: 25½ inches
COAT: Short; dense and fine
COLOR: White, with large brown patches;
heavy ticking gives the white a gray appearance
OTHER NAMES: Braque Belge
REGISTRY: FCI
GROUP: Gun Dog

This strong, clean-cut pointer from Belgium was known during the last century and was probably most closely related to the French braques. The 1960 edition of the official booklet of Belgian breeds listed him as very rare.

More recently, the FCI has listed the breed "in suspension," and a letter from the Societe Royale Saint Hubert (Belgian KC), dated 11/9/84, says he has "completely disappeared." This indicates no registrations have occurred for many years, and the breed may be extinct.

Bergamasco.

BERGAMASCO

COUNTRY: Italy
WEIGHT: 57–84 pounds
HEIGHT: 22–24 inches
COAT: Abundant, long, hanging in cords
COLOR: All shades of gray, flecked with black, tan or white
OTHER NAMES: Bergamaschi, Bergamese Shepherd, Cane da Pastore Bergamasco
REGISTRY: FCI
GROUP: Herding

These shaggy dogs were brought into Italy by ancient Phoenician merchants—from where, no one knows. We can speculate that the seamen traded for shaggy, corded sheep dogs from the Caucasus or farther east.

Concentrated in the Bergamo area, an old city situated in the north near Milan, the Bergamasco is an intermediate type: a large robust herding dog with flock-guarding ability. Developed by the shepherds of the Italian Alps, he has served his masters well over the centuries.

In his migrations northward, he may have been one progenitor of the shaggy European stock dogs (Briard, Nizinny, Bouvier, etc.). The breed is affectionate and loyal, with a long memory. Owners warn, however, of a natural stubbornness that must be overcome by training.

A thick, corded coat protects him from the elements and prevents injuries from kicks or from bites of wolves or other dogs. The back portion of the coat has a woolly consistency, with the front wiry and rough like goat hair. This hair cascades over his eyes. Like those of his ancestor, the Owtcharka, his cords are never combed out. The Bergamasco presents a unique picture in motion, similar to that of the Puli or Komondor.

The breed is adaptable to any habitat from the open Alpine pastures to a small yard and is devoted to its family but distrustful of strangers. He still demonstrates strong instincts to protect as well as to herd. During a storm, a shepherd encouraged his Bergamasco to sniff a lamb and then the mother of two lost lambs. The dog searched on its own for many hours, finally returning to lead his owner to the lambs, alive and well in a ravine.

Bergamasco.

Noted as easy keepers, they stay vigorous even on their usual pastoral diet of curds and whey. The Bergamasco possesses a heavier muzzle than other members of the herding group.

Until quite recently, he was rare almost to the point of extinction. Dog lovers in Italy, as in so many countries, have worked to save this piece of canine history. He is now promoted as a working dog and can be seen exhibited at Italian and Continental shows. A few specimens have reached other countries, but most of his numbers are still at home. A specialty club is based in Sondrio, on the Swiss border, and where there are dedicated fanciers, there is always hope.

Above and Below: Bergamascos.

Above: Bergamasco tending a flock on Italian landscape. **Below:** Bergamasco.

Berger de Beauce.

BERGER DE BEAUCE

COUNTRY: France
WEIGHT: 66–85 pounds
HEIGHT: 25–28 inches
COAT: Moderately short, close and dense
COLOR: Black/tan or harlequin; previously
known colors now unacceptable
OTHER NAMES: Beauceron, French Shorthaired
Shepherd, Bas Rouge
REGISTRY: FCI
GROUP: Herding

The earliest reference to the dog from La
Beauce plains near Paris appears to be in a Renaissance manuscript, dated 1578. Like their
cousin the Briard, this breed has shown its
strength, agility and adaptability in various employment. Originally hunters of wild boar, these
dogs turned to herding and livestock guarding
and eventually to K-9 dogs for the military and
police. The Beauce served its country by carrying messages during the Great Wars. A painting
at the British War Museum displays a Beauceron wearing a messenger cylinder attached to
his collar and leaping over soldiers in a foxhole.
The breed also acted as supply transports and
the detection of wounded and of mines. Other
capabilities are evident by the choice of Beaucer-
ons as dog guides for the blind and as guard
dogs. They have much the same versatility as
German Shepherds.

The Beauce is currently the second most popular sheep dog in France, following only his
countryman, the Briard. He carries strong herding traits, and will attempt to herd any group of
two or more. The Bas Rouge designation on the
Beauce signifies the reddish tan leg markings,
yielding the nickname "Red Stocking." The

harlequin coloring is a distinctive black/tan merle, also requiring the red markings. The Beauceron's ears are preferably cropped. In addition to the four regular toes, two large dewclaws are required on each hind foot.

They are aloof with strangers, and protective of their charges, including children. Parents are warned to remove a Beauce from the room if a disciplinary swat to a child is warranted. The breed is said to look kindly only upon its master.

It is an intelligent and calm dog, accepting new situations with aplomb. These dogs enjoy a run and need an outlet for their energy. A strong (not harsh) master is recommended; the Beauceron is not for the meek and mild.

Left: Head study of the Berger de Beauce. **Below:** Beauceron. Notice the prominent upright cropped ears.

BERGER DE PICARD

COUNTRY: France
WEIGHT: 50–70 pounds
HEIGHT: 21½–26 inches
COAT: Medium-long, hard and rough, heavy undercoat, not curly
COLOR: All shades of gray and fawn, no white, except on toes or chest
OTHER NAMES: Picardy Shepherd
REGISTRY: FCI
GROUP: Herding

One of the oldest French sheep-herding dogs, possibly introduced by the Celts, the Picardy is closely related to the Beauceron and Briard. The breed has been, for many years, and still is a flock worker in the Pas-de-Calais region by the Somme in the north of France. Although the breed became endangered during the two World Wars, its easy care and happy, though mischievous, temperament have started the Picardy back on the road to recovery. Nevertheless its numbers are still limited, even in its native country.

Berger de Picard.

Berger de Picard.

The rough, tousled coat does not mat or require special care, yielding a rustic appearance. The standard demands that the ears remain small, so they naturally stand erect.

Like many herding breeds, they require human companionship . . . lots of it, along with exercise . . . lots of it . . . and an owner who will provide both. They are rowdy in their play. The Picardy is a versatile worker. With intruders, they alert and stand their ground. Picardy Shepherds receive high ratings in the official French protection sport. A few specimens of this old breed can be found in the USA.

Berger du Languedoc.

BERGER DU LANGUEDOC

COUNTRY: France
HEIGHT: 16–20 inches
COAT: Usually short, sometimes medium length with short hair on head
COLOR: Various shades of fawn and black/tan
OTHER NAMES: Farou, Cevennes Shepherd
REGISTRY: None
GROUP: Herding

The Farou may be extinct or nearly so. It is smaller with a more pointed muzzle than the northern French sheep dogs; this southern relation otherwise has many similarities. His ears are cropped, and he may have one or two rear dewclaws. The hair can be fairly short or shaggy and moderately long. The face is short-coated in all varieties, similar to the Berger de Pyrenees. His tail is docked similar to the Bouvier's. FCI has recently dropped the breed from its official lists due to lack of registrations or interested breeders.

Berger de Pyrenees, long-haired variety, gray-fawn.

BERGERS DE PYRENEES

Berger de Pyrenees

COUNTRY: France
WEIGHT: 18–30 pounds
HEIGHT: 15½–19½ inches
COAT: Long—shaggy, will cord; Goathaired—medium-long, shaggy
COLOR: Fawn, gray, blue, brindle; black is acceptable; white points permissible but not preferable
OTHER NAMES: Pyrenean Shepherd Dog, Labrit
REGISTRY: FCI
GROUP: Herding

Berger de Pyrenees, Smooth Muzzled

COUNTRY: France
HEIGHT: 16–22 inches
COAT: Medium shaggy hair except on muzzle; there should never be hair covering the eyes
COLOR: Harlequin, brindle, fawn, blue and gray, with or without white markings
OTHER NAMES: Smooth Muzzled Pyrenean Shepherd Dog, Berger de Pyrenees a Face Race
REGISTRY: FCI
GROUP: Herding

As happened in so many European countries, the ancient occupation of raising sheep created a triad of shepherd, flock-guarding dog and sheep-herding dog in the Pyrenees mountains of France.

Thus, the history of the little Berger de Pyrenees traces back many years. It seems he was always there, and his characteristics have been set through necessity and use. He was quick and agile for pursuing sheep, and well covered with hair as protection from the elements. Highly resistant to both weather extremes and illness, the breed could go long periods without food. Although brave and ready to defend master and property, he did not need to be large—should an adversary appear to be too much for him to handle, the omnipresent Great Pyrenees was ready to close the gap.

Due to the isolation created by the rugged mountains which form a natural border between France and Spain, each valley individualized the sheep dogs, with small variations in coat length and texture, color and so on. Despite the variety of types, people referred to all of them with the patois name of Labrit, which is still often referred to as a "breed."

Today the breed is often called simply the *Petit Berger*, little shepherd. The French canine body recognized the Pyrenean Shepherd in 1926, and an eminent judge well known in the Great Pyrenees, B. Senac-Lagrange, drew up a standard which remains nearly intact today. At that time, the aforementioned types and valley names were consolidated into two breed classifications.

The Pyrenees sheep dog is slightly longer than tall, with a deep chest, keeping the center of gravity low to the ground. To facilitate all the steep climbing through the mountains, their hocks are a bit close. The thin-soled feet grip

Berger de Pyrenees, goat-haired variety, fawn.

185

slippery rocks. Their trot is close to the ground; in fact, the French say "he shaves the prairie."

The Berger de Pyrenees has both a longhaired and a moderately longhaired variety. The longer coat will cord if not combed, and is shaggy and long all over. The medium-length coat is called "goat-haired" and is the classic coat, a bit shorter overall, with "cuffs" and "breeches."

The Smooth Muzzled Berger de Pyrenees (literally, bare-faced) is shorter coated, and the hair is nearly smooth on the face and leg fronts. The smooth-faced variety also tends to be more square-bodied and up on leg than his shaggier brothers. They are exhibited in separate classes. Neither variety should have its eyes covered with hair. Working and show specimens have their ears cropped rather short and blunt, and their tails docked. Some pet owners, however, prefer to leave their dogs *au naturale*. The long tail has the shepherd's crook at the end.

The Pyr Shepherd is quite wary and independent, requiring patience and consistent firmness to fit into modern family life. Dogs not ade-

Left: Smooth Muzzled Berger de Pyrenees, blue with tan markings. **Below:** Berger de Pyrenees, goat-haired

quately socialized and trained can become quite unruly—even terrors—breeders warn, although when handled properly they are loyal guardians and a joy to their families. This guardianship is evidenced by a mountain climber's tale. A hiker became ill and had to stop at a Pyrenean shepherd's hut. When the shepherd and flock arrived with nine Pyr Shepherds, the climber was warned of a bear in the area. The shepherds were going down to the village that night for supplies, but planned to leave three dogs to watch the sheep. Three more were assigned to stay with the climber in the hut. Later, he related the dogs willingly came inside and calmly arranged themselves to watch both him and the outside. Although they did not growl or panic when he approached them, they would not let the stranger touch them. They would move silently away and rearrange themselves to continue their watch.

The Pyr Sheep dogs prefer to be with their people, so can be ideal companions for retired

Smooth Muzzled Berger de Pyrenees, harlequin.

Berger de Pyrenees, long-haired variety, black with white markings.

persons, the house-bound or those who enjoy taking a dog with them. They accept the family's children, but have a low tolerance for abuse, intentional or not. Socialization and training are recommended. Their energetic nature calls for long walks or frequent runs. These dogs thrive on having a job to accomplish, whether it be obedience, herding, avalanche and rescue work, or keeping an eye on the family. One dog gave the owner no peace until she entered an excavation she was passing and found an unconscious child. The same dog rejoices in finding lost items: watches, keys, etc. The Petit Berger is described in *The Pyrenean Shepherd Dog* as "a ball of fire . . . so vivacious and quick-witted that . . . . he can . . . perform any task."

Dogs of this breed still work in the Pyrenees, and a number of loyal fanciers promote the breed throughout Europe, as well as a handful doing so in the United States.

BERNESE MOUNTAIN DOG

COUNTRY: Switzerland
WEIGHT: 88 pounds
HEIGHT: 23–27½ inches
COAT: Moderate length hair, straight or wavy but never curly
COLOR: Classic Swiss coloring, black/tan with white markings
OTHER NAMES: Berner Sennenhund
REGISTRY: FCI, AKC, TKC, CKC
GROUP: Mastiff

The Bernese Mountain Dogs trace back to the Roman invasion of Helvetia (Switzerland) 2,000 years ago. Caesar's legions spread throughout Europe and needed guard dogs for their supplies and stations. Their mastiffs supplied the strength. Probable crosses with native flock-guarding dogs provided the ability to withstand the severe weather of the Alps, as well as softening temperaments.

Later used by the weavers of the Berne canton (district) as a draft dog, the Bernese Dog was also a general farm worker and flock guardian, although its benign temperament did not make it a suitable property protector. On market day, these great, patient dogs would be seen pulling

Bernese Mountain Dog.

carts piled high with dairy products or woven baskets into the villages.

The breed had nearly disappeared in the mid-1800s, due to a lack of concerted breeding efforts. Swiss interests had turned to other breeds, particularly the acclaimed St. Bernard, as well as imports that seemed more intriguing than the common native farm dogs. Around the turn of the century, a Swiss cynologist, Herr Franz Schertenleib, combed the countryside to find the last of these dogs his father had told him about. He had some success around the Durrbach district of Berne, which encouraged him to continue searching his country for good representatives of the breed. Zurich Professor Albert Heim joined his efforts. Thanks to the interest of these two men, the Bernese Mountain Dog made a comeback.

At first these dogs carried a variety of local and descriptive names, such as *Gelbbackler* (yellow cheeks), *Vierauger* (four eyes), cheese factory dogs or, most often, *Durrbachler*. Because they were from the entire canton of Berne, not just Durrbach, the club formed at that time changed the breed's name to Berner Sennenhund in 1908. By a 1910 exhibition of Bernese, 107 dogs were shown to judge Albert Heim. While many were without pedigree, three-quarters of the dogs were given the stamp of approval for breeding based on type. The Bernese was on its way!

In the 1930s, one faction made a push to make them seem fiercer, like a guard dog, with some breeding for very light eyes and the split nose. That soon ran its course like other fads, and common sense reigned again.

The Bernese has a huge body of supporters in its homeland, with a strong following in Continental Europe, in Scandinavia and, recognized by AKC in 1936, is steadily gaining ground in the USA. Canada took the breed into its fold in the 1970s, but it remains rare in Great Britain.

These dogs are not giants, and increased size is frowned upon by serious breeders. While the Bernese must be sturdy and strong, ability and soundness are equal prerequisites. Grooming is moderate, with a good brushing every couple weeks making the Bernese sleek and handsome. Their sweet, happy temperament has made them superb family dogs.

Bernese Mountain Dog.

BICHON FRISE

COUNTRY: France/Belgium
HEIGHT: 9–12 inches
COAT: Long, silky, loosely curled outer coat, with undercoat
COLOR: Pure white, although a bit of cream, apricot or gray on the head is allowed.
OTHER NAMES: Bichon Tenerife, Tenerife Dog, Bichon a Poil Frise
REGISTRY: FCI, AKC, TKC, CKC
GROUP: Gun Dog

Fourteenth-century sailors succumbed to the charms of the Bichon, bringing the little furry dog back to France from the shores of Tenerife, one of the Canary Islands in the Atlantic off the coast of Spain. The Bichon from Tenerife has been recorded for nearly as long as the Maltese. The two breeds are closely related, with the Bichon a bit larger. The island was certainly on the Phoenician trade route, and the dogs may have been brought there as items of barter. In Europe, his happy ways soon gained him friends in high places, and he enjoyed 400 years of living among kings and the aristocracy.

In the 1800s, their ride on the crest waned, and the royal whim turned to other dogs. The Tenerife Dog became a dog of the streets, a pet of the commoner. The little Bichon did not remain unemployed long, however. His winsome ways and agility soon gave him new employment as an organ grinder's dog or as a circus performer.

Again, it was servicemen who were entranced by the dog's soft, fluffy appeal. When they took specimens home from France after WWI, French breeders finally began taking the little dogs seriously and, in 1934, they obtained French Kennel Club recognition. They received the nod by the AKC to enter the Miscellaneous Class in 1971, and Canada followed suit in 1975.

Bichon a Poil Frise literally means bichon of the curly coat. The Bichon Frise is distinctive among the bichons, since it is the only one that is double-coated. His coat tends to puff out all over, rather than hang down like his single-coated cousins.

The Bichon is a comparative newcomer to AKC recognition, but is quickly becoming a source to be reckoned with in the show ring. Their sparkling white, poufy jackets and their gait, with a suggestion of a barely contained bounce, make them an attractive show contender.

Bichon Frise.

Bichon Frise.

Bichon Frise.

BILLY

COUNTRY: France
WEIGHT: 55–66 pounds
HEIGHT: 24–26 inches
COAT: Short and smooth
COLOR: Almost pure white, with orange or lemon spots on head and body
REGISTRY: FCI
GROUP: Hound

Developed in the last century by G. Hublot du Rivault, the Billy received its name from Rivault's Poitou estate. Rivault used three breeds, all of which are now extinct, in the development of his dogs. The Ceris was a small, graceful, bright orange-spotted hound used for hare and wolf. Montaimboeufs were large, strong, handsome, and fast dogs used for wild boar; they were also pale orange/white. The Larrye, noted for its exquisite nose, was the creation of Emile de Mauvisse, Count of Villars, in the early 1800s. This occurred in the region of Poitou. Mauvisse is believed to have used what was left of the Poitevins—and then named the breed after the Marquis de Larrye, who founded the Poitevin. Through careful linebreeding, these breeds became the Billy.

The Billy hound is lean-headed with a small, flat ear. He is resourceful and clever, a hound of acute scent, with a light and harmonious voice. He is a master deer hunter, and his pleasing bay—trumpeted through the valleys—differs in tone by the greatness of the game he has sighted. He is sensitive to cold and, when not working, is reported to be a bit quarrelsome with his fellow pack mates. Unknown outside his homeland, his current status in France is not well documented. Although nearly extinct after the last war, a group has fostered his comeback.

Billy.

Black Forest Hound.

BLACK FOREST HOUND

COUNTRY: Czechoslovakia
WEIGHT: 44–49 pounds
HEIGHT: 18–20 inches
COAT: Hard and wiry; ¾–2 inches in length, lying close to the body
COLOR: Black and tan
OTHER NAMES: Slovensky Kopov, Slovakian Hound
REGISTRY: FCI
GROUP: Hound

This Czech national hound is the only scenthound breed native to its country. Although known and used for centuries, formal recognition by the canine governing bodies did not occur until after WWII. He probably descended from dogs of Hungary or of the Balkans, with likely crosses to gun dogs or other non-hound breeds.

This is a distinctive hound. Tough and protective, he makes a diligent watchdog, as the Black Forest Hound lacks the tranquil, naturally obedient nature of most scenthounds. Although affectionate to his master, he requires rigorous early training to serve his purpose. This hound remains widespread throughout Czechoslovakia. The wild boar continues to be his natural prey and he is still hunted extensively in the mountainous regions of Czechoslovakia.

BLACK MOUTH CUR

COUNTRY: USA
WEIGHT: 40–95 pounds
HEIGHT: 16–25 inches
COAT: Short hair, either coarse or fine
COLOR: Reddish golden yellow to fawn or sandy yellow; with or without black muzzle or mask; small amount of white on toes, tip of tail or chest; no white on neck; no brindle or black allowed
OTHER NAMES: Southern Cur, Yellow Black Mouth Cur
GROUP: Hound

The Black Mouth Cur has a burning desire to please his master. A courageous, swift hunter of squirrel, coon, boar or bear, he never retreats. He runs to catch the game and catches to kill. On the track, trailing is semi-open or silent, with a chop or yodel acceptable on tree or at bay. Curs rarely trot, even while hunting, going from a walk to a ground-covering lope.

These dogs are avid hunters, yet work stock well too. Breeders say a pup will train himself—treeing, protecting and/or bunching and penning cattle by six months of age. They are used throughout the southern area of the USA.

The Black Mouth Cur owners claim "Old Yeller" as their property, and that is possible, although the dog in the book was bob-tailed. It is certain, whatever the breed, the family of the canine hero was cur.

Predictable, with even temperaments, the Southern Curs are loyal to their families, giving their lives, if necessary, to protect them. They are especially affectionate to women and children, and aloof with strange men. Some object to parents disciplining children which, of course, endears them to youngsters!

Black Mouth Cur.

BLACK RUSSIAN TERRIER

COUNTRY: USSR
HEIGHT: 25–28 inches
COAT: 2–4 inches, coarse, dense and bristly but close lying
COLOR: Black or salt/pepper
OTHER NAMES: Chornyi, Terrier Noir Russe
REGISTRY: FCI
GROUP: Terrier

In the 1960s, Soviet dog fanciers wished to create their own breed of large working terrier. Using mainly Giant Schnauzers crossed with Airedales, Rottweilers and other breeds, they fashioned a big, agile, tough and weather-resistant dog. It is interesting to note that in times past, the Giant Schnauzer was often called the Russian Bear Schnauzer, indicating the breed's widespread use in the USSR.

Type was fixed in a relatively short time and the Black Russian became widely known in its homeland. FCI has recently granted recognition to this newcomer. This international sanctioning denotes an established written standard and a stability and consistency of breed characteristics.

Many Black Russians are trained and used for professional guard work. They are large enough to be "manstoppers," with adequate coat to protect them from the Russian winters. But the majority of the breed are family pets. They are commonly seen in the larger urban areas, like Moscow and Leningrad, where they serve as companions and watchdogs. Although reliable with their masters, they are suspicious and have an active defense reaction. They are capable of being quite ferocious.

In appearance, they somewhat resemble an uncropped Giant, with a bit more bone and thickness of body as well as a wave to the coat, both gifts of their Airedale inheritance. Very few of the breed are found outside of its native land due to the fact the the Soviets have banned its export.

Black Russian Terrier.

Black Russian Terrier.

BLEUS DE GASCOGNE

Grand Bleu de Gascogne

COUNTRY: France
WEIGHT: 71–77 pounds
HEIGHT: 25–28 inches
COAT: Short and smooth, but not too fine
COLOR: Tricolor; body predominantly white, tan only above eyes, on cheeks and underside of ears, black on head with a few body spots; heavy roaning throughout the white creates the "blue" color
OTHER NAMES: Large Blue Gascony Hound
REGISTRY: FCI
GROUP: Hound

Petit Bleu de Gascogne

COUNTRY: France
WEIGHT: 44 pounds
HEIGHT: 19½–23½ inches
COAT: Short and smooth, but not too fine
COLOR: Tricolor; body predominantly white, tan only above eyes, on cheeks and underside of ears, black on head with a few body spots; heavy roaning throughout the white creates the "blue" color
OTHER NAMES: Small Blue Gascony Hound
REGISTRY: FCI
GROUP: Hound

Petit Griffon Bleu de Gascogne

COUNTRY: France
HEIGHT: 17–21 inches
COAT: Rough, wiry coat
COLOR: Tricolor; body predominantly white, tan only above eyes, on cheeks and underside of ears, black on head with a few body spots; heavy roaning throughout the white creates the "blue" color
OTHER NAMES: Small Blue Gascony Griffon
REGISTRY: FCI
GROUP: Hound

Basset Bleu de Gascogne

COUNTRY: France
WEIGHT: 35–40 pounds
HEIGHT: 12–14 inches
COAT: Short and smooth, but not too fine
COLOR: Tricolor; body predominantly white, tan only above eyes, on cheeks and underside of ears, black on head with a few body spots; heavy roaning throughout the white creates the "blue" color
OTHER NAMES: Blue Gascony Basset
REGISTRY: FCI
GROUP: Hound

Basset Bleu de Gascogne.

Gascony Province lies on the southwestern coast of France, near the Pyrenees Mountains and the Spanish border. Their hounds are of the classic French type, descending directly from the original scenting dogs of Gaul and the Phoenician hound trade. The Gascony stands beside the ancient French griffons as the two types from which most of the modern breeds developed. The Grand is one of the few modern breeds left from the Grand Chiens Courants of the past.

The Grand Bleu originally was used to hunt wolf and, like so many breeds for that purpose, nearly worked himself out of existence with his efficiency in making the European wolf extinct. France's King Henry IV, who reigned in the late 1500s and early 1600s, owned a renowned pack of this breed.

The Grand Bleu is one of the world's largest scenthounds. Only of moderate speed, he is known for his great ability to raise game by his tremendous endurance, his marvelous nose, and a strong and sonorous voice heard at great distance. A reputation as the "coldest nosed" dog is well earned, giving voice long after the "hot" scent has faded. He is built leggy and square, and is aristocratic looking, with no ponderance or heaviness. Many packs remain in France today, and are used on hare, deer and boar.

Many of this breed were brought to America and used in the development of American coonhound breeds. The Gascony probably first arrived in the late 17th century with French explorers. In 1785, General Lafayette gave seven purebred Grand Bleu Gasconies to General George Washington. Washington was known as a hound fancier and breeder, and he noted in his diary that, in October of that first year, one of the French Gascony bitches gave birth to 15 purebred puppies! He also remarked that their melodious voices were like the bells of Moscow. Gasconies were imported to America in the late 1800s and again during the mid-1900s. Because they lacked the trailing speed and the ability to locate quickly that was so desired for American coon hunting, they never gained a foothold as a pure breed in the Western World. But crossed with native hounds, they increased coldtrailing ability and endurance.

The Petit Bleu was bred down from the Grand to handle smaller quarry. Except for size,

Grand Bleu de Gascogne.

he is basically judged on the same standard as the Grand. He tends to be a bit more refined in head and compact of body. As a smaller dog, he is not only speedier but eats less, and is easier to keep and to transport. The breed is especially adept at finding and coursing rabbit, and it is said in France that "going hunting with a Petit Bleu means never coming home with an empty game bag."

The Basset version is a short-legged Grand, and is still a highly prized hunting companion. His handsome appearance, joyous and enthusiastic attitude to the hunt, as well as his pleasant and affectionate personality make him a pleasure to own. Some have found places as companion dogs.

Rarest of the Gascony hounds is the Petit Griffon Bleu, a product of the Petit crossed with wire-coated hounds. Except for his short, wiry jacket and slightly smaller size, he should be similar to the Petit in conformation and color. He is a rustic dog, and is a methodical and untiring worker with a keen nose.

Above Left: Petit Bleu de Gascogne. **Above Right:** Basset Bleu de Gascogne. **Below:** Grand Bleu de Gascogne.

BLOODHOUND

COUNTRY: Belgium
WEIGHT: 70–110 pounds
HEIGHT: 23–27 inches
COAT: Short, thick and hard
COLOR: Black/tan, red/tan, tawny; small amount of white on chest, feet and tip of tail allowed
OTHER NAMES: St. Hubert Hound, Chien de St. Hubert
REGISTRY: FCI, AKC, UKC, TKC, CKC
GROUP: Hound

The ancestry of the modern Bloodhound can be traced straight back to the monastery of St. Hu-bert and before. These were the ancient dogs called Segusius. The black hounds of the Ardennes were schweisshunds: slow, deliberate, heavy-skinned tracking dogs with persistence, exquisite noses and melodious voices. They originally coldtrailed game such as wolf, big cats or deer, or followed the trail of wounded game. The breed contributed to the development of many European hound breeds, especially the coldtrailing dogs.

When the Normans from France (Gaul) conquered England in 1066 AD, they undoubtedly introduced many of their dogs. The St. Hubert Hound was one of those brought to England, and figured in the formation of the Foxhound. But the original specimen refined with Talbot or

Bloodhound, black/tan.

201

Southern Hound and called Bloodhound in English also found favor in the British Isles and America.

His ability to discern a cold trail and persistently follow it for many hours gave rise to another profession. Law enforcement officials soon put him to work finding lost persons or trailing criminals. A documented story of a Kentucky Bloodhound named "Nick Carter" tells of the dog following a trail 104 hours old, leading to the discovery and arrest of a fugitive. This same dog's skill resulted in the capture and conviction of more than 600 criminals! Many other records

Bloodhound puppies.

of equally amazing feats are recounted among Bloodhound owners. Trails ranged from a short ten feet to 138 miles; one dog caught 23 escaped convicts in only a day-and-a-half of work.

This reputation as a tracker, especially of fugitives, is the one most people have in mind when they think of the Bloodhound. Movies and fictional stories encouraged the image of a fearsome, baying hound with fangs bared, pursuing escapees through the swamps.

Actually, the Bloodhound is a silent trailer, not announcing his presence. Although he certainly could track down a runaway, he might be more likely to greet the pursued with a licking tongue when he reaches his goal. The track is the only thing in his mind; he is not a pugnacious dog at all! In fact, the Bloodhound is much more frequently put to the trail of lost children or strayed hikers.

The modern Bloodhound is familiar around the world. Although not the identical dog of the monastery, he is officially named the Chien de St. Hubert in Belgium, after his ancient, extinct ancestors. This breed still may be referred to by this title in non-English-speaking countries. But whether Bloodhound or St. Hubert Hound, it is the same large, stolid dog with the long scrolled ears, sad countenance, facial wrinkles and hanging flews and dewlap.

Since he was bred to do his own thing rather than slavishly follow his master's every command, he may seem to be slow on the uptake. Training takes patience, and the instinct to track demands an enclosed yard. His single-mindedness means that, for his own safety, the "sniffer" should not be allowed off leash. Obedience is not his forte, but if you lay a track, you will be able to stand back in admiration. His sense of smell is so much more acute than a human's, it is difficult to fathom; it has been said to be two million times greater. Just think what a garbage can—or a frightened, sweating human—smells like to this breed—a veritable potpourri of scents!

Roger Caras, well-known animal lover and author of *A Celebration of Dogs*, considers "Yankee," the Bloodhound who shared his home, "vain, even arrogant . . . splendid, magnanimous, noble . . . superb . . . a blessing and a miracle."

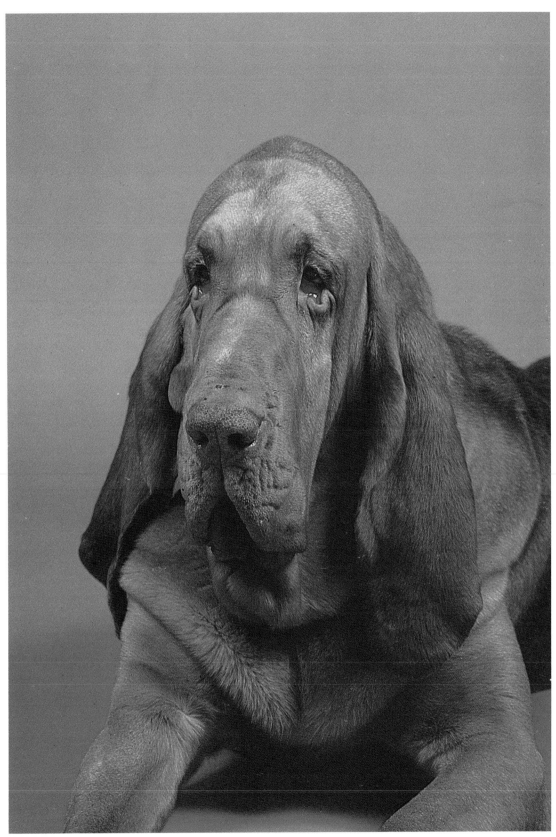

Bloodhound, red/tan.

BLUE LACY

COUNTRY: USA
WEIGHT: 40–50 pounds
COAT: Short, smooth
COLOR: Gunmetal gray, tan, yellow, cream, black; usually solid, but may have minimal white markings
REGISTRY: None
GROUP: Herding

The boast is that a Blue Lacy can do the work of five cowboys, and deluxe workers they are. They arrived "out West" by covered wagon from Kentucky in 1858, brought by the Lacy brothers.

These dogs are in the category of curs, with the emphasis on the herding/droving characteristics. They—like their relatives the Catahoulas—were created for specific needs of colonial Americans. Lacys are said to be the result of Greyhound/scenthound/ coyote cross. Droving dogs could have contributed to the breed as well. The origin of the unusual slate blue color (and blue nose) is a genetic rarity. Few dogs have this coloration—the Bearded Collie, the Neapolitan Mastiff, the Greyhound—so the Greyhound contribution to the Lacy's genetic make-up is a likely one. The so-called coyote in the cross could easily have been feral pariah dogs common in the southeastern United States.

Blue Lacy, gray.

Blue Lacy, black and tan.

Lacys were seen regularly on southwestern ranches for nearly a hundred years. Diane Gentry points out that they came close to disappearing when "modern cowboys on three-wheeled motorbikes" hit the trails.

H.C. Wilkes was determined to save the breed and has worked since 1975 to do just that. They are finding favor with ranchers due to their burning desire to work. A Lacy can handle the meanest longhorn cattle and take to the job instinctively, requiring no training. They can also tackle wild hogs, but can herd chickens in the barnyard as well. Their owners claim they're a good all-around dog, knowing just where to be at the appropriate time and diving into chores without being told to do so. Some will also tree game. They have a gentle nature and take direction with ease.

Bluetick Coonhound.

BLUETICK COONHOUND

COUNTRY: USA
WEIGHT: 45–80 pounds
HEIGHT: 21–27 inches
COAT: Short, dense; a bit coarse to the touch
COLOR: Tricolor, with heavy black ticking in white areas
REGISTRY: UKC
GROUP: Hound

The fine French hounds of the Gascogne, Porcelaine, Saintongeois and others had been brought to America even before colonial times. These patient, persistent, beautifully voiced hounds continued to be bred in fairly pure form in remote areas of the South.

During the early decades of this century, dog dealers made trips into the Louisiana bayou, the Ozark Mountains and other isolated areas,

Bluetick Coonhound.

bringing out hounds of remarkably pure type. These dogs, mainly of the heavily ticked blue color, were often referred to as Blue Gascons or French Staghounds. Crossed with various foxhounds and curs, they formed the basis of the UKC Bluetick Coonhound.

Because they were registered as English Coonhounds along with dogs of a very different type, distinct strains of these blue dogs became famous. The Ozark Mountain strain was said to be the closest to pure French and came to prominence in the 1930s. Famous dogs of this strain included "Missouri Valley Echo," "Bailey's Blue Dollar" and "Grant's King Bo."

In the 1920s, the Sugar Creek strain began, with dogs of this bloodline remaining today. They have some old-type Black and Tan in their makeup and are very like the French hounds in their style of hunting. Famous Sugar Creek hounds included the peerless "Blue Bones," who won the first field trial for coonhounds in 1924, and later "Top Notch Drum," "Huey Long," and the prepotent "Cornerstone." Bloodhound, Bluetick, and Porcelaine, as well as Gascogne blood, flowed through the veins of the Old Line strain, another very famous line which included the studs: "Lee's Troop," "Florida Blue" and

"Green's Panther." These dogs were much sought after during the late 1930s and the War years, but Old Line is simply gone. The Smokey River and Bugle strains were also prominent in the development of the breed.

Breeders of these blueticked dogs wanted to keep their old style of hunting. They feared a trend to make the majority of hounds registered as English faster and more hot-nosed. To maintain the old-fashioned type, they officially broke away in 1945 and established the breed known as the Bluetick Coonhound.

For a time, blueticked pups from a litter could be registered as Blueticks, and the redticked whelps became English Coonhounds. But soon the stud books were closed, and this practice was no more.

Blueticks still have devout followers and are fine coonhounds. But some owners feel these dogs recently have given way to the current trend of foxhound type and speed in order to participate in the competitive events, as the English hound did before them. Those who want the original big, cold-nosed, old-fashioned type have thus converted to the Blue Gascon and the Majestic.

BOLOGNESE

COUNTRY: Italy
WEIGHT: 5½–9 pounds
HEIGHT: 10–12 inches
COAT: Long, soft, tufty hair without undercoat
COLOR: White, some blond markings are allowed but not preferred
OTHER NAMES: Bichon Bolognese
REGISTRY: FCI
GROUP: Gun Dog

Bologna is a city of northern Italy, well known for centuries as a center of art and learning. The existence of the Bolognese has been recorded since the year 1200, most probably descended from bichon types brought in from southern Italy and Malta. By the Renaissance, the Bolognese had become a favorite of the nobility. Both the Gonzagas and the Medicis bred them and the Duke d'Este gave a pair to King Phillip II of Spain. Supposedly, he indicated that he had

Bolognese, white.

Bolognese, white.

never received a better gift. This breed was also a favorite with La Pompadour, Catherine of Russia, and the ladies-in-waiting of many European courts. Today it is less known, in fact, almost rare in its homeland. Nevertheless, dedicated breeders promote this ancient and admired dog, and there have been recent imports into the United States.

The Bolognese is a typical small bichon dog, intelligent, happy, faithful and companionable. While not hyperactive or high-strung, they are vivacious and full of fun. Breeders report that even ten-year-olds still play like puppies. They are quite fearless and love people.

Bred as companions, they need the attention and presence of their family. In fact, they become so attached to their owners they are like a shadow, following their idols from room to room. "To have a Bolognese in the house is to have someone to love and adore."

The cottony white coat requires daily brushing to keep it free of tangles. But apart from coat care, they are healthy, quiet dogs that make superb companions. They have acute hearing and eyesight, taking notice of anything new or unusual and notify their owners. So, while not barkers, they can be true watchdogs.

Above: Bolognese. **Below:** Bologneses, with blonde coloration.

Above: Border Collie, blue merle with tan points and white markings. **Below:** Border Collie, black with white markings, giving ample warning to the sheep in its herd.

BORDER COLLIE

COUNTRY: Great Britain
WEIGHT: 30–45 pounds
HEIGHT: 18–20 inches
COAT: Medium-long (up to 3 inches), thick, straight
COLOR: Black, blue, chocolate, red, with or without tan points and/or white markings—merle can occur in all colors
REGISTRY: FCI, AKC, UKC, TKC, CKC
GROUP: Herding

Border Collie, black with white markings.

The Border Collie probably remains closest in type to the generic "collie" of *auld* Scotland, originating in the border country between Scotland and England. One of the distinct features of the breed is its ability to "eye," a hypnotic stare which wills the sheep to move and turn. The Border was selected for its finesse at strong-eye, coming to prominence with the advent of sheep-herding trials, in which the breed excels. A Border of the early years, "Old Hemp," remains undefeated in English sheep dog trials to this day. Demonstrating his loyalty, another Border stood guard over his dead master for days after the shepherd died while in the hills with the flock.

Although type is distinct, size and coat variations always have been and are still less important than workability. Along with that vital quality, trainability is a prime consideration for the breed.

These dogs are often referred to as "farm collies" or "working collies" and remain excellent working dogs, aiding farmers and stock owners in sheep-herding. They are superb in obedience competition. Two types of temperament are apparent: the workaholic, driven to herd anything and everyone continuously, or the more laid-back family pet. Border Collies are happiest when given a chore and need to have an outlet for their energy. If thwarted in their herding opportunities, Borders will herd the neighbor's stock, other animals, the children—one, in Hawaii, even herds coconuts! A long-time breeder states, "To live with a Border collie is like having a shadow with you."

The Border is recognized throughout the world. The breed is highly exhibited in Australia and as part of the AKC and CKC Miscellaneous Classes. In North America many are registered within their own working-stock dog organizations, bypassing the official registries. Many Border owners fear emphasis on looks and beauty could lead to the breed's ruin. Instead these people encourage a stronger emphasis on working qualities.

BORDER TERRIER

COUNTRY: Great Britain
WEIGHT: 11–12 pounds
HEIGHT: 10 inches
COAT: Rough, wiry
COLOR: Red to wheaten, grizzle/tan or blue/tan allowed; any white other than small spot on chest undesirable
REGISTRY: FCI, AKC, TKC, CKC
GROUP: Terrier

The border area between England and Scotland is rocky with poor soil. Sheep raising is common, and the Border is one of many kinds of dogs developed for going after sheep-stealing foxes and other vermin. He is a small dog with an amazing amount of pluck for his size. The requirements for the Border called for a dog with legs long enough to enable him to cover territory swiftly and to follow a horse, but small enough to go to ground.

His ancestry is without written history, but stems from many of the same origins as the other terriers of northern England. He was previously known as the Reedwater Terrier or the Coquetdale Terrier for valleys or localities of his early existence. He acquired his present name in 1880, perhaps because he was so commonly worked with the Border Foxhounds.

The allowable color of blue and tan suggests a similar background to the Bedlington (whose original members were smaller than the present breed). He probably shares an ancestry with the Dandie Dinmont and the Lakeland as well. Even today an occasional whelp has the soft topknot.

The Border Terrier has not earned the recognition of some of his British relatives, but he is slowly gaining a foothold in the doggy community. In fact, when he was granted English Kennel Club acceptance in 1920, many terrier men were incensed, fearing he would be "prettified" into a show dandy. That fear has not been realized, and he retains his rough-and-tumble looks and qualities. Even though he is recognized by canine governing bodies, his lack of wide exposure in the show ring or as an over-popular pet has maintained his working attributes.

One advantage of the breed is the close, broken coat that affords him protection in the fields. It does not need to be stripped like that of the Wire Fox Terrier, Lakeland Terrier and many others. The standard states that a dog with correct coat should need but a slight "tidying-up of the head, neck, and feet" to go into the show ring. His small size and alert but obedient demeanor make him a marvelous watchdog and companion, as well as a competition-quality obedience dog. Although game, he is not quarrelsome with other dogs. His tail is undocked and carried gaily.

The Border's head should look "like that of an otter," with a broad flat skull, a gradual stop, and a semi-blunt muzzle. He should be built rather narrowly through the shoulder and rear to allow him access to the burrows of foxes and martens.

Border Terrier.

211

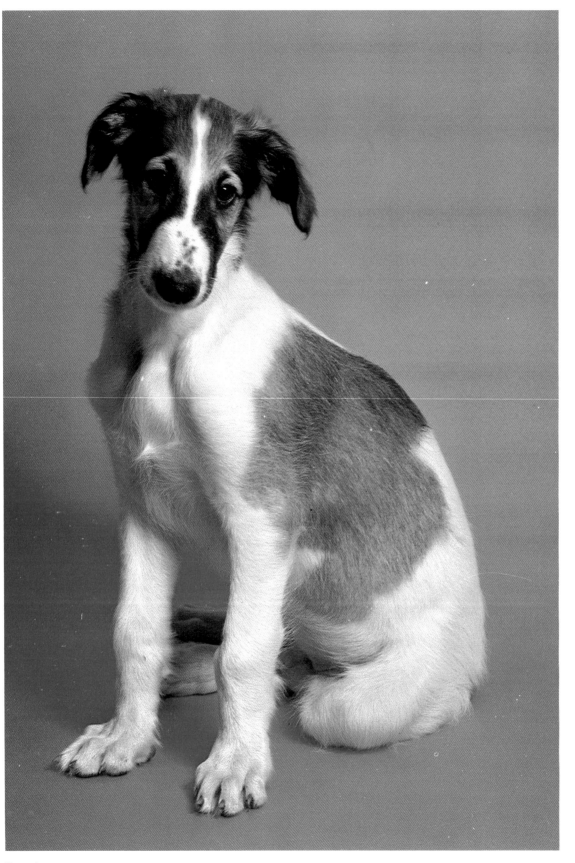

Borzoi, pup.

Borzois.

BORZOI

COUNTRY: USSR
WEIGHT: 75–105 pounds
HEIGHT: 28–31 inches
COAT: Moderately long, silky, flat, wavy or curly; short on head
COLOR: Any color—white usually predominates
OTHER NAMES: Russian Wolfhound, Psowaya Barsaya
REGISTRY: FCI, AKC, TKC, UKC
GROUP: Southern

The best-known Russian dog has been used in its motherland for coursing wolves since the early 17th century. A Russian duke imported several swift sighthounds from Arabia for hunting, but they succumbed almost immediately to the harsh winters. Trying a second time, he crossed the gazehounds with native coated breeds, probably Tartar coursing hounds or long-legged shepherd dogs, taking a step toward the modern Borzoi.

Ceremonial wolf hunts were a display of wealth beyond measure. Everything revolved around the killing of the wolf—from the pairs of aristocratic Russian Wolfhounds chosen from the vast kennels (identical in color and markings to please the noble's eye and equal in speed and strength to reach the wolf at the same time), to the quality horse flesh from the immense stables, the elegant dress of the noble hunters and their servants, and the accompanying opulent celebrations.

As soon as the wolf was sighted, a pair of dogs was unleashed—and the chase was on! It was imperative that the dogs reach the quarry at the same time, to attack from both sides. As the dogs held the wolf down, the nobleman finished off the kill with a flourish of his dagger.

The large, tough hunting dogs were, never-

213

theless, gentle in temperament and exotic in appearance, making impressive gifts from the czars to the crowned heads of Europe.

In 1903 an admirer of the breed, Joseph Thomas, undertook a pilgrimage to Russia to find the ideal Borzoi. He had little luck, even at the imperial kennels of the czar, until he found the original type in the kennels of Artem Balderoff at Woronzova and of His Royal Highness, the Grand Duke Nicholas at Tula. The dogs Thomas imported were the basis for breeding programs on both sides of the Atlantic.

After the Russian Revolution, many of the kennels were abandoned and breeding of the royal dog ceased. Dogs, through innocent association with the aristocracy, were slaughtered during the chaos. The breed survived through the previous gifts to the Western World and the few dogs that were smuggled out of the country.

Today, there is renewed Soviet pride for their magnificent hound, and they are used by practical hunters throughout southwestern Russia.

Although the Borzoi no longer hunts wolves, it is a competitive courser. Observers thrill to the magnificence of a Borzoi in full stride. Its large size, demand for exercise and great appetite still require more than a pauper's wages. The regal elegance of the breed stands them well in the world of advertising.

Indoors they are graceful and dignified, leaving no havoc behind them, despite their great size. A current breeder's ceramic business would be put to dust by most breeds, yet the Borzoi tiptoe through the shop filled with greenware with nary a mishap. Their calm demeanor and nobility make them an attractive pet for those with enough room.

Borzoi.

Borzoi.

BOSTON TERRIER

COUNTRY: USA
WEIGHT: 25 pounds maximum (classified as under 15, 15–20, or 20–25)
HEIGHT: 15–17 inches
COAT: Short, smooth
COLOR: Brindle with white markings preferred, black with white markings permissible
REGISTRY: FCI, AKC, UKC, TKC, CKC
GROUP: Mastiff

Bred down from pit-fighting dogs of the bull-and-terrier types, the Boston is one of the few breeds "made in the USA." Around 1893, a mixture of Pit Bull, Boxer, English Bull Terrier, French Bulldog and small English Bulldogs produced a pair—Hooper's Judge and Burnett's Gyp—who were the foundation of the Boston Terrier.

It is difficult to believe that these dapper little dogs were once tough pit-fighters. In fact, their weight classifications were once divided as light, middle and heavyweight. Their determination was remarkable, and they are still scrappy enough to defend themselves even with dogs many times their size.

In yesteryear, they were shown under the category of "Round-headed Bull and Terriers, any color." During the infancy of the breed, these little dogs were also called American Bull Terriers and Bullet Heads.

The Irish pattern is well established as the Boston's markings—i.e., white muzzle, blaze on skull, collar, and forechest; white paws and (if they had one) a white tip on tail. Markings are highly important in the show ring, with exact symmetry sought. The Boston's body proportions resemble those of the Staffordshire Terrier, while his short face and screw tail come from his Bulldog ancestors.

During the middle of the 20th century, the Boston Terrier reigned as the American king of purebreds, and his number one position lasted for many years. Because of the breed's large skull and small pelvis, however, many whelpings require Caesarean sections. Although he has stepped down from his throne to join the common dog, he retains his popularity as a pet by devoted enthusiasts of the breed.

Boston fanciers describe them as delightful dogs—keen and intelligent, not yappy. Their biddable nature produces good obedience workers and friends, making them an excellent choice for the elderly. The easily cared for coat and a need to be with their owners accentuate their selection as companions.

Boston Terrier, black with white markings.

Boston Terrier, brindle with white markings.

BOUVIER DE ARDENNES

COUNTRY: Belgium
WEIGHT: 55 pounds
HEIGHT: Medium—up to 24 inches; large—24 inches or more
COAT: 2 inches long, rough and wiry
COLOR: Any color
OTHER NAMES: Ardennes Cattle Dog
REGISTRY: FCI
GROUP: Herding

BOUVIER DES FLANDRES

COUNTRY: France/Belgium
WEIGHT: 88 pounds
HEIGHT: 22½–27½ inches
COAT: Medium length, rough, tousled, "steel wool" hair
COLOR: Fawn to black, pepper and salt, gray and brindle
OTHER NAMES: Belgian Cattle Dog
REGISTRY: FCI, AKC, UKC, TKC, CKC
GROUP: Herding

In times past, all dogs working with cattle were called *bouvier* (bovine herder), and each region throughout the area had its own type. From ancient rough-coated working stock, these dogs were prized as drovers and guardians. As the motorized age arrived, the need for driving cattle to market was gone and so was the call for the dogs that helped in the drives.

The Bouviers were almost eliminated during the long bloody fighting of WWI, and many of the rarer types were lost altogether. Sadly, breeds that are now but a memory include the Bouvier de Roulers, Bouvier de Moerman, and Bouvier de Paret. Still remaining are the Bouvier de Ardennes and Bouvier des Flandres. Both France and Belgium have claimed the dog of Flanders, and the FCI has actually dubbed it "Franco-Belgian." FCI recognizes the Ardennes, although the Belgian KC feels the breed may be nearing extinction—or already gone. A Belgian Army veterinarian, Captain Darby, can be credited with saving the Flandres through the War years. His outstanding Champion Nic de Sittengem won many exhibitions and proved

Bouvier des Flandres, black.

valuable as a sire, with most modern pedigrees tracing back to him.

The Bouvier is a tough, natural working dog, hardy enough to be kept outside all year. He has a forbidding countenance which tends to keep strangers at bay; he makes a good watch dog, but is obedient and affectionate with his master. The Flandres gained a respected reputation serving as an ambulance dog and messenger during World War I. In more recent years, the working Bouvier has served as a defense and military dog. In Belgium, a Bouvier cannot hold the title of show champion until it has passed a working test. He competes in schutzhund and obedience in North America and makes an excellent family guardian.

Ears are not cropped on the Ardennes, with an erect ear preferred. The Flandres' standard specifies cropped ears. Both breeds have short docked tails. The Bouviers' blocky strong head, rough jacket, beard and mustaches give them the appearance of a stern old grandfather. At one time, their harsh coat caused them to be called *pikhaar*, Flemish for hair which pricks, while another nickname *vuilbaard* (dirty beard) is self-evident.

Bouvier des Flandres.

Bouviers des Flandres, salt/pepper, black, and fawn.

Above: Bouvier de Ardennes. **Below:** In its native land, the Bouvier des Flandres is praised for its working abilities—usually.

BOXER

COUNTRY: Germany
WEIGHT: 53–71 pounds
HEIGHT: 22½–25 inches
COAT: Short, smooth
COLOR: Fawn or brindle, with or without white points
REGISTRY: FCI, AKC, UKC, TKC, CKC
GROUP: Mastiff

The Boxer is a refined version of the old *bullenbeisser* (literal translation bull-biter) which has been streamlined in body and sweetened in temperament. His ancestors are thought to have been early Great Danes and English Bulldogs. A similarity to the Boston Terrier, the French Bulldog and the old butcher's dog indicate a definite relationship.

He may have acquired his name through a variety commonly called the *boxl* or through a bastardization of *beisser*. Identifiable and in demand all over the world, the breed has been in its present form since the late 1800s. The promotion of the breed in 1894 by three Germans, Friedrich Robert, Elard Konig and R. Hopner, brought the Boxer to world prominence.

The breed has always been highly favored in its native land and, upon reaching America after the First World War, received steady admiration in the Western World.

White markings are considered "flashy," and should not cover more than one-third of the dog. Occasionally, however, an all-white puppy crops up in a litter of colored dogs. Boxer ears are cropped and the tail docked, but once these puppy cosmetics are performed, he demands little time for grooming. These dogs can be sensitive to extremely high or low temperatures; thus care must be taken during very hot or cold days.

The breed's clean-limbed sturdiness makes it a versatile worker. Boxers have served as police assistants, dog guides or simply defenders of their masters' property.

The stub of the tail wags the rest of the dog. Warm, sleek and loving, they are marvelous children's playmates. Boxers can be rowdy or well-behaved, depending on demeanor and owner demands, but they are always affectionate pets.

Boxer, fawn with white markings.

Boxer, brindle with white markings.

Boxer, fawn with white markings.

Boykin Spaniel.

BOYKIN SPANIEL

COUNTRY: USA
WEIGHT: 30–38 pounds
HEIGHT: 15–18 inches
COAT: Rather wavy or curly and waterproof
COLOR: Solid liver
REGISTRY: UKC
GROUP: Gun Dog

Just after the turn of the 20th century, Alexander White of Spartanburg, South Carolina, was attending Sunday services at church. As he was leaving, he saw a small brown spaniel wandering about and decided to take the tyke home as a pet for his family. The dog, a male, turned out to have some hunting aptitude and was later sent to White's hunting partner, L. Whitaker Boykin, of the Boykin community just outside Camden (South Carolina). With Boykin's schooling, the former stray became a first-rate turkey dog and waterfowl retriever. "Dumpy" was bred to various spaniel bitches who had similar aptitudes, and the little stray became the keystone sire of the Boykin Spaniel family history. Other spaniels, a Springer and an American Water Spaniel, Pointers and Chessies contributed to the breed make-up.

First a turkey dog, he was required to stay down and quiet in the blind while the hunter called the fowl; after the shot, the dog had to be ready to retrieve. The little spaniel fit "just right" into the small boats used on the Wateree River Swamp. As the century progressed, the little southern spaniel adapted well to small water and land birds, in dove hunting and duck shooting. The brown coloring camouflaged him in the woods, and his shortened tail, even if wagged in anticipation, made no sound in the underbrush to give the hunters away.

His area of origin for many years was a winter resort for northerners escaping the cold. Many of these vacationers saw the potential of these local dogs and took one or more home. Today he is used by hunters all along the Atlantic seaboard, with the majority of his admirers still in South Carolina. His history is entwined with that of his state of origin, and South Carolina has designated the Boykin Spaniel its official state dog.

In 1977, several lovers of this rare breed, concerned about indiscriminate breeding, formed the Boykin Spaniel Society to promote and foster him. Among the society's founding members were three descendants of Whit Boykin! They sponsor a field trial and festivities each year in South Carolina for the breed and its fanciers. His prowess is such that the retired head of AKC's Field Trials Department, Ham Rowen, owns a Boykin.

The Boykin is larger than the Cocker, with a smaller, higher set ear. He has considerably less hair and a straighter muzzle. Some coats may be a bit more curly than others, but the practical hunter knows these variations are inevitable and matter little as long as the dog has the abilities. He is a great swimmer and, because of his size, "easy to get in and out of a boat." Most owners report that each of these dogs has a unique personality and an enthusiastic field ability seldom matched by other dogs. His temperament is typically spaniel: docile, pleasant and obedient. Like all gun dogs, he does need abundant exercise, taken care of by long walks on leash or by romping with children in a large yard.

BRACCO ITALIANO

COUNTRY: Italy
WEIGHT: 55–88 pounds
HEIGHT: 22–26½ inches
COAT: Short, dense and fine
COLOR: All white, orange and white, orange roan, chestnut and white, or chestnut roan
OTHER NAMES: Italian Pointer
REGISTRY: FCI
GROUP: Gun Dog

The Italian Pointer is very old and houndlike, and, in fact, may be one of the earliest gun dog types. He has long, folded ears and a slight stop, with a nearly convex muzzle similar to that of the Segugio, and is most likely a descendent or from the same common progenitor. His body, however, is similar to other pointers. His tail is docked to about half its length. Although not known outside of Italy, he is admired at home as an all-purpose gun dog. He is tranquil, docile, obedient and loyal, making a fine family and house dog that doubles as a hunting companion.

Bracco Italiano.

BRAQUE D'ARIÉGE

COUNTRY: France
WEIGHT: 55–66 pounds
HEIGHT: 23½–26½ inches
COAT: Fine and short
COLOR: White, with orange or chestnut spots; may have some ticking
OTHER NAMES: Ariége Pointer, Braque de Toulouse
REGISTRY: FCI
GROUP: Gun Dog

The Ariége Pointer probably did not originate from the hound of the area (the Ariégois), since the hound is a breed of the 20th century. The Pointer is considerably older and came from stem hounds of the general area. Being near Italy and the Pyrenees Mountains, he traces back to the Spanish Pointer or Bracco Italiano, both of which he resembles as seen in 17th- and 18th-century paintings. About 60 years ago, the Ar-iége was modified by crossing with the racier Braque Saint-Germain and even the Braque Francais. These modifications were carried out by Monsieur de Morteau of the Chateau de Molestral in the Ariége during the time of Napoleon IV.

The dog is big and robust, the largest and most powerful of the French pointers. The hare feet, allowable dewlap, long "scrolled" ears and a square muzzle, which tends to the convex ram's shape, are all marks of the hound. For all its power, the breed is elegant and graceful, a tireless worker of slow pace for hunting in rough terrain. The tail is docked a bit in the fashion of many of the Continental pointers and is set on rather low.

The Braque d'Ariége is lively and independent, and needs a master who knows how to dominate him. Although a skilled retriever and hunting dog with a good nose, the breed is known only locally in France. Even at home, it is becoming a rarity.

Braque d'Ariége.

Braque d'Auvergne, black and white.

BRAQUE D'AUVERGNE

COUNTRY: France
WEIGHT: 49–62 pounds
HEIGHT: 22–24 inches
COAT: Short, fine, and shiny
COLOR: Black and white; roaning in the white is desirable to create a blue effect; black must appear on head, covering eyes and ears
OTHER NAMES: Bleu d'Auvergne, Auvergne Pointer
REGISTRY: FCI
GROUP: Gun Dog

Auvergne is in the central southwest of France, near enough to the Gascony region to assume that the Gascony was the hound ancestor of the Auvergne. During Napoleon's occupation of Malta, he decreed the dissolution of the Knights of Malta (*Chevaliers de Malte*). One story tells how the forbears of the Auvergne dogs were brought back to France when the knights returned to their country in 1798. His appearance, however, belies the story. Perhaps the knights brought back dogs who were crossed with local types. The Auvergne is a big, tough hunting dog, built for the Auvergne mountainous areas.

He is lively, sensitive, obedient and affectionate. Like his French hound progenitors, he is light and elegant in the chase. He wags a docked tail, and can be clear white with black spots, but the roaning is much preferred. The heavy roaning is called *charbonnee*, charcoaled. Ears and head should be a solid black and be clean, with no exaggeration and no flew. Among the disqualifications are the tan points, which are the stamp of the hound.

Braque du Bourbonnais.

BRAQUE DU BOURBONNAIS

COUNTRY: France
WEIGHT: 40–57 pounds
HEIGHT: 22 inches
COAT: Short, but hard
COLOR: White, with roaning all over; as few solid patches as possible is preferred; the color may be either liver, brown or orange
OTHER NAMES: Bourbonnais Pointer
REGISTRY: FCI
GROUP: Gun Dog

This provincial hunting dog descended from indigenous breeds of hounds and/or pointing dogs in its native area in central France. A woodcut done by Aldovrandi in 1580 shows a small-eared, short-coupled dog chasing a game bird. The dog is bob-tailed and smooth, with the ticking marks all over his body. Occasionally in times past, a tailless whelp appeared in Braque Francais litters, so some association between the two breeds is possible. Despite first-rate abilities and a good character, the Bourbonnais had never gained much recognition outside its homeland. Recently, however, through the efforts of M. Comte, of the French breed club, breeder M. Francoise Sarret, and the authors of this book, the breed has been introduced to the US. The first litter has been whelped and greeted with much anticipation. He is still a fine hunter of partridge, grouse and pheasant and can also be used on rabbit if trained for small game. French hunters find him a notable gun dog in shooting preserves, and say he is "born trained." A strong breed club now promotes him in France, and he is gaining in popularity, not only with practical hunters, but in field trials and exhibitions as well.

Often referred to as the tailless pointer, pups are usually born with a rudimentary tail. The tail should never be more than three inches in the adult dog. The Bourbonnais is of moderate size with a cobby body and cat feet. Some flew and dewlap are allowed. The standard calls the roan pattern *lie de vin*, a French color that describes wine dregs, while other writers describe the breed's pattern as "dressed like a trout."

Owners describe the breed as serene, sweet and affectionate. The long-time existence of a short-coupled pointing dog with the absence of a tail takes away some of the mystery of the Brittany. Even if one did not come from the other, the genes for cobby dogs with stubby tails were present in France for a very long time.

Braque du Bourbonnais.

BRAQUE DUPUY

COUNTRY: France
WEIGHT: 49–62 pounds
HEIGHT: 25½–27 inches
COAT: Short and fine
COLOR: White with chestnut markings, sometimes in a saddle or mantle
OTHER NAMES: Dupuy Pointer
REGISTRY: FCI
GROUP: Gun Dog

Since the early 17th century, Braques have dwelled in France. They were, at first, of an ancient gun dog prototype, very near the scenthound. Many forms were apparent, some of which, like the Braque Poitou, have disappeared. Others, such as the Braque Francais and perhaps the Dupuy, have survived to the present day.

Several stories concern the Dupuy's origin—and the truth may never be known. Since he is quite houndlike, however, he may go back to the earliest prototype from the hounds of Haut-Poitou. It is known that the breed existed in Poitou before 1808. Legend has it that the breed obtained its name from gamekeepers named Dupuy, who supposedly created it. The story goes that the Dupuy brothers (Homere and Narcisse) kept Braque Francais. A liver/white ticked bitch of theirs named "Miss" was crossed with a dog named "Zidar." Zidar was a *sloughi levrier,* a Sloughi type of Greyhound, brought from Africa by Monsieur Roy, a Lieutenant with the 33rd artillery regiment, garrisoned at Poitiers.

The Dupuy is big (the tallest of the French Braques), racy and elegant, with tight skin, very little stop, the ram's muzzle and a narrow head. His chest is deep and narrow, and there is an arch to the loin. All of these traits are reminders of the classic scenthounds of France, with a hint of the sighthound. Nevertheless, his modern use is for the gun, and he has an excellent nose and good speed over flat open terrain. He is still referred to as *le braque levrier* or Greyhound Braque.

His temperament is described as lively and intelligent, yet dignified. The tail is left intact. He can have patches, ticking or even a mantle of chestnut on his white coat, and the standard warns against the fault of the tan "tri" markings which are a stamp of the hound.

A written standard was published in 1963, but few specimens remain of this unique French breed.

Braque Dupuy.

Braque Saint-Germain.

BRAQUE SAINT-GERMAIN

COUNTRY: France
WEIGHT: 40–57 pounds
HEIGHT: 20–24 inches
COAT: Short, thick, but very fine
COLOR: White, with orange spots and ticking
OTHER NAMES: Saint-Germain Pointer, Compiègne Pointer
REGISTRY: FCI
GROUP: Gun Dog

In the early 1800s, two English Pointers were purchased from England as gifts for King Charles X of France. They were big running, yellow and white dogs with "grace . . . and elegance of form." They were entrusted to Baron de Larminat, who was the inspector of the forest of Compiègne, northeast of Paris. Although the dog, "Stop," soon died, the bitch was mated to a superior working French Braque. The seven offspring of this mating became the Braque Saint-Germain, an Anglo-French composition. Most of the puppies were given to the Compiègne forest wardens and, when some of these men were transferred to Saint-Germain, their choice working dogs went with them. Since

Saint-Germain was close to Paris, these dogs became the rage with Parisian hunters of the time. In fact, for a time, anything orange/white was called "Saint-Germain." Like the Braque Francais, this breed was also called the Braque Charles X, but confusion with the Small French Braque led the committee to drop this name in 1909. Because of his background, he was generally referred to as the *demi-sang*, half-blood braque. The name of his second home has been retained.

This pointer is an elegant, refined, fleet dog with strong searching instincts. The breed has the high headed, high-tailed style of its English heritage. He has a long tail and defined stop; his bright orange and white color also tends to hint at his British ancestors. The Saint-Germain is gentle and affectionate, intelligent and obedient. He is less useful in water due to his fine coat, but he is a first-rate pointer and retriever and competes in French field trials.

While the breed is not the most popular braque in France, it maintains a steady following. Modern owners say, "You only have to observe him to appreciate his elegance and balanced proportions."

Braque Francais, de Grande Taille.

Braque Saint-Germain.

BRAQUES FRANCAISES

Braque Francais, de Grande Taille

COUNTRY: France
WEIGHT: 45–71 pounds
HEIGHT: 22½–27 inches
COAT: Short, thick and dense
COLOR: White, with chestnut patches, with or without ticking
OTHER NAMES: Large French Pointer; French Pointer, Pyrenees type
REGISTRY: FCI
GROUP: Gun Dog

Braque Francais, de Petite Taille

COUNTRY: France
WEIGHT: 37–55 pounds
HEIGHT: 19½–23½ inches
COAT: Short, thick and dense
COLOR: White, with chestnut patches, with or without ticking; or the chestnut is a large mantle which may cover most of the body, but for white on the head and lower extremities
OTHER NAMES: Small French Pointer; French Pointer, Gascony type
REGISTRY: FCI
GROUP: Gun Dog

231

A very old gun dog from the Pyrenees area of France, the Large French Pointer is probably closely related to the Spanish and Italian Pointers and isn't too far from those early hound/gun dog prototypes. He has always been a prime working dog. It is likely that both sizes were used widely in the creation of other gun dog breeds. The smaller dog was merely bred down from his larger sibling. The large size was originally called *Braque du Pays*, meaning local or native, and the smaller version was known as *Braque de la Railliere* and later the Braque Charles X, after the monarch who was partial to him.

The old-style French Braque was losing favor to foreign breeds at the end of the 19th century, and he was scarce by 1900. Fortunately, two dog authorities, Dr. Castets and Monsieur Senac-Lagrange (later also involved with Great Pyrenees), and Dr. Jean Servier, a dynamic president of the current association, helped save the breed. The push by the Club du Braque Francais in the 1970s brought a modern renaissance to the breed which was rare just a scant 15 years before.

Braque Francais, de Petite Taille.

Braque Francais, de Petite Taille.

232

More than 500 were registered in 1980, and many have attained success at field trials and dog shows. The modern Braque Francais has recaptured the regard of hobby hunters. In the home, he is obedient, loyal and tranquil, and is good with family members.

The appearance includes a very strong head, with the convex muzzle and a bit of flew and dewlap. A muscular, strong body ends in a docked tail. Known at home as a good hunter, the breed has a stylish point and shows admirable instincts for retrieving and tracking. He works with the stylish "high nose" for air scent, especially in open fields, but can also pick up ground scent in heavy cover and marshes.

The Gascony variation is generally a proportionately smaller version of the Pyrenees type. It has a slightly more refined and tapering head, appearing to have a slightly convex face, and the ears are a bit shorter and higher set. The Gascony tends to be dryer of leg and throat. Its coloring is nearly a solid liver with small white points. Their hunting style is the same as the Pyrenees'.

Braque Francais, de Grande Taille.

Brazilian Terrier.

BRAZILIAN TERRIER

COUNTRY: Brazil
WEIGHT: 15–20 pounds
COAT: Short, smooth
COLOR: Tricolor
OTHER NAMES: Fox Paulistinha, Terrier Brasileiro
REGISTRY: None
GROUP: Terrier

The terrier from Brazil is one of only two native breeds, with the Fila Brasileiro being the other. Jack Russell Terriers, brought to Brazil from Europe in the 19th century, served as the nearest probable ancestor of the Fox Paulistinha. These dogs were crossed with the Pinscher and Chihuahua. Although the Terrier Brasileiro has been in existence for 100 years, the breed has just been registered since 1973.

Despite their size, they are tough, eager hunters and superb ratters. These terriers hunt in packs, surrounding and worrying the prey from all directions until the animal is exhausted.

The native terrier is most common on the outlying ranches and estates. With his alert bearing and bark, he warns of strangers. Lest intruders

Brazilian Terrier.

BRIARD

COUNTRY: France
WEIGHT: 75 pounds
HEIGHT: 23–27 inches
COAT: Long; slightly wavy, stiff
COLOR: All uniform colors except white—black, fawn, gray or tawny
OTHER NAMES: Berger de Brie
REGISTRY: FCI, AKC, UKC, TKC, CKC
GROUP: Herding

think they have only to deal with a noisy 20–pound terrier, the barking serves to wake up the tough 100–pound Filas which answer the alarm and handle any threat. The Fox Paulistinha can live in city or country, big or small homes; he "is happy to live with the person he likes."

The Brazilian Terriers are small, game and quick. They are excellent companions, with one fancier professing that "they spring and play all the time they are with the owner." Very intelligent, they "win the owner's heart" and are easily taught. Grooming is a simple chore, taken care of with a few flicks of the brush. Serving as great company for children and the elderly, the little terriers make good family pets. They quickly learn tricks and love to perform.

These smart little terriers of Brazil are unknown in other parts of the world. In their native land, however, they are second only to the Filas in registrations.

In many areas of the world, the large flock-guarding dog was partnered with a small herding dog. In England, after extermination of the wolves, the giant flock guard was not needed, and smaller herding dogs became the norm (an exception being the Old English Sheepdog). But in continental Europe, the demand was for a large herding dog that offered protection for the sheep, as well as controlling the flock. This type has been established since the Middle Ages, probably stemming from Oriental sheep-herding dogs with crosses to local guarding breeds for size and aggression.

In France this combination created the Briard, an old breed told about in legends. Among the many versions of an ancient tale, Aubry of Montdidier was murdered, with the only witness being his dog. The dog followed the killer, haunting his footsteps continually, making the man's life a misery. The king, being made aware of the situation, ordered a duel between the dog and the accused. (Trials by combat, even with animals, were known to occur in the Middle Ages.) The dog avenged his master's death.

Aubry's dog (in French, *chien d'Aubry*) was a dog of Briard type, and this is a probable source of the breed's name, although it could also be a derivative of the French region of Brie.

Charlemagne gave braces of Briards to friends, and Napoleon so relied on the breed that he took them with him on his military campaigns. Thomas Jefferson added his name to the list of their admirers and imported several dogs to aid the American farmer. Lafayette requested that Briards be sent to him at his American estate.

Briard, fawn.

The Briard is fearless and never timid, hardy and alert and possesses acute hearing. These attributes led the breed to gain a reputation as a noteworthy dog in combat, and to be named the official dog of the French army. The Briard Club of America recounts how these dogs carried supplies to the front lines, served as sentries and found the wounded. Their thick weather-protective coat and sturdiness enabled them to carry machine gun ammunition belts, wrapped around their bodies, to the gunning emplacements. They knew instinctively which soldiers required care and which would not survive. "It was said that any man the Briard passed by was beyond assistance." American soldiers were impressed with the breed, and it wasn't long before the dogs followed the "dog-faces" home.

The Berger de Brie, commonly known as the Briard, and the Berger de Beauce are closely related, with the coat being the major dissimilarity. Both these breeds sport an unusual ear crop, giving them a distinct appearance even today. The ear is shortened and rounded at the tip. The hair on the Briard cascades down off the upright ear, blending into the heavy beard and brows. Both breeds have a "crochet" hook at the end of the tail, which is carried low at rest. The Briard standard, as opposed to those of most breeds, requires the retention of the unusual double rear dewclaws. The best workers were reputed to be those with the extra rear toes, called "bastard fingers" in France.

Personalities are varied: clowns, teases, show-offs, gentlemen, or the "reserved philosophers." Their coarse double coat requires a thorough brushing weekly to remove dead, matting hair and tangles. Their movement is powerful and agile, likened to "quicksilver." They love being outdoors, and some prefer to lie in a snow drift. Briards are protective of their homes, stock and people. Socialization for the young pup is suggested.

Above Left: Briard. **Above Right and Below:** Briard, tawny.

Briard.

Brittany, orange/white.

BRITTANY

COUNTRY: France
WEIGHT: 35–40 pounds
HEIGHT: 19–20 inches
COAT: Flat, fine, only of moderate length, with a bit of a wave; some minimal fringe of ears, underside and back of legs
COLOR: Orange/white, liver/white in USA; International and French standards also allow black/white or tricolor; can have ticking, but clear colors preferred
OTHER NAMES: Epagneul Breton, Brittany Spaniel
REGISTRY: FCI, AKC, UKC, TKC, CKC
GROUP: Gun Dog

The "spaniels" of France are really all small setters. The Brittany may be close to the original couching dogs of medieval Europe. Except for his short tail, his similarity to the all-purpose setters of Germany and the Netherlands, and even the British setters, can be seen. The Brittany has a higher, smaller ear, lighter head and tighter skin than what is expected in flushing spaniels. Similar hunting dogs have been known for a long time in Brittany, and the presence of the Celts in Brittany, Wales and Ireland makes the origin of the red color an interesting topic. Hunting dogs born tailless have a French precedent in the Braque du Bourbonnais.

The modern history of the Brittany dates from the beginning of this century, when Arthur Enaud created a planned breeding program to restore this old, but waning, French breed. The Brit has become a popular hunting dog once again in France and, since its entry into the USA in the 1930s, has enjoyed remarkable success in the States as well.

American fanciers have recently dropped the word "Spaniel," changing the breed name to Brittany. The Brit works much the same as the pointers, the setters, and the *vorstehhunds*. He is an aggressive searching dog and can be pushed out to distance if the conditions warrant. A keen nose and classic point gives him style and dash and, after the point, he retrieves from land or water. His small size is ideal to minimize both the cost of feeding and the space needed to keep and transport him. The Brittany is immensely popular as a personal gun dog in the USA and consistently ranks well in AKC registrations. American Brittany field trials are well attended, and breeders are justifiably proud of a long list of dual champions. The breed also has shown an aptness for obedience competition.

Harsh training is not necessary as they are usually mild and obedient, often quite submissive and wanting to please. The Brit is a good choice for new hunters as the breed is a natural worker that handles easily. He has a tail either naturally short or docked, so that the adult length is never more than four inches. The American and Canadian standards allow only for the orange/white or the rarer liver/white; yet in his country of origin the black/white and tricolors also are recognized. Even the show specimens have not fallen into the trap of exaggerated coat, and grooming is minimal.

Above: Brittany, orange/white. **Below:** Brittany pups.

Above: Brittany, tricolor. **Below:** Brittany, liver/white.

Above: Brittany, tricolor. **Below:** Brittany, black/white.

Brittany.

Above Left: Brittany, black/white. **Above Right:** Brittany, tricolor. **Below Left:** Brittany, liver/white. **Below Right:** Brittany, tricolor.

Bulldog, brindle.

BULLDOG

COUNTRY: Great Britain
WEIGHT: 40–55 pounds
HEIGHT: 12–14 inches
COAT: Short, smooth
COLOR: Red brindle, other brindles, solid white, red-fawn or yellow, piebald (in descending order of preference); black undesirable
OTHER NAMES: English Bulldog
REGISTRY: FCI, AKC, TKC, CKC
GROUP: Mastiff

These dogs were first classified by cynologists as "bulldogs" in the 1630s, although mentioned earlier under "bandogge" or "butchers dogge." They probably shared a common ancestor with the Mastiff, through the Alaunt, which was described in *Master of Game* by Edward, second Duke of York, circa 1406: ". . . Alauntes are treacherous and evil . . . it is the best hound to hold and to nyme [seize] all manner of beasts and hold them fast."

During the heinous days of bull-baiting, dogs caught the bulls by the ear. The early Bulldog, more agile than other fighters, went for the nose and was not as likely to be hooked by a horn. Certainly, the higher legged "bulldogge" of yesteryear could harass the bull into lowering its head for the dog to grab a piece of anatomy, whether the ear or the tender nose. Rules stated that the dog then had to pull the bull backward around the ring—or to throw and pin the beast. Bears, lions, monkeys and badgers were also found worthy to meet the Bulldog in combat. As Pierce Egan recites, the sight brought forth patriotic utterances, as:

". . . What creature that, so fierce and
   bold,
That springs and scorns to leave his hold?
. . . It is the Bulldog, matchless, brave,
Like Britons on the swelling Wave."

Following the demise of this grisly sport, the old-fashioned Bulldog then waded through the bloodbath of the dog-fight pits. This encouraged crosses to various terriers to increase speed, which resulted in the creation of other well-known modern breeds.

The Bulldog of today is not the same as that of the 1600s. After bull-baiting was outlawed in 1835, the original dog evolved into the shorter faced, squattier version we know today, while retaining its powerful undershot jaw.

Bulldogs attained legitimacy in 1860 by entering a different arena—though not quite so bloody—that of the show ring. The bloodthirsty personality of its early years has mellowed into its even demeanor of modern times, while maintaining its threatening appearance. This has earned it the description of "beautiful in its ugliness." Bulldogs are popular mascots, demonstrating the toughness of a team, and have become a symbol of tenacity throughout the world.

The breed has widespread shoulders and a distinctive, rolling gait, making it recognizable anywhere. The exaggerated characteristics have made the Bulldog difficult to mate and whelp, often requiring human assistance through artificial inseminations and Caesarean sections. Care must be taken during hot weather, since the brachycephalic characteristics of the nose and throat tend to restrict air flow.

Bulldog temperament is loving, quiet and gentle. Docile and phlegmatic, their favorite activities are following their masters around the house and taking long naps at their feet.

Bulldog, fawn/white.

Bulldog, brindle/white.

Bulldog, brindle/white.

Bullmastiff.

BULLMASTIFF

COUNTRY: Great Britain
WEIGHT: 110–130 pounds
HEIGHT: 25–27 inches
COAT: Smooth, short
COLOR: Red, fawn or brindle, often with black mask
REGISTRY: FCI, AKC, TKC, CKC
GROUP: Mastiff

In an attempt to decrease the massive size of the English Mastiff, the Bullmastiff was created through crosses with the Bulldog during the late 1800s. This resulted in a more agile, quiet tracker, which retained much of his larger progenitor's power and enabled the Bullmastiff to cover short distances quickly. The Bullmastiff's similarity to the Dogue de Bordeaux, which is centuries older, brings to mind the various Mastiff crosses made throughout history.

These dogs were originally called Gamekeeper's Night Dogs and were set against poachers. Since poaching in England carried the death penalty, those choosing the profession were pre-pared to murder the gamekeepers pursuing them. This called for a tough, fearless, absolutely silent canine assistant.

As the 20th century approached, the need for gamekeepers and their dogs waned. Staged contests were still held, however, to see if a man could outwit the animal. The volunteer was given a head start in woods or moors and, after a few minutes, the muzzled pursuer was slipped off lead. Upon catching his quarry, the dog knocked down the poacher and kept his captive on the ground until the handler arrived. As far as the records show, it was always the dog that won.

Recognition in its homeland came in 1925, and AKC followed suit in 1933. The dark brindles so desirable for night work in its original profession gave way to fawns. British fanciers prefer a dog that appears to have half-Mastiff and half-Bulldog influence from the 19th-century crosses, while Americans seem to desire a 60/40 ratio, with the Mastiff dominating. Hollywood welcomed the Bullmastiff, with both Douglas Fairbanks and producer Harry M. Warner as admirers of the breed.

Nowadays, the Bullmastiff is a calm, though alert, pet. A young dog is often clumsy and demonstrates normal puppy naughtiness. These activities must be "nipped in the bud" before the dog's full size and strength are reached. He is protective of children, other pets and property. These tendencies require a firm, loving owner.

Bullmastiff.

Bullmastiff.

Bullmastiff.

BULL TERRIER

COUNTRY: Great Britain
WEIGHT: 52–62 pounds
HEIGHT: 21–22 inches
COAT: Smooth, short
COLOR: White, or any color other than white with or without white markings
REGISTRY: FCI, AKC, UKC, TKC, CKC
GROUP: Mastiff

Bull Terrier.

Bred from crosses of the bull-baiters and the now extinct English White Terrier, with a bit of Dalmatian, the Bull Terrier remains the closest to the original bull-and-terrier breeds. Size, color and head shape were in great variance during its development, and some authorities believe Pointers, Greyhounds and Whippets added their influence. The fighting dogs showed their prowess in the pits, with survivors continuing the fray—this time for ribbons—in the show ring, proudly bearing their battle scars.

Englishman James Hinks first standardized the breed, in the early 1850s, selecting for white color, gameness and the unique egg-shaped head. After type was fixed, the colored variety was added. Ears were originally cropped. Bull Terrier admirers formed a club in England in 1887, with Americans following in 1907.

Bull Terriers were rated by Colonel James Y. Baldwin, Commandant of the War Dogs Training Establishment, as the third most suitable breed in wartime achievements. General George Patton had a Bull Terrier, "Willie," as a companion and a mascot for his troops. One also followed President Theodore Roosevelt around the White House.

The Bull Terrier of today, although still strong and agile, is peaceful and tractable. Stories abound of famed pit-fighting dogs avoiding a confrontation when not "at work." One title-holder actually turned tail and headed for home when challenged by a street-tough cur, which was obviously beneath the champ's ability. Another, losing patience with a defiant Pekingese, picked up the annoyance and dropped it in a waste basket. Bred to defend himself and his human family but not to instigate hostility, he became known as the "white cavalier."

In 1895, when cropping was outlawed, the Bull Terrier suffered a setback while breeders attempted to obtain the required upright ears without losing other qualities. Naturally erect ears have now been fixed, along with his tiny triangular eyes, giving him a determined but jaunty air. His one-of-a-kind designer head adds to his distinctive appearance, which people seem to find variously exquisite or homely.

BTs are superb athletes, always eager for a game of ball or frisbee. As puppies, this bounding energy combined with amazing strength often makes them rowdy and in need of a firm hand. Their clowning antics have made them a subject of cartoonists and commercials. Like the AmStaff, the Bull Terriers are wonderful people dogs and long-suffering with children. (This, of course, does not mean abuse, but normal, active, clumsy behavior.) Today's Bull Terriers have been out of the pits for many years and most will tolerate family cats and dogs.

Bull Terrier, colored.

Above: Bull Terrier, colored. **Below:** Bull Terrier, white.

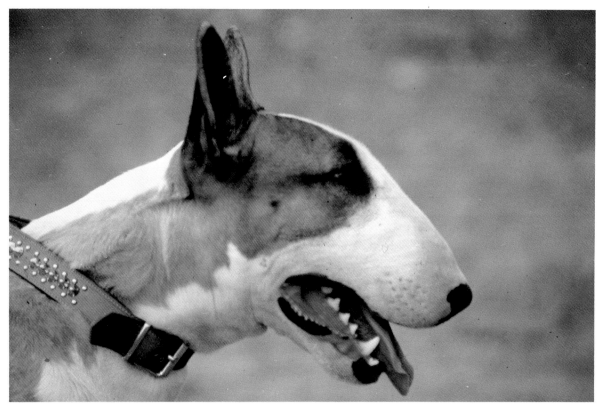

Above and Below: Bull Terrier, colored.

Above and Below: Bull Terrier, white.

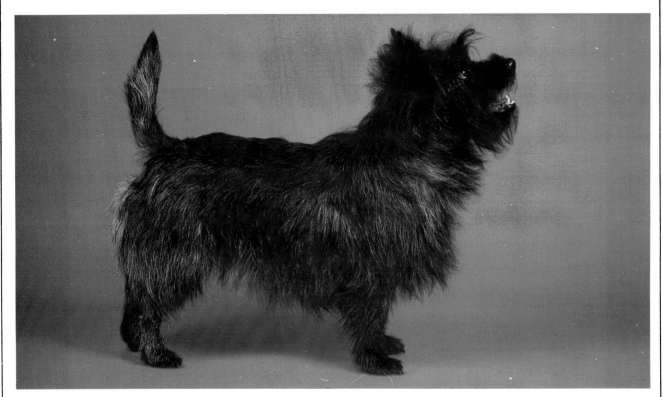

Cairn Terrier.

CAIRN TERRIER

COUNTRY: Great Britain
WEIGHT: 13–14 pounds
HEIGHT: 9½–10 inches
COAT: Rough, wire
COLOR: Any color except white
REGISTRY: FCI, AKC, UKC, TKC, CKC
GROUP: Terrier

The Cairn is a native of the western highlands of Scotland as well as the Isle of Skye, part of the Hebrides Islands, north of Scotland. The breed owes its name and its existence to the pile of rocks erected to identify a boundary or mark a grave. These cairns became favorite hiding places for foxes and other pests. A small but game terrier was needed to go into the cairns and rout out the vermin. The lairds of Scotland kept packs of the tousy terriers for hunting and extermination purposes.

This breed's history is parallel to that of the Skye, the West Highland White and the Scottish Terriers and goes back about 500 years. From a large variety of types in various locales, four distinct breeds slowly emerged: the Cairn, Skye, Westie and Scottie. When the Cairns were first exhibited in 1909, they were called Short-haired Skyes. This produced a howl from the Skye fanciers, resulting in the name Cairn.

Bursting with energy and a joy of life, the Cairn is independent in nature and intently curious, requiring firm instructions. Their terrier nature implores them to dig—whether in a burrow or a flower bed makes no difference to them.

The Cairn has been a neat, compact, cheerful and alert companion since the 1500s. These attributes have made them the favorite terrier in Great Britain, bringing them the honor of being called "the best little pal in the world" by the British Cairn Terrier Club. They reached American shores in 1913, where they have enjoyed a sensible middle-of-the-road status. The breed's sturdiness serves them in good stead as a child's dog.

The short muzzle and erect ears give the breed a keen expression. Its moderately short tail is carried gaily. Ring presentation calls for some "tidying up," since the Cairn's shaggy coat gives the dog a tousled appearance, much like "Toto" in *The Wizard of Oz*.

Cairn Terrier.

Cairn Terrier.

Canaan Dog, liver/white.

CANAAN DOG

COUNTRY: Israel
WEIGHT: 35–55 pounds
HEIGHT: 19–24 inches
COAT: Medium-short, harsh, straight; tail plumed
COLOR: White with large markings in either black, brown or red; browns and black, with or without white markings
OTHER NAMES: Kelef K'naani
REGISTRY: FCI, AKC,CKC
GROUP: Southern

The Canaan Dog has witnessed the birth of the world's greatest religions—Judaism, Islam and Christianity—and has followed the footsteps of Jesus of Nazareth and other Biblical prophets. Queen Jezebel is reputed to have had one of these dogs tied to her throne with a golden chain. They survived long years in the desert, longer even than the travail of Moses and his people. Some hunted with the Bedouins and herded their flocks; others were guards for the Druze on Mount Carmel. Cave drawings as far back as 2200 BC depict dogs resembling the modern Canaan.

When the Jewish people returned to the Promised Land in the 1930s, they discovered pariahs, living fossils, existing like the Dingoes of Australia in a feral state. These dogs were scavengers, surviving despite the hardships of intense heat and a scarcity of water and food. A definite "wild dog" pack order existed. Females left the pack to have their young either in a cave or a "dugout," returning to communal living when the pups were about seven months of age.

In the late 1930s, Dr. Rudolphina Menzel, an Israeli canine authority originally from Germany, was asked to develop a dog for guarding the kibbutz. She and her husband, also a doctor, had observed the pariahs and noted several varieties: *TYPE 1* is a heavier bodied dog, somewhat resembling the flock guards, with a double-coat. *TYPE 2* still has the double-coat and often a tail that tends to curl over the back, but he is lighter in body. This type has a vague resemblance to the northern dogs as well as the Dingo.

Still lighter in build and with a short smooth coat is the *TYPE 3* (the so-called collie-type) pariah, which, when redomesticated, became the Canaan Dog. The *TYPE 4* dog has the appearance of the sighthound, with more raciness and narrowing of the head and body. The wild Type 4 is nearly identical to the Portuguese Podengo and very similar to the Ibizan Hound.

Dr. Menzel cultivated the collie type, starting with "*Dugma*," meaning model or sample, and established the Canaan breed. Although capturing Dugma was a six-month challenge, once enticed to civilization, he was redomesticated with amazing ease.

The Canaan Dogs rose to high favor, due partly to their intelligence and high trainability. They served as sentry dogs and messengers and aided the Red Cross. During World War II, Dr. Menzel trained over 400 for mine detection. Her post-War efforts achieved recognition for the breed as a guide for the blind. They are popular dogs in their native country as companions and guards.

Today their versatility lends them to many tasks: herding, alerting and tracking, making them in demand for sheep dog trials, search-and-rescue, and obedience competition. Their sturdiness enables them to work into their teens.

Owners agree—they do bark, one of their guard attributes. In close proximity, barking can be a problem, and this natural tendency must be curtailed.

Canaan Dog, black with white markings.

Typical of the group, they tend to be aloof. Although they are devoted to their families, they maintain a strong flight reflex, "the highly developed caution toward humans that had allowed her [the breed] to survive in its native land for thousands of years." When confronted with a new or bewildering situation, such as a change in homes, dogs may bolt. Pursuit by well-meaning people seems to puzzle rather than frighten them. They are innately capable of caring for themselves in such a situation. In today's world of multi-lane, fast-moving traffic and dog-control laws, strong measures should be taken to prevent such an occurrence.

Canaans at play are a joy to watch, "boxing" and stalking one another and "talking" back to each other and their families. These dogs first entered the States in 1965. In just a few years, the Canaan has established type and a strong national club. The breed's Israeli standard includes a section on character, indicating that mistrust (of outsiders), endurance, reactability and tractability are all very high. The Canaan Dog is a member of both the AKC and CKC Miscellaneous Classes.

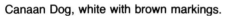
Canaan Dog, white with brown markings.

Above and Below: Canaan Dog, red.

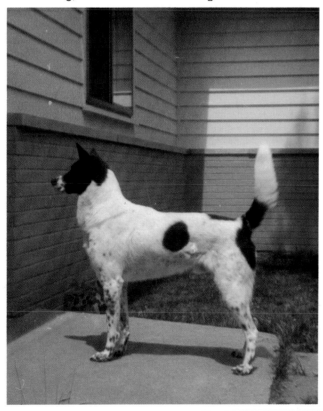

CÃO DA SERRA DE AIRES

COUNTRY: Portugal
WEIGHT: 26½–40 pounds
HEIGHT: 16–21½ inches (most 18 inches or over)
COAT: Long and slightly wavy, coarse goat hair; shaggy on head
COLOR: Shades of yellow, brown, fawn, gray, wolf or black
OTHER NAMES: Portuguese Sheepdog
REGISTRY: FCI
GROUP: Herding

An all-purpose herding and droving dog, the Cão is seen only in Portugal, mainly on the southern plains. It is very similar to the herding dogs of Catalan and to the Pyrenean Sheepdog, possibly crossed with the Briard. The Conde de Castro Guimaraes imported two Briards about 1900, furthering that theory. As with many working breeds, workability was more important than purity, and type was not fixed until 1930. The coat resembles that of the Briard, but carries no undercoat. Although their standard calls for a drop ear, the ears are sometimes cropped. They have long tails and rear dewclaws.

Cão da Serra de Aires.

Cão da Serra de Aires.

The Cão is called the "monkey dog" in his native land, due to his quaint expression. It is widely accepted in Alentejo as a sheep dog. But the breed guards as well as herds—not only sheep, but horses and pigs. These dogs are known for their quick, clever attitude and are particularly adept at bringing back strays. They love their master "above everything on earth," and tend to be a bit reserved with strangers. Adult males may challenge each other for supremacy; the breed requires a firm hand. As a working dog with a need for exercise, they prefer living outdoors, but enjoy an occasional visit in the house.

CÃO DE CASTRO LABOREIRO

COUNTRY: Portugal
WEIGHT: 44–88 pounds
HEIGHT: 20–24 inches
COAT: Medium, short
COLOR: Brindle, also gray and masked fawn
OTHER NAMES: Portuguese Cattle Dog
REGISTRY: FCI
GROUP Flock Guard

In their meanderings out of the Estrela range, many flocks moved to the flat lowlands of the north for winter grazing. The smaller, dark, smooth-coated Estrela dogs are believed to have been the stem of this breed, possibly crossing with native breeds long ago. His place of origin is in the very northern tip of Portugal where he took his name from the small village of Castro Laboreiro, meaning "village of the laborers." Not being part of the great migrations fending

Cão de Castro Laboreiro.

off wolves and bears, the Castro did not grow as large.

Today he is not limited to one village, but is found throughout the country, as one of the most favored of the Portugese guarding breeds. A few have reached other countries and some are used in American flock-guard programs. An owner states his opinion on the Laboreiro's ability: "I believe . . . the Castro could become for the livestock industry what the German Shepherd is to the military."

Due to his naturally suspicious and courageous character, he has adapted easily to police or guard work as well as protecting flocks, herds and isolated homesteads. The Laboreiro's threatening bark is frightening and singular, beginning with a rumbling baritone, quickly climbing the scales to a fortissimo finish.

The breed is bright and learns quickly, but uses its own judgment in decisions. Like many of the flock guards, he is constantly alert, protecting his flock or his family against threats. Totally dedicated to those he keeps safe, the dog is a good companion. Due to his thundering bark, a country home (or understanding neighbors) may be best. His sleek coat and tipped ears need little care other than a quick brush.

Cão de Castro Laboreiro.

CAROLINA DOG

COUNTRY: USA
WEIGHT: 30–40 pounds
HEIGHT: 22 inches
COAT: Short, dense
COLOR: Yellow-gold
REGISTRY: None
GROUP: Southern

Sometime, perhaps 8,000 years ago, dogs of the southern/pariah type migrated across the Bering Strait to the Western World with Asian travelers. These dogs spread the length and breadth of the Hemisphere, laying the foundation for a variety of types and breeds. In western Canada, the Tahltan Bear Dog was of pure pariah type. In the Maritime Provinces to the east, "Indian curs" contributed to the formation of the St. John's retrieving dogs. They also probably formed the basis for the miniaturized and hairless dogs of South America.

To show their widespread existence, a form of feral dog, very similar to the Dingo, lives on the black lava rocks and eats iguana lizards in the Galapagos Islands. His only adaptation is to the 130-degree heat. His ears have grown to im-

mense lengths, standing up like a jack rabbit's ears, to help dissipate body heat.

In what is now the USA, several types once lived. The so-called Basketmaker Dog, now extinct, was nearly a clone of the Dingo and was used by primitive Indians in the southeast. Another type, also lost, named for where his fossils were found, is the Kentucky Shell Heap Dog.

In the Deep South, yet another form of this ancient pariah lives on. Now called the Carolina Dog, because the last remaining specimens were found there, the breed is closely related, or perhaps identical to the other, now extinct, North American pariah breeds. The Carolina Dog was recognized by the Indians, the first explorers and early settlers in the South. Like the Dingo and pariahs before them, they have strong herding instincts. It is probable that the Carolina Dog, crossed with European hounds and other stock, was an ancestor for the American "cur" breeds. In fact, at home the Carolina Dog is of-

Carolina Dog.

Carolina Dog.

ten referred to as "Old Yaller" because of his yellow color.

The Carolina Dog could almost pass for the larger size Dingo with his wedged head, broad, pointed ears, light-boned unexaggerated body, and scimitar-shaped tail. They can be domesticated but, like so many pariah dogs, they have very strong flight reflexes. They tend to be shy and don't like much touching and handling, unless socialized at a very early age. When reared with proper handling, they make fine and well-adjusted family dogs.

Ecologists in the South, including Dr. I. Lehr Brisbin Jr., are searching for pure specimens still in the wild swamps and piney woods of the Savannah River basin. Pups are occasionally placed with selected families to be raised and trained as companions and hunters of small game. Brisbin defines his group's aim as promoting ". . . [the breed's] unique role in the development of today's modern breeds of purebred domestic dogs can be better understood."

265

Catahoula Leopard Dog, merle.

CATAHOULA LEOPARD DOG

COUNTRY: USA
WEIGHT: 40–50 pounds
HEIGHT: 20–26 inches
COAT: Short and dense
COLOR: Merle and black/tan
OTHER NAMES: Catahoula Hog Dog, Catahoula Cur
GROUP: Herding

Catahoula origin is lost in legends, but similar dogs have long been known in the southeastern United States. The breed is definitely a stock worker, although tougher and more aggressive than many of his shepherd relatives, but his ancestors remain a mystery. It is speculated that he is, in part, descended from the mastiff-type war dogs brought into the area with Spanish explorers. Cathy J. Flamholtz relates how Hernando de Soto cruelly set these dogs to attack the Indians of the area and then abandoned them to be cared for by their victims!

These, if crossed with shepherd dogs of either European or even Indian origin, could have been the breed's roots. There may also have been a drop of hound's blood. The breed will tree and trail although it does take after the shepherd side of the family in more traits. Many old timers still classify the breed as the Catahoula Cur (curs form a group of distinctly American dogs). Henri De Tonti, in 1686, told of seeing dogs with white eyes and mottled spots during his explorations. Jim Bowie owned a pair of Catahoulas, or "Cats" as they were frequently called, in the mid-1800s.

The breed's name comes from the Parish of Catahoula (meaning beautiful clear water), a swampy county in northeast Louisiana, where children went to school by boat rather than bus and where the Catahoula Hog Dog was best known. People from the bayous eked out a living from fishing, trapping, and running a few wild hogs and cattle back in the woods. This stock was wild and unruly, living off acorns and berries, not seeing humans except during the annual round-up.

The hogs, particularly, were nearly impossible to drive. They would turn on most herding dogs and fight rather than run. The Cats were essential to gathering and penning the pigs, and their herding techniques are described by H. Ellen Whiteley, DVM in her article "Catahoula Hog Dog Brings Back Memories of Home." Stragglers were picked out by the dogs and forced into a "fight." Distressed screams from the enraged boar brought the other hogs, especially the lead boar, to the rescue with champing jaws and raised back-bristles. The dogs then turned and ran, escaping the slashing tusks, just fast enough to tantalize the hogs into continuing the chase, which soon led directly into the waiting hog pens. The Cats deftly jumped the back fence, and the hogs were trapped!

Good dogs were worth their weight in gold. A natural selection of breeding stock occurred, since inept or slow specimens rarely made it through the first year of work.

When a person needed a working dog, one was received through a neighbor who had puppies. In the past, Catahoulas were generally not sold, due to the Bible verse in Deuteronomy, which states, "Thou shalt not bring . . . the price of a dog into the house of the Lord thy God . . . "

The modern Catahoula has been adapted for cattle as well as hogs, but he is still better for bringing semi-wild cattle out of the bush than for walking the tame dairy herd into the barn for milking. He is aggressive and heels hard, traits that are necessary for working wild stock, but can spook or injure placid barnyard animals. One breeder, as told to Dennis McClintic, refers to them as "walking sledgehammers." He is also valued for his ability to *wind* cattle (find them by scent) when they are scattered in heavy cover.

NALC (National Association of Louisiana Catahoulas) is the national organization working to standardize type and educate prospective buyers. In 1979, the Catahoula Dog was named the state dog of Louisiana.

Catahoulas use their deep bay to good advantage as watchdogs and hunting companions, even treeing coon. NALC ceased pitting Cats against coons in "Coon on a Log" trials, since it "wasn't fair for the coon to lose all the time." An owner describes her Cat as "strong, made of whipcord and leather," yet gentle with her other dog, though perpetually the "pack leader." The breed is strong-willed, yet sensitive to its owner's needs. They are affectionate and protective of their own family, but often do not welcome visitors.

Catahoula Leopard Dog, merle.

CATALAN SHEEPDOG

COUNTRY: Spain
WEIGHT: 40 pounds
HEIGHT: 18–20 inches
COAT: Long and wavy
COLOR: Fawn with black tips, black, black/tan, grizzle, brindle
OTHER NAMES: Perro de Pastor Catalan, Gos d'Atura Catala, Catalonian Shepherd
REGISTRY: FCI
GROUP: Herding

Catalan Sheepdog.

Catalan Sheepdog.

Catalonia is in the northeastern corner of Spain on the Mediterranean, just across the Pyrenees from France. The people who settled here are of French extraction—not Spanish—coming to Spain from the Pyrenees region. Physically the Catalan Sheepdog is similar to the Pyrenees Sheepdog. Ears may be cropped to stand. The beard, mustache and shaggy coat give them an appearance like the Portuguese Sheepdog or old-type Beardie. A rare, short-coated variety (similiar to that of the Shepherd), the Gos d'Atura Cerda, is noted as needing less care.

They herd horses as well as the sheep that are so abundant in Spain. Although some sources mention a nervous temperament, they are intelligent, vigorous and strong, and adapt well to police, army or guard work.

Caucasian Owtcharka, gray brindle.

CAUCASIAN OWTCHARKA

COUNTRY: USSR
HEIGHT: 24–26 inches minimum; usually much larger
COAT: Moderately short to medium; very thick fringing; some may have abundant ruff and fringe
COLOR: Usually gray, tan, fawn, white, brindle, piebald; any color except brown allowable
OTHER NAMES: Caucasian Sheepdog, Kawkasky Owtscharka, Kaukasische Schaferhund
REGISTRY: FCI
GROUP: Flock Guard

In both the Caucasus and Ural Mountains of the Soviet Union, flock-guarding dogs have long been utilized. Although fine-tuned within the USSR to suit local land and climatic conditions, they trace back to the same Asian/Middle Eastern sources of all flock guardians.

The Caucasus Mountains fill the long finger of land in southwestern Russia that reaches down between the Black Sea and the Caspian Sea to touch Turkey and Iran. In these high elevations (up to 18,000 feet), great flocks of sheep are kept and, for over 600 years, the Owtcharkas have protected them from wild animals and thieves.

Without kennel clubs and written history, there tends to be some variation in type throughout the mountain range.

Russians describe the massive, stocky Grusinian type; the taller, rangier Azerbeidjan from the south near Iran; the smaller, square-built Dagestanian from the southeast between the

Greater Caucasus and the Caspian Sea; and the big, strong Kangalian of the Turkish border. The best and most uniform modern examples are in the Georgian Republic. Despite regional differences, the desired Caucasian dog is large-boned, massive and strong, with the mental traits to do livestock guarding work. The proper Owtcharka is confident, strong-willed and fearless, with a large dose of independence. Russians describe him as ferocious and recommend approaching him with caution. He makes an extremely reliable guard dog, being able to naturally discriminate between true threat and benign interference. When real danger threatens, the Caucasian Sheepdog becomes "an incorruptible dare-devil," attacking without warning in utter silence.

Hair length varies with the elevations of lo-cale, and colors can be from the usual flock-guard white or gray/dun to reds, brindles and even piebalds. Ears are cropped short, not to a point, but horizontally and bluntly cut nearly off. Even modern exhibition specimens are still cropped. The tail is usually carried low with a hook at the end, but in excitement may be raised in a loose ring. In some areas of the USSR, tails are still docked.

The first Caucasian Owtcharkas outside their homeland were introduced to East Germany in 1969. By 1979, they had spread to West Germany, winning "the hearts of many dog fanciers by storm." There is now a specialty club in Germany, and these dogs are seen at international shows in Europe. At the present time, the exportation of this breed from the Soviet Union is forbidden.

Caucasian Owtcharka.

Cavalier King Charles Spaniels, Blenheim.

CAVALIER KING CHARLES SPANIEL

COUNTRY: Great Britain
WEIGHT: 10–18 pounds
HEIGHT: 12–13 inches
COAT: Long, silky, free from curl, ample feathering
COLOR: Black/tan, solid red (Ruby), red/white (Blenheim), and tricolor (Prince Charles)
REGISTRY: FCI, AKC, UKC, TKC, CKC
GROUP: Gun Dog

In the 1920s, Roswell Eldridge, an American, wondered if any of the original longer headed toy spaniels seen in early paintings still existed. For five years running, he offered first prizes of 25 pounds at Crufts, England's most prestigious dog show, to be awarded to "Blenheim Spaniels of the Old Type." Whether these types were still found in litters or skilled British breeders did some quick crossing, the prizes began to be claimed.

This revived breed became the Cavalier King Charles, achieving Kennel Club status in England in 1944. This spaniel has accomplished a most remarkable "comeback." Princess Margaret, of the British royal family, acquired one in the 1960s, and this boosted the breed's recognition even more. By the 1970s, this toy spaniel was nearing the top 20 in British registrations. He has been among Canada's recognized breeds since 1957. The American Kennel Club includes the breed in its Miscellaneous Class division. Dog lovers Nancy Reagan, wife of the US President, and Mordecai Siegal, award-winning author, are current fanciers.

The clamor for the breed in England was such that it reached a point of diminishing returns. Breed entries soared and breeders were concerned about the problems that occur at the public's whim. This demand has now sensibly leveled off. With the English passion for the Cavalier in mind and the fact that the breed is charming, one wonders why they haven't caught on more in America. Their coat is long enough for beauty, but isn't so abundant as to require excess care. A variety of colors allows for various tastes. The tail may be docked a bit, or not, allowing the length to balance with the body. In the particolor dogs, there should always be some white at the tip, thus the capriciousness of the color spots dictates whether one pup has his tail cut and another not.

Cavalier King Charles Spaniel.

271

Cavalier King Charles Spaniel, Prince Charles.

United States President Ronald Reagan with Cavalier King Charles Spaniel.

JR

Česky Fousek.

ČESKY FOUSEK

COUNTRY: Czechoslovakia
WEIGHT: 62–75 pounds
HEIGHT: 24–26 inches
COAT: 1 to 3 inches of bristly, rough outer hair, with thick, soft undercoat
COLOR: Liver or liver/white, with or without ticking
OTHER NAMES: Rough-coated Bohemian Pointer, Czech Coarsehaired Pointer, Slovakian Wirehaired Pointer
REGISTRY: FCI
GROUP: Gun Dog

The Česky Fousek is closely related to both the Drahthaar and the Stichelhaar, whom he resembles. The breed was very popular in the area of Bohemia between the mid-1800s and World War I but was almost lost during that war. He was revived in the 1930s, by using some German Shorthaired Pointer blood.

The tail is shortened to two-fifths of its full length. This pointer's rough coat is fairly long on underside and chest, beard and brows. He is described as an aristocratic and noble dog with good abilities. Today, Czechs say he is widespread and frequently hunted in their country.

CHESAPEAKE BAY RETRIEVER

COUNTRY: USA
WEIGHT: 64–75 pounds
HEIGHT: 23–26 inches
COAT: Moderately short, thick, and very coarse, with no beard or brow
COLOR: Dead grass most desirable, liver to hay color allowed
REGISTRY: FCI, AKC, UKC, TKC, CKC
GROUP: Gun Dog

The Chesapeake Bay area has been famous for its first-rate duck hunting ever since the first settlers set foot on shore. Retrievers have always been in demand by the Bay and, for many years, each hunter simply used the best dog he could find bred from other dogs who worked well. The Chesapeake dog was not an overnight creation, taking much of the 19th century to develop.

The oft-repeated story of the breed springing from two dogs saved from a shipwrecked brig is probably another doggy "tale." These two dogs, "Canton," a black female, and "Sailor," a dingy red male with yellow eyes, were probably of the early smaller Newfoundland type and certainly did contribute to the breed. But the fact that they were never bred to each other assures that there were other wellsprings. References point to imported Red Winchesters from Ireland, perhaps bearing some relationship to the breeds which spawned the Irish Water Spaniel. By the last third of the 1800s, owners had formed an organization to promote and standardize the "Chesapeake Bay Ducking Dog." Type was still a variant, with the modern breed taking shape over the next 20 years.

The Chesapeake Bay dog was a favorite of the commercial duck hunter who shot for the restaurant and market trade in the late 1800s and early 1900s. Well-documented records chronicle dogs who averaged a thousand ducks each fall. The icy water and rough waves of the saltwater bay necessitated a dog tough in mind and body who lived to retrieve. And the tougher the conditions, the more the Chessie seemed to enjoy the hunt.

The "dead grass" color was preferred, to provide a camouflage that blended with the fall landscape. His coat is very dense and harsh with an almost oily texture that sheds water and insulates from the wet and cold. The head has a tendency to be smoother than the rest of the body; just a hint of the possible stem to the European water dogs like the Curly-Coated Retriever, Wetterhoun and Irish Water Spaniel. Described as "utilitarian rather than beautiful" and "about as sensitive as a Sherman tank," the breed attracts serious duck hunters.

Bearing the reputation as a hard head, he retains the mental toughness and independent single-mindedness so necessary for his early work. Once the Chessie knows who is giving the orders, he is a hard and willing worker. There are excellent breed members in obedience and field trials, as well as weekend gunners' companions. This is a devoted family dog who loves children. Although most modern families could hardly provide the kind of work performed by one early dog, who "all his life worked an average of five days of every seven," it is necessary to provide a Chesapeake with adequate exercise and some kind of job to make him—and consequently his owner—content.

Chesapeake Bay Retriever.

Chesapeake Bay Retrievers.

Chesapeake Bay Retriever.

CHIEN D'ARTOIS

COUNTRY: France
WEIGHT: 40–53 pounds
HEIGHT: 20½–23 inches
COAT: Short and smooth
COLOR: Tricolor in a broken pattern
OTHER NAMES: Briquet
REGISTRY: FCI
GROUP: Hound

Northern France, bordering the English Channel, consists of the historical regions of Normandy and Artois. Normandy, Brittany's eastern neighbor, has the same rolling plains and poor soils. As one moves east into Artois right up on the Belgian border, however, fertile soils and forests abound. The Ardennes area of Belgium, where the St. Hubert was developed, is a near neighbor. Hounds from these regions stem from some of the earliest types.

The d'Artois dog was a favorite by the 17th century. The Prince Alexandre de Gray wrote to the Prince de Galle, in 1609, of his intention to "send a pack of little d'Artois dogs to the king . . . " In fact, this small French hound may have contributed to the formation of the Beagle in England.

By the 19th century, the curse of fashion was laid upon the breed. It became chic among French hunters to avail themselves of the dogs from the British Isles. With the importation of many British types, the inevitable crossbreeding resulted in the deterioration of the pure d'Artois. Crossing also took place with the taller, more elegant, longer, scroll-eared hounds called Normands (now extinct). During the 1800s, only the packs kept at Chantilly and those of the Prince de Conde retained the ancient type.

In the 1880s, Ernest Levair and his cousin, M. Therouanne, began a 20-year effort to breed the original d'Artois, removing the last of the Normand blood. Although their efforts resulted in great success, the war years again nearly destroyed the breed. Once thought to be extinct, there are now about 500 dogs registered in their stud books, making a strong comeback since 1975. They have the small size, shorter head, sturdy body with wide chest, and long, but very flat ears of the original type.

This breed is a supple, rustic hunting dog that is becoming increasingly available to French hunters. Used in small packs for rabbit, other small quarry, or even wild boar, he has a melodious, high bark.

Chien d'Artois.

Chien d'Artois.

CHIEN DE L'ATLAS

COUNTRY: Morocco
WEIGHT: 55 pounds
HEIGHT: 21–24 inches
COAT: Medium-short, dense
COLOR: White preferred; also appears in black; tawny; "washed out" red, black and white
OTHER NAMES: Atlas Sheepdog, Kabyle Dog, Aidi
REGISTRY: FCI
GROUP: Flock Guard

Whether the Aidi crossed into Africa from Spain or was carried from Italy (or beyond) by the globe-trotting Phoenicians matters little. He is a classic flock guard, although a bit smaller and with less coat due to his semi-arid environment.

This breed guards flocks, tents, camels and other belongings of the nomadic tribes in the northern African hills. Several are selected for their attentiveness and aggression, being staked out at night around the campsite. With each other and their masters, they are tractable.

They have exceptional noses, able to track even in the sands of the Sahara and join in the caravan's hunts. They are paired with a Sloughi, the Atlas dog finding the game by scent, then the Sloughi slipped for the chase. In the past he may have been used as a dog of war. The Atlas Sheepdog is versatile, performing as a shepherd, drover, gun, guard, war and police dog.

He is lively and high-strung, but with a job to do, he can be kept in the country or city, even though correspondents say the breed is a dog "of the rural zones." Confident and alert, the Aidi makes an outstanding watchdog.

Moroccans say that a club was organized to promote this national breed only recently. This group is proud of the breed's heritage and wants to preserve the purity of the Atlas Dog. The current standard supplied by the Moroccan Kennel Association describes the thick fur and heavy plume of tail as a sign of purity. Its thick "mane" and "fleece" shelter it from the arid heat and the mountain cold, also protecting the Aidi in fights with jackals and other predators. His ears are tipped to the front; sometimes dogs with cropped ears or a short tail are seen, although the natural condition is the only one recommended.

First-day cover issued by the Moroccan Post Service commemorating the Chien de l'Atlas.

Chien Francais Blanc et Noir.

CHIENS FRANCAISES

Chien Francais Blanc et Noir

COUNTRY: France
WEIGHT: 62–66 pounds
HEIGHT: 26–29 inches
COAT: Short and smooth
COLOR: Actually a tricolor, but the tan is reduced to marks on the head and ears
OTHER NAMES: French Black and White Hound
REGISTRY: FCI
GROUP: Hound

Chien Francais Blanc et Orange

COUNTRY: France
WEIGHT: 62–66 pounds
HEIGHT: 26–29 inches
COAT: Short and smooth
COLOR: Orange and white
OTHER NAMES: French Orange and White Hound
REGISTRY: FCI
GROUP: Hound

Chien Francais Tricolore

COUNTRY: France
WEIGHT: 60 pounds
HEIGHT: 25–28 inches
COAT: Short and smooth
COLOR: Tricolor in a broken pattern all over the body
OTHER NAMES: French Tricolor Hound
REGISTRY: FCI
GROUP: Hound

Besides the previously described French breeds, there are hundreds and hundreds of hound packs throughout France used strictly for hunting. Members of these packs are bred and selected for their abilities without great concern for appearance or type. With so many of the old classic "breeds" disappearing and the existence of all these other crossbred hounds, a committee of French cynologists conducted a survey in 1957 and inventoried all the extant packs. Many of the pack hounds were various crosses of

Chien Francais.

the French hounds) the tan is reduced to spots above the eyes, on the cheeks, and under the ears, so that the body appears to be black/white.

The Orange and White variety was described by the 1957 committee, which decided the breed was not sufficiently set in type to draw up a standard. If exhibited, these dogs are judged, except for color, by the same standard as the Black/White. They are, however, recognized by FCI.

A standard was set for the Tricolor variety after the survey. He is slightly smaller and has much more tan on the body. Otherwise, he is nearly a clone of the Black/White. The Tri is rarely exhibited, but the identification and description of a written standard aids in prevention of crossbreeding and loss of all these ancient types.

Chien Francais Blanc et Orange.

purely French breeds and were fairly similar in type. These were reclassified as the Chien Francais, or French Hound. Those dogs whose French ancestors had been crossed with English hounds for a more British build, were renamed Anglo-Francais (French-English Hound).

The Black and White French Hound is pure Gallic in type, and is mainly derived from crosses of the Gascon-Saintongeois and Levesque as well as others. He has a statuesque, elegant build with the French head and ears.

These dogs are "professional" hunters bred only for their work—yet they are affectionate, tranquil and obedient. Useful for any game, they are specialists on deer. They were the most prevalent of the three French varieties in the pack survey. They are not really black and white, but a tricolor in which (like so many of

Chihuahua, longcoated, black/tan.

CHIHUAHUA

COUNTRY: Mexico
WEIGHT: 1–6 pounds
COAT: Short and smooth; or long and soft with fringing
COLOR: Any color
REGISTRY: FCI, AKC, UKC, TKC, CKC
GROUP: Southern

The Chinese have long practiced the art of dwarfing animals, plants and fish. It is believed that Spanish traders traveled through Mexico on their returns from China and left behind some of their canine acquisitions. These, crossed with the native hairless breeds, made up the modern Chihuahua, which is the smallest dog in the world. Other cynologists have stated he is just a miniaturized version of native pariah dogs. His similarity to the small Podengo of Portugal (another dwarf pariah) is singular.

The tiny dogs may have been named for the State of Chihuahua in Mexico, and many tales lend belief of their existence there. No concrete evidence has been found to prove this theory; in fact, more recent research has provided evidence to the contrary. Explorers reporting the exis-tence of dogs called the Techichi are now be-lieved to have described a "prairie dog" type of rodent, which the natives "raised, castrated and ate." These little "dogs" lived in holes in the ground.

Whatever their beginnings, Chihuahuas first came to prominence in Mexico City around 1895, reaching El Paso, Texas, shortly thereaf-ter. Dog lovers in the USA refined and perfected the little dog of Mexico—and soon the breed was listed as the top toy in the States. He has maintained his appeal as a companion dog.

The long-coated version was probably pro-duced in the USA, crossing smooth Chihuahuas with other toys like the Papillon, Pomeranian and so on.

Their tiny bodies hide large hearts, making them a favorite for the elderly and those in apartments. They are playful and graceful, with large ears emphasizing their alert appearance. Due to their tiny size (some as small as one pound!), they are not the choice for rowdy fami-lies or outdoor living. Breeding and health prob-lems are accentuated in the tiniest specimens. The *mollera*, or open soft spot on the top of the skull, is usually found in the majority of Chihua-huas and is allowed by the standard.

283

Chihuahuas, longcoated, various colors.

Above: Chihuahua, longcoated, white. **Below:** Chihuahua, longcoated, particolor.

Above: Chihuahua pup, smooth, red.

Chihuahua.

Chihuahuas, particolors.

Chihuahua, orange with white markings.

Chihuahua, blue.

CHINESE CRESTED

COUNTRY: China/Africa
WEIGHT: 5–10 pounds
HEIGHT: Males 13 in. max, females 12 in. max
COAT: Hairless, except for tufts appearing on the head (crest), feet (socks), and tail (plume); Powderpuff—longish, double, soft, silky coat
COLOR: Skin from pink to black, mahogany, blue, lavender or copper, solid or spotted; Powderpuff—any color or combination
REGISTRY: FCI, AKC, TKC
GROUP: Southern

Hairless mutations have occurred in pariah-type litters, and from these the modern hairless breeds have evolved, likely first developing in Africa. Hairless dogs captivated the attention and fancy of ancient dog lovers in Africa, Mexico, Spain and China. During the Han dynasty, the Chinese Crested dogs were cultivated into two types: "treasure house guardians," or deer-type, and the larger, heavier cobby "hunting dog," which, when he didn't bring home meat, was the main ingredient in the cooking pot.

Other hairless varieties, like the African Elephant Dog, or the Abyssinian Sand Dog, developed in similar warm climates.

Fortunately for the breed, Chinese dogs accompanied their masters on trade vessels throughout the world, leaving mementos of their visits behind. True to the dominant genetics, hairlessness would show up in that first litter!

Chinese Cresteds, along with other lovely Chinese breeds, are now rarer than Cadillacs in their native land. Along with the belief of a "Chinese Crested in every pot," the Communist ideology against pets has nearly eliminated dogs on mainland China.

The breed enjoyed a brief stay in the AKC Miscellaneous Class and was exhibited at Westminster in 1885 and at the Sesquicentennial Exposition in Philadelphia in 1926. After a respite of several decades, fanciers organized the Chinese Crested Club of America in 1975, and the breed resumed competition in Miscellaneous Classes again in 1986.

A gay, loving personality, similar to the other hairless varieties, has endeared them to many. Their hair tufts are denser than the sparse wisps on other hairless dogs. They possess a hare foot and can grasp and hold their toys, food or people. Owners describe how they "hug" when held. Perhaps it was that quality or perhaps their "unclad" appearance that enamored Gypsy Rose Lee to their charms.

The powderpuff's veil coat has a soft undercoat with coarser guard hair, and may be short or long. Ears are erect on the hairless variety; the weight of the hair on the powderpuff may cause ears to drop.

Chinese Crested, blue spotted.

Above Left: Chinese Crested. **Above Right:** Chinese Crested powderpuff adult, white, and hairless pup, lavender. **Below:** Chinese Cresteds, pink spotted.

Above: Chinese Crested powderpuff. **Below:** Chinese Crested powderpuff pup, tricolor.

Chinook.

CHINOOK

COUNTRY: USA
WEIGHT: 65–90 pounds
COAT: Short, smooth, dense
COLOR: Tawny
GROUP: Northern

This sledding dog is an American creation, dating from 1915. Arthur Walden wanted to create a sled dog that had both the speed of Huskies and the strength of the larger sled dogs. He used his lead dog, "Chinook," meaning warm winds, as the keystone sire. Chinook, according to Walden, was "half-bred Eskimo" through his dam, whose pedigree led back to Admiral Robert E. Peary's lead dog on his North Pole expedition. Chinook's sire was ". . . mongrel . . . a trace of Saint Bernard."

In 1922 Walden's Chinook team beat three others to win the first Eastern International dogsled race. Walden was asked to be in charge of the teams on Admiral Richard E. Byrd's 1929 Antarctic expedition, and Chinook went with his master. The Admiral wrote in *Little America* that the dogs he prized most highly were the Chinooks. He said, ". . . Walden's team was the backbone of our transport." Loads averaged a remarkable 150 pounds per dog.

Chinook reached a sorrowful end on that trip, according to Admiral Byrd.

. . . the saddest . . . was the loss of Walden's famous lead dog, Chinook. Chinook was Walden's pride, and there was no doubting the fact that he was a great dog. He was old when brought to the Antarctic, too old for hard, continuous labor, and Walden used him as a kind of shock troop, throwing him into a team when the going turned very hard. Then the gallant heart of the old dog would rise above the years and pull with the glorious strength of a three-year-old. The affection between him and Walden was a beautiful thing to see: one sensed that each knew and understood the other perfectly, and it was Walden's rare boast that he never needed to give Chinook an order: the dog knew exactly what had to be done. A few days after his twelfth birthday, Chinook disappeared. We searched the camp for him, without success; in the trampled snow about the ship, it was impossible to find his tracks. . . . Whether he walked out alone to die, because his days of service were done, is something I cannot vouch for: this was the romantic theory advanced by several of the men. At any rate, his body was never found. . . . All this was a deep disappointment to Walden, who wanted to bury Chinook in his harness.

Chinook.

In 1940, ownership of the Chinook dogs was in the hands of Perry Greene, and he was challenged to prove his breed's superiority over the American Eskimo Dog, the Husky and the Malamute. Greene planned the longest race ever undertaken in the USA, 502 miles from northern to southern Maine. The sled was packed with 800 pounds of equipment and supplies topped by Greene's 13-year-old stepson. The journey was mostly by ice and snow-covered roads, allowing good sledding. Some roads, however, were bare. The seven-dog team arrived at their goal, Kittery, 90 hours later, with not a single dog limping. All were in excellent shape; some had gained weight! They achieved a measure of fame from several magazine features, including one in *The National Geographic* about the breed between the 1940s and 1960s, and the fact that one served as mascot of the Operational Chinook Helicopter Unit in Vietnam.

Greene refused to allow anyone else to breed the dogs, and only sold spayed females, fearing that others would ruin the breed. He, as Walden, kept the breeding combination to himself. Unfortunately, his misguided altruism caused a decline in the breed.

Chinooks remain in danger of extinction. *The Guinness Book of World Records* listed the Chinook as the world's rarest dog in 1966 when only 125 existed; now there are 150 dogs. Fanciers are working, through the Southern California Rare Breed Club, to gain more recognition, and are actively seeking sledders to work with breeders in programs that emphasize the working qualities. In addition, a breeding program has been charted by biogeneticists, and the Chinook Owner's Association maintains strict guidelines.

Chinooks offer several positive qualities other than the speed, endurance and strength demonstrated by their prowess as a sled dog. They are good, protective family dogs, though headstrong, needing a firm hand. For a large dog, the Chinook boasts a surprising record for good hips and a longevity of 10–15 years. The old-line Chinook's ears were drop, but many are carried erect today.

Chinook.

CHOW CHOW

COUNTRY: China
WEIGHT: 45–70 pounds
HEIGHT: 19–20 inches
COAT: Long coat—long, straight, spitzlike stand-off; smooth coat—shorter spitzlike, more plush, similar to the Siberian or Shiba
COLOR: Any solid color, as tan, red, cream, blue, black, silver gray, or white (rare)
REGISTRY: FCI, AKC, UKC, TKC, CKC
GROUP: Northern

Both the Chow Chow and the Shar-Pei are from mainland China. The Chow is certainly closely related to the other Nordic/spitz dogs, but may not be pure northern, having some sprinkling of mastiff types. This family introduced the heavier heads and thick, wrinkled skin, which some feel the Chow owes to crosses with the Tibetan Mastiff. It is possible some of the Nordic breeds owe their roots to the Chow, rather than the other way around.

Historians trace Chows to the 11th century BC when Tartar hordes invaded China. Art and literature of these eras were often destroyed by the succeeding emperors, and information is sketchy. During the Han dynasty, however, about 150 years BC, bas relief sculpture and pottery do depict Chowlike dogs hunting. Later, a T'ang emperor, circa 700 AD, boasted a kennel of 2,500 couples of Chows with a staff of 10,000 huntsmen!

The Chow Chow was relished throughout China as a delicacy, in addition to serving in other less fatal capacities, such as a draft, guard or flock dog. The eating of dog flesh was, and still is, common in Asia. The dogs were fed an all-grain diet and butchered while young. The fur of the longhaired Chow was made into clothing. *The Book of Marco Polo* tells of these dogs being utilized in a Nordic manner, drawing sledges through mire and mud.

Because China had a closed-door policy for centuries, these dogs did not make an appearance in other parts of the world until about 1780. Several types of Chinese dogs, including Pekingese and Chows, were smuggled out by sailors in the 1800s. It was a difficult task to convince these canine grain-eaters to eat the meat that was fed dogs in the Western World. These dogs were displayed in the London Zoo as the "Wild Dog of China" until dog lover and breed savior Queen Victoria took one into her fold.

In the early 1900s, the Chow was still a highly visible dog in China, being sold in market places, with puppies "sitting placidly" in large

Chow Chow, smooth coat, black.

Chow Chow, long coat, red.

blue and white jars on the doorsteps. Nevertheless, it was fortunate that the Chow left China when he did, as the Cultural Revolution declared dogs a useless commodity, and most have been destroyed. A recent visitor to China recorded seeing only three mongrels on her entire trip.

The breed's name is thought to be derived from the pidgin English term *chow chow*, which was a blanket description for the novelties, curios and dogs brought on ships from the Orient. Another theory is that *chou* is Chinese for edible. His Chinese name around Canton, where the breed was numerous, was *Hei She-t'ou* (black-tongued), *Lang Kou* (wolf dog), *Hsiung Kou* (bear dog) or *Kwantung Kou* (dog of Canton).

The breed quickly gained a following and the long, plush coat is admired throughout the world. With popularity ever growing, it is easily recognized and owned in many countries. The smooth coat is not as common, but a few of that variety are being shown in the USA.

As puppies, they have the appearance of live teddy bears. In fact, a belief that Chows descended from bears has been passed through generations. This legend persists not only due to their coat and sure-footedness, but because of the blue-black tongue peculiar to the polar bear and a few Asiatic bears located in the same vicinity. Like bear cubs, Chows do mature, and buyers should be aware that these cuddly pups will one day have their own minds in powerful bodies. Chows have an independent and rather suspicious nature and will guard their property—their family and all their possessions—to the death.

The Chow's black-pigmented tongue, lips, and gums are a stamp of the breed. The massive head and wrinkles make the dog appear to be scowling. Regular grooming is a necessity for the plush coat. Care must be taken in hot weather, especially during periods of high humidity, as the breed suffers greatly and may even be endangered by the combination of heat and humidity.

The breed personifies the one-man dog, and is extremely aloof with strangers. Attention forced on him by outsiders often results in aggressive behavior. But with his own family, he is predictable and loyal. Dangerfield and Howell attest to these characteristics in *The International Encyclopedia of Dogs* with the following statement: "It has been said that the Chow will die for his master but not readily obey him; walk with him but not trot meekly to heel; honour him, but not fawn on his friends and relations."

Chow Chows, long coat, black and red.

Chow Chows, adult and pup.

Cirneco dell'Etna.

CIRNECO DELL'ETNA

COUNTRY: Italy
WEIGHT: 18–26 pounds
HEIGHT: 16½–19½ inches
COAT: Short and smooth
COLOR: Fawn in all shades, white markings allowed
OTHER NAME: Sicilian Greyhound
REGISTRY: FCI
GROUP: Southern

This Pharaoh Hound look-alike was brought to Sicily in the Phoenician heyday, when dogs of this type were a hot item. He has been kept and bred in the shadow of Mount Etna for 3,000 years.

The large island of Sicily, located at the toe of Italy, is the major home of the Cirneco. In more ancient times the breed also was known further north on Corsica, and the Greek name for that latter island, *Cyrnecos*, may have contributed to his name. Mount Etna, the 10,000–foot active volcano on Sicily's eastern side, provides the other portion of his name. The roots and history of this breed are the same as the Pharaoh's and the Ibizan's, repeated on a different island. In fact, in times past the Cirneco was also called the Pharaoh Dog, due to its identical taproots in Egypt.

Even before recorded history, a temple dedicated to the local divinity has existed at Ardano on Sicily. This holy place was supposedly guarded by the Cirneco dogs who had "a supernatural instinct to attack the sacreligious and thief but to welcome enthusiastically the devout."

The breed is prevalent around Ardano, and it is now the only breed which hunts on the slopes of Mount Etna. They were officially recognized by the ENCI (the Italian Kennel Club) about 1940, due mainly to the efforts of Professor Giuseppe Solaro. The FCI has also recognized the breed as distinct from the Pharaoh Hound.

As hunters, they are smaller versions of their relatives from Malta and Ibiza. Although basically sighthounds of an ancient sort, they can also hunt by scent. The Cirneco is a specialist on rabbit and hare, but is so silent that it can also sneak up on any kind of feathered game. He is a lively and friendly companion not known outside of his localized area in Italy. Unfortunately, he is becoming extremely rare at home as well.

Cirneco dell'Etna.

Clumber Spaniel.

CLUMBER SPANIEL

COUNTRY: Great Britain
WEIGHT: 35–65 pounds
COAT: Thick, silky and straight, abundant feathering
COLOR: Lemon/white or orange/white, the more white the better
REGISTRY: FCI, AKC, TKC, CKC
GROUP: Gun Dog

This most distinctive flushing spaniel retained more hound genes than any of the others, except the Sussex, giving him the massive bone and heavy head that is his alone. His type was admired especially by the Duke of Newcastle in Nottingham more than a century ago. The Duke's estate, Clumber Park, was undoubtedly the source of the breed's name, but the breed's background is unknown. There are stories of hounds given to the Duke from French nobles. And yet, the traits may have been selected within the spaniels already extant. The characterization of the Field Spaniel, for example, was accomplished without crossbreeding!

These dogs have enjoyed quite some approval among British royalty. Prince Albert, consort of Queen Victoria, was the first to tout them, and his son, King Edward VII, was extremely proud of those he bred in his Sandringham kennels. As favorites of royalty, these spaniels quickly became fashionable. King George V, son of Edward VII, was a dedicated sportsman and hunter, and continued the tradition of using Clumbers. An interesting note is that this king never allowed his Clumbers to retrieve; his Labradors were brought in for that chore. King George continued to enjoy hunting into advanced old age and this may have contributed to the myth that the Clumber is a slow, plodding worker good only for "old men on shooting sticks " (i.e., hunting seats which are planted in the ground, and on which they waited for the game to come to them!).

The modern Clumber is a big fellow yet is anything but slow. He is birdy, active and can still put in a good day's hunt. Of course, he will not work at the pace of some of his lighter boned cousins, but he is especially useful in heavy cover, for the slower walking hunter, or where game is plentiful. Despite King George's desire to show off his Labradors, the Clumber is a fine retriever as well.

In both England and the USA, the dog is still rare despite his long and noble history. Dedicated fanciers keep his quality high, however, and he has never been in danger of disappearing. Tails, docked to the spaniel one-third, are carried low, never to be pegged in the show ring like a Boxer.

COLLIES

Collie, Rough

COUNTRY: Great Britain
WEIGHT: 50–75 pounds
HEIGHT: 22–26 inches
COAT: Long, dense
COLOR: Sable and white, tricolor, blue merle, white
OTHER NAMES: Scotch Collie
REGISTRY: AKC, UKC, TKC, FCI
GROUP: Herding

Collie, Smooth

COUNTRY: Great Britain
WEIGHT: 50–75 pounds
HEIGHT: 22–26 inches
COAT: Short, smooth, double
COLOR: Sable and white, tricolor, blue merle, white
OTHER NAMES: Scotch Collie
REGISTRY: FCI, AKC, TKC, CKC
GROUP: Herding

Rough Collie, sable and white.

The dog most widely recognized as and usually called simply Collie evolved from the same root stock as the other Scottish herding dogs. The breed often is referred to as the Scotch Collie. It is believed they are the descendants of dogs accompanying Roman invaders of 50 BC interbred with native Scottish dogs. When Queen Victoria visited Scotland in 1860, she first glimpsed the working Collie and brought several back with her to England. The royal stamp of approval skyrocketed the breed to instant fame. Over the next few years the points so admired—the elongated, narrow, chiseled head and the rough coat—were emphasized by breeders, creating the look we know today.

The Collie soon became "the dog of the moment," which accelerated with the Lad stories by Albert Payson Terhune and the Lassie films and television series. During their peak, Collies were a common sight on many farms. The breed rode the crest of popularity, but eventually stabilized to the moderate universal appeal it knows today.

Its sweet expression and tipped ears are considered the stamp of the breed and a highly important consideration in show dogs. The Smooth variety is judged by the same standard as the Rough, with the exception of coat. Their colors are rich and striking, often set off by the Irish pattern of white markings. The rough coat needs regular brushing to maintain its striking good looks; the smooth offers easy grooming.

The Collie is a superb children's loyal companion, always willing to give and accept adoration and to play when human playmates are more fickle. Universally gentle and docile with his family, he is an equally good choice for adults. The first recipient (in 1954) of the Dog Hero award, honored by the Quaker Oats Company Ken-L Ration division, was a Collie, and the breed has continued to garner its share of Dog Heroes since that first year.

Collies are so adoring of their families that they will endure incredible hardships to be with them. One, named "Bobbie," journeyed 2,000 miles to find his people again after being lost on the family's vacation trip!

Smooth Collie, tricolor (*left*); Rough Collie, blue merle (*right*).

Above: Rough Collie, blue merle. **Below:** Rough Collie, tricolor.

Above: Smooth Collie, sable and white. **Below:** Rough Collie, sable and white.

Rough Collie, blue merle.

Rough Collie, tricolor.

CONTINENTAL TOY SPANIELS

Continental Toy Spaniel, Papillon

COUNTRY: France/Belgium
WEIGHT: In proportion to height
HEIGHT: 8–11 inches
COAT: Long, fine and silky, with plenty of fringe on chest, ears, tail and legs
COLOR: Basically white, with patches of any color except liver; color should cover both eyes and ears, leaving a symmetrical white blaze down the face
OTHER NAMES: Papillon, Épagneul Nain Continental Papillon
REGISTRY: FCI, AKC, UKC, TKC, CKC
GROUP: Gun Dog

Continental Toy Spaniel, Phalene

COUNTRY: France/Belgium
WEIGHT: In proportion to height
HEIGHT: 8–11 inches
COAT: Long, fine and silky, with plenty of fringe on chest, ears, tail and legs
COLOR: Basically white, with patches of any color except liver; color should cover both eyes and ears, leaving a symmetrical white blaze down the face
OTHER NAMES: Épagneul Nain Continental, Phalene
REGISTRY: FCI
GROUP: Gun Dog

Continental Toy Spaniel, Papillon.

Continental Toy Spaniel, Phalene.

While the King Charles breed was developing in England, a slightly different toy spaniel was being created in continental Europe. He was more refined in bone, with a pointed head and tail curled over the back. Where he came from is conjecture, but miniature bichon dogs were highly esteemed in Europe at the time. Crossings of the more spaniellike miniatures with dogs of bichon type is a possibility. These little charmers created such a clamor that traders brought the dogs from one country to another on mule back and demanded high prices! One of these well-known dog merchants was a Bolognese, so the connection to the bichons cannot be ignored. Originally, all of the Continental "dwarf" spaniels had drooping ears, but later the erect-eared variety emerged.

The wealthy and noble of both Europe and England owned these Continental Toy Spaniels, and many a grand lady refused to have her portrait done unless her tiny dog was included. The breed was seen in paintings by many old masters, including Rubens, Van Dyke, Rembrandt, Fragonard, and others. Madame Pompadour had two Papillons, by name "Inez" and "Mimi." The English admired these little spaniels as well, and in the early days, crosses probably occurred between the English and Continental varieties.

By the time of organized kennel clubs in the late 1800s, the now well-known, prick-eared toy spaniel was universally known as the Papillon. This French word for butterfly aptly describes his large, upright ears which are set at the corners of his head. In fact, the dominant, erect ear became so widespread that many forgot the existence of the drop-eared variety. In the United States, the Papillon is a fairly well-known pet, and the standard describes the "correct" upright ear, but also allows for the drop-eared variety, called Phalene, or moth type. Thus, Americans have only the Papillon, allowing for two styles of ear carriages. In Europe, they also have one breed, but they call it Continental Toy Spaniel. This breed is divided into two varieties called Papillon (erect eared) and Phalene (drop eared). They are also affectionately called *Le Chien Ecureuil*, Squirrel Dog, in France, due to their lovely plumed tails.

Papillons are hardy dogs despite their small size. Their coat is beautiful and easy to care for. They know no enemy and are confident, outgoing, and friendly. Never wildly popular, there are numerous devoted adherents in Canada, America, England, throughout Europe and other countries around the world.

Continental Toy Spaniels, Phalene (*left*), Papillon (*right*).

Continental Toy Spaniel, Papillon.

Continental Toy Spaniel, Papillon.

Continental Toy Spaniel, Papillon.

COTON DE TULEAR

COUNTRY: Madagascar
WEIGHT: 12–15 pounds
HEIGHT: 10–12 inches
COAT: Long, cottony, no undercoat
COLOR: White, white with champagne head or body markings, black and white
REGISTRY: FCI
GROUP: Gun Dog

Bichon dogs from Tenerife were brought to Madagascar and nearby islands on trade ships, probably before the 17th century. From these original imports came the Coton de Reunion, an extinct breed once known on Reunion Island. The descendants of the Coton de Reunion became established near the city of Tulear, Madagascar, and developed into the breed known as the Coton de Tulear.

The Coton (French for cotton) became a favorite of the *merina*, the French nobility on the island during the colonial days. In fact, prior to the 20th century, it was considered criminal for a commoner to own a Coton. This canine social climber soon took on the title of the "Dog of Royalty" and, even today, only socially promi-nent Malagasy own a Tulear.

This breed is devoted to its masters, wanting always to be in their presence and trying its best to please. Because of these traits, the Coton requires little in the way of discipline to create a fine companion. He is a dog only for a house pet, as he is so happy and friendly that he will not defend himself. Like the other bichon dogs, however, he is alert and intelligent and will inform his master of unusual events. As long as he is primarily a house dog, he adapts well to almost any environment or climate. The breed is healthy and vigorous despite its small size, and requires only a bit of regular brushing to keep it handsome. One of their most endearing traits is a tendency to jump and walk on their hind legs.

Like the other bichons, the hair needs regular grooming to keep the dogs looking their cuddly best. Shedding on all the bichons is minimal and an advantage to allergic owners. The Coton's expression is "enquiring and adoring."

They achieved FCI recognition in 1970 and are being fostered by the Coton de Tulear Club of America. They are still rare throughout the world.

Coton de Tulear, white/champagne.

Croatian Sheepdog.

CROATIAN SHEEPDOG

COUNTRY: Yugoslavia
WEIGHT: 31–44 pounds
HEIGHT: 16–20 inches
COAT: 3–6 inches, soft, dense and wavy, except on the head and front of legs
COLOR: All black, small areas of white markings acceptable
OTHER NAMES: Hrvaški Ŏvcar
REGISTRY: FCI
GROUP: Herding

The Croatian is watchful and pugnacious, although amenable to training. It is only seen as a dog working with flocks and only in Yugoslavia. This is part of the common triumvirate of herding dog, flock guard and shepherd seen in so many European countries. In Yugoslavia, if he needs help protecting the sheep, the Karst Shepherd or Sarplaninac is there to lend a paw. He is still commonly seen among the flocks today.

His prick ears are set on at the corners of his head. If he is born with a tail, it is curled over his back in the style of the Puli, who is probably a close relative. Often the tail is docked. The coat is moderate in length, harsh and wavy, but smooth on the face and fronts of the legs. The body proportions are high on leg and square.

313

Curly-Coated Retriever, black.

breed historians state there were later introductions of Poodle to tighten the coat curl. The Curly-Coated Retriever became a popular hunting dog in Britain in the latter part of the 19th century. He was exported to Australia and New Zealand, where he has remained in demand as a working dog for quail hunting, as well as water birds. These two countries now claim more registrations of the breed than its native land does.

He is in his element in the water, but can retrieve handily on land as well. Owners say he is a natural retriever and easy to train, with a robust constitution and a sweet temperament. But he tends to be sober, independent and wary of strangers, and can be quarrelsome with his fellows in the field. The wonderfully short, waterproof and self-drying coat is a big plus for the sports enthusiast. The Curly-Coated Retriever is fearless, and often doubles as an excellent guardian for his family.

He is a big fellow, built square and up on leg. His tail is left at natural length, and tends to be rather short like a pointer's. There is no trimming required of his curly coat. The coat has no topknot or fringe on the ears, nor is there excess hair on the legs. The proper haircoat outlines the entire body with ringlets all over, like a flapper with a new perm and a tight cap of curls.

Curly-Coated Retriever.

CURLY-COATED RETRIEVER

COUNTRY: Great Britain
WEIGHT: 70–80 pounds
HEIGHT: 25–27 inches
COAT: Small, close, crisp curls all over, face smooth
COLOR: Solid black or solid liver
REGISTRY: FCI, AKC, UKC, TKC, CKC
GROUP: Gun Dog

The Curly is a fairly old breed, if not well-known. He began in the early 1800s from crosses of early British water spaniels with various retrievers or possibly even pointers. Some

CZESKY TERRIER

COUNTRY: Czechoslovakia
WEIGHT: 13–20 pounds
HEIGHT: 10½–14 inches
COAT: Long, fine and silky, with a tendency to wave
COLOR: Blue-gray (born black) or light coffee brown (born chocolate)
OTHER NAMES: Bohemian Terrier
REGISTRY: FCI
GROUP: Terrier

This handsome terrier is a modern development created by a Czechoslovakian breeder, Dr. Frantisek Horak. The Czesky is a superb ratter and alarm dog that will go to ground.

Dr. Horak was a knowledgeable geneticist and breeder of Scottish and Sealyham Terriers. He was also a sportsman and expected his terriers not only to win shows but to win trophies in the field. Horak crossbred his terriers, starting in 1949, and attained several positive qualities: the gameness and size to go to ground, and all the physical and mental attributes to participate in the hunt. He also attained a dog of style and beauty, accomplishing his purpose within just four breedings and in less than a decade! The first representative of the breed was Javor Lovu Zdar, who drew great attention in the dog world with his silvery blue jacket.

The breed has very slowly gained some

Czesky Terrier, blue-gray.

Czesky Terrier, light coffee.

ground, first in its homeland and now in a few other European countries. FCI recognized the Czesky in 1963, but the breed has been off and on in danger of disappearing.

Although Horak supposedly used only Scotties and Sealyhams, this combination creates many question marks. The Czesky has several traits that are quite uncommon in the majority of terriers. These distinctions include the low carried tail, extreme ratio of length to height, long silky coat, chocolate color, and the fading gene that lightens black to gray and brown to coffee. Both Scottish Terriers and Sealyhams have high-set, gaily carried tails, harsh and wiry broken coats, shortish legs without long bodies, and no hint of the chocolate color or fading factor. The Dandie Dinmont, however, carries most of these traits: the chocolate gene, silky coat, low tail and long, low body. Whether Dr. Horak was able to find these recessives in purely Scottie/Sealyham breeding stock or actually used some other crosses is an unknown.

An easygoing, obedient nature is typical, and he is a fine house dog and children's companion, residing in peace with other domestic animals. The long tail is carried rather low, and the ears fall forward in a semi-drop.

The Czesky has a lovely sheen to its coat, which is clipped on the upper body. A full underline and front is left, along with a profuse beard and eyebrows.

DACHSHUNDS

Dachshund, Miniature

COUNTRY: Germany
WEIGHT: Less than 9 pounds
COAT: Smooth, wire (like a German Wirehair), or long hair (like a setter)
COLOR: One color (includes reds or yellows, can have black tips or overlay); two-color (includes black/tan, chocolate/tan, gray/tan, or white/yellow); or dappled or striped, (includes merle, harlequin and brindle)
OTHER NAMES: Zwergteckel
REGISTRY: FCI, AKC, UKC, TKC, CKC
GROUP: Hound

Dachshund, Standard

COUNTRY: Germany
WEIGHT: 15–25 pounds
COAT: Smooth, wire (like a German Wirehair), or long hair (like a setter)
COLOR: One color (includes reds or yellows, can have black tips or overlay); two-color (includes black/tan, chocolate/tan, gray/tan, or white/yellow); or dappled or striped, (includes merle harlequin and brindle)
OTHER NAMES: Normalgrosse Teckel
REGISTRY: FCI, AKC, UKC, TKC, CKC
GROUP: Hound

While the French were developing their basset varieties for slower, closer hunting, the Germans created the Dachshunds. Short-statured hunting dogs have assisted Germans since the Middle Ages.

Their origin, like those of the bassets, is thought to be from dwarf mutations of the tall hounds. The Dachshund is basically a short-legged version of the schweisshund, although crosses may have been made to various terriers and/or spaniels to obtain the wire and long coats. The Dachsie is a true hound of German type, without exaggerated skin. He carries the ram's muzzle with very slight stop and the large high-set flat ear. *Dachs* means badger, another animal with a sturdy body on short, crooked legs. Therefore, the Dachsbracke is a bracke with short legs "like the badger," and the Dachshund is a tracking hound with similar appendages. Germans usually call the Dachshund a *Teckel*.

Dachshunds have been employed for many hunting chores: chasing rabbits, searching for various game and tracking. They are also small (and brave) enough to go into the lair to bolt hidden prey. To enable them to fill every hunting need, the breed was molded into a number of sizes and coat varieties as well as in a panorama of colors. The Standard, or largest size, was primarily a tracker, although he had ability

Dachshunds, smooth, wire, and long.

Smooth Dachshund.

Longhaired Dachshund puppy.

for searching as well. Smaller varieties were useful in searching, rabbit hunting and going to ground to chase out the quarry. The smallest ones were developed specifically to go into the rabbit warrens and put the inhabitants to flight.

During WWI, the breed was disparaged as was everything German, but he survived the prejudice. He is admired in Australia, the USA and many other countries around the world. The Smooth is a favorite hound in Great Britain, and in the States, Dachshunds cling firmly to their popularity.

In Germany, Dachshund sizes are separated not by weight, as in America, but by chest circumference—the division of classes based on what size hole they could enter! AKC recognizes two sizes, with the Miniature required to be nine pounds or under. FCI and Germany have the same Standard dog (called *Normalgrosse*), but describe two smaller versions. Their *Zwergteckel* (dwarf Dachshund) must not be more than 13.8 inches around the chest, and the little *Kaninchenteckel* (rabbit Dachshund) should not exceed 11.8 inches. All sizes appear in either a short, smooth; short, wiry; or a long, fringed coat. Colors commonly are according to the usual hound tones of black/tan, red or brindle, but more infrequent patterns of merle, blue/tan or gray with yellow markings are also allowed.

White markings are undesirable.

While most of the German hounds are not known outside their native land, the Dachshund has become widely popular throughout the world, fundamentally as a pet dog. In fact, in Gergweis, Germany, the "Dachshund Capital of the World," these little dogs outnumber people two to one. Here Dachsies are rented "by the hour" to tourists for walks. Affectionate and chipper, he is a fine companion and soul mate. Wary enough to be a watchdog, his devotion to his own family, especially to the children, is undying.

His novel shape lends itself to various nicknames: Weiner Dog, Sausage Dog or the Americanized "Hot Dog"! The length of body tends toward back problems, and owners should be careful about their dog's weight, which may intensify or contribute to this ailment.

His desire to hunt is still strong, and he well may excavate your petunia bed to reach a garter snake or gopher. He may even proudly present you with the rat he has killed in the backyard. But his energy and ability to have fun make up for any minor annoyances. All of this talent is bundled into a package with a selection of colors, coats and sizes, giving a prospective owner nearly unlimited choices!

Longhaired Dachshund.

Wire Dachshund.

Longhaired Dachshund.

Above: Longhaired Dachshunds, red. **Below:** Longhaired Dachshunds, dappled.

Above: Wire Dachshunds. **Below:** Dachshund with fallen deer, a large and unusual quarry for these dogs.

DALMATIAN

COUNTRY: Yugoslavia
WEIGHT: 50–55 pounds
HEIGHT: 19–23 inches, over 24 inches disqualifies
COAT: Short, hard, dense and glossy
COLOR: Pure white base, with round, distinct and well-defined spots of either black or liver evenly distributed all over the body
REGISTRY: FCI, AKC, UKC, TKC, CKC
GROUP: Gun Dog

This breed is so unique that it is hard to categorize. Dalmatian history is long and full of legends. His body type mimics both the pointers and the tight-skinned, small-eared hounds of eastern Europe. Since these types developed from one another, it may be a moot point. Since the breed is not used for either scent work or hunting with a gun, it is doubly hard to know his familial tree. Some histories show him used as a gun dog, a trail hound, a shepherd and guardian, a draft dog and even a ratter! Legend has him coming from northern India long ago, being brought to eastern Europe with bands of gypsies. Since some very early records of the breed are found in Dalmatia, from whence comes his name, the FCI lists him as a product of Yugoslavia.

Whatever his origin, the spotted dog that works with horses has been known in Europe since the Middle Ages. With his introduction into Britain, the aristocracy there found the perfect accent for their ornate carriages, liveried drivers and matched high-stepping horses. At first the Dal trotted alongside carriages on long treks to protect the travelers from highwaymen, but eventually the breed became more of an ornament for the wealthy. The Dalmatian dogs went ahead to "clear the way" in the streets or trotted decoratively under the front or rear axles. Popular also in the stables and liveries of the average man, they became known especially for their presence in the fire stations with horse-drawn water wagons. The sight of Dals running through the streets of London clearing the way for the firemen galloping to the scene of a fire gave the breed its nickname of "Firehouse Dog."

From his days in the carriage houses and fire stations of old England, he has made the transition to the modern mascot. A picture of an American firetruck and firefighter without the faithful spotted Dalmatian on the front seat just isn't complete. The breed remains friendly with horses, and he still carries out his task of accompanying horse-drawn equipage. Field events for modern fanciers test the abilities of the Dal to perform these duties. Although he enjoyed a steady, if moderate, popularity, the 1956 book *101 Dalmatians*, published in Britain and later made into a Walt Disney movie, thrust fame upon him!

The Dalmatian is a clean, quiet, discerning pet. He makes a fine watchdog, almost never barking unless there is evidence of something amiss. "Gentlemanly reserve" describes his character, for he has a highly tuned sense of who his master is. Despite good manners, he has a tough inner core and is not afraid to defend his own if pushed.

The breed's simple lines and lack of any need for clipping, grooming or docking appeals to many people. His repute has spread worldwide and he is found in homes, show rings and "on the job" in many countries.

Dalmatian puppies are born pure white, with the spots beginning to fill in during the first few weeks. This is one of the proofs that scientists have used to decide that the Dals' spots are genetically a form of large ticking. Just as the ticking on an Australian Cattle Dog or a German Shorthair doesn't show up until a few weeks or more after birth, such is the nature of the Dalmatian's adornment. Because of the white factor, a certain small percentage of Dalmatian puppies are born permanently deaf.

The Dal is a breed of almost incredible endurance, able to travel at a moderate pace almost indefinitely. Thus their need for exercise is more than casual, and prospective owners should keep that in mind.

Dalmatians.

Dalmatian.

Dalmatian.

DANDIE DINMONT TERRIER

COUNTRY: Great Britain
WEIGHT: 18–24 pounds
HEIGHT: 8–11 inches
COAT: Crisp mixture of hard and soft hair about 2" long
COLOR: Pepper (shades of blue black to light silvery gray) and mustard (reddish brown to pale fawn)
REGISTRY: FCI, AKC, TKC, CKC
GROUP: Terrier

Stemming from the same stock as the Border, Lakeland, Bedlington and Welsh, and from the north where England becomes Scotland, trotted the short-legged Dandie Dinmont. His coat's crisp mixture of hard and soft hair in the blue and liver shades, as well as the long drop ear, puts him very close to the Bedlington in ancestry. Yet crosses involving various hounds and running dogs are suggested because of his distinctive physical traits: the short, crooked legs, the arched loin, and the rounded head and large eye. The standard asks for a body that is one or two inches less in length than twice the height, making him long and not very tall.

This variety was developed as far back as the 1600s as a specialist for otter and badger in the Cheviot Hills and near Coquetdale. Most of these dogs were kept by a few families in the area, like the Allans. Willie "Piper" Allan, who died in 1704, kept an outstanding pack and refused to sell any despite handsome offers. His sons and grandsons continued the tradition, occasionally giving a pair to a friend or for favors. A tenant farmer, John Davidson, obtained a pair and bred them.

With these and similar breedings, the otter terriers were sprinkled sparingly throughout the area, without specific title or pedigree, when Sir Walter Scott chanced upon them in his travels. He immortalized them in his novel *Guy Mannering* (1814), in which one of the characters, a farmer named Dandie Dinmont (modeled after Davidson), kept this breed. Scott describes the attitude of Dinmont's famous six, "Auld Pepper," "Auld Mustard," "Young Pepper," "Young Mustard," "Little Pepper," and "Little Mustard," thus: "they fear naething that ever cam' wi' a hairy skin on't." From then on, the breed came to be known as Dandie Dinmont's Terrier. King Louis Phillipe of France owned a pair of Dandies in the 1840s.

The Dandie has the same intelligent character and guarding ability that make most terriers good companions. The Dandie does tend to be willful, however. His coat doesn't require a great amount of care, but does need combing out and an occasional plucking, especially to accentuate his distinctive soft, silky topknot.

A happy, loving family dog, the Dandie is indifferent to strangers. His serene disposition belies the dormant ratting instinct.

Dandie Dinmont Terrier, pepper.

DANISH BROHOLMER

COUNTRY: Denmark
HEIGHT: 27½–29½ inches
COAT: Short, harsh
COLOR: Light or brownish yellow, black; white marking on chest, feet and tail tip allowed
REGISTRY: FCI
GROUP: Mastiff

In the past, Broholmers attracted attention from royalty and from artists, and are portrayed in paintings of the Danish Renaissance kings, Frederik II and Christian IV. Mastiffs sent by the English to Danish courts were bred with local canines, probably of the early Great Dane type, producing the Broholmer. These dogs assisted in driving cattle to market and were often called *slagterhunden*, the butchers' dogs.

King Frederik VII and his consort, Countess Danner, owned several Broholmers. A painting of the couple completed around 1859 shows a favorite, "Tyrk," lying at their feet; Tyrk was immortalized at his death by being "stuffed" and donated to the Copenhagen Zoological Museum. About the same time, an archeologist, Count Niels Frederik Sehested of Broholm-Funen, began collecting and organizing the breed. This major source gave the breed its modern name. The Count presented numerous puppies to others who promised to support the breed and spent decades standardizing the Broholmer. For a time, the breed enjoyed the friendship of no-

Danish Broholmers, adult and pup.

bility, famed authors and commoners alike. Between the two World Wars, large dogs and their expensive feeding habits went out of fashion. Many thought this Danish dog just an antique.

Cynologist Jytte Weiss, however, stirred interest in restoring the native breed to its former status. In 1974, revival of the breed began with the Committee for National and Forgotten Breeds. The committee, appointed by the Danish Kennel Club, unearthed two quality Broholmers which matched the 1886 standard. Encouraged, committee members Weiss and Ole Staunskjar scoured the country for more, supported in their search by the press, veterinarians and dog lovers. Black variants were found in northern Seeland in the hands of peasants, farmers, lumberjacks and rangers. One of these blacks, named "Manne," became the cornerstone of the modern Broholmer.

The numbers are still not legion, but the Broholmer is gaining strength despite a narrow breed base. Breedings are still approved only through the committee. In 1982, FCI approved the standard and the breed can be exhibited in international shows.

In build, they are more elegant and not as massive as the English Mastiff, although they remain large and impressive. They have a massive, broad head, carried rather low when not alert. The chest is wide and rippling with muscles. The committee encourages the breeding of only steadfast, good-tempered dogs. These powerful dogs are naturally alert and make good watchdogs.

Danish Broholmer, red.

DEUTSCHE BRACKE

COUNTRY: Germany
HEIGHT: 16–21 inches
COAT: Short, smooth, hard and dense
COLOR: Tricolor; tan with black saddle; white limited to blaze, neck ring, chest and belly, feet, and tail tip
OTHER NAMES: German Hound, Deutsche Sauerlandbracke
REGISTRY: FCI
GROUP: Hound

Most German hounds are sturdily boned and a bit low-stationed, with the large but stiff-cartilaged ear that lies flat and wide instead of folding. They tend also to have the "ram's nose" profile with little stop.

The Deutsche Bracke evolved from generic all-purpose, hot-trailing Celtic hounds of varying type used for German forest work. Some earlier types were the Westphalian Bracke and the Sauerlander Holzbracke. These brackes were mainly promoted in the Sauerland and all of Westphalia, which are located in western Germany. For a while, there was some attempt to support the Steinbracke (or in Holland *Steenbrack*), a slightly smaller version of the bracke.

Stein, meaning stone, was an old German weight designation, one stone being about 22 pounds.

All of these fragmented varieties were finally gathered under one breed title, and the Deutsche Bracke is the only official Bracke now recognized in Germany. A club has fostered the type since 1896, although a written standard was not drawn up by the Deutsche Bracken Club until 1955.

In Germany, the Bracke is a dog promoted in the hills and low mountains for hare, fox, rabbit and boar. He is best on the hot scent, giving tongue with his melodious, bell-like voice. His long legs allow him to work quickly and cover a lot of territory.

A superb nose makes him capable of schweisshund work as well, working cold trails of wounded animals. This ability is required more and more, and at this he works silently. Old-time bracken hunters often feared that the use of a dog to trail the wounded deer would make him want to chase healthy ones. This has been proven to be untrue. With quality training methods, the Bracke quickly understands the difference between the hot track and the cold bloodtrail. Modern breeders say that it takes a good deal of patience to teach him to retrieve, but once he is trained, he is reliable.

Deutsche Bracke.

DEUTSCHER WACHTELHUND

COUNTRY: Germany
WEIGHT: 44–66 pounds
HEIGHT: 16–20 inches
COAT: Thick, longish; wavy enough that there is no fringe, smooth on head
OTHER NAMES: German Spaniel
REGISTRY: FCI
GROUP: Gun Dog

This spaniel was created from various breeds in the early 1900s. The "recipe" has been kept a secret, although the Wachtelhund undoubtedly owes much of his ancestry to the ancient European water dogs, as well as to other hunting breeds.

Not only is the Wachtelhund a fine retriever in wet or marshy areas, but he is also used for hare and fox, exhibiting the hound trait of giving tongue on the trail. Aggressive enough to face a fox or even a wolf, the German Spaniel naturally goes for the throat of his furred prey. As a flushing dog, he is useful in finding feath-

Deutscher Wachtelhund, brown.

Deutscher Wachtelhund.

ered game. His sensitive nose enables him to bloodtrail wounded game, such as deer or boar, in the forest.

He is particularly skilled in dense underbrush and areas with standing water. While obedient and affectionate with his master, he has *jagdpassion*, an intense desire to hunt. He is a choice dog for the professional hunter, such as the German forester. A sturdy fellow, a bit low on leg, his tail is docked by a small amount and is always carried low. Germans say he "should only be in sportsmen's hands."

Dingo, light fawn.

DINGO

COUNTRY: Australia
HEIGHT: 19–22 inches
COAT: Short, harsh, double
COLOR: Red to light fawn generally; other colors, such as white spotted or black/tan, exist
OTHER NAMES: Warrigal, Australian Native Dog
REGISTRY: None
GROUP: Southern

First skeletal evidence of the Dingo in Australia was dated about 3,000 years ago, indicating its progenitor probably trudged across the land bridge about the same time as the aborigine. The dogs and people made their trek before Australia was cut off from the mainland to be surrounded by water. The Dingo was first officially noted by Captain William Damphier, who wrote of the wild dog in 1699.

A direct descendant of the original pariahs from the Middle East and southeastern Asia, the

Dingo became feral and returned to the wild. There these canines have remained to the present as one of the only mammals native to Australia. Aborigines adopted pups into their tribes from time to time and raised them as pets and assistants in the hunt. Dogs occasionally interbred with the Dingoes, and the wild dog actually contributed to at least one modern breed: the Australian Cattle Dog.

Today interbreeding domestic dogs with the Dingo is frowned upon. The Australian Native Dog never stood in good favor, since so much of Australian economy is dependent on cattle and sheep production. The Dingo has received much bad press as a livestock killer and is classified as vermin in his homeland, to be killed (eliminated).

But a few people are now concerned with the native dog as a "living fossil" and are working toward studying and preserving him. The Australian Native Dog Training Society, based in New South Wales, has raised and trained many Dingoes. Their members put them on display and hold obedience and trick demonstrations, and the society's motto is: "A Fair Go for our Dingo." These dogs redomesticate quite easily if raised from a young age by a family, but retain the pariah traits of flight and wariness. Early and continued socialization is a must to overcome their shy and sensitive nature. Obedience training is best accomplished by kindness, patience, and a firm but gentle hand. The Dingo chooses a mate for life, sometimes mourning itself to death after the loss of its partner. Females whelp one litter a year in the spring, similar to many of the pariahs. Often a litter is found in the hollow of a tree, totally protected from all sides, with the dams guarding the front. Even so, whelps frequently fall prey to snakes.

Dingoes have strong cooperative instincts and live in small packs. These groups habitually hunt by night. They work silently and only learn to bark from association with other canines, but they do have a wide range of vocalizations, from high yodels to low crows and howls. To survive in the wilderness, they have learned to play possum, shamming death. These dogs' hardiness and resistance to heat have helped them exist in a land that does little to succor their survival. The Dingo has managed to exist without human intervention—and in spite of human dislike.

Dingo, red.

Doberman Pinscher, red.

DOBERMAN PINSCHER

COUNTRY: Germany
WEIGHT: 66–88 pounds
HEIGHT: 24–28 inches
COAT: Smooth, short
COLOR: Solid ground color (black, red, blue, or fawn), all with tan markings.
OTHER NAMES: Thuringer Pinscher, Plizeilich Soldatenhund, Dobermann
REGISTRY: FCI, AKC, UKC, TKC, CKC
GROUP: Mastiff

Herr Louis Dobermann was a tax collector cum dog-pound keeper who had to travel through dangerous areas. He needed assistants tough enough to protect him from bandits and to con-vince reluctant tax payers to cough up. He performed his duties with "a grave digger and a be-llringer"—and a few basic established breeds. In the late 1860s, he determined to create his own personal guardian, a dog that would look much like a large Miniature Pinscher.

Breed type was fixed in an amazingly short period of time. Dobermann utilized the old German Shepherd type for hardiness, intelligence and soundness, with German Pinscher blood for quick reaction and terrier fire. The Weimar Pointer donated hunting abilities and fine nose, as well as the dilute colors. Added to the strength, guarding instinct and courage of the Rottweiler, the breed needed only the English Greyhound for speed and the Manchester Terrier to give it a short, sleek coat. Dilution factors which produce the reds, blues, and fawns, despite their uncommon appearance, have been present in the general mastiff gene pool since the beginning.

In the early years of the breed, they were extremely sharp, willing to attack "even the devil himself." An early owner, Gottfried Liechti, recorded ". . . it required a good deal of courage to own one." In fact the breed's reputation preceded it to America. One early import won three Best in Shows before any judge had the courage to examine his mouth—only to find several missing teeth, a serious fault in the breed!

Some longhaired and natural bobtail pups were born in the early years. The bobtails were much admired, resulting in the current docking fashion. Earcropping in the long, stylish Ameri-

Doberman Pinscher, cropped ears.

Doberman Pinschers, black.

can show cut or the wider, shorter pet cut aided the ears to stand. Dewclaws were removed, completing the racy appearance.

After Dobermann's death, Otto Goeller continued promotion of the breed and is credited with improvement. Goeller's kennels produced the first notable stud dog, Hellegraf von Thueringen.

The breed began infiltrating American coastlines around the time of WWI. Many Dobermans left in Germany were drafted; others were euthanized, due to the scarcity of food. After the war, the breed's population once again began to rise in its homeland.

The Bulldog may be the official mascot of the US Marine Corps, but the Doberman has the

335

distinction of being named the Marine War Dog. The breed is loyal to its master and will do almost anything requested of it, from exciting drill team performances to schutzhund training. Dobermans have representatives in search-and-rescue, patrol or police dogs and as dog guides for the blind.

One of the breeds that strikes fear in the heart of many, the Dobe's reputation is generally unearned. It is a natural, loyal guard, but the breed has been mellowed to allow the approach of strangers. Socialization and authoritative discipline are recommended, along with a heritage of sound temperament. The Doberman of today is a handsome, light-footed aristocrat which prefers being with its owners to all other things. Owners suspect they must be part goat in their eating habits, swallowing anything in their path.

Above Right: Doberman Pinscher, red. **Below Right:** Doberman Pinscher, uncropped ears. **Below:** Doberman Pinscher, black.

Above: Doberman Pinscher. **Below:** Doberman Pinscher, red.

Above: Doberman Pinscher puppies, four colors. **Below:** Doberman Pinscher, white (*unacceptable color mutation*).

Doberman Pinscher

338

Doberman Pinscher

Dogo Argentino.

DOGO ARGENTINO

COUNTRY: Argentina
WEIGHT: 80–100 pounds
HEIGHT: 24-27 inches
COAT: Short, thick and smooth
COLOR: White
OTHER NAMES: Argentinian Mastiff
REGISTRY: FCI
GROUP: Mastiff

Distinguished as the only dog developed in Argentina, the Dogo Argentino was created in the 1920s, through the strategem of Dr. Antonio Nores Martinez. A dog lover and avid hunter, Martinez sought a tough guardian: a hunter who was a worthy opponent for wild boar, puma and jaguar. Nevertheless, he also desired a trustworthy family dog. Dr. Martinez believed, "A dog which attacks an intruder and then, at the first threat of injury, abandons its prisoner is worth nothing as a guardian."

The Old Fighting Dog of Cordoba, Spain, was the root stock of the recipe for the Dogo. The general type of the Cordoba was large, white and ferocious, with tremendous variation in appearance. These dogs were only interested in one thing—fighting; they were said to be so vicious, a male would attack bitches during the mating ritual! The Cordoba stemmed from Spanish Mastiff, Bull Terrier, old Bulldog of England and early Boxer.

The Cordoba's original mixture started the recipe for Martinez's "Super Dog" with plenty of spice and hot pepper. The Spanish Mastiff donated power, with the Bulldog contributing chest capacity, stoicism and tenacity. The Boxer's influence gave quiet confidence and trainability. Martinez blended the Cordoba

Dogs with the harlequin Great Dane for height and the Great Pyrenees to maintain the bulk and color. The Pyrenees also introduced hardiness in extreme weather. To heighten the hunting instinct, the English Pointer brought his fine nose and air-scenting ability, and the Irish Wolfhound added a dash of speed. Later crosses to the Dogue de Bordeaux intensified courage, along with body and jaw strength.

Over the next three decades, Martinez demonstrated the Dogo's versatility through its use as a sled dog and dog guide for the blind, as well as a great hunter and guardian. When Antonio Martinez died in 1956, his brother, Agustin, continued promoting and preserving the breed. His post as Ambassador enabled him to introduce the Dogo to other countries and to present these dogs as gifts to those in high positions.

Despite setbacks during political upheavals, the Dogo has achieved the recognition of the Argentina Kennel Club. The breed still hunts big game and guards homes. Argentinian hunts are held in strict silence—by both dogs and hunters. Dogos hunt in packs, ready to attack the tough big game. They are true dogs of heart, showing no hesitancy. The hunters value these dogs, caring for them first after a hunt, as a rider does for a horse.

The breed is well known throughout Europe, especially Germany, and was granted recognition by FCI in 1960. There is an active club in the United States where Dogo owners are encouraging their use as home protector, family dog, and in police or guide work.

The Dogo is loving to children and is a tireless playmate. The breed's stamina and longevity are remarkable, with some dogs still hunting at 16 years of age. In a home situation, if Dogos can't hunt pumas, they'll settle for mice. Their scenting ability was demonstrated by the bitch who picked her own pups out of the wet nurse's litter following her hospitalization. Extremely loyal, they are excellent guard dogs, requiring dominant masters.

Dogo Argentino.

DOGUE DE BORDEAUX

COUNTRY: France
WEIGHT: 80–100 pounds, minimum
HEIGHT: 23–27 inches
COAT: Short, smooth
COLOR: One color—dark auburn or fawn,
white on chest allowed
OTHER NAMES: French Mastiff
REGISTRY: FCI
GROUP: Mastiff

The Dogue de Bordeaux is similar to the Bullmastiff in size and type, yet is centuries older, being more closely related to the mastiff from Asia and the molossus that made the trek to Gaul from the Roman arenas. At one time, there were two varieties, the Doguin being the smaller version, which has since vanished into nothing but a sentence in reference books. Dogues have had wide and varied employment since their entrance into France after the fall of Rome. Originally, they served a dual purpose as war dogs and by guarding flocks from wolves and bears.

This was followed by the "glory" of combat with bears and bulls. After humane statutes outlawed the torture of the larger beasts, battles of Dogue against Dogue took the place of dog against bull. Spectators felt the French dog fights rivaled the bullfights in Spain for entertainment purposes. Occasionally, a dull match was sparked by tossing a jaguar in the pit.

This lack of concern for dogs and, in particular, for the Dogue de Bordeaux was written in the 1300s by Gaston Phoebus: ". . . with their thick heads, thick lips, and large ears, they are well suited to hunting bear and pigs because they are stubborn. But they are heavy and ugly and, if a wild boar were to kill them, it would be no great loss."

Following this era, near the end of the Middle Ages, the gladiator turned to cattle droving—not as "glorious" perhaps, but much safer. The breed served as personal protection when fighting was outlawed and the need for cattle drovers declined. His majestic presence decorated many estates. The French Revolution ended that occu-

Dogue de Bordeaux, auburn.

pation, with many of the noble guards giving their lives to protect their masters and property. Fortunately, enough survived to attract the attention of current French cynologists, and the Dogue is now found throughout France, with specimens also in Belgium, Germany, Switzerland, Japan, Africa and the States.

Professor Raymond Triquet headed the rebuilding of the breed during the mid-1960s and stressed that the dogs should be "superb athletes." The massive head is their trademark, with the jaw undershot and the muzzle masked in either black or red.

"Beauty is only skin deep" and despite the dogs' menacing appearance, they are sweet with their masters and children. They will, however, be aggressive with other dogs. The French expression *humeur de dogue* still refers to a person showing a bad temper.

Right: Head study of the Dogue de Bordeaux shows the tremendous size of the breed's skull compared to this youngster. **Below:** Body study of the Dogue de Bordeaux.

DRENTSE PATRIJSHOND

COUNTRY: Netherlands
WEIGHT: 50 pounds
HEIGHT: 22–25 inches
COAT: Thick and straight, with abundant feathering on legs, feet, tail and ears
COLOR: White with brown, orange, or, occasionally, brown/tan patches; with or without ticking or roaning
REGISTRY: FCI
GROUP: Gun Dog

Originating in the province of Drente, the source of his name, the Patrijshond appears in paintings done several centuries ago. He probably was created soon after the first use of firearms. His history is of the same pool of hawking or setting dogs, from which all of the setters and spaniels descended. Always a favorite dog for the weekend hunter in the Netherlands, there are about 6,000 of the breed, almost all in its native country.

He is a pointing dog and a fine retriever, as well as a quiet and well-mannered companion. Hunters also find him good for water work. His most admired quality is that he naturally hunts "under the gun."

Although searching thoroughly, he stays close to the hunter, never straying beyond gun range, and frequently looks to his master for direction. Partridge and quail are not so numerous as they once were in the Netherlands, but the dogs do not have to worry about unemployment—they have adapted well to hunting the still plentiful rabbit and pheasant. Due to his fine nature, he has gained some demand as a companion dog and house pet.

The name is often shortened to Drent (plural Drenten), which is also what people from this province are called. In body type, he is a heavier built dog than the Small Münsterländer, and perhaps most resembles the German Longhair, with a smaller and more refined head. His tail is left long in the style of the setter and, when on scent, is swung around circularly. Due to his gentle, obedient and meek nature, harsh training is unnecessary and, in fact, is counterproductive. The breed base is small, and there is nowhere to go for new blood, so the breed association is actively advising breeders and testing dogs in form and function to ensure all breeding stock is sound.

Drentse Patrijshond, white with brown.

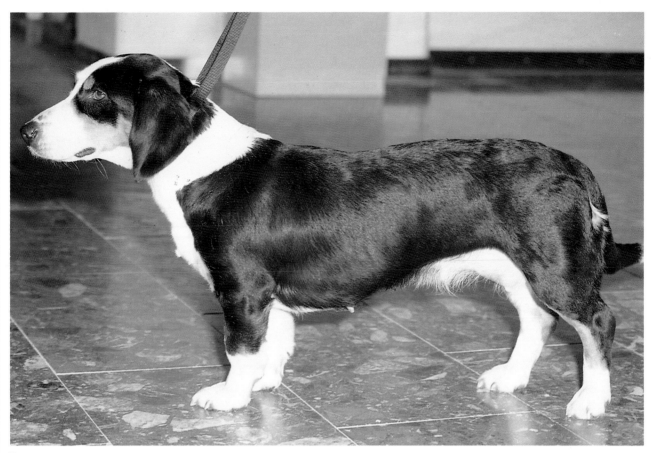

Drever.

DREVER

COUNTRY: Sweden
WEIGHT: 33 pounds
HEIGHT: 11½–15 Sweden; 12–16 inches Canada
COAT: Short, dense and hard
COLOR: Fawn, black, or black/tan; always with the white markings on face, feet, neck, chest and tail tip. Canada allows all colors
OTHER NAMES: Swedish Dachsbracke
REGISTRY: FCI, CKC
GROUP: Hound

Early in the 20th century, Westphalian Dachsbrackes were imported from Germany into Denmark and Sweden. They were appreciated for their hunting abilities. In Denmark, they were mated with Swiss hounds to create a Danish dachsbracke. When these Danish dogs were brought to Sweden, they were backcrossed again to Westphalian Dachsbrackes. This last cross created the breed known as the Drever.

Drev means to hunt in Swedish, and hunting was what the Drever did best. Officially named in 1947, the Swedish KC gave him the nod in 1949. Since then, the Drever has become one of the most popular breeds in his homeland.

He was also introduced to Canada, where he was officially recognized in 1956. But this breed is never seen in a show ring in either country. A slow, steady worker, he hunts hare, fox, and occasionally deer; but this dog has the courage to pit himself against even a wild boar. In such cases, he circles and dodges the prey, warning the hunter by barking furiously. The Drever has an excellent nose and his musical voice is "much larger than his size would seem to warrant."

White markings may appear on his face, neck, chest, feet and tail tip. His legs are straight, never bent like the Dachshund. The ever-wagging tail with its slight brush shows his affable, even temperament.

Dunker, black/tan saddled.

DUNKER

COUNTRY: Norway
WEIGHT: 35–49 pounds
HEIGHT: 18½–21½ inches; some well-built males may go to 22½ inches
COAT: Short, thick and straight
COLOR: Tan with large black saddle and small, symmetrical white markings; or the same color with the black being a splotched, marbled color by action of the harlequin (merle) gene
OTHER NAMES: Norwegian Hound
REGISTRY: FCI
GROUP: Hound

The Dunker was created in the 1820s, supposedly from indigenous dogs and Russian hounds. Although not heavy, he is a powerfully built hound designed for endurance. His name came from the man who originally created him. Today, the Dunker is probably the most numerous scenthound used in Norway and many good specimens can be found there, although he has found no following elsewhere.

The term harlequin refers to the marbled blue color pattern created by the merle gene. This is one of the few hounds carrying this color, along with the dappled Dachshund of Germany, the Irish Kerry Beagle and America's Mountain Cur. Glass (blue) eyes are allowed in the harlequin specimens. Breeding two harlequins is not recommended, as it produces dogs with a preponderance of white and sometimes defects of vision and hearing.

This hound is a robust, noble dog with clean lines and flat, smooth-lying ears. Depth of chest should equal one-half the height at the shoulders, giving plenty of lung power for endurance. Although the coat is described as short, it gives plenty of protection for northern winters. Thus a bit of brush on the tail and the back of the thighs is evidenced.

346

DUTCH SHEPHERDS

Longhaired Dutch Shepherd

COUNTRY: Netherlands
WEIGHT: 66 pounds
HEIGHT: 23–25 inches
COAT: Long, straight, flat and harsh; short on face and on leg fronts
COLOR: Various shades of brindle, including gray, yellow, silver, red or gold brindles; blue; color tends to lighten with age
OTHER NAMES: Langhaar Hollandse Herdershond
REGISTRY: FCI
GROUP: Herding

Roughhaired Dutch Shepherd

COUNTRY: Netherlands
WEIGHT: 66 pounds
HEIGHT: 23–25 inches
COAT: Medium long, wiry
COLOR: Various shades of brindle, including gray, yellow, silver, red or gold brindles; blue; color tends to lighten with age
OTHER NAMES: Ruwhaar Hollandse Herdershond
REGISTRY: FCI
GROUP: Herding

Shorthaired Dutch Shepherd

COUNTRY: Netherlands
WEIGHT: 66 pounds
HEIGHT: 23–25 inches
COAT: Short, dense
COLOR: Various shades of brindle, including gray, yellow, silver, red or gold brindles; blue; color tends to lighten with age
OTHER NAMES: Korthaar Hollandse Herdershond
REGISTRY: FCI
GROUP: Herding

The three varieties of the Dutch Shepherds are very similar (except for color) to the shepherds of nearby Belgium and early German shepherd varieties. They, like their Belgian cousins, are judged on the same physical standard. They have been known in their present form since the

Longhaired Dutch Shepherd, blue brindle.

early 1700s, when examples of the breeds were exported to Australia. The entire inland area of Holland, bordering on Germany, was mainly sheep-herding and flock-tending country. The Dutch Shepherd first came to the fore in Holland around 1870 from the north Brabant area. The dogs demonstrated superb herding abilities and were widespread at that time but, as the flocks dwindled, so did the dogs. Like other herding breeds, they lost more ground when the German Shepherd craze swept the world.

The Dutch Shepherds have been rediscovered in the last few decades and are quickly regaining popularity. Modern owners, proud of this breed's national heritage, are dedicated to retaining working qualities. These dogs have become competent in guard work, and occasionally schutzhund and obedience. But the inborn herding drive is still very acute, and that is what they do best. A few have been brought into the USA.

The rough coat was prevalent back in the 1940s, but today the smooth coat is seen almost universally, with the wire coat glimpsed but occasionally. The long coat, with shades of gold or silver brindle and liberal featherings on legs and tail, is disappearing. Only about 30 per year are registered in Holland. The simple reason for its rarity is that most of these dogs work out of doors, and the luxurious long coat requires too much care for practical owners who prefer the ease of grooming a short coat.

The Dutch Shepherd pup has indefatigable curiosity and is in perpetual motion, challenging its master to provide activity, new experiences and training. This dog possesses a keen and cunning intelligence. The adult is extremely possessive and territorial, and generally does not tolerate other dogs or thrive in close confinement. If raised with kids or in apartments, they accept the situation, but this is a working animal who is a workaholic and naturally wants to herd and defend. He is happiest in an environment where he has adequate exercise, a territory to defend and plenty of chores to keep both mind and body busy.

Above: Roughhaired Dutch Shepherd, brindle. **Below:** Shorthaired Dutch Shepherd, brindle.

Above: Roughhaired Dutch Shepherd. **Below:** Longhaired Dutch Shepherd.

Dutch Smoushond.

DUTCH SMOUSHOND

COUNTRY: Netherlands
WEIGHT: 20–22 pounds
HEIGHT: 14–16½ inches
COAT: Coarse, wiry, harsh, straight, medium length; leg furnishings, eyebrows, mustaches and beard are evident but never exaggerated. No topknot; no tendency to mat
COLOR: Solid yellow, with preference to dark straw color; ears, mustache, beard and eyebrows may be darker
OTHER NAMES: Hollandse Smoushond
REGISTRY: FCI
GROUP: Terrier

In the late 1800s the German Coarsehaired Pinscher, grandfather of the modern Schnauzer, was common throughout Germany. The Germans preferred the black or salt/pepper dogs and usually destroyed the red or yellow whelps which were common in litters at that time. An enterprising Dutch merchant named Abraas cleverly—and cheaply—bought these German "rejects" and brought them to Holland. They were sold on the streets of Amsterdam as *heerenstalhonden,* or gentlemen's stable dogs.

The yellow, roughhaired little charmers caught on and developed into the Smoushond. The breed enjoyed recognition from the FCI as well as the Dutch Kennel Club and was a popular family dog in the early part of the 20th century. In the years between the Wars, his numbers were greatly reduced, and he all but vanished during WWII. The last two litters were bred in 1949, with none following, and soon he was dropped from official roll calls and declared to be extinct.

In the early 1970s a Dutch woman, who had poignant memories of the Smoushonden owned by herself and friends in the 1940s, decided to recreate the breed. She advertised, asking for anyone owning a mongrel which bore resemblance to the accompanying photo to contact her. In a small country like the Netherlands, it was actually possible to go and check out each of these leads personally. If the "approved" dog was a female, this woman asked the owners to breed the dog once to a stud of her choice, and, of course, chose an appropriate male. She was dedicated to her task and went to look at *each* puppy born and still does even now, assisted by other breed wardens. In fact, this Dutch dog lover sees each Smoushond born in the Netherlands four or five times before breeding age, keeping photo records and recommending possible breeding partners.

By 1977, a specialty club had been refounded and recognition was forthcoming from the Raad van Beheer (Dutch KC) and the FCI. The breed is once again on fairly firm footing, and the modern proponents want to keep it that way. They are very cautious about breeding practices to forestall genetic problems and as yet have no interest in selling any outside the Netherlands.

The Smous is an affectionate and friendly fellow, totally devoid of nervousness, yappiness or wanderlust. His rough but short jacket is quite easy to care for and provides adequate protection. Although the standard allows for an uncut tail, most are docked, leaving one-third to be carried gaily. As the standard states, the Smous should be "a pleasant and easy family dog."

EAST EUROPEAN SHEPHERD

COUNTRY: USSR
WEIGHT: 75–105 pounds
HEIGHT: 24–28 inches
COAT: Moderately short, smooth
COLOR: Black, black/tan saddled, sable, rarely brindle or white
OTHER NAMES: Byelorussian Owtcharka
GROUP: Herding

These dogs are very similar in appearance to a German Shepherd Dog and developed directly from the GSDs brought to the Soviet Union in the 1920s. After over a quarter century of selection, especially for animals to withstand the Russian climate, the breed is distinctly different from the Shepherd known in the West. Although at first centered in Byelorussia and the far western provinces of the USSR, the EESKC has thousands of members all over Russia today. It is presently the leading breed in the USSR. Often dogs of this breed have longer soft hair on the ears, neck, limbs and tail. It is said that their Russian owners spin the cashmerelike wooly undercoat for use in garments.

They are a tough, aggressive guard dog, a favorite of the KGB. For Kremlin duty, the KGB insists on solid blacks. If only one pup of another color is whelped, the entire litter is destroyed, and the breeding is not repeated. Private breeders, however, allow more latitude in color.

Eyes may be brown, amber, blue or odd-eyed. Ears are long and upright, and the paws are large with long toes, giving a snowshoe appearance. Owners equate their temperament to that of a Doberman Pinscher.

The handful that are found in other areas of the world have been smuggled out of East Germany. A photo accompanying an article by Enid Bergstrom in the February 1983 issue of *Dog World* showed them to be a bit squarer in body and longer in muzzle than most modern German Shepherds.

East European Shepherd, black/tan.

East European Shepherd.

Tasy.

EAST RUSSIAN COURSING HOUNDS

Tasy

COUNTRY: USSR
HEIGHT: 22–28 inches
COAT: Short and silky, with fringing on tail and ears
COLOR: Tan, gray or black/tan; usually as spots with white
OTHER NAMES: Mid-Asiatic Borzoi
REGISTRY: None
GROUP: Southern

Taigan

COUNTRY: USSR
HEIGHT: 22–28 inches
COAT: Long, thick and double, sometimes wavy; heavy feathering on tail, ears, thighs, shoulder and front legs
COLOR: Solids in black, gray, fawn or white; can have white markings
OTHER NAMES: Kirghiz Borzoi, Tajgan
REGISTRY: None
GROUP: Southern

Among the lesser known and oldest of the Russian sighthounds are the Tasy and Taigan. The Tasy hails from the endless desert plains east of the Caspian Sea, where he is also an endurance dog. The ringed tail, tapering head and coat with heavy ear fringes—as well as his home area bordering on northern Iran and Afghanistan—may hint at his historical bonds. The fact that the Afghan Hound (who in his native working state had less hair) is sometimes called Tazi is even more intriguing.

Rural hunters have used the Tasy for coursing hare, marmot, fox, hooved game and even wolf. This dog is nimble and can even go into thicket and forest in pursuit. It has a capable nose as well and can search for game by scent before it sees the quarry and begins the chase. Asian hunters sometimes still use trained eagles in combination with the Tasy. These hunts were valuable sources of fur pelts as well as meat and, at one time, one purebred Tasy from the Kara-Tala River area was equated with 47 horses in a dowry. So high was the regard for the Tasy that he was allowed to sleep in the house.

Modern land reclamation and industrializa-

Above and Below: Taigan.

tion in these desert regions have forced the breed into remote areas, and today the purebred Tasy is quite rare. They are seldom exhibited, although a few breeders have taken up the banner of this breed and are determined not to see it disappear.

Even further east, in the high altitude Tien Shan region right on the Chinese border, the Taigan came to the fore. This unique breed is not found outside the borders of Kirghizia. It has been adapted for endurance work at six to ten thousand foot elevations and can do scent work as well as retrieve. Both commercial and amateur Kirghiz hunters used this dog for hunting fox, marmot, badger, hare, wildcat, wolf, and hooved game. Trained falcons were often used for the kill. This beautifully coated dog was full of hunting zeal and showed charm and grace with its handler.

Unfortunately, today the purebred Taigan is dwindling rapidly. In a 1986 count, most specimens had been mongrelized and, in the Talass Valley—forever a bastion of the breed—only a few dogs were left. Soviet authorities state that they hope this trend will be reversed.

Norwegian Elkhound.

ELKHOUNDS

Norwegian Elkhound

COUNTRY: Norway
WEIGHT: 44 pounds
HEIGHT: 20 inches
COAT: Short, thick, coarse, stand-off, double
COLOR: Any color of gray, shadings are usual
OTHER NAMES: Norsk Elghund (Gra), Grahund, Gray Norwegian Elkhound
REGISTRY: FCI, AKC, UKC, TKC, UKC
GROUP: Northern

Norwegian Elkhound, Black

COUNTRY: Norway
WEIGHT: 40 pounds
HEIGHT: 18–20 inches
COAT: Short, thick, coarse, stand-off, double
COLOR: Solid jet black
OTHER NAMES: Norsk Elghund (Sort)
REGISTRY: FCI
GROUP: Northern

Jämthund

COUNTRY: Sweden
WEIGHT: 66 pounds
HEIGHT: 23–25 inches
COAT: Short, thick, coarse, stand-off, double
COLOR: Any color of gray, shadings are usual
OTHER NAMES: Swedish Elkhound
REGISTRY: FCI
GROUP: Northern

The classic elkhound is probably very similar to the northern dog that first appeared at the side of humans during the Stone Age. Skeletons dating back to that era were found in Norway and are nearly identical to today's canine. These types have been selected for their hunting abilities, although at one time they probably were both herding and sledding dogs. In fact, the Norwegian Defense Minister was given the power to mobilize all privately owned elkhounds

Above: Jämthund. **Below:** Norwegian Elkhound.

for sledding hitches to carry military supplies over the snow in case of war. These breeds have remained remarkably the same through the millenia to the present time.

Throughout Scandinavia, dogs of the elkhound type were used and bred without pedigree or formal organizations. These dogs were good workers and bred fairly true, with some minor regional differences. When the FCI attempted to categorize the breeds, they separated them into the above three. The Black Elkhound of Norway is the smallest, with the gray Norwegian dog a bit bigger and the Jämthund the largest, raised and commonly used by the hunters of Jämtland district in Sweden. Although all are very popular dogs in their homelands, only the gray Norwegian Elkhound has achieved any popularity abroad.

Actually, *elghund* translates literally as moose dog, not elkhound, although they were used to hunt elk, lynx, bear and wolf as well as moose. In modern times, these breeds often hunt in pairs and assist sports enthusiasts by finding game and trying to drive it back toward the hunter or keep it within range of the gun. They are not chasers, following game over a great distance like the scenthounds, but work close to the hunter in the northern forests. Small game, such as marten, ermine or grouse, is approached by silently creeping up to it. The elkhounds attempt to block the animal's path or to turn it back toward the hunter. With larger prey, the elkhound feints attack, using this ploy to force the quarry to face the dog. A dog goes in, then dances away to protect himself, barking to keep the victim's attention until his master is within firing range.

Because of the spitz's long association with people, these dogs make fine companions and house dogs, and are especially good with children. They have the classic Nordic/spitz-type head and body, with the tail rolled up tightly on the back. Although lighter shades of gray are the norm of Elkhounds in America, at home they are often very dark gray, having a nearly black face with a mask. The smaller, solid black variety is still the rarest and, except for color, is judged by the same standard as the gray varieties.

Norwegian Elkhound, pup.

357

Norwegian Elkhound.

Norwegian Elkhound.

ENGLISH COCKER SPANIEL

COUNTRY: Great Britain
WEIGHT: 26–34 pounds
HEIGHT: 15–17 inches
COAT: Flat and silky on body; well, but not excessively, feathered
COLOR: Various solids, or those colors in a broken pattern with white; often have roan patterns
OTHER NAMES: Cocker Spaniel
REGISTRY: FCI, AKC, UKC, TKC, CKC
GROUP: Gun Dog

As the use of flushing spaniels became widespread in England, the smaller ones were called "cocking" spaniels. The name may have come from their use to spring or "cock" the game for the net and, later, the gun. Yet others feel it came from their usefulness on small game such as woodcock. At any rate, the merry little spaniels of England have been popular since the 19th century.

When the Kennel Club of England was cre-ated, just before the turn of the century, it soon recognized the Field, Springer and Cocker Spaniels as separate breeds. Each breed's individual development started from that time. The Cocker of England continued a rise to popularity that took him to the number one spot in his homeland during the 1930s and kept him there for 20 years. He also gained tremendous popularity in other Commonwealth nations.

While the Cocker Spaniel in England was rising to perfection, on the other side of the Atlantic, Americans using basically the same original breeding stock were developing a slightly different Cocker Spaniel. When imports from England were brought here during the 1930s, although there were separate classes for the English variety, there was still interbreeding between the English Cocker and the now native American Cocker. Because the two had become so divergent, most breeders felt that interbreeding was detrimental to both varieties. In 1940, the Kennel Club of England separated the breeds into the Cocker Spaniel and the Ameri-

English Cocker Spaniel, black.

can Cocker Spaniel. Soon after, the AKC followed suit but called the resulting breeds the English Cocker Spaniel (called Cocker in England) and the Cocker Spaniel (called American Cocker in England). FCI used great sense in defining both breeds by country, and the rest of the world calls one the English Cocker Spaniel and the other the American Cocker Spaniel.

The English Cocker in America holds a steady interest, mostly among exhibitors. He is a moderate dog, a bit larger, longer headed, and less coated than the American version. He sports the classic land spaniel tail which is level with the back and constantly wagging in extroverted joy of life. Neither the tail tucked in anxiety or pushed straight up, as seen with some misinformed handlers in the show ring, is typical of the breed. The breed's hunting instincts abound—if any would care to use them. He works close to the gun and uses his good nose to flush out a variety of game. Happy, willing and obedient, he is easy and fun to be with.

Tails are docked on pups. Coat care is a necessity but, if kept up, is not a problem.

Right and Below: English Cocker Spaniel.

English Cocker Spaniels. **Above Left:** Blue roan. **Above Right:** Particolor. **Below Left:** Red. **Below Right:** Buff roan.

English Cocker Spaniel.

English Cocker Spaniel.

English Cocker Spaniel puppy and feline friend.

English Coonhound, red tick.

ENGLISH COONHOUND

COUNTRY: USA
HEIGHT: 21–27 inches
COAT: Short, hard
COLOR: Mainly redtick, also bluetick, tricolor with ticks, white-red, white-black or white-lemon; brindle or too much red or black not acceptable
REGISTRY: UKC
GROUP: Hound

Tracing back to the Virginia hounds, the English Coonhound was bred to adapt to the rougher American climate and terrain. When the English was first recognized by the UKC, it was descriptively called the English Fox and Coonhound, alluding to its capabilities. In fact, at that time, the dogs were used more on fox than on raccoon. They were also capable of going after opossum, cougar and bear.

While the Redbone and Black and Tan were given separate breed status, all other treeing coonhounds were called English after the turn of the century. These included the blueticked dogs, the white tricolors and others, as well as those with redtick markings. There was also great variation in the history and in the style of hunting, from big, cold-nosed, patient trailing hounds to the refined, speedy hot-trailing dogs.

In 1945, the heavily ticked dogs split off from the English, registering themselves as the Bluetick Hound. Later, the tricolored hounds separated into the breed called Treeing Walker Coonhounds. Most modern English Coonhounds are of the redtick color, although they can be bluetick and other hound colors as well.

The breed is the extreme of the fast, hot-trailing competition-type coonhound. An English named "Bones," owned by Colonel Leon Robinson, won one of the first National Coonhound Championships. The breed is still used by practical hunters and competitive hound owners throughout the USA.

ENGLISH FOXHOUND

COUNTRY: Great Britain
WEIGHT: 55–75 pounds
HEIGHT: 23–27 inches
COAT: Very short and hard
COLOR: Bicolor or tricolor, usually with white predominating; blue not allowed
REGISTRY: FCI, AKC, CKC
GROUP: Hound

When fox hunting became the rage in England in the 13th century, a hound was needed specifically for trailing the fast and wily red fox. The trailing hounds of the St. Hubert/Bloodhound type were just too slow for this sport, although their blood formed the basis for the English Foxhound. Crosses were made to faster, lighter hounds and, some say, even to Greyhounds to increase speed.

In England, the foxhound is followed by mounted horsemen, and the dog must be fast with tremendous endurance. Fox scent is a "hot" trail and the hounds do not require the super-sensitive nose of the slow trailing hounds. But they do need good voice, drive and enthusiasm, as well as speed.

For many years each hunt developed its own style of hound, and type was not even. But by 1800, many large standardized packs existed, and the meticulous records kept by each individual Master of Hounds were incorporated in the Masters of Foxhounds Association formed around that time. Thus most Foxhounds in England can trace their pedigrees back, unbroken in written record, for over 150 years.

The first recorded importation of Foxhounds to the USA was in 1738; others soon came to American huntsmen with regularity. George Washington was an ardent hound fancier with many Foxhounds in his kennels. Some of these English dogs remain pure to the present time. Dozens of formal hunts, each with packs of pure English Foxhounds, are held in the eastern United States. Others of these early English imports formed the basis for the American Foxhound and other native coonhounds or scenthounds.

There is no doubt the breed can be prolific. A Foxhound, "Lena," holds the dubious honor of being tops in motherhood, whelping an astounding 23 puppies, with all surviving. Although it is assumed to be the drive to hunt that requires

English Foxhound, tricolor.

English Foxhound.

Owners of individually bred hounds do not practice this trimming. Therefore, in the show ring where both working hounds and home-raised dogs may be competing, a difference in ear lengths may be observed.

Most English Foxhounds who will be used in formal hunts are raised in large packs in kennels, and under those circumstances they tend to be "dog oriented," obstinately interested only in hunting. However, they are calm and affectionate hounds and, if raised within the family from the beginning, make fine companions. They are extremely strong and powerful for their size, and they need to learn discipline early. Supplying adequate exercise and proper training, many owners enjoy them as house pets. They are particularly gentle with children. Neither nervous nor yappy, their pack instincts cause them to enjoy being with their owners and to adapt easily to a human as "pack leader." Like with many of the smooth-coated scenthounds, grooming is almost non-existent. A fair number in the USA have found their way to the conformation and obedience show rings. Pack judging, even for non-hunters, is another outlet for competitive urges. These competitions and formal hunts provide a picturesque setting: scarlet coats (or "pinks") and packs of dogs bounding through grassy terrain.

Foxhounds preparing for a hunt in Great Britain.

the dam to be restrained from leaving the pups to join the pack, perhaps it is the size of her demanding family!

Physically, the English Foxhound is a square, strongly boned hound with tightly knuckled feet, medium flat ear and lack of any loose or hanging skin. His endurance is evidenced by the fact that many hunt packs are taken to the meet under their own power, which may mean a 10– to 15–mile walk from (and back to) the kennel, with as much as 50 miles of hard running in the interim.

They are described as symmetrical. It was said of "Belvoir Gambler," a great example of the breed in 1885 by Cuthbert Bradley, quoting poet Cannon Kingsley: "Next to an old Greek statue there are few such combinations of grace and strength as in a fine Foxhound."

The practice among formal hunters is not to register hounds until they are a year of age. By that time the qualities of the dog can be assessed and, if he proves to be a good worker, he is formally registered and his ears are "rounded." This process of trimming off the bottom inch or two of the ear length serves to prevent the common nicks and tears to the edge that can repeatedly open and bleed and are so hard to heal.

English Setter.

ENGLISH SETTER

COUNTRY: Great Britain
WEIGHT: 40–70 pounds
HEIGHT: 24–25 inches
COAT: Flat, of good length without curl, with feathering
COLOR: Tricolor, black/white, blue belton, lemon/white, lemon belton, liver/white, liver belton, orange/white, orange belton, all white
REGISTRY: FCI, AKC, UKC, TKC, CKC
GROUP: Gun Dog

The English Setter stemmed directly from those early couching and hawking dogs that were the basis for so many of the spaniels, as well as of the setters. In fact, the name "setter" derives from his old style of hunting. The breed still bears a strong tendency to creep catlike toward the bird, and may even sink slowly—just a bit—between the shoulder blades as they point. The modern development of the English Setter can be credited to Edward Laverack and Purcell Llewellin, who were contemporaries in mid-19th-century England.

Laverack obtained his foundation stock, "Ponto" and "Old Moll," from the Reverend A. Harrison, who had bred pure for 35 years. Laverack devoted his life and fortunes to developing the English Setter to his ideal. His strain was famous worldwide, and many were exported to the USA. An admirer of attractive appearance, his handsome "Laveracks" are behind many of today's best show strains. But, as with most gun dog breeders of the 19th century, Laverack's primary interest was field trialing and his dogs had these abilities. By the 1870s, long years of inbreeding had set some problems of temperament and infertility in his famous strain and, when outbreaks of distemper followed, the Laverack Kennels reached their nadir. But characteristics of the strain continued through other breeders, including Americans.

Llewellin started his famous field trial strain with high-strung Laverack bitches that, with their fire and high energy, could run to the edges of the course. He owned both Gordons and Irish Setters, and used them in various crosses. When he obtained his Duke-Rhoebes strain, consisting of coarse but sturdily practical English Setters, this proved the perfect nick with the Laverack blood—and made his strain and his name. The Llewellin strain became synonymous with field trial winners, and those imported to America dominated the circuit for many years in the early part of this century. So well known was the strain that there are still people who think the "Llewellin Setter" is a breed unto itself. The last of the straight-bred Llewellins was La Besita, who was the American National Champion of 1915. After that, Llewellins also degenerated by inbreeding, and the pointer soon supplanted the setter as the star of the All-Age Field Trials. Many of the Llewellins were lightly ticked tricolors, and some ill-conceived prejudice against this color remains in the show rings.

Besides these two pillars, whose individual ultimate good for the breed is occasionally—and heatedly—debated, there was a bevy of lesser known fanciers that kept these dogs. When the breed traveled across the seas, he gained the distinction of being America's first gun dog and attained quite a following. As *The New Dog Encyclopedia* attests: "The man who owns one English Setter shouts the praises of the breed to the housetops. The one who owns two English Setters does the same thing—only louder!"

Several of the breed set the tradition for top working field dogs. The modern English Setter is a handsome gun dog that often seconds as a pet. He is quite soft in nature and wilts under harsh treatment. His long coat does require a bit of care, and modern show style dictates some clipping of throat, head and ears. A host of attractive colors are allowed, with the solid white body covered with heavy ticking (called belton) preferred. The show type and field type are still quite far apart, although the breed has recently achieved its first dual championship. With the modern return of interest in the working qualities of many breeds, breeders may yet marry the two.

English Setters, liver belton, blue belton.

English Setter.

ENGLISH SHEPHERD

COUNTRY: USA
WEIGHT: 40–60 pounds
HEIGHT: 18–23 inches
COAT: Long, moderately coarse, dense; short on face, skull and legs
COLOR: Black/tan, tricolor, sable and white, black and white
REGISTRY: UKC
GROUP: Herding

Current owners believe the modern English Shepherd is still very similar to the Roman sheep and cattle dog which accompanied Caesar and his army to the British Isles in 55 BC. The forebears of this breed trotted off an English gangway to American soil, brought by early settlers to the shores of the United States. The English Shepherd was much admired and evolved to its modern type. American farmers found them agile, good workers and an answer to a farmer's prayers. They crossbred the varieties of old Scotch Collie, Border Collie and other

English Shepherd, tricolor.

English Shepherd, pup.

working types to produce today's dog. At first known as the "good ol' farm collie" or farm shepherd, the current name differentiates the breed from other collies. He is not exhibited, or even promoted, but is a simple working dog whose reputation has spread by word of mouth.

Like their cohort, the Australian Shepherd, they are active and good watchdogs. Weather-resistant and hardy, they may greet their owners in the morning from beneath a mound of snow, shaking off the flakes, ready to help with the chores.

They are natural drivers and heelers, good with cattle, sheep, hogs or even poultry. Bred to drive by nipping at heels, they are versatile, but should be started on the poultry or sheep, so they do not become too tough from learning on cattle or hogs. They differentiate between the young stock and adults and act accordingly. English Shepherds are "loose-eyed," in herding, as opposed to the "strong-eyed" Border Collie. The breed works well independently or under direction of a master.

The English Shepherd is a calm and steady all-purpose dog with keen senses. According to owner Diana L. Karr, they are particularly attuned to their family and some swear "by the time he is five or six, you can carry on a decent conversation with him." Owners find them able and eager hunters. They are good with children, pulling carts, helping them learn to walk and acting as referees in their squabbles. Although their tails are usually long, an occasional bobtail is whelped.

English Springer Spaniel, liver/white.

ENGLISH SPRINGER SPANIEL

COUNTRY: Great Britain
WEIGHT: 49–55 pounds
HEIGHT: 19–20 inches
COAT: Close and straight, with good feathering
COLOR: Black/white, liver/white, black tri, liver tri
REGISTRY: FCI, AKC, UKC, TKC, CKC
GROUP: Gun Dog

British flushing spaniels were often called "springing" spaniels, since they were used to spring the game from the cover. In the variety of spaniel sizes, sometimes in the same litter, the smallest were the Cockers, the medium-sized were the Fields and the larger ones became the Springers. Bede Maxwell illustrates the perfectly legal flexibility in those early days: the red/white dog, Corrin of Gerwin, was first registered as a Welsh Cocker, then re-registered as a Welsh Springer and his son became a registered English Springer! The first champion English Springer sired a daughter who was registered as a Field Spaniel.

Cockers and Springers from the same litter were classified by size. The confusion as to "when is a Cocker not a Cocker . . . when it's a Springer" finally led to complete separation of the breeds and a ban on interbreeding. The English gave the Springer official breed status in 1902, and under the direction of the English Springer Spaniel Field Trial Association, the breed became established in the USA.

Known under the pseudonym of Norfolk Spaniel for a time, English Springer Spaniel became the official name by 1900. Sir Thomas Boughey is credited with establishing the modern credentials; his family's stud books on the breed dated from 1812. The Springer is still a fine gunning dog, ideally suited for flushing birds, such as pheasants. The flashy dog show winner and the competitor at the AKC spaniel trials are at extremes of type for the breed. Many Springers show their skill in competition obedience.

The English Springer is not an exaggerated dog and is the leggiest of the flushing spaniels. His pleasant personality and good looks make him a fine house dog as well. The Springer tends to live a long life, staying active into his golden years.

Black/white English Springer Spaniel demonstrating the breed's excellence in obedience trial work.

English Springer Spaniel, liver tri.

English Springer Spaniel.

English Springer Spaniels, adult and pup.

ENGLISH TOY SPANIEL

COUNTRY: Great Britain
WEIGHT: 9–12 pounds
HEIGHT: 10–10½ inches
COAT: Long, wavy, silky and profuse
COLOR: Tricolor (Prince Charles), solid red (Ruby), red/white (Blenheim), or black/tan (King Charles)
OTHER NAMES: King Charles Spaniel
REGISTRY: FCI, AKC, TKC, CKC
GROUP: Gun Dog

Ever since there were spaniels, toy versions have curled in laps and warmed hearts. In England and on the Continent, the charming spaniel personality in a tiny package was valued as a pet. These dogs were selected for smaller and smaller size among the existing couching and setting dogs that established the type for the spaniels. Crosses to other tiny dogs may have occurred as well, but these were basically little gun dogs. Indulged and pampered by the wealthy, they were known as "comforters." Of course, they were mostly admired just for their companionship, but they were also useful as foot warmers in cold and drafty English castles!

Those in England took on the general appearance of a small Cocker Spaniel, and were illustrated frequently in literature and paintings. A medieval scoffer described the "Spaniell gentle . . . These dogs—pretty, proper and fine to satisfie the delicatenes of dainty dames and wanton women's wills . . ." A favorite legend tells that when Mary Queen of Scots was sent to her death in the 16th century, her executioner found one of her devoted little spaniels hidden in the folds of her skirt. To a happier end, in the late 1600s, they were favorites of King Charles II. He had many of them and they enjoyed full run of the palaces. Samuel Pepys, writing at the time, was critical of the king's devotion to them, noting that: "All I observed there was the silliness of the King playing with his dog all the while and not minding his business." Soon the little dogs were universally known as King Charles Spaniels, often referred to as Charlies.

Others who doted on the breed were noted: an advertisement appeared in the *Daily Courant* in 1720, promising a reward for the return of a King Charles Spaniel bitch. With a twisted sense of prideful ownership, one Duke of Norfolk would not sell or give his Toy Spaniels

English Toy Spaniel, Prince Charles.

English Toy Spaniel, King Charles.

away, but instead fed unwanted pups to his eagles!

Over the next century or so, the "King Charles Spaniel" began to change. Crosses to toy dogs from the Orient were likely. Soon the "comforters" became even smaller, with the extreme brachycephalic face, domed head, prominent eyes, and muzzle shortened so the nose was nearly flush to the face. They still had the charming spaniel personalities within a new contour. It is this short-faced version that has arrived at the present time as the English Toy Spaniel.

During the reign of King Charles, most of the specimens were black/tan and, thus, this color has taken on the king's name. The Blenheim color was named after the family estate of the Dukes of Marlborough, whose family owned many of the red/whites over the years. All colors are otherwise judged by the same standard of perfection. When The Kennel Club tried to classify all four colors under the title "Toy Spaniel," Edward VII, also a fancier, did not approve. Therefore, the breed is still also called the King Charles Spaniel—in deference to a king.

The breed is quiet and happy, content to be with its owners, and forgiving in nature. They are physically fastidious. Protruding eyes and hanging ears must be kept scrupulously clean, but otherwise care is minimal. Tails are docked like the other spaniels, and carried level with the back. Ears and their accompanying feathering are so long as to nearly brush the ground.

Above: English Toy Spaniel, Prince Charles. **Below:** English Toy Spaniel, Blenheim.

ENTELBUCHER

COUNTRY: Switzerland
WEIGHT: 55–66 pounds
HEIGHT: Under 20 inches
COAT: Short, smooth and dense
COLOR: Black and tan, with white at toes, tail tip, chest, and blaze. The tan always lies between the black and the white
OTHER NAMES: Entelbuch Mountain Dog, Entelbucher Sennenhund
REGISTRY: FCI
GROUP: Mastiff

The smallest of the four Swiss Mountain dogs, the Entelbucher is smooth-coated and bobtailed. *Sennenhund* means dog of the Alpine herdsman. This breed was used by these herdsmen to drive cattle to market.

One owner states the breed is quiet and easy-going. "Barrie does not bark just to hear his echo." He loves height and climbs on top the woodpile, doghouse and grooming table, "perhaps looking for the Alps." This owner sings praises of her dog, uttering only one complaint. Barrie likes to jump up and hit them with his body, even in play, which probably goes back to the dogs' hurling themselves at the cattle.

The breed is conscious of boundaries and is

Entelbucher.

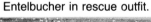

Entelbucher in rescue outfit.

territorial, protective but not aggressive. The dogs make good obedience workers since they love having a job to do. Entelbuchers are independent and self-confident, yet tuned in to their owners, as a Swiss owner demonstrates through the following statement: While her husband was in the hospital, her well-mannered four-year-old Entelbucher suddenly began crying, continuing for a half hour. Shortly thereafter, the family was notified of the master's death. The dog deteriorated and died four weeks later, seemingly of a broken heart.

Although the breed is exceptionally clean and requires little grooming, they enjoy it and demand their turn when others are groomed. All of the sennenhunds delight in the company of people and are friendly with other dogs. Entelbuchers are easy keepers and, in fact, tend to get a mite pudgy if given the opportunity.

Entelbucher.

ÉPAGNEUL FRANCAIS

COUNTRY: France
WEIGHT: 44–55 pounds
HEIGHT: 21–24 inches
COAT: Flat and straight, with feathering on legs, ears, belly and tail
COLOR: Clear white with liver markings
OTHER NAMES: French Spaniel
REGISTRY: FCI
GROUP: Gun Dog

The French Spaniel is a cousin to the Small Münsterländer and the Drentse Patrijshond setter type. The breed is quite old and, while boasting a long history in France, is unknown elsewhere. Fine pointing and retrieving dogs, they show a passion for their work.

They have a strong head that, in recent years, has shown some exaggerated flew and dewlap. As little ticking as possible is desired, with any tan marks disqualifying. The tail is left long, as with the setters. Personalities are—like so many of these breeds—docile, intelligent and trainable.

Épagneul Francais.

Épagneul Francais.

Épagneul Pont-Audemer, solid liver.

ÉPAGNEUL PONT-AUDEMER

COUNTRY: France
WEIGHT: 40–53 pounds
HEIGHT: 20–23 inches
COAT: Long all over and quite wavy, topknot on head, smooth face
COLOR: Solid liver, liver and white with or without ticking in the white
OTHER NAMES: Pont-Audemer Spaniel
REGISTRY: FCI
GROUP: Gun Dog

"He goes where the hunter can't go"—this old saying probably best describes the Pont-Audemer Spaniel, a specialist for water work. His origins most likely go back to the Poodle/Barbet, since they have both been in France for a long time. There may have been crosses to some of the French land spaniels, as well as to British and Irish spaniels, during his formation. He is a water dog of excellence and works the marshes for ducks; the breed has a dual purpose, as it is a fine pointing dog and can be used for other game.

Although a skilled hunter, he has not gained much prominence outside his native districts of Normandy and Picardy in northwestern France. With the invasion of English dogs on French shores and the apathy of French hunters, this breed is in danger of disappearing, perhaps due to its specialization. European hunters prefer a general-purpose dog. Due to the small numbers available for breeding following the War, it became necessary to cross to Irish Water Spaniels in the 1950s. Fewer than 100 registrations per year were recorded in the 1980s, with the numbers decreasing each year, and the breed is plagued with the problems that surface with the unavoidable inbreeding. Fortunately, the Society Havraise is dedicated to the renovation of the breed. The Pont-Audemer has joined forces with the Picardy and the Blue Picardy in a club for all three breeds.

His body is covered with gently curling locks which help him resist the cold, and his narrow, smooth face is topped with a jaunty toupee of curls. Ears are set rather high, and are long and hairy. The tail is docked to a third its original length. Midway between the smaller Brittany and the larger French Spaniel, the Audemer Spaniel is thick-set and robust.

Épagneul Pont-Audemer, liver and white with ticking.

ÉPAGNEULS PICARDIES

Épagneul Picard

COUNTRY: France
WEIGHT: 44 pounds
HEIGHT: 22–24 inches
COAT: Flat and straight with feathering on ears, legs, tail and belly
COLOR: Liver/tan/white tricolor, with heavy ticking
OTHER NAMES: Picardy Spaniel
REGISTRY: FCI
GROUP: Gun Dog

Épagneul Bleu de Picardie

COUNTRY: France
WEIGHT: 44 pounds
HEIGHT: 22–24 inches
COAT: Flat and straight with feathering on ears, legs, tail and belly
COLOR: Black/white, with heavy ticking; tan marks undesirable
OTHER NAMES: Blue Picardy Spaniel
REGISTRY: FCI
GROUP: Gun Dog

The time-honored spaniels of Picardy are closely related to the French Spaniel and others of his genre. At one time the Picard was under the threat of disappearing, but has recently gained a renewed interest among the hunters of France. He is a dog of natural abilities that can find and retrieve game under the most demanding and difficult conditions. If he has a specialty, it is probably marsh work for ducks, but owners say he is equally good for fur and feather in field or woods.

A dog of courage, the Picardy has an even temperament and is always in good spirits, making him a docile, amiable companion. French owners say he "loves to live in the house." He is devoted to his master and looks to his owner for direction. In appearance, he is a square-bodied setter, with the typically long tail and medium head without exaggeration. His colors, with the heavy ticking, are distinctive. With his chocolate/tan/white coat, the ticking throughout gives the Picard a two-tone brown roan jacket.

The soft-natured Blue was created by crossing Picards with British setters, probably blue belton English Setters in the late 1800s. Tan points called "fire marks" are not allowed; his black ticking creates the "blue" pattern. Modern owners say when the Blue accompanies a hunter, "he goes to work." His specialty is hunting the snipe in marshes. Considered a separate breed, the Blue Picardy is judged by nearly the same standard except for color.

Épagneul Bleu de Picardie.

384

Above Left: Épagneul Picard. **Above Right:** Épagneul Bleu de Picardie. **Below:** Épagneul Picard.

ESKIMO DOG

COUNTRY: Canada
WEIGHT: 60–105 pounds
HEIGHT: 20–27 inches
COAT: 3–6 inches, longer than some of the other sled dogs, thick with lots of undercoat
COLOR: Any color or combination of colors
OTHER NAMES: Husky, Esquimaux, Canadian Eskimo Dog
REGISTRY: FCI, TKC, CKC
GROUP: Northern

The Eskimo Dog has served as the only means of transportation for his people since 1000 BC. This far northern hauling dog—bred to haul sleds in winter, backpack in summer and hunt seals, oxen and bears all year—is closely related to the Greenland Dog. In fact, the Eskimo Dog Club of England considers them the same breed and registers canines imported from Scandinavia (where they are registered as Grønlandshund) as Eskimo Dogs. The FCI still recognizes two breeds, but they are very similar dogs, and there has been much crossing in the last 200 years. The Canadian version is native to the vast areas north of Hudson Bay and east of Alaska and the Mackenzie River—the Northwest Territories, stretching into the Arctic Circle, including Victoria Island, Baffin Island and even Greenland. Because the breed was fostered and saved by the interest of the Canadian KC, the FCI has dubbed it a Canadian breed.

The Eskimo Dog is a hardy, working breed, and has been known to withstand temperatures of -75 to -94 degrees Fahrenheit. The famed Arctic explorer MacMillan once drove a team of Eskimos 100 miles in a continuous run, taking less than 18 hours. The commander of the second Grinnell Expedition, Dr. Elisha Kent Kane, used a six-dog team, which hauled a fully-loaded sledge about 750 miles in two weeks. The packed sled weighed about 700 pounds, more than the usual average load of 100 pounds per dog.

Eskimo Dog, gray.

Eskimo Dog, black/white.

Because of their long history of survival in the harshest of environments, they have an extremely independent nature and go at everything "gung ho!"—fighting, eating, playing and working. They require firm, consistent handling from an owner who will earn their respect as the "lead dog." Owners report that the dogs have very strong pack instincts and that fights and challenges among their peers are common. By the same token, they need sufficient exercise and the company of other dogs. Most are kept outdoors because of their abundant energy, as well as to acclimate the working dogs during the cold months. They must be fenced constantly or walked on lead, since their wild instincts to run and chase are all but impossible to eradicate. In fact, there is some tendency to regard all other animals as food, and they are also inveterate food thieves, characteristics which assured survival in the bitter environs of their homeland.

Despite their strong working background, they are good tempered, affectionate and dignified with people. The mature dog has a certain aloofness similar to a cat and does not relish unsolicited attention. The breed doesn't bark but has a wide range of vocalizations that, owners say, can be quite explicit. The Canadian standard states: "The natural voice is a howl, not a bark. When in a group, the dogs often give voice in a chorus of strangely woven tones, and this is one of the thrilling sounds of the Arctic. A number of dogs will produce a mass crescendo persisting for varying periods until, as if cued by a special note, all will abruptly stop."

The Eskimo Dog is a primitive and natural working dog, representing an era long past. He is a dog only for those who understand his nature and who have the time and facilities to channel his energy. According to Sverdup,"they have the persistence and tenacity of the wild animal, the domestic dog's admirable devotion to their master; they are the wildest breath of nature, the warmest breath of civilisation."

Eskimo Dog, red.

ESTONIAN HOUND

COUNTRY: USSR
HEIGHT: 18–21 inches
COAT: Short, dense
COLOR: Black/tan usually; also tan saddled
OTHER NAMES: Gontchaja Estonskaja
GROUP: Hound

The Estonian Republic of the Soviet Union is in European Russia, straight north of Moscow on the Baltic Sea. In the early part of the 20th century, big fast hounds had begun decimating the population of wild goats that were abundant in the area where hare and fox were hunted. Hunters began working to develop a smaller, lower stationed hound that could stalk the small game but were outleagued by the pace of the wild goats.

First they crossed the smallest of the local hounds with English Beagles to reduce size and obtain strong feet, so necessary where snow falls heavily in February. Next into the mixing pot was the Swiss Neiderlaufhund, contributing his musical voice, persistence on the trail and, especially, his very early maturation (as young as five to six months!). A dash of Foxhound was added for endurance.

By 1954, the breed was introduced to the second Soviet Cynological Congress, where he was approved and a standard adopted. He was enthusiastically received by many hunters in other areas of Russia as well. So well had the Estonian breeders done their work that at the 1957 Moscow Exhibition, the Estonian Hound received a special award, and the founders were awarded gold medals.

The Estonian is a strong, rather low-stationed hound that is often ready to hunt effectively before his first birthday. Because of his smaller size and suspicion of strangers, he is often kept in a house or apartment, where he seconds as a watchdog.

Estonian Hound.

Estonian Hound.

ESTRELA MOUNTAIN DOG

COUNTRY: Portugal
WEIGHT: 66–110 pounds
HEIGHT: 24½–28½ inches
COAT: Medium-short or long; coarse and abundant, with dense feathering on tail; in long coats, dense feathering on chest and backs of legs and thighs
COLOR: Brindle, wolf gray and all shades of fawn; usually with black shadings and mask
OTHER NAMES: Portuguese Sheepdog, Cão da Serra da Estrela
REGISTRY: FCI, TKC
GROUP Flock Guard

The Estrela range in the central part of Portugal was the home of this ancient breed. One of the flock guards that spread from Asia to Iberia, the Estrela represents one of the Portuguese branches of the family. Flocks annually moved from the high Estrela plains where they grazed in summer to lower elevations where they stayed from October to March. These Portuguese *Transumancias*, like those in Spain, followed the same routes for centuries, and the migrations were always accompanied by large flock-guarding dogs. As they traveled in search of fresh pastures, the aristocracy confiscated a few of the dogs, finding them excellent guards for their large country estates.

The dogs that cast their lot with the wealthy naturally received better food and care—and more of it. Less agility was needed than that demanded in traipsing over mountains. The estate dogs grew larger, with bigger bone. Eventually, the herds diminished and the flock guards with them, so that the larger dog became more common. With the revival of interest in Portuguese native breeds in the 1930s, the Estrela found many friends, first at home, and later abroad.

The Estrela needs large doses of loving contact and should not be chained or isolated. Yet, they are not demanding of attention and accept what is given them with contentment. As these dogs watched over their flocks, they slept in whatever shelter they could find, often in the open, and they lived on shepherd's leftovers. Little wonder they are easily satisfied now.

As guard dogs, their bark is loud and threatening, and they are sometimes aggressive with

Estrela Mountain Dog, wolf gray.

other dogs of the same sex. Affectionate with their masters and good with children, Estrelas are suspicious of strangers. They can be obstinate and need to be handled with a firm hand, convinced that your way is better than theirs.

Outdoor activity is a necessity. Barking and a passion for wandering, even to jumping fences, can be annoying, both to owners and neighbors. For pet owners, some of this energy can be channeled into obedience work or other chores. Early socialization is recommended.

Planned breedings face "lousy" odds. As breeder/author Roger F. Pye said, "If you start trying when she is just . . . two, you may get her mated by the time she is three and a half."

A breed club fosters their preservation in Portugal, where they still guard flocks and estates. The first Portuguese show recording Estrela entries was Lisbon's in 1908 and a standard was published in 1933. Each year in the Serra da Estrela region, proud owners still gather to compare dogs and talk about their chosen breed at the *concursos* (rather like informal specialty shows). A good number of these dogs have been brought into England where they are exhibited at the larger shows.

Above: Estrela Mountain Dog, fawn. **Below:** Estrela Mountain Dog, reddish fawn.

EURASIAN

COUNTRY: Germany
WEIGHT: 40–70 pounds
HEIGHT: 19½–24 inches
COAT: Long, straight, abundant spitz type
COLOR: Red, fawn, wolfgray, black, or black with limited marks; white and pinto are not yet allowed for breeding
OTHER NAMES: Eurasier
REGISTRY: FCI
GROUP: Northern

The Eurasian is a modern breed developed in the 1960s. Julius Wipfel of Weinheim, Germany, wished to develop a large and distinctive spitz type of dog with all the beautiful colors plus a mellower character for modern times. He crossed Chow Chow males with large German Wolfspitz bitches. From the resulting puppies, he eliminated the Chowlike and more wild wolf-like types, keeping the intermediate, imposing spitz-type whelps. He called the new breed the "Wolf-chow." Later he crossed the Wolf-chow bitches with one Samoyed male, and that was the end of the crossbreeding. Good selection since that time has come to establish the breed, known since 1973 as the Eurasian, combining the best of the European and Asian spitz dogs to create a new one.

The Eurasian tends to bond very strongly with his owner and/or family. These dogs need to be with their people, and pine if chained or secluded away from family life or left in a boarding kennel. European owners advise that training should be done by the owner, not a hired trainer, as they respect only their own master. Even changing homes as an adult may be traumatic, if the binding ties are too strong.

Because of the bonding or pack instinct, the Eurasian is very reserved and even distrustful of strangers, making a natural watchdog. When he barks he has a reason to do so. Although friendly and quiet with his family and other dogs in his pack, he can become quite fierce if

Eurasian, wolfgray.

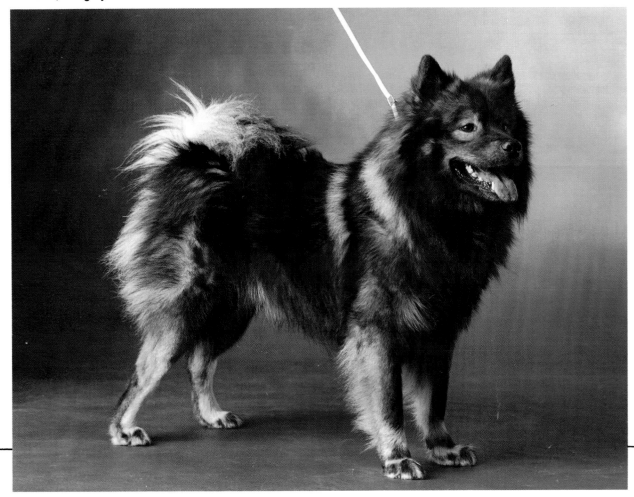

necessary. He will not hesitate to attack some-one threatening his people with harm, and is also quite capable of handling himself in a fight, even with larger dogs. Owners warn he must make up to new friends at his own pace, and thus strangers should not pet or handle him until he indicates he has accepted them.

Nevertheless, he is a sensitive dog that wants to please. He is an excellent lady's dog as he responds well to a light hand. Once he has his "pack," he is not a dog that requires constant reminders of who is the alpha animal. Any discord or arguing among his family members makes him truly uneasy, and he may run from one to another, whining and indicating that everyone should calm down and stop their bickering! Upon his family members' returning from even a short time away, the Eurasian will greet them with enthusiasm, dancing on his hind feet in great joy.

The Eurasian is a handsome and imposing spitz dog, gaining in favor all over Europe. They are recognized and shown throughout the Continent, and there are a few specimens in the United States.

Above and Below: Eurasian, red.

FAUVES DE BRETAGNE

Griffon Fauve de Bretagne

COUNTRY: France
WEIGHT: 44 pounds
HEIGHT: 20–22 inches
COAT: Rough, hard hair of medium to short length
COLOR: Solid, in various shades of wheaten to red; small white spot on chest allowed; black hairs highly objectionable
OTHER NAMES: Tawny Brittany Griffon
REGISTRY: FCI
GROUP: Hound

Basset Fauve de Bretagne

COUNTRY: France
WEIGHT: 20–35 pounds
HEIGHT: 13–15 inches
COAT: Rough, hard hair of medium to short length
COLOR: Solid, in various shades of wheaten to red; small white spot on chest allowed; black hairs highly objectionable
OTHER NAMES: Tawny Brittany Basset
REGISTRY: FCI, TKC
GROUP: Hound

The soil in Brittany is poor, and much of the agriculture is devoted to grazing, especially sheep. Brittany is a peninsula in the northwestern corner of France, reaching out into the Atlantic toward Britain. In times past, wolves posed a constant threat to the flocks. Dogs that could track down this predator were an economic necessity. An extra bonus was the diversion from the everyday farm routine provided by the wolf hunts.

The fawn-colored Griffons of Brittany were well chronicled as far back as the Middle Ages. Whether or not these dogs predate the Griffons of Vendee, which is the neighboring province to the south, is debatable. They go back to the same era, and facts of whether one contributed to the other or they came from some of the same stem breeds have been lost in the mists of time.

By 1885, the wolves were gone from Brittany and this breed fell into oblivion or was crossed carelessly with other hounds. Breeders of the present century have worked hard to save the tawny hound. This griffon was easily adapted to other game such as fox and wild boar and, although rarely seen outside of its native area, is still used by modern hunters. Because the breed was becoming bastardized, fanciers have applied a strict standard to eliminate animals that are not of correct type. They are about the same size

Basset Fauve de Bretagne.

as the Briquet Vendeen and are always of the solid fawn, tawny or wheaten color.

The Basset version was probably created from crosses of the large Griffon with bassets from Vendee or elsewhere. The smaller version is quite swift for his size and has a lively and enterprising personality. Brittany Bassets are generally hunted in packs of four, going after smaller prey such as rabbit, hare and wild boar. Along with many other bassets, this variety has achieved some standing in modern society as a companion. He makes a fine pet as long as his need for exercise and his passion for hunting are fulfilled. BFB s are bred and shown in England as well as in their homeland.

Right and Below: Griffon Fauve de Bretagne.

Field Spaniel.

FIELD SPANIEL

COUNTRY: Great Britain
WEIGHT: 35–50 pounds
HEIGHT: 18 inches
COAT: Fair length and density, flat or slightly wavy, silky in texture; with moderately abundant thick feathering on legs, ears, and belly
COLOR: Black, liver, golden liver or mahogany red, or any of these with tan markings; white markings are to be discouraged, and any present should contain roaning and not be clear white
REGISTRY: FCI, AKC, UKC, TKC, CKC
GROUP: Gun Dog

Spaniels were developed in the early 1800s from couching dogs and possibly hounds. Sussex types were the oldest. As the development of the spaniel continued, the Field Spaniel type emerged, with even less of the hound influence. They were first noted in the early 19th century and, in fact, early litters contained both Fields (the larger whelps used for grouse and quail) and Cockers (smaller dogs used for hunting woodcock). Sometime during the mid-1800s, show interests began to exaggerate and change the Field variety. Led by fancier Phineas Bullock, the whims of fashion nearly ruined the breed. The dog became a caricature, with cumbersome head, very short crooked legs, and elongated weak "hammock-slung" body. According to the *International Encyclopedia of Dogs*, descriptions of the breed at the time noted: ". . . sluggish and crocodile-like," "German sausage," "Caterpillars," with one wag suggesting they needed an extra pair of legs in the middle to keep their sagging bellies off the ground. One dog of the time purportedly was 12 inches at the shoulder and weighed 40 pounds!

As the Field Spaniel craze waned, dedicated owners brought the Field back to a sensible state by the turn of the century. English Springers and perhaps a dash of Cocker Spaniel had a hand in the refinement of the modern breed. The bad taste was not rinsed out of the public's mouth, however, and the Field slipped to the point of extinction. Even though the breed survived the two Wars, by the 1950s its numbers were so small in England that championship status was withdrawn. The breed was literally reduced to a handful of breeders. At a 1967 show in Birmingham, England, every Field in the country (with the exception of a few retirees) was on the bench that day. But numbers slowly increased, and the awarding of challenge certificates was restored in 1969.

Over the years, a few were brought to America. Those arriving in the late 1800s were still classed as Fields or Cockers, depending on weight. Thus, their history in America is tied closely to that of the Cocker Spaniel. After many years without any registrations, a few began to trickle in during the revival in the 1960s. Today, occasional specimens are seen on the show bench, both natives and imports. A handful of litters are registered by AKC each year, so the breed has a pawhold on both sides of the Atlantic.

A Field is the epitome of the basic spaniel, without any exaggeration. Moderate coat and feather, normal stop and flew, slightly more length than height; he stands out for his lack of overdone characteristics. A happy and levelheaded fellow, he has both perseverance and endurance in the field.

Field Spaniel.

Fila Brasileiro, brindle.

FILA BRASILEIRO

COUNTRY: Brazil
WEIGHT: Minimum 90 pounds female, 100 pounds male
HEIGHT: 24–29½ inches
COAT: Short, smooth
COLOR: Brindles and all solid colors, except white or mouse gray
OTHER NAMES: Brasilian Mastiff, Brasilian Molosser
REGISTRY: FCI
GROUP: Mastiff

The Fila Brasileiro's ancestors were brought into Brazil by the Portuguese conquistadores. The breed was created in the 19th century through existing mastiff and bullenbeisser stock, crossbred with Bloodhound. The introduction of scenthound into this molosoid blend gave the Fila its longer muzzle (equal in length to back skull), shallow stop and long, folded ear.

Brazilian ranchers of the 19th century were isolated, needing tough dogs for protection, to hunt jaguars and to track runaway slaves. The

Fila Brasileiro.

Filas were also intended to give assistance with the semi-wild cattle. When attempting to turn or stop a cow, they might bite and grasp the cheek or nose, but they generally grabbed the ear, just like their Alaunt ancestors. Although the breed has been utilized on ranches since its beginning, formal breeding—according to a standard—was augmented in the 1950s.

An abundance of loose skin hangs on the head and neck, denoting the hound ancestry. Although massive, they should be 40–50 pounds less than an English Mastiff of comparable height. The Fila's hind legs are lighter in bone, longer and less angulated than his front legs, giving him a downhill appearance. The dog sways in a "camel pace," causing a correct rocking and rolling motion to the gait. The pace is unique to the breed, unlike all others which are expected to trot. They are good jumpers, very agile and fast.

The Brazilian standard warns judges not to touch Filas if they wish to keep all their fingers,

since aggression is often encouraged. Dogs raised with firm corrections and socialization are shown without incident, however. These dogs are used successfully in schutzhund work in Germany, where they demonstrate their intelligence and ability to be controlled. Passing a shooting test, in which a blank pistol is fired five meters from the dog, is a requirement for all Brazilian champions. They must also pass a temperament test, where dogs (over 12 months) are approached aggressively with a stick. In both cases, the dog should express attention, showing self-confidence and assurance. The judge watches for the dislike the animal shows toward strangers and the self-assurance, courage, determination and bravery of each individual.

The Fila is the most popular breed in its native country. It has not been in the USA long, but has steadily gained ground. *Filar* in Portuguese means to hold or secure. "Faithful as a Fila dog" is an old Brazilian proverb; the Fila's temperament makes it totally loyal to owner and family and naturally distrustful of strangers. A breeder says, "This breed needs a home that understands and needs a dog that will not be friendly with strangers, even those allowed into the home. They should not attack viciously for no reason, but members outside the family should not expect to pet, play or be friendly with an adult." It is totally fearless in the face of danger. The Fila standard states the dog should have a calm, noble, self-assured expression when in repose and a determined, alert, firm one when at attention.

Filas do well in any climate, and their short coat is easily kept up. These dogs adore all members of their human families, including children, and love being close to them, even sitting on their feet. Caution must be taken with visitors, and early socialization is recommended for the pet or show dog. A breeder states the Fila is for "owners with responsible attitudes, not a macho personality."

Above: Fila Brasileiro, pup. **Below:** Fila Brasileiro, fawn.

FINNISH HOUND

COUNTRY: Finland
WEIGHT: 55 pounds
HEIGHT: 22–24½ inches
COAT: Short, but dense and coarse to the touch
COLOR: Tan with black saddle; small white markings on head, chest, feet and tail tip
OTHER NAMES: Suomenajokoira
REGISTRY: FCI
GROUP: Hound

Known since the 18th century, the Finnish Hound was developed by using a variety of English, German, Swiss and native Scandinavian hounds. Although the breed is popular and widespread in Finland, he is uncommon elsewhere. After hunting hare and fox with his master in the summer, he spends the long winters warm and cozy indoors with the family. He is rarely exhibited.

He is a rangy yet strongly boned hound much like a large foxhound. Probably a gift from his German ancestors, his singular ears are large with stiff cartilage, making them stand out somewhat from the head. He is friendly and calm in temperament, yet energetic in the hunt.

Above and Below: Finnish Hound.

Finnish Spitz, red.

FINNISH SPITZ

COUNTRY: Finland
WEIGHT: 25–30 pounds
HEIGHT: 15½–20 inches
COAT: Dense, moderately short, stand-off coat
COLOR: Chestnut red to pale red-gold, lighter shades on the undersides are allowed; puppies born brown
OTHER NAMES: Suomenpystykorva, Finsk Spets, Loulou Finnois
REGISTRY: FCI, AKC, TKC, UKC
GROUP: Northern

The Finnish Spitz is an old, northern breed native to Finland, and has had a written standard since 1812! This handsome red-gold-coated Norseman is the national dog of Finland and is mentioned in several national heroic songs. Improvement of the breed was expedited in the 1890s when forester Hugo Richard Sandberg successfully campaigned to have the barking dog recognized by the Finnish Kennel Club. Writing in *Sporten* that year, he characterized the Finnish Spitz:

"When living in close contact with a family, sharing its bright as well as cloudy days, the Finnish dog has features that resemble its owner, the Finn. The dog shows devotion and self-sacrificing faithfulness towards its master. It has also much more courage than one would expect of such a little dog. Under normal conditions it is a modest animal, but if fettered or shut into a kennel it easily becomes depressed and its fitness for use goes down. It seems to be like a pine: satisfied in poor soil with only a little food, but like a pine it demands air and freedom."

About the same time, Sandberg's cohort, Hugo Roos (another forester and hunter), was dedicated to finding and breeding typical specimens to maintain this handsome hunting dog. Titled English fanciers added support in the 1930s, particularly Lady Kitty Ritson.

In days of old, the Finnish Spitz was used by the Lapps for tracking bear and elk, but is now mainly used for bird hunting, especially capercaillie (similar to wild turkey) and black grouse, the game birds of Finland. His nickname, the

Finnish Spitz.

When a dog has three conformation certificates and either one first or two second prizes from a bird-hunting trial, he becomes a show champion. With a win in the open class at a bird-hunting trial and at least a second prize in a show, he becomes a trial champion. When he has won both titles, he is given the esteemed title of dual champion.

Hunting is considered so important in Finland that the status of the game bird population affects the breeding and registration of these dogs. The late 1970s were bad years for birds, and registrations of Finnish Spitz fell to their lowest level in many years. But when the bird population began recovering, interest in the red dog resumed. In 1980, registration of 1,087 Finnish Spitz was accomplished in Finland, and 116 hunting trials were held in which 579 dogs took part.

Finnish Spitz, pup.

barking bird dog, comes from his unique method of hunting. His lively manner of searching and acute scenting ability lead him to birds. Then by yodeling (barking continuously), he "enchants the bird to sit in the tree and watch the dog."

The dog is said to show "keen disappointment if the hunter misses. When the bird is shot the feet must be given to the dog as a prize, or legend has it, he will refuse to work for such an inconsiderate master."

Bird-hunting trials for the breed are common in Finland, and no Finnish Spitz can become a breed champion without winning a trial prize as well. The trials are set up with the judges following a dog and hunter into the forest. The dog is credited for finding and following birds, holding the bird in the tree, and the number of barks per minute (the more the better). It is claimed he must bark 160 times per minute. He is faulted for disobedience, "false barks" at a tree where there is no bird, ceasing to bark and/or leaving the bird, barking at squirrels or chasing elk or hare.

Finnish Spitz and owner on mountainside in Finland.

The best trial winners can compete in district championships, in the National Haukku contest, and the international contest between Finland and Sweden. Winner of the Haukku Trial is awarded the title "King of Barking" and victor of the international contest wins the crown of "Champion of The North." Breeders support these trials because of their strong desire to maintain working qualities. Because both hunting and the Finnish Spitz are essential parts of the history and culture of the Finnish wilderness, preservation and care of the breed are matters of honor for Finnish kennel clubs and Finnish hunters.

Watchful and alert, the Finnish Spitz makes a fine alarm dog, and is often kept in the home. He is built square and up on leg, with the lightness of build necessary for precise hunting. The tail comes up over the back and down the leg; it must end pressed against the thigh. The small, high-set, mobile ears are a trademark, the translation for his Finnish name, *Suomenpystykorva*, being Finnish cock-eared dog. In England, he is known affectionately as the "Finkie."

Since vocalization is part of their genetic make-up and barking is emphasized in trials, owners must not expect a silent companion. The dogs' beauty, size and happy temperament, as well as their cleanliness, sturdiness and easy care are pluses for family dogs.

The Finnish Spitz was added to AKC's Non-Sporting Group in 1988. He is also registered in Canada (since the '70s), England ('30s), Chile, Australia and several countries in continental Europe.

FLAT-COATED RETRIEVER

COUNTRY: Great Britain
WEIGHT: 60–70 pounds
HEIGHT: 22–23 inches
COAT: Dense, fine textured, as flat as possible, and of medium length, with feathering
COLOR: Solid black or liver
REGISTRY: FCI, AKC, UKC, TKC, CKC
GROUP: Gun Dog

Flat-Coated Retriever, black.

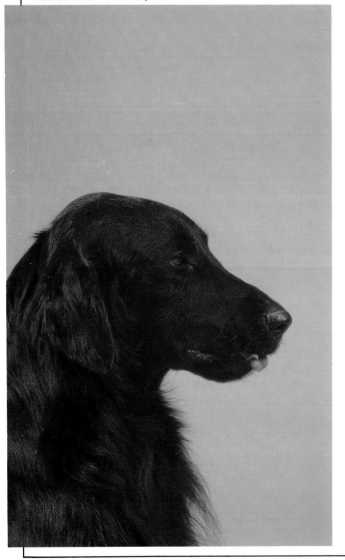

The Flat-Coat is one of the earliest "specialist" land retrievers created in Britain. In the latter half of the 19th century, the breed "appeared" and attracted immediate interest, and attained the reputation as the "game-keeper's dog" for its widespread use on British estates. Two of these dogs, "Old Bounce" and "Young Bounce," owned by game-keeper J. Hull, are credited with being the grande-dames of the modern breed. Very little else is known of his background, but he most likely stems from crossbreeding of trans-Atlantic imports with British setters. The imports were, undoubtedly, of the smaller Newfoundland-dog type, which was also the progenitor of the Labrador and Chesapeake Bay Retriever.

S.E. Shirley, MP, helped stabilize type in the 1880s. The Flat-Coat was a highly esteemed hunting and show dog until WWI. H.R. Cooke, a follower of Shirley, was a great patron of the breed. His Riverside Kennels dominated the breed for 60 years. This may have been the breed's downfall, as many less successful fanciers turned their attention to Labs and Goldens.

Perhaps to his benefit, however, this retriever has never been subject to the great popularity of some of his closely related kin, thus has not suffered the problems associated with "fad" breeds. Registrations are few in both England and the USA, and most dogs are associated with owners who utilize their abilities. The Flat-Coat is a fine land and water retriever with natural talent in marking, retrieving and delivering. He also doubles as a good flushing, upland game hunter. The Flat-Coat is a close-working, calm, biddable dog. Obedience enthusiasts are just beginning to discover his superior qualities of animation, trainability, and willingness to please that make him a top competitor.

The coat is without exaggeration, neither profuse nor over-long, and easy to care for. It has a tendency to wave—in fact, the original name was the "Wavy-Coated Retriever"—and the standard allows for the appearance of those long-ago genes, stating only that the coat should be "as flat as possible." An easygoing personality makes the Flat-Coat a pleasant companion dog, and he needs only adequate exercise to keep him fit.

Flat-Coated Retriever.

FOX TERRIER, SMOOTH

COUNTRY: Great Britain
WEIGHT: 16–18 pounds
HEIGHT: 15½ inches
COAT: Smooth, but hard and dense
COLOR: White predominates; liver, brindle or red objectionable
REGISTRY: FCI, AKC, UKC, TKC, CKC
GROUP: Terrier

FOX TERRIER, WIRE

COUNTRY: Great Britain
WEIGHT: 16–18 pounds
HEIGHT: 15½ inches
COAT: Hard, wiry
COLOR: White predominates; liver, brindle or red objectionable
REGISTRY: FCI, AKC, UKC, TKC, CKC
GROUP: Terrier

Familiar throughout the world, the Fox Terrier most likely came from the same types that produced the Bull Terrier and smooth Black/Tan (Manchester) Terrier. Many other additions, including scenthounds and sighthounds, are probable. Colonel Thornton's "Pitch," recorded in print and on canvas in the 1790s, was of remarkably modern type. Packs with a bit more influence from one breed or another were used by various hunt clubs.

The breed was first exhibited as a sporting dog, due to its remarkable eyesight, keen nose and staying power. Hunters on horseback carried feisty working terriers in a sack or box until the larger foxhounds had driven the quarry to hide. Once the fox was driven into its tunnel, the terriers were loosed and went to ground, routing out the fox.

Francis Redmond is credited for establishing uniform type in the last quarter of the 19th century. The original standard drawn in England in

Smooth Fox Terrier.

Wire Fox Terrier.

1876 has not been changed since, except for a two-pound drop in top weight for males. The dog remains unchanged as well, with his half-dropped ears and long docked tail.

The Wire variety is the same as the Smooth, except for his hard, wiry jacket. Although the rough coat was probably developed before the Smooth, the Wire made its debut into the show ring about 20 years after the Smooth. The rough variety was produced from crossing the Smooth Fox with broken-coated terriers. Reverend Jack Russell, who gave his name to another breed, was a devoted hunter and terrier man. Early Wires needed the elegance, narrow heads and predominance of white which the Smooth already possessed. The Reverend kept the rough-coat strain pure from 1815 to 1870, with one cross to the Smooth for improvement. Today both varieties are judged by the same standard except for coat.

Coat care on the Smooth variety is minimal, but the Wire needs to be "stripped" four times a year. Pet owners often have their Wires trimmed with electric clippers, rather than the time-consuming hand-stripping to remove dead coat.

Their personable and dapper appearance attracts attention whether the dog is in the show ring or playing in the park. Even non-terrier show enthusiasts recall the paragon of Fox Terriers, the remarkable Champion Nornay Saddler. The Fox Terriers are favorites in several countries, with the Smooth being the top terrier in Sweden and the Wire taking that honor in Belgium, Canada, Holland and Italy.

The terrier instinct of "going to ground" may erupt, leading to holes dug in a manicured yard. Given an outlet for their energy, they make sturdy companions for children and are good alarm and watchdogs.

Smooth Fox Terrier.

Above: Wire Fox Terrier puppies. **Below Left:** Smooth Fox Terrier puppy. **Below Right:** Wire Fox Terrier.

Smooth Fox Terrier.

FRENCH BULLDOG

COUNTRY: France
WEIGHT: Under 22 pounds or 22–28 pounds
HEIGHT: 12 inches
COAT: Short, smooth
COLOR: Brindle, fawn (with or without white markings); piebald or white
OTHER NAMES: Bouledogue Francais
REGISTRY: FCI, AKC, TKC, CKC
GROUP: Mastiff

During the 1860s, Bulldogs reached the height of popularity. Toy varieties appeared, which were highly favored, particularly around the English midlands where lace-making flourished. These diminutive Bullys may have been taken to France when some of the lacemakers moved there.

To say the Frenchie was developed totally from English stock is to ignore the fact that many other countries had, at this time, short-faced, bull-baiting and fighting dogs. Spain, especially, had erect-eared bull-baiting dogs. This new breed became highly visible in France, and visiting Americans brought it back to the USA.

Originally, many had the rose ear of their larger counterpart, but the erect, round-tipped "bat" ear has become their hallmark. Americans have been credited with fixing the bat ear. When this breed first "returned" to England to be shown, around 1900, a brouhaha arose. The English were highly insulted that the French had the nerve to use the name "Bulldog" since it was a symbol of Great Britain. Much controversy ensued: letters and editorials in the doggy press and opposition from the existing Miniature Bulldog faction. But despite all this, a specialty club was formed in England in 1903, and soon the Frenchie was recognized and is now known around the world.

Reliable sources on the sinking of the Titantic report a French Bulldog to be the only animal or pet to have perished in this historical disaster. The dog's owner sued for $1,500, a substantial sum for 1912.

The French Bulldog has less body bulk, exaggeration of wrinkle and bowing of legs than its English counterpart. He is born with a bobtail, eliminating the need for surgery. The breed standard is uniform throughout the world with the exception of color. The fawns and creams so favored in North America and Britain are disallowed in continental Europe.

The Frenchie has a bright, alert expression, conveying his fun-loving outlook. He enjoys a large or small family, adults or children. A delight in obedience, he is happy, bright and willing to please. The Frenchie character, alarm bark without yappiness and easy upkeep make these dogs a good choice as companions.

French Bulldog, brindle.

French Bulldog, piebald.

French Bulldog, white.

GALGO ESPAÑOL

COUNTRY: Spain
WEIGHT: 60–66 pounds
HEIGHT: 26–28 inches
COAT: Short, smooth
COLOR: Cinnamon, chestnut, red, black, brindle; solid or in combinations with white
OTHER NAMES: Spanish Greyhound
REGISTRY: FCI
GROUP: Southern

The Galgo has an ancient history. He is named for the Gauls, a Celtic tribe that inhabited the Iberian Peninsula six centuries BC. Celts always appreciated good dogs, and they acquired gazehounds from the Phoenician merchants who plied the Spanish shores. Caesar conquered the area just before the Christian era, and Roman writers of the first and second centuries AD describe the sleek Galgo. Spain was overtaken by the Moors in the eighth century, and additional sighthounds could have been introduced from Africa at that time.

After the Middle Ages, the Galgo maintained type for centuries, especially in Andalusia and Castile. Farmers used him for guard work or for hunting rabbits. Spanish nobility also favored these fleet hounds for formal coursing of live game. Those used for coursing remained the purest in type.

In the 20th century, the Spanish began using the Galgo on the racetrack. Although these coursing canines could "turn on a dime" and maneuver well following live hare through rough country, they were not as fast on the straightaway as their English racing cousins. Imported Greyhounds were crossed with the Galgo to obtain more speed, and large numbers of the ancient Spanish breed were altered by this dilution. Fortunately, fanciers maintained the cause of the old Galgo type.

Today the professional racing dog in Spain is called Galgo Inglés-Español (English-Spanish Galgo) and is *not* the same breed recognized by the FCI and breed purists in Spain. Spanish and European breed clubs formed for the Galgo Español are fostering the breed as a quiet aristocratic companion and a fine coursing dog. Specialty shows are offered for the breed. The Galgo is smaller than the English Greyhound, with a bit more stop and ears that hang straight down. He is a sturdier fellow, built for the demands of coursing and practical hunting.

Galgo Español, brindle.

Grand Gascon-Saintongeois.

GASCONS-SAINTONGEOIS

Grand Gascon-Saintongeois

COUNTRY: France
WEIGHT: 66–71 pounds
HEIGHT: 25–28 inches
COLOR: Tricolor; with tan only in spots on head, black restricted to head and a few body spots, and the white body having some black ticking throughout
OTHER NAMES: Virelade
REGISTRY: FCI
GROUP: Hound

Petit Gascon-Saintongeois

COUNTRY: France
HEIGHT: 22½–25 inches
COAT: Short, dense, and smooth
COLOR: Tricolor; with tan only in spots on head, black restricted to head and a few body spots, and the white body having some black ticking throughout
REGISTRY: FCI
GROUP: Hound

The Saintongeois region of France is on the western coast, just north of Gascony and below Poitou. Prior to the French Revolution, the famous hounds of Saintongeois were acclaimed for hunting the wolf. But following the fall of the nobility, the breed fell into disuse and only scattered specimens of the Saintongeois remained, along with tales of the breed's greatness. In the 1840s, Baron de Virelade crossed what few remaining specimens he could find with the robust Grand Gasconies to create the Gascon-Saintongeois breed. Although formally named for the breeds from which they came, this breed (especially the large size) is often called the Virelade after their creator.

These dogs are nearly as large as the Grand Bleu but are more powerful with a breathtaking, elastic gallop. Originally used for roe deer, they are strong enough for larger game, and today hunt deer, fox and boar. Their ultra-sensitive sense of smell makes them adaptable to and competent in all forms of hunting. A gentle and affectionate hound off the field, the breed is, unfortunately, quite rare today. In 1986, only ten packs were left in France.

415

Grand Gascon-Saintongeois.

The Petit Gascon-Saintongeois is a smaller version, developed specifically for rabbit or hare. Except for ten centimeters less in height, he has all the same qualities of his larger brother. Both varieties are of the classic French type. The colors are also the same: tricolor with the black restricted to head and a few body patches, topped off with bright ticking. The tan markings are restricted, as described: "On the hindfeet above the hock is a small gray-brown spot called *marque de chevreuil*," or the mark of the deer.

GERMAN HUNT TERRIER

COUNTRY: Germany
WEIGHT: 20–22 pounds
HEIGHT: 16 inches
COAT: Short and coarse, or harsh wire, broken
COLOR: Black/tan, chocolate/tan or red
OTHER NAMES: Deutscher Jagdterrier
REGISTRY: FCI
GROUP: Terrier

During the 1940s, four German sportsmen aspired to establish their own breed of all-purpose game terrier for hunting and going to ground. C.E. Gruenwald, Chief Forester R. Fiess, Dr. Herbert Lackner and Walter Zangenbert, who was also a writer on hunting, used dogs of the old Broken-haired Black and Tan type from England, probably similar to what is now called Patterdale. This type was crossed with German-bred Wire Fox Terriers. The progeny had both smooth and wire coats. With careful selection, type was quickly cemented. FCI recognized the Jagdterrier in a remarkably short period of time.

This breed is a pure hunting machine, not recommended for use as a house dog. He is so aggressive that some label him as cruel to prey. Any animal is fair game: badgers, fox, even the

German Hunt Terrier.

German Hunt Terrier.

dangerous wild boar. This belligerence can make him cantankerous with cats or other dogs. The German Hunt Terrier is also utilized for tracking and retrieving, as well as working underground. Guarding of his master's home and property comes naturally. Those who know him well warn that he may not tolerate friendly advances from anyone other than his master. He is a one-person dog, and even that person has to earn his respect, but once earned, he is devoted. This is a dog that can only fully be appreciated by serious hunters or professional foresters, who have great admiration for his courage and ability.

In Germany, specimens of this breed must pass working tests prior to being granted club approval to reproduce. With the breed club refusing to register offspring of non-working parents, casual fanciers are discouraged to insure maintenance of working qualities. The Jagdterrier is only rarely exhibited.

Some specimens were brought to the USA in the 1950s. For a time, a breed club was in existence, but interest does not seem to have been maintained.

The tail is usually docked to about half the original length, but the ears are left intact to tip forward. At this time, only the rough coat is acceptable.

German Hunt Terrier.

Above: German Hunt Terrier, coarse, black/tan. **Below:** German Longhaired Pointer, solid liver.

GERMAN LONGHAIRED POINTER

COUNTRY: Germany
WEIGHT: 55–77 pounds
HEIGHT: Minimum 21 inches, 25–27½ inches
COAT: Moderate length, wavy but tough in texture, never woolly or curly; not more than 2 inches in length, with some fringe on legs, ears, and underside
COLOR: Usually solid liver—can have white on chest and head; also liver/white spotted
OTHER NAMES: Deutscher Langhaariger Vorstehhund, Langhaar
REGISTRY: FCI, CKC
GROUP: Gun Dog

The Langhaar has been known for nearly as long as the other German *vorstehhunden*, as some of this variety were shown at an exhibition in Hanover in 1879. Longhaired gun dogs populated Europe, and the Longhaired Pointer was originally developed from among these. Later, as field work became emphasized over woods work, the breed was refined by crosses to setters from England. Despite the softer appearance of the flowing coat and liquid brown eyes, the breed is expected to perform all of the exacting hunting chores expected of German dogs—and does them well.

The Canadian Kennel Club recognizes the breed, but the numbers are small there, as they are in Germany today. Some breed interest is awakening in the Netherlands. As long as he has creative outlets for expending his energy (running, long walks, hunting), he is a sweet-natured dog that is "a big friend of the whole family." He enjoys feeling useful, and is easily trainable. An example of the enthusiasm is demonstrated by a female, "Niner," taught to bring the paper from the paperbox to the family in return for a dog biscuit. One morning, after receiving her treat, she returned with a second paper, and then another and another, until quite a heap was gathered. A little detective work showed the dog had "retrieved" all the papers from the neighborhood. The owners quietly returned the papers to their proper places, and ceased the exercise for a time. Niner, however, wasn't content, and ran beside the delivery car until the driver handed her a paper and Niner was again able to perform her task.

Their "long" coat is not so abundant as to require extensive grooming. The beautiful, flagged tail is left intact. They follow the other German utility dogs in conformation, with the high flat ear and the clean head, sans hanging lips.

German Longhaired Pointer, solid liver.

German Longhaired Pointer.

German Pinscher, black/tan.

GERMAN PINSCHER

COUNTRY: Germany
WEIGHT: 25–35 pounds
HEIGHT: 16–19 inches
COAT: Short, but coarse
COLOR: Black/tan or red
OTHER NAMES: Standard Pinscher
REGISTRY: FCI, TKC
GROUP: Terrier

As old as the British terriers, the German Pinscher does not possess the same immediate ancestors, although its prototypes probably converged in Europe prior to the Celtic invasion of the British Islands in the centuries before Christ. *Pinscher* means biter in German, referring not to the dog's temperament but to its abilities against adversaries. The German farmer's terrier was slightly larger than its English counterpart. It was a clean, alert guardian, used for home protection and vermin control. The German Pinscher was too large and long legged to go to ground but, nonetheless, could hold his own against anything above ground, even being a manstopper, if necessary.

The breed was officially recognized in Germany in 1879 and has been protected and promoted since 1894 by the German Pinscher-Schnauzer Club. During the years around the turn of the century, both smooth (pinscher) and coarsehaired (schnauzer) pups appeared in the same litters. The club initiated the policy of requiring proof of three generations of pure smooth coats for registration. This quickly helped set type and made them a distinct breed from the Schnauzer.

Over the years, new breeds were created in Germany and others introduced from foreign countries. The Doberman Pinscher and Miniature Pinscher gained acceptance worldwide, and the Standard Schnauzer found favor at home and abroad. The Standard Pinscher, however, fell into obscurity in its homeland and is now nearly unknown elsewhere. There were only ten litters registered in Germany in 1985. Despite the small numbers, interest has been growing lately to preserve this fine breed. There are a handful in the USA, where there is an organization to promote them, and their numbers are once again increasing.

German Pinscher, red.

German Pinscher.

German Pinschers are rough-and-tumble dogs who like a scrap and need a fair amount of exercise. They also need to know who is boss. But within these parameters, they are clean, alert and adaptable to new situations and are eager to please their "pack leader."

Great companions for children, the Pinschers are energetic and large enough for hours of play. Yet they are small enough for easy care, and grooming requires a minimum of fuss. American breeders state the dogs naturally maintain direct eye contact when playing, and are incredibly quick and fast, which means they have retained their capabilities as ratters as well.

Ears are traditionally cropped to a moderate length, much like a pet cut on a Doberman Pinscher, and the tail is docked short when the whelp is just a day or two old. The Pinscher's sleek coat usually is seen in the traditional black and tan, although various shades of red are also allowed.

GERMAN SHEEPPOODLE

COUNTRY: Germany
HEIGHT: 20–24 inches
COAT: Long, hard, shaggy
COLOR: White, also roan and pied
OTHER NAME: Schäfpudel
GROUP: Herding

This breed is unknown outside Germany and is rare, if not extinct, even at home. He had a wavy, poodlelike coat that tended to form in cords like the Poodle, Puli and Komondor. In fact, he was probably related to the Puli, as the importation and exportation of sheep between Germany and Hungary was common. And where the sheep went, the sheep dogs followed.

The Schäfpudel was a good herding dog with drop ears, long tail, and a gentle, tolerant and affectionate nature. Unfortunately, there has been no record of this breed for some time.

GERMAN SHEPHERD DOG

COUNTRY: Germany
WEIGHT: 75–95 pounds
HEIGHT: 22–26 inches
COAT: Moderately short, with dense undercoat
COLOR: Black/tan, sable, all black
OTHER NAMES: Deutsche Schaferhund, Alsatian
REGISTRY: FCI, AKC, UKC, TKC, CKC
GROUP: Herding

The German Shepherd Dog is one of the most widely recognized breeds in the world. The breed is known and favored in many countries for its intelligence, trainability, adaptability and fortitude.

The foundation of this breed is comparatively recent (1899), making the climb to its current numbers and status of renown even more amazing. Rittmeister Max von Stephanitz, proclaimed "the father of the breed," and his friend, Herr Artur Meyer, bought a working dog seen at a show in order to foster a strong, capable German herder. Von Stephanitz led the group that promoted German Shepherds from 1899 to 1935. During that time, he brought the breed to its current status of respect.

With less demand for herding over the years, von Stephanitz was determined not to let the Shepherd decline and encouraged its use by the police and the military. During World War I, there were 48,000 Shepherds "enlisted" in the German Army. Today, the GSD serves perhaps in more ways than any other breed: search-and-rescue (S&R), police, army and sentry, scent

German Shepherd Dog, black/tan.

discrimination and, of course, companion. They are superb dog guides for the blind and helpers for the handicapped.

Perhaps the best testimony to its S&R ability comes from the Hospice at St. Bernard, which still offers refuge to travelers. Today the Hospice raises Saint Bernards as a tourist attraction, but German Shepherds do the rescue work.

Despite fads, poor breeding practices, malignment of character as "attack" dogs, and discrimination against anything German during the years of and following World War I, the breed has thrived. During the German phobia, English owners refused to give up the breed they had come to admire. They did compromise and change the name to Alsatian, which prevailed for nearly 40 years after all hostilities ended. Their American counterparts, in a similar attempt to disguise the breed's origins, temporarily dropped the word "German" from the name. Two German Shepherds helped to soothe the post-War wounds. The film stars Rin Tin Tin and Strongheart reawakened interest in the breed, with their breath-taking adventures and thrilling rescues. During the Second World War, the Shepherd served the Allied forces in the fight against its homeland. These dogs have amazed even their trainers in feats of power and

German Shepherd Dog, solid black.

agility. A shepherd named "Max of Pangoula" scaled a high jump of 11 feet 5⅛ inches, and "Young Sabre" topped a ribbed wall of 11 feet 8 inches.

As late as 1915, there were three coat types—the smoothhaired, the longhaired and the wirehaired. The wirehaired has since disappeared; "long coats" are still born, but do not meet with approval in the conformation ring. They do, however, make fine companions, and there are admirers that prefer them.

Shepherds can tolerate extremes in weather conditions: barking with delight at a romp in below-zero temperatures, rolling in a snowbank; or withstanding the heat of a steamy jungle in a combat zone.

Their ears are required to stand erect naturally, although aid through taping may be given to youngsters with "lazy" ears. A correct, noble Shepherd head can best be described as possessing "the look of eagles." Their tails should reach long and be carried low, with the gentle curve of a saber at the end. All-white coloration is a disqualifying fault, and the Shepherd is one of the very few breeds that is disqualified for viciousness. This commendable practice has accomplished a great deal of good for the breed. It is a GSD, Champion Covy-Tucker Hill's Manhattan, who holds the honor of the most best in shows, over 200, carrying off prestigious wins at Westminster and the AKC Centennial.

The dog is sensible and has a devout loyalty to its family. Perhaps this is why the breed is so popular. Shepherd lovers seem to wear blinders when it comes to their favorite breed, thinking no other can compare. It is claimed the German Shepherd Dog has the intelligence of a seven-year-old child. Shepherds are often top contenders in the obedience ring.

As occurs with any breed that is so numerous, some poor breeding practices exist which perpetuate temperament and health problems. Buyers should study the dam and, if possible, the sire to see if they are physically sound and good-natured. A Shepherd is willing to do anything for the person he loves, to the point of giving his own life. The breed adores its own family and is naturally protective of it and of property. The standard stresses that it must stand its ground and be approachable in public situations.

German Shepherd Dog, black/tan.

German Shepherd Dog, pups.

German Shepherd Dog.

Above, Below, and Facing Page: German Shepherd Dog.

GERMAN SHORTHAIRED POINTER

COUNTRY: Germany
WEIGHT: 55–70 pounds
HEIGHT: 23–25 inches
COAT: Short, dense and hard
COLOR: Solid liver, or liver and white, with or without ticking or roaning
OTHER NAMES: Deutscher Kurzhaariger Vorstehhund, Kurzhaar
REGISTRY: FCI, AKC, UKC, TKC, CKC
GROUP: Gun Dog

The slow-working schweisshunds with their superb noses have been found in Germany for centuries. As early as the 1700s, dogs referred to collectively as *huehnerhunden*, bird dogs, were used. No specific types had yet evolved, but they stemmed directly from the existing brackes and schweisshunds present in Germany, refined with pointing dogs. By the 1800s, individual breeds of versatile gun dogs began to be fixed by German breeders.

Prince Albrecht zu Solms-Brauenfels, in the middle of that century, spearheaded a tireless effort to create the ultimate *vorstehhund*—the all-purpose hunting dog. Records show that the Prince owned good schweisshunds and fine Pointers imported from England, and these were probably the basis for the German Shorthaired Pointer.

Early Shorthairs were short and heavy bodied, long-eared and extremely slow-working, showing the strongest influence from the hounds. The oft-repeated story of the Shorthair springing from "Bloodhounds" is merely a lapse in translation. *Schweisshund* translates to "bloodhound," meaning a dog used to follow a bloodtrail, not the breed "Bloodhound." These dogs were long since separated from the Bloodhound (St. Hubert) that we know today. English Pointer blood was later added to existing Shorthairs to increase speed and style, but great care was taken to keep the desired talents in water work, retrieving and tracking, and in toughness.

German Shorthaired Pointer, liver and white with ticking.

German Shorthaired Pointer, solid liver with ticking.

German Shorthaired Pointer, solid liver with ticking.

When the breed was imported into the USA in the early 1900s, it was enthusiastically received by American hunters. In fact, since his official recognition by the AKC in the 1940s, the breed has fared well in AKC registrations. He is one of the favorites of the average weekend hunter because of his natural abilities, ease of training and adaptability to family life. The Shorthair is described as "all business, no frills." In addition, the breed has been successful in the AKC field trials, as well as in American show and obedience rings. The German Shorthaired Pointer Club of America, to its credit, has strongly supported all aspects of breed ability; hence, the Shorthair shows no sign of splitting into two distinct types as have some of the other gun dogs. The breed boasts the most dual champions of any breed in the USA.

His short coat requires little care, even after a day in the field. He is affectionate and good with children, fitting into the venue of pet as long as his basic nature is understood. A dog of immense energy and a desire to hunt, he does not recognize natural boundaries and may become destructive if bored by confinement and a lack of exercise. Behaviorists recommend an outdoor kennel when the owner is not at home.

Tail and dewclaws are clipped when the German Shorthaired Pointer pup is just a few days old. His expressive tail stub wiggles with excitement at his master's attention or becomes rigid on a point. His body, like most shorthaired dogs', is warm and comforting, as are his eyes. The Shorthair is very long-lived, often surviving past his 16th year.

German Shorthaired Pointers, adult and puppies.

German Shorthaired Pointer.

Above: German Shorthaired Pointer diving into water. **Below:** German Shorthaired Pointers holding retrieves.

GERMAN SPITZ

German Wolfspitz

COUNTRY: Germany
HEIGHT: 18 inches minimum
COAT: Long, dense, double, stand-off
COLOR: Wolf gray only
REGISTRY: FCI
GROUP: Northern

Giant German Spitz

COUNTRY: Germany
WEIGHT: 40 pounds
HEIGHT: 16 inches minimum
COAT: Long, dense, double, stand-off
COLOR: Solids only—black, white or brown
OTHER NAMES: Deutscher Grossspitz, Great Spitz
REGISTRY: FCI
GROUP: Northern

Standard German Spitz

COUNTRY: Germany
WEIGHT: 25 pounds
HEIGHT: 11½–14 inches
COAT: Long, dense, double, stand-off
COLOR: Solid colors—white, black, brown, orange, wolf gray
OTHER NAMES: Deutscher Mittelspitz
REGISTRY: FCI, TKC
GROUP: Northern

Small German Spitz

COUNTRY: Germany
WEIGHT: 7 pounds minimum
HEIGHT: 8½–11 inches
COAT: Long, dense, double, stand-off
COLOR: Solids in black, white, brown, wolf gray, or orange (in England particolors are also allowed)
OTHER NAMES: Deutscher Kleinspitz, Miniature German Spitz, Victorian Pom
REGISTRY: FCI, TKC
GROUP: Northern

Toy German Spitz

COUNTRY: Germany
WEIGHT: Under 7 pounds
HEIGHT: Under 8½ inches
COAT: Long, dense, double, stand-off
COLOR: All solid colors
OTHER NAMES: Zwergspitz
REGISTRY: FCI
GROUP: Northern

Besides the three traditional uses for the Nordic breeds, herding, hunting and hauling, spitz have become popular throughout the world as utility and companion dogs. Countries from all over the world have developed their own form, all of which are still similar to one another.

Giant German Spitz, brown.

Small German Spitz, black with white markings.

The German Spitz breeds descend directly from the profusely coated Nordic herding dogs, like the Samoyed or the Lapphund, that are so common in the North. They were probably brought to northern Germany and Holland by Viking plunderers and looters who plagued those areas during the Middle Ages. These dogs spread throughout Europe and even the British Isles, contributing to the development of the true herding and shepherd breeds, as well as being the progenitors of the Spitz.

The Spitz was mentioned in German literature and history as early as 1450. Count Eberhand Zu Sayre Buffon wrote in his 1750 *National History of Quadrupeds* that he believed the Spitz to be the ancestor of all domestic breeds. At the end of the 17th century, citizens of Pomerania were raising a large white Spitz, and those in Wurttemberg had black and brown varieties to watch over their farms and possessions.

These original Spitz dogs have evolved into several sizes and a bouquet of solid colors. Today, the FCI recognizes five varieties based on size. The Wolfspitz, the largest and in gray only, is a similar type to what became the Keeshond in Holland. The Giant is not really a giant, compared to some of the flock guards or mastiffs, and is reminiscent of a small Samoyed or a Lapphund in white, chocolate or black. Standard and Small Spitz, in a wider variety of colors, became much-loved companions with the more recent development of the tiny toy to satisfy the demand for an apartment or lap-sized Spitz. These breeds are popular in Germany and well known throughout Europe, but have not reached North American shores.

The Small Spitz was imported to England from Germany (Pomerania) over 100 years ago and adopted the pseudonym Pomeranian. It was a favorite of Queen Victoria and was occasionally called the Victorian Pom. Gainsborough admired the German Spitz and captured its beauty

437

on canvas.

The Pomeranian has developed separately and divergently with its own standard. These dogs are more refined and have an exaggerated coat. They closely resemble their cousin the Spitz, but are a breed of their own.

With the Pomeranians of the show ring becoming smaller and smaller, many English fanciers lamented the demise of the larger specimens. In fact, Pomeranian show classes for "over 7–pound" dogs had been discontinued in the 1940s. British breeders Janet Edmonds and Averil Cawthera brought in several Klein and Mittel German Spitz from the Continent in the mid-1970s, although they were registered as Poms in England and used in Pomeranian breeding programs.

With the desire to re-establish the larger type Spitz, a special arrangement was created with the Kennel Club of Great Britain. For a six-month period in 1985, any Pom with one or more of four imported Spitz dogs in their pedigrees could have their registries switched to that of German Spitz. After this initial six-month period, the stud books were closed to any further double registration. From this beginning, the German Spitz has been re-established in Great Britain and is now an official breed there.

Breeders say that these dogs are most adaptable, happily accompanying owners on a 30–mile walk or cuddling in front of the fire. They are described as being much like a young child, anxious to please—yet also wanting their own way and knowing how to obtain it. A structured family order exists among these breeds, with the youngest adult delegated to play with the puppies. Like so many of the other northern breeds, the German Spitzes are happy and buoyant, displaying charming smiles and seeming to laugh with you—or at you. They are excellent jumpers and like to stand on their hind legs to beg or to show off. They should never show any nervousness or aggression, being always equable and confident. The alert, watchful personality, needed long ago with the herds, is retained and now suits the watchdog and companion.

German Wolfspitz.

Above: Giant German Spitz. **Below:** Small German Spitz, white with black markings.

Above: Toy German Spitz, chocolate. **Above Right:** Small German Spitz. **Below Left:** Small German Spitz. **Below Right:** Toy German Spitz.

Above: Toy German Spitzes, five colors. **Below:** Small German Spitz.

German Wirehaired Pointer.

GERMAN WIREHAIRED POINTER

COUNTRY: Germany
WEIGHT: 60–70 pounds
HEIGHT: 24–26 inches
COAT: Harsh, wiry and flat lying outer coat, with good beard and brows, never so long as to hide the outline of the dog; plenty of underwool
COLOR: Solid liver, or any combination of liver and white
OTHER NAMES: Deutscher Drahthaariger Vorstehhund, Drahthaar
REGISTRY: FCI, AKC, UKC, TKC, CKC
GROUP: Gun Dog

German Wirehaired Pointer.

The history of the Wirehair in Germany is quite recent. An interest in gun dogs with bristly coats always existed, and several types were in evidence by the late 1800s. At first, the Wirehair Club in Germany fostered all hunting dogs with a wire coat, but the wide variation in types soon saw separate organizations for the Pudelpointer, the Griffon, the Stichelhaar, and the German Wirehaired Pointer. They may all have come from the same stock, as these breeds developed concurrently. From this time on, each breed became individualized.

Like the Shorthair, the Drahthaar was developed to be used as a utility hunting dog and still fills that capacity. Because of the diverse tasks the breed is expected to accomplish, the dog is ideally big and robust, with a coat that affords protection. Wirehairs lead all hunting dogs in German registrations.

The Wirehair came to America about the same time as the first Shorthairs, in the 1920s. But the Wirehair was later in achieving AKC recognition and has never become as widespread as his shorthaired cousins in the States. Wirehairs tend to be a bit more aloof, and sometimes are one-person dogs. Those who support the breed possess a fine, obedient companion and hunting dog.

His tail is docked, like the GSP, leaving about two-fifths. If the coat is proper, it requires very little care. The underwool sheds in the spring and requires bathing and brushing, as is true of most breeds. A good harsh coat will do well with occasional combing out of dead hair. Some slight stripping may be required to neaten him for exhibition, but the coat should never have to be clipped or scissored. Only when the coat is improperly long and woolly does excessive grooming become necessary to give him the proper outline. This improper coat also attracts burrs and sticks in the field, which is why it is discouraged.

Often a clown, the Wirehair provides entertainment for his family. His whiskery face can switch from an imp to a noble show dog or a stern uncle. Sufficient exercise is essential. If bored, his excess energy can turn to destructive entertainment. The more they are taught, the happier they are. The breed needs a mixture of firm training with all-out rough-housing.

443

German Wirehaired Pointer.

German Wirehaired Pointers.

GIANT SCHNAUZER

COUNTRY: Germany
WEIGHT: 70–77 pounds
HEIGHT: 23–27½ inches
COAT: Moderate length, hard, bristly, with woolly undercoat
COLOR: Black or salt and pepper
OTHER NAMES: Riesenschnauzer
REGISTRY: FCI, AKC, UKC, TKC, CKC
GROUP: Herding

Giant Schnauzer, black.

The Giant Schnauzer was developed in southern Germany as a cattle herder from smoothhaired droving dogs, a variety of rough-coated indigenous shepherd dogs and, perhaps, the black Great Dane. He was known as the Munchener Dog at one time, due to the area of origin near Munich. He was used from the 15th century until the arrival of the railroads, when the large cattle drives waned. Farmers then lost interest in feeding these big eaters, and the Giants moved into the towns to become the guardians and mascots of beer halls and butcher shops during the 19th century.

Theory has it that, during this era, breeders noted his similarity to the existing smaller Schnauzers and aimed their breeding programs toward increasing that likeness. This is when most breed historians feel a cross was made to the Standard Schnauzer. The results were called Munich Schnauzers for a time, until the imposing term "Giant" was adapted around the turn of this century.

Introduced to dog shows in Munich in 1909, they attracted immediate attention and a national club was formed. Although they landed on the American shores at about the same time as the German Shepherd, the Giants were simply overshadowed by demand for their native relative. The breed has never gained a large following in North America but, at home, it is still one of the principal breeds used for security work. During both World Wars, the Giant gave valiant service as a police and war dog, suffering so many casualties that many thought the breed was lost. Thankfully, dedicated breeders have maintained the Giant in many countries around the world.

Their coat is similar to that of the other Schnauzers, and requires stripping twice a year. A strong tendency exists to regress to a soft, woolly coat, and care must be taken by breeders to maintain the true Schnauzer "hard" terrier coat. This hair not only is easier to care for than the woolly coat but keeps the breed distinct from its distant relative, the Bouvier. Ears are cropped and the tail is docked. The Giants still retain their guardian instincts and do well in schutzhund trials.

Above: Giant Schnauzer, salt and pepper. **Below:** Giant Schnauzer, black.

Glen of Imaal Terrier, blue brindle.

GLEN OF IMAAL TERRIER

COUNTRY: Ireland
WEIGHT: 35 pounds
HEIGHT: 14 inches
COAT: Medium length, harsh-textured
COLOR: Wheaten or brindle blue
REGISTRY: FCI, TKC
GROUP: Terrier

Although the Glen Terrier is a new furry face to many dog fanciers, it is actually an old breed that was simply ignored for a long time by the dog fancy. The Glen area, in County Wicklow, Ireland, is a scenic but rather bleak area offering poor soil. Many of the local farmers descended from Lowland and Hessian soldiers who had been given the land in the 16th and 17th centuries for services to the crown. These determined, hard-working people had to eke out a living from the rocks and could ill afford a dog who couldn't earn its keep. The fact that the Glen Terrier flourished under such demanding conditions manifests the breed's attributes equal to that of its masters.

With shorter legs than the other Irish terriers, the Glen Terrier could go to ground for badger and fox—not just to put them to flight, for he is game enough to fight to the death. The rat population around homes and barns was kept to a minimum. Saturday nights found owners gathering at a remote spot to match the feisty Glen dogs one-on-one, accentuated by heated wagering.

Besides being good ratters, varmint dogs and Saturday-night entertainment, Glens served as "turn- spits" on the dog wheel. This device was a treadmill, propelled for hours by an energetic little dog, which turned the meat on the spit as it cooked. Their small size, low fronts and strong rears suited them for this task as cook's helpers, and the Glens trotted for miles going nowhere.

Their size is documented in an old story passed down to a current Irish owner from his father, who owned Glens for over 50 years.

Years ago, there were cannons at the Coolmoney Army Camp in County Wicklow, which was held by the British Army. Glen Terriers found their way into camp and were adopted by the men. The claim was that a Glen of Imaal Terrier could always fit into the barrel of those 14–inch cannons.

Folklore says that the Glen Terrier was the result of a cross between the great Celtic hounds and a mongoose, and that the offspring was saved from culling by St. Patrick. The yarn continues that the *Firbolgs*, half snake and half human, ate all the Irish babies and puppies in the land. Upon Patrick's return to Ireland, Glens assisted St. Patrick in ridding Ireland of the snake-people and the snakes. Although touched with the blarney, the tale typifies their prowess and their proud Irish owners.

The breed was recognized formally as recently as the 1930s. In the 1950s, Paddy Brennan and Willie Kane, both admirers of the breed, made a concerted effort to build its reputation and numbers.

To win a championship, the Glen not only had to be judged for conformation, but also had to earn his *teastas misneach* or dead game certificate, accomplished at a badger trial. The terrier was put into a winding tunnel, with his foe, a badger, furiously defending the other end. The dog had to draw or drag the badger out within a certain length of time. Any dog that barked was disqualified.

Modern English owners tell of the grit necessary to face a badger underground. The badger's method of biting can easily ". . . take the face off a terrier. Missing noses and lips, or broken and missing jaws are not unusual in terriers worked to badger." An Irish breeder states that when a Glen Terrier gets a grip on another animal, nothing will induce him to let go until he is "choked out of it" (pressing of the fingers on the dog's throat to loosen the grip). Glens don't shake the rat to break its neck like most terriers do but, with a mighty crunch, bite the rat in half. The Glen has even used its considerable talents to draw the badger from under concrete floors!

Trials with live badgers were outlawed in 1966 and, officially, the test was no longer necessary to make up a champion. But the dog is still a working dog and, no doubt, informal badger tri-

als are still held undercover to determine the gamest of possible breeding stock.

The Glen dog is low-stationed with slightly bowed front legs to give a mechanical advantage while digging. The harsh coat is weather-resistant. Because the "no barking" rule was absolute in trials, this terrier makes a quiet companion. Although the standard calls for a 35–pound dog, Irish breeders state that many Glens are heavier built—more in the 40–50-pound range. The reason for this probably stems back to the years that he was used for dog-fighting, when there were crosses to Bull Terrier, Staffordshire and other larger fighting dogs. Genes are carried forever; hence, the size problem still appears. Compared to some of his relatives, however, the Glen is still a rather moderately sized fellow. There are a handful of Glen enthusiasts in the United States.

Glen of Imaal Terrier, wheaten.

Golden Retriever.

GOLDEN RETRIEVER

COUNTRY: Great Britain
WEIGHT: 60–75 pounds
HEIGHT: 21½–24 inches
COAT: Dense and water repellent, lying flat to the body, flat or wavy, with some fringes—but not silky; good undercoat
COLOR: Various shades of lustrous golden
REGISTRY: FCI, AKC, UKC, TKC, CKC
GROUP: Gun Dog

The Golden is another product from the latter half of the 19th century, when so many of the gun dog breeds were formed. The breed owes much of its development to Sir Dudley Majoribanks (Lord Tweedmouth) whose records from his own meticulous stud books give a good basis of origins. Yellow recessives had always been present in the retrievers from Newfoundland and Labrador, even though in the 1850s the fashion in England was for black "Wavy-Coats" and Labradors. Lighter hues came to prominence later in the yellow Labs, as well in as the Chessie, and then the Golden.

Majoribanks took a liking to the yellow color and acquired a dog of that color, "Nous," from Flat-Coat breeding. To create good water retrievers, Nous was bred to Tweed Water Spaniel bitches, a now-extinct English retrieving dog that was close and curly-coated and a light liver color. Other crossings, of structured linebreeding, were recorded over a period of 20 years, including a Labrador or two, a red setter, possibly a Bloodhound, and other Wavy-Coats.

This, then, is the basic Golden's inheritance. Goldens were registered and shown as golden Flat-Coats until 1913, when they were listed as Golden or Yellow Retrievers and, finally, in 1920, took the name they bear today.

A legend still persists about Russian Sheep-

Golden Retriever.

dogs, acquired from a traveling circus, that contributed to the creation of the breed. No such information has been found among the Tweedmouth archives. Of course, others were breeding these golden-colored retrievers besides Majoribanks, so this strange mixture could have been introduced in other kennels. But most cynologists feel this was a contrived story, which the general public loved to believe. With the possible exception of trainability, the genetics of sheep dogs are diametrically opposed to the necessary abilities of the gun dog, and it is doubtful any knowledgeable dog breeder would have entertained the idea. Supporting this legend, however, the Golden was first exhibited under the name of Russian Retriever or Russian Retriever and Tracker. Thus, the story lives on.

Whatever its foundation, the modern Golden Retriever is a wonderfully versatile dog. He is a good retriever and upland game hunter, is used with increasing frequency as a guide for the blind and makes a loving, easygoing, pleasant companion. In the United States, the Golden dominates obedience competition with his flashy animation, quick reflexes, precision, trainability and intense desire to please. The same attributes

Golden Retriever with retrieved pheasant.

Golden Retriever performing in obedience trial.

stand him in good stead in the show ring.

A Golden requires sufficient exercise to overcome a tendency toward excess poundage. His beautiful coat requires only routine brushing, with a few grooming sessions during the spring when the undercoat is shed. The color can range from a soft, pale moon yellow to a lustrous burnished gold. It is as though the Golden has captured the warmth and beauty of sparkling sunshine in both his coat and temperament. He is a wonderful family pet, as he is loving and long-suffering with children, mannerly in the home, yet always ready to accompany any member in activities. A dog nearly void of guard instincts, his fringed tail always seems to be wagging. His expression is one of straightforward affection and trust.

452

Golden Retriever.

Golden Retriever on the retrieve.

Golden Retrievers, adults and pups.

Gordon Setter.

GORDON SETTER

COUNTRY: Great Britain
WEIGHT: 45–80 pounds
HEIGHT: 23–27 inches
COAT: Moderately long, flat and straight, long fine feathering
COLOR: Black/tan
REGISTRY: FCI, AKC, TKC, CKC
GROUP: Gun Dog

"Black and fallow" setting dogs have been known in Scotland for at least 350 years. They sprang from setting spaniels. These were crossed with local dogs to create a type for Scottish hunting conditions. In the 18th century, the present name was adapted because of the famed dogs kept by the Duke of Gordon.

An unknown writer in the late 1700s might well have been talking about a modern dog: "The Gordon Castle Setters are as a rule easy to break and naturally back well. They are not fast dogs but they have good staying powers and can keep on steadily from morning until night. Their noses are first class and they seldom make a false point or what is called at field trials a sen-sational stand . . . . [but] When they stand you may be sure there are birds."

Early kennels had black/whites, tricolors, and reds as well as the black/tan, but this last color soon became the most desired—and thus the mark of purity. Red whelps still may crop up occasionally in a litter, as the standard warns.

Because of their handsome looks as well as their field abilities, they were imported and welcomed into America in the mid-1800s. Their lack of breakneck speed and breathtaking style to compete with the English Setter and Pointer at the big Circuit Trials may have been their rescue from the breed split seen in other gun dogs. They remained a favorite with hunters who wanted a full game bag. The Gordon is a handsome competitor in the show ring. They make a good showing in the AKC field trials, and there are a few duals.

Gordons are the heaviest headed of the setters, showing some flew, and long, low-set ears. His typical setter nature allows the weekend hunter to have a house pet as well. He does tend to be a bit more suspicious of strangers than the other setters and serves well as a home guardian.

456

Gordon Setter.

GREAT DANE

COUNTRY: Germany
WEIGHT: 100 pounds or more
HEIGHT: Minimum 28–32 inches; 30–32 inches
or over preferred
COAT: Short, smooth
COLOR: Black, blue, fawn, brindle, harlequin
OTHER NAMES: Deutsche Dogge, German
Mastiff
REGISTRY: FCI, AKC, UKC, TKC, CKC
GROUP: Mastiff

Except for lacking the undershot jaw, the Great
Dane represents the closest modern example of
the Alaunt. In Italy, the breed is called *Alano*,
the Italian word for mastiff. Although not the
heaviest, they are the tallest of the mastiffs, and
their racier build may indicate a cross to hounds
in past centuries. Merle hounds or shepherd
dogs could have introduced the merle (harlequin) gene.

That the type is ancient is without question.
Dogs of Dane or Alaunt type are depicted in
drawings in the tombs of Beni-Hassan, dating

Great Dane, harlequin.

about 2200 BC. Some of these dogs are shown
as harlequins. Other pre-Christian replicas appear on coins, on bas reliefs and in paintings.

His name is the only thing about him that is
Danish. He is all German, used long ago by Germanic and Celtic tribes as a war dog, and is
called Deutsche Dogge by the FCI. Only in En-
glish-speaking countries is he still a "Dane."

At first a giant bull-baiter, he was also used as
a boarhound since the Middle Ages. In 1592, the
Duke of Braunschweig showed up for a boar
hunt with his pack of 600 male Danes! The
breed was declared the national dog of Germany
in 1876. A great favorite of the Iron Chancellor,
Bismarck, they were his body guards and constant companions. In modern times, the Dane
serves as a guardian and friend. His noble, statuesque appearance gives him the designation of
"Apollo of dogdom."

An early admirer and owner was William
"Buffalo Bill" Cody, when specimens were
brought to American shores in the mid-1800s.
Some of these early imports came directly from
German estates where they had been trained in
attack work. Thus the breed gained an early
false reputation for ferocity. Temperament was
soon "tempered." They were first shown under
the name of Siberian or Ulm Dog. The Dane
was introduced to British exhibitors in 1877,
where his great, majestic height amazed spectators.

As a giant, it is essential for buyers to research
their purchase, finding pups of strong, sound,
good-natured parents. Large males may often
reach as much as 180 pounds, though the tallest
dog on record, a Great Dane named Shamgret
Danzas, weighed 238 pounds at 41½ inches!

Although Danes are as content living in an
apartment as on an estate, it is necessary to allow them to stretch those long legs frequently.
Grooming, as with most of the mastiffs, is minimal—and feeding costs are maximum! They require involvement with family activities. If
bored, these giants can become destructive—
and a large dog can turn a table into toothpicks
in minutes.

Danes' ears have been cropped for many years
on the Continent and in the States; however, it
is becoming more common to see natural drop
ears even in the show ring.

Great Dane, black.

Great Dane, brindle, ears cropped.

Great Dane.

Great Dane.

Great Dane.

GREATER SWISS MOUNTAIN DOG

COUNTRY: Switzerland
WEIGHT: Around 130 pounds
HEIGHT: 23½–28½ inches
COAT: Short, dense
COLOR: Black and tan, with white at toes, tail tip, chest, and blaze. The tan always lies between the black and the white. Red tricolors do occur but are not acceptable.
OTHER NAMES: Grosser Schweizer Sennenhund
REGISTRY: FCI, AKC
GROUP: Mastiff

The "Swissy" is the largest—and probably the oldest —of the four Swiss varieties, bred from the mastiff types left behind by the Roman armies. It was used for centuries in rural cantons, with no formal breeding program, as a butcher's dog and as a draft dog pulling produce to market. Farmers loved them. The dogs worked as hard as horses but didn't eat as much, and litters were large—up to 18 pups!

At that time, he was referred to as "Old Blaze." He started to disappear as the popularity of the red/white St. Bernard soared in the mid-1800s. There were many crossbreedings, and anything with the dominant red and white was called St. Bernard. Likely, many Swissies became Saints in one generation!

Right after the turn of the century, only a few remained on isolated farms. Franz Schertenleib found one and bought it as a "white elephant." Eager to hear what the knowledgeable judge, Dr. Albert Heim, had to say about this find, he exhibited the dog at a 1908 show, entered in the Bernese class. Heim knew the history of the Swissy and—having thought the breed extinct—praised the dog and admonished Swiss dog lovers to scout the farms and find enough animals to revitalize the breed.

The Swiss took a renewed interest and worked to keep these dogs from dying out. In 1910, these breeders accomplished another goal when the GSMD was accepted by the Swiss registry. Today's Greater Swiss Mountain Dogs

Greater Swiss Mountain Dog.

Greater Swiss Mountain Dog.

trace back to seven or eight animals, a very narrow breed base. Up until the 1930s, "foundlings,"dogs which exemplified the breed but did not possess a pedigree, were still used in breeding programs. A problem with lack of size was conquered, possibly by crossbreeding with smooth Bernards.

Their natural protective instinct is demonstrated by the tale of "Nero." After an evening in the pubs, Nero's owner and his friends headed home. Instead of following his owner as usual, Nero chose to accompany a man who was in his cups. When the man fell in a creek, Nero fished him out, escorted him home and stayed overnight. When the gentleman came to his senses and opened the door the next morning, Nero immediately headed for home. This instinct is today channeled into schutzhund training and as watchdogs for the homes.

As peace loving as the Swiss people, the breed is calm, even-tempered and sturdy. Not a roamer, the Swissy hates to be tied or confined and is happiest with his family. He still loves to pull carts or sleds, especially if the passenger is a child.

The Swissy is an attractive, easily groomed show dog with an aptitude for obedience. The breed was introduced to the States in 1968, and in 1985 was accepted into the AKC Miscellaneous Group.

GREAT PYRENEES

COUNTRY: France
WEIGHT: 90–140 pounds
HEIGHT: 25–32 inches
COAT: Medium to medium-long
COLOR: White
OTHER NAMES: Pyrenean Mountain Dog, Chien de Montagne des Pyrenees
REGISTRY: FCI, AKC, UKC, TKC, CKC
GROUP: Flock Guard

Certainly the most recognizable and populous example of the flock-guarding breeds, the Pyr originated in the Pyrenees Mountains that separate France from Spain. The exact history of the dogs' arrival is not known, but they have been guarding the flocks in France for millenia. Fossils of the breed type have been found predating the Bronze Age (1800–1000 BC). "Discovered" by the French nobility before the Revolution, like the Maremma in Italy, they could be found guarding the large chateaux in southern France. Dauphin Louis XIV named the breed the Royal Dog of France.

Great Pyrenees.

This didn't secure the Pyr in the hands of royalty, however. The peasants continued to make use of his abilities as flock guard. Although physical characteristics such as strength, keen hearing, and big paws for sure-footedness were deemed highly preferable, the psychological aspects of the dog were considered of prime importance. If a dog didn't bond to the sheep and protect them despite his own discomforts, the dog was killed, abandoned or sold (at a steep price) to a tourist who didn't care about these attributes.

Pyrs also bore the ignominy of being dupes for smugglers. These majestic dogs wore a backpack stuffed with contraband, taking it across the border between France and Spain. Their sure-footedness enabled them to take roads impassable to humans, allowing the dogs to avoid detection by customs officials.

Early Pyrenees were brought to the Canadian Maritime Provinces by Basque fishermen and stayed long enough to mix their genes with local retrievers, creating a genetic base for the Newfoundland and Landseer. General Lafayette sent two of these dogs to a writer friend in America, touting the Pyrs' expertise in flock guarding.

The early 20th century found these dogs nearly extinct. Bernard Senac-Lagrange, a French aristocrat and well-known dog authority, can be credited with saving the breed. He consolidated various factions, went into the mountains to obtain good specimens and created the first written standard.

Imported into America soon after Lagrange's time, the Pyr achieved AKC recognition in 1933. During World War II, the breed carried messages and packs for the French troops. In America, deemed too large for military service, they were trained for pack work designed for an Alaskan campaign, if such a service was needed. When this idea was discarded, the Pyrs were "honorably discharged."

This lovely show dog has been sweetened considerably in temperament from the strong guarding dogs of the mountains, and has become one of the gentle giants. Specimens hailing directly from the Pyrenees may still have more of the typical independence and wariness.

Great Pyrenees.

Above: The Great Pyrenees, illustrated here with a young lamb, is a reliable and talented flock guard. **Below:** Great Pyrenees.

There is no need to feel that the breed has been ruined by exhibition, however. Because of his greater availability and higher profile, he is one of the breeds most commonly (and successfully) called upon for predator control. Farmers or ranchers introduce the puppy to the flock very early. By the time the pups are six months old, they are usually fully bonded to the sheep and are beginning to protect them. This breed does well with all livestock and with other dogs.

Pyrs have double dewclaws on the hind feet. A consistent regime of grooming is necessary to keep the dog shiny, unmatted and healthy. They are loving and protective of their home and family and need to be a part of activities. Lagrange said, "Only the true breed possesses this bewitching, almost indefinable expression in the eyes, both distant and caressing, contemplative and just a little sad. As you look in these eyes the immense moral value of the breed pierces your soul."

Above: Great Pyrenees puppies posing over mountainous terrain. **Below:** Body study of the Great Pyrenees—more commonly in Europe do beige patches appear on the breed's head and body.

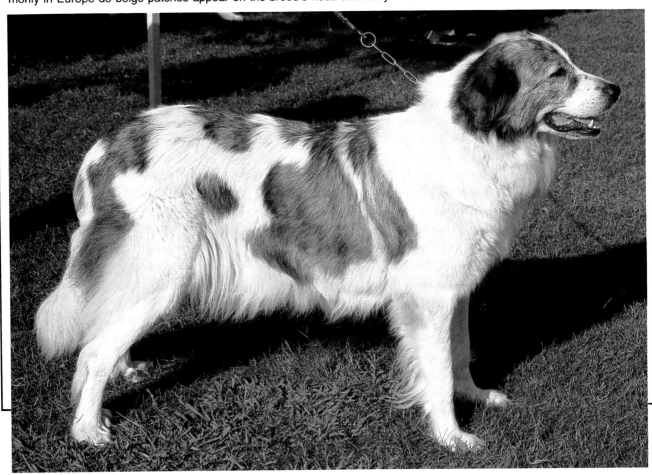

GREEK HAREHOUND

COUNTRY: Greece
WEIGHT: 38–44 pounds
HEIGHT: 18½–21½ inches
COAT: Very short; thick, a little coarse
COLOR: Black and tan saddled, with a white spot on chest allowed
OTHER NAMES: Hellinikos Ichnilatis, Hellenic Hound
REGISTRY: FCI
GROUP: Hound

Greek Harehound.

The native hound of Greece is very similar to the Yugoslavian Balkan Hound. Southern Yugoslavia borders on the north of Greece and forms the western edge of the Balkan Peninsula. The two breeds probably had similar origins or are actually two strains that have developed from the same ancient breed.

Although renowned locally for his skilled nose and resonant voice, the Greek dog is known only in his native land. Formal dog breeding and exhibiting is limited in Greece, but this type of hound has remained pure because of his abilities. Used especially over the rocky terrain so prevalent in his homeland, he is hunted singly, in pairs or in small packs.

Greek Sheepdog.

GREEK SHEEPDOG

COUNTRY: Greece
WEIGHT: 80–90 pounds
HEIGHT: 26 inches
COAT: Thick, dense
COLOR: White
GROUP: Flock Guard

Greece, just across the isthmus from Turkey, probably acquired its flock guards with early migrations of people to the West. These dogs have been used throughout Greece, particularly around the northern provinces in the Balkan foothills.

Said to look much like the Maremma or the Kuvasz, the breed is renowned for its ferocity. The dogs occasionally took it upon themselves to protect the whole countryside. A heavy log or other object attached to the collar curbed this zealotry. People walking in rural areas—sometimes even the shepherds—armed themselves with stout sticks or a pocketful of rocks.

According to Hughes, "Travels in Greece" (1800s), a traveler tells how he "was attacked by one of those fierce . . . dogs which shepherds use to protect their flocks. He flew at my horse's heels. I had to wheel the horse and discharge my fowling piece over his head."

Shepherds of the old school felt cropping the right ear improved the dog's hearing. This practice caused a peculiar lopsided look with a short stub on the right and a drop ear on the left.

Since there are no kennel clubs in Greece and few dogs are raised for pleasure, it is difficult to know the modern status of this ancient breed. They have never been introduced to any other country, but the great white dogs are still used by Greek shepherds. They breed them in the practical sense; best worker to best worker, with little regard for "fine points." But the type has remained pure. Modern Greek cynologists lament the fact that many Greeks feel imported breeds such as Dobermans and Rottweilers create more snob appeal and status that the native breeds.

GREENLAND DOG

COUNTRY: Scandinavian countries
WEIGHT: 66 pounds and up
HEIGHT: 24 inches
COAT: Medium, dense, stand-off
COLOR: Any color allowed, except albino
OTHER NAMES: Grønlandshund
REGISTRY: FCI
GROUP: Northern

The Greenland Dog is closely related to other northern hauling huskies. At one time, there were dozens of breeds and varieties, but many have disappeared due to modern use of snowmobiles and other machinery, which has supplanted the use of these dogs. Much crossing of types occurred as the modern settling of northern areas provided contact between previously remote areas. The Grønlandshund is one of the breeds saved and fostered by fanciers, especially in the Scandinavian countries. Sadly, the breed is no longer numerous even in its native environment.

Before use of the more recent method of chaining sled dogs when not working, the practice among the natives was to keep them tethered with thongs of seal hide. Of course, dogs chewed through their ties, so most working sled dogs had their incisors broken (the small cutting teeth in the front of the canines), which necessitated cutting their meat. Since most of the dogs were fed frozen meat or fish, the rations were chopped into small pieces which could be swallowed whole. In *The Voyage of the Fox*, McClintock recalls how he once cut 65 pounds of seal meat into small pieces, and his 29 hungry Eskimo dogs devoured every morsel in 42 seconds!

Greenland Dogs were also used by the natives as hunting dogs, utilizing their keen sense of smell to find seals' breathing holes in the ice. Once the hole was found, the dog and master sat back to wait, as sooner or later the seal came up for air and it would be speared. In the summer months, the dogs carried backpacks of supplies up to 33 pounds.

The breed remains principally a working dog. They have the typical, Nordic, good, loyal, affectionate temperament, but when the dogs work in teams, they don't have the opportunity to develop a relationship with one master. They are independent and self-willed, and rowdy and boisterous in their play. The thick, stand-off outer coat and dense underwool allow them to withstand constant outdoor living in temperatures that can reach -50 or even -75 degrees Fahrenheit.

Greenland Dog, fawn.

Above: Greenland Dogs pictured working on a snow-covered landscape in their homeland. **Below:** Greenland Dog.

472

Greenland Dog.

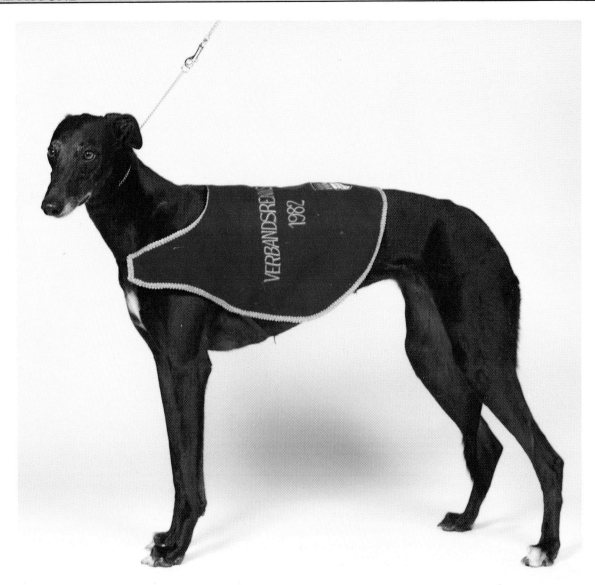

Greyhound.

GREYHOUND

COUNTRY: Great Britain
WEIGHT: 60–70 pounds
HEIGHT: 27–30 inches
COAT: Short, smooth
COLOR: Any color
REGISTRY: FCI, AKC, TKC, CKC
GROUP: Southern

> Heded like a Snake and necked like a
>   Drake.
> Foted like a Kat. Tayled like a Rat.
> Syded lyke a Teme.Chyned like a Beme.
>   *Boke of St. Albans,*Dame Berners, 1486

Edward, Duke of York, described the Greyhound in *The Master of Game* as "shuldres as a roe buck; the for legges stregth and grete ynow, and nought to hind legges; the feet straight and round as a catte, and great cleas, the boones and joyntes of the cheyne grete and hard as the cheyne of an hert; the thighs great and squarred as an hare, the houghs streight, and not crompying as an oxe."

This "duke's" mixture portrayed the sleek, muscled and racy Greyhound, admired for its speed for thousands of years. Tombs of Egypt from the Fourth dynasty, between 4000 and 3500 BC, show drawings of dogs similar to Greyhounds and Salukis, making it obvious that dogs of this type were much esteemed during this era. During the ensuing centuries, Greyhounds proved to be in great demand as an item of barter, and spread through the Near East and Europe. They were developed to standard in England, where they became a status symbol. A Welsh proverb states, "You may know a gentlemen by his horse, his hawk and his greyhound."

The source of the Greyhound name is accredited to various plausibilities: from as simple an explanation as the breed's early colors or the Latin word *gradus*, i.e., swiftness; to the Old English *grech* or *greg* meaning dog; or a corruption of "gazehound" or "great hound."

The dog was a favorite of English nobility, who limited ownership by the common folk under the *Laws of Canute* formulated in 1016: "No mean person may keepe any greyhounds, but freemen may keepe greyhounds so that their knees be cut before the verderors of the forest, and without cutting of their knees also, if he does abide 10 miles from the bounds of the forest." In wide flat expanses, a hunter was handicapped—no brushy forest to conceal the human presence or to hamper the animal as it attempted to bolt. With its powerful eyesight and great speed enabling him to overtake the quarry, the Greyhound proved an invaluable

Greyhound, brindle.

475

Greyhounds, fawn.

aid. One of them, "Bang" by name, jumped an astounding 30 feet while coursing a hare.

When dogs became more than a means to a full cooking pot, the Greyhound excelled in coursing, and later track racing, hitting a speed of nearly 45½ mph, maintaining its reputation as the fastest dog on earth. Only the cheetah tops him for speed in the animal world. His track abilities have given him an advantage over all other breeds. The racing Greyhound is the only recognized breed in America not afflicted with the curse of hip dysplasia. Several Greyhounds made their fame and their masters' fortune on the track, some winning as much as $50,000 during their racing peak. The sale of one dog, "Indian Joe," copped the biggest price in dogdom: $72,000.

"In 1867 a shiftless tenant of an Irish nobleman was sleeping off the effects of a drunken spree on the banks of a stream running through the estate when he heard muffled cries coming from a sack caught on the root of a rotting stump. Staggering to the stream's edge the tenant drew from the water a half-drowned Greyhound puppy. When grown this puppy . . . became the most famous of all racing greyhounds—Master McGrath . . . defeated but once in his entire racing career, and then only because he fell through the ice of a frozen stream during a course."

Modern Greyhounds make gentle, well-behaved, graceful pets, elegant show dogs or thrilling competitors. They are affectionate with their families and, like many sighthounds, aloof with strangers. An interesting piece of trivia is that a Greyhound named "Low Pressure" has the distinction of being the most prolific dog. During his eight-year breeding span, he sired 2,414 registered pups, with another 600 unregistered!

Greyhound, brindle with white.

Griffon Nivernais, blue-gray.

GRIFFON NIVERNAIS

COUNTRY: France
WEIGHT: 50–55 pounds
HEIGHT: 21-24½ inches
COAT: Long, hard, rough and bushy
COLOR: Preferably blue-gray, dark gray or wolf gray; roan, black/tan, tawny rarely seen
REGISTRY: FCI
GROUP: Hound

One of the oldest of the French hounds, the Griffon Nivernais originated in the Nivernais district of central France, just south of Paris. The genesis of the wire-coated hounds is un-known, although crosses to the Phoenician sighthound types could have introduced the wire gene. Shaggy coats were also exhibited by the Eastern-type herding or water dogs so these, too, could have been the source of the rough jacket. Whatever the origin, the wire coats furnished protection from the brush and rocky terrain. The bristly beard, mustache and body coat give the wire coats an unkempt, "devil-may-care" appearance.

The Nivernais can be traced back as far as the 1200s, when they were called the *Chien Gris de St. Louis* (St. Louis's Gray Dogs) as the favorites of Louis IX. These gray dogs probably came from the Balkans after the fourth Crusade. At home they were refined with crosses to other hounds. They remained in good standing, as they were also favored by the Sun King, Louis XIV, nearly 400 years later.

The breed was originally bred for hunting boar and wolves in packs and was the forerunner of many other scenthounds. Hunts, embellished with trumpeters and liveried beaters, involved hundreds of these hounds. These celebrated Nivernais packs were scattered following the Revolution. More than 100 years later, many dog lovers feared the noble Nivernais was gone forever, but a club founded in 1900 managed to gather remaining specimens and worked to restore the breed. Called *Chien de Pays*, meaning a local breed or native dog at home, he has made a comeback.

The breed is now used for smaller game and is particularly prized by "Sunday hunters" because of its ease of care, willingness to work and adaptability to any terrain including water. His expression should be "a little sad," but he should never be timid. The standard also demands a dog that is "simple and hardy," built for long hours of hard work rather than speed. Therefore the weekend hunter, who must follow the dog on foot, has a hunting companion that meets those needs. Four or five *barbouillards*, (nickname for the breed, meaning dirty and besmirched), are claimed to be better than a dozen hounds of other breeds. He is now utilized throughout France and has been exported to several countries, including Greece, as well as the United States and Canada, where he is used to hunt bear.

Above: A pack of Griffon Nivernais pictured with their masters in front of a castle in their native France. **Below:** Body study of the Griffon Nivernais.

479

GRIFFONS VENDEENS

Grand Griffon Vendeen

COUNTRY: France
WEIGHT: 66–77 pounds
HEIGHT: Minimum 23½ inches, larger
preferred
COAT: 1¼–2½ inches, hard and rough; never
soft
COLOR: Various shades of orange, gray, tawny,
or black/tan, usually as spots on white
background
OTHER NAMES: Large Vendeen Griffon
REGISTRY: FCI
GROUP: Hound

Grand Basset Griffon Vendeen

COUNTRY: France
WEIGHT: 40–44 pounds
HEIGHT: 15–16½ inches
COAT: 1¼–2½ inches, hard and rough; never
soft
COLOR: Various shades of orange, gray, tawny,
or black/tan, usually as spots on white
background
OTHER NAMES: Large Vendeen Basset
REGISTRY: FCI
GROUP: Hound

Briquet Griffon Vendeen

COUNTRY: France
WEIGHT: 35–53 pounds
HEIGHT: 20–22 inches
COAT: 1¼–2½ inches, hard and rough; never
soft
COLOR: Various shades of orange, gray, tawny,
or black/tan, usually as spots on white
background
OTHER NAMES: Medium Vendeen Griffon
REGISTRY: FCI
GROUP: Hound

Petit Basset Griffon Vendeen

COUNTRY: France
WEIGHT: 25–35 pounds
HEIGHT: 13–15 inches
COAT: 1¼–2½ inches, hard and rough; never
soft
COLOR: Various shades of orange, gray, tawny,
or black/tan, usually as spots on white
background
OTHER NAMES: Small Vendeen Basset
REGISTRY: FCI, TKC, CKC
GROUP: Hound

Grand Basset Griffon Vendeen, black/tan.

La Vendee is a district on the western coast of France, south of Brittany. The hounds of Vendee are some of the oldest varieties, bred directly from the white Southern Hound with crosses to rough-coated dogs reportedly from Italy. Crosses also occurred to the Griffon Nivernais. One of the first breeders was a king's recorder (clerk) in the 15th century. Clerk in French is *greffier*, and the reference to the "greffier's dogs" gradually became "griffon." The name was first used to describe these breeds and later to indicate many of the wire-coated hunting dogs. Several griffons were given to King Louis XII, bringing him much pleasure. In fact, the breed was once called *Chiens Blancs du Roi* or the King's White Hounds.

The French Revolution nearly sounded the death knell for these breeds, but they were fostered and revitalized by devoted breeders in the 20th century with the first club forming in 1907. The large (Grand) size was originally used in packs for big game such as boar and wolf. They were noted for their stamina and courage. The Grand is still a passionate and persistent hunter.

But hunting land in France, as in much of the world, is becoming restricted and is decreasing. This leaves a limited environment for the Grand, whose style is to follow the quarry for many hours. This variety is the rarest of the hunting Vendeens, and owners voice concern about "a dark future for this breed." Enthusiasts hope that more serious breeders will take up the banner of this old hound. One breeder in America has imported stock and is working to establish these dogs.

Briquet is the French term for a smaller hound used for hare coursing, and the Briquet version of the Vendeen Hound is just a slightly smaller variety. He is used today in small packs or singly as a personal hunting dog, literally beating the bushes for all types of game. Not a commonplace dog either, he has a wider appeal as a single hunter's dog, so is less likely to face extinction than the Grand.

There are two *Basset*, or short-legged, varieties of the Vendeen Griffons. The two sizes originally occurred even in the same litters, and interbreeding was allowed. It was 1950 before the Petit was given separate status, and 25 years later that crossing of the two sizes was forbid-

Petit Basset Griffon Vendeen, tawny.

den. These short-legged Bassets were ideal for the Vendee landscape, which is heavily interspaced with hedges and roads, making winter passage impossible on horseback. Hare-coursing is done on foot, and hounds that stayed close to the hunters were in demand. In both the large and small Basset varieties, the body retains its full size with only the legs being shortened by the dwarf mutation. In France and elsewhere the Vendeen Bassets are still used individually or in packs for hunting all sorts of quarry, including deer and wild boar, as well as smaller furred and feathered game.

Because of its extroverted, lively nature and jaunty expression, the Petit Basset has won some degree of popularity as a companion dog. Petit Basset Griffon Vendeens (often called *PeeBee-GeeVees* or just Petits in America to put a handle on their tongue-twister name) have been granted recognition in Canada, and there are a good number in the USA, including some hunt

A hunting pack of Grand Griffons Vendeens on lead with master.

packs. A PBGV baby, "Alexander," created a minor sensation by winning Best Puppy at the acclaimed 1983 Professional Handler's Super Match before most of America knew what the breed was. An American organization is fostering this breed, and their proponents hope for AKC recognition in the near future. Affectionately called Roughies in England and Griffons in Denmark, in French speaking countries they are still called PetitBassetGriffonVendeen, fluently rolled out as if it were all one word!

All these varieties are classic French hounds clad in a rough jacket, with lean heads and long folded ears. A lack of excessive loose skin, and the high-set, proudly carried saber tail completes the picture. The coat is medium length, rough and wiry, with plenty of undercoat for protection. It is not as long and shaggy as the Griffon Nivernais and is never trimmed, even for exhibition.

Although black/tan tricolors are allowed by the standard, the more commonly seen brighter shades of red, orange or tawny with the predominance of white sets these dogs apart from many hounds. The Grand Basset always has straight (albeit short) legs, while the Petit's legs may be either straight or a bit bowed.

Vendeens, like most scenthounds, are vocal when hot on a scent. Hunting is instinctive. So is digging. Non-hunters should be aware of these inclinations, never leaving these hounds loose—or they will be gone, over hill and dale!

All of the sizes are energetic, independent and—breeders warn—not naturally obedient. They must be taught control and be made to understand who is "top dog" from the beginning. Once that obstacle is overcome, they are nonstop tail waggers who win hearts wherever they go.

Above Left: Grand Griffon Vendeen, orange. **Above Right:** Briquet Griffon Vendeen, orange. **Below:** Petit Basset Griffon Vendeen, dark tawny.

483

Above: Petit Basset Griffon Vendeen, pups. **Below:** Grand Griffon Vendeen, orange.

Above: Petit Basset Griffon Vendeen. **Below:** Briquet Griffon Vendeen, orange.

Haldenstövare.

HALDENSTÖVARE

COUNTRY: Norway
WEIGHT: 44–55 pounds
HEIGHT: 19½–23½ inches
COAT: Short, shiny and dense
COLOR: Tricolor, with white predominating
OTHER NAMES: Halden Hound
REGISTRY: FCI
GROUP: Hound

Norwegian scenthounds have been popular hunting dogs in their native land since the 1800s, but have never gained a following elsewhere. The Haldenstövare was named after the town of Halden, where the breed was developed from indigenous hounds and foxhounds. A graceful and rather lightweight hunter, he is used especially for fast chases over wide open spaces—even in snow.

He has a clean, dry head and neck without excess skin, and moderately long ears that reach the middle of the muzzle when pulled forward. The body should give the impression of supple power, with a deep chest and ribs carried well back, wide muscular loin and straight, strongly boned legs. Feet are particularly important because of the terrain he must hunt. Toes are high and tight but long enough to grip the snow, and there must be dense hair between the toes for protection. In color, the white must predominate. Black patches occur on the head and body, and the tan is limited to the spots above the eyes, on the cheeks, legs and breast, and under the ears and vent. Color is quite important in this breed, since the predominantly white hound is distinctly different from most of the darker hued Scandinavian stövare.

Although a fine hunter, numbers of this native Norwegian hound are limited. Because of their relative scarcity, promoters warn that great care must be used in breeding programs to prevent various inheritable defects.

HAMILTONSTÖVARE

COUNTRY: Sweden
WEIGHT: 50–60 pounds
HEIGHT: 18–23½ inches
COAT: Short; very thick with lots of undercoat in the winter
COLOR: Tricolor: golden tan with black mantle, white on breast, muzzle, on feet and tip of tail; a partial collar is now permitted. No color should predominate.
OTHER NAMES: Hamilton Hound
REGISTRY: FCI, TKC
GROUP: Hound

About 100 years ago, Count A.P. Hamilton created the breed that carries his name. The Count was the founder of the Swedish Kennel Club and a connoisseur of hounds. His dog and bitch, "Pang" and "Stella," were basically of English Foxhound and/or Harrier breeding. Hamilton imported German hounds, like those of Hanover, Holstein and Curlandia, to cross with his British-bred dogs. From these hybrids came the Hamiltonstövare. Today it is a favored hunting dog in Sweden. Since 1968, a few have been imported into Britain, where they are slowly gaining a pawhold.

The Hamilton is always hunted singly, like the brackes of Germany. He accompanies the hunting parties into the vast Swedish pine forests, where he finds and flushes game back towards the guns, baying to indicate his whereabouts. Also adapted to snow cover, he is robust enough to trail large game.

His temperament is sweet and gentle, and he fits well into family life. However, the hunting instincts are strong and the need for activity is great. Those two factors must be kept in mind by prospective owners. Large space is necessary for long walks. Owners warn that, even when well trained, these dogs should be kept on leash in areas with game, as hunting instincts may override training. Once off on a scent, they will hunt for hours before returning to their original starting point, working up a hearty appetite. Owners describe them as real "chow hounds." But if enough physical activity is provided, these hounds are happy, bouncy and extroverted pals which relate well to people and other animals.

The Hamiltonstövare is popular enough in Sweden to be a part of the nation's folklore. A small elf, Tomten, is said to help Swedish homemakers in the house. He is accompanied by a Hamilton called "Karo."

Hamiltonstövare.

HANOVERIAN HOUND

COUNTRY: Germany
WEIGHT: 84–99 pounds
HEIGHT: 20–24 inches
COAT: Short, thick and shiny
COLOR: Light to dark red, more or less dark-streaked; face with or without dark mask
OTHER NAMES: Hannoverscher Schweisshund
REGISTRY: FCI
GROUP: Hound

Schweisshund literally means bloodhound, which is a generic term for a dog, such as the Hanoverian or Bavarian, that follows a bloodtrail. When large game is wounded during a hunt, it may travel many miles in heavy cover only to hide and die a long, slow death. The development of dogs for trailing the wounded animal are common on the Continent. The honor code of the German hunter demands an obligation to find all shot game—dead or wounded. A deer injured with an arrow or bullet may leave only occasional drops of blood many yards apart. The dogs, although brought in even hours later, can follow the cold trail for many miles and lead the hunter to the wounded animal. Sometimes the search goes on for days, but it is never abandoned until the wounded animal is found, dead or alive. This sort of hunting, actually trailing, is not often employed in the USA. It requires a dog with an excellent cold nose and great cold-trailing ability.

The Hanoverian was developed in the 19th century by gamekeepers around the city of Hanover in Upper Saxony, including the central plains of Germany. The breed fathers started with heavy tracking hounds known since the fifth century, like the Solling-Leitbracke, which was a close kin to the St. Hubert and other hounds of the Segusian type. These were crossed with lighter type Celtic Bracken, such as the Haidbracke and hounds from the Harz to create the modern form.

The Hanoverian is specifically a big-game tracking and trailing dog of superb nose, although quite slow on the move. His body is low on leg and heavy for his height. He carries some flew, but his hallmark is the huge stiff ear set rather high on the head. The Hanoverian has the marvelous nose necessary for bloodtrailing, and he is also an able assistant on live game. Although hunted in packs long ago, he is now usually worked singly. His blood flows in the veins of many of the European utility gun dogs, which is where these latter dogs inherited their nose, tracking ability and perseverance.

The Hanoverian is valued beyond rubies by gamekeepers and forest wardens. Even though gun dogs like the German Shorthair are trained to bloodtrail, if these non-specialists fail to find a wounded animal, the Hanoverian may be brought in—sometimes days later—and put on the trail. No wounded animal is left to waste in the forest.

One current German forester proudly tells of starting his Hanoverian on a track more than a week old. Over several days, they followed the trail 30 miles, finally successfully finding the quarry.

These dogs are calm, quiet, poised and very attached to their master and family. But when hunting, they are "hard, single-minded and persistent." They are highly specialized and must be worked steadily to bring out the best of their talents. Thus, they are not dogs for the casual hunter. Most are owned and utilized by foresters and game wardens.

Hanoverian Hound, brindle.

Above: Hanoverian Hound, red. **Below:** Hanoverian Hound.

HARLEQUIN PINSCHER

COUNTRY: Germany
WEIGHT: 22–26 pounds
HEIGHT: 12–14 inches
COAT: Short and smooth
COLOR: Variations of harlequin (merle blotching on either white or black)
OTHER NAMES: Harlekinpinscher
REGISTRY: FCI
GROUP: Terrier

The Harlequin Pinscher was selected from smaller specimens of the German Pinscher, specifically for the merle color. Since the merle gene is dominant and it is a color unknown in other terriers, a cross to another group is likely to have introduced this hue. Merle dogs show a preponderance of white, and many German breeders felt lack of pigment tended to introduce a multitude of problems. Thus the Pinscher-Schnauzer Club denigrated this variety and refused to recognize them.

Fanciers claimed the breed had outstanding temperament and made an ideal companion that thrived on indoor life. These factors suggest that small herding dogs, like the Sheltie or Berger de Pyrenees, may have contributed to the breed, introducing both the merle color and a more gentle personality. Hounds offer other possibilities, such as dappled Dachshunds. The Harlequin Pinscher is most likely now extinct. No formal registrations have been made since the 1930s, but there is some talk of a revival in the offing.

Harlequin Pinscher.

HARRIER

COUNTRY: Great Britain
WEIGHT: 48–60 pounds
HEIGHT: 19–22 inches
COAT: Short, coarse and hard
COLOR: Any hound color including blues
REGISTRY: FCI, AKC, CKC
GROUP: Hound

Harrier, brown and white, saddled.

The Harrier is, in actuality, a perfect small version of an English Foxhound: crosses of various old-style, heavy scenthounds with lighter, smaller hounds, such as the Beagle, with a dash of this 'n that. These dogs are the same in form and ability, and developed directly from the same stock that created the larger hound. Records show an established pack of Harriers was owned by Sir Elias de Midhope as early as 1260. The Cotley Pack of Somerset was organized by Thomas Deane in 1796, with many Harriers brought to the "colonies" during that time. Their original capacity was for following the large, slower European hare in front of their masters who hunted on foot. Later hunters on horseback followed the packs.

Like the English Foxhound, most Harriers were raised by specialized hunt clubs for use by their members. Many of these packs were renowned, their fame continuing for several generations. The Quarme Harriers, which have a distinctive pale color, were disbanded following the last World War, after a long and illustrious history. The Minehead Harriers still hunt in the County of Somerset. Other packs have been bred and hunted continuously for more than a hundred years. Pack Harriers in England are registered and regulated by the Association of Masters of Harriers and Beagles. This group's stud books have two sections—one for the English Harrier and one for the West Country Harrier, recognizing differences in type.

The sport of hound trailing is very popular in the Lake district and the area bordering England and Scotland. The hounds, following a drag track, are run for speed only; the first one arriving at the finish line is declared the winner. Since the sport attracts as much betting as the racing dog tracks, formal rules and regulations have been passed. For this activity, they use crossbred hounds that are basically Harrier, but with various surreptitious additions to create the necessary speed.

Harriers as a pure breed have subsisted in the United States although never in large numbers. If pack raised they are more dog-oriented, like the Foxhound. When reared in individual homes, they are like any other hound. The dogs are gentle, never biting nor snapping. Grooming is minimal, and they are healthy and hardy souls.

The hound stubbornness and single-mindedness do require firm, early discipline. A basic obedience course is recommended for any Harrier, even if the owner does not plan to pursue exhibiting in that arena. Training helps establish the proper relationship of who gives the orders.

This breed is a rough-and-tumble, independent lot, perfect for the family that works hard and plays hard. The Harrier thrives without pampering, and does well if the family is gone all day. Exercise is a must, however, making this dog an excellent companion for long hikes, bike rides or horseback jaunts.

491

HAVANESE

COUNTRY: Cuba
WEIGHT: 7–12 pounds
HEIGHT: 8–10½ inches
COAT: Profuse, wavy to curly, double-coated
COLOR: Wide variety of colors or color combinations
OTHER NAMES: Bichon Havanais, Havana Silk Dog
REGISTRY: FCI
GROUP: Gun Dog

These charmers descended from bichon types of the Old World, but there is some argument about which specific type was the origin. Most researchers say they came with the Spanish as they colonized the West Indies, which would probably point to Tenerife and the Bichon Frise as the progenitors. But Cubans seem to feel the dog originally came to their island with Italian sea captains, thus pointing to Malta or Bologna as the source. Captains often carried illegal contraband to be sold to wealthy Cuban families. "Hence, the entree gift of one of these precious little dogs to the wealthy Señoras [*sic*] opened the doors of her home to them."

The Havanese was soon a favorite of the very wealthy, and a frequent sight in the palaces and country estates. Catalina Laza, the wife of a wealthy Cuban sugar mill baron, raised the dogs for her own pleasure and to present to society friends. When the Cuban Revolution threatened the existence of these dogs and their owners, they were smuggled out by families fleeing their homeland. Quite rare today, they are now being revived and promoted by fanciers in the USA who have formed the Havanese Club of America.

Temperament for this breed is similar to all its bichon cousins—charming, intelligent and alert. Adults can be aloof with strangers. The Havanese has been known to guard children heroically and is a loving and devoted companion. Natural clowns, they are superb circus and trick dogs. Like the Bolognese, they make good watchdogs because of their alert demeanor and close relationship with their owners. One owner says they are "fantastic little friends." Their sturdiness and longevity make extra pluses as companions and their brilliance of colors, including cream, gold, silver, blue, black, chocolate (appropriately called "tobacco brown"), the rare white, or combinations of these adds to their appeal. Modern show dogs are kept free of tangles, but any trimming, fussing or coiffing is prohibited.

Havanese, white.

Above Left: Havanese, pup. **Above Right and Below:** Havaneses.

HAWAIIAN POI DOG

COUNTRY: USA
COAT: Short
COLOR: Variety
OTHER NAMES: Ilio
REGISTRY: None
GROUP: Southern

Pariah dogs came to Hawaii with the Polynesians during the first settlement more than 1,000 years ago. The dogs came under the care of the women and children, with a pup sometimes given as a present to an infant at birth. Nursing from the baby's mother supposedly gave the dog a protective instinct. If the child died, the dog was killed and buried with his tiny master. If,

Hawaiian Poi Dog, white.

as was often the case, the canine predeceased his young owner, his teeth were pulled and given to the child to wear as a necklace, continuing the "protection."

Unfortunately for the Poi Dog, writer Elinor Dewire observes, the island's people "made no distinction between the enjoyment of an animal's consumption and its companionship." Dogs played with during the day were fed as a delicacy to visiting chieftains and royalty that same night. The dogs were fed *poi* (a paste made from ground, baked and fermented taro root) to fatten them for eating.

Their vegetarian diet over a long period of time resulted in a change in the bones of their heads. The heads became large and flat, due to the disuse of the bones from a lack of chewing.

Not used for any purpose but to be eaten, the Poi Dogs gradually evolved into small, lazy animals, waddling around with distended bellies and shortened legs. These pariah types never reverted to the feral state, since the Hawaiian habitat was not suited to that lifestyle. Besides they probably were too lazy to bother scrounging for food when they could become fat on human handouts! They grew to be slow, lazy and dull witted, much like a slug in mind and body.

On one of his explorations in 1779, Captain James Cook described them, when he said the Poi Dogs seldom barked, came in many colors and ran with the hogs (which also held the dual role of pet/pork chop).

Early in the 19th century, other dogs had so intermingled with the Poi Dog that it was no longer pure. Years later two men conducted a breeding program at the Honolulu Zoo, attempting to reconstruct the breed. After 12 years, it was deemed to be a failure and the experiment was discontinued, and another breed was lost to the world of dogs.

HERTHA POINTER

COUNTRY: Denmark
WEIGHT: 45–60 pounds
HEIGHT: 23–25½ inches
COAT: Short and fine
COLOR: Yellow-orange; with small white markings on feet, tail tip, chest and muzzle
GROUP: Gun Dog

When the war between Germany and Denmark ended, the defeated Danish soldiers made their way home. Accompanying one group of veterans in 1864 was an orange-red pointer-type bitch. No one knew her origin or how she came to join the men, but they named her "Hertha" and she proved to be a fine gun dog. A sportsman bought her and presented her as a gift to his friend, a well-known hunter and supervisor in one of the great state forests of Jutland.

The island of Als has long been a political football for Denmark because of its position in the south of Jutland near the border of Germany. During the monarchy, the Dukes of Augustenborg made their home on this island. At the time of the Danish-German War, the Duke of Augustenborg was Frederik Christian, pretender to the Danish throne. He was a famous and daring breeder of quality hunting dogs and fine horses, and his kennel of (English) Pointers was renowned. Because of selective inbreeding, his dogs all had a solid orange-red color with distinctive small white markings. Although Hertha was of general gun dog type, she did not particularly possess the English Pointer look. But because of her color, many who saw her thought that she probably came from the Duke's kennels.

Hertha was bred to "Sport," who *was* a Pointer from the Duke's breeding, and the results of this pairing were the wellspring of the Hertha Pointer breed. For many years, hunters fostered the "Hertha dog" or "Hertha hound." Soon a breed club was formed, predating the Danish Kennel Club by 54 years (they changed the name to Hertha Pointer, which may have been an unforeseen mistake), and these dogs became common throughout Denmark. A standard has been in effect since 1897, and photos and description were included in the 1902 edition of Henri de Bylandt's book *Les Races de Chien.*

Hertha Pointer.

From this long history of breeding true to type, with pedigrees going back 123 years, the breed is as yet having a difficult time being accepted and recognized by the central canine authorities. The Pointer Club of Denmark and the Danish Kennel Club's official position is that the Hertha Pointer is merely a color variant of the English Pointer. In 1982 the Hertha Club was bitterly disappointed that, despite providing proof of what they felt were the criteria for what constitutes a breed, their petition for recognition was again denied.

There are perhaps some political stumbling blocks to the official acceptance of the breed. The tag of "Pointer" may have set in many people's minds that the dog *was* a Pointer. Over the years, most kennels that have Pointers have crossed their dogs to Herthas to gain the fine field abilities (Herthas, on the other hand, now are never bred to Pointers!). Therefore, while virtually all Pointers in Denmark today can find a trace of Hertha and Sport in their pedigrees, a multitude of purebred Herthas exist without Pointer blood! If the breed were declared a separate entity, this source of crossing would be closed to the Pointer fanciers, and some feel this is a motive for them to block the separation. The fact that the Duke of Augustenborg turned out to be an enemy of Denmark and lost his

dukedom to the Germans could also be a psychological factor against the breed. These and other problems, not of their own making, led to the creation of a group called the Committee for National and Forgotten Breeds, which fosters native breeds and works for their preservation and recognition. Cynologists everywhere would applaud this idea, which could be copied profitably elsewhere!

At any rate, the number of Herthas continues to climb slowly and their proponents are not daunted in the desire to have their breed recognized. These dogs have bred true for over one hundred years, with their sinewy aloofness and their distinctive color pattern. They are moderately sized, extremely athletic gun dogs with fine natural field abilities. The limited white markings remind one somewhat of those seen on the Perdigueiro Portugueso and, occasionally, the Small French Braque. The Hertha people find the presence of a small white spot on the forehead desirable. Although the standard warns against the purely self-colored individual (with no white), the presence of too much white is equally undesirable and untypical. The authors hope that the descendants of "Old Hertha" will soon find their place among the recognized breeds of the world.

HOVAWART

COUNTRY: Germany
WEIGHT: 65–90 pounds
HEIGHT: 24–28 inches
COAT: Long, thick with only slight wave
COLOR: Black, black/tan, red fawn
REGISTRY: FCI, TKC
GROUP: Herding

Dogs named *Hofewart*, meaning estate dog or farmyard warden, were mentioned and reproduced in documents and pictures since the 13th century. This dog was used to guard the courtyard, and a writer of that era told of his rescue as a baby by a wounded Hovawart. When the family castle was besieged, he was carried by the dog to a neighboring estate.

In those early times, stealing the Hovawart was penalized with a fine and a demand to replace the dog. The fine was higher for a nighttime theft than a day-time one because their worth as guards was so highly valued. The original Hofewart seemed to disappear with the German aristocracy. No mention of the breed was seen in formal dog circles for centuries. The breed reappeared around the turn of this century under the impetus of enthusiast Kurt Konig.

Much controversy exists over whether the 20th-century Hovawart was a "reinvented" breed or a resurrected one. Believers of the reinvention theory state that breeders used Leonbergers, German Shepherds, Newfoundlands, Kuvasz and the semi-wild African veldt dogs to create a tough working breed which looked like the Hofewart of old. It is hard to imagine type being established and dogs breeding true in a short period of time, after this extreme crossbreeding procedure—especially since neither the German Shepherd nor the Leonberger were themselves fixed in type at that time.

The resurrection proponents believe dogs of the old-type Hovawart survived on isolated farms and in remote rural areas of the Harz and Black Forest. These people contend that Konig and his cohorts scoured these areas, acquiring dogs that had the desired looks and temperament. It was these farm dogs that formed the base for the "new" breed.

Whatever the true story, type was well set in the early decades of this century and the German Kennel Club (VDH) recognized the Hovawart in 1937. The War years were hard on the breed. The new beginning of the breed had a tenuous hold, not only because of the cessation of breeding and scarcity of food during those years, but because many of the kennels were

Hovawart, black/tan.

Above: Hovawart, black/tan. **Below:** Tug o' war underway, Hovawart holding his own against worthy opponent.

designated as part of the eastern zone when Germany was divided in 1945. Interested owners reaffirmed their dedication, and the Hovawart—although not in large numbers—now is firmly established in Germany. In the 1960s, breed enthusiasts saw sponsoring organizations formed in Switzerland, the Netherlands, Austria, Denmark, Finland, Sweden and Scotland. Hovawarts were introduced to America in the 1980s.

Characterized as "weatherproof," intelligent, trustworthy and responsive to training, the Hovawart, however, tends to stay puppyish for a long time, and needs patience in training. Bred to protect their home and family, they are void of any hunting or roving tendencies. They work well with livestock in their role as farm dogs. Natural guardians even in puppyhood, the Hovawarts require a dominant hand. Care must be taken to assert the "pack leader" position of the human in this relationship. An aptitude for obedience and schutzhund work is apparent. A "job" and extensive exercise keeps them happy and fit. Hovawarts are good house dogs, being quiet in nature and requiring minimal coat care.

The breed is classified in Europe as a working dog, in the same group as German Shepherds, Boxers, Dobermans, Rottweilers and Giant Schnauzers. The breed organizations are very strict in selecting for good conformation, proper color, sound hips and health, and proper guardian temperament, which includes a gun shyness test. Puppies are guaranteed and German stock is 95-percent free of hip dysplasia.

Hygenhund, red/brown with white.

HYGENHUND

COUNTRY: Norway
WEIGHT: 44–53 pounds
HEIGHT: 18½–23 inches
COAT: Not too short; very dense
COLOR: red/brown or red/yellow, often with black tipping, with or without slight white markings; black/tan, usually with white symmetrical markings; or white with red/brown, red/yellow or black and brown spots and/or ticking
REGISTRY: FCI
GROUP: Hound

Norwegian breeder Hygen created his hound in the late 1800s from German Holsteiner hounds and various other hound breeds. The Hygenhund was bred as an endurance hunter which can go over the arctic snows for long periods without fatigue.

Structurally, they are quite short-coupled with a solid, tight build and no excess skin. Reminiscent of the Swedish Smålandsstövare, the head is a bit shorter and more wedge-shaped than most of the other Scandinavian hounds. In addition, the ears are smaller and higher set, allowing them to stand out slightly from the head instead of hanging straight down. The high-arched toes have plenty of protective hair between them. Tails are rather short, barely reaching to the hock, and carried in a slightly upward curve.

A happy dog, he is a serious hunter with great staying power. Like the Halden Hound, his population is small and strict breeding rules govern his sponsors. The standard warns that the wonderful characteristics of this native Norwegian cannot be retrieved from other breeds if lost, and thus a close eye must be kept on breeding programs to maintain his fine qualities.

IBIZAN HOUND

COUNTRY: Spain
WEIGHT: 42–55 pounds
HEIGHT: 22½–27½ inches
COAT: Shorthaired or wirehaired; short is close and hard, with perhaps a little brush on back of thighs and under tail; wire is hard, coarse, and 1–3 inches long, with a possible generous moustache and longer on back, thighs and tail. Neither coat is preferable to the other.
COLOR: Solid red or lion tawny, solid white or—more usually—a combination of the color with the white, either in a pied or an Irish pattern
OTHER NAMES: Podenco Ibicenco, Ca Eivissencs
REGISTRY: FCI, AKC, TKC, CKC
GROUP: Southern

Ibizan Hound, shorthaired.

In early times, the same ancient Middle Eastern, prick-eared dogs that created the Pharaoh Hound were brought by trading ships to the Balaeric Islands off the coast of Spain. One of these islands, Ibiza, gave this breed its name. Despite their isolated development, far from Malta, the dominance of their ancient characteristics allowed these two independently developed breeds to look very much alike even after many centuries. Ibizan Hounds were said to have ridden atop Hannibal's elephants when he invaded Italy; the fact that this Carthaginian general was actually born on Ibiza gives weight to the story. Ibizan Hounds have been known in their present form on the islands of Ibiza and its neighbor, Formentera, eight miles to the south, for more than 5,000 years.

The Ibizan was welcomed as an admirable hunter of rabbit and other small game on this poor island, where these prizes supplemented the diet of inhabitants whose food was scarce. Owners couldn't afford to feed many puppies, and often the weaker pups and most of the males were drowned in the sea. The survivors were easy keepers who could stay healthy and spirited on a diet of a few fish heads, an occasional bit of goat meat, and whatever game they could scrounge for themselves.

They were also known and worked in the nearby mainland provinces of Catalonia in Spain (where the breed is called in the Catalonian language, *Ca Eivissencs*) and the Provence and Roussillon area of France. Due to a silent style of hunting, the Ibizan or his crosses were often the choice of French poachers, who called him *Charnique* or *Charnegue*. These clandestine activities led to a declaration of this dog being banned in France.

Continuing in this vein as a simple hunting dog brought the Ibizan halfway through the 20th century. At that time, the breed came to the attention of a dog authority and judge from Spain, Doña Maria Dolores Olives de Cotonera, the *Marquesa de Belgida* of Barcelona. She wanted to save this now indigenous Spanish breed. Her kennel, located on the larger Balaeric island of Majorca (Mallorca), soon was producing high quality dogs which she promoted throughout Spain and the Continent. When interest generated in America, she per-in the air from a standstill. In straight-away racing, they have been clocked at 40 mph. The often-seen white mark on the head between the ears is called the "ax mark" and, probably due to an old superstition, is a highly prized characteristic.

Ibizan Hound, wirehaired, white with red.

Ibiizan Hound, shorthaired, white with red.

sonally saw that good quality representatives were sent to begin breeding programs in the USA.

Soon the Ibizan Hound was seen in many countries of the world, as a pet, as an exhibition dog, on race tracks, and in hunting or coursing competitions. In 1958, a special commission from the Egyptian government was sent to Ibiza and Formentera to see examples of the breed and bring specimens to their country. After 5,000 years, the Ibizan Hound returned home!

Their style of hunting utilizes scent and sound (with their huge antennae ears), as well as sight. They can follow their quarry in and out of brush, over walls and through any type of obstacle course. If they lose sight of their prey in heavy cover, they stand on their hind legs to relocate the game. Guns are unnecessary. When hunting to provide food for their masters' table, the Ibizans locate the prey by scent, flush and chase until they catch it and break its neck, then gently retrieve the prize to hand.

The American Kennel Club gave its official sanction to the Ibizan Hound in 1979. Ibizans are extremely hardy and agile. They are capable of jumping great distances both in height and width and can leap six to eight feet straight up

Iceland Dog.

ICELAND DOG

COUNTRY: Iceland
WEIGHT: 20–30 pounds
HEIGHT: 12–16 inches
COAT: Thick, coarse, quite short, stand-off
COLOR: Wheaten, black, wolf sable, "dirty" all-white; often with small symmetrical white markings, sometimes a black mask
OTHER NAMES: Icelandic Sheepdog, Iceland Spitz
REGISTRY: FCI
GROUP: Northern

There is probably no other country that has chronicled its history better than Iceland. The revered *Sagas* tell of Vikings bringing small herding dogs when they colonized Iceland in 880 AD. Actually just a smaller version of the Buhund, the Iceland Dog is directly descended from these dogs.

Pistol, a character in Shakespeare's *Henry IV* (ca. 1600), says, "Pish for thee, Iceland Dog. Thou prick-eared cur of Iceland." Sir Richard Burton wrote *A Summer in Iceland* in 1875, and made note that a good dog equaled the value of one horse. It was said that a dog can find a sheep buried under 11 yards of snow.

Denmark established a written standard for the Iceland Dog in 1898. The breed became rare in its native land after nearly all dogs in Iceland were destroyed by distemper near the end of the last century. In 1928, dog breeding was further curtailed by the ban on all importation of mammals into Iceland. The breed was reconstructed by British and Icelandic breeders by using what stock was left and carefully introducing other Nordic herding dogs. Mrs. Sigridur Petursdottir was instrumental in the revival of the breed, and in 1969, a club was formed to support the Iceland Dog.

The breed is void of hunting instincts, as it was developed exclusively as a herder like the Buhund. Lively, active, and affectionate, he is still developing mentally at 18 months. He needs to have close contact with his humans as well as calm, firm discipline to develop the desirable character. Naturally friendly, they are alert enough to be watchdogs. They have the same cleanliness and easy-care coat of the Buhund and bear the same lack of interest in hunting or wandering.

Iceland Dog.

INCA HAIRLESS DOG

COUNTRY: Peru
WEIGHT: Small 9–18 pounds; medium 18–26 pounds; large 26–55 pounds
HEIGHT: Small 10–16 inches; medium 16–20 inches; large 20–28 inches
COAT: Hairless; short fuzzy hair on top of head, edge of ears, feet and tail
COLOR: Solid dark skin
OTHER NAMES: Peruvian Hairless Dog
REGISTRY: FCI
GROUP: Southern

Hairless dogs have been bred in Peru since the time of the Incan civilizations. But today very few professional breeders of Inca Hairless Dogs live in Peru; only a handful breed dogs according to genetic studies and with careful planning.

Inca Hairless Dog.

Inca Hairless Dog, powderpuff variety.

A few of the Hairless dogs were sent to Germany, where rare breed club members helped the Peruvians draft a standard and obtain FCI recognition in 1985. A few are found in the United States.

Like the Inca Orchids, the Inca Hairless have missing premolars, often causing their tongues to hang out the side of their mouths. They also have the two coat varieties, with the same dominant hairless gene. In fact, owners say that the Peruvian dogs choose their canine friends on the basis of the length of their hair. Unlike their relatives of the night (Orchids), however, they have small eyes "from squinting in the sun."

Appreciation of their warmth was expressed by a peasant owner who said they are "nice to have in bed . . . warm as an oven on a chilly night. They are very clean, and they have no fleas."

They are agile dogs, with a light gait which comes "from centuries of walking the endless coastal sand." Two gaits are seen: the free trot and the restricted front rhythmic movement. Dogs with very straight fronts walk in tiny little steps, giving an impression of the Paso Fino horse.

IRISH RED AND WHITE SETTER

COUNTRY: Ireland
WEIGHT: 40–70 pounds
HEIGHT: 23½–27 inches
COAT: Flat, straight, and slightly coarse, longer for the feathering
COLOR: White ground color with clear red patches, roaning or ticking objectionable—but, if present, a minimum amount on face and below hock and elbow only
REGISTRY: TKC
GROUP: Gun Dog

The red/whites may actually predate the solid reds. The coat of arms of the Irish Nash family bears three red and white setters, and Sir Thomas Staples of County Tyrone and Evans of Gortmerron kept red/whites in the 18th century. Lord Rossmore of Monaghan can boast the same tradition and, indeed, the Red and White is, to this day, occasionally referred to locally as the Rossmore Setter.

Nevertheless, by the turn of the 19th century, while the solid red continued his rise to fame on

Irish Red and White Setter.

Irish Red and White Setter, pup.

both sides of the Atlantic, his spotted brothers retreated to remote areas of Ireland. They never completely disappeared, however. Being a recessive, the spotted dogs can, and still do, occasionally crop up in red litters. A few Irishmen, over the years, preferred to hunt over the more easily seen red/whites. A rare breeder or two also stubbornly continued to foster the type. The Reverend Noble Huston of County Down, Ireland, bred the variety in the early part of this century to keep the red-and-white flame alive.

In the 1940s, a breed club was formed, especially to foster the hunting qualities of the red-white. Shortly after, the Cuddys of County Cork, Ireland, began their interest in the breed; nearly all modern specimens trace their pedigree back to Cuddy dogs. In the early 1970s, the Irish Kennel Club awarded the task of monitoring the present-day revival to the Irish Red Setter Club. They created a committee to monitor all pups prior to registration, because the breed base was so small and crossings to the Red are close up in most pedigrees. From a low of seven registered animals at that time, the "Red-n-White" has begun a slow climb to full recognition. Owners of a red/white litter in Ireland, until recently, had to take them to the breed committee for the approval signature! To the credit of the Red Club and its wholehearted cooperation, the Red and White is now regarded as self-sufficient.

505

IRISH RED AND WHITE SETTER

A dog belonging to the Gormleys of County Dublin was entered at Crufts in 1980, in the "Any Variety Not Separately Classified" class. So unknown was the breed that the show committee tried to switch the entry into the Irish Red Setter class! Full championship status was given to the breed at Crufts in 1987, much to the pride of those who worked so hard for him. A few of the Red-n-Whites have been brought into the United States, where owners formed a breed club and interest is growing.

Character and appearance of the two breeds are very similar, with a few minor exceptions. The Red/Whites have a higher set ear, are a bit shorter, wider and sturdier of body, and have less of the long, heavy feathering. The practical hunter, unlike the show dog enthusiast, finds excessive feathering a bother. The Red/White probably looks very similar to the Irish (Red) Setter of 100 years ago! In temperament, the spotted dogs have "the same joyous exuberance as their Red cousins but are less forthcoming with strangers." Ann Millington interjects that "they are 'thinking' dogs and consider you well before deciding you are worthy of their friendship."

They still make good practical gun dogs and are particularly known for their stamina. Stories such as that of the field trial dog from bygone days, who ran ten miles behind his master's carriage to the trial grounds and then home again at night, are common. Color has to be carefully monitored, and dogs with an excess of ticking (roan, or belton, patterns like the English Setter) are faulted. A note of interest: 150 years ago there was described a third color of Irish Setter, called a "Shower of Hail" Setter, which was an all-over, heavily ticked pattern.

Irish Red and White Setter.

IRISH SETTER

COUNTRY: Ireland
WEIGHT: 60–70 pounds
HEIGHT: 25–27 inches
COAT: Moderately long, flat and straight, with abundant feathering
COLOR: Mahogany or rich chestnut red
OTHER NAMES: Irish Red Setter
REGISTRY: FCI, AKC, UKC, TKC, CKC
GROUP: Gun Dog

Irish Setter.

Setting dogs of both the solid red and the red-white spotted coats have existed in Ireland since the 1700s, when hawking was the fad. Development of a dog for wing shooting was accomplished from existing hawking dogs and other hunting types. The fact that the Celts, who settled Ireland, also populated Brittany is interesting with the existence of red or orange spaniels from the latter area. The Irish state their Setter is pure spaniel, the only setter with no crossing to pointer. Bede Maxwell, author of *The Truth About Sporting Dogs* says, "Irishophiles may prefer to believe their Setter sprung full-formed from among the shamrocks, but history yields no proof of it."

Yet the Irish Setter is physically the most pointerlike (i.e., houndlike) of all the setters. The Celts were famous for their scenthounds as well as their spaniels, so perhaps the crossing was among pure Celtic hounds, instead of the pointer breeds that sprang from them. Throughout the 18th—and for most of the 19th—century, the Setters bred in Ireland were still of both color types. In the late 1800s, several top winners, such as Ch. Palmerston, flaunted the solid red coat, and their popularity increased. When a club was formed for the breed in 1882, it took on the name of The Irish Red Setter Club and, from that time on, the red variety prospered while the red/white declined.

Irish Setters were brought to America in the late 1800s, mainly as gun dogs. They proved most useful, and many early ones were hunted as well as shown. Head types varied greatly, from the "dish" face, mimicking the English Pointer, to the stopless downface, like those found on the best German hounds. But the flashy red-jacketed bodies had great consistency and, as the show fraternity embraced the dashing redhead, they quickly succeeded in fixing head type.

The Red Setter became and has remained popular among both the show fancy and the pet-owning general public, due to his personality as well as his looks. Big, elegant and athletic, with his flowing red coat, and the happy, head-up, tail-wagging attitude, the Irish catches the eye of any judge. And that rollicking devil-may-care personality has captured the hearts of many owners. Like most all sporting dogs, however, he needs plenty of exercise, discipline, and a purpose to prevent his brain from finding other unwelcome activities to relieve his energy and boredom. More and more modern Irish owners and show fanciers are reemphasizing the hunting qualities that sometimes were forgotten in the race to fill the demand for puppies. There are dual champions, with more to come, and other owners are testing their dogs' abilities in non-competitive events like the new AKC hunting tests. The Irish Setter people have likewise used his trainability and verve to advantage in the competitive obedience ring. The breed is a sensitive one, and does not react well to harsh training methods.

Irish Setters.

Irish Setter.

Irish Terrier.

IRISH TERRIER

COUNTRY: Ireland
WEIGHT: 25–27 pounds
HEIGHT: 18 inches
COAT: Harsh, wire, broken coat
COLOR: Red to red wheaten
OTHER NAMES: Irish Red Terrier
REGISTRY: FCI, AKC, TKC, CKC
GROUP: Terrier

Called the Irish Red Terrier in the past to distinguish him from the other native terriers of Erin, this breed may be the oldest on the Isle. Dogs like these were known for centuries and were valuable only to poor Irish farmers with small holdings. Not much was written about them as they were not a dog of the aristocracy, who weren't in as dire need of ratting expertise. The type was descriptively mentioned in the Brehon laws (the earliest Irish legal code, first passed by word-of-mouth and then recorded in early medieval times) as the "dog of the dungheap." The dungheaps were the piles of manure that were inevitable in the farmyards and were breeding grounds for rats.

Dog expert, Stonehenge (J. H. Walsh), writing in 1887, shows his contempt for all things not inherently British with his refusal to believe that the Irish Terrier was a distinct breed from the "old Scotch terrier." But the differences were distinct. The truth might be that the raiding Irish could have introduced the prototype to Scotland many centuries ago. Or perhaps the Celts, who conquered both Scotland and Ireland four centuries before Christ, brought the archetypical terrier with them, and differences developed after that.

Whatever the early history, by the middle of the 1800s, the Irish Terrier, jacketed in black/-tan and brindle as well as the more desirable red, was a common sight. During these years, many of this breed were seen with cropped ears, a sure sign they were used for dog-fighting. The Irish Terrier's punishing jaws bode the end of many an Irish rat. But despite the instincts to destroy vermin, he could be a soft-mouthed retriever and often wore two hats: ratter and hunter. There was still variation in size and type at the breed's debut at an Irish show in 1875. Out of the 50 dogs that strutted the ring, entries included some in the under nine-pound division and one that was over 30 pounds; a pure white entry competed against many that would have passed for Cairns. These differences existed despite the rule that the dogs must have a pedigree to enter. Many had notes attached reading, "Breeding information available at such-and-such an address." The winner, "Boxer" by name, was brazenly labeled as "Bred by owner, pedigree unknown!" This mass confusion prompted the formation of a strong breed club still in existence today.

By the turn of the century, only the red dogs were accepted, type had become fairly well standardized and ear cropping (along with fighting) had been prohibited. The reputation of the breed was made during the First World War when the Irish Terriers were used as messenger dogs. The noise and confusion of trench warfare was no deterrent to the fearless Irisher, and many a soldier owed his life to these dogs.

A taller and racier dog than the Fox Terrier, the Irish still carries plenty of bone and substance. Always good-tempered, affectionate and loyal with his people, the breed should still show the characteristic fire, animation, and "heedless, reckless pluck" that has earned him the nickname daredevil. These dogs exude charm, and their cocksure strut belies the warmth within. They are particularly good with children and are said to be dogs "o'the little people." Writers Dangerfield and Howell, in their *Encyclopedia of Dogs*, noted, "A growing lad could wish no finer friend to grow up with; mischief overlooked by the one will certainly be exploited by the other!"

The Irish was the first native terrier from Ireland given Kennel Club recognition (19th century) and has gained worldwide acceptance since that time.

Irish Terrier.

Irish Water Spaniel.

IRISH WATER SPANIEL

COUNTRY: Ireland
WEIGHT: 45–65 pounds
HEIGHT: 21–24 inches
COAT: Tight, crisp ringlets on body, neck and 2 inches down tail, longer hair with loose curls on legs and topknot; smooth on face, remainder of tail, and back legs below hock
COLOR: Solid liver
REGISTRY: FCI, AKC, UKC, TKC, CKC
GROUP: Gun Dog

The exact origins of this most distinct breed are argued to this day. Several types of water retrievers coexisted in Ireland, but this specific breed appeared in the 1830s, mainly from the kennels of Justin McCarthy. His dog "Boatswain," whelped in 1834, is the acknowledged "sire" of the modern breed. McCarthy never revealed the sources of his breeding, and the Irishman kept his secret to the grave.

An ancestor of McCarthy fought with the Irish Brigade against England in France for Louis XII. Since several stem types have graced France since early times, specimens of the early Barbet/Poodle types could have been brought back to Ireland and later crossed with local Irish or British dogs. But those of the Portuguese Water Dog genus may have also been brought to British and Irish shores with Portuguese sailors. It is known that two types of water spaniels populated the Emerald Isle, the northern variety being small and particolored with a wavy coat. His southern counterpart was larger and sported a curly coat. This latter dog likely contributed to the modern IWS. Controversy notwithstanding, it is known he is from water dog stock and that his distinctive type, with high-held head and tail, long thighs and low hocks, and smooth tail, was fixed early.

Remarkably similar to the dogs of 150 years ago, he remains a popular working and show dog in his native Ireland. Although recognized in the USA since 1878 and supported by an active breed club, he is few in number. The breed was appreciated by hunters of waterfowl, who supplied American tables with various delicacies and who admired the breed's qualities of diligently working long hours day after day. The terrain and cover in Ireland were similar to those housing waterfowl in America, enabling the dog to do well in marshy bogs and making him a logical choice for the serious gunner.

He is a quality retriever in any cover and for a variety of game, but his real skills are seen in water, even in currents, where he is a strong swimmer and often dives to go after wounded ducks. His expertise lies in retrieving wounded fowl, which might otherwise escape the hunter. Large and strong enough to handle even geese with ease, his heavy coat affords him protection from long exposure in icy water. His coat needs to be groomed, but not clipped like a Poodle; it sheds water and doesn't become wet to the skin.

There are several well-known obedience workers in the breed, and the first sporting dog to win an obedience title in the USA was an Irish Water Spaniel. His nature is one of initiative and courage, yet he is innately trainable. Owners insist he is a dog with a sense of humor, and his enjoyment of games makes him a good family dog. He is, however, discerning with strangers. His head is capped with a characteristic topknot, and his expression is quizzical, adding to his appealing appearance.

Irish Water Spaniel.

IRISH WOLFHOUND

COUNTRY: Ireland
WEIGHT: Minimum 105 pounds for females and 120 pounds for males
HEIGHT: Minimum 30 inches for females and 32 inches for males, 32–34 inches more ideal
COAT: Rough and hard, especially wiry and long over eyes and on underjaw
COLOR: Gray, brindle, red, black, pure white, fawn, or any other color that occurs in the Deerhound
REGISTRY: FCI, AKC, TKC, CKC
GROUP: Southern

The Irish Wolfhound is the tallest of the running hounds, combining speed and power to the "nth" degree. Their history, equally sketchy, probably parallels that of the Scottish Deerhound. Imposing sighthounds have been recorded in Ireland since histories were kept. The Celts invaded Greece and sacked Delphi in 275 BC. There they could have acquired dogs of the Greyhound/Afghan type who accompanied them on their conquest of Europe. Celtic tastes in dogs ran to great speed and size, and these running hounds may have been crossed with rangy mastiffs even before they reached Ireland, the furthest reach of the Celtic migrations. The Romans found the dogs there when they invaded British shores in the first centuries AD.

A letter written in 393 AD by Roman consul Symmachus to his brother Flavianus, then stationed in Britain, thanked him for the seven Irish hounds sent previously. He states "All Rome viewed them with wonder"—this a jaded citizenship who regularly saw huge mastiffs and men fighting bears and lions in the arena! The Irish dogs must have been imposing figures even then.

In early times the great Irish hound came in smooth and rough coats as well as in a variety of dark and light colors. While type might have been quite variable, their qualities of heart, loyalty to master, strength and speed were universal and became legendary. From Ireland's heroic age of 200 BC to 200 AD, magnificent tales of these dogs abound.

One saga involves the hound "Ailbhe," who supposedly defended the entire province of the king of Leinster. The story says the dog was so fast that he could run around Leinster in a single day, and he possessed keen wisdom and supernatural intelligence. In one episode, Ailbhe is asked to decide whether the men of King Conor or those of Queen Maeve are more heroic. Unfortunately, the dog is killed while pursuing the frightened men of King Conor!

The bitch "Bran" was another famous legendary hound, the best of a famous pack of the 4th-century king of Ireland, Cormac. Cared for by Fionn MacCumhaill, the dogs in the pack supposedly were said to have magical powers. "Bran was especially prized for her incredible speed, her bravery in facing wild boars and her ability to warn Fionn and his men against enemy attacks." Fionn's men rescued Bran and other hounds when they were stolen by a servingman who intended to sell them in Britain.

From other written records of the fifth century, we know that dog breeding in Ireland was so organized and the dogs so valued that merchants sold them abroad by the shipload! At least the majority of the dogs to be sold were of the wolfhound type, and these Irish cargos may have contributed to the development of breeds in Europe.

In the 1100s, it was purported that the King of Ulster offered 4,000 cows for a coveted Wolfhound. When the offer for "Aibe" was refused, it started a war. A long Icelandic saga of the 13th century sets a dog in a prominent role. One of the principals, Gunnar, received an Irish hound as a gift from a friend, who said "he is a big animal and will make as good a comrade-in-arms as a powerful man. He has human intelligence and will bark at every man he recognizes as your enemy, but never at your friends; he can tell from a man's face whether he means you well or not. He would lay down his life rather than fail you. His name is Samr." In this tragedy of feuding and revenge, the dog serves Gunnar well. When enemies come to assassinate Gunnar, they pay a farmer to kill the dog first. Samr fights mightily and is killed only because they manage to drive an ax into his head. With his dying gasp, he emits an eerie howl which serves to warn Gunnar of the approaching enemies.

From this grim tale of the past, we know that

Irish Wolfhound, gray.

Irish Wolfhounds, fawn.

Irish dogs were already so exalted as to be featured in the literature of another country. It also shows they were regarded as princely gifts and the world knew of their strength and speed. The tale of the theft of Bran and her pack indicates how a poor man might make a few dollars selling these valuable dogs abroad.

Certainly a section on Wolfhounds would not be complete without the most famous—and true—story. In the 13th century, Llewelyn, prince of North Wales, had a place at Beddgelert, where he enjoyed hunting in the company of "Gelert, the Faithful Hound." One day, Gelert was unaccountably absent as the prince left on his hunt. On Llewelyn's return, the truant, stained and smeared with blood, joyfully sprang to meet his master. The prince, alarmed, hastened to find his son, and saw the infant's cot empty, the bed clothes and floor covered with blood. The frantic father drew his sword and plunged it into the bloody hound. The dog's dying yelp was answered by a child's cry. Llewelyn searched to discover his son unharmed, but lying near the body of a mighty wolf, which Gelert had slain. The prince, filled with remorse, is said never to have smiled again. Gelert's grave in northern Wales is marked by a monument that says: "He buried Gelert here. The spot is called Beddgelert."

From the medieval chores of battle, guarding, and hunting boar, stag and the long extinct Irish elk (which stood six feet high at the shoulder), the Wolfhound gradually turned to the specialized hunting of wolves by the 15th and 16th century. It was during this time that they became more consistent in type and more like the Wolfhound of today.

By the mid-1600s, Cromwell decreed the exporting of Wolfhounds to be illegal because wolves were still a major problem on the British Isles and the great hounds were not plentiful. The last wolf was killed in Ireland before 1800 and, within 50 years, the great hounds—having lost their purpose—were reduced to low numbers. The Great Irish Famine of the 1840s also took its toll on the large dogs. Because of the 150–year ban on exportation, there was nowhere else to go for new breeding stock.

Almost no one in the early 1800s had ever seen a live Wolfhound and, with their exagger-

Irish Wolfhounds, fawn.

ated tales in literature, there was much argument among period authorities over what a true Wolfhound had looked like. (Most assumed they were extinct.)

R.D. Richardson stirred some interest in the breed by writing articles in the 1840s. He also acquired a dog named "Bran" who was of the old type, and bred him to several wolfhounds and deerhounds, and their descendants became the ancestors of all modern Wolfhounds through the Kilfane and Ballytobin Kennels.

Finally in the latter half of the 1800s, Captain G.A. Graham made the restoration of this ancient Irish breed his life's work. He acquired descendants of Richardson's Bran and bred them to deerhounds of the Glengarry strain. With careful selection and occasional outcrosses to Borzoi or even Great Dane to increase size, he recreated the old type. It bred true. Shown successfully in the 1870s, the Irish Wolfhound was on the road to recovery and a breed club was formed in 1885.

The breed is admired and owned in many countries around the world, still prized for its gentleness and unswerving loyalty. His stature as the tallest dog in the world precludes him ever becoming a common pet, but he is a quiet house dog who can be successfully kept content if his regular need to run is met. The rough coat requires occasional combing only. Modern owners can take advantage of lure coursing and other running events.

Irish Wolfhound, gray.

Italian Greyhound.

ITALIAN GREYHOUND

COUNTRY: Italy
WEIGHT: Two varieties—8 pounds maximum; over 8 pounds
HEIGHT: 13–15 inches
COAT: Short, smooth
COLOR: All shades of fawn, red, mouse, blue, cream and white; black/tan not allowed
OTHER NAMES: Piccoli Levrieri Italiani
REGISTRY: FCI, AKC, TKC, CKC
GROUP: Southern

Evidence of miniature Greyhounds was found in the tombs of Egypt, but this exquisite version of its larger counterpart was bred to perfection during Roman times in Italy. Like many of the toy varieties, the little Italian was not bred to serve his masters in any way but as a lap dog. In fact, the miniature Greyhound may well be the first breed bred exclusively as a pet. Some believe that the Latin motto, *cave canem* (beware the dog), did not warn guests of the tough mastiff kept as a guard, but instead asked them to be careful not to harm the tiny Italian Greyhound.

The Italian Greyhound was fancied by the ladies of the court, quickly winning the hearts of Mary Queen of Scots and Anne of Denmark. King Lobengula, chief of a 19th-century Matabele tribe, was so entranced by their prancing movement he gave a breeder 200 head of cattle for one Italian Greyhound! Frederick the Great succumbed to their charms, as did countless others. The king carried his favorite pet with him, even into battle. It is said during the Seven Years' War that Frederick found it necessary to hide from the enemy under a bridge. If the dog had barked a warning or whined in fear, Frederick and Prussia would have met an early and tragic fate. But the dog hugged his master in silence.

During the 19th century, miniaturization of the breed was carried to grotesque extremes in Europe and Britain. The pathetic results were often sterile. Fortunately, by 1900, good sense again reigned. Although the two World Wars dealt harshly with the breed in Europe, good stock abounded in Canada and the USA to export, replenish and rejuvenate the Italian Greyhound.

Their current devotees sing praises of their easy care, their cleanliness, their quiet behavior. Owners are warned, however, to take care that they are not chilled. They definitely are house dogs, not candidates for kennels or cold outdoor living. Unlike most of the sighthounds, their size lets them receive plenty of exercise by following their people around the house. Their quiet demeanor invites gentle care.

Italian Greyhounds, mouse and white.

Italian Greyhound, fawn with white markings.

JACK RUSSELL TERRIER

COUNTRY: Great Britain
WEIGHT: 12–18 pounds
HEIGHT: Two sizes: 9–12 inches and 12–15 inches
COAT: Rough, broken (very short wire), or smooth
COLOR: At least 51 percent white (preferably more) with markings of tricolor, brown or black; brindle not allowed
REGISTRY: None
GROUP: Terrier

Jack Russell Terrier, broken, white with red.

Although a man of the cloth, the "Hunting Parson," Rev. Jack Russell, was a passionate fox hunter of the mid-1800s and pursued the sport until his death at age 88. Fox hunters needed small dogs to roust the foxes who had escaped to ground. Many hunters employed smaller or shorter legged terriers, which had to be carried on horseback to the fox's lair. But the Reverend Jack liked a longer legged type that could follow the hounds on foot. He developed his own strain, based on a crossbred terrier bitch, "Trump," which he bought from a milkman.

How Russell continued with the breeding program was never recorded, but even modern proponents of the breed admit a certain amount of crossbreeding occurred. First, fighting bull-and-terrier dogs were used to add the white color (easily differentiated by the hounds from the fox) and increase the aggression and tenacity. Unfortunately, this often resulted in a dog that silently killed the fox underground, thus spoiling the sport of the hunt for the others! Small "pocket" Beagles were used to temper this hard edge, as well as adding the tendency to give tongue. The result was a dog that was often one thought ahead of the fox.

Game to this day, a good Russell Terrier is still capable of going to ground. One owner described how her three JRTs chased a bull raccoon down a drain pipe near her home. When they hadn't emerged by the next morning, she had a backhoe brought in and started digging. The crew cut a ditch, reaching 300 feet, over the next 12 hours, and finally discovered the raccoon backed up against the cellar wall. Not only were the terriers none the worse for the ordeal,

they were still jockeying for position with one another to get closest to the prey. It is not unusual for this breed to forego food, water and other creature comforts once it has the whiff of the quarry.

Although the Parson never used his dogs for the purpose, the JRT is also a plucky ratter. In 1977, an Englishman and his team of four Jack Russells took three tons of rats out of chicken farms in just one day! Another modern JRT owner gave this practical advice to a writer from *Sports Illustrated* to pass on to anyone planning to take part in this sport with their dogs: "If you take your terrier ratting, always wear slacks or breeches tucked either into your Wellingtons or into your socks so that the rats cannot run up your trouser legs or skirt. This happens far more often than one might imagine, and, although it may be excruciatingly funny to the rest of the party, it is no joke for you."

Despite all this emphasis on its ability and desire to fight and kill pests, JRTs are excellent house dogs and children's pets. They have a unique sense of humor, are clean in their habits and are sweet and affectionate to people. They do require plenty of exercise. When there is more than one, they have a tendency to go off hunting on their own if not fenced. The old instincts to get down in the ground may cause some to be passionate diggers. But they are happy companions and their fans are delighted with them.

The Jack Russell Terrier has its own registering body in both Britain and the USA, but in neither country is there much desire for formal recognition of the breed. Owners prefer the unrefined nature of their dog. They worry about novice owners caring more about show points and good looks, allowing a loss of the working characteristics that have been so painstakingly kept over the years. A typical opinion is stated: "If these terriers ever become soft-bred show dogs, John Russell will turn over in his grave."

In fact, there is a reverse snob appeal about this breed, due to the fact that they do not want to be AKC recognized. This, in addition to the fact that they possess an affinity for horses, has made them a popular addition to many horse

A Jack Russell Terrier seated with master on horse while the hounds execute the initial task of scenting.

farms and estates of the wealthy, especially on the East Coast.

In all physical characteristics, form follows function. The size of a good Jack Russell should be about the same as that of a fox; if the fox can go down the hole, then the terrier should be able to follow without difficulty. The standard demands that the chest be narrow enough to be spanned by two hands behind the shoulder blades. Chests that are chunkier create a dog that can be stuck in the hole! The docked tail of an adult specimen should end up about four inches, just enough length to be able to grab in order to extract the dog from the burrow. The predominance of white differentiates him from the fox.

Most of the larger sized dogs sport the rough or broken coat (similar to a smooth, with fuller hair on the legs and a bit of wiry hair on the chin creating a beard), while the shorter legged variety, carrying more of the cross to the pocket beagle, are more often smooths. Although they often live to 16 years as a house pet, their fearless nature tends to shorten their lifespan in the country. One breeder estimates the average lifespan on a farm to be only six years.

Jack Russell Terrier, rough.

Above: Jack Russell Terrier, rough, white with brown. **Below:** Jack Russell Terrier, smooth, tricolor.

Japanese Chin, black and white.

JAPANESE CHIN

COUNTRY: Japan
WEIGHT: Two divisions—over 7 pounds; or
under 7 pounds, the smaller the better
COAT: Profuse, long, straight, and rather silky;
the abundant thick feathering tends to stand out,
creating a mane
COLOR: Black and white or red (includes all
shades of sable, brindle, lemon or orange) and
white in a broken pattern
OTHER NAMES: Japanese Spaniel
REGISTRY: FCI, AKC, TKC, CKC
GROUP: Herding

Although he has similarities to both of the other
two types of toy spaniels, the Japanese Chin
probably has an entirely different origin. He has
been known in Japan for many centuries, most
likely stemming from dogs of the Asian continent. Argument continues over whether they arrived as gifts to the Emperor with a Korean em-
issary of 732 AD or emigrated with Buddhist
monks and teachers from China, who taught
Zen Buddhism, as early as 520 AD. Perhaps
both are true. The Japanese Chin may share a
common ancestor with the Pekingese and Pug.

In Japan, they were owned only by nobility.
They were fed only rice and saki to stunt their
growth; some were so tiny that they were kept
in hanging cages like canaries! Dogs were protected from intentional injury by strict laws, and
special care and housing were given to sickly or
aged dogs. Dogs held a place of honor, perhaps
because the Emperor was born during the Year
of the Dog, and were considered gifts of high
value. When Perry opened Japan to the West in
1853, he brought some of these little dogs back
with him. Their appearance in Europe created a
great demand, and hundreds of Far Eastern
spaniels made the long journey by ship from the
Orient to the West. Ten of these little dogs appeared in an 1882 New York dog show. The
present Japanese Chin Club in America dates
from 1912, and the breed's entry into Canada
was about the same time. His ownership now
encompasses more than Japanese nobility. The
breed is a beloved pet in its homeland and other
countries.

The Chin is a charming and sensitive companion, adapting well to almost any indoor lifestyle.
He is clean and intelligent. The thickly feathered tail plumes up over the back.

Japanese Chin.

Japanese Chin.

Japanese Spitz.

JAPANESE SPITZ

COUNTRY: Japan
WEIGHT: 13 pounds
HEIGHT: 10–16 inches (English standard); often about 15 inches
COAT: Thick, long, and stand-off
COLOR: White only
REGISTRY: FCI, TKC
GROUP: Northern

The Japanese Spitz is a miniature lap spitz, descended from longer haired Nordic dogs brought to Japan in the early part of this century. The most likely type is the Siberian native Samoyed, which was bred smaller and smaller in size after arrival in Japan. This breed does not enjoy the wide acceptance of the Shiba, but has been exported into the Scandinavian countries. There these spitz were happily adopted and are shown.

In the 1970s, Dorothy Kenyon brought some from Sweden into England. They immediately became popular, and are allowed to compete for championships in British dog shows. They are very similar in size and appearance to the Miniature variety of the American Eskimo, which probably will preclude their ever developing any following in the USA.

Intelligent, bold, and lively, they have all of the character of the other spitz breeds. Their coat is self-cleaning, and they enjoy pleasing their owners. They are less suspicious in nature than some of their Nordic cousins, making them a true companion dog.

Their natural hunting instincts surface when they sight a squirrel or rabbit. Small enough to be a lap dog and large enough to enjoy a romp, the Japanese Spitz is an ideal choice for children or adults.

Above: Japanese Spitz, puppies. **Below:** Japanese Spitz.

527

JAPANESE TERRIER

COUNTRY: Japan
HEIGHT: 12–13 inches
COAT: Short, smooth
COLOR: Tricolor, with white predominating
OTHER NAMES: Nippon Terrier
REGISTRY: None
GROUP: Terrier

The Smooth Fox Terrier traveled all the way from Holland to Japan in 1702 to produce the first Japanese Terrier, bred from crossings with native breeds of that era. Type was refined in Yokohama and Kobe, harbor towns. They were designed exclusively as pets, to be carried about when their owners went out. Nicknames include *Oyuki* (snowy) Terrier and Mikado Terrier.

Very much like its progenitor (the Smooth Fox), the terrier from the Land of the Rising Sun has a certain elegance almost hinting of the Whippet. Its slick, smooth coat makes grooming an easy chore, and its lively terrier temperament makes it a spirited pet. Tails are docked and ears are set high and fold forward. It is unknown outside of Japan.

Japanese Terrier.

KANGAL DOG

COUNTRY: Turkey
WEIGHT: 75–150 pounds
HEIGHT: 28–34 inches
COAT: Short, smooth
COLOR: Chamois, dun or grayish dun; with a
black mask; white chest blaze and feet
characteristic; never white
OTHER NAMES: Karabash
GROUP: Flock Guard

These ancient guardians have served the shepherds of the mountains and plains in the Kangal district of eastern Turkey for thousands of years. In the Sivas area, the family headed by the Aga of Kangal has produced illustrious leaders in central Turkey since their ancestors, the Turkoman Beys, invaded Asia Minor around 1000 AD. They were a great land-owning family of the 16th through 19th centuries. These people were—and still remain—renowned breeders of beautiful animals: the Arabian horse, sheep and the Kangal Dog. The dogs were also owned by others in the area, but both the dogs and the region are named for the family.

Turkish natives all know and identify the Kangal Dog. When a traveler mentions Kangal, Turks answer, "big, thick head, black-masked dog." Their pride is such that the Kangal Dog is depicted on a national stamp. Yet, they are not found as pets in their homeland. As Moslems, most Turks do not allow dogs in their homes, and the majority of pets are owned by Europeans or Americans living in Turkey. Work is the only reason for the Kangal's existence, and to find a specimen, the shepherds and the flocks must be sought. Like other flock guards, the dogs are easy keepers and fierce, awesome guards. Nevertheless, children of the shepherd families can play with the dogs, with the little ones sometimes riding on the huge animals' backs.

The old term *karabash* means black head, and was sometimes used to describe this type. But the name Kangal is more accurate, both historically and geographically.

The nobility of the old Ottoman Empire strongly fostered the maintenance of purebred types. The sultanates and landed aristocracy fell

Kangal Dog, grayish dun.

in the 20th century, however, and this last vestige of support for pure dogs was lost. Despite the lack of regulatory groups, the dogs remain pure to type in the Kangal area. A recent non-doggy tourist to Turkey reported seeing the great dun-colored dogs among the flocks in the mountains north and east of Sivas.

Because there is no Turkish registry body nor dog shows, the dog remains a working animal in its native country. Ears are cropped or, more accurately, "chopped" by shepherds in Turkey. Kangals are now trickling into the United States and other countries, where they are used for guardians and livestock protection, in addition to being exhibited at rare breed shows.

Kangaroo Dog, brown and white.

KANGAROO DOG

COUNTRY: Australia
WEIGHT: 65–70 pounds
HEIGHT: 27½–29½ inches
COAT: Smooth and fine, sometimes coarser on the body
COLOR: All colors, black not desirable
OTHER NAMES: Kangaroo Hound, Australian Greyhound
REGISTRY: None
GROUP: Southern

Early Australian settlers used large sighthounds, such as Greyhounds, to hunt kangaroos, wallabies and Dingoes. Deerhound blood was added for increased size and power, and the resulting progeny were known as Kangaroo Dogs. In appearance, the Kangaroo Dogs resembled the English Greyhound, but were heavier.

These dogs did not have the fortune to attract the support and attention of breeders and have never reached registry status. With national protection of kangaroos and wallabies, the Kangaroo Dog became increasingly rare and is found only on remote sheep and cattle stations in Australia, and is possibly even extinct.

KARELIAN BEAR LAIKAS

Karelian Bear Dog

COUNTRY: Finland
WEIGHT: 44–49 pounds
HEIGHT: 19–23½ inches
COAT: Short, harsh, stand-off
COLOR: Black (preferably dull or with a brownish cast); white blaze, throat, chest, feet and tail tip
OTHER NAMES: Karelsk Bjornhund, Karjalankarhukoira, Karelischer Barenhund
REGISTRY: FCI, CKC
GROUP: Northern

Russo-European Laika

COUNTRY: USSR
WEIGHT: 45–50 pounds
HEIGHT: 21–24 inches
COAT: Short, harsh, stand-off
COLOR: Black, with symmetrical white markings
OTHER NAMES: Lajka Ruissisch Europaisch, Karelian Bear Laika
REGISTRY: FCI
GROUP: Northern

Large hunting laikas from Karelia and neighboring areas on the Russian/Finland border have become popular throughout European Russia as well as in Finland. The breed that the Finns fostered took on the name Karelian Bear Dog. In Russia (Karelia is now a territory of the Soviet Union), the breed is called Russo-European Laika, but they are much the same dog in background, appearance, and hunting style. The Russian strain called the Karelian Bear Laika is larger and more aggressive, creating a more specialized elk and bear dog. But all of them are big dogs, slightly longer than tall, and they boast a robust, athletic stature. Although the tail preferably plumes over the back, natural bobtails do exist and, while frowned upon, are still conceded by both the current Finnish and Soviet standards.

The dog always was employed for a variety of game, but interest was aroused in the breed by his reputation as a big game hunter. This was especially true of the Russian aristocracy in the last century. Bear Dog was accepted as its name, which gives the breed a certain dignity and stature. Although the breed remained fairly pure in backwoods villages for centuries, in the 1930s the Finnish Kennel Club took this breed into its

Karelian Bear Dog.

Russo-European Laika.

planned breeding programs, furnishing the boost needed to guarantee the breed's preservation.

The Winter War (between Russia and Finland in 1939–40) nearly decimated the breed and only a few fanciers remained. By the 1960s, the Karelian Bear Dog was seriously declining in Finland. Poor breeding practices—using parents without good abilities—were creating puppies which disappointed hunters. Conscientious breeders brought this laika back to today's strength in both numbers and abilities.

The Karelian Bear Dog in Finland has been used mainly as a hunter of elk. Now trials to choose breeding stock are held and are said to be very demanding on both dog and hunter. Erkki Tuominen, a Finnish breeder, says of the breed, ". . . its future depends on how we can retain and further develop its ability as an elkdog."

He described the dog eloquently in a letter: "A definite kind of abruptness, which could also be named self-respect, belongs to the tempera-

ment of the Carelian Bear Dog [Finnish spelling]. In a pinch it is unfailingly brave, never yielding, even merciless. This is the dog for a big-game hunter both in essence and character . . . . If one would have to describe the Carelian Bear Dog with a word, it would be *grand* . . . . Its black-white colour, the fiery look of . . . dark eyes and the stateliness and strength of its essence capture the eyes of a hunter . . . like a piece of wild and untamed wilderness . . . firm barking in [the] autumn landscape, the angrily puffing elk; that is Finnish big-game hunting at its best."

These big-game hunters are used for other types of quarry as well, depending on their owner. In Russia the laikas hunt squirrel, fowl and mink as well as bears, moose, boars and even wolves. American owners agree that the Karelians are excellent squirrel dogs. Contrary to the name, *laika* meaning barker, these dogs are always silent trailers, beginning their barking only when the game is treed or otherwise cornered. At that point, they begin their continuous barking to keep the quarry occupied until the hunter is within shooting range. They generally hunt singly, due to their aggressive tendencies.

Karelian Bear Dogs are owned and bred in Canada, America and other European countries as well as Russia and Finland. Owners emphasize they are a working breed and must have plenty of exercise, and that the dogs are most happy when owned by an outdoor enthusiast. Most are housed outside to keep them acclimated to the colder temperatures. They are tough and independent, but form a strong bond with their owner. These characteristics make them sharp guard dogs. The breed is aggressive with other dogs and will fight an intruder—human or canine—to the death, if need be. The Karelian does not make a good pet for those unable to control him. Training, socialization and leash control in public are advised.

Above: Russo-European Laika. **Below:** Karelian Bear Dog sounding a warning.

Karelo-Finnish Laika, fawn.

KARELO-FINNISH LAIKA

COUNTRY: USSR
WEIGHT: 25–30 pounds
HEIGHT: 15–19 inches
COAT: Dense, moderately short, stand-off
COLOR: Fawn in various shades, lighter tones on the undersides are allowed
GROUP: Northern Dog

The Karelo-Finnish Laika is very similar to the Finnish Spitz. Nordic hunting breeds developed long before current national boundaries. The red hunting dog fostered in Finland took on the name Finnish Spitz, and the same general type promoted in European Russia was named Karelo-Finnish for the area from which it came. The area called Karelia is actually a part of northwestern Russia, just east of Finland and south of the Barents seaport of Murmansk. The Russian term *laika* means barker or barking dog, similar to the term applied to his Finnish counterpart. All of the Nordic-type dogs from Russia are called laika, describing their distinctive hunting style. The actual Karelo-Finnish Laika is unknown outside of Russia, but at home he is very popular with hunters; in fact he is the most numerous of all the Russian laikas, due to his fine abilities and small size.

Maturing very early, he finds employment for various types of bird hunting—grouse, pheasant and duck—as well as squirrels. Many Soviet fur hunters also find this breed useful for trailing and entering fox, marten or raccoon burrows, and he is even brave enough to dance face to face with a bear. This energetic, small, quick dog is the least likely of the laikas to bog down and suffocate in the deep snow drifts.

In temperament, the Karelo-Finnish is high-strung and excitable. He is willing to please and cannot stand rudeness, punishment or unfair treatment. Russians say "everything about this dog, its eyes, ears, and tail, express joy and cheerfulness." But if ill-treated, the bond between Laika and hunter is broken, and the hunt will lose its joy.

Karelo-Finnish Laika.

Keeshond.

Keeshond.

KEESHOND

COUNTRY: Netherlands
WEIGHT: 55–66 pounds
HEIGHT: 17–19 inches
COAT: Long, dense, double, stand-off
COLOR: Wolf gray; lighter shadings on head and undersides, creating the typical spectacles around the eyes
OTHER NAMES: Wolfspitz, Chien Loup
REGISTRY: AKC, UKC, TKC, CKC
GROUP: Northern

Dogs of the spitz type have long been common in Friesland (northern Holland), left over from the Viking invasions. Legend tells of a Viking ship that went down at sea. The only survivor, a chieftain's son, was rescued during the storm by a Christian fisherman of Friesland and his dog. Wolfert (the fisherman) and the Viking finally landed in unknown territory and built a chapel to St. Olaf for their deliverance. This chapel became a village at the mouth of the Amstel River, where a dam was built in later years. The town was known as Amstelredam, later Amsterdam. The dog, a participant in the entire legend, was never forgotten. The seal of the city of Amsterdam shows an ancient vessel with a dog of definite spitz type watching over the side. Carrying a dog on board a vessel thus became a good omen, and later a custom. A ship's canines came under the sea laws, as the pets represented ownership. In the owner's absence, no one dared ransack a ship if there was a dog on board! So throughout Dutch history, boats and

537

Keeshond.

barges traditionally carried dogs on board, for vermin control, as watchdogs and simply for companionship and good luck.

Keeshonden are of the same stem stock as the German Spitz, but the Dutch seemed to espe-cially like and adopt the large, wolf gray type. The Dutch dearly loved their dogs and passed laws for their protection. One such law shows the value placed on companionship: "He who kills a hunting dog shall be fined eight pieces, but if he kills someone's pet dog the fine shall be twelve pieces."

Although known for centuries, he acquired his modern name from Cornelius de Gyselaer, a Dutch patriot at the time of the French Revolution. De Gyselaer's nickname was Kees (pronounced *kays*), and Kees's dog became a symbol of the common and middle-class Dutch Patriot Party that followed de Gyselaer. With the eventual defeat of de Gyselaer's cause, the dog fell into disrepute. Prominent people proved not to have the loyalties of their dogs—they did not want to be seen with a Kees dog. The breed dropped from sight among the urban and upper classes.

In 1920, nearly 150 years later, Baroness van Hardenbroek took an interest in the breed and began her search for good specimens. She was startled to find that among the bargemen, farmers and truckers of rural areas, there were still many enthusiasts of the breed. The dogs they had maintained were of remarkably good type, with many of these owners keeping their own rudimentary stud books. With the renewed interest that the Baroness stirred when she began breeding, the Keeshond again was seen throughout Holland. It was introduced in the 1930s into the USA and England simply as the Dutch Barge Dog. Never a dog of fads or crazes, the Keeshond has continued to have a steady and loyal following throughout the world. Although the FCI does not register the Keeshond, considering it the same breed as the German Wolfspitz, the USA, Canada and Great Britain consider him an entity.

Kees require only moderate grooming and are happy, family-oriented dogs, so much so they are sometimes called "the laughing Dutchman." They can be a bit self-willed, however, and may balk at being forced into doing things that they don't want to do. But with firm, consistent guidance, they prove compliant. The Kees is clean, personable and alert and has made the move from the boats of Holland to 20th-century apartments with ease.

Keeshonden.

Kerry Beagle, black/tan.

KERRY BEAGLE

COUNTRY: Ireland
HEIGHT: 22–24 inches
COAT: Hard, close and smooth
COLOR: Black and tan, blue mottled and tan, black/tan/white, or tan and white
OTHER NAMES: Pocadan
GROUP: Hound

From very early times, a large distinctive scent-hound has trod the Emerald Isle. He most likely arrived with the Celts and has been refined over the years with crosses to the Southern Hound and French hounds.

By the 18th and 19th centuries, their numbers had dwindled until they were primarily in only one kennel owned by the Ryan family of Scarteen, County Limerick. With interest in native breeds growing, however, there are now a good number of fine packs with Kerry Beagles hunted throughout rural Ireland. Many specimens came with Irish immigrants to the USA, where they contributed to the famous Trigg strain of American Foxhounds as well as being one of the major stems of the American Black and Tan Coonhound. The breed is unsponsored by any formal dog organization, even in its homeland.

The origin of his description as "beagle" is unknown, as he was never a small dog like the familiar Beagle. In fact, in earlier times, he was even larger, but has carried the label of Beagle for centuries. The present-day word for the breed in the Irish language is *pocadan*, which describes him as a hunting dog. In the beginning, he was mainly used for stag hunting, a sport requiring speed and stamina. He is now generally utilized for hare hunts as well as drag trials.

The exhilarating sport of foot hunting for hare is pursued in Ireland mainly for the enjoyment of following a fine pack of hounds. Watching these dogs from a high vantage point as they work the rocky mountainsides is a never-ending thrill, and listening to their beautiful voices echo across the valleys culminates the hunt. *The Native Dogs of Ireland* says that, "it is extremely rare if a hare is caught. The Hunt Master invariably calls off the hounds should the hare be in any danger or distress."

Drag trials are held in Ireland for the Kerry Beagle. The Kerry hounds fan out in a large circle when casting, and automatically turn to the first dog that finds the scent and indicates it by "opening" with a loud bay. They have astonishing speed and independence.

The Kerry Beagle sports long ears, full chops and a robust, athletic build. The black-and-tan jacketing is the classic coat, although a great variety of other "hound" colors as tan or red bicolors, tricolors, or even the very rare blue-mottled (merle) color, are seen and allowed. One 19th-century writer's description of him as "an indifferent bloodhound" was not meant to be unflattering, but merely indicated that they looked much like a Bloodhound without the exaggeration of bone and skin. One hopes that sufficient interest is maintained in this ancient Irish hound to ultimately find it included among the recognized and exhibited dogs of the world.

KERRY BLUE TERRIER

COUNTRY: Ireland
WEIGHT: 33–40 pounds
HEIGHT: 17½–19½ inches
COAT: Soft, profuse, dense and wavy
COLOR: Born black and clear to any shade of blue by the age of 18 months
REGISTRY: FCI, AKC, TKC, CKC
GROUP: Terrier

Like his cousin the Irish Terrier, the Blue Terrier of Eire has little literary reference before the 1800s. Oft repeated legends tell us that the Blue's ancestor swam ashore from a ship wrecked off Tralee Bay in the late 1700s, or even that it was from Spanish ships of the Armada in 1588. "This dark survivor was supposed to have mated with local terriers to produce a dog with a dark blue coat and the type and temperament of a terrier." There are also references to "blackish blue" terriers indigenous to County Kerry and other areas going back further that could have been the rootstock and to what the "dark survivor" was bred.

His rather soft wavy coat is distinct among the terriers. With all of the above evidence, even if the story of the shipwreck survivor is true, it is hard to know what type of dog he was. Would he have been a shaggy sheep dog type who instilled the herding ability and longer coat with fading pigment into the local terrier population? Or was it a water dog, of the type that produced the Poodles, Porties and Water Spaniels, who introduced the graying factor, soft wavy coat and water ability? All interesting speculation—the answer to which is lost in the mists of Irish lore.

Although used for all jobs required of terriers, the Kerry was said to be the only dog that "will tackle an otter, single-handed, in deep water." He also was used in his native land to tend stock.

This "true blue" native of the Emerald Isle enjoyed a peak in the 1920s, when no less than four clubs sponsored him in Ireland. The Kerry represented more than 25 percent of total Irish Kennel Club registrations in 1924. It was during this time that the struggle for national independence from Britain was going on, and the Kerry became a mascot for Irish patriots. His favor was such that, even during those bitter times, the Dublin Blue Terrier Club of 1920 was made up of members on both sides of the political fence. Politics were tolerated—or ignored—when it came to dogs, however. According to breed history, the first show held by the group was set up without permission of the ruling British KC. It was judged by Dan Nolan (at the time on the British authority "wanted" list for being a member of the Irish Republican Army). Among the spectators and competitors at this event were members of the English KC as well as an Inspector from the Constabulary. Yet all turned a blind eye while they competed for the Wyndham Quinn Challenge Cup for best Kerry!

American fanciers first exhibited the breed at Westminster in 1922. Among more contemporary owners, Mrs. William Randolph Hearst and heavy-weight champion Gene Tunney both owned Kerrys.

The Kerry in Ireland is required to be shown in an untrimmed, natural state. Elsewhere, the dog is exhibited with a sculptured, scissored coat. He is reported to be a long-lived dog. Like his close cousins, the Irish Terrier and the Soft-Coated Wheaten Terrier, he is a leggy, rangy dog.

Kerry Blues are born black and, if correct, have the dominant gene for coat fading. The color begins to fade to gray and acquires its adult solid slate gray color by 18 months. This is the same graying or fading gene seen in some Bearded Collies and Poodles.

While he sometimes suffers from an undeserved reputation for surliness, he can be described today as he was in 1922 by fancier E.M. Webb: "His temperament is well nigh faultless, if a slight tendency to diminish the cat population be excepted. He is . . . . unrivalled as a ratter, charming as a companion, trustworthy as a watchdog."

Kerry Blue Terrier, dark blue.

Kerry Blue Terrier, grayish blue.

Kerry Blue Terrier

Above: Kerry Blue Terrier, dark blue. **Below:** Kerry Blue Terrier, pups.

KOMONDOR

COUNTRY: Hungary
WEIGHT: 80–150 pounds
HEIGHT: 25½ inches minimum ("the bigger, the better")
COAT: Long, corded
COLOR: White
REGISTRY: FCI, AKC, UKC, TKC, CKC
GROUP: Flock Guard

A working flock guard in Hungary and a unique show dog of the United States and Great Britain, the Komondor serves as a link between yesterday and today.

Hungarian legend tells us that tenth-century Serb shepherds found a litter of wolf cubs and selected those that behaved most like dogs. These were trained to work with sheep, and crossed with native dogs, supposedly produced the Komondor.

Despite fanciful legends, the Komondor is directly descended from the Owtcharki brought to Hungary by the nomadic Magyars around 1,000 years ago. The source of his name cannot be pinpointed, but it may have been derived from the term *komondor kedvu* (meaning somber,

surly or angry), apt adjectives for the ancient flock guard.

A fixture in Hungary for centuries, the Kom has only been in North America since the 1930s. They are routinely seen in shows, besides participating in flock-guarding programs. Heavyweight boxer Gene Tunney owned an illustrious Komondor bitch. The breed, however, has never become well known in Great Britain.

The Kom protects and dominates whatever animals are under his care and includes children in that responsibility. He is an alert, tough guard and serves as a police dog in some areas.

Breeder and owner Joy C. Levy says, "The dog's protective instincts, and his instincts to make decisions for himself, have been selected for centuries. If we breed two imported dogs, their offspring carry on this temperament, which gets them into trouble in Modern American Society [*sic*]. This happens especially in modern suburbia, where fences do not exist and people regularly trespass in the eyes of the dog. Hordes of children rushing into houses without ringing or being let in often look as bad to a Komondor as that villain who steals his family's

Komondor.

Komondorok.

Komondor.

trash, or the one who comes into his house with a weapon, in the form of a plumber's wrench. In the USA some of the best dogs are put down as vicious, when all they did was try to defend their owner and his property."

True to the flock guards, they are not easy breeders. The bitches only cycle once a year, and the studs are not avid performers. As an additional hindrance, the long, corded coats make matings difficult.

The corded coat is not seen on more than a handful of breeds. Now a unique conversation piece, the cords served a purpose for the flock guard. These twisted ringlets were never combed and, in adulthood, served as armor, impervious to climate and predators' teeth. The cords also serve to make them look like one of the semi-wild sheep. In his native land, the working Kom is shaggy, heavily matted, and untidy. Show conditioning necessitates a neater appearance.

Cording takes special care, requiring meticulous training during puppyhood and from four to eight hours blow-drying the coat after bathing. In addition, owners spend up to two hours per week hand-separating the cords. Maintaining the white color complicates the care.

Outside the show ring, Koms serve as guardians for animals, property and families. They are part of several flock-guard programs in the USA. Breeders recommend obedience training, as the Kom likes to be the boss.

Kooikerhondje.

KOOIKERHONDJE

COUNTRY: Netherlands
WEIGHT: 20–24 pounds
HEIGHT: 14–16 inches
COAT: Moderately long, with slight wave; fringed, as a spaniel
COLOR: Red and white
OTHER NAMES: Kooiker Dog
GROUP: Gun Dog

Kooiker Dogs have been extant in the Netherlands for many years, helping the hunters draw the *kooikers,* a type of duck. It was a Kooiker that was credited with saving the life of Prince William of Orange (1533–1584). The dog barked at intruders, alerting the Prince to escape. Dutch artists Jan Steen and Jan Vermeer captured the breed in paintings during the 1600s.

History then skips any mention of the Kooiker Dog until the early 1940s when Baroness v. Hardenbroek van Ammerstol began her search for one of this native breed. The Baroness gave a likeness of the Kooiker Dog to a peddler and showed him the coat color, asking him to search for such a dog in his travels. The peddler was fortunate to find a Kooiker bitch, "Tommy," in the northern Netherlands. Two males, "Bobby" and "Bennie," were also found in the same area.

Tommy's first litter was born in 1943, and these three dogs set the foundation of the modern breed. Originally, tricolored dogs were allowed, but are now not permitted.

The Kooikerhondje is called the "decoy" in the Netherlands for its method of aiding the hunter. Pipes set with wire netting are placed around ponds and lakes. Feed is sprinkled near the end, with tame ducks eating the fodder and drawing the attention of the wild ducks. The Kooiker Dog leads the ducks in, attracting them with his bushy white tail. When they are under the netting, the hunter appears, frightening the birds into the netting. Young and rare birds are ringed and set free. The nature reserves in the

Netherlands employ about a hundred decoys.

Baroness v. Hardenbroek van Ammerstol received a gold pin of honor from the Council of Cynological Management for her work to solidify the futures of the national breeds including the Drent Partridge and the Dutch Kooiker Dog.

This old Dutch breed has only enjoyed an organized breed club since 1967; acknowledgement of the breed came in 1971. Fanciers feel FCI will accept the breed in the near future. Matings are still a problem, with strict breeding requirements and a narrow breed base. (All specimens are in the Netherlands.) However, those same regulations are improving soundness of the breed.

The Kooiker Dog is medium sized, very much like a small setter or spaniel in appearance. The tail must be long and bushy; hair on the ears is long, preferably with black tips called earrings. He is cheerful, easy to manage and affectionate with his owners. These qualities make him not only a good hunter's companion, but a delightful family and obedience dog.

Above: The Kooikerhondje demonstrating its obedience trial abilities. **Below:** A family of Kooikerhondjes from the Netherlands.

Krasky Ovcar.

KRASKY OVCAR

COUNTRY: Yugoslavia
WEIGHT: 55–88 pounds
HEIGHT: 20½–24 inches
COAT: Medium, dense and harsh
COLOR: Iron gray with shadings
OTHER NAMES: Karst Sheepdog, Istrian Sheepdog
REGISTRY: FCI
GROUP: Flock Guard

Nestled up against the Alps of Italy and Austria is the northern border of Yugoslavia. The area called Karst (or Kras) encompasses much of northern Yugoslavia, including the Istrian Peninsula jutting out into the Adriatic Sea. The local livestock-guarding dog is closely related to the Sarplaninac of the south. Both the Karst and the Sar are obviously related to the flock guards of Greece, Rumania and the eastern Balkans.

Americans, looking for examples of this breed in the late 1970s, were told that if any existed, "all the[se] dogs were now only in the south" of Yugoslavia. But their obituary was premature. A few lovers of this breed worked to see it saved in its homeland, Europe and even in America.

Most of these breeders were people of Yugoslavian descent who saw the Karst as a living piece of their country's history. The FCI has now granted international recognition to the breed.

The Krasky Ovcar is only seen in the iron gray color, preferably with darker shadings on the back and "spectacles" around the eyes. The ears are small and set fairly high, hanging down in a flat *v*. The long tail is heavy with hair, forming a flag. Muscles must be strong and well developed, giving an impression of mammoth strength. Its leathery footpads enable it to go over nearly impassable terrain and rocks.

A good domestic dog, the Karst has been described as a cheerful, delightful companion. He is wary of strangers and not easily won over, and these characteristics combined with abundant courage make him an excellent guardian. He is smaller and less aggressive than some of the other flock guards. Sporadically, a specimen of the breed is exhibited at rare breed shows in America and FCI events in Europe. The breed has not been promoted like the Sar for livestock guarding in America, but it has served in that capacity in its homeland for centuries.

Above: Kromfohrländer, wire. **Below:** Kromfohrländer, long straight.

552

KROMFOHRLÄNDER

COUNTRY: Germany
WEIGHT: 26 pounds
HEIGHT: 15–18 inches
COAT: Two types: rough wire; medium-long straight hair
COLOR: Mainly white with tan (light to very dark) markings in a broken pattern, including saddle and head
REGISTRY: FCI
GROUP: Terrier

The Kromfohrländer is a breed of the 20th century. In 1945, American soldiers marched into Germany from France. One group, arriving in the town of Siegen, Westphalia, was accompanied by a shaggy, tawny dog. Although his family tree was unknown, his appearance and French origin indicated a Breton Griffon (Griffon Fauve de Bretagne). The dog was taken in by a townswoman, Ilse Schleifenbaum. "Peter" became a beloved house pet and later "fell in love" with the next-door neighbor, "Fiffi," a fe-

Kromfohrländer, wire.

Kromfohrländer, medium straight.

male of uncertain pedigree, but possibly Fox Terrier extraction. The resulting puppies were uniform and so handsome that Mrs. Schleifenbaum decided to develop them into a new breed. Ten years later, in 1955, she succeeded in having the German Kennel Club officially recognize them, with the FCI giving them the stamp of approval shortly after.

Lively, loyal and obedient, the breed was developed specifically as a companion dog. The muzzle tapers slightly, ears are high and fall in a complete drop, and the happy tail is carried gaily, forming a loose ring over the back. This German terrier carries robust sporting dog proportions.

He is alert, watchful, devoted to his family and does not roam. Since the breed was a happy accident, these dogs do not hunt but are strictly companions and watchdogs. A current German owner relates how Kromfohrländers are a part of his family and says, "We did not know that dogs could be so intelligent."

KUVASZ

Country: Hungary
Weight: 110 pounds maximum
Height: 26 inches maximum
Coat: Wavy, medium length
Color: White to ivory
Registry: FCI, AKC, CKC
Group: Flock Guard

Kuvasz, white.

Many cynologists believe the Kuvasz was brought to Hungary by the Kumans, nomadic shepherds of Turkish origin in the 13th century. These dogs may have moved north with much earlier migrations, however. They are obviously part of the flock-guarding family, both as ancestors and descendants. Their similarity to the Akbash Dog is striking.

Kuvasz may have been derived from the Sumerians, ancient Eastern people who originally fostered dogs of this type. *Ku-assa*, in Sumerian, is dog horse, indicating a dog that guarded and ran along beside horses and riders. The term *ku-assa* is found on a clay board at the site of Akkad in northern Mesopotamia, circa 3000 BC. Most of the migrating peoples who came from Asia to populate eastern Europe were horse-riding tribes whose wealth was in large herds of range cattle. Those who settled what is now Hungary brought their white guard dogs with them.

The breed savored a moment of splendor in the 15th century in the court of King Matyas (Mathias) I, who claimed to trust his Kuvasz dogs more than his fawning courtiers. This king used his Kuvaszok for hunting wild boar and as personal guardians. The breed was never an exclusivity with royalty, however, and aided herdsmen and peasants in protection. He is still seen frequently in Hungary today.

The Kuvasz has been bred and exhibited in the United States since the 1920s. He successfully patrols American ranches for predator control. The breed has never become recognized in Great Britain.

A typical flock guard in temperament, he is wary and suspicious of that which is not familiar. This is correct temperament for the breed—and the group—as a whole.

Owners should be responsible, with enough experience and knowledge to control the macho temperament. The Kuvasz will continue to test his owner's dominance. Once he has given his devotion, he will be a one-family dog and will protect that family from all intruders, including a new neighbor or the toll-taker. The Kuvasz has an intense loyalty to that which is his own and needs proper socialization and control to become a dependable companion dog as well. The thick, white coat is also demanding of attention.

Kuvasz, ivory.

Kyi Leo, black/white particolor.

KYI LEO

COUNTRY: USA
HEIGHT: 8–12 inches, outside limits; 9–11 inches preferred
COAT: Long, thick and straight or slightly wavy, tends to part along the spine
COLOR: Usually black/white particolor, but also gold/white, or self colors, some dogs may fade from black to slate
REGISTRY: None
GROUP: Herding

In the 1950s, around the San Francisco Bay area of California, a few people experimented with crosses of Maltese dogs and Lhasa Apsos. Why this was begun is not recorded, but the result was small adorable dogs with sparkling personalties, causing people to succumb to their charms. One lady from San José linebred these shaggy dogs for many years, developing a type to her liking. When Harriet Linn acquired one of these Maltese/Lhasa Shaggies in 1965, little did she know that she was beginning a lifetime commitment. After breeding a litter from that first dog, she knew she was hooked. Mrs. Linn was the driving force behind the coalescing of this new breed. She acquired other specimens, including several from the San José kennel when it closed its doors in 1969. Three years later, sufficient interest in the breed brought owners and breeders together for a formal meeting.

They decided on the name Kyi Leo for their new breed. *Kyi* is Tibetan for dog, giving credit to the Lhasa, and *Leo* is Latin for lion, acknowledging the Maltese's contribution. A club was formed and an interim standard adopted. The breed club keeps detailed registration information on all Kyi Leos since the breed is not yet recognized by any formal kennel authority. A quarterly newsletter is sent out to all owners and interested parties, and the group sponsors an annual picnic (the Kyi Leo Get Together) for Kyi Leo lovers to meet one another and talk about their favorite subject!

Above: Kyi Leos, particolor. **Below:** Kyi Leo.

The Kyi Leo has many of the good points of both of his ancestors. Although a small dog, he is not as tiny and fragile as the Maltese. His muzzle is longer and lacks the underbite seen in most Lhasas. While his hair is long, it never reaches the excessive floor length of the show specimens of his forebears. Although other colors are seen and allowed, the black and white pied dogs are the trademark of the breed.

Known for their agility and catlike quickness, they are playful and people-oriented. These dogs are outgoing, happy and intelligent with an abundance of willingness to please. Yet they have a tendency to be a bit reserved with strangers, making them ideal small alarm dogs. Although, occasionally, they show a hint of stubbornness, most owners tolerantly see this as merely asserting their own characters. They charm their way into hearts. The breed is known in a dozen states, as well as Canada, and is growing in numbers each year.

Labrador Retrievers, yellow, chocolate, and black.

LABRADOR RETRIEVER

COUNTRY: Great Britain
WEIGHT: 55–75 pounds
HEIGHT: 21½–24½ inches
COAT: Moderately short, dense, hard and without wave; thick undercoat
COLOR: Solid black, chocolate, or yellow (from fox-red to light cream)
REGISTRY: FCI, AKC, UKC, TKC, CKC
GROUP: Gun Dog

As far back as the 17th century, water dogs were used by fishermen and hunters in Canada. These were called Newfoundland, Labrador (Greenland was once called Labrador) or St. John's Dogs, depending on their geographic location. These early dogs were moderate in size, had curled coats, carried the genetic factor to produce spotting, and tended to a high tail. Not much formal breeding was attempted, but from these eventually stemmed the modern Newfoundland and Landseer, as well as the Labrador, Flat-Coat and Chesapeake Bay Retrievers.

Throughout the world, fishing vessels, trading ships and exploratory expeditions provided continuous traffic. Most ships had dogs on board, and the crossing of various imported types with the native population of dogs was well documented. By 1800, these retrieving dogs were being sold into England by ships plying from the Canadian coast. But, later that century, a heavy dog tax caused a great reduction in the breed in Canada and, more importantly, the creation of the English quarantine laws essentially stopped further importation. Thus, although the root stock came from Canada, the modern development of the breed occurred in England.

Early Labs sported a large variety of types and colors, including spotted and brindle. The Flat-Coat was enjoying great favor during the 19th century, and the Labrador was not granted Kennel Club recognition until after the turn of the century. But, once he came to prominence, he stayed on top. Labs are now in the first five breeds in both England and America and maintain their popularity as duck dogs par excellence. In American retriever field trials, the Labrador dominates to the point of exclusion. He enjoys a sterling reputation as an upland bird flusher, companion, drug detector, obedience competitor and guide dog for the blind. In fact,

"Polly" lovingly served her blind master for a record 13 years! The Lab is well known and utilized also in Australia, Canada, and many other countries.

Willing-to-please perhaps best describes the Lab. The breed, overall, is sensible, even-tempered, intelligent, and possesses strong natural abilities in marking and retrieving. The short, easy-care coat and docile temperament make the Lab a favorite pet, who can—year round—run with the kids, catch a flying disc in the park, join the family by the fire, and still double as a hunting companion. Because of his fairly large size and his designated lifestyle as an active, athletic dog, soundness is of prime importance.

The ideal Lab is described as slightly longer than tall, with a robust, muscular build. His distinctive "otter" tail is covered by short, thick hair; he should *never* show any fringe on the underside of the tail! The double coat is quite waterproof, requiring frequent brushing only during the spring shedding season.

Labrador Retriever, yellow.

Labrador Retriever, chocolate.

Labrador Retriever, black, with a retrieved mallard.

Labrador Retriever, black.

Labrador Retriever, yellow.

LAKELAND TERRIER

COUNTRY: Great Britain
WEIGHT: 17 pounds
HEIGHT: 13–15 inches
COAT: Hard and wiry
COLOR: Blue, black, liver, black/tan, blue/tan, red, red grizzle, grizzle/tan, wheaten
REGISTRY: FCI, AKC, TKC, CKC
GROUP: Terrier

From solid-colored, broken-coated terriers of the lake districts of northern England, this fine working terrier emerged. The entire area—the northern counties of Cumberland, Northumberland and Westmoreland—was the fount of many terrier varieties. The dog that eventually developed into the Bedlington and Dandie Dinmont was probably the origin of the Lakeland and the Border Terrier as well. A century or more before organized dog shows, the Lakeland assisted in informal hunts. These were organized by farmers—with a couple of hounds and terriers—when foxes were raiding the sheepfolds.

These dogs were not like the "fox" terriers developed further south which were expected to bolt the quarry. The Lakelands were practical working terriers, required to face and kill the fox underground. When exhibited, they were still shown under the all-embracing term: Colored Working Terrier.

The breed was then called the Patterdale or Fell Terrier and came in a variety of colors as well as white. When they were first exhibited in the 1880s–90s, they were divided into white and colored dogs. Masters of Foxhounds judged the terriers not on their looks, but for their ability as working "fox" terriers. Soon the white terriers were used exclusively for otter work. (Young hounds, in their excitement, often mistook a dark dog for an otter and mauled the dog instead as both bolted from the hole.) The dark dogs were kept to hunt for foxes in the mountain rock piles.

Stories of Lakeland courage are plentiful. In 1871, Lord Lonsdale had a Lakeland that crawled 23 feet under rock after an otter. In order to extricate the dog, it was necessary to undertake extensive blasting operations. The dog was taken out, still in fine fettle, three days later. Still other dogs were recorded to have

Lakeland Terrier.

Lakeland Terrier.

LANCASHIRE HEELER

COUNTRY: Great Britain
WEIGHT: 6–12 pounds
HEIGHT: 10–12 inches
COAT: Short, smooth
COLOR: Black/tan
OTHER NAMES: Ormskirk Terrier, Ormskirk Heeler
REGISTRY: TKC
GROUP: Herding

Developed as a cattle dog during the 1960s–70s, the Lancashire still herds cattle, horses and goats in its namesake territory. The breed's roots trace back to Corgis and Manchester Terriers. Both ancestries are apparent in his skills and make the breed a perfect farm and family dog. Terrier attributes are evident in hunting rabbits, exterminating rats and alerting to intruders. Yet the little dog is a courageous heeler, built low to escape kicks. The Lancashire has such strong heeling instincts, one family says their dog even will try to round up cattle seen on television!

Lancashire Heeler.

been taken out alive after 10–12 days. Of course, many paid the ultimate penalty.

In 1921, a group of fanciers met to resume pre-War activities and dubbed the breed after its lake district. Seven years later, the name Lakeland became official. The first president of the breed club was Lord Lonsdale, whose family had raised Lakelands for 50 years.

The Lakeland coat must be groomed in a manner similar to that of the Wire Fox and other rough-coated terriers. Although not as well known as some other terriers, they are consistently successful in the show rings. One famous champion, Stingray of Derryabah, was Best in Show at Crufts in 1967, followed by a BIS at Westminster, in New York, the following year. He became the only dog to win these prestigious shows on both sides of the Atlantic. Actor Bill Cosby is an ardent terrier fan, co-owning several top-winning dogs, among them a Lakeland, a Wire Fox and a Welsh Terrier.

They capture more than shows, however, winning hearts as well. Lakelands are down-to-earth, level-headed dogs who make fine companions. The breed adores children and matches their energy step for step.

565

Small physiques encase a large dog personality, and these dogs are protective of their turf. Yet, Lancashires are playful, intelligent companions and excellent obedience dogs. Their small size belies their strength, agility and hardiness. Although rare in numbers and known only in England as yet, they are increasing in favor because of their versatility, happy temperament and ease of care. They are sturdy and long-lived and particularly good playmates for children.

The Lancashire is adaptable to new circumstances. Only recently entering the show ring, the breed has a good attitude and is athletic, showing high promise in that realm as well as the farm and home.

Lancashire Heeler.

Landseer.

LANDSEER

COUNTRY: Scandinavian countries
HEIGHT: 26–31½ inches
COAT: Moderate length, soft, fairly dense, fine to the touch; short on head and fronts of legs
COLOR: Clear white, with large distinct black spots on back and rump; head should be black with a symmetrical white blaze
REGISTRY: FCI
GROUP: Mastiff

The original "Newfoundland" imports from Canada were much different from our present breed. Sir Edwin Landseer created several famous paintings of "Newfoundland dogs" in the early part of the 19th century, and these gave the type its name. The painting *Off to the Rescue*, (1827) of "Bashaw," a black-and-white variety belonging to the Right Honorable Earl of Dudley, and *A Distinguished Member of the Humane Society*, (1838) of "Paul Pry" owned by Mrs. Newman Smith, were notable. The dogs were portrayed as spotted, having a tapering head, longer legs and a more "open" coat, with a tendency to curl.

As the century progressed, two quite different types of Newfies developed in Europe, not just in color but in other characteristics. In the 1881 edition of the official German stud books, two varieties of Newfoundland dogs were clearly described. The "wavy-haired" was solid black (white not desired), with a shorter nose, overhanging lips and more massive build. The "curly-haired" Newfoundland (i.e., Landseer) had the described spotted pattern and the longer, dryer and more tapering head. The latter type also stood higher on leg with a slightly lighter frame.

Fanciers on the Continent continued to breed this variety of the black and white Landseer Newfoundland. Although the First World War took its toll on giant breeds, efforts were made in the 1930s to re-establish the Landseer as a separate breed. Brothers Otto and Alfred Walterspiel spearheaded efforts in 1933 to bring the Landseer back to prominence. The breed base was so small that some crossing to the black Newfoundland occurred in the early days. At this time, the Landseer has been bred pure for many years.

FCI recognizes the two breeds and, in 1976, the German Landseer Club was born as the first organization promoting the Landseer separately from the Newfoundland. Holland and Belgium have joined in that premise.

Above and Below: Landseers.

567

LAPINPOROKOIRA

COUNTRY: Finland
WEIGHT: 66 pounds or less
HEIGHT: 19–22 inches
COAT: Medium short, stiff and coarse, dense undercoat
COLOR: Black, black/tan
OTHER NAMES: Lapland Reindeer Dog, Lapponian Herder, Lapponian Vallhund
REGISTRY: FCI
GROUP: Herding

For centuries the Laplanders of northern Finland hunted reindeer, using pure northern spitz dogs to assist them. As the wild herds disappeared, the Lapps changed to herding domesticated reindeer. With this modification of lifestyle, they needed a different kind of dog to assist them and crossed their native dogs with herding breeds brought in from Europe. The result was a strong, natural herding dog with a good nature.

The Lapinporokoira is a true intermediate between the Nordic and herding breeds—closer to the Nordic type—but with a bit more leg, less curl to the tail and a longer, less tapering head.

Originally the dogs worked outside in the elements throughout the year, keeping the herds together and bringing back strays. The Porokoira sometimes ran over 60 miles a day, usually through deep snow. Years later, in the 1960s, the snowmobile became very popular with the herdsmen, and nearly spelled the doom of the Lapponian Herder. It wasn't long before the high cost of the machine and its fuel made the Lapps take a second look at the old herding breed. The natural energy of the Lapp dog and its accompanying lower "fuel" bills acquired a greater appeal.

Olli Korhonen, chair of the Finnish KC in the 60s, spearheaded the creation of a standard (1966) and the organization of breeding the Lapponian Herder. Through these efforts, an efficient system has evolved. The Lapps want good working dogs, mostly males, and have little interest in raising litters. Many Porokoira fanciers in the south of Finland are attracted to the breed by its good nature, easy care and obedience. They cooperate with the herdsmen in the north, bringing the best working males south to breed with their females and sending the male pups north to work. This system also insures the retention of natural working qualities in the breed.

Lapinporokoira, black/tan.

Finnish Lapphund, sable.

LAPPHUNDS

Swedish Lapphund

COUNTRY: Sweden
WEIGHT: 44 pounds
HEIGHT: 17½–19½ inches
COAT: Long, thick stand-off, with heavy underwool, and fringing on leg backs, belly and tail
COLOR: Black or liver, usually solid but sometimes with symmetrical white marks
OTHER NAMES: Lapplandska Spetz, Swedish Lapp Spitz
REGISTRY: FCI
GROUP: Northern

Finnish Lapphund

COUNTRY: Finland
HEIGHT: 18–20½ inches
COAT: Long, thick, stand-off; heavy underwool, and fringing on leg backs, belly and tail
COLOR: Any color, as long as the color dominates, and any white markings are small and symmetrical
OTHER NAMES: Lapinkoira
REGISTRY: FCI
GROUP: Northern

These two breeds are almost identical, although the FCI recognizes both, and the Swedish and Finnish Kennel Clubs each recognize their own breed as distinct. The standard for the Finnish variety allows for a slightly larger size, although recent correspondence from Finland states that most dogs are in the smaller range and there is thought of changing the standard.

Part of the confusion lies with the Lapp people. They are an old group native to the Arctic Circle, and the area they populated has always been known as Lapland, although never comprising a separate country. The area called Lapland actually includes parts of northern Norway, Sweden, Finland and even northwest Russia. Thus, any dogs developed by the Lapps were named for them; those brought south into Sweden were called Swedish Lapphunds, and the ones coming into Finland became the Finnish Lapphund. Lapland is not far from the area of the Samoyede people in central Siberia, and the Lapland herding breeds bear much resemblance to the Samoyed dog.

The Lapphunds are natural herders of the ancient Nordic spitz type. Although much of reindeer herding has disappeared over the centuries, the dogs have adapted to work with sheep and cattle. Lapphunds were first brought to Finland from Pello in Lapland in the 1930s. These dogs were later bred with the longhaired Karelian Bear Dog, creating a breed called the Cockhill's Finnish Lapphound. When the Finnish Kennel Club decided to separate the Lapphound and the Lapponian Herder, the Cockhill variety was abolished, and breeders looked to Lapland to restore the original type.

Because of their moderate size and their courageous, affectionate nature, they make fine

Swedish Lapphund.

Above: Finnish Lapphund, black/tan. **Below:** Finnish Lapphund.

house pets that are natural alarm dogs. They have the longer coat and look very much like the German Spitz (i.e., Keeshond) as well as the Samoyed. Although the standards allow Irish white markings, self-colored dogs seem to predominate. The heavily plumed tail is carried up on the back.

The Finnish Kennel Club is concerned about preserving this breed, and notes particularly that breeding programs must emphasize the differences between the Lapinkoira and the Lapinporokoira. The Lapinporokoira (or Lapponian Herder) is larger, shorter coated, and has a body that is longer than tall. To keep the modern breeds distinct, the emphasis is on breeding Lapphunds that are moderate in size, nearly square-bodied, and long-coated.

LATVIAN HOUND

COUNTRY: USSR
HEIGHT: 16–19 inches
COAT: Short, dense
COLOR: Black and tan
GROUP: Hound

Latvia is another of the Russian Baltic states, where hunting is a passion in the heavy forests. The hunting of deer and boar in Latvia has followed an unusual format. The forest is blocked out into 1600-foot squares separated by wide clear-cut paths. Hunters may only shoot deer in the cut areas. During a hunt, each hunter is assigned a spot in the clearings, and beaters with dogs line up at the far side of the block. The hunting horn sounds, the hounds are slipped, and the chase is on. The dogs must be ultra-obedient to keep within the prescribed area, finding and flushing any game out to the waiting hunters in the clearings. These dogs needn't have the endurance or persistence, as they have to cover only the 1600 x 1600-foot block and are never expected to chase beyond that, even if the quarry is wounded.

Throughout the 19th century, Latvian gentry hunted deer with long-legged dogs called Curland Hounds, which had been created from a blend of Lucernese, English and Polish hounds. By WWI, good selection of these hounds had ceased, and they were often crossed with mongrels and Dachshunds. In 1920, the Latvian Department of Forestry banned the use of dogs larger than 20 inches, and hunters selected many of the Curland/Dachshund crosses, often blending them with English Beagles. It wasn't until 1947 that the Council of Hunters and Fishermen of the Latvian SSR resolved to fix the Latvian Hound as a specific breed. Despite great difficulty, they found and purchased 40 dogs of the desired type from private owners and began a breeding program. By 1971, type was fixed and a standard adopted.

The modern Latvian Hound is a dog of general basset type with cat feet, short straight legs, a strong arched back and a wedge-shaped, tight-lipped head. They are selected for their ability to raise game quickly and to be obedient to any of the handlers during the hunt.

Leonberger.

LEONBERGER

COUNTRY: Germany
WEIGHT: 80–150 pounds
HEIGHT: 25½–31½ inches
COAT: Medium-to-long thick hair on body, short on face and front of legs
COLOR: Lion-colored, golden yellow to red, with black mask
REGISTRY: FCI
GROUP: Mastiff

Mayor Heinrich Essig created the Leonberger in the 1840s to honor his German town. He wanted to produce a noble dog close in appearance to the lion in the Leonberg town crest. The monks at St. Bernard cooperated and encouraged him by sending some dogs for use in his breeding experiments. This proved to have a twofold benefit as the breeding program at the monastery had suffered severe setbacks from distemper outbreaks, as well as decreased vigor due to prolonged inbreeding. Some of Herr Essig's crosses were returned later to the monastery and incorporated into the monks' breeding program.

In the 1840s, Essig began by crossing a Landseer Newfoundland with a St. Bernard, then backcrossed to a Great Pyrenees. The results were large, strong dogs that quickly gained popularity as working animals and a leonine status symbol for the city of Leonberg and surrounding estates.

It is probable another solid-colored dog was incorporated into the base stock, as the Landseer and Saint are both particolored, and major white markings on the Leonberger are now undesirable. Conjecture has pointed to German or Austrian scenthounds, Greater Swiss Mountain Dogs or Kuvaszok contributing to the formation of the modern Leonberger.

The Leonberger displayed attributes from his progenitors: affection for people, great size, working aptitude, majestic appearance and, from the Newfoundland, his love for water. These qualities attracted attention from German breeders and from Austria's Empress Elizabeth, who quickly acquired one. There followed a parade of illustrious owners: the Prince of Wales, the King of Belgium, a Russian czar, Chancellor Otto Furst von Bismarck, Emperor Napoleon III, German composer Richard Wagner and Italian patriot Giuseppe Garibaldi.

The World Wars were devastating to the Leonberger. With owners barely able to obtain food for themselves and their families, feeding giant animals was out of the question. Breeders fled or were killed, leaving the dogs to fend for themselves and, in some instances, the animals

themselves were slain. At the end of WWI, only five dogs remained, and these were carefully nurtured and bred from until WWII, when the devastation struck again, leaving but eight Leonbergers to be found. Five litters were bred in 1945, resulting in 22 puppies. The following year, only 17 puppies survived. According to a present owner, it has taken 25 years to re-establish the breed.

While still considered a rare breed, the Leonberger is gaining ground and serves as a rescue dog and family watchdog, as well as companion. These dogs enjoy water—playing with it, being in it, or just lying in a child's wading pool, if there is no alternative. They even blow bubbles in their water bowls! The "Gentle Lion" is fascinated by and genial with small creatures—dogs, other animals and especially children. Most, given a choice, would prefer to be with children over anything else. Give them kids and a pool and they are in dog heaven! They will stand and watch for hours beside a playpen in utter contentment.

Due to the dogs' size and strength, owners stress the importance of human companionship and the need for early training, or you'll find yourself telling a new version of the old joke: Where does a 150-pound Leonberger sleep? . . . *Anywhere he wants!*

Leonberger.

LEOPARD CUR

COUNTRY: USA
WEIGHT: 45–70 pounds
COAT: Dense and smooth
COLOR: Leopard spotted (merle) or black/tan most common; occasional yellow, brindle, and blue (mouse color); all can have white points or neck rings
OTHER NAMES: Leopard Tree Dog
GROUP: Hound

The name "cur" to most of our minds, and according to *Webster's Dictionary*, is a mixed breed dog or a mongrel. Actually, Curs are a specific type of American dog with a long, proud history. Old-time coon hunters liked to say the word cur came from a dog that had been "cur-tailed" or docked since, at the birth of the breed, the Leopard Cur was born bob-tailed or was cur-tailed.

The early settler in the American South wanted a single dog of medium size that could hunt and tree the native game but also be aggressive and tough enough to guard against Indian attacks, work the semi-wild livestock and even fight if necessary. Probably originally created by crosses of various hounds, stock dogs, and possibly native American pariah dogs, these Cur types followed the pioneer into the American West. Curs had the natural inclination to tree their game, and thus figured prominently in the development of the coonhounds.

The Leopard Cur was probably the fountainhead of these types, beginning in eastern North Carolina in the early part of the 18th century. Spanish conquistadors had brought war dogs, often of the blue-splotched color, with them to America as early as 1542. The French, also, came to the southern region accompanied by their dogs, including not only their famous hounds but perhaps the big, bold Beauceron of the harlequin variety. The area was later settled by people of English, Scotch and Irish descent, who brought a variety of both hounds (including the mottled Kerry Beagle) and herding dogs (like the merle Collie). So, attempting to pinpoint the origin of the "leopard" color (blue merle) is impossible. It could have come from either the hound or the stock dog side.

In early pioneer times, the farmstead and

Leopard Cur, black/tan.

Leopard Cur, merle.

fields were fenced to keep the livestock *out*. The cattle and the semi-wild hogs ran free in the woods, fending for themselves and being rounded up once a year. For this task, the farmer needed a stock dog that was tough and aggressive and would go for the nose like the "bulldogs" of old. But he also wanted a hunting companion who would accompany him into the vast forests to shoot squirrel, raccoon, and other game as well as be tough enough for hunting big game like the panther (the eastern mountain lion). This type, called variously Leopard Dog, Leopard Cur, or just Cur, was well known before the American Revolution.

The Leopard Dogs moved west into Tennessee, Kentucky and beyond with the pioneers. Later, particularly after the Civil War, the dogs continued into the developing southwest of Texas and Oklahoma.

This creation was unique from the past hounds in two ways. First, their disposition was to want to please their master, while in general the pure hound is a more independent creature. This factor definitely came from those willing to please—the herding dogs. The second trait was the natural tendency and ability to tree game. Where this came from is pure conjecture. Perhaps it was from the war dog/bulldog mentality; perhaps it was just a happy accident. At any rate, the treeing instinct combined with the presence of the raccoon in America created a demand for this skill. Other hounds were just trailing dogs, but it was the addition of the Cur blood to those foxhounds and others that eventually created the treeing American Coonhounds.

By the early 20th century, the lifestyle of even the most remote mountain areas had changed enough that there was little need for the old style Leopard Dog. Few dogs of reasonable purity remained in the early 1950s.

About the same time, three men, working independently, began searches through remote areas. These men, J. Richard McDuffie, Leroy E. Smith and A.W. Carter, each established breeding programs to renew this old American breed. When they met in 1959, they created the American Cur Breeders Association to foster and promote the breed. They tried to register only dogs that traced back to the origins in North Caro-

575

lina. In 1974, McDuffie, the registrar, transferred the registration office to Billie Williams of Missouri. His organization, the ACBA, continues to promote the breed today. McDuffie and others became alarmed, however, that a few unscrupulous breeders were crossing the old-style Leopards with other hounds and, because the merle gene is dominant and mottled pups result, registering them as Leopard Curs. Thus these men began the Leopard Tree Dog Registration Office in 1977 to register only those dogs tracing back to original North Carolina pedigrees on both sides. Many modern breeders have their dogs double registered with both the ACBA and the LTD.

The true Leopard Cur has a look, a psychology and a hunting style that is distinctly "cur." They have fine noses and are open trailers capable of excellent speed on a cold track. But they are "chop-mouthed"; that is, they have more of a bark than the drawn-out bay of a hound. These dogs also "run for blood," which is defined as the fight at the end of the track as the primary interest. To the pure hound, following the trail is the prime motivation.

The Leopard Dog has small, shorter ears set fairly high on the head, and tight cat feet. Today, most Leopard pups are born with long tails, which are not docked. This Cur is very affectionate to his master and has an intense desire to please. He tends to be a one-man dog, wary of strangers and, although always preferring to run from someone not known to him, if cornered will turn and stand his ground. Highly muscled and alert, the Leopard gives the impression of a coiled spring, ready to bound into action. The breed is courageous, with great stamina, able to work in temperature extremes.

Breeding for color alone is highly discouraged, as the ability of the hound is far more important than his jacketing. The American Cur Breeders Association history states, "Regardless of color, if he did a superior job, he was used as breeding stock. If he didn't, he stopped a bullet." Plain and simple! The breeding of leopard to leopard color is never allowed, because of the possibility of white pups which may be deaf or blind.

Leopard Curs having successfully treed their game.

Levesque.

LEVESQUE

COUNTRY: France
WEIGHT: 55–66 pounds
HEIGHT: 26–28 inches
COAT: Short and smooth
COLOR: Tricolor; with the tan limited mainly to the head; the black occurs as a large mantle or blanket; white clear with no ticking
REGISTRY: FCI
GROUP: Hound

The hound bearing this name was created in 1873 by Rogatien Levesque. Levesque used Bleu Gascony, Virelade (Grand Gascon-Saintongeois) and English Foxhound to create a breed somewhat similar to the Grand Gascon in size, color and conformation. Originally bred to hunt in packs, the Levesque has a fine nose and is fast and sturdy. He is used for all types of game. The Levesque is a lighter built dog than some of the other large French hounds, even though still good sized. Today the Levesque is quite rare, having been crossed with other breeds, or may even be extinct. Many French cynologists feel that the remaining specimens were incorporated into the creation of the Chien Francais Blanc et Noir in 1957.

Lhasa Apso.

LHASA APSO

COUNTRY: Tibet (China)
HEIGHT: 10–11 inches for males, less for bitches
COAT: Heavy, straight, hard and dense
COLOR: Golden, sandy or honey (these preferably with black tips on ear, tail and beard hair); also grizzle, slate, smoke, particolor, black, white, or brown
OTHER NAMES: Tibetan Apso
REGISTRY: FCI, AKC, UKC, TKC, CKC
GROUP: Herding

Much of Oriental history has not become known to the Western Hemisphere, and the origins of Far Eastern dogs are sketchy. It is known, however, that the Tibetan Terrier, the shaggy herding dog of Tibet, was the basis for many other breeds and types.

Selection for giantism had long ago created the Tibetan Mastiff from large wolf dogs. A selection for dwarfism (brachycephalicism) among the Tibetan Terriers created a dog with slightly shortened muzzle and lower stationed, slightly bent legs. Maintaining the heavy coat and the tail up over the back, the result was a dog of the Lhasa Apso type. Small shaggy dogs were known in Tibet as far back as eight centuries before Christ.

These little "holy dogs" were presented to guests as tokens of luck or as "thank you" presents. They were welcomed not only for their alarm-dog tendencies, but because they were believed to bring peace and prosperity to their households. As the nomadic "guests" traveled through the Eastern Hemisphere into Europe, the appeal of their dogs spread also.

The impetus for fixing the Apso type, however, was the conversion of Tibet to Buddhism in the seventh century AD. Lions had been, even before Buddhism, a traditional symbol of Tibetan royalty, with their famous lion throne of the Dalai Lama and the flag displaying the king of beasts. This symbol of the mighty lion was used, in slightly modified form, to emphasize the power of Buddha. The god was said to have shown his complete domination over the animals by making the lion guard his temples and follow him around "like a pet dog." A leonine colored and shaped dog was a good example to show primitive people proof of this story.

Lhasas, "lion dogs," became fixtures inside the homes of Tibetan nobility and in lamas' monasteries. Of course, the little dogs were purported to be guardians which, with their wariness to strangers and sharp bark, they probably were. But, with a Tibetan Mastiff tied outside the dwelling to provide the heavy artillery, the Apsos were mainly the beloved companions and friends of people in an inhospitable part of the world. Legend says that lamas (priests) that failed to reach Nirvana came back reincarnated as Lhasa Apsos. With this prestigious background, it is obvious why they were treated so well by the Tibetans.

The origin of the breed's name is a matter of controversy. In Tibet, the Lhasa is called *abso seng kye*, which indicates a barking, sentinel lion dog. Most numerous around the religious capital of Lhasa, the resulting combination might have contributed to his Western name. There are those that feel the name came from the Tibetan word *rapso*, which means goatlike, a description of the coat. In Britain, he is sometimes called, more generically, the Tibetan Apso.

Documented evidence exists that, for centuries, the Dalai Lamas—the spiritual heads of Tibet—sent gifts of small lion dogs to the imperial courts of China as tokens of esteem and good fortune. These dogs were incorporated into the strains of Chinese dogs and helped in the formation of breeds such as the Shih Tzu and Pekingese. The last of the Manchu empresses was known to have bred the Lhasas into her Chinese dogs "to improve coat."

Lhasa dogs began to appear in the West around the turn of the century, brought back by British explorers, emissaries and other travelers to Tibet. There was much confusion at first, with shaggy Oriental dogs of a variety of sizes being called "Lhasa Terriers." It was only later

Lhasa Apso.

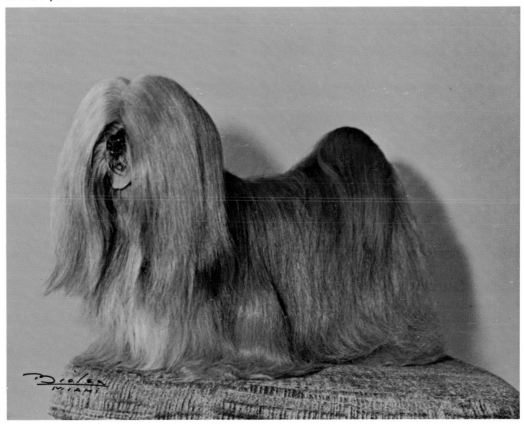

Lhasa Apso.

that authorities distinguished between the leggier and longer headed Tibetan Terrier and the smaller Lhasa Apso. Many early Shih Tzus also may have been a part of this confusion. But by the 1930s, the Lhasa Apso had his own identity and a supportive breed club in Britain. The breed was introduced into the United States about this same time, from an initial pair given as gifts by the 13th Dalai Lama to visiting Americans, the C. Suydam Cuttings, forming the famed Hamilton line. In fact, the dogs in Tibet were never sold, but given away to esteemed friends as good luck talismans that kept evil spirits away.

Later, when the Shih Tzu first arrived in the States, they were mistakingly registered as Lhasas. Some of these dogs were naturally bred to Lhasas, causing a great deal of trouble between breeders. Even today one will find stress placed on the "pure Hamilton line," indicating no Shih Tzu blood flows in their veins.

The Lhasa has become a favored companion dog in many modern nations. His small—but not toy—size combined with his surprising hardiness and ability to distinguish friend from foe have endeared him to many. Owners are amazed by his ability to adapt to a variety of climatic conditions and lifestyles, but he does need human contact to fulfill his destiny. Despite their natural companionability with man, some can be a bit strong-minded, and early introduction to rules and firm, loving discipline are recommended.

They are well known for their longevity; dogs of 18 are not uncommon and one champion of this breed lived to be 29! In the show ring, the Lhasa is the ultimate in coiffed glamour, with hair completely covering his eyes and head and reaching the floor. Even those specimens intended as pets require regular grooming to prevent a disaster of tangles and mats. Due to the brachycephalic nature of their genetic background, undershot jaws are the norm.

Lhasa Apso.

581

Lhasa Apso.

Lhasa Apso.

LITHUANIAN HOUND

COUNTRY: USSR
HEIGHT: 21–24 inches
COAT: Short and glossy
COLOR: Black with dapples
GROUP: Hound

This newest of the Russian scenthounds is a product of the present century. Lithuanian hunters crossed local big game hounds with Beagles, Bloodhounds (St. Hubert), Polish Hounds and later Russian Hounds, in an attempt to recreate the old-type Curland Hound (associated at one time with the Latvian Hound). Although progress was made at first, the breed was gasping for life in the 1970s and very low in numbers. During the 1976–77 hunting season, many fine dogs were killed by boars, and the breed was threatened with extinction. That year the Lithuanian Cynological Council appointed a specialist to be responsible for perpetuation of the breed, created a special kennel facility for raising them and adopted a standard. The breed seems to be on its feet now, although it is still found only in the Lithuanian Republic.

This hound is a good-sized, robust dog of clean, sleek, yet muscular proportions. He has the fervor, speed and persistence to track hare, fox and even boar, and is known for his glorious voice.

Lithuanian Hound.

Löwchen.

LÖWCHEN

COUNTRY: France
WEIGHT: 8–18 pounds
HEIGHT: 10–13 inches
COAT: Long, silky, wavy but not curly
COLOR: Any color or combination of colors
OTHER NAMES: Little Lion Dog, Petit Chien Lion
REGISTRY: FCI, TKC
GROUP: Gun Dog

Favorites of the Florentine nobles of the 15th century, the Löwchen catered to the whims of the elite. Ladies at court clipped the hair from the dogs' backs and used them as hot water bottles. Developed in Europe, the breed has been traditionally clipped similar to the Portuguese Water Dog in the "lion" trim. In fact, with his clip, his waving hair, his tail held high over his back and his color varieties, one can almost imagine him a miniature of that breed. This is probably not his immediate origin, but the simi-

larity of the bichon family and the water dogs is emphasized by these comparisons. The Little Lion Dog undoubtedly evolved from the family of bichons, as they traveled from the Mediterranean into Europe. Many feel that the breed was developed in Germany, but FCI lists France as the official country of development.

The Löwchen has been established in Spain, France and Germany since the 1500s. One of this type was painted by Goya in the late 18th century in a portrait of the beautiful Duchess of Alba. These dogs with the lion cut are often depicted at the feet of armored knights on tombs in old churches. The story goes that if a knight was killed in battle, he had a figure of a lion at his feet, demonstrating his courage. Otherwise he had the "little lion dogs," the Löwchens, as did the ladies—perhaps to provide them courage or comfort in their battles of the afterlife.

In more modern times, the Löwchen fell out of favor and nearly disappeared. The few that were left were turned out into the streets to fend

for themselves during the stress and uncertainty of the War years. Thanks to the post-war efforts of Madame M. Bennert of Brussels, a dedicated fancier, the Little Lion Dog was slowly brought back from obscurity. She combed the streets, collecting typical specimens. These contributed to the resurgence of the breed. Her work was carried on by a German, Dr. Richert, after her death. In 1960, the Löwchen was named the rarest breed by the *Guinness Book of World Records*.

They are now recognized in many countries of the world, including Great Britain, but are still fairly rare. No longer, however, do they win the dubitable claim to fame as the "rarest breed." Despite its diminutive size, the Löwchen is robust and full of energy, yet sensible and not hyperactive. A dog of intelligence and affection, he is exclusively a house pet and companion, and is winning admiration in the US.

Above: Löwchen, dark gray. **Below:** Löwchen, fawn.

Lundehund.

LUNDEHUND

COUNTRY: Norway
WEIGHT: 13–14 pounds
HEIGHT: 12½–14½ inches
COAT: Short, rough, stand-off
COLOR: Brown with black tipping and some white markings; rare blacks or white with black tipping allowed
OTHER NAMES: Norwegian Puffin Dog
REGISTRY: FCI
GROUP: Northern

This quaint dog is believed by some to have survived the Ice Age by feeding on sea birds. Its purity was assured by the isolation of Maastad and other Arctic islands. As early as 1591, Schonnebol told of these dogs in his travels.

The puffin (*lunde*) is a brightly colored bird which waddles on land, but fights fiercely to protect its young. Puffins breed in large colonies, with nests built deep in the rocky crevices on coastal islands in the Arctic seas. Nest rob-

bing is only for the very brave or foolhardy person, as the birds fight desperately to protect themselves with their vicious beaks and claws. Nevertheless, the young birds were sought to be salted, preserved and eaten during Lent. It is said they tasted enough like fish to satisfy even pious consciences. The puffin down and feathers were also valued.

When the fledglings were about 40 days old, the danger of the hunt was eased as the adults abandoned their young to the ways of the world. All that was left to battle was the folding, pleating and mutilating of oneself into the crevices. No human was up to that. Enter the Lundehund—physically a breed nonpareil—ideally suited to fit the job requirements.

The Puffin Dog is a typical Nordic dog, but with several modifications to fit his specialized job. His upright ears are placed so high and forward that, upon pricking them, they afford the added protection of almost closing to the front. This creates a shield from the constantly dripping water and dust in the caves. He is able to mold his body to fit in narrow passages because of the extraordinary range of motion in his joints. The head can be bent backwards, almost touching its back, and the forelegs can turn to the side at 90-degree angles.

The Lundehund certainly has the most interesting feet in dogdom. Small-bodied for agility among the rocks, the breed has been selected for polydactylism (supernumerary toes), so that it has at least two large functional dewclaws and up to eight plantar cushions per foot. The extra toes aid in the clamber up the rocks after the puffin. The standard states that there must be at least six toes on each foot and, of those, at least five toes on the forefoot and four on the hind foot should support the dog. On the front paw, five of those toes are triple-jointed, similar to our fingers, and one toe is double-jointed. Four toes on the rear foot have three joints, and one is split into two digits, each with two joints, all

giving the dog incredible grasping abilities, even on the rocky climbs. These characteristics must be on the judging table during competition.

Parson Petter Dass (1647–1708) wrote of the puffin hunt in a poem, *Nordlandstrompet*:

"A puffin hatches an only egg,
it is hidden in the scree as inside a wall
in the innermost caves of the rocks.
A nest is built so near the other,
that one bites the other's wing and feather
in the crevices, where they hide.
But the farmers who have a plan
know well to intrude upon those puffins
    with loot,
and that by trained dogs,
which by formation are supple and small,
so they can creep into the narrowest nook
and pull out live puffins.
When the dog snatches that puffin by the
    neck,

Lundehund modestly demonstrating his extraordinary flexibility.

which lies in front, whose life is for sale,
it begins straightway to set out.
At once the puffin, which sat behind
grasps the foremost by the tail and goes
    together,
whereas one is left behind.
By this it happens that a single dog
drags out at once from the darkest ground
twelve, thirteen—even fourteen and more,
and supplies its awaiting master
with so much booty, as he can handle,
whereby his profit may flourish.''

The little dog was considered as valuable as a cow, and neighbors squabbled over having more Lundehunds than each other. Around 1850, however, nets took the place of the Puffin Dogs. Dog enthusiast Sigurd Skaun read about the Lundehunds and tracked them down to the island of Veroy. He published an article on the breed in the Norwegian hunting and fishing union's 1925 periodical. Twelve years later Eleanor Christie read that article and began her search for the native dog. About 50 samples of the breed were finally found in Haastad on the southwestern part of Veroy.

Mrs. Christie obtained four pups from Monrad Mostad in 1939. In 1942, a severe distemper

Lundehund.

The Lundehund's double-jointed neck and closeable ears are mutations unique to the breed.

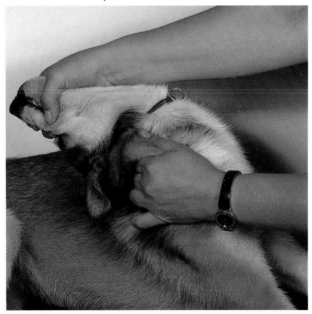

outbreak left only one survivor on Veroy. Christie came to the rescue with some of her breeding. One of these, although never hunted previously, took 14 puffins on his first outing.

It was impossible to obtain vaccine during the War years and, in 1944, distemper came to the Christies' kennel, leaving her with only an aged bitch. This time Mostad returned her generosity and supplied her with breeding stock. The breed was virtually down to the essentials, with only one bitch and one male in a breeder's hands. Eleanor Christie was determined not to let one of her country's national treasures become extinct, and has built the breed up to a respectable number today. Norwegian law now protects the colorful puffin and has exempted the Lundehund from taxation, allowing both species to flourish and multiply.

Despite the breed's odd proclivities, the Lundehund is perfectly normal when it comes to being friendly and enjoying his family. Though perhaps a bit obstinate, they make entertaining companions, joining in a variety of activities.

MAGYAR AGĂR

COUNTRY: Hungary
WEIGHT: 49–68 pounds
HEIGHT: 25–27½ inches
COAT: Short and a bit coarse
COLOR: All sighthound colors
OTHER NAMES: Hungarian Greyhound
REGISTRY: FCI
GROUP: Southern

When ninth-century Magyars invaded Hungary, they were accompanied by cattle/sheep herding dogs and running hounds from the steppes of Russia. During the early centuries, these dogs crossed with native sighthounds, present since Celtic times, and created the Agăr. These speedy and keen hounds were utilized for centuries by the nobility for formal hunts and coursing and by the peasants for poaching. In the 20th century, Greyhounds were introduced for greater speed and elegance. Many Hungarians felt this was destroying the old-type Agăr, diluting it until it is nothing more than a Greyhound's "poor cousin." In fact, the Agăr is often referred to today as a half-breed. But recognition by the FCI in 1966 revived interest in the true breed, both in its homeland and elsewhere in Europe.

The Agăr is used on hare and foxes in Hungary and chases the mechanical lure on the track. Although larger than the Galgo, he is still smaller than the Greyhound. Also distinguishing him from his English counterpart are a wide head and muzzle and the coarser haircoat for protection. He is a calm and affectionate dog.

Magyar Agăr, brindle/white.

Majestic Tree Hound, white with brown markings.

MAJESTIC TREE HOUND

COUNTRY: USA
WEIGHT: 75–110 pounds
HEIGHT: 24½–30 inches
COAT: Short, thick and dense
COLOR: Any color or combination of colors
GROUP: Hound

The creation of this breed is very recent, but the stem stock goes clear back to medieval northern France and the hounds of St. Hubert. The motives of this breed's creators were much the same as those who sponsor the American Blue Gascon Hound. These hunters wanted to save the large, cold-nosed, methodical working hound as a type in America, but the Majestic Tree Hound's forebear was the working Bloodhound.

Big game hounds of the old Bloodhound/Talbot/St. Hubert type inhabited American soil for

591

Majestic Tree Hound, pup, brown/white.

and jaguar, and are able to drive the big cats from their hiding places. Newhart offers a hunter's account of the scene: "It was a wild sight. The maddened hounds bayed at the foot of the pine. Above them in the lower branches stood the big horse-killing cat, the destroyer of the deer, the lord of stealthy murder, facing his doom with a heart both craven and cruel."

They also make superior coon hunters where the speed and numbers treed are not as important as the skill, voice and persistence of a fine hound. (This is true also of American Blue Gascon and Plott Hounds, both big game hunters.) An exquisite nose finds a track where other hounds would fail, and the coldtrailing ability keeps him on it long after others would have given up and gone home.

This is an extemely good-natured and affectionate hound, accepting equally both praise and correction. He is not quarrelsome with his fellows and has a noble and dignified expression.

Majestic Tree Hound, pup, tricolor.

many years, and these were crossed with a variety of other hounds for coldtrailing work. The Majestic people say they crossed these Bloodhounds with "western big-game hounds." These dogs may have been of the Gascon type like the Old Line dogs or even strains from those long ago Porcelaines that went west with the Rousseau family.

Lee Newhart, Jr., and several others created the National Majestic Tree Hound Association in 1980, and registered the first hounds in that year. These are *big* hounds with males averaging over 100 pounds. They have the long, low-set earage (with a minimum length specified), heavy flew and dewlap of their ancestors from the Ardennes. They carry more excess skin in general than the American Blue Gascon, and are noteworthy for their abundant flew and dewlap, as well as facial wrinkles.

Intended for rugged terrain and long endurance, they are most suited for lion, bear, bobcat

Maltese.

MALTESE

COUNTRY: Italy
WEIGHT: Less than 7 pounds, 4–6 pounds preferred
COAT: Long, flat silky hair hanging nearly to ground, no undercoat
COLOR: White; light tan or lemon on the ears only is allowed although not preferred
OTHER NAMES: Bichon Maltiase
REGISTRY: FCI, AKC, UKC, TKC, CKC
GROUP: Gun Dog

Small dogs referred to as "bichons" have been present and popular around the Mediterranean for thousands of years. The question of which breed is the oldest and which came first follows the puzzle of the chicken and the egg. They are all, essentially, miniaturized water retrievers,

coming from the same stock that produced the Portuguese Water Dogs, the Barbet, the Poodles and others. Those that lived on Tenerife were called Bichon Tenerife, those from Bologna called Bolognese and dogs on Malta were known as Maltese. Some may have developed independently, but all have similar type and character. All bichon varieties are cute, cuddly and coaty, giving them a winsome appeal.

Pets that fit the description of the Maltese have been known since very early times. The island of Malta, off the southern coast of Italy, was colonized by the Phoenicians about 1000 BC. These small, white dogs could have been brought to the area by the Phoenicians and/or spread elsewhere by them, since they sailed and traded around the known world. The Maltese dogs were entirely bred as companions and

Maltese.

Maltese.

"comforters," being especially favored by the ladies who often carried them in their sleeves or held them in their laps when in their carriages "taking air." But they won the hearts of more than the women; the Roman governor of Malta in the first century AD so adored his Maltese that he requested a portrait painted and poems written about her.

The Maltese maintained its demand as a companion through the centuries. Dr. Caius describes these small white dogs in the 1500s, and, in 1607, a writer described one that sold for $2,000! At that time, they were described as the size of a squirrel or a common ferret, as small as today's tiniest specimens.

The Maltese remains a much-loved pet and glamorous show dog. They are fastidious, refined and loyal. Devoted to their owners, they are friendly with everyone. Their snowy white, soft coat is without undercoat so they don't create yearly shedding problems, although they definitely require frequent combing to keep out tangles. Their tails are natural length and curve gracefully up over the back. The Maltese is playful and sturdy, despite its petiteness.

Maltese.

Malteses, adult and pups.

MANCHESTER TERRIERS

Manchester Terrier

COUNTRY: Great Britain
WEIGHT: 12–16 pounds; 16–22 pounds
COAT: Short, smooth
COLOR: Black/tan
OTHER NAMES: Black and Tan Terrier
REGISTRY: FCI, AKC, TKC, CKC
GROUP: Terrier

Toy Manchester Terrier

COUNTRY: Great Britain
WEIGHT: 7–12 pounds
COAT: Short, smooth
COLOR: Black/tan
OTHER NAMES: Black and Tan Toy Terrier,
English Toy Terrier
REGISTRY: FCI, AKC, TKC, CKC
GROUP: Terrier

Described by Dr. Johannes Caius's chronicle of English dogs (1570s), the Black and Tan Terrier was probably the original ratting terrier, highly skilled in his duty. The Black and Tan was coarser in head and body, and shorter on leg than many of our modern terriers and may have looked much like the modern smooth-coated Patterdale. The wellspring for many of the terrier breeds, these black/tan dogs also contributed to the formation of some fighting breeds.

The poor man's sports of rat killing and rabbit coursing reached a zenith in the Manchester district of England during the mid-1800s. John Hulme, as well as other sporting men, determined to produce a dog with "true grit" that could be used in both arenas, crossed the Black and Tan Terrier with the coursing Whippet. This combination created the breed now known as the Manchester Terrier. Backcrossing to fix type was mainly to more terriers, but the Whippet (sighthound) influence is evidenced still by

Manchester Terrier.

Toy Manchester Terrier.

the arched loin and slightly Roman nose with very little stop to the head. But grit they did have! The famed "Billy" was pitted against 100 rats, with a time limit of eight-and-a-half minutes. Billy killed them all in six minutes, 35 seconds, later lowering his time by another 22 seconds—only three-and-a-half seconds per rat!

Although the breed became celebrated, the name did not, many feeling it was too restrictive for a dog known throughout the British Isles. During his heyday in the Victorian era, he was often referred to as the "Gentleman's Terrier." For a time, around the turn of the present century, the original name (Black and Tan Terrier) was reintroduced.

With a great deal of size variation in the early Manchester stock, the Toy variety was created by selecting and breeding the smallest among them. Although called the Toy Manchester in the USA, the English version has retained the interim name of Black and Tan Toy Terrier. This smaller version also peaked in popularity during Queen Victoria's reign, with breeders fascinated with producing tinier and tinier specimens until health and normalcy were threatened. Two-and-a-half-pound adult dogs were not unusual.

Since ears always had been cropped, selection for ear size and carriage was unimportant. When ear cropping was outlawed in 1889, breeders of both varieties had difficulty in obtaining dogs of correct type that also had the good button ear. Also, the newly adopted standard required precise markings. This discouraged many breeders. By this time, ratting trials had been outlawed as well. The breeds lost favor and became quite rare. Due to the persistence of a few devotees, the Manchesters were maintained, without the size extreme favored in earlier times and with much-improved ears.

Manchester Terrier.

MAREMMA SHEEPDOG

COUNTRY: Italy
WEIGHT: 65–100 pounds
HEIGHT: 23½–29 inches
COAT: Profuse, long, never curly
COLOR: White, some yellow or pale orange tolerated on ears only
OTHER NAMES: Pastore Abruzzese, Cane da Pastore Maremmano-Abruzzese
REGISTRY: FCI, TKC
GROUP: Flock Guard

By 1923, American and English fanciers elected to stay with Manchester Terrier as a name for the breed. In the same year, the Manchester Terrier Club of America was formed.

Except for size and ears, the standard and Toy varieties are judged by the same standard. The larger is allowed folded ears, similar to those of the Fox and Lakeland Terriers, or erect ears, often cropped in a long cut (except in England). Ideally, the tan markings on the legs and toes should contain "pencil marks" of black. Any white in the coat is highly objectionable.

Their sleek beauty, graceful movement and intelligence make them a choice for the show ring. In the home, they are great friends with a long lifespan. All of these qualities, plus their easy-care coats and an alert bark, make them a good choice for the elderly.

Today, the Toy is a nearly identical smaller replica of the standard Manchester Terrier. The "little brother" has high-set erect ears that do not fold or drop, and cropping is a disqualification.

The Maremma is directly descended from the first flock guarders that migrated from the Middle East, probably across the Adriatic from Greece. A first-century writer, Lucius Columella, refers to the Maremma in his book on Roman rural affairs, and Marcus Terentius Varro, "most learned of the Romans," describes such a dog in 100 BC.

The breed was used all along the Apennine mountain range, the spine that runs the length of Italy. The pattern of the Tuscan farmers persisted for centuries. During the winter months, pasture was adequate in the dry, low areas (like Maremma) along the sea coast to support the flocks. White dogs protecting these animals were naturally called Maremmani. The summer heat dried up nearly every blade of grass in the lowlands so the shepherd, sheep and grand white dogs climbed the mountains to stay for many months in greener pastures.

Although many guarded flocks in the Abruzzi Mountains (and thus were called Abruzzese), they were also known further north and south along the Adriatic coast. When the shepherd went home at night, the sheep were left in a net enclosure to prevent wandering. The dogs never followed the master home, but stayed to protect the sheep. These dogs were also a traditional feature of the fine country houses of Tuscany. A story about British troops capturing some Italian soldiers with a Maremma tells of the dog placed in a pen with six trained Royal Air Force Alsatians (German Shepherds). In the morning, the white dog was calmly lying in the pen next to six dead Alsatians!

The Maremma is similar in type to the Great Pyrenees and Kuvasz, though without as great a

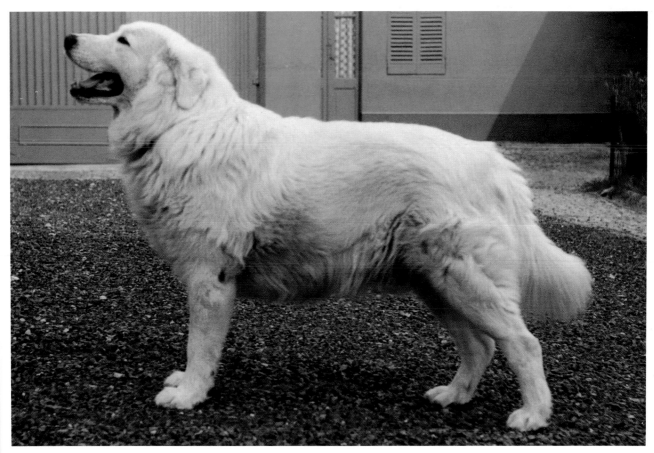

Maremma Sheepdog.

bulk. The dogs are often fed only curds and whey or a mealy pap, and yet they seem well nourished.

Fear of ruination by "improvement" kept the Maremma away from the public eye for many years. In the 1950s, a meeting finally took place in Florence, where a discussion of the types ensued. Although the Abruzzese was often considered a separate breed, sturdier with a more profuse coat, a decision was made that these were only normal variations based on climate. A standard was approved for a single breed, allowing for some variation of coat length. The official breed name in Italy includes both geographical labels to keep everyone happy.

These dogs have the typical flock-guard independence and must be handled with respect. While it is necessary to establish dominance, a Maremma that is beaten or ill-used will not hesitate to bite his master. They have a strong natural concept of their owners' belongings and feel the need to protect them. In a modern world, this encompasses home, grounds, cars and be-

longings, as well as family members. The Maremma will not allow anyone, even his master, to interfere with his guarding duties. He feels, often rightly so, that he knows best! As explained in the Maremma Sheepdog Club of Great Britain booklet, "It may be inconvenient if they [the children] deserve a spanking which he will not permit, or when he will not allow strangers to pick up their toys."

He has had an active following in Great Britain for more than 50 years, where the breed may compete for championships and is used to guard country estates. The Maremma has found favor in Sweden as well. Introduced into the United States in the 1970s, it serves only in the flock-guarding programs and is occasionally seen at rare breed shows. In just a short time, however, the breed has won the enthusiastic praise of stock owners. Some dogs, in fact, take their work too seriously. The Hampshire College program placed a six-month-old Maremma with a flock in Arkansas that had suffered losses from predators. The pup immediately took charge,

Maremma Sheepdog.

ending the kills. "Lady" became so attached to "her" sheep and their territory that when the sheep were sold and soybeans filled the pasture, she transferred her protection to the soybeans!

As with many of the flock-guarding breeds, the Maremma seems plagued with infertility and disinterest in breeding. Irregular heat cycles are reported, along with female aggression toward suitors. Researchers at Hampshire College have two bitches that have never had a litter, even though precautions were not taken to prevent matings. This modern breeder dilemma may actually have been a desirable trait in working dogs to prevent distractions from their duties. Once they conceive, they are likely to have good-sized litters. In their native land, working dams give birth under a tree or in some protective cavity.

They have a great instinct concerning "their" sheep. One working dog picked up an ill lamb in his mouth, and brought it to his master. An Italian breeder states, "In Italy sheep raising on the mountains would be practically impossible without these dogs."

The Maremma is not as large as some of the other flock guards and has the ability to appear larger or smaller than it is in reality. When unhappy, the dog will curl up and appear much smaller than normal. But when he is threatened or alerted, he draws himself to full size, flares his ruff, and holds his tail high over his back, seemingly increasing his bulk. The spiked collar, also used in Italy, increases the dog's aura even more.

Although the adult Maremma does not fawn on its master and is hesitant to show devotion, it will lay down its life to protect its family. It will remember its master "though many years may pass in his absence." It will also remember an unkindness.

MASTIFF

COUNTRY: Great Britain
WEIGHT: 175–190 pounds
HEIGHT: Minimum 27½–30 inches
COAT: Short, smooth
COLOR: Apricot, fawn or fawn-brindle, all with black mask
OTHER NAMES: Old English Mastiff
REGISTRY: FCI, AKC, TKC, CKC
GROUP: Mastiff

Early cynologists disagree just where the Mastiff originated, but they concur it is an ancient type. These dogs were depicted in bas reliefs as early as the Babylonian era, about 2200 BC, with their roots most likely leading back to the ancient Tibetan Mastiff. When the Romans arrived in England, the Mastiff had already preceded them, likely brought by ancient dog-traders. The English dogs' courage and power so impressed the Romans that they took examples of the breed back to Rome to fight in the arenas. These English powerhouses often defeated the homebred variety of molossus.

It was the Mastiffs' use as bandogs that brought them to prominence. Mastiffs, a derivative of the Latin *mastinus* meaning house-dog, roamed the grounds of estates and guarded castles, as well as lowly huts. Peasants were compelled to keep at least one Mastiff for every two serfs to ward off savage beasts and villains. The Legh family of Lyme Hall, Cheshire, is recorded to have kept Mastiffs since 1415. English kings showed their pride in the dogs and displayed generosity by gifting Spanish royalty with the breed. Henry VIII sent Charles V a battalion of 400 Mastiffs as war dogs. The mastiff type was so common in England at the time of the Norman invasion that the French word *dogue*, meaning mastiff, was incorporated into the English language to describe all of the canine species!

Mastiffs served time in the pits facing large, tough opponents during the Elizabethan era. Following the decline of the forbidden matches, these dogs entered a downward trend. During the mid-19th century, the breed was revitalized and believed to have been crossed with the Al-

Mastiff, fawn.

603

Mastiff, brindle.

pine Mastiff (St. Bernard). It was during this period that Mastiff fanciers "laid down the law" against the original longer head, now unfashionable. The wide use of one stud, with short, blocky head—but otherwise very faulty—created almost insurmountable problems.

Interest waned. From 63 Mastiffs at an 1871 English show, the entry dropped to zero just a few years later. The war years of the next century took further tolls on the breed. In 1945, only eight Mastiffs of breeding age were left in all of Britain! But a pair of fine pups, donated by a top Canadian kennel, helped restore the breed in its homeland, where it now is firmly entrenched.

In 1941, it was recognized in America and, currently, the Mastiff holds steady mid-way in AKC registrations. Throughout the years, Mastiffs have traveled the usual hills and valleys of popularity: large dog vs. small dog; hairy vs. smooth; tough vs. mellow.

Despite his giant size and forbidding appearance, the Mastiff is a good family pet, with those same qualities making him a worthy watchdog. He is a creature of habit and does not transplant easily, meaning that buyers who choose the Mastiff should plan to keep him for life. Tragically, like so many of the giants, he is not long-lived.

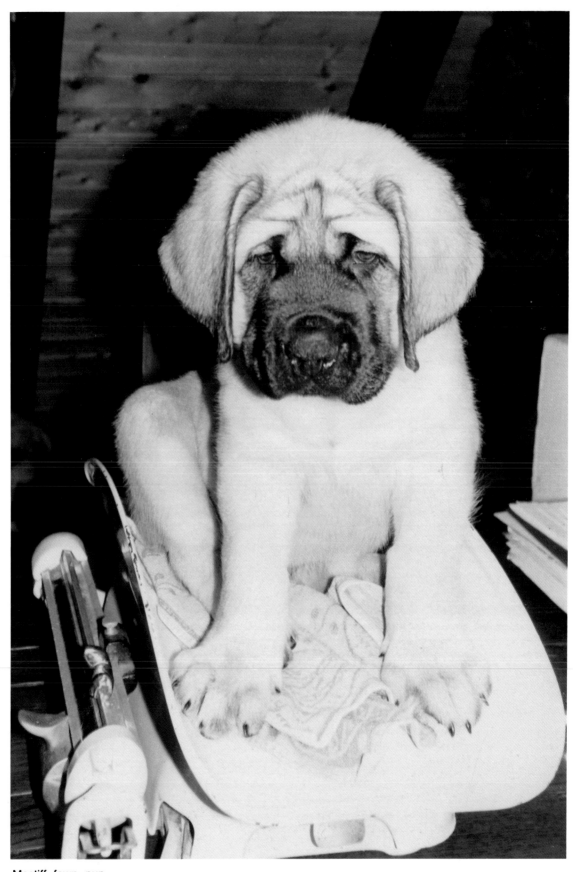

Mastiff, fawn, pup.

MIDDLE ASIAN OWTCHARKA

COUNTRY: USSR
HEIGHT 23½–25½ inches minimum; usually larger
COAT: Short and thick
COLOR: Black, white, gray or brindle; with or without white markings
OTHER NAMES: Mid-Asian Shepherd
GROUP: Flock Guard

The ancient home of the Middle Asian Owtcharka is east of the Urals into Siberia and even Mongolia. There he has aided and protected the nomadic tribes and their flocks for centuries. But modern changes in lifestyles have reduced the numbers of this breed. The best modern examples are in the Turkmen Republic, although he can be found in the Republics of Uzbek, Tadzhik, Kazakhstan and Kirgiz. He has never been exhibited nor been established outside mid-Russia.

Most are similar to the largest and thickest set of the Caucasian dogs, and they not only have their ears lopped off short, but have their tails bobbed as well. Many feel he resembles his ancestor, the Tibetan Mastiff, because of his thick skin with neck folds and facial wrinkles. He also comes in a variety of colors, but especially black. He is well adapted to the heat and scarce water conditions of Central Asia. Because of his strength and bravery he is sometimes used in hunting boar or snow leopards. In some areas he has been crossed with local Borzois to create a shepherd that seconds as a hunter. These crosses tend to be more refined in bone.

Middle Asian Owtcharka, black with white and tan markings.

Middle Asian Owtcharka.

Miniature Bull Terrier, colored.

MINIATURE BULL TERRIER

COUNTRY: Great Britain
WEIGHT: 10–40 pounds
HEIGHT: 10–14 inches
COAT: Short, harsh
COLOR: Solid white; white with head markings; brindle, red, fawn, black/tan, black brindle, with or without white markings in the Irish pattern
REGISTRY: FCI, AKC, TKC, CKC
GROUP: Mastiff

Good things come in small packages, and the Miniature Bull Terrier is all the fire and clowning of its larger version seen through the reverse side of a magnifying glass. Bred to aid their larger brothers in ratting duties, they were a great favorite of those who preferred a smaller, more manageable house pet. At one time, Bull Terriers ranged from as tiny as three pounds to a macho 30-plus. The Toy variety, under ten pounds, suffered the problems often seen in extreme miniaturization and has disappeared, but the Mini is picking up fans daily.

In 1938, Englishman Colonel Glyn founded the Miniature Bull Terrier Club, and the Minis were eligible for challenge certificates shortly after. Although they were shown in the United States early in the 1900s, they reached a lull and have only recently (1963) begun showing in the Miscellaneous Class again. The CKC also includes them in that class, while they merit full FCI recognition.

They adore their owners and are excellent playmates for children, as well as being good alarm dogs. Breeders warn owners to be careful not to leave precious or dangerous objects lying around, since the Mini thinks any object within his reach is fair game for lunch. Puppies are "energized" and can be destructive if left alone.

Strong and solid, the Minis can pull owners on skateboards or cross-country skis! They're adaptable to any lifestyle, from active to sedate, from large families with children to a single person or an elderly couple. These dogs enjoy being the center of attention, and will put up with a great amount of "foolishness" from children, including being dressed in doll clothes. All of this is often accompanied by a "Bully" smile.

This "pocket edition" of the Bull Terrier is even-tempered, but requires a controlling hand. Owners note that physical care is a breeze.

Miniature Bull Terrier, colored.

Miniature Pinscher

MINIATURE PINSCHER

COUNTRY: Germany
WEIGHT: 10 pounds
HEIGHT: 10–12½ inches
COAT: Short and smooth
COLOR: Black/tan, chocolate/tan or stag red
OTHER NAMES: Zwergpinscher
REGISTRY: FCI, AKC, UKC, TKC, CKC
GROUP: Terrier

The well-known "Min-Pin" has been bred for several hundred years, stemming directly from his larger cousin, the German Pinscher. Some feel that small Dachshunds and Italian Greyhounds were introduced to the smallest pinschers to obtain the diminutive size. These dogs are often called "Reh Pinscher," due to their resemblance to the small roe deer found in Rhineland forests.

When the German Pinscher-Schnauzer Club was formed in the 1890s, it embraced all pinscher sizes. For a time, the Miniature Pinscher's quest was for "the tinier, the better." These Lilliputian specimens were bedecked and bejeweled and were judged while lying on exquisite pillows or being held protectively in their owner's arms.

The club's influence helped establish type and spread interest. By WWI the breed had regained its soundness and was back on the ground, showing off its trademark: the high-prancing gait. Even with some reduction of breeding activities during the First World War, the breed continued to gain ground. It was first shown in American dog shows in small numbers during the 1920s, and has slowly increased its numbers in the United States since that time. Progress has been slower in Great Britain, due to strict quarantine laws as well as the ban on cropping. British breeders now are making good progress in breeding strains with small, naturally erect ears.

The Min-Pin was taken under the auspices of AKC in 1929 and first shown as a terrier. Now listed as a Toy, like the Yorkshire, he is all terrier! His natural presence makes him a born showman in the ring, giving him the title of "King of Toys." The Min-Pin is the top toy breed in Denmark, Holland and Italy.

Ears are usually cropped, and the tail is docked like the Standard Pinscher's. The similarity to their larger versions goes beyond mere looks, since guarding instincts and a robust and confident nature are evident, making them capable of biting an intruder—in the ankle. They can be suspicious and protective. Overall, they are fun-loving dogs who need little care to keep them in good condition.

Miniature Pinschers, red.

Miniature Pinschers, black/tan.

MOSCOW LONGHAIRED TOY TERRIER

COUNTRY: USSR
WEIGHT: 4½–6½ pounds
HEIGHT: 8–11 inches
COAT: Long and straight, with abundant fringe on ears, legs and neck ruff
COLOR: Black, brown, sable, fawn or tan, usually with tan points, but may be solid; merle also occurs
OTHER NAMES: Moscovian Miniature Terrier
REGISTRY: None
GROUP: Terrier

This newest of the Russian breeds is a definite charmer. Approved only in 1981, he is becoming the rage in the cities. The Longhaired Toy Terrier was developed especially as an urban pet, notably for senior citizens, which could withstand Russian winters. Limited information exists on which breeds were used, although it is thought that long-coated Chihuahuas and small English toys like the Yorkshire were used. The existence of the merle color, as well as good guarding ability, makes one think of small European terriers like the Harlequin Pinscher. The result is a gracious, aristocratic, lively and handsome dog that is easily trained and cared for.

His petite face tapers sharply, and the large ears cascade with flowing hair. His docked tail is held upright, and his every movement is light and quick. A wide range of colors adds to his appeal. He is unknown outside the Soviet Union. But at home, demand far outweighs supply due to their small litters.

Moscow Longhaired Toy Terrier, black with tan points.

MOSCOW WATCHDOG

COUNTRY: USSR
WEIGHT: 100–150 pounds
HEIGHT: 25–27 inches
COAT: Moderate length, thick with fringing
COLOR: Red/white
GROUP: Mastiff

This recent innovation was created by Moscow dog fanciers who wanted a large, strong watchdog that would be more receptive to taking and following orders. After World War II, breeders began with Caucasian Owtcharkas for wariness and ferocity. The St. Bernard was then chosen for its size and strength, but more benign temperament. A blend of the two has created the Moscow Watchdog, with the beautiful physical qualities of thick coat and strong muscles, as well as the mental characteristics these people wanted.

Moscow Watchdog.

Moscow Watchdog.

MOUNTAIN CUR

COUNTRY: USA
WEIGHT: 35–65 pounds
COAT: Short or slightly longer and heavy
COLOR: Brindle, yellow, black/tan or mouse blue; with or without white neck ring and points
GROUP: Hound

The Mountain Cur is of the same general gene pool as the Leopard Cur. They originated at the time the United States was new and were particularly common in the Ohio River Valley. As frontiersmen, followed by entire families, moved to open the West, their Cur dogs accompanied them. Those that foster this breed say that besides the herding dog and hound, there is a dash of "Indian cur" (a pariah-type dog) in their makeup. Although called "mountain" because of their particular advantage to settlers in wooded, wild areas, they were just as welcome in swampy or arid areas, or other places with harsh living conditions.

This breed tends less to the hound than some of the other Cur breeds, perhaps because of that elusive Indian background. He is very stocky, wide and muscular with a strong wide head and the short, higher set ear. Although the full length tail is allowed, many are born tailless.

Trailing ability varies with strains, but they have enough nose to follow game and are particularly strong in treeing ability. Usually they are silent trailers. And they are very tough, willing to face a squealing razorback or an angry wild cat when it is cornered. This breed does not have any of the blue-mottled color.

Mountain Cur, yellow.

Mountain Cur.

The book *Old Yeller*, about a boy growing up in frontier Texas and a dog for which the book is named, is a typical Mountain Cur (unlike the movie which starred a dog of Lab type). In the book, Old Yeller is a short-haired, yellow bobtailed dog that hunts and trees, naturally goes for the nose when he faces a mad bull, and isn't afraid to fight a full-grown bear when it threatens his own. The author is precise in describing this old-fashioned breed and its use to the pioneer, without ever naming the breed. Of course, in those days, the breed really didn't have a name or an individual identity.

The blanket name "cur" is slowly being sorted into individual types. The name Mountain Cur used to encompass what is now the Treeing Tennessee Brindle and the Stephens Stock as well, but these two have attained enough individual identity to justify their own registering groups.

By the end of the last war, there were very few of these old-time Mountain Curs left. A few die-hard owners still maintained some stock in isolated swamps and remote mountain regions of the southeast. Recently, they began to enjoy a modest revival, similar to the other Cur breeds. The Original Mountain Cur Breeders Association fosters and registers the breed today.

MUDI

COUNTRY: Hungary
WEIGHT: 18–29 pounds
HEIGHT: 14–20 inches
COAT: Short on head and fronts of legs, 2 inches on rest of body, coarse and bristly, with a tendency to curl.
COLOR: Black, white, pied
REGISTRY: FCI
GROUP: Herding

A truly rare breed, the Mudi has total accumulative registrations numbering only in the 300s. Despite the Mudi's small stature, he shows abundant courage in his duties as an all-around farm dog. The Mudi works the cattle, exterminates rodents—and hunts boar on his day off. The tail is usually docked. Almost all Mudis are in Hungary, although an occasional specimen is seen at European dog shows.

Mudi, black.

MÜNSTERLÄNDERS

Large Münsterländer

COUNTRY: Germany
WEIGHT: 50–70 pounds
HEIGHT: 23–25½ inches
COAT: Sleek, moderate length, with feathering
COLOR: Black and white, heavy ticking or roaning is preferred over the clear white patterns
OTHER NAMES: Grosser Münsterländer Vorstehhund
REGISTRY: FCI, TKC
GROUP: Gun Dog

Small Münsterländer

COUNTRY: Germany
WEIGHT: 33 pounds
HEIGHT: 19–22 inches
COAT: Sleek, moderate length, with feathering
COLOR: Liver and white, with ticking
OTHER NAMES: Kleiner Münsterländer Vorstehhund, Heidewachtel
REGISTRY: FCI
GROUP: Gun Dog

Back in the days of the generic *huenerhunden*, bird dogs in Germany came in all sizes and coat colors and textures. These were interbred, based on function only. In the latter part of the 19th century, the interest in individual breeds grew, and the types were separated.

When the club for the German Longhaired Pointer drew up its written standard, for some reason, it accepted only the liver/white dogs. Litters were often of mixed colors in those days, and the black/white pups denied registration were usually given away. Farmers and hunters, many from the Münster area, were the recipients of these well-bred gun dogs and cared little about their color or registration status. They continued breeding the black/white longhaired pointers, perhaps crossing to other dogs of the setter or spaniel type, and in 1919 formed a club for the Münsterländer.

The Münster has found friends throughout Germany and has been brought to England as well. He is an all-purpose pointing/retrieving gun dog and is expected to perform in the utility trials in Germany. In England, he competes with the other Continental gun dogs in the HPR (Hunt Point Retriever) Field Trials.

Large Münsterländer.

Although bred for training and ability to withstand the pressures involved, the breed wants to please and can be soft in nature. His beautiful, fringed coat is never exaggerated. The tail may be left intact or have just a tiny bit of the end removed. They love to retrieve, and naturally like to carry things about in their mouth.

As with all of their hunting relatives, they require sufficient exercise. But if walked or run enough, a Münster can adapt easily to indoor life, even in the city. He tends to be vocal and owner-oriented. Owners say if they are gone for even a moment, a Münster enthusiastically greets their return by "talking" in his low rumble and bringing them "their treasured possessions." The Münster does well in obedience, and is good with other animals and with children.

The smaller variety is of more recent origin, from the early 1900s; they are pointing dogs—as setters are—rather than flushers. The Small Münsterländer was the result of crosses of the German Longhair to Continental spaniels. This Münster appears only in the liver/white ticked color, and his tail is left long.

He is a good hunter, with a happy tail-wagging nature. Both the Large and Small Münsterländers are known in Canada, England, and in various European countries, although not in large numbers.

Above: Head study of the Large Münsterländer. **Below:** Small Münsterländer.

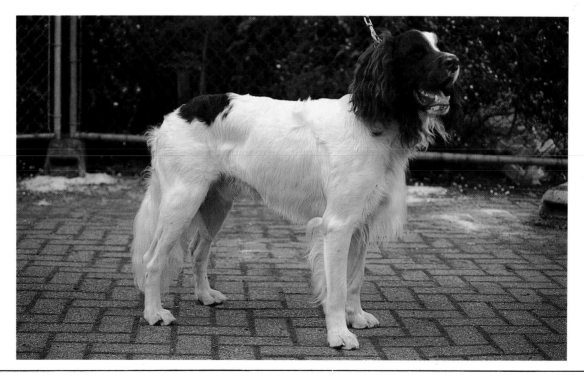

Neapolitan Mastiff, gray.

NEAPOLITAN MASTIFF

COUNTRY: Italy
WEIGHT: 110–150 pounds
HEIGHT: 23½–30 inches
COAT: Short, smooth
COLOR: Solid gray (in all shades), black, mahogany, blond
OTHER NAMES: Mastino Napoletano
REGISTRY: FCI, TKC
GROUP: Mastiff

Neapolitans are direct descendants of the molossus of the Roman arenas, probably very similar to the old type known 2,000 years ago. Over the centuries the dog has been used in war and for police, guard and draft work, as well as being a collaborator in crime. The Italian standard calls for a dog of "rustic but majestic appearance."

Although the breed has existed in southern Italy since Roman times, the Neapolitan was first presented to the general public at a Naples dog show in 1946. They so impressed a painter, Piero Scanziani, that he collected superior animals and started his own kennel. He is now considered the modern father of the breed. Scanziani set up the written standard, and obtained recognition for the breed from the Italian KC (ENCI).

Their appearance belies their affectionate temperament. Neos are gentle to friends, yet are natural guards and territorial, never wandering off their property. An owner of Neos says, "My husband would exercise our dogs by bicycle. All manner of dogs would come rushing off properties and out of driveways, challenging them as they passed. Surprisingly, the mastiffs would just stop and look, neither growling nor raising their hackles. It was almost as if the mastiffs were perplexed at the audacity and impudence of these up-starts!"

Although bred for combat, they are not pugnacious to other dogs and are good mothers. A

Neapolitan Mastiff.

breeder says that it is quite humorous to watch such a large dog tiptoeing with exaggerated daintiness amongst her pups in the whelping box.

As a fighting breed originally, the dogs were selected for their stoicism and still exhibit that trait today. Neapolitans are adaptable to various environments and climates, transferring smoothly from kennels in Italy to life as house dogs in North America. A Canadian breeder states, "It is always a little nerve-wracking arriving at the airport to collect a very large dog that you know nothing about temperament-wise, not to say . . . the apprehensiveness experienced driving home with a strange dog's head resting on your shoulder." This is especially true when it is a 130-pound dog, but there was no need for worry—as both she and the dog always arrived intact.

Neapolitan Mastiff.

Neapolitan Mastiff, mahogany.

The proper gait is typical of the larger mastiffs: slow, free and bearlike. Neos have distinctive physical traits, however. Skin hangs in exaggerated folds around the head, making it seem double or even triple-chinned. If the ears are cropped (as is the custom), they are "almost amputated, and docked to the point where it forms a nearly equilateral triangle." One-third of the tail is removed. Exhibiting an elegant and majestic aloofness, they give the appearance of someone you wouldn't want to meet alone at night in a dark alley. Neos enjoy a very active fancy in Italy, with growing numbers of good breeders in other countries. Enthusiastic programs can be found in Germany, France, Spain, England as well as other European nations, Canada, the USA, and Israel.

NEWFOUNDLAND

COUNTRY: Canada
WEIGHT: 110–150 pounds
HEIGHT: 26–28 inches
COAT: Medium length, very dense
COLOR: Solid black, bronze, particolor
(Landseer)
REGISTRY: FCI, AKC, UKC, TKC, CKC
GROUP: Mastiff

As canines were molded to fill whatever job was needed, residents of the banks of Labrador, St. John's and Newfoundland developed dogs for aiding the fishermen. The early history of these animals consists mainly of unsubstantiated stories and fanciful tales.

Newfoundland folklore tells of an early Tibetan Mastiff-type dog which accompanied Indians migrating across the polar region to the Maritime Provinces. Four thousand years later, in 1001 AD, when the Vikings arrived, they supposedly had "bear dogs" of similar origin. The fusion of these two "long-lost cousins" supposedly created the base for the Newfoundland breed.

By the 1600s, records show European fishing vessels were frequent visitors to the Maritimes and, since nearly all these fleets brought dogs with them, crosses probably occurred with various European breeds who "jumped ship" for a night on the town. Portuguese and Basque fishermen were the earliest, and both Portuguese Water Dogs and Great Pyrenees in turn probably contributed water-proofing, coat variations and water-working qualities, along with size and nobility.

Soon two distinct types developed: the so-called Lesser St. John's Dog (which developed into the Labrador Retriever) and the Greater St. John's Dog (which became the Newfoundland and Landseer).

Early Newfoundlands aided crews and became invaluable aboard ship, rescuing sailors and barking the danger of reefs. Newfies were strong swimmers, and retrieved both people and boats in distress. With the highest tides in the world (reaching 70 feet) in the Bay of Fundy near Newfoundland, it seems likely they were called upon frequently. Not all work was so romantic, however; daily duties found these dogs

Newfoundland, black.

swimming from ship to ship, carrying lines, or retrieving objects and drunken sailors who had fallen overboard.

By the 18th century, examples of these Newfoundland dogs were brought back to England on British trade ships. Early Newfs were a mixed lot, generally smaller and lighter boned than today's specimens, with a wide variance in colors (often spotted). Coat textures were rough, curly or long, and the high tail often curved in a circle.

Crossing may have occurred again in Europe, but type was eventually stabilized. The Newf evolved into a large, sturdily boned, low-tailed dog still in several colors and usually spotted. About the time a written standard was introduced in the late 1800s, the solid black variety became the rage in England, so much so that the black almost became known as the "only Newfoundland in Britain and North America." Today the spotted Newfoundland is considered a color variety, called Landseer, recognized by FCI as a separate breed. They also come in solid chocolate (bronze).

Nobility, peaceful personality, sleek good looks and superior strength attracted more than seafarers and Indians to the breed. None can forget Lord Byron's epitaph to "Boatswain," his Newfoundland:

Newfoundland, bronze.

Newfoundland backpacking in mountains.

When some proud son of man returns to
    earth,
Unknown to glory, but upheld by birth,
The sculptor's art exhausts the pomp of
    woe,
And storied urns record who rests below.
When all is done, upon the tomb is seen
Not what he was, but what he should have
    been.
But the poor dog, in life the firmest friend,
The first to welcome, foremost to defend.
Whose honest heart is still his master's
    own,
Who labors, fights, lives, breathes for him
    alone,
Unhonored falls, unnoticed all his worth,
Denied in heaven the soul he had on earth.
Ye who perchance behold this simple urn,
Pass on,—it honors none you wish to
    mourn;
To mark a friend's remains these stones
    arise;
I never knew but one—and here he lies.

Newfoundland, black and white particolor (Landseer).

Patriots, presidents and politicians have joined celebrities and royalty in their admiration for these dogs: Benjamin Franklin, Samuel Adams, George Washington, Robert Kennedy, Bing Crosby, King Edward VII, the Rumanian Queen Marie and her son King Michael, and, of course, Queen Victoria. A black Newfoundland named "Seaman" accompanied Meriwether Lewis on his boat, *Discovery*, up the Missouri River in 1804.

In 1886 Newfoundland owners formed a specialty club and drew up a standard. The gentle giant debuted in the show ring and enjoyed a small but respectable status. About 1935, the Newf began an upward climb, drawing a steady group of fanciers. The Newfoundland Club of America encourages the retention of natural ability by hosting water rescue tests. Basic tests include retrieves, find and retrieves, carrying lines, towing a boat, following instructions in the water, and lifesaving. Advanced dogs participate in more complex retrieves and lifesaving.

Their owners' only complaint is that the dogs don't know when the testing is over and "fun in the sun" time begins. Newfs tend to be overzealous in their rescues, occasionally dampening the fun of a swimming party by "rescuing" the swimmers.

For landlubber owners, the club also hosts draft-dog tests. The dogs are harnessed to carts and must back, follow commands, haul a load and maneuver an obstacle course. Breeders recommend Newfs be included in family activities and, if possible, water play. If ignored, they become bored and even depressed.

Like cuddly, sweet bear cubs, the Newfoundland pups grow to be large, impressive animals. Unlike the cubs, however, they retain the gentle demeanor and "benevolent expression." Surprisingly, the giant, economy-sized Newf eats only as much as most retrievers. Breeders credit this to his tranquil behavior and disposition. The breed is known to be easygoing and extremely patient with children and with animals.

623

Newfoundland.

NEW GUINEA SINGING DOG

COUNTRY: New Guinea
WEIGHT: 20 pounds
HEIGHT: 14–15 inches
COAT: Medium-short, dense
COLOR: Red; with or without symmetrical white markings
REGISTRY: None
GROUP: Southern

The island of New Guinea, second largest in the world, is home to many strange creatures. Its variation from the tropical clime in the lowlands to Alpinelike cold in the higher elevations is uncommon. Early domesticated southern dogs spread from the Middle East to southeastern Asia with various human migrations many thousands of years ago. Some drifted to Australia to become the Dingo and others to Malaysia (the Telomian).

Not far from Australia, a dingo-type dog took up residence in New Guinea. The torrid forests and chilled mountain peaks spawned a hardy animal called the New Guinea Singing Dog.

Many lived as pariah dogs with the village natives in the lower elevations. Other dogs climbed to the mountains, where they turned feral. In

New Guinea Singing Dogs.

New Guinea Singing Dog.

the cold climes, they developed a thicker, double, slightly longer coat than most pariahs. But curled tails, the foxy, wedge-shaped heads and high prick ears follow the usual pariah characteristics.

Although smaller than its near relative, the Singing Dog is similar to the Dingo but with unique propensities. It possesses the erect ears and is a swift hunter with social instincts. Unlike the Dingo, the New Guinea female cycles twice a year in captivity.

Its howl has an eerie yet synchronized quality which gives the breed its name. The howl can be spurred by agitation or excitement. One tone blends with the next, sending goosebumps up a listener's back.

In 1948, a pair of the dogs was brought to the Taronga Zoo in Sydney, Australia. Several other zoos clamored for the progeny, and pairs were brought to Europe and Russia in the 1950s–60s. For a time, the Singing Dogs fascinated the public. The interest in keeping and viewing a dog—albeit a feral dog—waned, although two pairs still live in zoos in the States.

"Singer" and "Dancer" sing for their supper at the Minnesota Zoo, with another pair at the Sedgwick County Zoo in Wichita, Kansas. The Minnesota duo once "accompanied" Metropolitan Opera star Benita Valente on television. The Singing Dogs are tame enough to be handled and petted, but don't tolerate these attentions for long. These dogs are believed to be scarce or even extinct in New Guinea.

Norbottenspets.

NORBOTTENSPETS

COUNTRY: Sweden and Finland
WEIGHT: 26–33 pounds
HEIGHT: 17 inches
COAT: Short and stand-off
COLOR: Basically white, with a few color spots preferably in yellow or brown; black spots permissible
OTHER NAMES: Nordic Spitz, Pohjanpystykorva
REGISTRY: FCI
GROUP: Northern

The little spitz of Sweden and Finland began long ago as a hunter of small game. Called the *Pohjanpystykorva* in Finland, it was taken by immigrant farmers to northern Sweden where it was given an even longer name, the *Norrbottens-skollandehund*. Although widespread for many years as a common hunting and farm dog, the average owner "didn't know that they had a breed," and breeding programs were not planned. As hunting with this dog waned and the popularity of foreign breeds increased, peo-ple lost interest.

The Norbottenspets was thought to be extinct and was dropped from the rolls of the Swedish KC in 1948. Lovers of the breed continued to scour both countries, discovering good speci-mens in remote villages and reestablishing breeding programs. It was reinstated by the ken-nel clubs in Sweden (1967) and in Finland (1970s) and is now quite popular again in both countries. His demand today is as a house com-panion and for hunting game birds such as grouse and hazel hens. A few have won high prizes in bird-hunting trials. The Norbottens-pets has a plus as a house pet—he is not the great barker that most of the other Nordic hunt-ers are.

His coat is quite short for a Nordic dog and his tail curves loosely over the back, turning down to lie against the thigh. He is square and firm bodied. His character is alert, lively, calm and friendly—also described as brisk—but never shy, nervous, or aggressive. The breed is particularly good with children. He is most happy when owned by a hunter, even if a hobby hunter.

NORFOLK TERRIER

COUNTRY: Great Britain
WEIGHT: 11–12 pounds
HEIGHT: 10 inches
COAT: Hard, wiry, broken, lies flat to the body
COLOR: Red to wheaten
REGISTRY: FCI, AKC, UKC, CKC, TKC
GROUP: Terrier

The Norfolk has many similarities to the Border in size, color and coat, but his head is more fox-like and he has the erect ear. His ancestors may have included some of the same brave fellows that produced the Border and his relative, the Cairn, in the north, and many cynologists feel that red terriers from Ireland figured in his history. The town of Norwich is in the county of Norfolk just north of London in the eastcentral area of England called East Anglia.

In the 1800s, there was no official recognition of the Norwich/Norfolk, which was just another general type farm dog and hunting terrier used in the area. In the 1880s, he became the rage with the undergraduates at Cambridge University and his popularity soared. Some even felt he should be called the Cantab Terrier in honor of the collegiate atmosphere which promoted him. In the early 1900s, the keystone sire was named "Rags." One of the prominent breeders after World War I was named Frank "Roughrider" Jones, a horseman, who had Glen of Imaal Terriers and a dark red brindle Cairn-type bitch. Some of these were bred to Rags, as was a terrier bitch named "Ninety," of Dandie Dinmont and hunting terrier stock. The harsh-coated red progeny were retained by Jones and these formed the foundation for the Norwich/Norfolk. Early specimens imported into the USA were often called Jones Terriers.

In America they were utilized by several Masters of Foxhounds for their original purpose of assisting the foxhound with the prey that had gone to ground. In fact, the Cheshire Hunt Club of Philadelphia and a few others of the 1920s maintained purebred kennels of Norwich to assist in their hunts. Bred to hunt in packs, they are sociable dogs. The breed obtained official recognition from English and American governing bodies in the 1930s.

Norfolk Terrier.

Like the Border, the Norwich is shown in a nearly natural coat. He is an alert, handsome, and charming fellow who makes a fine companion as well as a working terrier. Up until 1979, the breed was allowed to be shown in the USA with either a prick (erect) ear or a small forward-folding drop ear. At that time, AKC followed the example of The Kennel Club of England and called the prick-eared variety the Norwich Terrier and established a new breed name, the Norfolk Terrier, for the drop-eared variety. The town of Norwich is in the county of Norfolk; thus one was named for the town and the other for the whole county.

They are very similar except for the ears. "Wich" is the Norwich, and "wich" is the Norfolk? The Norwich has pointed ears like a *witch*'s hat, and the Norfolk's ears *fol*d.

Both terriers do fine in the house, with sufficient opportunity to "stretch their legs" outdoors. Responsive, but still scalawags, these little dogs bring to mind the warning of terrier man Jerome K. Jerome, "Terriers are born with about four times as much original sin in them as other dogs."

Norfolk Terrier.

NORTHEASTERLY HAULING LAIKA

COUNTRY: USSR
HEIGHT: 23–24 inches minimum
COAT: Medium, thick, double coat
COLOR: Any color
OTHER NAMES: Northeastern Sleigh Dog
GROUP: Northern

During the 1940s, Russian cynologists attempted to consolidate the multitude of existing Northern draft/hunting/herding type dogs from Siberia and the Soviet Union into six distinct breeds. This amounted to an exercise in "lumping." They established four hunting or hunting/sledding breeds, one sledding/ herding breed and one pure sledding breed, although they recognized there were other types that did not fit into these parameters.

The pure sledding breed is the Hauling Laika, which is probably an amalgamation of various native draft types. The standard established is one for a large hauling dog, very similar to the Eskimo Dog or the Malamute.

Soviet cynologists recognize the necessity for sled dogs in the most remote areas of Siberia and the Arctic. They say dogs and vehicular transportation, even in the 1980s, complement each other.

Should a visitor arrive in the lower Kolyman and Anadyr River areas of far east Siberia during their short summer, says a modern Soviet dog writer, he would immediately notice many idle, dirty dogs. They wander about, covered with clumps of shedding hair and mud, seeming quite useless to the visitor. But the locals know that the long, bitter winter is not far off. Then the dogs grow a beautiful winter coat and work constantly. They pull skiers (doing "skjoring") and haul sleds to all parts of the tundra. They deliver the physician and veterinarian and supplies as well as mail and news from afar.

This dog furnishes warmth to his master when, during a sudden blizzard, every living creature digs into a snow drift. And he can unerringly find his way home even in blinding snow. Hauling dogs often second as hunting dogs as well. A team of six to ten Hauling Laikas, pulling a load of 88–110 pounds per dog, may average three to four miles per hour. This figures to 40–48 miles a day for a four to six day trip in -40 to -50 degree weather, all on only about three pounds of fish a day per dog! Thus to this day, the northern peoples of the Soviet Union love and respect their amazing helpmates.

Northeastern Russian laikas slumbering on a snow covered peninsula.

NORWEGIAN BUHUND

COUNTRY: Norway
WEIGHT: 26–40 pounds
HEIGHT: 17–18 inches
COAT: Thick, harsh, short, and smooth-lying with a soft wool undercoat.
COLOR: Wheaten, black, wolf sable, small symmetrical white markings, and/or a black mask
OTHER NAMES: Norsk Buhund, Norwegian Sheepdog
REGISTRY: FCI, TKC
GROUP: Northern

Norwegian Buhund, wheaten.

The Buhund is one of the earliest known Nordic herding types, although it was not officially recognized until the 20th century. As humans from the North began to live in permanent settlements in the Scandinavian countries, they brought with them the hauling and reindeer-herding dogs used for centuries. This stock was used to create a herding dog for cattle, sheep and horses that doubles as an all-purpose farm dog. *Bu* in Norwegian means homestead or mountain hut and Buhund is the name given to their sheepdog. The Buhund was already widespread in the Middle Ages and has maintained a similar appearance ever since that time. John Saeland fostered the breed to recognition and formed a club in 1936.

Modern breeders state that the breed can be adapted not only for sheep and goat herding, but also for turkeys, ducks and domestic pheasant. The Buhund is now seen in several countries outside of Norway, and is a lively, courageous and energetic companion. He has become fairly numerous in Great Britain and is gaining a following in Australia as well. Quite adaptable to a variety of tasks, including child's companion, obedience dog, or hearing dog, he is a security guard that is never off-duty.

These dogs are in tune with owners, communicating with various noises and body language. They are highly trainable, great farm dogs and stay within call. The Buhund is a creature of habit and, as one owner said, knows the household routine and is usually one jump ahead.

An English owner tells of walking home from town after dark with her Buhund and another dog. She was attacked from behind and, while the other dog ran off, the Buhund sank its teeth into the aggressor's leg and doggedly held on, allowing her master to escape. In fact, even after the woman was safe, it took several calls for the dog to back off the attack and join her!

Another report tells of a bitch left alone in a home with her newborn pups. When fire broke out in the house, the bitch could have escaped, but chose to stay and protect her pups. Fortunately, she was discovered and saved by her 14-year-old owner.

Their herding and protective instincts come to the fore even when untrained and, occasionally, when unwanted. A town bitch was seen correctly and proudly herding sheep when she was a guest at a farm. Another "aided" her owner in a climb in Wales by tugging at her coat.

Like most of the Nordic dogs, Buhunds are clean, intelligent and fun. They also have the northern traits of great energy, the desire for human companionship, and the need for a firm, consistent master to overcome their strong will.

NORWICH TERRIER

COUNTRY: Great Britain
WEIGHT: 11–12 pounds
HEIGHT: 10 inches
COAT: Hard, wiry, broken, lies flat to the body
COLOR: Red to wheaten most common
REGISTRY: FCI, AKC, UKC, TKC, CKC
GROUP: Terrier

The Norwich was separated from the Norfolk only recently and has an identical history. It has many similarities to the Border in size, color and coat, but his head is more foxlike and he has the erect ear. His ancestors may have included some of the same brave fellows that produced the Border and his relative, the Cairn, in the north, and many cynologists feel that red terriers from Ireland figured in his history. The town of Norwich is in the county of Norfolk just north of London in the eastcentral area of England called East Anglia.

In the 1800s, there was no official recognition of the Norwich/Norfolk, which was just another general type farm dog and hunting terrier used in the area. In the 1880s, he became the rage with the undergraduates at Cambridge University and his popularity soared. Some even felt he should be called the Cantab Terrier in honor of the collegiate atmosphere which promoted him. In the early 1900s, the keystone sire was named "Rags." One of the prominent breeders after World War I was named Frank "Roughrider" Jones, a horseman, who had Glen of Imaal Terriers and a dark red brindle Cairn-type bitch. Some of these were bred to Rags, as was a terrier bitch named "Ninety," of Dandie Dinmont and hunting terrier stock. The harsh-coated red progeny were retained by Jones and these formed the foundation for the Norwich/Norfolk. Early specimens imported into the USA were often called Jones Terriers.

In America they were utilized by several Masters of Foxhounds for their original purpose of assisting the foxhound with the prey that had gone to ground. In fact, the Cheshire Hunt Club of Philadelphia and a few others of the 1920s maintained purebred kennels of Norwich to assist in their hunts. Bred to hunt in packs, they are sociable dogs. The breed obtained official recognition from English and American govern-

Norwich Terrier.

The Norwich Terrier and the Norfolk Terrier, once both called the Norfolk Terrier, are recognized today as two individual breeds. The Norwich Terrier is prick-eared (*left*) while the Norfolk is drop-eared (*below*). White is undesirable in both breeds but marks or patches are permissible in some standards.

BEST OF BREED

ASHBEY PHOTO

ing bodies in the 1930s.

Like the Border, the Norwich is shown in a nearly natural coat. He is an alert, handsome, and charming fellow who makes a fine companion as well as a working terrier. Up until 1979, the breed was allowed to be shown in the USA with either a prick (erect) ear or a small forward-folding drop ear. At that time, AKC followed the example of The Kennel Club of England and called the prick-eared variety the Norwich Terrier and established a new breed name, the Norfolk Terrier, for the drop-eared variety. One was named for the town and the other for the whole county.

They are very similar except for the ears. "Wich" is the Norwich, and "wich" is the Norfolk? The Norwich has pointed ears like a *witch*'s hat, and the Norfolk's ears *fol*d.

Both terriers do fine in the house, with sufficient opportunity to "stretch their legs" outdoors. Responsive, but still scalawags, these little dogs bring to mind the warning of terrier man Jerome K. Jerome, "Terriers are born with about four times as much original sin in them as other dogs."

Above and below: Norwich Terriers.

Nova Scotia Duck Tolling Retriever.

NOVA SCOTIA DUCK TOLLING RETRIEVER

COUNTRY: Canada
WEIGHT: 37–51 pounds
HEIGHT: 17–21 inches
COAT: Moderate length, lying close; thick, straight to slightly wavy, plenteous undercoat, fringing fairly abundant
COLOR: Red (from deep golden red to dark coppery red), usually with small white markings on feet, chest, tail tip and sometimes face
REGISTRY: FCI, CKC
GROUP: Gun Dog

The clever manner in which foxes work together to obtain a duck dinner has been observed over the centuries. While one of a pair conceals itself near the waterline, the other fox leaps and cavorts about on the shore, swishing his magnificent tail. The rafts of ducks out on the water soon become curious and move in closer and closer to see what all the commotion is. Soon, some are close enough to be caught by the undercover partner. Indians utilized this mesmerizing practice by stringing a fox skin across a length of shore and yanking it quickly back and forth, simulating the movement of the fox.

Dogs have been taught to draw ducks towards the hunter in the style of the fox. This process is called tolling, from the Old English *tollen*, to entice. Long ago, Europeans used tolling dogs to draw ducks into the net. For more than a hundred years, in the Little River district of Yarmouth County in southwestern Nova Scotia, hunters used tolling dogs, fashioned after the MicMac Indian Dog, which lured waterfowl in the manner of the fox.

These dogs were the result of various retriever crosses, estimated as Golden, Chesapeake, Labrador and Flat-Coat, with speculation of a dash of Cocker, Irish Setter (for its beautiful red coat) and various small farm collies and/or playful spitzlike dogs. Their unique hunting style has been set for more than a hundred years, but a formal registration and written standard is of recent date (1945). The breed used to be called the Little River Duck Dog or the Yarmouth Toller, but when the Canadian Kennel Club began registering them in the late 1950s, the present name was decreed. FCI gave them full international recognition in 1982. There are a fair number of Tollers and a breed specialty club in the United States.

The Duck Toller's unconventional style of hunting begins with the hunter concealed in a blind near the shore. A small stick or other retrieving item is tossed toward the water. The dog rushes out with tremendous animation, twirling and prancing as he retrieves the object and returns to the blind, tail wagging at all times. Some Tollers vocalize as they fetch. The object is thrown again and again. Sometimes the ducks are immediately curious. Other times they may watch the dog make 50 retrieves. The dogs must maintain the animation and enthusiasm for as long as it takes to draw the fowl. Sooner or later, ducks and geese become curious and move nearer, often hissing and beating the water with their wings as they approach the shore.

The properly trained tolling dog never breaks concentration to peer at the ducks as they inch closer, but continues his "game." When the ducks are within range, the hunter calls the dog back into the blind, stands up to put the ducks to flight and then shoots. After the shot, the Toller dons his other hat—that of a fine natural retriever.

Hunting with a Toller means being able to come home with a full game bag, even on those sunny, "blue bird" days that are notoriously poor for waterfowl hunting. A small 30–pound bitch is credited with retrieving a Canada goose (no small trophy) from the Atlantic Ocean during a storm. Another retrieved several of these geese, despite a face full of porcupine quills.

One breeder laughingly laments an over-enthusiastic dog, who thoroughly ruined his day's shooting, though providing her master a story for all time. This bitch persisted in catching quail on the wing, and brought the birds to him unharmed.

Tollers are like other retrievers in that they are companionable and easy to train, but as dogs of high energy they need a great deal of exercise. As long as an outlet is found to satisfy that need, they make fine house dogs. More and more owners are finding that obedience is another talent. The Toller's strong retrieving desire and playfulness are natural traits, both necessary for his tolling ability. Tolling is also a natural trait (like pointing) and cannot be taught. These dogs have an intense, natural excitement about their duty. Young dogs need to practice, but training sessions involve establishing a close relationship and having children throw sticks for them to retrieve. Nova Scotians still refer to working a tolling dog as "playing" the dog. Another owner says, "Tollers are retrieving fools. If anyone ever makes the mistake of throwing a ball for them, they will keep the unfortunate soul throwing until his arm gives out."

Nova Scotia Duck Tolling Retrievers.

The breed is sensible and devoted to its family. An owner in Michigan credits her well-being to her dog, after he twice saved her, once legitimately and more than once "illegitimately." The first instance occurred on a hiking expedition, when she ended on a precarious ledge. This medium-sized dog braced himself so that his owner could grasp his collar and pull herself to safety. The other instance involves her swimming attempts—he won't allow her deeper than ankle-high water!

The Toller may be a bit more reserved to non-family than the Golden Retriever. The coat requires the same care as other retrievers. Some Tollers have very little white, while others evidence the Irish pattern, even to a large facial blaze. The white tip of the tail is highly prized since it can be seen from a distance by the fowl, much like the white tip on Reynard's tail!

Above and Below: Nova Scotia Duck Tolling Retrievers.

Above: Nova Scotia Duck Tolling Retrievers burrowing in the snow. **Below:** Nova Scotia Duck Tolling Retriever.

Old Danish Bird Dog.

OLD DANISH BIRD DOG

COUNTRY: Denmark
WEIGHT: 40–53 pounds
HEIGHT: 20–23 inches
COAT: Short, dense, and tight
COLOR: Liver and white, a small amount of ticking allowed
OTHER NAMES: Gamle (or Gammel) Dansk Honsehund, Old Danish Pointer
REGISTRY: FCI
GROUP: Gun Dog

One of only two hunting dogs native to Denmark, this breed was developed in the early 1700s from various farm *blodhundes*, (probably a form of the St. Hubert Hound), and early pointing dogs brought from Spain by gypsies. The man most responsible for the breed's early development was Morten Bak, and the breed is sometimes still called the Bakhund locally.

The Old Danish Bird Dog was initially used as a retriever, but its skills as a close working gun dog increased over the years. Unfortunately, the breed began to wane and, in 1939, during the War, it nearly disappeared. Due to the persistence of a few enthusiasts, the Honsehund has gained steadily in popularity since that time. Today, in Denmark, its owners boast it is listed as third hunting dog in the number of registrations.

Modern Danish field trial standards for the breed demand a dog that works fairly close and takes direction from his handler while thoroughly hunting the terrain. He must have great stamina, clean retrieves and, although the high point is most desirable, the old style of creeping and/or dropping to a lying position is still seen and allowed. His tail moves eagerly and, upon scent, circles in full rotation. Because of the breed's superlative nose, many are trained for schweisshund work (seeking wounded deer) as well as for bomb detection.

Danish owners say that the breed's abilities are quite universal, with almost all dogs being used for hunting or some other form of work. But they also are a quiet, friendly family dog who can get by with a minimum of exercise. One fan says to live with a Honsehund is like having a "clever and good friend."

The heavy neck skin of the breed is a mark of its ancient hound lineage, but the standard warns against allowing too much exaggeration to creep in. His body proportions are that of a rectangle, being only slightly longer than tall, and his tapering tail is never docked. The Honsehund has had very little exposure outside Denmark, although recently, one was invited to compete in the European World Cup competition for all Continental pointing dogs.

Old Danish Bird Dog.

OLD ENGLISH SHEEPDOG

COUNTRY: Great Britain
WEIGHT: 66 pounds or more
HEIGHT: 22 inches or more
COAT: Long, profuse, hard texture, shaggy
COLOR: Any shade of gray, grizzle, blue or blue merle; with or without white markings
OTHER NAMES: Bobtail
REGISTRY: FCI, AKC, TKC, CKC
GROUP: Herding

Despite the name "Old English," evidence suggests the breed is neither old nor all English. An 1835 painting by Sidney Cooper gives us the first illustration of the Bobtail. Its ancestry is through the European shepherd dogs, such as the Bergamasco or Russian owtcharkas, bred to the sheep dogs of the British Islands. The body structure of the OES is more like that of the heavier shepherd dogs seen on the Continent.

Contrary to its nickname, the "Bobtail" was created (by docking), not born. In the 18th century, drovers' dogs, which helped drive the herds to market, were exempt from taxation. To mark these dogs, their tails were docked. The lack of a tail was not a hindrance to the drover's dog, which didn't require the quick turns and stops of the herder. The Bobtail made a good drover's dog: eager, protective of his charges and weather-resistant with his heavy, dense

Old English Sheepdog.

Old English Sheepdogs, adult and pups.

coat. No one spent time on grooming these dogs, however, and they were sheared down annually in the spring along with the sheep. Farmers' wives spun the dog shearings, as well as the sheep's wool, into warm clothing.

Everywhere the breed debuted in shows, it was received with delight. The OES won dedicated fanciers not only in England, but in Canada, the States and other countries around the world, due to its distinctive coat and its singular, rolling gait. That same coat with its time-consuming care, however, has kept its numbers sensible and has not allowed him to become a "dog of the moment." While the pet owner may still resort to the "shear down," the exhibition specimen requires hours of care.

The modern OES retains the appearance of a fluffy clown with the heart of a faithful guardian. The breed is a popular competitor with spectators in the obedience ring and scent hurdle races, and they perform well despite their veil of hair. They tend to be very protective of their possessions. Fanciers recognize the need for a firm hand in training to overcome their strong will.

Old English Sheepdog.

Otter Hound, grizzle.

OTTER HOUND

COUNTRY: Great Britain
WEIGHT: 65–120 pounds
HEIGHT: 23–27 inches
COAT: Medium length; hard and crisp in texture, with an oily waterproof nature and abundant underwool
COLOR: Generally grizzle or wheaten; black/tan, liver/tan, tricolor
REGISTRY: FCI, AKC, TKC, CKC
GROUP: Hound

To the American eye, the Otter Hound seems a bit of an oddity, with most hounds being of the smooth type like Beagles and Coonhounds—a shaggy dog seems out of sync. But in France, a wide variety of rough-coated hounds have hunted for centuries. The great Griffons of Nivernais, Brittany and, especially, Vendee are most surely the direct ancestors of the Otter Hound. He was perfected in England, with additions of various hounds (including Bloodhound) and water spaniels.

The greffier-type hound in France is a cold-trailer of great endurance, and these characteristics were useful in developing a dog to hunt otter. Otters, once in abundance, are predators that decimated the fish in English rivers. This furnished an excuse for avid hunters, since otters were the only game in season from April to September. Otter hunting thus became a minor sport during the 18th century.

European otters, weighing up to 24 pounds, live in holes dug in river banks with the entrance under the water surface. These otters can swim for great distances underwater, coming up only occasionally for air. The scent trail they leave on land is called a "drag" and on water is termed a "wash." The Otter Hound has an exquisite scenting ability like that of the Bloodhound, and he easily can pick up and follow a drag ten to twelve hours old. When pursuing a wash, the hounds sometimes swim as long as five hours, an activity requiring the ultimate in both nose and endurance. His oily, thick undercoat and webbed feet make him an Olympic-ability swimmer.

Several British monarchs carried the title of Master of Otterhounds: John; Richard III; Charles II; Edward II and IV; Henry II, VI, VII and VIII; and even Elizabeth I. During the height of otter hunting in the latter half of the 1800s, there were 18 to 20 packs in use throughout Britain each season. Famous hounds, such as the Hawkstone Pack of the Honorable Geoffrey Hill, killed more than 700 otters during a 20-year span. Squire Lomax of Clitheroe was a stickler for the formality of the hunt, and the manner in which his hounds worked was more important than the end result. During the late 1860s, his famous pack was so well trained that it was said they took their cues from him with only a minimal wave of his hand. Many of the major packs of those times would send a "couple" of hounds to the larger bench exhibitions, and the Carlisle and Kendal working packs were also noted for their show winners.

The Otter Hound, like previous hounds that hunted the wolf, was efficient enough to almost annihilate his own existence. The otter numbers were reduced so that fewer and fewer packs

Otter Hound, wheaten.

Otter Hound.

could be justifiably supported. In addition, many hunt clubs began crossing the shaggy Otter Hound with Foxhound to gain added speed. By 1900, there were very few purebred Otter Hounds left in England, although a number of good specimens had been exported to the United States. Today the breed is rare on both sides of the Atlantic, save a few fanciers who sponsor it at shows.

Otters are now a protected species in England, and otter hunting with dogs has never been practiced in the USA. This canine's background of persistence on a cold trail could perhaps make him useful on other game if anyone cares to try.

His rough, shaggy coat and large size make him the most distinctive of the hounds in America. He requires brushing about once a week. Sometimes the Otter Hound drinks by submerging his entire head in water. It is always at that moment that he decides to show his love for his master and lays his soggy beard in a lap!

These dogs have the independence of hounds yet possess great devotion to their masters. They are affectionate and boisterous, much like the children they enjoy playing with. Their hound attributes of a loud bugle and self-willed nature, combined with substantial size, need the skills of a knowledgeable trainer.

OWCZAREK PODHALANSKI

Country: Poland
Weight: 100–150 pounds
Height: 24–34 inches
Coat: Long, thick, hard, straight or wavy
Color: White
Other Names: Tatra Mountain Sheepdog, Owczarek Tatrzanski, Polish Mountain Dog
Registry: FCI
Group: Flock Guard

The Podhale, where this breed originated, is a small region in southern Poland, against the Tatra range, which are the highest peaks in the Carpathians. The Podhalanski's history follows that of similar dogs from Czechoslovakia, Hungary and Rumania, all of which trace back to the white guardian dogs of the Eastern World. The Polish *owca* (pronounced "ofsta") means sheep, and *owczarek* (pronounced "ofcharek") is the generic term for sheepdog. This is the same meaning as the Russian word *owtcharka* or the Yugoslavian *ovcar*.

This native Polish breed is an outstanding mountain worker. The tail is used as a handhold while following the dog through rough and steep terrain!

Beside the traditional use as a livestock guardian, the Polish people often use these dogs for personal protection and as guard dogs in factories. Much like the people who breed them, the Podhalanskis are independent, self-sufficient and courageous. They are coveted for their attributes: heartiness, adaptability and bravery. Their personalities are more easygoing than most of the flock guardians, with irritability or cowardice being a fault. This may be due to the dogs' use for hauling carts among the dairy, horticultural and bakery trades. The same dogs may be used in the mountains during the grazing season and in winter brought to town to help with other chores.

Young dogs that show high intelligence are selected for police, military or guide dog work. Every dog serves the people in some way, and is treated well in return. Even the dogs lacking in

Owczarek Podhalanski.

Owczarek Podhalanski.

talent are kept for their wool, with the combings used for upholstery and fine woolens!

Their owners claim the breed is easy to care for in both grooming and feeding. The coat is self-cleansing and "never requires bathing." Like many of the flock guards, Podhalanskis are surprisingly economical to feed.

The Podhalanski doesn't need people to be content. These dogs develop their own routines, and quickly attach themselves to environment, buildings, people or animals. As with the other flock-guarding breeds, dominance is exerted over another dog. The dominant one quietly puts his head on the other's shoulders as a reminder. Despite the more tractable tempera-

ment, proper dominance must be exerted by the master early in the relationship to overcome the dog's natural independence. Otherwise he might quietly put his head on the owner's shoulder!

The Podhalanski is placid and cheerful, but American owners warn about his tendency to bark if left outside alone at night. This breed is constantly on the alert.

The breed is popular in Poland and was introduced in the United States and Canada by a few imports in the 1980s. An American Foreign Service Officer stationed in Poland came to admire the breed. Once back in the States, he arranged to acquire three of these magnificent Polish dogs. They left Poland "by a whisker," leaving the very day martial law was declared in 1981. From this modest beginning, the Polish Tatra Sheepdog Club of America has been formed to help promote the breed and to bring owners together for a common cause.

Owczarek Podhalanski, pups.

PATTERDALE TERRIER

COUNTRY: Great Britain
WEIGHT: 12–13 pounds
HEIGHT: Less than 12½ inches
COAT: Short and coarse
COLOR: Black, red, chocolate or black/tan
OTHER NAMES: Black Fell Terrier
REGISTRY: FCI
GROUP: Terrier

Avid terrier people in Yorkshire and the lake districts to this day breed strictly working stock, often generally referred to as fell terriers. As is common with working dogs, they show physical variation, since mating is based only on working qualities and gameness. But one distinct type that emerged is the Patterdale Terrier, named for a village in Cumbria.

These dogs are particularly hard and tenacious. "Many [Foxhound] masters would not thank you for attempting to bolt his [sic] fox with a hard bitten Patterdale, for the dog is more likely to get hold and have a go, possibly kill the fox rather than allow him to bolt. . ."

thus spoiling the hunt with the hounds. The fells of the north country, with the protection afforded foxes in borrans, rock tips, mines and scree, created the need for a hard terrier able to scramble over the terrain and fearless enough to go to ground. The Patterdale filled—and still fills—that need.

Dan Russell of Shooting Times and Country Magazine relates the following story of having run a fox to ground in a rough place: "Turning to his terrier, Fury, Joe said 'Thee and me's bin good pals, but t'times come when we mun part, for if tha gaas in here ah'll nivver see thee agen.' In went Fury and soon there were sounds of a terrific battle underground. The fox refused to bolt and after a while Fury came out, badly bitten from ear to ear. The dog was sent to the nearest farm for treatment and tools were sent for. At the end of three hours digging an entrance was made into the borran and there, inside, were all the signs of an Homeric struggle and in the corner, piled on top of each other, were three big foxes."

Further testament to the high esteem in which Patterdales are held is evidenced in the

Patterdale Terriers, red and black.

647

following exchange reported by Nigel Hinchcliffe: "A Welshman once rang me and asked to buy a black terrier, preferably one fully working. When asked what kind of work, I was told 'a bit of ratting on the allotments and the occasional rabbiting in Pembrokeshire.' I declined him, advising him to buy locally, for buying a 'black-un' for such work was like buying a Rolls Royce in which to deliver milk."

The first Patterdales were brought to the USA in 1978. This dog is a laid-back terrier, not as yappy as some, who enjoys "curling up by the heat duct" in the house. Modern owners say he can be kenneled with two or three other terriers, as long as he has enough work and hunting to keep him exercised and content. If stale or bored, he may pick fights with a kennel mate.

They are game and tough when hunting, and hunters often take three or four dogs with them on a jaunt. In the States, these dogs hunt "anything with fur"—woodchuck (groundhog), fox, coon or even badger. An American Patterdale, aptly named "Rocky," a flyweight at 13 pounds, recently drew a 34-pound badger!

An owner says his Patterdales are sensible dogs. When they first enter a burrow, they'll bark and fuss, trying to incite the quarry to bolt. If the prey refuses to budge, only then will the terrier go in for a hold.

The Patterdale has a bit thicker and cheekier head than many of our modern show terriers, suggesting a hint of the Bull Terrier. This may have been what they looked like originally, or this look might have come from a later cross.

Patterdale Terrier, red.

PEKINGESE

COUNTRY: China
WEIGHT: 6 pounds, 6–8 pounds, and 8–14 pounds
COAT: Long, straight, harsh and profuse; heavy feathering and abundant undercoat
COLOR: All colors allowed: red, fawn, black, black/tan, sable, brindle, white and particolor (two colors evenly broken all over body); black masks and spectacles around the eyes and lines to the ears are desirable
OTHER NAMES: Peking Palasthund
REGISTRY: FCI, AKC, UKC, TKC, CKC
GROUP: Herding

The Pekingese may be the ultimately dwarfed version of the hairy dogs from Tibet. Or, like the Pug, it may contain some miniature versions of the brachycephalic mastiff dogs. A combination of these two sources could have resulted in this unique canine creation. Whatever the origin, similar miniature dogs have been known in China since the T'ang dynasty of the eighth century. In ancient superstitious times, the "terrifying" lionlike appearance of these dogs, and the "Fo Dog" idols that represented them, were supposed to frighten away evil spirits. The Peke was known by a variety of names: Lion Dog, like his close relatives the Lhasa and Shih Tzu; Sun Dog, for the prized golden color; or Sleeve Dog, when he was small enough to be carried around in a voluminous Chinese sleeve.

The Chinese emperor Ming Ti converted to Buddhism in the first century AD, and the leonine connection to Buddha was bestowed on the Pekingese, as well as others, to be protectors of the faith. As the centuries passed, the popularity of these and other types of small pet dogs among the wealthy ebbed and flowed. By the beginning of the 19th century, dogs of the Pekingese type had become the darlings of the Chinese imperial court and the next several decades saw them reach their zenith. There were thousands of them around the various imperial palaces, and 4,000 eunuchs were housed and employed in Peking solely for the purpose of breeding, raising and caring for the Pekingese dogs. Slave girls wet-nursed the imperial puppies after their own expendable daughters were slain. No one out-

Pekingese, sable.

side of the nobility was allowed to own one, and the dogs knew nothing but pampering and gentle care. Two little Pekes announced the appearance of the emperor with short, sharp barks; two more followed daintily carrying the hem of his imperial robe. Stealing one was punishable by death.

When Peking was sacked by the British in 1860, the imperial family gave instructions to destroy all the dogs so that none would fall into the hands of the "foreign devils." Nevertheless, soldiers found four guarding the body of the emperor's aunt, who had taken her own life. These small dogs (all "sleeves" under 6 pounds) were transported back to England where one was given to Queen Victoria who, with grim humor, called her "Looty." Others were soon obtained from Peking through more normal channels, and before long the breed became

fashionable and quickly rose to the esteemed position where it has remained. At the end of the 1800s, the regent dowager Empress T'zu Hsi presented a Pekingese to an American artist, Miss Carl, in return for a painting of her favorite dog. She also presented a dog to Alice Roosevelt upon her visit to Peking. J.P. Morgan was another admirer of these dogs and brought a pair home to America. The Peke was accepted by the AKC in 1909 and in England the following year.

The Dowager Empress is also credited with the following instructions concerning the little royal dog: it was to be fed sharks' fins and curlews' livers, breasts of quails, tea or milk of antelopes, broth made from the nests of sea swallows; if ill it was to be ". . . anointed with the clarified fat of the leg of a sacred leopard and give it to drink a throstle's egg shell—full of the juice of the custard apple in which has been dissolved three pinches of shredded rhinoceros horn. . . '' Her full description of the Pekingese included an ideal that "its forelegs be bent so that it shall not desire to wander far or leave the Imperial precincts."

In rural northern China today, a very small version of the Pekingese is still bred. This min-iscule canine, under one pound, is considered good luck. Always in the piebald pattern, their spotted coats are "read" like tea leaves.

The Pekingese does have rather distinctive physical characteristics that, while pleasing to some, may not be appealing to others. The ex-tremely shortened muzzle puts the nose directly between the eyes, creating a wide "smiling" mouth and a very flat face. This same character-istic causes them to suffer on hot, humid days. Pekingese eyes are prominent and prone to in-jury. The head is wide and flat, the neck short with relatively massive shoulders and chest, and front legs are short and crooked. Combined with a long body, short stature and rather narrow hips, the breed characteristically moves with a bit of a roll.

Pekingese do have marvelous personalities, exhibiting confidence, charm and a bit of stub-born independence. They are fearless but never aggressive, and their sole purpose in life is to give comfort and companionship to their owners.

Above: Pekingeses, particolor. **Below:** Pekingese, fawn.

Hunting instincts of the Portuguese are strong and natural. Owners say these dogs begin sight pointing and retrieving sticks and other objects by two or three months of age, without any training. As soon as they are taken to the fields for instructions, they naturally begin an intense searching pattern. They can withstand extremes of climate and do well in any terrain.

This dog is exceptionally sweet and affectionate to his master. In fact, the official standard says he can "go to extremes of affection, occasionally embarrassing, which can be easily corrected by . . . training." One current owner describes a female that would sit for hours in front of him, staring in adoration. His wife would jokingly say that the dog was the reincarnation of an old lover—the only way to describe the sweet, tender expression in the dog's eyes.

Obedience and sociability in large doses are built into this breed as well. Despite his abundance of attributes and his prestige at home, he has not gained a following outside Portugal.

Right: Perdigueiro Portugueso, longhaired, old type. **Below:** Perdigueiro Portugueso, smoothhaired.

653

Above: Perdigueiro Portugueso. **Below:** Perdiguero Navarro.

Perdiguero de Burgos.

PERDIGUERO DE BURGOS

COUNTRY: Spain
WEIGHT: 55–66 pounds
HEIGHT: 20–24 inches
COAT: Short and fine
COLOR: Liver and white, with ticking
OTHER NAMES: Perdiguero Burgales, Spanish Pointer
REGISTRY: FCI
GROUP: Gun Dog

PERDIGUERO NAVARRO

COUNTRY: Spain
WEIGHT: 55–66 pounds
HEIGHT: 20–24 inches
COAT: Short or long as a setter's
COLOR: Orange/white, liver/white
OTHER NAMES: Old Spanish Pointer, Navarra Pointer, Bracco Navarone, Pachon de Vitoria
GROUP: Gun Dog

The basis of the Spanish Pointer is unknown, but the breed has been known since the 1600s. A current breeder speculates that long ago hunters crossed Spanish breeds, such as the Pachon Iberico and the Sabueso Hound, to create a pointer. The breed maintains physical similarities to both of these.

Don Alonso Martinez, writing during the time of King Phillip VI (1700s), described dogs with characteristics of the Perdiguero de Burgos. Velasquez painted Prince Baltasar Carlos in hunting dress accompanied by Spanish Pointers of Burgos type. The Perdiguero hails from the provinces of Leon, Vitoria and Burgos in northern Spain.

During the Spanish Civil War (1936–39) and WWII (1939–45), the breed waned and came within a breath of extinction. Señor Ayza, a modern breeder, says it became a "forgotten breed. But thanks to a few people, such as Don Manuel Izquierdo, Don Gerardo Sadornil and others who with much self-denial and perse-

Perdiguero de Burgos.

verance, . . . won the revival of the breed."
There are now fine examples of the Burgos
throughout Spain once again.

He was used in times past by monarchs and
the nobility for large game such as deer. Nowadays, he is a specialist for smaller game, but still
demonstrates the bravery necessary for facing
larger prey. The Spanish Pointer is especially esteemed in the mountainous regions, where he is
tireless, although type varies according to the
terrain that is hunted.

He can do equally well finding and retrieving
rabbits, pointing quail, or bringing back ducks
no matter how deep and cold the water. His
crowning achievement is in assisting in hunts for
the famed Spanish red-legged partridge, the
Perdiz.

Sports enthusiasts come from all over the
world to hunt this bird that flies like a phantom
jet and is hard to shoot. The hunts, which are
organized with shooters in blinds in a line and
beaters to drive the birds toward them, still do
not guarantee birds. But if you hit them, the
Perdigueros are there to retrieve them. The au-

thors take this opportunity to note that the
Spanish government supports the maintenance
of Perdiz flocks by having their game wardens
keep track of the bird population. If the numbers on one farm are low, the government pays
the farmer market price for his crops so they
won't be harvested, leaving ground cover and
food for the Perdiz to prosper. This is decided
farm by farm, year by year. In a world where
game is disappearing, Spain has kept a large expanding population of these famed game birds.
Shooting is only done where permitted.

In hunting, the breed is only fast enough to
cover the terrain meticulously and methodically,
hunting with an elegant, high head. Keen on
scent, he points a fair distance from the game.
He is also noted for his soft mouth.

He has no following away from home; nevertheless, the breed is still very popular in Spain
because of its natural abilities, its resistance to
extremes of weather and terrain, and its docile,
affectionate and likable nature. He is good with
children, and most dogs are kept in the home as
pets.

This is a big dog, but not heavily boned. The
body is lean, muscular and tough, with a strong
head, noticeable dewlap, and prominent lips.
His tail is docked.

The Perdiguero de Burgos was already spread
throughout Spain when the Spanish Kennel
Club first recognized the Navarro in 1911. Yet
the Navarro is an ancient type of pointing dog,
and actually may have been the prototype for
other breeds. He was known in Spain for centuries, but was thought to be lost. A group of people in Navarra and Alava (Basque country) are
trying to revive and restore the breed.

Where he came from cannot be pinpointed,
but the breed always had both smooth and longhaired varieties. He may have figured in the
early development of the feathered setting dogs
of Europe, as well as of the vorstehhunds and
braques, because of the scope of Spanish influence in Europe during those times.

His distinctive feature is his split or double
nose, something mentioned in the histories of
other European hunting dogs, such as the German Shorthair. The Navarro is similar to the
Burgos in hunting style and is also used in the
Perdiz hunts.

Perdiguero Navarro.

PERRO DE PASTOR MALLORQUIN

COUNTRY: Spain
WEIGHT: 45–60 pounds
HEIGHT: 19–22 inches
COAT: Short (pelo corto) or medium (pelo largo)
COLOR: Usually dark brindle or black
OTHER NAMES: Ca de Bestiar
REGISTRY FCI
GROUP Flock Guard

This is a livestock guardian and farm dog originating on the Balearic Islands of Spain. He is a bit smaller than the Portuguese Cão de Castro Laboreiro, but otherwise closely resembles that breed and may, therefore, have a similar history. Their true background is unknown. They have the temperament and mental characteristics of the flock-guarding dogs, but are dark, small and smooth-coated.

The breed was brought to the Balearics on early trade routes through the Mediterranean. Since these dogs were isolated on islands, either crossing with other types occurred or a mutation appeared, giving the Perro de Pastor the ability to withstand extreme heat. Whether they were shipped around the Iberian Peninsula to Portugal or the other way around is unknown.

Unknown outside Spain, the Perro de Pastor is quite common there and is seen everywhere on farms and in rural villages. Farmers produce a litter when they need a replacement and give or barter the remainder to their neighbors. Although type is set, there are few breeders or exhibition dogs. In fact, the farmer who owns one might be quite surprised to find out he owns a pure breed. To him, it's just a "farm dog."

The Perro de Pastor is effective and extremely territorial, combining aggression and courage to make any rural family feel safe. He is good and loyal with his owners, but is rarely a house dog.

A limited number have been exported to Brazil and a few breeders support the Pastor dog there. No more than a handful of breeders who live on the Iberian Peninsula produce pedigreed specimens.

His dark coat requires little care, and the ears and tail remain natural. His rose ears fold back into his neck ruff. The FCI recognizes the breed, listing both the short-coated and long-coated varieties. Today, the long coat is rarely seen and may already be gone. The dogs are universally shorthaired and dark for ease of care.

Perro de Pastor Mallorquin.

Above Left, Above Right and Below: Perro de Pastor Mallorquin.

Perro de Presa Canario, brindle.

PERRO DE PRESA CANARIO

COUNTRY: Spain
WEIGHT: 84–110 pounds maximum
HEIGHT: 21½–25½ inches
COAT: Short, smooth, but coarse
COLOR: Brindles, fawn; some white permissible
OTHER NAMES: Canary Dog
GROUP: Mastiff

The Canario has recently been reborn, although once near extinction. The Canary Islands belonging to Spain were actually named for the fierce dogs found there, not for its little yellow singing birds. From the Latin *cane* came the "Island of the Dogs." These tough, smooth-coated, livestock and farm dogs, called Bardino Majero, were probably similar to the Perro de Pastor Mallorquin and the Cão de Castro Laboreiro and were present before Hispanic times.

When English settlers came to the archipelago in the 19th century, they brought mastiffs and old-style bulldogs which were crossed with these native dogs. The result was the Canary Dog.

This breed was selected and bred specifically for organized fights and became an extremely game, powerful and able fighting machine. Outlawed in 1940, dog-fighting continued as a clandestine activity, with the quality and purity of the breeding stock deteriorating.

By the 1960s, when the Canary Dog was at an all-time low, the German Shepherd Dog was introduced to the islands. The Shepherd became the breed in vogue, almost causing the demise of the native canine. In the early 1970s, however, interest was renewed in the native breeds, and Spaniards began to search for examples of the Canary Dog. Fortunately, pure specimens had been retained by farmers in rural and isolated areas where the Canario was found to be a good farm hand. Ten years later, breeders produced good examples of the breed, which can be seen today at dog shows. An active breed club is promoting him at home and elsewhere in Europe. Dr. Carl Semencic conducted research and introduced the breed to North America in recent years. Fanciers feel confident the breed is close to FCI recognition.

These dogs have a wide, solid head, often with an undershot jaw. A bit of loose, hanging skin appears on the chin and throat, and the ears are cropped to a point. The Canary Dog, despite his size, is quiet and subdued in the home. Devoted to his family, he makes an excellent home guardian.

Perro de Presa Canario.

Perro de Presa Canario pictured with child. The breed's tremendous size is evident.

PERRO DE PRESA MALLORQUIN

COUNTRY: Spain
WEIGHT: 150 pounds maximum
HEIGHT: 23 inches minimum
COAT: Short, smooth
COLOR: Yellow with black mask
OTHER NAMES: Ca de Bou, Mallorquin Bulldog
REGISTRY: FCI
GROUP: Mastiff

Ever since the days of the great Alaunts, the sports of bull-baiting, and later dog-fighting, have been notorious spectator sports in Spain. Large, agile fighting dogs were renowned in Spain, where they are generally called *Perro de*

Presa, meaning a gripping or holding dog and loosely translated as bulldog. Although bull-baiting is no longer practiced, dogfighting still has avid followers in Spanish rural areas and places settled by Spaniards (South America, Puerto Rico, etc.).

For many centuries the local fighting breeds were the white Cordoba Dog (see Dogo Argentino) and the dark-colored Perro de Presa España, the Spanish Bulldog, very like the original bulldogs of 16th-century England. The Presa had long, straight legs, even or slightly undershot mouth and great power with agility. He was around 100 pounds, with a long neck and a long tail held high; he was said to look much like the old smaller Doguin form of the Dogue de Bordeaux. He has long been extinct. The Cordoba Dog's influence is still seen in the Dogo Argentino and those brought to the Americas, forming various white dogs used to hunt wild boar.

As organized dog-fighting waned on the rest of the continent, it continued on the islands off the Spanish coast. On the Balearic island of Mallorca, one breed has been recognized by FCI. Officially called the Perra de Presa Mallorquin, much controversy exists over whether he is now extinct or not. Although he is still listed on the FCI roster, Spanish judges and dog breeders say the Mallorquin has completely disappeared. Americans at a recent rural Spanish show for Pit Bulls and other fighting dogs said, however, six times as many Mallorquin Bulldogs were entered as Pit Bulls. Whether these dogs represent a reconstruction of the breed or a revival is a matter to be settled in time.

The Mallorquin Bulldog was often called *Ca de Bou* in the native Catalan language. Up to a hefty and impressive 150 pounds, he had his ears cropped in a short, rounded cut to make him look like a panther. The Mallorquin Dog was brought in great numbers to Puerto Rico and other Spanish islands of the Caribbean where, in the early part of this century, dog-fighting was common. Although laws have not been passed against it, the "sport" is no longer organized. This breed was the fighting dog of the islands. Puerto Ricans say many Mallorquin crosses exist, but are not sure whether any pure specimens remain.

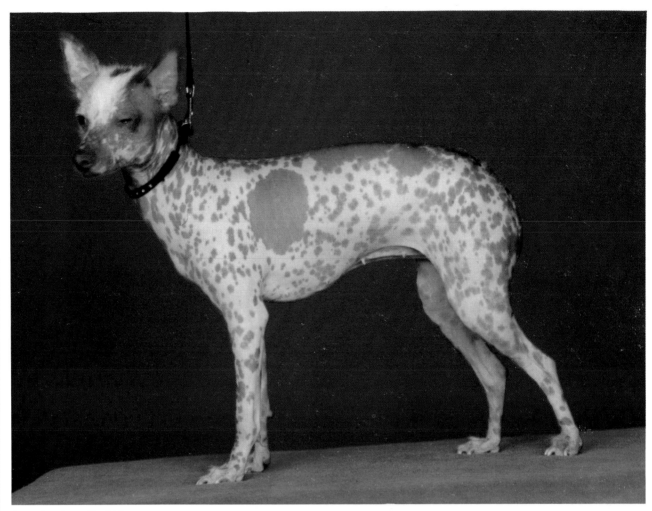

Peruvian Inca Orchid.

PERUVIAN INCA ORCHID

COUNTRY: Peru
WEIGHT: 20–38 pounds
HEIGHT: 15½–20 inches
COAT: Hairless—with crew-cut length hair on top of head permissible; Coated—with moderate length silky hair all over
COLOR: Heavy skin mottling of any color combination on pink or white background; or solid color
OTHER NAMES: Perro Flora, Moonflower Dog
REGISTRY: UKC
GROUP: Southern

Like their gentle Inca Indian masters, the Inca Orchid dogs are tranquil and intelligent. In the original Peruvian tongue, Oeuchua, the breed is called *caa-allepo*, which translates to dog without vestments.

When Spanish explorers landed in Peru, they found these hairless dogs in the homes of the Incan nobility, surrounded by orchids decorating the darkened rooms. The Inca Orchid dogs were kept inside during the day because of their sensitivity to the sun's rays. At night they ran free under the light of the moon—hence the origin of both names.

The Incans exercised selective breeding among their own people—even brother/sister marriages to assure purity and a predictable consistency—and carried over the practice to their animals. Incan nobility prized the light-colored dogs and rivaled among themselves for creating the palest hues. The common people strove to

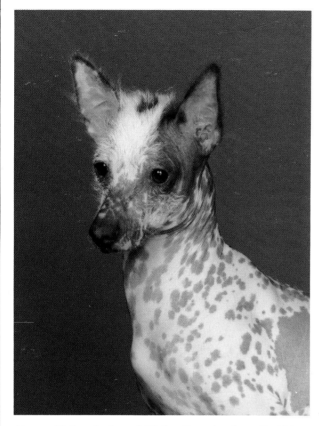

Above, Below Left and Right: Peruvian Inca Orchid.

breed the best quality dogs possible as a means of barter for favors from the nobility. Peruvian Indians still raise the dogs as beloved house pets but, reportedly, also as an occasional main dish.

The hairless head may be completely bald or be topped with a crew cut. The rarer powder-puff variety is not shown, but is kept for breeding purposes to correct teeth and skin problems that plague the hairless breeds. The ears of the hairless variety stand pricked at attention; the powderpuff's hair tips the ears forward, similar to a Sheltie's.

Oil is added to the dogs' food to keep the skin soft and healthy. The Inca Orchid must be protected from the sun, not only to ward off blisters and burns, but to prevent possible skin cancers. The Inca Hairless is dark-skinned, furnishing protection, and is considered the "daytime dog."

Deerlike in structure and movement, the breed is light boned but supple, lithe and swift. They are extremely sensitive in temperament and wilt under any roughness, even so much as a raised voice. They are laid back and unaggressive, and bloom with adult companionship. Kindness is repaid with utter devotion. The warmth received from their affectionate natures and heat-radiating bodies make them appealing to many as house pets. They can be found in America and Europe as well as in South America.

Above: Peruvian Inca Orchid, coated. **Below:** Fellow Peruvian, Inca Hairless Dog.

Pharaoh Hound

PHARAOH HOUND

COUNTRY: Malta
HEIGHT: 21–25 inches
COAT: Short and glossy; ranging from fine and close to slightly harsh with no feathering
COLOR: Self-colored tan, rich tan, or chestnut; white markings allowed only as follows—strongly desired white tip on tail and acceptable white on chest (called the star), toes, and slim snip on face
OTHER NAMES: Kelb-tal Fenek
REGISTRY: FCI, AKC, TKC, CKC
GROUP: Southern

Artifacts created in the Nile Valley during the Stone Age, perhaps as long ago as 4000 BC, display the image of a general type hound, such as the Pharaoh, Ibizan and Sicilian breeds. These dogs had the typical large, upright ears and descended from pariah-type southern dogs selected for their speed. Depicted widely during the Egyptian dynasties, these dogs bear a striking resemblance to the dog-god Anubis, who guided souls to their place in the afterworld.

But long before Egyptian times, the Phoenicians busily traded sighthounds of this kind around the known world. In most cases, these

Pharaoh Hound, chestnut.

dogs were molded and shaped into new breeds by crossing with native dogs. But, in certain cases, the canine cargo was left on isolated islands where they bred true for millenia. Such is the case with the Pharaoh Hound.

Phoenicians colonized the island of Malta about 1000 BC, probably bringing fleet hounds with them at that time. Over the years, the people of this poor-soiled rocky island learned to value the dogs for hunting rabbits. This is where they acquired the name Kelb-tal Fenek, or rabbit dog. After the decline of the Middle Eastern civilizations, Malta was left on its own for many centuries (although legend says that the Apostle Paul was shipwrecked near Malta in 60 AD when the inhabitants of these islands were converted to Christianity). For almost 2,000 years, the original dogs bred true on the island, without the introduction of any other type. Today the Pharaoh is the national dog of Malta and a piece of living history, showing us what dogs looked like thousands of years ago.

Although some Pharaoh Hounds were brought to Britain in the 1930s, they attracted little attention and soon disappeared. It wasn't until the breed was reintroduced in the 1960s that these dogs began to stir interest. A specialty club was organized in England as recently as 1968, with official Kennel Club recognition soon following. Specimens were introduced to North America in the late 1960s and gained much respect for their abilities in lure coursing and in field trials for sighthounds. Canada recognized the breed in 1979, with America following suit in 1983.

The Pharaoh is an unusual sighthound who can also competently hunt by scent. His temperament is friendly and affectionate, even playful. This, combined with his intelligence, often makes him a competitive obedience dog, a trait not common among the independent gazehounds. Despite his great speed and agility, his nature makes him quiet and unobtrusive in the home. The long, whiplike tail is carried high in a gentle curve when he is in action, very much like his ancient pariah ancestors and his cousin the Canaan Dog.

His alarm tendencies and easy care make him a viable choice for those who are willing to provide a workout. It has been noted by modern owners that Pharaohs lick rain water off each other, obviously a desert instinct to take advantage of any water. When excited, they blush a rosy pink, highlighting their faces and the inside of their ears. It is said "his face glows like a god."

Pharaoh Hound, pup.

Plott Hound, brindle.

PLOTT HOUND

COUNTRY: USA
WEIGHT: 50 pounds
HEIGHT: 22 inches
COAT: Short, thick and dense
COLOR: Usually brindle; from light golden brindle to "saddled" brindle with large black mantle and brindle only on the legs; occasional smokey blue dogs; buckskins barred from registration
REGISTRY: UKC
GROUP: Hound

The story of the Plott Hound parallels that of the Plott family and their neighbors in the Great Smoky Mountains that join North Carolina and Tennessee, in what was Cherokee territory. Sixteen-year-old Johannes Plott emigrated to this area from Germany in 1750 with his brother Enoch, who died on the journey. With them came their Hanoverian-type schweisshunds. The descendants of these hounds were fostered, bred and hunted by seven generations of Plotts.

As generations of Plotts married and began families in other parts of the mountains, their hounds spread with them. The Plott's hounds ran the mountainsides for over 200 years. Used on a variety of game, these hounds were bear dogs par excellence. They didn't carry any specific breed name in the early days. Those belonging to Plotts were called Plott's Hounds, those bred by the Cables of Swain County were named Cable Hounds, etc., even though the hounds were all basically the same type and breeding. The original schweisshunds were crossed with other hounds and with cur types especially for their treeing ability. At one time, the breed was even referred to as the Plott Cur. But through the years, each of these clans maintained the original type of a tough, persistent, coldtrailing hound. H.T. Crockett, the Hannahs, the Cruse family, the Reece brothers, the Will Orr family and Blain Blevins all had notable strains.

By the 1920s, the old strains of these brindle mountain-bear dogs needed a boost. The Blevins Hounds were a strain of black-saddled tan hounds also known in the Great Smokies. Gola Ferguson, who had bred hounds of the Plott type for many years, crossed some of his with those of Blevins' type. The result of this cross,

"Tige" and "Boss," was two legendary hounds that became known throughout the vast mountain range. Bred back to Plott types, they provided the boost that was needed to revive this old breed. Almost all modern registered Plotts trace to one or the other of these pillars. Even the Plott families, always able to appreciate a fine hound, bought dogs from Ferguson to improve their own stock. This cross also introduced the black-saddled brindle pattern.

When this breed was suggested for UKC registration in 1946, there were those that wanted them called Ferguson Hounds or Cable Hounds. Although many contributed to the breed, the Plott family received the honor in the final selection.

Plotts are very tough hounds who not only can coldtrail a 500–pound bear or a boar, but can stand up to that type of game when they have it cornered. As Ferguson said of one of his dogs, "Against bear, he was a one man army." One hunter's eager female Plott always tore up a bear's ear, which she'd grab and hang on to stubbornly. The Plotts are hounds of fine nose and beautiful voice, and are easily trained.

Hack Smithdeal, a well-to-do, avid bear hunter of Tennessee, did much to publicize the Plott breed. He claimed this breed to be the best he could find for bear hunting, and much of his famous pack came directly from John Plott and his son, George Plott, in the 1930s. A 1946 demonstration with Smithdeal's hounds for the Conservation Department opened bear hunting with dogs in Michigan. From Smithdeal dogs came the hounds of the Pioneer Kennel of Dale Brandenburg, who has produced many outstanding Plotts.

Although the lighter brindle color was common earlier, after the Blevins cross the most usual pattern was a black-saddled brindle, some almost a solid black with brindling only on the legs. Other colors appear in the breed, including slate blue from the Blue Delch strain and a very few buckskins. The buckskin color has recently been barred from registration due to the fact that some of that color had come from Redbone crosses. The Plott breeders, like the Blue Gascon and Majestic promoters, want to maintain the old hunting type without adulteration from hot-nosed speed hounds.

PODENGOS PORTUGUESOS

Podengo Portugueso Grande

COUNTRY: Portugal
WEIGHT: 66 pounds
HEIGHT: 22–28 inches
COAT: Short, coarse, longer than most of the sighthounds; Wirehaired—medium-long, shaggy and coarse
COLOR: Yellow, tan, dark gray with white markings
OTHER NAMES: Large Portuguese Hound
REGISTRY: FCI
GROUP: Southern

Podengo Portugueso Grande, wirehaired.

Podengo Portugueso Medio, shorthaired.

Podengo Portugueso Medio

COUNTRY: Portugal
WEIGHT: 35–44 pounds
HEIGHT: 15½–22 inches
COAT: Same as Grande
COLOR: Shades of fawn or gray, usually with white markings
OTHER NAMES: Medium Portuguese Hound
REGISTRY: FCI
GROUP: Southern

Podengo Portugueso Pequeño

COUNTRY: Portugal
WEIGHT: 10–12½ pounds
HEIGHT: 8–12 inches
COAT: Same as Grande
COLOR: Fawn and white combinations
OTHER NAMES: Small Portuguese Hound
REGISTRY: FCI
GROUP: Southern

Podengo Portugueso Pequeño, wirehaired.

Portugal's contributions to the sighthound classification can trace their ancestry to the running dogs of northern Africa. They are probably closely related to the Pharaoh Hound and most likely joined their relatives on board trading vessels, disembarking on Portuguese shores. Because they were not as isolated as those on islands, the availability of other breeding stock allowed for some variations over the years.

These dogs were most prevalent in northern Portugal where they were renowned rabbit dogs. Hunting singly or in packs, the Podengo developed into varieties allowing for the type of terrain to be covered. In more open country, the large size used its longer legs to overtake the prey with greater speed. Today the Grande is not seen as much as in times past. He is a natural dog, without docking or cropping. The Grande is an outstanding guard dog and an eager hunter.

Fitting snugly in between and bridging the gap is the Medio. While not as fast on the flat, he has more maneuverability in rougher cover and uneven terrain. It is the most common form seen with hunters in modern Portugal. His com-

paratively smaller size is easier to house and feed.

The Pequeño, looking much like a sturdy Chihuahua, still demonstrates the hunting instincts despite his diminutive size. He is touted as the world's smallest hunting dog, and is used (like the Kaninchen Dachshund) to enter the rabbit warrens and flush the prey into the open—either for the gun or for the larger Podengos to run down. The Pequeño is also commonly seen as a "crew member" on boats where his job is to dispatch rats. While all of the sizes can second as house pets, the small version fits best and most popularly into this venue.

These are breeds which have never been sponsored outside of their native Portugal. FCI recognizes all three varieties, and one sees them occasionally exhibited at Portuguese shows. Like the Ibizans and Pharaohs, they are quiet, easy keepers and simple to groom. The added value of filling the game bag has kept them in the forefront with Portuguese hunters. All three Podengos appear in both smooth and wire coats and are lively, affectionate companions.

Podengo Portugueso Pequeño, shorthaired.

Above: Podengo Portugueso Medio, wirehaired. **Below:** Podengo Portugueso Grande, wirehaired.

Pointer, black with white.

POINTER

COUNTRY: Great Britain
WEIGHT: About 44–66 pounds
HEIGHT: Around 21–24 inches
COAT: Short, dense, and smooth
COLOR: Liver, lemon, black, or orange, either solid or in combination with white
OTHER NAMES: English Pointer
REGISTRY: FCI, AKC, UKC, TKC, CKC
GROUP: Gun Dog

Pointing dogs popped up all over Europe around 1650, but the English version has remained the modern prototype. What exactly was used in its creation is not known, but development occurred within the British Isles; there was ample trade to Britain in dogs from all over the world. The strongest influence may have been the Portuguese Pointer, with his ancient lineage and his dished face.

The earliest Pointers were actually present before the age of wing shooting, assisting in the "hare-coursing" rage. The Pointer was sent out to find and "point out" the presence of a hare. Then Greyhounds were brought up and slipped as the hare bolted. When wing shooting came into vogue after 1700, the Pointer began to prove his real worth. The earliest Pointers really "set," dropping to the ground on the flush of game, a quality that has been bred out long since. Yet the ardent desire to hunt, speed of search, intense style, and exceptional nose have been retained to the present day. The Pointer has, over the years, been used in crosses in countries all over Europe to add elegance and dash to the native gun dogs.

The Pointer has remained in high esteem throughout the world. The great majority in the USA are registered with the Field Dog Stud Book, and have been bred for great speed and ground coverage, as well as tremendous courage and stamina for the required three-hour heats. This type now dominates the great Open All Age American Field Trial Circuit. Hunting of this sort, in front of mounted handlers covering vast acreages, is not available to most hunters. Therefore, the American Field type of Pointer may be "too much dog" for the average hunter who wants a pleasant day of sport and a full game bag. The AKC-registered Pointer, on the other hand, tends to be a closer working dog, competing in the AKC field trials, which are more the venue of the true gun dog.

The Pointer's distinctive "dished" face that hints of a mastiff background, the undocked tail of moderate length and taper, and his big, graceful elegance make him stand out among hunting dogs. He is especially known for his endurance in hot weather, but his longtime susceptibility to the cold and his reluctance in water remain a part of him. The breed is not always as enthusiastic and adept at retrieving as some of his Continental cousins. The passion to hunt is intense.

The classic good looks of the Pointer, with his proud bearing, demand attention at shows. Show Pointers do not often compete in field trials, making the first dual championship attained in the mid-1980s a piece of history. With adequate exercise, the Pointer makes an affectionate, clean and quiet companion dog.

Above: Pointer, liver with white. **Below:** Pointer, orange with white, in motion.

Above and Below: Pointer in field.

Above and Below: Pointer.

677

Pointer, liver with white.

Pointers.

POITEVIN

COUNTRY: France
WEIGHT: 66 pounds
HEIGHT: 24–28 inches
COAT: Short and glossy
COLOR: Tricolor or orange/white, with large body patches of both or all three colors; the tri has a black saddle
OTHER NAMES: Haut-Poitou
REGISTRY: FCI
GROUP: Hound

Wolves were plentiful in Poitou in the 1600s. This province on France's western coast is above Saintongeois and below Vendee and Brittany. In the 1690s, the Marquis Francois de Larrye of Poitou created a big, courageous hound specifically for wolf. Hunting in packs, these hounds were remarkable for their nose, voice and speed over rough ground. French hunters stated, "It was the best dog in the world for hunting wolves; capable of following its prey from sunrise to sunrise."

Most of the kennels were lost following the Revolution and an 1842 rabies outbreak decimated the last pack, leaving just one dog and two bitches. Determined fanciers of the 20th century have restored the breed, using some crosses including foxhound. Despite this revival, the Poitevin is still not widespread, perhaps because there is no demand for his "specialty." But he still has proponents in France, and recently there have been a handful of imports to an American hound fancier. An elegant and racy scenthound, he carries less ear than many of the classic French hounds.

Poitevin, tricolor.

Polish Hound, black and tan saddled.

POLISH HOUND

COUNTRY: Poland
WEIGHT: 55–71 pounds
HEIGHT: 22–26 inches
COAT: Short, smooth, and very dense, with a slight fringe on under side of tail
COLOR: Black and tan, or black and tan saddled
OTHER NAMES: Ogar Polski
REGISTRY: FCI
GROUP: Hound

The Polish indigenous hound, like so many of the European hounds, is unfamiliar outside his home borders. He is a big, slow, heavy dog, but without the ponderous head, long ears, and excessive skin of the St. Hubert type. He is proba-bly related to the deliberate tracking dogs of Germany and Austria. He has the German hound's large, stiff, flat ears with a bit of flew. In past centuries, he was highly prized for his superlative tracking ability. The War years decimated the breed, but it made a post-War comeback, achieving FCI recognition in 1966. At one time, a smaller version called the Gonczy Polski existed as well.

During the hunt he moves at a steady trot or a heavy gallop, and is highly prized for his perseverance and beautiful voice. Adapted to all terrain and weather, he is a dog of kind and gentle spirit. In recent years, he has again become scarce and is reputed to be quite rare.

681

POLSKI OWCZAREK NIZINNY

COUNTRY: Poland
WEIGHT: 30–50 pounds
HEIGHT: Maly—up to 14 inches; Sredni—16–18½ inches; Duzy Ponad—over 19 inches
COAT: Thick, long, with shaggy hair covering the face
COLOR: All acceptable, including piebald
OTHER NAMES: Valee Sheepdog, Polish Lowland Sheepdog
REGISTRY: FCI, TKC
GROUP: Herding

The Nizinny may well be the missing link between several modern, shaggy herding breeds and the ancient, corded herding dogs of the East. Of ancient lineage, bred from the Puli and the long-coated, medium-sized Hun herding dogs, some of these Nizinnys were traded by Polish sailors along their coastal destinations. Before long the sailors had a dog in every port. The Nizinny was instrumental in the ancestry of the Bearded Collie and Schapendoes.

Bred as a working dog since the 16th century by farmers and shepherds, the Nizinny was nearly extinct at the end of the Second World War. Most of the Polish people were concerned mainly with survival, not with the procreation and perfection of dogs, but—thankfully—a few breeders continued their lines from the scant six bitches and two dogs considered acceptable for breeding. A Polish veterinarian, Dr. Danuta Hrzniewicz, has been tireless in her efforts to rebuild the breed's foundation. These breeders' tough culling program produced today's version, which remains trainable, intelligent, and affectionate with children, yet alert to danger. Several of these dogs have been chosen to partici-

Polski Owczarek Nizinny.

pate as therapy dogs, visiting the hospitalized.

The sheepdog of Poland, divided into three sizes in its homeland, is best known in its medium-sized (Sredni) version. As with most breeds developed for working purposes, the Nizinny is wary of strangers. In Poland, a working certificate must be earned before a championship can be awarded, and the dogs are more populous in the country, where they still herd, than in the cities.

They have short tails, docked if necessary. Otherwise, in appearance, they are much like one of their descendants, the Bearded Collie. Their gaze is described as "penetrating," whereas the Beardie's is termed "inquiring," the end result being the same—that of being able to win the admiration of whosever eyes they captivate. According to breeders, the memory of a Nizinny is long, and years later, they will remember an offense or a caress. They have won friends in some countries outside of Poland, including a fair number in the United States.

Right: Polski Owczarek Nizinny. **Below:** Polish owners in traditional dress accompanied by Polish Lowland Sheepdogs and Owczarek Podhalanski pup.

POMERANIAN

COUNTRY: Great Britain
WEIGHT: 3–7 pounds
HEIGHT: 11 inches maximum
COAT: Very abundant spitz-type coat
COLOR: 12 allowed colors: black (and black/tan), brown, chocolate, beaver (dark beige), red, orange, cream, orange sable, wolf sable, blue, white, or particolor
REGISTRY: AKC, UKC, TKC, CKC
GROUP: Northern

The origins of this breed hail from European herding spitz dogs. When the first specimens were brought to England from the German province of Pomerania, they were larger (up to 30 pounds), usually white and less profusely coated than our modern specimens. Litters often included smaller pups, and soon the smallest species was preferred.

Queen Victoria fell in love with the tiny ball of fluff, bringing it home with her in 1888. She exhibited Poms extensively at British shows, and hers were generally in the 12–18 pound range. Large by modern standards, hers made the Poms of that day look monstrous by comparison. This encouraged an upsurge throughout England, where they were exhibited at that time as "spitzdogs." British breeders systematically bred them for smaller and smaller size, and more and more coat. Modern show specimens are usually four to five pounds! So, although they have been named for their homeland, they are considered to be an English breed, developed in Britain to their modern form. The FCI, however, does not separately register the Pomeranian, considering it the same breed as the German Zwergspitz. The Pomeranian came to North America around the turn of the century and quickly gained favor on that continent as well.

The Pom is a beloved companion dog throughout the world. Despite its diminutive size, the breed retains the spitz personality with a brilliance of colors. Pomeranians have the alert, active, and curious character of their larger brethren, and are useful alarm dogs and fine, accurate obedience dogs. The breed is "full of itself," and likes nothing better than to "strut its stuff" in a show ring or on a neighborhood walk.

Weekly grooming keeps Poms neat. They make wonderful playmates for children who are old enough to be considerate of their tiny stature. Their easy care, beauty and diminutive size suit them as companions to the elderly.

Pomeranian, black/tan.

Pomeranians, cream.

Pomeranian.

Pomeranian, red.

POODLES

Poodle, Standard

COUNTRY: France
WEIGHT: 45–70 pounds
HEIGHT: Over 15 inches
COAT: Profuse, dense, harsh, closely curling coat (will cord if not combed)
COLOR: Any solid color
OTHER NAMES: Caniche, Barbone
REGISTRY: FCI, AKC, UKC, TKC, CKC
GROUP: Gun Dog

Poodle, Miniature

COUNTRY: France
HEIGHT: 10–15 inches (USA), 11–15 inches (Great Britain)
COAT: Same as the Standard
COLOR: Same as the Standard
OTHER NAMES: Caniche, Barbone
REGISTRY: FCI, AKC, UKC, TKC, CKC
GROUP: Gun Dog

Poodle, Toy

COUNTRY: France
HEIGHT: Under 10 inches
COAT: Same as the Standard
COLOR: Same as the Standard
OTHER NAMES: Caniche, Chien Canne
REGISTRY: FCI, AKC, UKC, TKC, CKC
GROUP: Gun Dog

Where and when the Poodle breed developed remains a matter of controversy. Shaggy water dogs, often with the clipping which has become a tradition, were known in many countries predating the Christian era. These developed, over time, into the specific breeds we know today. Poodle types were depicted in artwork as early as the 15th century. Germany may have been the actual country of origin, where, known as the *pudel*, he was well established as a water retriever before that century. It is believed the breed entered France with German troops.

Standard Poodle, black.

Standard Poodle, white.

From the marshes of Germany, the Poodle climbed to world-wide popularity. Welcomed by the French, he is still called Caniche, from the French *chien canard* for duck dog. In France, he evolved into his modern form. His quick intelligence and charm soon found him favor as a performer, and since the dawn of European circuses, Poodles have entertained as trick dogs. One Poodle, named "Domini," was credited with telling time and playing a challenging game of dominoes. The exaggerated pompons were clipped to match those of the clowns. Small Poodles or Poodle crosses were also used extensively as truffle dogs, sniffing out the delectable underground fungus for their partners, the Dachshunds, who then unearthed the truffle.

The courts of Europe, especially in France, escalated the fad of the pampered pet, a position the Poodle has not lost to this day. Because he assumed most of his modern characteristics in France, FCI has identified that country as his place of origin.

The Standard Poodle may be the oldest of the varieties, but has always has been the least in numbers. His size and coat care require both space and time. To his credit, the modern Standard Poodle is an athletic yet urbane companion. He is still a hearty swimmer and can jog, hike, or compete in obedience with *joie de vivre*. Yet his long history as a companion enables him to be a gentleman in the home.

The Miniature variety appeared on the scene shortly after its larger siblings became celebrated. In circuses and homes, the smaller size was cheaper to feed and easier to care for. The Miniature has remained the most common of all the Poodle varieties. In fact, in the 1950s and 60s, he soared to a phenomenal popularity all over the world. The numbers were so great that inevitably, some genetic problems occurred. Today, however, the Poodle has returned to a position of security. The Miniature makes a lively, yet mannerly, companion for all lifestyles.

As the Poodle became the rage with the nobility in the 17th and 18th centuries, smaller and smaller specimens were desired, resulting in the birth of the Toy variety. Toy Poodles were portrayed by the German artist, Durer, circa 1500, and by Goya toward the end of the 18th century in Spain. Many in Louis XVI's court fancied the charming dog.

Miniature Poodle.

The Toy Poodle has all the same intelligence and friendliness of the two larger versions in a smaller package. As is true with any extreme miniaturization, a few more problems are inherent in the small size, such as in whelping puppies. The ideal for the breed defines a Toy as any Poodle under 10 inches—most show dogs, however, are around eight inches. Some breeders have attempted to produce even smaller specimens, calling them "Teacup" Poodles. No such variety is defined by the standard, and these very tiny dogs are prone to many more inborn problems.

People occasionally disparage the trim as an exaggerated bid for attention but, originally, the Poodle's clip had a practical purpose. The jacket was kept heavy around the joints and organs, for protection in cold water, and the remaining coat was shorn for efficiency. Following that sensible period, came an era of ridiculous embellishments. As revealed by Shirley Kalstone in "Origins of Trimming the Poodle" (AKC *Gazette*), groomers clipped the dog in any design the owner requested: a family coat of arms, monograms, fleurs-de-lis, with moustachios and imperiales (Van Dyke beards). If desired, they capped it off with a pompadour to match the owner's.

The Poodle coat requires either frequent home-grooming sessions or regular visits to professionals. The modern show ring allows only two coat clips—the English Saddle Clip and the Continental, with the pompons—both with full-length body hair requiring great attention. But most pet owners have their Poodles cut down into a kennel or Dutch clip, with shorter hair making care easier. Early show dogs were occasionally shown with a corded coat and, recently, this style has reappeared.

Poodles have their tails cut to about half-length when the whelps are just a few days old. Except for their size, all three varieties are judged by the same criteria. They move with a light, springy gait, almost as if they were dancing. The Poodle, in all of his varieties, probably remains the most popular companion dog in the world and jockeys with the Cocker Spaniel for AKC's top dog.

Standard Poodle.

Standard Poodles, white and apricot.

Above: Poodle, harlequin—particolor not recognized by any major registry. **Below:** Poodle in corded coat. Some fanciers have begun showing the breed in this style coat.

Poodle.

Miniature Poodle, light apricot.

Poodles, Standard and Miniature.

Miniature Poodles, apricot and silver.

PORCELAINE

COUNTRY: France
WEIGHT: 55–62 pounds
HEIGHT: 22–23 inches
COAT: Very short and fine
COLOR: Nearly solid white with a few spots of orange especially on the ears
OTHER NAMES: Chien de Franche-Comte, Franc Comptoise
REGISTRY: FCI
GROUP: Hound

The province of Franche-Comte is in the east in the French Alps up against the border of Switzerland. The hound from this district is very old, having descended from the Montaimboeufs, that ancient breed that stemmed directly from the Talbots. During his heyday in the 1700s, the Porcelaine or Comptoise was considerably larger than the modern breed. He is probably closely related to the Schweizer Laufhund of Switzerland. At first called by his area of origin, he began to be known locally, and finally universally, by his current descriptive name. During the French Revolution, he actually disappeared but was "reconstructed" in 1845 with the help of Swiss breeders and their Laufhunds.

During the Revolution or before, many of the French nobility fled France, often taking their hounds with them. A good number of this breed found its way to America. For example, a family named Rousseau was granted large tracts of land in the Louisiana Territory by King Louis XIV, and kept many hunting hounds there. Reportedly, just before the American Civil War, there were 250 Porcelaine hounds on the Rousseau plantations in the South. A painting owned by the family, and exhibited in Paris in 1906, shows 31 Porcelaines killing a panther in the Louisiana canebreak. After the Civil War, when the southern plantations were broken up, the descendants of the Rousseau family moved west into Texas. The pack of hounds was scattered as gifts to area ranchers. Although purebred Porcelaine breeding did not survive that move, the blood of these French hounds figured prominently in the creation of many of our native American hound breeds, especially in the southwest.

Bred to hunt hare and roe deer, the breed is energetic, impetuous, and fierce in the hunt, but serene when at home. He is a classic French hound in type with very long ears. The name Porcelaine came from his shining white coat which gives him the look of a porcelain statuette.

Porcelaine.

Portuguese Water Dog, white.

PORTUGUESE WATER DOG

COUNTRY: Portugal
WEIGHT: 35–55 pounds
HEIGHT: 16–22 inches
COAT: Shiny, wavy and loosely curled; or thick, with shorter curls
COLOR: White; black, liver, with/without white markings or spots in varying proportions
OTHER NAMES: Cão de Agua
REGISTRY: FCI, AKC, TKC
GROUP: Gun Dog

The Portie is from the same stem as other water dogs of Europe, with the speculation being that he arrived on the Iberian Peninsula with the Moors via northern Africa. They have the same body and coat type as the other water dogs, with a slightly different method of retrieving.

For centuries, the Portuguese fishermen of the Algarve area have found these dogs to be indispensable. Their great swimming ability and webbed feet enabled them to take messages between boats and to aid the villagers in handling the nets in the water, as well as "herding" the fish into the nets. They caught any fish that escaped from the nets, and would dive into deep water to retrieve lost articles and "men overboard." These dogs are credited with good sight and scent, announcing a school of fish from their place in the bow. At the end of the day, they guarded the catch and gear and were rewarded for their chores with a meal of fish.

Sitting in the bow during heavy fog, they served as a predecessor to the foghorn, barking continuously to warn others of the boat's presence. Their easygoing nature and trainability were a necessity in the tight quarters of the fishing boats. Size differences allow them to fit comfortably into all boats, from the smallest skiff to a larger vessel. So vital was their contribution to the fishing villages that one was actually put on a fisherman's payroll, and it was officially noted that anyone who harmed the Cão de Agua would be punished.

In more modern times with radios and other conveniences, this distinct dog has been disappearing from his native working environment. In 1960, only 50 specimens were believed to remain. Fortunately, the breed has found people to foster its perpetuation. In his native Portugal, the United States and other countries, dedicated breeders are demonstrating the great charm of the breed to others. Vasco Bensaud revived the breed when mechanical replacements threatened the robust, affable native dog. Deyanne Miller, a Connecticut breeder, is credited with introducing the breed to the USA, which may very well have served to rescue the Portie from anonymity or worse. A very adaptable dog to any environment, the Portie fits as well into a family situation as into the bow of a boat. His unique sense of humor makes him a valued family member, and he loves other dogs as well. His bark adds to the breed's individuality, by climbing "up and down an octave."

The Portie coat offers several solid colors and combinations, as well as two textures. The coat

Portuguese Water Dog, black.

can be clipped in both the traditional working retriever clip (moderately short all over) or the lion clip (trimmed short on abdomen, legs, tail and face, with the hair left long on the thorax and end of the tail). When excited or on the alert, his tail curls up over the back in a gentle curve.

He is a trainable, pleasant companion, yet athletic enough to be a retriever, obedience worker or walking companion. Recognized in several European countries, he was granted full AKC recognition in 1984. Famous admirers of the breed include a real "water man," Jacques Cousteau, as well as landlubber Raymond Burr. The Portie's coat is comparatively "non-shedding" and is not as aggravating as some other breeds' to people suffering from allergies. Breeders pass a word of warning to today's owners: guard against obesity and give sufficient exercise.

Portuguese Water Dog.

Above: Portuguese Water Dogs and masters outside castle in Portugal.
Below: Portuguese Water Dog, puppies.

Pudelpointer.

PUDELPOINTER

COUNTRY: Germany
WEIGHT: 55–70 pounds
HEIGHT: 24–26 inches
COAT: Hard, coarse and thick, but not very long, slight beard and brow
COLOR: Chestnut to dead leaf, solid with a small amount of white on paws and chest allowed
REGISTRY: FCI, CKC
GROUP: Gun Dog

A combination of pointers and "poodles" in name and genetic make-up, this breed was created in the late 1800s by Baron von Zedlitz. He started with 90 "pointers" (probably of the utility dog type, i.e., Shorthair, Wirehair, and others) and seven "poodles." Some who have stud-ied the breed espouse his use of the modern Poodle; however, others feel the breed's fore-bears were actually Barbets, ancestors of the Poodle. Nevertheless, the Pudelpointer inher-ited the intelligence, attachment and obedience to owners, love of water and natural retrieving ability demonstrated by Poodles. The pointers contributed other hunting skills, including the sensitive nose and fiery attitude toward game.

While working on establishing the mental characteristics and hunting attitude, physical type was slowly fixed. Today his short, rough, waterproof jacket with its camouflage coloring and other qualities enable him to figure promi-nently in German utility trials. The breed can-not achieve stud book status in its native land until the dog has passed these demanding ability tests. The dog must also pass a hip radiograph exam, as well as have a conformation rating.

Field trials in Germany demand formidable performance from the dogs. In the utility search competition, 25 requirements have to be passed. Judgment is made on work in the woods, water, field and in retrieving—and all dogs must have acquired at least a "good" rating in conformation before being allowed to compete.

The retrieving portion of the test necessitates finding and bringing back a hare and a fox; another fox must be retrieved over a high jump. Field work judging is based on nose, searching, pointing, retrieving of feathered game, and manners. The dog must not only track wounded duck but retrieve from deep water.

The difference between hunting styles becomes fully apparent in the woods. While the utility dog is never actually used to hunt deer, its ability to search for wounded game such as boar, hare, fox, and/or deer and stag is utilized throughout Europe. Especially in Germany, the sporting hunter makes every effort to find each piece of game that he wounds but fails to kill. As Dr. Fritz von Dewitz-Colpin relates, "All hunting is done under the motive: The subsequent search defines the value of the huntsman."

The dog must track a wounded hare and a fox, most preferably giving tongue while on the trail, and then retrieve the animal. He must find and put to flight furred game such as rabbits. And last, he is expected to follow the bloodtrail of a wounded deer or boar (in trials, simulated by dripping just one drop of blood every yard or so over a trail of 500 meters with a deer skin left at the end). To start, the dog tracks on lead, but as he becomes closer to the game and sure of his quarry, he is unleashed to go on by himself. When he reaches the dead game, he has to indicate his success. The *verbellen* (verbal) dog bays loudly to announce the find. This is the most desirable way since, in actual hunting situations, he may find the wounded deer alive and, having cornered it, bay until his master reaches him. Some dogs are naturally *verweisen* (mute), and these dogs usually are trained to take in their mouths a short strap, called a *bringsel*, that hangs from their collar, and return to the handler. This symbolic retrieve of the *bringsel*, literally "the bringing thing," indicates that the dog can lead the handler to dead game that is too

Pudelpointer.

large to retrieve.

Until 1933, the dog was also expected to pass a sharpness test in which he killed a "big cat" or a fox. These species preyed on both hare and birds, so it was important to game wardens that the numbers of cats and foxes be kept low. These tests have been outlawed, but owners of the utility breeds may find hints of this sharpness still present.

A limited number of Pudelpointers are in Canada and the USA, almost exclusively in the hands of hunters. Most comparable to the German utility tests are the trials sponsored by the North American Versatile Hunting Dog Association (NAVHDA), and the Pudelpointers perform commendably in these events. NAVHDA judges the dogs against a standard and expects them to perform a variety of hunting chores.

Pudelpointers do as well hunting in the desert as they do in a snowdrift. The breed has tremendous stamina and needs a large amount of exercise. Their tail is docked like that of a Shorthair.

PUG

COUNTRY: China
WEIGHT: 14–18 pounds
HEIGHT: 10–11 inches
COAT: Short, smooth
COLOR: Apricot or silver-fawn (both with black mask), black
OTHER NAMES: Mops, Carlin
REGISTRY: FCI, AKC, TKC, CKC
GROUP: Mastiff

The Pug is a miniature mastiff, with boxy head, large bone and typically thick, wrinkled skin. He hails originally from the Orient, where the Chinese have always favored the snub-nosed dog. This little dog could pass for a flat-faced miniature Tibetan Mastiff or a long-legged, smooth cousin of the Pekingese.

The Dutch East India Company traded around the world, including the Far East, where they found the Pug in China and brought it home to Holland, probably before the 16th century. By the time of William I, Prince of Orange (1533–1584), this breed was admired in the Netherlands. In fact, because the Prince had

Pug, black.

them, Pugs became the symbol of those who supported the royal family (the Orangists), just as the Keeshond was the mascot of the Patriots or commoner's cause. When William rose victorious after the unrest, the Pug soared in popularity.

When Protestant William III took over England's throne after Catholic James II was ousted, the Pug accompanied the Dutchman to the islands and to British favor. Thus, the Pug is not only a symbol of politics, but of religion. Years later, another famous couple, the Duke and Duchess of Windsor enjoyed the company of this miniature mastiff.

It is possible that the original Pug may have been larger, and it may have been he who contributed to the pushed-in faces of several breeds in Europe, i.e., the Affenpinscher and English Bulldog. His name source is controversial. Fanciers can make their own choice: the Latin *pugnus*, meaning fist, describes the dog's shape; the fact that many of the fighting breeds were descended from the Alaunt, which came down from the the Pugnaces; the old English term *pugg*, meaning someone tenderly loved, which was in general usage in England long before the breed's arrival.

Until the late 1800s the breed was only seen in fawn. The English Lady Brassey returned from the Orient in 1877 with a pair of black Pugs, introducing the second color.

Classified by AKC as a toy, the Pug is more solid than many others in the group and is sturdy enough to romp and play with children. His pushed-in nose and bright, button eyes give him a teddy-bear look. Children must be warned, however, that the little dog is not a teddy bear, but a living thing that can be hurt.

The breed motto is *multum in parvo*, a lot in a small package, which aptly describes the Pug. He has been the chosen companion of those who prefer a smaller dog that still evidences the character of a larger counterpart. Fanciers emphasize the Pug's laid-back temperament, cleanliness and affection for his master as attributes of the breed.

Quiet, but alert, affectionate and patient, they are true "gentlemen" and "ladies." If they attend too many tea parties, however, they tend to become grossly overweight.

Pug, apricot.

Pug, silver-fawn.

Pug, silver-fawn.

PULI

COUNTRY: Hungary
WEIGHT: 18–39 pounds
HEIGHT: 14–19 inches
COAT: Long, thick, coarse, wavy, forming cords
COLOR: Any solid colors–rusty black, black, all shades of gray, and white
REGISTRY: FCI, AKC, TKC, CKC
GROUP: Herding

Much of the Hungarian culture came from the Far East with invading Magyars, including its flock-guarding and herding breeds. The Puli is very much like the Tibetan Terrier in structure and instincts. It shows the Asian influence in its short-coupled body, the thick coat covering its body and, particularly, the tail curled over the back.

Its working abilities are of utmost importance. In fact, the dogs which do not measure up are not even given the breed name—they are just plain dogs and are not kept. The breed name is derived from the *Puli Hou*, the "Destroyer Huns" of Asia. One branch of these nomadic huns, the Magyars, migrated into eastern Europe with their sheep, dogs and horses in the ninth century and settled Hungary. In their native land, more than two dogs are called *Pulix*;

Puli.

in America the plural is *Pulik*. The Puli came close to being lost during the many wars that tore its country, but the breed has survived.

Recognizing the native breed's value as a herding dog, due to its intelligence and eagerness in performing its chores, Emil Raitsits brought the breed back from the edge of extinction.

The Puli coat is remarkable and resembles a rag mop. The idea that the coat is unkempt or not touched is a fallacy. Owners spend a great deal of time keeping their dogs' cords clean. The painstaking cording procedure is begun when the dog is a young puppy. Drying after a bath is time-consuming. Coats may be brushed into a woolly Afro, rather than corded in the States, but only corded coats may be shown in Hungary, Canada and Mexico.

A working Puli is a picture of agility and flying cords. The adult corded coat affords protection from the elements and a cushion from the hooves of cattle.

Pulik have been used for police work in some parts of the world. They have been successful in the show ring and obedience work in North America. In Hungary, these dogs are still seen with flocks.

Pulik.

Pulik.

PUMI

COUNTRY: Hungary
WEIGHT: 18–29 pounds
HEIGHT: 13–19 inches
COAT: Medium-long, curling hair, not felty like Puli type, never cording
COLOR: Solids—Black, all shades of gray, and reddish brown, white not favored
REGISTRY: FCI
GROUP: Herding

The Pumi was bred from Pomeranian or Hutes-pitz dogs brought from Germany and crossed with the Puli brought along with the merino sheep imported in the 17th and 18th centuries. This dog has evolved into a breed of its own over the last 300 years and is gaining popularity in its homeland. Developed to drive cattle, it is daring, energetic, mouthy and high-spirited. Its standard describes the Pumi as "unable to keep quiet." His character makes the breed a fine watchdog in remote areas.

The Pumi's tail is set high and carried gaily. One-third of the tail is removed. The ears are upright and tipped forward. The coat is distinct from the Puli's in that, although thick and long, the hair does not form into cords. The Pumi is considered the town dog in Hungary, while the Puli remains on the *puszta*, high plains.

Above and Below: Pumi.

710

Pyrenean Mastiff.

PYRENEAN MASTIFF

COUNTRY: Spain
WEIGHT: 120–155 pounds
HEIGHT: 28½–32 inches or more
COAT: Moderate length on the back; longer on tail, neck, chest and backs of legs
COLOR: Basically white with body or head markings of grays, brindle, black, orange or fawn obligatory
OTHER NAMES: Perro Mastin del Pireneo, Mastin d'Aragon
REGISTRY: FCI
GROUP: Flock Guard

Massive flock-guarding dogs arrived on the Iberian Peninsula over 30 centuries ago. Cargos of Assyrian and Sumerian-type dogs were traded around the Mediterranean by the Phoenicians. Many of these dogs were left in Spain, where they found ample employment with the great flocks. As they spread throughout the peninsula, the dogs developed several regional variations. Moving north into the ancient kingdom of Aragon, the Pyrenean Mastiff was born.

Until nearly 1500, Spain was divided into several small, ever-changing, often warring, principalities. But a most civilized system of sheep raising developed that transcended political and economical uncertainties.

The *Trashumante*, or the formal mass migration of flocks to and from grazing grounds, paralleled the history of the Pyrenean Mastiff. The Visigoth King Eurico created the first regulations for these migrations in 504 AD, which continued through the 18th century. The routes (always north and south from the mountains to the lowlands) for each grand flock were formally delineated, and the shepherds, sheep and sheepdogs were allowed to cross political barriers and to supersede wars in their search for grass. The

711

Pyrenean Mastiff.

sheep were divided into herds of 1,000 head, each assigned a shepherd and five mastins—no more—with the canines each receiving the same food allotment as each human. The dogs protected the flocks from wolves and bears and were highly esteemed.

Named for the area of the Trashumante source, dogs coming with flocks from Aragon were called Mastin d'Aragon. Those accompanying the migration from Navarre were dubbed Mastin Navarro, etc., with minimal type variations.

It wasn't until 1946 that any attempt at consolidation occurred. At that time, the smooth-coated, heavier headed, more solid-colored dogs from La Mancha, Extremadura, Castille and Leon were lumped together under the name Spanish Mastiff (Mastin de Español). The longer coated dogs with more white from the north and northeast were grouped as the Pyrenean Mastiff.

The Pyrenean dogs, once in danger of extinction, are now benefiting from a resurgence of pride in Spain for the native dogs of that country. They are magnificent companions and guardians, a living piece of Spanish history.

A proper Mastin del Pireneo should be distinctly different from both the Spanish Mastiff and the Great Pyrenees. The Spanish Mastiff is smooth-coated; has lower set, larger ears and more stop; and has more color—often solid-colored. Differing by his much more refined head, the Great Pyrenees is also rangier for his size and is all white. The Pyrenean Mastiff carries a very deep head frequently accompanied by a considerable wealth of dewlap, as well as "showing the haw." His ears often fold back into his neck ruff, like so many dogs in this group.

His temperament is benign, even with other animals, as long as property and beings under his watchful eye are not threatened—then he can be formidable. Owners say he has a "clear concept of his strength" and doesn't need to show it off. The breed has a good many proponents at home, with a fair amount of interest established in Sweden, Norway and Finland.

RAFEIRO DO ALENTEJO

COUNTRY: Portugal
WEIGHT: 95–110 pounds
HEIGHT: 30 inches maximum
COAT: Medium-short
COLOR: White with spots of black, red, yellow, gray or brindle
REGISTRY: FCI
GROUP Flock Guard

The Rafeiro was spawned from several breed sources in the Alentejo, the flat lowland area in southern Portugal. Some flocks from the Estrela Mountains came south to the Alentejo for the winter and contributed the genetic influence from their dogs. Other stems may have been the Mastin de Español from the other side of the border.

In the lowlands, the smooth-coated specimens gained favor. Used as estate guardians as well as shepherds' assistants, they tended to be large, with the massive head and rolls of dewlaps much like the Spanish mastins. The impassive appearance underscores their aggressive nature. These dogs are fierce as well as being willful and hard-headed.

This dog rarely makes a good house pet, being used to the space available outdoors; nor does he fit in well with necessary home routines. Some who have met the Rafeiro say he is too much dog for most people.

Americans searching for examples of this old breed were told the dogs still existed, but the travelers were unable to find pure specimens available for use in USA flock-guard programs. The Rafeiro is still raised and worked in the Alentejo, however, and a Portuguese specialty club today supports the breed.

Rafeiro do Alentejo, white with brindle.

Rat Terriers, tri.

RAT TERRIER

COUNTRY: USA
WEIGHT: 12–35 pounds; under 8 pounds; 4–6 pounds
HEIGHT: 14–23 inches; under 14 inches; 8 inches
COAT: Short, smooth
COLOR: Tri-spotted, red/white, solid red, solid black/tan, blue/white, red brindle
OTHER NAME: Feist
REGISTRY: None
GROUP: Terrier

The American Rat Terrier developed from crosses of Smooth Fox Terrier and Manchester Terrier. This mixture, started in England about 1820, proved to be one of the best in the rat-baiting pits. Contests fired bets on how many rats the dog could kill in a certain period of time. The record is held by a Rat Terrier that killed 2,501 rats found in an infested barn over a seven-hour span.

When brought to the USA in the 1890s, they were still their original black/tan. They became a favorite of Teddy Roosevelt, who gave them the name Rat Terrier, and who took them on several big game hunts. An old photo in *Outdoor Life* magazine shows this President with three of the black and tans. American breeders crossed them again with the Smooth Fox Terrier (thus introducing the modern predominance of white), as well as Beagle and Whippet. The Beagle increased bulk, trailing and hunting ability, along with the red color. Speed and agility were donated by the Whippet, who was also the probable source of both the blue and brindle colors.

In addition to its ratting chores, the standard or large-sized Rat Terrier is most used by American hunters for squirrel, coon, wild boar, varmints and deer. The medium size can be just as effective on the smaller quarry, but may not be able to tackle boar or deer. These terriers are sometimes put into dens in trees or in ground holes to eliminate their prey. The larger sizes are strictly hunting dogs and are quite fearless. A breeder reports that they are natural, tenacious hunters, with overwhelming instincts, making the dogs hyperactive and constantly eager. He says they should only be owned by those who hunt with them, as "they don't deserve to be ruined by people who might just want 'pets.'" They do make good farm and guard dogs.

Pups may be born tailless or are docked at two days. Ears are either upright or tipped. Breeders concerned with working dogs are not as fussy about the specifics of looks. Both of the larger varieties are extremely rugged and do fine outdoors. Although many of the small sizes are house dogs, they can do well outside too, with adequate protection during the coldest weather. A small or toy version was created by cross-breeding with Chihuahua and Toy Manchester.

The Toy Rat Terriers are commonly seen on farms and in homes as pets. They are excellent companions and are sturdy and robust. Despite their size, they are good guards who can (and often will) deliver a punishing bite if they deem it necessary.

Rat Terrier.

REDBONE COONHOUND

COUNTRY: USA
HEIGHT: 21–26 inches
COAT: Short, smooth and hard
COLOR: Solid red preferred; small amount of white on brisket or feet not objectionable
REGISTRY: UKC
GROUP: Hound

In the 18th and 19th century, breeders began creating faster, hotter nosed coonhounds that were quicker to locate and faster to tree. Using the available foxhound strains as well as other hounds, and perhaps a little dash of cur, the specific treeing coonhound breeds were born. All of these hounds were more American Foxhound type than any other, exhibiting strong, moderately sized bodies and clean heads with smaller ears.

Red hounds have been common in America since very early times, when the pioneers' essential tools were: an axe, a spade, a saw, a gun and a "huntin' dawg." Records show Scottish immigrants bringing red hounds to the States in the late 1700s and the importation of red Irish hounds to an American hunter before the Civil War. Colonel George F.L. Birdsong is known to have acquired red hounds that figured in his strain as well as the subsequent July line of foxhounds. Although the exact origin of the red coonhound is based on speculation, there were certainly plenty of European hounds of that color to choose from.

Early hounds were often given the name of their breeder, strain or color. Some say Peter Redbone, a Tennessee promoter of this type of hound, gave his name to the hound, while others feel the name evolved from its color. At any rate, by the latter part of the last century, a well-known treeing dog called a Redbone Hound was available in solid red, red with white marks, red with a black saddle (called Saddlebacks) or, occasionally, even black and tan. Registration began shortly after 1900, with some attempt to breed only red hounds with white trim.

One of the early greats was a dog named "Midnight Flyer," bought in 1920 from breed promoter Sam Stephenson. In 1927, the first Leafy Oaks Coonhound Field Trial Champion-

715

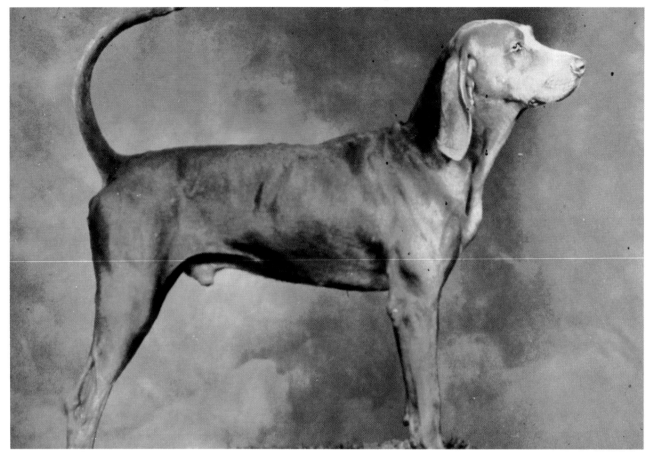

Redbone Coonhound.

ship was won by a Redbone named "Little Sheik," who pocketed a $1,000 prize. "Jungle Jim," a great-great-grandson of Midnight Flyer, born in 1938, put the Redbone name on the map. His owner Brooks Magill was a dedicated supporter of the breed and the originator of the "Nite Hunt." Jim's good looks, fine abilities and his prepotency as a sire made him a household word in the breed. He lived until 1950, and most modern Redbone pedigrees contain his name.

UKC began formal registration of the American coonhound breeds in 1940. Stephenson backed the breed saying, "He is always ready for a hunt, no woods is strange to him, no night too dark or water too deep or too cold. He will stop at nothing until the coon is safely up a tree and will stay and bark at the tree for hours or until you go to him." With the adoption of a written standard for the Redbone, breeders made an even greater effort to eliminate the white markings and soon had a nearly solid red dog. The concentration on color set the breed back a bit, but dedicated hunters demanded performance as well as color, and soon both attributes were set in.

Redbones are a widely used hound, blessed with a marvelous nose and voice, trailing ability and a strong desire to tree their game. Owners feel they have a good-looking dog that pleases the eye but, most especially, one that has the talent to make the hunter proud. As breed historian Col. Dorman W. Clouse states, "They have proved their greatness in the swamp lands in the deep south to the mountains in California to have the guts, grit and desire to please their master."

The even-tempered Redbone Coonhound is no longer only a breed of the USA; it has spread into Canada and Mexico, and traveled across the seas to Japan, South Africa and South America. It received some fame in the Walt Disney production, *The Hound That Thought He Was a Coon.*

RHODESIAN RIDGEBACK

COUNTRY: South Africa
WEIGHT: 65–75 pounds
HEIGHT: 24–27 inches
COAT: Short, dense, sleek and glossy
COLOR: Light to red wheaten, a little white on toes and chest allowed
OTHER NAMES: African Lion Hound
REGISTRY: FCI, AKC, TKC, CKC
GROUP: Southern

This breed is one of those conglomerates that makes it hard to classify. Dutch, German and Huguenot immigrants came to South Africa in the 16th and 17th centuries to start new lives.

Rhodesian Ridgeback.

Rhodesian Ridgeback.

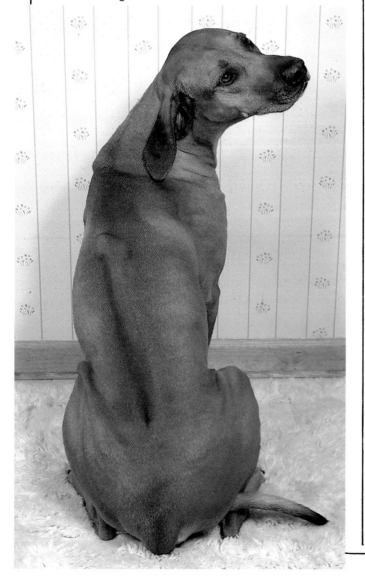

With them came their mastiffs (like the Great Dane), scenthounds and other dogs. The Hottentots (or Khoikoi, the name preferred by anthropologists) were a tribe of this area who had, over the previous thousand years, migrated from northern Africa. With them came dogs of the sighthound type that had a distinctive ridge of hair growing the opposite way down their backs. Anthropologists have placed similar dogs bearing a ridge and of a fiercely loyal type in South Africa prior to 1505.

The Phu Quoc Dog, from its namesake island near Thailand, was said to be pariah/hound type. This dog, now probably extinct, is the only other purebred to bear the distinctive ridge. The Phu Quoc could have been brought to Africa aboard Phoenician ships and passed its trait to African dogs.

The European emigrants came to be known as Boers, who were mostly farmers. They needed large, brave dogs which would protect their families and stock from wild animals and marauders, and could also be used for hunting deer and feather. Of necessity, the breed had to be able to withstand the harsh climate, as well as the deadly tropical diseases and parasites in the African *veldt*, or grassland. For a hundred years after

717

Rhodesian Ridgeback.

1700, European immigration was closed, so breeding had to be accomplished with what was available. Dogs brought originally with the first emigration from Africa were crossed with the native ridged dogs, and the distinctive Rhodesian Ridgeback was formed. The Ridgeback had the courage, solid body and good nose of the European hound/mastiff but retained the ridge, speed and acclimation to the African environment from the Hottentot dogs.

In the 1870s, the Reverend Helm brought a few of these dogs into Rhodesia (now Zimbabwe), an area where the big game hunters were active. Famous hunters of the day, such as Selons, Upcher and especially, Van Rooyen, found these South African Boer dogs to be outstanding for the sport of hunting lions on horseback. The Ridgeback had the nose and trailing ability to follow the giant cats and the heft and courage to face a quarry of that size. Cornelius Van Rooyen, living in the Bulawayo area, refined and perfected his pack over a period of 35 years, with the breed often being called Van Rooyen Dogs in those early days.

In 1922, after Van Rooyen's death, a group of fanciers created a club to standardize and foster the breed. At first this group asked the South African Kennel Club for the name Rhodesian Lion Dog, but because of the fierce connotation of the moniker, it was soon changed to Rhodesian Ridgeback. The breed first came to England in 1928 and was recognized by the AKC in 1959.

He is a powerful dog without being cumbersome, and is known for his clean, quiet and obedient nature. The ridge is his hallmark: a line of hair growing in the opposite direction from the other hair, up the center of the back with two whorls (called crowns) on either side of it near its beginning between the shoulder blades. For show specimens, the exact length, symmetry and shape of this ridge is of the utmost importance. Inheritance of the ridge is very dominant, and one can see mongrels in Africa today that look very much like shepherds, Boxers, Great Danes or others, all carrying the ridge up their back.

The Ridgeback is known in countries throughout Europe and North America with a small but loyal following. The breed can be headstrong and easily bored. The ideal owner will provide an outlet for his energy and train with a firm but fair hand.

Russian Harlequin Hound.

RUSSIAN HARLEQUIN HOUND

COUNTRY: USSR
HEIGHT: 22–26 inches
COAT: Short, dense
COLOR: Tricolor, white predominant
OTHER NAMES: Russian Piebald Hound,
Gontchaja Russkaja Pegaja
GROUP: Hound

English Foxhounds were brought into Russia during the reign of Empress Anne (1730–1740), and by the latter part of the 19th century, these English dogs had been blended with the Russian Hound to form a breed called the Anglo-Russian. After 1951, it was renamed the Russian Harlequin Hound.

In those early days, hounds were valued just for their voice and fierce speed as they tracked the quarry only until sighted, at which time the Borzoi were slipped. For this, the Foxhound excelled. But as hunting changed over to using only the scenthound, this blend of English and Russian dogs created an outstanding dog for the Red Chase, so called because of the traditional term red game for fox or wolf.

This hound had the beautiful voice, speed, size, persistence and endurance of both its ancestors, plus the Foxhound's smart, visible color. This color was important to be able to distinguish the game from the hound, even in heavy cover.

The Harlequin Hound is squarer in build than the Russian Hound, carrying a strong head, with a well-defined stop and plenty of flews.

Today, the Harlequin Hound is being improved in type and uniformity. The members of the Dynamo Sport Society of Tula have produced a particularly fine, uniform pack of Harls used for wolves. In the 1980s hunters from Moscow and its suburbs began to utilize the best Tula dogs to upgrade their own stock. At current Soviet dog shows, the quality of the Harlequin is now considered equal to the best Russian Hounds.

RUSSIAN HOUND

COUNTRY: USSR
HEIGHT: 22–27 inches
COAT: Moderately short, very dense
COLOR: Yellow/red; may or may not have a black saddle and/or small white markings
OTHER NAMES: Kostroma Hound, Russian Drab Yellow Hound, Gontchaja Russkaja
GROUP: Hound

Scenthounds have been used in Russia as far back as any European country, probably before the Middle Ages. In fact, the Russians feel that their indigenous Russian Hound was crossed with the laikas many years ago to obtain the smaller ears, oblique eyes, thick grayish undercoat and more wedge-shaped head. By the early 16th century, writings confirmed the presence of fine hounds with "loud and melodious baying" that were used for hunting hare.

Although the Russian Hound has changed gradually over its long history through the introduction of European hounds and selective breeding, it maintains many of its earlier qualities. It is the hound most suited to the Russian hunt, as well as the country's climate, and hunting with hounds is the Russian national sport.

In the early 20th century, the Russian Hound had many minor regional differences based on its locale or breeder, and was often named for these places or people. The first Soviet Cynological Congress adopted a standard for the breed in 1925, based on the dogs bred in the Kostroma region. Soon regional distinctions were obliterated, and today the Russian Hound is one of the most populous breeds in the country, with many thousands registered. These dogs are slightly longer than tall and thick set, with a quiet, even temperament.

Although at one time hunted in packs, modern dogs are usually hunted singly. They are hounds with a keen nose and particularly great persistence and endurance in pursuing game (mainly hare, but occasionally fox). Their voices are rich and melodious and must carry across vast distances. Soviet hunters say they can recognize individual dogs from afar by their distinctive sound, either bass, baritone, tenor, alto or a high-pitched treble. As the Russian dog researcher Dmitri Dimov describes, the hound's voice is the symbol of the hunt, "singing to the glory of the joyous hunt in the autumn Russian forest. In these moments, a true hunter forgets about his gun. Tears come to his eyes, and emotions take his soul. . . . For such moments, do the true fanciers keep their hounds."

Russian Hound.

Russian Spaniel, white with black.

RUSSIAN SPANIEL

COUNTRY: USSR
HEIGHT: 15–17 inches
COAT: Silky, with fringing ears, belly and back of legs
COLOR: Variety of colors allowed
GROUP: Gun Dog

Following WWII, urban Russian hunters sought a small hunting companion. To fill this demand, they created the Russian Spaniel, using a variety of European spaniel breeds. Their invention was recognized by Soviet dog authorities in 1951. In the 1970s, a few were exported to East Germany, where a following has ensued.

This dog is not well suited to areas poor in game or very dense or harsh conditions. He is small and can become exhausted. But, in areas with plentiful game, he has plenty of verve and ability to search, flush and retrieve feathered or small furred game. Although regions rich in waterfowl are dwindling in the USSR today, the Russian Spaniel can make a good duck dog as well. Hunters use his abilities in hunting quail, corncrake and sandpiper or in flushing hare and wild goats from the forests. This spaniel is also talented in trailing wounded game, often successfully following a track as old as 36 hours. When the dead game is found, he either bays or brings back the *bringsel* strap, indicating that he can lead the handler to game too large to retrieve.

His handsome appearance and agreeable nature make him a good companion, and most are kept at home. In general appearance, he is reminiscent of a robust and leggy Springer Spaniel. Easy to train, he is devoted to his master, never letting him out of sight. The Russian Spaniel is also amiable with children and serves as an alarm dog when the need arises.

Saarlooswolfhond.

SAARLOOSWOLFHOND

COUNTRY: Netherlands
WEIGHT: 79–90 pounds
HEIGHT: 27½–29½ inches
COAT: Short, dense
COLOR: Agouti, wolf gray, woods brown, may have small areas of white markings
REGISTRY: FCI
GROUP: Herding

As a student of genetics, Leendert Saarloos studied various species, including several breeds of dogs. In the 1930s, Saarloos entered a cooperative effort with a Dutch zoo. He obtained a female wolf which he intended to cross with his German Shepherd, attempting to bring purebred dogs back to their "natural ability and sturdiness." His belief was that the domesticated dog had "degenerated" to an animal full of diseases and softness. He thought that the germs which were so debilitating and even fatal to dogs would not affect the wolf, but his theory was immediately proven wrong when the zoo animal succumbed to a virus. Fortunately for his program, the zoo provided another wolf, and his plan began to unfold.

Over the years, he selected for health and character from the wolf/dog progeny, breeding the get back to German Shepherds. Despite setbacks, he persisted, seeking the advice of a Dutch geneticist, Professor Hagendorn. Saarloos achieved some small successes in using these "European Wolfdogs" as dog guides for the blind. His faith in the breed was such that he also tried to encourage their use as police and rescue dogs, but to no avail. He fought a continual battle against the wild wolf characteristics of caution, reserve and flight in his breeding program. Several thwarted attempts were made to obtain recognition of the breed. Others noted his efforts, but he discouraged their interest, wishing to monopolize control of the program.

Saarloos died in 1969 before his dream of a newly recognized breed was realized. Not much improvement was attained until after his death when the genetic base expanded. Other inter-

728

ested owners created a strong club and finally attained recognition from the Dutch Kennel Club for these dogs in 1975. They honored the father of the breed by changing the name to Saarlooswolfhond. The association is very strict in its requirements against hip dysplasia, spondylosis of the spine and other health and temperament problems. Casual breeding is discouraged.

Saarlooswolfhonds are exceptionally strong-willed and do not take well to obedience or schutzhund work. They are still pack-oriented and need a strong alpha leader and a social atmosphere. Seclusion intensifies anti-social behavior, and the dogs panic if locked in an enclosure. Owners must establish the dominant alpha position, be willing to spend a great deal of time with them and train with patience. The breed is quiet, seldom barking, alerting homeowners in other ways. They do well in packs, with a leader emerging and keeping order. Problems can occur, however, if a dog who does not understand the established order is introduced to the pack. The club's publication notes that most owners of the breed have at least two to provide the necessary "pack." The Saarlooswolfhond is not known outside the Netherlands.

Above and Below: Saarlooswolfhond.

729

Sabueso Español de Monte, white with red.

SABUESOS ESPAÑOLES

Sabueso Español de Monte

COUNTRY: Spain
WEIGHT: 55 pounds
HEIGHT: 20–22 inches
COAT: Short and glossy
COLOR: Basically white, with red or black patches distributed evenly all over
OTHER NAMES: Large Spanish Hound
REGISTRY: FCI
GROUP: Hound

Sabueso Español Lebrero

COUNTRY: Spain
HEIGHT: Under 20½ inches for males or 19½ inches for females
COAT: Short and glossy
COLOR: Nearly solid red; with white usually reduced to an Irish pattern of blaze, neck ring, socks, belly and chest patch, and tail tip
OTHER NAMES: Small Spanish Hound
GROUP: Hound

Brought to Spain long ago by the Celts and isolated on the Iberian Peninsula, this breed has remained fairly pure. The Sabueso is a classic mastiff or St. Hubert-type hound with heavy bone, large ponderous head, long pendulous ears, lots of flew and dewlap, low-set tail and short on leg.

Hunted in packs at one time, these dogs are now used mostly by law enforcement authorities for tracking. They are particularly adapted for long hours of work in the heat, and have an abundance of energy. The breed needs discipline in training since it can be temperamental and self-willed. But these same qualities have given this dog the perseverance necessary to follow cold trails for many hours. They are loyal and affectionate to their masters. The two types are similar with the exception of size and minor color differences.

SAINT BERNARD

COUNTRY: Switzerland
WEIGHT: 110–200 + pounds
HEIGHT: 25½–27½ inches minimum
COAT: Two varieties—short and smooth or medium-long
COLOR: Red and white
OTHER NAMES: St. Bernhardshund
REGISTRY: FCI, AKC, UKC, TKC, CKC
GROUP: Mastiff

High in the Swiss Alps is the Hospice du Grand St. Bernard. Located at St. Gotthard's pass near the Italian border, this monastery is one of the highest and oldest human settlements in Europe. The Romans erected a temple to Jupiter there as they marched north to conquer Europe.

In the tenth century, Bernard of Menthon (later canonized St. Bernard) built a Hospice over the old ruins and dedicated his life to helping the poor and needy pilgrims who traveled through the pass on their way to Rome, often on foot.

The monks at St. Bernard's worked to aid travelers and to rescue victims of avalanches and bitter winters. By 1707, the overworked monks soon realized that dogs, with their superior noses, strength and weather-resistant coats, were better equipped to guide and rescue travelers. Humans couldn't follow the treacherous narrow trails when deep snow covered them, and often plunged to their death. But the sure-footed dogs showed them the way. The dogs' amazing sense of direction was a godsend in blizzards, when even the native monks became lost and disoriented.

Initial attempts utilized a hodge-podge of mastiff cast-offs from the Roman era. But by 1800, the monks had established a kennel and their own breeding program, generally calling the dogs Alpine Mastiffs.

Edwin Landseer, at the age of 17, immortalized

Saint Bernard.

Saint Bernard.

Tales of their great rescues abound, with 2,500 lives credited to the dogs. One of the most famous dogs, "Barry," reportedly saved 40 lives. On his 41st mission, his rescue attempt ended in tragedy when the person killed Barry in a misbegotten "fit of cowardly terror." Around 1810, the breed was often referred to as Barry hounds.

They were, at first, all moderately sized and shorthaired. In the 1830s the canine population at the Hospice was decimated by losses, disease, inbreeding and bad winters. Over the next few decades, the monks outcrossed to other breeds to regain vigor and establish the St. Bernard as we know it today. As a side effect, crosses to larger breeds, such as the Newfoundland, increased the size and introduced the longhaired variety. Today the St. Bernard dogs are still mascots at the monastery.

The Reverend J.C. Macdona, an English owner, brought the breed before the public around 1870. He and other fanciers of that time standardized the St. Bernard. It never takes long for a breed creating a sensation to reach America, and the first Saints competed at Westminster Kennel Club in 1877. Asking prices were listed for a few of the dogs in the Westminster catalog, with some of the St. Bernard price tags greater than $1,000.

These dogs are gargantuan in size and in accomplishments, with three listed in the *Guinness Book of World Records*. "Benedictine" won the honor of the largest dog on record by tipping the truck scales at 305 pounds. A Saint named Ayette's Brandy Bear shifted the heaviest load, 6,400½ pounds of steel on a wheeled cart, for 15 feet in less than 90 seconds. And a bitch, appropriately named "Careless Ann," tied the record for the largest litter with 23 puppies whelped.

As true giants, they have the physical problems associated with the other large breeds. Their gait is lumbering, they slobber and are expensive to feed. Families that are willing to cope with these aspects have majesty at their feet.

Saints are not always "saints," but they are always large. The combination takes an owner who is willing to discipline that adorable ball of fluff right from the start. Responsible breeders urge buyers to be selective, choosing from sturdy-bodied parentage with gentle temperament.

these dogs on canvas, and established not only their fame but his own as a dog portraiteur. One work, entitled *Alpine Mastiffs Reanimating a Distressed Traveler*, portrays two dogs standing over a fallen traveler. One of the rescuers bayed its alarm, and the other, with the all-important brandy cask around its neck, attempted to revive the man by licking his hand. Landseer's whimsical addition of a non-existent brandy keg has carried through the years as a symbol.

The youngsters accompanied adult dogs on their missions, learning from their experienced elders. It is said if a person were found, one Saint lay down on each side, furnishing body heat. Another licked the face, attempting to revive the victim, and yet a fourth dog returned to the monastery for assistance.

Saint Bernard.

SALUKI

COUNTRY: Iran
HEIGHT: Males 23–28 inches; bitches may be considerably smaller
COAT: Smooth and silky, with feathering on legs, back of thighs, under tail and on ears; or a smooth variety which is void of feathering
COLOR: White, cream, fawn, golden, red, grizzle/tan, tricolor, black/tan
OTHER NAMES: Persian Greyhound
REGISTRY: FCI, AKC, UKC, TKC, CKC
GROUP: Southern

The Saluki and the Sloughi have parallel histories and most likely date back to the same stem in the ancient Middle East. Some of the very earliest representations of running gazehounds include those with the attractive fringing of tail, ears and thighs. A painting at Hierakonapolis, dated 3600 BC, shows a Salukilike dog. The breed's ancient name may have come from the long-disappeared southern Arabian city of Saluk, with its reputation for fine armor and dogs, or it may be derived from the town of Seleukia in the old Greek empire of Syria.

A translation from the Diwan of Abu Nuwas, court poet and jester, 800, AD says: "It is as though behind the place where his eyelashes meet there are burning coals constantly kindled . . . Like a hawk swooping on sand-grouse, he peels the skin of the earth with four feet. He runs so swift! They do not touch the earth as he runs . . . "

These graceful dogs were esteemed by sheiks of the desert throughout the centuries and called *El Hor*, the noble one. The Salukis coursed gazelles and other game, either alone or as an adjunct to the falcon. Like their near relative, the Azawakh, they were slipped loose when near the quarry, enabling them to run down game and hold it for the arrival of the master who made the kill. Training for their part in the hunt began when the pups were four months old.

These dogs held places of honor in the tents of the Bedouins. The breeding of fine Arabian horses and gazehounds was an art taught to sons by their fathers. Pedigrees, kept pure for thousands of years, were never written down but were committed to memory and passed to each new generation by word of mouth. A Saluki was

Saluki, grizzle/tan.

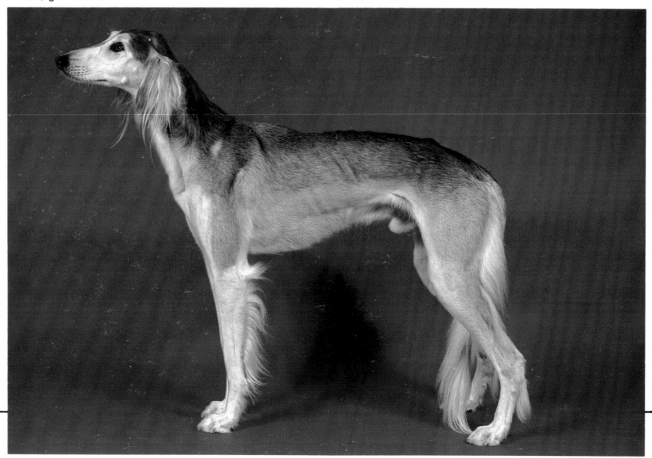

Saluki, tricolor.

Saluki, fawn.

never sold, but given as a treasured gift or as a trade for favors. Some were obtained in this fashion by Europeans during the Crusades (11th–13th centuries), but were absorbed into the native dog populations when returned to Europe.

A pair of these desert hounds was presented to Lady Florence Amherst in the late 1800s, and she was so taken with the dogs that she strove to have the breed recognized in England. But it wasn't until after the end of WWI that the breed made any headway in the British Isles, with the Saluki recognized there in 1923. Breeding stock came to the USA from England at this time and the AKC recognized the breed in 1927. In the late 1930s, Esther Bliss Knapp of Ohio took up the breed and imported many lovely specimens from England, Arabia, Egypt and Persia into her Pine Paddock Kennels. This stock, directly from the desert, was the basis for quality breeding programs that have continued in America. Canada followed with recognition in 1938. In fact, such good specimens are produced in America and in England that oil-rich sheiks have been known to come to the Western World today to buy Salukis. Despite the modern trap-

pings of luxury cars and business suits, these desert men can still compare the current pedigrees and the dogs to those legendary ancestors of yesteryear.

One of the common practices in the desert was the cropping of Saluki ears. While the thought of chopping off those lovely graceful appendages seems a crime, it was done to prevent injury and infection in a climate where flies and disease abound. Many of the first specimens brought in from the deserts were cropped, thus precluding their being shown in the States. It was their offspring who first made appearances in American dog shows.

Like all sighthounds, the Saluki is a fine pet and companion but not for everyone. Exercise is a must, but so is control over their excursions. They are generally very hardy dogs, having been selected by nature's cruel "survival of the fittest" for so long. Indoors they are like cats, clean, quiet and enjoying attention when they feel like it. Heavy feathering between the toes protects the feet from the heat of the sand. The smooth version is sometimes called Shami, although it was also called *slughi* at one time.

Saluki.

SAMOYEDS

Samoyed

COUNTRY: Scandinavian countries
WEIGHT: 50–65 pounds
HEIGHT: 19–23½ inches
COAT: Long, stand-off, with dense underwool
COLOR: White, white with biscuit, cream, all biscuit
REGISTRY: FCI, AKC, UKC, TKC, CKC
GROUP: Northern

Nenets Herding Laika

COUNTRY: USSR
WEIGHT: 40–50 pounds
HEIGHT: Over 18 inches for males, over 16 inches for females
COAT: Long, stand-off, with dense underwool
COLOR: White, gray, black or tan, either solid or piebald pattern with white
OTHER NAMES: Russian Samoyed Laika, Reindeer Herding Laika
GROUP: Northern

The herding-type dogs of the North were used by many ancient peoples for their reindeer. These dogs were chosen for demonstrating *no* hunting instincts, since the practice of leaving the dogs untied, especially in the summer, meant that dogs with hunting urges could kill the reindeer. These northern herding dogs were the basis of several breeds later developed in Europe. Some of them have remained pure herders while others were also adapted for sledding.

The Samoyedes and Nentsy, ancient nomadic tribes of northcentral Siberia, have always relied on their dogs. Many of the inland northern nomadic peoples used their dogs for herding reindeer, and the dog of the Samoyedes started out in that role. Never a hunter, he was later adapted for pulling and as a guard and companion. His close association with people, even sharing the *choom*, or portable tent, made him the friendly dog he remains today.

The first European explorers in the area described the longhaired white or black dogs. The adventurer Tooke wrote, in 1779, that the Samoyede people "used their dogs to haul sledges

Samoyed.

Samoyeds.

and . . . wore clothes of shaggy dog skins." In his first polar expedition in the 1890s, Fridtjof Nansen used white and black/white Samoyed dogs. Fur traders traveling to Siberia for sable brought the first samples of the breed back to England. Ernest Kilburn-Scott brought one home with him in 1889, and he and his wife became great admirers and breeders of the Samoyed. A Sam named "Etah" led his team on the first trip to the South Pole for Norwegian explorer Roald Amundsen in 1911. The breed was also established early in Australia, being brought there after Scott used them in his second attempt to reach the South Pole.

Only 12 dogs are credited as the foundation of the Samoyed breed today. Most were obtained through explorers and a handful of English breeders who traveled to the region.

The black colors were soon eliminated, and the pure, sparkling white is nearly universal today. The proper outer coat is harsh and straight, never wispy, silky or wavy, and is longer than other Arctic breeds. This hair texture provides the maximum protection from the elements, while demanding minimum care. Even though white, a properly coated Sammy stays very clean looking, with mud simply brushing off as it dries. The correct coat has a glorious silver sheen. His very dense double coat does require regular brushing, especially in the spring and summer. Shedding of the heavy underwool, if not removed from the coat, can cause matting and subsequent skin problems. This hair can be turned to positive purposes and spun into elegant wool.

Because of the centuries of working and living closely with humans, the Samoyed is exceptionally people-oriented. The breed quickly caught on as a beautiful and charming companion dog. He happily tackles any task or game with a carefree air and typically joyous abandon. The Sammy "smile" is a mark of the breed and of his cheerful personality.

During the creation of the six amalgamated laikas of the Soviet Union, the Nenets was the only sledding/herding breed established. The Nenets Herding Laika is probably very similar to the Samoyed the rest of the world knows and loves. It is possible that the Russian breed represents the dog in its native land, where color variation is still allowed. Early imports of the same stem became the Samoyed of today.

The Nenets dog, unlike the hunting laikas who need to be independent thinkers, looks to his master for direction. He is a cheerful, devoted dog willing to work long hours on the tundra, rounding up strays, bringing in weak calves which have fallen behind, or huddling the herd when necessary.

His longer coat, like the Samoyed's, forms a face ruff and thick trousers on the thighs. Not only is this protection in the winter when he works all day and sleeps all night in a snowbank, but it is a barrier to the biting mosquitos and midges of the short Arctic summer.

A variety of colors exists, since this breed has never been selected for color, and pure white dogs often have blue eyes.

Modern Soviet cynologists have encouraged the continued use of these ancient herding dogs and have recently introduced them as herders into reindeer breeding programs in Eastern Siberia and the Kamchatka Peninsula.

Nenets Herding Laika, black.

Samoyed.

SANSHU DOG

COUNTRY: Japan
WEIGHT: 44–55 pounds for large size
HEIGHT: Small size 16–18 inches, large size 20–22 inches
COAT: Short, harsh; stand-off, abundant
COLOR: Red, black/tan, tan, fawn, salt/pepper, or pied
GROUP: Northern

Breeders developed the Sanshu Dog about 1912 on Honshu, Japan's main island where all of the major cities and population centers are located. They started by crossing indigenous middle-sized Japanese dogs with the Chow Chow from China.

The robust Sanshu looks very much like a small Akita (or a large Shiba), but his tail tends to curl more loosely over the back.

He comes in a wide range of attractive colors. Both varieties are popular as companion dogs throughout Japan. Despite this, he has never achieved any official recognition.

Sanshu Dog, salt/pepper.

Sarplaninac, tan.

SARPLANINAC

COUNTRY: Yugoslavia
WEIGHT: 55–80 pounds
HEIGHT: 22–24 inches
COAT: Dense, medium length (about 4 inches), rough or smooth
COLOR: Tan, iron gray, white or black
OTHER NAMES: Sar Planina, Illyrian Sheepdog
REGISTRY: FCI
GROUP: Flock Guard

Pronounced "shar-pla-née-natz," the breed name is taken from the mountain range in the south of Yugoslavia which is the dog's home. This geographical area was once known as Illyria, the original name given to the breed. The region is now called Macedonia, but the dogs worked mainly in the mountains and were renamed for the range. One of the oldest breeds in Yugoslavia, the "Sar" is one of only two breeds officially recognized by the Yugoslavian Kennel Club.

These dogs are similar to their probable ancestors, the Greek Sheepdogs and Akbash Dogs to the east. As various western migrations penetrated southeastern Europe, they were accompanied by their flocks and their guardian dogs. Numerous in its homeland, the Sarplaninac is still part of the great flocks. It is versatile and occasionally works cattle or serves as guard. In fact, a military line of Sars was created in Marshall Josip Tito's kennels.

The Sar holds allegiance to only one master; everyone else is the enemy. They are aggressive in defending their flocks and are dedicated to their charges. A traveler relates: "One of these dogs just jumped off a high embankment on the side of the trail onto my horse's back. I might have been dragged from the saddle, but I beat on his head with my iron handled whip . . . . They are of mastiff size with thicker hair, brown to dun, long fine muzzle and magnificent tail."

The first Sar in America, a pure white bitch, was imported into the USA in 1975. She was brought down from the Yugoslavian mountains by muleback and shipped to California. The Hampshire College Livestock Dog Project brought in several more in 1977. From these beginnings, the Sarplaninac has infiltrated farms

and ranches all over the States and Canada. Sheep and goat raisers are discovering advantages to owning a Sar when the majority of their predator problems disappear.

One six-month-old Sar in a USA flock-guarding program began working with sheep in a barn, and couldn't be coaxed away from "his" barn, even to play. In the spring, however, some sheep were sold, others purchased and the flock was put out to pasture. "Bruno" was the ideal employee, happily adapting to new sheep and new quarters.

The Sarplaninac is one of the few flock guards that comes in solid colors other than white. Although a bit smaller than some of the other related breeds, these dogs have the natural guarding qualities and independent thinking typical of the group. Their temperaments are calm, contrasting sharply to the ferocity that can quickly erupt when the situation warrants. A Missouri sheep rancher and Sar owner summed it up: "Owning a Livestock Guardian Dog can be a rewarding experience if placed in the proper perspective. The use of any of the[se] unique breeds . . . . is not to be taken lightly, it requires work, time and, like anything else on a farm, proper management."

They tolerate family members including children if raised with them, but remain aloof with outsiders. The Sar's protection incorporates all of its territory and living creatures within it.

Above: Sarplaninac.
Left: Sarplaninac puppy with sheep.

Schapendoes.

SCHAPENDOES

COUNTRY: Netherlands
WEIGHT: 33 pounds
HEIGHT: 17½–20 inches
COAT: Long, dense, harsh, with a tendency to wave
COLOR: All colors acceptable, blue gray to black preferred
OTHER NAMES: Dutch Sheepdog
REGISTRY: FCI
GROUP: Herding

The Schapendoes is the shaggy sheep dog of Holland. With the rough, dense, long coat and drop ears, the breed is physically similar to the Beardie, Puli, Nizinny and other European varieties. Root stock is believed to be the same as that of Briard, Bearded Collie and Bergamasco.

Although the Dutch Sheepdogs have been in existence for many centuries, they are not well known. They did not attract the attention of royalty but remained a dog of the common people; therefore they were rarely immortalized in art or literature. More recently, small flocks of sheep in Holland were subsidized by the government as "show" for tourists, presenting a pretty picture of green pastures dotted with white sheep. The native sheep dogs did not reap the same government benefits as their charges. Due to a lack of interest in the native breed and the importation of English Border Collies, the Schapendoes dwindled into small numbers prior to the Second World War.

Dutch inspector and publicist P.M.C. Toepoel discussed the dog's characteristics with others who were interested in the breed and became the driving force behind preserving the Schapendoes. Following his lead, a few enthusiastic Dutch owners became dedicated to resurrecting the breed and, in the 1940s, the first specimens were shown. Their cheerful temperaments, coupled with a rough-and-tumble appeal, stirred in

Schapendoes.

noses and shoulders. They are lively, courageous and intelligent, although a bit high-strung. Daily running expends energy and aids in keeping them fit. Their tireless playfulness makes the Schapendoes an ideal children's companion and, since they are alert without aggression, they also serve as watchdogs. Their herding instincts, like many of their counterparts, are such that they will herd anything—even children, if necessary.

Owners say they are sweet, merry buddies, a "flower for the future." They are meant to look like a shaggy dog, not plush and sleek like a Tibetan Terrier or to be only a decoration. During puppyhood some mats form; a routine brushing schedule removes them.

Schapendoes.

terest in the Schapendoes. Growth in numbers has been tempered with caution by wise breeders. Even large kennels only keep four or five dogs with a few pups, and waiting lists are long. The breed is known in several European countries.

The weather-resistant coats serve them in good stead in inclement weather, although like many modern dogs, they much prefer being indoors with their people to being kept outdoors. Thoroughly brushing the hair to the roots every two weeks is recommended for adults, with puppies requiring a bit more care. The finished product should appear clean, but a bit unkempt. Their feet are lighter in color than the body coat. The tail is all-expressive, carried high (but not curled over the back) when trotting or in his usual gallop; while jumping it serves as a helm. Although slightly elevated at attention, the tail is carried low when at rest.

These sheepdogs are still worked in their native land, firmly nudging the animals with their

Schillerstövare.

SCHILLERSTÖVARE

COUNTRY: Sweden
WEIGHT: 40–53 pounds
HEIGHT: 19½–24 inches
COAT: Short, but very thick with plenty of undercoat
COLOR: Self-colored tan with a black saddle; no white desired
OTHER NAMES: Schiller Hound
REGISTRY: FCI
GROUP: Hound

The Schillerstövare's ancestors have hunted the Swedish forests since the 1400s. The modern breed evolved through crossing these native dogs with scenting hounds from Germany, Austria and Switzerland.

Per Schiller, the father of the breed, showed two of his dogs at the first Swedish dog show in 1886. These two hounds, "Ralla I" and "Tamburini," became the pillars of the breed. The Swedish registering body did not recognize the breed, however, until 1952.

Of only moderate size, he is strongly boned and sturdily made. He carries no exaggeration in earage, skin or head. His square body contains tremendous power, and he is noted for his speed. The Swedish KC booklet says he is the fastest of all the Scandinavian hounds. He is self-colored tan with the black saddle or mantle and no white.

These dogs are particularly useful in hunting snow hare, as they seem to be immune to the cold suffered during long hunts in deep snows.

Schipperke.

SCHIPPERKE

COUNTRY: Belgium
WEIGHT: 18 pounds maximum
COAT: Abundant, harsh and straight, with ruff, cape, jabot, and culotte, (terms for the stand-off hair on parts of the body, with the ruff describing the neck, the cape for the shoulder, the jabot for the chest, and the culotte for the backs of the rear legs; jabot means a lace frill on the front of a shirt and culottes are trousers that are full in the leg)
COLOR: In USA, solid black only; FCI allows other solid colors such as chocolate, sable or cream, but black preferred
REGISTRY: FCI, AKC, UKC, TKC, CKC
GROUP: Northern

These small watchdogs from the Belgian province of Flanders have been known for many hundreds of years. Although there are those today who say the Schip is a miniature version of the black Belgian Sheepdog, it is more probable that he evolved from northern spitz dogs of early Viking days. Since the shepherd dogs trace their family tree to the same stock, one could still claim an ancient relationship.

The Schipperke's legend tells of a shoemaker who, in 1609, became irritated at the persistent thieving of his neighbor's dog and, after finally catching him at it, cut off his tail. The much improved appearance of the mutilated thief supposedly was copied, starting the trend for docking. In those days, the breed was still called *spits* or *spitske* and was immensely popular among shoemakers and other tradesmen. In the years before 1700, it was the custom of these crafts-people to parade their little black, tailless dogs on alternate Sundays. The dogs wore wide brass collars worked with intricate designs, perhaps done by a metal worker. This may have led to the Sunday dog show custom! At any rate, the Schipperke may be credited with the first specialty (one breed) show, an exhibition put on for them in 1690 by the "Guild Workmen."

It was his common presence on the canal boats of Flanders, however, that earned the breed its modern name of Schipperke, Flemish for little boatman. A barge owner named Reussens promoted the breed in the 19th century, using the dogs as guards on his canal trips between Brussels and Antwerp. The frugal Belgians liked this small guardian who alerted them to trouble, yet ate little and occupied minimum space.

Queen Marie Henriette, wife of Belgian King Leopold II, saw a victorious Schipperke at a show in 1885 and acquired it, thus starting its rise to favor as a fashionable pet.

The Schip remains a welcome house dog today, with a sharp, perky personality and kind nature. The breed displays tendencies of alarm dogs, however, investigating every noise or movement. Schips have even been known to hunt small game with their owners and to be good mousers. Their intelligence and alert, athletic bearing make them potentially good obedience workers.

While the tail is usually entirely removed at birth, a Schipperke who has the tail left intact has a beautiful plume that curves up over its back. Proponents of the natural look feel the tail acts as a barometer of the dog's mood. The breed is a perfect miniature Nordic dog, like a small Buhund or Elkhound. With his standard's requirement for the jabot, culottes, cape and ruff, he's a dandy in full dress on the runway at the dog show. He requires only a minimum of care and generally provides his family with many years of mutual affection.

Schipperke, black.

SCHNAUZER, MINIATURE

COUNTRY: Germany
WEIGHT: 13–15 pounds
HEIGHT: 12–14 inches
COAT: Wiry, rough
COLOR: Salt and pepper, black or black/tan
OTHER NAMES: Zwergschnauzer
REGISTRY: FCI, AKC, UKC, TKC, CKC
GROUP: Terrier

SCHNAUZER, STANDARD

COUNTRY: Germany
WEIGHT: 33 pounds
HEIGHT: 18½–19½ inches
COAT: Wiry and rough
COLOR: Salt/pepper or black
REGISTRY: FCI, AKC, UKC, TKC, CKC
GROUP: Terrier

Schnauze means muzzle in German. Early smooth-coated Standard Pinschers were crossed to obtain a wiry coat. What they were crossed with remains a matter of controversy, with claims being made for black Poodles, gray Wolfspitz, "dog of Bologne," or even shepherd's dogs like the extinct Schafpudel. Possibly they were all used. Whatever the source, the type has been recognized for many centuries. Artist Albrecht Durer owned a Schnauzer-type and painted the dog in several works, including the 1492 watercolor *Madonna with the Many Animals*.

The Standard Schnauzer filled many needs: ratter, drover's dog, stock tender, and guardian in the home and stables. He pulled carts loaded with produce to market and watched the children in his spare time, causing him to be called a *kinderwachter*. In other words, the Schnauzer was an all-around farm dog.

Standard Schnauzer, salt and pepper.

Miniature Schnauzer, salt and pepper.

Originally, wires and smooths sometimes occurred in the same litter and the "pinscher" and "schnauzer" were not considered separate breeds. In 1880 the medium-sized Schnauzer club published its first breed standard. Within ten years, the Pinscher-Schnauzer Club of Germany had separated the two coat varieties. Still called a Wire-haired Pinscher, the winner of the first classes for the breed in 1879 was named "Schnauzer." Possibly this was the source for the breed's name.

The Standard Schnauzer was the earliest of the three varieties. Brought to the USA in 1925,

he was first classified as a terrier. He now competes in the Working Group. Today he is a spirited and courageous companion as well as a fine obedience worker.

The Miniature version was created either from the Standard Schnauzer or Min-Pin crossed with Affenpinschers or perhaps both. He debuted in the show ring in 1899 and reached the States around the same time as his larger brother. He is a popular and much-loved companion dog throughout the world. His terrier background makes him alert and spunky, not a mellow lap dog. Today's Miniature Schnauzer temperament has been softened so that he is a delightful and charming companion. He also makes a sparkling obedience competitor.

Schnauzers are lively and demanding of owners' time for game-playing and coat care. Some people elect to have the jacket professionally groomed—leaving *all* their time for games. The broken coat requires periodic stripping or clipping; routine care allows for a smart appearance and a pet that does not smell doggy. The Schnauzer trim leaves an abundant beard, mustache and eyebrows, and furnishings on the legs and feet.

Miniature Schnauzer.

Miniature Schnauzer, black with white markings.

Miniature Schnauzer.

Standard Schnauzer, puppy.

Standard Schnauzer.

SCOTTISH DEERHOUND

COUNTRY: Great Britain
WEIGHT: 75–110 pounds
HEIGHT: 28–32 inches
COAT: Harsh, wiry, crisp and 3–4 inches long, softer on head, belly and breast; a slightly silky coat is preferable to the highly objectionable woolly coat
COLOR: A variety of dark self colors, as dark blue-gray, dark or lighter grays and brindles, or the yellow, sandy red or red fawn with black mask and ears. A small amount of white on breast and toes allowed, but the less the better.
REGISTRY: FCI, AKC, TKC, CKC
GROUP: Southern

Exactly when the first sighthounds came to the British Islands is lost in the mists of the moors. The Phoenicians sailed as far as Britain ten centuries before Christ and could have brought their famous trade goods. Celts conquered areas of the Middle East and probably acquired dogs of this sort before migrating to the British Isles. Whatever their original source, great running hounds were well known there by the time of the Roman invasions.

In the harsh environment of the Scottish Highlands, the early silken-skinned African Greyhounds (forerunner of the Deerhound) were at a great disadvantage. They were probably crossed with shaggy native breeds to acquire weather protection. Beneath that wiry coat remains an almost classic Greyhound outline. A historical monument, the Hilton of Cadboll stone, eighth century AD, shows two hounds attacking a deer, and early English literature tells of "highland Greyhounds" with long, rough hair.

Under the feudal system of the Middle Ages, the great lords of Scotland had the time and wherewithal to pursue the sport of "deer driving," using packs of these fleet hounds to run down the quarry. The dogs' use and ownership by the highland clan chieftains became so exclusive that, at one time, laws were passed preventing anyone below the rank of earl from owning a Deerhound. This may have been a ploy to insure that there were adequate deer for the noble-bred Scots to hunt! At any rate, it also insured

that there were very few of these stately dogs. "A leash of Deerhounds was held the fine whereby a noble lord condemned to death might purchase his reprieve."

By the 18th century, three factors combined to nearly spell the end of this great breed. The invention of firearms made hunting with large packs of running hounds unnecessary, as well as drastically reducing the numbers of the large Scottish stag. The increased use of land for agriculture deprived hunters of the vast unfenced spaces necessary for running down a stag with hounds. Those huge hunts became but a memory. And after 1745, when the Scots lost the Battle of Culloden to the British, the clan system collapsed and disappeared. Thus the dogs lost their purpose as well as their sponsors, and their days in the highlands seemed numbered.

It wasn't until the early 1800s that two brothers, Archibald and Duncan (Lord Colonsay) McNeill, undertook the task of the revival of this great Scottish hound. These gentlemen began a search for good specimens, followed by careful breeding for the lost ideal. Their success is demonstrated by this period being called the "Colonsay revival." As the numbers slowly increased, several prestigious English persons took up the banner of the Deerhound. Queen Victoria, who could—and did—gainsay the popularity of a breed by her interest alone, became a patron. The Deerhound was often painted by the famous dog artist, Landseer, who was so expert at "capturing all the essentials of the breed: gentleness, strength, dignity and courage."

Sir Walter Scott called his Deerhound, "Maida," "the most perfect creature of heaven." After the great hound's death, Scott buried his dog with a monument bearing this inscription:

Beneath the sculptured form
which late you wore,
Sleep soundly, Maida, at your
Master's door.

The breed was brought to North America during this Victorian resurrection of the late 1800s. Canada had a total of seven Deerhounds registered during 1888–89. There were nine entered in the first Westminster Kennel Club show of

Scottish Deerhound.

1877, two of which had been bred by Queen Victoria and were offered for sale, carrying the royal price tag of 10,000 pounds sterling each!

Typical of dedicated dog lovers, during the difficult years of the Second World War, Norah Hartley of Peterborough, England, struggled to keep her Deerhounds going. She carefully put aside some food and bred an occasional litter. She told an inspector, "A lot of people are having their dogs destroyed, but I'm not going to have mine destroyed until I must. Put one box of cartridges on the top shelf, and that will be one for each of the Rotherwoods [her kennel name] that remain if the occasion becomes necessary to use them. If I can't feed them, they'll be shot. If I can feed them, then I shall keep them." The box of cartridges remained on the top shelf.

Dedicated promoters of the Deerhound still reside on both sides of the Atlantic, and the breed is in no danger of extinction. Due to the dogs' size, however, the cost of feeding and pro-

viding the necessary space will always keep the breed limited, and they remain near the bottom of AKC registrations—which satisfies their fans just fine. The Deerhound has the gentle, quiet nature of most sighthounds, silently curling up or tiptoeing around the house. Once outside, the urge to run can carry them great distances in a short span of time. Grooming is at a minimum; all that is required is an occasional brushing to remove dead hair. Some modern owners compete in the lure-coursing events to test their hounds' instincts and to give the great beasts a chance to do what their inner natures tell them to do—run full out after an object. At least an hour daily of trotting, alternated with galloping, is necessary to keep the breed in good physical and mental conditioning.

The Deerhound adores his family in a quiet, dignified manner. He is a good pet for those who are willing to fulfill his needs. The breed found fame in the film *Out of Africa* as one of Baroness Karen Blixen's Deerhounds.

Scottish Terrier, black.

SCOTTISH TERRIER

COUNTRY: Great Britain
WEIGHT: 19–23 pounds
HEIGHT: 10–11 inches
COAT: Wiry as bristles
COLOR: Black, brindle, wheaten, grays, or grizzled
REGISTRY: FCI, AKC, TKC, CKC
GROUP: Terrier

The Scottish Terrier seemed to appear from the mists of the moors. Until 1859, no mention of the breed was recorded and, yet, that year Scotties were exhibited as a pure breed. For a time, they were dubbed the Aberdeen, due to the central locus of the breed in that area. It is certain the West Highland White and Scottish Terriers are closely related, the ancestors of both centralizing in the Blackmount region of Perthshire and the Moor of Rannoch. Although the hunters of the era, like the shepherds, were more interested in ability than purity, certain families had a pride in developing and retaining their own pure strain—and this is where the various types blossomed into specific breeds.

Those that favor the "Scottie" prefer to believe that the hairy beast described by Caius was the old version of the Scottish Terrier. Untrimmed, he would, indeed, be covered with hair. Another very old type—perhaps a prototype of the Scottie *and* the Cairn—crossed with a shipwrecked Maltese, created the more glamorous Skye that we now know. Wire-coated terriers could have all come originally from the Far North where their foundation Nordic breeds lived.

In 1881, a standard was drawn and shortly after, a club was organized. One scant year later, the Scottish Terrier landed in Canada, where the breed is now firmly entrenched. The first Scottie registered in the USA was Canadian bred. After the breed's initial introduction, it became a common sight.

True terrier temperament is apparent to the extreme in the Scottie, causing him to be alert, quick and feisty. These qualities make him an ideal watchdog and varmint controller. Unfortunately, this "killer" tendency sometimes extends to the neighbor's cat or an unwary bird. Without proper firmness, he can become a bossy brat and even a biter, but consistent discipline allows his great character and loyalty to shine.

It is startling to some that Scotties are not always black. That image has been perpetuated through Franklin Roosevelt's Scottie, "Fala," as well as the famous Black and White™ Scotch advertising. Early specimens were often red with a black mask, and today a wide variety of colors can and do occur.

The prominent eyebrows and mustaches draw attention to the elongated head and give him a scowling appearance. Stripping takes care of the show dog coat, with pets usually being clipped. Owners should be aware, however, that clipping softens terrier coats and lightens colors, so if they change their minds and decide to show their companion, a lengthy process of coat repair is involved. The Scottish Terrier is a frequent winner in shows throughout the world.

Above: Scottish Terrier, gray. **Below:** Scottish Terrier, wheaten.

Scottish Terrier, black.

Scottish Terrier, wheaten.

Sealyham Terrier.

Sealyham Terrier.

SEALYHAM TERRIER

COUNTRY: Great Britain
WEIGHT: 22–25 pounds
HEIGHT: 10–11 inches
COAT: Wiry outer coat with undercoat
COLOR: White, although lemon, tan or badger markings are allowed on the head and ears
REGISTRY: FCI, AKC, TKC, CKC
GROUP: Terrier

Bred in Wales in the mid-1900s, the Sealyham went after badgers, foxes and other vermin, including polecats. Captain John Owen Tucker Edwardes of Sealyham, Pembrokeshire, determined to produce his idea of a perfect terrier. He wanted a breed that was small enough to go to ground after badgers and be courageous enough to fight otters with the Captain's pack of Otterhounds. He is believed to have begun with the Corgi and incorporated the Dandie for short legs and pluck. The West Highland White Terrier, Bull Terrier, Wire Fox Terrier and the extinct Old English White Terrier are all possible contributors to the type known today. There is also speculation about an infusion of "Flander's Basset," one of the low-stationed hounds of northern France. Edwardes's survival-of-the-fit-test breeding program trained pups on rats, and his tough culling methods selected the "keepers."

Captain Edwardes placed his puppies with his tenant farmers to work rats and other vermin in the barnyards while the pups matured. When he went around later to visit the pups, he was accompanied by a pair of his most belligerent adult terriers and a shotgun. He expected the youngster on the farm to firmly stand his ground when approached by the aggressive older dogs. If they gave an inch (backed up or turned), a shot ended the cowardice.

Those that passed this test faced a second one at a year of age. A live polecat (skunk) was hidden in a burrow after being dragged in a sack for some distance. The prospective yearlings were placed at the start of the drag. Spiritedly, they had to follow the scent trail to the burrow opening, enter without any hesitancy and dispatch the dangerous and furious animal. The Captain waited by the entrance with his trusty shotgun for the faint of heart or those with second thoughts. Others with slow reflexes or a lack of strength were also culled—by the polecat. Obviously, the Edwardes strain became extremely game and aggressive.

Since this was the breed of only one man, it was fortunate that, after Edwardes's death in 1891, other people took up the cause of the Sealyham. One of these was Fred Lewis, whose tireless work in promoting the Sealyham and sponsoring an organization gained him the label of father of the breed, although there is no doubt the actual "father" was Edwardes. The British canine authority recognized the Sealyham in 1911, the same year the USA recognized the breed.

Independent and long-living pets, Sealyhams need frequent brushing and occasional trimming and plucking. Even more grooming is necessary for the show dog. The breed has rather low-set, drop ears and a docked tail. Despite their past history of toughness, the modern breed has mellowed considerably. He is still game and self-assured, but certainly more peaceful. Firm, fair discipline is the best way to approach training.

Sealyham Terrier.

Segugio Italiano a Pelo Raso, fawn.

SEGUGIOS ITALIANOS
Segugio Italiano a Pelo Forte

COUNTRY: Italy
WEIGHT: 40–62 pounds
HEIGHT: 20½–23 inches
COAT: Hard, wiry and dense; lying close to the body, without bushy brows and very little beard; hair never to exceed 2 inches
COLOR: Black/tan or fawn (from deep red to very pale wheaten); any white is to be discouraged
OTHER NAMES: Roughhaired Italian Hound
REGISTRY: FCI
GROUP: Hound

Segugio Italiano a Pelo Raso

COUNTRY: Italy
WEIGHT: 40–62 pounds
HEIGHT: 20½–23 inches
COAT: Very short, thick and shiny
COLOR: Black/tan or fawn (from deep red to very pale wheaten); any white is to be discouraged
OTHER NAMES: Shorthaired Italian Hound
REGISTRY: FCI
GROUP: Hound

The Italian hound is a distinct type, as an intermediate between sighthound and scenthounds. He probably originated from crossing early Celtic hounds in southern Gaul with sighthounds of the Phoenicians. Two ancient statues, *Diana The Huntress* in the Naples Museum and *Diana With Bow and Arrow* at the Vatican Museum, display dogs of the classic Segugio type.

The Segugio's appearance and abilities were improved and fixed during the Renaissance, when the breed was in demand by all classes of society for hunting. At the Segugio's apex, the pomp and circumstance of the Italian nobility's hunts included participants with finely appointed horses, as well as trumpeters and beaters in full livery, with hundreds of these hounds.

As the grand hunts ended, the breed fell into a period of neglect for several hundred years, with much crossbreeding done by those "just wanting a good rabbit dog." Fortunately, the 20th century brought a renewed interest in fostering this unique Italian breed. The Segugio is now one of the most numerous dogs in Italy and, under the guidance of the Societa Italiana Pro Segugio, quality continues to improve.

The Segugio is a large but refined dog of moderately light bone and a racy body with "no fat." The muzzle is long, tapering and slightly convex with very little stop and no excessive skin. The unique and characteristic ear is very long, narrow, low-set and folded toward the tip. No surplus skin appears anywhere on the body. The tail is carried like a saber, high in a sickle curve.

Fanciers in Italy are divided equally among those preferring the wire coat and those with smooth-haired stock. The smooth coat is described as being "like glass."

Temperaments are mild but vivacious. These are sociable dogs, as are most hounds, and they are ardent in the hunt. Today the Segugio hunts rabbit, hare and wild boar, and expertly handles these chores in both flat, open country and in mountainous areas with heavy cover. Especially noted for their endurance and "steel legs," these dogs often hunt a full 12-hour day without a rest, willing and able to repeat the performance the next day—and the day after that! A pleasing harmonious bark rounds out the hunting attributes. Although a streak of stubbornness may surface, this can be eliminated by initiating training as a young pup.

Segugio Italiano a Pelo Forte, fawn.

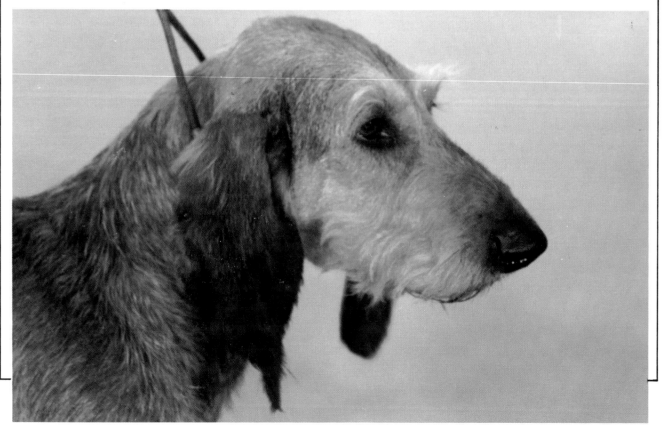

Above: Segugio Italiano a Pelo Raso, fawn. **Below:** Segugio Italiano a Pelo Forte, black/tan.

Shar-Pei, fawn.

SHAR-PEI

COUNTRY: China
WEIGHT: 45–55 pounds
HEIGHT: 18–20 inches
COAT: Short, bristly, stand-off outer coat; very short, called *horse* coat; slightly longer, called *brush* coat; no undercoat
COLOR: Fawn, cream, red, black or chocolate
OTHER NAMES: Chinese Fighting Dog
REGISTRY: FCI, AKC, UKC, TKC
GROUP: Northern

Although the breed gained recognition as a fighting breed with obvious mastiff characteristics, the Shar-Pei also attributes its background to the Nordic genes and perhaps others. Chow-type dogs may have been crossed with Western mastiffs brought in on the early trade routes. The pariah may have even added a drop or two of its blood.

Whatever his background, the Shar-Pei has existed for centuries in the southern provinces near the South China Sea, with Dah Let, Kwan-tung Province given as its source. The breed aided the peasants through hunting, herding and protection—and provided them entertainment through dog fighting.

The loose skin enabled the dog to turn on its opponent even when grasped firmly in his enemy's teeth. He was said to be capable of turning around in his own skin. The tiny ears and deep-set eyes were other qualities much desired to prevent injury. His short, bristly coat was distasteful in an opponent's mouth.

While the Chow Chow was gaining popularity abroad, the Shar-Pei breed was being decimated at home in China. They finally disappeared in mainland China, and only a few remained in Hong Kong. It was during that time a clever owner, Matgo Law, became concerned that his beloved breed might disappear entirely. He wrote to an all-breed dog magazine, beseeching Americans to become involved with the plight of the Shar-Pei. His impassioned plea and the accompanying photos brought immediate response from the Western Hemisphere.

Shar-Pei, brown.

Shar-Pei, fawn.

When a few specimens were brought to the United States in the 1970s, they were considered the rarest dog in the world. Their unusual features swiftly made them the darling of the talk shows which, in turn, ignited the excitement among those people craving the unique and eclectic. Shar-Pei numbers are increasing rapidly and they have been accepted for registration with the UKC and the AKC's Miscellaneous Class.

Except for even more skin, the very tiny drop ear (like no other breed of dog), and the thicker padding of the muzzle, they are much like a very smooth-haired Chow. They also have the black mouth pigment and tongue, making the relationship obvious. The tail may be carried in a tight curl, loose curl or arched.

Breeders describe the head as being "reminiscent of a hippopotamus," with a broad muzzle padded with flesh and described as a meatmouth. The horse coat is preferred over the slightly longer brush coat, solid colors chosen over "flowered" (spotted) and solid black tongues chosen over flowered ones.

All pups are cute and tempting, but there is perhaps none more fascinating than a baby Shar-Pei clad in skin many sizes too large for him and definitely not permanent-pressed. Prospective

Shar-Pei, cream.

Shar-Peis.

buyers must be aware of the breed's idiosyncracies and be prepared to deal with them. The skin requires as much attention as a heavy-coated dog, since the wrinkles make them prone to skin disease. Eye problems can also result, and some breeders have the abundant eye skin "tacked" by the veterinarian at three or four weeks until about 8–10 weeks of age. Adults grow into their over-sized coat and wrinkles often appear only on the face and shoulders when mature.

Their mastiff heritage contributed dominant temperaments, and they may pick fights among their housemates. Their strong personalities require firm training and socialization. They want to be with their people, and their early housebreaking habits assure acceptance in the home. A kennel existence is torture for them.

Shetland Sheepdog, sable.

SHETLAND SHEEPDOG

COUNTRY: Great Britain
HEIGHT: 13–16 inches
COAT: Long, dense, harsh with abundant undercoat
COLOR: Black, blue merle or sable, marked with varying amounts of white (in Irish pattern) and/or tan
REGISTRY: FCI, AKC, UKC, TKC, CKC
GROUP: Herding

During the 1700s fishing boats arrived regularly on the Shetland Islands, bringing black and tan King Charles Spaniels, "Yakki" dogs from Greenland and spitz-type herding dogs from the Scandinavian countries. These dogs were allowed to "stretch their legs" during their on-shore leave, and often left little remembrances of their visit on the islands. The Shetland Sheepdog is obviously related to the other collies, either directly or through a common ancestor. The progeny of these "sailors" and the native island dogs proved to be alert, eager working stock and came to be known as *Toonie* dogs, for the *toon* or town (or from *tun*, Norwegian for farm). Obviously, they were good workers in town or on the farm.

The Shetland Islands are bare and rugged. The terrain furnishes inhospitable territory for raising stock, but its natives were rugged, too, and developed animals that didn't need lush flora to survive. Their miniature cattle, dwarf sheep and tiny Shetland ponies were herded by correspondingly small sheep dogs. The small farms were known as crofts, and the crofters thought highly of their gentle little herding dogs. The Shelties' gait carried them lightly over rough terrain, and their easygoing manner made them gentle with stock.

Early literature refers to the dogs as "nondescript." Eventually a Shetlander named Loggie standardized type for the show ring, and the breed was entered in Crufts in 1906, where they were shown with the Collies, as miniatures. After the destructive years of WWI, a fancier introduced a Collie into the surviving lines, and created the type known at this time.

Quick workers, Shelties are highly intelligent and willing to please, making them one of the outstanding obedience breeds in the ring today. These "apartment-size" collies make ideal pets—they are amiable, healthy, docile and great with children. As with the other collies, a regular grooming schedule keeps their plush coats looking attractive.

The Sheltie standard is precise in height and marking requirements. Due to the relatively recent cross with the Rough Collie, a tendency exists for some specimens to be larger than desired. Puppies termed as "mismarks" and youngsters that go over-size, however, still make delightful companions.

772

Above: Shetland Sheepdog, blue merle. **Below:** Shetland Sheepdog, sable.

Above and Below: Shetland Sheepdog, sable.

Shetland Sheepdog, sable.

SHIBA INU

COUNTRY: Japan
WEIGHT: 20–30 pounds
HEIGHT: 13½–15½ inches
COAT: Fairly short, harsh, plush, straight, stand-off, double
COLOR: In order of Japanese preference—deep red, red sesame (red and black hairs with the red predominating), black/tan, black sesame (same as red sesame, except here the black hairs predominate), white, lighter red. American standard has no order of preference and also includes brindles and white markings.
REGISTRY: FCI
GROUP: Northern

In Japan, a small package filled with a keen disposition and talent is generally compared to the Japanese pepper. This term fits the Shiba dog, spicy though small. His name literally means small dog. The Shiba should look like a small version of the Akita.

Wending its way through the southern regions, perhaps over land bridges from Korea and China, Shibas originated in the mountainous landlocked areas of Japan, where the type has been known for nearly 3,000 years. The Shiba is a result of interbreeding ancient types: the Sanin, the Mino and the Shinshu.

Shibas were used as hunters of ground birds and small game. The little dog occasionally assisted the hunter for boar, bear and deer, as well. Originally, more than one type were bred in different areas. Modern breeders have combined the various types, selecting from among them for the desired qualities of small size, curled tail, triangular-set "Oriental" eyes, deep red color, and warmth and affection for the master.

Because of its native ability and environment, the modern Shiba enjoys the out-of-doors and cold weather. In fact, some Japanese owners put their dogs on ice and blow fans on them to grow lush coats!

Agile and quick, they delight in a good run with owners. A warning to use a leash accompa-

Shiba Inu.

nies this suggestion, for it is said, "you can never outrun a Shiba." They are catlike in their cleanliness and have the northern dog tendency of aloofness to strangers and an independent nature, being natural guardians. Although affectionate to their family, they are sometimes scrappy with other dogs.

Owners describe their cunning intelligence, saying that they could charm a stone! Breeders warn they are not a dog for everyone, even though many who see one find it appealing. Prospective owners must understand the spitz-type personality and be prepared to deal with it before they will truly enjoy owning one. They are perky and sturdy for their size, making them ideal children's playmates. If there are no children around, nor adults available, a Shiba is perfectly able to entertain himself for long periods. They are loving and ready for fun, but are not always underfoot when their people are busy. An owner says, they "love to live and live to love."

The Shiba has been the most popular dog in Japan for a number of years, where his size is welcome in a small country with a high population. The Shiba is making headway in the USA, with at least two organizations promoting and registering the breed, and the breed has a good number of enthusiasts in other countries.

Above: Shiba Inu. **Below:** Shiba Inu with three Japanese girls in traditional dress.

777

Shih Tzu.

SHIH TZU

COUNTRY: Tibet (China)
WEIGHT: 9–16 pounds ideal, 19 pounds maximum
HEIGHT: 8–11 inches
COAT: Long and dense; appearing harsher than it feels
COLOR: All colors allowed, but white blaze and tail tip are highly prized
OTHER NAMES: Chrysanthemum Dog
REGISTRY: FCI, AKC, UKC, TKC, CKC
GROUP: Herding

Although the Shih Tzu's roots are in Tibet, his perfection occurred in China. If the Lhasa is a mildly dwarfed Tibetan Terrier, the Shih Tzu is a slightly more exaggerated dwarf form of these breeds. The Chinese prized the smaller individuals from the Lhasas sent to China and pre-ferred the very shortened face. Although some writers feel crossing to the Pekingese occurred, simple selection for the most dwarfed forms of the Lhasas could easily have created this charmer.

To further link the two breeds, the Chinese call their version *Shih Tzu,* which means lion dog, the same label that the Lhasa dog bears in Tibet. The scenario can easily be imagined: Tibetans sent pairs of charming smallish lion dogs to the imperial court of China. The Chinese also called them lion dogs (in Chinese, of course). Over the centuries the smaller, shorter legged and shorter faced specimens were selected or crossed with native toy breeds, and the result evolved into our modern Shih Tzu.

The dogs lived lives of luxury in the palaces of China, and were bred as loving companions. After China became a republic in 1912, occasional specimens made their way into Britain. Fortunately, enough were brought to England and Norway, and later North America, to begin good breeding programs prior to the Communist takeover when dogs were virtually eliminated in China.

The British awarded championship status to the breed in 1949 but it was not recognized in North America until the 1960s. When allowed to be shown in America in 1969, one of the specimens exhibited went all the way to Best in Show the first time he was shown. The breed is well known for its marvelous movement, with tremendous reach and drive pushing that little body smoothly ahead like a locomotive. Shih Tzus have enjoyed tremendous success in show rings all over the world. In Canada, where their standard allows for a slightly larger specimen, they are a part of the Non-Sporting Group. The

Shih Tzu.

Shih Tzu.

Shih Tzu is shown in the Toy Group in the United States.

The Shih Tzu is also being "discovered" as a fine companion dog. Less suspicious of strangers than his erstwhile cousin, the Lhasa, he is vivacious and athletic for his small size, and very people-oriented. Full of confidence and self-importance, his arrogant carriage is described in the standard. His beautiful, flowing coat does require a fair amount of grooming to look its best. It is the hair that grows upward from the short nose that gives the Shih Tzu the "chrysanthemum" look described by the Orientals. In fact, the original standard issued by the Peking Kennel Club may have been the most descriptive in dogdom. Included in the requirements were a "lion head, bear torso, camel hoof, feather-duster tail, palm-leaf ear, rice teeth, pearly petal tongue and movement like a goldfish." Shih Tzus consider themselves extremely dignified, yet can be charming clowns.

Shih Tzu.

Shih Tzu.

SHIKA INUS

Kishu

COUNTRY: Japan
HEIGHT: 17–22 inches
COAT: Short, coarse and straight, soft, dense undercoat, fringe on cheeks and tail
COLOR: White most common, but can be red, sesame or brindle
REGISTRY: FCI
GROUP: Northern

Kai Dog

COUNTRY: Japan
HEIGHT: 18–22½ inches
COAT: Short, straight and coarse with soft, dense undercoat, hair longer on the tail
COLOR: Black brindle, red brindle or brindle
OTHER NAMES: Tora (Tiger) Dog
REGISTRY: FCI
GROUP: Northern

Kishu, white.

Kai Dog, brindle.

Shikoku

COUNTRY: Japan
HEIGHT: 17½–22 inches
COAT: Short, harsh and straight with soft, dense undercoat
COLOR: Brindle or red
REGISTRY: FCI
GROUP: Northern

The Kishu, Kai Dog and Shikoku fall into the category of Shika Inu, or medium-sized Japanese dogs. They are very similar with overlapping colors and have only small differences in size and other fine points. Originally, these were all dogs that assisted the *matagi*, the professional hunters, with wild boar or deer. Known for their bravery, it is said that the Shika dog "will

Shikoku, red.

not concede a step before danger."

Although mainly working dogs, they all have been more or less adapted as companions and guardians since the matagi profession has nearly disappeared.

The Kishu is the matagi's dog from the mountainous regions of Wakayama and Mie prefectures and has been known since before the Christian era. Although previously used for deer, it was best known for boar hunting. The hunter's weapon was the firelock, which could be fired only once before reloading. If a wild boar was wounded, it could fatally charge the hunter, and the dog was expected to courageously run interference until the hunter could reload. It is not difficult to discern why the breed was noted for its "scarred glory."

These dogs are clean, silent and docile. Although they are useful in herding, as watchdog, fishermen's helpers, or hunters' aides, many are also kept in the home. The Kishu is distinguished from the Ainu Dog because he is a bit longer in body proportions and, although cautious, is more benign of temperament. The white coat tends to disappear in the snow, but has the advantage of being easily distinguished from his dark-colored prey.

Used more for deer, the Shikoku and the Kai are other varieties of the Shika (mid-sized) dogs. As former hunting dogs of the matagi, they were often referred to as "deerhounds." Coming from the mountains around Fuji and the southern Alps region of Yamanishi prefecture, the Kai was considered too rough to make a good house pet, being close to the wild in temperament. Modern dogs are milder and some are now seen in homes. He is, however, loyal to his master and a fine hunter. The Japanese say he is a one-man dog with people. Hunted in packs, he is companionable with other dogs. Brindling may not be apparent until after six months of age.

The Shikoku is the final variety of Shika dogs, and is similar to the other two. His home is Shikoku Island, across the inland sea from Osaka, where he was also used for hunting. This smallest of the middle-sized dogs comes only in solid reds and brindle color. None of the Shika dogs are known outside Japan.

Siberian Husky, gray.

SIBERIAN HUSKY

COUNTRY: USA
WEIGHT: 45–60 pounds
HEIGHT: 21–23½ inches
COAT: Thick, peltlike, stand-off; dense undercoat
COLOR: Any color acceptable, grays, blacks, reds, and even pied are common, usually with light shading around the head and underside
OTHER NAMES: Arctic Husky
REGISTRY: FCI, AKC, TKC, CKC, UKC
GROUP: Northern

A variety of primitive paleo-Asiatic tribes have been present in Siberia for half-a-million years, during the time when the vast North was a warmer and more hospitable hunting ground. These tribes continued to live much as they had during the Stone Age. Each group relied on dogs as helpers, and each developed a specific

Siberian Husky, black.

type, based upon such factors as hunting requirements and snow cover, terrain and temperature.

The Chukchi tribe, often referred to as the "Dog Breeding" Chukchi, was based along the coasts of the Arctic and Pacific Oceans on the peninsula that reaches out from Siberia toward Alaska. When a harsh cold settled into the area about 3,000 years ago, the Chukchi people adapted by creating a culture based on the long-distance sled dog. The tribe lived in permanent inland settlements and had to go long distances to hunt the sea mammals which fed both people and dogs. A small sledding dog was ideal, one that could exist on very little food. Neither sprinters nor freighters, these dogs were endurance animals and could pull light loads of killed game at moderate speeds over incredible distances. When a Chukchi needed to haul something heavier, he merely borrowed extra dogs from friends and harnessed up 16 or 18 instead of the usual six-to-eight hitch.

All males except the finest lead dogs were castrated after a year in harness, not only to control the breeding urges but to help maintain fat on their bodies. By keeping all but the unneutered lead dogs tied during the winter when the bitches came in heat, a workable system of line-breeding was established. Because the Chukchi women did most of the dog care and selection, these dogs were used to children and were accustomed to being a part of the family.

Siberian Chukchis were brought into Alaska in the early 1900s, and quickly gained a reputation for sledding. The Chukchi dog in pure form, or crossed with other native sledding breeds, became universal, especially in chores where speed with endurance was of utmost importance, such as mail delivery and long-distance sled dog racing. He was, at that time, still called Chukchi or "husky," a generic term for a sled-pulling dog.

Siberian Husky.

As the breed gained a foothold with American dog fanciers, the name Chukchi was replaced by the more general term Siberian Husky, and that became his official name. Thanks to the Chukchi selection for good temperament, he is people-oriented and a popular companion dog—thus not a very good guard dog. Nevertheless, he is a working dog and, if not given adequate attention, exercise, training and discipline, can be stubborn and easily bored. The Siberian Husky is still the most popular breed for modern "mushers" or owners who want to try him with a sled, since the breed happily ignores frigid temperatures and deep snows. He has tiny, high-set erect ears and a plush coat. Because of their long association with people, they still maintain the fastidious cleanliness which was always demanded of them. The United Kennel Club recognizes the breed as the Arctic Husky.

Siberian Husky.

Siberian Husky, copper.

SIBERIAN LAIKAS

West Siberian Laika

COUNTRY: USSR
WEIGHT: 40–50 pounds
HEIGHT: 21–24 inches
COAT: Short, stand-off
COLOR: Solid or piebald in white, gray, tan, red or black
REGISTRY: FCI
GROUP: Northern

East Siberian Laika

COUNTRY: USSR
WEIGHT: 40–50 pounds
HEIGHT: 22–25 inches
COAT: Short, stand-off
COLOR: Usually black or black piebald; tan or white allowed
REGISTRY: FCI
GROUP: Northern

These are the other two breeds (in addition to the Karelo-Finnish and the Russo-European Laikas) established by the Russian council in 1947 as hunting/sledding laikas. They are combinations of types from various native tribes throughout Siberia.

The West Siberian Laika is the most numerous of the two, in fact, outnumbering all hunting dogs registered in the USSR, except the Russian Hound. They are bred by Khantu and Mansi hunters throughout the giant upper Irtysh River basin in the eastern slopes of the Ural Mountains. These vast forest areas are hunted for their valuable fur animals: mink, sable, marten, squirrel, otter and even bear. As the local hunters say, "Without a dog, there is no hunter!" The most valuable of the dogs hunt sable (in winter called ermine), the prize termed the "white gold."

This takes tremendous speed and endurance over snow or in forests littered with fallen trees. The praiseworthy dog must take one stride for

West Siberian Laika, tan.

East Siberian Laika, piebald.

each four or five bounds of the sable, continuing for long hours. Thus, these Laikas are selected for size and power with emphasis on being tall and a bit light to work in deep snow. Even the most accomplished workers "earn retirement after eight years of hunting," so demanding is their chore. Temperaments are calm and even.

The last 25 years have seen tremendous progress in the number of uniform specimens, as well as in the high level of quality work of the West Siberian.

The East Siberian Laika, on the other hand, is still considered more of a conglomerate with only a temporary standard in existence. Many laikas are used in Eastern Siberia, but the vast territory has created a large variety of types and strains, each with slightly different appearance and style of hunting. These dogs are generally larger and tougher than the Western Laikas.

Large scale breeding programs for the Eastern form began in the 1980s, and Soviet breeders hope to consolidate type and improve the skill level of this breed in the future. Although the overwhelming majority are hunting dogs, some of these are seen in the cities as companions.

Above: West Siberian Laika. **Below:** East Siberian Laika.

Silky Terrier.

SILKY TERRIER

COUNTRY: Australia
WEIGHT: 8–10 pounds
HEIGHT: 9 inches
COAT: 5–6 inches, flat, fine, glossy and silky
COLOR: Blue/tan
OTHER NAMES: Australian Silky Terrier,
Sydney Silky, Silky Toy Terrier
REGISTRY: FCI, AKC, TKC, CKC
GROUP: Terrier

The histories of the two native Australian terriers are tied inextricably—one to the other. Both the Australian Terrier and the Silky Terrier were developed in the 19th century by Australians using various British terrier breeds. Records show that blue and tan broken-coated terriers of about ten pounds were renowned watchdogs around Tasmania, even in the early 1800s. Other terriers of that era in Australia were sandy colored.

Sometime in the 1820s, one of those early small-sized blue/tan bitches was taken to England and bred to a Dandie Dinmont. The result-

793

Silky Terrier.

ing progeny eventually returned to Australia and became the foundation for the Silky Terrier. The Dandie imparted the silkier coat and back length, as well as the tendency to an arched back and high rear still seen in modern specimens. Not all of the credit for silky coat belongs to the Dandie, however, since Skyes, used in the make-up of the Aussie, sometimes produce a faulty predisposition to silky coats. Selection for the Skye's faulty trait contributed to the desirable coat of the Silky. Additional backcrosses to Yorkshire Terriers may have fixed the small size and blue color.

MacArthur Little was an early prominent breeder of these "silkys," and when he migrated to Sydney with his kennel, the name of Sydney Silky Terrier was adopted. Because the "Silky" was not accepted as an official name until 1955, the term Sydney Silky is heard still.

The Silky standard was accepted in 1906 in New South Wales, and another—different—standard was drawn in Victoria. It wasn't until 1959 that all discrepancies were smoothed out, and AKC recognized the Silky shortly after the revised standard was approved. Although officially the Silky Terrier in the USA, he is called Australian Silky Terrier in his native Australia and Silky Toy Terrier in Canada.

The Silky was developed as a pet and house dog and needs only regular brushing to keep his coat in good condition. The Silky's coat is long and soft, but is never intended to cascade clear to the floor like that of the Yorkie's. It must stop at about knee level, leaving feet and pasterns exposed.

Modern dogs all have the erect ear, although for many years both prick and drop ears were allowed. This was probably another throwback to the Skye, which has both ear carriages. The Silky, like his cousin the Australian Terrier, has his gaily carried tail docked short. Although the Aussie is still classified by AKC as a Terrier, the Silky is in the Toy Group. Despite his diminutive size, he is still capable of killing rodents and snakes and shrilly announcing the presence of intruders.

Australian judge, Frank Longmore, describes the Silky, as "The little dog that fits into our hearts and homes, no matter how large the former nor how small the latter . . . ."

SKYE TERRIER

COUNTRY: Great Britain
WEIGHT: 25 pounds
HEIGHT: 9½–10 inches
COAT: Hard, but long (5½ inches) and straight
COLOR: Solid black, grays (from platinum to dark blue), fawn or cream
REGISTRY: FCI, AKC, TKC, CKC
GROUP: Terrier

One historian says the Skye hailed from the Isle of Skye more than 400 years ago, and was described by Caius nearly in its present form, ". . . brought out of barbarous borders fro' the uttermost countryes northward . . . which, by reason of the length of heare, makes showe neither of face nor of body." Another theory suggests that shipwrecked Maltese types from the ill-fated Spanish Armada mated with local terriers (probably Cairns or Cairn prototypes) to create the breed in the 1600s. Certainly, other breeds added their influence to create the extreme ratio of length to height. Once called the Terrier of the Western Islands, he evolved to his present form isolated on the rocky Isle of Skye.

Whatever his history, he is a distinctive terrier. His silken beauty has given him the nickname of the "heavenly breed." Queen Victoria added the Skye to her kennel, and its reputation was established. The coat was silky on the original working dog, although not as long.

The Skye has not changed much over the years, and has not followed the whims of fashion. The motto of the Skye Club of Scotland is: *Wha daur meddle wi' me*. This could refer to the fact that the tough terrier dares anyone to challenge him, but it could also be a warning to future owners and breeders not to meddle with a good thing! The only variable has been the ears. Prior to 1890, most Skyes had drop ears, but the prick ear became more prevalent. Although either type is allowed, the pendant ear is rarely seen today.

Around 1858, an Edinburgh shepherd died without family or friend—other than a little Skye Terrier named "Bobby." The little gray dog took up vigil on the shepherd's grave in Greyfriars' churchyard. Although he was coaxed from the graveyard time after time and offered the comforts of a home, he preferred to stay

Skye Terrier, gray.

Skye Terrier.

with his master. Finally, Bobby was given a permanent license and allowed to stay in the graveyard. Fed by the townspeople, he continued his vigil until his death, ten years after his owner's. A monument was later erected at the cemetery gate, paying tribute to his loyalty and steadfastness.

Still loyal and predictable in demeanor, Skyes are gentle and tuned into their owners, but reserved with others. They often loathe being touched by strangers, especially without a proper introduction, and their terrier nature may make them answer a casual pat with a bite. Pluses for the breed are its longevity and contentment with only small amounts of exercise.

The Skye has a longer, stronger muzzle than the Cairn and larger ears. He carries his tail low, which is an oddity among terriers. The long coat parts down the back and hangs, spilling over the ears and face, necessitating regular brushing.

SLOUGHI

COUNTRY: Morocco
WEIGHT: 45–60 pounds
HEIGHT: 24–28½ inches
COAT: Short, fine and dense
COLOR: Sand, sable, red sable, charcoal sable, brindle; with or without black mask and/or black manteau (saddle or black tipped hairs on back)
OTHER NAMES: Slougui, Arabian Greyhound
REGISTRY: FCI, TKC
GROUP: Southern

While several of the gazehounds claim the distinction of being the world's oldest breed, the point may be moot. "Breeds" as such did not exist in those ancient times, and types tended to mold and change over the years and with transitions to other environments. The Sloughi, however, is certainly one of the oldest types, and is still being used in the same area in which he began. The breed is found throughout the Sahara in what are now portions of Morocco, Tunisia, Algeria and Libya. Due to its modern presence and promotion there, the breed was declared by the FCI to be of Moroccan origin, although it is still often called the Arabian Greyhound.

There are rock engravings of dogs manifesting the Sloughi/gazehound type found in North Africa that date back to the Neolithic Period (8000–6000 BC). The old Berber culture of the Sahara worked hounds of this type. As civilizations arose, these dogs were in demand by the wealthy for organized hunting. Supposedly the Sloughi was Tutankhamen's favorite dog and many were depicted in paintings and artifacts found in his tomb. Hannibal was accompanied by Berber cavalry when he crossed the Alps and, since these horsemen were never without their hunting dogs, Sloughis (as well as the previously mentioned Ibizans) may well have been introduced to southern Europe at that time. Crossed with native scenthounds, these dogs would account for some of the sighthound characteristics seen in the hounds of Italy.

But their main role was as dogs of the desert tribes. They have lived for literally thousands of years with their nomadic masters, chasing down desert game and guarding the encampments.

Their long webbed toes enabled them to grip the hot desert sands while running.

The Moslem culture generally denigrated the dog as "unclean," especially the detested pariah dog. One of the greatest fears for people of these areas was the fate of non-burial after death, with their bodies being eaten by the scavenging pariahs. But the gazehounds had become an exception to the hatred of dogs. These sighthounds were highly valued and shared their masters' tents.

Such was the bond between Sloughi and nomad that these beloved dogs are, even to the present time, treated like members of the family—at least male members of the family! The birth of a Sloughi litter is cause for celebration among friends, treated with the same joy as the birth of a son. Sugar or a lamb, the traditional funeral offerings, are brought as solace when a Sloughi dies. Photo albums are kept of the dogs and their ancestors and shown to friends. One modern enthusiast describes the usual scene of a Sloughi and his master comfortably relaxing in the living room, while the wife and daughters are stuck working in the kitchen!

In the mountains, the brindle color camouflaged the Sloughi; in the desert, the coloring was like that of sand. Saluki and Sloughi enthusiasts debate whether or not they are the same breed. Saluki owners dismiss the Sloughi as a smooth-coated member of their breed, while Sloughi fanciers insist their dogs have distinct differences. The Sloughi is larger and heavier boned.

Sloughis are quiet, sensitive dogs that bond strongly and early with their masters. This trait makes it very difficult for them to change homes as adults. Their gentle manners and fastidiousness make them welcome in the home, which is where they must be to satisfy their great need for human companionship. They do need adequate outlets for their energy, and a place for regular gallops or long walks is necessary. Digging can be a problem, as they once dug holes to the cooler sand for relief from the heat.

In their homeland, their qualities are not al-

Sloughis with owners at meeting of Club for Native Moroccan Breeds.

ways looked upon by the townspeople with the same fatherly affection as by the nomads. Because of their instinct to chase, they are considered a predator, and hunting with Sloughis is now regulated in most areas. The modern world contains small pet cats and dogs and fenced livestock that the Sloughi may view as rabbits or gazelles. Therefore, care and control must always be used. It stands to reason that chase games are favorites when two or more can join the fun.

The breed is not numerous, but enthusiasts in both Morocco and abroad are keeping the Sloughi from slipping away to extinction. The CRCN (Club for National Dog Breeds) in his homeland has published a standard, holds exhibitions, and in other ways promotes this old, native breed. The Sloughi has found enthusiasts in several European countries and Great Britain, with a few appearing in the USA as well. Sloughis may be seen competing in Continental dog shows.

Sloughi, sand.

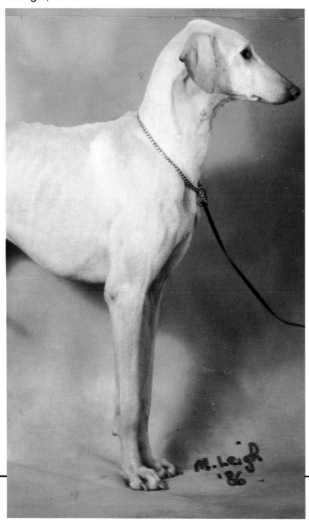

Slovak Cuvacs.

SLOVAK CUVAC

COUNTRY: Czechoslovakia
WEIGHT: 85–105 pounds
HEIGHT: 25–28 inches
COAT: Medium length; thick and wavy
COLOR: White
OTHER NAMES: Slovensky Tchouvatch, Liptok
REGISTRY: FCI
GROUP: Flock Guard

The Carpathian mountain chain originates in Rumania and skirts Hungary, filling much of eastern Czechoslovakia as it pushes north, ending in the Liptok Mountains of the High Tatra range in the southeastern corner of Poland. The great white guardian prototype followed the mountains northward. The Czechoslovakian flock guard could easily pass for a Kuvasz, a Rumanian Sheepdog or a Podhalanski. Their histories are undoubtably similar. The breed name is spelled *Cuvac* in Czechoslovakian, but the English and German spelling, *Tchouvatch*, reflects the pronunciation (chew-votch).

The breed has been well documented as far back as the 17th century. But as the wolves slowly disappeared from the European mountains and modern herding practices were instituted, the Cuvac also began to be a relic from the past. What few specimens were left in the 1950s were bred carelessly. Credit for reviving the breed and fixing characteristics is due Dr. Antonin Hruza, in cooperation with the Veterinary School of Brno. A written standard was established and approved in 1964.

Currently, a few breeders of the Cuvac are scattered throughout Czechoslovakia and other European countries, as well as the USA. The Cuvac is still quite rare, but at least fanciers are working to save the breed. An owner in Germany describes her dogs' marvelous temperaments with children. Yet she warns about the Cuvac's stubborn, independent nature which must be overcome with proper training. Once they have learned something, she says, they never forget it.

Their tremendous speed for their size and bulk is noteworthy. This is probably the origin of the Czech lore that says the Cuvac was the result of crossing a Greyhound and a wolf.

The Cuvac is a dog requiring adequate space, and thus owners should have a good-sized yard for exercise. These dogs thrive best in an environment of a large family, children and livestock to care for. Farms and ranches make the best homes. These dogs are natural animal guardians and children watchers, taking to this busy lifestyle like a junkfood junkie to a bowl of peanuts. They are gentle and loyal to their family and its possessions. This handsome white flock guard has diversified from slaying wolves or hunting big game to border patrol or search-and-rescue.

Regular grooming keeps the white coat clean and attractive—and furniture free from white "mohair." The annual shed of the dense underwool requires vigorous brushing and bathing sessions in the spring.

Slovak Cuvac.

Smålandsstövare.

SMÅLANDSSTÖVARE

COUNTRY: Sweden
WEIGHT: 33–40 pounds
HEIGHT: 17 inches
COAT: Thick and heavy, but short
COLOR: Black with tan markings; any white to be discouraged
OTHER NAMES: Smålands Hound
REGISTRY: FCI
GROUP: Hound

Like the Schillerhound, the Smålandsstövare is a Swedish hound that traces its roots back to ancient periods. They were probably used as far back as the Middle Ages. The hound of Smålands is indigenous to central Sweden and possesses some singular physical traits.

Although the occasional hock-length tail is conceded, it is universally born (never docked) with a short tail; no other scenthound sports the short version. The head is shorter and more wedge-shaped than most hounds, with the ears very small and flat; the body is cobby and small, all of which indicate that a long-ago cross of hounds to native Nordic-type dogs may have occurred to produce this breed. But he has keen scenthound abilities and is used in all terrain and weather for trailing game. They are most commonly employed in the hunting of fox and hare throughout the dense forest of Smålands district in southern Sweden.

SOFT-COATED WHEATEN TERRIER

COUNTRY: Ireland
WEIGHT: 35–45 pounds
HEIGHT: 18–19 inches
COAT: Profuse, soft and silky, not harsh
COLOR: Any shade from light wheaten to golden reddish
REGISTRY: FCI, AKC, TKC, CKC
GROUP: Terrier

In times past, all of the terriers of Ireland were known collectively as Irish Terriers, so it is hard to know whether ancient references to this strain are about the generic type or specifically about the red breed known today. People who foster the Wheaten feel that he is as old or older than the red "daredevil," both coming from the same stem breed. Actually, the Wheaten, Kerry and Irish Terriers share a similar leggy, racy, square terrier appearance that stamps them with generally analogous origins.

The Wheaten Terrier of 200 years ago was also a dog of the poor, and was so common that few considered it worth notice. There are some references to wheaten-colored, open-coated dogs with punishing jaws, mainly in the Kerry and Cork areas. These dogs were used especially for otter and badger. Under the Irish penal laws of the 1700s, tenant farmers were prohibited from owning a dog worth more than five pounds, and thus the soft-coated dog was the bargain basement one commonly owned.

He had no wealthy aristocrats to foster him and was only recognized as a separate breed when the Wheaten was issued its present name in 1937. Around that time, a group of fanciers wanted to save this historic Irish breed. So, although the Wheaten is a very old breed, it is a latecomer to the modern world of purebred dogs. Irish canine authorities recognized the breed in 1937; AKC approval did not come until 1973, with Canada following in 1978.

His temperament can best be described as "defense with aggression"; however, he is not a fellow who picks a fight. Having lived in homes with families for hundreds of years, he is a gentle and loyal pet. He is lively and puppyish all his 10–14 years, and firm—but fair—discipline is necessary.

The breed is noted for its late maturity, with dogs rarely at their best for exhibition until two years of age. Although pets and show dogs should be trimmed for best appearance, this should be accomplished only with scissors, not clippers. Although the original Irish standard admonished a sculptured appearance, modern show specimens are exhibited more and more this way. When the coat is properly cared for, the dead hair is brushed out rather than falling all over the carpeting, a fact pleasing to most homemakers.

Soft-Coated Wheaten Terrier.

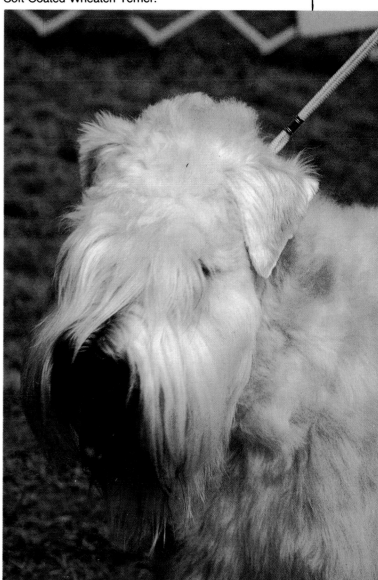

Soft-Coated Wheaten Terrier.

Above: Soft-Coated Wheaten Terrier. **Below:** Soft-Coated Wheaten Terriers, bitch and pups.

SOUTH RUSSIAN OWTCHARKA

COUNTRY: USSR
WEIGHT: 110–155 pounds
HEIGHT: 25–26 inches minimum; 30-34 inches usual
COAT: Long, dense, silky with woolen undercoat
COLOR: Pure white; white with head spots in shades of fawn or gray
OTHER NAMES: Ovtcharka de Russie Meridionale, South Russian Sheepdog
REGISTRY: FCI
GROUP: Flock Guard

In the inhospitable elevations of the mountains, a larger and heavier coated dog evolved. This giant pastoral guarding breed has a long history in the steppes of the Ukraine in European Russia. The old-style Owtcharka, originally with a heavy-corded coat, probably stemmed from large dogs of a similar type from Tibet or elsewhere in the East. These dogs were brought west with the migrations centuries before Christ. Some were left in the Ukraine, while others accompanied the nomads further west into Hungary to form the basis of the Komondor.

In 1797, shepherds' dogs were brought to the Ukraine from Spain with imported merino

South Russian Owtcharka, white.

South Russian Owtcharkas.

sheep, but proved too small (at 20 inches) and weak to protect the flocks from the Russian wolves. These Spanish dogs were crossed with the original corded Owtcharkas to begin the breed now known as the South Russian Owtcharka.

In the early part of this century, representatives of the breed were brought to England via Baltic trade ships. Some reached the USA and enjoyed a brief stay in AKC's Miscellaneous Class. Not long after that they disappeared into the Russian interior and were lost to the West. Those at home became scarce as well, although a few are seen at the larger dog shows in Russia. The majority in their homeland are bred by the Red Army, who found the breed useful for guard work. They are often left to guard isolated facilities or industrial plants, or used on duty with troops. The military, naturally, selects the more aggressive tendencies and forbids the exportation of these dogs.

Recently, several of these closely guarded white giants have been secreted out of Russia, reintroducing them to Europe and the West. A Swiss couple, who own three of these Owtcharki and praise their qualities, encountered "James Bond" adventures smuggling their dogs out of Moscow and Leningrad. They emphasize that,

although not as aggressive as the Red Army dogs, this breed is extremely protective and intelligent, requiring a strong-minded "alpha" owner. They have a quicker trigger than many other guardian breeds, giving very little warning before attacking when they perceive danger to their owner. With a firm, but loving hand and proper early socialization, the breed can be a desirable companion and guardian. But a breeder warns this animal is not for a novice or timid dog owner: "You can spoil this breed into a murderer."

He does require sizeable outdoor room, not only for adequate exercise, but because "he needs a kingdom to keep intruders out." Modern Russian owners say he is ever vigilant, "although it may seem that his eyes are closed, he does see everything." The modern SRO, although his coat is long, shaggy and profuse, does not cord like the old-style Owtcharka. It does need extensive grooming to maintain his appearance and good health. His speed is amazing for a dog of giant size, and he has lightning reflexes. The Swiss have found this dog to be a natural as *Katastrophen Hund*, a dog used in emergencies, such as finding avalanche victims or persons trapped in earthquake rubble.

Spanish Mastiff, reddish.

SPANISH MASTIFF

COUNTRY: Spain
WEIGHT: 110–132 pounds
HEIGHT: 26–28 inches
COAT: Short, very thick
COLOR: Reddish, wolf gray, fawn, white and black, white and golden yellow, white and gray, grizzle
OTHER NAMES: Mastin de Español, Mastin de Extremadura, Mastin de Leon, Mastin de La Mancha
REGISTRY: FCI
GROUP Flock Guard

The Spanish Mastiffs, although named mastiff, fill flock-guard positions. They share a similar history to all flock-guarding dogs from Spain and Portugal. Landing with the Phoenicians, they were part of the tradition of the Trashumante (flock migrations) in the southern routes of Spain. Those that spilled over into Portugal became the Estrela and the Rafeiro do Alentejo.

Still found guarding cattle and sheep in the hills of Spain, this dog is a powerful, protective animal with infinite color variance. As is true of many large animals (and humans), he does not feel the need to show his obvious strength. He is alert, but calm and unruffled. The stock guardian sounds the alarm to the shepherd, then becomes quiet and attentive, not attacking.

The breed is still natural in its behavior and instincts. Expectant dams find a secluded place to bear and raise their puppies.

The Spanish Mastiff is gentle with other animals—even cats—and loving to his owners. He enjoys being with his family and doing a job for them. This dog is easily satisfied with minimal exercise and grooming. Owners that do not raise stock find them apt family guardians, search-and-rescue dogs or obedience workers. Currently, there are breeders in Switzerland and Germany, and the dogs are beginning to infiltrate the USA and other countries. They are seen occasionally at international dog shows.

Above: Spanish Mastiff, grizzle. **Below:** Spanish Mastiff, pup.

Spinone Italiano, chestnut roan.

SPINONE ITALIANO

COUNTRY: Italy
WEIGHT: 71–82 pounds
HEIGHT: 24–26 inches
COAT: Hard, dense and shaggy
COLOR: All white, orange and white, orange roan, chestnut and white, or chestnut roan
OTHER NAMES: Italian Coarsehaired Pointer
REGISTRY: FCI, AKC, TKC, CKC
GROUP: Gun Dog

The Spinone is truly an antique. Although he stemmed from native hounds, probably of Segugio type, as did the Bracco, his history is not complete. For instance, what gave him his wiry coat? This may be evidence that the griffons of France and the Spinone are closely related, with the griffons springing from early Spinones—or both coming from common ancestors. The pres-ence of the corded shepherd dogs in Italy could have accounted for the bristling wiry coats on these breeds. He is also credited with being a very old blend of coarsehaired setters from Italy, bred with those left by Greek traders and others from the Adriatic coast, and a cross to white mastiff. The truth in dog histories is entwined with legends.

The breed is noted for its superior nose and ultra-soft mouth. The Spinone is especially good in heavy cover or cold, wet conditions where his protective coat serves him well.

Even dogs that do not hunt are served well by their coat, as evidenced by a 12-week-old pup exposed to the cold and damp after falling into a well shaft and spending ten hours there. This same inquisitive pup enjoyed a tastier experience when he discovered the milkman's delivery and "was soon having his extra pint."

Still hunted throughout Piedmont in Italy, he is beginning to be appreciated and fostered in England, in other European countries and the USA. There seems to be a split in his homeland between show and field interests, with a separate standard for each of the two types.

The Italian working standard specifies: "When the quarry tries to get away, the Spinone steers it downwind, mastering the direct emanation of the scent . . . he moves forward with extreme caution, avoiding as far as possible dry branches or crackling leaves." Despite his size and usual "long, tidy trot," the Spinone can turn into a powerful, swift hunter should the quarry take flight.

He is given credit by various sources as a "thinker," and will use this ability to adapt to various conditions. He is called "Nature's gentleman." His expression toward his master is lowering of the head, with an upward look in "silent communication."

The Spinone is big but docile and affectionate. They love playing with other dogs, but in play they can "crush all opponents by using their considerable weight." They can be stubborn, however, and need training and direction. With careful selection and proper socialization, they are "big cuddly teddy bears." In fact, owners have few complaints, other than his "wet beard in their faces." The bristly head gives the appearance of a wise, old, whiskery grandfather. His tail is docked to about half its natural length.

Above: Spinone Italiano, orange and white. **Below:** Spinone Italiano pointing.

Stabyhoun, black with white markings.

STABYHOUN

COUNTRY: Netherlands
WEIGHT: 33–44 pounds
HEIGHT: 19½–21 inches
COAT: Moderately long and sleek, no curl although a bit of wave over the croup is acceptable; the "feathering" on tail and breeches is thick so it appears bushy; ear feather is long at the base of the ear, decreasing to short hair at the tip
COLOR: Black, chocolate, or orange, with white markings, in which there may be ticking and roaning
REGISTRY: FCI
GROUP: Gun Dog

Like the Dutch Wetterhoun, the Stabyhoun originated in Friesland, where he has been known since the 1600s. The Spanish occupied the Netherlands until the mid-16th century, and there is speculation that they brought setting and couching dogs from other parts of Europe. These imports developed into the native spaniel/setters: the Drentse Patrijshond, the Kooikerhondje, and the Stabyhoun in Holland, as well as the German Longhaired Pointer, Large Münsterländer and Small Münsterländer of Germany. Frisian writers of the early 1800s describe the Stabyhoun in his present form. Similar dogs are depicted in early Dutch paintings. Exhibition of the breed didn't begin until the 1940s, and soon after, official recognition was granted by both the Dutch and international dog organizations.

The "*Bijke*," as he is affectionately called at home, is a quality pointing and retrieving dog, doubling as a mole and polecat catcher, guard and children's companion around the home. He is used in duck and pigeon hunting, calmly staying down and unobserved until called upon to make the retrieves. Wounded game is searched out and returned in his soft mouth. In field and woods, he enthusiastically searches for game and is an excellent pointer. As one owner says, "His nose never lies."

The larger specimens have also been used as

draft dogs, undoubtedly because of the breed's calm and even temperament. The mole-catcher needed to be of a size to be carried "in a basket on the back of a small man's bicycle." With children, even those not known to them, they are soft and gentle. Its good temperament is described in brief by the Dutch Stabyhoun Wetterhoun Club as "A spontaneous Frysk . . . (that) wears its heart on its sleeve."

The bushy feathering of the tail and breeches, and the ear that is fringed at the base but smooth haired at the tip, are distinctive breed characteristics. The low-set tail is not docked.

To maintain his good qualities, the Dutch Club has very strict breeding policies. Before dogs can be bred, they must have hips radiographed free of dysplasia, receive an excellent or very good rating at a conformation show, have prior permission granted by the breed committee, and meet other restrictions to insure the production of quality puppies. The Stabyhoun is promoted by Dutch breeders, not only because of his character and abilities but also because of their desire to protect a native breed with a long and proud history.

Stabyhoun.

Staffordshire Bull Terrier, red.

STAFFORDSHIRE BULL TERRIER

COUNTRY: Great Britain
WEIGHT: 24–38 pounds
HEIGHT: 14–16 inches
COAT: Short, smooth
COLOR: Red, beige (fawn), white, black, blue or brindle; with or without white markings
REGISTRY: AKC, FCI, TKC, CKC
GROUP: Mastiff

This was the original "Bull-and-Terrier." Crossing the 19th century bulldog with the old English Terrier produced the modern Staffordshire Bull, which still looks very much like its bull/-terrier ancestor. Upon arrival in the United States in the early 1800s, the breed was crossbred to become larger and taller. The results were the American Staffordshire Terrier and the American Pit Bull Terrier. Those which remained in England retained their original form, and came to the United States about 1870, where they were recognized as the Staffordshire Bull Terrier.

Staffordshire Bull Terrier, red with white markings.

During these early years, the Staff was bred and used for dog-fighting but, by the 1930s, the law had begun to make this activity disappear. Rather than see his beloved dogs vanish with their profession, fancier Joseph Dunn organized a club and worked to have this breed recognized by The Kennel Club of England. Another name besides Bull-and-Terrier had to be chosen (since the Bull Terrier had already assumed that one), so the locale of greatest interest, Staffordshire, was chosen as its dog tag.

After official acceptance in 1935, the breed's good qualities elevated these dogs to a position of popularity in their homeland, and they have retained that favor. Most Staffs brought to North America came after World War II. The breed was recognized in Canada in 1952, fol-lowed by American acceptance in 1974.

The basic difference between the Staff, AmStaff and Pit Bull, other than size, is the fact that ear cropping is not allowed on the Staff. A folded-back "rose" or half-drop ear is required.

These dogs need activity to keep their hard-muscled physique and are happy to join their owners in jogging or other sports. Like similar breeds, they are devoted to their families, are gentle with children and accept other pets.

The Staff does require firm, consistent handling as a pup. With maturity, he is laid back, loves social contact and is a real "character." He can competently defend his own if necessary, and he knows it. Thus he rarely shows any bravura of snapping or snarling. He is quiet and calm—until needed.

Staffordshire Bull Terrier.

STEPHENS STOCK

COUNTRY: USA
WEIGHT: 35–55 pounds, over 55 pounds disqualifies
HEIGHT: 16–23 inches, over 23 inches disqualifies
COAT: Short, smooth
COLOR: Black, a few white markings permissible
OTHER NAMES: Stephens Cur
GROUP: Hound

In the years after World War II, five strains of mountain curs were recognized. Hugh Stephens's family, of southeastern Kentucky, had owned one strain for over 100 years, always preferring their "Little Blacks." Stephens was first Vice President of the Mountain Cur Club but, in 1970, it was felt the Stephens strain and the McConnell lines were distinct enough to form their own registry.

At that time the name Stephens Stock was chosen for the breed, honoring the Stephens family. These curs were more houndlike than many of the others, as they worked a cold track and opened on the trail. Several hunters preferred them, due to the dogs' sound on the trail, good change of voice at the tree and their competitive hunting spirit. Colors other than black do occur but are not registerable.

Stephens dogs are quick, sensible and easy to train. Natural at treeing, they are specialists at squirrel and coon. Although Stephens Stock are too small to go after big game alone, they are very courageous and will work as a team on mountain lions and bears. These dogs are very responsive to kindness and are family-oriented but wary of strangers.

Hugh Stephens, founder of the breed, with "Jack," a black Stephens Stock.

Stichelhaar.

STICHELHAAR

COUNTRY: Germany
WEIGHT: 44 pounds
HEIGHT: 22–26 inches
COAT: 1½ inches, hard and bristly, but lying close to the body; only a moderate amount of mustache, eyebrows, and feathering of belly, chest, legs and tail
COLOR: Brown and white, in a roan or spotted pattern
OTHER NAMES: Deutscher Stichelhaariger Vorstehhund, German Brokencoated Pointer
REGISTRY: FCI
GROUP: Gun Dog

The history of the Wirehair in Germany is quite recent. An interest in gun dogs with bristly coats always existed, and several types were in evidence by the late 1800s. At first, the Wirehair Club in Germany fostered all hunting dogs with a wire coat, but the wide variation in types soon saw separate organizations for the Pudelpointer, the Griffon, the Stichelhaar, and the German Wirehaired Pointer. They may all have come from the same stock, as these breeds developed concurrently. From this time on, each breed became individualized.

The Stichelhaar, meaning broken hair, carries a very harsh, short, but flat-lying coat. Except for his beard and brow, the wire jacket is not noticeable until it is touched. His similarity to the German Wirehaired Pointer in both appearance and hunting style blurred the lines between the two breeds. Most dogs that were once of Stichelhaar breeding are now under the label of Drahthaar. The FCI and the German authorities do still recognize the Stichelhaar. Currently, the breed is quite scarce, with only 10 to 15 registrations per year.

Strellufstöver

STRELLUFSTÖVER

COUNTRY: Denmark
HEIGHT: 12–15 inches
COAT: Short, straight and dense; slight fringe on tail
COLOR: Any color, with white markings
OTHER NAMES: Danish Dachsbracke
REGISTRY: FCI
GROUP: Hound

The Strellufstöver is a 20th-century creation. Frands Christian Frandsen, of Holsted, Jutland, envisioned a hound with the persistence and independence to hunt a variety of game in the Holsted area. About 1912, he acquired Smålandsstöveren from Sweden, Westphalian Dachsbracken from Germany and Berner Laufhunds from Switzerland, and crossbred these hounds, selecting the desired traits from the progeny.

By the mid-1920s, Frandsen had fixed the type he wanted, and hunters from all over Denmark were using the new Danish Dachsbracke.

By 1929, fanciers formed the Dansk Stovarklub, which still supports the breed, soon named Strelluf after Frandsen's kennel. FCI recognized the new hound in 1937, seven years before his benefactor's death.

Later, the Danish Dachsbracke moved on to Sweden, where these dogs contributed to the makeup of the Drever. By 1960, Scandinavian dog authorities agreed that the Drever and Strellufstöver were so close as to be essentially the same breed. They are now listed as one breed with one standard, but in Denmark his advocates still prefer to call him Strelluf. He has a slow, steady following (500) in his homeland, as compared to 11,000 Drevers in Sweden!

The Strellufstöver is used for fox, deer and hare. He works slowly over large estates, baying constantly and driving the game out to the hunter.

This dog is watchful, calm, never nervous or aggressive. His bold white markings must be visible from both sides, as well as from the front and back.

STUMPY-TAIL CATTLE DOG

COUNTRY: Australia
WEIGHT: 35–45 pounds
HEIGHT: 17–20 inches
COAT: Medium-short, harsh, straight, dense
COLOR: Blue speckled with black markings on head; red speckled with darker red markings on head
GROUP: Herding

Sharing much of the same history and appearance as the Australian Cattle Dog, the Stumpy-Tail Cattle Dog is a cross of the Smithfield and Dingo, accomplished by a drover named Timmons. The Smithfield was a longhaired, black and white bobtail, similar to a small Old English Sheepdog. The first samples of Stumpy-Tails were red in color, bob-tailed and were tabbed Timmons Biters. A later influx of Blue-Merle Collies added the blue coloration. The Stumpy-Tail was bred selectively for the three to four inch bobs.

Like the AuCaDo, the Stumpy bites low—at the foot still touching the ground—and immediately crouches to avoid the ensuing kick. A natural selection was easily accomplished by the cattle themselves. A bite to the heel of the hoof in the air, or a tendency to stay erect, served only to lay open the skull of the under-achiever.

The tail must be a natural bob of less than four inches. The Stumpy's close relative, the Australian Cattle Dog, is sometimes born tailless as well. The Stumpy-Cattle Dog is unknown outside Australia and is becoming rare in its native land as well.

Stumpy-Tail Cattle Dog, blue speckled.

STYRIAN ROUGHHAIRED MOUNTAIN HOUND

COUNTRY: Austria
WEIGHT: 33–40 pounds
HEIGHT: 17½–23 inches
COAT: Rough but not wiry; short and straight, without shine
COLOR: Red or reddish yellow
OTHER NAMES: Steirischer Rauhaarige Hochgebirgsbracke, Peintinger Bracke
REGISTRY: FCI
GROUP: Hound

Ancient Middle Eastern hounds aboard Phoenician and Greek vessels were traded to Celtic and Germanic tribes. This stock, coming down through the centuries, is the basis for these and other Austrian hounds.

Much of Austria is mountainous with extreme climatic variations, and the Austrian hounds have been adapted for these conditions. *Hochgebirgs* means high mountains, and the Rauhaarige is especially adapted to that environment. Styria, the land of *lederhosen* and embroidered capes, is in the south of Austria on the Yugoslavian border. The rough-coated hound from that area is a cross of schweisshund-type trackers with the wirehaired hounds of Istria. This blend created a tough utility scenthound for use in the highest elevations.

One of the first crosses was done by Herr Peintinger in 1870, through mating his Hanoverian bitch, "Hela I," to an Istrian dog. Many other crosses and experiments occurred before the breed was stabilized, but soon Peintinger was exhibiting and hunting the third-generation pure type. The breed was recognized by its official name in 1889, but is still often called by the name of its founder.

The Styrian is of robust build, and is muscular and sturdy. The head is straighter with a bit more stop than the Brandl. He has small feet with high, arched toes. The rough hair is never very long and he sports no moustaches. His head and coat give him "a serious . . . nearly a threatening facial expression." Yet, he is not a vicious dog at all, but calm and gentle.

Competent in silent trailing as well as the vocal pursuit on a hot scent, he is both serious and intelligent. He is particularly noted for being an easy keeper and for his ability to overcome cold, damp, heat, thirst and other discomforts while following his prey through the mountains. Modern hunters from Austria and Yugoslavia prize this resistant, tough, but good-natured hound.

A strict breed club that requires proof of ability as well as health and soundness before approving a breeding helps to assure that these dogs retain their attributes.

Styrian Roughhaired Mountain Hound.

Sussex Spaniel.

SUSSEX SPANIEL

COUNTRY: Great Britain
WEIGHT: 40–45 pounds
HEIGHT: 13–15½ inches
COAT: Flat, silky and moderately long, with abundant feathering
COLOR: Solid golden liver, white spot on chest faulty
REGISTRY: FCI, AKC, TKC, CKC
GROUP: Gun Dog

While the rest of Europe was developing the pointing spaniels, the British created their equivalent in the form of the flushing land spaniel. Although the flushing spaniel owes most of his inheritance to the couching dogs of early days, other additions changed his size and style of hunting. What these crossings were is a matter of conjecture, but they may have come from the small, though massive, heavy-skinned influence of the low-stationed hound. The result was a passionate and happy hunting dog that flushed rather than pointed. These dogs became very popular with British gunners, and a variety of sizes and color types developed.

The Sussex is probably a remnant of the oldest type, maintaining a hint of hound in both his heavy-skinned appearance and his urge to give tongue when on scent (especially fur). His earliest proponent, in the 1790s, was A.E. Fuller of Rosehill Park, in the British county of Sussex. By 1803, the British dog press was praising "the golden Spaniel of Sussex, the largest and strongest of the Spaniels." This proves that not only was the Sussex in England at that time, but other types of spaniels also existed with which to compare him.

Since its original introduction, this rare spaniel has constantly verged on extinction. Despite fine abilities and the beautiful golden color, the breed has never attracted a wide circle of fanciers. British breeder Joy Freer may have held the longest interest, acquiring her first Sussex in 1923 and maintaining her sponsorship until her death in 1984. She literally carried the breed through the Second World War, borrowing a little of her hogs' rations here and butcher's scraps there to maintain her eight dogs through the years of food rationing. She continued a limited breeding program through those difficult years, regimentally and carefully placing the one litter a year with others who loved the breed. Nearly all modern dogs trace to these eight survivors of the War.

To say the breed base is narrow does not begin to define the problems. With so few in existence, all closely inbred through necessity, it has been a difficult task to upgrade stock. But much to the credit of fanciers on both sides of the Atlantic, improvement is being accomplished. Great care is taken with the placement of each precious puppy, since every dog may be needed for promotion of the breed or for breeding stock.

In appearance, the Sussex has a tendency to loose skin, heavy and long, low-set ears and prominent flew, reminiscent of the hound—with the setter's heavy fringed coat and merry, docile disposition. The breed is a sturdy hunter with great stamina, though not quick. This probably proved its downfall in later years, against the more agile swift retrievers and setters.

This is a laid-back spaniel who, while friendly, is a bit more territorial than most others of his group. Devoted to his family, he rarely lets them out of his sight. Owning one means having a shadow around the house. Sussex Spaniels take correction well and learn quickly. Many have the endearing habit of "smiling" when excited, or when asking forgiveness after a scolding. Swimming is a passion taken to naturally. If not hunted, the Sussex will find his own quarry: birds, insects and butterflies.

Joy Freer described them like this: "There is no other animal which has his coloring except the lion . . . [the Sussex] also have the same big bone and big feet, and something of the same steady way of regarding you that the lion does."

SWISS LAUFHUNDS

Schweizer Laufhund

COUNTRY: Switzerland
WEIGHT: 34–44 pounds
HEIGHT: 18–23 inches
COAT: Short, thick and hard
COLOR: White with orange, yellow or sometimes red markings
OTHER NAMES: Swiss Hound
REGISTRY: FCI
GROUP: Hound

Schweizer Laufhund, white with orange.

Schweizer Neiderlaufhund

COUNTRY: Switzerland
WEIGHT: 30–40 pounds
HEIGHT: 13–16½ inches
COAT: Short, thick and hard
COLOR: White with orange, yellow or
sometimes red markings
OTHER NAMES: Small Swiss Hound
REGISTRY: FCI
GROUP: Hound

Bruno Jura Laufhund

COUNTRY: Switzerland
WEIGHT: 34–44 pounds
HEIGHT: 18–23 inches
COAT: Short, thick and hard
COLOR: Tan with black saddle, or black with
tan points
OTHER NAMES: Jura Hound, Bruno de Jura
REGISTRY: FCI
GROUP: Hound

St. Hubert Jura Laufhund

COUNTRY: Switzerland
WEIGHT: 34–44 pounds
HEIGHT: 18–23 inches
COAT: Short, thick and hard
COLOR: Tan with black saddle, or black with
tan points
OTHER NAMES: Jura Hound
REGISTRY: FCI
GROUP: Hound

Jura Neiderlaufhund

COUNTRY: Switzerland
WEIGHT: 30–40 pounds
HEIGHT: 13–16½ inches
COAT: Short, thick and hard or short wire
COLOR: Tan with black saddle, or black with
tan points
OTHER NAMES: Small Jura Hound
REGISTRY: FCI
GROUP: Hound

Berner Laufhund

COUNTRY: Switzerland
WEIGHT: 34–44 pounds
HEIGHT: 18–23 inches
COAT: Short, thick and hard
COLOR: Tricolor; white ground color with
black head and body spots and tan markings
above eyes, on cheeks, under ears and on legs;
very little ticking in the white
OTHER NAMES: Bernese Hound
REGISTRY: FCI
GROUP: Hound

Berner Neiderlaufhund

COUNTRY: Switzerland
WEIGHT: 30–40 pounds
HEIGHT: 13–16½ inches
COAT: Short, thick and hard
COLOR: Tricolor; white ground color with
black head and body spots and tan marking
above eyes, on cheeks, under ears and on legs;
very little ticking in the white
OTHER NAMES: Small Bernese Hound
REGISTRY: FCI
GROUP: Hound

Luzerner Laufhund

COUNTRY: Switzerland
WEIGHT: 34–44 pounds
HEIGHT: 18–23 inches
COAT: Short, thick and hard
COLOR: Tricolor; with heavy ticking in the
white creating a blue effect
OTHER NAMES: Lucernese Hound
REGISTRY: FCI
GROUP: Hound

Luzerner Neiderlaufhund

COUNTRY: Switzerland
WEIGHT: 30–40 pounds
HEIGHT: 13–16½ inches
COAT: Short, thick and hard
COLOR: Tricolor; with heavy ticking in the
white creating a blue effect
OTHER NAMES: Small Lucernese Hound
REGISTRY: FCI
GROUP: Hound

Schweizer Laufhund, white with orange.

The scenthounds of Switzerland are called *lauf-hunds* (walking dogs), or dogs to follow on foot. As with the French hounds, the Swiss hounds' history leads back to the Celtic/Phoenician connection, with varieties established during the Middle Ages. Twelfth-century Zurich cathedral art shows hounds of quite good modern type. Correspondence between parties in Milan, Italy, and Switzerland in the 1500s recounts the fine nose and grand tracking ability of the "famous" Swiss hounds. These dogs have come down to the present time with the same appearance and abilities and are still used on hare, fox, stag and roe deer by practical hunters throughout Switzerland.

The Swiss hounds are all very similar, excepting color and size, and strongly resemble the classic French hounds in type. All of them have an intense love of hunting and for this reason are not recommended as just watchdogs or pets. Hunting and chasing instincts are strong, and if these are not satiated, the dogs must be taken out on leash for plenty of supervised exercise.

When a laufhund comes to a fresh trail, he announces it with a "rare hauling bark." In fact, the voice that is so important in the hunt may cause his owners trouble if he is kept in town. Because of this mouthiness, his ownership is forbidden in some populated areas. However, if given a supervised outlet for energy, he is a friendly, gentle and loyal friend for the home as well as the hunt. Besides practical hunting, the Swiss breed organization holds tests for both hunting and coldtrailing to assess abilities.

With its geographic distribution near the French border, the richly colored Schweizer Hound shows a close relationship to the Porcelaine of Franche-Comte and other orange-and-white French hounds from which the breed stemmed. In repayment, the Schweizer was used in the reconstruction of the Porcelaine.

The Jura Mountains run along the western edge of Switzerland bordering on France. The hound that developed there had no white and is a bit more akin to the old-style pure Celtic hound. He probably developed from French and Belgian dogs of the St. Hubert type. There are two distinct varieties of the Jura. The Bruno variety, often called the Bruno de Jura, is very like the French hounds and the other Swiss hounds, while the St. Hubert variety has a big head, exaggerated heavy ears, and an abundance of loose skin on the head, lips and neck.

Lucerne is in the northcentral lake region of Switzerland, the home of the Lucernese Hound. He probably stemmed from the French Petit Bleu de Gascognes and is very similar to them in appearance.

The Bernese variety was probably named, not for the city of Bern, but for the Bernese Alps which are further south. He is closely akin to French hounds like the Ariége and Artois, with their moderate size and clear white without ticking.

The short-legged hound varieties that the French call *basset* and the Germans name *dachshund*, the Swiss term *Neiderlaufhunds*. Each of the Swiss hound varieties comes in "petit" as well as "tall," which are otherwise judged by the same standard as the large sizes. The Neiderlaufhunds are especially noted for their full-bodied voices which resound pleasantly during the hunt. The Neider variety of the Jura is more like the Bruno than the St. Hubert type. The Berner Neiderlaufhund is the only one of the Swiss hounds that can be seen in a rough wiry coat. These dogs are all gentle and patient with children. Given sufficient exercise and an outlet for hunting instincts, they are good, sturdy companions. One, which fell into a hole in rocks, was finally rescued after ten days of working to retrieve him. He was still alive although he had no food or water available!

Bruno Jura Laufhund.

Above: Bruno Jura Laufhund, tan with black saddle. **Below:** Jura Neiderlaufhund, black with tan points.

Above: Berner Laufhund. **Below:** Berner Neiderlaufhund.

825

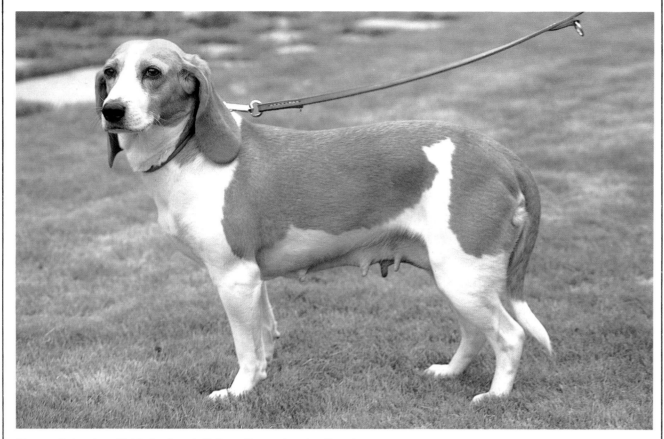

Above: Schweizer Neiderlaufhund. **Below:** Bruno Jura Laufhunds.

Above: Luzerner Laufhund. **Below:** Luzerner Neiderlaufhund.

TAHLTAN BEAR DOG

COUNTRY: Canada
WEIGHT: 15 pounds maximum
HEIGHT: 15 inches maximum
COAT: Short, dense, close-coated, with bushy tail
COLOR: Black or blue with small white markings
REGISTRY: CKC
GROUP: Southern

Raised by the Tahltan Indians to hunt bear, the Tahltan Bear Dog was a mighty power in a small package. Before a hunt, the dogs were ceremonially bled by stabbing them in the hindquarters with the fibula bone of a fox or wolf. The morning of the hunt, two dogs were carried in a sack over the Indian's shoulder until fresh bear tracks were sighted. Upon release, these little dogs moved lightly over the crust of snow while the bear was slowed down by the deep drifts. Their foxlike staccato yaps harassed the bear into submission or confused him until the Indians could come close enough for a kill. To prepare for a foray against big cats, a claw from a dead lynx was used to ceremonially mark the dog's face.

The Tahltan Bear Dog had the courage to face a bear, but was friendly and gentle with smaller animals and with humans. They lived in the tent with the family, sharing bed and board. A Jesuit of the 17th century described the Indians' communal houses in winter, saying he "could not decide which was worse—the smoke, the fleas or the dogs."

Descended from pariah-type dogs that had come with prehistoric migrations, the Tahltan Dogs were centralized in the remote mountainous areas of northwestern British Columbia and the southern Yukon. Their usual diet was small bits of birds, meat and fish, and they flourished in the bitter cold. Outside their native environment, they succumbed to distemper, heat prostration and problems due to dietary changes. As white explorers came into the territory, bringing a variety of other dogs, the Tahltan Dog became diluted.

Like others of their group, they had a peculiar yodel. Foxy in appearance, their main distinction among dogs is their novel tail. Short, bushy and carried erect, it has been described variously as a shaving brush or a whisk broom.

The CKC has recognized the breed for many years, but it has been over 20 years since the last Tahltan Bear Dog was registered. In 1984, only two spayed bitches of this type were recorded as living in Canada. Sadly, it appears the breed may be doomed.

Tahltan Bear Dog, blue.

Telomian.

TELOMIAN

COUNTRY: Malaysia
WEIGHT: 18–28 pounds
HEIGHT: 15–19 inches
COAT: Short, smooth
COLOR: Any shade of sable, with white in Irish pattern or piebald, occasional black mask
REGISTRY: None
GROUP: Southern

As pets of the aborigines, the Telomians were an integral part of their lives, protecting the villagers from snakes. The dogs were sight hunters of small game and caught fish in the midst of a stream. These natives ate mostly tapioca, rice and a small amount of fish and fruit, a diet shared with their pets. The masters' huts were built on six-to-eight foot stilts, and the Telomians climbed the ladders to the quarters to sleep. Entering first, a dog chased out and killed any snakes and small animals that had taken up residence during the family's absence. Today, the breed retains that climbing agility and is difficult to confine.

The breed reached the public eye in 1963 when anthropologist Dr. Orville Elliot discovered specimens protected by aborigines in the jungles of Malaysia. The Telomian was named for the Telom River near their source. Due to increased access to the jungles, the little dog's lifestyle was changing and threatened. The natives communicated their concern for their beloved dogs to the doctor and his wife. To prevent dilution or extinction of the breed, the Elliots obtained a pair.

Dr. Elliot sent this pair to Dr. J.P. Scott, at Jackson Laboratory in Maine, for inclusion in his study on animal behavior. They were bred in laboratory situations until their introduction to the public in 1970 by research assistant Audrey Malone Palumbo. That year the Telomian Dog Club was formed and became interested in obtaining another pair of dogs, as the current stock was intensely inbred. Elliot once again traveled to Malaysia to search for a pair, which arrived in 1973.

The Telomians carry many similarities to the Basenji and other pariah dogs: the wrinkled brow, almond eyes, light square body structure and annual estrus cycle. They vocalize in the same manner—a unique howl/growl/crowing effect.

Telomians love to play and run, needing to work off energy, making them excellent pets for children. Similar to their playmates, they are attracted to almost anything—balls, sticks, frisbees, toads, skunks. A characteristic of the breed is the use of their paws, opening doors, holding toys and chewbones, much like a human infant.

They require a maximum amount of human handling at four-to-eight weeks of age, starting earlier than the peak socialization period of other breeds. Without this bonding, they remain aloof to people and unable to adjust to new situations. If socialized, Telomians become marvelous and fascinating friends.

Mostly companion dogs, they are lure-coursed and do well in coursing trials. At 35 mph, they are swift competitors. The Telomian Dog Club, based in the United States, helps place Telomian puppies in appropriate homes. All Telomians existing today in America stem back to only two original pairs.

TIBETAN MASTIFF

COUNTRY: Tibet (China)
WEIGHT: 180 pounds or more
HEIGHT: 22–28 inches
COAT: Thick, medium length, double
COLOR: Gold and black/tan most common; also black, grizzle, sable, brown, blue/tan and others
REGISTRY: FCI, TKC
GROUP: Mastiff

It is highly possible that the Tibetan Mastiff is the missing link between the flock guard and the mastiff breeds. He is from the area which gave us the stem of the original mastiff; yet he has a longer coat than most, and a tail curled over the back. It is possible that the Tibetans crossed the original archetype with other dogs to obtain today's breed. While the answer is lost in

Tibetan Mastiff, black/tan.

Tibetan Mastiff.

the mystery of Tibet, the breed, thankfully, has survived. It has been around since recorded history—or before—and is just now gaining some acceptance in the West, primarily in the US and Europe. The Tibetan Mastiff certainly is the forebear of several modern breeds.

Two types of mastiffs originally aided the lamas and villagers of Tibet: the Bhotia, an agile livestock guardian, and the Tsang Kyi, a larger territorial sentinel. The latter dog has for centuries protected nobility and religious orders. A pup was kept tied from two months of age to make him fierce; in fact, the Tibetans' name for their mastiff is the *Do-kyi*, dog you can tie up. Chaining or tying intensifies aggression, and these dogs bear the reputation of guarding an entire village. Like the bandogs of England, he was secured during the day and set free at night. Because of this habit, the breed tends to be sociable with other dogs and livestock, though he will defend himself if challenged.

The Tibetans say that a white spot on the chest is a good sign, signifying a brave heart. A white tail tip, however, is cut off as it denotes weakness. Tibetan natives make their dogs a protective woolly collar from the finest stiff hairs of a yak's tail. The hair is dyed red, and

when a TM is wearing the collar, he appears even larger and more threatening.

Tibetan dogs traveled with Alexander the Great from "the roof of the world" to European countries, where they planted the seed for so many of today's mastiff and flock-guarding breeds.

The modern Tibetan Mastiff has been known outside Tibet for more than a century. The Prince of Wales owned at least one specimen in the 1880s, and a British standard for the breed was in existence in the 1930s. President Eisenhower received two as gifts from the Dalai Lama. Yet others reached America in the early 1970s through drug smugglers who placed packets of illegal substances under false bottoms in dog crates. These dealers then shipped the largest and toughest Tibetan Mastiffs to the States, where no customs inspector dared to inspect their crates!

A positive aspect of this crime is that many specimens escaped Communist China and reached the hands of concerned breeders. Others were brought in by more conventional routes. The TM is now recognized in many European and Asian countries, and there are national organizations for the breed in both North

Above: Tibetan Mastiff, gold. **Below:** Tibetan Mastiff.

America and Europe. In the US they have been used as guard and sled dogs, as well as family companions.

The American Tibetan Mastiff Association recommends mating only genetically sound animals. Besides physical soundness, breeders are advised to choose stock with proper guardian tendencies and a stable family-oriented temperament. Bitches cycle only once a year.

The breed has incorporated many of the giant attributes of "impressive stature, formidable appearance and great strength." A controlled environment with moderate weight gain and adequate exercise is recommended by breeders to forestall many of the problems that often plague large breeds. The eight-week-old fluffy clown, often described as a teddy bear, will grow into a large, aloof adult with a strong sense of territory and an instinct to defend it. Socialization, discipline and routine grooming should begin early.

Despite their tough, protective instincts, they are gentle with their own families. In their homeland, they are controlled by even the smallest child, who can handle them and call them off intruders with ease. The Tibetan Mastiffs were bred to withstand the extreme temperatures of their native mountain land and are still capable of playing in a snowdrift in below zero temperatures or of performing an obedience routine at 90 degrees.

Tibetan Spaniel.

TIBETAN SPANIEL

COUNTRY: Tibet (China)
WEIGHT: 9–15 pounds
HEIGHT: 10 inches
COAT: Moderately long, silky, double; shorter on face and front of legs, heavy feathering on tail, breeches and ears
COLOR: All colors and combinations of colors permitted
REGISTRY: FCI, AKC, TKC, CKC
GROUP: Herding

As with other Oriental dogs, mystery surrounds this old, but only lately unveiled, little breed. It is known that, just as the Tibetan Terrier isn't a terrier, the Tibetan Spaniel isn't a spaniel. So much for nomenclature! The breed's close relative, the Pekingese, didn't reach its state of "perfection" until about 150 years ago. Prior to that time, based on what is depicted in Chinese art, the Peke was less exaggerated in coat and body form. In fact, many paintings of the period depicting palace dogs show a type very similar to the modern Tibetan Spaniel. Early Pugs, long known in China, had lengthier muzzles and also appeared much like smooth versions of the "spaniel" from Tibet.

The close political ties between ancient Tibet and China resulted in a steady stream of trade between the two nations. Just as the Shih Tzu was created from dogs that came from Tibet to China, the Tibetan Spaniel may have resulted from dogs going in the other direction. Early Chinese Pekingese-type dogs that were given as gifts to Tibetan officials formed the stem from which the Tibetan Spaniel developed. As the dogs that were left in China slowly evolved into our modern Pekingese, those that went to Tibet maintained the older type. An exaggerated brachycephalic dog, with the short face causing restricted nasal capacity, could not survive in the high altitude of Tibet.

The Tibetan Spaniel was fostered and loved in the monasteries of Tibet for many centuries. Monks carried the little dogs under their flowing robes in the winter, with both benefiting from the additional warmth. The spaniels reputedly turned the prayer wheels for the monks, in

Above: Tibetan Spaniels, adults and pups, various colors. **Below:** Tibetan Spaniel.

addition to serving as alarms. Like the Lhasas that the lamas also favored, these dogs were considered to bring good luck. The first examples of this breed were brought back to Great Britain by medical missionaries in the 1920s. The great popularity of the Pekingese seemed to have left no room for these plainer brothers. But they had established a toehold and, after WWII, the Tibetan Spaniel finally became firmly established in England, gaining distinction as both a show dog and family pet. The first specimens were brought to Canada in the mid-60s and the CKC recognized the breed in 1979. Their introduction to the USA came later and was slower; AKC finally recognized this breed in 1983.

While the unknowledgeable might view this relative newcomer to the Western dog scene as a poor quality or crossbred Pekingese, he is his own dog, with distinctive appearance and character. One of the things his adherents like about him is the very lack of exaggeration. He has the exotic charm of so many of the Oriental breeds without any gross distortion of body or a plethora of coat. Full of intelligence, owners find the breed gay and assertive. None of the delicate, fragile toy is displayed in him, and he enjoys an energetic romp. Affectionate with his own family, he tends to be a bit aloof with strangers.

TIBETAN TERRIER

COUNTRY: Tibet (China)
WEIGHT: 18–30 pounds
HEIGHT: 14–16 inches
COAT: Long, shaggy, covering face
COLOR: White, gray, black, golden, with or without white or tan
OTHER NAMES: Dhokhi Apso
REGISTRY: FCI, AKC, TKC, CKC
GROUP: Herding

Despite his name, this ancient Tibetan is not a terrier, but a true herding dog. The spunky lit- tle animal developed through ancient breeds, the North KunLun Mountain Dog and the Inner Mongolian Dog, which resembled a Poodle and stemmed back to the owtcharkas. Others believe this breed to be one of the prototypes of the herding family.

One talent specifically mentioned by Margareta Sundqvist is the Tibetan Terrier's ability to assist the shepherds on their journeys down from the mountains, by leaping to the backs of the sheep and down again in narrow passages.

They also served as alarm dogs in remote Tibetan villages, alerting the Tibetan Mastiffs of

Tibetan Terrier, black with white marking.

Tibetan Terrier, gray with white marking.

intruders. Tibetans that were too small for such a rigorous life were given to the lamas and utilized and bred by the Tibetan monks for many centuries, developing into Lhasa Apsos.

Brought into Europe by the Magyars, the TT is a likely contributor to the Puli's makeup, being similar in size, shape, tail carriage and working traits. Other modern breeds acquired some of his qualities as he made his way through Europe.

The triad of shepherd, flock guard and herding dog has worked as a partnership throughout the world and over the centuries. None thrives alone in its sheep tending, so each has learned to rely on the other. Ancient Tibetan natives conceived this workable arrangement, with their Tibetan Mastiff doing the guarding and the Tibetan Terrier taking care of the actual herding. As the barbarians of the East invaded Europe, their families and flocks came with them, along with their two types of dogs. These Mastiffs and herders were left in all countries which absorbed these migrations, where they became individualized for the local region.

Poland developed the mighty Podhalanski and the shaggy Nizinny; in Hungary, the corded Komondor watched the flocks while the Puli did the footwork; northern Italy brought forth the Maremma and the accompanying Bergamasco. Spain boasts the Spanish Mastiff and the Gos d'Atura. Even tiny Portugal, on the coast, has the Estrela Mountain Dog which works with the Cão de Serra de Aires. And the French Great Pyrenees plays guard while the Berger de Pyrenees runs interference.

In each of these regions, the flock-guarding dogs have remained very similar. The sheepherding dogs have retained many characteristics that lump them together with the sheepdogs of the East, rather than those that came by way of the North. These sheep dogs tend to be shaggy all over their bodies. Many have the tail that tends to curl over the back. Grizzled colors of grays and fawns predominate, rather than the black/tans so common in the northern shepherd dogs.

An English physician, Dr. H.R. Grieg, saved a Tibetan citizen's life and was honored with one of these shaggy Tibetan herding dogs. She later obtained another and brought them back to England; although she was not successful in breeding them, her dogs did serve to introduce the breed to the Western World. The Tibetan Terrier has been recognized in India since 1920, and in England since 1937, where they compete in the Utility Group. A comparative newcomer to the United States, they have been shown in Non-Sporting since 1973.

While the Tibetan Terrier of past centuries was tousled and shaggy-coated, today's show dog is adorned by an elegant coat necessitating hours of skillful grooming. Their long, elegant tails wrap protectively around themselves while sleeping. Another charming characteristic is that of using their paws in a catlike manner, holding, grasping and batting at balls. They can be stubborn if pushed into compliance. The Tibetan makes a merry household pet, small enough for apartments and sturdy enough for children's roughhousing.

Tibetan Terrier.

TOSA INU

COUNTRY: Japan
WEIGHT: 100–200 pounds
HEIGHT: 24½–25½ inches minimum (usually much larger)
COAT: Short, smooth
COLOR: Solid red preferred; brindle, dull black, fawn and white markings permitted
OTHER NAMES: Tosa Ken, Tosa Token
REGISTRY: FCI
GROUP: Mastiff

Tosa Inu, red.

Dog-fighting has been a passion in Japan for many years, and the Tosa was bred particularly to fill that demand, coming from Tosa, Kochi prefecture. After the National Isolation Policy was lifted in 1854, original spitz-type fighters, such as the Akita, habitually were defeated by European breeds. Fighting enthusiasts wouldn't put up with such loss of face and bred the native dogs to St. Bernards, Mastiffs, Great Danes, Bulldogs and Pointers from the West. This increased size and strength, creating the modern Tosa, a dog similar in type and ability to the European "heavyweights."

The dogs were trained with two whips: one had a loud snap but a small sting and the other was used for punishment, inflicting pain. These canine "sumo wrestlers" were chosen for their silent and stoic fighting—they would not scream or utter a whimper though fighting to the death.

Fights were ceremonial occasions, with the dogs paraded to the ring. They were controlled by thick white ropes tied around their necks and held by strong men bracing their legs. Fights were usually stopped if one combatant eased up or gave ground. Contests for top national honors, however, were sometimes allowed to go the bitter and deadly end. Winners received ceremonial aprons, beautiful and valuable, with some priced at $31,000!

The breed suffered setbacks during World War II, as did other large dogs around the world. Favorites were sent to isolated areas in northern Japan, where they continued to be bred. Later fighting enthusiasts standardized appearance and revived the breed to its former glory. They have been exported, in small numbers, to other areas, including the USA and Germany, where they exist as companions and guards only.

The standard notes its aggression toward other dogs. The Tosa gives no ground; it attacks head on. Although massive, the Tosa is agile and athletic, requiring an owner willing to discipline and capable of physically handling and mentally dominating a large, powerful dog. Nevertheless, if properly handled, the Tosa Inu is a quiet, well-behaved breed and is a good family companion.

Tosa Inu in traditional Japanese festival dress.

Toy Fox Terrier.

TOY FOX TERRIER

COUNTRY: USA
WEIGHT: 3½–7 pounds
HEIGHT: 10 inches
COAT: Short, smooth
COLOR: Tri preferred, with white predominating
OTHER NAMES: AmerToy
REGISTRY: UKC
GROUP: Terrier

The Toy was bred directly from the Smooth Fox Terrier, which was brought to the USA from England in the 1870s. At that time, size varied considerably. Although AKC only recognizes the standard size, UKC registered both sizes as Fox Terriers until 1936. The breed then was divided into two varieties: the Fox Terrier and the Toy Fox Terrier.

The AmerToy is widely known in America, with several clubs and organizations fostering him. He has all of the desirable terrier attributes in a small, attractive package. Many people from rural backgrounds recall having these little dogs around the farm "forever." Often appearing in Fox Terrier litters, they were termed runts.

In today's apartment and condo, the AmerToy finds himself equally at home, although the instincts remain. One breeder was called by a farmer who had purchased a pup as a pet for his wife some time earlier. The dog had been exclusively a spoiled house dog all of its life. One day the dog accompanied the farmer out to the silo where it spotted a rat. This tiny, pampered pet ran to the rat, grabbed and killed it with a quick shake, as though he had been doing it all of his life. The farmer related that the dog now serves dual duty, and the farm is nearly rat-free!

AmerToys have also proven their worth as Handi-Dogs, which are trained to assist the deaf and handicapped. These dogs can pick up and return a dropped pencil, fetch a shoe or the paper, and bark on command to indicate the need for help. For people with limited abilities of their hands or who are confined to a wheelchair, Handi-Dogs give their masters increased independence.

The AmerToy is a breeze to groom, and provides its own exercise. Ears are erect, and the tail is docked. His frisky clowning endears him to his owners.

TRANSYLVANIAN HOUNDS

Transylvanian Hound, Short

COUNTRY: Hungary
HEIGHT: 18–22 inches
COAT: Short and coarse
COLOR: Red and tan (with a brown nose); small amounts of white acceptable
OTHER NAMES: Erdelyi Kopo, Short Hungarian Hound
GROUP: Hound

Transylvanian Hound, Tall

COUNTRY: Hungary
WEIGHT: 66–77 pounds
HEIGHT: 22–26 inches
COAT: Short and coarse
COLOR: Black and tan
OTHER NAMES: Erdelyi Kopo, Tall Hungarian Hound
REGISTRY: FCI
GROUP: Hound

When the Magyars invaded the Carpathian Mountains of eastern Hungary in the ninth century, they brought hounds with them. Crossbred with native or Polish dogs, the Transylvanian basis was formed. The Carpathians are heavily forested, so thick that by the time a young hunter on foot walked through the woods, he would be an old man. Therefore, the dogs of the area were strong, bred to go after game following mounted riders.

Heavy winter snows and sultry summers required hounds that were particularly adapted to extremes of climate. In the past, they were used extensively by Hungarian kings and princes for hunting wolf and bear in the mountains. In more modern times, the long-legged variety was used on stag, lynx and boar, while the shorter legged version kept pace with the fox and hare.

The Transylvanian is known for its keen sense of direction and orientation to the environment, vital in mountainous and forested cover. This is a dog without exaggeration, moderate in bone and head with tight skin and a medium flat ear. Prized as an obedient, trainable, good-natured hound who is an easy keeper, he was never known outside Hungary. Recent reports indicate that the Transylvanian dogs face extinction, with their numbers dangerously low.

Tall Transylvanian Hound.

TREEING TENNESSEE BRINDLE

COUNTRY: USA
WEIGHT: In proportion to height, around 45 pounds
HEIGHT: 16–24 inches
COAT: Short, dense and smooth
COLOR: Brindle, or black with brindle trim; small amount of white on breast or feet allowed
GROUP: Hound

Treeing Tennessee Brindle, brindle.

The second of the "mountain" curs is the Treeing Tennessee Brindle. As opposed to the Mountain Cur, this breed tends a lot more to the hound. His roots are the same as the other coondogs, and the rather honest statement of the Association sums up this dog's history. "Our original breeding stock came from outstanding brindle tree dogs from every part of the country." The Plott dogs as well as the Curs may have played prominently in the formation of the Tennessee dog.

Hunters used the small brindle hounds for generations. They didn't have a name for them then; they just knew that these unpretentious dogs were fine open trailers and were superb locators, fearless with game such as coon and squirrel but very companionable with men and dogs.

It wasn't until 1967 that a group formed to foster and register the breed and give it an official name. Founded by the Reverend Earl Phillips who is in his late 90s and still working his dogs, the Treeing Tennessee Brindle Breeders Association has grown from modest beginnings to over 500 members in 30 states. In 1978, the TTBBA turned its registry over to the American Coon Hunters Association and the Treeing Brindle was recognized as this group's ninth breed of coonhound. The TTBBA has recently applied to AKC for Miscellaneous Class status for their breed.

Hunting characteristics are much like the other coonhound breeds, with ample nose for trailing game, open trailers with a coarse chop mouth, and fine treeing ability. Small hounds, they have tight cat feet and small ears. They are fast and courageous hunters and, as companions, are intelligent, affectionate and easygoing. Their promoters say these dogs have "heart and try" in abundance.

Puppy buyers are encouraged to look for one that is happy, bold, confident and inquisitive. The breed is particularly sensitive to neglect or abuse, and breeders warn that care must be taken in training not to destroy that heart—"You can take it out, but you can *never* put it back!" Traits such as large size, long low ears, stub tails and colors other than brindle are warned against, since all would put him into another canine category.

TREEING WALKER COONHOUND

COUNTRY: USA
WEIGHT: 45–70 pounds
HEIGHT: 20–27 inches
COAT: Short, smooth and glossy
COLOR: Tricolored preferred; bicolors allowed
REGISTRY: UKC
GROUP: Hound

Like the other coonhounds, the Treeing Walker has the Virginia hounds to thank for its beginnings. From the English Foxhounds, the Virginia hounds begat the Walker Foxhound, which in turn begat the Treeing Walker. Sometime in the 1800s, a dog known as "Tennessee Lead," a stolen dog of unknown origin, was crossed into the Walker Hound. He was a pre-potent dog, excelling in game sense, drive and speed, and having a clear, short chop mouth.

This breed has a higher percentage of foxhound and is swift and hot-nosed. The breed broke off from the English Coonhound in 1945. One owner says he believes they are the best breed for coonhound field trials because of their speed, ability to locate quickly and good treeing ability.

Treeing experts like the Redbone, these dogs can be used for other game, but specialize in raccoon and opossum. They learn their trade early and adjust easily to most living conditions. Another owner says his hounds have brought him many hours of enjoyment while hunting and showing in field trials, as well as for "the pure pleasure of going out in the stillness of the night and treeing a coon." Almost all of these dogs are working hounds.

High-strung but loving and eager to please, the Treeing Walker is intelligent and confident. Although there are tan and white dogs in the breed, they must never be called "red," most likely to distinguish them from the Redbone.

Treeing Walker Coonhound, tricolor.

843

Tyroler Bracke, black/tan.

TYROLER BRACKE

COUNTRY: Austria
WEIGHT: 33–48 pounds
HEIGHT: 16–19 inches
COAT: Short; very tough and dense hair
COLOR: Self-colored in black, black/tan, red or yellow; small white markings allowed
OTHER NAMES: Tyrolean Hound
REGISTRY: FCI
GROUP: Hound

Celtic brackes, known throughout the Alps since the Middle Ages, were the basis for many German and Austrian hounds. These Alpenbracken slowly developed into many modern breeds. By 1860, hunters in the Tyrol began to select their own specific type, and this developed into the modern, capable Tyroler Bracke. The first specimen was exhibited at Innsbruck in 1896, after which the standard was accepted.

The Tyrol is the long western finger of Austria, bordering on the Swiss and Italian Alps. Its high altitude mountains have frigid winters and steamy summers, and the Tyrolean Hound is perfectly adapted to this harsh environment.

These dogs are used for hunting rabbit and fox, but can be utilized as a *Nachsuchenhund* (that is, to search for sick or wounded deer). They are especially adapted for tracking and trailing after the shot has been fired.

Most common in the Tyrol, modern hunters in other parts of Austria and in a few other countries have recognized the Tyroler Bracke's outstanding qualities. He is an ideal companion for the hunter, especially in high elevations.

He works the hot trail *spurlaut,* (i.e., he gives tongue to let the hunter know he is on to a scent), what American hound owners call "opening" on trail. He is a lively and spirited dog, with a superb nose and great endurance during the hunt. Intelligent and easygoing, the Tyrolean is tractable and fits into home life well. He is most happy, however, when he is used for his intended work.

A tracker, the Tyroler is built with much the same lines as the Bavarian dogs with strong bodies, but rather short legs. This Austrian hound is smaller than his German cousins. Owners say too many white marks on the limbs are frowned upon.

VASGOTASPETS

COUNTRY: Sweden
WEIGHT: 20–32 pounds
HEIGHT: 13–16 inches
COAT: Medium length, thick and hard
COLOR: Shaded gray preferred, followed by shaded red, then brindle, blue-gray; white markings, if any, must be less than 40 percent
OTHER NAMES: Swedish Vallhund, Swedish Cattledog
REGISTRY: TKC
GROUP: Herding

An old, indigenous breed from the Vastergotland plains of Sweden, known for its cattle herds, the Vallhund's similarity to the Welsh Corgis—especially the Pembroke—is intriguing. Pembrokeshire is accessible to the coast, and Viking raiders struck along the Irish and Welsh coast. Whether the Vikings introduced the short-legged dog to the Welsh or seized the hard-working little dog as part of their spoils is speculated, but uncertain, and tends to be colored by whether it is a Vallhund or Corgi owner telling the story.

The Vasgotaspets, meaning spitz of the West Goths, was known at one time as the Vikingarnas Dog. It has very small prick ears and a natu-ral bobtail (more than four inches is a standard disqualification, as is docking). This Corgi-type dog is higher on leg and shorter in body than its close relative in Great Britain. Its head is foxy, even more so than the Corgi's. The breed is used on farms, not only for cattle droving, but also as a vermin catcher, watchdog and over-all farm dog.

With the *Vallhund*, forest dog, in danger of extinction in the 1930s, dedicated Swedish breeders, led by Count Bjorn von Rosen, motivated a comeback for this handsome little dog. Officially recognized by the Swedish KC in 1948, the breed is now quite popular in its homeland and has found some following in other countries. A good number live in England where it was granted recognition in 1984, and the Swedish herding dog has recently been introduced to America.

Exhibiting a unique sense of humor, he is a natural showoff. Once he realizes a particular stunt brings laughter or applause, he will repeat it over and over. Affectionate and sensitive to his owner's mood, the Swedish herder reflects joy or quiet contemplation. The Vasgotaspets is intelligent and spirited and does not hesitate to vocalize his joy at being alive. He is a sturdy little dog and is easy to care for.

Vasgotaspets.

VIZSLA

COUNTRY: Hungary
WEIGHT: 49–62 pounds
HEIGHT: 22–24 inches
COAT: Shorthaired—smooth and fine; Wirehaired—bristly but quite short (1–1½ inches) and conforming to the outline of the dog, some beard and brow desirable
COLOR: Various shades of gold to sandy yellow
OTHER NAMES: Magyar Vizsla
REGISTRY: FCI, AKC, UKC, TKC, CKC
GROUP: Gun Dog

The exact origin of this striking Hungarian hunting dog is difficult to pinpoint. Some historians think the Vizsla goes back in pure line to the days of the Magyar hordes that overran Hungary from the East. Others feel it is a creation of the present century! Perhaps the reality is somewhere between.

The home of the Vizsla is the hot central plain of Hungary, the Puszta, an area of rich and diverse agriculture and plentiful game. Etchings of nearly a thousand years ago show Magyar huntsmen with dogs and falcons. It is known that they had good hounds (such as the Transyl-vanian), and they must have used these hounds in selective breeding for dogs to use with the falcon. Legends persist about the "Yellow Turkish Hunting Dog" used in the Vizsla's development. This will continue to be a mystery, as there is no modern equivalent of this type, and it isn't known even what kind of "hunting" dog the extinct breed was. Of course, it is only logical to assume that good hunting dogs were brought with the migrating Magyars as they left Asia Minor for Europe. But the modern fine tuning of this breed as an all-purpose hunting dog probably occurred fairly recently, possibly with crosses to other established European breeds.

The Vizsla suffered greatly between the two Great Wars, and much of the modern breed is based on dogs taken out of Hungary by owners emigrating to other countries. The breed has gained some following in several European countries, as well as in North America. Because of his origin on the hot plains, he has been noted for his stamina in hot weather. Some Vizsla historians note that at some point during the 1930s, after crosses were made to the German Wirehair, the Drotszoru or wirehaired ver-

Vizsla, wirehaired.

Vizsla, shorthaired.

sion appeared. This variety has not been officially recognized in the USA, but the wire coat is encouraged in Hungary since it can better withstand the winter weather, especially while retrieving ducks from ice-cold water and sitting (wet) for hours in a boat.

The Hungarian pointer is expected to be an all-rounder, searching diligently, not ranging too far, and marking and retrieving from land and water. These are gentle dogs, willing to please but not adapting well to a harsh hand. Their character is defined by their Hungarian name, *Vizsla*, meaning alert and responsive.

The breed is more refined than many of the other European utility dogs, only moderate of bone, standing high on cat feet, with a hint of an arch to the loin. Perhaps that "yellow dog

from Turkey" had some of the sighthound in him! But breeders are warned to avoid letting their dog degenerate into one too refined and shelly to stand up to the work expected of him.

The Vizsla is making a good name for himself among American hunters, and his bright gold color stands him well in the show ring. A steady trickle of dual champions is being produced by dedicated breeders who don't want a breed split. Obedience has also found him a capable participant. In 1987, a Vizsla captured the first and only triple American championship, a special award created by AKC for a dog that has won his bench title for the ideal appearance, his field trial championship, and an obedience trial championship won after the UD title is obtained.

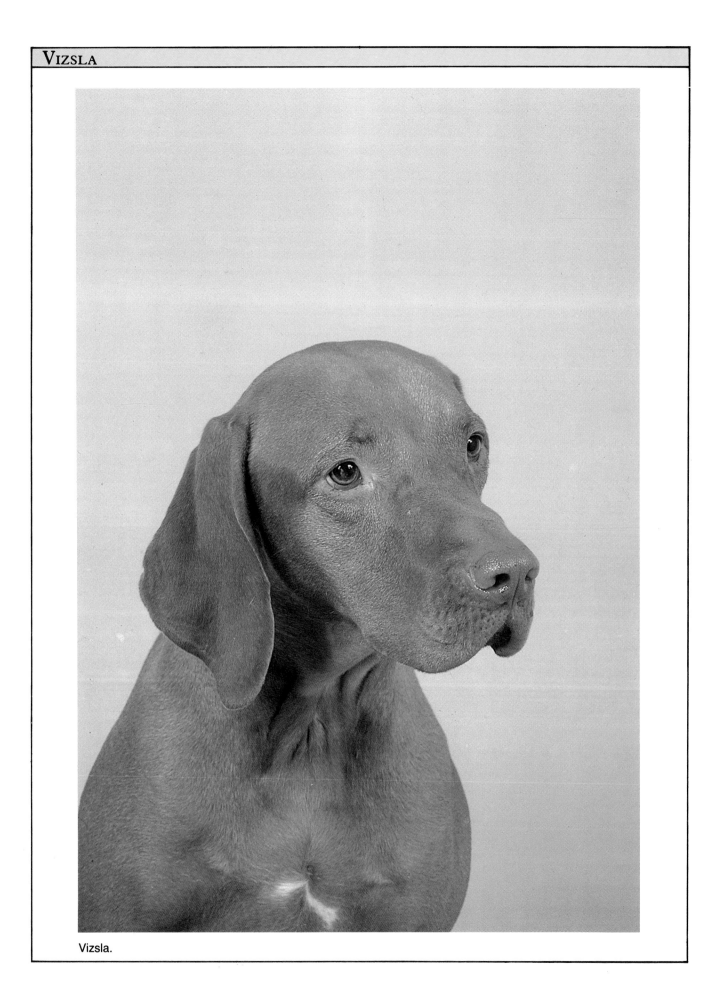

Vizsla.

Vizsla.

VOLPINO ITALIANO

COUNTRY: Italy
WEIGHT: Less than 10 pounds
HEIGHT: 11–12 inches
COAT: Long, thick spitz coat
COLOR: Pure white or sable (rare)
OTHER NAMES: Florentine Spitz, Cane de Quirinale
REGISTRY: FCI
GROUP: Northern

Spitz types were found throughout the ancient world. Specimens from this group have been found preserved in European peat bogs which anthropologists trace to 4000 BC. The remains—with curly tails, foxy heads and small erect ears—have been found, dating back over 5,000 years. These little pets wore decorative ivory bracelets and collars. Engravings of similar dogs were found in Greece, and these have been determined to date about 400 BC.

The Volpino has been known and loved by Italian royalty for centuries, being an especial favorite of the ladies. Although bearing a strong resemblance to the Pomeranian, the breed is much older and thus has a different background. The northern dogs found their way south very early in canine history. The Italian word for wolf is *lupo*, and the Keeshond is called both Lupino and Volpino in Italian, so Volpino may be an old term for wolfdog or wolfspitz. Despite his long history, the Volpino is unknown outside of Italy and is now quite rare even in his homeland.

Volpino Italiano, white.

Weimaraner, shorthaired.

WEIMARANER

COUNTRY: Germany
WEIGHT: 70–85 pounds
HEIGHT: 23–28 inches
COAT: Shorthaired—short, fine and hard;
Longhaired—1–2 inches and fringed as a setter
COLOR: Solid light gray
REGISTRY: FCI, AKC, UKC, TKC, CKC
GROUP: Gun Dog

The Weimaraner, favored at the court of Weimar, also looks to the brackes and schweisshunds of Germany for his ancestry. Pointers, a little heavier, a little slower than those used to develop the Shorthair, contributed to his genealogy. Although a dog of Weimaraner type appeared in a Van Dyke painting of the early 1600s, the breed was closer to hound type at that time, and was used for tracking and hunting large game such as bear, wolves and big cats.

As wing shooting began to displace hunting of the diminishing big game, the Weimaraner was crossed with "huenerhunden" to secure more bird dog characteristics. The Weim is a true versatile gun dog, still carrying more of the ancestral hound stamp than many of his German cousins. The large, stiff, flat ear is very similar to the type seen on the German schweisshunds. He is a tough and able hunter, carrying out all of the desirable "after-the-shot" jobs so important to the European hunter.

Breeding of the gray dog was kept close to the vest in Germany for many years by a very strict breed club. Although quality was high, there was never a large number of the breed, even in its homeland.

Only a few were brought to the USA prior to the War but, in the 1940s, interest grew both in America and in other European countries. Unfortunately, the Weim's introduction in the US was accompanied by much hoopla and media hype about his natural all-around abilities. The promoters failed to mention the rigorous training necessary to develop the finished German utility dog. Many gullible new owners were dis-

appointed that the "Gray Ghost" wasn't a wonder dog who came pre-trained! Fortunately, his modern fanciers are following a more prudent path of hunting, showing, field trialing and obedience training their dogs—creating a showcase for the dog-owning public to see. Weims are fine companions and hunting dogs and have accomplished much in the way of obedience and tracking titles as well as a good number of duals. They are resilient enough to be trained in schutzhund protection work.

The longhaired variety is well known and accepted in Europe, although it constitutes a disqualification in the AKC standard. Governed by a recessive gene, the longhairs still, legitimately, pop up now and then in American litters. Although they are prohibited from registration, the longhairs still make fine hunting dogs or obedience prospects. Several Americans have imported registered German Longhaired Weimaraners into the USA in an attempt to have the variety recognized. Although the shorthaired variety has the tail docked to about half the original length, the long coats often are left undocked, more in the venue of the setter.

Weimaraner, longhaired.

Weimaraner.

Weimaraner.

Weimaraner.

Cardigan Welsh Corgi, brindle.

WELSH CORGIS

Welsh Corgi, Cardigan

COUNTRY: Great Britain
WEIGHT: 28–30 pounds maximum
HEIGHT: 12 inches
COAT: Medium-short, harsh and dense
COLOR: Red, sable, brindles, black, tricolor, blue merle, usually with white in Irish pattern; predominant white is a serious fault
REGISTRY: FCI, AKC, UKC, TKC, CKC
GROUP: Herding

Welsh Corgi, Pembroke

COUNTRY: Great Britain
WEIGHT: 24–28 pounds
HEIGHT: 10–12 inches
COAT: Medium-short, dense
COLOR: Red, sable, fawn, black/tan; self-colored or with white markings on legs, chest and neck, and a minimal amount on the head
REGISTRY: FCI, AKC, UKC, TKC, CKC
GROUP: Herding

Although the Cardigan is not as well known as the Pembroke variety, the Cardi is thought to be the older, being brought to Wales with the Celts (about 1200 BC). The Pembroke is a comparative newcomer to the Welsh, entering with Flemish weavers around the tenth century. Another theory contends that both breeds descended from Swedish Vallhunds brought to the Welsh coast by Viking invaders in the ninth century.

The derivation of the name Corgi is attributed to the Celtic word for dog (*corgi*). Other tales passed on through generations say that the little dogs were named for *cor*, dwarf, and *gi*, dog, or for *cur*, watch over.

The crofters of Wales had no land of their own to graze their cattle, as they were allowed to fence only small areas around their dwelling. These poor farmers were granted, however, the liberty of driving their cattle to pasture on the Crown's open range. An intelligent, hard-working droving dog was an asset. Corgis met those requirements and gave an added benefit: they were short-legged, cattle-heeling dogs, developed to run under the legs, avoiding dangerous kicks.

The two breeds are very similar to each other with a few minor differences. In fact, until the 1930s, Pembrokes and Cardigans were interbred. Since that time, each breed's fanciers have emphasized the individualities. The Cardigan is a bit larger, heavier boned and longer bodied, and displays a long, low tail. The Cardi has been called the "yard-long" dog, being the same length from the tip of its nose to the end of its outstretched tail as a Welsh yard. His ears are larger and set wider than the Pembroke's. Color and coats also differ. Legend says that the blue-merle color of the Cardi was brought by fairies one dark night.

The dog from Pembrokeshire has straighter legs and is known for its foxier look, due to its more wedge-shaped head and smaller, higher earset. Occasionally, their pups are born tailless. Those that aren't are docked flush with the body, leaving not even a stump to wag. To remember which is which, word association can help: the Cardigan has a long tail, like the long sleeves in a cardigan sweater, and the Pembroke has a "broke" tail.

Cardigan Welsh Corgi, blue merle.

Pembroke Welsh Corgi, sable.

Although the Cardigan has never become as prevalent, the Pembroke has been in vogue, due to being a favorite of the British royal family. The latter breed has become one of the most prominent dogs in England and Australia.

Both are handsome, loving, learn quickly and are good obedience workers. They are often chosen as small companions by large breed fanciers, because Corgis possess the heart of a larger dog. Full of their own self-importance, they are jaunty little characters. Their working background and sturdy bodies allow them to handle the roughhousing of large, rowdy dogs—or large, rowdy families.

Pembroke Welsh Corgi, red with white.

Cardigan Welsh Corgi.

WELSH SPRINGER SPANIEL

COUNTRY: Great Britain
WEIGHT: 35–45 pounds
COAT: Straight and flat, with moderate feathering
COLOR: Red and white
REGISTRY: FCI, AKC, TKC, CKC
GROUP: Gun Dog

Wales's distinctive red/white spaniel has been portrayed by artists even earlier than the other British spaniels. The Celts originally settled Wales, Ireland and Brittany, and some relationship to the red/white hunting dogs of those areas could easily be established. He was also part of that happy mixture of British spaniels prior to the 20th century. Consequently, a long and pure history is not pretended. His standardization coincided with the time period of the Cocker and the Springer. Breeder A.T. Williams, around 1900, promoted the breed both on the bench and at working trials.

The Welsh differs from the English Springer by reason of his more tapered head, the body, which is lower on leg, the smaller and higher set ear, as well as his clear red and white jacket. A true individual, he should not be dismissed as a "dumpy English Springer" or a "big coarse Cocker." He doesn't show any exaggeration of feathering or coat, which may carry a bit of a wave.

A natural flushing spaniel, he is a keen and tireless worker, and is particularly good in water. In Wales, he is also known as a "Starter." The breed has never become numerous in the United States or in any other country. But his happy spaniel temperament has won loyal friends who continue to foster the breed.

Welsh Springer Spaniels.

Welsh Springer Spaniel.

Welsh Terrier.

Welsh Terrier.

WELSH TERRIER

COUNTRY: Great Britain
WEIGHT: 20 pounds
HEIGHT: 15 inches
COAT: Wire
COLOR: Black/tan
REGISTRY: FCI, AKC, TKC, CKC
GROUP: Terrier

The old black and tan Broken-Coated Terrier (or Old English Terrier) of northern England was used in the foundation of so many of our modern terriers. Today's modern Welshie is probably the closest and the most direct descendant of this ancient strain, with legs stretched and head elongated a bit. They were all shown under the same classification until 1888. One dog, "Dick Turpin," won prizes over a three-year period in both breeds. English owners wanted the type called English Broken-haired, and the Welsh wanted to retain their claim. The Welsh terrier-like persistence won over The Kennel Club.

Used for ratting and for badger and otter hunting like so many other terriers in the last century, the breed is also known for its good nature and ease of handling. To be most efficient in the Welsh hills, he had to be long-legged enough to climb and to run after a horse. He has been compared in general appearance to a small version of the Airedale.

He is broader headed than his cousin, the Wire Fox Terrier, and is always wire-jacketed in black and rich tan. The breed requires stripping four times a year to retain its smart appearance. His tail is docked.

A Welshie has an almost catlike curiosity, which can cause him—and his owners—problems at times. His playfulness and energy call for a firm hand and an outlet such as swimming (which he enjoys immensely), obedience training or romping with older children. He is affectionate and calm in the home.

863

WEST HIGHLAND WHITE TERRIER

COUNTRY: Great Britain
WEIGHT: 15–22 pounds
HEIGHT: 10–11 inches
COAT: Rough, wiry
COLOR: White
REGISTRY: FCI, AKC, UKC, TKC, CKC
GROUP: Terrier

From the general rough-coated terrier stock of Scotland, white whelps were selected to form this breed. Colored pups were culled, just as the whites were given away or destroyed when creating the purebred Cairn and Scottish Terrier. Like all the other terriers, the Westie was used for vermin control.

These white dogs were easy to distinguish from their surroundings and the wildlife. Thus, white terriers have run the Scottish Highlands for over 300 years. Records show that King James I, a Stuart who ruled England in the 1620s, requested some game "little white earth dogges" out of Argyleshire—possibly Westies.

Colonel Malcolm of Polltalloch, Argyleshire, Scotland, accidentally shot and killed his favorite terrier (a dark-colored one) on an 1860 hunting excursion, and determined to have only white dogs from then on. The Malcolms may have been the originators of the Highland Terrier—as game white terriers were kept by this family since the 18th century or before. At that early time, they were often called Polltalloch Terriers.

Others in this shire also fostered the breed. The Duke of Argyll's estate at Dumbartonshire (Scotland) was called Roseneath. In the 19th

West Highland White Terriers, adult and pup.

West Highland White Terrier.

century, Westies became generally known as Roseneath Terriers, indicating the Duke's patronage and interest. The breed was also known as the White Scottish Terrier in the first organized dog shows in the late 1800s. In 1904, they were first classified under the name of West Highland White Terrier. Westies first charmed Westminster spectators in 1906.

The breed has survived fads exaggerating certain breed points, such as the straight short forelegs, and returned to the sensible structure of today. Its shaggy white coat, small erect ears and black button nose give the Highland Terrier a cute and cuddly image. But it is all terrier with too much energy and spirit for much of that "cuddling nonsense"!

The Westie resembles a Cairn more than the Scottie. Modern show dogs have taken on a clip that accentuates the head. The hard-textured hair causes mud to just fall off when dry. They clean up with a few strokes of the brush, so keeping the coat white is not a major problem.

The breed is hardy, devoted and happy-go-lucky, exhibiting typical terrier tendencies: sturdiness, alarm barks, digging, cock-of-the-walk strutting and one-upmanship with other dogs (especially males). But this dog is not as volatile as some of the others in his group. In fact, the Westie standard warns against excessive pugnacity. Inclement weather is no deterrent to his energetic personality, and he makes a fine family pet.

Westphalian Dachbracke, red with white markings.

WESTPHALIAN DACHSBRACKE

COUNTRY: Germany
HEIGHT: 12–15 inches
COAT: Short, smooth, hard and dense
COLOR: Tricolor, as the Deutsche Bracke, or red with the described white markings
OTHER NAMES: Westfälische Dachsbracke, Sauerlander Dachsbracke
REGISTRY: FCI
GROUP: Hound

Just as the French developed their bassets for closer or slower hound work, the Germans created their dachshunds and dachsbrackes. Short-legged versions of the bracke have been known for a very long time in the western German areas of Westphalia and the Sauerland. Modern authorities feel his development included short-legged mutations of the larger brackes, as well as crosses to the dachshunds of the time. Cynologists Ludwig Beckmann and Otto Grashey first

officially described and named the breed in 1886, although portraits from the Middle Ages show the little dog. The Westphalian Dachsbracke was recognized by the German Kennel authorities in 1935, and is fostered and protected today under the umbrella of the Deutsche Bracken Club.

This Dachsbracke has been recruited for hunting hare, fox, wild boar and rabbit in the central high mountains. Hunting in the mountain woods is impossible without dogs. He searches for game, is especially good for the "circle chase" with rabbits and is employed for blood-trailing as well. Often the prey is not as fearful of the smaller Dachsbracke and allows the dog to approach closer before fleeing.

This short hunter performs well unless the snow is very deep. He must be willing to give tongue, but only when sure of his quarry. This vocal attribute is highly desirable, and silent dogs are neutered. The "loud" hunting is utilized only for short distances, often when he chases the quarry around in a circle and back to the waiting hunter. More and more, the Westphalian dog is also used for schweisshund trailing work. This is a pleasant and companionable dog.

Westphalian Dachsbracke, tricolor.

WEST RUSSIAN COURSING HOUNDS

Chortaj

COUNTRY: USSR
HEIGHT: 25–26 inches
COAT: Thick and smooth
COLOR: Many colors allowed, often solids
OTHER NAMES: Eastern Greyhound
REGISTRY: None
GROUP: Southern

South Russian Steppe Hound

COUNTRY: USSR
HEIGHT: 24–28 inches
COLOR: Solid colors
OTHER NAMES: Steppe Borzoi
REGISTRY: None
GROUP: Southern

While the AKC Borzoi has had all the world-wide publicity because of his association with royalty, the lesser known *borzoi* (sighthounds) of the Soviet Union are far older and are still widely bred and hunted. In the northern half of Russia, hunting is done either with scenthounds or laikas. But in the south, across the vast plains and steppes, the villagers still hunt on horseback with one or two sighthounds and sometimes an eagle or falcon instead of a gun. This is a centuries old tradition of the Tartars and Cossacks who settled these regions. The proximity of this area to the Middle East probably answers the question of source, although these dogs came into the area so long ago, they are now considered indigenous breeds.

On the immense steppes from the north Caucasus Mountains, west of the Caspian Sea, up through the Volga and Don River estuaries, abundant game flourished, allowing the continuation of the Cossack tradition of coursing.

In these areas, hunters use both the Chortaj (pronounced *hortai*) and various strains of the South Russian Steppe Hound. They ride out looking for game, depending on the Chortaj, who has eyesight keen enough to spot game up to 280 yards away. Once seen, the pursuit is on. These dogs are endowed with tremendous endurance to withstand the lengthy chases which fi-

Chortaj, gray.

Chortaj.

WETTERHOUN

COUNTRY: Netherlands
WEIGHT: 33–44 pounds
HEIGHT: 21½–23¼ inches
COAT: Thick, tight curls all over, except smooth on the head, bottom third of the ears and the legs
COLOR: Liver, liver/white, black, or black/white; ticking or roaning may appear in the white
OTHER NAMES: Otterhoun, Dutch Spaniel
REGISTRY: FCI
GROUP: Gun Dog

Friesland is a county in the northwestern corner of the Netherlands. The Frisian people have their own culture and language, and have developed two of the native Dutch hunting dogs. The Wetterhoun is one of these distinctive Frisian breeds. The breed's history goes back to the

Wetterhoun, black/white.

nally exhaust the game. A Borzoi, although possessing greater speed, would be worn out himself before the fox, hare or antelope could be run down on the spacious steppes. The Steppe Borzoi can, however, put on short bursts of tremendous speed to turn the quarry before it is able to find safety in a thicket or heavy brush. Young dogs are coupled with experienced ones to train them; those that don't make the grade are shot.

Modern Russian cynologists admit that many dogs of these two breeds have, until very recently, been kept and trained under exceedingly primitive conditions and poor nutrition. Often they roamed at will in the villages. The authorities are diligently working to educate the South Russian hunters in the practical value of proper care and selection. Now more and more of the dogs are being kept penned or leashed. Russians emphasize the importance of dog shows and field trials to compare quality and learn how to improve the breed. A few Chortaj have been exhibited at Moscow shows recently and type is improving. The Chortaj looks very much like a smooth Borzoi, with a stopless down face and rosed ear, while the Steppe Borzois (those that are fixed in type) often are reminiscent of a Sloughi.

Wetterhoun, black/white with roaning.

1600s, or earlier, although their exact origin is unknown. It is surely related to the generic water dogs of Europe, but the tail curled over the back suggests a possible cross to dogs of Nordic type.

Originally, the Wetterhoun (literal translation from the Frisian is water dog) was used to find and kill otters in the lake district of his homeland. For this chore he needed to be tough and fearless. There is little present-day need for an otter dog, but the Wetterhoun is also an excellent close-working flushing dog. He works like many of our modern land spaniels, searching for game and indicating its presence. After the shot, he retrieves well from land or water. Breeders say that while hunting in heavy cover the Wetterhoun "goes like a tank." They love the water and happily swim even in freezing weather. When thwarted in hunting, a pet may turn to stalking moles and mice.

The breed is quite distinctive as a gun dog in both appearance and character. He has a rather wide and powerful body with a strong head and a tightly spiraled tail. The coat must never be woolly, the curls correctly being large bundles of hair with an almost greasy, waterproof texture. An admirer says, "It is a go-getter and goes up to the fish-otter without any fear at all, just like it approaches the polecat and the wildcat as if they didn't bite at all. The Musks even fear the Wetterhoun. . . . "

The Dutch say these dogs are much like the Frisian people, obstinate but, once their hearts are won, loveable and loyal. His standard calls for him to be of stubborn character and reserved with strangers. The Dutch Wetterhoun Club describes the breed: "A cautious Frysk with a heart of gold." While quiet in the home, loving with their people and excellent with children, they do need plenty of daily exercise for their energies. Their reticent nature also makes them natural watchdogs. With their masters, they learn quickly and take well to training, as they love their work.

WHIPPET

COUNTRY: Great Britain
WEIGHT: 28 pounds
HEIGHT: 18–22 inches
COAT: Short, fine and close
COLOR: Any color
REGISTRY: FCI, AKC, UKC, TKC, CKC
GROUP: Southern

English miners loved to gamble, but didn't have the finances for horses or even large dogs, so these sportsmen turned to the "snap" dog trials in the 1800s. Rabbits released in an enclosure were chased down and killed by dogs racing against the clock. The English terriers were outstanding at killing rats, but suffered embarrassment when pitted against the speed of rabbits. They couldn't catch them to kill them!

These terriers were modified with Greyhound blood to increase speed, and some say the Whippet was the result. Later humane laws put a crimp in the gambler's "fun," and the passion turned to racing. Lure or "rag racing" was substituted for the live rabbit. At that time, small greyhound types, such as the Italian Greyhound, added refinement to the terrier blend. Lancashire textile workers, immigrating to New England in the early 1900s, introduced the Whippets and their racing to North America.

Whippet, brown brindle.

Whippets.

As the poor man's race horse, Whippets served the purpose of the working class, who wanted a piece of the racing action. Because these men didn't have fancy oval tracks, and had to arrange their races in back alleys and empty lots, the Whippet became a straight-away sprinter. His acceleration ability gives him jackrabbit starts, covering 200 yards in 12 seconds! Whippets have been clocked at up to 37 mph.

They have a fragile appearance, but that is belied on the track. Slim and powerful as a marathoner, Whippets have the clean lines and dignity of their larger half-brothers the greyhounds. Many breed champions also hold a racing merit award. They make quiet, sturdy and affectionate pets and obedience dogs, delighting in the company of people and other dogs—especially other Whippets!

Recently the appearance of a longhaired version has stirred much controversy. The American parent club has denied them status.

Whippet, brindle.

WIREHAIRED POINTING GRIFFON

COUNTRY: France
WEIGHT: 50–60 pounds
HEIGHT: 22–24 inches
COAT: Hard and coarse, "like a wild boar" with heavy beard and eyebrows
COLOR: Solid chestnut or chestnut with white or steel gray (roan) markings
OTHER NAMES: Korthals Griffon, Griffon d'Arret a Poil Dur
REGISTRY: FCI, AKC, CKC
GROUP: Gun Dog

Edward K. Korthals, a Dutchman who later moved to Germany, created this versatile hunting breed. Its development took place in the 1860s–70s, when so many of the shooting dogs were being developed. Korthals's basic stock started with a bitch named "Mouche," and continued with other griffons of Barbet origin for coat, love of water and intelligence. What he

Above: Wirehaired Pointing Griffon, chestnut with roaning. **Below:** Wirehaired Pointing Griffons.

Wirehaired Pointing Griffon.

crossed the griffons with is not known for sure. Experts speculate that he used various setters or pointers for pointing ability and air scenting; German Shorthairs, Small Münsterländers and others of this type were in abundance in Germany at this time. Many feel he used the Braque Francais. Herr Korthals served as an agent to the Duke of Penthievre in France. Interest soon generated a following for his new breed in that country. Thus, France was the source of much crossbreeding and the area of first interest, which is the reason FCI lists the breed as French.

The Pointing Griffon was brought to the USA in the very early years of this century, and, in fact, was the first of the Continental "all-purpose" breeds to gain official recognition here. But, like so many of the excellent working Continental breeds that followed him, he tended to be denigrated by the American dog press as too slow and unstylish. The United States, at that time, was still a nation of abundant game and vast, unfenced spaces, where the big running pointer/setter was at his glory. Only recently has the modern American hunter had to come to grips with the commonplace situation in Europe

a century ago: urban expansion, increased use of all land for crops and livestock, and shrinking habitat for wild game. Therefore, only lately have American hunters begun to appreciate the Continental breeds, which may be slower but never miss a "single"—dogs who work closer and are more biddable in small farm fields, who trail a wounded running bird so it won't be lost, and retrieve in water as well as on land.

Even though the Korthals breed has been a long-term resident of the USA, it has never reached great heights of popularity, which is acceptable, perhaps preferable, to those who foster it. He has maintained a steady, if small, following among practical hunters. His keen nose and passion for the hunt are still present. Only a few are ever seen in American show rings. The breed club in America is adamant in stressing working qualities and soundness. The Korthals is still bred in Europe as well.

His tail is docked to leave a third, and his wiry, bristly coat requires a minimum of brushing. He is an intelligent, affectionate dog, but is also active and energetic. The Pointing Griffon needs plenty of exercise, especially if he is to be kept in the house.

XOLOITZCUINTLIS

Xoloitzcuintli

COUNTRY: Mexico
HEIGHT: 13–22½ inches (Standard and Miniature)
COAT: Hairless, with a wisp of short, thin hair on head and nape, feet and tail tip; Powderpuff variety
COLOR: Skin can be dark solid charcoal, slate, reddish gray, liver or bronze preferred; pink or coffee colored spots are permissible
OTHER NAMES: Standard Mexican Hairless
REGISTRY: FCI
GROUP: Southern

Xoloitzcuintli, Toy

COUNTRY: Mexico
HEIGHT: 11–12 inches (size of small Fox Terrier)
COAT: Hairless, with a wisp of short, thin hair on head and nape, feet and tail tip; Powderpuff variety
COLOR: Skin can be dark solid charcoal, slate, reddish gray, liver or bronze preferred; pink or coffee colored spots permissible
OTHER NAMES: Mexican Hairless, Tepeizeuintli
REGISTRY: CKC
GROUP: Southern

Ancestors of the Aztec Indians brought hairless dogs called *Biche*, meaning naked, with them when they arrived in Mexico from Asia. The Aztecs enjoyed the hairless dogs as pets, but also found them useful as bedwarmers and sacrificial offerings. The Mexican Hairless and the larger variety, Xoloitzcuintli (pronounced *show-low-eats-QUEEN-tlee*), warmed their stomachs—inside and out. Clay figures and remains of these dogs, dating from 300 to 900 AD, have been found in burial sites, where the dogs guided the souls to a happy afterlife—and furnished nourishment until it was reached.

After the Spanish conquest, the great Aztec society disappeared, and with it the pampered pet/culinary delicacy. Small numbers of Xolos survived in remote villages. They were not forgotten, however. Famed Mexican artist Diego Rivera captured them in his murals. In the 1950s, the Mexican Kennel Club made a concerted effort to re-establish this distinct national breed.

The toasty warm body heat of these hairless dogs made them in demand as ancient hot-water bottles, relieving stomach pains and rheumatic joints, or simply warming chill nights. Extreme cold made for a "Three Dog Night." The breed's palliative qualities magnified until its "healing powers" became a panacea. The

Toy Xoloitzcuintli, charcoal with white.

warmth from these dogs is still enjoyed today, particularly by the elderly.

The Xolo and Mexican Hairless are identical except for size. The Mexican KC feels that the size variation is acceptable and recognizes them as one breed, the Xolo. In the USA, however, the smaller variety has been renamed the Mexican Hairless. The ancient link of both varieties to the pariahs and sighthounds is evident in the racy, elegant body, streamlined head and lighter bone. Ears must be erect. Structurewise the Xolo is similar in appearance to the standard Manchester Terrier.

Their character is one of happy, though calm, temperament without fear. In fact, the Xolo makes a good alarm dog, noisy only when necessary. Considered totally hairless, he sometimes has a bit of fuzz on the top of the head and a hair or two on the tail. They are admired for their elegance, unique appearance, personality—and hairlessness. The very fact that they have no hair makes them a choice for allergic owners,

Toy Xoloitzcuintli, slate.

Toy Xoloitzcuintli.

with the side benefits of cleanliness, no doggy odor and no fleas!

Time saved on coat grooming, however, is spent on skin care. The fragile skin is susceptible to sunburn, drying irritations and tears from other dogs and objects. All hairless breeds must be protected from the cold by providing the knit sweater or coat that Nature left off. Although powderpuff coats occur in about one of three, they are disqualified and may not be shown.

The Mexican Hairless was recognized by AKC until 1959, when a lack of registrations and show entries caused it to be dropped. The CKC still recognizes the breed, and a nucleus of dedicated fanciers in North America still promote the small Mexican.

Above: Toy Xoloitzcuintli, coated variety. **Below:** Xoloitzcuintli, slate.

Above: Toy Xoloitzcuintli, coated variety, charcoal and white. **Below:** Toy Xoloitzcuintli, reddish gray.

YORKSHIRE TERRIER

COUNTRY: Great Britain
WEIGHT: Under 7 pounds
HEIGHT: 9 inches
COAT: Long, straight; glossy, fine and silky
COLOR: Blue/tan
REGISTRY: FCI, AKC, UKC, TKC, CKC
GROUP: Terrier

The Yorkshire came from the same district as the Airedale, appearing for the first time around 1850, with "Huddersfeld Ben" listed as the first Yorkie. His background is not well documented, although speculation says Old English Black/Tan Terriers contributed the general terrier outline and mental qualities. Maltese donated the long, silky coat and petite face. The Skye fixed terrier temperament while retaining the coat. Each breeder, however, may have used a different "recipe."

These small, silky-coated terriers were in great demand by the wealthy families of Yorkshire. Poor farmers and workers occasionally established a lucrative sideline by producing puppies to fill that demand, and the competition to "corner the market" made these breeders closed-mouthed about their formulas.

Yorkshire Terriers, adult and pup.

They were originally called Broken-haired Scotch or Yorkshire Terriers, although their coat is not similar to the other brokenhaired terriers. About 1870, the breed became known as the Yorkshire Terrier. He was promoted in the eastern US by Americans who adored the little sprite, as well as in England. The size of today's toy was set by choosing the smaller specimens of the original 12–14 pound variety. While the selective breeding was occurring, size varied from under three to 13 pounds. Coat, too, was much shorter, though silky even at that time. Terrier advocates of the time degraded the "dresser drawer dog" and predicted little future for him. How wrong they were! By the 20th century, he was prized throughout the world.

Yorkies are spunky, which was aptly evidenced by "Smokey," spoils of WWII. American William Wynne found the Yorkie in a shell hole near Japanese lines in New Guinea. Nobody claimed her, and she seemed not to understand either Japanese or English. Smokey backpacked through the rest of the war, accompanying Wynne on 150 air raids and 12 air-sea rescue missions. She even survived a typhoon at Okinawa. In between these feats, she learned tricks which entertained the troops and enabled her to assist the Signal Corps by carrying a telegraph wire through a 70–foot, eight-inch pipe. No timid toy, Smokey also jumped from a 30–foot tower with her specially made parachute. After the War, Smokey and Wynne were a hit at veterans' hospitals. A few years later, another Yorkie entered politics when "Pasha" trotted the halls of the White House with the Nixon family.

Their handy, pick-me-up size makes them ideal travel companions. As with most tiny toys, the Yorkie is not the best choice for young children. The smallest dog ever recorded, according to the *1985 Guinness Book of World Records*, is "Sylvia," a Yorkie adult, at ten ounces. Despite their size, however, they possess the typical terrier temperament and are spirited and self-assured. Affectionate and devoted to their owners, they won't hesitate to sound the alarm if danger lurks. Born black/tan, the black slowly changes to a dark steel blue by adulthood, enhanced by the rich tan markings. Routine grooming is necessary.

Yorkshire Terrier.

Trio of Yorkshire Terriers.

Yorkshire Terrier.

YUGOSLAVIAN HOUNDS

Balkan Hound

COUNTRY: Yugoslavia
WEIGHT: 44 pounds
HEIGHT: 18–21 inches
COAT: Short, but coarse, thick and flat
COLOR: Black and tan saddled
OTHER NAMES: Balkanski Gonič
REGISTRY: FCI
GROUP: Hound

Bosnian Roughhaired Hound

COUNTRY: Yugoslavia
WEIGHT: 35–53 pounds
HEIGHT: 18–22 inches
COAT: Long (4 inches); hard and bristly, with a thick undercoat
COLOR: Grain yellow, reddish yellow, earth gray, blackish; bicolors and tricolors also acceptable
OTHER NAMES: Bosanski Barak
REGISTRY: FCI
GROUP: Hound

Balkan Hound.

Yugoslavian Mountain Hound.

Istrian Hound, Smoothhaired

COUNTRY: Yugoslavia
WEIGHT: 35–50 pounds
HEIGHT: 18–21 inches
COAT: Short and fine
COLOR: White; orange or yellow markings mainly on ears, with a few markings allowed on body, especially at base of tail
OTHER NAMES: Kratkodlaki Itrski Gonič
REGISTRY: FCI
GROUP: Hound

Istrian Hound, Wirehaired

COUNTRY: Yugoslavia
WEIGHT: 35–53 pounds
HEIGHT: 18–23 inches
COAT: 2–3-inch wiry outer coat, close to the body; with eyebrows and beard; woolly undercoat
COLOR: White; orange or yellow markings mainly on ears, with a few markings allowed on body, especially at base of tail
OTHER NAMES: Resasti Itrski Gonič
REGISTRY: FCI
GROUP: Hound

Posavac Hound

COUNTRY: Yugoslavia
WEIGHT: 40 pounds
HEIGHT: 18–23 inches
COAT: ¾–1½ inches, thick, hard and wiry
COLOR: Shades of wheaten or red; white on chest, abdomen and paws allowed
OTHER NAMES: Posavski Gonič
REGISTRY: FCI
GROUP: Hound

Yugoslavian Mountain Hound

COUNTRY: Yugoslavia
WEIGHT: 44–55 pounds
HEIGHT: 18-22 inches
COAT: Thick, flat, short but coarse
COLOR: Black and tan
OTHER NAMES: Jugoslavenski Planinski Gonič
REGISTRY: FCI
GROUP: Hound

Posavac Hound.

Yugoslavian Tricolor Hound

COUNTRY: Yugoslavia
WEIGHT: 44–55 pounds
HEIGHT: 18–22 inches
COAT: Thick, flat, short but coarse
COLOR: Tricolor with lots of tan, white only on face, chest, tail tip, feet and legs
OTHER NAMES: Jugoslavenski Tribarvni Gonič
REGISTRY: FCI
GROUP: Hound

Although Yugoslavia was designated a country only in this century, the Slavic people who live there have an ancient history. Because the Yugoslavian ports on the Adriatic were on the major trade routes of the Phoenicians, all Slavic hounds have long roots reaching back to ancient times. They most likely are a mixture of the early sighthounds, which were almost pariah in type, crossed with the scenthounds of Europe.

These Yugoslavian dogs (and their Greek

Yugoslavian Tricolor Hound.

885

Smoothhaired Istrian Hound.

pitched, full voice.

The dogs of Istria differ from the other hounds of Yugoslavia because of their distinctive white-and-orange color. The lighter the shade of orange-yellow spots, the purer the dog is considered. They have a racier build, cat feet, a head with less stop and a higher set ear. The thinner the tail, the more valued the dog. The Wirehaired version, with his beard and brows, is slightly larger but judged by the same standard as the smooth. In recent years, the Wirehaired Istrian has been gaining proponents among nonhunters in Yugoslavia. His peaceful character makes him a fine house companion, and his striking appearance draws attention at dog shows.

The fertile northcentral plains along the Sava River of Yugoslavia are the home of the Posavac Hound. Little known outside its own locale, this dog is an esteemed hunting companion at home and is used for hare and deer. His bright red wheaten color creates a handsome effect. Much like the other Yugoslavian hounds, he is a bit low on leg. He is obedient and affectionate with the family.

Bosnia marks the beginning of the mountainous inland area in northcentral Yugoslavia. In the last century, the rough-jacketed Bosnian Hound was bred especially for withstanding bad weather and going over rough terrain. He is unknown outside his native country. The standard calls for a body length ten percent greater than height, a strong muzzle with beard and moustaches, heavy ears, and the four-inch rough coat.

The last three smooth-coated hounds of Yugoslavia are all from the south and are quite similar. The Mountain Hound is from the Planina range in southwestern Yugoslavia, the Balkan Hound is from the eastern regions near the Bulgarian border and the Tricolor is also from the south. Used over hostile terrain, they are all strong and untiring hunting "pros" for hare, fox, deer and even boar. The Balkan is known particularly for his high-pitched voice and his ability as a tracking dog. These breeds are not promoted outside their specific areas. Current correspondence from Yugoslavian breeders indicates that the Tricolor and Mountain Hounds are now very rare.

cousins) are the sole scenthounds of southeastern Europe and the Balkans. All are quite similar in type. They are moderate in size, slightly longer than tall and possess fairly good bone. The squarish head has no loose skin and moderate flat ears. While they are passionate hunters, untiring even over the roughest terrain, they all seem to be tranquil, good-natured and affectionate in the home.

Istrian dogs were probably the oldest of these, or at least most like the original type. Istria is a peninsula in the northwestern corner of Yugoslavia jutting out into the Adriatic Sea. Hounds from this area, now called Slovenia, are hunted in small packs or pairs over rough and heavy terrain for fox and hare and are especially sharp against the wild boar. The Istrian Hound is also a talented bloodtrailer and is known for his low-

Above: Smoothhaired Istrian Hound. **Below:** Wirehaired Istrian Hound.

Glossary

AKC. The commonly used abbreviation of American Kennel Club.

American Kennel Club. The official registry for purebred dogs in the United States. Publishes and maintains the Stud Book and handles all litter and individual registrations, transfers of ownership, and so on. Keeps all United States dog show, field trial, and obedience trial records; issues championships and other titles in these areas as they are earned; approves and licenses dog show, obedience trial, and field trial judges; licenses or issues approval to all championship shows, obedience trials, and recognized match shows. Creates and enforces the rules, regulations, and policies by which the breeding, raising, exhibiting, handling, and judging of purebred dogs in the United States are governed. Clubs, not individuals, are members of the American Kennel Club, each of which is represented by a delegate selected from the club's own membership for the purpose of attending the quarterly American Kennel Club meetings as the representative of the member club, to vote on matters discussed at each meeting and to bring back a report to the individual club of any decisions or developments which took place there.

Angulation. The angles formed by the meeting of the bones, generally referring to the shoulder and upper arm in the forequarters and the stifle and hock in the hindquarters.

Autosomal. All genes that are inherited on the regular chromosomes (NOT on the X/Y chromosome). Thus, they follow the regular rules of Mendelian dominance and recessiveness.

Balance. Symmetry and proportion. A wellbalanced dog is one in which all of the parts appear in correct ratio to one another: height to length, head to body, skull to foreface, and neck to head and body.

Beard. Long, thick hair growth on muzzle, especially the lower jaw.

Bench Show. A show where dogs are judged on their appearance. Although most modern shows allow the exhibitor to show his dog and then leave, in the past the dogs were put on display on a "bench" all day for spectators. Thus the term bench showing has remained as a general synonym for conformation showing.

Best in Show. The dog or bitch chosen as the most representative of any dog in any breed from among the group winners at an all-breed dog show. (The dog or bitch that has won Best of Breed next competes in the group of which its breed is a part. Then the first-prize winner of each group meets in an additional competition from which one is selected the Best in Show.)

Bitch. A female dog.

Bite. The manner in which the upper and lower jaws meet.

Black/Silver. A true black and silver has the solid black body with grayish silver markings above the eyes, on the cheeks, under the ears, on the forechest, on the feet and inside of the legs, and under the tail (e.g., Schnauzer).

Black/Tan. Just like the black/silver except the grayish silver points are tan in color (e.g., Rottweiler).

Black/Tan Saddled. The tan marks, as in the black/tan, are much larger including much of the head, upper legs, neck, and belly, and leaving the black only as a "saddle" on the back, as well as on the top of the neck and tail (e.g., German Shepherd Dog).

Blue. There are four distinct colors that are called "blue;" all are inherited differently:
1) *Blue (dilute):* Dogs born a solid steel or gun metal gray, *always* with a gray nose and paw pads (e.g., blue Great Dane or Chow). 2) *Blue (silvering, graying):* There is another "blue" that starts black and fades to a blue-gray in adulthood, *always* with a black nose (e.g., Kerry Blue Terrier). 3) *Blue (ticking):* Another "blue" is created by black roaning on white, *always* with a black nose (e.g., Grand Bleu de Gascogne). 4) *Blue Merle:* This is a marbled gray on black, *always* with a black nose, sometimes with blue eyes. Can also be called harlequin or mottled (e.g., merle Collie).

Bone. Refers to the girth of a dog's leg bones. A dog called "good in bone" has legs that are correct in girth for its breed and for its own general conformation. Well-rounded bone is roundish in appearance, flat bone rather flattish. Light bone is very fine and small in diameter, almost spindle-like in appearance; legs are extremely slender. Heavy bone refers to legs that are thick and sturdy.

Breed. Purebred dogs descended from mutual ancestors refined and developed by man.

Breeder. A person who breeds dogs.

Brisket. The forepart of the body between the forelegs and beneath the chest.

Brood bitch. A female dog used primarily for breeding.

CACIB. A Challenge Certificate offered by the Federation Cynologique Internationale towards a dog's championship.

Canadian Kennel Club. The principle dog registry in Canada. Formed in 1887, the organization devoted itself to the promotion of breeding and exhibiting 'thoroughbred' dogs in Canada, the formulation of rules for the governing of dog exhibition, as well as the recommendation of able judges and the official opening of a registry for purebred dogs.

Canines. Dogs, jackals, wolves, and foxes as a group.

Cat foot. The short-toed, round tight foot similar to that of a cat.

Ch. Commonly used abbreviation of champion.

Challenge Certificate. A card awarded at dog shows in Great Britain by which championship there is gained. Comparable to our Winners Dog and Winners Bitch awards. To become a British champion a dog must win three of these Challenge Certificates at designated championship dog shows.

Champion. A dog or bitch that has won a total of fifteen points, including two majors, the total number under not less than three judges, two of whom must have awarded the majors at AKC point shows.

Character. Appearance, behavior, and temperament considered correct in an individual breed of dog.

Cheeky. Cheeks which bulge out or are rounded in appearance.

Chest. The part of the body enclosed by the ribs.

Chiseled. Clean-cut below the eyes.

Chop Mouth. A hound that does not have a long, drawn out bay, but more of a short, choppy bark as he follows the scent trail.

Chops. Pendulous, loose skin creating jowls. *See* Flews.

CKC. Abbreviation for the Canadian Kennel Club.

Close-coupled. Compact in appearance. Short in the loin.

Closed Trailing. Refers to a dog that follows a scent trail silently.

Coarse. Lacking in refinement or elegance.

Coat. The hair which covers the dog.

Cold Nosed. Refers to a hound that is capable of following a "cold" scent, one that is either very old and/or one that is very difficult to find and follow.

Cold Trailer. Refers to a hound, usually slow working, that has the inherent ability of nose as well as the desire, endurance and tenacity to follow a cold trail.

Condition. General health. A dog said to be in good condition is one carrying exactly the right amount of weight, whose coat looks alive and glossy, and that exhibits a general appearance and demeanor of well-being.

Conformation. The framework of the dog, its form and structure.

Couching. This is a very old term describing hunting dogs that, when they scented game, slowly crept nearer while lowering themselves to the ground. This was a trait desired when birds were captured with nets, or when the dog found birds for the falcon.

Coupling. The section of the body known as the loin. A short-coupled dog is one in which the loin is short.

Crest. The arched portion of the back of the neck.

Crop. Cut the ear leather, usually to cause the ear to stand erect.

Croup. The portion of the back directly above the hind legs.

Cynology. A study of canines.

Dam. Female parent of a dog or bitch.

Dentition. Arrangement of the teeth.

Dewclaws. Extra claws on the inside of the legs. Should generally be removed several days following the puppy's birth. Required in some breeds, unimportant in others, and sometimes a disqualification—all according to the individual breed standard.

Dewlap. Excess loose and pendulous skin at the throat.

Dish-faced. The tip of the nose is placed higher than the stop.

Disqualification. A fault or condition which renders a dog ineligible to compete in organized shows, designated by the breed standard or by a leading dog registry.

Dock. Shorten the tail by cutting it.

Dog. A male of the species. Also used to describe male and female canines collectively.

Dog show. A competition in which dogs have been entered for the purpose of evaluation and to receive the opinion of a judge.

Domed. A top-skull that is rounded rather than flat.

Double coat. A coat consisting of a hard, weather-resistant, protective outer covering over a soft, short, close underlayer which provides warmth.

Down-faced. A downward inclination of the muzzle toward the tip of the nose. Also called a "ranis nose."

Drag. A trail having been prepared by dragging a bag, generally bearing the strong scent of an animal, along the ground.

Drive. The powerful action of the hindquarters which should equal the degree of reach of the forequarters.

Drop ear. Ears carried drooping or folded forward.

Dry head. One exhibiting no excess wrinkle.

Dry neck. A clean, firm neckline free of throatiness or excess skin.

Dual champion. A dog having gained both bench show and field trial championships.

Elbow. The joint of the forearm and upper arm.

Even bite. Exact meeting of the front teeth, tip to tip with no overlap of the uppers or lowers. Generally considered to be less serviceable than the scissors bite, although equally permissible or preferred in some breeds. Also known as level bite.

Expression. The typical expression of the breed as one studies the head. Determined largely by the shape of the eye and its placement.

Fancier. A person actively involved in the sport of purebred dogs.

Fancy. The enthusiasts of a sport or hobby. Dog breeders, exhibitors, judges, and others actively involved with purebred dogs as a group comprise the dog fancy.

Fawn. There are two different colors which can be referred to as "fawn."
1) *Fawn* (*brown*): A tan color ranging from light chamois to red wheaten, often with shadings of the red or even black tips on the hairs. *Always* with a black nose. Genetically, this color is the same as sable (e.g., Boxer). 2) *Fawn* (*gray*): There is another color sometimes called "fawn" which is a pale grayish brown dilution of brown and blue. These dogs *always* have a pale gray to flesh-colored nose (e.g., Weimaraner).

FCI. Abbreviation of the Federation Cynologique Internationale.

Feathering. The longer fringes of hair that appear on the ears, tail, chest, and legs.

Federation Cynologique Internationale. A canine authority representing numerous countries, principally European, all of which consent to and agree on certain practices and breed identifications. Recognizing each breed of the countries it includes, the FCI registers about 400 breeds—each of the breeds that are federated are thusly eligible for International Championship.

Fetch. Retrieving of game by a dog, or the command for the dog to do so.

Field champion. A dog that has gained the title field champion has defeated a specified number of dogs in specified competition at a series of American Kennel Club licensed or member field trials.

Field trial. A competition for specified Hound or Sporting breeds where dogs are judged according to their ability and style on following a game trail or on finding and retrieving game.

Finishing a dog. Refers to completing a dog's championship, obedience title, or field trial title.

Flank. The side of the body through the loin area.

Flat bone. Bones of the leg which are not round.

Flat-sided. Ribs that are flat down the side rather than slightly rounded.

Fld. Ch. Abbreviation of field champion, used as a prefix before the dog's name.

Flews. A pendulous condition of the skin at the corners of the mouth.

Flush. To drive birds from cover. To spring at them. To force them to take flight.

Flying ears. Ears correctly carried dropped or folded that stand up or tend to "fly" upon occasion.

Foreface. The muzzle of the dog.

Front. The forepart of the body viewed head-on. Includes the head, forelegs, shoulders, chest, and feet.

Gait. The manner in which a dog walks or trots.

Gallop. The fastest gait. Never to be used in the show ring, but often used when hunting, racing, etc.

Game. The animals or wild birds which are hunted.

Gay tail. Tail carried high.

Gazehound. A general name for the swift hounds that run by sight; a synonym for sighthound or windhound.

Get. Puppies.

Groom. To bathe, brush, comb, and trim your dog.

Groups. Refers to the variety groups in which all breeds of dogs are divided.

Gun Dog. One that has been specifically trained to work with man in the field for retrieving game that has been shot and for locating live game.

Guns. The persons who do the shooting during field trials.

Gun-shy. Describes a dog that cringes or shows other signs of fear at the sound or sight of a gun.

Hackney action. High lifting of the forefeet in the manner of a hackney pony.

Hard-mouthed. A dog that grasps the game too firmly in retrieving, causing bites and tooth marks.

Hare foot. An elongated paw, like the foot of a hare.

Haw. This is the red membrane (third eyelid) in the inner corner of a dog's eye. When a dog has a lot of heavy facial skin or loose hanging lids, the haw is more apparent.

Hock. The joint between the second thigh and the metatarsus.

Honorable scars. Those incurred as a result of working injuries.

Hot nosed. Refers to a dog that can follow a fresh trail, one made by an animal that has a scent that is easy to follow (like a fox).

Hot trailing. Refers to a hound that follows a hot scent, usually at much greater speed than the cold nosed dog.

Int. Ch. An abbreviation of International Champion.

International Champion. A dog awarded four CACIB cards at F.C.I. dog shows.

Jowls. Flesh of lips and jaws.

Kennel. The building in which dogs are housed. Also used when referring to a person's collective dogs.

Kennel Club. The Kennel Club of Great Britain is the principle dog registering organization in the country and was founded in 1873. The registry's objective and purpose is set forth in its rule number I as "promoting the improvement of Dogs, Dog Shows, Field Trials, Working Trials and Obedience Tests." Functioning in an advisory capacity to the organization is an elected body of persons with similar objectives to the club, breeding, training and exhibiting purebred dogs.

Layback. 1) Describes correctly angulated shoulders. 2) Describes a short-faced dog whose pushed-in nose placement is accompanied by undershot jaw.

Leather. The ear flap. Also the skin of the actual nose.

Level bite. Another way of describing an even bite, as teeth of both jaws meet exactly.

Lippy. Lips that are pendulous or do not fit tightly.

Liver. A brown color ranging from reddish to chocolate, *always* with a brown nose and paw pads (e.g., Irish Water Spaniel).

Loin. Area of the sides between the lower ribs and hindquarters.

Loose-eyed. Refers to sheep-herding dogs that can direct sheep by eye contact (see strong-eyed) but can also round up by heeling; their eye contact is not as intense as the strong-eyed dog.

Lumbering. A clumsy, awkward gait.

Lure coursing. Sighthounds used to course after live game, but most modern contests use a rag or mechanical lure for the dogs to chase.

Mane. The long hair growing on the top and upper sides of the neck.

Mate. To breed a dog and a bitch to one another. Littermates are dogs which are born in the same litter.

Merle. *See* Blue Merle.

Miscellaneous Class. A class provided at AKC point shows in which specified breeds may compete in the absence of their own breed classification. Dogs of breeds in the process of becoming recognized by AKC may compete in this class prior to the eventual provision of their own individual breed classification.

Mustache. Long, thick hair growth on the upper muzzle.

Muzzle. 1) The part of the head in front of the eyes. 2) To fasten something over the mouth, usually to prevent biting.

Nick. A successful breeding that results in puppies of excellent quality.

Non-slip retriever. A dog not expected to flush or to find game; one that merely walks at heel, marks the fall, then retrieves upon command.

Nose. Describes the dog's organ of smell, but also refers to his talent at scenting. A dog with a "good nose" is one adept at picking up and following a scent trail.

Obedience trial. A licensed obedience trial is one held under AKC rules at which it is possible to gain a "leg" towards a dog's obedience title or titles.

Obedience trial champion. Denotes that a dog has attained obedience trial championship under AKC regulations by having gained a specified number of points and first place awards.

Occiput. Upper back point of skull.

O.F.A. Commonly used abbreviation for Orthopedic Foundation for Animals.

Open trailing: Refers to a hound that begins baying as soon as he has found the scent (opens) and continues as long as he is on the trail.

Orthopedic Foundation for Animals. This organization is ready to read the hip radiographs of dogs and certify the existence of or freedom from hip dysplasia. Board-certified radiologists read vast numbers of these files each year.

O.T. Ch. An abbreviation of the obedience trial champion title.

Pad. Thick protective covering of the bottom of the foot. Serves as a shock absorber.

Parti-colored. A spotted dog, *see* Pied.

Patterned white. White markings restricted to a symmetrical pattern on feet, tail tip, chest mark, facial blaze, and sometimes a collar, also called "Boston" or "Irish" spotting (e.g., Boston Terrier).

Pied. Patches of color on a white background, also called piebald, parti-color, or "broken" pattern. When there are two colors, it is called bi-colored and, if there are three, the dog is referred to as tri-color (e.g., Pointer).

Pile. Soft hair making a dense undercoat.

Plume. A long fringe of hair on the tail.

Poach. To trespass on private property when hunting.

Police dog. Any dog that has been trained to do police work.

Quality. Excellence of type and conformation.

Racy. Lightly built, appearing overly long in leg and lacking substance.

Rangy. Excessive length of body combined with shallowness through the ribs and chest.

Reach. The distance to which the forelegs reach out in gaiting, which should correspond with the strength and drive of the hindquarters.

Register. To record your dog with your dog-registering organization.

Roach back. A convex curvature of the top-line of the dog.

Roan. Individual colored hairs in the white markings. Red hairs create a "red roan" and black hairs give a steel gray appearance called "blue" or "blue roan" (e.g., Australian Cattle Dog).

Rolling gait. An aimless, ambling type of action correct in some breeds but to be faulted in others.

Sable. A rich reddish brown with shadings of color, may or may not have black tipping on each hair. Genetically it is the same as tan fawn (e.g., Rough Collie).

Scissors bite. The outer tips of the lower incisors touch the inner tips of the upper incisors. Generally considered to be the most serviceable type of jaw formation.

Self-colored. When a dog is a solid color, without white markings.

Semi-open trailing. Refers to a dog that will bark some of the time on trail (e.g., chop mouth), but really begins howling when he has the quarry treed.

Shelly. A body lacking in substance.

Shoulder height. The height of the dog from the ground to the highest point of the withers.

Sire. The male parent.

Soundness. Mental and physical stability. Sometimes used as well to denote the manner in which the dog gaits.

Stake. A class in field trial competition.

Standard. The official description of the ideal specimen of a breed. The Standard of Perfection is drawn up by the parent specialty club (usually by a special committee to whom the task is assigned), is approved by the membership and by the American Kennel Club, and then serves as a guide to breeders and to judges in decisions regarding the merit, or lack of it, in evaluating individual dogs.

Stifle. The joint of the hind leg corresponding to a person's knee.

Stop. The step-up from nose to skull; the indentation at the juncture of the skull and foreface.

Straight behind. Lacking angulation in the hindquarters.

Strong-eyed. Refers to sheep-herding dogs who have intense qualities of staring down and almost hypnotically directing sheep by eye contact.

Stud. A male dog that is used for breeding.

Stud book. The official record kept on the breeding particulars of recognized breeds of dogs.

Substance. Degree of bone size.

Tail set. Manner in which the tail is placed on the rump.

Thigh. Hindquarters from the stifle to the hip.

Throatiness. Excessive loose skin at the throat.

Ticking: Small dots of color in the white markings, "freckles" (e.g., English Springer Spaniel).

TKC. Abbreviation for The Kennel Club of Great Britain employed in this atlas. *See* Kennel Club.

Tongue: This term is used as a synonym for bay, howl or "open," all terms meaning the dog is vocal when he is following a scent trail.

Topline. The dog's back from withers to tail set.

Trail. Hunt by following a trail scent.

Tricolor. Indicating black/tan or chocolate/tan in combinations of white. There are several forms of the color.

1) *Pied tricolor*: White and black spots broken over the entire body, plus tan marks over eyes, on cheeks, under ears, on feet and around vent (e.g., English Toy Spaniel, Prince Charles variety). 2) *Saddled tricolor*: White and tan spots evenly distributed, plus the black saddle (e.g., Foxhound). 3) *Patterned tricolor*: A true black/tan color plus white blaze, chest, feet, tail tip (e.g., Bernese Mountain Dog).

Trot. The gait at which the dog moves in a rhythmic two-beat action, right front and left hind foot and left front and right hind foot each striking the ground together.

Tuck-up. The amount of "waist line" behind the rib cage, measured as the depth of body at the loin. The Greyhound has a large amount of tuck-up, while the Mastiff has very little.

Type. The combination of features which makes a breed unique, distinguishing it from all others.

UKC. Abbreviation for the United Kennel Club.

Undershot. The front teeth of the lower jaw reach beyond the front teeth of the upper jaw.

United Kennel Club. United Kennel Club (UKC) was established in 1898 by Mr. Chauncey Z. Bennett and is the second largest all-breed registry in the United States. It is privately owned and controlled, and has developed the only complete computer registry system. Through its outstanding registration system, the UKC offers a six- or seven-generation pedigree to qualifying registrants. The UKC is the first registry to recognize all six breeds of Coonhound.

Upper arm. The foreleg between the forearm and the shoulder blade.

Vent. A synonym for the anus, or the area under the tail.

Walk. The gait in which three feet support the body, each lifting in regular sequence, one at a time, off the ground.

W.C. An abbreviation of Working Certificate.

Withers. The highest point of the shoulders, right behind the neck.

Working Certificate. An award earned by dogs who have proven their hunting ability and who are not gun-shy.

Bibliography

Alzugaray, Domingo and Catia, eds., *Fox Paulistinha*, Editora Tres Ltda, Sao Paulo, SP.

American Chinese Crested Club official brochure.

American Kennel Club official publication, *The Complete Dog Book*, Doubleday & Co., Inc., Garden City, NY, 1968.

American Kennel Gazette, "Dogs from the Roof of the World," 3/37.

Anatolian Shepherd Dog Club of America Newsletter, 2/84.

Anatolian Shepherd Dog Club of America official pamphlet.

Archer, Colleen, "Canada's Native Dog," *Dog World*, 8/85, p. 22.

Arnold, Cecilia, "A Tribute to History," *Pure-Bred Dogs/-American Kennel Gazette*, 12/86, pp. 34-41.

Ash, Edward C., *Dogs: Their History and Development*, Vol. I, 1st published London, 1927, reissued by Benjamin Blom, Inc., New York, 1972.

_____. *The New Book of the Dog*, MacMillan Co., New York, 1939.

v. August Grimpe, Druck, Deutsches Hunde-Stamm Buch, Hannover, 1881.

Australian Kennel Control Council official publication, *Dogs of Australia*, Hedges and Bell Printing, Singapore, 1984.

Balmain, Margot, "The True Blue Australian," *Dog Fancy*, 3/87, p. 44.

Barker, A.J. and H.A., *The Complete Book of Dogs*, Bison Books, Ltd., London, 1982.

Barnard, Charles N., "The Descendants of Walden's Dog," *True*, Feb. 19??, pp. 37-38, 62-63.

Beresford, Pat, "A Golden Jubilee," *Pure-Bred Dogs/American Kennel Gazette*, 11/86, pp. 70-73.

_____. "Duality of Purpose," *Pure-Bred Dogs/American Kennel Gazette*, 1/87, p. 61.

Bergstrom, Enid S., "Ovcharka—the 'New' Police Dog?" *Dog World*, 2/83, pp. 14-15.

Berners, Dame Juliana, *Boke of St. Albans*, 1486.

Bernues, Juan Fernando, Carlos Contera Alejandre, et al., *El Libro del Mastin del Pirineo*, Guara Editorial, Zaragoza, Spain 1983.

Bixler, Alice, "The Loverly Lowchen," *Dogs in Canada*, 12/81, pp. 14-15.

Bobb, Maggie, "Confessions of a Filaphile," *Dog World*, 1/86, pp. 26, 83-86.

The Borzoi Club of America, Inc., official publications.

Boxhall-James, Betty, "Chinese Crested Powderpuff and Hairless," English Club Newsletter.

Boykin Spaniel Society official brochure, Camden, SC.

Brandenburger, Dale, *Plott Hound History*.

Braund, Kathryn, *The Uncommon Dog Breeds*, Arco, New York, 1975.

Braund, Kathryn and Deyanne F. Miller, *The Complete Portuguese Water Dog*, Howell Book House, NY, NY, 1986.

Brearley, Joan McDonald, *The Book of the Afghan Hound*, T.F.H. Publications, Inc., Neptune City, NJ, 1978.

_____. *The Book of the Akita*, T.F.H. Publications, Inc., Neptune City, NJ, 1985.

_____. *The Book of the Bulldog*, T.F.H. Publications, Inc., Neptune City, NJ, 1985.

_____. *The Book of the Cocker Spaniel*, T.F.H. Publications, Inc., Neptune City, NJ, 1982.

_____. *The Book of the Maltese*, T.F.H. Publications, Inc., Neptune City, NJ, 1984.

_____. *The Book of the Yorkshire Terrier*, T.F.H. Publications, Inc., Neptune City, NJ, 1984.

The Briard Club of America official brochure.

Brisbin, Dr. I. Lehr, Jr., "Primitive Dogs," *Pure-Bred Dogs/American Kennel Gazette*, 3/87, p. 79.

Brown, E. Jane, "Polish Pup Shows Pizzazz," *Dog World*, 7/83, p. 132.

Browne, A. Gondrexon-Ives, *The Hamlyn Guide to Dogs*, Hamlyn Pub. Group, Ltd., London, 1974.

Bruce, James Jr., "Early History," Redbone Coonhound Club of America Yearbook.

Burger, Carl, *All About Dogs*, Random House, 1962.

Burgoin, Gillian, *Guide to the Weimaraner*, The Boydell Press, Suffolk, England, 1985.

Butrick, Carol, "A Tervriffic Event, An Historic Perspective," *Pure-Bred Dogs/American Kennel Gazette*, 11/86, p. 63.

Byrd, Richard Evelyn, *Little America*, G.P. Putnam's Sons, New York, 1930.

Caius, Iohannes (Johannes), *Of English Dogges*, London, 1576; modern reproduction DaCapo Press, NY, 1969.

Calif, Lee, "Keeping the Memories Alive," *Canine Chronicle*, 5/31/86.

Calkins, Diane, "Pit Bulls," *Dog Fancy*, 8/86, pp. 36-37, 41-43.

Canaan Club of America, Inc., brochure, "Canaan Dog."

Canadian Kennel Club official publication, *The Canadian Kennel Club Book of Dogs*, General Publishing Co., Ltd., Toronto, Canada, 1982.

Canine Chronicle, "Chinese Crested to Rejoin Miscellaneous Group Feb. 1," 1/4/86, p. 32.

Canine Chronicle, "Petit Basset Griffon Vendeen Find a

New Home with CKC," 7/31/85, p. 26.

Canine Classified, ed. Anne Page, "Petit Basset Griffon Vendeen," Vol. IV, issue 3, 3/86, pp. 16, 18, 20.

Caras, Roger, *A Celebration of Dogs*, Times Books, 1982.

———. "A Plea for the Chinook," *Long Island Newsday Magazine*, 3/20/84.

Cavill, David, *All About the Spitz Breeds*, Pelham Books Ltd., England, 1978.

Clouse, Col. Dorman W., "History of the Redbone," Redbone Coonhound Club of America Yearbook.

Cooper, Mrs. B.M., "The Origin and Development of the Australian Kelpie."

Coppinger, Lorna and the International Sled Dog Racing Assoc., *The World of Sled Dogs*, Howell Book House, NY, NY, 1977.

Coppinger, Lorna and Raymond, "So Firm a Friendship," *Natural History*, Vol. 89, No. 3, 3/80.

———. "Livestock-Guarding Dogs," *Blair & Ketchum's Country Journal*, Vol. VII, No. 4, 4/80, pp. 68-77.

———. *Livestock Guarding Dogs for U.S. Agriculture*, Livestock Dog Project, Montague, MA, 1978.

Crisp, W.G., "Tahltan Bear Dog," *Dogs in Canada*, 12/56, pp. 13-15.

Dangerfield, Stanley and Elsworth Howell, eds., *The International Encyclopedia of Dogs*, Rainbird Reference Books, Ltd., London, 1971.

Dannen, Kent and Donna, "The Samoyed," *Dog Fancy*, 2/87, pp. 36, 41.

Darwin, Charles, *The Zoology of the Voyage of H.M.S. Beagle*, Nova Pacifica Pub., Wellington, NZ, 1833.

Davis, Henry P., revised and updated, *The New Dog Encyclopedia*, Stackpole Books, Harrisburg, PA, 1970.

De Bernes, Suzanne, "The Italian Spinone," *Our Dogs*, England, 5/20/82, p. 10.

Debo, Ellen Weathers, *The Shar-Pei*, T.F.H. Publications, Inc., Neptune City, NJ, 1986.

Demidoff, Lorna and Michael Jennings, *The Complete Siberian Husky*, 1st Ed., Howell Book House, NY, NY, 1978.

Deutscher Landseer Club (1976-1981), E.V. Zuchtbuch, Netherlands, 1983.

Dickerson, S.M., *Chinese Crested*.

Diwan of Abu Nuwas, Court Poet and Jester, 800 A.D.

Dimov, D., *Dogs of the Soviet Union*, Vadim Yudin, translator, unpublished manuscript.

Dogo Argentino Club of America, Goodland, IN, "The Dogo Argentino," *Canine Chronicle*, 12/17/86, p. 4a.

Dogs USA, Susan Pearce, ed., Elizabeth Dunn, pub., Ontario, Canada, 10/86.

Dog World Magazine, official standards issue, Maclean Hunter Publishing Corp., Chicago, IL, 6/86.

Donahue, Jane B., "Puli Power," *Pure-Bred Dogs/American Kennel Gazette*, 1/84, p. 41.

Donovan, John A.K., *The Irish Wolfhound—the Great Symbol of Ireland*, Alpine Publication, Inc., Loveland, CO, 1986.

Dorl, J., "The 'Imperial' Pekingese," *Pure-Bred Dogs/American Kennel Gazette*, 5/86, p. 37.

Draper, Dr. Samuel and Joan M. Brearley, *The Book of the*

Chow Chow, T.F.H. Publications, Inc., Neptune City, NJ, 1977.

Drury, Mrs. Maynard K., *This is the Newfoundland*, T.F.H. Publications, Inc., Neptune City, NJ, 1978.

Dullinger, Betty R., "The Yorkshire Terrier," *Dog Fancy*, 5/87, pp. 36, 41.

Durant, John, "Prodigious Perry Greene," *The Saturday Evening Post*, 1/11/17, pp. 26-27, 63, 66, 68-69.

The Dutch Sheepdog Club official brochure, Kloosterburen, Netherlands.

Egan, Pierce, "The Bull Bait," *Sporting Anecdotes*, 1820.

English, Dorothy, "Can You Name This Dog?" *Dog Fancy*, 1/87, p. 60.

Eskimo Dog Club of Great Britain, *The Eskimo Dog*.

Fiennes, Richard and Alice, *The Natural History of Dogs*, Bonanza Books, New York, 1968.

The Finnish Spitz Club of America official publication.

Fiorone, Fiorenzo, *The Encyclopedia of Dogs; The Canine Breeds*, Thomas Y. Crowell Company, New York, (first pub. in Italy as *Enciclopedia del Cane* in 1970), translation copyright 1973 by Rizzoli Editore.

Flamholtz, Cathy J., *A Celebration of Rare Breeds*, OTR Publications, 1986.

Foy, Marcia, *The Basset Hound*, T.F.H. Publications, Inc., Neptune City, NJ, 1985.

Foy, Marcia and Anna Katherine Nicholas, *The Beagle*, T.F.H. Publications, Inc., Neptune City, NJ, 1985.

Fraser, Jackie, "Chow Mania, An Ancient History," *Pure-Bred Dogs/American Kennel Gazette*, 8/86, p. 65.

———. "Dignified and Loving," *Pure-Bred Dogs/American Kennel Gazette*, 1/85, p. 37.

———. "The Early Days," *Pure-Bred Dogs/American Kennel Gazette*, 2/86.

———. "Evolution of the Miniature Pinscher," *Pure-Bred Dogs/American Kennel Gazette*, 6/86, p. 55.

Freedman, Alix M., "Rabbits Can Relax When a Basset Pack is Hunting for Them," The *Wall Street Journal*, 11/19/85.

Gentry, Diane K., "Blue Lacys—Instinctive 'Cowboys'," *Dog Fancy*, 3/87, pp. 46-47.

Gordon, J.F., *An Illustrated Guide to Some Rare and Unusual Dog Breeds*, John Bartholomew & Son, London, 1975.

Great Lakes Canaan Club official brochure, Hoffman Estates, IL.

Green, Jeffrey S. & Roger A. Woodruff, *Guarding Dogs Protect Sheep From Predators*, U.S. Sheep Experiment Station, Dubois, Idaho, 1/83.

Guillet, Dr. Emile, *Les Chiens Courants D'Aujour D'Hui*, ed. du Passage, Paris.

Gyes, Nancy, "Introducing the Hovawart," *Animal Times*, Palo Alto, CA, 9/86.

Hancock, David, "Saving the Danish Breeds," *Pure-Bred Dogs/American Kennel Gazette*, 7/86.

Harling, Donn and Deborah, *Australian Cattle Dogs—The First 5 Years 1980–1985*, Sun Graphics, Parsons, KS, 1986.

Hart, Ernest H., *Encyclopedia of Dog Breeds*, T.F.H. Publications, Inc., Neptune City, NJ, 1975.

———. *The German Shepherd Dog*, T.F.H. Publications, Inc., Neptune City, NJ, 1985.

Hartop, Judith J., "Man & Animals," *Pure-Bred Dogs/American Kennel Gazette*, 11/84, pp. 54-57.

Helle, Nancy, "The Portuguese Water Dog Makes Waves in America," *The Greenwich Review Magazine*, 3/77, pp. 18-21.

Hinchliffe, Nigel, "The Patterdale Terrier," *The Working Terrier Yearbook*, Vol. 3, 1985.

Holler, Heinz, *Schnauzer und Pinscher*, Eugen Ulmer GmbH & Co., 1986, pp. 42-43.

Hovawart Club of Germany, *Unser Hovawart*.

Howe, Dorothy, *The Labrador Retriever*, T.F.H. Publications, Inc., Neptune City, NJ, 1985.

Hubbard, Clifford L.B., *Dogs in Britain*, MacMillan & Co., Ltd., London, 1948, pp. 291-293.

———. *Working Dogs of the World*, Sidgwick and Jackson Ltd., London, 1947.

Huddleston, Arthur, *The Boston Terrier*, Denlinger's Publishers, Ltd., Fairfax, VA, 1985.

Irick, Mackey J. Jr., *The New Poodle*, 6th Ed., Howell Book House, NY, NY, 1986.

Jerome, Jerome K. in Wood, Margaretta, "Norfolk/Norwich Terrier column," *Pure-Bred Dogs/American Kennel Gazette*, 2/87, p. 156.

Junko, Fujino, "The Dogs of Japan," *The East*, Vol, VIII, No. 3, 3/72, pp 28-35.

Kaleski, Robert, *Australian Barkers and Biters*, The Endeavor Press, Sydney, Australia, 1933.

Kalstone, Shirlee, "Origins of Trimming the Poodle," *Pure-Bred Dogs/American Kennel Gazette*, 4/87, pp. 14-15.

Kanzler, Kathleen, Sheila Balch, Dolly and Robert Ward, "The Arctic Breeds—The Similarities and the Differences," *Kennel Review*, 10/81, pp. 1-3.

Karr, Diana L., "The English Shepherd as a Watchdog," *Bloodlines*, 7-8/81, pp. 30-31.

Kenyon, Dorothy and Ann, *Japanese Spitz*, E.G. Parrott, Torquay, 1979.

Kline, David Van Gordon, "The Border Terrier," *Dog Fancy*, 5/87, pp. 42-43.

v. Kramer, Eva Maria, "Der Schapendoes aus Holland," *Hendewelt*, 9/86, pp. 270-271.

Lane, Marion S., ed., *Pure-Bred Dogs/American Kennel Gazette*, Anniversary Issue, 2/87.

———."To the Harness Born," *Pure-Bred Dogs/American Kennel Gazette*, 7/86, pp. 42-43.

Lanting, Fred, "An American Dog Watcher in Japan," *Dog World*, 8/85, pp. 12-13, 135, 137, 146-147, 149.

Large Munsterlander Club brochure, Bishop's Stortford Herts., England.

Larsen, Linda and Richard W. Eichhorn, *The Tibetan Mastiff Owner's Manual*, Drakyi Tibetan Mastiffs, Sherman Oaks, CA, 1982.

Laws of Canute, No. 31, 1016 A.D.

Lehman, Patricia F., "The West Highland White Terrier," *Dog Fancy*, 1/87, pp. 36-41.

Levy, Joy C., "Problems in a Rare Breed," *The World of the Working Dog*, 7-8/76, pp. 21-22.

Litell, Richard J., "The Puffin Dog," *SAS Magazine Scanorama*, 4-5/76.

Llewellyn, Zell, "An Introduction to the Shar-Pei," *Bloodlines*, 11-12/82.

———. "The Barbet Dog—National Water Dog of France," *Portuguese Water Dog Cruise Lines*, 1-2/87, pp. 14-15.

Lorenz, Karl, *Man Meets Dog*, Penguin Books, 1973.

MacLeod, Norm and Altoona, *The Australian Kelpie Handbook*, Victoria, Australia, 2nd Ed., 4/85.

McLeroth, Diane, *The Briard: A Collection*, Aubry Assoc. and The Briard Club of America, Baraboo, WI, 1982.

McLoughlin, John, *The Canine Clan: A New Look at Man's Best Friend*, The Viking Press, NY, 1983.

McWhirter, Norris and Ross, David A. Boehm, Maris Cakars, *Guinness Book of World Records*, Special Edition, Sterling Publishing Co., Inc., New York, 1985.

Malo Alcrudo, Rafael, et al., eds., *El Libro del Mastin del Pireneo*, Guara Editorial, Zaragoza, Spain, 1983.

Mansencal, Guy, "Pyrenean Sheepdog," Tarbes, France.

The Maremma Sheepdog Club of Great Britain, official booklet.

Martin, Bobi, "Chinooks: Fighting to Survive," *Dog World*, 10/85, pp. 14, 118.

Martin, Inge, "The Inca Hairless Dog," *Americas*, 7/-8/83, pp. 26-29.

Maxwell, C. Bede, *The Truth About Sporting Dogs*, Howell Book House, Inc., New York, NY.

Menzel, Drs. R. & R., *Pariah Dogs: A History of the Canaan Dog Breed*, translated by Bryna Comsky, 1982.

Messerschmidt, Donald A., PhD, "The Tibetan Mastiff Color, Coat and Collar," *Dog World*, 9/83.

Middle Atlantic States Komondor Club, Inc., booklet, 1980.

Miller, Felicity, "Letters," *The Sled Dog*, Glemsford, Suffolk, England, 8/86, pp. 15-17.

Millington, Ann, "A Very Rare Breed, Indeed!" *Canine Chronicle*, 4/84.

Miniature Bull Terrier Club of America pamphlet.

Mondador, Arnoldo, ed., *Le Enciclopedic di Arianna*.

Mureen, Sigrid, "Island Working Dogs," *Pure-Bred Dogs American Kennel Club*, 9/86, p. 71.

Nederlandse Vereniging Voor Stabij-En Wetterhounen, *De Fryske Hounen*, n.d.

Nelson, David D., "The Kangal Dog of Turkey," *Dog World*, 3/85.

Nelson, David D. and Judith N., "Akbash Dog, A Turkish Breed for Home and Agriculture," The Akbash Dog Assn. Intl. Inc., Wilmington, DE, 1983.

Nicholas, Anna Katherine, *The Book of the English Springer Spaniel*, T.F.H. Publications, Inc., Neptune City, NJ, 1983.

———. *The Book of the German Shepherd Dog*, T.F.H. Publications, Inc., Neptune City, NJ, 1983.

———. *The Book of the Miniature Schnauzer*, T.F.H. Publications, Inc., Neptune City, NJ, 1986.

———. *The Book of the Shetland Sheepdog*, T.F.H. Publications, Inc., Neptune City, NJ, 1984.

———. *The Boxer*, T.F.H. Publications, Inc., Neptune City, NJ, 1984.

――――. *The Boston Terrier*, T.F.H. Publications, Inc., Neptune City, NJ, 1988.

――――. *The Chihuahua*, T.F.H. Publications, Inc., Neptune City, NJ, 1988.

――――. *The Chow Chow*, T.F.H. Publications, Inc., Neptune City, NJ, 1985.

――――. *The Collie*, T.F.H. Publications, Inc., Neptune City, NJ, 1986.

――――. "The Collie," *Dog Fancy*, 12/86, p. 36.

――――. *The Dachshund*, T.F.H. Publications, Inc., Neptune City, NJ, 1987.

――――. *The Dalmatian*, T.F.H. Publications, Inc., Neptune City, NJ, 1986.

――――. *The Fox Terrier*, T.F.H. Publications, Inc., Neptune City, NJ, 1989.

――――. *The German Pointer (Shorthaired and Wirehaired)*, T.F.H. Publications, Inc., Neptune City, NJ, 1985.

――――. *The Great Dane*, T.F.H. Publications, Inc., Neptune City, NJ, 1988.

――――. *The Keeshond*, T.F.H. Publications, Inc., Neptune City, NJ, 1985.

――――. *The Lhasa Apso*, T.F.H. Publications, Inc., Neptune City, NJ, 1989.

――――. *The Maltese*, T.F.H. Publications, Inc., Neptune City, NJ, 1984.

――――. *The Pekingese*, T.F.H. Publications, Inc., Neptune City, NJ, 1989.

――――. *The Poodle*, T.F.H. Publications, Inc., Neptune City, NJ, 1984.

――――. *The Weimaraner*, T.F.H. Publications, Inc., Neptune City, NJ, 1986.

――――. *The World of Doberman Pinschers*, T.F.H. Publications, Inc., Neptune City, NJ, 1986.

Norwegian Buhund Magazine of Great Britain, "The Buhund Nature," 1980.

Norwegian Lundehund Club, "The Lundehund."

Pagel, Adrienne, "Vive La Difference," *Pure-Bred Dogs/-American Kennel Gazette*, 11/86, pp. 66-68.

Parsons, A.D., *The Working Kelpie*, Nelson Pub., Melbourne, Victoria, Australia, 1986.

Peterson, Clementione, *The Complete Keeshond*, Howell Book House, NY, NY.

Pielanen-Degenhardt, E., "De Saarloos Wolfhond," *De Hondenwereld*, Asten, Netherlands, November, 1985.

――――. *Nederlandse Vereniging van Saarlooswolfhonden*, Oud-Beyerland, Netherlands.

Pugnetti, Gino, *Guide to Dogs*, ed., Elizabeth Meriwether Schuler, Simon & Schuster, NY, NY, 1980.

Pye, Roger F. F.S.A., *The Estrela Mountain Dog and Its Background*, Oporto, 1980.

Raber, Hans, *Die Schweizer Hunderassen*.

Rahn, Mike, "For Whom the Dog Tolls," *Fins and Feathers*, Vol. 14, No. 2, 2/85, pp. 48-49, 51-52.

Redditt, JoAnne, *The Chinese Shar Pei Puppy Book*.

Riddle, Maxwell, *Dogs in History*, Denliger's Ltd., Fairfax, VA, 1987.

――――. "My Portuguese Castro Laboreiros," *Dog World*, 1/84, pp 20, 47, 48.

Rine, Josephine, *The World of Dogs*, Doubleday & Co., Garden City, NY, 1965, Dolphin Books Edition 1973.

Robinson, Jerome B., "Decoy Dogs," *Sports Afield*, 8/81, pp. 64, 106-109.

Rorem, Linda, "Three American Herding Breeds," *Dog Fancy*, 3/87, pp. 42-43.

Rutledge, Richard, "Skye Terrier Column - Vocabulary Lesson," *Pure-Bred Dogs/American Kennel Gazette*, 11/86, p. 140.

Sammon, Edy, "Pure-bred World. The Pit Bull Controversy," *Dog Fancy*, p. 54, 8/86.

Scott, Willie and Edwin, "The American Hairless Terrier, *Bloodlines*, 5-6/86, pp. 16-17.

Seiger, Herr H.F. and Dr. F. von Dewitz-Colpin, *The Complete German Shorthaired Pointer*, Howell Book House Inc., NY, NY, 1951.

Semencic, Carl, PhD, "The Canary Dog," *Dog World*, 11/86.

――――. "Introducing the Dogo Argentino," *Dog World*, 11/85.

――――. *Man-Stopping Guard Dogs*, T.F.H. Publications, Inc., Neptune City, NJ, 1989.

――――. *The Tosa Ken*, Tosa Ken Assoc. of America.

――――. *The World of Fighting Dogs*, TFH Publications, Neptune City, NJ, 1984.

Semencic, Carl, PhD and Don Fiorino, "A New Look at the Contribution of the Eastern Brachycephalic Breeds to 'Bull Breed' History," *Dog World*, 3/84.

Smith, A. Croxton, *Dogs Since 1900*, Andrew Dakers, Ltd., London, 1950.

Spencer, James B., "Newfies to the Rescue," *Dog Fancy*, 11/86.

――――. "The Noble Newfoundland," *Dog Fancy*, 11/86, pp. 36, 41-43.

Steele, Ernie, "How St. Patrick and His Little Dogs Rid Ireland of Snakes," *Canine Chronicle*, 3/15/86, pp. 18, 22.

Stodghill, Tom D., *Stodghill's Animal Research Magazine*, issues fall '69, spring '66, fall-winter '72-'73.

Strang, Alison, "The Nova Scotia Duck Tolling Retriever, Canada's Own All-around Dog," *Show Ring*, 1978.

Strang, Paul D., ed., "The Pyrenean Shepherd Dog," Pyrenean Shepherd Dog Club of America Newsletter, 1981.

Stratton, Richard F., *The Rottweiler*, T.F.H. Publications, Inc., Neptune City, NJ, 1985.

――――. *The World of the American Pit Bull Terrier*, T.F.H. Publications, Inc., Neptune City, NJ, 1983.

Sundqvist, Margareta, "Tibetan Terrier column—A Swedish View," *Pure-Bred Dogs/American Kennel Gazette*, 12/81, p. 173.

Sverdrup, Otto, *New Land: Four Years in the Arctic Regions*.

Swift, E.M., "The Mutt with a Touch of Class," *Sports Illustrated*, 11/81, pp. 92-102.

Tanner, Renee, "The Dynamic Dobermans," *Dog Fancy*, Oct. '86, pp 36.

The Telomian Dog Club of America official brochure, Grand Rapids, OH.

Thornton, Kim, "The American Eskimo Dog," *Dog Fancy*, 2/87, p. 59.

Tobias, John, "Singing Dogs of New Guinea," *Dog Fancy*, 5/87, pp. 33-35.

Topsell, Edward, *The Historie of the Foure-Footed Beastes*, Wm. Iaggard, London, 1607.

Treen, Esmeralda, "Where Are They Now?" *Pure-Bred Dogs/American Kennel Gazette*, 11/84, pp. 72--79.

Triebels, Dr. L.F., *De Hollandse Herder*, Nederlandse Herdershonden Club.

United Kennel Club, *American Pit Bull Terrier*, Kalamazoo, MI.

United Kennel Club, *Early Days of U.K.C. Registered Redbone Coonhound*, Kalamazoo, MI.

Vlanin, Nina, "Are There Dogs in Russia?" *Pure-Bred Dogs/American Kennel Gazette*, 7/87, pp. 28-31.

Walker, Tom T., Ed.D, "Introducing the Finnish Spitz," *Dog World*, 2/84, pp. 14, 42.

Walkowicz, Chris, *The Bearded Collie*, Denlinger's Ltd., 1987.

Walkowicz, Chris and Bonnie Wilcox DVM, *Successful Dog Breeding*, Arco, 1985.

Walsh, J.H., (Stonehenge) *The Dogs of the British Islands*, 1878.

Warwick, Helen, *The New Complete Labrador Retriever*, 3rd Edition, Howell Book House, NY, NY 1986.

White, H. Ellen DVM, "Catahoula Hog Dog Brings Back Memories of Home," *DVM Newsmagazine*, 3/85, pp. 36-37.

Williams, Jill, "What's a Pudelpointer?," *Dog Fancy*, 1/87, pp. 44-45.

Wolk, Bruce Harold, "Herr Essig and His Leonberger," *Dog World*, 3/84.

———. "The Spaniels of Joy," *Dog World*, 1/84, pp. 24, 49-51, 55.

Zilberman, Gisele, "Teamwork and Responsibility."

Contributors

Photographers

Isabelle Francais, as the principal photographer for this Atlas, has traveled throughout Europe and North America capturing the dogs of the world on film. Ms. Francais has focused her dedicated effort on this project over the past five years. The success of her efforts is evident: for the first time ever have over 400 breeds been assembled in full-color in one captivating, all-encompassing volume.

We also acknowledge the contribution of Vladimir Pcholkin who provided the outstanding photography of the dogs of the Soviet Union. Other contributing photographers include: Alton Anderson, John L. Ashbey, Maria Carlos, Bryna Comski, Jay Lorenz Corvallis, Lloyd Donner, Michael Gilroy, Rich Johnson, Ron Moat, M. Montoya, Robert Pearcy, Fritz Prenzel, Ron Reagan, A. & J. Riely, Joe R. Rinehart, Vincent Serbin, Robert Smith, Pete Souza (the White House), Sandra E. Tucker, Marianne von der Lanken, Ken Walters and Irene Weidler.

Translators

Lilianne Black; Taylor Ridge, Illinois. Lea Gut; Siglistorf, Switzerland. Kiyoko Kibble, Spring Valley, New York. Julie McFarland, Rock Island, Illinois. Elleka Mesdag; Normal, Illinois. Karen Pouder; Eli-Fran Cockers, Silvis, Illinois. Dr. Lars Scott; Augustana College, Rock Island, Illinois. Helga Steiner; Friendship Farm West, Milan, Illinois. Thomas Swegle; Sherrard High School, Sherrard, Illinois. Marsha Winters; Rockridge High School, Edgington, Illinois.

Dog Owners & Correspondents

The following compilation represents the owners of the dogs portrayed in this book as well as the authors' correspondents. The authors are deeply indebted to these persons who willingly shared first-hand experience and information. The editorial staff of T.F.H. congratulates all dog fanciers associated with this Atlas and extends a sincere apology to anyone who may have been accidentally excluded from this list. Much thanks to all!

Aboczky, Maria; Upper Saddle River, New Jersey. Abraham, Lee; New Jersey. Accrudo, Rafael; Zaragoza, Spain. Aceto, Gratia; Torino, Italy. Aigeldinger, Ingrid; Siglistorf, Switzerland. Albaronte, Juan A.C.; Madrid, Spain. Alderfer, J. Ralph; Souderton, Pennsylvania. Allen, Peggy; Centre, Alabama. Alstede, Joanne; Chester, New Jersey. Althaus, Fritz; Kirchberg, Switzerland. Amyot, Gilbert; Quebec, Canada. Andersen, Chickie; Brooklyn, New York. André, Pioc; Vilaine, France. Andrews, Bill & BJ; Ashville, North Carolina. Andrews, Gayle; St. Augustine, Florida. Andrews, Miss Valerie; Hampshire, England. Animals Unlimited; USA. Armor, Rallye; Plesidy, France. Ashbey, Janet; Stewartsville, New Jersey. Attalla, Anthony; Rutland, Massachusetts. Augustowski, Kaz & Betty; Severn, Maryland. Austin, B.M.; Leicester, England. Australian National Kennel Council; Victoria, Australia. Aveaux, Carpe; Paris, France. Avery, Sarah; Bristol, England. Ayza, Jose Drago; Peniscola, Spain. Back, Nancy; Hedgesville, West Virginia. Backa-Greeven, M.; Holland. Bailey, Eunice; Allendale, New Jersey. Bakelaar, D.C.; Amsterdam, Holland. Barger, Stephen W.; Old Chatham, New York. Barhammar, Bertil; Thorsby, Sweden. Barlow, Dianne; USA. Barth, Dr. Wolf-Eberhard; St. Andreasberg, Germany. Bayly, Judith A.; Ellsworth, Maine. Beakes, Louise D.; Quebec, Canada. Beaupre, Bob & Judy; Aliquippa, Pennsylvania. Bello, Hose; San Tander, Portugal. Belmont Jr., Peter; Kansas City, Kansas. Belson, Mr. & Mrs. G.J.; Norfolk, England. Benis, Les; Playa Del Ray, California. Benjamin, Carol Lea; New York City, New York. Berger, Jill; Speonk, New York. Bergeron, France; Quebec, Canada. Bergman, Hinda; Raleigh, North Carolina. Berkel, Mark J.; Floral Park, New York. Bernhardt, Valerie; Milford, Pennsylvania. Bessa, Joao; Peco d'Arcos, Portugal. Bett, Leta; Ashton, Ontario, Canada. Bickel, Elizabeth; Kansas City, Missouri. Bierwirth, Wolfgang; Wehretal, Germany. Bigot, Hubert; La Bourbonnaise, France. Blanck, Doris; Mainhardt-Hütten, Germany. Blankenagel, M.; Krefeld, Switzerland. Blankenship, John & Pauline; Christiana,

Tennessee. Blao, Robert; Dorylaton, New York. Blom-Meijer, Mrs. A.; Ede, Netherlands. Bloom, Robert; Douglastown, New York. Bodier, M.; Cosne d'Allier, France. Bodine, Nan; Lakewood, New Jersey. Boegli, A. Jean-Pierre; Delemont, Switzerland. Boel, D.V.; Holland. Boelte, P.; Valhalla, New York. Boerkamp, E.; Budapest, Hungary. Bolle, Frau; Kelsterbach, Germany. Bolzmann, Kurt; Witten, Germany. Book, Maureen; Havelock, North Carolina. Botega, Joann; Brooklyn, New York. Boxer, Shirley; Skillman, New Jersey. Braginton, Edith M.; Spotswood, New Jersey. Bramblett, Susan; New Jersey. Brandenburger, Dale; Millspadt, Illinois. Brasier, Rodger; Moreno Valley, California. Brennan, Mr. Sean; Kilkenny, Ireland. Breton, Denise; Quebec, Canada. Breum, Robert L.; Omaha, Nebraska. Brewster, Joy; Newtown, Connecticut. Brisbin Jr., Dr. I. Lehr; Aiken, South Carolina. Brody, Irene; Richmond, Texas. Brookes, Marjorie; Santa Rosa, California. Brown, Gerald & Patricia; Honeybrook, Pennsylvania. Brubaker, Joyce K.; Bernville, Pennsylvania. Brügger, Bernadette; Romanshorn, Finland. Bryan, C.; New South Wales, Australia. Bryant, Mildred; North Central Texas. Burg, C.; Amsterdam, Holland. Butterklee, Arlene; Nesconset, New York. Cabezas, Juan Antonio; Madrid, Spain. Cadwell, Julia; Santa Rosa, California. Cahill, Mr. & Mrs. George; Merseyside, England. Campagne, Dr. Y.; Sainte Maure, France. Canadian Kennel Club; Ontario, Canada. Caporale, Janet A.; Hammonton, New Jersey. Capstick, Beverly; USA. Carberry, Mary Jane; Pennington, New Jersey. Carnathan, Howard; Tupelo, Mississippi. Carpenter, Jim; Waxhaw, North Carolina. Caruso, Victoria; Cedar Grove, New Jersey. Casper, Ursula; Schwetzingen, Germany. Cavalchini, Dr.; Bergamo, Italy. Cawthera, Averi; Durham, England. Chalain, Nadine; Saint Gemmes, France. Chamberland, Mme. Louise; Quebec, Canada. Chaplain, Alain; Ste. Cernin, France. Chataigner, Jean. Chathos, Bobbie; Rutland, Massachusetts. Chorn, Donly; Deerfield, Illinois. Ciceri, Paolo; Milano, Italy. Cinofilla Italiana Ente Nazionale; Milan, Italy. Clark, Jean; Franklin, New Hampshire. Clark, Tom & Judy; Edmonds, Washington. Clarke, Robert N. & Bonnie S.; Ellington, Connecticut. Club for Native Moroccan Breeds. Cock 'N' Bull Kennels; Bloomington, California. Cocuzza, Patti; Jeffersonton, Virginia. Cohen, Dorothy; Las Vegas, Nevada. Coia, Arthur; Barrington, Rhode Island. Colburn, Mr. & Mrs. P.; Milton Keynes, England. Collins, Gerarda; Old Greenwich, Connecticut. Comski, Bryna; Hoffman Estates, Illinois. Cone, Susan; Livingston, New Jersey. Connelly, William; Dumont, New Jersey. Conner, Eileen & Wm.; Jerome, Idaho. Consolazio, Monique; Putnam Valley, New York. Coonhunters Assoc. Professional; Memphis, Tennessee. Coppinger, Lorna; Amherst, Massachusetts. Cornelissen, C.; West Germany. Cornwell, Sandy; Potomac, Illinois. Corrone, Susan; Bethany, Connecticut. Cottrell, Lynda; Pompano, Florida. Cowell, Robert P.; Bridgeport, Connecticut. Cruz, Hector; Humacao, Puerto Rico. Curley, Peter; Columbia, Missouri. Cynologique International Federation; Thuin,

Belgium. Cynologique Swisse Societe; Bern, Switzerland. Da Costa Botto, Hose Manuel; Sousel, Portugal. Danish Kennel Club; Solrodstrand, Denmark. Darkrooms Plus; USA. Davidson, Dr. & Mrs. John; Dunlap, Illinois. Davidson, Henry & Gabe; Annandale, Minnesota. Davis, Bob; San Diego, California. Davis, Helen T.; Hillside, New Jersey. Davis, Karla; Woodlake, California. De La Rochefoucauld, M.; Combreux, France. De Palma, Victoria K.; Milford, Connecticut. De Paula Bessa, A.; Voluntaris, Portugal. Dean, Mrs. P.A.; Hampshire, England. Deavers, Ruth A.; New York, New York. Defois, Aime; St. Armez, France. Dejaeger, Erik; Northwest Territories, Canada. Delhorne, C.; Bouc Bel Air, France. Demary, Allen; Valatic, New York. Derraugh, Mrs. C.; Orleans, Ontario, Canada. Dervin, Irene; Philadelphia. Deutsche Hunderassen e. V. Verband fur das; Dortmund, Germany. DeVore, Mrs. Pat; Birch Tree, Missouri. Dickson, Alice; Green Village, New Jersey. DiGiacomo, Kathy; Fair Lawn, New Jersey. Dijkmans, A.F.; Someren, Holland. Dixon, Alice; Green Village, New Jersey. Dobbyn, Mr. E.; County Cork, Ireland. Dobish, Denise; Garfield, New Jersey. Döbler, E.; Roesbenberg, Austria. Dokter, Kim; Stadskandal, Finland. Doniere, Pat & Judy; Holland, Ohio. Donyer, M.; Holland. Dremaux, Jacques; Gambersart, France. Dridrit, Klaus; Reukingen, West Germany. Droz, Paul; Switzerland. Duede, Daniel; St. Maurice, France. Dueker Schaffner, Nancy; Schwenksville, Pennsylvania. Duff, Robert; Davenport, California. Duryea, Carolyn S.; Riverside, New Jersey. Dusoux, Laurent; Douvaine, France. Eckes, Mrs. Charles R.; Denver, Colorado. Edwards, Alida; Frankville, Ontario, Canada. Eggers, Lynn; North Central Texas. Eichhorn, Richard; Simi Valley, California. Eisenberg, Nancy L.; Merrick, New York. Eisenolbe, J.; Riyswijk, Netherlands. El Yamani, M. Fatmi El Kadiri; Rabat, Morocco. Elitz, E.; Great Britain. Elly, Englebert; Amsterdam, Holland. Equipage de Bramofam; Vienna, Austria. Erny, Andrew & Nancy; Mahwah, New Jersey. Ervin, Mercer Russo; Patterson, New York. Erwin, Florence; Scarborough, Ontario, Canada. Esteban, Julio & Isabel; Towson, Maryland. Evans, Mrs. J.; Purcell Bucks, England. Fairbanks, Mrs. Richmond; Greenville, South Carolina. Fajfar, Joze; Radovljica, Yugoslavia. Fargas Caribra, Miguel; La Margosta, Spain. Farley, John; Gig Harbor, Washington. Farr-Williams, Leah; Allentown, Pennsylvania. Farrar, P.; USA. Fasoli, Bruno; Tourville, Germany. Fassi-Fehri, Docteur Mahi; Rabat, Morocco. Fernandez, Amy & Mary; Forest Hills, New York. Field Sports Society; London, England. Fielder, Stephen (UKC); Kalamazoo, Michigan. Filiatrault, Raymond; Quebec, Canada. Fillenberg, Heinz; Roding, Germany. Filleul, M. Paul; Rochechouart, France. Findlay, Ann; Sussex, England. Fink, Wolfgang; Moers-Kapellen, Germany. Finkelstein, Barbara; Hewlett, New York. Finnegan, Edward J., Jr.; Monroe, New York. Fischer, Elyse; Port Washington, New York. Fisher, Betty; El Cajon, California. Fitt, Kevin; Marino Valley, California Fonda, Cathy; Rialto, California. Fontaine, Mariette; Chassy, France. Ford, Judith E.; Wallkill, New York.

Fortin, Martin; Montreal, Quebec, Canada. Franzen, Christa; Rosrath, Germany. Fraser, Jocelyn; Cornwall, Ontario, Canada. Freeman, Edith L.; Ontario, Canada. French, Virginia, USA. Frenzel, Madame Edith; Riehen, Switzerland. Froats, Brad & Carol Ann; Ontario, Canada. From, Per-Alrik; Tarnaby, Sweden. Galera Ibanez, Albert; Spain. Galibois, Richard; Lauzon, Quebec, Canada. Gallantry Giant Schnauzers; Warminster, Pennsylvania. Gammons, David J.; White Plains, New York. Gannon, Dee; Wenonah, New Jersey. Garding, Dieter; Schiedsberg, Holland. Garrick, John; New York City, New York. Gascoigne, Mr. & Mrs. E.; Essex, England. Gaston, Daniel; Neuchâtel, Switzerland. Gebied in Nederland Raad v. Beheer op Kynologisch; Emmalaan, Netherlands. Genovese, Mary; Bristol, England. Genzâlez, Beatriz; San Tander, Portugal. Gerber, Fritz; Bretzwil, Switzerland. German Club for Pekes, Chins & Toy Spaniels. Getter, Lorraine; Old Tappan, New Jersey. Gettings, Ruth M.; Staten Island, New York. Gilat, Josette; Remasoble, France. Gioia, Margaret; Beechhurst, New York. Giuntini, Francesco; Firenze, Italy. Goby, Roger; Imphy, France. Goldsmith, Carol; Montpelier, Virginia. Gonzaga de Oliveira, Prof. Luiz; São Paulo, Brazil. Goodale, Dorothy; Montrose, Colorado. Gordon, Fred & Sandra; Ontario, Canada. Gormley, Mr. A. & Mrs. A.; County Dublin, Ireland. Goucher, Mary "Skeeter"; Bradley, Oklahoma. Grechko, Valerie; Wolcott, Connecticut. Green, Sheila; Mahwah, New Jersey. Greene, Forrest & Beverly; Houston, Texas. Greenwood, Nancy E.; Nashua, New Hampshire. Grey, Denise; USA. Grossenbacher, Evelyn; Bern, Switzerland. Grossman, Laura; Roeland Heights, California. Grouf, Joy; Dancer Poodles, New York. Gryzlo, Janet; Queens Village, New York. Guénolé, Patrick; Plougasnou, Switzerland. Guerin, Ana Filomena; Sesimbra, Portugal. Guerrini, Nadir; Vercelli, Italy. Guimard, M.; Lavardens, Belgium. Guinard, Maurice; Plourivo, France. Gunnell, Mrs. J.; Sussex, England. Guthier, Marie; Telford, Pennsylvania. Guyonard, Maurice; Berrien, France. Gyes, Nancy; San Jose, California. Haan, S.; Amsterdam, Holland. Haarlem, A.; Amsterdam, Holland. Haggkvist, Olle B.; Sveg, Sweden. Hagland, Rudolf; Haugesund, Norway. Haight, Judy; Lake Ronkonkoma, New York. Hailes, Helen; Ringoes, New Jersey. Hall, Robert & Laura; Aiken, South Carolina. Hamer, Sandra; Quebec, Canada. Hamilton Ed., Ferelith; Kent, England. Hampton, Suzanne H.; Fort Lee, New Jersey. Hansen, Dr. Jens; Bremervorde, Germany. Harmand, Daniel; Contreyeville, France. Harned, Quinn & Marilyn; Alpine, California. Harrison, J.C.; Mt. Horeb, Wisconsin. Hayden, Betty; Forestville, Connecticut. Healy, Leslie; San Angelo, Texas. Hecker, Heinrich; Wald-Michelbach, Germany. Heidenrijk, Ferry Bruhwiler & Marijke; Siegershausen, Switzerland. Heiderer, Fritz; Herzogenburg, Austria. Helbig, Maureen B.; Irvington, New York. Helén, Anne, Vantua, Finland. Helm, E.; Oranjewand, Poland. Henaff, Bruno; LaMontagne, France. Henderson, Karen Abbott; Duxbury, Massachusetts. Herschman, Patricia; Hewlett, New York. Hess, Irene; Wustenrot-Neulautern, Germany. Higgins,

Dorothy; Brooklyn, New York. Hodges, Shirley; New Jersey. Hoff, Graciela; Rio Grande, Puerto Rico. Hoffman, Mrs. J. Frederick; Lafayette, Indiana. Hofman, Nancy J.; Norwalk, California. Holler, Heinz; Alsdorf, Germany. Hollmann, Keistin; Aulendorf, Holland. Hood, Katherine; Altamont, Illinois. Houdou, Mr. & Mrs. Maurice; Lake Grove, New York. Hrabak, J. U. O.; Worms-Weinsheim, Germany. Huber, Dennis; USA. Hugo, Frank; Marlton, New Jersey. Huisman, J.; Leiden, Holland. Humphrey, Curtis; London, Ohio. Humphreys, Jim; Stuarts Draft, Virginia. Hunter, Mrs. Dorothy; Lincoln, England. Ibanez, Hugo J.; Charlotte, North Carolina. Impey, Gillian ; Little Silver, New Jersey. Irish Kennel Club, Department of Publications; Dublin, Ireland. Irish Kennel Club; Dublin, Ireland. Irwin, Carroll Ann; North Hollywood, California. Israel, Edward; Atco, New Jersey. Jacques, Marie; Ontario, Canada. Jameson, Jean K.; Deep River, Connecticut. Jawzky, Tizsf; Budapest, Hungary. Jefferey, Richard C.; Frederick, Maryland. Jester, Carolyn; Stroud, Oklahoma. Joffe, Grace & Jeff; Ft. Lauderdale, Florida. Johle, Helmut; Vohrenbach, Switzerland. Johnson, John D.; Summerville, Georgia. Jones, Brenda; Tulsa, Oklahoma. Jones, Jacque & Ray; Coolville, Ohio. Jones, Kenneth C.; Adolphus, Kentucky. Joss, Helen; Hiuberbenzring, Switzerland. Joyal, Jeannine; St. Felix De Kingsley, Canada. Kaiser, Mrs. Henry J.; Alekai Kennels, USA. Karr, Diana; Arbutus, Maryland. Katz, Charlotte; Woodbine, Maryland. Kauen, Samuel; Lucerne, Switzerland. Keim, Margaret E.; Sacramento, California. Kellerman, Wendy L.; Glen Oaks, New York. Kennel Club, The; London, England. Kenyon, Dorothy; Devon, England. Kerkhof, E.P.; Vlaardingen, Switzerland. Kiaulenas, Laura; Farmingville, New York. Kiefer, Claus; Romerberg-Berghausen, Germany. King, Eileen J.; Philadelphia. Kirk, Mr. A.; Herfordshire, England. Klose, Ingeborg; St. Johann Tirol, Austria. Knight, James; Beeville, Texas. Knight, James H.; Hanna City, Illinois. Kolster-Reckman, Mrs. Th. F. M.; Emmer-Compascuum, Netherlands. Koppel, Robert A. Koul, C. Kerl; Austria. Kovakova M.V. Dr., Alzbeta; Kosice, Czechoslovakia. Kovalic, Virginia & Frank; Detroit, Michigan. Kristensen, Villy G.; Sonderborg, Denmark. Kroll, Kurt; Hawthorne, New Jersey. Krom, Esther C.; Clifton, New Jersey. Kruel, Clelia; Campinas, Brazil. Krukar, John & Linda; Bethlehem, Pennsylvania. Kuberski, Elaine B.; Englishtown, New Jersey. Kuczynski, Lynne; Emmaus, Pennsylvania. Kuehl, Elke; Juliustown, New Jersey. Kuenzle, Dr. Clive; Zurich, Switzerland. Kwait, Kathy; Fairlawn, New Jersey. Labaire, Beverly; Rutland, Massachusetts. Lacchia, Linda; Whitestone, New York. Laemmle, Cheryl; New York City, New York. Laflamme, Sandra; Manassas, Virginia. Lamoureus, Sarole; Sherbrooke, Canada. Lamphere, Al & Cindy; Sparta, New Jersey. Lang, Christen; Oslo, Norway. Langevin, Pauline; Sherbrooke, Quebec, Canada. Larsen, Poul; Skjern, Denmark. Lassagne, P.; Longpre Les Corps Saints, France. Lawler, Alice S.; Cream Ridge, New Jersey. Le Blanc, Joe; Telford, Pennsylvania. Le Fevre, Betty; Processieweg, Belgium. Le Pennec, Henry;

899

France. Lebris, Nane; Loudeac, France. Lecki, Irene & Tom; Philadelphia, Pennsylvania. Leclerc, Steve; Hampden, Massachusetts. Lee Jr., Donald T.O.; Honolulu, Hawaii. Lenz, Annette; Holland. Leone, Pat; Califon, New Jersey. Leroy, Jacques; Saint Chairsurelle, France. Les Loge Marchis; France. Leseigneur, Madame; Bernay, France. Leutenegger, A.; Eichtenstr, Holland. Lewis Jr., John R.; Natural Bridge, Virginia. Libson, Paul; Patchogue, New York. Linders, Ch.; Oudenbosch, Holland. Lindinger, Hans; Geroiering, Germany. Lingmont, Erik; Amsterdam, Holland. Link, Valerie; Pleasant Hill, California. Linn, Harriet; Concord, California. Little Mountain Kennels; Port Angeles, Washington. Liukkonen, Outi; Espoo, Finland. Ljungren, Doug & Penny; Kent, Washington. Llewellyn, Dick & Zella; Alvin, Texas. Lockquell, Lise; Quebec, Canada. Lopez, A.D.; Madrid, Spain. Loureiro Borges, Dr. J. M.; Lisbon, Portugal. Lowery, Dr. John C.; Muscle Shoals, Alabama. Luburich, Ms. Felicie E.H.; East Brunswick, New Jersey. Lucero, Michael; New York City, New York. Ludenberg, H.; Tilburg, Belgium. Lussion, R.A.; Wilberham, Massachusetts. Luttikhuis, Mr. K.G.M.; Rijn, Netherlands. Lyons, Joy; Pompano Beach, Florida. McCarthy, Sean & Elizabeth; USA. McCormack, Mary M.; Doylestown, Pennsylvania. McDuffie, J. Richard; Columbia, South Carolina. McGregor, Mrs. Freda; Kent, England. Machenaud, M.; Le Petit Bois, France. McKeever, M. Barbara; Malvern, Pennsylvania. McNeal, Jo Ann; Old Chatham, New York. McNeil, Germain; Richmond, Quebec. McNeil, Germaine; Quebec, Canada. Maggard, Stephen B.; Charlotte, North Carolina. Magowits, New York City, New York. Malloy, Mrs. Heidi; Bernardsville, New Jersey. Malone, Mary; Alliance, Ohio. Malone, Thomas Jr.; County Wicklow, Ireland. Mandarino, Sandy; Bergenfield, New Jersey. Mangold, Theodor; St. Leonhard, Austria. Mannings, Dr. Michael; Staten Island, New York. Mannlein, Stan & Sue; Staten Island, New York. Mansencal, Guy; Tarbes, France. Marburger, Sylvia; Truckee, California. Marcelle, Robin; Jonzic, France. Marks, Robert J.; Dundee, Illinois. Martin, Dawn; Windgap, Pennsylvania. Martin, Mona; Dover Plains, New York. Martin, Nancy; Spring House, Pennsylvania. Martinez, Antonio; Madrid, Spain. Martinez, Marie-Pierre; Chantoiseaux, France. Masse, Ives; Perpignan, France. Matalouge, Pepa; Barcelona, Spain. Matenaar, Frau Christa; Konigswinter, Germany. Matunas, Tom & Judy; New Jersey. Mauldin, Guy & Thelma; Richmond, Texas. Maus-Vickus, Elisabeth; Overath, Germany. Mazo, Hose; San Tander, Portugal. Mazurkiewicz, Linda; New Jersey. Mazzarella, Angelica C.; Syosset, New York. Merson, Shelly & Ron; New City, New York. Mertens, Joe & Jackie; Elgin, Illinois. Meyer, J. & J.; La Cibourg, Switzerland. Milliand, Claude; Yugoslavia. Mills-De Hoog, Mrs. W.H.; Kent, England. Milor, M.; Honfleur, France. Mitchell, Page; Ojai, California. Miyama, Tetsuo; Old Chatham, New York. Mohr, Terre, Newburgh, New York. Mollet, Janice; Holtsville, New York. Mollusky, Debbie; Staten Island, New York. Monadnock Kennels; Fitzwilliam, New

Hampshire. Monaghan, Kay; Woodlawn, Maryland. Moore, William E.; Trenton, New Jersey. Morneau, Louise; Quebec, Canada. Moron, Jean; St. Joachim, France. Morrissey, Michael J.; Middletown, Delaware. Moser, Silvia; Bigenthal, Switzerland. Mott, Margaret; Harris, New York. Mott, William J.; Glen Oaks, New York. Mousley, Greg; USA. Moyette, Gabriel; Ontario, Canada. Mulder, J.; Amsterdam, Holland. Mulder, Saskia; Haag, Netherlands. Munroe, Marilyn C.; Jeffersonville, New York. Munz, Ruth; Basel, Switzerland. Murphy, Pat; West Chicago, Illinois. Murray, Mignon; Jacksonville, Florida. Myre, Martha; Merrickville, Ontario, Canada. Nathan, Jody; Tulsa, Oklahoma. Nathanson, Amy; Lawrenceville, New Jersey. Navrotil, Huguette; Quebec, Canada. Nelinson, Leslie; Hackensack, New Jersey. Nelson, David & Judith; Chevy Chase, Maryland. Newhart Jr., Lee; Ithaca, New York. Nichol, Diana; Kent, England. Niederhauser, Mrs. Elizabeth; Mas Campiroi, Switzerland. Nijssen, Christina; Mallorca, Spain. Norden Laboratories; Lincoln, Nebraska. Normand, Claude; Dreuil, France. Norsk Kennel Klub; Oslo, Norway. Norstrom, Richard & Marjorie; Honolulu, Hawaii. Norton, Kirk & Anne; Herron, Michigan. Noyelle, Laureys; Edegem, Belgium. Noyelle, Rita; Paris, France. Nunez, Ojeda; Barcelona, Spain. Nysen, Willy; Brasschaat, Belgium. Obee, C.; Emmelwoord, Holland. Olciua, Manuel Maria; Alicante, Spain. O'Neil, George & Dorothy; Westwood, Massachusetts. O'Neill, Marie E.; Hewlett, New York. Oqueranza, R.; Alava, Spain. Orlik, Jo Ann; Jackson, New Jersey. Ostiguy, Louise; Montreal, Quebec, Canada. O'Weill Wagner, Beverly; Joppa, Maryland. Palmeiri, Frank; East Haven, Connecticut. Paludi, Gail & Carmen; Verona, New York. Pare, Mario; Fleurimont, France. Parker, Robert; Old Greenwich, Connecticut. Parkyns, Mrs. J.S.; Buckingham, England. Parr, Judith A.; West Islip, New York. Parrinha, Francisco; Barrvudo, Portugal. Paton, Jeanette; Kilmar Nock, Scotland. Pauciello, Rita A.; Hopatcong, New Jersey. Paule, Frances & Ruth; Riverton, Indiana. Paulsen, Patrick J.; New Jersey. Pedron, Jean; St. Brieu, France. Peek, Larry & Terri; Clearfield, Utah. Pellegrini, Melle; Le Puy, France. Perez, Ginette; Westbrookville, New York. Petersen, B. Kirkegaard; Vejenbrødvej, Denmark. Pfeister, Larry; Mt. Carmel, Illinois. Phillips, Mary; Little Silver, New Jersey. Pielanen-Degenhardt, E.; Beijerland, Netherlands. Pilat, Josette; Rémalard, France. Pinkus, Susan; West Orange, New Jersey. Pitts, Chuck & Marilyn; Lehi, Utah. Pober, Stacy; Roslyn, New York. Pohn, Hermann; Vöcklabruck, Austria. Pohoreau, B.; Lyon, France. Poisson, Anita; Katevale, Quebec, Canada. Pompeo, Patrick J. & Carol; Fairlawn, New Jersey. Pontois, Yves; Championne, France. Poole, Mrs. Jack A.; Johnstown, Pennsylvania. Porreca, Pat; Pleasanton, California. Pratt, Betty; Napa, California. Princehouse, Miss Patricia; Kent, Ohio. Purves, Mr. G. & Mrs. J.; Newcastle, England. Pye, Roger F.; Porto, Portugal. Quadri, Mario; Brescia, Italy. Quaintance, Judy; Lafayette, Indiana. Radonis, Virginia; Flushing Meadow, New York. Rafeio, F.A.; Faro-Allarve, Portugal.

Rahaman, Cheryl; New Paltz, New York. Ramalho, F.F.; Sintra, Portugal. Rancourt, Marcel; Quebec, Canada. Randall, Robert M.; USA. Rasch-Gründing, Fritz & Helga; Bramsche, Germany. Ratzlaff, Doris; Oakland, New Jersey. Rayner, Jacqueline; Hamilton, New Jersey. Rayner, Kenneth; Hopewell, New Jersey. Rector, Claas; Dornum, Germany. Redditt, JoAnn; Alexandria, Virginia. Reder, Marianne; Cuyahoga Falls, Ohio. Reed, Mauren L.; Baltimore, Maryland. Reed, Sharon D.; Bloomfield, New Jersey. Rees, W. Valerie; Doylestown, Pennsylvania. Regan, Martin; Richwood, New Jersey. Regelman, Kristin; Ridgewood, New Jersey. Reingold, Suzy A.; New York City, New York. Renaud, Danielle; Quebec, Canada. Resch, Helene; Piscataway, New Jersey. Ressa, Elaine; Neptune City, New Jersey. Reynolds, Richard L.; New York City, New York. Reyns, Frans; Olen, Belgium. Ricci, Dennis G. & Ruth Ann Freer-; Vincentown, New Jersey. Richter, Dr. Paul; Dreistetten, Austria. Ridgeway, Margaret; Haverford, Pennsylvania. Riederer, Rene & Sonja; Wila, Switzerland. Roadhouse, Donna; Aldergrove, British Columbia, Canada. Roberts Dumont, Karen; Quebec, Canada. Roberts, Dot; New City, New York. Roby, JC; Whitesville, Kentucky. Rodgers, Mary; Hamilton, Montana. Roeder-Thiede, Dr. M.; Munchen, Germany. Rogers, Amelia F.; Hampstead, Maryland. Roossien-Bruggink, Mrs. A.J.; Deventer, Netherlands. Roques, Cyrille; Aix-en Provence, France. Rosen, Betty & Herbert; Lutherville, Maryland. Roth R.Ph., Ann H.; Wilmington, North Carolina. Roth, Walter; Speonk, New York. Rowland, Mrs. B.; Surrey, England. Ruiz, Eduardo Benito; Madrid, Spain. Russell, J. Lewis; Marlton, New Jersey. Russell, Robert Jay; Torrance, California. Rutten, Andre; Veldwezelt, Austria. Ryan, James L.; Woodstown, New Jersey. Sachs, Lisa; Huntington, New York. Saint-Hubert Union Cynologique; Brussels, Belgium. Saint-Jean, Marcel; Simorre, France. Saintoingois, Rallye; La Treublade, France. Samson, Miss R.J.; Kent, England. San Diego Spuds; San Diego, California. Santiago, Rick & Brenda; Pearl River, New York. Sarret, Francoise; Ferrand, France. Sarttila, Reino; Helsinki, Finland. Saunders, Alex; Kingston, Ontario, Canada. Saunders, Ann; New Jersey. Saunders, Miss Jacky; Avon, England. Scagliotti, Patricia; Bergenfield, New Jersey. Scalzo, Gail; Nutley, New Jersey. Scheer, D.; Steenberger, West Germany. Schetters, C.; Laagboss, Holland. Schinz-Graf, Frau Dorothea; Gruningen, Switzerland. Schmid-Joggi, F. & L.; Wallbach, Switzerland. Schonheyder, Mrs. Sofie; Oslo, Norway. Schrage, Bill; Spokane, Washington. Schreurs, Joan A.; Edison, New Jersey. Schriber-Schar, Edy & Regina; Bern, Switzerland. Schultze, Ilse; Hamburg, Germany. Schutz, Pauline; Alvin, Texas. Schwartz, Barbara; Hollis, New Hampshire. Schwartz, Shirley; Little Neck, New York. Schwarz, Jane A.; Wyckoff, New Jersey. Scott, Edwin & Willie; Trout, Louisiana. Scott, Willie; Trout, Louisiana. Seiler, Regula Pales; Bern, Switzerland. Sellers, Monica; Lancester, California. Semencic, Carl; West Hempstead, New York. Sentis, Richard; Rouergue, France. Serman, Mrs. Chris; Erdington, England. Shannon, Ellen J.; Farmingdale, New York. Sherling, Kristina; Saugus, California. Shushunov, Sergey; Jacksonville, Florida. Siegenthaler-Eggiman, Dr. Margret; Zollbruck, Switzerland. Silkworth, Mary M.; Jackson, Michigan. Simard, H.; Agen, France. Simpson, Mrs. N.C.; New Plymouth, New Zealand. Sinnema, H.; Amsterdam, Holland. Skeen, Susan; Long Beach, California. Skilton, Donald & Louise; Weymouth, Massachusetts. Slater, Rachel; South Granby, Quebec, Canada. Slaughter, Bill; Land-O-Lakes, Florida. Smith, Mrs. M.M.; Watford, England. Smith, Susan & Daniel; Newtown, Connecticut. Snizer, Ed; Lincoln, New Jersey. Solarski, Diane E.; Wrightstown, New Jersey. Solinsky, Barbara; Nesco, New Jersey. Sombach, David E.; Schwenksville, Pennsylvania. Soriano, Pedro Pérez; Tarragona, Spain. Sorkin, Dr. Arthur; Los Gatos, California. Sorrentino, Diane; Bogota, New Jersey. Sottile, Michael; Bridgewater, New Jersey. Sousa Mendes, José; Portugal. Spannagl, Leopold; Zwettl, West Germany. Spesak, Barbara; Spring Valley, Ohio. Spies, K.; New Jersey. Spitz Club of Finland. Spurrell, Mrs. P.V.; Wiltshire, England. Squire, Karen; Valatie, New York. St. Onge, Jacqueline; Quebec, Canada. Stachel, Ernst; Franental, Austria. Stadler, W.; Germany. Stampe, Annelise Juul; Viborg, Denmark. Stanton, Kenneth & Charlotte; Westwood, Massachusetts. Starkweather; Patricia; Haverford, Pennsylvania. Steen, Mrs. Wiebke; Hamburg, Germany. Steghofer, Andreas; Vienna, Austria. Steidel, Kitty; Scottsdale, Arizona. Stein, Angela; New Jersey. Stein, Kathy & Louis; Icard, North Carolina. Stelql, Pia Maria; Wienfelden, Switzerland. Stephens, Jim; Beaver Dam, Kentucky. Stephens, Lorraine; Newcastle, Oklahoma. Stiles, Barbara; Newton, New Jersey. Stodghill, Tom; Quinlan, Texas. Stoeckli, Hans-Rudolf; Langenthal, Switzerland. Stone, Faye & Myrl; USA. Storace, Dr. Antonio; Genova, Italy. Storholm, Mr. Karl; Elverum, Norway. Strang, Alison & Roy; British Columbia, Canada. Streeter, Mrs. Elizabeth; Chester Springs, Pennsylvania. Stroink-Schreuder, Mrs. A.; Heerhugowaard, Netherlands. Strowe, Margaret & John; Sparta, New Jersey. Summons, Dr. Howard & Gretel; Sinking Spring, Pennsylvania. Sunzer, Ed; Lincoln Park, New Jersey. Sutter, Joseph; Waldkirch, Switzerland. Swanberg, Roberta; Stanfordville, New York. Tabor, Joan; Upper Montclair, New Jersey. Tapp, Susan; Washington, New Jersey. Tavernese, Yuan; D'Aigues, France. Terrada, Alejandro Malter; Argentina. Terry, Herb & Ruth; Weston, Connecticut. The Boykin Spaniel Society; Camden, South Carolina. Thiery, Michel; Puymirol, France. Thomas, Amanda; Clinton, New York. Thomas, Joan; Scarborough, Ontario, Canada. Thomas, Patricia A.; Lansing, Michigan. Thompson, Clarence E.; Macon, North Carolina. Thompson, Dottie; Bloomingdale, Illinois. Thompson, Robert; Brooklyn, New York. Thordsen, Carol; Andover, New Jersey. Thorp, Susan; Oskaloosa, Iowa. Tipoin, Albert; Beause, France. Tirry, R.; Hoboken, Belgium. Tomita, Rick Jacquet; Paramus, New Jersey. Touf, Alfonso; Barcelona, Spain. Toze, Zajtar; Radovljica, Yugoslavia. Trabiley, E.T. & L.J.; Brick Township, New Jersey. Trainor, William J.; Oxford,

Massachusetts. Trama, Noreen; Richmond, Texas. Travers, Garry & Lynn; Ontario, Canada. Traverse, E.S.; Castleton, Vermont. Trowbridge, Marjorie; Madison, Connecticut. Tschopp, Ilse E.; Forch, Switzerland. Tucker, Ron; Pennsburg, Pennsylvania. Tveter, Mr. Oddvar; Sarpsborg, Norway. Tyson, Miss Valerie; Coventry, England. Umlaas, Rod; Clinton, New York. Ungar, Kathy & Maurice; Valencia, California. United Kennel Club, USA. Vael, F.W.A.; Holland. Vallet, Alfred; Chevreuse, France. Van Abeelzoom Kennel; Kilburg, Holland. Van Benthem, Cees; Elst, West Germany. Van der Ende, H.; Mülheim-Ruhr, Germany. Van der Raadt, T.; Amsterdam, Holland. Van Elsbergen, Heimo; Bonn, Germany. Van Gelder, Ferdinand Nuyts & Lea; Averbode, Belgium. Van Huffel, Danny; Amsterdam, Holland. Van Vliet, Mr.; Connecticut. Vansteenkiste, Deleu; Klemskerke, Holland. Varese, Rosanna; Italy. Vasconcelos Pres., Señor; Lisbon, Portugal. Vaudo, Joseph & Mary; Newton, Connecticut. Verheugen, Mr. J.; Biezen-mortel, Netherlands. Vines, G.S.; Bretforton, England. Vittorio, Merigo; Issiglio, Italy. Vlanin, Nina; San Francisco, California. Voillot, Mr. Marcel; Montigny/Aube, France. Voorhees, Mr.; Edwardsburg, Michigan. Vooris, Donna; Shirley, New York. Vulvin, M.; La Geney Touse, France. Vutela, Paivi; Inkeroinen, Finland. Walker, Darlene; Kemah, Texas. Walschaerts, Mrs. A.; Lucca, Italy. Walters, Berenice; Bargo, Australia. Ward, Dr. Craig; Columbia, South Carolina. Ward, Jeanette & Joel; Wiscosville, Pennsylvania. Ward, Mrs. Janet; Suffolk, England. Wasserman, Ann; Pompton Lakes, New Jersey. Watson, Mrs. M.; Norwich, England. Wear, Mrs. W.P.; Cecilton, Maryland. Weber, Felix & Tina; Rickenbach, Switzerland. Weikel, John; Mt. Vernon, Indiana. Weiss, Jytte; Soro, Denmark. Werk, C.; Vlaardingen, Hungary. White, Lisa; Dickinson, Texas. Whitely, Dr. H. Ellen; Amarillo, Texas. Whitman, Janet & Marvin; Spring Valley, New Jersey. Wilkes, Paul & Pam; Hardwick, Massachusetts. Williams, Kenneth; Hempstead, Maryland. Wills, Angela; Spencer, Oklahoma. Wilson, Jeanne Kundell; Westford, Vermont. Wilson, Leon J.; Patterson, New Jersey. Wilson-Smith, Miss Kayte; Herfordshire, England. Winston, Ruth; Lido Beach, New York. Wöhry, Victor; Kapfenberg, Austria. Wojculewski, Stephen; Coram, New York. Wolforth, Gwendolyn; Icard, North Carolina. Wollpert, Neil & Marra; Kettering, Ohio. Wood, Barbara; Cranford, New Jersey. Wunsch, Nete; Naestved, Ontario, Canada. Wurgler, L.; Zollbruck, Switzerland. Wurtenberger, Heinz; Ludwigshafen-Oggersheim, Germany. Wuthrich, Hansruedi; Bernes Oberland, Switzerland. Yanoff, Arthur; Concord, New Hampshire. Yntema, R. & E.; British Columbia, Canada. Young, Fredricka; Fairfax Station, Virginia. Yrza, J.D.; Castellon, Portugal. Yuspa, Rochelle; Baltimore, Maryland. Zarko, Bengić; Pazin, Yugoslavia. Zarobinski, Karen M.; Dover, New Jersey. Zazempa, Daniel; Pontheirry, France. Zingler, Marcy; Fort Lee, New Jersey. Zollo, Michael; Bernardsville, New York.

Index

Page numbers in bold indicate major breed articles.